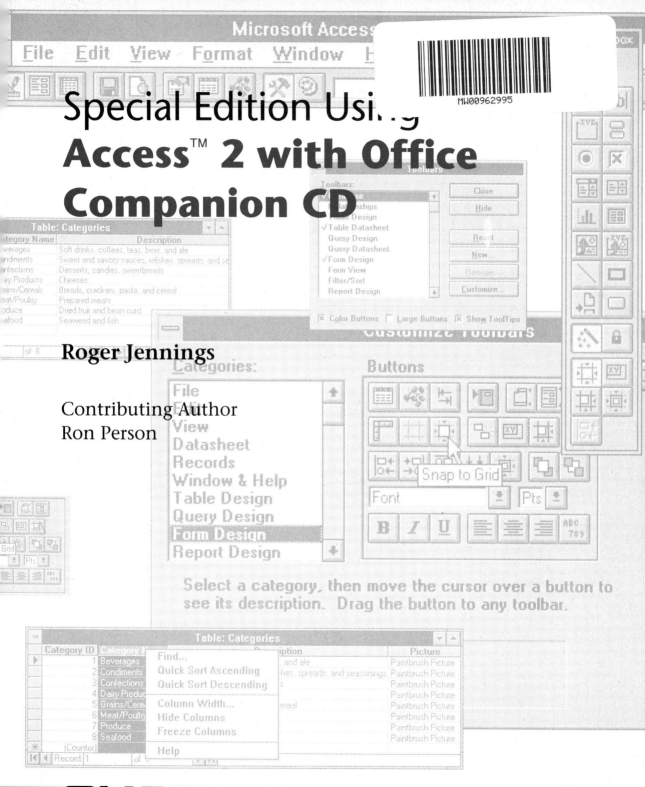

Special Edition Using
Access™ 2 with Office
Companion CD

Roger Jennings

Contributing Author
Ron Person

Special Edition Using Access 2 with Office Companion CD

Library of Congress Catalog No.: 95-68264

ISBN: 0-7897-0350-5

97 96 95   10 9

Interpretation of the printing code: the rightmost double-digit number is the year of the book's printing; the rightmost single-digit number, the number of the book's printing. For example, a printing code of 94-1 shows that the first printing of the book occurred in 1994.

Screen reproductions in this book were created using Collage Plus from Inner Media, Inc., Hollis, NH.

Special Edition Using Access 2 with Office Companion CD, is based on Microsoft Access version 2 for Windows.

Publisher: David P. Ewing

Associate Publisher: Michael Miller

Managing Editor: Michael Cunningham

Product Marketing Manager: Ray Robinson

Credits

Publishing Manager
Don Roche

Acquisitions Editor
Sarah Browning

Product Director
Steven M. Schafer

Production Editors
Chris Nelson
Patrick Kanouse

Editors
Elsa Bell
Danielle Bird
Geneil Breeze
Judy Brunetti
Barry Childs-Helton
Barb Colter
Thomas F. Hayes
Jeanne Lemen
Rhonda L. Rieseberg
Alice Martina Smith

Technical Editors
Brian Blackman
Jim Ferguson

Figure Specialist
Wilfred R. Thebodeau

Book Designer
Amy Peppler-Adams

Editorial Assistants
Theresa Mathias
Jill L. Stanley
Michelle Williams

Production Team
Angela Bannan, Katy Bodenmiller,
Ayrika Bryant, Kim Cofer,
Juli Cook, Lisa Daugherty,
Karen Dodson, Terri Edwards,
Kimberly K. Hannel,
Angela P. Judy, Greg Kemp,
Jamie Milazzo, Ryan Rader,
Beth Rago, Nanci Sears Perry,
Tonya R. Simpson, Kim Scott,
Susan Shepard, SA Springer,
Rebecca Tapley, Suzanne Tully,
Elaine Webb, Dennis Wesner

Indexers
Charlotte Clapp
Jeanne Clark
Rebecca Mayfield
Johnna VanHoose

Composed in *Stone Serif* and *MCPdigital*
by Que Corporation

Dedication

This book is dedicated to my wife, Alexandra.

About the Author

Roger Jennings is a consultant specializing in Windows database and multimedia applications. He was a member of the Microsoft beta-test team for Microsoft Access 1.0, 1.1, and 2.0, Excel 4.0 and 5.0, Word for Windows 2.0 and 6.0, Project 4.0, Windows 3.1, Windows for Workgroups 3.1 and 3.11, Video for Windows 1.0 and 1.1, Visual Basic for DOS, Visual Basic 2.0 and 3.0 for Windows, and the Microsoft Professional Toolkit for Visual Basic 1.0. He is the author of Que Corporation's *Discover Windows 3.1 Multimedia* and *Access for Windows Hot Tips,* and is a contributing author to Que's *Excel Professional Techniques, Killer Windows Utilities*, and *Using Visual Basic 3.0.* He has written two other books about creating database applications with Access and Visual Basic, is a contributing editor of the Smart Access newsletter, and is a frequent contributor to the *Visual Basic Programmer's Journal* and the *Microsoft Developer Network News* and *CD-ROMs.*

Roger has more than 25 years of computer-related experience and has presented technical papers on computer hardware and software to the Academy of Sciences of the former USSR, the Society of Automotive Engineers, the American Chemical Society, and a wide range of other scientific and technical organizations. He is a principal of OakLeaf Systems, a Northern California software development and consulting firm; you may contact him via CompuServe (ID 70233,2161), the Internet (70233.2161@compuserve.com), or fax (510-839-9422).

Acknowledgments

Ron Person, the author of Part IV of this book, has written more than a dozen books for Que Corporation, including *Using Windows 3.1*, Special Edition; *Using Excel Version 5 for Windows*, Special Edition; *Using Word Version 6 for Windows*, Special Edition; and *Windows 3.1 QuickStart*. Ron is the principal consultant for Ron Person & Co., a San Francisco-based consulting firm that operates nationwide. He is a Microsoft consulting partner for Microsoft Excel and Microsoft Word. Ron's firm helps corporations develop in-house programming skills and support expertise for the embedded macro languages of Microsoft Access 2.0 and Word 6.0, and the Excel 5.0 version of Visual Basic for Applications. You may contact Ron at

Ron Person & Co.
P.O. Box 5647
3 Quixote Court
Santa Rosa, CA 95409
Fax: (707) 538-1485

Thanks to Monte Slichter, Kim Hightower, Gary Yukish, and all of the other members of Microsoft Corporation's Product Support Staff (PSS) for Access 2.0 during its beta-testing period. The PSS staff's prompt replies to questions concerning the prerelease versions of Access are especially appreciated. Scott Fallon, the Access product manager who represented the marketing group in the beta forum, provided valuable insight on Microsoft Corporation's marketing strategy for Access 2.0 and the Access Distribution Toolkit (ADT). Scott's consistent good humor and unflagging diplomacy, while under bombardment by an untold number of messages, made a major contribution to the success of the Access 2.0 test program.

Steve Schafer, product director, provided valuable insight and suggestions for the development of this book's content and organization. Sarah Browning, acquisitions editor, made sure that I did not fall too far behind the manuscript submission schedule. Chris Nelson, production editor, put in long hours to add last-minute changes incorporated in the testing releases of Access and still met a tight publication schedule. Technical editing was done by Brian Blackman and Jim Ferguson, each of whom is an Access expert. Their contributions to this book are gratefully acknowledged. The responsibility for any errors or omissions, however, rests solely on my shoulders.

Trademarks

Contents at a Glance

Contents

2 Up and Running with Access Tables   67

3 Navigating within Access   83

II Querying for Specific Information   285

8 Using Query by Example   287

9 Understanding Operators and Expressions in Access   315

III Creating Forms and Reports   437

12 Creating and Using Forms   439

V Integrating Access with Other Applications 699

24 Working with Structured Query Language   883

32 Migrating Access 1.x Applications to Access 2.0   1155

Appendixes   1163

A Glossary   1165

B Naming Conventions for Access Objects   1205

Introduction

Microsoft Access 2.0 is a mature, stable relational database management system (RDBMS) for creating Windows 3.1 and higher desktop and client-server database applications. Version 1.0 of Access revolutionized the Windows database market and achieved a new record for the sales of a Windows application—Microsoft Corporation received orders for more than 750,000 copies of Access 1.0 between its release data in mid-November, 1992, and January 31, 1993. Access 1.1, introduced in May, 1993, solved some of the shortcomings in Access 1.0, and the Access 1.1 Distribution Kit (ADK) gave developers the ability to release royalty-free, run-time versions of their Access applications. When *Using Access 2 for Windows,* Special Edition, was written, Microsoft had sold more than 1 million copies of Access 1.0 and 1.1, not counting upgrades from version 1.0 to 1.1.

One of the primary reasons for Access's initial success is that Access duplicates most of the capabilities of client-server relational database systems. Client-server RDBMSs are leading the way in transferring database applications from mini-computers and mainframes to networked PCs—a process called *downsizing.* Despite Access's power, the system is easy for nonprogrammers to use. Access 2.0 has a new, intuitive user interface, similar to that of Excel 5.0 and Microsoft Word for Windows 6.0. Buttons on new multiple toolbars offer shortcuts for menu commands; and wizards handle most of the mundane chores involved in creating new tables, queries, forms, graphs, and reports. Builders aid you in creating complex controls on forms and reports, as well as in writing expressions. *Cue Cards*, introduced in Access 1.0, help you quickly learn the basic operations of Access. Cue Cards now have found their way into other Microsoft applications for Windows.

Microsoft Access 1.0 introduced a new approach to writing macros that automate repetitive database operations. Access 2.0 extends version 1.x's full-featured programming language, *Access Basic*, which is modeled closely on Visual Basic 3.0 and Visual Basic for Applications. The syntax is easy to learn, yet Access Basic provides a vocabulary rich enough to satisfy veteran xBase and Paradox application developers. Access Basic is a dialect of Microsoft's *Object Basic*, the common application programming language class that includes Visual Basic, Word Basic, and Visual Basic for Applications (VBA). Microsoft Excel 5.0 and Project 4.0 now use VBA as their programming language. VBA is destined to be incorporated in all mainstream Windows applications published by Microsoft. You can expect future versions of Access to substitute an application-specific dialect of VBA for Access Basic. Fortunately, the Access Basic of version 2.0 and VBA are almost identical in their structure and syntax.

Access 2.0 now supports Object Linking and Embedding (OLE) 2.0 as a client application, giving you the benefits of in-place activation of objects, such as Excel 5.0 worksheets and Microsoft Word 6.0 documents stored in Access databases. Access 2.0 is the first application to use Microsoft's new OLE 2.0 server for creating graphs and charts, MSGraph5. Access 2.0 also lets you manipulate objects created by other recently released Microsoft applications for Windows using OLE Automation. Access is the first Microsoft product to take advantage of the new OLE 2.0 Custom Controls that Microsoft, third-party add-in software publishers, and you can create with Microsoft Visual C++ 1.5, the Microsoft Foundation Class Libraries, and the new OLE 2.0 Control Development Kit (CDK).

Access is specifically designed for creating multiuser applications where database files are shared on networks, and Access incorporates a sophisticated security system to prevent unauthorized persons from viewing or modifying the databases you create. Access 2.0 simplifies the labyrinthine security model employed by versions 1.x and makes creating secure Access applications much easier. In addition, you can alter permissions for your database objects using Access 2.0's new Documents collections.

Access has a unique database structure that combines all related data tables and their indexes, forms, reports, macros, and Access Basic code within a single .MDB database file. Access has the capability to import data from and export data to the more popular PC database and spreadsheet files, as well as text files. Access also can attach dBASE, FoxPro, Paradox, and Btrieve table files to databases and manipulate these files in their native formats. You also can use Access on workstations that act as clients of networked file and database servers in client-server database systems. Access, therefore, fulfills all the requirements of a professional relational database management system, as well as a front-end development tool for use with client-server databases. Microsoft has made many improvements to these features in Access 2.0. The most important new features of Access 2.0 are discussed in Chapter 1, "Access 2.0 for Access 1.1 Users—What's New."

The contributors to this book are seasoned users of database management systems and Windows. The author, Roger Jennings, has more than 10 years of experience in developing database systems for personal computers and is the author of several other books about Access and Windows database development. Contributing author Ron Person, who wrote Part IV of this book, "Powering Access with Macros," has written more than a dozen books for Que Corporation, including *Using Excel Version 5 for Windows*, Special Edition, and *Using Word Version 6 for Windows*, Special Edition. This book, therefore, isn't just a recompilation of the manuals that are shrink-wrapped with the installation disks. *Using Access 2 for Windows*, Special Edition, makes comparisons between Access and other popular database management applications when such comparisons are appropriate. This feature makes the book a useful tool in determining whether Access 2.0 is the appropriate database manager for you or the organization for which you work.

This book provides extensive coverage on using your existing database files in their native formats—alone or with those in Access's own file structure. Many readers have used the dBASE dot prompt and programming language, Paradox macros and PAL (the Paradox Application Language, including Object PAL), or both of these desktop database management systems. References to both *xBase* (the name applied to applications that use dialects of the dBASE programming language) and PAL appear throughout this book. If you aren't an xBase or Paradox user, just skip these references. You don't need experience in using a relational database management program, however, in order to create useful, even complex, database applications with what you learn in this book.

Several chapters of this book are devoted to using Access with other Windows applications, such as Microsoft Excel 5.0 and Microsoft Word 6.0, and the *applets* supplied with Windows 3.1 and Access 2.0: Paintbrush, Microsoft Graph 5, and WordArt. Applets are small but useful applications supplied as components of major applications; Paintbrush, for example, is a Windows OLE 1.0 applet. Using the multimedia features found in Windows 3.1 and Windows for Workgroups 3.11 with Access also is covered.

Who Should Read This Book?

Using Access 2 for Windows, Special Edition, takes an approach that is different from most books about database management applications. This book doesn't begin with the creation of a database for Widgets, Inc., nor does it require you to type a list of fictional customers for their new Widget II product line in order to learn the basics of Access. Instead, this book makes the following basic assumptions about your interest in Microsoft's relational database management system:

- You have one or more PCs operating in a business, professional, institutional, or government agency setting.

- You are using or have decided to use Microsoft Windows 3.1, Windows for Workgroups 3.11, or Windows NT 3.1 as the operating environment for at least some, if not all, of your PCs.

- You are able to navigate Microsoft Windows 3.1 using the mouse and keyboard. Books about DOS database managers no longer attempt to teach you DOS, nor does *Using Access 2 for Windows*, Special Edition, try to teach you Windows fundamentals.

- You aren't starting from "ground zero." You now have or will have access via your PC to data that you want to process with a Windows database manager. You already may have acquired Access and want to learn to use it more quickly and effectively. Or you may be considering using Access as the database manager for yourself, your department or division, or your entire organization.

- Your existing data is in the form of one or more database, spreadsheet, or even plain text files that you want to manipulate with a relational database management system. Access can process the most common varieties of all three types of files.

- If your data is on a mini- or mainframe computer, you are connected to that computer by a local area network and a database gateway or through terminal emulation software and an adapter card. Otherwise, you are able to obtain the data on PC-compatible disks; some people call this method *SneakerNet* or *FootWare*.

If some or all of your data is in the form of ASCII or ANSI text files, or files from a spreadsheet application, you need to know how to create an Access database from the beginning and import the data into Access's own .MDB file structure. If your data is in the form of dBASE, FoxPro, Paradox, or Btrieve files, you can attach the files as tables and continue to use them in the format native to your prior database manager. (The Microsoft ODBC Desktop Database Driver kit lets you attach Excel and text files to Access databases.) The capability to attach files in their native format is an important advantage to

have during conversion from one database management system to another.
Each of these subjects receives thorough coverage in this book.

Using Access 2 for Windows, Special Edition, is designed to accommodate readers who are new to database management; who are occasional or frequent
users of dBASE for DOS, FoxPro, or Paradox for DOS or Windows; or who are
seasoned database application developers.

How This Book Is Organized

Using Access 2 for Windows, Special Edition, is divided into eight parts that are
arranged in increasing levels of detail and complexity. Each division after Part
I draws on the knowledge and experience you have gained in the prior parts,
so use of the book in a linear, front-to-back manner through Part IV, "Powering Access with Macros," is recommended during the initial learning process.
After you have absorbed the basics, *Using Access 2 for Windows*, Special Edition, becomes a valuable reference tool for the advanced topics.

As you progress through the chapters in this book, you create a model of an
Access application called *Personnel Actions*. In Chapter 4, "Working with Access Databases and Tables," you create the Personnel Actions table. In the
following chapters, you add new features to the Personnel Actions application until, when you reach Chapter 18, "Creating Macros for Forms and
Reports," you have a complete, automated method of adding and editing
Personnel Actions data. When you are learning Access, therefore, it is important that you read this book in a sequential manner, at least through Chapter
18. Make sure to perform the example exercises for the Personnel Actions
application each time you encounter them, because succeeding examples
build on your prior work.

The eight parts of *Using Access 2 for Windows*, Special Edition, and the topics
they cover are described in the following sections.

Part I

Part I, "Learning Access Fundamentals," introduces you to Access and many
of the unique features that make Access the easiest to use of all database managers. The chapters in Part I deal almost exclusively with tables, the basic
elements of Access databases.

Chapter 1, "Access 2.0 for Access 1.1 Users—What's New?," provides a
summary of the most important new features of Access 2.0 and a detailed
description of each of these additions and improvements. Much of the
content of this chapter is of interest primarily to readers who now use

Access 1.x, but readers new to Access will benefit from the explanations of why many of these features are significant in everyday use of Access 2.0.

In Chapter 2, "Up and Running with Access Tables," you learn how to open an Access database, view a table, use a typical query, add a few new data items, view the results of your work, and finally print a formatted report.

Chapter 3, "Navigating within Access," shows you how to navigate Access by explaining its toolbar and menu choices and how they relate to the structure of Access.

Chapter 4, "Working with Access Databases and Tables," delves into the details of Access tables, how to create tables, and how to choose the optimum data types from the many new types Access offers.

Chapter 5, "Entering, Editing, and Validating Data in Tables," shows you how to arrange the data in tables to suit your needs and limit the data displayed to only that information you want. Finding and replacing data in the fields of tables also is covered here.

Chapter 6, "Sorting, Finding, and Filtering Data in Tables," describes how to add new records to tables, enter data in the new records, and edit data in existing records.

Chapter 7, "Attaching, Importing, and Exporting Tables," explains how you import and export files of other database managers, spreadsheet applications, and even ASCII files you may download from information utilities such as Dow Jones News Service or government-sponsored databases.

Part II

Part II, "Querying for Specific Information," explains how to create Access queries to select the way you view data contained in tables and how you take advantage of Access's relational database structure to link multiple tables with joins.

Chapter 8, "Using Query by Example," starts you off with simple queries created with Access's graphic query-by-example (QBE) design window. You learn how to choose the fields of the tables that are included in your query and return query result sets from these tables.

Chapter 9, "Understanding Operators and Expressions in Access," introduces you to the operators and expressions that you need to create queries that provide a meaningful result. You use the Immediate Window of the Access Basic code editor to evaluate the expressions you write.

In Chapter 10, "Creating Multitable and Crosstab Queries," you create relations between tables, called *joins*, and learn how to add criteria to queries so that the query result set includes only those records you want. Chapter 10 also takes you through the process of designing powerful crosstab queries to summarize data and to present information in a format similar to that of worksheets.

Chapter 11, "Using Action Queries," shows you how to develop action queries that update the tables underlying append, delete, update, and make-table queries. Chapter 11 also covers Access 2.0's new cascading update and cascading deletion features.

Part III

Part III, "Creating Forms and Reports," is your introduction to the primary application objects of Access. (Tables and queries are considered database objects.) Forms make your Access applications come alive with the control objects you add using Access 2.0's new toolbox. Access's full-featured report generator lets you print fully formatted reports or save reports to files that you can process in Excel or Word.

Chapter 12, "Creating and Using Forms," shows you how to use Access's Form Wizards to create simple forms that you can modify to suit your particular needs.

Chapter 13, "Designing Custom Multitable Forms," shows you how to design custom forms for viewing and entering your own data with Access's advanced form design tools.

Chapter 14, "Printing Basic Reports and Mailing Labels," describes how to design and print simple reports with Access's Report Wizard and how to print preformatted mailing labels using the Mailing Label Wizard.

Chapter 15, "Preparing Advanced Reports," describes how to use more sophisticated sorting and grouping techniques, as well as subreports, to obtain a result that exactly meets your detail and summary data reporting requirements.

Part IV

Part IV, "Powering Access with Macros," written by contributing author Ron Person, is your introduction to the first level of programming provided by Access 2.0.

Chapter 16, "Automating Applications with Macros: An Overview," is an introduction to Access macros. This chapter shows you how to write simple macros that run queries and open other forms when you click a command button control you place on a form.

Chapter 17, "Understanding Access Macros," explains how you create the macros that automate your applications, and gives you examples of combining Access 2.0's standard macro actions into macro objects that take the place of programming code required by other desktop database management applications.

Chapter 18, "Creating Macros for Forms and Reports," gives you specific examples of useful macros that you can use for tasks such as opening a form, changing a form's size, adding and deleting records, and printing a form.

Part V
Part V, "Integrating Access with Other Applications," shows you how to use the new Object Linking and Embedding (OLE) 2.0 features of Access 2.0 with Microsoft Graph 5.0, Excel 5.0, and Word 6.0.

Chapter 19, "Using OLE 2.0," explains Object Linking and Embedding, the new principles that make OLE 2.0 a major advance in Windows application development, how these principles apply to your Access database applications, and how you use OLE 2.0 server applications with Access 2.0.

Chapter 20, "Adding Graphics to Forms and Reports," describes how to take best advantage of Access OLE Object field data type and bound object frames to display graphics and play multimedia objects stored in your Access tables. Adding static graphics to forms and reports with unbound object frames is also covered.

Chapter 21, "Using Access with Microsoft Excel," gives you detailed examples of exchanging data between Access and Excel 5.0 workbooks by using OLE 2.0 and the dynamic data exchange functions that you can use with Access forms and reports without employing Access Basic code.

Chapter 22, "Using Access with Microsoft Word and Mail Merge," shows you how to store documents in OLE Object fields, and how to use Access's OLE Automation Mail Merge Wizard to interactively create form letters and envelopes addressed with data from your Access applications.

Part VI
Part VI, "Using Advanced Access Techniques," covers the theoretical and practical aspects of relational database design and Structured Query Language

(SQL), and then goes on to describe how to set up and use secure Access applications on a local area network. Part VI also describes how you use the Open Database Connectivity (ODBC) Application Programming Interface (API) to create Access front-ends for client-server databases.

Chapter 23, "Exploring Relational Database Design and Implementation," describes the process you use to create relational database tables from real-world data—a technique called *normalizing the database structure*. This chapter explains how to use the Database Documentor add-in included with Access to create a data dictionary that fully identifies each object in your database.

Chapter 24, "Working with Structured Query Language," explains how Access uses its particular dialect of SQL to create queries and how you write your own SQL statements. Special emphasis is given to the extensions to Access SQL included in Access 2.0, such as UNION queries and subqueries, as well as Access 2.0's new implementation of SQL's Data Definition Language (DDL).

Chapter 25, "Securing Multiuser Network Applications," explains how to set up Access to share database files on a network and how to use the security features of Access to prevent unauthorized viewing of or tampering with your database files.

Chapter 26, "Connecting to Client-Server Databases," introduces you to the ODBC API and shows you how to create ODBC data sources from client-server databases and Excel .XLS files, as well as the basics of designing Access front-ends for client-server databases.

Part VII

Part VII, "Programming with Access Basic," assumes that you have no programming experience in any language. Part VI explains the principles of writing programming code in Access Basic and applies the principles to using OLE Automation and Dynamic Data Exchange (DDE) and OLE Automation to exchange data with an Excel 5.0 worksheet.

Chapter 27, "Writing Access Basic Code," describes how to use Access Basic to create user-defined functions and to write simple procedures that you activate with macros or directly from events. Access 2.0's newly-implemented Code Behind Forms feature that lets you store event-handling code in Form and Report objects is also described.

Chapter 28, "Understanding the Data Access Object Class," shows you how to declare and use members of the Access database engine's object collections, such as TableDefs, to create new tables and modify the properties of tables with Access Basic code.

Chapter 29, "Exchanging Data with OLE Automation and DDE," gives you a complete, working application that uses either OLE Automation or Access Basic DDE commands to transfer data to and from an Excel 5.0 worksheet.

Part VIII

Part VIII, "Completing an Access Application," is oriented toward adding the finishing touches to applications you create for others to use and converting your existing Access 1.1 database applications to Access 2.0 standards.

Chapter 30, "Using the Access 2.0 Developer's Toolkit," describes the content of the ADT, which replaces Access 1.1's Distribution Kit, and how to design applications for use with the run-time version of Access 2.0.

Chapter 31, "Adding On-Line Help for Users," outlines the techniques you use to create applications for others to use, including how to write help files to answer users' questions about how the application works. This chapter also describes how you use the help compiler (HC31.EXE) included with the ADT.

Chapter 32, "Migrating Access 1.x Applications to Access 2.0," tells you what changes you need to make your current Access 1.1 database applications to assure compatibility with and to take full advantage of the new features of Access 2.0.

Appendixes

Appendix A, the "Glossary," presents a glossary of the terms, abbreviations, and acronyms used in this book that may not be familiar to you and cannot be found in commonly used dictionaries.

Appendix B, "Naming Conventions for Access Objects," incorporates a proposed set of standardized naming conventions for Access objects and Access Basic variables.

Appendix C, "Data Dictionary for the Personnel Actions Table," shows you how to implement the Personnel Actions table that is used for many of the examples in this book.

How This Book Is Designed

The following special features are included in this book to assist readers:

- Readers who have never used a database management application are provided with quick-start examples to gain confidence and experience while using Access with the Northwind Traders demonstration data set.

Like Access, this book uses the *tabula rasa* approach: each major topic begins with the assumption that the reader has no experience with the subject. Therefore, when a button from the toolbar or control object toolbox is used, its icon is displayed in the margin.

■ Users of the two major DOS database managers will find marginal icons that identify important points of similarity with or departures from xBase and Paradox methodologies. These icons are accompanied by brief explanations and, where necessary and possible, short workarounds (methods of implementing the equivalent of xBase and Paradox commands not available in Access). Many of these icons also will apply to other RDBMSs that have related macro or programming languages.

■ Notes offer advice to aid you in using Access, describe differences between Access 2 and 1.x, and explain the few remaining anomalies you find in version 2.0 of Access. In a few instances, notes explain similarities or differences between Access and other database management applications.

■ Tips describe shortcuts and alternative approaches to gaining an objective. These tips are based on the experience the authors gained during more than two years of testing successive alpha and beta versions of Access and the Access Distribution Kit.

■ Cautions are provided when an action can lead to an unexpected or unpredictable result, including loss of data; the text provides an explanation of how you can avoid such a result.

■ Features that are new or have been modified in Access 2.0 are indicated by the version 2.0 icon in the margin, unless the change is only cosmetic. Where the changes are extensive and apply to an entire section of a chapter, the icon appears to the left or right of the section head.

■ Tips, techniques, and cautions that apply to the design of applications you plan to run under MSARN200.EXE, run-time Access, are indicated by the ADT 2.0 marginal icon. You are likely going to need to change the design of your Access applications to obtain a satisfactory result under run-time Access.

■ All sample databases and associated queries, forms, reports, and the like, used in this book will be posted to the Prentice Hall Computer Publishing forum on CompuServe. GO PHCP while on-line with CompuServe and browse the Libraries using the keywords USING ACCESS.

▶ "Starting
Access," p. 68

Most software manuals require you to wade through all the details relating to a particular function of an application in a single chapter or part, before you progress to the next topic. In contrast, *Using Access 2 for Windows*, Special Edition, first takes you through the most frequently used steps to manipulate database tables and then concentrates on using your existing files with Access. Advanced features and nuances of Access are covered in later chapters. This type of structure requires cross-referencing so that you can easily locate more detailed or advanced coverage of the topic. Cross-references to specific sections in other chapters occur in the margins next to the material they pertain to, such as in the sample reference next to this paragraph.

Typographic Conventions Used in This Book

This book uses various typesetting styles to distinguish between explanatory and instructional text, text you enter in dialogs, and text you enter in code-editing windows.

Typefaces and Fonts

Terms employed by the graphics profession are used in this book to designate typefaces and fonts used in forms and reports. The terms *typeface* and *face* are substituted interchangeably for the term *font* when referring to multiple sizes of the same typeface. *Font* is used to indicate type in a single size, such as Courier New 12, indicating the Courier New (TrueType) family, 12-point size, roman (regular) style. A typeface *family* includes all available styles of a face: black, bold, normal, light, condensed, expanded, italic, oblique, and so on.

The term *font* is used by printers to mean a collection of characters of a single typeface, style, and size. In the days of metal type, these characters were stored in trays with compartments of varying sizes proportional to the frequency of use of the character. When Hewlett-Packard introduced its first LaserJet series of laser printers, the term *font* was properly applied to the choices offered because each was a bit map of a specific family, style, and size, like Courier 10 Italic. Printers using the Adobe PostScript page description language, which introduced scalable typefaces, used *font* instead of *typeface* or *face* to describe the outline used to create typefaces. This transgression was perpetuated by the Microsoft/Apple TrueType products designed to compete with PostScript.

Key Combinations and Menu Choices

Key combinations that you use to perform Windows operations are indicated by joining the keys with a plus sign: Alt+F4, for example. This indicates that you press and hold the Alt key while pressing the function key F4. In the rare cases when you must press and release a control key, and *then* enter another key, the keys are separated by a comma without an intervening space: Alt,F4, for example. Key combinations that perform menu operations that require more than one keystroke are called *shortcut keys*. An example of such a shortcut is the Windows 3.1 key combination, Ctrl+C, which substitutes for the **C**opy choice of the **E**dit menu in most Windows applications.

To select a menu option with the keyboard instead of the mouse, you press the letter that appears in boldface type in the menu option. Sequences of individual menu items are separated by a space: **E**dit **C**ut, for example. The Alt key required to activate a choice from the main menu is assumed and not shown.

Successive entries in dialogs follow the tab order of the dialog. *Tab order* is the sequence in which the caret moves when you press the Tab key to move from one entry or control option to another, a process known as *changing the focus*. The entry or control option that has the focus is the one that receives keystrokes or mouse clicks. Command buttons, option buttons, and check box choices are treated similarly to menu choices, but their access key letters aren't set in bold type. Text box entries for choosing files sometimes are shown with the menu choices that precede them, as in the example **F**ile **O**pen DATABASE.MDB.

When, for example, you must substitute a name of your own making for a text box entry, lowercase italic type is used for the substitutable portion, as in the example **F**ile **S**ave **A**s *filename*.MDB. Here, you substitute the name of your file for *filename*, but the .MDB extension is required because it is in a roman (standard) face. File and path names are capitalized in the text and headings of this book, but conform to standards established by Windows 3.1 common dialogs—all lowercase—in code examples.

SQL Statements and Keywords in Other Languages

SQL statements and code examples in other languages, including dialects of Object Basic other than Access Basic, are set in a `monospace` font. Keywords of SQL statements, such as `SELECT`, are set in all uppercase, as are the keywords of foreign database programming languages when they are used in comparative examples, such as `DO WHILE…ENDDO`. Ellipses indicate intervening programming code that isn't shown in the text or examples.

Square brackets in `monospace boldface` type (`[]`) that appear within Access Basic SQL statements don't indicate optional items as they do in syntax descriptions. In this case, the square brackets are used in lieu of quotation marks to frame a literal string or to allow use of a table and field names, such as `[Personnel Actions]`, that include embedded spaces or special punctuation, or field names that are identical to reserved words in Access and Access Basic.

Typographic Conventions Used for Access Basic

This book uses a special set of typographic conventions for references to Access Basic keywords in the presentation of Access Basic examples:

- Monospace (MCPdigital) type is used for all examples of Access Basic code, as in the following statement:

  ```
  Dim NewArray ( ) As Long
  ReDim NewArray (9, 9, 9)
  ```

- Monospace type also is used when referring to names of properties of Access database objects, such as `SourceConnectStr`. The captions for text boxes and drop-down lists in which you enter values of properties, such as Source Connect Str, are set in the proportionally spaced font (Stone Serif) of this book.

- `Bold monospace` type is used for all Access Basic reserved words and type-declaration symbols (which are seldom used in the code examples in this book), as shown in the preceding example. Standard function names in Access Basic also are set in bold type so that reserved words, standard function names, and reserved symbols stand out from variable and function names and values you assign to variables.

- *Italic monospace* type indicates a replaceable item. For example,

  ```
  Dim DataItem As String
  ```

- ***Bold italic monospace*** type indicates a replaceable reserved word, such as a data type, as in

  ```
  Dim DataItem As DataType
  ```

  `DataType` is replaced by a keyword corresponding to the desired Access Basic data type, such as `String` or `Variant`.

- An ellipsis (. . .) substitutes for code not shown in syntax and code examples, as in `If. . .Then. . .Else. . .End If`.

- French braces ({}) surrounding two or more identifiers separated by the pipe symbol (¦) indicate that you must choose one of these identifiers, as in

  ```
  Do {While¦Until}...Loop
  ```

  In this case, you must use either the **While** or the **Until** reserved word in your statement.

- Square brackets ([ ], not in bold type) surrounding an identifier indicate that the identifier is optional, as in

  ```
  Set tblName = dbName.OpenTable(strTableName[, fExclusive])
  ```

  Here, the fExclusive flag, if set **True**, opens the table specified by strTableName for exclusive use. fExclusive is an optional argument.

System Requirements for Access

Access 2.0 is a very resource-intensive application. Access must be installed on an 80386- or 80486-based IBM-compatible PC with a fixed disk drive capable of running Windows 3.0 or higher in standard or enhanced mode. You will find execution of Access on computers using the 80386SX CPU to be quite slow, and operation may be glacial with large tables. Although the documentation accompanying Access 1.1 said that you could use Access 1.1 on a computer with only 4M of RAM, a bare minimum of 6M to 8M is now required for Access 1.1. If you plan to use Access for extensive handling of graphic images or run it often with other applications using object linking and embedding (OLE), 8–12M of RAM should be installed. Using OLE 2.0 to manipulate complex objects, such as large bitmaps, requires substantial amounts of memory. (16M of RAM is recommended if you plan to make extensive use of OLE 2.0 or OLE Automation.) As a rule, adding more RAM, at least to 16M, is more cost-effective than increasing processor speed or power.

A complete installation of Access 2.0 requires a total of about 20M of free disk space, and you should reserve at least 5M to store the new databases you create. You also should have a permanent Windows swap file of at least 9M (Microsoft recommends a total of 25M of RAM plus permanent swap file space for best performance.) Access also make use of temporary files in the directory you specify with the SET TEMP= entry in your AUTOEXEC.BAT file. About 12.5M is required in your \ACCESS directory, and the sample applications require about 2.5M in \ACCESS\SAMPAPPS. An additional 1.2M of files associated with the setup application are stored in \ACCESS\SETUP. The remaining 4M or so of files are copied to subdirectories of your \WINDOWS directory. The additional space occupied by this group of files depends on whether you have installed other OLE 2.0-compatible applications. Plan on reserving 10M for the Access 2.0 Developers Toolkit if you plan to distribute applications that operate with run-time Access. Access 2.0, Windows 3.1, and Windows for Workgroups 3.11 have been tested under Stac Electronics' Stacker 2.x and 3.x fixed disk file compression application during the course of writing this book. Stacker or DoubleSpace reduce the physical fixed disk space required to install Access 2.0 by a factor of about 1.5 to 1.7. Access 2.0 and the Access 2.0 ADK have been found to operate satisfactorily with Stacker 3.0 and 3.1.

Note

Fixed disk compression utilities such as Stacker and the DoubleSpace compression utility supplied by Microsoft with MS-DOS 6.x do not compress encrypted Access .MDB files. Compression utilities rely on creating *tokens* that represent repeating groups of bytes in files. The utility stores the tokens and a single copy of the translation of each token. Encryption removes most, if not all, of the repeating groups of bytes in the file. More forceful compression techniques, such as those employed by PKWare's PKZIP utility, can achieve some (but usually not worthwhile) compression.

A mouse or trackball isn't a requirement for using the Access applications you create, but you need one of these two pointing devices to select and size the objects that you add to forms and reports using Access's toolbox. Because a pointing device is required to create Access applications, this book dispenses with the traditional "Here's how you do it with the mouse..." and "If you want to use the keyboard..." duplicate methodology in step-by-step examples. Designing your Access applications with shortcut keys to eliminate mouse operations, however, speeds keyboard-oriented data entry by enabling the operator to keep his or her fingers on the keyboard during the entire process.

Chapters 21 and 29 use data from a large worksheet of stock prices created by Ideas Unlimited that is available for downloading from CompuServe Information Services. The name of the file is STOCK.ZIP, and it is located in Library 3 (Excel for the PC) of CompuServe's Microsoft Excel Forum (GO MSEXCEL). STOCK.ZIP is compressed with PKWare's shareware archiving program, PKZIP.EXE. You need a modem, communication software, and a CompuServe account to obtain the data and a copy of PK204G.EXE that contains

PKUNZIP.EXE to decompress STOCK.ZIP. Information on obtaining a CompuServe account is provided in a section later in this introduction. If you don't have a modem, now is the time to install one. An external 9,600- or 14,400-bps modem is recommended for users who are new to PC telecommunications because the light-emitting diodes let you know what is happening (or not happening), and external modems don't occupy a valuable adapter card slot. External 14,400-bps fax modems now are available in the $150–$200 range.

Although upgrading to Windows 3.1 wasn't necessary to use Access 1.x, you'll need Windows 3.1 or Windows for Workgroups 3.11 or higher to use the OLE 2.0 features of Access 2.0. The principal advantage of Windows for Workgroups 3.11 or higher, aside from its improved networking capabilities, is faster disk operation if you use the 32-bit disk access option offered by Windows for Workgroups 3.11. (Unfortunately, 32-bit disk access is not available with Windows for Workgroups 3.11 if you use SCSI fixed disk drives.)

Other Sources of Information for Access

SQL and relational database design, which are discussed in Chapters 19 and 20, are the subject of myriad guides and texts covering one or both of these topics. Articles in database-related periodicals and files you download from on-line information utilities, such as CompuServe, provide up-to-date assistance in using Access 2.0. The following sections provide a bibliography of database-related books and periodicals, as well as a brief description of the CompuServe forums of interest to Access users.

Bibliography

Introduction to Databases, by James J. Townsend, gives a thorough explanation of personal computer databases and their design. This book is especially recommended if the subject of PC databases is new to you. (Indianapolis, 1993, Que Corporation, ISBN 0-88022-840-7.)

Using SQL, by Dr. George T. Chou, provides a detailed description of SQL, concentrating on the dialects used by dBASE IV and ORACLE databases, and explains the essentials of the design of relational database systems. (Indianapolis, 1990, Que Corporation, ISBN 0-88022-507-6.)

Understanding the New SQL: A Complete Guide, by Jim Melton and Alan R. Simpson, describes the history and implementation of the American National

Standards Institute's X3.135.1-1992 standard for the latest official version of Structured Query Language, SQL-92. Jim Melton of Digital Equipment Corp. was the editor of the ANSI SQL-92 standard, which consists of more than 500 pages of fine print. (San Mateo, CA, 1993, Morgan Kaufmann Publishers, ISBN 1-55860-245-3.)

American National Standards Institute (ANSI) supplies copies of its standards and those originating from the International Standards Organization (ISO), headquartered at the United Nations facility in Geneva. You can get copies of ANSI Standard X3.135.1-1992 by writing to the following address:

American National Standards Institute
11 West 42nd Street
New York, NY 10036
(212) 642-4900 (Sales Department)

SQL Access Group (SAG) is a consortium of users and vendors of SQL database management systems. SAG publishes a number of standards that supplement ANSI X3.135. The Open Database Connectivity (ODBC) API developed by Microsoft Corporation is derived from SAG's Call-Level Interface (CLI) standard.

SQL Access Group
1010 El Camino Real, Suite 380
Menlo Park, CA 94025
(415) 323-7992 x221

Periodicals

The following are a few of the magazines and newsletters that cover Access exclusively or in which articles on Microsoft Access appear on a regular basis:

- *Access Advisor*, published by Advisor Communications International, Inc., is a full-color, bi-monthly magazine intended to serve Access users and developers. You can supplement your subscription with an accompanying diskette that includes sample databases, utilities, and other software tools for Access.

- *Data Based Advisor* is published by Data Based Solutions, Inc., a firm related to the publishers of Access Advisor. John Hawkins, Editor-in-Chief of *Data Based Advisor*, holds the same position with *Access Advisor* and *FoxPro Advisor* magazines. *Data Based Advisor* covers the gamut of desktop databases, with emphasis on xBase products, but Access receives its share of coverage, too.

- *DBMS* magazine, published by M&T, a Miller-Freeman company, is devoted to database technology as a whole, but *DBMS* concentrates on the growing field of client-server RDBMS. *DBMS* covers subjects, such as SQL and relational database design, that are of interest to all developers, not just those who use Visual Basic.

- *Inside Microsoft Access* is a monthly newsletter of Access tips and techniques of the Cobb Group, a subsidiary of Microsoft Corporation, which publishes a variety of newsletters on products such as Visual Basic and Paradox.

- *Smart Access* is a monthly newsletter of Pinnacle Publishing, Inc., which publishes several other database-related newsletters. *Smart Access* is directed primarily to developers and Access power users. This newsletter tends toward advanced topics, such as creating libraries and using the Windows API with Access Basic. A diskette is included with each issue. Like other publications directed to Access users, much of the content of *Smart Access* is of equal interest to Visual Basic database developers.

- *Visual Basic Programmer's Journal* (formerly *BasicPRO*) is a bi-monthly magazine from Fawcett Technical Publications that covers all of the dialects of the BASIC language, with emphasis on Visual Basic, Visual Basic for Applications, and Access Basic. *Visual Basic Programmer's Journal* has a monthly column devoted to database topics.

On-Line Sources

Your modem-equipped PC enables you to tap the resources of on-line commercial and government databases, as well as special-interest electronic bulletin board systems (BBSs) run by individuals and organizations.

CompuServe

Microsoft provides technical support of Access and the ADK in the MSACCESS forum (GO MSACCESS) on CompuServe Information Services. The MSACCESS forum is one of the most active application forums on CompuServe, and a substantial number of Microsoft Product Support Specialists are available to answer technical questions on Access topics. Many authors of books about Access and contributors to publications that feature Access, as well as professional Access developers, participate regularly in this forum. A variety of useful utility and sample applications written by Microsoft staff members and third-party developers also are available for no charge other than the cost of connection time to CompuServe. For information on joining CompuServe, which costs about $10 per hour at 2,400 bps, call (800) 848-8199.

The Microsoft Knowledge Base (GO MSKB) contains text files of technical tips, workarounds for bugs, and other useful information about Microsoft applications. Use "Access" as the search term, but remember to turn on your communication software's capture-to-file feature because the information is in the form of messages that scroll down your screen, not in the form files.

Support for Windows for Workgroups is provided in the Windows for Workgroups forum (GO MSWRKGRPS). The ODBC Library (Lib 10) of the Windows Extensions forum (GO WINEXT) provides technical assistance in using the ODBC API and the Microsoft ODBC Desktop Database Drivers kit.

Data Based Advisor magazine operates a forum on CompuServe (GO DBA) that covers a wide range of database topics, including client-server systems. One section of the DBA forum is devoted to Microsoft Access. *DBMS* magazine also has its own forum (GO DBMS) on CompuServe. Both of these forums cover Access development topics.

Other On-Line Sources of Information

Private electronic bulletin boards (BBSs) are a rich source of information on database topics in general. As use of Access becomes widespread, you can expect several BBSs across the country to specialize in Access application development, or at least devote a conference or a files section to Access. The telephone numbers and the subjects in which BBSs specialize are listed in local computer-based periodicals and magazines devoted to on-line telecommunication.

Part I

Learning Access Fundamentals

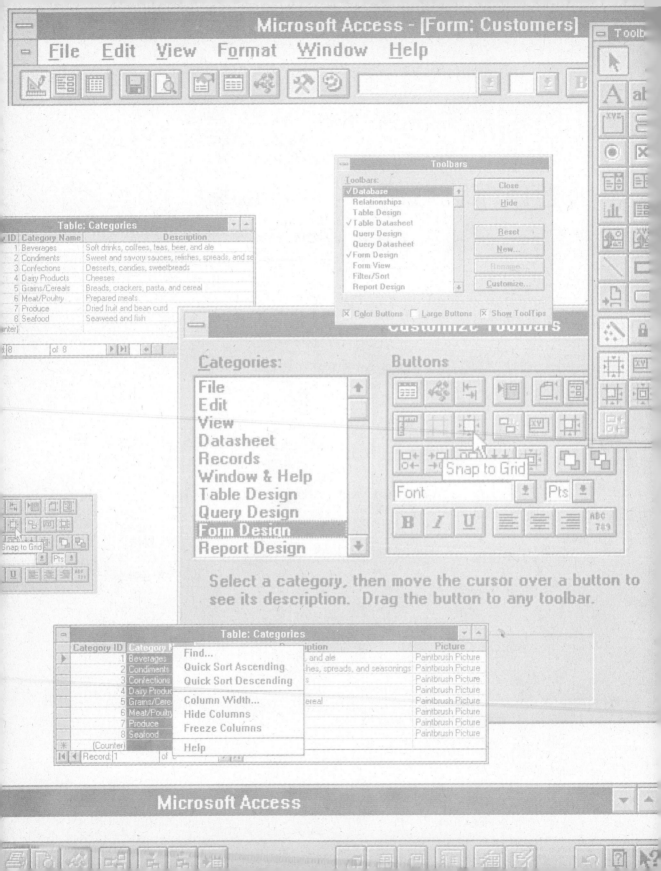

Chapter 1

Access 2.0 for Access 1.1 Users—What's New?

Access 2.0 is a *major* upgrade from Access 1.1. Most of the features that database end-users and developers requested during the beta testing programs for both Access 1.0 and Access 1.1 have been incorporated in Access 2.0. The JET (Joint Engine Technology) database engine of Access 1.x, now referred to simply as *Jet,* has undergone a major upgrade in version 2.0. Many of the new features of Access 2.0, such as its more versatile toolbars and tab-style dialogs, are evident when you launch Access 2.0. Incremental improvements, such as Jet's faster query processing, are more subtle and depend on your application's table and query design.

This chapter includes a categorized summary of what's new in Access 2.0; it also includes a detailed description of each of the major new features and improvements found in Access 2.0, and why these new elements are important. Microsoft has made several hundred additions and changes to Access 1.1; the changes are about evenly divided between modifications to the user interface and additions of elements designed to accommodate the growing Access developer community. In all of the following chapters of this book, the "New in Access 2.0" icon, shown here in the margin, indicates a new or altered feature. Because this chapter is devoted entirely to the new features of and improvements to Access 2.0, the icon only appears once in this chapter.

Access

2.0

Some of the main topics in this chapter are

- Access 2.0's new user interface

- The Add-In Manager

- Using OLE 2.0 and OLE Automation with Access 2.0

- Additions to Access 2.0 SQL

- New features for Access developers

- The Access 2.0 Developer's Toolkit

Summarizing Access 2.0's New Features and Improvements

Access 2.0's new features and improvements and a new Access product offered by Microsoft fall into the nine categories of the following list:

- *User interface* (UI) modifications make Access 2.0 conform to recently released versions of other mainstream Microsoft applications for Windows, such as Excel 5.0 and Microsoft Word 6.0. The primary changes to the UI include new customizable toolbars, floating shortcut menus that appear when you click the right mouse button, and a variety of new and improved wizards and builders to make creating new Access 2.0 applications faster and easier. The Properties window now groups object properties by type; this is important because Access 2.0 objects have many new properties.

- *Add-in management* for library databases is now an integral part of Access 2.0, emulating Excel 5.0's Add-ins feature. Access 2.0's Add-In Manager controls the attachment of library databases by adding or removing entries in the Access private initialization file, MSACC20.INI (the new name for Access 1.x's MSACCESS.INI). In addition to wizards, Access 2.0 includes new add-ins for documenting your applications, managing attached tables, importing objects from other Access databases, and creating menu macros. (The Menu Builder add-in is a builder, so it is described in the section devoted to Access 2.0 builders.) Although not technically an add-in, Access 2.0's new built-in telephone AutoDialer feature replaces third-party autodial libraries.

- *Data integrity maintenance* is strengthened by enforcing domain integrity (data validation) rules at the table level. In other words, you can't violate a data validation rule that you establish for the field of a table with an update query or when you enter data in a form. Referential integrity (preventing orphan records) now is maintained on attached Access 2.0 tables, and Access 2.0 provides optional automatic cascading updates and deletions. The new graphic Relationships window makes establishing relations and enforcing referential integrity easier. Input masks for text boxes and the new Input Mask Wizard makes entering valid data faster.

- *Application interoperability* enhancements include in-place activation (also called *in-place* or *in situ* editing) of OLE objects you create with OLE 2.0 server applications, OLE Automation to manipulate objects created by OLE 2.0 servers, and support for mail-enabled applications.

(*OLE* is an acronym for Object Linking and Embedding.) Operations that export reports to other applications in .XLS, .RTF, and .TXT file formats also have been enhanced. A new driver supports the Paradox 4.x file structure, and you can export mailing lists directly to Microsoft Word 6.0's Mail Merge window.

- *Performance improvements* make Access 2.0 applications run substantially faster than preceding versions if you have 8M or more of RAM. The Access 2.0 database engine sports an improved query optimizer (QJet). FoxPro's Rushmore methodology speeds queries against large Access tables with indexes on all fields included in SQL WHERE criteria. The remote query optimizer (RJet) has a variety of new features that increase the efficiency of client-server decision support and transaction processing systems. The new System Info dialog displays more than you may want to know about your computer's use of resources.

- *Structured Query Language (SQL) extensions* let you create UNION queries and add subqueries to your SELECT queries. TOP *n* and TOP *nn* PERCENT queries return only rows for the highest-valued members of a query set. Access SQL now supports SQL's Data Definition Language (DDL) so that you can create new tables in an Access database with simple SQL statements. SQL pass-through for client-server database front-ends is now a built-in feature of Access 2.0. You need to use the SQL window to write SQL statements that create SELECT queries with the new UNION, TOP, and subquery features, so Microsoft enhanced Access 1.1's SQL window to make writing SQL statements in Access 2.0 easier.

- *Multiuser and security functions* have been enhanced in version 2.0. A new Workgroup Administrator application, WRKGADM.EXE, lets you join an existing workgroup or create a SYSTEM.MDA file for a new workgroup. An expanded collection of permissions lets you assign new Administer, Update Data, Insert Data, and Delete Data permissions for groups and individual users.

- *Developer features* focus on bringing Access 2.0 into conformance with the database programmability standards established by Visual Basic 3.0. You now can alter the values of most form and report properties in run mode. More events (still called *properties* in Access 2.0) have been added, and you can write event-handling procedures (called *event handlers* in this book) that are stored with the form or report. Visual Basic 3.0's data access object (DAO) class has been added to Access 2.0, together with Access-specific objects (such as the Users and Groups collections) that are not available in Visual Basic 3.0.

■ *Microsoft Access Solutions Pack*, which is sold separately by Microsoft, includes four Access 2.0 applications that serve as examples or starting points for creating your own Access database applications. The Access Solutions Pack provides a Sales Contact Manager, Registration Desk, Asset Management, and PC Help Desk application. These applications illustrate a variety of database design and programming techniques that use macros, Access Basic code, or a combination of the two, to handle events. Each application can be used in a stand-alone or multiuser environment.

The sections that follow describe the new and improved features of Access 2.0 in detail and place these features in perspective for both new and seasoned users of Access.

Improvements to the User Interface

The current trend is to purchase Windows applications in *suites* that include at least spreadsheet, word processing, database, and presentation graphics applications. Earlier versions of Microsoft Office included Excel, Word, PowerPoint, and a Microsoft Mail client application. When this edition was written, more than 50 percent of Microsoft's Windows application sales were reported to come from suite sales. Now that Access 2.0 has become a member of the Microsoft Office suite (in the Professional Edition only), over the next few years millions of Windows users will experience their introduction to relational database management systems through Access 2.0 and future versions.

One of the principal benefits that accrue to purchasers of Windows application suites is a consistent user interface for each of the applications included. The major cost of adopting new Windows applications in large organizations is the training of prospective users; a consistent UI shortens the learning curve for each application. Access 1.x's user interface was quite different from the UI of other popular Microsoft applications for Windows, such as Excel and Microsoft Word 6.0. Thus, Microsoft needed to bring the UI of Access 1.x into line with the UIs of Excel 5.0, Word 6.0, and, to a lesser extent, PowerPoint 4.0. The sections that follow describe the changes you see in the new user interface of Access 2.0.

Access 2.0 Toolbars and Shortcut Menus

Windows applications, such as Microsoft Word and Excel, feature multiple rows of toolbars, each having many buttons that provide shortcuts for commonly used menu choices. Access 1.x's toolbars were quite sparse compared to Word's and Excel's toolbars. Microsoft added many new buttons to each Access 2.0 toolbar to minimize the need to make two-step (or more) choices from menus.

Access 2.0 also adds a new **T**oolbars choice to the **V**iew menu. The Toolbars dialog, shown in figure 1.1, lets you choose the toolbar(s) that, by default, appear at the top of Access 2.0's main window, directly below the title bar. In addition to the standard toolbar that appears during the design and run modes of each database object, you can add other toolbars at the top of the main window. After you add a new toolbar, you can drag it to any edge of the window and drop it there. When you drop the toolbar, it rearranges itself to conform to the location you chose; then it anchors itself in place, a process called *docking the toolbar*.

▶ "The Toolbar in Table View," p. 93

Access Fundamentals

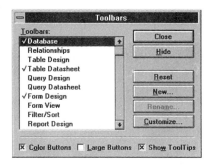

Fig. 1.1
Access 2.0's
Toolbars dialog.

If you drop the toolbar in the center of the window, it becomes a *floating toolbar* that you can move by dragging the small title bar. You can change the aspect ratio of (resize) the floating toolbar by dragging its borders. Figure 1.2 shows Access 2.0's Form Design window with toolbars docked on each edge and a floating toolbar. The Form Design toolbar appears at the top of the window, the Database toolbar at the left, the Table toolbar at the right and the Macros toolbar at the bottom. (It is unlikely that you want all these toolbars to appear simultaneously in a real-life situation.)

Figure 1.2 also illustrates Access 2.0's new shortcut menus. Place the mouse pointer on an object and then click the left mouse button. A floating pop-up menu appears, providing choices applicable to the object you selected. For example, choosing **B**uild Event invokes the Choose Builder dialog that lets you choose an Access builder to provide the value for a property. (Builders are discussed in the "Builders for Creating Expressions and Setting Property Values" section, later in this chapter.)

Fig. 1.2

Form design mode with the shortcut menu and four docked and one floating toolbar.

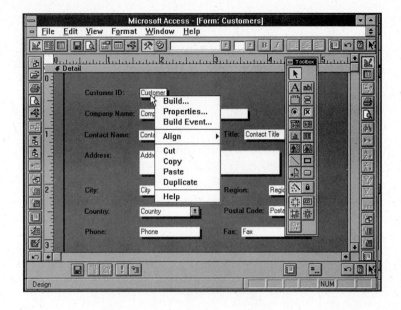

Access 2.0 lets you customize the standard toolbars in the Toolbar dialog's list box and even create your own toolbars for Access applications. (Standard toolbar definitions are stored in SYSTEM.MDA; application toolbar definitions are stored in your application's .MDB file.) Figure 1.3 shows the Customize Toolbars dialog that lets you add or delete toolbar buttons.

Fig. 1.3

Access 2.0's new Customize Toolbars dialog.

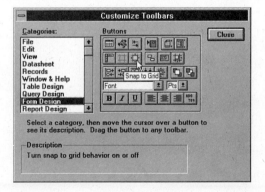

Access 2.0 Wizards

Relational database management systems (RDBMSs) are the least familiar and the most complex of all mainstream Windows applications. The *blank page* metaphor of word processing applications and the grid-like windows of spreadsheets have physical manifestations in everyday life. Almost everyone with a PC has had at least some experience using one or more word processing and spreadsheet applications. The container for your data appears when you launch the application, and you can start typing on the empty page or enter data in the blank cells without knowing a great deal about how the application works. This is not the case with RDBMSs; you must create the container(s) for your data (tables in a database) before the RDBMS becomes a useful application. Thus, users who are new to RDBMSs need more assistance in getting started than word processing or spreadsheet users.

You'll find the new and improved Access 2.0 wizards make creating tables, some queries, and most forms and reports quick and easy processes. Access 1.x provided wizards for creating forms, reports, and graphs. Access 2.0 adds the following new wizards:

- *Table Wizards* create new tables based on a variety of predefined table types, both business and personal. Each predefined table has a collection of fields that you can select for your new table. The opening window of the Table Wizards is shown in figure 1.4.

▶ "Using the Table Wizard to Create New Tables," p. 149

- *Query Wizards* design special types of queries (such as crosstab) find duplicate values, find unmatched values, and archive data queries. For example, the Archive Wizard helps you design a query to make a table from selected records, and then optionally remove the archived records from the table(s) that underlie your archive query.

▶ "Creating an Archive Query with the Query Wizards," p. 431

- *Control Wizards* help you design more complex control objects for forms. You enable the Control Wizards by clicking the Control Wizards button of the toolbox in form design mode. Command Button, List Box, Combo Box, and Option Group Wizards appear when you add a new command button list box, drop-down combo list, or option group control object to your form.

▶ "Access Control Wizards," p. 491

- *Input Mask Wizard* helps you create masks, similar to xBase's `@xx, yy` `GET` *FieldName* `PICTURE` *MaskString* statement that controls how users enter data and how the data appears in a text box. The Input Mask Wizard is discussed in the "Using the Input Mask Wizard" section later in this chapter.

- *Mail Merge Wizard* uses OLE Automation to create Microsoft Word 6.0 form letters directly from your tables or queries. This wizard is described in the "Direct Mail Merge with Microsoft Word" section later in the chapter.

Fig. 1.4
The opening
window of the
new Table Wizard.

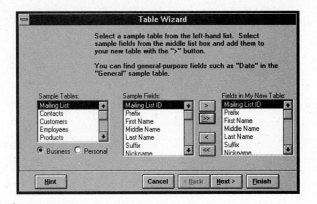

Builders for Creating Expressions and Setting Property Values

Access 1.x incorporated the Builder feature that lets you assign the value of a property from the content of a text box in another window or a value defined by an Access Basic function. When one of Access 2.0's new, full-featured builders is available for a property, an ellipsis button appears to the right of the property value text box you select. When you click the ellipsis button, either the builder itself or, if you select an *event property*, the Choose Builder dialog appears, as shown in figure 1.5. This book uses the Windows term *event*, rather than *event property*; the latter term implies that events have properties (which they do not).

Fig. 1.5
Selecting an event
handler with the
Choose Builder
dialog.

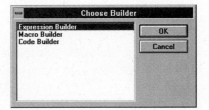

▶ "Adding Table-
Level Valida-
tion Rules and
Using the
Expression
Builder," p. 195

▶ "Using the
Expression
Builder to Add
Query Crite-
ria," p. 349

The following list provides a brief description of each of Access 2.0's new builders and the properties to which these builders are applicable:

■ *Expression Builder* lets you create complex expressions by selecting operands from list boxes and clicking command buttons to add operators, as shown in figure 1.6. You also can type your own expression in the text box. When you close the Expression Builder's dialog, the expression appears as the value of your selected property. Expression Builder is applicable to any property that can accept an Access expression as its value. (Expression Builder is one of the choices offered by the Choose Builder dialog for events.)

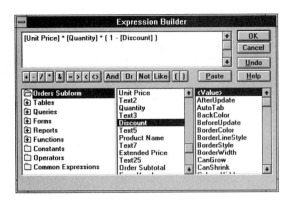

Fig. 1.6
Using the Expression Builder to create a default value.

■ *Color Builder* lets you select one of 48 preselected colors (including the 16 Windows system colors) or design a custom color using the common color dialogs. Color Builder returns the Windows RGB value (a long integer) of the color you choose or design, when you close the dialog.

■ *Query Builder* displays a modified version of the Query Design window to supply an SQL statement as the value of, for example, the RecordSource property of a form or the RowSource property of a drop-down combo list. When you close the Query Builder's window, the SQL statement created by Access's graphical QBE window is inserted into the selected property's text box.

■ *Macro Builder* is one of the options for handling Access events. Selecting Macro Builder from the Choose Builder dialog displays a modified version of the Macro Design window. After you write your macro and close the Macro Builder menu, the name under which you save the macro appears in the text box for the event.

▶ "Attaching a Macro to an Event," p. 663

■ *Picture Builder* is designed to add bit-mapped images to command buttons. You can select images from a list of more than 50 icons supplied with Access (see fig. 1.7), or you can click the Browse button to add an image from a Windows bit-map (.BMP) or icon (.ICO) file to the button.

■ *Menu Builder* is an add-in that automates the process of designing custom menus for applications. Menu macros remain the only method of customizing menus for Access applications. Prior to Access 2.0, creating custom menus was a tedious process. The Menu Builder, which you open by choosing Add-ins from the File menu and then choosing Menu Builder from the submenu, lets you edit an existing menu or create a

▶ "Running Macros from Custom Menu Commands," p. 664

new menu, either from scratch or based on an existing standard Access system menu. Figure 1.8 shows the Menu Builder's editing dialog, which is based on Visual Basic's Menu Editor. (The Add-In Manager is discussed later in this chapter.)

Fig. 1.7
Adding an icon to a command button with the Picture Builder.

Fig. 1.8
Editing a custom menu based on the Forms menu bar.

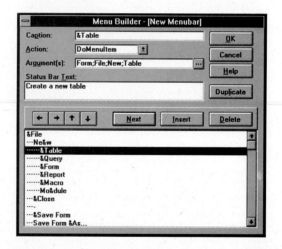

■ *ODBC Connect String Builder* provides a dialog in which you create the value of the SourceConnectStr property needed to open a client-server database. Access passes the information contained in the ODBC source connect string to the ODBC driver in use when opening a connection to the database server.

▶ "Writing Code Behind Forms with the Code Builder," p. 1032

■ *Code Builder* creates an Access Basic event-handling procedure stub, consisting of **Sub** *ObjectName_EventName*. . .**End Sub** statements that surround the Access Basic code you write to process the event, and displays a code editing window for the container object, either a form or report. Figure 1.9 shows the prenamed event-handler for the DblClick event of the Categories button of the Forms Switchboard form. Except for the need to choose the Code Builder from the Choose Builder dialog, opening an Access event-handling code window is identical to writing event-handling procedures in Visual Basic. When you use the Code Builder, your event-handling code is stored with the form (called *Code Behind Forms* or *CBF* by Microsoft). Like Visual Basic, event-handlers are subprocedures, rather than Access Basic functions. (If you want to handle events with code in Access Basic modules, you continue to use the **Function** *FunctionName*. . .**End Function** structure of Access 1.x and type **=FunctionName( )** in the text box for the event.)

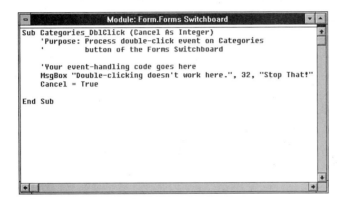

Fig. 1.9
Writing Access Basic CBF subprocedures to handle events.

Improved Properties and Events Window

Database objects in Access 2.0 have many new properties and events. This is especially true for forms, reports, and control objects, which now have a wider variety of events that you can use to trigger macros, CBF subprocedures, or functions contained in modules. (Adding more events is called *increasing event granularity*, a term that means you have finer control over which event you want to use to trigger your event-handler.) To solve the problem of the lengthening list of properties and events of forms, reports, and controls, Microsoft added a drop-down list to the Properties window. In this window, you can select the category of properties you want. Figure 1.10 shows the events list for the Categories command button of the Forms Switchboard form. Notice that the event-handler subprocedure described in the preceding section appears in the On DblClick event text box as [Event Procedure].

▶ "Selecting, Editing, and Moving Form Elements and Controls," p. 460

> **Note**
>
> The `OnClick` event replaces the `OnPush` event of Access 1.x. Access 2.0, and Visual Basic 3.0 events now have the same names, with the exception of Access's `On` prefix. Notice that the `On` prefix does not appear in the name of the event-handling subprocedure shown in figure 1.9, which is the same as the name of the equivalent Visual Basic event handler.

Fig. 1.10

Access 2.0's new Properties window.

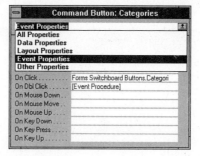

Properties are divided into three categories: Data, Layout, and Other. Events have their own list, and you can elect to see all the properties of an object. Some objects, such as lines and shapes, don't have Data properties; if an object doesn't possess properties of a given category, the Properties list for the category is empty. All Access form, report, and control objects respond to at least a few events. Layout properties include dimensions, colors, and other visible properties of a form, report, or control. Other is a catch-all category for miscellaneous properties, such as the `Name` of the control, `TabOrder`, and `HelpContextID`.

Access 2.0's Add-In Manager and New Add-Ins

Library databases are a unique and valuable feature of Access. Library databases let you attach one or more additional databases to your Access application. All the Access wizards are contained in library databases that, by convention, use the .MDA file extension. Library databases let you create your own wizards, builders, or provide a common database that contains, for example, a ZIP Code lookup table that can be used simultaneously by several different applications.

After you create a library database, you attach the library to Access by adding an entry, lib_name.mda=ro (for read-only permissions) or lib_name.mda=rw (for read-write permissions), to the [Libraries] section of MSACC20.INI. You can invoke features of your library database from a menu choice by adding an entry to the [Menu Add-Ins] section of MSACC20.INI. Open MSACC20.INI in Windows Notepad and scroll to these two sections to see the entries for the wizards and add-ins provided with Access 2.0.

Microsoft Excel pioneered the add-in concept with an Add-In Manager that determines which .XLA files are loaded when Excel opens. Access 2.0 has adopted Excel's approach with a new Add-In Manager that you open by choosing Add-ins from the **F**ile menu, as discussed in connection with the Menu Builder, earlier in the chapter. When you choose Add-In Manager from the Add-ins submenu, the Add-In Manager dialog appears, as shown in figure 1.11. You can uninstall add-ins you don't need by selecting the add-in and then clicking the Uninstall button. (Minimizing the number of add-ins makes Access load faster and consume fewer memory resources.) To add your own or a third-party library database to Access, click the Add New button and select the library file from the list of .MDA files in the Add New Library dialog.

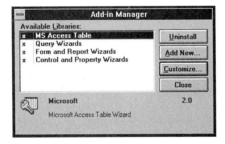

Fig. 1.11
Access 2.0's Add-In
Manager dialog.

The sections that follow describe how you can customize the standard wizards and the new add-ins of Access 2.0. The Menu Builder add-in is described in the "Builders for Creating Expressions and Setting Property Values" section earlier in this chapter.

Customizing Access 2.0 Wizards

Access 2.0 lets you customize features of each of the wizard add-ins, except the Query Wizards. For example, you can customize the features of the Table Wizards by selecting MS Access Tables and then clicking the Customize button to display the Customize Add-in dialog shown in figure 1.12. Double-click the Customize Table Names item in the Customize list to display the

Customize Table Wizard Tables dialog, as illustrated by figure 1.13. This dialog lets you edit the names and sequence of existing fields of the sample table, as well as add or delete fields from the table.

Fig. 1.12

Selecting a wizard feature to customize.

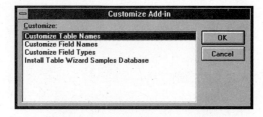

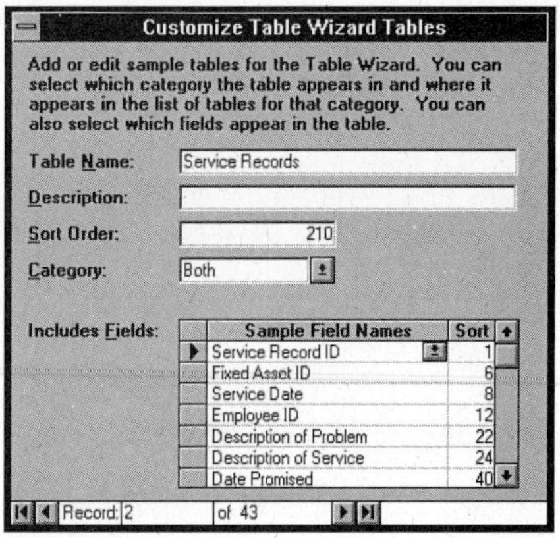

Fig. 1.13

Customizing the fields of a Table Wizard sample table.

It's unlikely that you want to customize the Table Wizard's sample tables. Customizing the Form Wizards and Report Wizards to alter the templates employed by the wizards to create new forms and reports is useful when your organization has a standard style for these objects.

Using the Database Documentor

▶ "Access's New Integrated Data Dictionary System," p. 866

Access 1.x included a library database, ANALYZER.MDA, that created a rudimentary listing of the properties of database objects. Access 2.0's Database Documentor add-in is a substantial improvement on Access 1.x's Database Analyzer. You can generate a complete data dictionary for your database using Database Documentor. You launch the Database Documentor by choosing Add-ins from the **F**ile menu and then **D**atabase Documentor from the submenu to open the Database Documentor dialog shown in figure 1.14.

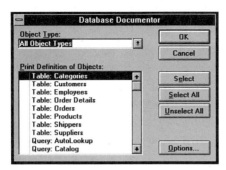

Fig. 1.14
The Database
Documentor's
main dialog.

You can select a specific class of objects to document, or select All Object
Types from the Object Type drop-down list. You select specific objects, such
as a table or a query, in the Print Definition of Objects list and then click the
Select button to add the object to the internal list of objects whose properties
are included in the report. Select Tables and click the Select All button to
create a data dictionary. If you want your report to include all the objects in
the Print Definition of Objects list, click the Select All button.

The Options button lets you select the properties of an object to include in
the report. Figure 1.15 shows the Print Table Definition dialog with the optional properties for table objects selected. Click the OK button to generate
the report. If you include all the options for tables and print all the tables in
NWIND.MDB, the Northwind Traders sample database, your report is about
38 pages long. Printing all the properties of all the objects in NWIND.MDB
results in a several-hundred-page report that takes a *very long time* to create,
even on a fast computer. Figure 1.16 shows the first part of Data
Documentor's report for the Customers table of the Northwind Traders
sample database in print preview mode.

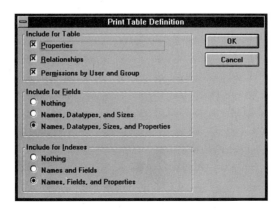

Fig. 1.15
The Database
Documentor's Print
Table Definition
dialog.

Fig. 1.16
Part of the data
dictionary report
for the Customers
table.

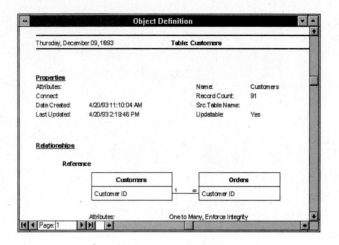

Managing Attached Tables

Tip
The
SOLUTION.MDB
and ORDERS.MDB
databases in your
\ACCESS\SAMPAPPS
directory are
examples of Ac-
cess applications
with attached
tables.

It is a good database design practice to use two database files for your Access application: one .MDB file (the database) contains the tables and, perhaps, query definitions for your application; and another .MDB file (the application) contains application-specific objects, such as forms, reports, macros, and modules. You then attach the tables in the database file to the application file. This allows you to update the application components of your database by replacing the application's .MDB file without affecting the data managed by the application. In multiuser applications, it is a common practice for users to run a local copy of the application .MDB file with retail or run-time Access and share the database file located on a file server. This method can improve the performance of multiuser applications greatly.

The drawback to using this recommended design method is that the well-formed path (including the drive designator) to the database file is stored in your application database's system tables. Thus, if you move the database file or a user of your application installs the database file on a different drive or in a different directory, the application database can't find the database file and displays an error message. With Access 1.x, you had to manually delete the existing table attachments and then reattach the tables from their actual location.

▶ "Using the
Attachment
Manager Add-
In to Reattach
Tables," p. 243

> **Note**
>
> The Attachment Manager can't load if you don't have attached tables in your application .MDB file.

Access 2.0 includes an Attachment Manager add-in that simplifies the task of re-attaching tables that your application can't find in their specified location. To see the Attachment Manager in action, open the SOLUTION.MDB example database in \ACCESS\SAMPAPPS. All the tables of the Solutions application, except the Sales Goals table, are attached from NWIND.MDB. When you choose Attachment Manager from the File Add-ins submenu, the Attachment Manager's dialog appears. Mark the check boxes of the tables that you want to reattach, as shown in figure 1.17. When you click the OK button, the Attachment Manager refreshes (clears and re-creates) each attachment. If NWIND.MDB were located in a directory other than that shown in the Attachment Manager's list, a common File Open dialog appears so that you can specify the correct .MDB file name and directory for the attached tables.

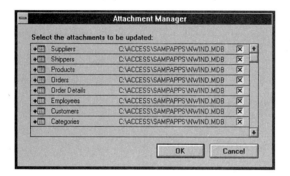

Fig. 1.17

Selecting tables to reattach to an application database.

Changing Ownership by Importing an Access Database

When you create an object in an Access database, you become the owner of the object. (Access calls the object owner the "Creator" of the object.) The concept of database and object ownership is derived from client-server RDBMSs, such as the Microsoft and Sybase versions of SQL Server, where table names are prefixed with the table owner's ID. (An example is the dbo.authors table of the pubs sample database, where "dbo" represents "database owner.") One of the characteristics of Access's labyrinthine security system, which is modeled on that of SQL Server, is that no one, including members of the Admins group, can revoke full permissions from the owner of an object. (Members of the Admins group and others with the appropriate permissions can delete the object, however.)

▶ "Understanding Database Object Ownership," p. 942

The only method of changing the ownership of an Access database object is to import the object into a new database. Imported objects are owned by the user of Access who imports them. If you are distributing an Access application for others to use and you created your application with the default

Admin user name and no password (to avoid the logon process), you have an *unsecure* database. Anyone using the default logon has full permissions to modify every object of your unsecure database application, even if you attempt to explicitly revoke permissions of the Admin user for some objects.

In Access 1.x, you had to import objects into the new database manually, one at a time. Access 2.0's Import Database add-in automatically imports all the objects from the database file you select in the Import Database dialog, which appears when you choose Import Database from the File Add-ins submenu. If you import objects from an Access 1.x database, the objects are automatically converted to Access 2.0 format.

The Built-In Telephone AutoDialer

Telephone autodialers that use your Hayes-compatible modem to dial telephone numbers stored in table fields are one of the most needed features of database applications. You can download several different telephone autodialer libraries for Access 1.x from the MSACCESS Forum of CompuServe. Now Access 2.0 has its own built-in telephone autodialing feature.

To try the Access AutoDialer, follow these steps:

1. Open the Customers table of NWIND.MDB in Datasheet View.

2. Choose Toolbars from the View menu to display the Toolbars dialog.

3. Select the Table Datasheet item of the Toolbars list.

4. Click the Customize button to display the Customize dialog.

5. Choose Records from the Categories list to display the available buttons.

6. Click the telephone button and drag it to the empty position of the Table Datasheet toolbar between the Datasheet View and Print buttons.

7. Click the Close button to return to Access.

8. Move to the Phone field of the Customers table and select the first North American number you find (assuming you're in North America).

9. Click the AutoDialer button of the toolbar to display the AutoDial dialog. The telephone number appears in the Number text box, and you can add a prefix you specify in the Prefix text box when you mark the Use Prefix check box (see fig. 1.18).

You need to set up the AutoDialer to correspond with your modem's COM port assignment and speed. The default values for tone or pulse dialing (pulse), your modem's COM port (2), and the baud/bps communication rate (1200) appear when you click the Setup button (see fig. 1.19). Change the COM port value as necessary; you don't need to change the speed if you have a 1200-baud or faster modem.

10. Click OK to dial the number. A message box appears instructing you to pick up the phone. Clicking OK without picking up the phone puts the line back on the hook (hangs up). Click Cancel if you don't have a modem.

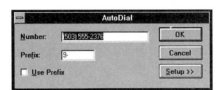

Fig. 1.18
The Access 2.0
AutoDial dialog.

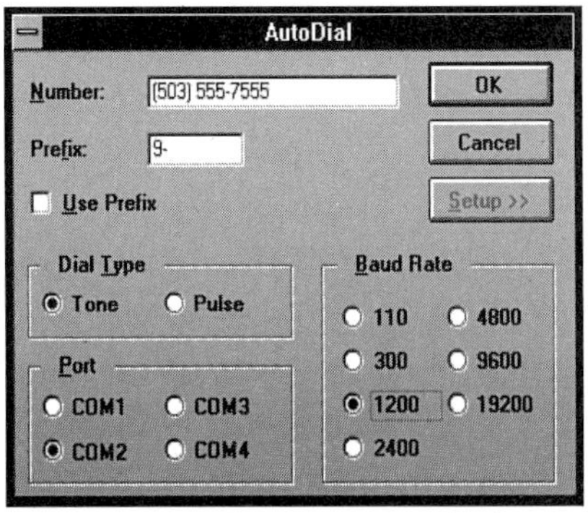

Fig. 1.19
The AutoDial
dialog expanded to
display modem
setup options.

You need to enter telephone numbers in a format suited to dialing from your local area; there is no provision to enter your local area code to strip the local area code from the field value. You need to write some Access Basic code to format the number as a dialing string in a text box on a form to make the Access AutoDialer a truly functional component of your application.

Enhanced Data Integrity

The ability to automatically maintain the integrity of data in tables is one of the characteristics that distinguishes client-server RDBMSs from conventional desktop databases. Two of the principal complaints of Access 1.x developers were the failure of version 1.x to enforce domain integrity at the table level and its failure to maintain referential integrity within attached Access tables. These two features and cascading updates and cascading deletions of dependent records have been added to Access 2.0. These new features are described in the sections that follow.

Enforcing Table-Level Domain Integrity

The *domain* of a table field is the range or set of values that is allowed in a table's field. You establish the domain of a field by entering an expression as the value of the ValidationRule property that defines the domain. (Validation rules often are called *business rules*.) Examples are <= **Date**(), which restricts date values to today's date or earlier, or "A" Or "B" Or "C" Or "D", which restricts the entry to one of the characters A through D.

Access 1.x only enforced the ValidationRule property when data was entered in Table or Query Datasheet View. Thus, it was necessary to add the ValidationRule property to each text box or other control bound to the field in every form that updated the field value. This violates a cardinal rule of database design: do not depend upon applications to maintain domain integrity. This rule applies to all databases not just relational databases.

▶ "Adding Field-Level Validation Rules," p. 193

Access 2.0 now enforces domain integrity at the field *and* the table level. This distinction is important. *Field-level* validation rules relate only to the values of the field itself. The preceding examples of ValidationRule expressions apply at the field level. You add field-level validation rules in the Validation Rule text box of the Field Properties pane of the selected field, as shown in figure 1.20. Access 2.0 has two new field properties, Required, which applies to all field data types, and AllowZeroLength, which applies only to fields of the Text field data type. A Yes (**True**) value of the Required property is the equivalent of the **Is Not Null** expression and a No (**False**) value of the AllowZeroLength property is the same as <> "". (An empty string, "", and the **Null** value are not the same values.) The Order Date value should be entered for any order received, so the value of the Required property is set to Yes in figure 1.20.

▶ "Adding Table-Level Validation Rules and Using the Expression Builder," p. 195

Troubleshooting

When importing or converting Access 1.1 tables, a message box with an "Errors occurred converting N validation rules and default values. See error table 'Convert Errors' for errors" message.

Importing or converting Access 1.x tables with now-illegal field-level validation rules and default values requires that you re-create the validation rule at the table level in Access 2.0. Open the Convert Errors table to determine the *ValidationRule* or *DefaultValue* property that you need to re-create in your Access 2.0 database.

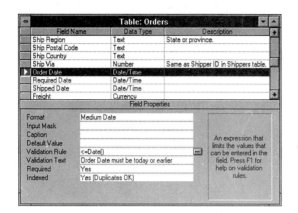

Fig. 1.20

Entering a field-level validation rule for a table.

Table-level validation rules allow you to make the domain of one field dependent on the value in another field of the table. In the case of the Orders table of NWIND.MDB, the `ValidationRule` value `[Shipped Date] >= [Order Date]` **Or IsNull**(`[Shipped Date]`) is a table-level validation rule because it involves a comparison of the values of two fields of the table. Access 2.0 requires that you enter table-level validation rules as the value of the `ValidationRule` property of the *table* in the Table Properties window (see fig. 1.21). You can no longer enter a `ValidationRule` value in the Field Properties pane that contains a literal reference to the field itself or to another field. (This was allowed in Access 1.x.) If, for example, you attempt to save your design with `>= [Order Date]` **Or Is Not Null** as the value of the `ValidationRule` property for the Shipped Date field, you receive an error message.

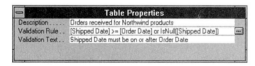

Fig. 1.21

Entering table-level validation rules in the Table Properties window.

Relationship and Referential Integrity Enhancements

Access 2.0's new graphical Relationships window makes establishing default relationships between tables in Access databases a quick and easy process. With the NWIND.MDB sample database open, choosing **R**elationships from the **E**dit menu displays the graphical Relationships window shown in figure 1.23. (Access 1.x users will notice the similarity to the Database Diagram query in Design View.) Enhancements to relationship diagramming in Access 2.0 include indication of one-to-many relations with a 1 adjacent to the primary key field of the base (or primary) table and an ∞ (infinity) symbol adjacent to the foreign key field of the related table. (One-to-one relations are indicated by a 1 adjacent to the primary key field of each of the related tables.)

▶ "Establishing Relationships between Tables," p. 164

Fig. 1.22
Access 2.0's new graphical Relationships window.

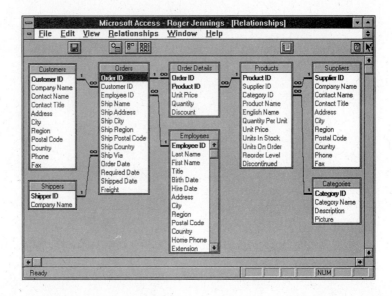

To establish default relationships for tables that you create in Access 2.0, follow these steps:

1. Open the Relationships window, and add each of the tables in your database with the Add Table dialog in the same manner you add tables to queries.

Tip
Make sure you drag the base table's primary key field to the corresponding key field of the foreign table. If you reverse the procedure, you can't enforce referential integrity for the relationship.

2. Drag the field name of the primary key field from the field list window of the base table and drop it on the foreign key field in the field list window of each related table. A line with dots at each end joins the two fields.

3. Double-click the join line to display the Relationships dialog shown in figure 1.23. The Relationships dialog has three check boxes that are not present in Access 1.x's Relationships dialog: Inherited Relationships, Cascade Update Related Fields, and Cascade Delete Related Fields. These controls are disabled when the Relationships dialog opens.

4. Enforcing referential integrity prevents orphan records in the related table. (An *orphan record* is a record in a related table with no corresponding record in a base table.) Mark the Enforce Referential Integrity check box. The Cascade Update Related Fields and Cascade Delete Related Fields check boxes are now enabled.

5. If you want to delete records in the related table automatically when you delete the corresponding record in the base table, mark the Cascade Delete Related Fields check box.

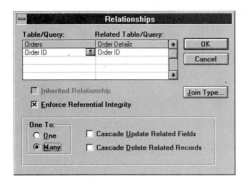

Fig. 1.23
The initial appearance of the Relationships dialog after creating a default relationship by the drag-and-drop method.

I

Access Fundamentals

6. If you want to change the value of the foreign key field of the records in the related table that correspond to a change you make to the value of the primary key field in the base table, mark the Cascade Update Related Fields check box.

7. Click the Create button to establish the default relationship with the added referential integrity properties and close the Relationships dialog.

If your tables are attached from another database, the Inherited Relationships check box is enabled and marked by default. The ability to enforce referential integrity with attached databases is a very important new feature of Access 2.0. As discussed in the previous section, "Managing Attached Tables," most Access developers use separate databases to contain data and application objects. The ability to maintain referential integrity in attached databases now makes Access 2.0 applications with attached tables behave identically to those with tables contained in the application database.

Using the Input Mask Wizard

Access 2.0 provides a new property of text boxes, `InputMask`, that gives you precise control of the formatting of data entry in text boxes. Adding values to the `InputMask` property of an Access 2.0 text box creates the equivalent of Visual Basic 3.0's masked edit custom control. (The masks you create with Access 2.0 do not have the problems with **Null** values and other defects associated with Visual Basic 3.0's masked edit control.) You can apply masks, such as `!(999) 000-0000;;_`, to enter telephone numbers in the standard North American format. The Input Mask Wizard, shown in figure 1.24, helps you create the proper value for the `InputMask` property for a variety of commonly used fields. To display the Input Mask Wizard, select the Input Mask text box for a text box control with a Text or Date/Time field data type and then click the ellipsis button.

▶ "Using Input Masks," p. 146

Fig. 1.24
The Input Mask
Wizard's opening
dialog.

OLE 2.0 and New Data Export Features

As noted earlier in this chapter, Microsoft Corporation's strategy for its mainstream Windows applications is to maximize interoperability of these products. The goal is to let you create large-scale *workflow* applications using Microsoft Excel, Word, Access, and Project as building blocks. (The new classification of these applications is *productivity products*.) Workflow applications are designed to automate business processes by providing a means for participants in a particular activity (the *workgroup*) to contribute their input electronically. Creating workflow applications is one of the elements of business *re-engineering*, a popular buzz-word of the "information age" that does not yet have a precise definition. Part of the plan is to use Microsoft Mail as the communication link between participants in the workflow process. One of Microsoft's primary objectives is to create a viable competitor to Lotus Development Corporation's Notes, a client-server workgroup application with a database at its core and cc:Mail for communication. The sections that follow describe the new features of Access 2.0 that enable it to be one of the cornerstones of Microsoft's workflow strategy.

In-Place Activation of OLE 2.0 Objects

▶ "Activating OLE 2.0 Objects in Place," p. 717

Using existing Windows productivity products as building blocks for larger applications without large-scale, complex programming projects requires that one application be capable of easily manipulating objects created by another application. OLE 1.0, which as formally introduced by Windows 3.1, was a step in the right direction. OLE 1.0 lets you launch an OLE server application, such as Windows Paintbrush, Excel 4.0, or Word 2.0, by double-clicking an

OLE object, such as a bound or unbound OLE object frame in an Access 1.x form. The OLE 1.0 server's window appears, and you can edit the object or, in the case of multimedia objects such as sound and video, play the object using the OLE server application. Incorporating one object, such as a Microsoft Word document, in another object, for instance an Access table or form, is called creating a *compound document*. Microsoft Word is the OLE server, Access is the OLE client, and your table or form becomes the compound document.

Access 2.0 is an OLE 2.0 client application. (OLE clients are now called *container applications* in OLE 2.0 parlance.) This means that you can create compound Access documents using OLE servers, such as Excel and Microsoft Word. You cannot create a Microsoft Word or Excel compound document that contains an Access 2.0 object because Access 2.0 is not an OLE server. OLE 2.0 is backward-compatible with OLE 1.0, so Access 2.0 can employ both OLE 1.0 (Paintbrush) and 2.0 (Excel and Word) server applications. Microsoft Graph 5.0 (MSGraph5), which is included with Access 2.0, is an OLE 2.0 server *applet*. A Windows applet is an application that you can run from another application; you cannot execute an applet directly. OLE server applets can only be executed from within an OLE client application. Many software publishers, including Microsoft, were busily adapting their OLE 1.0 applications to provide OLE 2.0 conformance while this edition was being written.

OLE 2.0 makes the process of creating and manipulating compound documents easier and more transparent to the user than OLE 1.0. One of the principal improvements is called *in-place activation*, also known as in situ or in-place editing. In-place activation means that the OLE 2.0 server does not appear in its own window; it temporarily takes over your application's window. As an example, you can embed an Excel 5.0 worksheet in an OLE Object field of an Access table and display the worksheet object in a form. (In-place activation works with embedded but not linked OLE 2.0 objects.) When you double-click the bound OLE object frame, Excel 5.0 takes over the menus of Access 2.0's main (parent) window and Excel's familiar row and column headers appear in the frame. Excel 5.0 toolbars appear as floating toolbars on top of your form. Figure 1.25 shows an activated Excel 5.0 workbook object that replaces the photo that usually appears in the Employees form of NWIND.MDB. Figure 1.25 was created by adding another record to the Employees table, then inserting the \EXCEL\EXAMPLES\BOOKST.XLS worksheet object into the Photo field of the new record by choosing Insert Object from the Edit menu and embedding (not linking) the workbook object from the file.

Fig. 1.25

A demonstration of in-place activation of an Excel 5.0 work-book object.

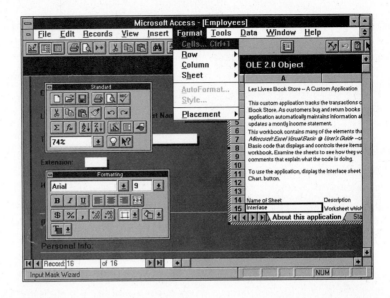

OLE Automation

▶ "Taking Advantage of OLE Automation," p. 718

For Access developers, OLE Automation is a more important feature of OLE 2.0 than in-place activation. OLE Automation, commonly abbreviated OA, lets you manipulate objects created by OLE 2.0 server applications with Access Basic code. Most, but not all, OLE 2.0-compliant server applications support OLE Automation. Microsoft Excel 5.0, Word 6.0, and Project 4.0, and Shapeware Corporation's Vision 2.0 template-based drawing application let you create new objects or open existing objects with OA methods. OLE Automation is designed to replace dynamic data exchange (DDE) as the primary method of interprocess communication (IPC, sometimes called *interapplication communication,* or IAC) between Windows applications.

Unlike DDE, which you can execute over a network using Windows for Workgroups' and Windows NT's NetDDE feature, IPC with OLE Automation presently is limited to applications that reside on the same computer. Future versions of Windows and OLE will let you transport objects over networks and exchange objects with other operating systems, such as Apple's System 7+, UNIX, and NextStep. Despite the current transport limitation, OLE Automation is a very important new feature of Access 2.0. The next two sections describe how database application developers use OLE Automation with Access 2.0.

Creating OLE Automation Objects with Access Basic. OLE Automation server applications expose *collections* of objects, together with the properties and methods that are applicable to each object in the collections. A collection is similar to an array; the Worksheets collection of an Excel Workbook object is an ordered list of the worksheets contained in an .XLS file. You use the new Access Basic **CreateObject()** and **GetObject()** functions (methods) to create a new object or open an existing object, respectively, and assign the object to a variable of the **Object** data type. Your new **Object** variable gives you access to all the objects that the OA server application exposes. You can alter the properties of the object or apply methods to the object with code in Access Basic functions and subprocedures.

▶ "Manipulating an Excel 5.0 Workbook Object," p. 1060

Access 2.0's Mail Merge Wizard, described in the "Direct Mail Merge with Microsoft Word" section that follows shortly, uses OLE Automation for creating Microsoft Word 6.0 form letters from within Access. OA lets you transfer the values of worksheet cells between Excel and your Access 2.0 application by specifying or reading the value of the Cell(*RowColumn*) object of the Cells collection. OLE Automation is a much more robust method of interprocess communication than DDE; DDE has been likened to *throwing a ball over a fence and seeing if anyone catches it.*

Adding Custom Controls to Access 2.0 with OLE 2.0. One of the features that has made Visual Basic successful as a programming language for creating Windows applications is its extensibility. *Extensibility* means the ability to add new features to an application or programming language without having to upgrade the product. Visual Basic's custom controls, in the form of .VBX files that you include with your application, are an excellent example of extensibility; Microsoft and third-party suppliers provide a broad assortment of custom controls that you can add to your Visual Basic forms. Access developers who also are experienced in Visual Basic requested (to no avail) that Microsoft include the ability to use Visual Basic custom controls in Access 1.x.

Now OLE 2.0 and OLE Automation let you add the equivalent of Visual Basic's .VBX custom controls to your Access 2.0 applications. Using Microsoft's OLE 2.0 Control Development Kit (CDK) and the Professional Edition of Visual C++ 1.5, that incorporates the Microsoft Foundation Class Library for OLE 2.0, you can create your own custom controls for Access 2.0. The Calendar OLE 2.0 custom control created as an example for Access 2.0 by Microsoft is shown in figure 1.26. If you're not an accomplished C++ programmer, you can expect many of the publishers of Visual Basic .VBX custom controls to provide equivalents as OLE 2.0 Custom Controls. Access 2.0 is the first Microsoft application to support OLE 2.0 Custom Controls.

Access Fundamentals

Fig. 1.26
Microsoft's
Calendar OLE 2.0
Custom Control
contained in an
unbound object
frame.

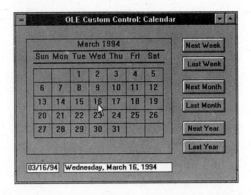

> **Note**
>
> Example OLE Custom Controls and the files necessary to use OLE Custom Controls
> with Access 2.0 are part of the Microsoft Access Developer's Toolkit (ADT). The retail
> version of Access 2.0 does not include the files required to support OLE custom
> controls.

Exporting Reports to Files

► "Copying, Ex-
porting, and
Mailing Sorted
and Filtered
Data," p. 221

Access 1.x included a library database called OUTPUTAS.MDA and an accompanying dynamic link library, OUTPUTAS.DLL, that attempted to export the
content of reports to worksheet (.XLS), word processing (.RTF), and plain text
(.TXT) files. Access 2.0 has a new Output **T**o choice of the **F**ile menu and also
has the Output to Excel and Output to Word buttons of the Print Preview
toolbar that provide a slightly improved version of the Output As library.
Sending files created by the Output To feature as attachments to Microsoft
Mail messages is discussed in the "Mail-Enabled Access Applications" section
that follows shortly.

► "Sending Re-
ports by
Microsoft
Mail," p. 599

When you click the Output to Excel button of the toolbar, Access prints the
report to an .XLS file, launches Excel, and displays the newly-created
worksheet. (Choosing Output **T**o from the **F**ile menu creates the file, but does
not launch the application.) Figure 1.27 shows Northwind Traders' Sales by
Year report printed as an .XLS file and opened in Excel 5.0. Click the Output
to Word button to print the report to an .RTF file and open the file in Word.
You also can use Output To feature to create an .XLS, .RTF, or .TXT file from
the data contained in table, query, or form objects of your database. The
advantage to using the menu command is that you can choose the name for
your file; Access automatically names your file, shortening the object name to
eight characters, replacing any spaces in the object name with underscore
characters.

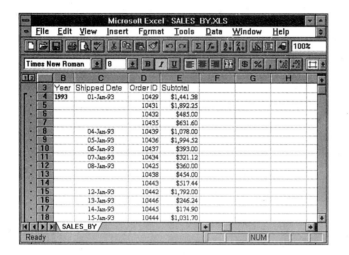

Fig. 1.27
The Sales by Year report of NWIND.MDB created by the Output to Excel feature and displayed in Excel 5.0.

Note

Files you create with the Output To feature do not include data contained in subreports or subforms. If you plan to use Output To to create files from either forms or reports, you need to design special forms or reports so that the information you want to include in the file is not derived from a subform or subreport.

Direct Mail Merge with Microsoft Word

If you've installed Microsoft Word 6.0, you can use the Mail Merge Wizard to create form letters or address envelopes directly from Access 2.0. The Mail Merge Wizard uses dynamic data exchange (DDE), not OLE Automation, to communicate with Microsoft Word 6.0. If you haven't created the form letter, the Mail Merge Wizard lets you open a new Microsoft Word document to create one. When you create a new form letter with Access 2.0's Mail Merge Wizard, the Wizard creates an object of the Word.Basic class, opens Microsoft Word's main window, and then uses WordBasic menu commands to display Microsoft Word's Mail Merge toolbar and add the field names of the table or query to the Insert Merge Fields menu. (Spaces in field names are converted to underscore characters to comply with Microsoft Word's Merge Field syntax.) Figure 1.28 shows the process of adding Mail Merge fields to a Microsoft Word 6.0 form letter from NWIND.MDB's Customers table.

▶ "Using the Access Mail Merge Wizard," p. 810

Fig. 1.28
Creating a form
letter in Microsoft
Word 6.0 with
Access 2.0's Mail
Merge Wizard.

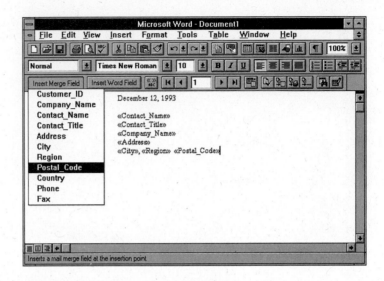

Mail-Enabled Access Application

If you're running Access 2.0 under Windows for Workgroups 3.1+ or Windows NT 3.1, or you have the Microsoft Mail client application installed, you can send report files or the content of tables, queries, and forms, as files attached to Microsoft Mail. The Send choice of the File menu creates an .XLS, .RTF, or .TXT file from the table, query, form, or report and then attaches the file to a Microsoft Mail message. (The file is created as described in the previous section, "Exporting Reports to Files.") Mail's window opens with the attachment indicated by an icon so you can address the message and add comments. Figure 1.29 shows a message with an attachment consisting of CUSTOMER.XLS, an Excel file created from the Customers table of NWIND.MDB.

Tip
If you regularly
use the Send
feature, you
can add the
Send Mail
button to your
toolbars from
the File cat-
egory of the
Customize
Toolbars
dialog.

Performance Improvement

Microsoft Access is a very large, complex application that uses a variety of sizable Windows dynamic link libraries (DLLs) to perform specific functions. The executable file for Access 2.0, MSACCESS.EXE, has a size of about 2M. You can see the names of some DLLs used by Access with the new Microsoft System Info application that is a component of all recently-released Microsoft products. Choose About Microsoft Access from the Help menu to display the copyright notice; then click the System Info button to run MSINFO.EXE. Select System DLL's from the Choose a Category drop-down list. A list of the

DLLs in your \WINDOWS\SYSTEM directory appears. Most of the DLLs required by Access 2.0 begin with "MSA" and include "20" in their file names. Figure 1.30 shows the Microsoft System Info dialog with a beta version of MSAJT200.DLL selected. MSAJT200.DLL, about 1M in size and in memory whenever Access is running, is the DLL for the Jet database engine that provides the connection to Access and other databases.

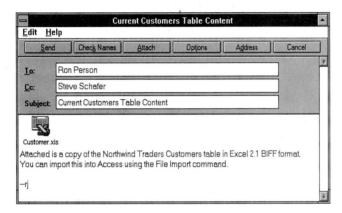

Fig. 1.29
A Microsoft Mail message with an attached file in Excel 3.0 BIFF format.

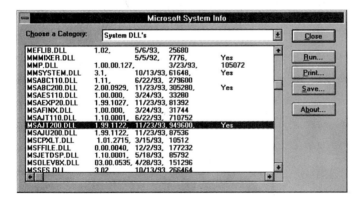

Fig. 1.30
Displaying some of the DLLs that support Access 2.0.

As a general rule, the larger the application, the slower it runs. Programmers can overcome the size-versus-speed problem by optimizing the source code used to create the application. Optimizing the code for an application such as Access is a lengthy and tedious process. Microsoft's programmers have made a substantial improvement to the speed of operation of Access 2.0 compared to Access 1.x; you'll find your Access 1.x applications have more *snap* when you run them under Access 2.0 if you have 8M or more of RAM in your computer.

> **Note**
>
> Microsoft specified 2M as the minimum requirement for Access 1.0, but 4M was the practical lower limit to run Access 1.0 and 1.1. For Access 2.0, Microsoft recommends a 6M minimum, but you need 8M of RAM to run Access 2.0 applications with more than trivial content. 12M to 16M of RAM delivers substantial improvements in application operating speed. As a rule, you gain more "bang for the buck" by adding memory (at least up to 8M) than by replacing your computers 80X86 microprocessor with a faster version of the same chip.

Rushmore Query Optimization

Improved query optimization methods make a further contribution to Access 2.0's performance. The designers of the FoxPro database development application for DOS created a method, called *Rushmore technology*, to optimize queries that return information from large database tables. FoxPro DOS applications that use Rushmore are renowned for their blazing speed. Microsoft acquired the FoxPro product line in 1992 and has added the Rushmore query optimizing methodology to Access 2.0.

▶ "Using Access Indexes," p. 869

The basis of Rushmore optimization is the restructuring of the sequence of execution of SQL statements, where necessary, to take maximum advantage of indexes on table fields. You need to create indexes on most or all the fields that serve as the criteria for the rows your query returns (the SQL WHERE clause) to gain the benefits of Rushmore optimization. Although adding a number of indexes to your Access tables substantially increases the size of the .MDB file, the improved performance is usually worth the loss of free disk space. You'll find that adding several indexes to a table slows update and append processes, because changing the values of indexed fields also requires that the indexes be updated.

Optimization of Remote Queries

The basic principle of client-server RDBMS operation is that queries are executed by the database application that runs on the server. The client application sends the SQL statement to the server over the network; the server processes the SQL statement and then sends the rows of data that comprise the query result set back to the client. This method minimizes the amount of processing on the client side and reduces network traffic. The computers on which the server runs often have much higher speed processors and more memory, so remote queries execute faster, even taking into account the time required to send the data over the network.

If you're using Access 2.0 as the client of a client-server RDBMS, such as Microsoft SQL Server or ORACLE, you'll find that Access 2.0 takes better advantage of the server's processing power to minimize network traffic and, thus, speed performance. The Remote Jet (RJet) features of Access 2.0 have been overhauled so that, in many cases, the entire query is processed on the server. If you use a feature of Access, such as creating a crosstab query, that is not supported by the server, RJet executes as much of the query as possible on the server and then manipulates the returned data on the client side as necessary. *SQL pass-through,* where you send the SQL statement directly to the server, is now a native feature of Access 2.0. SQL pass-through methods are discussed in the "Built-In SQL Pass-Through for Client-Server Systems" section that follows shortly.

Extensions to Access SQL

Behind every query you create with Access, there is an English-language statement that fully describes the query. As you add tables, fields, and criteria to your graphical QBE (query-by-example) queries in Access's Query Design window, Access writes an SQL statement. SQL is the standard language for executing queries against almost all client-server databases and has been adopted both in the U.S. (by the American National Standards Institute, ANSI) and internationally (by the International Standards Organization, ISO). Access 2.0's dialect of SQL conforms, in most part, to the ANSI/ISO standards. You don't have to be able to read or write Access SQL to create most Access queries, but you need to do so to take advantage of Access 2.0's new implementation of and extensions to ANSI/ISO SQL that are described in the following three sections.

▶ "What Is Structured Query Language," p. 884

Access 2.0's Data Definition Language

The SQL dialect of Access 1.x did not include ANSI/ISO SQL's data definition language (DDL) statements. To create a new empty table or add indexes to an existing table under program control with Access 1.1 required an add-in DLL called MSADDL11.DLL whose functions you had to declare and then call in an Access Basic module. (Microsoft calls this process creating or modifying objects "programmatically.") Using MSADDL11.DLL effectively was not an easy task, even for experienced Access Basic programmers.

▶ "Creating Tables with Access DDL," p. 894

Access 2.0 SQL now includes the CREATE TABLE, CREATE INDEX, DROP TABLE, DROP INDEX, and ALTER TABLE reserved words of SQL's data definition language. CREATE INDEX supports the UNIQUE, KEY, PRIMARY, and FOREIGN modifiers to define index type and key fields. If you want to require entry in the field of a table, you can add the NOT NULL modifier. You can use the CONSTRAINT and REFERENCES modifiers to establish default relationships between tables and use CONSTRAINT on a table field to set a primary key or to enforce domain integrity rules. Access 2.0's DDL implementation is almost fully SQL-92 compliant. (Some CONSTRAINT modifiers, such as CHECK and CASCADE, are not included.) Although you don't need to be a programmer to use Access 2.0's new DDL reserved words, you do need to be able to be fully conversant with writing SQL statements. You only can create DDL queries in Access 2.0's improved SQL window.

Subqueries and *UNION* Queries

▶ "Implementing Subqueries," p. 908

SQL subqueries are useful when a query is dependent upon the result set returned by another query. You could create an approximation of SQL subqueries in Access 1.x by executing one query and then executing another query on the result set from the first query. (This process is called *nesting* queries.) Subqueries usually are more efficient and faster than nested queries, especially with large tables or against client-server databases. You can add subqueries as a calculated field expression in Access's Query Design grid or as a criterion (part or all of the SQL WHERE clause) to select records returned by the main query. The SQL syntax of queries with subqueries can become quite complex.

▶ "Using *UNION* Queries," p. 906

> ### Note
> You can't include *UNION* or crosstab queries in subqueries, and you can't create *UNION* queries in Access's Query Design window.

UNION queries let you combine the result of two or more SELECT queries in a single query result set, providing that each of the queries return the same number of columns and that the table fields specified in the UNION SELECT query have the same field data types as the first SELECT query. If you need to include the UNION reserved word in your query, you must do so in the SQL window. However, you can use Access Query Design window to create the primary query and then add your UNION SELECT statement in the SQL window after the primary query but before the terminating semicolon.

TOP n and *TOP* nn *PERCENT* Queries

There are many cases where you want a query to return only the *big picture* and disregard trivial data. For example, you may want to determine the sales of the top 10 products for the month or year but no other products. Access

2.0 adds the TOP *n* and TOP *nn* PERCENT modifiers, where n is the maximum number of records to be returned and *nn* is the percent of the total number of records in the query that are actually returned. The SQL syntax for these Access-specific reserved words is SELECT TOP *n* `FieldNames`... and SELECT TOP *nn* PERCENT `FieldNames`. ... Both *n* and *nn* must be integers.

If you know the total sales for the month, you can create a pie chart that shows the distribution of sales between the TOP n products, with another wedge for "Other." You have to do some OA programming of the MSGraph5 object to accomplish this, however, because Microsoft didn't implement TOP *n* PLUS OTHER or similar syntax that groups the *Other* total in an *n* + 1th record. You would think that returning only the first few records speeds the execution of your query against tables with large numbers of records. This does not occur because the ORDER BY clause used with TOP. . . queries requires that QJet examine each row of the query result set before concluding which rows qualify for inclusion in the final set.

Tip
You need to add an ORDER BY (sort) clause to your SELECT TOP. . . query so that the QJet query parser knows what constitutes *top*.

Built-In SQL Pass-Through for Client-Server Systems

You can attach tables from client-server databases to an Access database using the Microsoft ODBC API (Open Database Connectivity application programming interface) and then execute queries you create in the graphical Query Design window against the attached client-server tables. Attached server database tables behave as if the tables were native to your Access database, except that scrolling through the records of a remote table in Datasheet View often is slower because of the need to send the data to display the records over the network. One of the advantages of attaching client-server database tables to your Access database is that, in most cases, you can update the data in the attached tables.

▶ "Using Access 2.0's SQL Pass-Through Queries," p. 975

To take maximum advantage of the capabilities of client-server databases, however, you must use SQL pass-through methods. SQL pass-through lets you send SQL statements directly to the server, effectively bypassing the QJet engine. SQL pass-through lets you take advantage of *stored procedures* of database servers, such as Microsoft and Sybase SQL Server, that support this feature. Stored procedures are preprepared queries that are precompiled and stored on the server; you execute stored procedures by name. You can send parameters to stored procedures to customize the query so that it returns rows for, as an example, a particular accounting period or range of dates. SQL pass-through also lets you take advantage of server-specific language extensions to SQL. SQL Server's Transact-SQL, for example, lets you use IF. . .ELSE, WHILE, and BEGIN. . .END constructs for conditional execution and looping within an SQL statement. These constructs are not permissible in ordinary ANSI/ISO SQL statements.

Tip
Query result
sets from SQL
pass-through
SELECT queries
are not
updatable; that
is, you cannot
change values
in the underly-
ing tables by
editing query
data. Use pass-
through UPDATE
queries to
change table
values.

Access 1.x used a DLL, MSASP110.DLL, to implement SQL pass-through. As
with MSADLL11.DLL, using MSASP110.DLL required using Access Basic code
to declare and call its functions. Data returned from the server by
MSASP110.DLL calls appended one record at a time to a newly created table,
a slow process at best. Although MSASP110.DLL lets you minimize the
amount of data sent over the network, the savings in data transmission time
was often lost by the time required to add records to the table.

Now Access 2.0 lets you add the SQL pass-through option to queries you
write in the SQL Pass-Through Query window. (Native SQL pass-through first
appeared in Visual Basic 3.0.) Instead of adding records to a physical table,
Access creates a virtual table (a **Recordset** object of the **Snapshot** type) in
memory and adds the query result set's rows to the virtual table. If you have
enough free memory to hold part or all of the returned data, this is a much
faster process than adding records to a physical table. (Data that can't be held
in memory spills over to a temporary table in your \WINDOWS\TEMP directory.) To write an SQL pass-through query, you choose **SQL** Specific from the
Query menu and then choose **P**ass-Through from the submenu, without
adding any tables to your query. Figure 1.31 shows an SQL pass-through
query that calls a Microsoft SQL Server stored procedure, total_sales, in a
test database, CT_01,CA, 1/1/94, and 3/31/94 are parameters passed to the
stored procedure to specify the query criteria: state, beginning date, and ending date.

Fig. 1.31
Access 2.0's SQL
Pass-Through
window and
Query Properties
window for a
Microsoft SQL
Server for Win-
dows NT database.

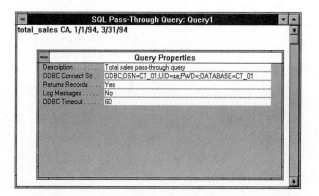

System-stored procedures, which take the prefix sp in SQL Server, return information about the database and the tables, stored procedures, and other
objects it contains. You also can use SQL pass-through queries to control
permissions for objects in the server database using the SQL GRANT and REVOKE
reserved words. (You must have administrative privileges for the database to
alter permissions.) Controlling access to database objects is part of SQL's Data
Control Language (DCL), which is not supported in Access SQL.

New Features for Access Developers

Everyone who creates an Access application automatically becomes an Access developer. This book, however, uses the term *developer* in a more restrictive sense; developers are persons who design and develop database applications as independent consultants or entrepreneurs, or who specifically have been assigned database application development responsibility by their employer. The sections that follow describe some new features of Access 2.0 that are of interest primarily to Access developers and those users who make regular use of Access Basic code in their applications.

Object Variables and Collections

The OLE 2.0 API specifies a standard methodology for organizing the objects created by a Windows application into a hierarchical structure of object *collections*. A collection of objects, as mentioned earlier in the chapter, is similar to an array; the principal difference between a collection and an array is that the number and order of the elements of a collection changes as you create or destroy objects in your application. The elements of the collection consist of pointers (memory addresses) to instances of objects. Each object has its own collection of properties and methods. You refer to members of collections by their position within the array (index) or by the name of the object. Collections are *enumerations* of the objects they contain. Listing the objects in a collection with a **For. . .Next** loop is called *enumerating* the collection.

▶ "Data Types and Database Objects in Access Basic," p. 993

One purpose of the hierarchy of collections is to provide a standard method by which applications can expose their objects to other applications through OA. Another purpose is to create a structure that is compatible with a common application programming language, Visual Basic for Applications (VBA). Version 2.0 of Access does not expose its objects and, thus, is not an OLE Application server, nor does Access 2.0 use VBA as its programming language. These features are expected to be incorporated into future versions of Access. Many of Access 2.0's additions to Access Basic appear to be designed to streamline future transition to VBA and OA server status.

Access 2.0 includes a number of objects and collections that do not appear in Access 1.x. An example is the Application object that is at the top of the hierarchy. You can apply the new **Echo**, **GetOption()**, **SetOption()**, and **Quit** methods to the Application object. The **Echo** and **Quit** methods substitute for macro actions. Application.**Echo False** is equivalent to the **DoCmd** Echo **False** statement to prevent screen repainting; the **Quit** method substitutes for a **DoCmd** DoMenuItem statement that closes Access. New methods for Access objects often can take the place of the more cumbersome execution of macro actions. Application.**GetOption**(str*OptionName*) returns the value of settings in the Options dialog. You can set the value of an option with the Application.**SetOption**(str*OptionName*) statement. (Options set from list boxes require that you substitute int*OptionNumber* for str*OptionName*.)

Although the OLE 2.0 API does not specify names of application objects and collections, it recommends terms to describe objects that are commonly found in Windows applications. All Microsoft OA-compliant applications use these common terms (to the extent possible) to maintain Object Basic code consistency between applications. *Object Basic* is a term used in this book to refer collectively to all dialects of Basic in Microsoft applications for Windows, with the present exception of WordBasic. The data access objects and collections added in Access 2.0 are described in a separate section that follows shortly.

Modifying Application Object Properties with Access Basic Code

One of the principal complaints of Access 1.x developers was the *read-only in run mode* characteristic of the majority of the application objects' properties. You had to write code to change to design mode, alter the property value, and then change back to run mode to display the revised form or report. Creating a new subform to display the result of a user-definable crosstab query, for example, was a major coding exercise. Changing to and from design mode caused a significant performance problem.

Access 2.0 lets you alter many more properties, such as the Height and Width properties of a control object, in run mode. Although you still can't create new application objects in run mode, you can now create continuous subforms with variable numbers of columns by hiding unneeded text boxes and setting the Width property of the visible text boxes to the required dimension. The ability to set most of the properties of application objects unifies programming methods for Access Basic 2.0 and Visual Basic 3.0.

Access 2.0's Data Access Object Class

The most important set of new object collections in Access 2.0 is the data access object (DAO) class. *Data access objects* is a term used to refer collectively to the objects and collections of objects created by the Jet database engine. The **DBEngine** object tops the hierarchy of DAOs and refers to the Jet database engine itself. The Workspaces collection of **Workspace** objects define sessions (instances) of Jet engine use. (You can open multiple Jet engine sessions with Access Basic code.) **Workspace** objects include the Users and Groups collections for establishing permissions for **Workspace** objects. Within each **Workspace** you have the Databases collection that enumerates the **Database** object(s) opened in the **Workspace**. The difference between DAOs and application objects is that you can apply the **Append** or **Open***Object*() methods to DAOs to add a new member to the collection. (You can't use **Append** to add a new member to the Forms or Reports collection or add a new control to a form or report, unfortunately.)

Access 2.0 adds the TableDefs collection to the **Database** object. Visual Basic programmers were introduced to the TableDefs collection in Visual Basic 3.0, which includes the Access 1.1 version of the Jet engine. The TableDefs collection, which enumerates each table of a **Database** object, lets you add new tables to a database, define fields, create indexes, and modify existing tables. The Relationships collection, which is not available in Visual Basic 3.0, defines the default relationships between the tables in an Access 2.0 database.

The **DBEngine** object also has **Container** objects that are members of the Containers collection. **Container** objects enumerate the types of Access objects: Databases, TableDefs (tables), Relationships, QueryDefs (queries), Forms, Reports, Scripts (macros), and Modules. Each **Container** object has a Documents collection that enumerates the saved application and database objects in your application. In addition to providing the data to populate the Database window's list, **Container** objects let you set permissions for each member of the Documents collection with Access Basic code.

Access Basic Code Behind Forms

Code Behind Forms, mentioned earlier in the chapter, brings Visual Basic's event-handling methodology to Access 2.0. Access 2.0 application objects have many more events than their Access 1.x equivalents. For example, text box controls now have 15 events, whereas only 5 events were offered by Access 1.x text boxes. Developers experienced in writing Visual Basic applications, who generally prefer using Access Basic code rather than macros for handling events, will appreciate the similarity between Access 2.0's code behind forms (CBF) and Visual Basic's event-handling code for forms. Both applications now store form-level event-handling code with the form itself. Thus, if you import a form into another database, the event-handling code comes with it. Another benefit of CBF is that you now can import Visual Basic 3.0 event-handling code to Access without making major changes. (Unfortunately, you can't import Visual Basic 3.0 forms into Access 2.0.)

The Access Developer's Toolkit

Most Access 1.1 applications created by developers are distributed as run-time versions that use MSARN110.EXE, instead of MSACCESS.EXE for execution. Many run-time Access applications are installed as client applications in a multiuser (network) environment. The Access Distribution Kit (ADK) for Access 1.1 provided MSARN110.EXE and a Setup Wizard to create application distribution diskettes. In addition, the ADK included a booklet, *The Secrets of Access Wizards*, that described the more arcane methods used in Access Basic to create new application objects programmatically in design mode.

Access 2.0 substitutes the Access Development Toolkit for the ADK. The Access Development Toolkit includes the following components:

- MSARN200.EXE, the run-time executable file for Access 2.0, and other distributable files that you supply with your run-time applications.

- The Microsoft Help Compiler and the *Help Compiler Guide*, which shows you how to use the help compiler, HC31.EXE, with .RTF files you create with Microsoft Word.

- An improved Setup Wizard for creating distribution disks for your run-time applications.

- Several example applications, including versions of Access wizards that contain fully commented code.

- Three OLE Custom Controls: Calendar, Scrollbar, and Data Outline. The OC1016.DLL file, required to use Microsoft and third-party OLE Custom Controls, also is provided.

- A replacement for Visual Basic 3.0's VBDB300.DLL that provides Visual Basic developers with a *mapping layer* between Visual Basic 3.0 and Access 2.0's new .MDB file structure. The mapping layer detects whether the .MDB file is version 1.1 or 2.0, and automatically uses the appropriate Jet DLLs for the .MDB. The Jet DLLs required by Visual Basic 3.0 developers also are included in the ADT.

- The *Access Basic Language Reference*, which is no longer included as a component of the Access 2.0 documentation. You can purchase the *Language Reference* manual directly from Microsoft Corporation if you want to experiment with Access Basic but do not want to purchase the ADT.

- An *Advanced Topics* book describes how to design Access applications for the run-time environment, as well as how to use the components of the ADT. *Advanced Topics* also describes how to use the new OLE 2.0 custom controls with Access 2.0 applications.

The new additions to Access 1.1's ADK make the ADT a virtual necessity for those who develop Access 2.0 applications on a regular basis, whether these applications run under the retail version or the run-time version of Access.

The Microsoft Access Solutions Pack

One of the problems that besets publishers of database development applications such as Access is providing examples of real-world database applications that take full advantage of the features of the publisher's product. Sample databases, such as the Northwind Traders database, do not fulfill this need because sample databases must be designed expressly for entry-level users. Sample databases also are designed to provide example objects for use in conjunction with the product documentation; such databases are subject to modification during the learning process. Modifying the properties of database objects in a real-world application can lead to unexpected behavior. Unexpected behavior is exactly what you *don't want* in a learning environment.

To fill this void, Microsoft offers the Microsoft Access Solutions Pack, a collection of four sample applications that have real-world application. Each of these sample applications consists of a database that holds the tables, an application database, and a help file for the application. The databases are secure and are designed for a networked multiuser environment, but you can use the applications equally well in single-user mode. You can use the applications *as-is* or modify them to suit your particular requirements. The Solutions Pack applications are valuable to developers because they can be used to demonstrate the capabilities of Access to potential clients or to your employer.

Following is a brief description of each of the Solutions Pack applications:

- *Microsoft Access Sales Manager* is designed to store data on sales contacts, track sales opportunities, and find information on both contacts and opportunities. Sales Manager has a built-in time-scheduling system, lets you maintain a history of customer contacts, and can generate mailing lists for form letter preparation with Microsoft Word. Sales Manager provides an excellent demonstration of the use of drill-down methods in a transaction-processing application. Figure 1.32 shows the Contact Overview window of the Sales Manager application.

Fig. 1.32

The Contact Overview window of the Sales Manager application.

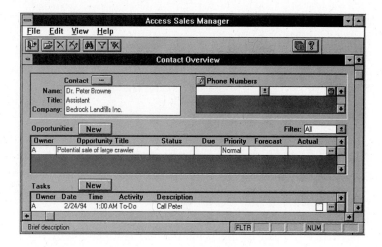

- *Microsoft Access Registration Desk* automates the registration process for seminars, training programs, and similar events. You can preregister attendees and add on-site registrations, and account for paid and owed registration fees. Registration Desk lets you print badges for attendees and create a mailing list to send them letters. You also can compile an on-line survey of attendees responses to the event.

- *Microsoft Access Asset Tracker* is aimed at determining the location of and valuing fixed assets. You can use Asset Tracker to answer one of the questions that plague large corporations: "It's 3:00 p.m. of the last business day of the year. Where are your personal computers and laser printers?" Asset Tracker also lets you maintain records on maintenance cost, depreciation, and asset status.

- *Microsoft Access Service Desk* is an application that maintains queues of service requests and documents the current status and resolution of the service requests. Although the sample data supplied with Service Desk is PC-related, you can use this application for any similar type of activity or business.

From Here...

This chapter has given you an overview of the new and improved features that Microsoft incorporated in Access 2.0, and why these upgrades to Access 1.x are significant to both new and seasoned users of Microsoft Access. There is little question that Access 2.0 is the undisputed victor in the Windows database war that has raged since the introduction of Access 1.0 in November, 1992. It remains to be seen whether promised improvements to competitive products can match Access 2.0's combination of ease of use and remarkably flexible programmability.

- Chapter 2, "Up and Running with Access Tables," gives you a quick introduction to the use of Access 2.0's database and table objects so that you become accustomed to Access's user interface and obtain a foundation in handling the primary objects of relational databases: tables.

- Chapter 8, "Using Query by Example," describes how to create queries in Access's graphical QBE window, and shows how Access translates the query design into Access SQL.

- Chapter 12, "Creating and Using Forms," introduces you to Access's form design environment to create the graphical user interface for Access applications.

- Chapter 19, "Using OLE 2.0," is an overview of how Access 2.0's implementation of in-place activation and OLE Automation makes integrating OLE 2.0 servers with database applications a reality.

- Chapter 28, "Understanding the Data Access Object Class," defines the structure of the new DAOs of Access 2.0 and how to manipulate the members of the DAO class with Access Basic code.

Access Fundamentals

Chapter 2

Up and Running with Access Tables

This chapter is designed to give you an overview of Access's two most important database objects: databases and tables. Even if you're well acquainted with Access 1.x, you might want to browse this chapter for the Access 2.0 icon in the margin that indicates a description of a new feature or an improvement over version 1.x. You'll see the Access 2.0 icon at each location in this book where a new or improved feature is discussed except in Chapter 1, which is devoted to the novel elements of Access 2.0. The examples in this chapter, like most other examples in this book, use the Northwind Traders sample database, NWIND.MDB, that is supplied with Access. *Northwind Traders* is a fictitious wholesaler of specialty food products whose accounting system is an Access database application created by Microsoft. The sample database includes tables, forms, and reports that a small firm might use to automate its invoicing, inventory control, ordering, and personnel operations. The remainder of Part I (Chapters 3 through 7) expands on the subjects you learn in this chapter using NWIND.MDB and describes in detail how you create and use Access database tables.

Access

2.0

In this chapter, you learn to

- Launch Access and open the Northwind Traders database

- Open a table and view its contents

- Select records and edit the data they contain

- Use design mode to view the properties of a table and its fields

- Print the contents of a table

Note

This chapter assumes that you have installed Access. If you haven't installed Access, refer to your Access documentation for instructions on setting up Access on your fixed disk.

Starting Access

To start Access and open the Northwind Traders database, NWIND.MDB, perform the following steps:

1. Double-click the Access icon in the Access application group.

   As Access is loading, a copyright notice (called a *splash screen*) appears with the name and organization that was entered during the installation process. Then Access's sparse opening window appears, as shown in figure 2.1.

Fig. 2.1
Access 2.0's blank
opening window.

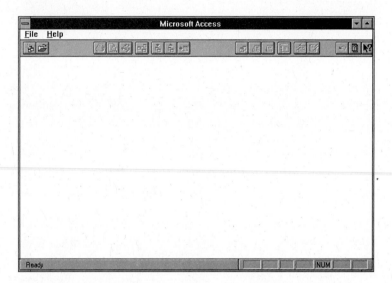

2. Click the Open Database button of the toolbar, or choose **F**ile from the main menu bar. If you use the menu to open a database, the **F**ile menu appears (see fig. 2.2).

   If you have run Access previously, the file names of up to four Access database files you have opened may appear above the **E**xit command in the **F**ile menu.

   The screen shown in figure 2.2 and the other screens throughout this chapter have sizable borders. When you launch Access, its display is *maximized*—it fills your entire display. Figure 2.2 shows Access operating in a normal, sizable window. To change to a sizable window, click the Application Control-menu box at the upper-left corner of the display, and then choose **R**estore. Click and drag the sides of Access's window to make it the size you want.

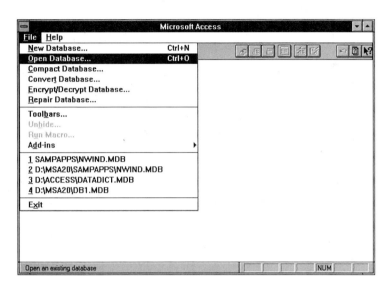

Fig. 2.2
The Access **F**ile menu.

3. Choose the **O**pen Database command from the **F**ile menu to display the Open Database dialog.

4. Double-click sampapps in the Directories list to change the directory to \ACCESS\SAMPAPPS. The Open Database dialog appears, as shown in figure 2.3.

5. Double-click nwind.mdb in the File Name list to open the Northwind Traders sample database.

The Database window for the Northwind Traders database appears, as shown in figure 2.4.

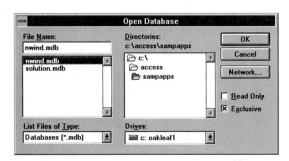

Fig. 2.3
The Open Database dialog.

Note

Toolbar buttons of Access 2.0 now provide *ToolTips.* ToolTips are small captions that appear under a button after the mouse pointer has rested on a button for more than about 0.5 seconds. If you find ToolTips to be distracting, you can turn off this feature by choosing Tool**b**ars from the **V**iew menu to display the Toolbars dialog. Click the Show ToolTips check box to remove the check mark and click the Close button. If you are using SVGA mode (800×600 pixels) or UVGA mode (1,024×768 pixels), you may want to try clicking the Large Buttons check box of the Toolbars dialog. The icons of larger buttons are easier to discern in SVGA mode and especially UVGA mode.

Fig. 2.4

The Database Window for the Northwind Traders sample database.

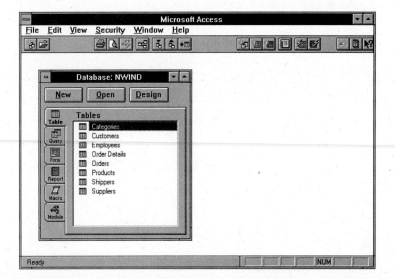

Note

You can use several other methods to open a file in the common Open Database dialog. You can click nwind.mdb to place it in the File Name text box and then click OK. Or you can type **nwind** in the File Name text box and click OK. Access adds the default .MDB extension for you. Double-clicking is the fastest and most mistake-proof method of opening a file.

The Database window is your "home base" for all operations with the sample database or databases you create. Almost every operation you perform with Access begins with a choice you make from the Database window.

After you open a database file, the three groups of buttons to the right of the New Database and Open Database buttons of the Database toolbar (under the main menu bar) are enabled. *Toolbar buttons*, a common feature of new Windows applications, are shortcuts for menu choices. Any operation you can perform by clicking a toolbar button can be performed by making two or more menu choices. Access 2.0 has 19 standard toolbars; Access displays the appropriate toolbar for the database object in the active window. You can customize the standard toolbars or create your own special-purpose toolbars. Using the toolbar buttons is much quicker and, once you learn what the symbols mean, more intuitive than using Windows' standard menu structure. Chapter 3, "Navigating within Access," describes the use of Access 2.0's new toolbars in detail.

Access
2.0

▶ "The Toolbar in Table View," p. 93

▶ "Customizable Toolbars," p. 491

Using Database Tables

This chapter is devoted to exploring tables, which are the basic elements of all databases and the portion of the Access database file where data is stored.

▶ "Understanding Access's Table Display," p. 87

Viewing Data in Tables

To display the contents of the Categories table, which describes the types of products in which Northwind trades, double-click Categories in the Database window's list of tables. The Categories table appears, as shown in figure 2.5.

The normal method of displaying the information contained in relational database tables is the familiar row-column technique used by spreadsheet applications. Every widely used PC RDBMS uses row-column presentation for data contained in tables. The rows of a table are known as *records*, and the columns are referred to as *fields*. A record contains information on a single object, such as one class of product or a particular invoice. A field contains the same type of information, such as a product code, for all records in a table. In this book, the intersection between a row and a column—a single field of a single record—is called a *data cell*. A data cell contains a single piece of information. The terms *data item* and *data entity* often are used as synonyms for *data cell*.

Figure 2.5 shows the data in the Categories table in what Access calls *Datasheet View*—the default method of displaying a table. You select the Datasheet View, if another type of view is active, by clicking the Datasheet button, which resembles a spreadsheet, on the toolbar. You also can choose **D**atasheet from the **V**iew menu. Datasheet View also is the default for viewing the results of queries; you can see a Datasheet View of the table or query when you are creating an Access form.

Tip
You also can display the Categories table by clicking Categories and then clicking the Open button or pressing Enter. The double-clicking method is quicker, however.

Fig. 2.5

The Datasheet display of the records in the Categories table.

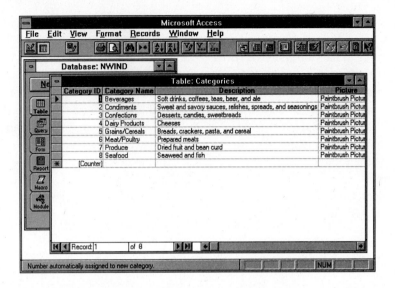

Selecting and Editing Data Records

To change the data contained in any cell of the table (other than in OLE Object fields that are used to display pictures), select the cell by clicking it with the mouse or by using the arrow keys. Selected content is indicated by the white on black (reverse) appearance of the cell. The default selected cell is the first field of the first record of the table. All contents of that cell are selected when you first display the table.

> **Caution**
>
> If you type a character into a cell when its entire content is selected, the character you type replaces what was in that cell. You can recover from an accidental replacement by pressing Esc; this action restores the original content, but *only* if you have not yet selected a different cell. When you make a change in a data cell and then move to a new data cell, the change is made to the content of the table. Click the selected data cell to deselect the entire contents of the cell.

> **Note**
>
> See Chapter 5, "Entering, Editing, and Validating Data in Tables," for detailed information on editing data records.

You can select any cell to edit by positioning the mouse pointer at the point within a cell where you want to make the change and then clicking your mouse. The mouse pointer resembles an I-beam when it is located within the contents of data cells. The editing cursor, a thin vertical line called the *caret* by Windows and this book, often referred to as the *insertion point* in other texts, appears.

The conventional text-editing functions of Windows applications apply to Access. At this point, you shouldn't change the data, called *values*, of the data cells. Changes to values may affect the appearance of examples in later chapters. If you do make a change, a pencil symbol appears in the gray box at the left of the window corresponding to the record whose value you have changed. You can return to the original value by pressing Esc. If you click an OLE Object field, indicated in figure 2.5 by a cell containing the words Paintbrush Picture, the cell has a thick, gray border and the caret does not appear. You cannot edit the text of an OLE Object field.

You use the empty record at the bottom of the table, indicated by the asterisk (*) in the selection button column for the record, to add a new record to the table. If you enter any data into a cell of this record, a new record containing the data you entered is added to the table. If you accidentally add data in this *tentative append* record, click the Record Selection button to select the record, and then press Delete. A dialog appears requesting confirmation of your deletion. Click OK.

If you use the arrow keys to select a data cell, all contents of the cell are selected. You cannot click the corner of a cell and drag the mouse pointer to a cell in the opposite corner of an imaginary rectangle to select a group of cells, as you do with Excel. You can, however, select an entire record by clicking the selection button for that record, or you can select a group of records by dragging the mouse down the selection button column. Records and groups of records most often are selected in order to copy the records to the Windows Clipboard. Notice that when you select a cell with the keyboard or the mouse, the triangular arrow moves to the selected record. The button with the triangular arrow is called the *current record pointer*.

You use the left set of buttons in the bar at the bottom of the datasheet window to position the current record pointer within the bounds of the table. Click the left-arrow button to position the current record pointer at the first record in the table, and click the right-arrow button to move to the last or bottom record of the table. The left- and right-arrow buttons move the pointer one record at a time in the direction indicated. You can enter a record number in the Record text box or use the vertical scroll bar to position the active record pointer. The vertical scroll bar appears only if more records are present than can fit in the vertical dimension of the Datasheet window.

 The horizontal scroll bar enables you to view fields that lie to the right of the far right visible field. Use the left and right arrows for small movements, or use the scroll box to make large moves to the left or right. You also can traverse several fields by clicking the region of the scroll bar between the scroll box and the arrow.

 To select all data cells in a field, click the button containing the field name at the top of the datasheet. When the mouse pointer is over a field name, the pointer changes to a down arrow. You can search for cells within the field you select that contain a particular group of characters by clicking the toolbar's Find button—a pair of binoculars. The Find dialog appears (see fig. 2.6).

Fig. 2.6
The Find dialog.

Enter the characters you want to find in the Find What text box. Then open the Where drop-down list by clicking the down arrow, and select Any Part of Field. You can search up or down from the position of the current record by selecting the Up or Down Direction option buttons. Click the Find First button to search for the first occurrence of a match, and then click the Find Next button to locate other matches. After you find all matching records or no matching records, a dialog appears stating that you have reached the end of the table. Click the Close button to return to the Table window.

Viewing and Editing Graphics

One of the reasons for choosing the Categories table for this chapter is that it
includes bit-mapped graphic images stored in an OLE Object field. If you
double-click one of the Paintbrush Picture data cells, Windows 3.1's Paintbrush window appears with the bit-mapped image displayed, as shown in
figure 2.7. You can use Paintbrush to display the image or to edit. Because
Windows 3.1's Paintbrush is an OLE 1.0 server, all of Paintbrush's bit-mapped
image display and editing capabilities are available to you while you are using
Access. (Paintbrush is not an OLE 2.0 server, so you are not able to take advantage of in-place editing with embedded Access OLE objects created with
Paintbrush.)

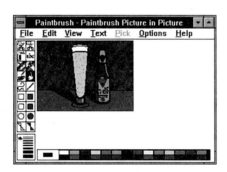

Fig. 2.7

A bit-mapped
image displayed
using Windows
Paintbrush.

When you're finished viewing an image, double-click the Application
Control-menu box in the upper left corner of Paintbrush's window to close
the image. You also can exit an OLE server by choosing E**x**it & Return from
the server's **F**ile menu. If you have made any changes to the image, a dialog
appears asking whether you want to update the Access table. In this case,
click No to retain the original image.

Using Design Mode

Design mode for tables displays the characteristics of each field in the table in
a grid format similar to a spreadsheet. To view the design of the Categories
table, click the Design View button, which appears as an architect's triangle   ▶ "Defining Access
and pencil, at the left end of the toolbar. Design mode appears, as shown in   Operating
figure 2.8. Alternatively, you can choose Table **D**esign from the **V**iew menu   Modes," p. 87
or select the table name in the Database window and click the Design button.

You can view and edit the properties that apply to the table object as a whole in the Table Properties window, as shown in figure 2.9. Click the Properties button on the toolbar (a hand pointing to a window) or choose Table Proper**t**ies from the **V**iew menu to display the Table Properties window. The Table Properties window enables you to enter a text description of the table and assign a value to the `ValidationRule` property of the table. Table-level validation rules, which are new with Access 2.0, can contain a rule that applies to more than one field in a table. The `ValidationText` text property is the message that appears if you attempt to violate the validation rule.

Click the Indexes button or choose **I**ndexes from the **V**iew menu to display the Indexes window, which also is new in Access 2.0. The Indexes window, shown in figure 2.10, displays each of the fields of the table and identifies the *primary-key field*, which is the field with the symbol of the key in its selection button column. The primary-key field is the field or combination of fields that is used to uniquely identify each record in the table. Most tables are indexed on a single primary-key field, and primary-key field indexes do not permit duplicate keys. *Indexes* are internal tables that speed the creation of query result tables by simulating the sorting of the table on the value of the key field. Key fields establish the relations by which multiple tables of a database are linked when you create a query. The term *relational database* indicates database management applications that are capable of linking tables by key fields.

▶ "Using Access Indexes," p. 869

Fig. 2.8
The Design View
of a table.

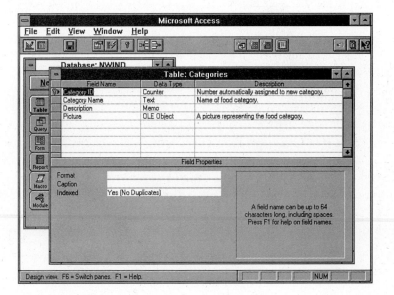

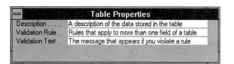

Fig. 2.9
The Table
Properties
window.

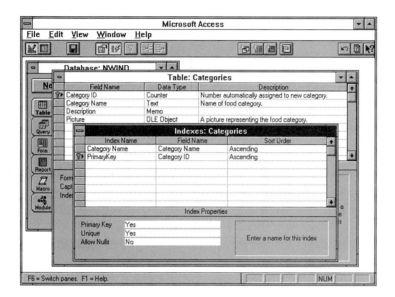

Fig. 2.10
The Indexes
window.

Each field in a table requires a unique name and must be assigned a field data type. Field names, data types, and an optional text description of the field are entered in the design grid. (Click the Indexes button or double-click the Application Control-menu box of the Indexes window to close it so that the entire design grid is visible. Do the same to close the Properties window.) Text is the most common type of data in tables; therefore, Text is the default data type. Many other field data types are available in Access; you already have been introduced to the OLE Object field data type. Click one of the Data Type cells, and then click the down-arrow to open the Data Type drop-down list to display the Data Type choices offered by Access. Click the arrow again to close the list. Field data types in Access include various numeric formats, date and time, and other types that you learn about in later chapters of this book. Now click the Datasheet View button to display the Datasheet View of the Categories table in run mode.

Printing the Contents of a Table

Access enables you to print the contents of your table without creating a fully formatted report. You may want to print raw table data to proofread the new records you have created or the old ones you have edited. The Print Preview window is much like the one offered by Microsoft Word and Excel. The Print Preview window enables you to see how tables, forms, and reports will appear if printed.

 To see how the Categories table will appear if printed, click the toolbar's Preview button (the page symbol with the magnifying glass). The Print Preview window appears, as shown in figure 2.11. The title bar of the Print Preview window reflects what you're preparing to print. In this example, the title bar shows Table:Categories. You also can choose the Print Preview option from the File menu to display the Print Preview window.

 To see a magnified view of how the printed version of your table will appear, click the surface of the simulated sheet of paper in the Print Preview window. When the mouse pointer is on the paper, the pointer turns into the shape of a magnifying glass, as shown in figure 2.11. Place the magnifying glass over the image; otherwise, when the window is magnified, the view is of a blank page and you wonder where the table went. Figure 2.12 shows the magnified (zoomed) view of the Categories table. Click again to restore the original, unreadable version of the report. The Zoom button has an effect similar to clicking the mouse on the surface of the preview image.

Fig. 2.11

The Print Preview window for a table.

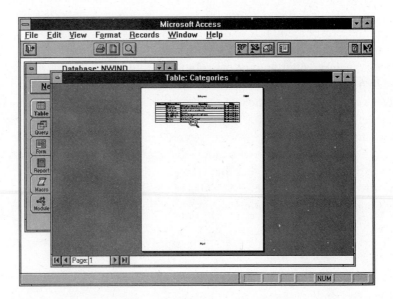

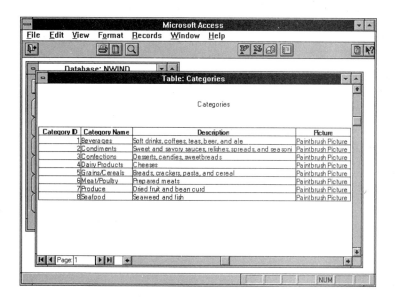

Fig. 2.12
A magnified view
of the Categories
table.

Access Fundamentals

When you are ready to print, click the Print button (with the symbol of a printer) on the toolbar. The Print dialog appears, as shown in figure 2.13.

To print in landscape mode with your laser printer or to otherwise change your printer's settings, click the Setup button and make the appropriate changes in the Print Setup dialog, as shown in figure 2.14. You can reset the printing margins by entering different values in the Margins text boxes. Click OK to reopen the Print dialog, and click OK to print the table.

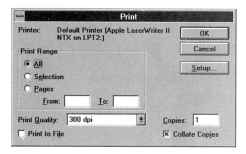

Fig. 2.13
The Print dialog.

Now that you have run the gamut of the basic operations available for Access tables, double-click the Document Control-menu box to close the Print Preview window and return to the Database window. Now, you may open one or more of the other tables that comprise the Northwind Traders database to learn a bit more about their contents. The Employees table includes scanned images of photographs of the fictional staff of Northwind Traders. The Suppliers table lists an eclectic group of food-processing firms from many points on the globe. You can see most of the international characters, such as umlauts and tildes, in Windows' ANSI character set in the supplier name and address fields. Both Access and Windows 3.1 are available in a wide range of languages in addition to British, Canadian, and U.S. English.

Fig. 2.14
The Print Setup
dialog.

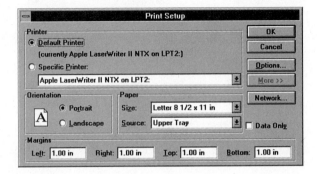

From Here...

This chapter gave you a feel for the methods you can use to view and manipulate the data contained in tables. The basic operations you learned in this chapter are applicable, in general, to all other functions of Access, as should be the case with any well-designed Windows application.

Your next step is to learn more about the overall plan that Microsoft drew up for the user interface of Access. The plan was implemented by changing toolbar buttons and menu choices depending on whether you are viewing or creating tables, queries, forms, reports, macros, or modules.

- Chapter 3, "Navigating within Access," describes how Access is organized, as well as how you manage multiple document windows, keyboard commands, and Access's context-sensitive help system.

- Chapter 4, "Working with Access Databases and Tables," has you begin to apply what you learned in this chapter in order to work with Access tables. The majority of the examples in Chapter 4 continue to use the Northwind Traders database, but you add your own tables to expand its capabilities.

- Chapter 5, "Entering, Editing, and Validating Data in Tables," shows you how to add records to tables, edit data in the records, and add validation rules to your tables to ensure that data values fall within accepted limits.

- Chapter 6, "Sorting, Finding, and Filtering Data in Tables," describes how to use Access's built-in sorting, search, search and replace, and filters to locate records meeting criteria you set, and how to make bulk changes to field data.

- Chapter 7, "Attaching, Importing, and Exporting Tables," explains how to import data from your existing database tables, worksheets, or text files, and how to export table data in a variety of useful formats.

- Chapter 20, "Adding Graphics to Forms and Reports," shows you how to display and print OLE objects contained in OLE Object fields of Access tables and in OLE control objects you place on forms and reports.

Access Fundamentals

Chapter 3

Navigating within Access

This chapter describes how Access is structured and organized to expedite the design and use of the database objects it offers. A substantial portion of this chapter consists of tables that list the functions of window Control-menu boxes, toolbar buttons, and an array of function key combinations. Many function and key assignments are derived from other Microsoft applications, such as Excel (F2 for editing) and Word for Windows (Shift+F4 to find the next occurrence of a match). These assignments don't duplicate those key assignments to which you may have become accustomed when using dBASE, xBase, or Paradox.

This chapter is a reference to which you can return when you conclude that a keystroke combination may be a better choice for an action than a mouse click, but you cannot remember the required combination. (Refer to Chapter 5, "Entering, Editing, and Validating Data in Tables," for details of the key combinations you use to edit data in tables and queries.) An explanation of the structure and content of the help system for Access also is included in this chapter.

In this chapter, you learn to

- Use Access 2.0's new toolbars with tables

- Use global function keys to perform common operations

- Set your own default options for Access 2.0

- Use Cue Cards and the Access help system

- Compact and repair Access 2.0 databases

Understanding Access's Functions and Modes

Access, unlike word processing and spreadsheet applications, is a truly multi-functional program. Although word processing applications, for example, have many sophisticated capabilities, their basic purpose is to support text entry, page layout, and formatted printing. All of a word processing application's primary functions and supporting features are directed to these ends. All word processing operations are performed using views representing a sheet of paper—usually 8 1/2 inches by 11 inches. Most spreadsheet applications use the row-column metaphor for all their functions—even for writing highly sophisticated programs in their macro languages. The sections that follow describe Access's basic functions and operating modes.

Defining Access Functions

To qualify as a full-fledged relational database management system, an application must perform the following four basic, but distinct functions, each with its own presentation (called a *view*) to the user:

■ *Data organization.* Involves the creation and manipulation of tables that contain data in conventional tabular (row-column or spreadsheet) format, called *Datasheet View* by Access.

■ *Table linking and data extraction.* Links multiple tables by data relationships to create temporary tables stored in your computer's memory or temporary disk files that contain the data you choose. Access uses *queries* to link tables and to choose the data to be stored in a temporary table called a **Recordset** object in Access 2.0. (Access 1.x's **Dynaset** and **Snapshot** objects, which are both **Recordset** objects, are supported in Access 2.0 for backward compatibility.) A **Recordset** object consists of the data that results from running the query; **Recordset** objects are called *virtual tables* because they are stored in your computer's memory, rather than in database files. The capability to link tables by relations distinguishes relational database systems from simple list-processing applications, called *flat-file managers.* Data extraction limits the presentation of dynasets to specific groups of data that meet criteria you establish. *Expressions* are used to calculate values from data, such as an extended amount by multiplying unit price and quantity, and to display the calculated values as if they were a field in one of the tables.

■ *Data entry and editing.* Requires design and implementation of data viewing, entry, and editing forms as an alternative to tabular presentation. A form enables *you*, rather than the *application*, to control how the data is presented. Forms are much easier than recordsets in tabular format for most persons to use for data entry, especially when many fields are involved. The capability to print forms, such as sales orders and invoices, is a definite benefit to the user.

■ *Data presentation*. Requires creation of reports that are capable of summarizing the information in recordsets that you can view and print (this is the last step in the process). The capability to provide meaningful reports is the ultimate purpose of any database management application. Also, the management of an enterprise usually lends more credence to reports that are attractively formatted and contain charts or graphs that summarize the data for those officials who take the "broad brush" approach.

The four basic functions of Access that are implemented as views are organized into an application structure represented graphically in figure 3.1. If you are creating a new database, you use the basic functions of Access in the top-down sequence shown in the illustration. You choose the function to be performed by clicking a button in the Datasheet window, except for security and printing operations, which are menu choices. In most views, you can use the Print Preview window that leads to printing operations by clicking the Print Preview button of the toolbar.

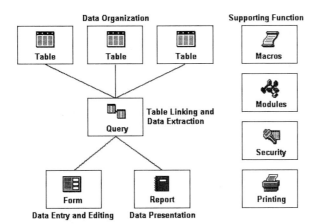

Fig. 3.1
The basic and supporting functions of Access.

Four supporting functions apply to all the basic functions of Access:

■ *Macros*. A sequence of actions that automate repetitive database operations. You create a macro by choosing actions from a list of available actions in Access, in the order in which you want them to appear. You can use a macro, for example, to open a report, print the report, and then close the report. The terms *open* and *close*, as they are used in Access, are explained in the next section.

■ *Modules*. Functions and procedures written in the Access Basic programming language. You use Access Basic functions to make calculations that are more complex than those that can be expressed easily by a series of conventional mathematical symbols, or to make calculations that require decisions to be made. Access Basic procedures are written to perform operations that exceed the capabilities of standard macro actions. You run Access Basic procedures by invoking them with the macro action RunCode or directly from events, such as clicking a command button with the mouse, that can occur when a form or report is the active object.

■ *Security*. Functions available as menu choices only. Security functions enable you to give permission for other people to use your database in a multiuser environment. You may grant access to user groups and individuals, and you may restrict their ability to view or modify all or a portion of the tables in the database.

■ *Printing*. Enables you to print virtually anything you can view in Access's run mode. You can print your Access Basic code, but not the macros you write, from the toolbar. (You can use the Database Document add-in to print the content of your macros.)

The terms *open* and *close* have the same basic usage in Access as in other Windows applications, but usually involve more than one basic function:

■ Opening a database makes its content available to the application through the Database window described in Chapter 2. You may open only one database at a time during ordinary use of Access. Writing Access Basic code enables you to operate with tables from more than one database. You can achieve the equivalent of multiple open Access databases by attaching tables from other databases.

■ Opening a table provides a Datasheet View of its contents.

■ Opening a query opens the tables involved but does not display them. Access then runs the query on these tables to create a tabular **Recordset**. Changes made to data in the **Recordset** cause corresponding changes to be made to the data in the tables associated with the query, if the **Recordset** is updatable. (Access 1.x's **Table** and **Dynaset** objects usually are updatable, but **Snapshot** objects are never updatable.)

■ Opening a form or report automatically opens the table or query with which it is associated. Both forms and reports usually are associated with queries, but a query also can employ a single table.

■ Closing a query closes the associated tables.

■ Closing a form or report closes the associated query and its tables.

Defining Access Operating Modes

Access has three basic operating modes:

■ *Startup.* Enables you to compress, encrypt, decrypt, and repair a database by commands from the **F**ile menu prior to opening a database. These commands, discussed at the end of the chapter, aren't available after you have opened a database.

■ *Design.* Enables you to create and modify the structure of tables and queries, develop forms to display and edit your data, and format reports for printing. Access calls design mode *Design View*.

■ *Run.* Displays your table, form, and report designs in individual document windows (run is the default mode). You execute macros by choosing one and then selecting run mode. Run mode is not applicable to Access Basic modules, because functions are executed when encountered as elements of queries, forms, and reports. Procedures in modules are run by macro commands, or directly from events of forms and reports. Run mode is called *Datasheet View* for tables and queries, *Form View* for forms, and *Print Preview* for reports.

You can select design or run mode by choosing command buttons in the Datasheet window, buttons on the toolbar, or commands from the **V**iew menu.

You can change the default conditions under which Access displays and prints your tables, queries, forms, and reports by choosing the **V**iew **O**ptions menu command. Options that are applicable to Access as a whole, and those that apply only to tables, are described in the section, "Setting Default Options," near the end of this chapter.

Understanding Access's Table Display

You probably are familiar with the basic terms for many of the components that comprise the basic window in which all conventional Windows applications run. The presentation of Access windows differs with each of the basic functions Access performs. Because Part I of this book deals almost exclusively with tables, Table View is used in the examples that follow. Figure 3.2 shows Access for Windows' basic display for operations with tables. The individual components of the window are described in table 3.1.

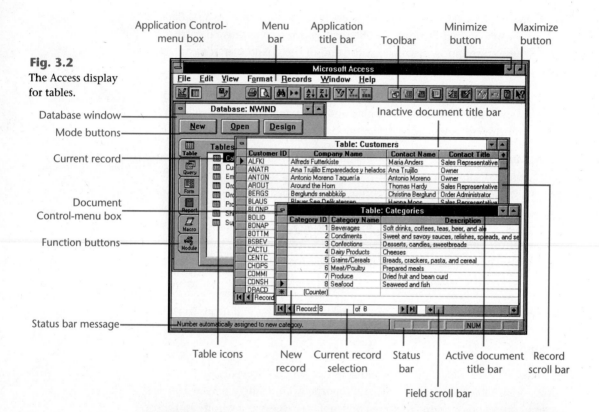

Fig. 3.2
The Access display for tables.

Table 3.1   Components of the Access Display for Tables

Term	Description
Active window	The window to which all mouse and keyboard actions are directed. When an application or document is active, its title bar appears in color (dark blue, unless you have changed your Windows color scheme). If both the application title bar and a document title bar are active, the document title bar receives the mouse and keyboard actions.

Access Fundamentals

Term	Description
Application Control-menu box	The box, or button, for the Application Control menu that controls the presentation of the Application window. You display the Application Control menu by clicking the box or pressing Alt+space bar.
Application title bar	A bar at the top of the application's window that displays its name. You can move the entire application, if it isn't maximized, by clicking the application title bar and dragging it to a new position.
Application window	The window within which Access is displayed. Each application you launch runs within its own application window.
Caret	A vertical flashing line that indicates the insertion point for keyboard entry in areas of a window that accept text.
Current Record button	Indicates a single selected record in the table. When you are editing the current record, the button icon becomes a pencil, rather than a triangular arrow. The Current Record button also is called the *record pointer*.
Current Record selection buttons and window	Buttons that position the record pointer to the first, next, preceding, and last record number in the table. If a key field has been specified, the current record number is not the record number corresponding to the sequence of its addition to the database (as is the case with xBase and Paradox), but the sequence of the record in the sorting order of the primary key.
Database window	The window that controls the operating mode of Access and selects the current function of the active document window. You select the component of the database to display in the document window, such as a particular table, from those displayed in the Database window.
Document Control-menu box	The box, or button, for the Document Control menu that controls the presentation of a document window. You access the Document Control menu by clicking the box or pressing Alt+- (hyphen).
Document title bar	A bar at the top of each document's window that displays the document's name. You can move the document, if it isn't maximized, by clicking the application title bar and dragging the document to a new position.

Record Number

(continues)

Table 3.1 Continued	
Term	**Description**
Document window	The window in which a component of an Access database is displayed. Tables, queries, forms, reports, macros, and modules are referred to as *documents* in Windows terminology. You can have multiple Access documents of any type open simultaneously. These windows are called *multiple document interface (MDI) child windows*, because the Access application window is their *parent*.
Field scroll bar	Enables you to view fields of tables that are outside the bounds of the document window. Record scroll bars provide access to records located outside the document window.
Function buttons	Six buttons that choose whether the active document window displays tables, queries, forms, reports, macros, or modules.
Inactive window	A window in the background, usually with a white or grayed title bar. Clicking the surface of an inactive window makes it the active window and brings it to the front. If an inactive window is not visible because other windows obscure it, you can make the window active by choosing the window's name from the **W**indow menu.
Maximize button	Clicking the *application's* Maximize button causes Access to occupy your entire display. Clicking the *document's* Maximize button causes the document to take over the entire display. Figure 3.3 shows a maximized table document.
Menu bar	A horizontal bar containing main menu choices. These choices remain constant, but the choices in the drop-down menus corresponding to the main menu selections change, depending on Access's status.
Minimize button	Collapses the application or document window to an icon at the bottom of your display.
Mode buttons	Three buttons that determine the operating mode of Access. *Open* places Access in run mode. *New* or *Design* puts Access in design mode, where you can create or edit tables.
New record	A button with an asterisk that indicates the location of the next record to be added to a table. Entering data in the new record appends the record to the table and creates another new record.

Term	Description
Restore button	A double set of triangular arrows that, when clicked, returns the window from full display to its normal size, with moveable borders. When displayed, the Restore button takes the place of the Maximize button in the window's upper right corner.
Status bar	A bar located at the bottom of the application window that displays prompts and indicators, such as the status of the Num Lock key.
Toolbar	A bar containing command buttons that duplicate the more commonly used menu choices. The number and type of toolbar buttons change depending on which basic function of Access you are using.

Maximized Document Windows

Access uses a windowing technique that you should know about before you accidentally minimize or close Access when you intended to minimize or close a maximized document. After you click the Maximize button of a document window, the document window takes the place of the application window and occupies the entire display, except for the menu bar and toolbar (see fig. 3.3). Most other Windows applications that display multiple documents, such as Word for Windows and Excel, have a similar capability to expand a document to occupy the entire window.

The Document Control-menu box and Document Restore button move to the extreme left and right, respectively, of the menu bar. The title of the document takes the place of the application title in the title bar at the top of the display. To return the document window to its original size, established when the application window was first active, click the Document Restore button; or click the Document Control-menu box and then choose **R**estore from the Document Control menu. You can close the document window by double-clicking the Document Control-menu box. If you accidentally double-click the Application Control-menu box just above the Document Control-menu box, however, you close Access for Windows. You receive no warning that you are about to exit Access unless you have changed the design of an object.

Document Control-menu box

Application Control-menu box

Document Maximize button

Document Minimize button

Document Restore button

Fig. 3.3

An Access table in
a maximized
document
window.

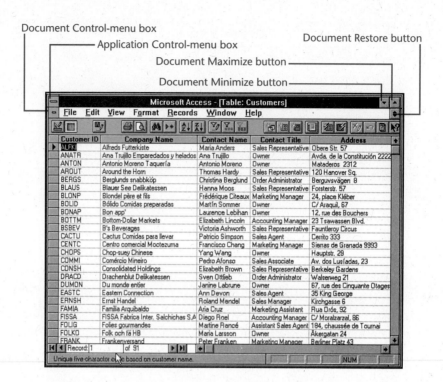

Document Windows Minimized to Icons

Working with several overlapping windows limits each window to a size that
enables you to select another by clicking its surface with the mouse. This
overlapping may overly restrict your view of the data the windows contain.
You can minimize Access document windows and the Database window to
icons that remain within the application window, as shown in figure 3.4. If
you minimize a document window to an icon, rather than closing it, you
quickly can return the window to its original size by double-clicking the icon.
If you single-click the icon, you can choose how the window reappears by
using the Document Control menu, as shown for the Database window in
figure 3.4.

If you choose to display your document window in maximized form by
choosing Maximize from the Document Control menu that appears when
you click the icon, the document hides the icons at the bottom of the
application window. In this case, use the **W**indow menu and choose the
document you want. If you size your document windows like the window
in figure 3.4 by dragging their borders, you can avoid the substantial mouse
movement and two-step menu-selection process to select the active document.

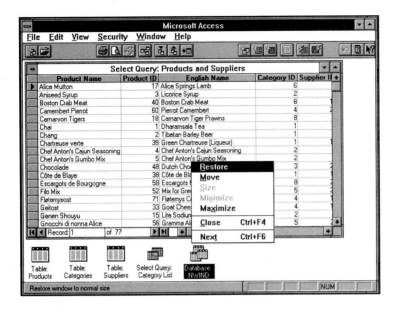

Fig. 3.4
Tables, a query, a form, and the Database window minimized to icons within the application window.

The Toolbar in Table View

The buttons that appear in Access's toolbar change according to the function that Access is performing at the time. When you are working with tables in run mode, the toolbar appears, as shown in figure 3.5. Many additional menu shortcut buttons have been added to the toolbars of Access 2.0. The toolbar buttons that appear in table run mode (Datasheet View) are described in table 3.2.

Access
2.0

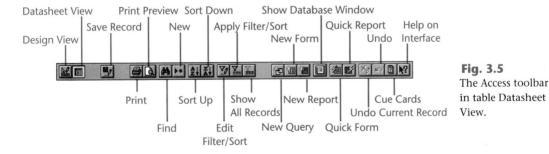

Fig. 3.5
The Access toolbar in table Datasheet View.

Toolbar buttons represent shortcuts to traditional selection methods, such as choosing menu commands or choosing command or option buttons in a particular sequence. The Alternate Method column of table 3.2 lists how you can achieve the same effect as clicking a toolbar button by using the menus or the command buttons in the Database window.

Table 3.2 Appearance and Functions of Buttons and Other Elements of the Table Toolbar

Icon	Button	Alternate Method	Function
	Design View	**V**iew **T**able Design	Changes table display to design mode. In design mode, you specify the properties of each field of the table.
	Datasheet View	**V**iew Data**s**heet	Returns table display to run mode (Datasheet View) from design mode.
	Save Record	**Fi**le Save Rec**o**rd	Saves changes to the current record.
	Print	**Fi**le **P**rint	Prints the table.
	Print Preview	**Fi**le Print Pre**v**iew	Displays the contents of a table in report format and enables you to print the contents of the table.
	Find	**E**dit **F**ind	Displays the Find in Field dialog that locates records with specific characters in a single field or all fields.
	New	**R**ecords **G**o to Ne**w**	Selects the tentative append record.
	Sort Up	**R**ecords **Q**uick Sort **A**scending	Sorts the records in ascending order.
	Sort Down	**R**ecords **Q**uick Sort **D**escending	Sorts the records in descending order.
	Edit Filter/Sort	**R**ecords Edit **F**ilter/Sort	Creates or changes a filter or sort order.
	Apply Filter/Sort	**R**ecords Apply Filter/Sort	Applies a filter or sort order to a table.
	Show all records	**R**ecords **S**how All Records	Removes an applied filter.

Icon	Button	Alternate Method	Function
	New Query	Database window, Query New	Changes to design mode and creates a New Query window displaying the field list box for the first table on the table list or the table you have opened in Datasheet View.
	New Form	Database window, Form New	Changes to design mode and displays a dialog that enables you to select whether to use the Form Wizard or a blank form to create a new form for data entry or display.
	New Report	Database window, Report New	Changes to design mode and displays a dialog that enables you to select whether to use the Report Wizard or a blank report to create a new report for summarizing data or printing.
	Show Database Window	**W**indow **1**	Displays Database window.
	Quick Form	New Form with Wizard	Equivalent to clicking the New Form button, and choosing Single-column as the form type and Embossed as the form style.
	Quick Report	New Report with Wizard	Equivalent to clicking the New Report button, and choosing Single-column as the report type and Presentation as the report style.
	Undo Current	(None)	Returns the Record current record to its state prior to editing.

(continues)

Table 3.2	Continued		
Icon	**Button**	**Alternate Method**	**Function**
	Undo	**E**dit **U**ndo	Returns you to the status immediately preceding the last action you took. The Undo button is inactive if there is no action to undo. Access provides a single-level Undo feature; it will repeal only one action.
	Help on User	Shift+F1	Turns the mouse interface pointer into a ? symbol with a pointer. Placing the pointer on a toolbar button and clicking the mouse button displays the help window for the button or the corresponding menu choice.

Access's toolbar has a fixed width, anchored at its left edge. If you reduce the width of Access's application window by dragging either vertical border inward, you first lose the Help button, then the Undo and Quick buttons, and finally the New buttons from right to left. Operating Access in a maximized window usually is best, because all the toolbar buttons are easily accessible when you use the default in-line horizontal toolbar.

Access

2.0

Manipulating Access 2.0 Toolbars

The toolbars of Access 1.x were Access forms stored in the UTILITY.MDB file, and were firmly anchored to the area immediately below the menu bar. Access 2.0 has adopted the resizable, customizable, floating toolbars of the current crop of Microsoft applications, such as Excel 5.0 and Microsoft Word 6.0. Access 2.0's new **V**iew **T**oolbars menu choice opens the Toolbars dialog (see figure 3.6) that lets you display as many toolbars at once as will fit in your display.

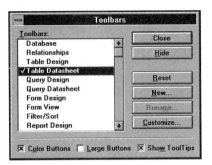

Fig. 3.6
Access 2.0's new
Toolbars dialog.

In addition to displaying multiple toolbars, you can reshape the toolbars to suit your own taste. Click a blank area of the toolbar and hold the left mouse button down to drag the toolbar to a new location. The toolbar turns into a *pop-up* floating toolbar, similar to the toolbox that you use to add control objects to forms and reports. Pop-up toolbars always appear on top of any other windows open in your application. Figure 3.7 shows two floating toolbars, the Table Datasheet toolbar and the Microsoft toolbar. The Microsoft toolbar lets you launch Microsoft Word, Excel, Mail, PowerPoint, FoxPro, Project, and Schedule+ by clicking a button, if these applications are installed on your computer.

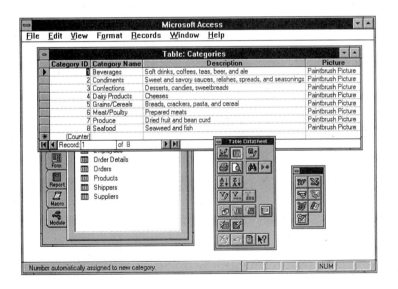

Fig. 3.7
Two floating
toolbars dragged
from below the
menu bar.

Right Mouse Button Shortcut Menus

Another feature introduced by Access 2.0 is the shortcut menu that appears when you click the right mouse button with the mouse pointer located on the surface of an Access database object. Shortcut menus (also called *floating menus*) present choices that depend on the type of object you click. Figure 3.8 shows the shortcut menu for a field of a table that was selected by clicking the field name header. If you select a single data cell, the shortcut menu gives you the option of displaying the data in the Zoom dialog, copying the selection to the Clipboard, or obtaining help on editing data in tables.

Fig. 3.8

The shortcut menu for a selected field of a table.

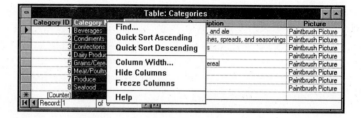

Using the Function Keys

All 12 function keys of the 101-key extended keyboard are assigned to specific purposes by Access. Some keys, such as Shift+F4 (which you press to find the next occurrence of a match with the Find dialog), are derived from other Microsoft applications—in this case, Word for Windows. You use function keys with the Shift, Alt, and Ctrl keys to enable users to perform up to 96 functions by using the 12 keys.

Global Function Keys

Global function key assignments, except for F11 and Alt+F1, are used by Windows, rather than by Access, to perform functions that are identical in all Windows applications. Table 3.3 lists the global function key assignments.

Table 3.3 Global Function Key Assignments	
Key	**Function**
F1	Displays context-sensitive help related to the present basic function and status of Access.
Shift+F1	Adds a question mark to the mouse pointer. Place the mouse pointer with the question mark over an object on-screen for which you want help, and click the mouse.

Key	Function
Ctrl+F4	Closes the active window.
Alt+F4	Exits Access or closes a dialog if one is open.
Ctrl+F6	Selects each open window in sequence as the active window.
F11 or Alt+F1	Selects the Database window as the active window.
F12 or Alt+F2	Opens the File Save As dialog.
Shift+F12 or Alt+Shift+F2	Saves your open database; the equivalent of the **F**ile **S**ave menu choice.

Function Key Assignments for Fields, Grids, and Text Boxes

Access assigns function key combinations that aren't reserved for global operations to actions that are specific to the basic function you are performing at the moment. Table 3.4 lists the function key combinations that are applicable to fields, grids, and text boxes. You may see some repetition of information from the previous tables; this repetition is unavoidable if the tables are to be complete.

▶ "Using Keyboard Operations for Entering and Editing Data," p. 184

Table 3.4 Function Keys for Fields, Grids, and Text Boxes	
Key	**Function**
F2	Toggles between displaying the caret for editing and selecting the entire field.
Shift+F2	Opens the Zoom box for entering expressions and other text.
F4	Opens a drop-down combo list or list box.
Shift+F4	Finds the next occurrence of a match of the text entered in the Find or Replace dialog, if the dialog is closed.
F5	Moves the caret to the record-number box. Enter the number of the record you want to display and press Enter.
Ctrl+F5	Adds a new record to the table.
Shift+F5	Saves a record to the database.

(continues)

Table 3.4 Continued	
Key	**Function**
F6	In Design View, cycles between upper and lower parts of the window. In Datasheet View and Form View, cycles through the header, body (detail section), and footer.
Shift+F6	In Datasheet View and Form View, cycles through the footer, body (detail section), and header.
F7	Opens the Find dialog.
Shift+F7	Opens the Replace dialog.
F8	Turns on extend mode. Press F8 again to extend the selection to a word, the entire field, the whole record, and then all records.
Shift+F8	Reverses the F8 selection process.
Esc	Cancels extend mode.

Function Keys in the Module Window

▶ "Exploring the Module Window," p. 1014

The Module window is designed for writing Access Basic code, the subject of Part VII of this book. Table 3.5 lists the purposes of the function keys. The Module window shows many of the characteristics of Windows' Notepad applet, including the F3 key, which you use for searching.

Table 3.5 Function Keys in the Module Window	
Key	**Function**
F2	Views procedure.
Shift+F2	Goes to procedure selected in Module window.
F3	Finds next occurrence of text specified in the Find or Replace dialog.
Shift+F3	Finds preceding occurrence of text specified in the Find or Replace dialog.
F5	Continues execution of code after a break condition.
F6	Cycles between upper and lower panes (if you have split the window).
F7	Opens the Find dialog.

Key	Function
Shift+F7	Opens the Replace dialog.
F8	Single step.
Shift+F8	Procedure step.
F9	Toggles a breakpoint at the selected line.

Setting Default Options

You can set about 100 options that establish the default settings for the system as a whole, and also those for the six functions defined by the buttons in the Database window. You aren't likely to change default options until you are more familiar with Access, but this book is both a tutorial guide and a reference, and options are a basic element of Access's overall structure.

You set defaults by choosing **V**iew from the main menu and then choosing **O**ptions. The Options dialog appears, as shown in figure 3.9. General, Keyboard, and Printing category options apply to the system as a whole. Datasheet options apply to both forms and queries. The remainder of the option categories are specific to other basic functions.

You select a category by clicking it with the mouse or by using the up- and down-arrow keys. As you change a category, the options for that category appear in the Items list. Most of the items require Yes/No or multiple-choice entries that you select from drop-down lists which you open by clicking the drop-down button to the right of the entry fields. In some cases, you must enter a specific value from the keyboard. After you complete your changes, click OK to close the dialog. If you decide not to implement your changes, click Cancel to exit the Options dialog.

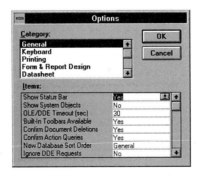

Fig. 3.9
The Options dialog
displaying the
General options
category.

System Defaults

▶ "Sharing Your Access Database Files with Other Users," p. 919

Access uses a special Access database, SYSTEM.MDA, to store all default properties for displaying and printing the contents of tables, queries, forms, reports, and modules for each user of Access. Access stores these properties in tables, along with other tables that determine the behavior of Access, in SYSTEM.MDA. SYSTEM.MDA also is used to store user names and passwords when you secure your Access database or use Access 2.0 in a multiuser environment.

> **Note**
>
> SYSTEM.MDA is vital to the proper operation of Access. You should keep a backup copy of SYSTEM.MDA on a disk. If you make changes to any options or implement the security features of Access, you should create an updated backup when your changes or additions are complete.

General Options

General options, as described in table 3.6, consist of choices that apply to Access as a whole. Several new general options have been added in Access 2.0. Default values established by Access are shown in bold type in the table. You probably will not need to change any of these options, with the possible exception of the default database directory. When you create your own databases, you should store them in a directory dedicated to databases in order to simplify backup operations. A dedicated database directory also is a good place to keep a backup copy of SYSTEM.MDA.

Table 3.6   General Options for the Access System

Option	Value	Function
Show Status Bar	**Yes**/No	Displays (**Yes**) or hides (No) the status bar at the bottom of the window.
Show System Objects	Yes/**No**	Displays (Yes) or hides (**No**) system objects in the Database window.
OLE/DDE Timeout	0-300 (**30**) seconds	Determines the time after which Access stops retrying failed OLE or DDE operations.

Option	Value	Function
Built-in Toolbars Available	**Yes**/No	Displays (**Yes**) or hides (No) the built-in toolbars.
Confirm Document Deletions	**Yes**/No	Displays (**Yes**) or doesn't display (No) a confirmation message box before deleting an object from the database.
Confirm Action Queries	**Yes**/No	Displays (**Yes**) or doesn't display (No) a confirmation message box before Access runs an action query.
New Database Sort Order	**General** and other languages	Sets the alphabetical sort order used for new databases. You can change the sort order for an existing database by selecting a different sort order setting and then compacting the database by choosing **F**ile Compact.
Ignore DDE Requests	Yes/**No**	Ignores (Yes) or doesn't ignore (**No**) DDE requests from other applications.
Default Find/Replace Behavior	**Fast** Search or General Search	Use **Fast** Search or General Search as the default for **E**dit **F**ind and **E**dit Replace operations. **Fast** tests the current field and requires a match of the entire field. General tests all fields and matches any part of the field. Changes you make don't take effect until your next Access session.
Default Database Directory	A valid (**working**) directory	Changes the default directory for the File Open Database dialog. The default is the Access working directory, indicated by a period.
Confirm Record Changes	**Yes**/No	Displays (**Yes**) or doesn't display (No) a confirmation message box before deleting or pasting records, or before changes are made with the **E**dit R**e**place command.
Can Customize Toolbars	**Yes**/No	Allows you to modify the standard toolbars supplied with Access 2.0.
Enable DDE	**Yes**/No	Lets you specify whether or not the data is refreshed at specific intervals during DDE operations.

(continues)

Access Fundamentals

Option	Value	Function
Table 3.6 Continued		
Refresh		
First Weekday	**Sunday**	The day of the week that corresponds to Day = 1.
First Week	Starts on **Jan 1**	The week that corresponds to Week = 1 (allows use of fiscal instead of calendar week numbers).
Show Tool Tips	**Yes**/No	Displays (**Yes**) or doesn't display (No) captions for toolbar buttons.
Color Buttons	**Yes**/No	Displays color (**Yes**) or monochrome (No) toolbar buttons. (Use No for monochrome laptop computers.)

Keyboard Options

Keyboard options, as listed in table 3.7, are especially important if you are accustomed to a particular type of arrow-key behavior. Bold type indicates the default value established by Access. You probably will want to change keyboard options more than any of the other categories, except perhaps printing. You can make the arrow keys behave as if you are editing xBase fields, rather than using their default behavior, which duplicates that of Excel, for example.

xBase

Keyboard Behavior

▶ "Data Entry and Editing Keys," p. 185

▶ "Running Macros from a Shortcut Key," p. 669

Printing Options

You use printing options to set default margins for printing datasheets, the code in modules, or new forms and reports. Table 3.8 lists the available options, with their default values in bold type. Changes you make to the printing options don't affect existing forms and reports. You must modify the printing properties of each existing form and report in Design View in order to change the printing margin.

Margins usually are expressed in inches. If you are using an international version of Access, margin settings are in centimeters. You also can specify margin settings in *twips*, the default measurement of Windows. A twip is 1/20 of a printer's point. A point is 1/72 inch, so a twip is 1/1440 inch.

Table 3.7 Keyboard Options for the Access System

Option	Value	Function
Arrow Key Behavior	**Next Field**/Next Character	The right- or left-arrow key selects the next or preceding field (**Next Field**) or moves the insertion point to the next or preceding character (Next Character). Select Next Character if you want to duplicate the behavior of xBase.
Move After Enter	No/**Next Field**/Next Record	Enter does not move the insertion point (No), it moves the insertion point to the next field (**Next Field**), or it moves the insertion point to the next record (Next Record).
Cursor Stops at First/Last Field	Yes/**No**	Pressing the right- or left-arrow keys, Enter, or Tab cycles (Yes) or does not cycle (**No**) the insertion point from the first to the last or the last to the first field in a row.
Key Assignment Macro	A valid macro name	Establishes the name of the key assignment macro. Use this name when you assign a macro to a key combination. The default name of the key assignment macro is *AutoKeys*.

Table 3.8 Printing Options for All Access Functions

Option	Value	Function
Left Margin	0-page width (**1**")	Establishes the default left margin.
Top Margin	0-page height (**1**")	Establishes the default top margin.
Right Margin	0-page width (**1**")	Establishes the default right margin.
Bottom Margin	0-page height (**1**")	Establishes the default bottom margin.

The one-inch default margins are arbitrary; you may want to reset them to your preference before creating any forms or reports of your own. If you are using a laser printer, refer to its manual to determine the maximum printable area. The printable area determines the minimum margins you can use.

Defaults for Datasheet View

You use Datasheet View options to customize the display of all query datasheets, and new table and form datasheets (see table 3.9). As with printing options, to change the display format of existing table and form datasheets, you must edit the appropriate properties of the table or form in Design View. The options you set here don't apply to forms and reports created with Access wizards. Each wizard has its own set of default values. In table 3.9, default values appear in bold type.

Table 3.9 Options for Datasheet Views

Option	Value	Function
Default Gridlines Behavior	**On**/Off	Shows (**On**) or hides (Off) gridlines in datasheets, duplicating the **L**ayout **G**ridlines menu choice.
Default Column Width	0 to 22 in. (**1 in.**)	Sets the width of columns in datasheets. You adjust the column width of datasheets by dragging the dividing lines between column names with the mouse.
Default Font Name	Name of a typeface on your system	Sets the typeface of field names and data in datasheets, duplicating the **L**ayout **F**ont menu choice. The default is MS Sans Serif.
Default Font Size	Varies with typeface	Sets the size of field names and data in datasheets, duplicating the **L**ayout **F**ont menu choice. The default is **8**-point type.
Default Font Weight	All common weights	Sets the weight of field names and data in datasheets. Choices are Thin, Extra Light, Light, Normal, Medium, Semibold, Bold, Extra Bold, or Black. Few typefaces, however, offer all these weights. The default is **Normal**.
Default Font Italic	Yes/**No**	Displays field names and data in italic style.
Default Font Underline	Yes/**No**	Underlines field names and data.

> **Note**
>
> The remaining option categories, Form & Report Design, Query Design, Macro Design, Module Design, and Multiuser/ODBC, are discussed in the chapter(s) of this book that are devoted to the subject of the particular option category.

Using Cue Cards

Cue Cards are a unique feature of Access, and you can expect to see them in future versions of many Microsoft applications. Cue Cards are designed to interactively guide you through the basic operations of Access. You choose a topic by clicking a button. Then a new series of buttons displays dialogs with text and graphic images that explain elements of the topic you chose.

To examine some of the Cue Cards that are provided with Access, perform the following steps:

1. Close all document windows, but leave the Database window open.

2. Choose **C**ontents from the **H**elp menu. The Help Table of Contents window appears, as shown in figure 3.10.

3. Click the Cue Cards button. The Cue Cards main menu appears, as shown in figure 3.11. You can choose **C**ue Cards from the **H**elp menu as a shortcut to this point. To learn more about Cue Cards, click the *hot spot*, "Help Features", near the top of the help window. Then click the "About Cue Cards" hot spot to display the help window that describes how Cue Cards work.

> **Note**
>
> When you click *hot-spot* text, usually shown in green, you receive an explanation of the hot-spot topic. Hot-spot topics in regular text open small pop-up windows that ordinarily define the hot-spot term. Hot spots in green, underlined, bold text are links to windows in the Help file related to the topic of the hot spot.

Fig. 3.10
The Help Table of
Contents window
for Access 2.0.

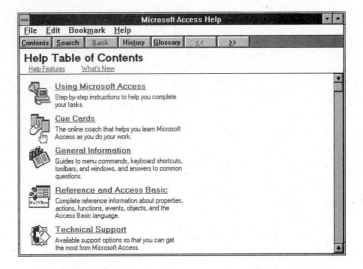

Fig. 3.10
The Help Table of
Contents window
for Access 2.0.

Fig. 3.11
The Cue Cards
main menu.

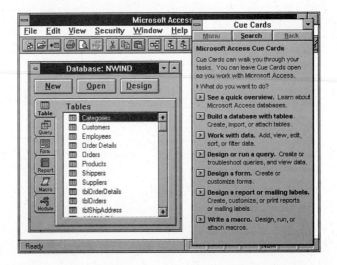

4. Because this is your introduction to Access, and possibly to the subject of databases as a whole, click the See a Quick Overview button to display the Quick Overview menu.

5. Click the Databases button to display cue cards that describe databases (see fig. 3.12).

6. Click the Next button to display the next card in the deck, shown in figure 3.13, which describes Access databases in more specific terms.

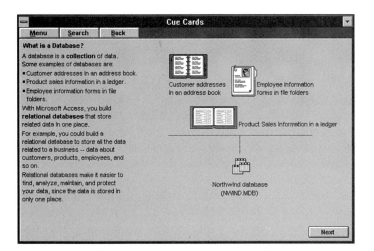

Fig. 3.12
The Cue Card that
defines databases
in general.

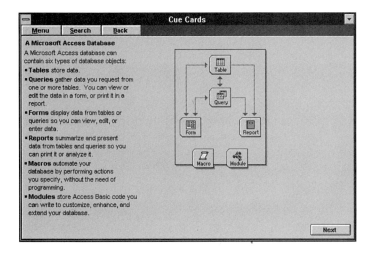

Fig. 3.13
A Cue Card
describing Access
databases.

7. As you continue to click the Next button, the information contained in
the successive Cue Cards becomes increasingly specific until you run
out of cards and are returned to the preceding Cue Card menu. You can
return to the preceding card or menu by clicking the Back button, or
you can go to the top of the deck by clicking the Menu button. Close
the Cue Card window or menu by double-clicking the Control-menu
box in the upper left corner of the card. You also can click the Control-
menu box once, and then select **C**lose from the menu to close the Cue
Card window.

Troubleshooting

After clicking the Cue Cards button of the toolbar, a message box appears that says "There was an error while attempting to communicate with Cue Cards."

The problem is most likely a lack of available system resources. Close other open applications to regain their system resources, then click the Cue Cards button again. Program Manager can show you the current amount of free memory and the percentage of free system resources. Choose **A**bout from Program Manager's **H**elp menu. If free system resources is less than about 35%, you probably won't be able to open Cue Cards or Access's help file.

Using Access Help

The Access help system is extensive and easy to use. All the new help functions incorporated in Windows 3.1's WinHelp Engine are used by Access's help system.

This section discusses methods of getting help with specific functions and objects of Access. Chapter 31, "Adding On-Line Help for Users," describes how you can aid users of your applications by writing help files of your own to accompany your Access applications.

Context-Sensitive Help

Context-sensitive help tries to anticipate your need for information by displaying help windows related to the operating mode, function, and operation in which you are involved or attempting to perform. You can get context-sensitive help in two ways: by pressing the F1 key, or by using the help mouse pointer that appears after you press Shift+F1.

If, for example, a dialog is open when you press F1, you receive information on the purpose of the dialog and the effects of your entries and choices. Figure 3.14 shows the help window for the Find dialog, which also is applicable to the **E**dit **F**ind command.

You can reposition and resize the help window by dragging its borders with your mouse. Click and drag the help title bar to reposition the help window. If more information is in the help file on the topic you selected than will fit in the window, a vertical scroll bar appears at the right of the window. Drag the scroll box down to display additional text.

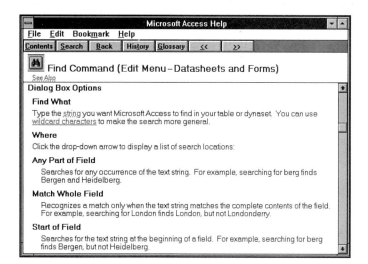

Fig. 3.14
The help window for the Find command and dialog.

Most of Access's help windows include hot spots that provide additional information about a topic. Hot spots with dotted underlines, such as "See Also" in figure 3.14, display definition windows that generally are used to define terms used in the window, but they also can be used to create *jumps* to other related topics. If you click the "See Also" hot spot, the definition window of figure 3.15 appears. You can click any of the hot spots in that window to *jump* to the topic shown with the solid underline in the figure.

If you click the "string" hot spot in figure 3.14, the definition of the term *string* appears in the definition window, as shown in figure 3.16.

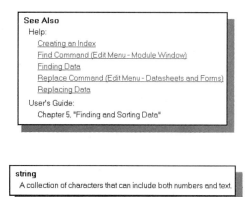

Fig. 3.15
The definition window displayed by the "See Also" hot spot.

Fig. 3.16
The definition window for the word "string."

Clicking the "wildcard characters" hot spot in figure 3.14, which has a solid underline, results in a jump to the help window for the Wildcard topic, displayed in figure 3.17.

Fig. 3.17

A related help window displayed by clicking a topic hot spot.

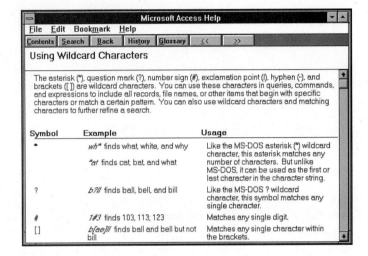

After you read the help window for the topic to which you jumped, click the Back button to return to the preceding help window. Each of the help buttons is explained later in this chapter.

The second method of getting context-sensitive help is to press Shift+F1 and then place the mouse pointer with the question mark on the item with which you need help. Click the mouse button; the topic related to the object appears. Figure 3.18 shows an example that explains the toolbar when a database is open but no database object is present in a document window.

The help window in figure 3.18 shows a different method of creating hot spots. Bit-mapped icons can be used in help files as a substitute for the green, underlined text for topic jumps. Here you click the image of the toolbar button to get help on how to use the button.

Help Menu

An alternative to the use of context-sensitive help is provided by Access's **H**elp menu. Table 3.10 lists the options presented by the **H**elp menu.

You can get a more general form of help by choosing **C**ontent from the **H**elp menu. In this case, you always start from square one—the table of contents of the entire help system shown in figure 3.10, earlier in this chapter. You click the hot spot or icon that represents the subject about which you want to learn. This action causes a jump to the first help window for the subject, which often provides several additional choices for more detailed help on a specific topic.

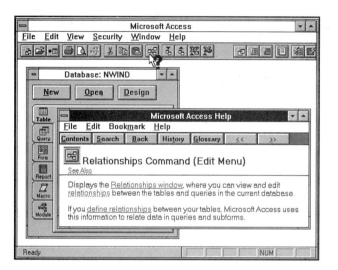

Fig. 3.18
The help mouse pointer and help window for the toolbar.

Table 3.10 Access's Help Menu Options	
Option	**Function**
Contents	Displays the table of contents of the Access help system (refer to fig. 3.17).
Search	Displays a Search dialog that enables you to enter a search term to find topics that include the term (refer to fig. 3.18).
Cue Cards	Displays the first Cue Card in the deck (see "Using Cue Cards," earlier in this chapter).
Technical Support	Displays a window that lists sources of technical support for Access in North America and throughout the world.
About Microsoft Access	Displays the copyright notice for Microsoft Access, the name and organization you entered during setup, and the serial number of your copy of Access. Effective with Windows 3.1, you also are told the mode in which Windows is running, how much conventional memory you have installed, whether you have a math coprocessor in your computer, and the amount of remaining disk space.

Access

2.0

Contents

You can return to the table of contents window at any time by clicking the Contents button.

Search

The Windows 3.1 WinHelp engine has a useful function that enables you to search the contents of the help system based on a word or fragment of a word you enter in a text box. Click the Search button to display the Search dialog shown in figure 3.19.

Fig. 3.19
The Search dialog.

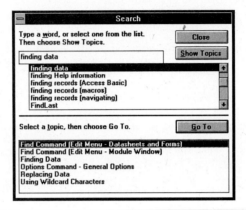

In the text box, enter a word you want to search for, and press Enter or click OK. If Access finds matches among the help topics, it displays the matches in the list portion of the Search Topic combo list. Subjects shown in lowercase letters are index entries for groups of topics that appear in the Select a Topic list. Double-click the topic you want to display, or click the topic and then click the Go To button. The example in figure 3.19 is the result of entering **find** and clicking finding data in the Search list. After you double-click Find Command, the help window shown in figure 3.14 (earlier in this chapter) appears.

Back

The WinHelp engine keeps a history of each help window you have viewed, as illustrated in figure 3.20. You can locate any of the subjects that you have reviewed previously in your present Access session by dragging the scroll box, if your list of selections exceeds the depth of the window. When you find the prior topic that you want to review, double-click the entry. Or, you can use the multistep approach by clicking the Back button. If this is your first help window in a sequence, the Back button is inactive.

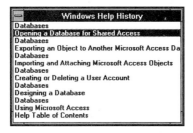

Access Fundamentals

Fig. 3.20
The Windows Help
History window
for an Access
session.

You can use the two directional buttons in the help window, backward (<<) and forward (>>), to scroll through topics related to the topic you selected. Topics are assigned context numbers, and the << and >> buttons display windows in the sequence of their help context numbers assigned by Microsoft's authors.

The Access 2.0 help system adds a Glossary button to its help window. When you click the Glossary button, the Glossary help window for the letter *A* appears. Click one of the 26 buttons to display all terms defined by the Access 2.0 glossary, then click the hot spot corresponding to the term for which you want a definition. The pop-up help window that defines the term *foreign key* appears in figure 3.21.

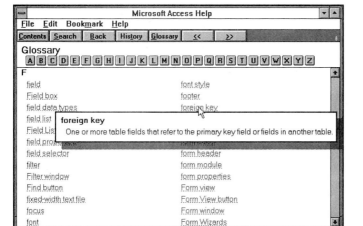

Fig. 3.21
The Glossary help
window of Access
2.0.

Help Window Menu Choices

In addition to the buttons, the help window includes a menu with the choices shown in table 3.11.

Table 3.11	**Options for Datasheet Views**
Option	**Function**
File **O**pen	Enables you to select a different help file. The default extension of help files is .HLP.
Print Topic	Prints the currently visible help topic on your printer.
P**r**int Setup	Displays the Printer Setup dialog to change printer settings.
E**x**it	Closes the help window.
Edit **C**opy	Opens a text box in which you can select all or a portion of the help text and copy it to the Windows Clipboard.
Annotate	Enables you to add your own comments to the current help topic.
Bookmark **D**efine	Displays a dialog in which you can enter an alias for the current help topic for quick access.
Bookmark Names	Choices representing the bookmarks you have created. (This choice does not appear unless you have added bookmarks.)
Help **H**ow to Use Help	Help windows containing instructions on how to use the WinHelp Engine (also called **H**elp on Help in some applications). Select this topic to get additional information on **H**elp menu choices.
Always on **T**op	Makes the window the topmost window at all times when open.
About Help	Displays the copyright notice for the current version of Windows installed, the version of the WinHelp Engine in use, the licensing boilerplate, the mode in which you are operating Windows, the amount of free memory (including virtual memory), and the percentage of both RAM and virtual memory presently consumed by Windows and running applications.

Troubleshooting

When I press the F1 key, a message box appears that reads "Help isn't available due to a lack of available memory or improper installation of Windows or Microsoft Access."

This problem is related to the problem with Cue Cards described earlier in the chapter. If Access's **H**elp menu choices have worked previously, the problem is usually not a lack of "available memory," which consists of the sum of free RAM and free space in your Windows swap file. The problem is probably a lack of available system resources. Close other open applications to regain the system resources they consume, then try again. You can see the current amount of free memory and the percentage of free system resources by choosing **A**bout from Program Manager's **H**elp menu. If free system resources are less than about 35%, you probably will not be able to open Access's help file.

Using Database Functions in Startup Mode

Four functions exist that you can perform only when you are in Access's startup mode with no database open. You access the database functions from the **F**ile menu. If you have a large database, these operations will take a considerable amount of time. Each of the operations described in the following paragraphs involves two dialogs. In the first dialog, you select the database in which the operation is to be performed; in the second dialog, you enter the name of the file that is to be created by the operation. Default file names for new files are DB#.MDB, where # is a sequential number assigned by Access, beginning with 1.

Compacting Databases

After you have made numerous additions and changes to objects within a database file, especially additions and deletions of data in tables, the database file can become disorganized. Like xBase files, when you delete a record, you don't automatically regain the space in the file that the deleted data occupied. You must compact the database, the equivalent of xBase's PACK command, to optimize both its file size and the organization of data within the tables that the file contains. When you pack an Access file, however, you regain space only in 32K increments, not in fixed disk cluster increments (usually 2K) that you regain by packing xBase files.

xBase

PACK

To compact a database, perform the following steps:

1. From the **F**ile menu, choose **C**ompact Database. The Database to Compact From dialog appears, as shown in figure 3.22.

2. Double-click the name of the database file you want to compact. Or click the name and then click OK. The Database to Compact Into dialog appears, as shown in figure 3.23.

3. Enter the name of the new file that is to result from the compaction process in the File Name text box. If you choose to replace the existing file with the compacted version, you see a message box requesting confirmation of your choice. Click OK.

> ### Caution
>
> If the compaction process fails, your database may be damaged. Databases damaged in the compaction process are unlikely to be repairable (see the "Repairing Databases" section that follows). Thus, it is not a good practice to compact the database into a new database with the same name. Do so only if you have made a backup copy of your database with a different name, in a different directory, or on a floppy disk.

4. Access creates a compacted version of the file. The progress of the compaction is shown in a blue bar in the status bar. If you decide to use the same file name, after compaction, the new file replaces the preceding file.

Fig. 3.22
The Database to Compact From dialog.

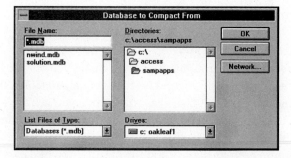

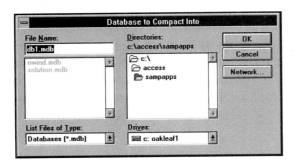

Fig. 3.23
The Database to
Compact Into
dialog.

Periodically compacting files generally is the duty of the database administrator in a multiuser environment, usually in relation to backup operations. It is a good practice to back up your existing file on disk or tape before creating a compacted version.

Converting Databases to Access 2.0 Format

Access 2.0 uses the Conver**t** Database choice of the **F**ile menu to convert Access .MDB database files and .MDA library files created with Access 1.x to the new database format of Access 2.0. The new conversion process differs from that used by Access 1.1 to convert Access 1.0 database files to the format of version 1.1. (There was very little difference between the file structures of versions 1.0 and 1.1, but major differences exist between Access 2.0 and 1.x database files.) The process of converting database files from Access 1.x formats to Access 2.0 is almost identical to the process for compacting files described in the preceding section. The only difference you'll observe is that the names of the dialogs are Database to Convert From and Database to Convert Into. (Chapter 32, "Migrating Access 1.x Applications to Access 2.0," covers the conversion process in detail.)

Access

2.0

> **Caution**
>
> Although you can convert an Access 1.x .MDB or .MDA file into Access 2.0 format, Access 2.0 does not provide a means of converting back from Access 2.0 format to Access 1.1 or 1.0 formats. If you attempt to open an Access 2.0 database or library file with the Convert Database menu choice, you receive a message stating, "Can't convert this database. It is not version 1.0 or version 1.1." Thus, if you must support users of Access database applications that do not have Access 2.0, you need to separately maintain two sets of database files. This means you must have the retail versions of both Access 1.x and Access 2.0 available to maintain your application. You also need both versions of the Access Distribution Kit if your applications use run-time Access.

Encrypting and Decrypting Databases

If other persons have access to your database, either from a file server or within a workgroup using peer-to-peer networking systems, encrypting the file prevents unauthorized persons from reading its contents with a text editor or file-editing application. You use the same process as that for file compaction to create a new encrypted file or to replace the "clear" version with the encrypted file. If you select **E**ncrypt/Decrypt Database from the **F**ile menu and the database you open has been encrypted previously, you are given the opportunity to obtain a decrypted version. File security is the subject of Chapter 25, "Securing Multiuser Network Applications."

Repairing Databases

A database can become corrupted as the result of the following problems:

- Hardware problems in writing to your database file, either locally or on a network server

- An unrecoverable application error (UAE) in Access or another application running in Windows 3.0 when an Access database file is open and has been modified

- A general protection fault (GPF), the equivalent of a UAE in Access with Windows 3.1

- A power failure that occurs after you have made modifications to an Access database file

Access includes a database repair facility that you can use to recover a usable database file from the majority of corrupted files resulting from the preceding list of events. The process is the same as that for creating compacted and encrypted versions of the file.

Occasionally, a file may become corrupted without Access detecting the problem. This lack of detection is more often the case with corrupted indexes. If Access or your application behaves strangely when you open an existing database and display its contents, try repairing the database. Choose **R**epair Database from the **F**ile menu, and then follow the same steps as described for compacting the database.

From Here...

This chapter explained the structure of Access 2.0 for Windows, the shortcut keys, and the terminology and appearance of your display. Options for establishing the default methodology for Access as a whole and the table function were discussed. An explanation of the extensive, context-sensitive help authored by Access was included so that users not familiar with the new features of the Windows 3.1 WinHelp engine can take full advantage of these features. You also learned how to use Access's Cue Cards to get additional help.

Refer to the following chapters for more information related to the topics covered in this chapter:

- Chapter 4, "Working with Access Databases and Tables," has you begin to apply what you learned in this chapter in order to work with Access tables. The majority of the examples in Chapter 4 continue to use the Northwind Traders database, but you add your own tables to expand its capabilities.

- Chapter 5, "Entering, Editing, and Validating Data in Tables," and Chapter 6, "Sorting, Finding, and Filtering Data in Tables," show you how to manipulate data contained in tables.

- Chapter 7, "Attaching, Importing, and Exporting Tables," starts you working with tables created from your existing database or spreadsheet applications by using the Import and Attach functions of Access 2.0.

Chapter 4

Working with Access Databases and Tables

The traditional definition of a database is a *collection of related data items that are stored in an organized manner*. Access is unique among desktop database development applications for the PC because of its all-encompassing database file structure. Unlike conventional desktop databases, such as dBASE, FoxPro, and Paradox, a single Access .MDB file can contain data objects—tables, indexes, and queries—as well as application objects: forms, reports, macros, and Access Basic code modules. Thus, you can create a complete Access database application that is stored in a single .MDB file. Most Access developers use two .MDB files: one to contain data objects and the other to hold application objects. The reason for using two .MDB files are explained in this chapter and in Chapter 25, "Securing Multiuser Network Applications." Regardless of which approach you choose, Access's all-encompassing .MDB file structure makes creating and distributing database applications simpler.

Defining the Elements of Access Databases

Access databases include the following elements in a single .MDB database file:

- *Tables* that store data items in a row-column format similar to that used by spreadsheet applications. You may include up to 32,768 tables in an Access database, and you may work on (open) up to 254 tables at one time if you have sufficient available resources. You can import tables from other database applications (such as xBase and Paradox),

In this chapter, you learn about

- Elements of Access database files

- Creating new databases

- Adding tables to a database

- Creating default relations between database tables

- Enforcing referential integrity rules

- Copying and pasting tables

client-server databases (such as Microsoft SQL Server), and spreadsheet applications (such as Microsoft Excel and Lotus 1-2-3). In addition, you can attach Access databases, other types of database tables (dBASE, FoxPro, and Paradox tables, for example), and formatted files (Excel worksheet and ASCII text) to Access databases. Attaching, importing, and exporting tables is the subject of Chapter 7.

■ *Queries* that display selected data contained in up to 16 tables. Queries enable you to determine how data is presented by choosing the tables that comprise the query and up to 255 specific fields (columns) of these tables. You determine the records (rows) that are displayed by deciding the criteria that the data items in the query data must meet in order to be included in the display. Creating queries is explained in Part II of this book.

■ *Forms* that display data contained in tables or queries and enable you to add new data and update or delete existing data. You can incorporate pictures and graphs in your forms, and, if you have a sound card, include narration and music in your form. You learn how to create forms in Chapters 12 and 13, and you learn how to add graphics to forms in Chapter 20. Access 2.0 forms also can incorporate Access Basic code, a feature called Code Behind Forms (CBF), to provide event-handling subprocedures for forms and the controls that appear on forms.

■ *Reports* that print data from tables or queries in virtually any format you want. Access enables you to add graphics to your reports so that you can print a complete, illustrated catalog of products from an Access database. Access's report capabilities are much more flexible than those of most other relational database management applications, including those designed for mini- and mainframe computers. Like forms, you can include Access Basic event-handling subprocedures in Access 2.0 reports. Creating reports is covered in Chapters 14 and 15.

■ *Macros* that automate Access operations. Access macros take the place of programming code required by other database applications, such as xBase, to perform specific actions in response to user-initiated events, such as clicking a command button. In most cases, you can create a fully functional database application without writing any programming code at all. Macros are the subject of Chapters 16 through 18.

■ *Modules* that contain Access Basic code you write to perform operations that the standard collection of macros included in Access does not support. You learn how to write Access Basic code stored in modules or behind forms and reports in Chapter 27.

A better definition of an Access database may be *a collection of related data items and, optionally, the methods necessary to select, display, update, and report the data*. This is a very important distinction between Access and other database management applications. Even client-server database systems, such as Microsoft SQL Server, that include all related tables within a single database do not include the equivalent of forms and reports within the database. You must use another application, called a *front-end*, to display, edit, and report data stored in client-server databases. You can use Access to create front-ends for client-server databases by attaching tables from the client-server database to your Access database. Creating front-ends for client-server databases is one of the major applications for Access in medium- to large-size firms.

▶ "Defining the Client-Server Environment," p. 958

> **Note**
>
> As mentioned in prior chapters, it is a good database application development practice to maintain tables that store your application's data in one Access database (.MDB) file and the remainder of your applications objects, such as forms and reports, in a separate .MDB file. This chapter uses the Northwind Traders sample database, which is a self-contained application with a single .MDB file. Chapter 7, "Attaching, Importing, and Exporting Tables," describes how to use or create separate .MDB files to store data and application objects.

This chapter introduces you to Access databases and tables—the fundamental elements of an Access application. You will see many references in this book to the term *Access application*. An Access application is an Access database that has the following characteristics:

- It contains the queries, forms, reports, and macros necessary to display the data in a meaningful way and update the data as necessary. These are called *application objects* in this book. A self-contained (single-user) Access application includes tables in the application database. Multiuser Access applications usually consist of two .MDB files, one containing the tables shared by users (*database objects*) and the other consisting of the Access application that manipulates the data. If you are creating a front-end application, tables usually are attached from the client-server database. Some front-end applications, however, also use tables stored in the application database file.

- It does not require that users of the database know how to design any of its elements. All elements of the database are fully predefined during the design stage of the application. In most cases, you want to restrict other users from intentionally or unintentionally changing the design of the application.

■ It is automated by Access macros or Access Basic code so that users make choices from command buttons or custom-designed menus, rather than from the lists in the Database window you used in Chapter 2.

As you progress through the chapters in this book, you create a model of an Access application called *Personnel Actions*. Later in this chapter, you create the Personnel Actions table. In the following chapters, you add new features to the Personnel Actions application until, when you reach Chapter 18, you have a complete, automated method of adding and editing Personnel Actions data. When you are learning Access, therefore, it is important that you read this book in a sequential manner, at least through Chapter 18. Make sure to perform the example exercises for the Personnel Actions application each time you encounter them because succeeding examples build on your prior work.

Understanding Relational Databases

All desktop database managers enable you to enter, edit, view, and print information contained in one or more tables that are divided into rows and columns. At this point, the definition of a database manager doesn't differ from that of a spreadsheet application—most spreadsheets can emulate database functions. Three principal characteristics distinguish relational database management systems (RDBMSs) from spreadsheet applications:

■ All RDBMSs are designed to deal efficiently with very large amounts of data—much more than spreadsheets can handle conveniently.

■ RDBMSs easily link two or more tables so that they appear to the user as if they are one table. This process is difficult or impossible to accomplish with spreadsheets.

■ RDBMSs minimize information duplication by requiring repetition of only those data items, such as product or customer codes, by which multiple tables are linked.

Database managers that cannot link multiple tables are called *flat-file managers* and are used primarily to compile simple lists such as names, addresses, and telephone numbers. The Windows Cardfile applet is an example of a rudimentary, but useful, flat-file manager.

Because relational databases eliminate most duplicate information, they minimize data storage and application memory requirements. Figure 4.1 shows a typical relational database that a manufacturing or distributing firm may use. This database structure is similar to that of the Northwind Traders sample database provided with Access.

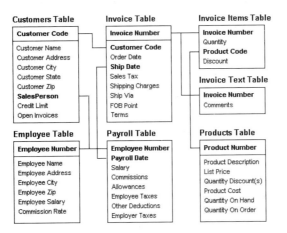

Fig. 4.1
A portion of a typical database for a manufacturing or distributing firm.

If your job is to create an invoice-entry database, you don't need to enter a customer's name and address more than once. Just assign each customer a unique number or code and add a record containing this information to the Customers table. Similarly, you don't need to enter the names and prices of the standard products for each invoice. You assign unique codes to products, and then add records for them to the Products table. When you want to create a new invoice for an existing customer, you enter the customer code and type the codes and quantities for the products ordered. This process adds one record (identified by an automatically assigned sequential numeric code) to the Invoices table and one record for each different item purchased to the Invoice Items table.

▶ "The Process of Database Design," p. 838

Each table is related to the other by the customer, invoice, and product codes and numbers, shown by the connecting lines between the tables in figure 4.1. The codes and numbers shown in boxes are unique; only one customer corresponds to a particular code, and one invoice or product corresponds to a given number. When you display or print an invoice, the Invoice table is linked (called a *join*) with both the Customers and Invoice Items tables by their codes. In turn, the Invoice Items table is joined with the Products table by the common value of a Product Code in the Invoice Items table and a

▶ "Joining Tables to Create Multitable Queries," p. 356

Product Number in the Products table. Your query (view) of the desired sales order(s) displays the appropriate customer, invoice, items, and product information from the linked records. (Queries are explained in the following section.) You can calculate quantity-price extensions, including discounts, by multiplying the appropriate values stored in the tables. You can add the extended items, sales taxes, and freight charges; you also can calculate the total invoice amount. These calculated values need not be included (and in a properly designed database never are included) in the database tables.

Using Access Database Files and Tables

Access has its own database file structure, similar to that used by client-server RDBMSs, and uses the .MDB extension. As discussed in the introduction to this chapter, Access differs from traditional PC databases in that all the related tables, indexes, forms, and report definitions are contained in a single file. Even the programming code you write in Access Basic is included in the .MDB file. You don't need to be concerned with the intricacies of the .MDB file structure because Access handles all the details of file management for you.

All the field data types familiar to xBase and Paradox users are available in Access, as well as some new and useful field data types, such as Currency for monetary transactions. dBASE users need to learn to use the term *table* for file and *database* to indicate a group of related tables or files, the equivalent of dBASE's CATALOG. *Records* commonly are called *rows*, and *fields* often are called *columns*. This book uses records and fields when referring to database tables and rows and columns for sets of records returned by queries. Users with Paradox, Excel, or 1-2-3 experience should find the terminology of Access quite familiar. Paradox and FoxPro users will appreciate dealing with only one .MDB file, instead of the myriad files that make up a multitable Paradox or FoxPro database.

The Access System Database

◀ "Setting Default Options," p. 101

In addition to database files with the .MDB extension, Access includes a master database file named SYSTEM.MDA. This file contains information about the following:

■ Names of users and groups of users that are allowed to open Access

- User passwords and a unique binary code, called a System ID (SID), that identifies the current user to Access

- Operating preferences you establish by choosing **O**ptions from the **V**iew menu

- Definitions of customized Access 2.0 toolbars created by each user

Sharing database files and granting permission for others to use the files is covered in Chapter 25, "Securing Networked Multiuser Applications."

Access Library Databases

Another category of Access database files is *libraries*. Libraries are Access databases, usually having an .MDA extension to distinguish them from user databases, that you can attach to Access through an entry in the MSACCESS.INI file in your \WINDOWS directory. When you attach an Access library, all the elements of the library database are available to you after you open Access. The Access 2.0 wizards, which you use to create forms, reports, and graphs, are stored in an Access library database file, WZFRMRPT.MDA. Another wizard, WZDOC.MDA, lets you create data dictionaries for Access databases. A *data dictionary* is a detailed written description of each of the elements of a database. Library databases are an important and unique feature of Access. Microsoft and other third-party firms provide a wide range of Access libraries to add new features and capabilities to Access.

Creating a New Database

If you have experience with relational database management systems, you may want to start building your own database as you progress through this book. In this case, you need to create a new database file at this point. If database management systems are new to you, it is better to explore the sample databases supplied with Access as you progress through the chapters of this book, and design your first database using the principles outlined in Chapter 23, "Exploring Relational Database Design and Implementation." Then come back to this point and create your new database file.

To create a new database, follow these steps:

1. If Access is not running, launch Access and skip to step 3.

Access

2.0

▶ "Creating a Transaction Form with the Form Wizard," p. 442

▶ "Access's New Integrated Data Dictionary System," p. 866

Access

Access Fundamentals

2. If Access is running and the Database window is visible, click its title bar to make the Database window the active window. If the Database window is not visible, click the Show Database Window button of the toolbar, choose **1** Database from the **W**indow menu, or press the F11 key.

This action is called giving the Database window the *focus*. When a window has the focus, the background of its title bar is usually blue; when a window does not have the focus, it is inactive and its title bar is usually white. If you have changed from the default Windows color scheme by using the Control Panel's Colors function, these colors are different.

3. Click the New Database button of the toolbar, or choose **N**ew Database from the **F**ile menu.

The Access application window must be empty or the Database window must be active in order for the Database toolbar to be visible and the **N**ew Database and other database file options to be present when you select the **F**ile menu. The New Database dialog appears as shown in figure 4.2.

Access supplies the default file name, DB1.MDB, for new databases. (If you have previously saved a database file as DB1.MDB, Access proposes DB2.MDB as the default.)

Fig. 4.2
The New Database dialog used to create and name a new Access database.

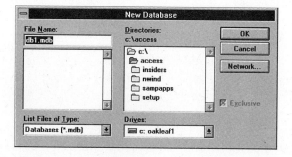

4. Enter a file name for the new database in the File Name text box, using conventional DOS file-naming rules (you cannot use spaces or punctuation in the name, other than the period used as the extension separator). You can use any extension you want for an Access database, but only files with the .MDB extension are associated with Access by the File Manager.

5. Click OK to create the new database.

   If a database was open when you created the new database, Access closes any windows associated with the database and the Database window. During the process of creating the database, the following message appears in the status bar:

   Verifying System Objects

   Whenever you open a new or existing database, Access checks to see whether all the elements of the database are intact. Access's main window and the Database window for the new database (named NEW.MDB for this example) appears as shown in figure 4.3.

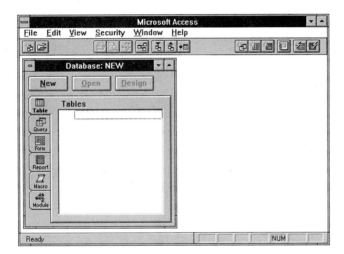

Fig. 4.3

Access's main window and the Database window are displayed for a newly created database.

Your new database has a number of hidden system tables but no other database objects. Adding tables to a database is explained in the "Adding a Table to an Existing Database" section later in this chapter.

Each new database occupies 64K of disk space when you create it. Most of the 64K is space reserved for adding the information necessary to specify the names and locations of other database elements that are contained in the database file. Because of the way data is stored in Access tables, what appears to be an excessive amount of reserved space quickly is compensated for by Access's more efficient data storage methods.

Understanding the Properties of Tables and Fields

Before you add a table to a new database you create or to one of the sample databases supplied with Access, you need to know the terms and conventions used by Access to describe the structure of a table and the fields that contain the data items that comprise the information stored in the table. With Access, you specify properties of tables and fields.

Properties of Access tables apply to the table as a whole. Entering table properties is optional. You enter properties of tables in text boxes of the Table Properties window, which you display by clicking the Properties button on the toolbar in Table Design View (see fig. 4.4). The three properties of Access tables follow:

► "Working with Data Dictionaries," p. 864

- *Description.* An optional explanation of the purpose of the table for use with a data dictionary. Data dictionaries are used to document databases and database applications.

- *Validation Rule.* An optional ValidationRule property value that lets you establish domain integrity rules with expressions that refer to more than one field of the table. Validation rules that apply to the table as a whole, rather than to a single field, are a new feature of Access 2.0. Validation rules are described in the "Validating Data Entry" section later in this chapter.

- *Validation Text.* An optional ValidationText property value that specifies the text of the message box that appears if you violate a table's ValidationRule expression.

Fig. 4.4
The Table Properties window for the Order Details table.

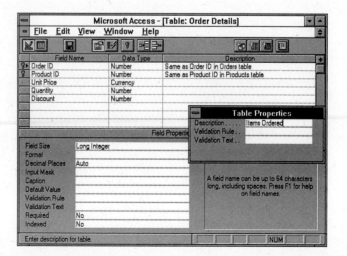

Access 1.x used the Properties window to define the table's primary-key field(s) and composite indexes on table fields. Access 2.0 provides a separate Indexes window to specify the primary key and all table indexes. Use of the Indexes window is described in the section, "Adding Indexes to Tables," later in this chapter.

▶ "Using Access Indexes," p. 869

You assign each field of an Access table a set of properties from the following list. The first three field properties are assigned within the *Table Design grid*, the upper pane of the Table Design window shown in figure 4.4. The PrimaryKey property is assigned by selecting the field and clicking the Primary Key button on the toolbar. The remaining property values in the lower Field Properties pane of the Table Design window are selected from drop-down or combo lists or by typing values in text boxes.

- *Field Name.* You enter the name of the field in the first column of the Table Design grid. Field names may contain up to 64 characters and may include embedded (but not leading) spaces and punctuation— except periods (.), exclamation marks (!), and square brackets ([ ]). Field names are mandatory, and you cannot assign the same field name to more than one field. It is a good database programming practice not to include spaces in field names. (Substitute an underscore (_) for spaces to improve the readability of field names.) Minimizing the length of field names conserves resources and saves typing when you refer to the field name in macros or Access Basic code.

- *Data Type.* You select data types from a drop-down list in the second column of the Table Design grid. Data types include Text, Number, Currency, Date/Time, Yes/No, Memo, and OLE Object. Choosing a data type is the subject of the next section of this chapter.

- *Description.* You can enter an optional description of the field in the text box in the third column of the Table Design grid. If you add a description, it appears in the status bar at the lower left of Access's window when you select the field for data entry or editing.

- *Primary Key.* To choose a field as the primary-key field, select the field by clicking the field selection button to the left of the Field Name column, and then click the Primary Key button on the toolbar. The Order Details table has a composite primary key, consisting of the Order ID and Product ID fields. (See "Selecting a Primary Key," later in this chapter, for instructions on how to create a composite primary key.)

- *Field Size.* You enter the field size for the Text data type in the Field Size text box. (See "Fixed-Length Text Fields," later in this chapter, to learn how to choose a text field size.) For Numeric data types, you choose the field size by making a selection from a drop-down list. Field size is not applicable to the Counter, Currency, Memo, or OLE Object data type.

- *Format.* You can select a standard, predefined format in which to display the values in the field from the drop-down combo list applicable to the data type you chose (except Text). Alternatively, you can enter a custom format in the text box (see "Custom Display Formats" later in this chapter). The Format property does not affect the data values; it affects only how these values are displayed.

- *Decimal Places.* You can select Auto or a specific number of decimal places from the drop-down combo list, or you can enter a number in the text box. The Decimal Places property applies only to Number and Currency fields. Like the Format property, the Decimal Places property affects only the display, not the data values, of the field.

- *Input Mask.* Input masks are character strings, similar to the character strings used for the Format property, that determine how data is displayed during data entry and editing. If you click the Ellipsis button for a field of the Text or Date/Time field data type, the Input Mask Wizard appears to provide you with a predetermined selection of standard input masks, such as telephone numbers with optional area codes.

- *Caption.* If you want a name (other than the field name) to appear in the field name header button in Table Datasheet View, you can enter an alias for the field name in the Caption list box. The restrictions on punctuation symbols do not apply to the Caption property. (You can use periods, exclamation points, and square brackets.)

- *Default Value.* You can specify a value that is entered automatically in the field when a new record is added to the table by entering the value in the Default Value text box. The current date is a common default value for a Date/Time field. (See "Setting Default Values of Fields," later in this chapter, for more information.) Default values are not applicable to fields with Counter or OLE Object field data types.

- *Validation Rule.* Validation rules are used to test the value entered in a field against criteria you supply in the form of an Access expression. Expressions are explained in Chapter 9, "Understanding Operators and Expressions in Access." The ValidationRule property is not available for fields with Counter, Memo, or OLE Object field data types. Adding validation rules to table fields is one of the subjects of the next chapter, "Entering, Editing, and Validating Data in Tables."

- *Validation Text.* You enter the text that is to appear in the status bar if the value entered does not meet the Validation Rule criteria.

- *Required.* If you set the value of the Required property to Yes, you must enter a value in the field. Setting the Required property to Yes is the equivalent of entering **Is Not Null** as a field validation rule. (You do not need to set the value of the Required property to Yes for fields that are included in the primary key because Access does not permit **Null** values in primary-key fields.)

- *Allow Zero Length.* If you set the value of the AllowZeroLength property to Yes, the field must contain at least one character. The AllowZeroLength property applies to the Text field data type only. (A zero-length string ("") and the **Null** value are not the same.)

- *Indexed.* You can select between an index that allows duplicate values or one that requires each value of the field to be unique from the drop-down list. You remove an existing index (except from a field that is a single primary-key field) by choosing No. The Indexed property is not available for Memo or OLE Object fields. (See "Adding Indexes to Tables," later in this chapter, for more information on indexes.)

Adding your first table, Personnel Actions, to the Northwind Traders database, requires that you choose appropriate data types, sizes, and formats for the fields of your table.

Choosing Field Data Types, Sizes, and Formats

You must assign a field data type to each field of a table, unless you want to use the Text data type that Access assigns as the default. One of the principles of relational database design is that all the data in a single field consists of one type of data. Access provides a much wider variety of data types and formats to choose from than most PC database managers. Besides the data type, you can set other field properties that determine the format, size, and other characteristics of the data that affect its appearance and the accuracy with which numerical values are stored. Table 4.1 lists the field data types you can select for data contained in Access tables.

Table 4.1   Field Data Types Available in Access

Information	Data Type	Description of Data Type
Characters	Text	Text fields are most common, so Access assigns Text as the default data type. A Text field can contain up to 255 characters, and you can designate a maximum length less than or equal to 255. Access assigns a default length of 50 characters. A fixed-length Text data type is similar to xBase's Character field and Paradox's Alphanumeric field.
	Memo	Memo fields can contain up to 32,000 characters and are used for descriptive comments. Memo fields are similar to those of xBase, except that the data in the Memo field is included in the table rather than in a separate file. The contents of Memo fields are displayed in Datasheet View. A Memo field cannot be a key field, and you cannot index a Memo field.
Numeric Values	Number	A variety of numeric data subtypes are available. You choose the appropriate data subtype by selecting one of the FieldSize property settings listed in table 4.2. You determine how the number is displayed by setting its Format property to one of the formats listed in table 4.4.
	Counter	A *counter* is a numeric (Long Integer) value that is incremented by one for each new record you add to a table. A Counter field creates a value that is similar to xBase's and Paradox's record number. The maximum number of records in a table that uses the Counter field is slightly more than 2 billion.
	Yes/No (Logical fields)	Logical (Boolean) fields in Access use numeric (integer) values: –1 for Yes (**True**) and 0 for No (**False**). You use the Format property to display Yes/No fields as Yes or No, True or False, On or Off, or –1 or 0. (**True** also can be represented by any nonzero number.) Logical fields cannot be key fields, and they cannot be indexed.
	Currency	Currency is a special fixed format with four decimal places designed to prevent rounding errors that would affect accounting operations where value must match to the penny (similar to the Paradox Currency data type).

Information	Data Type	Description of Data Type
Dates and Times	Date/Time	Dates and times are stored in a special fixed format. The date is represented by the whole number portion of the Date/Time value, and the time is represented by its decimal fraction. You control how dates are displayed by selecting one of the Date/Time Format properties listed in table 4.4.
Large Objects	OLE Object (BLOBs, binary large objects)	Includes bit-mapped graphics, vector-type drawings, waveform audio files, and other types of data that can be created by an OLE server application, some of which are listed in table 4.3. You cannot assign an OLE object as a key field, and you cannot include an OLE field in an index.

Regardless of the length that you set for Text fields in Access, they are stored in the database file in variable-length records. All trailing spaces are removed. This technique conserves the space that is wasted in xBase files, for example, where text is stored in fixed-length character fields. Fixed-length character fields in conventional PC RDBMSs waste the bytes used to pad short text entries in long fields.

Character Fields

Choosing Field Sizes for Numeric and Text Data

The FieldSize property of a field makes the final determination of the data type that is used by Number fields or the number of characters for fixed-length text fields. Field Size properties are called *subtypes* to distinguish them from the *data types* listed in table 4.2. For numbers, you select a FieldSize property value from a list provided by the Field Size drop-down list in the lower Field Properties pane of the Table Design window (see fig. 4.5).

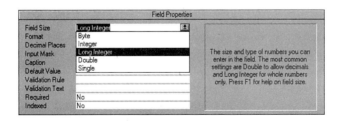

Fig. 4.5
Selecting a subtype for the Number data type from the Field Size list.

Subtypes for Numeric Data

The Number data type of table 4.2 isn't a fully specified data type. You must select one of the subtypes from those listed in table 4.3 for the Field Size property to properly define the numeric data type. To select a data subtype for a Number field, follow these steps:

1. Select the Data Type cell of the Number field for which you want to make the subtype selection.

2. Click the Field Size text box in the Field Properties window. You also can press F6 to switch windows, and then use the arrow keys to position the caret within the Field Size text box.

3. Click the drop-down arrow to open the list of choices shown in figure 4.5. You can press the F4 key to open the list, if you prefer.

4. Select the data subtype. Data subtypes are described in table 4.3. Making a selection closes the list.

After you select a Field Size property, you select a Format property from those listed in table 4.4 to determine how the data is displayed. The Currency data type is included in table 4.4 because it also can be considered a subtype of the Numeric data type.

Regardless of how you format your data for display, the number of decimal digits, range, and storage requirement remains that chosen by Field Size. With the exception of the Byte data type, these data types are available in most dialects of Basic, including Visual Basic 3.0. All the data types listed in table 4.2 are included in Access Basic and are reserved words of the language. You cannot use a reserved data type word for any purpose in Access Basic functions and procedures other than to specify a data type.

Table 4.2   Subtypes of the Number Data Type Determined by the Field Size Property

Field Size	Decimals	Range of Values	Bytes	xBase	Paradox
Double	15 places	$-1.797 * 10^{308}$ to $+1.797 * 10^{308}$	8	Numeric	Numeric
Single	7 places	$-3.4 * 10^{38}$ to $+3.4 * 10^{38}$	4	N/A	N/A
Long Integer	None	$-2,147,483,648$ to $+2,147,483,647$	4	N/A	N/A
Integer	None	$-32,768$ to $32,767$	2	N/A	Short Number
Byte	None	0 to 255	1	N/A	N/A

Field Size	Decimals	Range of Values	Bytes	xBase	Paradox
Currency (a data type, not a subtype)	4 places	−922337203685477.5808 to +922337203685477.5808	4	N/A	N/A

The xBase and Paradox columns of table 4.2 indicate the Access data types that correspond to data types in common use with these two types of DOS RDBMSs.

Both xBase RDBMSs and Paradox store numbers with 15 significant-digit precision. Neither xBase nor Paradox, however, offers the full range of values of numbers having Access's Double Field Size property. All references to Paradox in this book apply to version 3.5. Paradox 4.0 had just been released and Paradox for Windows was in the beta test stage when this book was written, and version 1.0 of Access is compatible only with Paradox 3.5 (and earlier) tables.

Numeric Data Type

Numeric and Short Number Data Types

As a rule, you select the Field Size property that results in the smallest number of bytes that encompasses the range of values you expect and that expresses the value in sufficient precision for your needs. Mathematical operations with Integer and Long Integer proceed more quickly than those with Single and Double data types (called *floating-point* numbers) or the Currency and Date/Time data types (*fixed-point* numbers).

Fixed-Width Text Fields

You can create a fixed-width Text field by setting the value of the FieldSize property. Access creates a 50-character-wide Text field by default. Enter the number, from 1 to 255, in the Field Size cell corresponding to the fixed length you want, as shown in figure 4.6. Data that you import to the field that is longer than the field size selected are truncated, meaning that the far right characters beyond the limit you set are lost. You, therefore, enter a field length value that accommodates the maximum number of characters you expect to enter in the field. Fixed-width Text fields behave identically to the Character and Alphanumeric field data types of xBase and Paradox applications.

Character Fields

Alphanumeric Fields

> **Note**
>
> The term fixed-width and fixed-length have two different meanings in Access. Even if you specify a fixed-width for a field of the Text field data type, the data in the field is stored by Access in variable-length format.

Fig. 4.6
Assigning a fixed-width to a Text field in the Field Size cell.

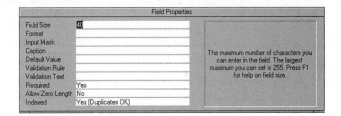

Subtypes for the OLE Object Data Type

Fields that have data types other than characters and numbers must use the OLE (object linking and embedding) Object data type. Object linking and embedding is described in Chapter 19, "Using OLE 2.0," and the OLE field data type is explained in Chapter 20, "Adding Graphics to Forms and Reports." Because many subtypes of OLE data exist, this data type enables you to violate the rule of database design that says all data in a field must be of a single data type. Typical OLE Object subtypes are listed in table 4.3. To avoid breaking the rule, separate OLE Object fields should be created for different OLE data subtypes.

Table 4.3   Subtypes of the OLE Object Data Type and OLE Servers That Create Them

OLE SubType	File Format	Created by OLE Servers
Bit-mapped graphics	.BMP, .DIB, .TIF	Windows 3.1 Paintbrush, Micrografx Picture Publisher 3.1
Vector-based drawings	.WMF	Microsoft Draw, Windows DRAW! with OLE, CorelDRAW!, PowerPoint
Formatted text	.RTF	Windows 3.1 Write, Word for Windows 2.0, Lotus Ami Pro

OLE SubType	File Format	Created by OLE Servers
Unformatted Text	.TXT	Object Packager (with Windows Notepad as the application)— Memo fields are a better choice
Spreadsheet	.XLS, .DIF	Microsoft Excel 3.0 and later
Waveform Audio	.WAV	Sound Recorder, Media Player 3.1, Media Vision Pocket recorder
MIDI Music Files	.MID	Media Player 3.1

In the case of OLE Object fields, the data subtype is determined by the OLE server used to create the data, rather than by an entry in a text box or a selection from a list box. Windows 3.1's Object Packager OLE server enables you to embed files created by applications that aren't OLE servers. You can, for example, embed .TXT files and .MID files with Object Packager.

Selecting a Display Format

You establish the Format property for the data types you select so that Access displays them appropriately for your application. You select a format by selecting the field and then clicking the Format text box in the Field Properties window. Figure 4.7 shows the choices Access offers for formatting the Integer data type. You format number, Date/Time, and Yes/No data types by selecting a standard format or creating your own custom format. The two methods are described in sections that follow.

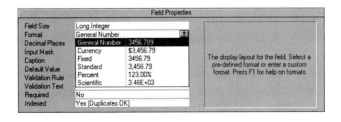

Fig. 4.7
Assigning one of the standard formats to an Integer field from the Format list.

Standard Formats for Number, Date/Time, and Yes/No Data Types

Access provides 17 standard formats that are applicable to the numeric values in fields of the Number, Date/Time, and Yes/No data types. The standard formats shown in table 4.4 probably meet most of your needs.

Table 4.4 Standard Display Formats for Access Number, Date/Time, and Yes/No Data Types

Data Type	Format	Appearance
Number	General Number	1234.5
	Currency	$1,234.50
	Fixed	12345
	Standard	1,234.50
	Percent	0.1234 = 12.34%
	Scientific	1.23E+03
Date/Time	General Date	10/1/92 4:00:00 PM
	Long Date	Thursday, October 1, 1992
	Medium Date	10-Oct-92
	Short Date	10/1/92
	Long Time	4:00:00 PM
	Medium Time	04:00 PM
	Short Time	16:00
Yes/No	Yes/No	Yes or No
	True/False	True or False
	On/Off	On or Off
	None	–1 or 0

xBase

Date Data Type
and TIME()

PDOX

Currency Data Type
and Date Formats

The Short Date format is similar to the Date data type in xBase and Paradox, except that leading zeros for months and days having a value less than 10 aren't displayed. The 4 date formats are included in the 11 date formats offered by Paradox; the other 7 Paradox formats can be created by using custom formats described in the next section. The Short Time format is equivalent to what you obtain from an xBase SUBSTR(TIME(),5) expression. A Double data type with Currency format appears identical to Paradox's Currency data type.

The *Null* Value in Access Tables

Fields in Access tables can have a special value, **Null**, which is a new term for most users of PC-based database management systems. The **Null** value indicates that the field contains no data at all. **Null** isn't the same as a numeric value of zero, nor is it equivalent to blank text that consists of one or more spaces. **Null** is similar but not equivalent to an empty string (a string of zero length, often called a *null string*). For now, the best synonym for **Null** is *no entry*. (**Null** is set in monospace bold type because it is a reserved word in Access Basic.)

The **Null** value is useful for determining whether a value has been entered in a field, especially numeric fields where zero values are valid. Until the advent of Access, the capability to use Null values in database managers running on

PCs was limited to fields in the tables of client-server database systems, such as Microsoft SQL Server. The `Null` value is used in the "Custom Display Formats" and "Setting Default Values of Fields" sections later in this chapter.

Custom Display Formats

To duplicate precisely the format of xBase's Date data type or one of the seven date formats offered by Paradox that is not a standard format in Access, you must create a custom format. You create a custom format by creating an image of the format using combinations of the special set of characters, called *placeholders*, listed in table 4.5. An example of a custom format for date and time is shown in figure 4.8. If you enter **mmmm dd**", "**yyyy - hh:nn** as the format, the date 03/01/94 displays as March 1, 1994 - 00:00.

Fig. 4.8
Creating a custom date and time format from entries in the Format text box.

Except as noted, the example numeric value used in table 4.5 is 1234.5. Bold type is used to distinguish the placeholders you type from the surrounding text. The resulting display is shown in monospace type.

Table 4.5 Placeholders for Creating Custom Display Formats	
Placeholder	**Function**
Empty string	Displays the number with no formatting. Enter an empty string by deleting the value in the Format Text field of the Field Properties window.
0	Displays a digit if one exists in the position or a zero if not. You can use the 0 placeholder to display leading zeroes for whole numbers and trailing zeros in decimal fractions. **00000.000** displays 01234.500.
#	Displays a digit, if one exists in the position; otherwise, displays zeros. The # placeholder is equivalent to 0, except that leading and trailing zeros aren't displayed. **#####.###** displays 1234.5.

(continues)

Table 4.5   Continued

Placeholder	Function
$	Displays a dollar sign in the position. **$###,###.00** displays $1,234.50.
.	Displays a decimal point at the indicated position in a string of 0 and # placeholders. **##.##** displays 1234.5.
%	Multiplies the value by 100 and adds a percent sign in the position shown with 0 and # placeholders. **#0.00%** displays 0.12345 as 12.35% (12.345 is rounded to 12.35).
, (comma)	Adds commas as thousands separators in strings of 0 and # placeholders. **###,###,###.00** displays 1,234.50.
E– e–	Displays values in scientific format with sign of exponent for negative values only. **#.###E–00** displays 1.2345E03. **0.12345** displays 1.2345E–01.
E+ e+	Displays values in scientific format with sign of exponent for positive and negative values. **#.###E–00** displays 1.2345E+03.
/	Separates the day, month, and year to format date values. **mm/dd/yy** displays 06/06/92. You can substitute hyphens to display 06-06-92.
m	Months placeholder for dates. **m** displays 1, **mm** displays 01, **mmm** displays Jan, and **mmmm** displays January.
d	Days placeholder for dates. **d** displays 1, **dd** displays 01, **ddd** displays Mon, and **dddd** displays Monday.
y	Years placeholder for dates. yy displays 92, and yyyy displays 1992.
: (colon)	Separates hours, minutes, and seconds in format time values. **hh:mm:ss** displays 02:02:02.
h	Hours placeholder for time. **h** displays 2, and **hh** displays 02. If an AM/PM placeholder is used, **h** or **hh** displays 4 PM for 1600 hours.
n	Minutes placeholder for time. **n** displays 1, and **nn** displays 01. **hhnn "hours"** displays 1600 hours.
s	Seconds placeholder for time. **s** displays 1, and **ss** displays 01.
AM/PM	Displays time in 12-hour time with AM or PM appended. **h:nn AM/PM** displays 4:00 PM. Alternate formats include am/pm, A/P, and a/p.

Placeholder	Function
@	Indicates that a character is required in the position in a Text or Memo field. You can use @ to format telephone numbers in a Text field, as in @@@-@@@-@@@@ or (@@@) @@@-@@@@.
&	Indicates that a character is optional in the position in a Text or Memo field.
>	Changes all text characters in the field to uppercase.
<	Changes all text characters in the field to lowercase.
*	Displays the character following the asterisk as a fill character for empty spaces in a field. **"ABCD"*x** in an eight-character field appears as ABCDxxxx.

The Format drop-down combo list is one of the few examples in Access where you can select from a list of options or type your own entry. Format is a true drop-down combo list; lists in which you can only make a choice from the list are called *drop-down lists*. You don't need to enter the quotation marks shown in figure 4.8 surrounding the comma and space in the Format text box (**mmmm dd", "yyyy - hh:nn**) because Access does this for you. The comma is a nonstandard formatting symbol for dates (but it is standard for number fields). Nonstandard formatting characters automatically are enclosed in double quotation marks when you create them in the Field Properties window.

When you change the Format or any other property of a field, and then change to Datasheet View in run mode to view the result of your work, you need to save the updated table design first. You are asked to confirm the design change(s) with the dialog shown in figure 4.9.

Fig. 4.9
The confirmation dialog for changes to the format of a field.

If you apply the custom format string **mmmm dd", "yyyy - hh:nn** (shown in fig. 4.8) to the Birth Date field of the Employees table, the Birth Date field entries appear as shown in figure 4.10. For example, Nancy Davolio's birth date appears as December 08, 1948 - 00:00. The original format of the Birth Date field was Medium Date, the format also used with the Hire Date field.

You need to expand the width of the Birth Date field to accommodate the additional characters in the Long Date format. You increase the width of the field by dragging the right vertical bar of the field name header to the right to display the entire field. Date fields are right-justified in Access.

Birth Date field with custom format

Fig. 4.10
The Birth Date field when formatted with the custom format shown in figure 4.8.

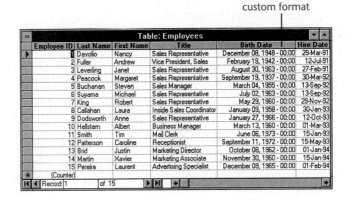

The time of birth is displayed as 00:00, because the decimal fraction that determines time is 0 for all entries in the Birth Date field.

Following is an example that formats negative numbers enclosed in parentheses and replaces a **Null** entry with text:

```
$###,###,##0.00;$(###,###,##0.00);0.00;"No Entry Here"
```

The entries 1234567.89, –1234567.89, 0, and a **Null** default value appear as follows:

```
$1,234,567.89
$(1,234,567.89)
0.00
No Entry Here
```

Using Input Masks

A feature of Paradox and xBase that was missing in Access 1.x is the capability to restrict entries in Text fields to numbers or to otherwise control the formatting of entered data. Access developers missed xBase's PICT[URE] expression used to format telephone numbers, social security numbers, ZIP codes, and similar data. Although Access 1.x allowed you to display data in accordance with the value of the Format property, as soon as you edited the data, the formatting characters disappeared. Access 2.0's new InputMask property, which closely resembles dBASE's PICT statement, solves this problem. Access's

InputMask property is based on the Masked Edit custom control of Visual Basic 3.0, but the InputMask property accommodates **Null** values and offers several improvements over the quirky Masked Edit control.

Table 4.6 lists the placeholders that you can use in character strings for input masks in fields of the Text field data type.

Table 4.6 Placeholders for Creating Input Masks	
Placeholder	**Function**
Empty string	No input mask.
0	Number (0–9) or sign (+/–) required.
9	Number (0–9) optional (space if not entered).
#	Number (0–9) or space optional (space if not entered).
L	Letter (A–z) required.
?	Letter (A–z) not required (space if not entered).
A	Letter (A–z) or number (0–9) required.
a	Letter (A–z) or number (0–9) optional.
&	Any character or a space required.
C	Any character or a space optional.
. , : ; – / ( )	Literal decimal, thousands, date, time, and special separators.
>	All characters to the right of > are converted to uppercase.
>	All characters to the right of < are converted to lowercase.
!	Fill mask from right to left.
\	Precede above characters with \ to include the literal character in a format string.

As an example, entering **\(000"**) "**000\-0000** as the value of the `InputMask` property causes results in the appearance of (___) ___-____ for a blank telephone number cell of a table. Entering **000\-00\-000** creates a mask for social security numbers, ___-__-____. When you enter the telephone number or social security number, the digits you type replace the underscores.

> **Note**
>
> The \ characters (often called *escape* characters) that precede parentheses and hyphens specify that the following character is a literal, not a formatting character. If spaces are included in the format, enclose the spaces and adjacent literal characters in double quotes.

 Access 2.0 includes an Input Mask Wizard that appears when you place the cursor in the Input Mask text box for a field of the Text or Date/Time field data type and click the ellipsis button at the extreme right of the text box. Figure 4.11 illustrates the opening dialog of the Input Mask Wizard, which provides 11 common input mask formats from which you can choose.

Fig. 4.11

The Input Mask Wizard for Text and Date/Time field data types.

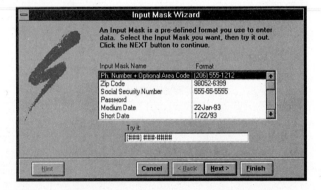

Using the Northwind Traders Sample Database

One of the fundamental problems with books about database management applications is the usual method of demonstrating how to create a "typical" database. You are asked to type fictitious names, addresses, and telephone numbers into a Customers table. Next, you must create additional tables that relate these fictitious customers to their purchases of various widgets in assorted sizes and quantities. This process is unrewarding for readers and authors, and few readers ever complete the exercises.

Access includes a comprehensive and interesting sample database; therefore, this book takes a different tack. Instead of creating a new database at this point, you create a new table as an addition to the Northwind Traders database. Adding a new table minimizes the amount of typing required and requires just a few entries in order to make it functional. The new Personnel Actions table demonstrates many of the elements of relational database design. Before you proceed to create the Personnel Actions table, try the quick example of adding a new table to the Northwind Traders sample database that is given in the section that follows.

Using the Table Wizard to Create New Tables

Access includes a variety of wizards whose services simplify the creation of new database objects. Wizards lead you through a predetermined set of steps that determine the characteristics of the object you want to create. Access 2.0 includes a Table Wizard that you can use to create new tables based on prefabricated designs for 26 business-oriented and 17 personal-type tables. Many of the business-oriented table designs are based on tables contained in NWIND.MDB.

The Table Wizard is one of the simplest of the wizards supplied with Access 2.0. Thus, the Table Wizard serves as an excellent introduction to the use of Access wizards in general. Follow these steps to create a new Access table that is designed to catalog a music collection:

1. If the Employees table is open, close it by double-clicking the Document Control-menu box to make the Database window active. Alternatively, click the Show Database window button of the toolbar.

2. Click the Table button of the Database window, if it isn't selected, and then click the New button to display the New Table dialog shown in figure 4.12.

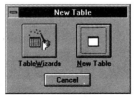

Fig. 4.12
The New Table dialog lets you elect to use the Table Wizard for table design.

3. Click the Table Wizard button to display the opening dialog of the Table Wizard. (If you click the New Table button, a blank Table Design grid appears.)

4. Click the Personal option button to display a list of tables for personal use in the Sample Tables list, and then use the vertical scroll bar to display the Music Collection entry in the list.

5. Click the Music Collection entry to display the predetermined set of field names for the new table in the Sample Fields list.

6. Click the >> button to add all of the fields from the Sample Fields list to the Fields in My New Table list. (The > button adds a single selected field from the Sample Fields list, the < button removes a single selected field from the My New Table list, and the << button deletes all the fields in the My New Table list.) The Table Wizard's dialog now appears as in figure 4.13.

Fig. 4.13
Adding fields to the new Music Collection table.

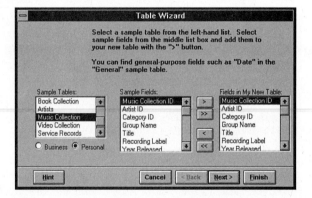

7. Click the Next > button to display the second Table Wizard dialog in which you select the name for your new table, and select how the primary-key field for the table is determined. Accept the default table name or enter a name of your choice, and then click the Define My Own option button in the Primary Key option group. The second dialog of the Table Wizard now appears (see fig. 4.14).

Fig. 4.14
Choosing a table name and how to determine the table's primary key.

8. Click the Next > button to display the dialog shown in figure 4.15 that lets you select the primary-key field and the data type for the field. The Music Collection ID field is the logical choice for a primary key and the Counter field data type, which automatically creates a sequential number for the Collection ID is appropriate in this case. Thus, you can accept the default values determined by the Table Wizard.

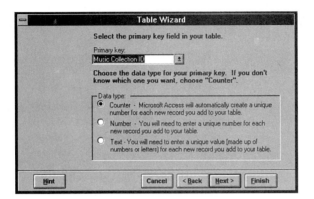

Fig. 4.15
The primary-key dialog of the Table Wizard.

9. Click the Next > button to complete the table design definition process. The Table Wizard's last dialog appears (see fig. 4.16). Click the Design button to display your new table in design mode, as illustrated by figure 4.17.

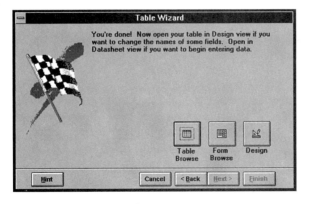

Fig. 4.16
The last Table Wizard dialog.

If you want to delete the Music Collection table from NWIND.MDB, click the Show Database Window button of the toolbar, click the Table button if the Tables list is not open, and then click the Music Collection entry in the Table list to select (highlight) it. Press Delete; click OK when the message box asks you to confirm the deletion.

Fig. 4.17
The new Music
Collection table in
design mode.

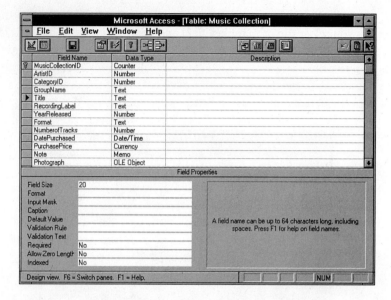

> **Note**
>
> Creating tables based on the sample tables provided by the Table Wizard has limited usefulness in real-life business applications. In the majority of cases, you probably import data from another database or spreadsheet application to create your Access tables. If you can't import the data, you probably need to define the fields of the tables to suit particular business needs. Thus, the remainder of this chapter is devoted to designing a new database table by the traditional method of manually adding fields to a blank table design and then specifying the properties of each field.

Adding a New Table to an Existing Database

The Northwind Traders database includes an Employees table that provides most of the information about the employees of the firm that is typical of personnel tables. This chapter explains how to add a table called *Personnel Actions* to the database. The Personnel Actions table is a record of hire date, salary, commission rate, bonuses, performance reviews, and other compensation-related events for employees. Because Personnel Actions is based on information in the Employees table, the first step of this process is to review the structure of the Employees table to see how you can use it with your new table. The structure of tables is displayed in design mode. You add validation rules to the table and enter records in the table when you reach the next chapter, "Entering, Editing, and Validating Data in Tables."

To open the Employees table in design mode, follow these steps:

1. Close any Access document windows that you have open, and then click the Table button in the Database window to display the list of tables in the NWIND.MDB database.

2. Click Employees in the Database window, and then click the Design button. You also can open the Employees table by double-clicking the Database window entry, and then clicking the Design View button on the Tables toolbar.

3. The Design grid for the Employees table appears. Maximize the document window to the size of your Access window by clicking the document's Maximize button.

4. Close the Properties window, if it appears, by double-clicking its Application Control-menu box. Alternatively, you can choose Table Properties from the **V**iew menu.

The Table Properties command toggles the visibility of the Table Properties window. A check mark next to Table Properties indicates that the window is always visible in Table Design View. At this point, your display resembles that shown in figure 4.18.

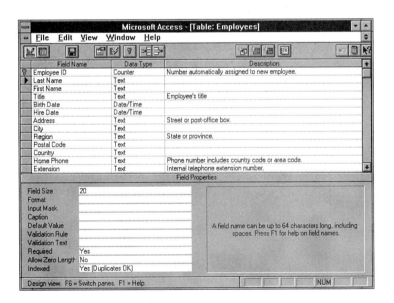

Fig. 4.18
The Employees table of the Northwind Traders database in Table Design View.

The Table Design window displays the field names and the field data types and provides a third column for an optional description of each field in the table. This display is called a *grid* rather than a *datasheet* because the display doesn't contain data from a table. A scroll bar is provided, regardless of whether more fields exist in the table than can be displayed in the window. The Field Properties pane enables you to set additional properties of individual fields and provides a brief description of the purpose of each column of the grid and of the Field Properties entries as you select them. You cannot resize this pane.

  One field is conspicuous by its absence: the social security number that is used by most firms to identify their personnel in databases. The Employee ID field is an adequate substitute for the social security number for an example table because a unique sequential number (the Counter field data type) is assigned to each employee. Click the Datasheet View button to display the data in the Employee ID field, and then return to design mode by clicking the Design View button.

Designing the Personnel Actions Table

You should place employee remuneration data in a table of its own, rather than adding fields for entries (such as salary, commission rate, and bonuses) to the Employees table for the following reasons:

- Multiple personnel actions are taken for individual employees over time. If these actions are added to records in the Employees table, you are forced to create many additional fields to hold an arbitrary number of personnel actions. If, for example, quarterly performance reviews are entered, you are forced to add a new field for every quarter to hold the review information. In this situation, flat-file managers encounter difficulties.

- Personnel actions can be categorized by type so that any action taken can use a common set of field names and field data types. This feature makes the design of the Personnel Actions table simple.

- Employees can be identified uniquely by their Employee ID numbers. Therefore, records for entries of personnel actions can be related to the Employees table by an Employee ID field. This feature eliminates the necessity of adding employee names and other information to the records in the Personnel Action table. You link the Employees table to the Personnel table by the Employee ID field, and the two tables are joined; they act as if they are a single table. Minimizing information duplication to only what is required in order to link the tables is your reward for choosing a relational, rather than a flat-file, database management system.

■ Personnel actions usually are considered confidential information and are made accessible only to a limited number of people. Although Access enables you to grant permission for others to view specific fields, restricting permission to view an entire table is simpler.

The next step is to design the Personnel Actions table. Chapter 23, "Exploring Relational Database Design and Implementation," discusses the theory of database design and the tables that make up databases. Because the Personnel Actions table has an easily discernible relationship to the Employees table, the theoretical background isn't necessary for this example.

Determining What Information Should Be Included

Designing a table requires that you identify the type of information the table should contain. Information associated with typical personnel actions might consist of the following items:

■ *Important dates.* The date of hire and termination, if applicable, are important dates, but so are the dates when salaries are adjusted, commission rates are changed, and bonuses are granted. Each action should be accompanied by the date when it was scheduled to occur and the date when it actually occurred.

■ *Types of actions.* Less typing is required if personnel actions are identified by a code character, rather than a full-text description of the action. This feature saves valuable disk space, too. First-letter abbreviations used as codes, such as *H* for *hired, T* for *terminated,* Q for *quarterly review,* and so on, are easy to remember.

■ *Initiation and approval of actions.* As a rule, the employee's supervisor initiates a personnel action, and the supervisor's manager approves it. Therefore, the Employee ID number for a supervisor and manager must be included.

■ *Amounts involved.* Salaries are assumed to be based on monthly payment, bonuses are paid quarterly with quarterly performance reviews, and commissions are paid on a percentage of sales made by the employee.

- *Performance rating*. Rating employee performance by a numerical value is a universal, but somewhat arbitrary, practice. Scales of 1 to 9 are common, with exceptional performance ranked as 9 and candidacy for termination as 1.

- *Summaries and comments*. Provision should be made for a summary of performance, explanation of exceptionally high or low ratings, and reasons for adjusting salaries or bonuses.

If you are involved in personnel management, you probably can think of additional information that might be included in the table, such as accruable sick leave and vacation hours per pay period. The Personnel Actions table is just an example; it isn't meant to add full-scale human resources development capabilities to the database. The limited amount of data described serves to demonstrate several uses of the new table in this and succeeding chapters.

Assigning Information to Fields

After you determine the types of information, called *data entities* or *entities*, to be included in the table, you must assign each data entity to a field of the table. This process involves choosing a field name that must be unique within the table. Table 4.6 lists the candidate fields for the Personnel Actions table. *Candidate fields* are written descriptions of the fields that are proposed for the table. Data types have been assigned from those listed in table 4.7 in the following section.

> **Note**
>
> The table name and fields names of the Personnel Actions table contain spaces. As mentioned earlier in this book, it is not a good database design practice to include spaces in table names or field names. In this case, spaces are included in both the table name and field names to demonstrate the special rule (enclosing the name within square brackets) that you need to observe when referring to object names that include spaces. The Northwind Traders sample database includes spaces in many of its table and field names, so the use of spaces here is consistent with the other tables in the database.

Table 4.7   Candidate Fields for the Personnel Actions Table

Field Name	Data Type	Function of Field
PA ID	Number	Identifies the employee to whom the action applies. PA ID numbers are assigned based on the Employee ID field of the Employee table (to which the Personnel Table is linked).
PA Type	Text	Code for the type of action taken. H=hired, C=commission rate adjustment, Q=quarterly review, Y=yearly review, S=salary adjustment, B=bonus adjustment, and T=terminated.
PA Initiated By	Number	Employee ID number of the supervisor who initiates or is responsible for recommending the action.
PA Scheduled Date	Date/Time	The date when the action is scheduled to occur.
PA Approved By	Number	Employee ID number of the manager who approves the action proposed by the supervisor.
PA Effective Date	Date/Time	The date when the action occurred. The effective date remains blank if the action has not occurred.
PA Rating	Number	Performance on a scale of 1 to 9, with higher numbers indicating better performance. A blank indicates no rating; 0 is reserved for terminated employees.
PA Amount	Currency	Salary per month, bonus per quarter, commission rate as a percent of the amount of the order, expressed as a decimal fraction.
PA Comments	Memo	Abstracts of performance reviews and comments on actions proposed or taken. No limit exists for the length of the comments; the supervisor and manager can contribute to the comments.

> **Note**
>
> Use distinctive names for each field. In this example, each field name is preceded by the abbreviation PA to identify the field with the Personnel Actions table. When designing xBase databases, for example, a common practice is to use the same name for fields that contain identical data but are located in different tables. Because of the way Access uses these names in expressions for validating data entry and calculating field values (discussed later in this chapter and in Chapter 9), a better practice is to assign related, but distinctive, names to such fields.

Creating the Personnel Actions Table

Now you can put to work what you have learned about field names, data types, and formats by adding the Personnel Actions table to the Northwind Traders database. The field names, taken from table 4.7, and the set of properties you assign to the fields are shown in table 4.8. The text in the Caption property column substitutes for the Field Name property that is otherwise displayed in the field header buttons.

Table 4.8   Field Properties for the Personnel Actions Table

Field Name	Caption	Data Type	Field Size	Format
PA ID	ID	Number	Long Integer	General Number
PA Type	Type	Text	1	@> (all caps)
PA Initiated By	Initiated By	Number	Integer	General Number
PA Scheduled Date	Scheduled	Date/Time	N/A	Short Date
PA Approved By	Approved By	Number	Integer	General Number
PA Effective Date	Effective	Date/Time	N/A	Short Date
PA Rating	Rating	Number	Integer	General Number
PA Amount	Amount	Currency	N/A	#,##0.00#
PA Comments	Comments	Memo	N/A	(None)

The Field Size property of the PA ID field must be set to the Long Integer data type, although you might not expect Northwind Traders to have more than the 32,767 employees that is allowed by an integer. You need to use the Long Integer data type because the Counter field data type of the Employee ID field of the Employees table is a Long Integer. The reason that the data type of PA ID must match that of the Employee ID number field of the Employees table is explained in the "Enforcing Referential Integrity" section later in this chapter.

To add the new Personnel Actions table to the Northwind Traders database, complete the following steps:

1. Close the Employees table, if it is open, by double-clicking the Document Control-menu box to make the Database window active.

2. Click the Table button of the Database window, if it isn't selected, and then click the New button. Click the New Table button of the New Table dialog. Access enters design mode and opens a blank grid where you enter field names, data types, and optional comments. The first cell in the grid is selected automatically by Access.

3. Enter **PA ID** as the first field name. Press Enter to accept the field name. The caret moves to the Data Type column; Access adds the default field type, Text.

4. Press F4 to open the Data Type list. The function keys, rather than the mouse, are used here because your entries are from the keyboard.

5. Use the arrow keys to select the Number data type, and press Enter to accept your selection (see fig. 4.19).

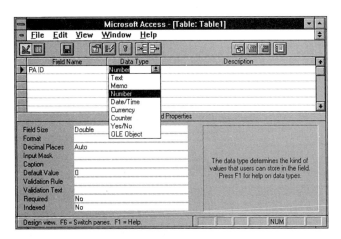

Fig. 4.19
Entering the field data type for the PA ID field in the Personnel Actions table.

6. Press F6 to move to the Field Size text box in the Field Properties window. Access has entered Double as the value of the default `FieldSize` property. To learn more about the `FieldSize` property, press F1 for help.

7. Press F4 to open the Field Size list. Select Long Integer, and press Enter (see fig. 4.20).

Fig. 4.20

Adding the Long Integer subtype (Field Size property) for the PA ID field.

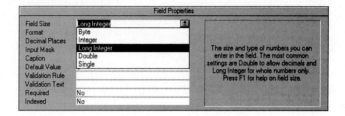

8. Press the down arrow to select the Format text box. You can press F1 for context-sensitive help on the `Format` property.

9. Press F4 to open the Format list, select General Number from the list, and press Enter (see fig. 4.21).

Fig. 4.21

Assigning the General Number format to the PA ID field.

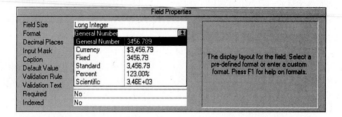

10. Press the down-arrow key twice to bypass Decimal Places and select the Caption text box. Integers cannot have decimal fractions, so Decimal Places can remain set to Auto.

11. Enter **ID** as the caption, and press Enter. ID is used as the Caption property to reduce the column width necessary to display the PA ID number.

12. Press F6 to return to the Table Design grid. The caret is located in the Comments column. The remaining properties for each field will be completed after the basic properties shown in table 4.8 have been completed.

13. Comments are used to create prompts that appear in the status bar
    when you are adding or editing records in run mode's Datasheet View.
    Although comments are optional, a good database design practice is to
    enter the purpose of the field if its use isn't obvious from its Field Name
    or Caption property. You can skip the Caption property entries now;
    then refer to table 4.8 and enter the captions as a group when you have
    completed the basic steps described here.

14. Press the down-arrow key to select the next row of the grid.

15. Repeat steps 3 through 13, entering the values shown in table 4.8 for
    each of the eight remaining fields of the Personnel Action table. N/A
    means that the entry in table 4.8 isn't applicable to the data type for
    the field.

Your Table Design grid now appears (see fig. 4.22). You can double-check
your properties entries by selecting each field name with the arrow keys and
reading the values shown in the properties text boxes of the Field Properties
window.

Field Name	Data Type	Description
PA ID	Number	Linked to Employee ID of Employees table
PA Type	Text	H = hired, S = salary adjustment, Q = quarterly review, Y
PA Initiated By	Number	Employee number of supervisor
PA Scheduled Date	Date/Time	Date on which action is scheduled to occur
PA Approved By	Number	Employee number of approving manager
PA Effective Date	Date/Time	Date action is to be effective (requires approval)
PA Rating	Number	Employee performance rating, 0 to 9, 0 for terminated em
PA Amount	Currency	Amount of increase (or decrease) in salary, bonus or com
PA Comments	Memo	Comments by supervisor or manager

Fig. 4.22
The initial design
of the Personnel
Actions table.

Click the Datasheet toolbar button to return to Datasheet View in run mode
to view the results of your work. You receive a "Must save table first. Save
now?" message. Click OK, and a Save As dialog appears, with the default table
name, Table1, requesting that you give your table a name. Type **Personnel
Actions**, as shown in figure 4.23, and press Enter or click OK.

Fig. 4.23
The dialog for
naming the
Personnel Actions
table.

The Datasheet View of your table appears, with its first default record. To
view all the fields of your new table, narrow the field name header buttons by
dragging to the left the right vertical bar that separates each of the headers.

When you have finished adjusting the display widths of your fields, your Datasheet View of the Personnel Actions table appears as in figure 4.24. Only the empty tentative append record (a new record that will be added to your table if you enter values in the cells) is present. You have more property values to add to your Personnel Actions table, so don't enter data in the tentative append record at this point.

Fig. 4.24

The tentative append record of the Personnel Actions table.

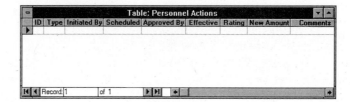

Setting Default Values of Fields

Access 1.x assigned your fields default values, such as 0 for Number and Currency fields and No for Yes/No fields. Access 2.0 does not assign default values to Number and Yes/No fields automatically. Text, Memo, and Date fields in all versions of Access are empty by default. You can save data entry time by establishing your own default values for fields. The default values for the fields of the Personnel Actions tables are listed in table 4.9.

Table 4.9	**Default Field Values for the Personnel Actions Table**	
Field Name	**Default Value**	**Comments**
PA ID	No entry	0 is not a valid Employee ID number.
PA Type	Q	Quarterly performance reviews are the most common personnel action.
PA Initiated By	No entry	0 is not valid.
PA Scheduled Date	Date( )	The expression to enter today's (DOS) date.
PA Approved By	No entry	0 is not valid.
PA Effective Date	Date( )+28	Today's (DOS) date plus 28 days.
PA Rating	No entry	In many cases, a rating is not applicable. A 0 rating is reserved for terminated employees.

Field Name	Default Value	Comments
PA Amount	No entry	If a salary, bonus, or commission has no change, no entry should appear. 0 would indicate no salary, for example.
PA Comments	No change	For now, Access's default is adequate.

No entry in the Default Value text box creates a `Null` default value. `Null` values can be used for testing whether a value has been entered into a field to ensure that required data has been entered. (This subject is discussed in the following section.) The Date+28 default is an *expression* that returns the DOS date plus four weeks. Expressions are used to enter values in fields, make calculations, and perform other useful duties, such as validating data entries. Expressions are discussed briefly in the next section and in greater detail in Chapter 9, "Understanding Operators and Expressions in Access." Expressions used to establish default values always are preceded by an equal sign.

To assign the new default values from those of table 4.9 to the fields of the Personnel Actions table, complete these steps:

1. Change to design mode by choosing Table **D**esign from the **V**iew menu. The PA ID field is selected automatically. Select the PA Type field.

2. Press F6 to switch to the Field Properties window, and then move the caret to the Default Value text box. Enter **Q** as the default value.

3. Press F6 to switch back to the Table Design grid. Move to the next field, and press F6 again.

4. Create the default values for the eight remaining fields from the entries shown in table 4.9, repeating steps 2 through 4. Enter **Date** for the AP Scheduled Date field and **Date+28** for the AP Effective Date field. Delete any default values that may appear in the other fields that call for No Entry in table 4.9.

5. When you have completed your default entries, choose Data**s**heet from the **V**iew menu to return to run mode. A dialog requesting confirmation of the changes you made appears. Click OK. The Design View of the Personnel Actions table now appears as shown in figure 4.25 with the new default entries you have assigned.

Fig. 4.25
The first record of the Personnel Actions table with the new default entries.

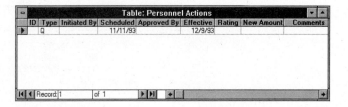

Working with Relations, Key Fields, and Indexes

Your final tasks before adding records to the Personnel Actions table are to determine the relationship between Personnel Actions and an existing table in the database, assign a primary-key field, and add indexes to your table.

Establishing Relationships between Tables

Relationships between existing tables and your new table determine the field used as the new table's primary key. The following four possibilities exist for relationships between tables:

- *One-to-one* relationships require that the value of the key field in one and only one record in your new table match a corresponding value of the related field in the existing table. In this case, the key field in your new table must be unique; duplicate values aren't allowed in the key field. A one-to-one relationship is the equivalent of a table that contains all the fields of the existing table and the new table. Tables with one-to-one relationships are uncommon.

- *Many-to-one* relationships allow your new table to have more than one value in the key field corresponding to a single value in the related field of the existing table. In this case, duplicate key field values are allowed. Many-to-one relationships are the most common type found; the capability to create many-to-one relationships is the principal reason for choosing a relational system, rather than a flat-file application, to manage your databases.

- *One-to-many* relationships require that your new table's key field be unique, but the values in the key field of the new table can match many entries in the related field of the existing database. In this case, the related field of the existing database has a many-to-one relationship with the key field of the new database.

■ *Many-to-many* relationships are free-for-alls in which no unique relationship exists between the key fields in the existing table or the new table, and both of the tables' key fields contain duplicate values.

Keep in mind that the many-to-one and one-to-many relationships apply to how your new table relates to an existing table. When viewed from the existing table's standpoint, the relationships to your new table are one-to-many and many-to-one, respectively. Chapter 23, "Exploring Relational Database Design and Implementation," provides a more comprehensive explanation of the four types of relations.

▶ "Types of Relationships," p. 859

Many entries in the Personnel Actions table may apply to a single employee whose record appears in the Employees table. A record is created in Personnel Actions when the employee is hired, and a record is created for each quarterly and yearly performance review. Also, any changes made to bonuses or commissions other than as the result of a performance review are entered, and employees may be terminated. Over time, the number of records in the Personnel Actions table is likely to be greater by a factor of 10 or more than the number of records in the Employees table. Thus, the records in the new Personnel table have a many-to-one relationship with the records in the Employees table. Establishing the relationships between the new and existing tables when you create the new table enables Access to reestablish the relationship automatically when you use the tables in queries, forms, and reports.

Access requires that the two fields participating in the relationship have exactly the same data type. In the case of the Number field data type, the Field Size property of the two fields must be identical. You cannot, for example, create a relationship between a Counter type field (which uses a Long Integer data type) and a field containing Byte, Integer, Single, Double, or Currency data. On the other hand, Access enables you to relate two tables by text fields of different lengths. Such a relationship, if created, can lead to strange behavior when you create queries, which is the subject of Part II. As a rule, the relationships between text fields should use fields of the same length.

Access 2.0 introduces a new graphical Relationships window that replaces the Relationships dialog of Access 1.x. To establish the relationships between two tables using Access's Relationships dialog, follow these steps:

Access

2.0

1. Close the Personnel Actions table by double-clicking the Document Control-menu box. If the Employees table is open, close it. You cannot create or modify relationships between tables that are open.

2. If the Database window isn't the active window (indicated by a colored title bar), click the Database window, click the Show Database Window button of the toolbar, or choose **1** Database from the **W**indows menu. Up to nine of the windows for database objects you have opened appear as numbered choices in the **W**indows menu. (The Database window is always number 1.) The Database window must be active in order to establish relationships.

3. Click the Relationships button of the toolbar or choose **R**elationships from the **E**dit menu. The Relationships window for the Northwind Traders database appears (see fig. 4.26). All of the tables for which relationships have been defined appear in the Relationships window.

Fig. 4.26
The Relationships window of Access 2.0.

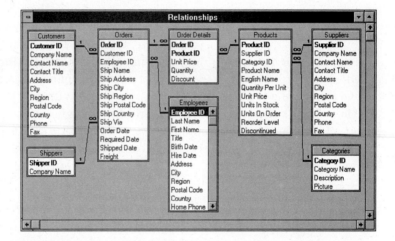

4. Click the Add Table button of the toolbar or choose **A**dd Table from the **R**elationships menu to display the Add Table dialog shown in figure 4.27.

Fig. 4.27
Adding a new table to the Relationships window.

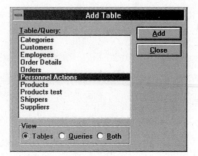

5. Double-click the Personnel Actions entry in the Table/Query list to add the Personnel Actions table to the Relationships window or click the entry to select it; then click the Add button. Click the Close button to close the Add Table dialog.

6. The relationship of the Personnel Actions table with the Employees table is based on the PA ID field of the Personnel Actions table and the Employee ID field of the Employees table. Click the Employee ID field of the Employees table and, holding the left mouse button down, drag the field to the PA ID field of the Personnel Actions table. Release the left mouse button to drop the field symbol on the PA ID field. When you drag-and-drop a new relationship, the Relationships dialog appears (see fig. 4.28).

Note

The sequence of the drag-and-drop operation to create a new relationship is important. Drag the field from the *one* side of a one-to-many relationship and drop it on the *many* side. This sequence assures that the primary (or base) table for the *one* side of the relationship appears in Table/Query list and that the table for the *many* side appears in the Related Table/Query list. If you reverse the relationships (creating a many-to-one relationship) and attempt to enforce referential integrity, you receive an error message in the final step of the process when you attempt to create the relationship.

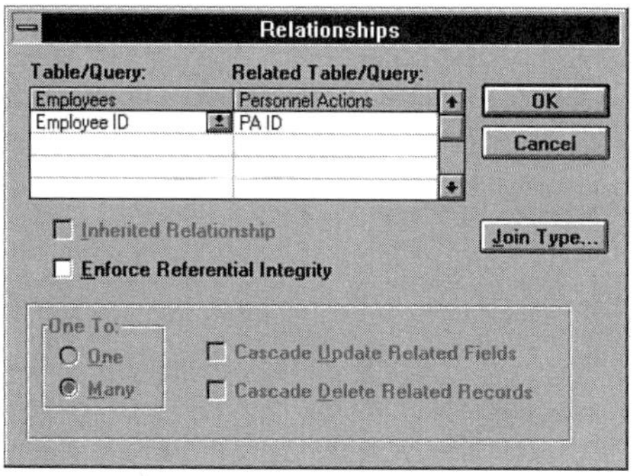

Fig. 4.28
Defining a relationship with the Relationships dialog.

7. Click the Join Type button to display the Join Properties dialog shown in figure 4.29. You want to create a one-to-many join between the Employee ID field (the *one* side) of the Employees table and the PA ID field (the *many* side) of the Personnel Actions table. Thus, you want to include *all* Personnel Actions records for a single employee. To do so, click option 3 in the Join Properties dialog. Click OK to close the dialog.

Fig. 4.29
Choosing the type
of join for the
Personnel Actions
and Employees
tables.

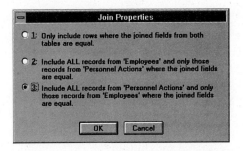

8. The Enforce Referential Integrity check box is provided so that Access can perform validation testing for you and accept entries in the PA ID field that correspond to values for Employee IDs in the Employees table. This process is called *enforcing* (or maintaining) referential integrity. Referential integrity is discussed in the following section. Enforced referential integrity is required here, so make sure that the box is checked. The Relationships dialog now appears as shown in figure 4.30.

> **Note**
>
> Access 2.0 lets you automatically maintain referential integrity of tables by providing check boxes that you can mark to cause cascading updates to and cascade deletions of related records when changes are made to the primary table. Cascading updates and deletions are discussed in the section that follows. The cascade check boxes are enabled only if you elect to enforce referential integrity.

Fig. 4.30
Relationships
dialog entries for
a one-to-many
relationship with
referential in-
tegrity enforced.

9. Click the OK button to accept the new relationship and display the relationship in the Relationships window as shown in figure 4.31.

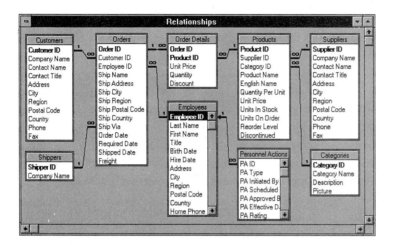

Fig. 4.31
The Relationships window with the new Personnel Actions relationship added.

10. Click the Document Control-menu box to close the Relationships window and return to the Database window. Click Yes when asked to confirm that you want to save the layout changes to the Relationships diagram.

The relationship you have created is used by Access when you create queries and design forms and reports that require data in the Personnel Actions table.

The relationship is equivalent to that which is created by the following xBase statements:

```
SELECT 1
USE employee INDEX emp_idno
SELECT 2
USE pers_act
SELECT employee
SET RELATION TO emp_idno INTO employee
```

xBase

SET RELATION TO

The difference between Access and xBase relationships is that the related table in xBase, pers_act, must be indexed on the key expression of the primary table, Employee ID, but Access does not require that the related table be indexed.

Enforcing Referential Integrity

The ability to automatically enforce referential integrity is an important feature of Access; few other PC relational database managers include this feature. Referential integrity prevents the creation of "orphan records" that have no connection to a primary table. An example of an orphan record is a record for a personnel action for PA ID 10 when you have records in the Employees file only for employees numbered 1 through 9. You would never know who employee 10 might be until you entered the next employee hired. Then the orphan record, intended for some other employee, is attached, improperly, to the new employee's record.

How Referential Integrity Is Enforced

Referential integrity enforcement prevents you from deleting or modifying values of a primary table's record on which related records depend. If you terminate an employee and then try to delete the employee's record from the Employees table, Access prevents you from doing so. Access displays a message box informing you that you must delete all records related to the primary table's record before you can delete the primary record. You can't change a value in the Employee ID field of the Employees table because the field data type is Counter. If the data types are such that you can change the value of an Employee ID on which related records depend, however, Access also displays a warning message.

In the same vein, if you attempt to change an employee ID value in the PA ID field of the Personnel Actions table to a value that does not exist in the Employee ID field of the Employees table, you also incur an error message. Thus, enforcing referential integrity eliminates the need to validate entries in the PA ID field using the ValidationRule property. With referential integrity enforced, Access automatically makes sure that the value you enter corresponds to a valid Employee ID value when you save the new or edited record.

**Access
2.0**

Cascading Updates and Deletions

Prior to Access 2.0, you had to implement the series of actions that are required to maintain referential integrity by writing macros or Access Basic code. As an example, to delete a record in the Employees table, you needed to test to determine if related records existed in any other table that depended on the Employee ID field. Then you had to delete the dependent records. If you wanted to change the Customer ID of a record in the Customers table, the situation became more complex: You couldn't change the related records to a new Customer ID that isn't yet in the table, nor could you change the Customer ID in the primary table because it has dependent records. You could resolve this dichotomy by a variety of methods, but none of the methods were simple.

Access 2.0's cascading deletion and cascading update options for tables with referential integrity enforced makes maintaining referential integrity a simple process: just check the Cascade Update Related Fields and Cascade Delete Related Records check boxes. Access 2.0 does all of the work for you.

> **Note**
>
> Enforcing referential integrity automatically is usually, but not always, a good data-base design practice. An example of where you would not want to employ cascade deletions is between the Employee ID fields of the Orders and Employee tables. If you terminate an employee and then attempt to delete the record for the employee, you might accidentally choose to delete the dependent records in the Orders table. Deleting records in the Orders table could have very serious consequences from a marketing and accounting standpoint. (In the real world, however, it is unlikely that you would delete a terminated employee's record.)

Selecting a Primary Key

You do not need to designate a primary-key field for a table that is never used as a primary table. A *primary table* is a table that contains information repre-senting a real-world object, such as a person or an invoice, and has just one record that is uniquely associated with that object. The Personnel Actions table can qualify as a primary table because it identifies an object—in this case, the equivalent of a paper form representing the outcome of two actions: initiation and approval. Personnel Actions, however, probably is not used as a primary table in a relationship with another table.

Using a key field is a simple method of preventing the duplication of records in a table. Access requires that you specify a primary key if you want to create a one-to-one relationship or update two or more tables at the same time; this subject is covered in Chapter 10, "Creating Multitable and Crosstab Queries."

The primary table participating in relations you set with the Relationships dialog must have a primary key. Access considers a table without a primary-key field to be an oddity; therefore, you often are prompted by a message that a key field hasn't been created when you make changes to the table and re-turn to Design View. (Access 2.0 asks you only once whether you want to add a primary-key field.) Related tables can have primary-key fields and often do; a primary-key field is useful to prevent the accidental addition of duplicate records.

Primary keys can be created on more than one field. In the case of the Per-sonnel Actions table, a primary key that prevents duplicate records must consist of more than one field, because more than one personnel action for an employee can be scheduled or approved on the same date. If you establish the rule that no more than one type of personnel action for an employee can be scheduled for the same date, you can create a primary key that consists of the PA ID, PA Type, and PA Scheduled Date fields. When you create a primary key, Access creates an index based on the primary key. Indexes are the subject of the next section and are discussed in detail in Chapter 23, "Exploring Relational Database Design and Implementation."

To create a multiple-field primary key and index for the Personnel Actions table, follow these steps:

1. Open the Personnel Actions table from the Database window in design mode.

2. Click the selection button for the PA ID field.

3. Hold down the Ctrl key and click the selection button for the PA Type field. In most instances, when you hold down Ctrl and click a selection button, you can make multiple selections.

4. Hold down Ctrl and click the selection button for the PA Scheduled Date field.

   If you accidentally select one of the other fields, release Ctrl and click the field's selection button to deselect it.

5. Click the Key Field button on the toolbar. Symbols of keys appear in each of the selected fields, indicating their inclusion in the primary key (see fig. 4.32).

Fig. 4.32
Setting a multiple-field primary key for the Personnel Actions table.

Primary key indicators —

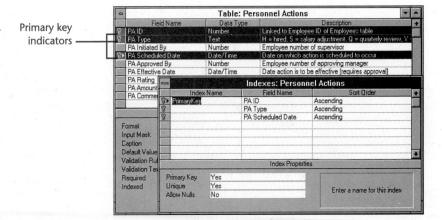

6. To determine the sequence of the fields in the primary key, click the Index button of the toolbar to display the Indexes window, as shown in figure 4.32.

In Access, you can create multiple-field primary keys and indexes with fields of different data types, without resorting to xBase-type changing functions. The entry in the Primary Key text box is the equivalent of the following xBase statement:

INDEX Expressions

```
INDEX ON STRZERO(pa_id,2) + pa_type + DTOS(pa_sced)
TO whatever
```

The capability to concatenate different data types to form an index instruction or a string is the result of Access's Variant data type discussed in Chapter 27, "Writing Access Basic Code."

You now have a multiple-field primary key and a corresponding index to the Personnel Actions table that precludes the addition of records that duplicate records with the same primary key.

Adding Indexes to Tables

Although Access creates an index on the primary key, you may want to create an index on some other field or fields in the table. Indexes speed searches for records that contain specific types of data. You may want to find all personnel actions that occurred in a given period and all quarterly reviews for all employees in PA Scheduled Date sequence, for example. If you have many records in the table, an index speeds up the searching process. A disadvantage of multiple indexes is that data entry operations are slowed by the time it takes to update the additional indexes. You can create up to 32 indexes for each Access table, and 5 of those can be of the multiple-field type. Each multiple-field index can include up to 10 fields.

To create a single-field index for the Personnel Actions table based on the PA Effective Date field, and a multiple-field index based on the PA Type and the PA Scheduled Date fields, follow these steps:

1. Select the PA Effective Date field by clicking its selection button.

2. Select the Indexed text box in the Field Properties window.

3. Open the Indexed drop-down list by clicking the arrow button or pressing F4. The list appears as shown in figure 4.33.

4. In this case, duplicate entries are acceptable, so click Yes (Duplicates OK) and close the list. You can create only a single-field index by using this method.

Fig. 4.33
Creating a single-field index on the PA Effective Date field.

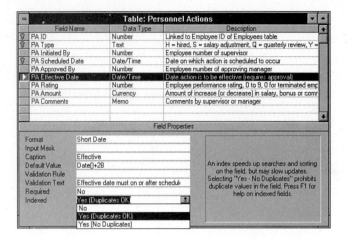

 5. Click the Indexes button if the Indexes window is not open. The Primary Key and PA Effective Date indexes already created appear in the list boxes. Enter **PA Type/Date** as the name of the composite index, and then select PA Type and PA Scheduled Date from the Field Name drop-down list to create a multiple-field index on these two fields, as shown in figure 4.34.

Fig. 4.34
Creating a multiple-field index on the PA Type and PA Scheduled Date fields.

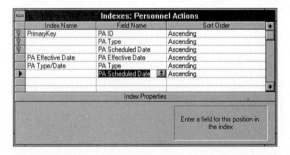

 6. Click the Datasheet View button to return to run mode. Click OK when the message box asks if you want to save your design changes. A message in the status bar indicates that the new indexes are being created as you leave design mode.

You now have three indexes for the Primary Key table: the index automatically created for the primary key, the single-key index on PA Effective Date, and the multiple-key index on PA Type and PA Scheduled Date.

Altering Fields and Relationships

When you are designing your own database, you often will discover that the original choices you made for the sequence of fields in a table, data types, or relationships between tables must be altered. One of the reasons for adding substantial numbers of records to tables during the testing process is to discover any changes that are necessary before putting the database into daily use.

You can change formats, change validation rules and text, change lengths of Text fields, and make other minor modifications to the table by changing to design mode, selecting the field to modify, and making the changes in the properties boxes. Changing data types can cause a loss of data, however, so be sure to read "Changing Field Data Types and Sizes," later in this chapter, before you attempt to make these changes. Changing relationships between tables is considered a drastic action if you have entered a substantial amount of data, so this subject also is covered in a later section, "Changing Relationships between Tables."

> **Note**
>
> Avoid changing field names if you have created data entry forms or reports that use the data in the field. Although Access performs many operations automatically, it does not change the field names that you have assigned to text boxes and other objects in forms or the groups in reports. The time to finalize field names is while creating your tables; a bit of extra thought at this point saves hours of modification when you are well into creation of a complex application.

Rearranging the Sequence of Fields in a Table

If you are manually entering historical data in Datasheet View, you can find that the sequence of entries isn't optimum. You may, for example, be entering data from a printed form with a top-to-bottom, left-to-right sequence that doesn't correspond to the left-to-right sequence of the corresponding fields in your table. Access makes rearranging the order of fields in tables a matter of dragging and dropping fields where you want them. You can choose whether to make the revised layout temporary or permanent when you close the table.

To rearrange the fields of the Personnel Actions table, follow these steps:

1. Click the Datasheet View button. This is the only table design change you can implement in Access's Datasheet View.

2. Click the field name button of the field you want to move. This action selects the field name button and all the data cells of the field.

3. Place the mouse pointer on the field name button and press the left mouse button. The mouse pointer turns into the drag-and-drop symbol, and a heavy vertical bar marks the far left position of the field. Figure 4.35 shows the PA Scheduled Date field being moved to a position immediately to the left of the PA Effective Date field.

Fig. 4.35

Dragging a field to a new position in run mode.

ID	Type	Initiated By	Scheduled	Approved By	Effective	Rating	New Amount	Comments
1	H	1	4/1/87		4/1/87		2,000.00	Hired
2	H	1	7/15/87		7/15/87		3,500.00	Hired
3	H	2	3/1/88		3/1/88	2	2,250.00	Hired
4	H	2	4/1/88		4/1/88	2	2,250.00	Hired
5	H	2	9/15/89		9/15/89	2	2,500.00	Hired
6	H	5	9/15/89		9/15/89	2	4,000.00	Hired
7	H	5	12/1/89		12/1/89	2	3,000.00	Hired
8	H	2	2/1/90		2/1/90	2	2,500.00	Hired
9	H	5	10/15/91		10/15/91	2	3,000.00	Hired
*	Q		11/11/93		12/9/93			

Record: 1 of 9

4. Move the mouse pointer and vertical bar combination to the new position for the selected field and release the mouse button. The field assumes the new position shown in figure 4.36.

Fig. 4.36

The PA Scheduled Date field dropped into a new position in Datasheet View.

ID	Type	Initiated By	Approved By	Scheduled	Effective	Rating	New Amount	Comments
1	H	1		4/1/87	4/1/87		2,000.00	Hired
2	H	1		7/15/87	7/15/87		3,500.00	Hired
3	H	2	2	3/1/88	3/1/88		2,250.00	Hired
4	H	2	2	4/1/88	4/1/88		2,250.00	Hired
5	H	2	2	9/15/89	9/15/89		2,500.00	Hired
6	H	5	2	9/15/89	9/15/89		4,000.00	Hired
7	H	5	2	12/1/89	12/1/89		3,000.00	Hired
8	H	2	2	2/1/90	2/1/90		2,500.00	Hired
9	H	5	2	10/15/91	10/15/91		3,000.00	Hired
*	Q			11/11/93	12/9/93			

Record: 1 of 9

5. When you close the Personnel Actions table, you see the familiar Save Changes message box. To make the modification permanent, click OK; otherwise, click No.

MODIFY STRUCTURE

Dragging and dropping fields to a new location is a much simpler process than the MODIFY STRUCTURE operations required by xBase to achieve the same result. You can reposition fields in design mode by clicking the select button of the row of the field to be moved and then dragging the row vertically to a new location. Changing the position of a field in a table doesn't change any of its other properties.

Changing Field Data Types and Sizes

You may find it necessary to change a field data type as the design of your database develops or if you import tables from another database, a spreadsheet, or a text file. If you import tables, the data type automatically chosen by Access during the importation process cannot be what you want, especially with Number fields. Importing and exporting tables and data from other applications is the subject of Chapter 7. Another example of altering field properties is changing the number of characters in fixed-length Text fields to accommodate longer than expected entries, or converting variable-length Text fields to fixed length.

> **Caution**
>
> Before making changes to the field data types of a table that contains substantial amounts of data, make a backup copy of the table by copying or exporting it to a backup Access database. If you accidentally lose parts of the data contained in the table, such as decimal fractions, when you make the conversion, you can import the backup table to your current database. The simple and quick process of exporting Access tables is covered in Chapter 7. After you create a backup database file, you can copy a table to Windows Clipboard and then paste it to the backup database. Copying and pasting tables to and from the Clipboard is discussed in the "Copying and Pasting Tables" section later in this chapter.

Numeric Fields

Changing a data type to one that requires a larger number of bytes of storage is, in almost all circumstances, safe. You do not sacrifice the accuracy of your data. Changing a numeric data type from Byte to Integer to Long Integer to Single and, finally, to Double, does not affect the value of your data because each change, with the exception of Long Integer to Single, requires more bytes of storage for a data value. Changing from Long Integer to Single and Single to Currency involves the same number of bytes and only decreases the accuracy of the data in exceptional circumstances. The exceptions can occur when you are using very, very large numbers or extremely small decimal fractions, such as in some scientific and engineering calculations.

On the other hand, your data may be truncated if you change to a data type with fewer data bytes required to store it. If you change from a fixed-point format (Currency) or floating-point format (Single or Double) to Byte, Integer, or Long Integer, any decimal fractions in your data are truncated. *Truncation* means reducing the number of digits in a number to fit the new Field

Size property you choose. If you change a numeric data type from Single to Currency, for example, data in the fifth, sixth, and seventh decimal places (if any exists) of your Single data is lost because Single provides up to seven decimal places and Currency provides only four.

RECNO(), PACK

You cannot convert any type of field to a Counter-type field. The Counter field is restricted to use as a record counter and enables entry only by the appending of new records; you cannot edit a record number field. When you delete a record in Access, the Counter values of the higher numbered records are not reduced by 1. Access record numbers are assigned to records in the order of the primary key not in the order in which the records were entered. If your table doesn't have a primary key, the record numbers represent the order in which the records were created.

Text Fields

You can convert Text fields to Memo fields without Access truncating your text. Converting a Memo field to a Text field, however, truncates characters beyond the 255 limit of Text fields. Similarly, if you convert a variable-length Text field to fixed length, and some records contain character strings that exceed the length you chose, these strings are truncated.

Conversion between Number, Date, and Text Field Data Types

Access makes many conversions between Number, Date, and Text field data types for you. Conversion from Number or Date to Text field data types does not follow the Format property you assigned to the original data type. Numbers are converted using the General Number format, and dates use the Short Date format. Access is quite intelligent in the methods it uses to convert suitable Text fields to Number data types. Access accepts dollar signs, commas, and decimals during the conversion, for example. Access ignores trailing spaces. Access converts dates and times in the following Text formats to internal Date/Time values that you then can format the way you want:

```
1/4/93 10:00 AM
04-Jan-92
January 4
10:00
10:00:00
```

> **Caution**
>
> You cannot change the Data Type or Field Size property of a field designated as the primary-key field, included in a composite primary key, or having a designated relationship with a field in another table. If you try to change a Data Type or Field Size in this case, you receive the message shown in figure 4.37.

Fig. 4.37
Attempting to
change a data
type or field.

Changing Relationships between Tables

Adding new relationships between tables is a straightforward process, but changing relationships can require you to change data types so that the related fields have the same data type. To change a relationship between two tables, complete the following steps:

1. Close the tables that are involved in the relationship.

2. If the Database window is not active, click it and then click the Show Database Window button, or choose Database from the **W**indows menu.

3. Click the Relationships button of the toolbar, or choose **R**elationships from the **E**dit menu to display the Relationships window.

4. Click the join line that connects to the field whose data type you want to change. When you select the join line, the line becomes darker (wider) as shown in figure 4.38.

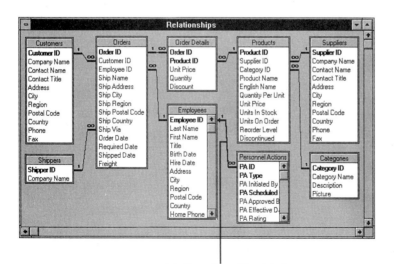

Fig. 4.38
Deleting a
relationship before
changing a data
type in a related
field.

Join line selected for deletion

5. Click Delete to clear the existing relationship. Click OK when the message box asks you to confirm your deletion.

6. If you are changing the data type of a field that constitutes or is a member field of the primary key of the primary table, delete all other relationships that exist between the primary table and every other table to which it is related.

7. Change the data types of the fields in the tables so that the data types match in the new relationships.

8. Re-create the relationships, using the procedure described in the earlier section, "Establishing Relationships between Tables."

Copying and Pasting Tables

You can copy a complete table or records of a table to the Windows Clipboard with the methods applicable to most other Windows applications. (Using the Clipboard to paste individual records or sets of records into a table is one of the subjects of the next chapter.) You use Clipboard operations extensively when you reach Part V of this book, "Integrating Access with Other Applications." You can copy tables into other databases, such as a general purpose back-up database, by using the Clipboard; however, exporting a table to a temporary database file, described in Chapter 7, is a more expeditious method.

To copy a table to another Access database, a destination database must exist. To create a backup database and copy the contents of the Personnel Actions table to the database, follow these steps:

1. Make the Database window active by clicking it, if it is accessible, or by choosing Database from the **W**indows menu.

2. Click the Table button, if necessary, to display the list of tables.

3. Select the table you want to copy to the new database.

4. Press Ctrl+C, or choose **C**opy from the **E**dit menu.

5. If you plan to copy the table to your current database, skip to step 8.

6. If you have created a destination backup database, choose **O**pen from the **F**ile menu and open the database; then skip to step 8.

7. To create a backup database, choose **N**ew from the **F**ile menu and type **backup.mdb** or another appropriate file name in the Files combo list, and then click OK. Access creates your BACKUP.MDB database, which occupies 64K without any tables (this is called 64K of overhead). Your new database now is active.

8. Press Ctrl+V, or choose **P**aste from the **E**dit menu. The Paste Table As dialog shown in figure 4.39 appears.

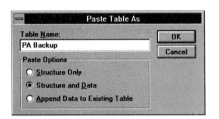

Fig. 4.39
The Paste Table As dialog used to create a backup table.

9. You have three options for pasting the backup table to the destination database. You can create a new table or replace the data in a table of the name you enter in the Table Name text box by selecting Structure and Data, which is the most common choice. You can paste the structure only and then append data to the table later by selecting Structure Only, or you can append the records to an existing table of the name you enter. For this example, accept the default: Structure and Data.

10. Your current or backup database now has a copy of the table you selected, and the name you entered appears in the backup's Database window. You can save multiple copies of the same table under different names if you are making a series of changes to the table that may affect the integrity of the data it contains.

To delete a table from a database, select the table name in the Database window, and then press Delete. A confirmation message box appears. Click OK to delete the table forever. You cannot choose **E**dit, **U**ndo after you have deleted a table.

From Here...

Tables are the core elements of the databases you create. The capability to segregate data of different types into individual tables and then relate the tables by common fields or combinations of fields is central to the concept of relational databases.

The techniques you used in this chapter to add the Personnel Actions table to the Northwind Traders database are typical of those techniques you use when you create databases from the information you have stored in other types of databases, spreadsheets, or text files, or from information that you or others enter manually.

For information related to the topics discussed in this chapter, refer to the following chapters:

■ Chapter 5, "Entering, Editing, and Validating Data in Tables," shows you how to add records to tables, edit data in the records, and add validation rules to your tables to ensure that data values fall within accepted limits.

■ Chapter 6, "Sorting, Finding, and Filtering Data in Tables," shows you how to sort data in tables and how to apply filters to display or print records that meet the criteria you enter in the Filter window. Filters are queries in disguise; when you add a filter to a table, you create a query that Access calls a filter.

■ Chapter 23, "Exploring Relational Database Design and Implementation," gives you an in-depth description of how you design tables that conform to the rules of relational databases. This chapter also explains how Access and other database indexes work.

Chapter 5

Entering, Editing, and Validating Data in Tables

Ease of data entry is a primary criterion for an effective database development environment. Most of your Access database applications probably use forms for data entry. In many instances, however, entering data in Table Datasheet View is more expeditious than using a form, especially during the database development cycle. For example, it is a good idea to test your proposed database structure before you commit to designing the forms and reports. Changing table and field names or altering relationships between tables after you create a collection of forms and reports involves a substantial amount of work to reenter ControlSource property values. Thus, you often need to enter test data to verify that your database design is workable. Even if you import data from another database type or from a worksheet, you likely need to edit the data to make it compatible with your new application. The first part of this chapter concentrates on data entry and editing methods.

Another important factor in a database development environment is the capability to maintain domain integrity of your data. Domain integrity rules limit the values you enter in fields to a range or set of values you specify. Domain integrity rules complement the referential integrity rules described in the preceding chapter. As mentioned in Chapter 1, Access 2.0 enables you to enforce domain integrity rules (often called *business rules*) at the field and table levels. You enforce domain integrity by entering expressions as the value of the ValidationRule property of fields and tables. This chapter uses simple expressions for domain integrity validation rules. After you master Access operators and expressions, the subject of Chapter 9, you can write complex validation rules that minimize the possibility of erroneous data in your tables.

In this chapter, you learn to

- Use shortcut keys to enter repetitive data

- Change the default behavior of data entry keys

- Add new records to a table

- Edit the data in new and existing records

- Add validation rules to enforce domain integrity

- Test your validation rules to make sure that they work

Using Keyboard Operations for Entering and Editing Data

Although Access is oriented to using a mouse to make selections, keyboard equivalents are provided for the most common actions that seasoned Windows users perform using the mouse. One reason for providing keyboard commands is that many data entry operators aren't accustomed to using a mouse, trackball, or other pointing device. Constant shifting of the hand from a keyboard to mouse and back can reduce data entry rates by more than half. Shifting between a keyboard and mouse also can lead to or aggravate repetitive stress injury (RSI), of which the most common type is carpal tunnel syndrome (CTS).

Data entry operators are likely to expect your Windows database applications to behave identically to those of the DOS data entry screen of xBase or Paradox applications to which they are accustomed. Keyboard operations, therefore, are as important in a data entry environment as in word processing applications. Consequently, the rather dry exposition of key combinations for data entry appears here rather than being relegated to fine print in an appendix. The data entry procedures you learn in the sections that follow prove quite useful when you come to the "Entering Personnel Actions Table Data and Testing Validation Rules" section near the end of the chapter.

Creating an Experimental Copy of NWIND.MDB

Tip

If you're short on fixed disk space, open a new database and copy the NWIND.MDB Customers and Orders tables to your new database as described in the "Copying and Pasting Tables" section of Chapter 4.

If you want to experiment with the various keyboard operations described in the following sections, you are wise to work with a copy of the database. When you're using a copy, you don't need to worry about making changes that affect the sample database. Experimenting also gives you the opportunity to try the Access database-compacting operation described in Chapter 3, "Navigating within Access."

To compact NWIND.MDB to a new copy of NWIND.MDB, follow these steps:

1. Close all open document windows. You can leave the Database window open.

2. Choose **C**lose Database from the **F**ile menu. Access reverts to its blank opening window.

3. Choose **C**ompact Database from the **F**ile menu to open the Compact From dialog. In this case, the file is compacted to make a copy of the NWIND.MDB file.

4. Double-click NWIND.MDB in the Database to Compact From dialog. The Compact To dialog appears. You can double-click the default file name, DB1.MDB, in the Filename text box, or you can enter a more creative name, such as **ILLWIND.MDB**, and click OK. Compacting a database file with a new name creates a new, compacted database that you can use for testing.

5. Choose **O**pen Database from the **F**ile menu, and double-click DB1.MDB or the name of your file.

6. Open the Customers table by double-clicking its entry in the Database window.

In the tables that follow, the term *field* is used in place of the more specific description, *data cell* or *cell*, to maintain consistency with Access's documentation and the Help windows. A *field*, in conventional database terminology, indicates the collection of data consisting of the contents of that field in each record of the table.

Data Entry and Editing Keys

> ### Note
>
> Most keyboard operations described in this section apply to tables and updatable queries in Datasheet View, text boxes on forms, and text boxes used for entering property values in Properties windows and in the Field Properties grid of Table Design View. The examples are for the `ArrowKeyBehavior` property set to the Next Character value, rather than the Next Field value (the default). See the "Setting Data Entry Options" section that follows for changing the value of the `ArrowKeyBehavior` property. When the `ArrowKeyBehavior` property is set to Next Field, the arrow keys move the caret from field to field. You are likely to find data entry operators accustomed to DOS or mainframe database applications prefer the Next Character approach.

Editing Keys

Arrow keys and combinations are, for the most part, identical to those used in other Windows applications. Little resemblance exists between these combinations and the key combinations used by DOS database managers. The F2 key, used for editing cell contents in Excel, has a different function in Access—it toggles between editing and select mode. *Toggle* means to alternate between two states. In the editing state, the caret indicates that the insertion point in the field and the key combinations shown in table 5.1 are active. If the field is selected (indicated by a black background with white type), the editing keys behave as indicated in table 5.2. The term *grid* in the tables that follow indicates a display in tabular form that doesn't represent fields and records. The list of fields and their descriptions in table design mode is an example of a grid.

Table 5.1 Keys for Editing Fields, Grids, and Text Boxes	
Key	**Function**
F2	Toggles between displaying the caret for editing and selecting the entire field. The field must be deselected (black type on a white background), and the caret must be visible for the following examples to operate as shown.
→	Moves the caret right one character until you reach the last character in the line.
Ctrl+→	Moves the caret right one word until you reach the last word in the line.
End	Moves the caret to the end of the line.
Ctrl+End	Moves the caret to the end of a multiple-line field.
←	Moves the caret one character to the left until you reach the first character in the line.
Ctrl+←	Moves the caret one word to the left until you reach the first word in the line.
Home	Moves the caret to the beginning of the line.
Ctrl+Home	Moves the caret to the beginning of the field in multiple-line fields.
Backspace	Deletes the entire selection or the character to the left of the caret.
Delete	Deletes the entire selection or the character to the right of the caret.
Ctrl+Z or Alt+Backspace	Undoes typing, a replace operation, or any other change to the record since the last time it was saved. An edited record is saved to the database when you move to a new record or close the editing window.
Esc	Undoes changes to the current field. Press Esc twice to undo changes to the current field and to the entire current record, if other fields were edited.

Operations that select the entire field or a portion of the field, as listed in table 5.2, generally are used with the Windows Clipboard operations described in table 5.3 of the next section. Selecting an entire field and then pressing Delete or typing a character is a quick way of ridding the field of its original contents.

Table 5.2 Keys for Selecting Text in Fields, Grids, and Text Boxes

Selection	Key	Function
Text within a field	F2	Toggles between displaying the caret for editing and selecting the entire field. The field must be selected (white type on a black background) for the following examples to operate as shown.
	Shift+→	Selects or deselects one character to the right.
	Ctrl+Shift+→	Selects or deselects one word to the right.
	Shift+←	Selects or deselects one character to the left.
	Ctrl+Shift+←	Selects or deselects one word to the left.
Next field	Tab or Enter	Selects the next field. The "Setting Default Data Entry Options" section later in this chapter tells you how to change the effect of the Enter key.
Record	Shift+space bar	Selects or deselects the entire current record.
	↑	Selects the preceding record when a record is selected.
	↓	Selects the next record when a record is selected.
Column	Ctrl+space bar	Toggles selection of the current column.
	→	Selects the column to the right (if a column is selected and there is a column to the right).
	←	Selects the column to the left (if a column is selected and there is a column to the left).
Fields and records in extend mode	F8	Turns on extend mode. You see EXT in the status bar. In extend mode, pressing F8 extends the selection to the word, field, record, and all records.
	Shift+F8	Reverses the last F8 selection.
	Esc	Cancels extend mode.

Key Combinations for Windows Clipboard Operations

**Access
2.0**

In Table Datasheet View, the Windows Clipboard is used primarily for transferring Access data between applications. However, you also can use the Clipboard for repetitive data entry. Access 2.0 enables you to select a rectangular block of data cells of a table and copy the block to the Clipboard. (Access 1.x enabled you to select only a single cell or one or more entire rows for copying operations.) To select a block of cells, follow these steps:

1. Position the caret at the left edge of the top left cell of the block you want to select. The caret (shaped like an I-beam until this point) turns into a northeast-pointing arrow.

2. Hold the left mouse button down and drag the mouse pointer to the left edge of the bottom right cell of the desired block.

3. The selected block appears in reverse video (white on black). Release the left mouse button when the selection meets your requirement.

A selected block of data in the Customers table appears in figure 5.1. You can copy but not cut data blocks.

Fig. 5.1

Selecting a rectangular data block in Access 2.0's Table Datasheet View.

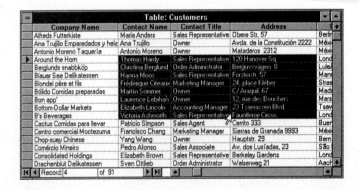

Table 5.3 lists the key combinations for copying or cutting data to and pasting data from the Clipboard. When you paste data from the Clipboard, all the data in the Clipboard is pasted to a single cell if the Clipboard data is of the correct data type and fits within the size of the field. You also can use the three clipboard buttons of the toolbar—Cut, Copy, and Paste—as a substitute for the key combinations. Another alternative is to choose Cu**t**, **C**opy, or **P**aste from the **E**dit menu.

Table 5.3   Key Combinations for Windows Clipboard Operations

Key	Function
Ctrl+C or Ctrl+Insert	Copies the selection to the Windows Clipboard.
Ctrl+V or Shift+Insert	Pastes the contents of the Clipboard at the location of the caret.
Ctrl+X or Shift+Delete	Copies the selection to the Clipboard, and then deletes it. This operation also is called a *cut*. You can cut only the content of a single cell you select with the caret.
Ctrl+Z or Alt+Backspace	Undoes your last Cut, Delete, or Paste operation.

Note

If you attempt to paste a rectangular block into a cell, you receive a "Data too long for field" error message. Access then creates a Paste Errors table that contains the content of the rectangular block. This is a quick way of creating a new table from a block selection.

Shortcut Keys for Fields and Text Boxes

You use shortcut keys to minimize the number of keystrokes required to accomplish common data entry tasks. Most shortcut key combinations use the Ctrl key with other keys. Ctrl+C, Ctrl+V, and Ctrl+X for Clipboard operations are examples of global shortcut keys in Windows 3.1. Table 5.4 lists shortcut keys applicable to field and text box entries.

Table 5.4   Shortcut Keys for Fields in Tables and Text Boxes

Key	Function
Ctrl+; (semicolon)	Inserts the current date.
Ctrl+: (colon)	Inserts the current time.
Ctrl+' (apostrophe) or Ctrl+" (quote)	Inserts the value from the same field in the preceding record.
Ctrl+Enter	Inserts a newline character (carriage return plus line feed) in a text box.

(continues)

Table 5.4	Continued
Key	**Function**
Ctrl++ (plus)	Adds a new record to the table.
Ctrl+– (minus)	Deletes the current record from the table.
Shift+Enter	Saves all changes to the current record.

Setting Data Entry Options

Tip

Emulating the data entry key behavior of DOS RDBMs can make a major difference in the acceptance of your database applications by data entry operators who have years of experience with DOS database applications.

You can modify the behavior of the arrow keys and the Tab and Enter keys by choosing **O**ptions from the **V**iew menu and choosing Keyboard from the Categories list. Table 5.5 lists the available options with the default values shown in bold type. (This table also appears in Chapter 3.) These keyboard options enable you to make the behavior of the data entry keys similar to that of DOS database managers, such as dBASE and Paradox.

Table 5.5	Keyboard Options for the Access System	
Option	**Value**	**Function**
Arrow Key Behavior the	**Next Field**/Next Character	The right- or left-arrow key selects the next or preceding field (**Next Field**) or moves insertion point to the next or preceding character (Next Field). Select Next Character if you want to duplicate the behavior of xBase.
Move After Enter	No/**Next Field**/ Next Record	Enter does not move the insertion point (No); it moves the insertion point to the next field (**Next Field**), or it moves the insertion point to the next record (Next Record).
Cursor Stops at First/Last Field	Yes/**No**	Pressing the right- or left-arrow keys, Enter, or Tab cycles (Yes) or does not cycle (**No**) the insertion point from the first to the last or the last to the first field in a row.
Key Assignment Macro	A valid macro name	Establishes the name of the key assignment macro. Use this name when you assign a macro to a key combination. The default name of the key assignment macro is *AutoKeys*.

Adding Records to a Table

When you create a new table, it contains a single blank record with an asterisk (*) in its selection button. Record selection buttons are the gray buttons in the leftmost column of Table Datasheet View. A similar blank record also appears at the end of an existing table if the table is *updatable*. If you open a database for read-only access by marking the Read Only check box of the Open Database dialog, the tentative append record does not appear. Tables attached from other databases also can be read-only; the updatability of attached tables is discussed in Chapter 7, "Attaching, Importing, and Exporting Tables."

This book refers to the blank record as the *tentative append* record. The term *tentative* is used because the record is appended to the table only after you enter data in one of the fields and then save the changes you make to the record. You can save changes to a record by moving the record pointer to a different record or by choosing Save Record from the **F**ile menu. The location of the record pointer is indicated by an arrow symbol in the record selection button. The record with the arrow symbol is called the *selected record*.

When you place the caret in a field of the tentative append record, the record selection button's asterisk symbol turns into the selected record symbol. When you add data to a field of the selected tentative append record, the selected record symbol changes to the edit symbol (a pencil), and a new tentative append record appears in the row after your addition. Figure 5.2 shows a new record in the process of being added to the Customers table. The Customer ID field has an input mask that requires you to enter five letters, which are capitalized automatically as you enter them. The input mask changes the caret from an I-beam to a reverse-video block.

Tip

To go to the tentative append record quickly, click the New Record button of the toolbar.

◀ "Using Input Masks," p.146

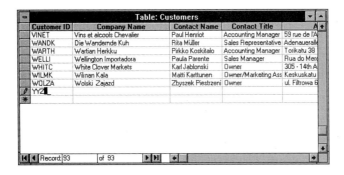

Fig. 5.2

Adding a new record to the Customers table.

You can cancel the addition of a new record by deleting all the entries you made in the record before moving the record pointer. If you edited only the first field and did not move the record pointer, you can press the Esc button to cancel the addition.

Selecting, Appending, Replacing, and Deleting Table Records

 You can select a single record or a group of records to copy or cut to the Clipboard, or to delete from the table, by the following methods:

- To select a single record, click its record selection button.

- To select a contiguous group of records, click the first record's selection button and then drag the mouse pointer along the record selection buttons to the last record of the group.

- Alternatively, to select a group of records, click the first record's selection button, hold down the shift key, and then click the last record to include in the group.

You can cut or copy and append duplicate records to the same table—if appending the duplicate records does not cause a primary-key violation—or to another table. You cannot cut records from a primary table that have dependent records in a related table if you enforce referential integrity. The following methods are applicable to appending or replacing the content of records with records stored in the Clipboard:

- To append records from the Clipboard to a table, choose Paste Append from the Edit menu. (No shortcut key exists for Paste Append.)

- To replace the content of a record(s) with data from the Clipboard, select the record(s) whose content you want to replace and then press Ctrl+V or choose Paste from the Edit menu. Only the number of records you select or the number of records stored in the Clipboard, whichever is fewer, is replaced.

To delete one or more records, select the records you want to delete and press Delete. If deletion is allowed, a message box asks you to confirm your deletion. You cannot undo deletions of records.

Validating Data Entry

The data entered in tables must be accurate if the database is to be valuable to you or your organization. Even the most experienced data entry operators occasionally enter incorrect information. You can add simple tests for the reasonableness of entries by adding short expressions to the Validation Rule text box. If the data entered fails to conform to your validation rule, a message box informs the operator that a violation occurred. Validating data maintains the domain integrity of your tables.

Expressions are the core element of computer programming. Access enables you to create expressions without requiring that you be a programmer, although some familiarity with a programming language is helpful. Expressions are statements used to calculate values using the familiar arithmetic symbols, **+, -, *** (multiply), and **/** (divide). These symbols are called *operators* because they operate on (use) the values that precede and follow them. The symbols are printed in monospace bold type because they are reserved symbols in Access Basic. The values operated on by operators are called *operands*.

You can use operators to compare two values; the **<** (less than) and **>** (greater than) symbols are examples of *comparison operators*. **And, Or, Is, Not, Between,** and **Like** are called *logical operators*. Comparison and logical operators return only **True, False,** and unknown (the **Null** value). The **&** operator combines two text entries (character strings or just strings) into a single string; **&** is the equivalent of the **+** used to join (concatenate) character strings in xBase, Excel, and other related applications. (You can use **+** in Access to concatenate strings, but **&** is the preferred symbol.) To qualify as an expression, at least one operator must be included. You can construct complex expressions by combining the different operators according to rules that apply to each of the operators involved. The collection of these rules is called *operator syntax*.

Data validation rules use expressions that result in one of three values: **True, False,** or **Null.** Entries in a data cell are accepted if the result of the validation is true and rejected if it is false. If the data is rejected by the validation rule, the text you enter in the Validation Text text box appears in a message box. Chapter 9 explains the syntax of Access validation expressions.

▶ "Understanding the Elements in Expressions," p. 316

Adding Field-Level Validation Rules

Validation rules that restrict the values entered in a field based on only one field are called *field-level validation rules*. Table 5.6 lists the simple field-level validation rules used for some of the fields of the Personnel Actions table you created in Chapter 4.

Access Fundamentals

I

Table 5.6 Validation Criteria for the Fields of the Personnel Actions Table		
Field Name	**Validation Rule**	**Validation Text**
PA ID	>0	Please enter a valid employee ID number.
PA Type	"H" **Or** "S" **Or** "Q" **Or** "Y" **Or** "B" **Or** "C"	Only H, S, Q, Y, B, and C codes can be entered.
PA Initiated By	>0	Please enter a valid supervisor ID number.
PA Scheduled Date	**Between Date**() -3650 **And Date**() +365	Scheduled dates cannot be more than 10 years ago or more than one year from now.
PA Approved By	>0 **Or Is Null**	Enter a valid manager ID number or leave blank if not approved.
PA Rating	**Between** 0 **And** 9 **Or Is Null**	Rating range is 0 for terminated employees, 1 to 9, or blank.
PA Amount	N/A	N/A
PA Comments	N/A	N/A

The validation rules for fields that require employee ID numbers are not, in their present form, capable of ensuring that a valid ID number is entered. You could enter a number greater than the total number of employees in the firm. The validation rule for the PA ID field tests the Employee ID number field of the Employees table to determine whether the PA ID number is present. You don't need to create this test because the rules of referential integrity, discussed in the "Enforcing Referential Integrity" section in Chapter 4, perform this validation for you. Validation rules for PA Initiated By and PA Approved By require tests based on entries in the Employees table.

To add the validation rules to the Personnel Actions table, follow these steps:

1. Return to design mode by clicking the Design View button. The PA ID field is selected.

2. Press F6 to switch to the Field Properties window, and then move to the Validation Rule text box.

3. Enter **>0**. Press Enter to accept the entry and move to the Validation Text text box.

4. Type **Please enter a valid employee ID number** in the Validation Text text box. The text scrolls to the left when it becomes longer than can be displayed in the text box. To display the beginning of the text, press Home. Press End to position the caret at the last character. Press Enter to complete the operation.

5. Move to the Required text box and enter **Yes**, or open the drop-down list and click Yes. Figure 5.3 shows your entries in the Field Properties text boxes.

6. Press F6 to switch back to the Table Design grid. Move to the next field, and press F6.

7. Enter the validation rule and validation text for the six remaining fields listed in table 5.6 that use data entry validation, repeating steps 2 through 5. Square brackets ([]) enclose field names that include punctuation or spaces. Enter **Yes** in the Required text box for the PA Type, PA Initiated By, and PA Scheduled Date fields.

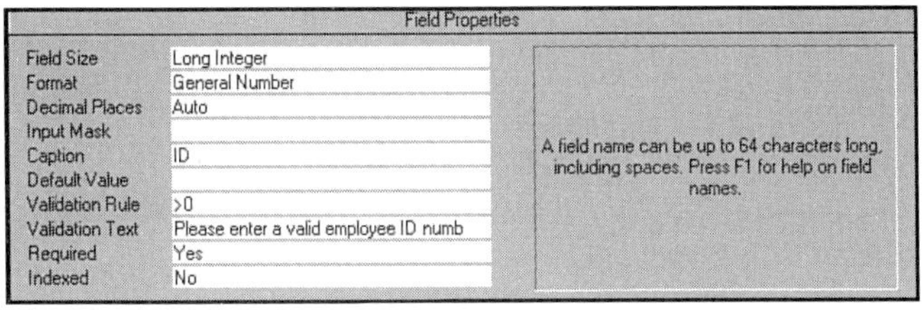

Field Properties	
Field Size	Long Integer
Format	General Number
Decimal Places	Auto
Input Mask	
Caption	ID
Default Value	
Validation Rule	>0
Validation Text	Please enter a valid employee ID numb
Required	Yes
Indexed	No

A field name can be up to 64 characters long, including spaces. Press F1 for help on field names.

Fig. 5.3
The Field Properties text boxes showing your first validation entries.

You test your validation rule entries in the "Entering Personnel Actions Table Data and Testing Validation Rules" section later in this chapter.

Adding Table-Level Validation Rules and Using the Expression Builder

Access
2.0

One of the fields, PA Effective Date, requires a validation rule that depends on the value of PA Scheduled Date. The effective date of the personnel department's action should not be prior to the scheduled date for the review that results in the action. Access 1.x enabled you to refer to one or more field names when creating a field-level validation rule expression. You cannot refer to other field names in a validation rule expression in Access 2.0; instead, you enter the validation rule in the Table Properties dialog. Validation rules in which the value of one field depends on a previously entered value in another field of the current record are called *table-level validation rules*.

The following steps create a table-level validation rule for the PA Effective Date field:

1. Click the Properties button of the toolbar to display the Table Properties dialog (see fig. 5.4).

2. Enter **Personnel Department Actions** in the Description text box, as shown in figure 5.4.

3. Move the caret to the Validation Rule text box. Click the ellipsis button that appears to right of the Validation Rule text box (see fig. 5.4) to display the Expression Builder dialog. The current table, Personnel Actions, is selected in the left list, and the fields of the table appear in the center list.

Fig. 5.4
Adding a table description in the Table Properties dialog.

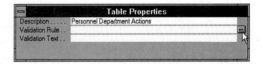

4. Double-click `PA Effective Date` entry in the center list to place `[PA Effective Date]` in the expression text box at the top of the dialog.

5. Enter `>=` in the expression text box and double-click `PA Scheduled Date` in the center list to add `[PA Scheduled Date]` to the expression.

6. You also want to accept a blank entry if the effective date of the personnel action is not scheduled, so add `Or [PA Effective Date] Is Null` to the expression. Your expression appears as shown in figure 5.5.

7. Click OK to add the table-level validation rule and close the Expression Builder dialog.

8. Move to the Validation Text text box and enter **Effective date must be on or after scheduled date**. Your Table Properties dialog appears as shown in figure 5.6.

9. Double-click the Document Control-menu box of the Table Properties dialog or click the Properties button in the toolbar to close the dialog.

> **Note**
>
> You can create more than one table-level validation rule by using the **And** reserved word and then adding another expression that involves the relationship between other fields of the table. However, Access only provides a single Validation Text message that appears when you violate any of the table-level validation rules.

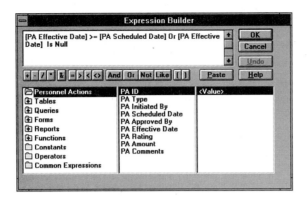

Fig. 5.5
Creating a
validation rule
with the Expres-
sion Builder.

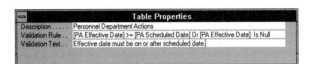

Fig. 5.6
Adding Validation
Text to a table-
level validation
rule.

Adding Records to the Personnel Actions Table

Now you have a chance to test your work in creating the Personnel Actions table and to check whether Access is enforcing referential integrity. The initial entries for each of the nine employees of Northwind Trading are shown in table 5.7. The entries for PA Scheduled Date and PA Effective Date are taken from the Hire Date field of the Employees table. The Hire Date field of the Employees table now is superfluous because it duplicates the data in the Personnel Actions table. You delete the Hire Date field in a later chapter. Feel free to be as generous or as parsimonious as you want with the monthly salaries shown in the PA Amount field.

Table 5.7   First Nine Entries for the Personnel Actions Table

ID	Type	Initia-ted By	Sched-uled	Approved By	Effective Rating	New Amount	Com-ments
1	H	1	01-Apr-87		01-Apr-87	2,000	Hired
2	H	1	15-Jul-87		15-Jul-87	3,500	Hired
3	H	2	01-Mar-88	2	01-Mar-88	2,250	Hired
4	H	2	01-Apr-88	2	01-Apr-88	2,250	Hired

(continues)

Table 5.7	Continued						
ID	Type	Initia-ted By	Sched-uled	Approved By	Effective Rating	New Amount	Com-ments
5	H	2	15-Sep-89	2	15-Sep-89	2,500	Hired
6	H	5	15-Sep-89	2	15-Sep-89	4,000	Hired
7	H	5	01-Dec-89	2	01-Dec-89	3,000	Hired
8	H	2	01-Feb-90	2	01-Feb-90	2,500	Hired
9	H	5	15-Oct-91	2	15-Oct-91	3,000	Hired

Entering historical information in a table in Datasheet View is a relatively fast process for an experienced data entry operator. This process also gives you a chance to test your default entries and Format properties for each field. You can enter bogus values that don't comply with your validation rules to verify that your rules are operational. To add the first nine historical records to the Personnel Actions table using the data from table 5.7, follow these steps:

1. Click the Datasheet button on the toolbar to return to Datasheet View in run mode if necessary. The caret is positioned in the PA ID field of the default first record.

2. Enter the PA ID of the employee. Press Enter, Tab, or the right-arrow key to move to the next field. When you do this, a new default blank record is added to the view but not to the content of the table. A new record is added to the table only when a value is entered in one of the fields of the default blank record.

3. Type the numeric value for the PA Initiated By field. (You need a value in this field for each employee because of the field's validation rule.) Press Enter, Tab, or the right-arrow key to move to the next field.

4. Type the PA Scheduled Date entry. You don't need to delete the default date value. When you type a new date, it replaces the default value. Then press Enter, Tab, or the right-arrow key.

5. If a value is in the table for PA Approved By, type the value. Then press Enter, Tab, or the right-arrow key.

6. Type the PA Effective Date entry. Press Enter, Tab, or the right-arrow key twice to skip the Rating field, which is inapplicable to newly hired employees.

7. Enter the PA Amount of the monthly salary at the time of hiring. Press Enter, Tab, or the right-arrow key.

8. Type **Hired** in the PA Comments field, or any other comment you care to make. Press Enter, Tab, or the right-arrow key. The caret moves to the PA ID field.

9. Press the down-arrow key to move the caret to the default blank record.

10. Repeat steps 2 through 9 for eight more employees in table 5.7. (You can add similar records for employees 10 through 15 if you want.)

When you complete your entries, your table appears as shown in figure 5.7.

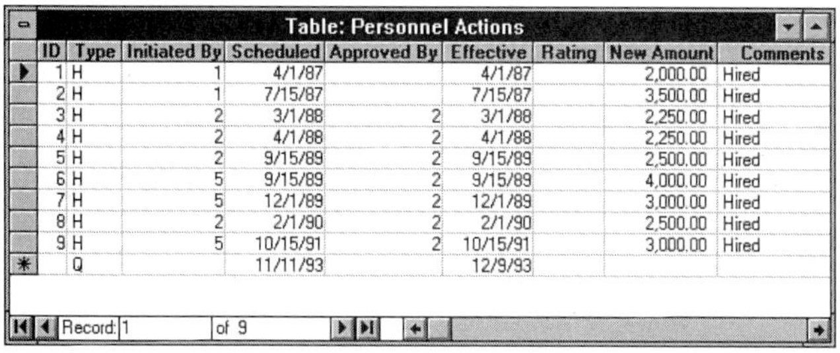

ID	Type	Initiated By	Scheduled	Approved By	Effective	Rating	New Amount	Comments
1	H	1	4/1/87		4/1/87		2,000.00	Hired
2	H	1	7/15/87		7/15/87		3,500.00	Hired
3	H	2	3/1/88	2	3/1/88		2,250.00	Hired
4	H	2	4/1/88	2	4/1/88		2,250.00	Hired
5	H	2	9/15/89	2	9/15/89		2,500.00	Hired
6	H	5	9/15/89	2	9/15/89		4,000.00	Hired
7	H	5	12/1/89	2	12/1/89		3,000.00	Hired
8	H	2	2/1/90	2	2/1/90		2,500.00	Hired
9	H	5	10/15/91	2	10/15/91		3,000.00	Hired
	Q		11/11/93		12/9/93			

Record: 1   of 9

Fig. 5.7
The first nine records of the Personnel Actions table.

Troubleshooting

Error messages appear when attempting to enter data in fields with validation rules.

Edit or reenter the data to conform to the data types and validation rules for the field. Error messages that appear when you enter the data correctly indicate that something is amiss with your validation rules. In this case, change to design mode and review your validation rules for the offending fields against those listed in table 5.7. You may want to remove the validation rule temporarily by selecting the entire expression and cutting the rule to the Clipboard. (You can paste the expression back into the text box later.) Return to run mode to continue with your entries.

Entering Personnel Actions Table Data and Testing Validation Rules

You can experiment with entering table data and testing your validation rules at the same time. Testing database applications often requires much more time and effort than creating them. The following basic tests are required to confirm your validation rules:

■ *Referential integrity.* Type **25** in the PA ID field and **2** in the PA Initiated By field of the default blank record, record number 10, and then press the up-arrow key. Pressing the up-arrow key tells Access that you are finished with the current record and to move up to the preceding record with the caret in the same field. Access then tests the primary-key integrity before enabling you to leave the current record. The message box shown in figure 5.8 appears. Click OK, or press Enter.

Fig. 5.8

The message box indicating that an entry violates referential integrity rules.

■ *No duplicates restriction for primary key.* In the record just added, attempt to duplicate exactly the entries for record number 9, and then press the up-arrow key. You see the message box shown in figure 5.9. Click OK, or press Enter.

Fig. 5.9

The message box that appears when a record with a duplicate key is added to a field indexed with the No Duplicates option.

■ *PA Type validation.* Type **x** and press the right-arrow key to display the message box with the validation text you entered for the PA Type field, shown in figure 5.10. Click OK, or press Enter.

Fig. 5.10

A message box created by an entry that violates a validation rule.

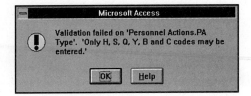

Type **q**, and move to the PA Initiated By field. When the caret leaves the PA Type field, the q changes to Q because of the > format character used. Type **0** (an invalid employee ID number), and press the right-arrow key to display the message box shown in figure 5.11. Click OK, or press Enter.

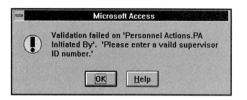

Fig. 5.11
The message box that appears in response to an invalid employee ID number entry.

Continue with the testing. Type a date, such as **1/1/80**, for the PA Scheduled Date, and type the same date for the PA Effective Date to display the error message boxes with the validation text you entered. Enter a valid date after the test. To edit a field rather than retype it, press F2 to deselect the entire field and display the caret for editing. F2 toggles selection and editing operations.

When you finish your testing, click the selection button of the last field you added, and then press Delete. The confirmation message box shown in figure 5.12 appears.

Fig. 5.12
The confirmation box for deletion of one or more records.

From Here...

This chapter outlined the various key combinations you can use to make keyboard-oriented data entry more efficient. The basic procedures for selecting, adding, editing, and deleting records also were covered in detail. The methods are applicable not only to tables but also to updatable queries in Datasheet View and text box controls you add to forms. You learned how to use the Windows Clipboard to cut, copy, and paste fields and entire records or groups of records. Adding and testing validation rules for data entry completed the chapter.

See the following chapters for information related to the topics covered in this chapter:

- Chapter 6, "Sorting, Finding, and Filtering Data in Tables," describes how to use Access's built-in sorting, search, search and replace, and filters to locate records meeting criteria you set, and how to make bulk changes to field data.

- Chapter 7, "Attaching, Importing, and Exporting Tables," explains how to import data from your existing database tables, worksheets, or text files, and how to export table data in a variety of useful formats.

Chapter 6

Sorting, Finding, and Filtering Data in Tables

Microsoft Access provides a variety of sorting and filtering features that make customizing the display data in Table Datasheet View a quick and simple process. Sorting and filtering records in tables is quite useful when you use data in a table to create a mailing list or print a particular set of records.

Access also includes versatile search (find) and replace facilities that enable you to locate every record that matches a value you specify, and then, optionally, change that value. If you have a large table, Access's find facility enables you to quickly locate the needles in the haystacks. Search and replace often is needed when you import data from another database or a worksheet, which is the subject of the next chapter.

The sorting, filtering, searching, and replacing features of Access actually are implemented by behind-the-scenes queries that Access creates for you. When you reach Part II of this book, which deals exclusively with queries, you'll probably choose to implement these features with Access's graphical query-by-example (QBE) methods. Learning the fundamentals of these operations with tables, however, makes understanding queries easier. You also can apply filters to query result sets, use the find feature with queries in Datasheet View, and use search and replace on the result sets of updatable queries. For readers who are xBase users or know SQL, statements in these two languages equivalent to the operation being performed are given where applicable.

Sorting Table Data

A fundamental requirement of a database development environment is the capability to sort records quickly so that they appear in the desired sequence.

In this chapter, you learn to

- Sort tables on one or more fields
- Show and hide columns of tables
- Find records matching values you enter
- Search for and replace data in table fields
- Apply filters so that only certain records appear
- Customize your Table Datasheet View
- Export sorted and filtered data to a file

Early desktop database managers, such as dBASE II and III/III+, required that you create a new copy of a table if you wanted physically to sort the table's records in a new order. Creating and specifying an index on a field table enabled you to display or print the table in the order of the index. If you wanted to sort the data by two or more fields, however, you either had to create a composite index on the fields, or pre-sort the data in the order of one or more fields, and then apply the single-field index.

Modern desktop database development systems, such as Access, never require that you physically sort the table. Instead, the physical location of the records in the file is the order in which the records were entered. By default, Access displays records in the order of the primary key. This behavior is similar to that of Borland's Paradox. If your table doesn't have a primary key, the records display in the order you enter them. Unlike dBASE and its clones, you cannot choose a specific Access index to alter the order in which the records display in Table Datasheet View of the user interface (UI). You can, however, specify an index to order records of tables you manipulate with Access Basic code. Access uses sorting methods to display records in the desired order. If an index exists on the field in which you sort the records, the sorting process is much quicker. Access automatically uses indexes, if indexes exist, to speed the sort. This process is called *query optimization*. Access's indexes and query optimization methods are discussed in Chapter 23, "Exploring Relational Database Design and Implementation."

The following sections show you how to use Access's sorting methods to display records in the sequence you want. The Customers table of NWIND.MDB is used for the majority of the examples in this chapter because it is typical of a table whose data you can use for a variety of purposes.

Freezing Display of a Table Field

If the table you are sorting contains more fields than you can display in Access's Table Datasheet View, you can freeze one or more fields to make viewing the sorted data easier. Freezing a field makes the field visible at all times, regardless of which other fields you display by manipulating the horizontal scroll bar. To freeze the Customer ID and Company Name fields of the Customers table, follow these steps:

1. Open the Customers table in Datasheet View.

2. Click the field header button of the Customer ID field to select the first column.

3. Hold the Shift key down and click the Company Name field header button. Alternatively, you can drag the mouse from the Customer ID field to the Company Name field to select the first and second columns.

4. Choose Free**z**e Columns from the F**o**rmat menu. (The F**o**rmat menu was the **L**ayout menu in Access 1.x.)

When you scroll to fields to the right of the frozen columns, your Datasheet View of the Customers table appears as illustrated in figure 6.1. A solid vertical line replaces the half-tone grid line between the frozen and thawed (selectable) field columns.

Customer ID	Company Name	Region	Postal Code	Country	Phone
ALFKI	Alfreds Futterkiste		12209	Germany	030-0074321
ANATR	Ana Trujillo Emparedados y helados		05021	Mexico	(5) 555-4729
ANTON	Antonio Moreno Taquería		05023	Mexico	(5) 555-3932
AROUT	Around the Horn		WA1 1DP	UK	(71) 555-7788
BERGS	Berglunds snabbköp		S-958 22	Sweden	0921-12 34 65
BLAUS	Blauer See Delikatessen		68306	Germany	0621-08460
BLONP	Blondel père et fils		67000	France	88.60.15.31
BOLID	Bólido Comidas preparadas		28023	Spain	(91) 555 22 82
BONAP	Bon app'		13008	France	91.24.45.40
BOTTM	Bottom-Dollar Markets	BC	T2F 8M4	Canada	(604) 555-4729
BSBEV	B's Beverages		EC2 5NT	UK	(71) 555-1212
CACTU	Cactus Comidas para llevar		1010	Argentina	(1) 135-5555
CENTC	Centro comercial Moctezuma		05022	Mexico	(5) 555-3392
CHOPS	Chop-suey Chinese		3012	Switzerland	0452-076545
COMMI	Comércio Mineiro	SP	05432-043	Brazil	(11) 555-7647
CONSH	Consolidated Holdings		WX1 6LT	UK	(71) 555-2282
DRACD	Drachenblut Delikatessen		52066	Germany	0241-039123

Record: 1   of 91

Fig. 6.1
The Customers table of NWIND.MDB with the Customer ID and Company Names fields frozen.

Note

If you frequently freeze columns, you can add the Freeze Columns button from the Datasheet collection to your Datasheet toolbar. See Chapter 13 for how to customize your toolbars.

Sorting Data on a Single Field

When creating a mailing list, a standard practice in the United States is to sort the records in ascending ZIP Code order. This practice often is observed in other countries that use postal codes. To sort the Customers table in the order of the Postal Code field, follow these steps:

1. Select the Postal Code field by clicking the field header button of the Postal Code field.

2. Click the Sort Ascending (A-Z) button of the toolbar or choose **Q**uick Sort from the **R**ecords menu, and then choose **A**scending from the submenu.

▶ "Writing Select
Queries in
SQL," p. 896

Your Customers table quickly is sorted into the order shown in figure 6.2. Sorting a table is equivalent to specifying the selected field as the table name of the ORDER BY clause of an SQL statement, as in

```
SELECT * FROM Customers ORDER BY [Postal Code]
```

To perform the same operation with xBase, use the following statements at the command line:

```
USE customer INDEX cust_zip
{LIST¦BROWSE}
```

Fig. 6.2

Applying an
ascending sort
order to the Postal
Code field of the
Customers table.

Customer ID	Company Name	Region	Postal Code	Country	Phone
HUNGO	Hungry Owl All-Night Grocers	Co. Cork		Ireland	2967 542
WOLZA	Wolski Zajazd		01-012	Poland	(26) 642-7012
QUICK	QUICK-Stop		01307	Germany	0372-035188
QUEDE	Que Delícia	RJ	02389-673	Brazil	(21) 555-4252
RICAR	Ricardo Adocicados	RJ	02389-890	Brazil	(21) 555-3412
MORGK	Morgenstern Gesundkost		04179	Germany	0342-023176
GOURL	Gourmet Lanchonetes	SP	04876-786	Brazil	(11) 555-9482
ANATR	Ana Trujillo Emparedados y helados		05021	Mexico	(5) 555-4729
CENTC	Centro comercial Moctezuma		05022	Mexico	(5) 555-3392
ANTON	Antonio Moreno Taquería		05023	Mexico	(5) 555-3932
PERIC	Pericles Comidas clásicas		05033	Mexico	(5) 552-3745
TORTU	Tortuga Restaurante		05033	Mexico	(5) 555-2933
COMMI	Comércio Mineiro	SP	05432-043	Brazil	(11) 555-7647
FAMIA	Família Arquibaldo	SP	05442-030	Brazil	(11) 555-9857
HANAR	Hanari Carnes	RJ	05454-876	Brazil	(21) 555-0091
QUEEN	Queen Cozinha	SP	05487-020	Brazil	(11) 555-1189
TRADH	Tradição Hipermercados	SP	05634-030	Brazil	(11) 555-2167

Record: 1 of 91

Sorting Data on Multiple Fields

Although the sort operation in the preceding section accomplishes exactly what you specify, the result is less than useful because of the vagaries of postal code formats used in different countries. What's needed here is a multiple-field sort on the Country field first and then the Postal Code field. Thus, you might select both the Country and the Postal Code fields to perform the multi-column sort. The Quick Sort technique, however, automatically applies the sorting priority to the leftmost field you select, Postal Code. Access offers two methods of handling this problem: Reorder the field display or specify the sort order in a Filter window. Filters are discussed in the "Filtering Table Data" section, later in this chapter, so follow these steps to use the reordering process:

1. Select the Country field by clicking its field header button.

2. Hold the left mouse button down and drag the Country field to the left of the Postal Code field. Release the left mouse button to drop the field in its new location.

3. Press the Shift key and click the header button of the Postal Code field to select both the Country and Postal Code columns.

4. Click the Sort Ascending button of the toolbar or choose **Q**uick Sort from the **R**ecords menu, and then choose **A**scending from the submenu.

The sorted table, shown in figure 6.3, now makes much more sense. Applying a multi-field sort on a table (sometimes called a *composite sort*) is the equivalent of the following SQL statement:

```
SELECT * FROM Customers ORDER BY Country, [Postal Code]
```

If you had a composite xBase index derived from the `country` and `post_code` fields, the statements in xBase to achieve the same result are the same as those in the preceding section.

Customer ID	Company Name	Region	Country	Postal Code	Phone
OCEAN	Océano Atlántico Ltda.		Argentina	1010	(1) 135-5333
CACTU	Cactus Comidas para llevar		Argentina	1010	(1) 135-5555
RANCH	Rancho grande		Argentina	1010	(1) 123-5555
PICCO	Piccolo und mehr		Austria	5020	6562-9722
ERNSH	Ernst Handel		Austria	8010	7675-3425
MAISD	Maison Dewey		Belgium	B-1180	(02) 201 24 67
SUPRD	Suprêmes délices		Belgium	B-6000	(071) 23 67 22
QUEDE	Que Delícia	RJ	Brazil	02389-673	(21) 555-4252
RICAR	Ricardo Adocicados	RJ	Brazil	02389-890	(21) 555-3412
GOURL	Gourmet Lanchonetes	SP	Brazil	04876-786	(11) 555-9482
COMMI	Comércio Mineiro	SP	Brazil	05432-043	(11) 555-7647
FAMIA	Família Arquibaldo	SP	Brazil	05442-030	(11) 555-9857
HANAR	Hanari Carnes	RJ	Brazil	05454-876	(21) 555-0091
QUEEN	Queen Cozinha	SP	Brazil	05487-020	(11) 555-1189
TRADH	Tradição Hipermercados	SP	Brazil	05634-030	(11) 555-2167
WELLI	Wellington Importadora	SP	Brazil	08737-363	(14) 555-8122
MEREP	Mère Paillarde	Québec	Canada	H1J 1C3	(514) 555-8054

Record: 1   of 91

Fig. 6.3
The effect of a multiple-field sort on the Country and Postal Code fields of the Customers table.

Removing a Table Sort Order and Thawing Columns

After you freeze columns and apply sort orders to a table, you might want to return the table to its original condition. To do so, Access offers you the following choices:

- To return to the Datasheet View of an Access table with a primary key to its original sort order, select the field(s) that comprise the primary key (in the order of the primary key fields).

- To return to the original order when the table has no primary key field, close and reopen the table.

- To thaw your frozen columns, choose **U**nfreeze All Columns from the **Fo**rmat menu.

- To return the sequence of fields to its original state, either drag the fields you moved back to their prior position or close the table without saving your changes.

If you make substantial changes to the layout of the table and apply a sort order, it usually is quicker to close and reopen the table. (Don't save your changes to the table layout.)

Removing the sort order from a field is the equivalent of issuing the following SQL statement:

```
SELECT * FROM Customers
```

Finding Matching Records in a Table

To search for and select records with field values that match (or partially match) a particular value, use Access's Find feature. To find Luleå—a relatively large city in northern Sweden close to the Arctic Circle—in the City field, follow these steps:

1. Select the field—City—you want to search. You can select the City field by either clicking the header button or placing the caret in the field.

2. Click the Find button of the toolbar or choose **F**ind from the **E**dit menu to display the Find in Field dialog shown in figure 6.4.

Fig. 6.4
Opening the Find in Field dialog with the City field selected.

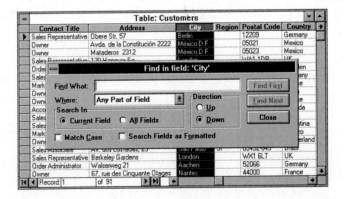

3. Type the name of the city, **Lulea**, in the Find What text box (see fig. 6.5). When you make an entry in the Find What text box, the Find First and Find Next command buttons are enabled.

4. Select Match Whole Field from the Where drop-down list. (The other choices, Start of Field and Any Part of Field, are just as effective in this case.)

5. The default values of the Search In and Direction option buttons are satisfactory, and matching case or format is not important here.

6. Click the Find First button. If you do not have a Scandinavian keyboard, Access displays the "end of records" message box shown in figure 6.6.

Fig. 6.5

Attempting to find Luleå in the City field.

Fig. 6.6

The message box that appears when Access cannot find a match to the content of the Find What text box.

The "end of records" message indicates that the Find feature did not locate a match between the present position of the record pointer and the last record of the table. The reason Access missed your entry is that the Scandinavian diacritical "°" is missing over the *a* in *Lulea*. In the ANSI character set, "a" has a value of 97, and "å" has a value of 229.

Note

You can enter international (extended) characters in the Find What text box by typing the English letters and then using Windows 3.1's Character Map (CHARMAP.EXE) applet to find and copy the extended character to the Clipboard. (Don't worry about choosing the correct font.) Paste the character into the Find What text box at the appropriate location.

If the letters preceding an extended character are sufficient to define your search parameter, follow this set of steps to find Luleå:

1. Type **Lule**, or delete the *a* from *Lulea*, in the Find What text box.

2. Select Start of Field from the Where drop-down list.

3. Click the Find First button. Access finds and highlights *Luleå* in the City field, as shown in figure 6.7.

You also can find entries in any part of the field. If you type **ule** in the Find What text box and choose Any Part of Field from the drop-down list, you get a match on *Luleå*. However, you also match *Thule*, the location of the Bluie West One airfield (AKA Thule AFB) in Greenland.

Fig. 6.7
Finding a record that contains a special character.

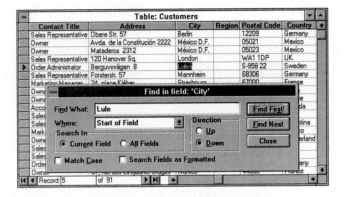

> **Note**
>
> Searching all fields for an entry is usually much slower than searching a single field, especially if you have an index on the field being searched. Unless you specify the Any Part of Field option, Access uses the index to speed the searching operation.

Following is a list of the options available in the Find in Field dialog:

- To specify a case-sensitive search, mark the Match Case check box.

- To search using the field's format, mark the Search Fields as Formatted check box. This enables you to enter a search term that matches the formatted appearance of the field rather than the native (unformatted) value if you applied a Format property value to the field. Using the Search Fields as Formatted option slows the search operation; indexes are not used.

- To find additional matches, if any, click the Find Next button. Clicking the Find First button starts the search at the first record in the table, regardless of the current position of the record pointer.

- To start the search at the last record of the table, click the Up option button.

SQL has no direct equivalent to a Find First or Find Next operation. SQL is a set-oriented language, so the following SQL statement:

```
SELECT * FROM Customers WHERE City = "Luleå"
```

returns the set of all records that meet the criterion. The SQL CURSOR construct enables you to move between records of a set, but the CURSOR reserved word is not supported in Access SQL and its use is beyond the scope of the SQL discussion in this chapter.

The following statements in xBase find the first and second records meeting the criteria:

```
LOCATE FOR city = "Luleå"
CONTINUE
```

Neither xBase's FIND or SEEK commands, both of which require an index on the field, provide the Find Next function. FIND and SEEK only duplicate the effect of the Find First button.

Replacing Matched Field Values Automatically

A variation on the Find in Field dialog's theme—the Replace in Field dialog—enables you to replace values selectively in fields that match the entry in the Find What text box. To display the Replace in File dialog, choose **R**eplace from the **E**dit menu. (No button on the standard Table Datasheet toolbar exists for the search and replace feature.) The derivation of the shortcut key combination for **E**dit **R**eplace, Ctrl+H, is a mystery.

The entries to search for *Luleå* and replace with *Lulea* appear in figure 6.8. To replace entries selectively, click the Find Next button, and then click the Replace button for those records in which you want to replace the value. You can do a bulk replace in all matching records by clicking the Replace All button.

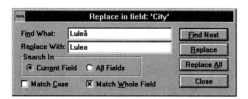

Fig. 6.8
The Replace in Field dialog.

In SQL, the statement to replace all occurrences of *Luleå* with *Lulea* is as follows:

```
UPDATE Customers SET City = 'Lulea' WHERE City = 'Luleå'
```

▶ "Updating Values of Multiple Records in a Table," p. 422

▶ "Specifying
Action Query
Syntax," p. 908
The xBase dot prompt command to replace the first or all instances of *Luleå*—
if you have the appropriate Scandinavian code page loaded in DOS—is as
follows:

```
REPLACE [ALL] city WITH 'Lulea' FOR city = 'Luleå'
```

Filtering Table Data

Access enables you to apply a filter to specify the records that appear in the
Datasheet View of a table or a query result set. An Access filter can do double-
duty because you also can add a sort order on one or more fields. Filters in
Access, as mentioned previously, are queries in disguise. The basic differences
between the Filter design window and the Query design window are as follows:

- The Add Table dialog does not appear.

- The SQL button is missing from the toolbar, so you can't display the
  underlying SQL statement.

- The Show row is missing from the Filter Design grid.

Filters are limited to using one table or query that Access automatically specifies when you enter filter design mode. You can save a filter you create as a
query, but Access has no provision for saving a filter as a filter. The sections
that follow describe how to add criteria to filter records and to add a sort
order in the Filter design window.

Adding a Multi-Field Sort and Compound Filter Criteria

Toolbar buttons provide the fastest access to the three filter operations: Edit
Filter/Sort, Apply Filter/Sort, and Show All Records. Each of these operations
also is a choice of the **R**ecords menu. To create a filter on the Orders table,
which provides more records to filter than the Customers table, follow these
steps:

1. Open the Orders table in Datasheet View.

2. Click the Edit Filter/Sort button of the toolbar or choose **E**dit Filter/Sort
from the **R**ecords menu to display the Filter window. The Filter window
appears as shown in figure 6.9. The default filter name, Filter1, is concatenated with the table name to create the default name of the first
filter, OrdersFilter1. The field list window for the Orders table appears in
the upper pane of the Filter window.

3. One of the fields that you might want to sort or limit displayed records is Order ID. Click the Order ID field in the Orders field list window in the upper pane and drag the field to the first column of the Fields row of the filter design grid in the lower pane and drop it. (When your mouse pointer reaches the lower pane, it turns into a field symbol.)

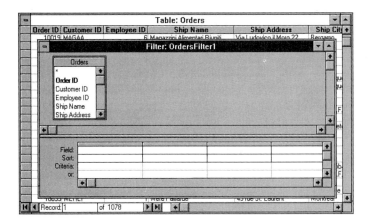

Fig. 6.9
The Filter design window opened by clicking the Edit Filter/Sort button.

4. Repeat step 3 for other fields on which you want to sort or establish criteria. Candidates are Customer ID, Ship Company, Ship Country, Ship Postal Code Order Date, and Ship Date fields.

5. Add an ascending sort to the Ship Country and Ship Postal Code fields to check the sorting capabilities of your first filter. Your Filter design window appears as shown in figure 6.10.

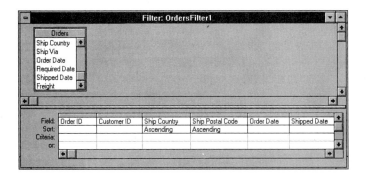

Fig. 6.10
Adding fields and sort orders to the Filter design window.

6. Click the Apply Filter/Sort button of the toolbar, or choose Apply Filter/Sort from the **R**ecords menu.

Access Fundamentals

7. Use the horizontal scroll bar of the datasheet to reveal the Ship Country and Ship Postal Code fields. Your sorted table appears as shown in figure 6.11.

8. Click the Edit Filter/Sort button to display the Filter design window.

Fig. 6.11
The Orders table ordered by the Ship Country and Ship Postal Code fields.

	Ship Address	Ship City	Ship Region	Ship Postal Code	Ship Country
▶	Av. del Libertador 900	Buenos Aires		1010	Argentina
	Cerrito 333	Buenos Aires		1010	Argentina
	Cerrito 333	Buenos Aires		1010	Argentina
	Av. del Libertador 900	Buenos Aires		1010	Argentina
	Av. del Libertador 900	Buenos Aires		1010	Argentina
	Ing. Gustavo Moncada 858	Buenos Aires		1010	Argentina
	Ing. Gustavo Moncada 858	Buenos Aires		1010	Argentina
	Ing. Gustavo Moncada 858	Buenos Aires		1010	Argentina
	Cerrito 333	Buenos Aires		1010	Argentina
	Cerrito 333	Buenos Aires		1010	Argentina
	Cerrito 333	Buenos Aires		1010	Argentina
	Av. del Libertador 900	Buenos Aires		1010	Argentina
	Ing. Gustavo Moncada 858	Buenos Aires		1010	Argentina
	Ing. Gustavo Moncada 858	Buenos Aires		1010	Argentina
	Ing. Gustavo Moncada 858	Buenos Aires		1010	Argentina
	Ing. Gustavo Moncada 858	Buenos Aires		1010	Argentina
	Cerrito 333	Buenos Aires		1010	Argentina
	Av. del Libertador 900	Buenos Aires		1010	Argentina
	Geislweg 14	Salzburg		5020	Austria
	Geislweg 14	Salzburg		5020	Austria
	Geislweg 14	Salzburg		5020	Austria

Record: 1 of 1078

9. Type **USA** in the Criteria row of the Ship Country column to limit records to those with ship to address in the United States. Access automatically adds double-quotes (") around "USA", indicating that the entry is text, not a number.

10. Click the Apply Filter/Sort button of the toolbar or choose App**l**y Filter/ Sort from the **R**ecords menu and scroll to display the sorted fields. Only records with destinations in the United States appear, as shown in figure 6.12. (The width of the fields to the left of the Ship Country field have been reduced so that the Ship Country field appears as in figure 6.12.)

Fig. 6.12
The result of applying a "USA" criterion to the Ship Country field.

Table: Orders

	Order	Custom	Emp	Ship Name	Ship Address	Ship City	Ship	Ship	Ship Country
▶	10057	THECR	4	The Cracker Box	55 Grizzly Peak Rd.	Butte	MT	59801	USA
	10624	THECR	4	The Cracker Box	55 Grizzly Peak Rd.	Butte	MT	59801	USA
	10775	THECR	7	The Cracker Box	55 Grizzly Peak Rd.	Butte	MT	59801	USA
	11003	THECR	3	The Cracker Box	55 Grizzly Peak Rd.	Butte	MT	59801	USA
	10271	SPLIR	6	Split Rail Beer & Ale	P.O. Box 555	Lander	WY	82520	USA
	10329	SPLIR	4	Split Rail Beer & Ale	P.O. Box 555	Lander	WY	82520	USA
	10349	SPLIR	7	Split Rail Beer & Ale	P.O. Box 555	Lander	WY	82520	USA
	10369	SPLIR	8	Split Rail Beer & Ale	P.O. Box 555	Lander	WY	82520	USA
	10385	SPLIR	1	Split Rail Beer & Ale	P.O. Box 555	Lander	WY	82520	USA
	10432	SPLIR	3	Split Rail Beer & Ale	P.O. Box 555	Lander	WY	82520	USA
	10756	SPLIR	8	Split Rail Beer & Ale	P.O. Box 555	Lander	WY	82520	USA
	10821	SPLIR	1	Split Rail Beer & Ale	P.O. Box 555	Lander	WY	82520	USA
	10974	SPLIR	3	Split Rail Beer & Ale	P.O. Box 555	Lander	WY	82520	USA
	10052	SAVEA	7	Save-a-lot Markets	187 Suffolk Ln.	Boise	ID	83720	USA
	10065	SAVEA	1	Save-a-lot Markets	187 Suffolk Ln.	Boise	ID	83720	USA
	10098	SAVEA	1	Save-a-lot Markets	187 Suffolk Ln.	Boise	ID	83720	USA
	10167	SAVEA	3	Save-a-lot Markets	187 Suffolk Ln.	Boise	ID	83720	USA
	10168	SAVEA	6	Save-a-lot Markets	187 Suffolk Ln.	Boise	ID	83720	USA
	10193	SAVEA	1	Save-a-lot Markets	187 Suffolk Ln.	Boise	ID	83720	USA

Record: 1 of 149

Using Composite Criteria

You can apply composite criteria to expand or further limit the records that display. Composite criteria are applied to more than one field. To display all orders received on or after 1/1/94 with destinations in North America, try the following:

1. Click the Edit Filter/Sort button to display the Filter design window.

2. Type **Canada** in the second criteria line of the Ship Country column and **Mexico** in the third line, and then move the caret to a different cell. When you add criteria under one another, the effect is to make the criteria alternative. (Adding criteria in successive rows is the equivalent of using the OR operator in SQL.)

3. Type **>=#1/1/94#** in the first criteria line of the Order Date field. When you add criteria on the same line as another criterion, the criteria is additive; that is, orders for the United States placed on or after 1/1/94. (Adding criteria in the same row is the equivalent of using the SQL AND operator.) The # symbols indicate to Access that the enclosed value is of the Date/Time data type.

4. Press F2 to select the entry of step 2, and then press Ctrl+C to copy the expression to the Clipboard. Position the caret in the second row of the Order Date column, and press Ctrl+V to add the same expression for Canada. Repeat this process to add the date criterion for Mexican orders. Your Filter Design grid now appears as shown in figure 6.13. You need to repeat the date criterion for each country criterion because of a limitation in constructing SQL statements from QBE grids, which is discussed shortly.

5. Click the Apply Filter/Sort button to display your newly filtered datasheet (see fig. 6.14).

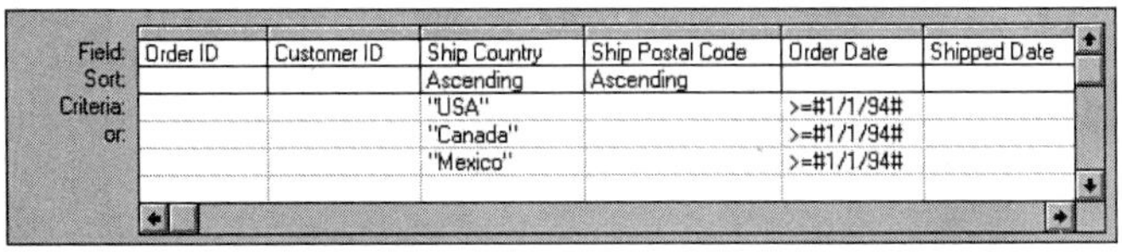

Field:	Order ID	Customer ID	Ship Country	Ship Postal Code	Order Date	Shipped Date
Sort:			Ascending	Ascending		
Criteria:			"USA"		>=#1/1/94#	
or:			"Canada"		>=#1/1/94#	
			"Mexico"		>=#1/1/94#	

Fig. 6.13
The Filter grid with composite criteria added.

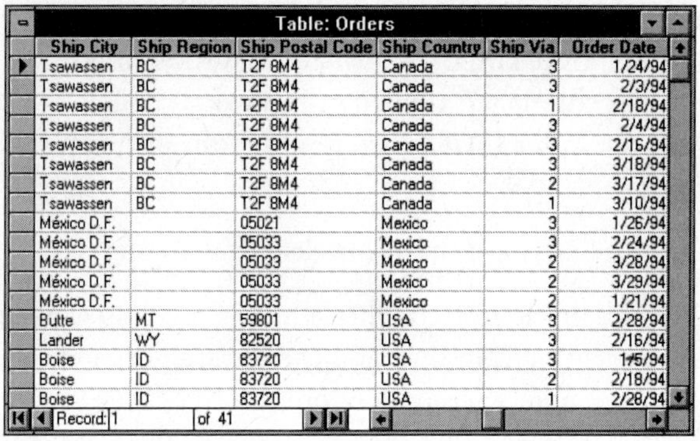

Fig. 6.14

The result of the filter of figure 6.13 applied to the Orders datasheet.

Ship City	Ship Region	Ship Postal Code	Ship Country	Ship Via	Order Date
Tsawassen	BC	T2F 8M4	Canada	3	1/24/94
Tsawassen	BC	T2F 8M4	Canada	3	2/3/94
Tsawassen	BC	T2F 8M4	Canada	1	2/18/94
Tsawassen	BC	T2F 8M4	Canada	3	2/4/94
Tsawassen	BC	T2F 8M4	Canada	3	2/16/94
Tsawassen	BC	T2F 8M4	Canada	3	3/18/94
Tsawassen	BC	T2F 8M4	Canada	2	3/17/94
Tsawassen	BC	T2F 8M4	Canada	1	3/10/94
México D.F.		05021	Mexico	3	1/26/94
México D.F.		05033	Mexico	3	2/24/94
México D.F.		05033	Mexico	2	3/28/94
México D.F.		05033	Mexico	2	3/29/94
México D.F.		05033	Mexico	2	1/21/94
Butte	MT	59801	USA	3	2/28/94
Lander	WY	82520	USA	3	2/16/94
Boise	ID	83720	USA	3	1/5/94
Boise	ID	83720	USA	2	2/18/94
Boise	ID	83720	USA	1	2/28/94

Record: 1 of 41

The SQL statement equivalent to this filter/sort combination is as follows:

```
SELECT * FROM Orders
    WHERE ([Ship Country] = 'USA' AND [Order Date] >= #1/1/94#)
        OR ([Ship Country] = 'Canada' AND [Order Date] >= #1/1/94#)
        OR ([Ship Country] = 'Mexico' AND [Order Date] >= #1/1/94#)
ORDER BY [Ship Country], [Ship Postal Code]
```

The following is a more efficient SQL statement that accomplishes the same objective:

```
SELECT * FROM Orders
    WHERE ([Ship Country] = 'USA'
        OR [Ship Country] = 'Canada'
        OR [Ship Country] = 'Mexico')
    AND [Order Date] >= #1/1/94#
ORDER BY [Ship Country], [Ship Postal Code]
```

A statement using the SQL IN predicate is even simpler:

```
SELECT * FROM Orders
    WHERE [Ship Country] IN('USA', 'Canada', 'Mexico')
        AND [Order Date] >= #1/1/94#
ORDER BY [Ship Country], [Ship Postal Code]
```

You can't generate either of the more efficient forms of the SQL statement with QBE because Access has to take into consideration that you might want a different range of order dates for each country.

The xBase equivalent of the preceding SQL statement is as follows:

```
USE orders INDEX ctry_zip
LIST FOR AT(country, 'USACanadaMexico') > 0 .AND. ord_date >=
➥CTOD('01/01/94')
```

Alternatively, you can use xBase's SET FILTER TO command to apply the filter, and then LIST the records.

Saving Your Filter as a Query and Loading a Filter

Access does not have a persistent Filter object. A *persistent* database object is an object you create that is stored as a component of your database's .MDB file. All persistent database objects appear as items in one of the list boxes of the Database window. A *filter* is the equivalent of a single-table query, so Access lets you save your filter as a `QueryDef` object. Access saves the names of the filters associated with each table in the system tables of your database when you save a filter as a query. This is the principal advantage of using a filter rather than a query when only a single table is involved.

To save your filter and remove the filter from the Orders table, follow these steps:

1. Choose Save **A**s Query from the **F**ile menu to display the Save As Query dialog.

2. Enter a descriptive name for your filter in the Query Name text box. Using the `flt` prefix distinguishes the filters you save from conventional queries (see fig. 6.15).

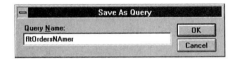

Fig. 6.15
Naming the `QueryDef` object that contains a filter.

3. Click OK to save the filter.

4. Double-click the Document Control-menu box to close the Filter window.

5. Click the Show All Records button of the toolbar or choose **S**how All Records from the **R**ecords menu to remove the filter from the Orders datasheet.

6. A filter remains in memory while the table to which it applies is open. To close the filter, double-click the Document Control-menu box to close the Orders table.

Re-creating a filter from the filter you saved as a query requires the following steps:

1. Reopen the Orders table in Datasheet View.

2. Click the Edit Filter/Sort button of the toolbar to open the Filters window with an empty filter.

3. Choose **L**oad from Query from the **F**ile menu to display the Applicable Filter dialog, shown in figure 6.16.

Fig. 6.16

A saved filter listed in the Applicable Filters dialog.

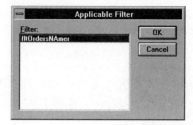

4. Double-click the fltOrdersNAmer filter to load the saved query into the Filter window.

5. Click the Apply Filter/Sort to display the resulting filter set in the Orders datasheet.

You can save the preceding steps by simply executing the saved query. You execute a query the same way you open a table:

1. Close the Orders table.

2. Click the Query tab of the Database window to list the saved queries.

3. Double-click the fltOrdersNAmer item. The datasheet of the Select Query:fltOrdersNAmer window that appears is identical to the datasheet you created in step 5 of the preceding operation.

4. Click the Design View button of the toolbar to display the query design, shown in figure 6.17. Notice that the columns of your original filter, in which no criteria were entered, are empty.

5. Click the SQL button of the toolbar to display the SQL statement behind the query, illustrated by figure 6.18.

Access adds a multitude of parentheses, plus table name qualifiers, to the field names of the statements created from QBE grids. Most of the parentheses are superfluous. (They are present to help the QJet engine's query parser execute more complex queries.) Table name qualifiers are not necessary in a SQL statement when only one table is included in the FROM clause.

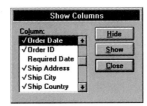

Fig. 6.19
The Show
Columns dialog
that lets you show
and hide datasheet
fields.

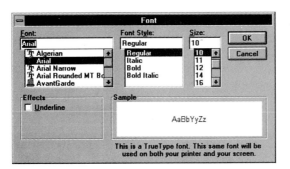

Fig. 6.20
Choosing a display
and printing font
for datasheets.

Fig. 6.21
A customized
version of the
Orders datasheet.

Order ID	Ship Name	Ship City	Ship Region	Ship Postal Code	Shi
10918	Bottom-Dollar Markets	Tsawassen	BC	T2F 8M4	Car
10944	Bottom-Dollar Markets	Tsawassen	BC	T2F 8M4	Car
10982	Bottom-Dollar Markets	Tsawassen	BC	T2F 8M4	Car
10949	Bottom-Dollar Markets	Tsawassen	BC	T2F 8M4	Car
10975	Bottom-Dollar Markets	Tsawassen	BC	T2F 8M4	Car
11048	Bottom-Dollar Markets	Tsawassen	BC	T2F 8M4	Car
11045	Bottom-Dollar Markets	Tsawassen	BC	T2F 8M4	Car
11027	Bottom-Dollar Markets	Tsawassen	BC	T2F 8M4	Car
10926	Ana Trujillo Emparedados	México D.F.		05021	Me:
10995	Pericles Comidas clásica:	México D.F.		05033	Me:
11069	Tortuga Restaurante	México D.F.		05033	Me:
11073	Pericles Comidas clásica:	México D.F.		05033	Me:
10915	Tortuga Restaurante	México D.F.		05033	Me:

Record: 1   of 41

Copying, Exporting, and Mailing Sorted and Filtered Data

A primary use for filters and customized datasheets is so that you can export
the filtered records to another application, such as Microsoft Excel or Word.
A variety of methods for exporting filtered and custom-formatted records is
available, each of which is described in the following list:

▶ "Exporting Data
from Access
Tables," p. 278

■ Copy the entire datasheet to the Clipboard, and then paste it into the
other application. Hidden columns don't appear, but formatting (font,
font attributes, and row height) is not preserved.

■ Use the Output To feature to export the datasheet to an Excel worksheet (.XLS) or a rich text format (.RTF) file for Word or other Windows word processing applications. (Choose Output **T**o from the **F**ile Menu, and then select the file type you want in the Output To dialog.) Output To preserves the attributes you use to customize the filtered and sorted data when you choose Excel format. Hidden columns, however, appear when you open the resulting file in any version of Excel.

  ■ Click the Analyze It with MS Excel or Publish It with MS Word button. (If these buttons do not appear in your Table Datasheet View toolbar, you need to customize your Table Datasheet menu and add the two buttons.)

 ■ Click the Merge It button to create form letters with Microsoft Word 6.0. (You may need to customize your Table Datasheet toolbar by adding the Output To Mail Merge button.) Using Mail Merge with Microsoft Word is discussed in Chapter 22.

 ■ Send the file as an attachment to a Microsoft Mail message. Hidden columns don't appear, but formatting is not preserved. (The attached file is in Excel 3.0 format.)

If you make the Database window the active window and choose **E**xport from the **F**ile menu, the entire content of the table is exported without regard to the filter you added.

Troubleshooting

When attempting to use the Mail Merge with Word feature, a "Must save object first" or "Name not found in this collection" message box appears.

You applied a filter or created a query for your Mail Merge operation that you did not save before clicking the Merge It button. The filter or query object (filters are saved as **QueryDef** objects) must be a member of a the QueryDefs collection before the DDE conversation between Access and Word commences. Save the filter or the query, and then try clicking the Merge It button again. Chapter 28, "Understanding the Data Access Object Class," provides detailed information on database objects and object collections.

From Here...

Microsoft provided table sorting and filtering features so that Access can duplicate the functions of other less-powerful desktop database managers, such as dBASE, that presently do not provide a graphical QBE environment to perform these operations. Some of the examples give you insight into the simple SQL statements used to create filters/queries. The find and the search and replace features of Access also are offered as macro actions, and you execute these macro actions from Access Basic code.

- Chapter 8, "Using Query by Example," shows you how to use Access's graphical QBE design window to create queries that can act as filters.

- Chapter 17, "Understanding Access Macros," describes how to use Access macro actions to apply filters and execute queries.

- Chapter 24, "Working with Structured Query Language," provides an in-depth analysis of Access SQL's SELECT query syntax.

Access Fundamentals

Chapter 7

Attaching, Importing, and Exporting Tables

Undoubtedly, more than 90 percent of personal computer users have data that can be processed by database management techniques. Any data a computer can arrange in tabular form, even tables in word processing files, can be converted to database tables. The strength of a relational database management system (RDBMS) lies in its capability to handle large numbers of individual pieces of data stored in tables and to relate the pieces of data in a meaningful way.

PC users acquire RDBMSs when the amount of data created exceeds the application's capability to manipulate the data effectively. A common example of this situation is a large mailing list created in a word processing application. As the number of names in the list increases, using the word processor to make selective mailings and maintain histories of responses to mailings becomes increasingly difficult. A PC RDBMS is the most effective type of application for manipulating large lists.

One of Access's strong points is its capability to transform existing database table, spreadsheet, and text files created by other DOS and Windows applications into the Access .MDB format—a process called *importing* a file. Access can *export* (create) table files in any format in which it can import the files. Most PC RDBMSs share this capability, but Access can import and export Borland Paradox files, whereas many other systems cannot. Most client-server RDBMSs can import and export only text-type files.

Access can attach a database table file created by Access or another RDBMS to your current Access database; Access then acts as a database front end. Because Access has an attaching capability, it can use a file created by another RDBMS in its native form. This capability is far less common in other PC and

In this chapter, you learn to

- Attach tables from Access and other desktop databases

- Use the Attachment Manager add-in to alter where Access looks for attached files

- Attach Excel worksheets using the Microsoft ODBC Desktop Database Drivers

- Import and export files from worksheet, text, and database files in other formats

client-server RDBMSs. When you attach a database table from a different RDBMS, you can display and update the attached table as if it were an Access table contained in your .MDB file. If the file containing the table is shared on a network, other users can use the file with their applications while it is attached to your database. This capability to attach files is an important feature for two reasons: you can have only one Access database open at a time, and you can create new applications in Access that can coexist with applications created by other database managers.

This chapter deals primarily with what are called *desktop database development applications*—a term used to distinguish them from client-server RDBMSs, such as Microsoft and Sybase SQL Server, ORACLE, Informix, and Ingres databases. (Client-server RDBMSs are designed specifically for use with networked PCs and, with the exception of Microsoft SQL Server for Windows NT, require you to set aside a PC for use as a file server to store the database files.) Desktop RDBMSs, such as dBASE, FoxPro, and Paradox, are much more widely used than client-server systems. The majority of desktop RDBMSs can share files on a network, but several publishers require that you purchase a special multiuser version of the RDBMS to do so. Multiuser desktop RDBMSs, while accommodating the workstation-server configuration required by conventional networks such as Novell NetWare, Microsoft LAN Manager, and Windows NT Advanced Server, are especially well suited to the peer-to-peer networks discussed in Chapter 25, "Securing Multiuser Network Applications," such as Windows for Workgroups 3.11, NetWare Lite, and LANtastic. Chapter 25 explains how to use Access with shared database files in general, and Chapter 26 deals with client-server databases in particular.

Learning How Access Handles Tables in Other Database File Formats

Conventional desktop database development applications maintain each table in an individual file. Each file contains a *header* followed by the data. A header is a group of bytes that provides information on the structure of the file, such as the names and types of fields, the number of records in the table, and the length of the file. When you create a table file in dBASE, FoxPro, or Paradox, for example, the file contains only a header. As you add records to the file, the file grows by the number of bytes required for one record, and the header is updated to reflect the new file size and record count. Novell Btrieve files are slightly different from the files created by dBASE and Paradox because Btrieve files use variable-width records for storing text data.

Desktop RDBMSs create a variety of supplemental files—some of which are required to import, attach, or export RDBMSs:

- Paradox stores information about the primary-key index file (.PX) in the associated table (.DB) file; the .PX file for the .DB file must be available in order for Access to open a Paradox .DB file. Access attaches the .PX file automatically.

- dBASE and FoxPro store memo-type data in a separate .DBT file. If a dBASE table file contains a memo field, the .DBT file must be available. If the .DBT file is missing, you cannot import or attach dBASE or FoxPro tables that contain a memo field.

- Use of .NDX (dBASE III), .MDX (dBASE IV), or .IDX or .CDX (FoxPro) index files is optional. You should always use index files when you have them. If you do not attach the index files when you attach an indexed .DBF table file, modifications you make to the attached tables are not reflected in the index. This causes errors to occur when you attempt to use the indexed tables with dBASE or FoxPro.

- Opening Btrieve files requires having FILE.DDF and FIELD.DDF data dictionary files for the database that contains the table file. You need a copy of Novell's WBTRCALL.DLL in your \WINDOWS\SYSTEM directory to open or create a Btrieve table. WBTRCALL.DLL is not supplied with Access 2.0. (You can purchase a license for WBTRCALL.DLL from Novell, Inc. WBTRCALL.DLL usually is included with third-party Btrieve utilities.) You also need the correct entry in the [btrieve] section of your WIN.INI file.

All supplemental files must be in the same directory as the related database file to be used by Access.

The header of an Access .MDB file differs from conventional PC RDBMS files in that an .MDB header consists of a collection of *system tables* that contain information on all the tables, indexes, macros, and Access Basic functions and procedures stored in a single Access file. The Access system tables also contain information on the location and characteristics of other PC RDBMS files that you have attached to your Access database. Access's system tables are similar to the tables used in client-server databases to maintain information on the content of database devices (files).

◄ "Understanding
Relational
Databases,"
p. 126

Identifying PC Database File Formats

Access can import, attach, and export the following types of database table files used by the most common PC database managers:

- *dBASE .DBF table and .DBT memo files, and dBASE III .NDX and dBASE IV .MDX index files.* dBASE III files and indexes are the standard language of the PC RDBMS industry. The majority of PC RDBMSs, as well as all common spreadsheet applications, can import and export .DBF files. Most of these RDBMSs can update existing .NDX and .MDX index files, and some RDBMSs can create these index files.

  The .DBF file structure is native to other xBase clone applications such as FoxPro, but not all these RDBMSs create fully compatible dBASE file structures. Compilers like CA-Clipper and Arago have their own native index file structures, but they can use .NDX indexes when necessary. The capability to use .MDX multiple-index files is less widespread.

  Access can attach but not create .NDX and .MDX files. Access updates both types of dBASE index files when you edit or add records to an attached .DBF file. The section "Setting Primary Keys and Using Index Files" later in this chapter discusses index files in attached tables. When you export an Access table with a memo field, a .DBT memo file with the same name you assign to the dBASE file is created.

- *FoxPro 2+ .DBF table files.* You can import, export, and attach FoxPro 2+ .DBF files and files created by earlier versions of FoxPro. The procedures for handling FoxPro 2+ .DBF files are the same as those for dBASE III and IV. Access 1.1 maintains the currency of FoxPro 2+ .IDX (single) and .CDX (multiple) index files.

- *Paradox 3.x and 4.0 .DB table and .PX primary key files.* You can attach Paradox for DOS 3.x and 4.x table and index files but not files created by Paradox for Windows. The next section presents the specific limitations applicable to Paradox files.

- *Btrieve table and .DDF data definition files.* The Btrieve file structure is one of the first RDBMSs used by PC applications written in the C language. The Btrieve table file contains the indexes; they are not in separate files. A number of PC-based accounting applications use Btrieve files but do not advertise this fact. If the application you are using creates databases and the files are not dBASE or Paradox files, they may be Btrieve files. If the directory containing the database files includes a .DDF file, you probably can attach the tables to an Access database. If the directory does not contain a .DDF file, you can contact the publisher of the application to determine whether the files are in Btrieve format and whether a data definition file with a disguised extension exists.

The majority of applications that use table and index files also use the standard file extensions presented in the preceding paragraphs. The dBASE memo file, for example, requires a standard extension, .DBT. Using the standard extensions for all types of files, however, is not a requirement. Some developers of xBase applications disguise their files by using arbitrary extensions. You may have to do a bit of detective work to determine which files contain data and which are indexes.

> **Note**
>
> If you are working in a multiuser environment, you must have exclusive access to the file you intend to import. No other user can have that file open when you initiate the importing process, and other users are denied access to the file until you close the Import dialog.

> **Caution**
>
> Make sure that you work on a backup copy of the attached file, not the original, until you are certain that your updates to the data in the attached table are valid for the existing database application.

To attach or import an xBase, Paradox, or Btrieve file as a table in an open Access database, such as NWIND.MDB, follow these steps:

1. Click the Show Database Window button of the toolbar or choose 1 Database from the **W**indow menu. Access does not require that all open tables be closed before you attach or import a table.

2. If you created a test database that can be used for this procedure, click the Open Database button of the toolbar or choose **O**pen Database from the **F**ile menu; then select the test database, open it, and skip to step 7.

3. If you do not have a test database, create a sample to use throughout this chapter. Click the New Database button of the toolbar or choose **N**ew Database from the **F**ile menu.

4. In the File Name text box, type a name, such as **MDB_TEST.MDB,** for your test database, and click OK. You must wait while Access creates and tests the new database.

5. In this example, you attach a table. Click the Attach button of the toolbar or choose **A**ttach Table from the **F**ile menu. The Attach dialog appears (see fig. 7.1). If you click the Import Table button or choose **I**mport Table, the Import dialog appears.

Fig. 7.1

Selecting the type of file to attach as an Access table.

6. Use the arrow keys or the scroll bar slider to select the data source. (If you have a suitable Paradox table to attach, select Paradox. Otherwise, select dBASE III, dBASE IV, or Btrieve as appropriate to the format of your table file.) Click OK. The Select File dialog appears (see fig. 7.2).

Fig. 7.2

Choosing the file to attach.

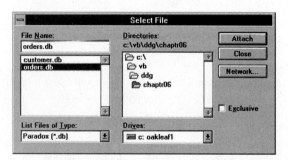

7. From the list in the File Name combo, select the table you want to attach or import. Access supplies the standard extensions for dBASE, FoxPro, and Paradox table files and the .DDF extension for Btrieve data definition files. Click the Attach button. If you have no other tables of the selected type to attach, click the Close button.

> **Note**
>
> You can attach Access 1.1 files to an Access 2.0 database. Attaching Access 1.1 files solves the problem of not being able to convert an Access 2.0 .MDB file to the Access 1.1 .MDB format for backward compatibility. This is one more reason to always use one .MDB file for tables and another .MDB file for your application database objects.

If you are attaching a Btrieve file, the Attach Tables dialog appears (see fig. 7.3). Select the table to attach, and then click the Attach button.

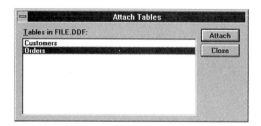

Fig. 7.3
Choosing the Btrieve tables to attach.

8. If the file you choose is encrypted (coded) and requires a password to decrypt it, the Password Required dialog appears. Type the password in the box and press Enter.

9. After you successfully attach or import the file, a dialog appears confirming this operation (see fig. 7.4). If you attach more than one table with the same name, Access automatically appends a sequential digit to the table name.

Fig. 7.4
Confirming that Access has attached a table.

10. In the Select File dialog, click Close. The selected table is now listed in the Database window. If you attached a file, Access adds an icon indicating the type of database table and an arrow indicating that the table is attached (see fig. 7.5).

11. Select the table you attached, and then click the Open button to display the records in Table Datasheet View (see fig. 7.6).

Open

Fig. 7.5
The Database
window after
attaching four
types of tables.

Fig. 7.6
The Datasheet
View of a Btrieve
file that Access
attached to a test
database.

Order_ID	Cust_ID	Empl_ID	Ship_Name	Ship_Addr	Ship_City
10000	FRUGF	6	Frugal Feast Comestibl	Evans Plaza	Eugene
10001	MERRG	8	Merry Grape Wine Mer	304 King Edward Pl.	East Vancouver
10002	FOODI	3	Foodmongers, Inc.	418 - 6th Ave.	Walla Walla
10003	SILVS	8	Silver Screen Food Ge	12 Meikeljohn Ln.	Helena
10004	VALUF	3	ValuMax Food Stores	986 Chandler Dr.	Austin
10005	WALNG	5	Walnut Grove Grocery	33 Upper Arctic Dr.	Buffalo
10006	FREDE	8	Fred's Edibles, Etc.	1522 College Blvd.	Bellingham
10007	RATTC	0			
10008	FUJIA	3	Fujiwara Asian Special	72 Dowlin Pkwy.	Phoenix
10009	SEVES	8	Seven Seas Imports	90 Wadhurst Rd.	London
10010	SILVS	8	Silver Screen Food Ge	12 Meikeljohn Ln.	Helena
10011	WELLT	6	Wellington Trading	16 Newcomen Rd.	Sevenoaks
10012	LIVEO	6	Live Oak Hotel Gift Sh	7384 Washington Av	Portland
10013	RITEB	3	Rite-Buy Supermarket	2226 Shattuck Ave.	Berkeley
10014	GRUED	4	Gruenewald Delikatess	3344 Byerly St.	Berkeley
10015	PICAF	6	Picadilly Foods	12 Ebury St.	London
10016	FRUGP	3	Frugal Purse Strings	418 Datablitz Ave.	Pocatello
10017	BLUMG	4	Blum's Goods	The Blum Building	London

Record: 1   of 499

Note

To import, export, or attach Btrieve files, you need the following entries in your
WIN.INI file:

```
[btrieve]
tasks=10
access-options=/m:64 /p:4096 /b:16 /f:20 /l:40 /n:12
➥/t:C:\ACCESS\BTRIEVE.TRN
```

The value of the /t: parameter should point to the location of your BTRIEVE.TRN file
used to manage transactions in a multiuser environment. (If you do not have a
BTRIEVE.TRN file, you need to omit the /t: parameter.) You might need to increase
the value of the tasks= entry in networked Btrieve applications. Access 2.0 automatically adds the access-options= entry to the [btrieve] section of WIN.INI if the
[btrieve] section exists. If an Access 1.x options= entry exists, the values for the
options= entry are copied to the access-options= entry.

After you attach an external file as a table, you can use it almost as if it were a table in your own database. The only general limitation is that you cannot change the structure of an attached table: field names, field data types, or the FieldSize properties. In attached Paradox files, Access prevents you from changing a table's primary-key field that has been defined because this property determines the contents of the associated .PX index file.

Solving Problems with Importing or Attaching Files

Access detects problems with attached or imported tables that might cause errors when you try to use the tables with Access. The following sections describe these problems and how to overcome most of them.

The Incorrect Password Dialog

If you enter a wrong password or just press Enter, Access informs you that it cannot decrypt the file. It gives you another opportunity to enter the password or to click Cancel to terminate the attempt (see fig. 7.7).

Fig. 7.7
The dialog resulting from an incorrect password entry for a Paradox 3.x table.

The Null Value in Index Dialog

Occasionally, Paradox .PX index files do not have an index value for a record; when this happens, you receive a warning dialog (see fig. 7.8). In most cases, you can disregard the message and continue attaching or importing the file. The offending record, however, might not appear in the table; fixing the file in Paradox and starting over is better than ignoring the message.

Fig. 7.8
The dialog indicating a null value in a Paradox primary-key index file.

The Missing Memo File Dialog

If Access cannot open a dBASE memo file because it does not exist, it is not in the same directory as the .DBF file with which it is associated, or it contains nontext data. A dialog appears, and Access cancels the attachment or importation (see fig. 7.9).

Fig. 7.9
The dialog that
appears if Access
cannot open a
required dBASE
memo file.

The Graphics Field Type Restriction

If the successful-attachment dialog does not appear, your table or its accompanying dBASE memo file probably contains a graphics field type. The following section discusses modifying files with graphics content so that you can attach them or import them as Access tables.

Dealing with Graphics in External Files

Most database managers designed for Windows include some form of graphics field data type. Superbase, Paradox 4.0, and Paradox for Windows provide a special field data type for graphics. Although dBASE IV does not have a field data type for graphics, third-party software firms publish applications that enable you to store graphic images in dBASE memo fields. A variety of add-on applications enables CA-Clipper programmers to display and edit graphic images. The images are usually in individual files, but a few third-party applications place images in memo files. CA-dbFast, for example, can display but not edit images stored in Windows bit-map (.BMP) files. CA-dbFast does not add a graphics field type to store bit-mapped data within tables.

> **Note**
>
> Although Visual Basic 3.0 enables you to manipulate Access 1.1 database files with the Access database engine, Visual Basic 3.0 does not support the OLE Object field data type of Access tables. You need a third-party custom control, such as ImageKnife/VBX from Media Architects, Inc. (Portland, OR), to create OLE-compatible graphics to make Access tables with graphics compatible with Access 1.1. You can attach the Access 1.1 tables to Access 2.0 databases to maintain compatibility with Visual Basic 3.0.

When you attempt to import or attach Paradox 4.0, Paradox for Windows files, or dBASE .DBT files that contain images or other binary data, you receive an error message that the memo file is corrupted or a message that you cannot import the .DB or .DBF file that contains the offending memo or graphics field (see fig. 7.10). In rare cases, usually involving tiny images, you can import the .DBF and .DBT files, but you see random characters in the Access memo field.

Fig. 7.10

The dialog that indicates a graphic or other nonstandard field.

If the dialog in figure 7.10 (or a dialog indicating a similar type of problem) appears, the attachment or importation process is canceled.

The following recommendations can help you deal with graphic images processed with other RDBMSs and add-on applications:

- Use add-on applications for xBase clones and compilers that operate with the original graphics files in their native format, such as .TIF, .PIX, .GIF, or .TGA. In nearly all cases, the original graphics file is on your computer's fixed disk or on a file server. You can link or embed the graphics file in an Access OLE Object field by using the techniques described in Chapter 20.

- Do not use add-on applications that incorporate graphics in .DBT files. If you are committed to this approach, use the method that follows to place the offending memo file in a new file.

- If you are using Paradox 4.0 or Paradox for Windows with application development in Access, maintain files with graphics fields (as well as any OLE fields in Paradox for Windows tables) separate from those containing conventional data types.

- Use an OLE server that can process the graphics file type of the original image. Windows Paintbrush is limited to Windows bit-map files (.BMP and .DIB) and .PCX files. To display the image in a form or report, you can create a reduced-size, 16-color or 256-color, Windows bit-map file to be displayed as a bound object. Chapter 20, "Adding Graphics to Forms and Reports," discusses methods of handling images in this way.

To attach or import an xBase file containing a memo field or a Paradox file containing graphics fields, you must be familiar with file-restructuring methods for dBASE or Paradox. To restructure an xBase file with a memo file containing graphic images, follow these steps:

1. Make a copy of the file and give the file a new name.

2. Modify the structure of the original file by deleting all but the related fields and the memo or graphics field of the original file. Modifying the new file with Modify Structure creates a backup of the original file with a .BAK extension.

3. Modify the structure of the new file by deleting the memo or graphics field.

4. Add a field for the path and file name of the original graphics file, if it is not already included. Access then can use the location of the original graphics file to pass the file name to an OLE server. You must write a bit of Access Basic code to do this, however. See Chapter 27 for examples of writing Access Basic code.

5. Modify the source code of your original application, establishing a one-to-one relationship between the new files.

Converting Field Data Types to Access Data Types

When you import or attach a file, Access reads the header of the file and converts the field data types to Access data types. In most cases, Access is quite successful in this conversion; Access offers a greater variety of data types than any other widely used PC RDBMS. Table 7.1 shows the correspondence of field data types between dBASE, Paradox, Btrieve, and Access files.

Table 7.1   Field Data Type Conversion between Access and RDBMSs

dBASE III/IV	Paradox 3.0 and 4.x	Btrieve	Access
Character	Alphanumeric	String, lstring, zstring	Text (Specify Size property)
Numeric, Float*	Number, Currency	Float or bfloat (8-byte) Float or bfloat (4-byte) Integer (1-byte)	Number (Double) Number (Single) Number (Byte)
	Short Number	Integer (2-byte) Integer (4-btye)	Number (Integer) Number (Long)

dBASE III/IV	Paradox 3.0 and 4.x	Btrieve	Access
Logical			Yes/No
Date	Date		Date/Time
Memo	Memo		Memo

*Sometimes two types of field data, separated by commas, are shown within a single column in table 7.1. When Access exports a table containing a data type that corresponds with one of the two field data types, the first of the two data types is assigned to the field in the exported table. The Float data type is available only in dBASE IV.

If you are importing tables, you can change the field data type and the `FieldSize` property so that they are more suitable to the type of information contained in the field. When you change a data type or `FieldSize`, however, follow the precautions noted in Chapter 4, "Working with Access Databases and Tables." Remember that you cannot change the field data type or `FieldSize` property of attached tables. You can use the `Format` property with imported or attached tables, however, to display the data in any format compatible with the field data type of imported or attached files. You can change any remaining properties applicable to the field data type, such as validation rules and text. Using the `Caption` property, you can give the field a new and more descriptive name.

◀ "Choosing Field Data Types, Sizes, and Formats," p. 135

◀ "Adding Indexes to Tables," p. 173

Setting Primary Keys and Using Index Files

Methods of setting primary keys and creating indexes differ according to the type of file you use to attach a table. Tables based on Paradox, Btrieve, and client/server RDBMS files usually have predefined primary-key fields and are indexed on the key fields. Files based on dBASE structures, however, do not have fields specified as primary-key fields and use separate index files. The following two sections discuss the effects these differences have on the tables you create.

Establishing Key Fields in Attached Paradox and Btrieve Tables

When you attach or import a Paradox or Btrieve table that has a primary-key index, Access establishes this primary key as the primary key for the new table. To verify that Access establishes a primary key for an attached Paradox or Btrieve table, click the Design View button on the toolbar. A dialog informs you that you cannot modify some properties of the table (see fig. 7.11). Click OK.

The table appears in design mode. If the Table Properties window is not displayed; choose Table Properties from the **V**iew menu.

Fig. 7.11
The dialog reminding you, when you enter design mode, that a table is attached.

When you attach a Paradox .DB table file that has a primary key, Access uses the Paradox .PX file to establish the primary key. (With Btrieve, Access uses the .DDF and database files.) If you modify the values in a key field, the .DB and .PX files simultaneously reflect that modification. The Table Properties window text box shows the primary key.

Attaching dBASE Index Files

Key-field indexing is not automatic with dBASE files attached as tables; dBASE file headers do not include data about the indexes used by the application that has the .DBF file. The first time you attach the .DBF file as an Access table, you must manually attach the index files associated with a dBASE file. Then when you open the Access database with the attached table again, Access attaches the indexes you specify.

> **Note**
>
> Access cannot open or update index files in proprietary formats of xBase clones and compilers. You cannot, for example, attach CA-Clipper .NTX files. Current versions of CA-Clipper (5+), however, can create and maintain .NDX files, as an addition to or a substitute for their original index structures. Access cannot use secondary indexes of Paradox tables. If you created or commissioned custom database applications that use nonstandard or secondary indexes and you plan to use Access to update these files while they are attached, you must modify your applications so that they use only .NDX or .PX indexes. You probably do not have to make a major revision of the source code, but you might find that your present applications run more slowly with .NDX indexes.

When you attach a dBASE file as a table in your database and select the file name for the table, Access displays a Select Index Files dialog (see fig. 7.12). When you import a dBASE file, this dialog does not appear.

If you select a dBASE III source file, Access supplies the default .NDX file extension. Your dBASE III file might have one or more .NDX index files associated with it. The four indexes that appear in figure 7.12 with the cust_ prefix are for the CUSTOMER.DBF table; the two indexes beginning with ordr_ are for the ORDERS.DBF table shown attached as the ORDERS2 table earlier in the chapter.

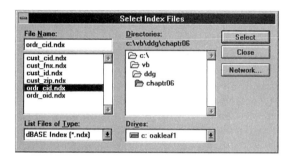

Fig. 7.12
The dialog for selecting dBASE III index files.

dBASE IV can create a multiple-index (.MDX) file that includes all the indexes associated with the .DBF file. The .MDX file usually has the same file name as the .DBF file. Access supplies both .MDX and .NDX as default index-file extensions when you select a dBASE IV file.

To attach index files to tables created from dBASE files, follow these steps:

1. From the list in the File Name of the Select Index Files dialog, select the index file name, and then click Select. A dialog appears, prompting you to confirm the addition (see fig. 7.13).

Fig. 7.13
The dialog confirming that Access added an attached index to an attached table.

> **Caution**
>
> Access does not test to determine whether the table's .NDX or .MDX index file matches the structure of its associated Access .DBF file. If the index file does not match the Access file, Access does not update the index file. Unfortunately, Access does not advise you that it is ignoring the nonconforming index. If you add records to the table in Access and then attempt to use the table with an xBase application that uses the proper index, you receive the following error message: "Index does not match database." You then must reindex the .DBF file.

If more than one index file is associated with the dBASE.DBF file, you must repeat this step for each .NDX file.

> **Caution**
>
> When you attach a dBASE III file used by another application, you must select *all* indexes associated with that file if your Access application modifies fields in the index expressions of each index file. If you do not update all the associated index files while updating the .DBF file with Access, the other application might display the following error message: "Index does not match file." Worse yet, the application might produce erroneous or unpredictable results. If the message or errors occur, you must reindex the file in the other application.

2. After you add the names of all the indexes required for your Access table, click the Close button in the Select Index Files dialog.

3. Click the Close button in the Select File dialog.

4. Click the Design button in the Database window to display the structure of your attached dBASE table.

5. If the Indexes window is not visible already, click the Indexes button on the toolbar or choose **I**ndexes from the **V**iew menu. The field names that are the basis for any attached single- or multiple-field indexes appear in the Index Name text boxes of the Indexes window (see fig. 7.14).

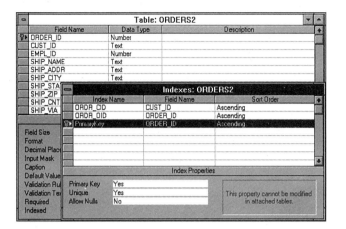

Fig. 7.14
An Access table
with an attached
dBASE file and its
associated index
files.

Caution

Access does not distinguish between dBASE indexes created with SET UNIQUE ON
and SET UNIQUE OFF. In the case of the Invoice database of figure 7.14, the index
on the FINV_NO field was created with SET UNIQUE ON. Access indicates, however,
that duplicates are OK in the Indexed text box.

Caution

Access 2.0 enables you to designate a primary-key field for dBASE and FoxPro tables,
although primary-key fields are not supported by these types of tables. Although the
PrimaryKey entry appears in the Index Name text box, Access 2.0 disregards the
entry and does not display the table in the order of the bogus PrimaryKey index.
You also can enter duplicate values, despite the fact that the Unique property in the
Index Properties pane displays the Yes value.

If you try to modify the primary-key field or change the data type or the
FieldSize property of an attached table and then click the Datasheet button
in run mode, Access displays a dialog (see fig. 7.15). Click OK. (Choosing
Cancel restores the original values.) Access does not change the properties in
the attached file, although the Design and Datasheet windows display the
changes.

Fig. 7.15
The dialog
indicating that
Access is ignoring
changes made to
restricted table
properties.

Creating Access .INF Files for dBASE Indexes

When you attach one or more indexes to a table created from a dBASE file,
Access creates a file with the same file name as the .DBF file but with an .INF
extension. The *FILENAME*.INF file contains the path and the file name of the
index you attached in a format identical to the format used for Windows .INI
files, such as this WIN.INI file:

```
[dBASE III]
NDX1=C:\UMC\DBASE\INV_AREA.NDX
NDX2=C:\UMC\DBASE\INV_CITY.NDX
NDX3=C:\UMC\DBASE\INV_NUMB.NDX
NDX4=C:\UMC\DBASE\INV_PHON.NDX
[dBASE III]
NDX1=C:\VB\DDG\CHAPTR06\ORDR_CID.NDX
NDX2=C:\VB\DDG\CHAPTR06\ORDR_OID.NDX
```

The .INF file is located in the same directory as the .DBF file you are attaching. If you create an invalid .INF file, or the .INF file is not found in the specified location, Access terminates the current attach operation, and you must
attach the dBASE file again. Figure 7.16 shows the message you receive if
Access can't find the specified .INF file. When you reattach index files to
correct a prior error, a message box indicates that an .INF file exists (see
fig. 7.17). Click Yes to create a new .INF file if the indexes have changed
or you moved the .INF file.

Fig. 7.16
The message box
informing you of a
duplication in an
attachment of a
dBASE index file.

Fig. 7.17
The message box
warning that you
already have
attached indexes
for an attached
dBASE file.

Attaching Tables from Other Access Databases

The procedure for attaching a table from one Access database to another Access database is like the procedure for attaching other tables. If you want to attach a table from NWIND.MDB to your test database, for example, follow these steps:

1. Select Access Table, the default, from the Attach dialog. The Attach Tables dialog appears.

2. Select the name of the table you want to attach from the Tables in NWIND.MDB list that displays the names of tables in the other Access database. Then click Attach (see fig. 7.18).

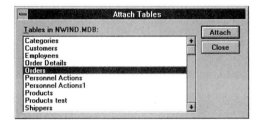

Fig. 7.18
The dialog for choosing another Access database table to be attached to the current Access database.

3. Click Close in the Attach Tables dialog. The name of your attached Access table appears in the Database window.

Access maintains a record of the drive and directory containing the files responsible for your attached tables. If you rename or change the location of a file that you attached as a table, Access is no longer able to find the file and displays the error dialog (see fig. 7.19).

Fig. 7.19
The dialog indicating that Access cannot find an attached file.

Using the Attachment Manager Add-In to Reattach Tables

Before Access 2.0, if you moved a file that was attached to or contained objects attached to an Access 1.x database, you had to delete the attached tables, and then reattach the tables from their new location. Access 2.0 provides an add-in assistant called the Attachment Manager that simplifies

Access
2.0

reattaching tables. If you move an Access, dBASE, FoxPro, or Paradox file that provides a table attached to an Access 2.0 database, choose **Ad**d-Ins from the **F**ile menu, and then choose **A**ttachment Manager from the submenu. The Attachment Manager's window lists all the attached tables (except attached Btrieve and ODBC tables). Click the check box of the file(s) whose location(s) changed (see fig. 7.20).

Fig. 7.20
Changing the location of a table with the Attachment Manager add-in.

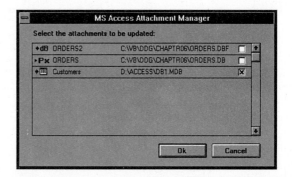

Click OK to display the Select New Location of *TableName* dialog shown in figure 7.21. Select the directory and file where the table is located, and then click OK to change the attachment reference and close the dialog. Click the OK button of the Attachment Manager to close the add-in.

Fig. 7.21
Changing the location of a table with the Attachment Manager add-in.

Importing versus Attaching Database Files as Tables

The preceding examples demonstrate the differences between the behavior of Access with attached and imported database files. You should attach tables contained in another database file if any of the following conditions are present:

■ You share the file with other users who are allowed to update the file, or you make your updates of the file available to other users.

- You use another RDBMS to modify the file in any way.

- The file is resident on another computer, such as a server, and its size is larger than fits comfortably on your fixed disk.

- You observe the recommended database application development practice of maintaining separate .MDB files for tables and your application's objects.

You should import a table when one of the following conditions is present:

- You are developing an application and want to use data types or `FieldSize` properties different from those chosen for you by Access.

- You or the users of your application do not have on-line access to the required database files and cannot attach them.

- You want to use a key field different from the field specified in a Paradox, Btrieve, or client-server table. This situation can occur when the structure of one or more of the files you plan to use seriously violates one or more of the normalization rules described in Chapter 23, "Exploring Relational Database Design and Implementation."

- You need Access to allow duplicate values in your table when a primary-key field precludes duplicate values.

If you decide to use a temporarily imported table in an application that, when completed, will also use an attached table, make sure that you do not change any of the field names, field data types, or `FieldSize` properties after you import the table. If you change `FieldName` properties, you might have to make many changes to forms, reports, macros, and Access Basic code when you change to an attached table. If your application involves Paradox, Btrieve, and client-server database tables, do not change the primary-key fields of these tables. With dBASE tables, make sure that the indexes you create correspond to those of the associated .NDX or .MDX files.

Importing and Attaching Spreadsheet Files

Access can import files created by spreadsheet and related applications, such as project management systems, in the following formats:

- Excel 2.x, 3.0, 4.0, and 5.0 .XLS files and task and resource files created by Microsoft Project for Windows 1.0 and 3.0 in .XLS format.
- Lotus 1-2-3 .WKS (Release 1 and Symphony), .WK1 (Release 2), and .WK3 (Release 3) files. Most spreadsheet applications can export files to at least one of these Lotus formats.

You can embed or link charts created by Microsoft Excel that are stored in files with an .XLC extension. Copy the contents of the file to the Windows Clipboard (either from Excel or the Windows 3.1 Object Packager). Then embed or link the chart in fields of the OLE object type, and display the chart on a form or print it on a report as an unbound object. Similarly, you can embed or link views displayed in Project for Windows 3.0 or 4.0, which also uses the Microsoft Chart applet, except task and resource forms and the Task PERT chart. Chapters 19 through 22 describe linking and embedding techniques.

Creating a Table by Importing an Excel Worksheet

Figure 7.22 illustrates the preferred format for exporting data from Excel and other spreadsheet applications to Access tables. Most spreadsheet applications refer to the format as a *database*. The names of the fields entered in the first row and the remainder of the database range consist of data. The type of data in each column must be consistent within the database range you select.

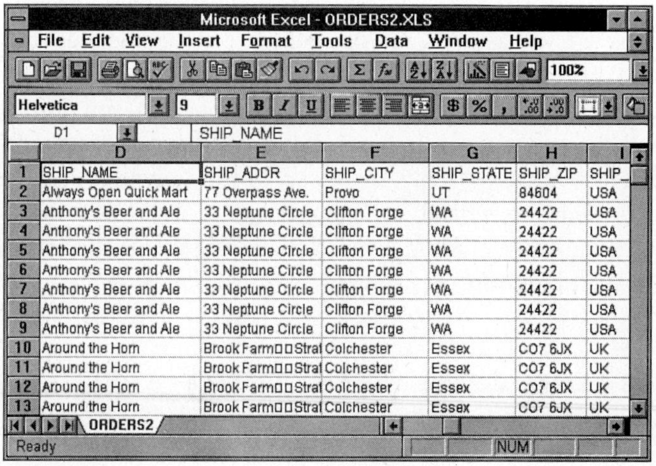

	D	E	F	G	H	I
1	SHIP_NAME	SHIP_ADDR	SHIP_CITY	SHIP_STATE	SHIP_ZIP	SHIP_
2	Always Open Quick Mart	77 Overpass Ave.	Provo	UT	84604	USA
3	Anthony's Beer and Ale	33 Neptune Circle	Clifton Forge	WA	24422	USA
4	Anthony's Beer and Ale	33 Neptune Circle	Clifton Forge	WA	24422	USA
5	Anthony's Beer and Ale	33 Neptune Circle	Clifton Forge	WA	24422	USA
6	Anthony's Beer and Ale	33 Neptune Circle	Clifton Forge	WA	24422	USA
7	Anthony's Beer and Ale	33 Neptune Circle	Clifton Forge	WA	24422	USA
8	Anthony's Beer and Ale	33 Neptune Circle	Clifton Forge	WA	24422	USA
9	Anthony's Beer and Ale	33 Neptune Circle	Clifton Forge	WA	24422	USA
10	Around the Horn	Brook Farm□□Strat	Colchester	Essex	CO7 6JX	UK
11	Around the Horn	Brook Farm□□Strat	Colchester	Essex	CO7 6JX	UK
12	Around the Horn	Brook Farm□□Strat	Colchester	Essex	CO7 6JX	UK
13	Around the Horn	Brook Farm□□Strat	Colchester	Essex	CO7 6JX	UK

Fig. 7.22 Invoice data in a Microsoft Excel 5.0 worksheet.

> ### Caution
>
> All the cells that comprise the range of the worksheet to be imported into an Access table must have *frozen values*. Frozen values substitute numeric results for the Excel expressions used to create the values. When cells include formulas, Access imports the cells as blank data cells. Freezing values causes Access to overwrite the formulas in your spreadsheet with the frozen values. If the range to be imported includes formulas, save a copy of your .XLS file with a new name. Using the worksheet window with the new file name, select the range to be imported and freeze the values by choosing **C**opy from the **E**dit menu, or by pressing Ctrl+C. Choose Paste **S**pecial from the **E**dit menu, select the Values option, and click OK. Save the new spreadsheet by its new name and use this file to import the data. The "Using the Clipboard to Import Data" section, later in this chapter, presents an alternative to this procedure.

To import data from an Excel spreadsheet into an Access table, follow these steps:

1. Launch Excel, and open the .XLS file that contains the data you want to import.

2. Add field names above the first row of the data you plan to export (if you have not done so). Field names cannot include periods (.), exclamation points (!), or brackets ([ ]). You cannot have duplicate field names. If you include improper characters in field names or use duplicate field names, you receive an error message when you attempt to import the worksheet.

3. If your worksheet contains cells with data not to be included in the imported table, select the range that contains the field names row and all the rows of data needed for the table. Choose **D**efine Name from the Fo**r**mula menu and name the range.

4. If the worksheet cells include expressions, freeze the values as described in the caution preceding these steps.

5. Save the Excel file (using a different file name if you froze values), and exit Excel to conserve Windows resources for Access if your computer has less than 8M of memory.

Tip
Access 1.0 does not accept Excel's Database range name for importing table data, but both Access 1.1 and 2.0 enable you to import the Database name range.

Access

2.0

6. Launch Access, if it is not running, and open the database to which you want to add the new table. The Database window must be active (with a dark title bar, usually blue) for you to be able to import a file.

7. Choose **I**mport from the Access **F**ile menu. The Import dialog appears (see fig. 7.23). The Data Source list provides several more formats for importing tables than it provides for attaching files.

8. Select Microsoft Excel from the list and click OK.

9. Select the drive, directory, and file name of the spreadsheet to import from the Select File dialog and then click OK. The Import Spreadsheet Options dialog appears (see fig. 7.24).

Fig. 7.23

The dialog for selecting an Excel spreadsheet as the import file source.

Fig. 7.24

The dialog for selecting options for importing spreadsheets.

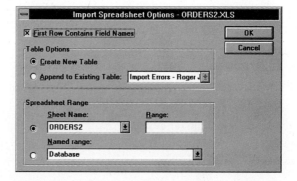

10. Your spreadsheet range contains field names in the first row, so click the First Row Contains Field Names box. You have the option of creating a new table or appending records from the spreadsheet to an existing table. Create New Table is the default. If you named the range in your spreadsheet that contains the data to import, enter the range name in the Spreadsheet Range text box. Or you can enter the range in standard row-column format. Then click OK.

11. Access imports the field names and data from the .XLS file. When the operation is complete and error-free, the Import Results dialog displays a message confirming the importation and telling you how many records were imported (see fig. 7.25).

Fig. 7.25
The Import Results dialog when no errors occur.

If every cell in a column has a numeric or date value, the columns convert to Number and Date/Time field data types, respectively. A single text entry in a column of your spreadsheet causes Access to display a message reporting that errors occurred and to change the field data type to Text (see fig. 7.26). The five errors reported were deliberately introduced in another imported Excel file named INV_ERRS.XLS.

If you received an error message similar to the one shown in figure 7.26, Access creates an Import Errors table with one record for each error (see fig. 7.27). You can review this table, select the records in which the errors are reported, and fix them. A better approach, however, is to correct the cells in the spreadsheet, resave the file, and import the corrected data.

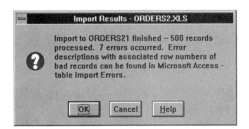

Fig. 7.26
The Import Results message box that reports errors.

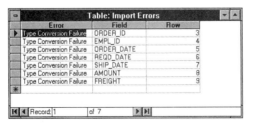

Fig. 7.27
The Import Errors table that Access creates when inconsistent field data types occur.

The Database window now contains a new table with the name of your file, minus the extension as the default. If you import another file with the same name as your spreadsheet file name, Access adds the number 1 to the file name.

To verify that you obtained the result you wanted, double-click the name of the imported table in the Database window to display the new table in Datasheet View. Figure 7.28 illustrates a portion of the Access table created from the ORDERS2.XLS spreadsheet file of figure 7.22. The **Null** values that appear in the second row of the ORDER_ID field and the third row of the EMPL_ID field result from two of the errors deliberately introduced in the .XLS file to create the Import Errors table of figure 7.27. Access names the table created from the ORDERS2.XLS worksheet ORDERS21 because an at-tached ORDERS2 table existed in the MDB_TEST.MDB database.

Fig. 7.28

The Excel spreadsheet data of figure 7.22 imported to the Invoice table.

ORDER_ID	CUST_ID	EMPL_ID	SHIP_NAME	SHIP_ADDR	SHIP_CITY
10062	ALWAO	5	Always Open Quick Mart	77 Overpass Ave.	Provo
	ANTHB	3	Anthony's Beer and Ale	33 Neptune Circle	Clifton Forge
10028	ANTHB		Anthony's Beer and Ale	33 Neptune Circle	Clifton Forge
10101	ANTHB	8	Anthony's Beer and Ale	33 Neptune Circle	Clifton Forge
10137	ANTHB	9	Anthony's Beer and Ale	33 Neptune Circle	Clifton Forge
10142	ANTHB	5	Anthony's Beer and Ale	33 Neptune Circle	Clifton Forge
10218	ANTHB	8	Anthony's Beer and Ale	33 Neptune Circle	Clifton Forge
10365	ANTHB	3	Anthony's Beer and Ale	33 Neptune Circle	Clifton Forge
10144	AROUT	7	Around the Horn	Brook Farm	Colchester
10355	AROUT	6	Around the Horn	Brook Farm	Colchester
10383	AROUT	8	Around the Horn	Brook Farm	Colchester
10453	AROUT	1	Around the Horn	Brook Farm	Colchester
10212	BABUJ	2	Babu Ji's Exports	Delhi House	London
10190	BABUJ	8	Babu Ji's Exports	Delhi House	London
10362	BABUJ	3	Babu Ji's Exports	Delhi House	London
10340	BABUJ	1	Babu Ji's Exports	Delhi House	London
10331	BABUJ	9	Babu Ji's Exports	Delhi House	London
10470	BABUJ	4	Babu Ji's Exports	Delhi House	London
10045	BERGS	9	Bergstad's Scandinavian	41 S. Marlon St.	Seattle
10158	BERGS	6	Bergstad's Scandinavian	41 S. Marlon St.	Seattle
10171	BERGS	6	Bergstad's Scandinavian	41 S. Marlon St.	Seattle
10213	BERGS	7	Bergstad's Scandinavian	41 S. Marlon St.	Seattle

Table: ORDERS21 — Record: 1 of 500

 To display the .XLS file data types that Access has chosen, click the Design View button on the toolbar. Figure 7.29 shows the structure of the new Invoice table.

To change the table name from the default assigned by Access, close all open tables and activate the Database window, if necessary. Choose Rename from the File menu. The Rename dialog appears with the default table name (see fig. 7.30). In the text box, type the new name for the table and then press Enter or click OK. You cannot rename an open table, and you cannot rename a table created from an attached file.

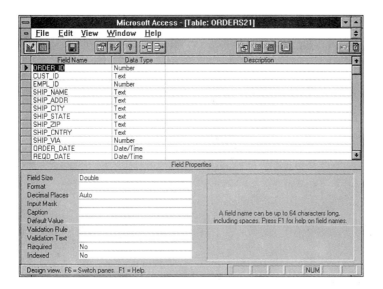

Fig. 7.29
The structure of
the Invoices table
imported from
Excel.

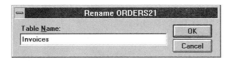

Fig. 7.30
Renaming a table.

After you successfully import the table, you might want to change the properties of the fields. Unlike the procedure with attached files, Access places no restrictions on altering the field properties of imported files. The section "Modifying Attached and Imported Tables," later in this chapter, discusses changing the default field data types of tables created by imported files.

Attaching an Excel Worksheet using the ODBC API

If you have Excel 5.0 or you purchased the Microsoft ODBC Desktop Database Drivers kit or Q+E Software's ODBC Driver Pack, you can attach Excel worksheets to your Access database files. Attaching an Excel worksheet has the advantage of providing up-to-date information if the data in the worksheet is subject to periodic updates. You use the ODBC Administrator application supplied with Access 2.0, Excel 5.0, or Word for Windows 6.0 to create an ODBC *data source* from your Excel worksheet. Data source is a synonym for database when you use the ODBC API to attach tables. Unlike Access 1.x, which installed ODBCADM.EXE, an executable version of the ODBC Administrator application, Access 2.0 and Excel 5.0 install the ODBC Administrator (ODBCINST.DLL) as a function of Windows Control Panel. (Windows NT 3.1 uses ODBCADM.EXE as the ODBC Administrator application.)

To attach an Excel worksheet to an Access database, assuming that you have previously installed the ODBC Administrator application, follow these steps:

ODBC

1. Open the Control Panel and double-click the ODBC icon to display the Data Sources dialog (see fig. 7.31). If you haven't set up any ODBC data sources, the Data Sources (Driver) list is empty. The data sources shown in figure 7.31 are used in later chapters of this book.

2. Click the Add button to display the Add Data Source dialog (see fig. 7.32). Click the Excel Files (*.xls) item (if you are using the Microsoft ODBC driver) or Q+E ExcelFile (for the Q+E ODBC Drivers Pack) in the Installed ODBC Drivers list, and then click the OK button to display the setup dialog for Excel files.

Fig. 7.31

The ODBC Administrator's Data Sources dialog.

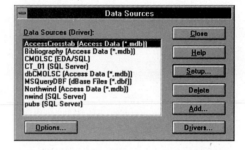

Fig. 7.32

Adding an ODBC data source.

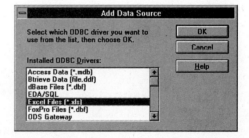

3. Click the Options button of the ODBC Microsoft Excel Setup dialog (if you are using the Microsoft driver) to expand the dialog to show the Driver options of figure 7.33. The Rows to Scan text box specifies the number of rows that the ODBC driver tests to determine the data type of each column (by majority rule).

4. Enter a short name for the worksheet in the Data Source Name text box and a longer description in the Description text box; then click the Select Directory button to display the Select Directory dialog.

5. Select the drive, directory, and Excel worksheet file you want for your data source, as shown in figure 7.34. Click the OK button of the Select Directory dialog to add the new ODBC data source and close the Select Directory dialog.

Fig. 7.33
Setting up an Excel worksheet as an ODBC data source.

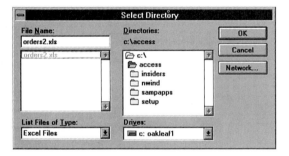

Fig. 7.34
Choosing the .XLS file to use as the ODBC data source.

6. Your new ODBC data source appears in the Data Sources dialog (see fig. 7.35). Click the OK button to close the dialog and then close Control Panel.

7. Launch Access and open a database file, if necessary. Choose A**t**tach Table from the **F**ile menu to display the Attach dialog (see fig. 7.36).

8. Double-click <SQL Database> to display the SQL Data Sources dialog shown in figure 7.37. Double-click the name you gave your new data source to display the Attach Tables dialog.

9. If you attach an Excel workbook with more than one worksheet, each worksheet appears in the Tables in <SQL Database> list. Select the worksheet(s) you want to attach as table(s), and then click the Attach button (see fig. 7.38). A message box confirms that each worksheet is attached as a table. When you've attached all the tables, click the Close button.

Fig. 7.35
The Data Sources
dialog with a new
data source added.

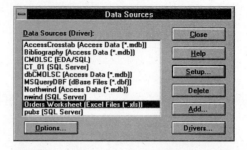

Fig. 7.36
Selecting ODBC
data sources in the
Access Attach
dialog.

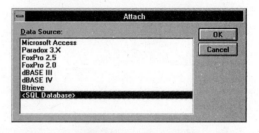

Fig. 7.37
Choosing the
ODBC data source
to attach.

10. Your attached worksheet table appears in the Database window (with the ODBC globe turned to display Africa), as shown in figure 7.39.

Fig. 7.38
Selecting the
worksheet to
attach as a table.

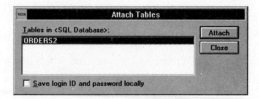

Fig. 7.39
Access's Database
window with
the attached
worksheet
added as a table.

Access Fundamentals

Click the Open button of the Database window to display your attached
worksheet. The appearance of the worksheet as an attached table is identical
to a table imported from a worksheet with one major difference: you cannot
update an attached worksheet. When you attach a table to an Access database
using the ODBC API and the Microsoft ODBC drivers, you only can update
the table if the table has a designated primary-key field. (The imported table
is represented by a read-only **Recordset** object of the **Snapshot** type.)

> **Note**
>
> The Q+E ODBC drivers in the ODBC Driver Pack have an option that enables you to
> edit Excel worksheet and text files that you attach to Access tables. Add the line
> WorkArounds=1 to the entry for your ODBC data source in ODBC.INI to take advan-
> tage of this option. For further information on the ODBCINST.INI and ODBC.INI files,
> see Chapter 26, "Connecting to Client-Server Databases."

Importing Text Files

If the data you want to import into an Access table was developed in a word
processor, database, or other application that cannot export the data as a
.DBF, .WK?, or .XLS file, you need to create a text file in one of the text formats supported by Access. (A *text file* is a file with data consisting of characters that you can read with a text editor, such as Windows Notepad or the
DOS EDIT.COM text editor.) Most DOS-compatible data files created from
data in mainframe computers and files converted from nine-track magnetic
tapes are text files, and Access imports these files in various formats.

> **Note**
>
> EBCDIC (Extended Binary-Coded-Decimal Interchange Code) is a proprietary format used by IBM to encode data stored on nine-track tape and other data interchange media. EBCDIC is similar to the ANSI (American National Standards Institute) and ASCII (American Standard Code for Information Interchange) codes. You need to convert EBCDIC-encoded data to ANSI or ASCII code before the data can be imported into an Access table. Nine-track tape drives designed for PC applications and service bureaus who provide tape-to-disk conversion services handle the EBCDIC-ASCII conversion. The printable (text) characters with values 32 through 127 are the same in ANSI and ASCII, so conversion from ASCII to ANSI, the character set used by Windows and Access, is seldom necessary.

Access refers to the characters that separate fields as *delimiters* or *separators*. In this book, the term *delimiter* refers to characters that identify the end of a field; the term *text identifiers* refers to the single and double quotation marks that you can use to distinguish text from numeric data.

The following list details the formats that Access supports:

Format	Description
Comma-delimited text files (also called CSV [Comma-Separated Value] files)	Commas separate (delimit) fields. The *newline pair*, carriage return (ASCII character 13), and line feed (ASCII character 10) separate records. Some applications enclose all values within double quotation marks; this format often is called *mail-merge* format. Other applications enclose only text (strings) in quotation marks to differentiate between text and numeric values, the standard format for files created by the xBase command COPY TO *FILENAME* DELIMITED.
Tab-delimited text files	These files treat all values (also called ASCII files) as text and separate fields with tabs. Records are separated by newline pairs. Most word processing applications use this format to export tabular text.
Space-delimited files	Access can use spaces to separate fields in a line of text. The use of spaces as delimiter characters is uncommon because it can cause fields, such as names and addresses, to be divided inconsistently into different fields.

Format	Description
Fixed-width text files	Access separates (parses) the individual records into fields based on the position of the data items in a line of text. Newline pairs separate records; every record must have exactly the same length. Spaces pad the fields to a specified fixed width. Using spaces to specify field width is the most common format for data exported by mainframes and minicomputers on nine-track tape. Unlike the delimited and tab-separated files, Access requires that you create an import/export specification before you import a fixed-width text file.

Access requires that you define how text files are to be imported. For delimited files of any type, you first can select the file and then provide the setup parameters. Fixed-width files, however, require that you prepare and save a setup specification before you select the text file to import.

To create an import specification before you select the text file to import, complete the following steps:

1. Activate the Database window to make the import/export commands appear in the **F**ile menu.

2. Choose Imp/Exp **S**etup from the **F**ile menu. The Import/Export Setup dialog appears (see fig. 7.40).

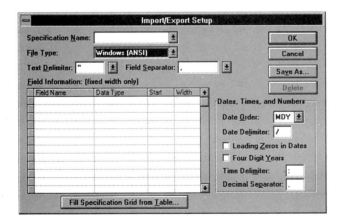

Fig. 7.40
Using the Import/ Export Setup dialog to specify parameters for imported text files.

3. Select the formatting you want for date, time, and decimal fields in the Date, Times, and Numbers frame.

4. If you are importing delimited files, select the field-separator character (usually a comma or a tab character) from the drop-down list box. Select the quotation mark (") as the text delimiter if you are importing files that distinguish between text and other field data types by enclosing text fields in double quotation marks. (The .SDF text files created by xBase applications use double quotation marks surrounding text fields.) Skip to step 8.

5. If you are importing a fixed-width text file, you are required to assign field names, data types, starting positions, and field widths at this point. Text-delimiter and field-separator characters are ignored when fixed-width text files are imported.

Access

2.0

6. If you have a table with a structure the same as or similar to the fixed-width file you plan to import, click the Fill Specification Grid from Table button to display the Fill Specification Grid From Table dialog (see fig. 7.41). Filling the Field Information grid automatically is a new feature of Access 2.0.

Fig. 7.41

Selecting the table on which to model the import specification.

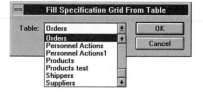

7. Double-click the name of the table whose structure you want to use in the Table list box to add the structure data to the Field Information grid (see fig. 7.42). You can edit the data in the grid if the specification does not match your fixed-width file exactly. If you don't have a table with a format similar to the file you want to import, you need to enter the data in the grid manually.

8. Click Save As. The Save Specification As dialog appears (see fig. 7.43).

9. Enter a descriptive name for the specification in the dialog. Click OK.

After you create and save an import/export setup, you can reuse the setup by choosing Import/Export **S**etup from the **F**ile menu to display the Import/Export Setup dialog. This dialog is the only place where you can select or delete an existing specification that you created. You can select one of your customized setups from the Specification Name drop-down list.

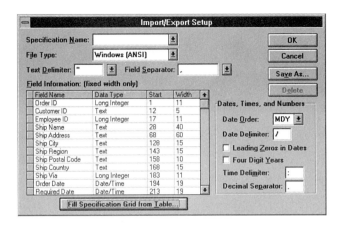

Fig. 7.42
The Import/Export
Setup dialog with
an imported set of
field specifications.

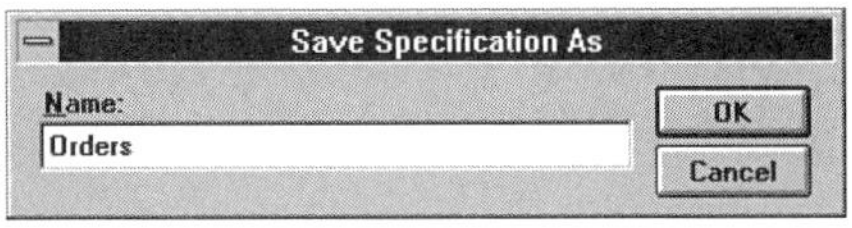

Fig. 7.43
Assigning names
to import/export
specifications.

The specific values of the parameters to be used and the method of calculating field starting points for delimited and fixed-width text file types are described in the two sections that follow.

Using Delimited Text Files

Delimited files can accept a wide variety of field- and record-delimiting characters. The native format (used by files created within WordPerfect) of WordPerfect secondary merge files, for example, uses control characters to separate fields and records. Access provides commas, tabs, and spaces as standard field delimiters. You can type any printable character (such as an asterisk or a dollar sign) in the text box as a delimiter. Because spaces and other special-character delimiting is seldom used, only comma-delimited (.CSV) and tab-delimited files are presented in this chapter.

Word processing applications use both commas and tabs as delimiters in the mail-merge files that they or other applications create for personalized documents. The newline pair is universally used to indicate the end of a record in mail-merge files; a record always consists of a single line of text.

Comma-Delimited Text Files without Text-Identifier Characters

Comma-delimited files come in two styles: with or without quotation marks surrounding text fields. The quotation marks, usually the standard double quotation marks ("), identify the fields within them as having the Text data type. Fields without quotation marks are processed as numeric values. Not all applications offer this capability; for example, .CSV files exported by Excel do not enclose text within quotation marks. Figure 7.44 shows a typical Excel .CSV file opened in the Windows Notepad applet.

Fig. 7.44
A comma-
delimited Excel
file displayed in
the Windows
Notepad applet.

```
                    Notepad - ORDERS.CSV
 File   Edit   Search   Help
 Order ID,Customer ID,Employee ID,Ship Name,Ship Address,Ship City,Ship
 10000,FRANS,6,Franchi S.p.A.,Via Monte Bianco 34,Torino,,10100,Italy,3,
 10001,MEREP,8,Mère Paillarde,43 rue St. Laurent,Montréal,Québec,H1J 1C3
 10002,FOLKO,3,Folk och Fä HB,Åkergatan 24,Bräcke,,S-844 67,Sweden,3,5/1
 10003,SIMOB,8,Simons bistro,Vinbæltet 34,København,,1734,Denmark,1,5/15
 10004,VAFFE,3,Vaffeljernet,Smagsløget 45,Århus,,8200,Denmark,2,5/16/91,
 10005,WARTH,5,Wartian Herkku,Torikatu 38,Oulu,,90110,Finland,3,5/20/91,
 10006,FRANS,8,Franchi S.p.A.,Via Monte Bianco 34,Torino,,10100,Italy,1,
 10007,MORGK,4,Morgenstern Gesundkost,Heerstr. 22,Leipzig,,04179,Germany
 10008,FURIB,3,Furia Bacalhau e Frutos do Mar,Jardim das rosas n. 32,Lis
 10009,SEUES,8,Seven Seas Imports,90 Wadhurst Rd.,London,,OX15 4NB,UK,1,
 10010,SIMOB,8,Simons bistro,Vinbæltet 34,København,,1734,Denmark,1,5/28
 10011,WELLI,6,Wellington Importadora,"Rua do Mercado, 12",Resende,SP,08
 10012,LINOD,6,LINO-Delicateses,Ave. 5 de Mayo Porlamar,I. de Margarita,
 10013,RICSU,3,Richter Supermarkt,Starenweg 5,Genève,,1204,Switzerland,3
 10014,GROSR,4,GROSELLA-Restaurante,5ª Ave. Los Palos Grandes,Caracas,DF
```

> **Note**
>
> Using Notepad to view files that fit within its 60K file size limitation is a quick way to determine the type of text file that you are dealing with. If the file is longer than 60K, you can use Windows Write to view the file. Make sure, however, that you do not save the file as a .WRI file after you view or edit it. If you used Write to edit the file, choose Save **A**s from the **F**ile menu and specify a .TXT file.

To import values in a comma-delimited (.CSV) file into an Access table, follow these steps:

1. Activate the Database window, making the **F**ile menu's import commands available.

2. Choose **I**mport from the **F**ile menu to display the Import dialog (see fig. 7.45).

Fig. 7.45
Selecting a
delimited text file
in the Import
dialog.

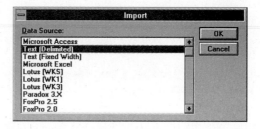

3. Select Text (Delimited) and then click OK. The Select File dialog appears (see fig. 7.46).

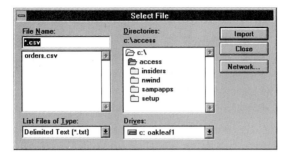

Fig. 7.46
Choosing the .CSV file to import.

4. Select the drive, directory, and file name of the .CSV file from which the values are to be imported. Click OK. (Enter ***.csv** to display only .CSV files in the File Name list.) The simplified version of the Import Text Options dialog appears. Click the Options button to display the complete dialog (see fig. 7.47).

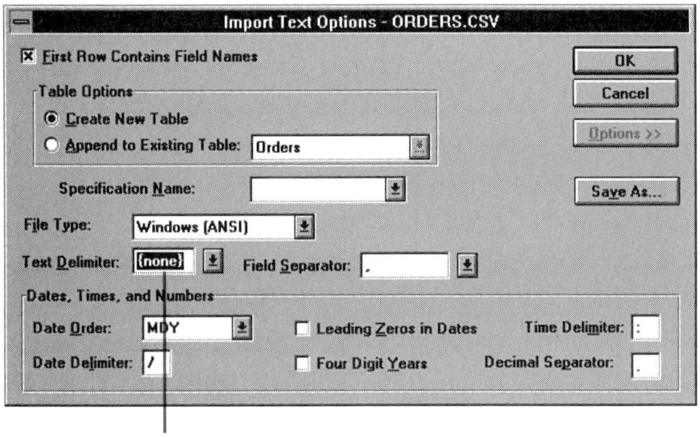

No text delimiter

Fig. 7.47
The detailed version of the Import Text Options dialog.

5. Because the .CSV file includes the field names, click the First Row Contains Field Names check box. Access offers to append records to an existing table, Orders. In this case, accept the default, Create New Table. You do not have a specification name yet for .CSV files, so accept the blank default. Excel uses the ANSI character set so the default value, Windows (ANSI), for the file type is correct.

6. Because Excel .CSV files do not use text-delimiter characters, open the Text Delimiter combo list and select **{none}**. Accept the default Field Separator, a comma.

7. Make any changes you need to the controls in the Dates, Times, and Numbers frame, and then click the Save As button. The Save Specification As dialog appears (see fig. 7.48). Enter a descriptive name and then click the OK button to return to the Import Text Options dialog.

Fig. 7.48

The Save Specifications As dialog.

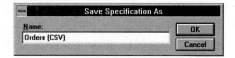

8. Click the OK button of the Import Text Options dialog to create the new ORDERS1 table from the .CSV file.

From this point, the procedure for importing text files is the same as the procedure for importing spreadsheet files. If no errors occur during importation, you receive the Import Results dialog with the number of records imported.

Caution

If you export the Orders table from NWIND.MDB to Excel and then use Excel to create an ORDERS.CSV file and import the file into an Access table, you may receive an extraordinary number of errors. Most of such errors are due to a mixture of numeric values for United States ZIP codes and alphanumeric values used for Canadian, U.K., and European postal codes. The first data cell in the Postal Code column is a number, so the Access import procedure determines that the field should have the Number field data type. Thus, mixed value fields (letters and numbers) cause import errors. A wise policy is to not import delimited text files without text identification characters to Access tables.

Comma-Delimited Text Files with Text-Identifier Characters

The default delimited text file type of dBASE, called .SDF for Standard Data Format, created by the COPY TO *FILENAME* DELIMITED command, creates comma-delimited files with text fields surrounded by double quotation marks. (Date and Numeric field types do not have quotation marks.) This type of delimited file is standard in many other database systems, as well as project and personal information management applications. Figure 7.49 shows an example of an .SDF text file created by dBASE III+.

> ### Note
>
> The dBASE III+ table ORDERS.DBF, used to create ORDERS.SDF, was created by exporting the Orders table of NWIND.MDB in dBASE III format. When you create a dBASE III file from an Access file, Access translates characters with ANSI values 128 through 255 to the PC-8 character set used by character-based DOS and OS/2 applications. Letters with diacriticals and special characters of Scandinavian and romanized Slavic languages do not have the same values in the PC-8. These letters and characters appear as black rectangles in figure 7.49 because the PC-8 values do not correspond to printable ANSI values.

The specification for double quotation marks as the text identifier is one of the differences between the Import Text Options dialog entries of the ORDERS.CSV and ORDERS.SDF files (compare figs. 7.47 and 7.50). The first row of data exported by dBASE in .SDF format does not contain field names. dBASE uses the PC-8 character set, therefore you need to select "DOS or OS/2 (PC-8)" from the File Type drop-down list. If you fail to do so, black rectangles similar to those shown in figure 7.49 appear in your Access table if your .SDF file contains special characters.

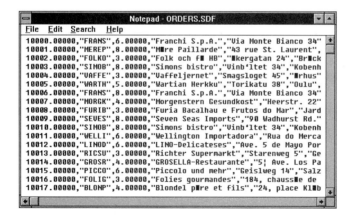

Fig. 7.49
A comma-delimited text file with PC-8 characters and text identifiers using double quotation marks.

Fig. 7.50
The Import Text
Options dialog for
files with text-
identification
characters.

PC-8 ——
conversion

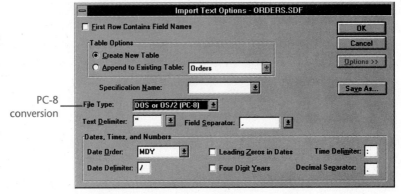

Note

If you have a table that corresponds to the structure of the delimited text file you're importing and you don't want to append the text records to that file, create a "structure-only" (no records) copy of the table with a different name. Import the delimited text file into the new table. If you don't create a table into which to import a delimited text file that does not have field names in the first record, Access names the fields 1, 2, 3, and so on up to the number of fields in the text file.

Tab-Delimited Text Files

Word processing applications often use tab characters to separate fields in mail-merge files. These tab characters usually define the fields of tables when you convert conventional text to tabular format (and vice versa) in word processors such as Word for Windows. Figure 7.51 shows a tab-delimited text file in Windows Notepad. Tab-delimited text files rarely use text-identification characters; however, the ORDERS.WWM file of figure 7.51 was created by exporting the Orders table of NWIND.MDB in Word for Windows Merge format. (Exporting table data is discussed later in this chapter.) Access adds double quotation marks as text-identifier characters so that Word does not interpret embedded newline pairs (carriage return and line feed, or CR/LF) in text fields as the end of the record. (Allowing embedded newline pairs in text fields is not a recommended database design practice.)

Many organizations acquire RDBMSs because the amount of their data is too large for their word processing application to maintain mailing lists for direct-mail advertising and other promotional and fund-raising purposes. RDBMSs also enable you to create specialized merge data files for specific types of customers, ranges of ZIP codes, and other parameters you select.

Figure 7.52 shows a conventional Word for Windows merge data file displayed in Word 2.0.

```
=                    Notepad - ORDERS.WWM                    ▼ ▲
File  Edit  Search  Help
"Order_ID"     "Customer_ID"   "Employee_ID"    "Ship_Name"      "S ▲
10000  "FRANS" 6       "Franchi S.p.A."        "Via Monte Bianco
10001  "MEREP" 8       "Mère Paillarde"        "43 rue St. Lauren
10002  "FOLKO" 3       "Folk och Fä HB"        "Åkergatan 24"   "B
10003  "SIMOB" 8       "Simons bistro" "Vinbæltet 34"  "København
10004  "VAFFE" 3       "Vaffeljernet"  "Smagsløget 45" "Århus"
10005  "WARTH" 5       "Wartian Herkku"        "Torikatu 38"   "O
10006  "FRANS" 8       "Franchi S.p.A."        "Via Monte Bianco
10007  "MORGK" 4       "Morgenstern Gesundkost"        "Heerstr.
10008  "FURIB" 3       "Furia Bacalhau e Frutos do Mar"        "J
10009  "SEVES" 8       "Seven Seas Imports"    "90 Wadhurst Rd."
10010  "SIMOB" 8       "Simons bistro" "Vinbæltet 34"  "København
10011  "WELLI" 6       "Wellington Importadora"        "Rua do Me
10012  "LINOD" 6       "LINO-Delicateses"      "Ave. 5 de Mayo Po
10013  "RICSU" 3       "Richter Supermarkt"    "Starenweg 5"   "G
10014  "GROSR" 4       "GROSELLA-Restaurante"  "5ª Ave. Los Palos
10015  "PICCO" 6       "Piccolo und mehr"      "Geislweg 14"   "S
10016  "FOLIG" 3       "Folies gourmandes"     "184, chaussée de ▼
←                                                              →
```

Fig. 7.51
A tab-delimited text file with text-identification characters displayed in the Notepad applet.

Fortunately, Access has a simple process for converting the merge data files used by most word processors to text files that can be imported and maintained by an Access database application. In Word for Windows, for example, you simply open the merge data file in whatever format you use (usually the native .DOC) and save the document in Text Only (.TXT) format with a different file name. WordPerfect 5+ (using CONVERT.EXE) and WordPerfect for Windows offer a variety of export formats for their secondary merge files. Unless you have a specific file type in mind, select the tab-delimited format for these files.

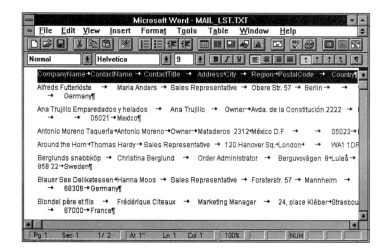

Fig. 7.52
A Word for Windows 2.0 merge data file that you can export as a text file.

Handling Fixed-Width Text Files

If you have a choice of text file formats for the data you plan to import into Access, avoid using fixed-width text files by choosing a delimited file format. If you are importing data created by a mainframe or minicomputer, however, it is likely that the data is in fixed-width format. Fixed-width text files require that you enter a complete specification for the location and width of each field. As mentioned earlier in this chapter, you must name the fields, rather than rely on the first line of the text file to provide names for you. Fixed-width text files seldom come with a field name header in the first line.

A fixed-width text file looks like the file in figure 7.53. Fixed-width text files often contain more spaces than data characters. In a tab-delimited file, the spaces between fields are not included in the file itself but are added by the text editor (see the Notepad in fig. 7.37) when tab characters (ASCII or ANSI character 9) are encountered. In a fixed-width file, each space is represented by ASCII or ANSI character 32.

> **Note**
>
> The fields of fixed-width text files often run together; the first four fields of the ORDERS.TXT file shown in figure 7.53 are Order ID (five digits), Customer ID (four letters), Employee ID (one digit), and Ship Name (40 characters). The Ship Name field is padded with spaces to a width of 40 characters. The appearance of the data in figure 7.53 is typical of COBOL "text dumps" from mainframe and minicomputer tables. If you have the COBOL file description for the fixed-width table, it is much easier to complete the import specification.

Fig. 7.53

A fixed-width text file displayed in Notepad.

To import a fixed-width text file into an Access table, complete the following procedure:

1. Choose Import/Export **S**etup from the **F**ile menu. The Import/Export Setup dialog appears without the Field Information entries. Access requires an import specification before you can select the fixed-width text file for importing. You can disregard the field delimiters and text-identification characters when you are working with fixed-width text files.

2. In the Field Information text boxes, enter the field name and data type for each field contained in the records. With fixed-width fields, you can select data types from a drop-down list that includes the standard field data types and those defined by the FieldSize property, such as Integer.

3. In the Start box, enter the beginning position of the first character of the field. Then, in the Width text box, enter the number of characters in the field. You often can obtain the required entries from a file-specification sheet provided with the disk or tape on which the file was stored originally. If you do not have a specification sheet, add the values of the starting position to the field width of the last field you entered in order to find the starting position of the next field.

4. Repeat steps 2 and 3 until you fully specify each field. Figure 7.54 shows the specification for the ORDERS.TXT file. Note that the width of the text fields containing digits does not necessarily correspond to the actual width of the field size of the Number field data type into which the text fields containing digits are converted.

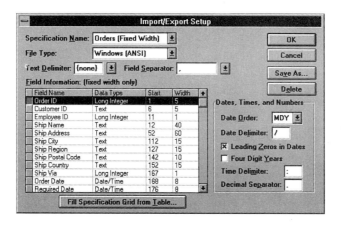

Fig. 7.54
The file specification for the fixed-width ORDERS.TXT file.

5. Save your import specification by clicking the Save As button. The Save Specification As dialog appears.

Caution

If you do not save your specification, you will lose all your work.

---

6. In the Save Specification As dialog, enter a name for your format.

7. Choose **I**mport from the **F**ile menu. The Import dialog appears.

8. Select Text (Fixed Width) from the Data Source list of the Import dialog. Another variation of the Import/Export Options dialog appears—this time with a Specification Name drop-down list (see fig. 7.55).

Fig. 7.55
The Import Text Options dialog after you create a file import/export specification.

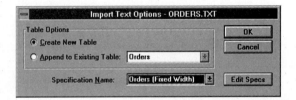

9. Select the name you assigned to the import specification for the fixed-width file, and click OK.

From this point, the import procedure is the same as that for spreadsheets and delimited text files.

Troubleshooting

When importing tables created from fixed-width text files, a large number of errors occur.

You probably have miscalculated one or more of the starting positions of a field. Locate the first field name with a problem; the names following it usually have problems, too. Choose Import/Export **S**etup from the **F**ile menu to correct the errors in field position. Close all open tables. From the Database window, select the table you imported and press the Delete key. If you have an Import Errors table, delete it, too. You cannot delete an open table.

Appending Text Data to an Existing Table

If the data you are importing is provided on a floppy disk, you might need several disks to store the data. Fixed-width text files especially require more floppy disks because they usually are derived from data on mini- and mainframe computers, and the fixed-width format is quite inefficient. If you have imported multiple-disk data into dBASE files, for example, you probably learned that you must concatenate all the files on your hard disk into one large text file. You concatenate files by using the DOS COPY *file1+file2 file3* command or by appending each file to a separate dBASE file and then appending the remaining dBASE files to the file created from the first disk. This is a very tedious process.

Access enables you to append data from text files to an existing table. In addition to simplifying the process described in the preceding paragraph, you can update an imported file with new text data by appending it directly from the source text file, instead of by creating a new Access table, and then appending the new table to the existing one.

If you saved the import/export specifications when you first created the table from a text file, you can append a text file to an existing table by following these steps:

1. Make a backup copy of your table in the same database or another database in case an error occurs during the Append operation.

2. Choose **I**mport from the **F**ile menu.

3. Select the type of source data from the Import dialog.

4. In the Import Options dialog, click Append to Existing Table.

5. From the drop-down list of existing tables, select the table to which you want to append the data.

6. Open the Specification Name drop-down list, select the import specification that applies to the table, and then click OK.

At the end of the appending process, a message box appears reporting the number of new records added to your table. The Import Errors table displays any errors made.

> ### Note
>
> Maintaining a backup copy of the table to which you are appending files is very important. If you accidentally select the wrong import specification for the file, you can end up with one error for each appended record. Then, if you do not have a backup file, you must delete the appended records and start over. To use a backup table file, close and delete the damaged table. Then choose Rena**m**e from the **F**ile menu to change the name of the backup table to the name of the damaged table.

Using the Clipboard to Import Data

If another Windows application generates the data you want to import, you can use the Windows Clipboard to transfer the data without having to create a file. This technique is especially useful for making corrections to a single record with many fields or for appending new records to a table. This process requires a table with the proper field structure so that you can paste the data copied to the Clipboard in the other application. Pasting rows from an Excel spreadsheet, for example, requires a table with fields containing data types that correspond to those of each column that you copy to the Clipboard. Other Windows applications that can copy tabular data to the Clipboard use similar techniques.

Pasting New Records to a Table

To import data from the Clipboard and then append the data to an existing table or table structure, use the following procedure:

1. Open the application you are using to copy the data to the Clipboard—in this case, Microsoft Excel. Then open the file that contains the data. If you have less than 3M of memory, you might have to close Access before you can open Excel.

2. Select the range to be appended to the table (see fig. 7.56). The Excel columns you select must start with the column that corresponds to the first field of your Access table. You do not, however, need to copy all the columns that correspond to fields in your table. Access supplies blank values in the columns of your appended records that are not included in your Excel range. Remember that, if any of the columns you select contain formulas, the values must be frozen.

Fig. 7.56
Cells selected in Excel to be appended to an Access table using the Clipboard.

Selected — fields

	A	B	C	D	E	F	G	H	I
1	Order ID	Customer	Employee	Ship Nam	Ship Addr	Ship City	Ship Regi	Ship Post	Ship Cc
2	10000	FRANS	6	Franchi S.	Via Monte	Torino		10100	Italy
3	10001	MEREP	8	Mère Pail	43 rue St.	Montréal	Québec	H1J 1C3	Canada
4	10002	FOLKO	3	Folk och f	Åkergatan	Bräcke		S-844 67	Swede
5	10003	SIMOB	8	Simons bi	Vinbæltet	København		1734	Denma
6	10004	VAFFE	3	Vaffeljerne	Smagsløg	Århus		8200	Denma
7	10005	WARTH	5	Wartian H	Torikatu 3	Oulu		90110	Finland
8	10006	FRANS	8	Franchi S.	Via Monte	Torino		10100	Italy
9	10007	MORGK	4	Morgenste	Heerstr. 22	Leipzig		04179	German
10	10008	FURIB	3	Furia Bac	Jardim da	Lisboa		1675	Portuge
11	10009	SEVES	8	Seven Se	90 Wadhu	London		OX15 4NB	UK
12	10010	SIMOB	8	Simons bi	Vinbæltet	København		1734	Denma
13	10011	WELLI	6	Wellingtor	Rua do M	Resende	SP	08737-363	Brazil
14	10012	LINOD	6	LINO-Deli	Ave. 5 de	I. de Marg	Nueva Es	4980	Venezu
15	10013	RICSU	3	Richter Su	Starenwec	Genève		1204	Switzer
16	10014	GROSR	4	GROSELL	5ª Ave. Lo	Caracas	DF	1081	Venezu
17	10015	PICCO	6	Piccolo un	Geislweg	Salzburg		5020	Austria
18	10016	FOLIG	3	Folies gou	184, chaus	Lille		59000	France

ORDERS.XLS

3. To copy the selected cells to the Clipboard, press Ctrl+C or choose **C**opy from the **E**dit menu.

4. Launch Access, and open the table to which you are appending the records in Datasheet View.

5. Choose Paste Appen**d** from the Access **E**dit menu. If no errors occur during the pasting process, a message box reports how many new records you added (see fig. 7.57). Click OK. The records are appended to the bottom of your Access table (see fig. 7.58). Choose **S**how All Records from the **R**ecords menu to place the appended records in the correct order.

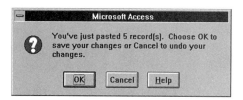

Fig. 7.57
The message box that follows a successful appending operation.

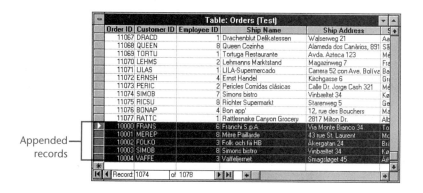

Fig. 7.58
Records appended to an Access table.

Troubleshooting

Paste errors occur when pasting spreadsheet cells into a table.

Errors usually occur during the Paste/Append process for one of two reasons: the data types in the Excel cells do not match those in the corresponding fields of your Access table, or you attempted to paste records with data that duplicates information in key fields of the table. Both types of errors result in Access creating a Paste Errors table containing information on the records with the errors. The Paste Errors table for field type mismatches is similar in purpose and appearance to the Import Errors table described earlier in this chapter.

Errors caused by duplicate primary-key violations result in the following series of cascading message boxes:

1. Figure 7.59 shows the first message you receive indicating a primary-key violation. Access does not offer a Cancel option; therefore, you must click OK.

Fig. 7.59

The dialog indicating that an attempt was made to paste a record with a duplicate key value.

2. Next, a message box appears enabling you to suppress further error messages (see fig. 7.60). If you want to cancel the append operation, click Cancel. Otherwise, click Yes to attempt to paste the remaining records without reporting further errors. If you want to see which errors occur as they are encountered, click No.

Fig. 7.60

The message box enabling you to continue pasting records without reporting more errors.

3. A message box reports how many records were pasted successfully (see fig. 7.61). Click OK.

Fig. 7.61

The message box indicating that some records were pasted.

4. Finally, a message box reports where the records that couldn't be pasted were placed (see fig. 7.62). Click OK.

Fig. 7.62
The message that
some records could
not be pasted.

Figure 7.63 illustrates the result of this Pandora's box of messages. The set of
five records copied to the Clipboard from Excel contained two records that
duplicated key-field values in the existing table. Access pasted the remaining
three records and inserted the two records with duplicate key values into a
Paste Errors table.

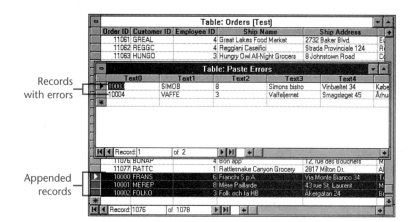

Fig. 7.63
Tables showing
pasted records and
key-field index
errors.

If you specified one or more primary-key fields for your table, records that
duplicate key field values are not appended. Tables without primary-key fields
do not preclude adding duplicate records. The capability to index a nonkey
field with the condition "no duplicates allowed" is useful when you make
new entries into a spreadsheet or word processing document, and you want
to append the new entries as records to a table. You preserve the uniqueness
of the records by preventing the addition of records that duplicate records
already in your table.

> **Note**
>
> When pasting or importing large numbers of records to a table, you must specify primary-key fields or a no-duplicates-allowed index for fields that later may become the primary key before you import any data. If you import the data before you create the primary-key fields index, you may find many duplicate records in the table. Then when Access attempts to create a no-duplicates index on the key fields, you receive the following message: "Can't have duplicate key." You must manually review all the added records for duplicates because Access does not create an Errors table in this case. If, on the other hand, the data you are importing contains redundant information that you ultimately will remove to one or more secondary tables, you must import every record. Do not assign key fields or no-duplicates indexes in this case. The section "Deleting Redundant Fields in Imported Tables," later in this chapter, discusses the requirement to import every record when records contain one-to-many relations.

Replacing Records by Pasting from the Clipboard

You can replace existing records in an Access table by pasting data in the Clipboard over the records. This process is useful when you are updating records with data from another Windows application. The data you paste must have a one-to-one column-to-field correspondence and must begin with the first field of the table. You need not, however, paste new data in all the fields. If no data is pasted in a field that is not included in the copied data's range, that field retains its original values.

To use data in the Clipboard to replace existing records in a table, follow this procedure:

1. Select and copy the data from the other application that you want to paste to the Clipboard, using the method previously described for appending records from Clipboard data.

   If you choose more than one row of data in Excel, for example, the rows must have a one-to-one correspondence with the records to be replaced in the Access table. The one-to-one correspondence is likely to occur only if the table is indexed and the source data you are copying is sorted in the same order as the index. You can paste only contiguous rows from Excel.

2. Open your Access table. To select the records to be replaced by the Clipboard data, click the selection button for a single record or drag the mouse across the buttons for multiple records.

If you are replacing multiple records, the number of records you select must be equal to or exceed the number of rows you copied to the Clipboard. If the number of records selected is less than the number of rows, the remaining rows are ignored.

If you are replacing records in a table with key fields or a no-duplicates index, the columns of the replacement data corresponding to the key or indexed fields of the table must match exactly the key fields of the selected records. Otherwise, you receive the key duplication error message sequence.

3. From the Access **E**dit menu, choose **P**aste. In this case, instead of appending the records, the contents of the existing records are overwritten, and you see a dialog telling you how many records were replaced successfully.

When you use **P**aste for a replacement record rather than Paste Appen**d** for a new record with an identical key field value, Access suppresses the key violation error messages.

> **Note**
>
> If you do not select one or more records to be replaced by the Pasting operation, and the caret is located within a data cell of one of your records or a data cell is selected, Access attempts to paste all the data in the Clipboard to this single cell, rather than to the records. If the data does not create a mismatch type error or exceed 255 characters (if the caret is in a Text field), you do not receive a warning message. If you notice unexpected data values in the cell, Access has pasted all the data to a single cell. Press Esc before selecting another record; Access restores the original value of the data cell.

Modifying Attached and Imported Tables

Access provides a great deal of flexibility in the presentation of the Datasheet View of tables. You can rearrange the sequence of fields in Datasheet View without changing the underlying structure of the database. You also can alter the Caption property of the fields to change the names of the field name buttons. Although you cannot modify the field names, field data types, or FieldLength properties of attached tables, you can use the Format property to display the data in attached or imported tables in various ways.

Restructuring the Presentation of Tables

The basic structure of the tables you attach or import is controlled by the structure of the files from which the table was created. The original structure, unfortunately, may not be in the sequence you want to use for data entry. Database design, for example, often displays the key fields in a left-to-right sequence, starting with the first field. This sequence may not be the best sequence for entering data. You can change the order of the fields displayed by dragging and dropping the field name buttons of attached or imported tables to new locations, using the method described in Chapter 5, "Entering, Editing, and Validating Data in Tables."

Adding Fields to Tables with Imported Data

You can add fields to tables that use imported data. During the development of your database application, you may need to repeatedly import data into your table. Therefore, you should append new fields to the end of the field list in Design View rather than insert them between existing fields. The imported data fills the fields in the sequence of the rows in the field list, and the added fields contain null values. You then can rearrange the display position of the new fields in Design View, as described in the preceding section.

Changing Field Data Types of Imported Files

Access converts all numeric data within imported files to the **Double** data type. The only exception is Btrieve files, where Access assigns Byte, Integer, Long Integer, and Single data types when you attach or import Btrieve files that include these data types. The following list contains recommendations for field data type changes for data imported from any type of source file:

- Use *Integer* or *Long Integer* field data types for numeric fields that do not require decimal values. Your database files consume less disk space, and your applications run faster.

- Change the data type of values that represent money to the data type *Currency* to eliminate rounding errors.

- Assign FieldLength property values to text-type fields. You should assign FieldLength values no greater than the longest text entry you expect to make. If you assign a FieldLength value less than the number of characters in the field, characters in positions beyond the FieldLength value are lost irretrievably.

Because Paradox 3+ does not provide a memo field data type, you often can find comments in large, fixed-width alphanumeric fields. If you are importing Paradox files that contain fields of comments, you should convert the fields to memo fields unless you plan to export the data back to a Paradox 3+ file. (You cannot export a table containing a memo-type field to Paradox 3+ files.) The same recommendation applies to comments in variable-length string fields of Btrieve files.

Adding or Modifying Other Field Properties

The following list includes properties of both attached and imported tables that you can change:

Property	Description
Caption	Use this property to change the caption of the field name buttons when using attached files. You can assign any FieldName property to imported tables.
DecimalPlaces	You can specify the number of decimal places to be displayed for numeric values other than Byte, Integer, and Long Integer.
DefaultValue	Default values are substituted for data elements missing in the imported or attached file. The default values, however, do not replace zeros and blank strings that represent "no entry" in the fields of most PC database files.
Format	You can create custom formats to display the data in the most readable form.
ValidationRule	Validation rules do not affect importing data; they affect only editing the data or appending new records in Access. You cannot use a validation rule to filter imported records. Filtering, in this case, means importing only those records that meet the validation rule.
ValidationText	Prompts created from validation text assist data entry operators when they begin using a new table.

Deleting Redundant Fields in Imported Tables

The purpose of a relational database is to eliminate redundant data in tables. If you design a database that does not use data imported or attached from existing databases, you can eliminate data redundancy by following the normalization rules of relational database design described in Chapter 23, "Exploring Relational Database Design and Implementation." When you attach files, however, you are at the mercy of the database designer who originally created the files. Any redundant data the attached file contains is likely to remain a permanent characteristic of the file. Existing database structures are substantially inert; developers of applications that work usually are reluctant to make changes. Changes may introduce new problems that can come back to haunt the developers later.

If you import table data from a file or append records by pasting from the Clipboard, you can eliminate data redundancy by restructuring the resulting tables. The Invoice tables used for the examples of this chapter contain one record for each invoice. When a customer makes more than one purchase, the customer information is duplicated in the invoice file for each purchase. You need to create separate tables for customers and invoices. The Customer table should contain one record per customer, with name and address information. The Invoice table should contain one record per customer with date, amount, and other information specific to the transaction.

The process of removing redundancy from existing tables by dividing them into two or more related tables is not a simple task. You must create a query that establishes the relationship between two tables that contain one record for each invoice based on a new primary-key field. Then you delete the duplicate records from the Customer table. Fortunately, the Import Errors table can do much of the work for you; import the data into a new table with primary-key fields or a no-duplicate index on the customer name and address.

Another type of redundancy is the presence of fields in tables that have values calculated from other fields, either within the table itself or in the fields of related tables. Any field with values derived from combinations of values within the table or accessible in any other related table within the database or attached to the database contains redundant data. In this case, you simply can remove the redundant field and perform the calculation with a query. You should not remove redundant fields, however, until you verify that your calculated values match those in the redundant field to be replaced.

You need to learn about queries and joining tables, the subject of the next four chapters, to know how to eliminate redundancy in imported tables. The point of this discussion is to let you know that you can perform much of the restructuring by using specialized Access operations, and to caution you not to attempt to remove duplicate data from imported tables prematurely.

Exporting Data from Access Tables

▶ "Joining
Tables to Create Multitable
Queries,"
p. 356

You can export data contained in Access tables in any format you can use to import data. The most common export operation with PC RDBMSs is the creation of mail-merge files, used with word processing applications and spreadsheet files, for data analysis. In most cases, you may want to export the result of a query, enabling you to select specific records to export rather than the entire contents of a file. Exporting tables created from action queries is discussed in Chapter 11, "Using Action Queries."

Exporting Data through the Windows Clipboard

If a Windows application is to use your exported data, the simplest method to export data is to copy the records you want to export to the Windows Clipboard and then paste the data into the other application. You can copy specific groups of contiguous records to the Clipboard by using the techniques described in Chapter 5, "Entering, Editing, and Validating Data in Tables."

To create a merge data file from the Customers table of the Northwind sample database for use with Word for Windows, follow these steps:

1. Activate the Database window, and then open the NWIND.MDB database.

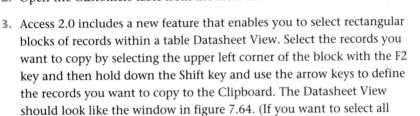

2. Open the Customers table from the table list.

3. Access 2.0 includes a new feature that enables you to select rectangular blocks of records within a table Datasheet View. Select the records you want to copy by selecting the upper left corner of the block with the F2 key and then hold down the Shift key and use the arrow keys to define the records you want to copy to the Clipboard. The Datasheet View should look like the window in figure 7.64. (If you want to select all fields of all records in the table, choose Select **A**ll Records from the **E**dit menu.)

4. Press Ctrl+C or choose **C**opy from the **E**dit menu to copy the selected records to the Clipboard.

5. Open Word for Windows, and choose **N**ew from the **F**ile menu to create a new window for your merge data file.

6. Press Ctrl+V or choose **P**aste from the **E**dit menu to paste the records from the Clipboard into your new document. Access 2.0 pastes the records as a fully-formatted table in Word for Windows, as illustrated by figure 7.65. The column widths you select in Access are used to define the column widths of the Word table. This makes Access 2.0 more compatible with Excel; when you paste a group of Excel worksheet cells to Word, you create an unformatted table. (Access 1.x pastes unformatted records in tab-delimited format.)

When you copy Access records to the Clipboard, the first line contains field names, no matter what group of records you select. If you append individual records or groups of records to those already pasted to a document in another application, you must manually remove the duplicated field names.

Fig. 7.64

Customer records
selected for
copying to the
Clipboard.

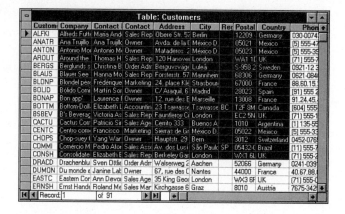

Fig. 7.65

Data in figure 7.64
imported into a
Word for Win-
dows document.

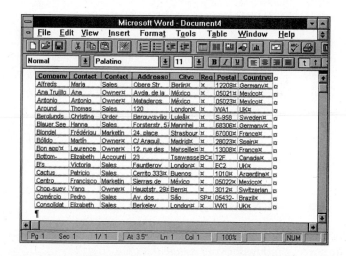

Note

The field names pasted into the Word for Windows documents contain spaces.
Spaces, however, are not allowed in the first (field names) row for merge data documents. Delete the spaces or replace them with underscores so that Word for Windows accepts the names. If you do not remove the spaces, you receive an error
message when you try to use the document during the Merge operation.

Exporting Data as a Text File

Exporting a table involves a sequence of operations quite similar to importing a file with the same format. To export a table as a comma-delimited file that you can use as a merge file with a wide variety of word processing applications, complete these steps:

1. Activate the Database window.

2. Choose **E**xport from the **F**ile menu. The Export dialog appears, enabling you to select the type of file to which the table is to be exported (see fig. 7.66).

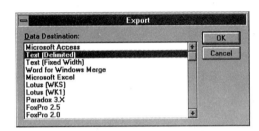

Fig. 7.66
The dialog for choosing the file format of an exported table.

3. Select Text (Delimited), and click OK. The Select Microsoft Access Object dialog appears, enabling you to select the table to export (see fig. 7.67). Select the Customers table for this example, and click OK.

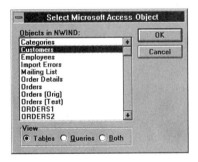

Fig. 7.67
The dialog for selecting the table to export.

Access provides a default file name with the extension .TXT for all text files (see fig. 7.68). The file name consists of the first eight characters of the table name, with any spaces or other punctuation (except underscores) removed.

4. Edit the file name, if necessary, to properly identify the file and choose the destination drive and directory. Then click OK. The abbreviated Export Text Options dialog appears.

Fig. 7.68
The File Save As dialog disguised as the Export to File dialog.

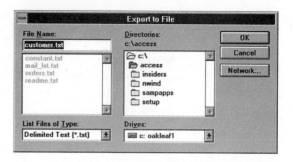

5. Click the Options button to display the full Export Text Options dialog (see fig. 7.69). The defaults shown in the Export Text Options dialog are standard for comma-delimited files with text-identification characters.

Fig. 7.69
The full Export Text Options dialog for delimited files.

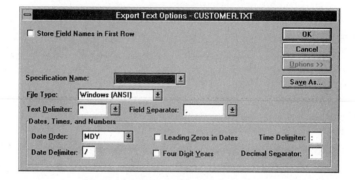

6. Click OK. Access creates the comma-delimited file, consisting of all records in the table. A portion of a comma-delimited file exported from the Customers table and displayed in the Notepad applet is shown in figure 7.70.

> **Note**
>
> The two highlighted lines in figure 7.70 are a single record from the Access table that has been split into two text records during the export process. A newline pair is included in the Address field of the record for Blum's Goods. The purpose of the newline pair is to separate a single field into two lines, The Blum Building and 143 Blum Rd. Use of newline pairs within fields causes many problems with exported files. As mentioned earlier in this chapter, use of embedded newline pairs in text fields in not a good database design practice. Use two address fields if you need secondary address lines.

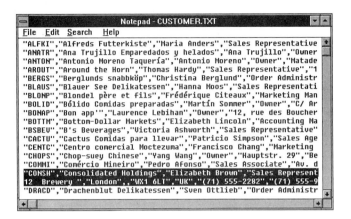

Fig. 7.70
The comma-delimited file created from Northwind's Customers table.

The records in files created by Access are exported in the order of the primary key. Any other order you may have created is ignored. If you do not assign primary-key fields, the records are exported in the sequence that you entered them into the table.

Exporting Data in Other File Formats

In addition to text files, you can export data to any other file format that Access can import. Access supports export to Excel .XLS files (in formats for versions 2.0 through 4.0 and a new format for version 5.0), Lotus 1-2-3 and Symphony .WK? format, rich-text format (.RTF) files for Microsoft Word and other Windows word processing applications, Btrieve, Paradox for DOS 3.x and 4.x formats, and dBASE III/III+ and IV formats.

> **Note**
>
> When you export a dBASE file, Access does not create .NDX files corresponding to the primary key or any additional indexes you might have created in Access. Similarly, exporting a Paradox .DB file does not create an associated .PX file to accompany it. You must use dBASE, one of its clones, or Paradox to re-create any index files required for your application in the other RDBMSs.

As mentioned near the end of the preceding chapter, you can export the content of tables and queries with the Output To choice of the File menu or the Output to Excel, Output to Word, Output to Notepad, and Output to Mail Merge buttons. The File, Output To command is not the same as the buttons; the buttons transfer data from your object via DDE or OLE Automation to the specified application. Using Output to Excel is discussed in

Chapter 21, and using Output to Word and Output to Mail Merge is covered in Chapter 22.

From Here...

Importing data created by other applications is one of the most important subjects when explaining how to use an RDBMS with a new and, for PC RDBMSs, unusual file structure. Fortunately, with Access you can attach dBASE, Paradox, and even Btrieve files; Btrieve file compatibility is uncommon in PC RDBMSs. After you create your database applications using Access forms, reports, and macros and change over to Access as your primary RDBMS, you probably will choose to import all your files into the Access native .MDB structure.

The next four chapters deal with *queries*—the method used by Access to enable you to select the specific data you need from one or more tables:

- Chapter 8, "Using Query by Example," introduces you to Access's graphical QBE design window.

- Chapter 9, "Understanding Operators and Expressions in Access," shows you how to create expressions that you use to add criteria to your queries.

- Chapter 10, "Creating Multitable and Crosstab Queries," explains how to join two or more tables based on primary- and foreign-key fields, and how to rearrange your query result set into a spreadsheet-like format.

- Chapter 11, "Using Action Queries," describes how to create queries that alter the data in tables or create new tables from a query result set.

A few of these chapters are extensive; you don't have to remember all the nuances of these chapters. You do need to remember where the instructions for performing specific types of operations are presented so that you can return to that point in the book when you create your initial database applications.

Part II

Querying for Specific Information

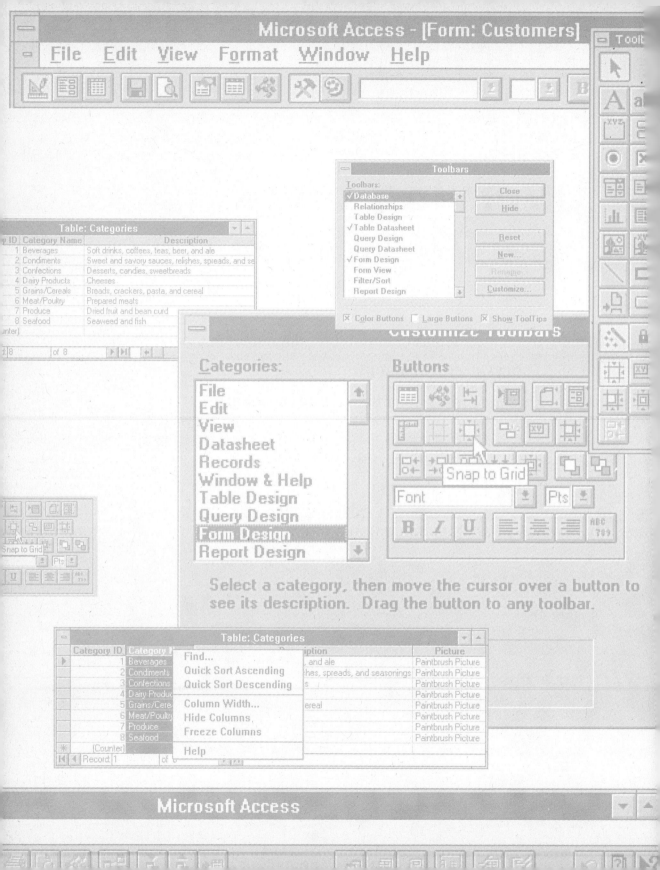

Chapter 8

Using Query by Example

Query by Example, usually abbreviated QBE, was originally developed to enable users of mainframe-computer database applications to find and display pieces of data (or collections of data) without requiring them to know a computer language. Many database management systems eventually came to use QBE in one form or another. (In fact, dBASE, the first commercially successful PC database manager, uses a variant of QBE for its dot-prompt commands.)

At a command prompt, for example, QBE users entered such statements as this:

```
LIST ALL lastnames LIKE Lin* WITH state IL IN us_hist
```

These are known as *give me an example of* statements. The QBE application program then searched the lastnames field of the us_hist table file for all names beginning with Lin. The program disregarded the remaining characters in the names and displayed only those records having a state field containing the value IL.

As computer display terminals became more sophisticated, *graphical QBE* developed as the preferred method of creating queries. Graphical QBE displays the field names of one or more database tables as headers of a column. Users can type partial example statements, or *expressions*, in these columns to create a query. Because terminals capable of displaying actual graphics were a rarity when graphical QBE was developed, the standard 80-character by 25-line text mode was used. The term *graphical* is a misnomer, therefore, in today's world of truly graphical user environments like Windows. In the original version of graphical QBE, the preceding example statement might resemble the following display:

```
LASTNAME FIRSTNAME ADDRESS CITY STATE
Like LIN*                        IL
```

In this chapter, you learn to

- Create a simple select query for a single table

- Print your query as a report

- Create a simple make-table action query

- Add user-entered parameters to queries

- Understand simple SQL statements

II

Querying

Fields corresponding to the columns in which no expressions are entered are not checked for compliance with the query.

After the designated fields are checked and all matches within the searched file are found, the application displays those addresses containing matching values. The parts of each address appear in their respective columns, as in the following example:

```
LASTNAME   FIRSTNAME      ADDRESS        CITY          STATE
Lincoln    Abraham        123 Elm St.    Springfield   IL
Lincoln    Mary Todd      123 Elm St.    Springfield   IL
Lincoln    Todd           123 Elm St.    Springfield   IL
```

Learning to type query expressions in graphical QBE columns proved easier for most computer users than typing QBE expressions at a prompt. The user had to know the syntax of only a few expressions to create relatively complex queries. The use of graphical QBE was one feature that made Ansa Software's original Paradox RDBMS a success in the PC desktop RDBMS market, dominated at the time by dBASE II and dBASE III+.

The advent of Microsoft Windows introduced a graphical user environment ideally suited to a truly graphical QBE database management system. Microsoft has taken full advantage of the wide range of graphical features incorporated in Windows 3.x, as you see when you create your first true Access query.

Creating Your First Real Query

Chapter 6, "Sorting, Finding, and Filtering Data in Tables," introduced you to the concepts of creating queries when you applied a sort order to tables and added record selection criteria to filters for data contained in tables. Access's Query Design window, however, gives you greater flexibility than the Filter window because it lets you choose the fields that appear in the query result set. You also can create more complex queries by joining primary and related tables. This chapter is designed to teach you the basics of QBE; you learn to create multitable queries in Chapter 10, "Creating Multitable and Crosstab Queries"—after you learn the details of how to use operators and create expressions in Chapter 9, "Understanding Operators and Expressions in Access." Expressions often are used as criteria for more complex queries.

To devise a simple query that enables you to customize mailing lists for selected customers of Northwind Traders, for example, follow these steps:

1. Open the Northwind Traders database (file name NWIND.MDB in the \ACCESS\SAMPAPPS directory of Access 2.0 or in the \ACCESS directory of Access 1.x). The NWIND Database window appears.

2. Click the New Query button in the toolbar; alternatively, click the Query button in the Database window and then click the New button. The New Query dialog appears (see fig. 8.1). This dialog lets you choose the Query Wizards button to design specialized queries or the New Query button to design your own query. Click the New Query button to display the Query Design window.

Fig. 8.1
Choosing between Query Wizards and New Query to create your own query design.

3. The Add Table dialog is superimposed on the Query Design window, as shown in figure 8.2. The Table/Query list in the Add Table dialog lets you select from all existing tables, queries, or a combination of tables and queries. You can base a new query on one or more previously entered tables or queries. (The tables and queries listed in the Add Table list come with Access as samples for the Northwind Traders database.)

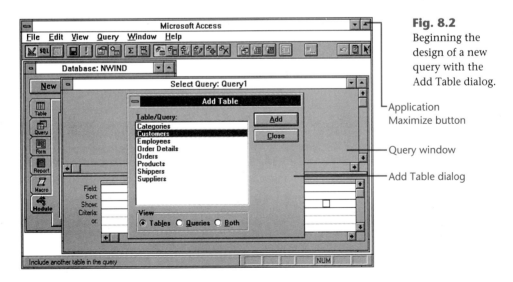

Fig. 8.2
Beginning the design of a new query with the Add Table dialog.

Application Maximize button

Query window

Add Table dialog

II

Querying

4. For this example, only tables are used in the query, so accept the default selection of Tables in the View frame. Click (or use the down-arrow key to select) Customers in the Add Table list to select the Customers table, and then click the Add button. Alternatively, double-click Customers to add a table to the query. You can use more than one table in a query by choosing another table name from the list and clicking Add again. In this example, however, only one table is used. When you have selected the table or tables you want to use, click Close. The Add Table dialog disappears.

5. Now maximize the size of the Query Design window by clicking the Document Maximize button in the window's upper right corner. The Field list for the Customers table appears at the left in the upper pane of the Query Design window, and a blank Query Design grid appears in the lower pane, as shown in figure 8.3. The Field list displays all the names of the fields listed in the Customers table.

Fig. 8.3

Displaying the Field list box of the Customers table in a Query Design window.

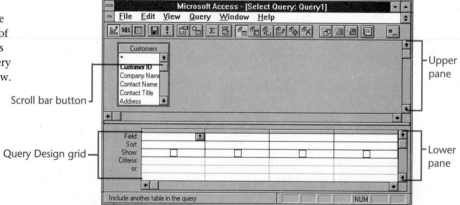

By clicking the Query and New buttons in the NWIND Database window, you entered Access's query design mode. Access assigns a default name, Query1, to the first query you create (but have not yet saved) in this mode. You assign your own names to queries when you save them. If you create additional queries without saving the first query, Access assigns them the default names Query2, Query3, and so on, in sequence.

Choosing Fields for Your Query

After you choose a table from the Add Table dialog, the next step is to decide which of the table's fields to include in your query. Because you plan to use this query to create a customer mailing list, you must include the fields that make up a personalized mailing address.

As explained in the introduction to this chapter, the first row of any graphical QBE query contains the names of each field involved in the query. (These field names also are called *field headers*.) The sample query you are creating, therefore, must include in its first row the names of all the fields that constitute a mailing address.

To choose the fields you want to include in the Query Design grid, follow these steps:

1. When you open the Query Design window, the insertion point (also called the *caret*) is located in the Field row of the first column. Click the List Box button that appears in the right corner of the first column, or press F4, to open the Field Name list (see fig. 8.4).

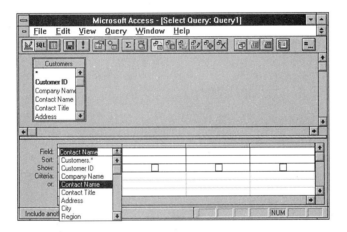

Fig. 8.4

The first step in creating a query design: entering a field name.

2. Click the Contact Name field to choose it as the first field header of the query, or use the down-arrow key to highlight the name and press Enter. The Field list in the lower pane closes.

3. Move the insertion point to the second column by using the right-arrow or Tab key. (Notice that the List Box button moves to the second column along with the insertion point.) Double-click Company Name in the Customers field list in the upper pane to add Company Name as the second field of your query. Double-clicking entries in the list in the upper pane is the second method Access uses to add fields to a query.

Access offers a third method of adding fields to your query: the *drag-and-drop* method. You can add the Address, City, and Region fields to columns 3 through 5, respectively, in one step by using the drag-and-drop method (refer to steps 4 and 5).

4. To use the drag-and-drop method of adding fields, you must first select the fields. In the Customers field list in the upper pane of the Query Design window, click Address and hold the Shift or Ctrl key as you click City and Region. Alternatively, select Address with the down-arrow key, hold the Shift or Ctrl key, and press the down-arrow key twice more. You have selected the Address, City, and Region fields, as shown in figure 8.5.

Fig. 8.5
Selecting multiple fields and using the drag-and-drop method to add the fields to the query.

International Do Not Enter symbol —

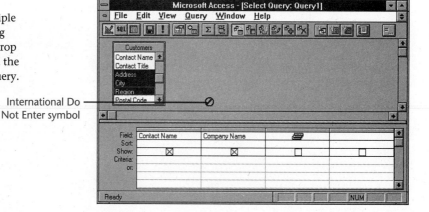

5. Position the mouse pointer over the selected fields, and click the left mouse button. Your mouse pointer turns into a symbol representing the three selected field names. Drag the symbol for the three fields to the third column of your query's Field row, as shown in figure 8.5, and release the left mouse button.

Access adds the three fields to your query, in sequence, starting with the column in which you drop the symbol. When the mouse pointer is in an area where you cannot drop the fields, it becomes the international Do Not Enter symbol shown in the upper pane of the Query Design window.

6. The Query Design grid in the lower pane can display a maximum of five columns (in the default width) at a time when both Access's main window and the Query Design window are maximized. This query uses seven fields, so you need to move the grid's display to expose two addi-

tional empty fields. You can reduce the width of the columns by dragging the divider of the grid's header bars to the left. Click the scroll-right button (on the horizontal scroll bar at the bottom of the window) twice to display two blank fields, or you can drag the scroll bar slider button to the right to expose empty fields as necessary.

7. Click the scroll-down button in the Customers field list to display the Postal Code and Country fields. Hold the Shift or Ctrl key and select Postal Code and Country. Drag the symbol for these two fields to the first empty field cell (column 6), and drop the two fields there. Your Query Design window appears similar to the one shown in figure 8.6. (Notice that the check boxes in the Show row for the columns that contain a field name now are marked.)

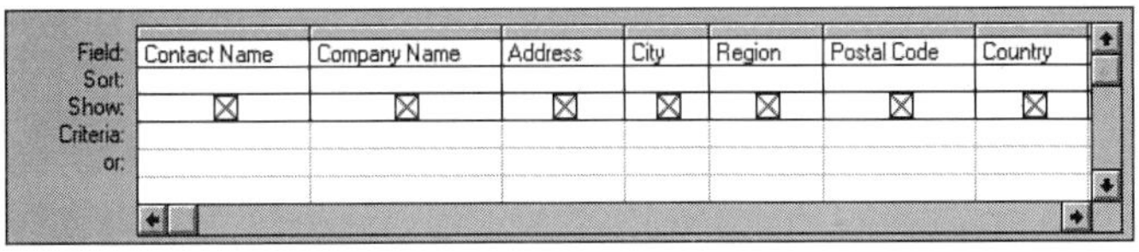

Field:	Contact Name	Company Name	Address	City	Region	Postal Code	Country
Sort:							
Show:	☒	☒	☒	☒	☒	☒	☒
Criteria:							
or:							

Fig. 8.6
The seven field names included in the new query.

> ### Note
>
> Many figures in this book are created with Access's main window in *Normal* style, which occupies a portion of the display, rather than *Maximized* style, which occupies all of the display. Normal style is used so that figures can be reproduced on a larger scale, which improves legibility.

8. Click the Query Datasheet View button on the toolbar to enter run mode. Expect a brief waiting period while Access processes your query on the Customers table. Alternatively, click the Run Query button on the toolbar to run your query against the Customers table.

Because you have not yet entered any selection criteria in the Criteria row of the Query Design grid, your query results in a display of all records in the Customers table. These records appear in the order of the primary key index on the Customer ID field because you have not specified a sorting order in the Sort row of the design. (The values in the Customer ID field are alphabetic codes derived from the Company Name field.) The result of your first query is shown in figure 8.7.

Querying

Fig. 8.7
A list of all
records contained
in the table.

Contact Name	Company Name	Address	City	Region	Postal Code	Country
Maria Anders	Alfreds Futterkiste	Obere Str. 57	Berlin		12209	Germany
Ana Trujillo	Ana Trujillo Emparedado	Avda. de la Constituc	México D.		05021	Mexico
Antonio Moreno	Antonio Moreno Taquerí	Mataderos 2312	México D.		05023	Mexico
Thomas Hardy	Around the Horn	120 Hanover Sq.	London		WA1 1DP	UK
Christina Berglund	Berglunds snabbköp	Berguvsvägen 8	Luleå		S-958 22	Sweden
Hanna Moos	Blauer See Delikatesser	Forsterstr. 57	Mannheim		68306	Germany
Frédérique Citeaux	Blondel père et fils	24, place Kléber	Strasbourg		67000	France
Martín Sommer	Bólido Comidas preparad	C/ Araquil, 67	Madrid		28023	Spain
Laurence Lebihan	Bon app'	12, rue des Bouchers	Marseille		13008	France
Elizabeth Lincoln	Bottom-Dollar Markets	23 Tsawassen Blvd.	Tsawasse	BC	T2F 8M4	Canada
Victoria Ashworth	B's Beverages	Fauntleroy Circus	London		EC2 5NT	UK
Patricio Simpson	Cactus Comidas para lle	Cerrito 333	Buenos Ai		1010	Argentina
Francisco Chang	Centro comercial Mocte;	Sierras de Granada 9!	México D.		05022	Mexico
Yang Wang	Chop-suey Chinese	Hauptstr. 29	Bern		3012	Switzerland
Pedro Afonso	Comércio Mineiro	Av. dos Lusíadas, 23	São Paulo	SP	05432-043	Brazil
Elizabeth Brown	Consolidated Holdings	Berkeley Gardens	London		WX1 6LT	UK
Sven Ottlieb	Drachenblut Delikatesse	Walserweg 21	Aachen		52066	Germany

Record: 1   of 91

Datasheet View   NUM

◀ "Working with
Relations, Key
Fields, and
Indexes,"
p. 164

Selecting Records by Criteria and Sorting the Display

The mailing for which you are creating a list with your sample query is to be
sent to U.S. customers only, so you want to include in your query only those
records that have USA in their Country fields. Selecting records based on the
values of fields—that is, establishing the criteria for the records to be returned
(displayed) by the query—is the very heart of the query process.

Perform the following steps to establish criteria for selecting the records to
comprise your mailing list:

1. Click the Design View button on the toolbar to return to design mode.
   The partially filled Query Design grid replaces the mailing list on-
   screen.

2. To restrict the result of your query to firms in the United States, type
   the expression **USA** in the Criteria row of the Country column. Entering a criterion's value without preceding the value with an operator
   indicates that the value of the field must match the value of the expression USA. You do not need to add quotation marks to the expression;
   Access adds them for you (see the Country column in fig 8.8).

Access
2.0

> **Note**
>
> Access 1.x required that an equal operator (=) precede the value of a criterion
> to specify an exact match. In Access 2.0, the equal operator is optional. You
> use other comparison operators (<, <=, <>, >=, >) identically in criteria cells of
> Access 1.x and 2.0.

3. Click the Show check box in the Country column to remove the X that appeared when you named the column. After you deactivate the Show check box, the Country field is not displayed when you run your query. (You do not need to include the Country column in your mailing list address if you are mailing from a U.S. location to other U.S. locations.) If a Show check box is not deactivated, that field in the query displays by default.

4. Move the insertion point to the Sort row of the Postal Code column, and press F4 to display the sorting options for that field: Ascending, Descending, and (not sorted). Choose the Ascending option to sort the query by Postal Code from low codes to high.

   At this point, the Query Display grid appears as shown in figure 8.8.

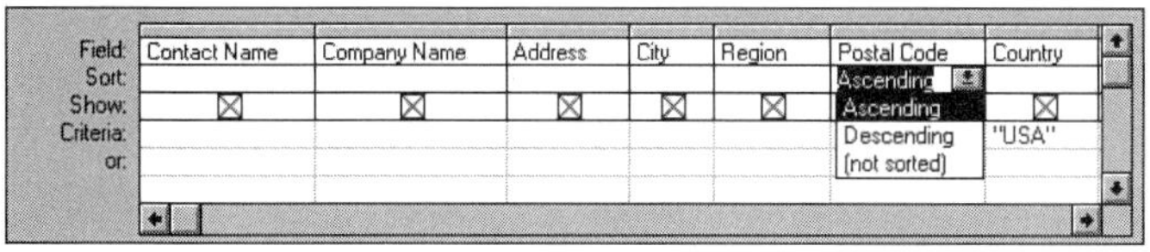

Field:	Contact Name	Company Name	Address	City	Region	Postal Code	Country
Sort:						Ascending	
Show:	☒	☒	☒	☒	☒	Ascending	☒
Criteria:						Descending	"USA"
or:						(not sorted)	

Fig. 8.8
Adding the Ascending sort order to the Postal Code field.

5. Click the Query Datasheet View button on the toolbar to display the result of your criterion and sorting order. Use the horizontal scroll bar to display additional fields. (The NWIND.MDB file supplied with Access 2.0 has fewer U.S. firms in the Customers table than the NWIND.MDB file included with Access 1.x.)

Figure 8.9 displays the query result table (also called a *query result set*) that Access 2.0 refers to as an updatable **Recordset** (a **Recordset** object of the **Dynaset** type, to be more precise). A **Recordset** object is a temporary table stored in your computer's memory—it is not a permanent component of the database file. A **Recordset** object differs from the conventional view of an object created by the SQL VIEW reserved word because you can update the data in a **Recordset** object of the **Dynaset** type. Only the design specifications of the query—and not the values the query contains—are saved in the NWIND.MDB (the Northwind Traders database) file after you save the query. The query design specification is called a **QueryDef** object.

II

Querying

Fig. 8.9

Sorting the query
in numeric order
by Postal Code
values.

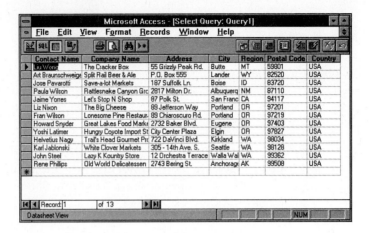

Creating More Complex Queries

To limit your mailing to customers in a particular state or group of states, you
can add a Criteria expression to the Region or Postal Code field. To restrict
the mailing to customers in California, Oregon, and Washington, for example, you can specify that the value of the Postal Code field must be equal
to or greater than 90000. Alternatively, you can specify that Region values
must be CA, OR, and WA.

Follow these steps to restrict your mailing to customers in California, Oregon,
and Washington:

1. Click the Design View button on the toolbar to return to design mode.

2. Use the right-arrow or Tab key to move the insertion point to the Region column. If the Region column is not on-screen, click the scroll-
   right button until that column appears.

3. Type **CA** in the first criteria row of the Region column. Access adds the
   quotation marks around CA (as it did when you restricted your mailing
   to U.S. locations with the USA criterion).

4. Press the down-arrow key to move to the next criteria row in the Region
   column. Type **OR**, and then move to the third criteria row and type
   WA. Your query design now appears as shown in figure 8.10. Access
   adds the required quotation marks to these criteria also.

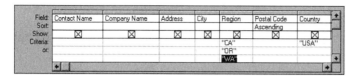

Fig. 8.10
Adding criteria to
the Region field of
the Query Design
grid.

> **Note**
>
> After you type a criterion on the same line as a previously entered criterion in
> another field, only those records that meet *both* criteria are selected for dis-
> play. In the preceding example, therefore, only those records with Region
> values equal to CA *and* Country values equal to USA are displayed. Records for
> Region values OR and WA need not have Country values equal to USA to be
> displayed because the USA criterion is missing from the OR and WA rows. This
> omission does not really affect the selection of records in this case because all
> OR and WA records are also USA records.
>
> (Note that the remaining criteria rows in the different columns on the Query
> Design grid enable you to enter additional criteria to further qualify which
> records are displayed. In the current example, no additional criteria are
> needed, so these cells are left blank.)

5. Click the Query Datasheet View or Run Query button on the toolbar to
return to run mode. The query result set appears as shown in figure
8.11.

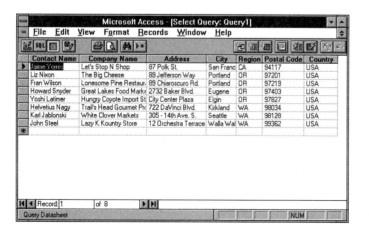

Fig. 8.11
Running the query
for customers in
California,
Oregon, and
Washington.

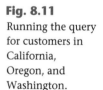

Editing Table Data in Query View

You can edit the data in any visible fields of the table in the query display. Changes you make to data cells in an updatable **Recordset** object are reflected in the table(s) that underlie the **Recordset**. To edit an entry in a query and then verify the change to the corresponding record in the underlying table, perform these steps:

1. Use the right-arrow or Tab key to move the insertion point to the first row of the Company Name column (Let's Stop N Shop).

2. Press F2 to deselect the field and to enter edit mode.

3. Use the arrow keys to position the cursor to immediately before the *N* and add an apostrophe to change the Company Name value to **Let's Stop 'N Shop**.

4. Press Enter or move the insertion point down another line to make the change for Let's Stop 'N Shop permanent. (Data in the underlying table is not changed until you press Enter or move to a different record.)

> **Note**
>
> Unlike edits made to values in indexed fields in dBASE's browse mode, changes made to sorted fields in Access do not actually move the edited records to their correct locations in the query tables until you press Shift+F9 to rerun the query.

5. Click the Show Database Window button of the toolbar, or choose **1** Database from the **W**indow menu and then click the Table tab of the Database window.

6. Double-click the Customers table to display the table in Datasheet View. Scroll down to verify that the update made to the query data is reflected in the underlying Customers table (see fig. 8.12).

Changing the Names of Query Column Headers

You can substitute the field header names in a query with column header names of your choice. If you are a U.S. firm, for example, you may want to change Region to State and Postal Code to ZIP Code. (Canadian firms may want to change Region to Province.) Another reason to alter field names is to make the field names correspond to the merge field names used in mail merge documents. (Spaces usually are not permitted in merge field names.)

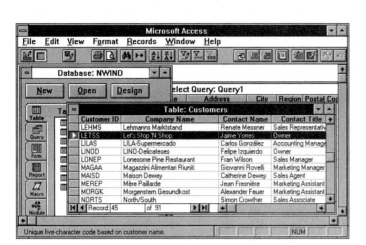

Fig. 8.12
Rerunning the
query after
correcting the
Company Name of
a record.

To change the query column header names, perform the following steps:

1. Switch to design mode by clicking the Design View button. Then use the right-arrow or Tab key to move the insertion point to the Field column containing the field header name you want to change—in this case, the Region column.

2. Press F2 to deselect the field; then press Home to move the insertion point to the first character position.

3. Type the new name for the column and follow the name with a colon (no spaces): **State:**. The colon separates the new column name you type from the existing table field name, which shifts to the right to make room for your addition. The result, in this example, is `State:Region` (see fig. 8.13).

4. Use the arrow key to move to the Postal Code field and repeat steps 2 and 3, typing **ZIPCode:** as that header's new name. The result, as shown in figure 8.13, is `ZIPCode:Postal Code`.

Tip
If you already
have a main
document for
the merge
operation,
substitute the
merge field
names of the
main merge
document for
the table's field
header names
in your query.

Field:	Company: Company	Address	City	State: Region	ZIPCode: Postal Code	Country
Sort:					Ascending	
Show:	☒	☒	☒	☒	☒	☐
Criteria:						"USA"
or:						

Fig. 8.13
Changing the
names of the
Region and Postal
Code column
headers.

5. Change the column header for the Contact Name field to Contact; change the column header for the Company Name field to Company (refer to steps 2, 3, and 4).

6. Delete the CA, OR, and WA criteria from the State:Region column so that all records for the U.S. appear.

7. Your mailing list is for the U.S. only, so you do not need to display the Country column. Click the Show button to remove the X from the Show check box for that column.

8. Click the Query Datasheet View or Run Query button to return to run mode and execute the query. Verify that the change or changes have been made to the column headers (see fig. 8.14).

Fig. 8.14
The query result set
with new column
headers.

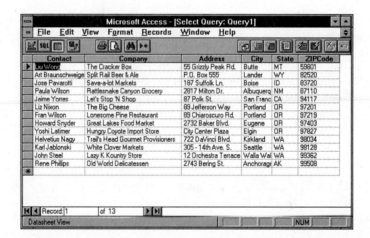

Contact	Company	Address	City	State	ZIPCode
Liu Wong	The Cracker Box	55 Grizzly Peak Rd.	Butte	MT	59801
Art Braunschweige	Split Rail Beer & Ale	P.O. Box 555	Lander	WY	82520
Jose Pavarotti	Save-a-lot Markets	187 Suffolk Ln.	Boise	ID	83720
Paula Wilson	Rattlesnake Canyon Grocery	2817 Milton Dr.	Albuquerq	NM	87110
Jaime Yorres	Let's Stop 'N Shop	87 Polk St.	San Franc	CA	94117
Liz Nixon	The Big Cheese	89 Jefferson Way	Portland	OR	97201
Fran Wilson	Lonesome Pine Restaurant	89 Chiaroscuro Rd.	Portland	OR	97219
Howard Snyder	Great Lakes Food Market	2732 Baker Blvd.	Eugene	OR	97403
Yoshi Latimer	Hungry Coyote Import Store	City Center Plaza	Elgin	OR	97827
Helvetius Nagy	Trail's Head Gourmet Provisioners	722 DaVinci Blvd.	Kirkland	WA	98034
Karl Jablonski	White Clover Markets	305 - 14th Ave. S.	Seattle	WA	98128
John Steel	Lazy K Kountry Store	12 Orchestra Terrace	Walla Wal	WA	99362
Rene Phillips	Old World Delicatessen	2743 Bering St.	Anchorage	AK	99508

Printing Your Query as a Report

Access
2.0

Queries are often used to print quick, *ad hoc* reports. Access 2.0 lets you print your report to a Word for Windows .RTF (rich-text format) file, Excel worksheet .XLS file, a DOS text .TXT file, or as an attachment to a Microsoft Mail message. (Access 1.x required an add-in library, OUTPUTAS.MDA, and a Windows dynamic link library, OUTPUTAS.DLL, to create .RTF, .XLS, and .TXT files from reports.) Printing reports to .RTF and .XLS files and as attachments to Microsoft Mail messages is described in Chapter 14, "Printing Basic Reports and Mailing Labels."

Previewing the appearance of your query table to see how the table will appear when printed is generally a good idea. After you determine from the preview that everything in the table is correct, you can print the finished query result set in a variety of formats.

To preview a query result set before printing it, follow these steps:

1. In Query Datasheet View, click the Print Preview button on the toolbar. A miniature version of the query table appears in report preview mode.

2. Position the *Zoom mouse pointer* (the magnifying glass button) at the upper left corner of the miniature table and click the left mouse button or the Zoom button above the window to view the report at approximately the scale at which it will print.

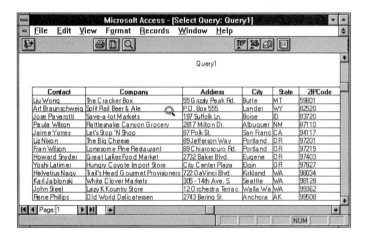

Fig. 8.15
A preview of the Mailing List query table in zoomed scale.

3. Use the vertical and horizontal scroll bar buttons to position the preview in the window (see fig. 8.15).

> **Note**
>
> Field width in the query table is based on the column width you last established in run mode. You may have to drag the right edge of the field header buttons to the right to increase the width of the columns so that the printed report does not truncate the data. If the width of the query data exceeds the available printing width (the paper width minus the width of the left and right margins), Access prints two or more sheets for each page of the report.

4. Click the Close button and then alter the width of the columns in run mode so that all seven columns of the query fit on one sheet of paper when you print it. Return to report preview mode after you finish this process.

> **Note**
>
> Adjust the displayed width of query fields in the same manner that you adjust table fields (described in Chapters 4 and 6). Access 2.0 stores query column widths as properties of the query; if you use Access 1.x, the widths revert to their default values when you change to design mode.

To print a query table after you have previewed it and determined that all the data is correct, follow these steps:

1. Click the Print button while you are in report preview mode. The standard Print dialog appears.

To change the default printing margins of one inch on all sides of the sheet (or any revised defaults you may have set earlier by choosing the Options command from the View menu), or to print only data (but not field header names), follow steps 2 and 3. If you don't want to change anything, skip to step 4. (You can display the Print Setup dialog by clicking the Page Setup button of the Print Preview window.)

2. Click the Setup button. The Print Setup dialog appears, as shown in figure 8.16. (The Network button of the Print Setup dialog appears only if you are running Windows for Workgroups, Windows NT, or another Windows network client application.)

Fig. 8.16
The Print Setup dialog.

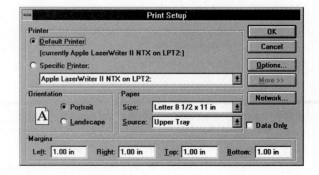

3. Enter any changes you want to make to the margins; click the Data Only check box if you do not want to print the field header names. Then click OK.

   You return to report print preview mode; click the Print button to display the Print dialog.

4. Click the OK button in the Print dialog to print your query data.

Using the Data from Your Query

Occasionally, you may want to use data from your query as part of a different Windows application without printing the data in a report. The simplest technique for transferring data in your query to another Windows application is to use the Clipboard. Clipboard operations for data in query tables are identical to those operations for tables described in Chapter 7, "Attaching, Importing, and Exporting Tables."

◄ "Printing Options," p. 104

To create a merge data file for Word for Windows directly from a query, for example, follow these steps:

1. In Query Datasheet View, choose Select All Records from the Edit menu.

   For a partial mailing, such as to firms in California only, you can choose the individual records by dragging the mouse over the records' selection buttons.

2. Press Ctrl+C or choose Copy from the Edit menu to copy the selected records to the Clipboard.

3. Run Word. Press Ctrl+Esc to display the Windows Task Manager's list. If Word is running, double-click its name to display its window. If Word is not running, double-click Program Manager to launch Word. Choose New from the File menu to open a new window.

4. Press Ctrl+V, or choose **P**aste from the Word for Windows Edit menu. Your Access mailing records are added as a table to the Word for Windows file (see fig. 8.17).

5. Convert the table to the tab-delimited format necessary for Word merge data files. Place the insertion point in one of the cells of the table and choose Select Table from the Table menu to select all the rows and columns of the table.

Querying

Fig. 8.17

The query result set copied to a Word for Windows document.

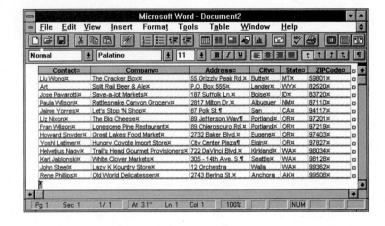

6. Choose Convert Table to Text from the Table menu to display the dialog that lets you choose the field delimiter character. Accept the default Tab selection in the Convert Table to Text dialog and click OK. Your merge data file appears as shown in figure 8.18.

Fig. 8.18

A Microsoft Word merge data file with extra newline pairs embedded.

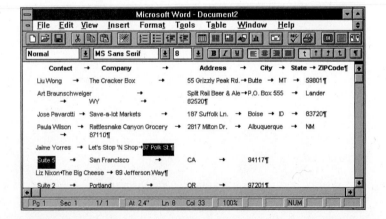

> **Note**
>
> Some of the records of this query also contain *newline pairs* (paragraph marks) embedded in fields that result in premature ends of these records. An example of a spurious newline pair in the Address field is highlighted in figure 8.18. Replace the extra newline pairs with commas and spaces, and delete the quotation marks that enclose fields containing extra headline pairs before using the document in a merge operation.

If you use a DOS word processor and want to import query data into a merge data file, save the query in the form of a table and export the table as a file in a format compatible with that of your word processor. This process requires that you create an action query to create a table. Then export the data from the table in a compatible format, as described in Chapter 7. Action queries are discussed briefly in "Creating and Using a Simple Make Table Action Query," later in this chapter, and in Chapter 11, "Using Action Queries."

Saving and Naming Your Query

After completing your query, save it as an element of your database file, giving the query its own descriptive name.

Follow these steps to save and name your query:

1. Close your query by double-clicking the Document Control-menu box. Access prompts you with a message box to save the new or modified query, as shown in figure 8.19.

2. Click the Yes button in the message box to save your query. Because Access has already assigned a default name to your query, the Save As dialog appears (see fig. 8.20). If you choose Cancel or press Esc, Access does not save your query.

3. Type a descriptive name for your query in the Query Name text box, in this case qryUSMailList, and press Enter or choose OK. Your query now is saved under the name you assigned it rather than under the default name.

Fig. 8.19
A message box reminding you to save a newly created or modified query.

Fig. 8.20
The Save As dialog.

As an alternative, you can save your query by choosing Save As from the File menu.

Querying

To rename a saved query, follow these steps:

1. Close the query by double-clicking the Document Control-menu box. (You cannot rename an open query.)

2. Select the query you want to rename from the Database window.

3. Choose Rename from the File menu.

4. Type the new name in the text box of the Rename dialog that appears after you choose Rename.

5. Press Enter or choose OK. Access saves your query with the new name you assigned.

Creating Other Types of Queries

Access enables you to create the following four basic types of queries to achieve different objectives:

- *Select*. Extracts data from one or more tables and displays the data in tabular form.

- *Crosstab*. Summarizes data from one or more tables in the form of a spreadsheet. Crosstab queries are useful for analyzing data and creating graphs or charts based on the sum of the numeric field values of many records.

- *Action*. Creates new database tables from query tables or makes major alterations to a table. Action queries enable you to add or delete records from a table or to make changes to records based on expressions you enter in a query design.

- *Parameter*. Repeatedly uses a query and makes only simple changes to its criteria. The mailing list query you created in the first part of this chapter is an excellent candidate for a Parameter query because you can change the criterion of the Region field for mailings to different groups of customers. When you run a Parameter query, Access prompts you with a dialog for the new criterion. Parameter queries are not actually a separate query type because you can add the parameter function to select, crosstab, and action queries.

Chapters 10 and 11 explain how to create each of the four query types. Creating a table from the mailing list query to export to a mail merge file is an example of an action query. (In fact, this is the simplest example of an action query and also the safest because make-table queries do not modify data in existing tables.)

Creating and Using a Simple Make-Table Action Query

To create a table from your mailing list query, you first must convert the query from a select to an action query. Follow these steps to make this change:

1. Open your mailing list query in design mode by selecting the name you gave the query in the Database window and clicking the Design button.

2. Choose Make Table from the Query menu. (The Query menu is accessible only in query design mode.) The Query Properties dialog appears, as shown in figure 8.21.

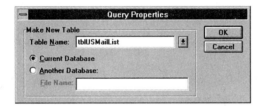

Fig. 8.21
The Query Properties dialog.

3. Type a descriptive table name for your query table in the Table Name text box.

   The Query Properties dialog enables you to further define your query table's properties in several ways. You can add the table to the Northwind Traders database by choosing the Current Database option (the default). You also can choose the Another Database option to add the table to a different database.

4. Choose OK. Access converts your select query to the make-table type of action query. The Datasheet View of your query is no longer available, as indicated by the inactive status (gray color) of the Query Datasheet View button on the toolbar.

5. Close your query by double-clicking the Document Control-menu box. Your query name in the Database window now is prefixed by an exclamation point, as shown in figure 8.22. An exclamation point indicates that the query is an action query.

Now that you have converted your query from a select query to an action query, you can create a new U.S. Mailing List table. To create the table, follow these steps:

1. Run the newly converted action query table to create your mailing list by double-clicking its name in the Queries list of the Database window (see fig. 8.22).

Fig. 8.22
A highlighted action query in the list of queries.

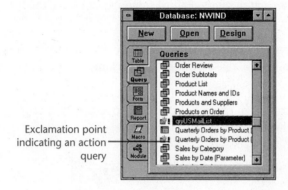

Exclamation point indicating an action query

After you open an action query table, it performs the desired action—in this case, creating the tblUSMailList table—instead of simply displaying a select query result set. Before Access carries out the action, however, a message box (see fig. 8.23) appears and warns you that the data in the tblUSMailList table will be modified (despite the fact that the table has yet to be created).

Fig. 8.23
The message box that appears after you open an action query.

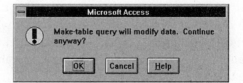

2. Click OK to dismiss the message box and continue the operation. A second message box, shown in figure 8.24, appears to tell you what happens after you execute the action query.

3. Click OK. Because you have not run this action query before, running it now creates the new tblUSMailList table.

Fig. 8.24
A second message
indicates the
effects of running
the action query.

4. Click the Table button in the Database window. Access adds the new
tblUSMailList table to the list of tables in the NWIND database, as
shown in figure 8.25.

Fig. 8.25
The new table
added to the
NWIND database's
table list.

5. Open the tblUSMailList table. Its contents may appear as they do in
figure 8.26.

Contact	Company	Address	City	State	ZIPCode
Liu Wong	The Cracker Box	55 Grizzly Peak Rd	Butte	MT	59801
Art Braunschweiger	Split Rail Beer & Ale	P.O. Box 555	Lander	WY	82520
Jose Pavarotti	Save-a-lot Markets	187 Suffolk Ln.	Boise	ID	83720
Paula Wilson	Rattlesnake Canyo	2817 Milton Dr.	Albuquerque	NM	87110
Jaime Yorres	Let's Stop 'N Shop	87 Polk St.	San Francisco	CA	94117
Liz Nixon	The Big Cheese	89 Jefferson Way	Portland	OR	97201
Fran Wilson	Lonesome Pine Re	89 Chiaroscuro Rd.	Portland	OR	97219
Howard Snyder	Great Lakes Food I	2732 Baker Blvd.	Eugene	OR	97403
Yoshi Latimer	Hungry Coyote Imp	City Center Plaza	Elgin	OR	97827
Helvetius Nagy	Trail's Head Gourm	722 DaVinci Blvd.	Kirkland	WA	98034
Karl Jablonski	White Clover Marke	305 - 14th Ave. S.	Seattle	WA	98128
John Steel	Lazy K Kountry Sto	12 Orchestra Terra	Walla Walla	WA	99362
Rene Phillips	Old World Delicate	2743 Bering St.	Anchorage	AK	99508

Record: 1   of 13

Fig. 8.26
Running a
Datasheet View of
the records in the
new table.

After you create the new table, you can export its data to any of the other file
formats supported by Access by using the methods described in Chapter 7,
"Attaching, Importing, and Exporting Tables."

Adding a Parameter to Your Make-Table Query

◀ "Setting De-
fault Op-
tions," p. 101

A simple modification to your mailing list query enables you to enter a selection criterion, called a *parameter*, from a prompt created by Access. Follow these steps:

1. Close the tblUSMailList table by double-clicking the Document Control-menu box; then click the Query button in the Database window.

2. Choose the qryUSMailList query you created earlier in the chapter, and then click the Design button to display your make-table action query in design mode.

3. Type [**Enter the state code:**] in the first criteria row of the State:Region column, as shown in figure 8.27. The enclosing square brackets indicate that the entry is a prompt for a parameter after you run the action query.

Fig. 8.27
Entering a
parameter prompt
as a criterion in
Query Design
View.

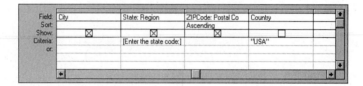

4. Close the action query, select the qryUSMailList query, and choose Rename from the File menu. The Rename dialog appears.

5. Rename your query by typing **qryStateMailList** in the text box and clicking OK.

6. Select the renamed qryStateMailList query from the list in the Database window, and then click the Open button. You see the message box indicating that data will be modified (refer back to fig. 8.23).

7. Choose OK; another message box appears. This message warns you that you are about to overwrite the data in the table created by the last execution of your query (see fig. 8.28).

Fig. 8.28
The message box
warning that data
is about to be
overwritten.

8. Click the Yes button. Access displays the Enter Parameter Value dialog. This dialog contains a prompt for you to enter the State criterion, as shown in figure 8.29.

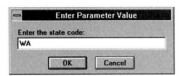

Fig. 8.29
The text box for entering a parameter to be used as a select criterion.

9. Type **WA**, and press Enter or choose OK. (You do not need to type an equal sign before the state code here because Access enters the equal sign for you.)

   Another message box appears, similar to the one in figure 8.24, indicating the number of records in the new version of the tblUSMailList table that have a value in the Regions field matching your state parameter entry.

10. Click OK. The message box closes and the Database window shows tblStateMailList as one of its options.

11. Click the Table button in the Database window, and select tblUSMailList. Click the Open button. Records for customers in Washington appear in the table.

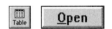

You can delete the new table from the Northwind Traders database by closing the table, selecting the tblUSMailList table in the Database window, and then pressing the Delete key. (Access requests that you confirm your deletion. Click OK and Access removes the table from the database.)

Translating Graphical QBE to Structured Query Language

Structured Query Language, or SQL, is a standard set of English words used to describe a query. Access translates the QBE expressions you type in the Query Design grid into a series of statements in Structured Query Language. Access then carries out these instructions on any tables that contain fields matching those specified in your query.

Access's use of SQL is important when you are dealing with client-server databases that process SQL statements on the server's computer. After the query is processed, the server sends the data for the query result table to your Access client application for further processing.

To display the SQL statements created from your mailing list query, perform the following steps:

1. Open the mailing list query in design mode by selecting the name you gave the query in the Database window and clicking the Design button.

2. Click the SQL button of the toolbar, or choose SQL from the View menu.

3. The SQL window, which acts as a multiline text box, appears, as shown in figure 8.30. (Access 1.x's SQL window was a dialog with a size that made it difficult to view all of a complex SQL statement without using the vertical scroll bar.)

Fig. 8.30

Graphical QBE expressions translated by Access into SQL.

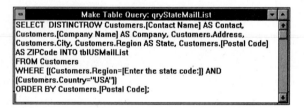

```
Make Table Query: qryStateMailList
SELECT  DISTINCTROW Customers.[Contact Name] AS Contact,
Customers.[Company Name] AS Company, Customers.Address,
Customers.City, Customers.Region AS State, Customers.[Postal Code]
AS ZIPCode INTO tblUSMailList
FROM Customers
WHERE [[Customers.Region=[Enter the state code:]] AND
[Customers.Country="USA"]]
ORDER BY Customers.[Postal Code];
```

SQL *reserved words* are displayed in uppercase letters. SQL reserved words are the instructions or the actions to be performed by the query. The names of the objects in your query appear in uppercase and lowercase letters. The meanings of the reserved words used in your query are explained in the following list:

- SELECT is usually the first reserved word in an SQL statement that returns records to a query result set. The expressions that follow specify the fields involved in the query. Fields are identified by the name of the table followed by a period and the name of the field.

- DISTINCTROW causes only unique records to be included in the query result table. DISTINCTROW is an Access SQL (and Transact-SQL) reserved word and is not included in ANSI SQL-92.

- AS establishes the alias for the field name preceding the alias. ZIPCode, for example, is the *alias* for the Postal Code field. The alias is the caption that appears in the field header for the Postal Code field.

- INTO specifies the name of the table into which the results of the query are to be placed. INTO is applicable only for action queries.

- FROM is the name of the table in which the fields are located.

- WHERE identifies the expressions that follow as the selection criteria for the query.

- AND is a logical operator that results in records that meet both the criterion that precedes the AND *and* the criterion that follows the AND.

- ORDER BY specifies the field(s) by which the query result table is to be sorted.

When you are finished viewing the SQL statements, close the SQL dialog by choosing Cancel.

Only a brief glimpse of SQL is provided here and in Chapter 6, and only a small cross-section of the reserved words of SQL are used in this example. The syntax used to edit and create SQL statements is explained in detail in Chapter 24, "Working with Structured Query Language."

▶ "What Is Structured Query Language," p. 884

From Here...

This introduction to query-by-example gave you insight into the methods used by Access to choose data from tables and to organize the selected data into query result sets (called **Recordset** objects of the **Dynaset** and **Snapshot** type by Access 2.0). Even when you are not concerned with creating Access forms and reports, you can use queries to display data in tabular form for analysis or to export to other Windows and DOS applications.

- Chapter 10, "Creating Multitable and Crosstab Queries," expands on the query designs described in this chapter to create query result sets based on more than one table and to rearrange your data into a format similar to that associated with spreadsheets.

- Chapter 12, "Creating and Using Forms," and Chapter 13, "Designing Custom Multitable Forms," show you how to use queries as the RecordSource property value for forms.

II

Querying

■ Chapter 24, "Working with Structured Query Language," describes Access 2.0's dialect of SQL.

To create more sophisticated queries than those covered in this chapter, you must learn more about the syntax of the expressions that you need to choose records. As you become increasingly specific in the selection of records for your queries, the complexity of these expressions increases. For this reason, the next chapter, "Understanding Operators and Expressions in Access," precedes the chapter in which you actually learn the detailed procedures for creating queries based on more than one table and optimizing your queries.

Chapter 9

Understanding Operators and Expressions in Access

In this chapter, you learn to

- Distinguish between the elements of expressions

- Use operators, literals, and identifiers to create expressions

- Create expressions for default values and validating data

- Write expressions for query criteria

- Use expressions to create calculated query columns

You were introduced briefly to operators and the expressions that use them in Chapter 5, "Entering, Editing, and Validating Data in Tables," when you added validation rules to table fields. Expressions were touched on again in Chapter 8, "Using Query by Example," when you devised selection criteria for the query you created. You must use expressions with the forms (Chapters 12 and 13), reports (Chapters 14 and 15), and macros (Chapters 16 through 18) you combine in creating custom Access applications; furthermore, expressions are used extensively in programming with Access Basic (Chapters 27 through 29). To work effectively with Access, therefore, you must know how to create simple expressions that use Access's group of functions and operators.

If you use spreadsheet applications, such as Microsoft Excel or Lotus 1-2-3, you may be familiar with using operators to create expressions. In spreadsheet applications, expressions are called *formulas*. As discussed in Chapter 4, the syntax for expressions that create default values, such as =**Date**() + 28, is similar to formula entries in Excel. Conditional expressions that use the =IF() function in Excel use the **IIf**() function in Access.

Much of this chapter is devoted to describing the functions available in Access for manipulating data of the Numeric and Text field data type. Functions play important roles in every element of Access, from validation rules for tables and fields of tables to the control of program flow in Access Basic. You use functions in the creation of queries, forms, reports, and macros. To use Access effectively, you must know that functions are available to you.

Understanding the Elements in Expressions

An *expression* is a statement of intent. If you want an action to occur after meeting a specific condition, your expression must specify that condition. To select records in a query that contains ZIP Code field values of 90000 or higher, for example, you type the expression **ZIPCode>=90000**. You also can use expressions in arithmetic calculations. If you need an Extended Amount field in a query, for example, you type **[Extended Amount]: Quantity * [Unit Price]** as the expression to create calculated values in the data cells of the Extended Amount column.

To qualify as an expression, a statement must have at least one operator and at least one literal, identifier, or function. The following list describes these elements:

- *Operators* include the familiar arithmetic symbols +, −, * (multiply), and / (divide), as well as many other symbols and abbreviations. Most other operators available in Access are equivalent to those operators found in traditional programming languages, such as BASIC, but some are specific to Access or SQL, such as the **Between**, **In**, **Is**, and **Like** operators.

- *Literals* consist of values you type, such as 12345 or ABCDE. Literals are used most often to create default values and, in combination with field identifiers, to compare values in table fields.

- *Identifiers* are the names of objects in Access (such as fields in tables) that return distinct numeric or text values. The term *return*, when used with expressions, means that the present value of the identifier is substituted for its name in the expression. As an example, the field name identifier [Company Name] in an expression returns the value (a name) of the Company Name field for the currently selected record. Access has five predefined named constants that also serve as identifiers: **True**, **False**, Yes, No, and **Null**. Named constants and variables you create in Access Basic also are identifiers.

- *Functions*, such as **Date**() and **Format$**(), which are used in the examples in Chapter 5, return a value in place of the function name in the expression. Unlike identifiers, most functions require that you supply with parentheses an identifier or value as an argument. Functions and their arguments are explained in the "Functions" section later in this chapter.

When literals, identifiers, or functions are used with operators, these combinations are called *operands*. These four elements of expressions are described more thoroughly in the following sections.

> **Note**
>
> Expressions in this book appear in `monospace type` to distinguish expressions from the explanatory text of the book. Operators, including symbolic operators, built-in functions, and other reserved words and symbols of Access Basic are set in `monospace bold type`.

Operators

Access provides six categories of operators you can use to create expressions:

- *Arithmetic operators* perform addition, subtraction, multiplication, and division.

- *Assignment and comparison operators* set values and compare values.

- *Logical operators* deal with values that can only be true or false.

- *Concatenation operators* combine strings of characters.

- *Identifier operators* create unambiguous names for database objects so that you can assign the same field name, for example, in several tables and queries.

- *Other operators* simplify the creation of expressions for selecting records with queries.

Operators in the first four categories are available in almost all programming languages, including xBase and PAL. Identifier operators are specific to Access; the other operators of the last category are provided only in RDBMSs that create queries using QBE or SQL. The following sections explain how to use each of the operators in these categories.

Arithmetic Operators

Arithmetic operators operate only on numeric values and must have two numeric operands, with the following exceptions:

- When the minus sign (-) changes the sign (negates the value) of an operand. In this case, the minus sign is called the *unary minus*.

- When the equal sign (=) assigns a value to an Access object or an Access Basic variable identifier.

Table 9.1 lists the arithmetic operators you can use in Access expressions.

Table 9.1	Arithmetic Operators	
Operator	**Description**	**Example**
+	Adds two operands	[Subtotal] + [Tax]
-	Subtracts two operands	**Date**() - 30
- (unary)	Changes sign of operand	-12345
*	Multiplies two operands	[Units] * [Unit Price]
/	Divides one operand by another	[Quantity] / 12.55
\	Divides one integer operand by another	[Units] \ 2
Mod	Returns remainder of division by an integer	[Units] **Mod** 12
^	Raises an operand to a power (exponent)	[Value] ^ [Exponent]

Access operators are identical to operators used in Microsoft QuickBASIC, QBasic (supplied with DOS 5.0 and later), and Visual Basic. If you aren't familiar with BASIC programming, the following operators deserve further explanation:

\   The integer division symbol is the equivalent of *goes into*, as used in the litany of elementary school arithmetic: *Three goes into 13 four times, with one left over.* When you use integer division, operators with decimal fractions are rounded to integers, but any decimal fraction in the result is truncated.

Mod   An abbreviation for *modulus*, this operator returns the *left over* value of integer division. Therefore, 13 **Mod** 4, for example, returns 1.

^   The exponentiation operator raises the first operand to the power of the second. For example, 2 ^ 4, or two to the fourth power, returns 16 (2*2*2*2).

These three operators seldom are used in business applications but often are used in Access Basic program code.

Assignment and Comparison Operators

The equal sign associated with arithmetic expressions is missing from table 9.1 because it is used in two ways in Access—neither of which falls into the arithmetic category. The most common use of the equal sign is as an *assignment operator*; = assigns the value of a single operand to an Access object or to a variable or constant. When you use the expression = "Q" to assign a default value to a field, the equal sign acts as an assignment value. Otherwise, = is a comparison operator that determines whether one of two operands is equal to the other.

Comparison operators compare the values of two operands and return logical values (**True** or **False**), depending on the relationship between the two operands and the operator. An exception is when one of the operands has the **Null** value. In this case, any comparison returns a value of **Null**; because **Null** represents an unknown value, you cannot compare an unknown value with a known value and come to a valid **True** or **False** conclusion. The **Null** value is a very important concept in database application, but few desktop RDBMSs support **Null** values.

Table 9.2 lists the comparison operators available in Access.

Table 9.2 Comparison Operators			
Operator	**Description**	**Example**	**Result**
<	Less than	123 < 1000	**True**
<=	Less than or equal to	15 <= 15	**True**
=	Equal to	2 = 4	**False**
>=	Greater than or equal to	1234 >= 456	**True**
>	Greater than	123 > 123	**False**
<>	Not equal	123 <> 456	**True**

The principal uses of comparison operators are creating validation rules, establishing criteria for record selection in queries, determining actions taken by macros, and controlling program flow in Access Basic.

Logical Operators

Logical operators (also called *Boolean operators*) are used most often to combine the results of two or more comparison expressions into a single result. Logical operators can combine only expressions that return the logical values `True`, `False`, or `Null`. With the exception of `Not`, which is the logical equivalent of the unary minus, logical operators always require two operands.

Table 9.3 lists the Access logical operators.

Table 9.3	Logical Operators		
Operator	**Description**	**Example 1** **Example 2**	**Result 1** **Result 2**
And	Logical and	`True And True` `True And False`	`True` `False`
Or	Inclusive or	`True Or False` `False Or False`	`True` `False`
Not	Logical not	`Not True` `Not False`	`False` `True`
Xor	Exclusive or	`True Xor False` `True Xor True`	`True` `False`

The logical operators `And`, `Or`, and `Not` are used extensively in Access expressions. `Xor` is seldom used in Access. `Eqv` (equivalent) and `Imp` (implication) are rarely seen, even in programming code, so these two operators are not included in the table.

Concatenation Operators

Concatenation operators combine two text values into a single string of characters. If you concatenate ABC with DEF, for example, the result is ABCDEF. The ampersand (`&`) is the preferred concatenation operator in Access because `&` is the standard concatenation symbol in SQL. Although you can use the `+` operator to link two strings of characters as in BASIC, using the `+` operator for concatenation can lead to ambiguities because the operator's primary purpose is adding two operands.

Identifier Operators

The identifier operators, `!` (the exclamation point, often called the *bang character*) and `.` (the period, called the *dot operator* in Access), are separators and perform the following operations:

- Combine the names of object classes and object names to select a specific object or property of an object. For example, the following expression identifies the Personnel Actions form:

```
Forms![Personnel Actions]
```

This identification is necessary because you may also have a table called Personnel Actions.

■ Distinguish object names from property names. Consider the following expression:

```
TextBox1.FontSize = 8
```

TextBox1 is a control object and FontSize is a property.

■ Identify specific fields in tables, as in the following expression, which specifies the Company Name field of the Customers table:

```
Customers![Company Name]
```

You use the ! symbol to separate object references; the general syntax is *ObjectClass!ObjectName*. The . symbol separates objects and their properties or methods, as in *ObjectClass!Object.Property* or *ObjectClass!ObjectName.Method*().

Other Operators

The remaining Access operators are related to the comparison operators. These operators return **True** or **False**, depending on whether the value in a field meets the chosen operator's specification. A **True** value causes a record to be included in a query; a **False** value rejects the record. When used in validation rules, entries are accepted or rejected based on the logical value returned by the expression.

Table 9.4 lists the four other operators used in Access.

Table 9.4	Other Operators	
Operator	**Description**	**Example**
Is	Used with **Null** to determine whether a value is **Null** or **Not Null**	`Is Null` `Is Not Null`
Like	Determines whether a string value begins with one or more characters (you need to add a wild card, *, or one or more ?s for **Like** to work properly)	`Like "Jon*"` `Like "FILE????"`
In	Determines whether a string value is a member of a list of values	`In("CA", "OR", "WA")`
Between	Determines whether a numeric value lies within a specified range of values	`Between 1 And 5`

The wild-card characters * and ? are used with the `Like` operator the same way they are used in DOS. The * (often called *star* or *splat*) takes the place of any number of characters. The ? takes the place of a single character. For example, `Like` `"Jon*"` returns `True` for values such as `"Jones"` or `"Jonathan"`. `Like` `"*on*"` returns `True` for any value that contains `"on"`. `Like` `"FILE????"` returns `True` for `"FILENAME"`, but not `"FILE000"` or `"FILENUMBER"`. Wild-card characters may precede the characters you want to make, as in `Like` `"*son"` or `Like` `"????NAME"`.

With the exception of `Is`, the operators in the other category are equivalent to the reserved words `LIKE`, `IN`, and `BETWEEN` in SQL and are included in Access to promote compatibility with SQL. You can create each of these operators by combining other Access operators or functions. `Like` `"Jon*"` is the equivalent of Access Basic's `InStr`(`Left$`(*FieldName*, 3), `"Jon"`); `In`(`"CA"`, `"OR"`, `"WA"`) is similar to `InStr`(`"CAORWA"`, *FieldName*), except that no matches occur for the ambiguous `"AO"` and `"RW"`. `Between` 1 `And` 5 is the equivalent of `>=` 1 `And` `<=` 5.

Literals

Access provides three types of literals you can combine with operators to create expressions. The following list describes these types of literals:

- *Numeric literals* are typed as a series of digits, including the arithmetic sign and decimal point, if applicable. You don't have to prefix positive numbers with the plus sign; positive values are assumed unless the minus sign is present. Numeric literals can include `E` or `e` and the sign of the exponent to indicate an exponent in scientific notation—for example, `-1.23E-02`.

- *Text literals* (or *string literals*) can include any printable character, plus unprintable characters returned by the `Chr$()` function. The `Chr$()` function returns the characters specified by a numeric value from the ANSI character table (similar to the ASCII character table) used by Windows. For example, `Chr$`(9) returns the Tab character. Printable characters include the letters A through Z, numbers 1 through 0, punctuation symbols, and other special keyboard symbols such as the tilde (~). Access expressions require that string literals be enclosed within double quotation marks (""). Combinations of printable and unprintable characters are concatenated with the ampersand. For example, the following expression separates two strings with a newline pair. (`Chr$`(13) is the carriage return (CR), and `Chr$`(10) is the line feed (LF) character; together they form the *newline pair*.)

    `"First line" & Chr$(13) & Chr$(10) & "Second line"`

When you enter string literals in the cells of tables and Query Design grids, Access adds the quotation marks for you. In other places, you must enter the quotation marks yourself.

■ *Date/time literals* are enclosed within number or pound signs (#), as in the expressions #1-Jan-80# or #10:20:30#. Access adds the enclosing pound signs if the program detects that you are typing into a Design grid a date or time in one of the standard Access date/time formats.

Numeric and string literals have exact equivalents in BASIC, xBase, and PAL, but the date/time literal is a literal data type defined by Access.

Identifiers

An *identifier* is usually the name of an object; databases, tables, fields, queries, forms, and reports are objects in Access. Each object has a name that uniquely identifies that object. Sometimes, to identify a subobject, an identifier name consists of a *family name* (object class) separated from a *given name* (object name) by a bang symbol or a period (an identifier operator). The family name of the identifier comes first, followed by the separator and then the given name. SQL uses the period as an object separator. An example of an identifier in an SQL statement is as follows:

```
Customers.Address
```

In this example, the identifier for the Address field object is contained in the Customers table object. *Customers* is the family name of the object (the table), and *Address* is the given name of the subobject (the field). In Access, however, the ! symbol is used to separate table names and field names. (The period separates objects and their properties.) If an identifier contains a space or other punctuation, enclose the identifier within square brackets, as in this example:

```
[Personnel Actions]![PA ID]
```

You cannot include periods or exclamation points within the names of identifiers; [PA!ID], for example, is not allowed.

In simple queries that use only one table, identifiers are usually the name of a field. You use identifiers to return the values of fields in form and report objects. The specific method of identifying objects within forms and reports is covered in Chapters 12 through 15.

Functions

▶ "Using DDE Links with Excel," p. 802

▶ "Modules, Functions, and Procedures," p. 989

Functions return values to their names; functions can take the place of identifiers in expressions. One of the most common functions used in Access expressions is **Now()**, which returns to its name the date and time from your computer's internal clock. (The empty parentheses are optional for the **Now** function.) If you type **Now()** as the DefaultValue property of a Date/Time field of a table, for example, 5/94 9:00 appears in the field when you change to Datasheet View (at 9:00 A.M. on March 15, 1994). Access has defined about 140 individual functions. The following list groups functions by purpose:

- *Date and time functions* manipulate date/time values in fields or date/time values you enter as literals. You can extract parts of dates (such as the year or day of the month) and parts of times (such as hours and minutes) with date and time functions.

- *Text-manipulation functions* are used for working with strings of characters.

- *Data-type conversion functions* enable you to specify the data type of values in Numeric fields instead of depending on Access to pick the most appropriate data type.

- *Mathematic and trigonometric functions* perform on numeric values operations beyond the capability of the standard Access arithmetic operators. You can use simple trigonometric functions, for example, to calculate the length of the sides of a right triangle (if you know the length of one side and the included angle).

- *Financial functions* are similar to functions provided by 1-2-3 and Excel. Financial functions calculate depreciation, values of annuities, and rates of return on investments. To determine the present value of a lottery prize paid out in 25 equal yearly installments, for example, you can use the **PV()** function.

- *General-purpose functions* don't fit any of the preceding classifications—you use these functions in creating Access queries, forms, and reports.

- *Other functions* include functions to perform dynamic data exchange (DDE) with other Windows applications, domain aggregate functions, SQL aggregate functions, and functions used primarily in programming with Access Basic.

The following sections describe these functions more fully.

You can create user-defined functions by defining them with Access Basic programming code. Creating user-defined functions is the subject of Chapter 17, "Understanding Access Macros."

Using the Immediate Window

When you write Access Basic programming code in a module, the Immediate window is available to assist you in debugging your code. You also can use the module's Immediate Window to demonstrate the use and syntax of functions.

To experiment with some of the functions described in the following sections, perform these steps:

1. Click the Module tab in the Database window.

2. Click the New button to create a temporary module. Access assigns the default name Module1 to the temporary module.

3. Click the Document Maximize button in the upper right corner of the Module window, if the window is not already maximized.

4. Click the Immediate Window button of the toolbar or choose **I**mmediate Window from the **V**iew menu. The Immediate Window appears, as shown in figure 9.1. The entries shown in figure 9.1 aren't visible at this point. You can create similar entries by using the functions for date and time described later in this chapter.

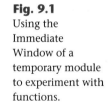

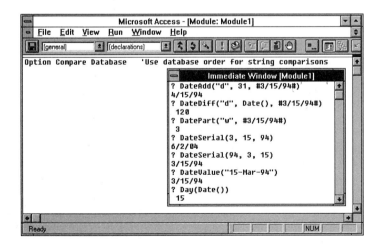

Fig. 9.1
Using the Immediate Window of a temporary module to experiment with functions.

5. Type **?Now()** and press Enter. The date and time from your computer's clock appear on the next line. The **?** is shorthand for the **Print** statement (which displays the value of a function or variable) and must be added to the **Now( )** function to display the value of the function.

6. If you neglected to precede the function entry with **?** or **Print**, an error message appears, indicating that Access expected you to type a statement or an equal sign. Choose OK and type **?** before the function name in the Immediate Window. Press End to return the caret to the end of the line and then Enter to retry the test.

The following sections contain descriptions of the various functions available to Access users and provide the correct syntax for these functions. This information is designed to help acquaint you with the use of functions with queries, forms, and reports. These descriptions and syntax examples are brief compared to the information available from the Access on-line Help system and in the *Microsoft Access Language Reference*.

One way to learn more about functions is to choose **S**earch from the **H**elp menu and type the name of the function for which you want more information in the text box of the Search dialog. For a faster method to learn more about a particular function, however, follow these steps:

1. Click the surface of the Module1 window anywhere outside the Immediate Window to make the Module1 window active. (This procedure is commonly called *giving it the focus*.)

2. Press Enter to move the caret to the beginning of a new line.

3. Type the name of the function; select the name by clicking it or by pressing Shift+left-arrow key (as shown for the **Format** function in fig. 9.2).

4. Press F1. The Help window opens. If a function and a property or event share the same name, as is the case with **Format**, an intermediate Help window appears that enables you to choose the function, the event, or the property. Click Format, Format$ Functions. The Format, Format$ Functions Help screen appears (see fig. 9.3).

5. Click See Also. Related Help topics appear in a pop-up help window (see fig. 9.4). Click the See Also window to make the window disappear.

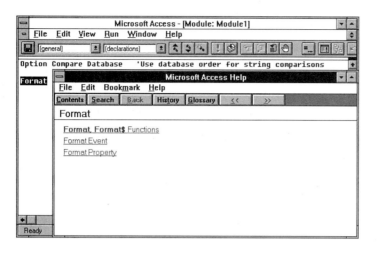

Fig. 9.2
The Help window leading to a description of the *Format* function.

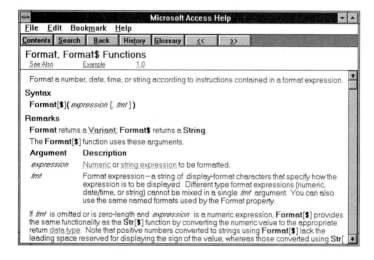

Fig. 9.3
The *Format, Format$* Functions Help window.

II

Querying

Fig. 9.4
The See Also pop-up window.

6. After you review the syntax and other information concerning the function, close the Help window by double-clicking its Application Control-menu box. Then press Delete to delete the selected function name. (This step prevents any error messages that may result from leaving an incomplete line of code in the Module1 window.)

Help windows for functions have a standard format, as shown in figure 9.3. If you click Example in any function Help window, another window displays an example of the function used in Access Basic code. These examples show the syntax of the functions and appropriate arguments.

The *Variant* Data Type in Access

The **Variant** data type is a special data type unique to Microsoft Object Basic dialects. No equivalent of the **Variant** data type exists in xBase, Paradox 3+, or other BASIC dialects. The **Variant** data type enables you to concatenate values that ordinarily have different data types, such as an integer and a character string. The capability to concatenate different data types is called *turning off data type checking*. **Variant** values are related to the **As Any** data type used by Access Basic to turn off data type checking when declaring external functions contained in Windows Dynamic Link Libraries (DLLs).

The **Variant** data type enables you to concatenate field values of tables and queries that have unlike data types without BASIC's data type conversion functions such as **Str$()** or xBase's **DTOC()**. (**Str$()** converts numeric values to the **String** data type; **DTOC()** converts xBase date values to the character, or string, data type.) The **Variant** data type also simplifies expressions that combine field values to create concatenated indexes. Specifying a composite (concatenated) index on customer number (Long Integer) and date (Date/Time) in Access 2.0's Indexes window, for example, is much simpler than using the expression **STRZERO (Cust_Num,6) + DTOC(Order_Date)** required to create a similar index in xBase. The **Variant** data type also accommodates the Structured Query Language requirement that values of different data types can be concatenated with the **&** symbol.

Table 9.5 lists the nine subtypes of the **Variant** data type.

Table 9.5	Subtypes of the *Variant* Data Type	
Subtype	**Corresponds To**	**Stored As**
0	Empty (uninitialized)	Not applicable
1	**Null** (no valid data)	Not applicable
2	**Integer**	2-byte integer
3	**Long**	4-byte long integer
4	**Single**	4-byte single-precision floating point
5	**Double**	8-byte double-precision floating point

Subtype	Corresponds To	Stored As
6	`Currency`	4-byte fixed point
7	Date/Time	8-byte double-precision floating point
8	`String`	Conventional string variable

You can concatenate **Variant** values with any of the nine **Variant** subtypes listed in table 9.5. You can concatenate a subtype 8 **Variant** (**String**) with a subtype 5 **Variant** (**Double**), for example, without receiving from Access the Type Mismatch error message you receive if you attempt this with conventional **String** (text) and **Double** data types. Access returns a value with the **Variant** subtype corresponding to the highest subtype number of the concatenated values. This example, therefore, returns a subtype 8 (**String**) **Variant** because 8 is greater than 5, the subtype number for the **Double** value. If you concatenate a subtype 2 (**Integer**) value with a subtype 3 (**Long**) value, Access returns subtype 3 **Variant** data.

Distinguishing between the Empty and **Null Variant** subtypes is important. Empty indicates that a variable you create with Access Basic code has a name but doesn't have an initial value. Empty applies only to Access Basic variables (see Chapter 27, "Writing Access Basic Code"), but Empty is not a reserved word or a keyword in Access Basic. **Null** indicates that a data cell doesn't contain an entry. You can assign the **Null** value to a variable, in which case the variable is initialized to the **Null** value, **Variant** subtype 1.

You can experiment with **Variant** subtypes in the Immediate Window to become more familiar with using the **Variant** data type. Access provides a function, **VarType()**, that returns the integer value of the subtype of its argument. Figure 9.5 shows the data subtype values returned by **VarType()** for four variables (A to D) and the result of the concatenation of these variables (E).

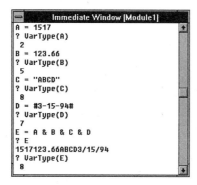

Fig. 9.5
The *Variant* subtypes return values for four variables and the result of the concatenation.

Functions for Date and Time

◀ "Choosing Field
Data Types,
Sizes, and
Formats,"
p. 135

Access offers a variety of functions for dealing with dates and times. If you have used Visual Basic, you probably recognize most of the functions applicable to Date/Time field data types shown in table 9.6. Access has added several new Date/Time functions, such as **DateAdd()** and **DateDiff()**, to simplify the calculation of date values.

◀ "Adding Indexes
to Tables,"
p. 173

All Date/Time values are stored as double-precision values but are returned as **Variant** subtype 7 unless you use the **String** form of the function. The **String** form is identified by the **String** data type identification character, **$**, appended to the end of the function name. Both ? **VarType(Date$())** and ? **VarType(Time$())** return a subtype 8 (**String**) **Variant**.

> **Note**
>
> The Immediate Window in figure 9.1 shows a few of the entries used to test the syntax examples of table 9.6.

Table 9.6   Access Functions for Date and Time

Function	Description	Example	Returns
Date(), **Date$()**	Returns the current system date and time as a subtype 7 date **Variant** or a standard date **String** subtype 8	**Date()**	4/15/94 15-Apr-94
DateAdd()	Returns a subtype 7 date with a specified number of days weeks ("ww"), months ("m"), or years ("y") added to the date	**DateAdd ("d",31, #4/15/94#)**	15/Apr/92
DateDiff()	Returns an **Integer** representing the difference between two two dates using the d/w/m/y specification	**DateDiff ("d",Date(), #4/15/94#) (assuming Date () = 5/15/94)**	30
DatePart()	Returns the specified part of a date such as day, month, year, day of week, ("w"), and so on, as an **Integer**	**DatePart ("w",#4/ 15/94#)**	6 (Friday)
DateSerial()	Returns a subtype 7 **Variant** that represents the number of days since December 31, 1899	**DateSerial (94,4,15)**	4/15/94

Function	Description	Example	Returns
`DateValue()`	Returns a subtype 7 **Variant** that corresponds to a date argument in a string format	`DateValue ("15-Apr-94")`	`4/15/94`
`Day()`	Returns an **Integer** between 1 and 31 (inclusive) that represents a day of the month from a Date/Time value	`Day(Date())` (assuming the date is the 15th of the month)	`15`
`Hour()`	Returns an **Integer** between 0 and 23 (inclusive) that represents the hour of the Date/Time value	`Hour(#2:30 PM#)`	`14`
`Minute()`	Returns an **Integer** between 0 and 59 (inclusive) that represents the minute of a Date/Time value	`Minute(#2:30 PM#)`	`30`
`Month()`	Returns an **Integer** between 1 and 12 (inclusive) that represents the month of a Date/Time value	`Month(#15-Apr-94#)`	`4`
`Now()`	Returns the date and time of a computer's system clock as a **Variant** of subtype 7	`Now()`	`4/15/94 11:57:28 AM`
`Second()`	Returns an **Integer** between 0 and 59 (inclusive) that represents the second of a Date/Time value	`Second (Now())`	`28`
`Time()`, `Time$()`	Returns the Time portion of a Date/Time value from the system clock	`Time()` (returns subtype 7) `Time$()` (returns string)	`11:57:20 AM`
`TimeSerial()`	Returns time serial value of time expressed in integer hours, minutes, and seconds	`TimeSerial (11,57,20)`	`11:57:20 AM`
`TimeValue()`	Returns time serial value of time (entered as **String** value) as a subtype 7 **Variant**	`TimeValue ("11:57")`	`11:57`
`Weekday()`	Returns day of the week (Sunday=1) corresponding to date as an integer	`Weekday (#4/15/94#)`	`6`
`Year()`	Returns the year of a Date/Time value as an **Integer**	`Year (#4/15/94#)`	`1994`

II

Querying

Text-Manipulation Functions

Table 9.7 lists the functions that deal with the Text field data type, corresponding to the **String** data type or **Variant** subtype 8. Most of these functions are modeled on basic string functions and have similarly named equivalents in xBase and PAL.

Table 9.7	**Functions for *String* and Subtype 8 *Variant* Data Types**		
Function	**Description**	**Example**	**Returns**
Asc()	Returns ANSI numeric value of character as an integer	Asc("C")	67
Chr(), Chr$()	Returns character corresponding to the numeric ANSI value as a string	Chr(67) Chr$(10)	C (Line feed)
Format(), Format$()	Formats an expression in accordance with appropriate format strings	Format(Date(), "dd-mm-yy")	15-Mar-94
InStr()	Returns position of one string within another	InStr("ABCD","C")	3
LCase(), LCase$()	Returns lowercase version of a string	LCase("ABCD")	abcd
Left(), Left$()	Returns leftmost characters of a string	Left("ABCDEF",3)	ABC
Len()	Returns number of characters in string as an integer	Len("ABCDE")	5
LTrim(), LTrim$()	Removes leading spaces from string	LTrim(" ABC")	ABC
Mid(), Mid$()	Returns a portion of the string from a string	Mid("ABCDE",2,3)	BCD
Right(), Right$()	Returns rightmost characters of string	Right("ABCDEF",3)	DEF
RTrim(), RTrim$()	Removes trailing spaces from string	RTrim("ABC ")	ABC
Space(), Space$()	Returns string consisting of a specified number of spaces	Space(5)	
Str(), Str$()	Converts numeric value of any data type to a string	Str(123.45)	123.45
StrComp()	Compares two strings for equivalence and returns the integer result of comparison	StrComp("ABC", "abc")	0

Function	Description	Example	Returns
String(), **String$()**	Returns a string consisting of specified repeated characters	**String**(5, "A")	AAAAA
Trim(), **Trim$()**	Removes leading and trailing spaces from a string	**Trim**(" ABC ")	ABC
UCase(), **UCase$()**	Returns uppercase version of a string	**UCase**("abc")	ABC
Val()	Returns numeric value of a string in data type appropriate to the format of the argument	**Val**("123.45")	123.45

Two versions of most of the functions are shown in table 9.7: one with, and one without, a string-identifier character (**$**). In these cases, the function without the **$** returns a **Variant** subtype 8 (**String**); the function with the **$** returns the Text field data type (**String** in Basic). Figure 9.6 shows tests of a few of the string functions in the Immediate window.

Access's **Format()** and **Format$()** functions are identical to the **Format()** and **Format$()** function of Visual Basic 3.0 (see Chapter 4, "Working with Access Databases and Tables," for the arguments of these functions). Table 9.7 doesn't include the **Tab()** and **Spc()** functions because these functions are used primarily to format the printing of text strings; printing text strings is handled by Access's built-in report-generation feature.

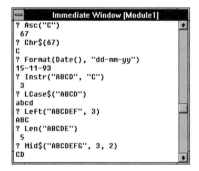

```
Immediate Window [Module1]
? Asc("C")
 67
? Chr$(67)
C
? Format(Date(), "dd-mm-yy")
15-11-93
? Instr("ABCD", "C")
 3
? LCase$("ABCD")
abcd
? Left("ABCDEF", 3)
ABC
? Len("ABCDE")
 5
? Mid$("ABCDEFG", 3, 2)
CD
```

Fig. 9.6
Testing the string-manipulation functions.

Numeric, Date/Time, and *String* Data-Type Conversion Functions

You can assign a particular data type to a numeric value with any of the data-type conversion functions. After you *freeze* a data type with one of the numeric data-type conversion functions, you cannot concatenate that data type with the **String** data type or data **Variant** subtype 7. Table 9.8 lists the eight numeric data-type conversion functions. The *NumValue* argument in the Syntax column can be any numeric or **String** value. However, if a **String** value is used as the argument of a numeric-type conversion function, the first character of the argument's value must be a digit, a dollar sign, a plus symbol, or a minus symbol.

Table 9.8 Data-Type Conversion Functions for Numeric, Time/Date, and *String* Values

Function	Description	Syntax
CCur()	Converts numeric value to **Currency** data type	CCur(*NumValue*)
CDbl()	Converts numeric value to **Double**-precision data type	CDbl(*NumValue*)
CInt()	Converts numeric value to **Integer** data type	CInt(*NumValue*)
CLng()	Converts numeric value to **Long** integer data type	CLng(*NumValue*)
CSng()	Converts numeric value to **Single**-precision data type	CSng(*NumValue*)
CStr()	Converts numeric value to **String** data type	CStr(*NumValue*)
CVar()	Converts numeric value to **Variant** data type	CVar(*NumValue*)
CVDate()	Converts numeric value to **Variant** subtype 7	CVDate(*NumValue*)

Mathematic and Trigonometric Functions

Access provides a sufficient number of mathematic and trigonometric functions to meet most scientific and engineering requirements. You can create additional trigonometric functions with more complex expressions. If you are interested in more obscure transcendental functions, such as cosecants or hyperbolic functions, choose the **S**earch command from the **H**elp menu, enter **math functions** and then click Derived Math Functions from the Math Functions Help menu. Table 9.9 lists the mathematic and trigonometric functions available directly in Access.

Table 9.9 Mathematic and Trigonometric Functions

Function	Description	Example	Returns
Abs()	Returns absolute value of numeric value	**Abs**(-1234.5)	1234.5
Atn()	Returns arctangent of numeric value, in radians	**Atn**(1)	.7853982
Cos()	Returns cosine of angle represented by numeric value, in radians	**Cos**(p/4)	.707106719949
Exp()	Returns exponential (antilog) of numeric value	**Exp**(2.302585)	9.9999990700 (rounding errors)
Fix()	Identical to **Int()** except for negative numbers	**Fix**(-13.5)	13
Int()	Returns numeric value with decimal fraction truncated, data type isn't changed unless argument is a string	**Int**(13.5) **Int**(-13.5)	13 14
Log()	Returns natural (Napierian) logarithm of numeric value	**Log**(10)	2.302585
Rnd()	Creates random single-precision number between 0 and 1 when no argument is supplied	**Rnd**() (varies)	.533424
Sgn()	Returns sign of numeric value: 0 if positive, -1 if negative	**Sgn**(-13.5)	-1
Sin()	Returns sine of numeric value, in radians	**Sin**(p/4)	.707106842423
Sqr()	Returns square root of numeric value	**Sqr**(144)	12
Tan()	Returns tangent of numeric value, in radians	**Tan**(p/4)	1.0000001732 (fraction because of rounding)

The angles returned by the trigonometric functions are expressed in radians, as is the argument of the arctangent (**Atn()**) function shown in the table. In the examples, the expression Pi = 3.141593 was typed in the Immediate Window before entering the syntax example expressions. The returned values of the trigonometric functions are for an angle of approximately 45 degrees, corresponding to p/4 radians.

II

Querying

> ### Note
>
> Because a circle of 360° contains 2π radians, you convert radians to degrees with the expression radians * 360/2p. Because Pi is a rounded value of π and the trigonometric functions round results, you usually obtain values with rounding errors. The cosine of 45 degrees, for example, is 0.7070707. . . but Access returns 0.7071067. . . . These rounding errors are not significant in most applications.

Int() and Fix() differ in the following way: Fix() returns the first negative integer *less than or equal to* the argument; Int() returns the first negative integer *greater than or equal to* the argument. Int() and Fix(), unlike other mathematic and trigonometric functions, return the integer value of a string variable but not the value of a literal string argument. Entering **?** **Int("13.5")**, for example, returns a data-type error message; however, if you type **A = 13.5** and then **? Int(A)**, Access returns 13.

Financial Functions

You may be interested in the financial functions of Access because you have used similar functions in Excel or 1-2-3 spreadsheets. The financial functions of Access (listed in table 9.10) are identical to their capitalized counterparts in Excel and employ the same arguments. If you have a table of fixed asset records, for example, you can use the depreciation functions to calculate monthly, quarterly, or yearly depreciation for each asset and then summarize the depreciation schedule in an Access report.

> ### Note
>
> A full description of the use and syntax of these functions is beyond the scope of this book. If you are interested in more details about these functions, choose **S**earch from the **H**elp menu and enter the function name.

Table 9.10   Financial Functions for Calculating Depreciation and Annuities

Function	Description
DDB()	Returns the depreciation of a fixed asset over a specified period by using the double-declining balance method
FV()	Returns the future value of an investment based on a series of constant periodic payments and a fixed rate of interest

Function	Description
IPmt()	Returns the amount of interest for an installment payment on a fixed-rate loan or annuity
IRR()	Returns the internal rate of return for an investment consisting of a series of periodic incomes and expenses
MIRR()	Returns the modified internal rate of return for an investment consisting of a series of periodic incomes and expenses
NPer()	Returns the number of payments of a given amount required to create an annuity or to retire a loan
NPV()	Returns the net present value of an annuity paid out in equal periodic installments
Pmt()	Returns the amount of the periodic payment that must be made to create an annuity or to retire a loan
PPmt()	Returns the amount of principal in an installment payment on a fixed-rate loan or annuity
PV()	Returns the present value of an annuity paid out in equal periodic installments
Rate()	Returns the interest rate of a loan or annuity based on a constant interest rate and equal periodic payments
SLN()	Returns the depreciation of a fixed asset over a specified period by using the straight-line method
SYD()	Returns the depreciation of a fixed asset over a specified period by the sum-of-the-years'-digits method

General-Purpose Functions

Access provides seven functions that don't fit in any of the preceding categories but that you can use for creating queries, validating data entries, or with forms, reports, and macros. Table 9.11 lists these general-purpose functions.

Table 9.11 General-Purpose Access Functions

Function	Description	Syntax
Choose()	Returns a value from a list of values, based on the position of the value in the list	Choose([Unit of Measure], "Each", "Dozen", "Gross")
IIf()	Returns one value if the result of an expression is True, another if the result is False	IIf([Order Quantity] Mod 12 = 0, "Dozen", "Each")

(continues)

Table 9.11 Continued		
Function	**Description**	**Syntax**
`IsDate()`	Returns **True** if argument is the Date/Time field data type; otherwise, returns **False**	`IsDate(FieldName)`
`IsEmpty()`	Returns **True** if argument is a noninitialized variable; otherwise, returns **False**	`IsEmpty(FieldName)`
`IsNull()`	Returns **True** if argument is **Null**; otherwise, returns **False**	`IsNull(FieldName)`
`IsNumeric()`	Returns **True** if argument is one of Number field data types; otherwise, returns **False**	`IsNumeric(FieldName)`
`Partition()`	Returns a string value indicating number of occurrences of a value within a range of values	`Partition (Number,Start, Stop, Interval)`
`Switch()`	Returns the value associated with the first of a series of expressions evaluating to **True**	`Switch([Unit of Measure], "Each", 1, "Dozen", 12,"Gross", 144)`

Choose() creates a lookup table that returns a value corresponding to a position from a list of values you create. **Choose**() is related closely to the **Switch**() function, which returns a value associated with the first of a series of expressions evaluating to **True**. In the **Choose**() example of table 9.1, if the value of the Unit of Measure field is 1, Each is returned; if the value is 2, Dozen is returned; and if the value is 3, Gross is returned. Otherwise, **Null** is returned.

The **Switch**() example returns a divisor value for an order. If the value of the Unit of Measure field is Each, **Switch**() returns 1. If Unit of Measure is Dozen, 12 is returned; and 144 is returned if Unit of Measure is Gross. **Null** is returned for no matching value. **Choose**() and **Switch**() have similarities to the **Select Case** statement in Access Basic and other BASIC dialects (**Null** is the **Case Else** value).

The **IIf**() function is called *in-line If* because it substitutes for the multiline **If...Then...Else...End If** structure of the Access Basic conditional expression. In the example shown in table 9.1, the **IIf**() function returns Dozen if the quantity ordered is evenly divisible by 12; otherwise, the function returns Each.

The **Partition**() function creates histograms. A *histogram* is a series of values (usually displayed in the form of a bar chart) representing the frequency of events that can be grouped within specific ranges. A familiar histogram is a distribution of school examination grades, indicating the number of students who received grades A, B, C, D, and F. The grades may be based on a range of test scores from 90 to 100, 80 to 89, 70 to 79, 60 to 69, and less than 60. You establish the upper and lower limits of the data and then add the partition value.

Effective use of the **Partition**() function requires typing or editing an SQL statement; the result of the query is most useful if presented in graphical form. Adding a histogram chart to a form is much easier than using the **Partition**() function.

The four **Is*DataType***() functions determine the type or value of data. You can use **IsNull**() in validation rules and query criteria of one field to determine whether another field—whose field name is used as the argument—contains a valid entry. Although *FieldName* is the argument in the example syntax in table 9.11, you can substitute an Access Basic variable name.

Other Functions

Descriptions and syntax for special-purpose functions are explained in the chapters covering the Access database object in which the following special-purpose functions are used:

- *SQL aggregate functions* are described in Chapter 10, "Creating Multitable and Crosstab Queries," because these functions are used most often with multiple-table queries that provide the data source forms. SQL aggregate functions return statistical data on the records selected by a query. You cannot use these functions in macros or call them from Access Basic modules, except within quoted strings used to create SQL statements to populate **Recordset** objects.

- *Domain aggregate functions* perform the same functions as the SQL aggregate functions, but on calculated values rather than the values contained in query fields. Chapter 12, "Creating and Using Forms," covers these functions. One domain aggregate function, **DCount**(), is useful in validating entries in tables; this function is explained later in this chapter in the section "Expressions for Validating Data."

- The two dynamic data exchange functions, **DDE**() and **DDESend**(), are used to transfer data from and to other applications, respectively. The use of **DDE**() and **DDESend**() is covered in Chapter 21, "Using Access with Microsoft Excel."

II

Querying

■ The remaining Access functions are used exclusively or almost exclusively in Access Basic modules, and are described in Part VII of this book, "Programming with Access Basic."

Constants

Access Basic has five predefined named constants. The names of these constants are considered *keywords* because you cannot use these names for any purpose other than returning the value represented by the names: -1 for **True** and Yes, 0 for **False** and No. (*True* and *Yes* are synonyms, as are *False* and *No*, and can be used interchangeably.) As mentioned earlier in the chapter, **Null** indicates a field with no valid entry.

Named constants return a single, predetermined value for the entire Access session. You can create constants for use with forms and reports by defining them in the declarations section of an Access Basic module. Chapter 27, "Writing Access Basic Code," describes how to create and use constants such as π (used in the examples of trigonometric functions).

Creating Access Expressions

Chapter 4, "Working with Access Databases and Tables," uses several functions to validate data entry for most fields in the Personnel Actions table. Chapter 7, "Attaching, Importing, and Exporting Tables," uses an expression to select the states to be included in a mailing list query. These examples provide the foundation on which to build more complex expressions that can define more precisely the validation rules and query criteria for real-life database applications.

The topics that follow provide a few examples of typical expressions for creating default values for fields, validating data entry, creating query criteria, and calculating field values. The examples demonstrate the similarity of syntax for expressions with different purposes. Part III, "Creating Forms and Reports," of this book provides additional examples of expressions designed for use in forms and reports; Part IV, "Powering Access with Macros," explains the use of expressions with macros.

Expressions for Creating Default Values

Expressions that create default field values can speed the entry of new records. Assignment of values ordinarily requires you to use the assignment operator (=). When you are entering a default value in the Properties pane for a table in design mode, however, you can enter a simple literal. An example is the **Q** default value assigned to the PA Type field in Chapter 4, "Working with Access Databases and Tables." In this case, Access infers the = assignment operator and the quotation marks surrounding the **Q**. To adhere to the rules of creating expressions, the default value entry must be = "Q". Access often enables you to use shorthand techniques for typing expressions by inferring the missing characters. If you enter = **"Q"**, you achieve the same result; Access doesn't infer the extra characters.

You can use complex expressions for default values if the result of the expression conforms to or can be converted by Access to the proper field data type. You can enter =**1** as the default value for the PA Type field, for example, although 1 is a Numeric field data type and PA Type is a Text type field.

Expressions for Validating Data

The Personnel Actions table uses a number of expressions to validate data entry. The validation rule for the PA ID field is > **0**; the rule for the PA Type field is **"S" Or "Q" Or "Y" Or "B" Or "C"**; the rule for the PA Approved By field is >**0 Or Is Null**. The validation rule for the PA ID field is equivalent to the following imaginary in-line **IIf**() function:

```
IIf(DataEntry > 0, [PA ID] = DataEntry, MsgBox("Please enter a
valid employee ID number."))
```

Access tests *DataEntry* in the validation rule expression. If the validation expression returns **True**, the value in the field of the current record is replaced by the value of *DataEntry*. If the expression returns **False**, a message box displays the validation text you typed. **MsgBox**() is a function used in Access Basic programming to display a message box on-screen. You cannot type the imaginary validation rule just described; Access infers the equivalent of the imaginary **IIf**() expression after you add the ValidationRule and ValidationText properties with entries in the two text boxes for the PA ID field.

The validation rule for the PA ID field isn't a valid test because you can type a value greater than the number of employees in the firm. You can determine the number of employees only from the Employees table. One way you can test for a valid PA ID number entry is to retain the > **0** restriction and make sure that the maximum value of the entry is less than or equal to the number of records in the Employees table. This procedure is close to a valid test because the Employee ID field of the Employees table is of the Counter field data type, which numbers appended records consecutively. But how do you determine the number of employees in the Employees table?

The domain aggregate function **DCount**() is useful for performing validations that involve testing entries in other tables. **DCount**() returns the number of records in a domain that meet a particular criterion. A *domain* can be a table or the result of a query. The syntax of the **DCount**() function follows:

DCount("[*FieldName*]", "*DomainName*", "*Criterion*")

FieldName is the name of the field to be tested—in this case, Employee ID. *DomainName* is the name of the table containing the Employees field. *Criterion* is an optional expression you can use to count records containing values that cause the expression to return **True**. If you need to count only the number of entries in the Employee ID field, you can omit the *Criterion* argument. After you use **DCount**(), the function creates and runs the equivalent of the following SQL statement:

SELECT Count([*FieldName*]) FROM *DomainName* WHERE *Criterion*

Although SQL is the subject of Chapter 24, "Working with Structured Query Language," examples of simple SQL statements are shown here so that you can become familiar with the syntax of these statements. If you program with Clipper, you can see that the use of **DCount**() is much simpler than VALID *UserFunction()*, which requires you to write a user-defined function to count the records.

To improve the Validation Rule for the PA ID field, follow these steps:

1. Open the NWIND.MDB database, if necessary.

2. Open the Personnel Actions table in design mode. The PA ID field is selected after you enter design mode. Because

Between *Value1* **And** *Value2*

is a more expressive syntax for

>= *Value1* **And** <= *Value2*

replace >**0** in the Validation Rule text box with the following statement:

Between 1 **And DCount**("[Employee ID]", "Employees")

Typing this entry fills the Validation Rule text box. Access has a solution for this problem: the Zoom box for expressions. Press Shift+F2 to open the Zoom box (see fig. 9.7).

3. Complete the expression in the Zoom box. Then click OK to move the completed entry into the Validation Rule text box.

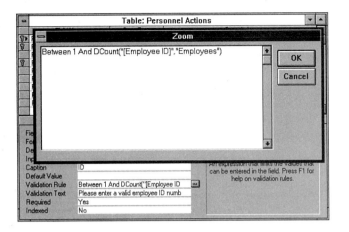

Fig. 9.7
The Zoom box for entering complex expressions.

4. The new validation rule isn't tested for syntax errors until you change to run mode. Click the Datasheet button on the toolbar and click Yes when the message box informs you that you must save the table before changing to run mode.

    If you make spelling errors or miss quotation marks when you type the validation rule, a Syntax Error message box appears. Open the Zoom box to correct the entry.

5. Access 2.0 adds a new feature that tests your Validation Rule statement with the data in table. Before changing to run mode, the message box shown in figure 9.8 appears. Click Yes to test the data you entered in the Personnel Actions table.

    The field and table names you type in the validation rule aren't tested unless you have records in the table. If you have records in the table, the **DCount**() function opens the Employees table, counts the number of records with **Not Null** values in the Employee ID field, and returns the count to the expression.

Fig. 9.8
The message box that gives you the option of testing your validation rule against existing data.

Access 2.0

> **Note**
>
> If you made an error in the field name or the table name, a "Can't evaluate expression" message box appears (similar to the one shown in fig. 9.9) when you test the expression against existing data or attempt to enter a new record in run mode. If the error is encountered when Access 2.0 is testing the expression, click OK. You see the "Errors were encountered during save. Properties were not updated" message box. (Access 1.x provided a more informative message box than "Can't evaluate expression.") The most common cause of this message is an incorrectly spelled field or table name, but invalid syntax or argument values of functions also result in the "Can't evaluate expression" message.

Fig. 9.9

A message box announcing an error in the syntax of an expression.

For this exercise, try entering employee ID numbers such as 0 and 25, which are outside the valid range. You receive the message box containing the following validation text:

Please enter a valid employee ID number.

Using **DCount**() to validate employee numbers doesn't provide a foolproof test. If you delete records for employees terminated from your employee list, for example, some employee numbers will be missing and a count no longer gives the proper upper limit for employee numbers. If you don't delete records for terminated employees, you can enter actions for persons no longer employed. It is useful if the **DCount**() function accepted a *Criterion* argument such as the following that would test for the existence of the Employee ID value you enter in the Initiated By field:

```
Between 1 And DCount("[Employee ID]", "Employees", "[Personnel
Actions]![PA ID] = [Employee ID]")
```

Entering this expression results in a "Can't evaluate expression" message because you cannot refer to a field that is not in the table specified by the *TableName* argument.

The expression "S" **Or** "Q" **Or** "Y" **Or** "B" **Or** "C" used to test the PA Type field is another candidate for change. The **In**() function provides a simpler expression that accomplishes the same objective:

```
In("S", "Q", "Y", "B", "C")
```

Alternatively, you can use the following validation expression:

```
InStr("SQYBC",[PA ID]) > 0
```

Both expressions give the same result.

Expressions for Query Criteria

When creating the qryUSMailingList query (in the "Creating More Complex Queries" section of Chapter 8) to select records from the states of California, Oregon, and Washington, you enter **="CA"**, **="OR"**, and **="WA"** on separate lines. A better expression is **In**("CA", "OR", "WA"), entered on the same line as the **="USA"** criterion for the Country field. This expression corrects the failure to test the Country field for a value equal to USA for the OR and WA entries.

You can use a wide range of other functions to select specific records to be returned to a query table. Table 9.12 shows some typical functions used as query criteria applicable to the Northwind Traders tables.

Table 9.12   Typical Expressions Used as Query Criteria

Table	Field	Expression	Records Returned
Customers	Country	**Not** "USA" **And** **Not** "Canada"	Firms other than those in the U.S. and Canada
Customers	Country	**Not** ("USA" **Or** "Canada")	Same as preceding; the parentheses apply the **Not** condition to both literals
Customers	Company Name	**Like** "[N–Z]*"	Firms with names beginning with _N_ through _Z_, outside the U.S.
Customers	Company Name	**Like** S* **Or** **Like** V*	Firms with names beginning with _S_ or _V_ (Access adds **Like** and quotation marks)
Customers	Company Name	**Like** "*shop*"	Firms with _shop_, _Shop_, _Shoppe_, or _SHOPPING_ in the firm name

(continues)

Table 9.12   Continued

Table	Field	Expression	Records Returned
Customers	Postal Code	`>=90000`	Firms with postal codes greater than or equal to 90000
Orders	Order Date	`Year([OrderDate]) = 1994`	Orders received to date, beginning with 1/1/1994
Orders	Order Date	`Like "*/*/94"`	Same as preceding; using wild cards simplifies expressions
Orders	Order Date	`Like "1/*/94"`	Orders received in the month of January 1994
Orders	Order Date	`Like "1/?/94"`	Orders received from the 1st to the 9th of January 1994
Orders	Order Date	`Year([OrderDate]) = 1994 And DatePart("q", [OrderDate]) = 1`	Orders received in the first quarter of 1994
Orders	Order Date	`Between #1/1/94# And #3/31/94#`	Same as preceding
Orders	Order Date	`Year([OrderDate]) = 1994 And DatePart("ww", [OrderDate]) = 10`	Orders received in the 10th week of 1994
Orders	Order Date	`>= DateValue ("1/15/94")`	Orders received on or after 1/15/94
Orders	Shipped Date	`Is Null`	Orders not yet shipped
Orders	Order Amount	`>= 5000`	Orders with values greater than or equal to $5,000
Orders	Order Amount	`Between 5000 And 10000`	Orders with values greater than or equal to $5,000 and less than or equal to $10,000
Orders	Order Amount	`< 1000`	Orders less than $1,000

The wild-card characters used in **Like** expressions simplify the creation of criteria for selecting names and dates. As in DOS, the asterisk (*) substitutes for any legal number of characters and the question mark (?) substitutes for a single character. When a wild-card character prefixes or appends a string, the matching process loses its default case sensitivity. If you want to match a string without regard to case, use the following expression:

    UCase$(FieldName) = "MATCH STRING"

Note

The Orders table of the Northwind Traders sample database supplied with versions 1.0 and 1.1 of Access included an Order Amount field. The value in the Order Amount field was set equal to the sum of the products of the Quantity and Unit Price fields, less the Discount percentage, of the records in the Order Details table. Including the Order Amount field violates the rule of relational databases that requires that all data in the fields of primary tables (Orders is a primary table) be dependent on the primary key and independent of other fields, either in the table or in other tables. The value of the Order Amount field is dependent on entries in the Order Details table. If you are using Access 1.x, you can substitute the Order Amount field of the Orders table for the calculated Amount field created in the query in the following section.

Entering a Query Criterion

To experiment with query criteria expressions, follow these steps:

1. Click the Query tab of the Database window, and then click the New button to open a new query.

2. Select the Customers table from the Add Table list box, and click the Add button. Repeat this process for the Orders and Order Details table. Click the Close button to close the Add Table dialog box. The Customer ID fields of the Customers and Orders tables and the Order ID fields of the Orders and Order Details tables are joined; *joins* are indicated by a line between the fields of the two tables. (The next chapter covers joining multiple tables.)

3. Add the Company Name, Postal Code, and Country fields of the Customers table to the query. You can add fields by selecting them from the field drop-down list in the Query Design grid or by clicking a field in the Customers Field list above the grid and dragging the field to the desired Field cell in the grid.

4. Add the Order ID, Order Date, Shipped Date, and Freight fields of the Orders table to the query. Use the horizontal scroll bar slider under the Query Design grid to expose additional field columns as necessary. Click the Table Names button of the toolbar or choose Table **N**ames from the **V**iew menu to display the table names in the Tables row of the Query Design grid. Place the caret in the Sort row of the Order ID field, press F4 to open the Sort list box, and choose Ascending Sort.

5. Click the Totals button of the toolbar or choose **T**otals from the **V**iew menu to add the Total row to the Query Design grid. The default value, Group By, is added to the Total cell for each field of your query.

6. Scroll the grid so that the Freight column appears. Click the selection bar above the Field row to select the Freight column and press the Insert key to add a new column.

7. Type **Amount: CCur([Unit Price]*[Quantity]*(1–[Discount]))** in the Field cell of the new column (see fig. 9.10). This expression calculates the net amount of each line item in the Order Details table. Using expressions to create calculated fields is discussed in the next section of this chapter.

Fig. 9.10

The query design for testing the use of expressions to select records with values that meet criteria.

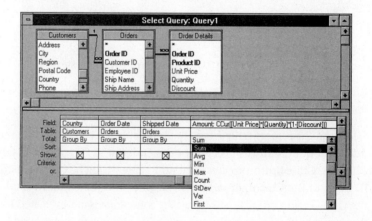

8. Move the caret to the Total row of the new column and press F4 to open the drop-down list. Choose Sum from the list (see fig. 9.10). The Sum option totals the net amount for all the line items of each order in the Orders table. You learn the details of how to create queries that group data in the next chapter.

The Total row for all the other columns of the query shows Group By. Make sure that the Show check box is marked so that your new query column appears when you run the query. (Do not make an entry in the Table row of your new query column; if you do, you receive an error message when you run the query.)

9. Click the Run Query or Datasheet View button of the toolbar to run your new query. Your query appears as shown in figure 9.11.

Select Query: Query1							
Company Name	Order ID	Postal Code	Country	Order Date	Shipped Date	Amount	Freight
Franchi S.p.A.	10000	10100	Italy	5/10/91	15-May-91	$108.00	$4.45
Mère Paillarde	10001	H1J 1C3	Canada	5/13/91	23-May-91	$1,363.15	$79.45
Folk och fä HB	10002	S-844 67	Sweden	5/14/91	17-May-91	$731.80	$36.18
Simons bistro	10003	1734	Denmark	5/15/91	24-May-91	$498.18	$18.59
Vaffeljernet	10004	8200	Denmark	5/16/91	20-May-91	$3,194.20	$20.12
Wartian Herkku	10005	90110	Finland	5/20/91	24-May-91	$173.40	$4.13
Franchi S.p.A.	10006	10100	Italy	5/21/91	24-May-91	$87.20	$3.62
Morgenstern Gesun	10007	04179	Germany	5/22/91	11-Jun-91	$1,405.00	$36.19
Furia Bacalhau e Fi	10008	1675	Portugal	5/23/91	29-May-91	$1,171.00	$74.22
Seven Seas Import	10009	OX15 4NB	UK	5/24/91	31-May-91	$1,530.00	$49.21
Simons bistro	10010	1734	Denmark	5/28/91	30-May-91	$470.00	$3.01
Wellington Importac	10011	08737-363	Brazil	5/29/91	03-Jun-91	$589.05	$31.54
LINO-Delicateses	10012	4980	Venezuela	5/30/91	03-Jun-91	$1,057.60	$102.59
Richter Supermarkt	10013	1203	Switzerland	5/31/91	07-Jun-91	$560.40	$50.87
GROSELLA-Restau	10014	1081	Venezuela	6/3/91	12-Jun-91	$192.10	$17.67
Piccolo und mehr	10015	5020	Austria	6/5/91	20-Jun-91	$1,423.50	$22.10
Folies gourmandes	10016	59000	France	6/6/91	11-Jul-91	$2,052.68	$113.01
Blondel père et fils	10017	67000	France	6/7/91	10-Jun-91	$1,148.00	$111.81

Record: 1 of 1078

Fig. 9.11
The query result set for the query design of figure 9.10.

Using the Expression Builder to Add Query Criteria

Once you've created and tested your query, you can apply criteria to limit the number of records returned by the query. You can use Access 2.0's Expression Builder to simplify the process of adding record-selection criteria to your query. To test some of the expressions listed in table 9.12, follow these steps:

Access
2.0

1. Click the Design View button of the toolbar to change to query design mode.

2. Place the caret in the Criteria row of the field for which you want to establish a record-section criterion.

3. Click the Expression Builder button of the toolbar to display the Expression Builder's window.

4. In the expression text box at the top of Expression Builder's window, type one of the expressions from table 9.12. Figure 9.12 shows the sample expression **Like** "*shop*" that applies to the Criteria row of the Company Name column. You can use the Like button under the expression text box as a shortcut for typing **Like**.

Fig. 9.12

Entering a criterion in Expression Builder to create a criterion to match "shop."

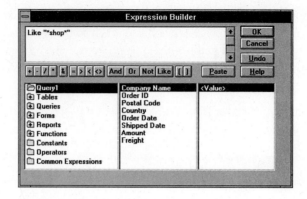

5. Click OK to return to the Query Design grid. Expression Builder places the expression you build into the field where the caret is located (see fig. 9.13).

Fig. 9.13

The Query Design grid with the expression created by the Expression Builder.

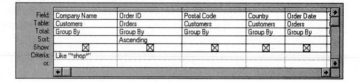

6. Click the Run Query button of the toolbar to test the expression. The query result for the example in figures 9.12 and 9.14 appears as shown in figure 9.14. (If you are using Access 1.x, your query returns many more records for **Like** "*shop*" because the Customers table of Access 1.x has more entries for North American firms that use the terms *shop* or *Shop* in their company names.

7. Return to query design mode; select and delete the expression by pressing the Delete key.

8. Repeat steps 2 through 7 for each expression you want to test. When you test expressions using Date/Time functions, sort the Order Date field in ascending order. Similarly, sort on the Order Amount field when queries are based on amount criteria. You can alter the expressions and try combinations with the implied **And** condition by entering criteria for other fields in the same row. Access warns you with an error message if you make a mistake in the syntax for an expression.

9. After you finish experimenting, save your query with a descriptive name, such as qryOrderAmount.

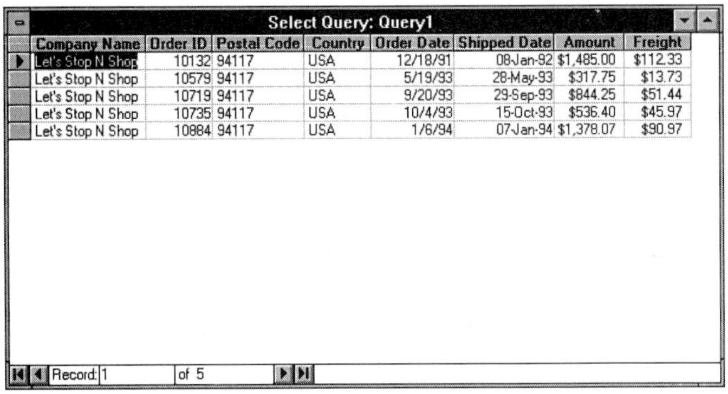

Fig. 9.14
The query result set resulting from adding the *Like "*shop*"* criteria to the Company Name field.

Expressions for Calculating Query Field Values

The preceding section demonstrated that you can use expressions to create new, calculated fields in query tables. Calculated fields display data computed based on the values of other fields in the same row of the query table. Table 9.13 shows some representative expressions you can use to create calculated query fields.

Table 9.13 Typical Expressions to Create Calculated Query Fields		
Field Name	**Expression**	**Values Calculated**
Total Amount	[Amount] + Freight	Sum of Order Amount and Freight fields
Freight Percent	100 * Freight/[Amount]	Freight charges as a percent age of the order amount
Freight Pct	**Format**([Freight]/[Amount], "Percent")	Same as above, but with formatting applied
Sales Tax	Format([Amount] * 0.05, "$#,###.00")	Sales tax of 5 percent of the amount of the order added with display similar to the Currency data type

To create a query containing calculated fields, follow these steps:

1. Move to the first blank column of the query you created in the preceding section. Type the field name shown in table 9.13, followed by a colon and then the expression. Press Shift+F2 to use the Zoom box to enter the expression, as shown in figure 9.15. If you don't type the field name and colon, Access provides the default Expr1 as the calculated field name.

Fig. 9.15
Entering an
expression in the
Zoom box to
create a calculated
field in a query.

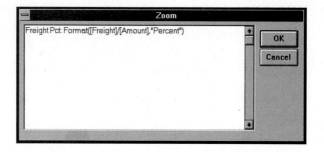

2. Place the caret in the Total cell of the calculated field and choose Expression from the drop-down list, as shown in figure 9.16. (If you don't enter Expression, your query returns an error message when you attempt to execute it.)

Fig. 9.16
The query design
for two of the
calculated fields of
table 9.13.

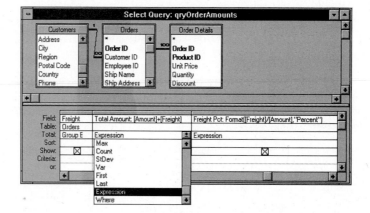

3. Run the query. The result set for the query with the calculated field appears as shown in figure 9.17.

4. Repeat steps 1, 2, and 3 for each of the four examples in table 9.13.

You use the **Format**() function with your expression as its first argument to display the calculated values in a more readable form. When you add the percent symbol **(%)** to a format expression or specify "Percent" as the format, the value of the expression argument is multiplied by 100, and the percent symbol preceded by a space is appended to the displayed value. (Access 2.0 introduces "Percent" as a new format specifier equivalent to entering **"0.00%"**)

Fig. 9.17
The query result set displaying order total and freight charges as a percent of order amount.

Figure 9.18 shows the rather complex SQL statement that creates the query with three calculated fields in Access 2.0's new and improved SQL window. (Click the SQL button of the toolbar to display the SQL window.) Note that you cannot include periods indicating abbreviations in field names. Periods and exclamation points are identifier operators and they cannot be included within identifiers.

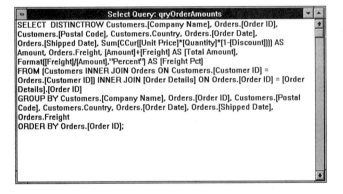

Fig. 9.18
The SQL statement used to create a query with three calculated fields.

II

Querying

Troubleshooting

When attempting to execute a query that contains an expression, a "Can't evaluate expression" or "Wrong data type" message box appears.

The "Can't evaluate expression" message usually indicates a typographic error in naming a function or an object. Depending on the use of the function, an Enter Parameter Value dialog may appear if the named object does not exist. The "Wrong data type" message is most likely to occur as a result of attempting to use mathematic or trigonometric operators with values of the Text or Date/Time field data types. If your expression refers to a control contained in a **Form** or **Report** object, the form or report must be open when you execute the function.

Other Uses for Expressions

You can use expressions with update queries, as conditions for the execution of a macro action, or as an argument for an action such as RunMacro (see Chapter 17, "Understanding Access Macros"). Expressions are used in SQL SELECT statements, such as the following:

```
WHERE [Birth Date] >= #1/1/60#
```

See Chapter 24, "Working with Structured Query Language," for more information. Expressions also are used extensively in Access Basic code to control program flow and structure. These uses for expressions are described in the chapters devoted to macros, SQL, and Access Basic programming (Parts IV, VI, and VII).

From Here. . .

Expressions you create with Access operators, identifiers, constants, and functions—and the literals you supply—are used in every aspect of an Access database application. Although the emphasis in this chapter is on using expressions to validate data entry in tables and creating query tables, expressions also are basic elements of forms, reports, macros, and modules.

- Chapter 10, "Creating Multitable and Crosstab Queries," you learn how to join tables in one-to-many relationships using Access's Query Design window.

- Chapter 11, "Using Action Queries," deals with queries that update data in tables, delete and add table records, and create new tables.

- Chapter 24, "Working with Structured Query Language," shows you how to use expressions in WHERE clauses that serve as query criteria and to create joins between tables.

Chapter 10

Creating Multitable and Crosstab Queries

Your purpose in acquiring Access is undoubtedly to take advantage of this application's relational database management capabilities. To do so requires that you be able to link related tables based on key fields that have values in common, a process known as a *join* in database terms. Chapters 8, "Using Query by Example," and 9, "Understanding Operators and Expressions in Access," showed you how to create simple queries based on a single table. If you tried the examples in Chapter 9, you saw a glimpse of a multiple-table query when you joined the Order Details table to the Orders table that you then joined to the Customers table to create the query for testing expressions. The first part of this chapter deals exclusively with queries created from multiple tables related through joins.

This chapter provides examples of queries that use each of the four basic types of joins you can create in Access's Query Design View: equi-joins, outer joins, self-joins, and theta joins. Two of the three new query features introduced by Access 2.0, subqueries and UNION queries, cannot be used in the queries you design in Access's graphic QBE window. These two new query features only can be implemented by writing SQL statements, the subject of Chapter 24, "Working with Structured Query Language." Some of the example queries in this chapter use the Personnel Actions table you created in Chapter 4, "Working with Access Databases and Tables." If you didn't create the Personnel Actions table, refer to the "Creating the Personnel Actions Table" section of Chapter 4 or to Appendix C, "Data Dictionary for the Personnel Actions Table," for instructions to build this table. Other example queries build on queries you create in preceding sections. You will find, therefore, that reading the chapter and creating the example queries sequentially, as the queries appear in text, is more efficient.

In this chapter, you learn to

- Join tables with queries

- Design queries that establish indirect relationships between tables

- Format the data in query result sets

- Summarize data with crosstab queries

- Design parameter queries

II

Querying

This chapter also includes descriptions and examples of the five categories of queries that you can create with Access: select, summary, parameter, crosstab, and action queries. Four types of action queries exist that you can use to create or modify data in tables: make-table, append, delete, and update. The chapter presents typical applications for and examples of each type of action query.

Joining Tables to Create Multitable Queries

Before you can create joins between tables, you must know the contents of the fields of the tables and which fields are related by common values. As mentioned in Chapter 4, "Working with Access Databases and Tables," assigning identical names to fields in different tables that contain related data is a common practice. This approach was followed when Microsoft created the Northwind Traders database and makes determining relationships and creating joins between tables easier. The Customer ID field of the Customers table and the Customer ID field of the Orders table, for example, are used to join orders with customers. The structure of the Northwind Traders database, together with a graphical display of the joins among the tables, is shown in figure 10.1. Joins are indicated in Access query designs by lines between field names of different tables. Primary-key fields are indicated by bold type. At least one primary-key field is usually involved in each join.

Fig. 10.1
The joins among the tables of the Northwind Traders sample database.

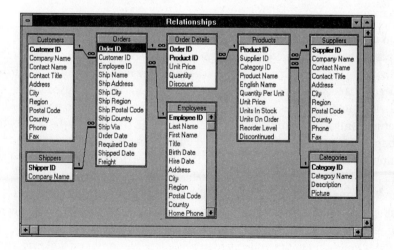

You can display the structure of the joins between the tables in the North-wind Traders database of Access 2.0 by giving the Database window the focus (click the Show Database Window button of the toolbar) and then clicking the Relationship button of the toolbar or choosing **R**elationships from the **E**dit menu. The "1" above the line that shows the join between two tables in figure 10.1 indicates the "one" side of a one-to-many relationship; the infinity symbol (∞) indicates the "many" side. If you're using Access 1.x, click the Query button in the Database window, select the Database Diagram query, and click Design. (If you open Access 1.x's Database Diagram in Datasheet View, only a single field header appears; this query was designed as a diagram, not to be run.)

Four types of joins are supported by Access in the graphical QBE design mode:

- *Equi-joins* (also called *inner joins*) are the most common join in creating select queries. Equi-joins display all the records in one table that have corresponding records in another table. The correspondence between records is determined by identical values (= in SQL) in the fields that join the tables. In most cases, joins are based on a unique primary-key field in one table and a field in the other table in a one-to-many relationship. If no records in the table that act as the *many* side of the relationship have field values that correspond to a record in the table of the *one* side, the corresponding records in the *one* side don't appear in the query result.

  Access creates the joins between tables if the tables share a common field name and this field name is a primary key of one of the tables or if you previously specified the relationships between the tables in the Relationships window.

- *Outer joins* are used in database maintenance to remove orphan records and to remove duplicate data from tables by creating new tables that contain records with unique values. Outer joins display records in one member of the join, regardless of whether corresponding records exist on the other side of the join.

- *Self-joins* relate data within a single table. You create a self-join in Access by adding a duplicate of the table to the query (Access provides an alias for the duplicate) and then creating joins between the fields of the copies.

II

Querying

■ *Theta joins* relate data by using comparison operators other than =. Theta joins include *not-equal joins* (<>) used in queries designed to return records that lack a particular relationship. Theta joins are implemented by WHERE criteria rather than by the SQL JOIN reserved word. Theta joins aren't indicated by lines between field names in the Query Design window, nor do theta joins appear in the Relationships window.

Creating Conventional Single-Column Equi-Joins

◄ "Establishing Relationships between Tables," p. 164

Joins based on one column in each table are known as *single-column equi-joins*. Most relational databases are designed to employ single-column equi-joins only in one-to-many relationships. The basic rules for creating a database that enables you to use simple, single-column equi-joins for all queries are detailed in the following list:

■ Each table on the *one* side of the relationship must have a primary key with a No Duplicates index to maintain referential integrity. Access automatically creates a No Duplicates index on the primary-key field(s) of a table.

■ Many-to-many relationships, such as the relationship of Orders to Products, are implemented by an intermediary table (here, Order Details) having a one-to-many relationship (Orders to Order Details) with one table and a many-to-one relationship (Order Details to Products) with another.

■ Duplicated data in tables, where applicable, is extracted to a new table that has a primary-key, no-duplicates, one-to-many relationship with the table from which the duplicate data is extracted. Using a multicolumn primary key to identify extracted data uniquely often is necessary because individual key fields may contain duplicate data. The combination (also known as *concatenation*) of the values of the key fields, however, must be unique. Extracting duplicate data from tables is described in the "Creating New Tables with Make-Table Queries" section in Chapter 11.

All the joins in the Northwind Traders database, shown by the lines that connect field names of adjacent tables in figure 10.1, are single-column equi-joins between tables with one-to-many relationships. Access uses the ANSI SQL-92 reserved words INNER JOIN to identify conventional equi-joins, and LEFT JOIN or RIGHT JOIN to specify outer joins.

Among the most common applications for queries based on equi-joins is matching customer names and addresses with orders received. You may want to create a simple report, for example, that lists the customer name, order number, order date, and amount. To create a conventional one-to-many, single-column equi-join query that relates Northwind's customers to the orders the customers place, sorted by company and order date, follow these steps:

1. If NWIND.MDB is open, close all windows except the Database window by double-clicking the Document Control-menu box. Otherwise, open Access's **F**ile menu and click NWIND.MDB to open the Northwind Traders database.

2. Click the Query button of the Database window, and then click New to create a new query. The New Query dialog appears. Click the New Query button. Access displays the Add Table dialog superimposed on an empty Query Design window.

3. Select the Customers table from the Add Table list, and click the Add button. Or, you can double-click the Customers table name to add the table to the query. Access adds the Field Names list for Customers to the Query Design window.

4. Double-click the Orders table in the Add Table list, and then click the Close button. Access adds the Field Names list for Orders to the window, plus a line that indicates a join between the Customer ID fields of the two tables, as shown in figure 10.2. The join is created automatically because Customer ID is the key field of the Customers table and Access found a field with the same field name in the Orders table.

5. To identify each order with the customer's name, select the Company Name field of the Customers table and drag the field symbol to the Field row of the first column of the Query Design grid.

6. Select the Order ID field of the Orders table and drag the field symbol to the Field row of the second column. Drag the Order Date field to the third column. If you are using Access 1.x, you also can drag the Order Amount field to the fourth column. (Access 2.0's Orders table does not include the Order Amount field because inclusion of this field violates one of the rules of relational database design; don't include calculated values in fields of tables.) The query design appears as shown in figure 10.3.

II

Querying

Fig. 10.2
A join between fields of two tables with a common field name, created by Access.

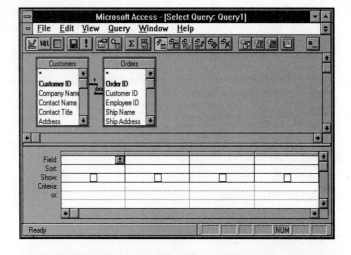

Fig. 10.3
Designing a query to display orders placed by customers, sorted by company name and order date.

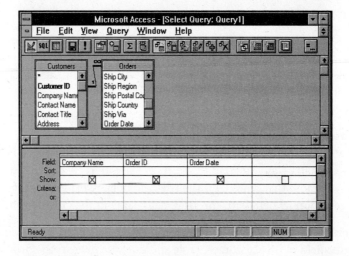

7. Click the Run Query or Datasheet View button to display the result of the query, the **Recordset** shown in figure 10.4.

Specifying a Sort Order for the Query Result Set

◄ "Adding Indexes to Tables," p. 173

Access displays query result sets in the order of the index on the primary-key field. If more than one column represents a primary-key field, the query result set is sorted in left to right key field column precedence. Because Company Name is the farthest left primary-key field, the query result set displays all orders for a single company in order number sequence. You can override the primary-key display order by adding a sort order. As an example, if you want to see the latest orders first, you can specify a descending sort by order date. To add this sort sequence to your query, follow these steps:

1. Click the Design View button to return to query design mode.

2. Place the caret in the Sort row of the Order Date column of the Query Design grid and press F4 to open the drop-down list.

3. Select Descending from the drop-down list to specify a descending sort on date—latest orders first (see fig. 10.5).

4. Click the Run Query button or the Datasheet View button to display the query result set with the new sort order (see fig. 10.6).

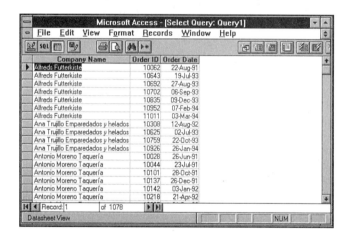

Fig. 10.4
The result of the query design of figure 10.3 that joins the Customers and Orders tables.

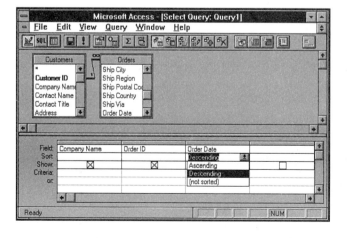

Fig. 10.5
Adding a special sort order to the query.

II

Querying

Fig. 10.6
The result of adding a descending sort on Order Date to the query.

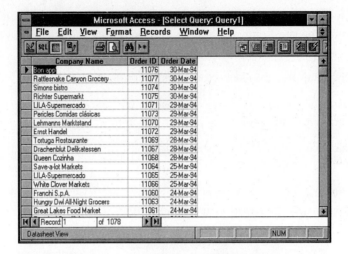

Company Name	Order ID	Order Date
Bon app	11076	30-Mar-94
Rattlesnake Canyon Grocery	11077	30-Mar-94
Simons bistro	11074	30-Mar-94
Richter Supermarkt	11075	30-Mar-94
LILA-Supermercado	11071	29-Mar-94
Pericles Comidas clásicas	11073	29-Mar-94
Lehmanns Marktstand	11070	29-Mar-94
Ernst Handel	11072	29-Mar-94
Tortuga Restaurante	11069	28-Mar-94
Drachenblut Delikatessen	11067	28-Mar-94
Queen Cozinha	11068	28-Mar-94
Save-a-lot Markets	11064	25-Mar-94
LILA-Supermercado	11065	25-Mar-94
White Clover Markets	11066	25-Mar-94
Franchi S.p.A.	11060	24-Mar-94
Hungry Owl All-Night Grocers	11063	24-Mar-94
Great Lakes Food Market	11061	24-Mar-94

Creating Queries from Tables with Indirect Relationships

You can create queries that return indirectly related records, such as the categories of products purchased by each customer. You need to include in the query each table that serves as a link in the chain of joins. If you are creating queries to return the categories of products purchased by each customer, for example, include each of the tables that link the chain of joins between the Customers and Categories tables. This chain includes Customers, Orders, Order Details, Products, and Categories. You don't need to add any fields, however, from the intermediate tables to the Query Design grid; the Company Name and the Category Name are sufficient.

To modify your customers and orders so that you create a query that displays fields of indirectly related records, follow these steps:

1. Delete the Order ID column of the query by clicking the thin bar above the Field row to select (highlight) the entire column. Then press Delete. Perform the same action for the Order Date columns so that only the Company Name column appears in the query.

2. Click the Add Table button of the toolbar or choose **A**dd Table from the **Q**uery menu and add the Order Details, Products, and Categories tables to the query, in sequence, then click the Close button of the Add Table dialog. The upper pane of figure 10.7 shows the chain of joins that Access creates between Customers and Categories based on the primary-key field of each intervening table and the identically named field in the adjacent table.

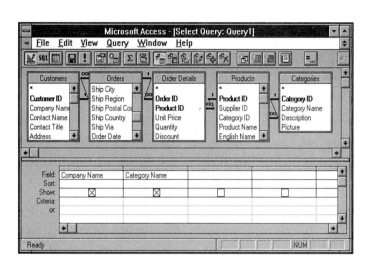

Fig. 10.7
The chain of joins
required to create
queries from tables
that have an
indirect
relationship.

3. Drag the Category Name from the Categories field list to the Field row
   of the second column of the grid.

4. If you want to see the SQL statement that Access uses to create the
   query, click the SQL button of the toolbar or choose **S**QL from the **V**iew
   menu to display Access 2.0's new SQL window shown in figure 10.8.
   The joins of the table appear as INNER JOIN...ON... clauses. Cascaded
   joins use the INNER JOIN...ON...ON... syntax, which is explained in
   Chapter 24, "Working with Structured Query Language."

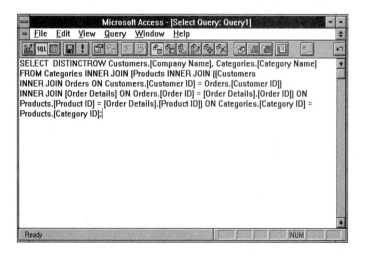

Fig. 10.8
The SQL statement
that creates the
query to determine
customers
purchasing
categories of
products.

5. Click the Design View button or double-click the Document Control-menu box to close the SQL window, and then click the Run Query button on the toolbar. The query result set shown in figure 10.9 appears.

6. Click the End of Table button to determine the number of rows in the query table. When this chapter was written, the number of rows (Records) was 643. Because databases are dynamic objects and Microsoft may continue to add new records to the tables during the beta-testing process, your query result set may have more rows.

7. Close the query by double-clicking the Document Control-menu box. This query is only an example, so you don't need to save the query.

Queries made on indirectly related tables are common, especially when you want to analyze the data with SQL aggregate functions or Access's crosstab queries. For more information, see the sections "Using the SQL Aggregate Functions" and "Creating Crosstab Queries" in this chapter.

Fig. 10.9
The Customers-Categories *Recordset*, resulting from the query of figure 10.7.

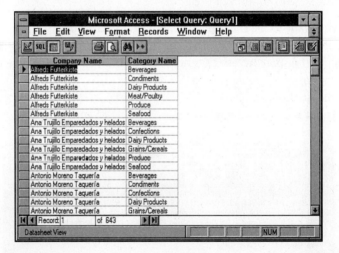

Creating Multicolumn Equi-Joins and Selecting Unique Values

You can have more than one join between a pair of tables. You may, for example, want to create a query that returns the names of customers for which the billing and shipping addresses are the same. The billing address is the Address field of the Customers table, and the shipping address is the Ship Address field of the Orders table. Therefore, you need to match the Customer ID fields in the two tables and `Customers.Address` with `Orders.[Ship Address]`. This task requires a *multicolumn equi-join*.

To create this example of an address-matching multicolumn equi-join, follow these steps:

1. Create a new query by giving the Database window the focus and clicking the New Query button of the toolbar. Alternatively, click the Query button and then the New button in the Database window.

2. Add the Customers and Orders tables to the query by selecting each table in the Add Table dialog and clicking the Add button. Click Close.

3. Click and drag the Address field of the Field List box for the Customers table to the Ship Address field of the Field List box for the Orders table. Another join is created, indicated by the new line between Address and Ship Address (see fig. 10.10). The new line in Access 2.0's graphical QBE window has dots at both ends, indicating that the join is between a pair of fields that do not have a specified relationship, the same field name, or a primary-key index.

Access 2.0

4. Drag the Company Name and Address fields of the Customers table to the Field row of the first and second query columns and drop the fields. Drag the Ship Address field of the Orders table to the third column of the query and drop the field in the Field row.

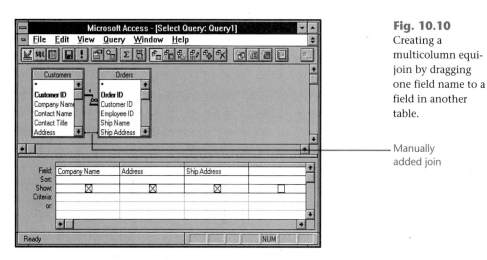

Fig. 10.10
Creating a multicolumn equi-join by dragging one field name to a field in another table.

— Manually added join

5. Add an ascending sort to the Company Name column.

6. Click the Run Query button on the toolbar. The result of the query is shown in figure 10.11.

Fig. 10.11
A query result set of orders for customers who have the same billing and shipping addresses.

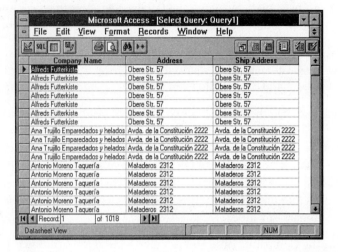

7. To eliminate the duplicate rows, you must use Access 2.0's new Query Properties window's Unique Values option. To display this window, which is shown in figure 10.12, click the Design View button, and then click the Properties button on the toolbar or double-click an empty area in the upper pane of the Query Design window. If the Properties window's title bar displays Field Properties or Field List, click an empty area in the upper pane of the Query Design window so that the title bar displays Query Properties.

Fig. 10.12
Using the Query Properties dialog to display only rows with unique values.

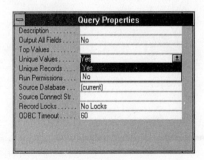

8. The `UniqueRecords` property is set at **True** (Yes) and the `UniqueValues` property is set at **False** (No) by default. The default settings add the Access SQL `DISTINCTROW` keyword to the SQL statement that creates the query (see fig. 10.8). Place the caret in the Unique Values text box, and press F4 to open the drop-down list. Select Yes and close the list. Setting the `UniqueValues` property to **True** substitutes the ANSI SQL reserved word `DISTINCT` for Access's `DISTINCTROW`. Click the Properties button again to close the Properties window.

9. Click the Run Query button of the toolbar. The result set no longer contains duplicate rows, as demonstrated by figure 10.13.

Fig. 10.13

The query result set after duplicate rows are removed.

10. Click the SQL button of the toolbar to display the SQL statement (see fig. 10.14). The `DISTINCT` modifier of the `SELECT` statement causes the query to display only those records whose fields values that *are included in the query* differ.

11. Double-click the Document Control-menu box to close the query, without saving it. You then avoid cluttering the Queries list of the Database window with obsolete query examples.

Because most of the orders have the same billing and shipping addresses, a more useful query is to find the orders for which the customer's billing and shipping addresses differ. You cannot create this query with a multicolumn equi-join, however, because the `INNER JOIN` reserved word in Access SQL doesn't accept the `<>` operator. Adding a not-equal join uses a criterion rather than a multicolumn join, as explained in the "Creating Not-Equal Theta Joins with Criteria" section later in this chapter.

Fig. 10.14

The SQL statement that results in the query result set of figure 10.13.

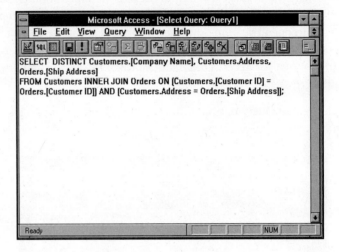

Troubleshooting

When I run my query, an Enter Parameter Value dialog appears that asks me to enter a value. I hadn't specified a parameter for the query.

The Enter Parameter Value dialog appears when the Jet engine's query parser cannot identify an object specified in the query or can't evaluate an expression. In the majority of cases, the appearance of the Enter Parameter dialog appears as a result of a typographic error. Creating parameter queries intentionally is the subject of the "Designing Parameter Queries" section, later in this chapter.

Outer, Self, and Theta Joins

The preceding sections of this chapter described the equi-join or, in the new parlance of SQL-92, an inner join. Inner joins are the most common type of join in database applications. Access also lets you create three other joins: outer, self, and theta. These three less common types of joins are described in the sections that follow.

Creating Outer Joins

Outer joins enable you to display fields of all the records in a table participating in a query, regardless of whether corresponding records exist in the joined table. With Access, you can select between left and right outer joins.

In diagramming database structures, a subject of Chapter 23, "Exploring Relational Database Design and Implementation," the primary *one* table traditionally is drawn to the left of the secondary *many* table. A left outer join (LEFT JOIN or *= in SQL) query in Access, therefore, displays all the records in the table with the unique primary key, regardless of whether matching records exist in the *many* table. Conversely, a right outer join (RIGHT JOIN or =*) query displays all the records in the *many* table, regardless of the existence of a record in the primary table. Records in the *many* table without corresponding records in the *one* table usually, but not necessarily, are orphan records; these kinds of records may have a many-to-one relationship to another table.

To practice creating a left outer join, follow these steps to detect whether records are missing for an employee in the Personnel Actions table:

1. Open a new query and add the Employees and Personnel Actions tables. Drag the Employee ID field symbol to the PA ID field of Personnel Actions to create an equi-join between these fields if Access didn't create the join. (Access automatically creates the join if you established a relationship between these two fields when you created the Personnel Actions table in Chapter 4.)

2. Select and drag the Last Name and First Name fields of the Employees table to columns 1 and 2 of the Query Design grid. Select and drag the PA Type and PA Scheduled Date fields of the Personnel Actions table to columns 3 and 4.

3. Click the *line* joining Employee ID with PA ID to select it, as shown in figure 10.15. The thickness of the center part of the line increases to indicate the selection. (The two field list boxes have been separated in figure 10.15 so that the thin section of the join line is apparent.)

4. Choose **J**oin Properties from the **V**iew menu. (The **J**oin Properties command is active only after you select an individual join with a mouse click.) You also can double-click the *thin section* of the join line. (Double-clicking either of the thick sections of the line displays the Query Properties window.) The Join Properties dialog of figure 10.16 appears. Type 1 is a conventional inner join, type 2 is a left join, and type 3 is a right join.

Fig. 10.15
Selecting a join to change the join's property from an inner to a left or right outer join.

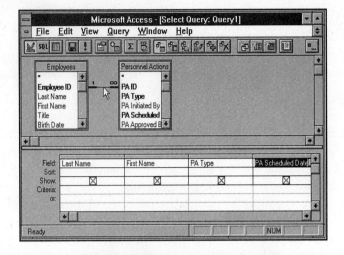

Fig. 10.16
The Join Properties dialog for choosing inner, left, or right joins.

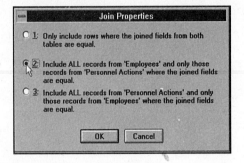

5. Select a type 2 join, a left join, by clicking the 2 button. Click OK to close the dialog.

    Note that an arrowhead is added to the line that joins Employee ID and PA ID. The direction of the arrow, left to right, indicates that a left join between the tables was created.

6. Click the Run Query button of the toolbar to display the result of the left join query. The five employees without a record in Personnel Actions appear in the last rows of the result table, as illustrated by figure 10.17. (Microsoft added these five employees to the Employees table of Access 2.0; Northwind had only nine employees in Access 1.x.)

7. Close, but don't save, the query.

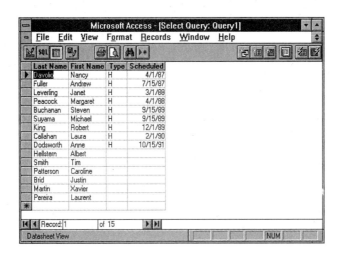

Fig. 10.17
The result of creating a left join between the ID fields of the Employees and Personnel Actions tables.

If you could add a personnel action for a nonexistent Employee ID (the validation rule you added in Chapter 9, "Understanding Operators and Expressions in Access," prevents you from doing so), a right join shows the invalid entry with blank employee name fields.

Creating Self-Joins

Self-joins relate values in a single table. Creating a self-join requires that you add a copy of the table to the query and then add a join between the related fields. An example of the use of a self-join is to determine whether supervisors have approved personnel actions that they initiated, which is prohibited by the imaginary personnel manual for Northwind Traders.

To create this kind of self-join for the Personnel Actions table, follow these steps:

1. Open a new query and add the Personnel Actions table.

2. Add another copy of the Personnel Actions table to the query by clicking the Add button again. Access names the copy Personnel Actions_1.

3. Drag the PA Initiated By field of the original table to the PA Approved By field of the copied table. The join appears as shown in the upper pane of figure 10.18.

Click the Table Names button of the toolbar to add the Table row to the query design grid so that you can distinguish between fields added from the original and copied tables.

Fig. 10.18
Designing the query for a self-join on the Personnel Actions table.

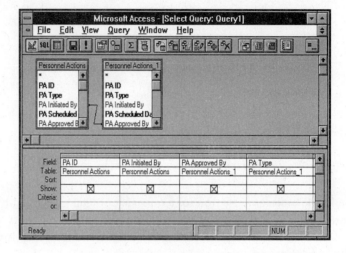

4. Drag the PA ID and PA Initiated By fields of the original table, and the PA Approved By and PA Type fields of the copy of Personnel Actions, to the Field row of columns 1 through 4, respectively, of the Query Design grid.

5. With self-joins, you must specify that only unique values are included. Click the Properties button on the toolbar or double-click an empty area in the upper pane of the Query Design window, and set the value of the UniqueValues property in the Query Properties window to Yes. Click the Properties button again to close the Query Properties window.

6. Click the Run Query button of the toolbar to display the records in which the same employee initiated and approved a personnel action, as shown in figure 10.19. In this case, Employee ID 2 (Mr. Fuller) is a vice-president and can override personnel policy.

In this example, you can add the Employees table to the query to display the employee name. Adding the Employees table creates an additional join between the PA ID field of the original Personnel Actions table and the Employee ID field of the Employees table. You then need to drag the Last Name field to the fifth column of the Query Design grid. Because this join includes a primary-key field, Employee ID, the default DISTINCTROW process yields unique values. To verify that the values are unique, click the Properties button of the toolbar or double-click an empty area in the upper pane of the Query Design window, and set the value of the UniqueValues property to Yes, and then rerun the query.

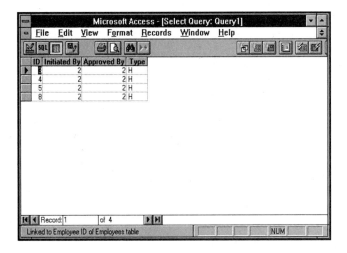

Fig. 10.19
The result of a self-join that tests for supervisors approving personnel actions they initiated.

Self-joins are seldom used in full-fledged relational database applications because the types of problems self-joins can detect can be (and should be) eliminated by validation criteria and enforcement of referential integrity.

◄ "Validating Data Entry," p. 193

◄ "Enforcing Referential Integrity," p. 169

Creating Not-Equal Theta Joins with Criteria

Most joins are based on fields with equal values, but sometimes you need to create a join on unequal fields. Joins you create with graphical QBE in Access are restricted to conventional equi-joins and outer joins. You can create the equivalent of a not-equal theta join by applying a criterion to one of the two fields you want to test for not-equal values.

Finding customers that have different billing and shipping addresses, as mentioned previously, is an example in which a not-equal theta join is useful. To create the equivalent of this join, follow these steps:

1. Create a new query and add the Customers and Orders tables.

2. Select and drag the Company Name and Address fields from the Customers table, and the Ship Address field from the Orders table, to the first three columns of the Query Design grid, respectively.

3. Type **<> Orders.Address** in the Criteria row of the Ship Address column. (Access automatically adds square brackets surrounding table and field names regardless of whether the names include spaces or other punctuation.) The Query Design window appears as shown in figure 10.20. This criterion adds the WHERE Orders.[Ship Address] <> Customers.Address clause to the SQL SELECT statement shown in figure 10.21.

Fig. 10.20

Designing the query for a not-equal theta join.

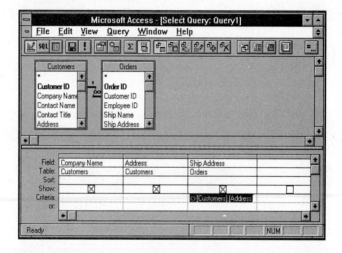

Fig. 10.21

The SQL statement for a not-equal theta join.

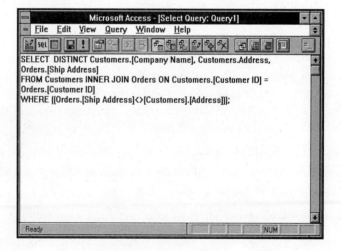

Typing **<> Customers.[Ship Address]** in the Address column gives an equivalent result. This criterion adds a WHERE Customers.Address <> Orders.[Ship Address] clause to the SQL SELECT statement.

4. Click the Properties button or double-click an empty area in the upper pane of the Query Design window to open the Query Properties window and set the value of the UniqueValues property to Yes.

5. Run the query. Only the records for customers that placed orders with different billing and shipping addresses appear, as shown in figure 10.22.

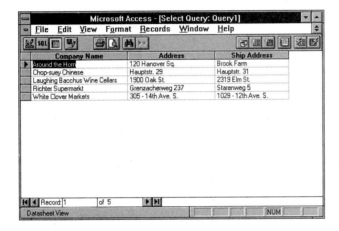

Fig. 10.22
The result of a not-equal theta join designed to identify different billing and shipping addresses.

Updating Table Data with Queries

Many of the queries you create with the UniqueRecords property set to **True** (Yes) are updatable because the queries are created using Access SQL's DISTINCTROW modifier. These queries create **Recordset** objects of the **Dynaset** type (called **Dynaset** objects in Access 1.x). You cannot update a query unless you see the tentative (blank) append record (with the asterisk in the select button) at the end of the query result table. Queries you create with the UniqueValues property set to **True** (Yes) create **Recordset** objects of the **Snapshot** type (called **Snapshot** objects in Access 1.x) by substituting ANSI SQL's DISTINCT modifier. You cannot edit, add new records to, or otherwise update a **Recordset** object of the **Snapshot** type. The next few sections describe the conditions under which you can update a record of a table included in a query and how to use the Output Field Properties window to format query data display and edits.

> **Note**
>
> **Dynaset** and **Snapshot** objects are types of Access 2.0's new **Recordset** object. Although Microsoft states that the reserved words **Dynaset** and **Snapshot** are included in Access 2.0 only for compatibility with Access 1.x, their distinctive terminology makes it unlikely that these two terms will disappear from common use among Access developers.

Characteristics That Determine If Queries Can Be Updated

Adding new records to tables or updating existing data in tables included in a query is a definite advantage in some circumstances. Correcting data errors that appear when you run the query is especially tempting. Unfortunately, you cannot append or update records in most of the queries you create. The following properties of a query *prevent* you from appending and updating records:

- Unique values are set with the check box in the Query Properties dialog.

- Self-joins are used in the query.

- SQL aggregate functions, such as Sum(), are employed in the query. Crosstab queries, as an example, use SQL aggregate functions.

- No primary-key field(s) with a unique (No Duplicates) index exists for the *one* table in a one-to-many relationship.

When designing a query to use as the basis of a form for data entry or editing, make sure that none of the preceding properties apply to the query.

If none of the preceding properties apply to the query or to all tables within the query, you can append records to and update fields in the following listing:

- A single-table query

- Both tables in a one-to-one relationship

- The *many* table in a one-to-many relationship

- The *one* table in a one-to-many relationship if none of the fields of the *many* table appear in the query

Updating the *one* table in a one-to-many query is a special case in Access. To enable updates to this table, follow these steps:

1. Add the primary-key field(s) of the *one* table and additional fields to update to the query.

2. Add the field(s) of the *many* table that correspond to the key field(s) of the *one* table; this is required to select the appropriate records for updating.

3. Add the criteria to select the records for updating to the fields chosen in step 2.

4. Click the Show box so that the *many* table field(s) doesn't appear in the query.

After following these steps, you can edit the *nonkey* fields of the *one* table. You cannot, however, alter the values of key fields that have relationships with records in the *many* table. Such a modification violates referential integrity. You also cannot update a calculated column of a query; calculated values are not allowed in tables.

Formatting Data with the Output Field Properties Window

The display format of data in queries is inherited from the format of the data in the tables that underlie the query. You can override the table format by using the **Format**(*ColumnName*, *FormatString*) function described in Chapter 9 to create a calculated field. Access 2.0 provides an easier method: it adds a Field Properties window that you can use to format the display of query data. You also can create an input mask to aid in updating the query data. To open the Field Properties window, place the caret in the Field cell of the query column you want to format and then click the Properties button of the toolbar or double-click an empty area in the upper pane of the Query Design window. Figure 10.23 shows the Field Properties window for the Order Date column of a simple one-to-many query created from the Customers and Orders tables.

Access
2.0

Fig. 10.23

Changing the display format for a query column of the Date/Time field data type.

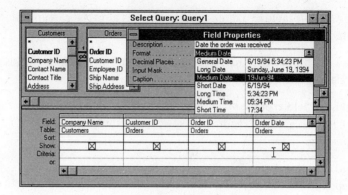

The Field Properties window displays the following subset of the properties that are applicable to fields of a table:

- *Description.* For entering the text to appear in the status bar when you select the field in Datasheet View

- *Format.* For controlling the appearance of the data in Datasheet View, such as Medium Date

- *Decimal Places.* For setting the precision with which Number fields are displayed

- *Input Mask.* For establishing the format for entering data, such as 90/90/00

- *Caption.* For changing the query column heading, such as Received for the Order Date column

Each of the above query properties follows the rules described in Chapter 4, "Working with Access Databases and Tables," for setting table field properties. Adding a value for the Caption property is the equivalent of adding a column alias by typing **Received:** as a prefix in the Field cell of the Order Date column. The value of the InputMask property need not correspond to the value of the Format property. For example, the Received (Order Date) field in figure 10.24, which shows the effect of setting property values shown in the preceding list, has a Medium Date format and an input mask for Short Date format.

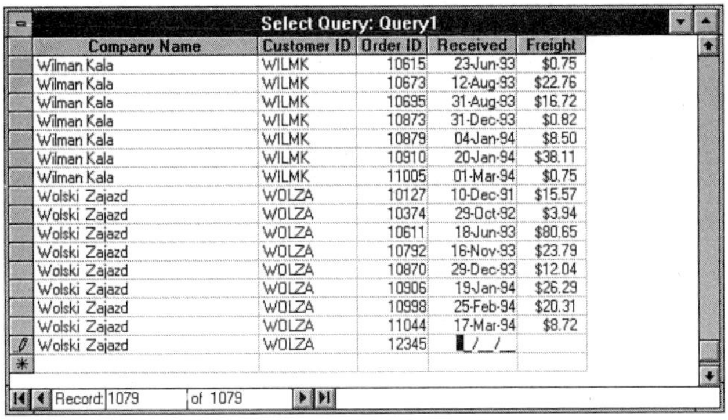

Fig. 10.24
Adding a new order record with an Order Date input mask.

Troubleshooting

I can't create an updatable one-to-many query with my attached dBASE tables, despite only displaying fields from the "many" side of the relationship.

You need to specify (or create) primary-key indexes for each dBASE table that participates in the query. The field(s) you choose must uniquely identify a record; no duplicate values are allowed in the index. Delete the attachment to the dBASE tables, and then re-attach the table with the primary-key indexes. Make sure you specify which index is the primary-key index in the Select Unique Record Identifier dialog that appears after you attach each table.

Make sure you don't include the field of the *many-side* table on which the join is created in the query. If you add the joined field to the field list, your query is not updatable.

Making All Fields of Tables Accessible

Most queries you create include only the fields you specifically choose from or type into the drop-down combo list in the Field row of the Query Design grid or by dragging the field names from the field lists to the appropriate cells in the Field row. You can, however, include in a query all the fields of a table. Access provides three methods, which are covered in the following sections.

Using the Field List Title Bar to Add All Fields of a Table

One way to include all the fields of a table in a query is to use the field list title bar or asterisk. To use this method to include all fields, together with their field name headers, in your query, follow these steps:

1. Open a new query and add the required tables.

2. Double-click the title bar of the field list of the table for which all fields are to be included. All the fields in the field list are selected.

3. Click and drag a field name to the Field cell of the Query Design grid and drop the field name where you want the first field to appear. An example of the result of the preceding steps for the Customers table is shown in figure 10.25.

Adding all the fields to the table by this method creates an SQL statement equivalent to

```
SELECT DISTINCTROW TableName.FirstField, TableName.SecondField, ...
TableName.LastField FROM TableName.
```

Fig. 10.25

Adding all fields of the Customers table to a query by double-clicking the header of the Customers field list.

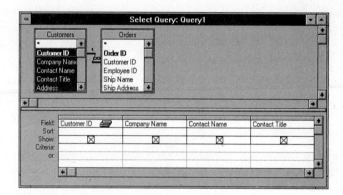

Using the Asterisk to Add All Fields without Field Names

To include in the query all fields of the table without displaying their field names, click and drag the asterisk to the first Field cell of the Query Design grid and drop the asterisk where you want all the fields to appear in the query result table. The asterisk column is equal to the Access SQL statement SELECT DISTINCTROW * FROM *TableName*.

You cannot sort on a column with an asterisk in the Field cell, nor can you establish criteria. If you choose the asterisk approach, you can sort or apply criteria to one or more fields in the table by following this technique:

1. After you add the asterisk to the Field cell, drag and drop the name of the field you want to sort or to which you want to apply a criterion to the Field row of the adjacent column.

2. Add the sort specification to the Sort cell or the criterion to the Criteria cell.

3. Click the Show box, which removes the check mark, so that the field doesn't appear twice in the query. The resulting query design with the Customers table is shown in figure 10.26.

You can use this method to add to the query as many columns from the asterisk table as you need. The field on which you sort the data is added to the SQL statement as a SORT BY `TableName.FieldName` clause, and a criterion is added in a WHERE `CriterionExpression` clause.

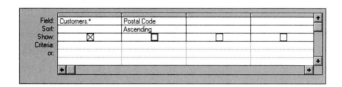

Fig. 10.26

Adding all fields of the Customers table with the asterisk field and providing a hidden column for sorting by Postal Code.

Selecting All Fields with the Output All Fields Property

Usually, only the fields whose names appear in the query are available for updating in forms or including in reports. All other fields are excluded from the result set. You can make all the fields in every table used in the query available to the forms and reports you create—even though the fields are not included by name in the query design—by setting the OutputAllFields property to **True**. (This is the equivalent of turning off the Restrict Available Fields option (turned on by default) in the Query Properties dialog of Access 1.x.) To use the OutputAllFields property to make all table fields available, follow these steps:

1. Open a new query and add the table(s) that participates in the query.

2. Click the Properties button of the toolbar or double-click an empty area in the upper pane of the Query Design window to display the Query Properties window.

3. In the Query Properties window, place the caret in the Output All Fields text box, press F4 to open the drop-down list, and change the default value, No, to Yes.

4. If the Unique Values text box displays Yes, you cannot update fields if the Unique Values Only option is chosen.

5. Click OK to close the Query Properties dialog.

Turning off the Restrict Available Fields option adds an all-fields asterisk to the list of specified fields in the SQL statement, as in the following example:

```
SELECT DISTINCTROW Customers.[Company Name], Categories.
➡[Category Name], *
```

When you include all fields in your queries, you may find that running the query takes longer, especially with queries that create a large number of rows in the result set.

Making Calculations on Multiple Records

One of the most powerful capabilities of QBE is the capability of obtaining summary information almost instantly from specified sets of records in tables. Summarized information from databases is the basis of virtually all management information systems (MIS). Management information systems usually answer questions, such as "What are our sales to date for this month?" or "How did last month's sales compare with the same month last year?" To answer these questions, you must create queries that make calculations on field values from all or selected sets of records in a table. Making calculations on table values requires that you create a query that uses the table and employ Access's SQL aggregate functions to perform the calculations.

Using the SQL Aggregate Functions

Summary calculations on fields of tables included in query result tables use the SQL aggregate functions listed in table 10.1, which are known as *aggregate functions* because these functions apply to groups (aggregations) of data cells. The SQL aggregate functions satisfy the requirements of most queries needed for business applications. You can write special user-defined functions with Access Basic code to apply more sophisticated statistical, scientific, or engineering aggregate functions to your data.

Table 10.1	SQL Aggregate Functions	
Function	**Description**	**Field Types**
Avg()	Average of values in a field	All types except Text, Memo, and OLE Object
Count()	Number of **Not Null** values in a field	All field types

Function	Description	Field Types
First()	Value of field of the first record	All field types
Last()	Value of field of the last record	All field types
Max()	Greatest value in a field	All types except Text, Memo, and OLE Object
Min()	Least value in a field	All types except Text, Memo, and OLE Object
StDev(), StDevP()	Statistical standard deviation of values in a field	All types except Text, Memo, and OLE Object
Sum()	Total of values in a field	All types except Text, Memo, and OLE Object
Var(), VarP()	Statistical variation of values in a field	All types except Text, Memo, and OLE Object

StDev() and Var() evaluate population samples. You can choose these functions from the drop-down list in the Total row of the Query Design grid. (The Total row appears when you click the Sum button of the toolbar or choose **T**otals from the **V**iew menu.) StDevP() and VarP() evaluate populations and must be entered as expressions. If you are familiar with statistical principles, you recognize the difference in the calculation methods of standard deviation and variance for populations and samples of populations. The method of choosing the SQL aggregate function for the column of a query is explained in the following section.

> **Note**
>
> ANSI SQL and most SQL (client-server) databases support the equivalent of Access SQL's Avg(), Count(), First(), Last(), Max(), Min(), and Sum() aggregate functions as AVG(), COUNT(), FIRST(), LAST(), MAX(), MIN(), and SUM(), respectively. ANSI SQL and few, if any, SQL databases provide equivalents of the StDev(), StDevP(), Var(), and VarP() functions.

Making Calculations Based on All Records of a Table

Managers, especially sales and marketing managers, are most often concerned with information about orders received and shipments made during specific periods of time. Financial managers are interested in calculated values, such as the total amount of unpaid invoices and the average number of days between the invoice and payment dates. Occasionally, you may want to make calculations on all the records of a table, such as finding the historical average value of all invoices issued by a firm. Usually, however, you apply criteria to the query to select specific records that you want to total.

 Access considers all SQL aggregate functions to be members of the Totals class of functions. You create queries that return any or all SQL aggregate functions by clicking the Totals button (with the Greek sigma, Σ, which represents summation) on the toolbar.

 The Orders table of Access 2.0's NWIND.MDB sample database does not include an Order Amount field that represents the total amount of the order, less freight. (If you're using Access 1.x's NWIND.MDB, you can skip the following steps because the Order Amount field is included in the Orders table.) To create a sample query that uses the SQL aggregate functions to display the total number of orders, total sales, and the average, minimum, and maximum order values, you need a field that contains the total amount of each order. If you're using Access 2.0, follow these steps to create a new table that includes an additional field with a computed Order Amount:

1. Create a new query, and add the Orders and Order Details tables to it.

2. Drag the Order ID field of the Orders table to the first column of the Query Design grid, and then drag the Order Date field to the second column.

3. Type **Order Amount: Sum([Quantity]*[Unit Price]*(1-[Discount]))** in the Field row of the third (empty) column. This expression sums the net amount of all line items for each order, as demonstrated in Chapter 8, "Using Query by Example." Click the Properties button of the toolbar or double-click an empty area in the upper pane of the Query Design window, and select Currency from the drop-down list of the Format property to format your new column.

4. Click the Totals button on the toolbar. A new row, Total, is added to the Query Design grid. Access adds Group By, the default action, to each cell in the Totals row. The following section discusses the use of Group By.

5. Move to the Total row of the second column, and press F4 to display the drop-down list of SQL aggregate functions. Select Expression from the list. Your Query Design grid appears as shown in figure 10.27.

6. Click the Run Query button of the toolbar to test your initial entries. Your query in Datasheet View appears as in figure 10.28.

Fig. 10.27
The Query Design grid to create a calculated field with the *Sum()* function.

Fig. 10.28
Running the query design of figure 10.27.

7. Click the Design View button of the toolbar, and then click the Make-Table button of the toolbar to display the Query Properties dialog for make-table queries.

8. Type **Orders2** in the Table Name text box of the Query Properties dialog, and then click OK. (Make-table queries are described in detail later in this chapter.)

9. Click the Run Query button of the toolbar to create the new table. Click OK when the message box appears that informs you of the number of rows that will be copied into your new Orders2 table.

10. Open the Orders2 table in design mode and set the Format property of the Order Amount field to Currency. You are warned by a message box that changing the field data type may cause you to lose data. Only decimal digits in the fifth decimal place and beyond are lost, so click OK.

11. Click the Datasheet View button to confirm that the Orders2 table appears similar to the Datasheet View of your original SELECT query (see fig. 10.28), differing only in the formatting of the data. Close the make-table query without saving it.

II

Querying

> **Note**
>
> When you apply the Format property to the Order Amount column by selecting
> Currency in the Field Properties window, the value of the Format property is not
> inherited by the table you create (the default Format value, Double, is applied). If
> you type **Order Amount: CCur(Sum([Quantity]*[Unit Price]*(1-[Discount])))**
> in the Field row of the Order Amount column, however, the Format property of the
> Order Amount field of the table you create is set to Currency.

Follow these steps to apply the SQL aggregate functions to the Order
Amounts field of the Orders2 or Orders table:

1. Open a new query, and add the Orders2 table if you are using Access 2.0
   or Access 1.x's Orders table. Drag the Order ID field to the first column,
   and then drag the Order Amount column four times to the adjacent
   column to create four Order Amount columns.

2. Move to the Total row of the Order ID column and press F4 to display
   the drop-down list of SQL aggregate functions. Choose Count as the
   function for the Order ID, as shown in figure 10.29.

Fig. 10.29

Choosing the SQL
aggregate function
for calculations
based on multiple
records in a table.

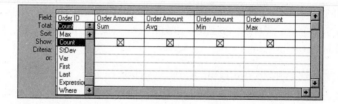

3. Move to the first Order Amount column, open the list, and choose Sum
   from the Total drop-down list. Repeat the process, choosing Avg for the
   second Order Amount column, Min for the third, and Max for the
   fourth.

4. Place the caret in the Count field, and click the Properties button of the
   toolbar or click the right mouse button, and then click Properties in the
   pop-up menu to display the Field Properties window. Type **Count** as
   the value of the Caption property.

5. Repeat step 4 for the four Order Amount columns, selecting Currency
   for the Format property and typing **Sum**, **Average**, **Minimum**, and
   Maximum as the values of the Caption property for the four columns.
   (You don't need to set the Format property if you used the **CCur()** function in the make-table query for the Orders2 table.)

6. Click the Run Query button of the toolbar to display the result of the query. You haven't specified criteria for the fields, so the result shown in figure 10.30 is for the table as a whole. Notice that each field name button caption is prefixed with the name of the function employed. (The values in the result may differ from the values in figure 10.30 because of records added by Microsoft to the sample database after this book was written.)

7. Save your query with a descriptive name, such as **qrySQLAggregates**, because the query is used in the two sections that follow.

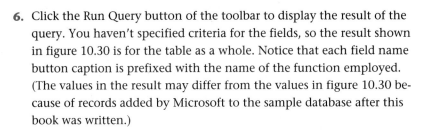

Fig. 10.30
The result of the all-records query of figure 10.29.

Count	Sum	Average	Minimum	Maximum
1078	$1,534,351.86	$1,423.33	$12.50	$16,387.50

Making Calculations Based on Selected Records of a Table

The preceding example query performed calculations on all orders received by Northwind Traders that were entered in the Orders table. Usually, you are interested in a specific set of records—a range of dates, for example—from which to calculate aggregate values. To restrict the calculation to orders Northwind received in March 1994, follow these steps:

1. Click the Design View button on the toolbar to return to design mode so that you can add criteria to select a specific group of records based on the date of the order.

2. Drag the Order Date field to the Order ID column to add Order Date as the first column of the query. The Order Date field is needed to restrict the data to a range of dates.

3. Open the Total drop-down list in the Order Date column, and choose Where to Replace the Default Group By. Access erases the mark in the Show box of the Order Date column. (If you attempt to show a column that provides the SQL WHERE restriction, you receive an error message when you run your query.)

4. Move to the Criteria row of the Order Date column and type **Like "3/*/94"** to restrict the totals to orders received in the month of March 1994 (see fig. 10.31). When you use the **Like** criterion, Access adds the quotation marks if you forget to type them.

Fig. 10.31
Adding a *WHERE* criterion to restrict the totals to a range of records.

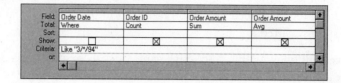

5. Click the SQL button of the toolbar to display the SQL statement for your query. The Where criterion in the Total row adds a WHERE clause to the SQL statement, here WHERE ((Orders.[Order Date] Like "3/*/94")), to restrict the totaled records to the records for the date range specified. If you don't add the Where instruction to the Total row, the query result consists of rows with the totals of orders for each day of March 1994, not the entire month.

6. Click the Run Query button on the toolbar to display the result: the count, total, and average value of orders received during the month of March 1992 (see fig. 10.32).

Fig. 10.32
The result of adding the *WHERE* criterion to the query.

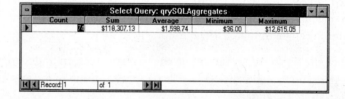

You can create a more useful grouping of records by replacing the field name with an expression. As an example, you can group aggregates by the year and month (or year and quarter) by grouping on the value of an expression created with the **Format**() function. The following steps produce a sales summary record for each month of 1993:

1. Click the Design View button of the toolbar, and then click the header bar of the Order Date column of the query to select the first column. Press the Insert key to add a new, empty column to the query.

2. Type **Month: Format([Order Date],"yy-mm")** in the Field row of the first (empty) column. (You use the **"yy-mm"** format so that the records sort in date order. For a single year, you also can use **"m"** or **"mm"**, but not **"mmm"** because **"mmm"** sorts in alphabetic sequence starting with Apr.)

3. Change the Where criterion of the Order Date column to **Like "*/*/93"**. Your query design appears as shown in figure 10.33.

<table>
<tr><td>Field:</td><td>Month: Format([Order Date],"yy-mm")</td><td>Order Date</td><td>Order ID</td><td>Order Amount</td></tr>
<tr><td>Total:</td><td>Group By</td><td>Where</td><td>Count</td><td>Sum</td></tr>
<tr><td>Sort:</td><td></td><td></td><td></td><td></td></tr>
<tr><td>Show:</td><td>☒</td><td>☐</td><td>☒</td><td>☒</td></tr>
<tr><td>Criteria:</td><td></td><td>Like '*/*/93'</td><td></td><td></td></tr>
<tr><td>or:</td><td></td><td></td><td></td><td></td></tr>
</table>

Fig. 10.33
Designing a query for a yearly sales summary by month.

4. Click the Run Query button to display the result of your query (see fig. 10.34). The query creates sales summary data for each month of 1993.

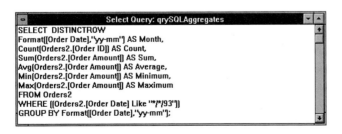

Select Query: qrySQLAggregates

Month	Count	Sum	Average	Minimum	Maximum
93-01	30	$40,003.57	$1,333.45	$156.00	$4,924.13
93-02	29	$36,602.04	$1,262.14	$147.00	$10,495.60
93-03	32	$59,260.71	$1,851.90	$136.80	$9,921.30
93-04	32	$54,845.66	$1,713.93	$110.00	$10,191.70
93-05	30	$30,929.65	$1,030.99	$23.80	$3,120.00
93-06	31	$50,275.18	$1,621.78	$48.75	$6,475.40
93-07	37	$55,177.62	$1,491.29	$55.80	$5,510.59
93-08	36	$65,482.39	$1,818.96	$45.00	$10,164.80
93-09	37	$51,833.64	$1,400.91	$93.50	$4,451.70
93-10	35	$49,889.40	$1,425.41	$28.00	$4,529.80
93-11	50	$82,994.77	$1,659.90	$12.50	$10,952.84
93-12	58	$95,519.06	$1,646.88	$98.40	$16,387.50

Record: 1   of 12

Fig. 10.34
The result set of the query design of figure 10.33.

5. Click the SQL button of the toolbar to display the SQL statement that created the query result set. The SQL statement in the SQL window of figure 10.35 has been reformatted for clarity. (Formatting an SQL statement with spaces and newline pairs does not affect the execution of the statement.)

```
Select Query: qrySQLAggregates
SELECT DISTINCTROW
Format([Order Date],"yy-mm") AS Month,
Count[Orders2.[Order ID]] AS Count,
Sum[Orders2.[Order Amount]] AS Sum,
Avg[Orders2.[Order Amount]] AS Average,
Min[Orders2.[Order Amount]] AS Minimum,
Max[Orders2.[Order Amount]] AS Maximum
FROM Orders2
WHERE [[Orders2.[Order Date] Like '*/*/93']]
GROUP BY Format([Order Date],"yy-mm");
```

Fig. 10.35
The SQL statement for a yearly sales summary by month.

6. Choose Save **As** from the **F**ile menu and save it under a different name, such as **qryMonthlySales**, because you modify the query in the next section.

Designing Parameter Queries

If you expect to run a summary or another type of query repeatedly with changes to the criteria, you can convert the query to a *parameter query*. Parameter queries, explained briefly in Chapter 8, enable you to enter criteria with the Enter Parameter Value dialog. You are prompted for each parameter required. For the example qryMonthlySales query that you created previously in this chapter, the only parameter likely to change is the range of dates for which the product sales data is to be generated. The two sections that follow show you how to add a parameter to a query and how to specify the data type of the parameter.

Adding a Parameter to the Monthly Sales Query

To convert the qryMonthlySales summary query to a parameter query, you need to begin by creating prompts for the Enter Parameter Value dialog that appears when the query is run. Parameter queries are created by substituting the text with which to prompt, enclosed within square brackets, for actual values. Follow these steps:

1. Open the qryMonthlySales query you created in the preceding section in design mode.

2. With the caret in the Field row of the Month column, press F2 to select the expression in the Field cell and then press Ctrl+C to copy the expression to the Clipboard.

3. Move the caret to the Field row of the Order Date column, and press Ctrl+V to replace Order Date with the expression used for the first column.

4. Move to the Criteria cell of the Order Date column and replace Like "*/*/93" with **[Enter the year and month in yy-mm format:]** (see fig. 10.36).

5. Click the Run Query button of the toolbar. The Enter Parameter Value dialog appears with the label you assigned as the value of the criterion in step 4.

Fig. 10.36
The expression to
create the Enter
Parameter Value
dialog with boxes
for the year and
month.

6. Type **93-06** in the text box to display the data for June 1993, as illustrated by figure 10.37.

7. Click OK to run the query. The result appears as shown in figure 10.38.

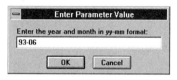

Fig. 10.37
The Query
Parameters dialog
for entering the
year and month.

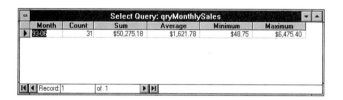

Fig. 10.38
The query result
for the *93-06*
parameter.

Specifying the Parameter's Data Type

The default field data type for parameters of Access queries is Text. If the
parameter creates a criterion for a query column of the Date/Time or Number
field data type, you need to assign a data type to each entry that is made
through an Enter Parameter Value dialog. Data types for values entered as
parameters are established in the Query Parameters dialog. Follow these steps
to add an optional data type specification to your parameter:

1. Use the mouse to select Enter the year and month in yy-mm format: in
the Criteria cell of the Month column (without the square brackets) and
copy the text of the prompt to the Clipboard by pressing Ctrl+C.

2. Choose Para**m**eters from the **Q**uery menu to display the Query Parameters dialog.

3. To insert the prompt in the Parameter column of the dialog, place the
caret in the Parameter column and press Ctrl+V. The prompt entry in
the Parameter column must match the prompt entry in the Criteria
field exactly; copying and pasting the prompt text ensures an exact
match. The square brackets are not included in the Parameter column.

4. Press Tab to move to the Data Type column, press F4 to open the Data Type drop-down list, and choose Text (see fig. 10.39). Click OK to close the dialog.

Fig. 10.39
The Query
Parameters dialog
for assigning
data types to
user-entered
parameters.

> ### Note
>
> Complete your query design and testing before you convert any type of query to a parameter query. Using fixed criteria with the query maintains consistency during the testing process, and repeated changes between design and run mode are speeded if you don't have to enter one or more parameters in the process. After you complete testing the query, edit the criteria to add the Enter Parameter Value dialog.

The parameter-conversion process described in this section applies to all types of queries you create, providing that one or more of the query columns includes a criterion expression. The advantage of the parameter query is that you or a user of the database can run a query for any range of values, in this case dates, such as the current month to date, a particular fiscal quarter, or an entire fiscal year.

Creating Crosstab Queries

Crosstab queries are summary queries that enable you to determine exactly how the summary data appears on-screen. Crosstab queries display summarized data in the traditional row-column form of spreadsheets. Crosstab queries use the Access SQL TRANSFORM keyword to indicate that the statements that follow the keyword are for a crosstab query. With crosstab queries, you can perform the following processes:

■ Specify the field that creates labels (headings) for rows by using the Group By instruction.

■ Determine the field or fields that create column headers and the criteria that determine the values appearing under the headers.

■ Assign calculated data values to the cells of the resulting row-column grid.

The following list details the advantages of using crosstab queries:

■ You can display a substantial amount of summary data in a compact format familiar to anyone who uses a spreadsheet application or a columnar accounting form.

■ The summary data is presented in a format ideally suited for creating graphs and charts automatically with the Access Graph Wizard.

■ Designing queries to create multiple levels of detail is quick and easy. Queries with identical columns but fewer rows can represent increasingly summarized data. Highly summarized queries are ideal to begin a drill-down procedure by instructing the user, for example, to "Click the Details button to show sales by product."

The only restriction imposed by using crosstab queries is that you cannot sort your result table on calculated values in columns. You cannot, therefore, create a query in which products are ranked by sales volume. Columns are likely to have values that cause conflicts in the sorting order of the row. You can choose an ascending sort, a descending sort, or no sort on the row label values in the first column.

One of Access 2.0's Query Wizards is designed to help you create crosstab queries. However, the Crosstab Query Wizard is limited to creating crosstab queries for a single table. If your database follows the rules of relational database design, it's far more likely that a usable crosstab query is based on at least two tables. Thus, you create the examples of crosstab queries in the next two sections with help from this book, instead of from the Query Wizard.

Access

2.0

Creating a Monthly Product Sales Crosstab Query

To create a typical crosstab query that displays products in rows and monthly sales volume for each product in the corresponding columns, follow these steps:

1. Open a new query and add the Products, Order Details, and Orders tables to it.

2. Drag the Product ID and English Name fields from the Products table to the first two columns of the query, and then drag the Order Date field of the Orders table to the third column.

3. Choose **C**rosstab from the **Q**uery menu. The title bar of the query changes from Select Query: Query1 to Crosstab Query: Query1, and another row, Crosstab, is added to the Query Design grid.

4. Open the drop-down list of the Crosstab row of the Product ID column and select Row Heading. Repeat this process for the English Name column. These two columns provide the required row headings for your crosstab.

5. Open the drop-down list of the Order Date column and select Where. Type **Like "*/*/93"** in the Criteria row of this column to restrict the crosstab to orders received in 1993.

6. Move to the Field row of the next (empty) column and type

   Sales: Sum([Order Details].[Quantity]*[Order Details].[Unit Price])

   Move to the Total row, choose Expression from the drop-down list, and then move to the Crosstab row and choose Value. The expression calculates the gross amount of the orders received for each product that populates the data cells of your crosstab query. (You need to specify the Orders Detail table name; if you don't, you receive an "Ambiguous field reference" error message.)

7. Move to the Field row of the next (empty) column and type **Format([Order Date], "mmm")**. Access adds a default field name, Expr1:. Accept the default because the Format() function you added creates the column names, the three-letter abbreviation of the months of the year ("mmm" format), when you run the query. The months of the year, Jan–Dec, are your column headings, so move to the Crosstab row and choose Column Heading from the drop-down list. The design of your crosstab query appears as shown in figure 10.40.

8. Click the Run Query button on the toolbar to execute the query. A period of disk activity occurs, followed by a display of the result of the crosstab query, shown in figure 10.41.

Notice that the crosstab query result contains a major defect: The columns are arranged in alphabetical order by month name rather than in calendar order. You can solve this problem by using fixed column headings, which you learn about in the following section.

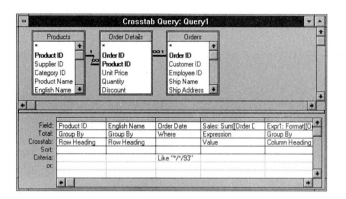

Fig. 10.40
The design of a crosstab query for monthly sales of products.

Fig. 10.41
The first result set from the crosstab query design of figure 10.40.

Using Fixed Column Headings with Crosstab Queries

◀ "Functions for Date and Time," p. 330

Access uses an alphabetical or numerical sort on row and column headings to establish the sequence of appearance in the crosstab query result table. For this reason, if you use short or full names for months, the sequence is in alphabetic rather than calendar order. You can correct this problem by assigning fixed column headings to the crosstab query. Follow these steps to modify and rerun the query:

1. Return to query design mode and click the Properties button of the toolbar or double-click an empty area in the upper pane of the Query Design window. The Query Properties window has an option only for crosstab queries: Column Headings.

2. Type the three-letter abbreviations of all 12 months of the year in the Column Headings text box (see fig. 10.42). You must spell the abbreviations of the months correctly; data for months with spelling mistakes do not appear. You can separate entries with commas or semicolons,

and you don't need to type quotation marks because Access adds them. Spaces are unnecessary and undesirable between the Column Headings values. After you complete all 12 entries, close the Query Properties window.

Fig. 10.42
Entering fixed column headings in the crosstab Query Properties window.

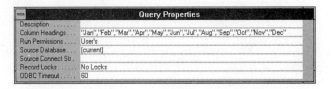

3. Click the Run Query button of the toolbar. Now the result table, shown in figure 10.43, includes columns for all 12 months, but only January through May appear in figure 10.43. (Scroll to the right to see the remaining months.) If the crosstab appears different, check to see if you entered the Fixed Column Headings in the Query Properties window properly. A misspelled month causes Access to omit the month from the query result set.

Fig. 10.43
The result table from the crosstab query design with fixed column headings and a date-limiting criterion.

Product ID	English Name	Jan	Feb	Mar	Apr	May
1	Dharamsala Tea		$216.00	$864.00		$540.00
2	Tibetan Barley Beer	$684.00	$912.00	$228.00		
3	Licorice Syrup		$160.00		$600.00	$140.00
4	Chef Anton's Cajun Seasoning	$281.60		$2,200.00	$1,100.00	
5	Chef Anton's Gumbo Mix					
6	Grandma's Boysenberry Sprea					
7	Uncle Bob's Organic Dried Pe.	$384.00	$720.00	$1,500.00	$300.00	$300.00
8	Northwoods Cranberry Sauce			$1,360.00		
9	Mishi Kobe Beef			$1,552.00		
10	Fish Roe	$843.20	$496.00	$558.00		$155.00
11	Cabrales Cheese	$772.80	$336.00	$63.00	$1,890.00	$1,050.00
12	Manchego La Pastora Cheese	$456.00			$1,710.00	
13	Kelp Seaweed	$4.80		$120.00	$48.00	
14	Bean Curd		$223.20	$1,627.50	$697.50	$604.50
15	Lite Sodium Soy Sauce			$186.00		$155.00
16	Pavlova Meringue Dessert	$1,181.50	$736.70	$872.50	$1,465.80	$209.40
17	Alice Springs Lamb	$312.00		$975.00	$1,872.00	$1,326.00
18	Carnarvon Tiger Prawns		$1,500.00	$1,562.50		$3,625.00

Record: 1 of 77

4. Choose Save Query As from the File menu and save the query with an appropriate name, such as **qry1993MonthlyProductSales**.

You can produce a printed report quickly from the query by clicking the Print Preview button on the toolbar and then clicking the Print button.

Note

You may want to use fixed column headings if you use the Group By instruction with country names. U.S. users will probably place USA first, and Canadian firms will undoubtedly choose Canada as the first entry. If you add a record with a new country, you need to remember to update the list of fixed column headings with the new country value. Fixed column headings have another, hidden benefit of usually speeding the operation of crosstab queries.

Decreasing the Level of Detail in Crosstab Queries

The result table created by the preceding example query has a row for every product for which Northwind Traders received an order in each month of 1993. Higher-level management usually wants information in the form of a graph or chart to use to analyze trends in the data. You, therefore, need to reduce the number of rows and columns so that you can create a readable graph from the values in the query result table.

To create a summary query that reports quarterly gross sales of products by category (rather than by Product ID), follow these steps:

1. Choose Save Query **A**s from the **F**ile menu, and save a copy of the query you created in the preceding section with a descriptive name, such as **qry1993QuarterlyCategorySales**.

2. Choose **A**dd Table from the **Q**uery menu and add the Categories table to the query.

3. To make the relationships among the tables more clear, click the title bar of each of the field lists in the upper pane and drag the field lists to the positions shown in figure 10.44.

4. Drag and drop the Category ID and Category Name fields of the Categories table to the Field cell of the first column, which contains Product ID. New Category ID and Category Name columns are added to the query. Move down to the Crosstab cell and choose Row Heading from the drop-down list for both new columns.

5. Click the selection bar above the Product ID cell of the third column, and then press Delete to delete this column. Repeat this process for the English Name column. The crosstab Query Design grid then appears as shown in figure 10.44.

Fig. 10.44
The design of a summary query for quarterly sales by product category.

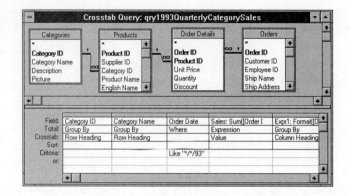

6. Edit Expr1:, which creates the column headings, so that the expression appears as **Format([Order Date],"""Quarter ""q")**. This results in column headings of Quarter 1–Quarter 4. (The multiple quotes are necessary to specify Quarter and a space as literals and q as a formatting character.)

7. Click a blank area in the upper pane of the Query Design window, and then click the Properties button or double-click an empty area in the upper pane of the Query Design window to open the Query Properties window. Delete the Column Headings entries for the month abbreviations, then close the Query Properties window. (If you don't delete the fixed column headings, your query can't return any rows. You can add the four Quarter # headings, separated by commas or semicolons, as the value of the ColumnHeading property in the Query Properties window to speed operation of your query.)

8. Click the Run Query button on the toolbar. The query result set appears as shown in figure 10.45.

9. Click the SQL button of the toolbar to view the SQL statement that creates the crosstab query (see fig. 10.46). The Access SQL TRANSFORM clause, which corresponds to the Values crosstab property, defines the values that appear in the data cells. The PIVOT statement defines the column headings. (The IN predicate following the PIVOT statement specifies the fixed column headings, if any.) TRANSFORM and PIVOT are not reserved words of ANSI SQL. The ANSI SQL IN predicate is interpreted differently by Access crosstab queries and by conventional SQL SELECT queries.

Crosstab Query: qry1993QuarterlyCategorySales				
Category ID	Category Name	Quarter 1	Quarter 2	Quarter 3	Quarter 4
1	Beverages	$23,615.10	$25,398.00	$21,953.25	$62,639.25
2	Condiments	$15,527.30	$15,064.35	$14,041.65	$16,039.40
3	Confections	$23,808.55	$16,873.43	$24,002.60	$29,078.64
4	Dairy Products	$22,484.80	$34,135.60	$34,054.50	$42,643.10
5	Grains/Cereals	$12,788.20	$14,799.00	$13,332.00	$25,219.25
6	Meat/Poultry	$19,590.49	$12,033.90	$33,121.41	$21,272.00
7	Produce	$12,512.70	$11,362.20	$16,223.25	$16,607.20
8	Seafood	$12,656.00	$15,977.90	$26,307.55	$31,406.10

Record: 1 of 8

Fig. 10.45
The result set of the query design for quarterly sales by product category.

Crosstab Query: qry1993QuarterlyCategorySales

```
TRANSFORM Sum([Order Details].[Quantity]*[Order Details].[Unit Price]) AS Sales
SELECT Categories.[Category ID], Categories.[Category Name] FROM
Categories INNER JOIN [Orders INNER JOIN [Products INNER JOIN [Order Details]
ON Products.[Product ID] = [Order Details].[Product ID]] ON Orders.[Order ID] =
[Order Details].[Order ID]] ON Categories.[Category ID] = Products.[Category ID]
WHERE [[Orders.[Order Date] Like '*/*/93'])
GROUP BY Categories.[Category ID], Categories.[Category Name]
PIVOT Format([Order Date],'"*"Quarter "*"q') In ("Quarter 1","Quarter 2","Quarter
3","Quarter 4");
```

Fig. 10.46
The SQL statement that creates the quarterly sales by product query.

10. Choose **S**ave from the **F**ile menu to save your query. The
qry1993QuarterlyCategorySales query is used for many different
purposes in later chapters of this book.

Crosstab queries that display time-series data, such as monthly and quarterly
sales for products or categories of products, often are used as the basis for
graphs. Chapter 20, "Adding Graphics to Forms and Reports," uses the
qry1993QuarterlyCategorySales query to create two types of Access graphs.

Creating Queries from Tables in Other Databases

Access
2.0

Access 2.0's Query Properties window includes two new properties that let
you create a query based on tables contained in a database other than the
current database. Access calls the database you open after you launch Access
the *current* database. Databases other than the current database commonly are
called *external* databases. The use of these two new properties is as follows:

■ The value of the SourceDatabase property for desktop databases is the
path to the external database and, for Access databases, the name of the
database file. To run a query against tables contained in the
SOLUTIONS.MDB sample database, type

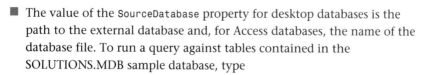

c:\access\sampapps\solution.mdb

in the Source Database text box, as shown in figure 10.47. To run a query against a set of Paradox tables in the *D*:\PARADOX directory, you type the path only (***d*:\paradox**). If you're using the ODBC API to connect to a client-server database, you leave the Source Database text box empty.

■ The value of the SourceConnectStr property also depends on the type of external database. If your external Access database is not secure, you leave the Source Connect Str text box empty, otherwise, you type **UID=UserID;PWD=Password** to specify the user ID and password needed to open the external database. For other desktop databases, you type the product name, such as **Paradox 3.5** or **dBASE III**. ODBC data sources require the complete ODBC connect string. Using ODBC databases is one of the subjects of Chapter 25, "Securing Multiuser Network Applications."

Fig. 10.47
Setting the
SourceConnectStr
property for a
query against an
external database.

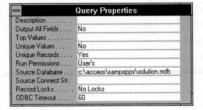

Running a query against an external database is related to running a query against attached tables. When you attach tables, the data in the tables is available at any time your application is running. When you run a query against an external database, the connection to the external database is open only while your query is open in design or run mode. There is a slight performance penalty for running queries against an external database; each time you run the query, Access must make a connection to (open) the database. The connection is closed when you close the query.

Figure 10.48 shows a query design based on tables contained in the SOLUTIONS.MDB sample database that accompanies Access 2.0. In this case, NWIND.MDB is the current database. The lines indicating joins between the native tables of SOLUTIONS.MDB have dots at their endpoints indicating that referential integrity is not maintained by your application. Figure 10.49 shows the result of executing the query design of figure 10.48 against the Example Objects, Examples, and Example Topics tables of SOLUTIONS.MDB.

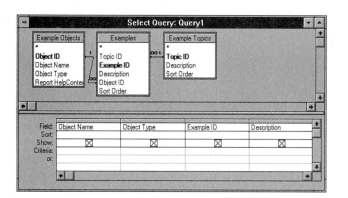

Fig. 10.48

A query design based on tables in an external Access database.

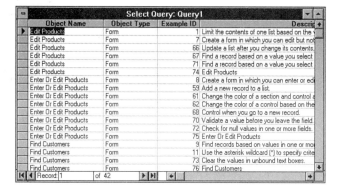

Fig. 10.49

The query result set of the query design of figure 10.48.

Nesting Queries

The example queries presented so far in this chapter have been based exclusively on data contained in tables. You can, however, create queries based on data created by a previously saved query. Queries based on data created by other queries, rather than in tables, are known as *subqueries* or *inner queries* in SQL. Access 1.x only executed subqueries as *nested queries*. A nested query requires execution of the query on which the subquery is based and then execution of the subquery. Access 2.0 lets you create SQL statements with subqueries, but you cannot create subqueries with Access 2.0's graphical QBE window. (You write your own SQL statements if you want to use subqueries and Access 2.0's new UNION queries. Chapter 24, "Working with Structured Query Language," shows you how to write these queries.) This chapter deals only with queries you can create in Access's Query Design window.

Access

2.0

II

Querying

Access allows you to have up to 50 levels of nested queries. The initial query is the first level; a query based on the initial query is the second level; a query based on the second-level query is the third level; and so on. Nested queries are especially useful for analyzing data created by summary queries. A nested query is useful, for example, in determining the level of current inventory for products included in orders that have not yet been shipped. If more units of a product are on order than are available from inventory, orders for the product must be placed with suppliers.

The Northwind Traders database includes a Products and Suppliers query that relates the name of the supplier to each of the products Northwind sells. This query can be used as the first-level query because it includes the Product ID, English Name, supplier Company Name, Units In Stock, Units on Order, and Reorder Level fields that you need to display inventory levels by product and make decisions on what products to purchase. The design of the Products and Suppliers query is shown in figure 10.50.

Fig. 10.50

The design of the Products and Suppliers query of the Northwind Traders database.

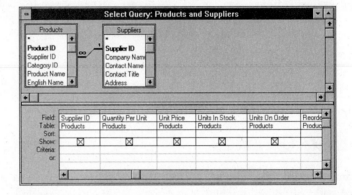

You need to create a summary query that displays the number of units of each product for which open orders exist so that the quantity on order can be compared to the quantity in stock. (It is assumed that the Units In Stock value is updated each time a product is shipped to a customer or received from a supplier.) This second-level query is a useful query in its own right because it gives an overall comparison of open orders versus inventory levels. Finally, you need to create a third-level select query with the criteria that displays only the products whose inventory levels are insufficient to meet open order requirements.

To create the second-level summary query to compare units in stock with units required for open orders, follow these steps:

1. Open a new query, and add the Products and Suppliers query from the Add Tables dialog. (Click the Tables and Queries option button so that queries display in the list.) Add the Order Details table because this table includes the Quantity Ordered field that you need to compare with the Quantity in Stock field of the Products and Suppliers query. Add the Orders table because this table includes the Shipped Date field that has a `Null` value for orders that have not yet been shipped. Click the Close button.

   Access creates the joins between the Product ID field of the Products and Suppliers query to the Product ID field of the Order Details table, and the Order ID field of the Order Details table and the Order ID field of the Orders table. Notice that none of the fields in the Products and Suppliers Field list are in bold type because queries don't have key fields and the join between the Product ID fields doesn't maintain referential integrity because query columns don't have primary-key fields.

2. Drag the Product ID, English Name, Company Name, and Units in Stock fields from the Products and Suppliers query to the Field row of columns 1, 2, 3, and 4 of the Query Design grid, respectively. Drag the Quantity field of the Order Details table and the Shipped Date field of the Orders table to the Field row of columns 5 and 6 of the Query Design grid. Drag the Discontinued field of the Products and Suppliers to column 7.

3. Click the Summary Query button on the toolbar to create a summary query. You need a summary query because totals of the Quantity on Order field of the Order Details table are required for each product. The default Group By function is assigned to the Total row of each column of the grid.

4. In this example, aliases have been added to each Field cell to reduce the width of the field names. Select each field cell in sequence and prefix the field names with ID:, Product:, Supplier:, Stock:, and Required:, from left to right. The Shipped Date and Discontinued columns are not displayed, so these columns do not need an alias.

5. Click the Total cell for the Required: Quantity field and choose Sum from the drop-down list because you want to compare the total of the units of a product required to fill orders with the number of units in stock and, ultimately, on order from the supplier.

6. Type **Is Null** in the first Criteria row of the Shipped Date column. The value of the Shipped Date field is `Null` for orders than have not been shipped.

7. Type **False** in the first Criteria row of the Discontinued column. You don't want to test order quantities for discontinued items. Your nested query design appears as shown in figure 10.51.

8. Run the query. The inventory status of all products on order and not shipped is displayed, as shown in figure 10.52.

9. Close the query and save it with a descriptive name, such as **qryOpenOrderTest**, because you must save a query before it can be employed by a subquery.

Fig. 10.51

The query design for the second-level nested query.

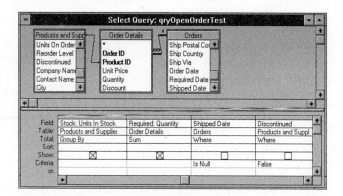

Fig. 10.52

The query result set that compares units of products required to fill open orders with units in inventory.

ID	Name	Supplier	Stock	Required
1	Dharamsala Tea	Exotic Liquids	39	40
2	Tibetan Barley Beer	Exotic Liquids	17	62
3	Licorice Syrup	Exotic Liquids	13	4
4	Chef Anton's Cajun Seasoning	New Orleans Cajun Delights	53	1
6	Grandma's Boysenberry Spread	Grandma Kelly's Homestead	120	21
7	Uncle Bob's Organic Dried Pears	Grandma Kelly's Homestead	15	16
8	Northwoods Cranberry Sauce	Grandma Kelly's Homestead	6	2
10	Fish Roe	Tokyo Traders	31	1
11	Cabrales Cheese	Cooperativa de Quesos 'Las Cabras'	22	10
12	Manchego La Pastora Cheese	Cooperativa de Quesos 'Las Cabras'	86	2
13	Kelp Seaweed	Mayumi's	24	44
14	Bean Curd	Mayumi's	35	21
16	Pavlova Meringue Dessert	Pavlova, Ltd.	29	46
19	Teatime Chocolate Biscuits	Specialty Biscuits, Ltd.	25	10
20	Sir Rodney's Marmalade	Specialty Biscuits, Ltd.	40	1
21	Sir Rodney's Scones	Specialty Biscuits, Ltd.	3	23
23	Thin Bread	PB Knäckebröd AB	61	2
30	Nord-Ost White Herring	Nord-Ost-Fisch Handelsgesellschaft mbH	10	4

Record: 1 of 45

Although you could review each of the records of the Open Orders against Inventory query to determine which products are in short supply, a simple third-level nested select query can do this. Another advantage of an Access nested query is that you can sort the nested query in a different order than the higher-level query on which the nested query is based. Also, you can add calculated fields to the nested query that may not be applicable in the higher-level queries.

To create a third-level nested query that limits the display to products for which the quantity on hand is less or equal to than the quantity on order, follow these steps:

1. Open a new query, and add the qryOpenOrderTest query and the Products tables to the query. Drag the ID field of the qryOpenOrderTest query to the Product ID field of the Products table to create an equi-join between these fields.

2. Drag the * field (all fields) to the Field cell of the first column, and then drag the Stock and Required fields to the second and third columns, respectively. You need to add these two fields so that you can compare their values. Click the Show button of the Stock and On Order columns to prevent their duplication in the query result set.

3. Type **>=[Stock]** in the Criteria row of the Required column. This expression selects only the product records of the qryOpenOrderTest result set where the number of unfilled orders for a product is greater than or equal to the inventory level.

4. Create a calculated field by typing **Short: [Required]–[Stock]** in the first empty column (6), and then add a Descending Sort property so that the records for the largest shortages are displayed first. The addition of the Descending Sort property proves that Access can sort nested queries and demonstrates the use of calculated fields to sort any type of query. The query design appears as shown in figure 10.53.

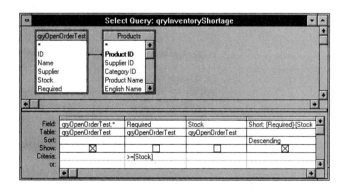

Fig. 10.53
The design for the third-level nested query that displays products with shortage status.

5. Run the query. The resulting third-level subquery result set appears as shown in figure 10.54. The records are sorted in order of the severity of the shortage.

The query result set of figure 10.54 includes two additional columns that don't appear in the query design of figure 10.53: On Order and To Order. The On Order Field is the Units on Order field of the Products table with an alias. The To Order field is calculated by the expression `To Order: [Required]-[Stock]-[Units On Order]`.

Fig. 10.54

The query result of the third-level nested query that displays product shortages sorted by severity.

ID	Name	Supplier	Stock	Required	Short	On Order	To Order
64	Wimmer's Delicious Bread	Plusspar Lebensmittelgroß	22	132	110	80	30
60	Pierrot Camembert	Gai pâturage	19	73	54	0	54
49	Licorice	Karkki Oy	10	62	52	60	-8
2	Tibetan Barley Beer	Exotic Liquids	17	62	45	40	5
31	Gorgonzola Telino	Formaggi Fortini s.r.l.	0	20	20	70	-50
21	Sir Rodney's Scones	Specialty Biscuits, Ltd.	3	23	20	40	-20
13	Kelp Seaweed	Mayumi's	24	44	20	0	20
43	Malaysian Coffee	Leka Trading	17	36	19	10	9
16	Pavlova Meringue Dessert	Pavlova, Ltd.	29	46	17	0	17
51	Manjimup Dried Apples	G'day, Mate	20	24	4	0	4
35	Steeleye Stout	Bigfoot Breweries	20	24	4	0	4
7	Uncle Bob's Organic Dried	Grandma Kelly's Homeste	15	16	1	0	1
1	Dharamsala Tea	Exotic Liquids	39	40	1	0	1

Record: 1 of 13

6. Save the nested query with an appropriate name, such as **qryInventoryShortage**, if you want to keep it for further reference.

You should consider using nested queries whenever you create several queries based on the same or a similar set of records in more than one table. Nested queries save time when you create drill-down applications that progressively display more detail about categories of data. For example, you may create a parameter query that displays all orders for the month you enter as a parameter. You can then create several nested queries based on the parameter query to display additional details of the orders received for the month.

From Here. . .

Queries are the foundation on which you build most of the forms and reports you design to create full-scale applications in Access. One of the principal features of Access, however, is its capability to select, display, and print both detailed and summary information without the need to design forms or reports. In many cases, a simple query can answer *ad hoc* requests for status reports. The printed output of the query does not have a slick format, but the data is what counts.

The section of this chapter on crosstab queries, for example, demonstrates that you can design a query to display and print a time-series area chart for trend analysis in less than five minutes. This area is where Access shines in comparison with conventional spreadsheet applications; using Access, you can select and process the data required to produce a time-series chart in a tenth or so of the time required to produce the equivalent spreadsheet. Although the new Pivot feature of Excel 5.0 makes creating crosstab worksheets easier, Access still wins hands down when you have a large number of records to process.

- Chapter 9, "Understanding Operators and Expressions in Access," provides a complete description of the functions and operators that you can use in creating queries.

- Chapter 11, "Using Action Queries," describes how you use action queries to update, append, and delete table records. Action queries also let you create new tables from query result sets.

- Chapter 24, "Working with Structured Query Language," delves deeper into the use of SQL and how to write queries in the SQL window, rather than using Access's query-by-example method.

II

Querying

Chapter 11

Using Action Queries

Action queries create new tables or modify the data in existing tables. Four types of action queries are available in Access:

- *Make-table queries* create new tables from the data contained in query result sets. One of the most common applications for make-table queries is creating tables to export for use by other applications. A make-table query is a convenient way of copying a table to another database. In some cases, you can use make-table queries to speed the generation of multiple forms and reports based on a single, complex query.

- *Append queries* add new records to tables with data created by the query.

- *Delete queries* delete records from tables that correspond to the rows you delete from the query result set.

- *Update queries* change the values of existing fields of table records corresponding to rows of the query result set.

This chapter shows you how to create each of the four types of action queries and how to try Access 2.0's new cascading deletions and cascading updates of related records. It also shows you how to use the Archive Query Wizard to copy query result sets to a new archive table and to remove the copied records from the original table. Cascading deletions and cascading updates are covered in this chapter because these features are related to delete and update action queries, respectively.

Creating New Tables with Make-Table Queries

In the following sections, you learn how to use a make-table query to create a new table, Shipping Address, for customers that have different shipping and

In this chapter, you learn to

- Design queries that create new tables

- Append records to existing tables with queries

- Delete selected records from tables with queries

- Update values in tables with queries

- Use the Query Wizard to create archive queries

II

Querying

billing addresses. This process allows the deletion of the shipping address data that, in most of the records in the Orders table, duplicates the address data in the Customers table. Removing duplicated data to new tables is an important step when you are converting data contained in a flat (nonrelational) database to a relational database structure.

Caution

Always make a backup copy of a table that you are going to modify with an action query. Changes made to table data with action queries are permanent; an error can render a table useless. Invalid changes made to a table with an action query containing a design error often are difficult to detect.

The example you create in the following sections extracts data from the Orders table based on data in the Customers table and creates a new table, tblShipAddress. A modification of the query that you created in the "Creating Not-Equal Theta Joins with Criteria" section of Chapter 10 generates the data for the new table. Make-table queries are useful in converting flat-file tables that contain duplicated data, including tables created by spreadsheet applications, to relational form.

Designing and Testing the Select Query

To create the new shipping address table from the data in the Orders table, first you need to build a select query. To build a select query, follow these steps:

1. Create a new query, and add the Customers and Orders tables to it.

2. Click the Table Names button of the toolbar, or choose Table **N**ames from the **V**iew menu to add the Table row to the Query Design grid.

3. Drag the Customer ID field from the Customers table and drop it in the first column of the query. The Customer ID field is the field that links the Shipping Address table with the Orders table.

4. Drag the Ship Name, Ship Address, Ship City, Ship Region, Ship Postal Code, and Ship Country fields and drop them in columns 2 through 7, respectively. You use these fields, in addition to Company ID, to create the new Shipping Address table.

   Next, you want to add only the records of the Orders table for which the Ship Name doesn't match the Company Name or the Ship Address doesn't match the Address of the Customers table.

5. In the first Criteria row of the Ship Name column, type

   <>[Customers].[Company Name]

6. Move to the next row of the Ship Address column and type

   <>[Customers].[Address]

   in the cell. This entry must be in a different Criteria row than the Company Name criterion so that the Or operator is applied to the two criteria. The Query Design grid appears as shown in figure 11.1.

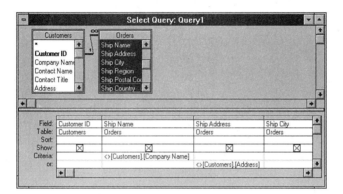

Fig. 11.1
Creating the select query for the new Shipping Address table.

II

Querying

Note

A more precise approach is to add additional **Or** criteria to test for not-equal cities, regions, postal codes, and countries. A customer having exactly the same address in two different cities, however, is highly improbable.

---

7. Click the Properties button of the toolbar or double-click an empty area in the upper pane of the Query Design window to open the Query Properties window. Open the Unique Values drop-down list and select Yes.

8. Click the Run Query button to run the select query. Data for customers that placed orders with different billing and shipping addresses appears, as shown in figure 11.2.

Customer	Ship Name	Ship Address	Ship City	Ship Region	Ship Post	Ship Country
ALFKI	Alfred's Futterkiste	Obere Str. 57	Berlin		12209	Germany
AROUT	Around the Horn	Brook Farm	Colchester	Essex	CO7 6JX	UK
CHOPS	Chop-suey Chinese	Hauptstr. 31	Bern		3012	Switzerland
GALED	Galería del gastrol	Rambla de Cataluña,	Barcelona		8022	Spain
LAUGB	Laughing Bacchu	2319 Elm St.	Vancouver	BC	V3F 2K1	Canada
LETSS	Let's Stop N Shop	87 Polk St.	San Francisc	CA	94117	USA
RICSU	Richter Supermark	Starenweg 5	Genève		1204	Switzerland
WHITC	White Clover Mark	1029 - 12th Ave. S.	Seattle	WA	98124	USA
WOLZA	Wolski Zajazd	ul. Filtrowa 68	Warszawa		01-012	Poland

Fig. 11.2
The data to be added to the new Shipping Address table.

Converting the Select Query to a Make-Table Query

Now that you have tested the select query to make sure that it creates the necessary data, you can create the table from the query. To create the table, follow these steps:

1. Click the Make Table button of the toolbar or choose Ma**k**e Table from the **Q**uery menu. A variation of the Query Properties dialog appears. Type the name of the table, **tblShipAddress**, in the Table Name text box (see fig. 11.3). Click OK.

Fig. 11.3

The Query Properties dialog for make-table queries.

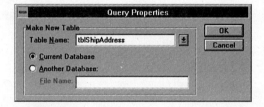

2. Click the Run Query button on the toolbar. A message box confirms the number of records that you are adding to the new table (see fig. 11.4). Click OK to create the new Shipping Address table.

3. Click the Show Database Window button of the toolbar to activate the Database window, click the Table button, and open the new Shipping Address table. The entries appear as shown in figure 11.5.

Fig. 11.4

The confirmation message box that precedes creation of the new table.

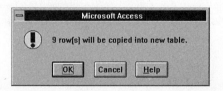

Fig. 11.5

The Shipping Address table created from the make-table query.

Customer	Ship Name	Ship Address	Ship City	Ship Reg	Ship Postal	Ship Country
ALFKI	Alfred's Futterki	Obere Str. 57	Berlin		12209	Germany
AROUT	Around the Hor	Brook Farm	Colchester	Essex	CO7 6JX	UK
CHOPS	Chop-suey Chir	Hauptstr. 31	Bern		3012	Switzerland
GALED	Galería del gas	Rambla de Catal	Barcelona		8022	Spain
LAUGB	Laughing Bacc	2319 Elm St.	Vancouver	BC	V3F 2K1	Canada
LETSS	Let's Stop N Sh	87 Polk St.	San Francisc	CA	94117	USA
RICSU	Richter Superm	Starenweg 5	Genève		1204	Switzerland
WHITC	White Clover M	1029 - 12th Ave.	Seattle	WA	98124	USA
WOLZA	Wolski Zajazd	ul. Filtrowa 68	Warszawa		01-012	Poland

Now, complete the design of the new Shipping Address table by following these steps:

1. Click the Design View button of the toolbar. The basic design of the table is inherited from the properties of the fields of the tables used to create the new table. Shipping Address does not, however, inherit the primary key assignment from the Customer ID field of the Customers table.

2. Click the Properties button of the toolbar or double-click an empty area in the upper pane of the Query Design window to display the Table Properties window. Type **Shipping addresses different from billing addresses** as the description in the Description text box of the Table Properties window, as shown in figure 11.6.

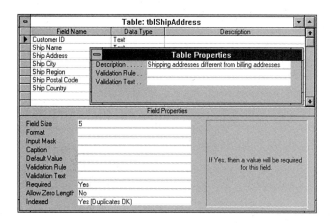

Fig. 11.6

The design of the newly created Shipping Address table.

3. The Shipping Address table presently has a one-to-one relationship with the Customers table because only one shipping address record exists for each customer who has different shipping and billing addresses. Customers may have a number of different shipping addresses, however, so the relationship of Customers to Shipping Address is one-to-many, and duplicate values in the Customer ID field of Shipping Address must be allowed. You cannot, therefore, create a primary key for the Shipping Address table unless you include three fields—Customer ID, Ship Name, and Ship Address—to make multiple entries for one customer unique. In this example, no primary key is used. Choose the Customer ID field, open the Indexed property drop-down list, and choose the Yes (Duplicates OK) value. Indexing improves the performance of queries when you have many different shipping addresses for customers.

4. The Customer ID, Ship Name, Ship Address, Ship City, and Ship Country fields are required, so set the value of the Required property for each of these fields to Yes. (Many countries do not have values for the Ship Region field, and a few countries do not use postal codes.)

Establishing Relationships for the New Table

Access
2.0

Now you need to complete the process of adding the new table to your database by establishing default relationships and enforcing referential integrity so that all records in the tblShipAddress table have a corresponding record in the Customers table. Access 2.0's new graphical relationships window makes this process simple and intuitive. To establish the relationship of tblShipAddress and the Customers table, follow these steps:

1. Close the tblShipAddress table, and click the Show Database Window button of the toolbar to make the Database window active.

2. Click the Relationships button of the toolbar or choose **R**elationships from the **E**dit menu to open the Relationships window that establishes the default relationships between tables. Click the Add Table button of the toolbar and double-click the tblShipAddress table to add the table to the relationship window; then click the Close button. Move the field list to the position shown in figure 11.7. (Drag the bottom of the Orders field list up to make room for the tblShipAddress field list.)

3. Click the Customer ID field of the Customers table and drag the field symbol to the Customer ID field of the tblShipAddress table and drop it. The table names are emphasized here because the direction in which you drag the field is important. The Relationships dialog appears (see fig. 11.8). The field that you select to drag appears in the Table/Query list (the "one" side of the relationship), and the field on which you drop the dragged field appears in the Related Table/Query list (the "many" side of the relationship).

4. Click the Enforce Referential Integrity check box. The default relation type, one to many, is set for you and is the correct choice for this relation. Access also establishes a conventional equi-join as the default join type, so you don't need to click the Join Type button to display the Join Properties window in this case.

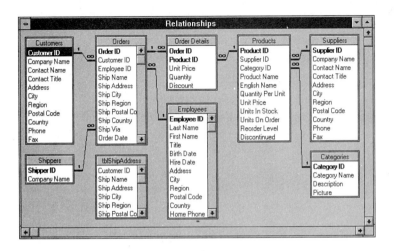

Fig. 11.7
Adding the tblShipAddress table to the Relationships window.

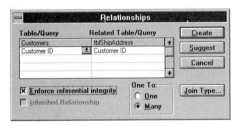

Fig. 11.8
The Relationships dialog for the new shipping address table.

5. Click the Create button of the Relationships dialog to close it. Your Relationships window appears as shown in figure 11.9.

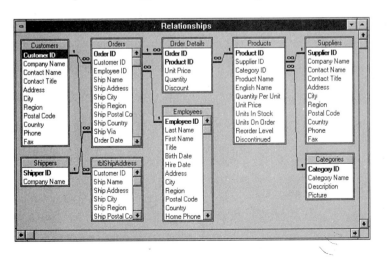

Fig. 11.9
The Relationships window showing referential integrity enforced for the new table.

II

Querying

6. Close the Relationships window and click OK to save your changes. Save your make-table query with an appropriate name, such as **qryMakeShipAddress**.

Using the New tblShipAddress Table

After creating a new table from a make-table query, you must take care of a number of "housekeeping" chores before you can take advantage of your new table. The purpose of creating the new shipping address table is to eliminate the data in the Orders table that duplicates information in the Customers table. The additional steps you must take to use the new table include the following:

- You need a new Number (Integer) field, Ship ID, for the tblShipAddress and Orders tables. A value of 0 in the Ship ID field can be used to indicate that the shipping and billing addresses are the same. You then assign a sequential number to each shipping address for each customer. (In the present case, the value of the Ship ID field is 1 for all records in tblShipAddress.) Adding the Ship ID field to the tblShipAddress table lets you create a composite primary key on the Customer ID and Ship ID fields. The no-duplicates index on the composite primary key prevents accidental duplication of a Ship ID value for a customer.

- Do not delete fields that contain duplicate data that was extracted to a new table until you confirm that the extracted data is correct and modify all the queries, forms, and reports that use the table. You use the update query described later in this chapter to assign the correct Ship ID field value for each record in the Orders table. After you verify that the correct value of the Ship ID field has been assigned, you can delete the duplicate fields.

- Add the new table to any queries, forms, reports, macros, and modules that require the extracted information.

- Change references to fields in the original table in all database objects that refer to fields in the new table.

During this process, you have the opportunity to test the modification before deleting the duplicated fields from the original table. Making a backup copy of the table before you delete the fields also is a low-cost insurance policy.

Creating Action Queries to Append Records to a Table

A make-table query creates the new table structure from the structure of the records that underlie the query. Only the fields of the records that appear in the query are added to the new table's structure. If you design and save a Shipping Address table before extracting the duplicated data from the Orders table, you can use an *append query* to add the extracted data to the new table.

Another situation in which append queries are useful is during the process of removing duplicate data from a table currently in use. In this case, you use make-table queries to create the related tables and then change them to append queries. You change the type of query by choosing **S**elect, **C**rosstab, Ma**k**e Table, A**p**pend, or **D**elete from the **Q**uery menu, or by clicking the appropriate button of the toolbar while in design mode.

An append query also differs from a make-table query because an append query may have fewer fields than the table to which the data is to be appended. Otherwise, the make-table and append processes are basically identical. To append records to the tblShipAddress table, for example, follow these steps:

1. Open the tblShipAddress table in Datasheet View, choose Select **A**ll Records from the **E**dit menu, and then press the Delete key to delete all the records from the table. Click Yes when asked to confirm the deletion, and then close the table.

2. Open your make-table query from the Database window in design mode (or choose it from the **W**indow menu if it is open). If you double-click qryMakeShipAddress or open qryMakeShipAddress in Datasheet View, you run the make-table query.

3. Click the Append Query button of the toolbar, or choose **A**ppend from the **Q**uery menu. The append variant of the Query Properties dialog appears with tblShipAddress as the default value in the Table Name drop-down list, as shown in figure 11.10. Click the OK button to close the Query Properties dialog.

Fig. 11.10
The Query
Properties dialog
for an append
query.

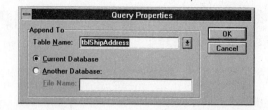

> **Note**
>
> To append data to a table, the field names of the query and those of the table to which the records are to be appended must be identical, or you must specify the field of the table to which the append query column applies; data will not be appended to fields in which the field name differs by even a single space character. The Query Design grid for append queries has an additional row, Append To, shown in figure 11.11, that Access attempts to match by comparing field names of the query and the table. Default values appear in the Append To row of columns for which a match occurs. If a match does not occur, open the drop-down list in the Append row and choose the field of the table from the list.

Fig. 11.11
The Append Query
Design grid with
the Append To
row added.

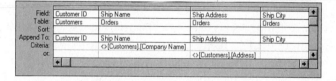

4. Click the Run Query button of the toolbar to execute the append query. A message box displays the number of records that will be appended to the table (see fig. 11.12). Click the OK button to append the records.

5. Open the tblShipAddress table to verify that the records have been added.

Fig. 11.12
The message that
announces an
impending
append.

Troubleshooting

After I append records to the existing table, I can't create a primary key on the table.

The Unique Values Only test that you specify in the Query Properties dialog applies only to the query, not to the table to which the records are being appended. If you want to exclude the possibility of appending duplicate records to the tblShipAddress table, you must first create the composite primary key, discussed in the preceding section, which creates a No Duplicates index on the primary key; then append the records.

If you attempt to append records that contain values that duplicate the values of the key fields in existing records, these records aren't appended. You see a message that indicates the number of records that cause key field violations. Unlike the Paste Append operation described in previous chapters, however, a Paste Errors table that contains the unappended records isn't created.

Deleting Records from a Table with an Action Query

Often, you may need to delete records from a table. You may, for example, want to delete records for orders that were canceled, or records for customers that have made no purchases for several years. Deleting records from a table with a *delete query* is the reverse of the append process. You create a select query with all fields (using the * choice from the field list) and then add the individual fields to be used to specify the criteria for the deletion of specific records. If you don't specify any criteria, all the records in the table are deleted when you convert the select query into a delete query and run it against the table.

To give you some practice at deleting records—you stop short of actual deletion in this case, however—suppose that the credit manager for Northwind Traders has advised you that Ernst Handel (Customer ID ERNSH) was declared insolvent by the Austrian authorities and that any orders from Ernst Handel

Tip

It is a good practice to run a select query to show the records you are about to delete, and then convert the select query to a delete query.

II

Querying

not yet shipped are to be canceled and deleted from the table. To design the query that selects all of Ernst Handel's open orders, follow these steps:

1. Open a new query and add the Orders table to it.

2. Drag the * (all fields) item from the field list to the Field cell of the first column of the query.

3. Drag the Customer ID field to the Field cell of the second column. This field is required to provide record selection for a specific customer. The fields that comprise the query must be exactly those of the Orders table, so click the Show box to hide the Customer ID field. This field is included in the * (all fields) indicator in the first column.

4. Move to the Criteria cell of the Customer ID field and type **ERNSH** to represent Ernst Handel's ID.

5. Orders that have not shipped are indicated by a `Null` value in the Ship Date field. Drag the Ship Date field from the field list to the Field cell of the third column. Click the Show box to hide the Ship Date field because it too is included in the first column.

6. Type **Is Null** in the Criteria cell of the Ship Date field. This criterion must be on the same line as the criterion for the Customer ID field so that only records for Ernst Handel *and* those that have not been shipped are deleted. The select query design for the delete query appears as shown in figure 11.13.

Fig. 11.13
The select query design for a delete query.

7. Run the select query to display the records to be deleted if you run the delete query. The query result set appears in figure 11.14.

Fig. 11.14
The unshipped orders for Ernst Handel to be deleted from the Orders table.

To proceed with the simulated deletion, follow these steps:

1. Click the Show Database Window button of the toolbar to activate the Database window; then click the Table button to display the table list. Create a copy of the Orders table by clicking the Orders table entry and pressing Ctrl+C to copy the table to the Clipboard. Press Ctrl+V and type **tblOrders** as the name of the new table copy. Repeat this process for the Order Details table, naming it **tblOrderDetails**. These two tables are backup tables in case you actually delete the two records for Ernst Handel.

2. Activate your select query and click the Design button of the toolbar to return to design mode. Click the Delete Query button of the toolbar or choose **D**elete from the **Q**uery menu. The Sort and Show rows of the Select Query grid are replaced by the Delete row, as shown in figure 11.15. The From value in the first column of the Delete row, Orders, indicates that records that match the Field specification will be deleted from the Orders table. The Where values in the remaining two cells indicate fields in which the deletion criteria are specified.

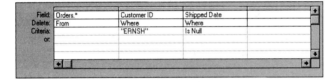

Fig. 11.15
The delete query design created from the select query of figure 11.1.

3. Click the Run Query button. The message box shown in figure 11.16 appears, asking you to confirm the deletion of the rows. Click the OK button.

4. The message shown in figure 11.17 appears indicating that you cannot delete the two records because of key violations. Click the Cancel button to terminate the attempt to delete the records.

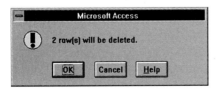

Fig. 11.16
The deletion confirmation message box.

Note

Deleting records in a *one* table when records corresponding to the deleted records exist in a related *many* table violates the rules of referential integrity; the records in the *many* table would be made orphans. In this situation, referential integrity is enforced between the Order Details and Orders table, preventing the creation of orphan Order Details records for the two records of the Orders table you attempted to delete. To delete the two records of the Orders table requires a process called *cascading deletion*. First you delete the Order Details records; then you delete the Orders records. Creating a macro for cascading deletions is one of the subjects of Chapter 18, "Creating Macros for Forms and Reports."

Fig. 11.17
The message box
that indicates a
violation of the
rules of referential
integrity.

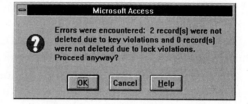

If you accidentally delete records for Ernst Handel because you removed the referential integrity requirement from the Order Details and Orders tables, reverse the process you used to make the backup tables: copy the backup tables, tblOrders and tblOrderDetails, to Orders and Order Details, respectively.

Updating Values of Multiple Records in a Table

Update queries change the values of data in a table. Update queries are useful when field values of a large number of records must be updated with a common expression. For example, you may need to increase or decrease the unit prices of all products or products within a particular category by a fixed percentage.

To see how an update query works, you perform some of the housekeeping chores discussed earlier in the chapter that are associated with using the tblShipAddress table. To implement this example, you must have created the tblShipAddress table, as described in the "Creating New Tables with Make-Table Queries" section earlier in the chapter. You also must modify the

tblOrders and tblShipAddress tables to include a field for the Ship ID code by
following these steps:

1. Click the Table button in the Database window and open the tblOrders
   table in design mode. If you didn't create the tblOrders table as a
   backup table for the example of the preceding section, do it now.

2. Select the Ship Name field by clicking the selection button with the
   mouse and press Insert to add a new field between Employee ID and
   Ship Name Freight. (Fields are inserted in tables above the selected
   field.)

3. Type **Ship ID** as the field name; then pick Number as the field data
   type and Integer as the description of the field. Set the value of the
   Required property to Yes. The table design pane appears as shown in
   figure 11.18 (the new Ship ID field is shown selected).

4. Close the tblOrders table and save the changes to your design. You
   changed the domain integrity rules when you added the Required property, so the message box of figure 11.19 appears. Click the No button to
   avoid the test, which will fail because no values have been added to the
   Ship ID field.

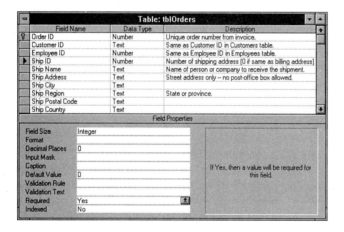

Fig. 11.18
Adding the Ship ID
field to the
tblOrders table.

Fig. 11.19
Choosing whether
to test changes to
domain integrity
rules.

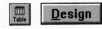

5. Open the tblShipAddress table in design mode and add the Ship ID field between the Customer ID and the Ship Name field. Set the properties of the field the same as in preceding step 3 for the Ship ID field of the tblOrders table.

6. Change to Datasheet View and type **1** in the Ship ID cell for each record of the tblShipAddress table.

7. Change to design mode, and select both the Customer ID and the Ship ID field by clicking and dragging the mouse.

8. Click the Set Primary Key button of the toolbar to create a composite primary key on the Customer ID and Ship ID fields, and then close the tblShipAddress table. This time you test the changes you made to the table.

Now you need to set up a query to select the orders to which you want to add a value of 1 to the Ship ID field to indicate use of data from the tblShipAddress table. This query is very similar to that which you used to create the tblShipAddress table earlier in the chapter. Follow these steps to design your update query:

1. Click the New Query button with the Database window active. Add the Customers and tblOrders tables to the query.

2. Drag the Company Name and Address fields of the Customers table to columns 1 and 2, and the Ship Name and Ship Address fields of the tblOrders table to columns 3 and 4 of the Query Design grid.

3. Type **<>[Customers].[Company Name]** in the first Criteria row of the Ship Name column and **<>[Customers].[Address]** in the second Criteria row of the Ship Address column. Your query design appears as shown in figure 11.20.

4. Run the query to verify that the set of records to be updated is selected correctly. If you changed the name of Let's Stop N Shop to Let's Stop 'N Shop in the "Editing Table Data in Query View" section of Chapter 8, the five records for orders placed by this firm appear when you run the query (see fig. 11.21). Checking for errors of this type is one of the reasons for running the select query before you run the update query. If these records appear, however, you also have a tblShipAddress record for the firm. This is only an example, so you can proceed with the update.

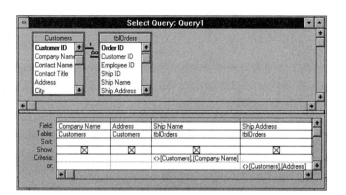

Fig. 11.20
The select query to test for orders that will require *1* as the value of Ship ID.

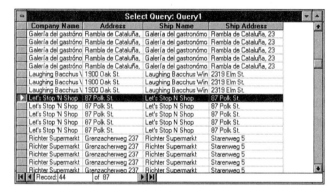

Fig. 11.21
The result of the select query used to test the records to be updated.

After making sure that the appropriate records of the tblOrders table have been selected for updating, you are ready to convert the select query to an update query by following these steps:

1. Return to design mode and drag the Ship ID field of the tblOrders table to the first column of the query.

2. Click the Update Query button of the toolbar or choose Update from the **Q**uery menu. A new Update To row replaces the Sort and Show rows of the Select Query Design grid.

3. Type **1** in the Update To cell of the Ship ID column to set the value of Ship ID to 1 for orders that require use of a record from the tblShipAddress table. The update Query Design grid appears as shown in figure 11.22. The Update To cells of the remaining fields are blank, indicating that values in these fields are not to be updated.

Fig. 11.22
The completed
update Query
Design grid.

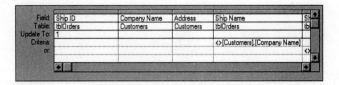

 4. Run the update query. The number of records that will be updated is
indicated by a message box like the one shown in figure 11.23. (The
query may return a different number of records because of changes to
the sample database since this book was written.)

Fig. 11.23
The message box
that indicates the
number of records
to which the tax
will be added.

 5. Click the Show Database Window button and open the tblOrders table.
Check a few records to see that the Ship ID value of 1 has been added
correctly.

 6. You need to add 0 values to the Ship ID cells of records that have the
same shipping and billing addresses. Close the update query and create
a new query, and add only the tblOrders table.

 7. Drag the Ship ID field to the first column of the query and click the
Update Query button of the toolbar.

 8. Type **0** in the Update To row and **Is Null** in the Criteria row, then click
the Run Query button to replace **Null** values in the Ship ID column
with **0**.

After you check the tblOrders table to verify the result of your second update
query, you can change to table Design mode and safely delete the Ship Name,
Ship Address, Ship City, Ship Region, Ship Postal Code, and Ship Country
fields. Later chapters in this book show you how to link the tblShipAddress to
the tblOrders table to choose shipping addresses.

Testing Cascading Deletion and Updating

Access

2.0

Access 2.0 provides two new features that were requested by users of Access 1.x: cascading deletion and cascading updating of records having a many-to-one relationship. When you delete a record in a primary or base table on which records in a related table depend, cascading deletion automatically deletes the dependent records. Similarly, if you modify the value of a primary key field of a table and there are records in a related table that are related by the value of the primary key field, cascading updating changes the value of the related foreign key field for the related records to the new primary key field value.

Cascading deletions and cascading updates are special types of action queries executed for you by the Jet engine. The following three sections show you how to use Access 2.0's new cascading deletion and cascading updating features with a set of test tables copied from the Orders and Order Details tables of NWIND.MDB.

Creating the Test Tables and Establishing Relationships

When you experiment with database features, it is a good practice to work with test tables, rather than on "live" data. As mentioned in the note at the beginning of this chapter, using copied test tables is particularly advisable when the tables are participants in action queries. The remaining sections of this chapter use the two test tables, tblOrders and tblOrderDetails, that you create in the following steps:

1. Click the Table tab of the Database window, and then select the Orders table from the list.

2. Press Ctrl+C to copy a reference (pointer) to the table to the Clipboard.

3. Press Ctrl+V to display the Paste Table As dialog.

4. Type **tblOrders** in the Table Name text box; then click OK or press Return to create the test tblOrders table.

5. Repeat steps 1 through 4 for the Order Details table, naming the copy **tblOrderDetails**.

II

Querying

Cascading deletions and updates require that you establish a default relationship between the primary and related tables, and enforce referential integrity. To add both cascading deletions and updates to the tblOrderDetails table, follow these steps:

1. Click the Relationships button of the toolbar to display the Relationships window.

2. Click the Add Table button of the toolbar to display the Add Table dialog.

3. Select tblOrders from the Table/Query list and click the Add button.

4. Double-click the tblOrderDetails item in the list, and then click the Close button to close the Add Table dialog.

5. Use the vertical scroll bar of the Relationships window to make the tblOrders and tblOrderDetails field lists fully visible. Move the two field lists to an empty area at the bottom of the window.

6. Click the Order ID field of tblOrders; then drag the field symbol to the Order ID field of tblOrderDetails to establish a join on the Order ID field. The Relationships dialog appears.

7. Click the Enforce Referential Integrity check box to enable the two Cascade check boxes.

8. Click the Cascade Update Related Fields and Cascade Delete Related Records check boxes, as shown in figure 11.24.

9. Click the OK button of the Relationships dialog to make your changes to the join effective, and then double-click the document control symbol to close the Relationships window, saving your changes to the window's layout.

Troubleshooting

When I try to enforce referential integrity, I get a "Can't create relationship to enforce referential integrity..." message.

You dragged the field symbols in the wrong direction when you created the relationship. The related table is in the Table/Query list and the primary or base table is in the Related Table/Query list. Close the Relationships dialog, click the thin area of the join line to select the join, and then press the Delete key to delete the join. Make sure you drag the field name you want from the primary table to the related table.

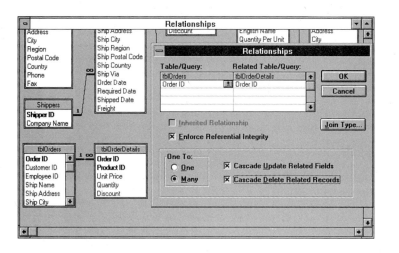

Fig. 11.24
Setting the cascading deletions option.

Testing Cascading Deletion

To try cascading deletion with the test tables, follow these steps:

1. Open the tblOrders and tblOrderDetails tables in Datasheet View.

2. Click the surface of the tblOrders datasheet to make it the active window, and then click a record selection button to pick an order in tblOrders to delete.

3. Press the Delete key to tentatively delete the selected records and the related order line item records in tblOrderDetails.

4. The message box shown in figure 11.25 appears requesting confirmation of the deletion. Click the OK button to delete the records.

Fig. 11.25
Confirming the cascading deletion.

You can verify that the related records have been deleted by scrolling to the related record(s) for the order you deleted in the tblDetails table. If you opened tblOrderDetails in step 1, the data cell values for the deleted related records are replaced with #Delete.

II

Querying

Testing Cascading Updates

Cascading updates to the foreign key field of records that depend on a primary key value that you want to change in a primary table is a very valuable feature of Access 2.0. Performing updates of primary key values while enforcing referential integrity is not a simple process; the problems associated with performing such updates manually is discussed briefly in Chapter 4, "Working with Access Databases and Tables." To see how Access 2.0 takes the complexity out of cascading updates, follow these steps:

1. With the tblOrders and tblOrderDetails windows open, size and position the two datasheets as shown in figure 11.25; then click the surface of the tblOrders datasheet to make it the active window. Positioning the two table datasheet windows as shown in the illustration lets you see the cascading updates in the tblOrderDetails window as they occur.

2. Change the value of the Order ID cell of the first record to the order number you deleted in the preceding section. Alternatively, change the value of the Order ID cell to a value, such as 20000, that is outside the range of the values of the test table.

3. Move the caret to another record to cause the cascading update to occur. You see the changes in the Order ID foreign key field of the related dependent records immediately (see fig. 11.26).

Fig. 11.26
An example of a cascading update.

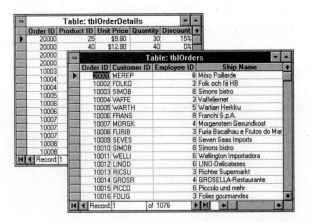

No confirmation message appears when you execute a cascading update, because the effect of a cascading update is reversible. If you make an erroneous entry that causes an undesired cascading update, you can simply change the entry to its original value by choosing **U**ndo Saved Record from the **E**dit menu. Alternatively, you can simply reenter the original or the correct value manually.

Creating an Archive Query with the Query Wizards

Microsoft includes four Query Wizards with Access 2.0 that you can use to create the following types of queries:

- *Find Duplicates Query.* A query that locates records with duplicate values in a particular field. The Find Duplicates Query is most useful when you want to specify a field as the primary key, but duplicate records prevent you from doing so.

- *Find Unmatched Query.* A query that creates a right outer join to locate related records that do not have a corresponding primary record (or-phan records).

- *Crosstab Query.* A summary crosstab query in which all of the column headers represent values in table or query fields, rather than months or quarters. The Crosstab Query Wizard is not capable of creating time-series crosstabs.

- *Archive Query.* An action query that copies unneeded records to a new table and then optionally deletes the unneeded records from the source table.

The types of specialty queries created by the first three Wizards are discussed in the preceding two chapters. Although these three Wizards are useful, learning to write your own versions of these three types of queries is an important step in gaining familiarity with query methodology. Once you learn the fundamentals of query design, it is unlikely that you will use the first three Wizards.

The Archive Query Wizard creates two-stage queries that are useful in a production database environment. The purpose of an archive query is to append a specified set of obsolete records to a new or existing destination table and to delete the original records from the source table. The following steps show you how to use the Archive Query Wizard to delete records for pre-1993 orders from the tblOrders and tblOrderDetails test tables:

1. Click the Queries tab of the Database window, and then click the New button to display the wizard selection dialog shown in figure 11.27.

2. Double-click the Archive Query item in the list box to display the Archive Wizard's opening dialog (see fig. 11.28).

Fig. 11.27
Choosing the type of Query Wizard to employ.

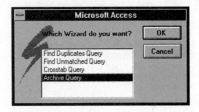

Fig. 11.28
Choosing the table that contains the records you want to archive.

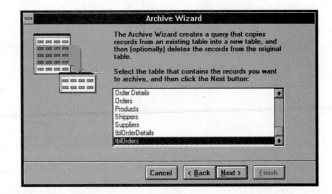

3. Select the tblOrders table in the list box and click the Next > button to display the criteria entry dialog shown in figure 11.29.

Fig. 11.29
Entering the archiving criteria.

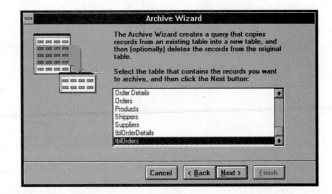

4. Open the This Value drop-down list and select the Shipped Date field.

5. Type **<** in the Is drop-down combo, or select the < symbol from the list.

6. Type **1/1/93** in the This Value text box. Your entries are designed to archive all orders shipped prior to 1993.

7. Click the Next > button to display the records to be archived in a datasheet (see fig. 11.30).

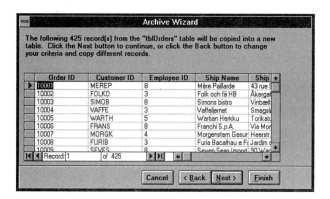

Fig. 11.30

The records to be archived in Datasheet View.

8. Click the Next > button to display the Wizard's dialog that lets you elect to delete the original record(s), as shown in figure 11.31. Click the Yes, I Want to Delete the Original Record(s) option button.

9. Click the Next > button to display the final dialog that lets you assign the name to the table to receive the archived records (see fig. 11.32). Type **tblOrdersArchive** in the drop-down combo list to create a new archive table. If you already have an archive table for orders, you can append the records to the existing archive table by selecting the table from the combo list.

10. Click the Archive the Records option button, and then click the Finish button to execute the query.

11. Click Yes to confirm that you want to copy the records to the destination table in the message box of figure 11.33.

12. When the message box of figure 11.34 appears, click Yes to confirm that you want to delete the records from the source table.

13. The message box of figure 11.35 confirms that the archived records were deleted from the source table. Click OK to complete the archiving process.

Fig. 11.31
Electing to delete
the original
records from the
source table.

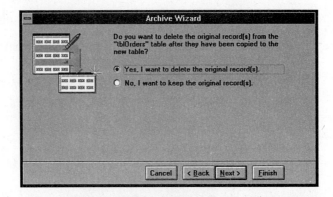

Fig. 11.32
Naming or
selecting a name
for the destination
table.

Fig. 11.33
Confirming
archiving of the
records.

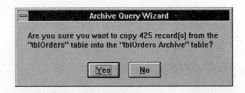

Fig. 11.34
Confirming
deletion of the
archived records.

Fig. 11.35
Final confirmation that the archiving process is completed.

The Archive Query Wizard adds two new queries to the Database window: tblOrdersArchive_DelQ and tblOrdersArchive_MovQ, representing the delete query and the make-table or append query, respectively (see fig. 11.36).

Fig. 11.36
The two archive queries added to the list of queries in the Database Container.

From Here...

This chapter demonstrates the power of action queries to update, append, and delete records in tables. Action queries are the foundation of Access transaction processing applications. Access executes each of the action queries described in this chapter with the SQL Data Manipulation Language (DML) statements that are described in Chapter 24, "Working with Structured Query Language."

For more information related to the topics addressed in this chapter, refer to the following:

■ Chapter 9, "Understanding Operators and Expressions in Access," explains how to write expressions to create criteria for action queries.

■ Chapter 10, "Creating Multitable and Crosstab Queries," explains how to design select queries that you easily can convert to action queries.

■ Chapter 24, "Working with Structured Query Language," shows you how to write action queries using SQL instead of employing Access's graphical Query Design window.

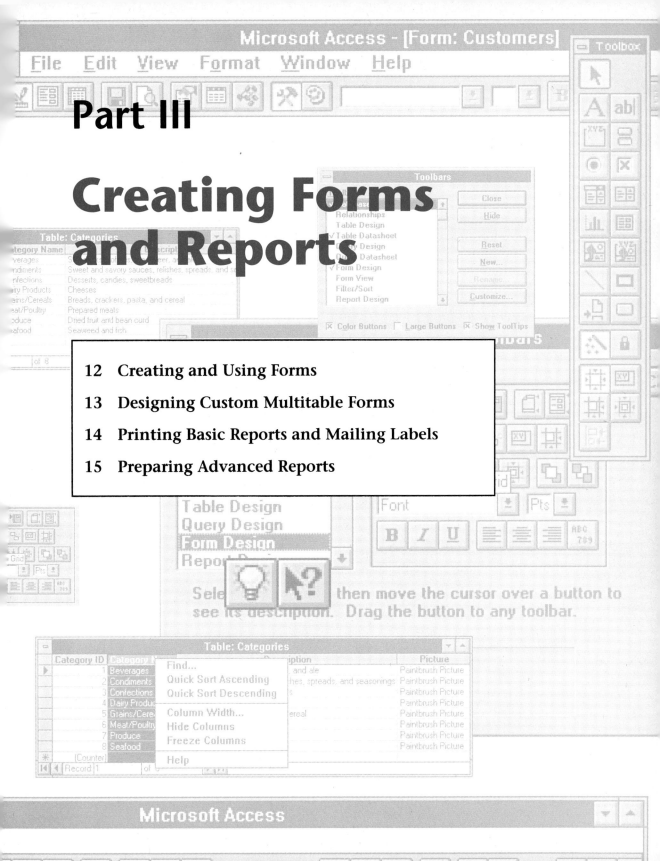

Part III

Creating Forms and Reports

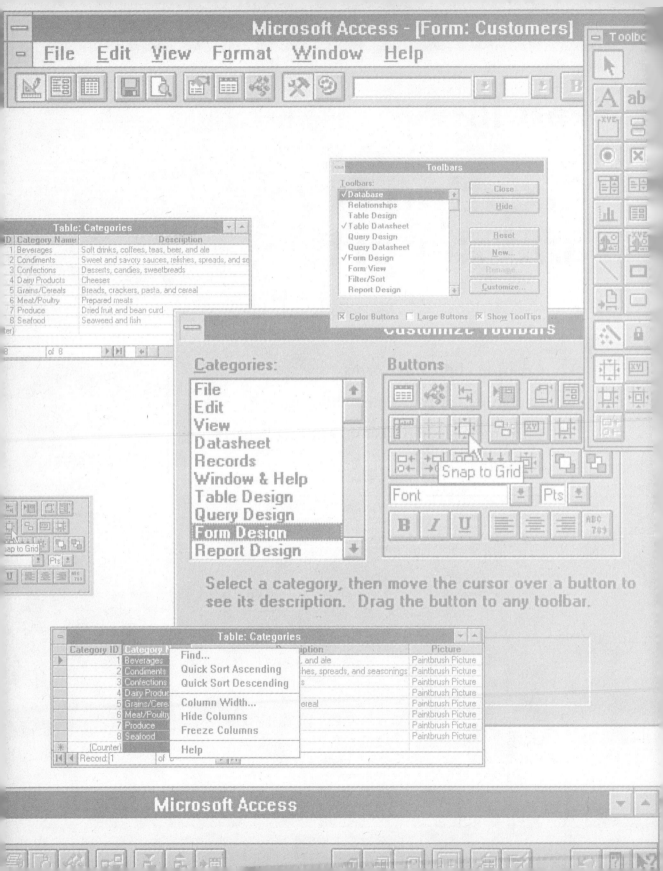

Chapter 12

Creating and Using Forms

Access forms create the user interface to your tables. Although you can use table and query views to perform many of the functions provided by forms, forms offer the advantage of presenting data in an organized and attractive manner. You can arrange the location of fields on the form so that the data entry or editing operations for a single record follow a left-to-right, top-to-bottom sequence. Forms enable you to create multiple-choice selections for fields that use shorthand codes to represent a set of allowable values. A properly designed form speeds data entry and minimizes operator keying errors.

Forms are constructed from a collection of individual design elements, called *controls* or, more properly, *control objects*. Controls are the components you see in the windows and dialogs of Access and other Windows applications. You use text boxes to enter and edit data, labels to hold field names, and object frames to display graphics. A form consists of a window in which you place a group of controls that display the data in your tables and other controls that display static data that Access provides, such as labels or logos that you create.

This chapter concentrates on creating forms that consist only of text-type controls. Part V, "Integrating Access with Other Applications," provides explanations of object linking and embedding (OLE), the method used by Access to incorporate graphs and other graphical elements in forms and reports.

Access forms are versatile; they enable you to complete tasks that you cannot complete in Table or Query Views. You can validate entries based on information contained in a table other than the one you are editing. You can create forms that incorporate other forms. A form within a form is called a *subform*. Forms can calculate values and display totals. This chapter shows you how to

In this chapter, you learn to

- Use the Form Wizard to create a new form

- Modify the design of a form

- Relocate and resize controls on forms

- Modify the foreground and background colors of controls

- Change the formatting of text in controls

III

Forms and Reports

create a form using the Access Form Wizard and how to modify the form to speed data entry. Chapter 13, "Designing Custom Multitable Forms," explains how to use the form toolbox to add controls to forms and how to establish default values and validation rules with forms.

Identifying Types of Forms

The content and appearance of your form depend on its use in your database application. Database applications fall into three basic categories:

- *Transaction processing.* Add new records to the tables and edit existing records. Transaction processing applications require write access to (permissions for) the tables that underlie the form.

- *Decision-support.* Supply information in the form of graphs, tables, or individual data elements, but don't enable the user to add to or edit the data. Decision-support applications only require read permissions for the tables that supply the data.

- *Database maintenance.* Administrative functions that relate to creating databases and the tables they contain, and to controlling database access by users, security assurance by encryption, periodic database compaction, and backup operations. Database maintenance applications require full permissions for all the objects in the database.

Forms are key elements in transaction processing and decision-support applications, which are described in sections that follow. Common database maintenance operations don't require forms, but forms can be useful for maintaining records of database maintenance activities.

Forms for Transaction Processing

Forms for transaction processing usually operate directly on tables when only one table is involved. If a single form is intended for adding or editing information in more than one table, you create a query that includes all the fields that you want to add to or edit and then base the form on the query. Your primary form also can use a single table as its data source and use another form, incorporated in the basic form and called a *subform*, that has a related table as its data source. An example of a transaction processing form that uses the subform approach is the Orders form of the Northwind Traders sample database (see fig. 12.1). The datasheet subform that appears below the Order ID text box is used to display and add line items to an invoice.

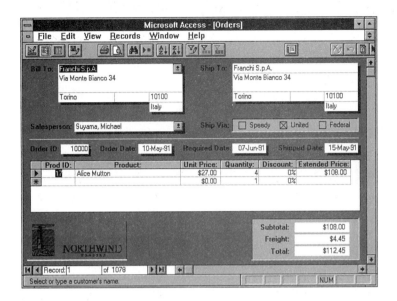

Fig. 12.1

The Orders form of the Northwind Traders database.

This chapter concentrates on forms used for transaction processing, but the techniques you learn are applicable to forms used for any other purpose.

Forms for Decision Support

Forms designed only to present information fall into the category of decision support; these forms provide historical data that managers and supervisors use to determine a course of action. You can design decision-support forms for long-range planning or for short-term (or *ad hoc*) decisions. Short-term decisions relate to a single action, such as granting a larger credit line to a customer or sending a sales representative to determine why the customer's purchases have declined. An example of a form to support a short-term decision is Northwind's Quarterly Orders form, which appears in figure 12.2.

The Quarterly Orders form consists of a main form that displays Customer ID, Company Name, City, and Country, and a subform that displays quarterly sales of products to the customer. The main form is based on the Customers table. The subform consists of the Quarterly Orders subform (a separate form), which is based on the Quarterly Orders by Product crosstab query. Access enables you to include subforms within forms and even subforms within subforms. This feature is called *nesting*. You can nest forms in up to three levels: main, subform, and sub-subform.

Forms that support short-term decisions often are based on crosstab queries that summarize data in a time series, such as sales to a customer totaled by

months, quarters, or years. A table used to support the decision to grant additional credit to a customer might list by quarters the number of invoices issued to the customer, total purchases, and average payment times in days.

Fig. 12.2

The Quarterly Orders form.

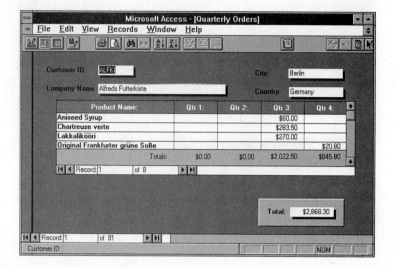

Creating a Transaction Form with the Form Wizard

The form that you create in this example is typical of the transaction-processing forms used to add new records to the many sides of a one-to-many relationship. Adding line items to an invoice is an example for which a form of this kind, called a *one-to-many form*, is necessary. The object of the Personnel Actions form is to add new records to the Personnel Actions table or enable you to edit the existing records. If you didn't add the Personnel Actions table shown in figure 12.3 to the Northwind Traders database in Chapter 4 "Working with Access Databases and Tables," and Chapter 5, "Entering, Editing, and Validating Data in Tables," do so before proceeding with this example. The structure of the Personnel Actions table also is provided in Appendix C, "Data Dictionary for the Personnel Actions Table."

Besides basic data entry and editing, the Personnel Actions form has a subform that displays all the previous personnel actions for a given employee. The majority of the forms found in common database applications are one-to-many forms, and most one-to-many forms require a subform to display data from the many side of the relationship.

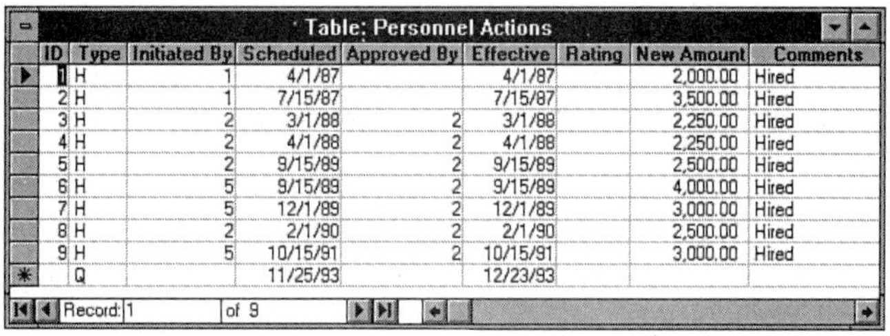

Table: Personnel Actions

ID	Type	Initiated By	Scheduled	Approved By	Effective	Rating	New Amount	Comments
1	H	1	4/1/87		4/1/87		2,000.00	Hired
2	H	1	7/15/87		7/15/87		3,500.00	Hired
3	H	2	3/1/88	2	3/1/88		2,250.00	Hired
4	H	2	4/1/88	2	4/1/88		2,250.00	Hired
5	H	2	9/15/89	2	9/15/89		2,500.00	Hired
6	H	5	9/15/89	2	9/15/89		4,000.00	Hired
7	H	5	12/1/89	2	12/1/89		3,000.00	Hired
8	H	2	2/1/90	2	2/1/90		2,500.00	Hired
9	H	5	10/15/91	2	10/15/91		3,000.00	Hired
	Q		11/25/93		12/23/93			

Record: 1 of 9

Fig. 12.3
The Personnel Actions table with a single entry for the first nine employees.

You can take two approaches to designing a form that accomplishes the objectives of the Personnel Actions form:

- Use the Employees table as the source of the data for the main form, and use the subform to display, add, and edit records of the Personnel Actions table. This method enables you to add a new employee to the Employees table, but the data of primary interest is relegated to a datasheet in the subform.

- Use the Personnel Actions table as the source of data for the main form and the subform. In this case, you cannot add a new employee because the Employees table has a one-to-many relationship with the Personnel Actions table you are editing.

Because the Northwind Traders database includes an Employees form that you can use to add a new employee, this example form uses the Personnel Actions table as its primary source of data. If you were creating a full-scale human resources database application, you might choose the Employees table as the data source for the form and design a subform for editing the Personnel Actions table with the history displayed in a subform of the subform.

Creating the Query on Which to Base the Form

The Personnel Actions table identifies employees only by their ID numbers, located in the PA ID field. You need to display the employee's name and title on the form to avoid entering records for the wrong person. To obtain the employee's name and title data for the form, you need to create a one-to-many query that joins the Employees table, which has only one entry per employee, with the Personnel Actions table, which can have many entries for one employee.

To create the Personnel Actions query that serves as the data source for your main form, follow these steps:

1. Close any open forms, click the New Query button of the toolbar; then click the New Query button of the New Query dialog. Double-click the Personnel Actions table item in the list of tables in the Add Table dialog to add the Personnel Actions table to your query.

Alternatively, you can bypass the Add Table dialog step by clicking the Table button of the Database window and then selecting (highlighting) Personnel Actions in the table list. When you click the New Query button with a table selected, the table is added automatically to the new query.

2. Double-click the Employees table in the table list and then click Close. The field list windows for the Personnel Actions and Employees tables appear in the upper pane of the Query Design window.

If you used the alternative method to add the Personnel Actions table to the query described in step 1, you need to click the Add Table button of the toolbar to open the Add Table dialog to add the Employees table to your query.

3. Click the Table Names button of the toolbar to add the Tables row to your Query Design grid.

4. Click the PA ID field in the Personnel Actions Field List dialog and drag it to the Employee ID field of the Employees Field List dialog to create a join between these two fields (see fig. 12.4).

Fig. 12.4

The upper pane of the Query Design window for the Personnel Actions query.

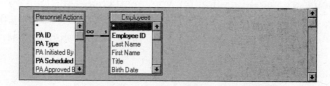

5. Click the * field of the Personnel Actions table, drag it to the first column of the Query grid, and drop it in the Personnel Actions column. This adds all the fields to the Personnel Actions table to your query.

6. Click the Employee ID field of the Employees table, drag it to the Query grid, and drop it in the second column.

7. From the Employees table, click and drag the Last Name, First Name, and Title fields, and drop them in columns 3, 4, and 5 of the Query grid, respectively, as shown in figure 12.5.

Fig. 12.5
The Query grid for the Personnel Actions query.

8. To simplify finding an employee, click the Sort row of the Last Name column and select an Ascending sort.

9. Close the new query. Click Yes when the message box asks if you want to save the query.

10. In the Save As dialog, give the query a name, such as **qryPersonnelActions**, and then click OK (see fig. 12.6).

Fig. 12.6
The Save As dialog.

If you didn't add records to the Personnel Actions table when you created it in Chapter 4, you can add them with the Personnel Actions form you create with the assistance of Access's Form Wizards.

Creating the Basic Form with the Form Wizards

Form Wizards create the basic design of the form and add the text box controls to display and edit the values of data items.

To create the Personnel Actions form with the Form Wizards, follow these steps:

1. Click the Form button of the Database window, and then click the New button. The New Form dialog appears, as shown in figure 12.7.

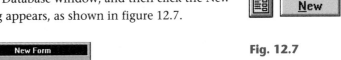

III

Fig. 12.7
The New Form dialog.

Forms and Reports

2. Click the arrow to open the drop-down list of existing tables and queries that may serve as a source of data for a form. The qryPersonnelActions query that you just created is the basic source of data for your form, so select it and then click the Form Wizards button. The first Form Wizards dialog appears, as shown in figure 12.8.

Fig. 12.8
The types of forms the Form Wizards can create.

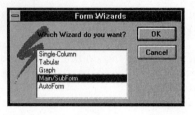

3. Because your form is to include a Personnel Actions history subform, select Main/Subform and click OK. (Single-column creates a simple data-entry form without a subform, Tabular creates a form with a row-column grid, Graph uses the Graph Wizard to add a graph or chart to your form, and AutoForm automatically creates a single-column form with an embossed style. AutoForm is a new feature of Access 2.0.)

    The second Form Wizard dialog appears and prompts you to choose the table or query that contains the data for the subform (see fig. 12.9).

4. Select qryPersonnelActions from the Tables/Queries list, and click the Next button.

    The next Form Wizard dialog appears and asks which Personnel Actions fields should be included on your main form.

> **Note**
>
> Creating a form and subform, both of which are based on the same underlying table, in this example the Personnel Actions table, is a somewhat unconventional but totally acceptable database application design method. Most forms that employ subforms employ a base table (such as Employees) or a query whose data source is a base table as the RecordSource of the main form. A related table or a query based on a related table serves as the RecordSource of the subform. Many of the forms of NWIND.MDB demonstrate the conventional form-subform design. The form example, frmPersonnelActions, uses a common underlying table for both the form and subform to illustrate some of the unique characteristics of this approach to one-to-many form design.

Fig. 12.9
Selecting the
source of the data
for the subform.

5. You need to be able to edit all the fields of the Personnel Actions table, so click the >> button to add all the fields to the Fields On Main Form list, as shown in figure 12.10. Click the Next > button.

The next dialog appears and asks you to choose the fields to appear on the subform (see fig. 12.11).

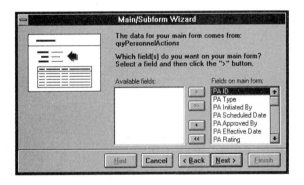

Fig. 12.10
Selecting the
Personnel Actions
fields to include
on the main form.

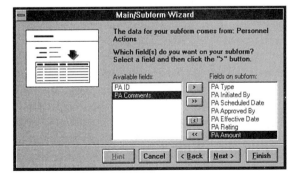

Fig. 12.11
Selecting the
Personnel Actions
fields to include
on the subform.

III

Forms and Reports

> **Note**
>
> If you make an error or change your mind, you can click the < Back button, when it is enabled, to modify your previous choices. Cancel takes you back to the Database window without completing the form-creation process.

6. The PA ID field is included in the Personnel Actions query, so you don't need to include the PA ID field in the subform. For this example, reviewing previous comments isn't necessary. To expedite the addition of fields, click >> to add all the fields. Choose PA ID and click the < button. Then choose PA Comments and click the < button again. This process removes the PA ID and PA Comments fields from the subform. The Available Fields and Fields On Subforms lists appear as illustrated by figure 12.11.

   Double-check the items in the two lists to verify that the fields on the subform are correct, and then click the Next > button. The list of tables used in the forms appears, as shown in figure 12.12.

Fig. 12.12
Specifying the table that contains the fields in the main form and the subform.

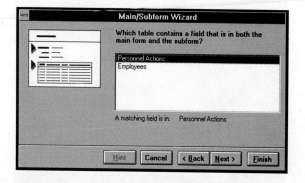

7. Access needs to know which of the two tables that supply data for the form is the source of data for the main form and the subform. Tables in subforms must be related to the main form. Select Personnel Actions from the list of tables, and click the Next > button. The dialog shown in figure 12.13 appears.

   This dialog enables you to apply a style to your form. This form is for use by a data-entry operator and doesn't need special effects to highlight or decorate the fields.

Fig. 12.13
Selecting the style
for your form.

8. Select Standard style and click the Next button. A dialog appears, as shown in figure 12.14, asking you for a title for your form. (A special area for the title, the form header, is included at the top of the form you create.)

Fig. 12.14
Giving your form
a title.

9. Type **Personnel Action Entry** as the title of the form in the text box. Click the Open button to allow the Form Wizard to create the new form. If you click Design, you can change the design of the new form without viewing it in run mode.

   A message box appears indicating that the main form must be able to open the subform before the subform can appear in the Forms window (see fig. 12.15). Access cannot open a form that hasn't been saved.

10. Click OK. The Save As dialog appears (see fig. 12.16).

11. Subforms are like any other main form; they are included in the list of forms displayed in the Database window. Enter a title for the subform, such as **sbfPersonnelActions**, in the Save As dialog, and click OK.

III

Forms and Reports

Fig. 12.15

The message box indicating that you must save your subform.

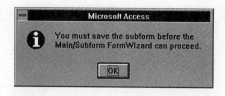

Fig. 12.16

The Save As dialog used to name your subform.

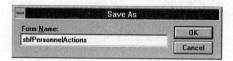

12. In one-to-many forms, the subform needs to be linked to the main form so that records in the subform are related to the current record displayed in the main form. The Form Wizard could not divine a suitable field in the subform to link to a field in the main form, so the message box of figure 12.17 appears. (The Access 1.x Form/Subform Wizard created links with any field(s) common to the form and subform. This often led to problems. The Access 2.0 Wizard is more selective.) Later in this chapter, you create the linkage between the main form and the subform manually, so click OK.

The new form created by the Form Wizard appears as a normal-sized window.

Fig. 12.17

The message box that advises you need to set the subform linkage yourself.

13. Click the Document Maximize button to expand the form's window to fill the available area (see fig. 12.18).

The Form Wizard creates a single column of text boxes with associated labels for entering or editing the values of data items in each of the fields you specified in step 5. The vertical distance required for a single column of text boxes causes the subform to be pushed to the bottom of the window. In the next section, you learn how to rearrange the controls created by the Form Wizard so that all the controls, including the subform, easily fit in a single window.

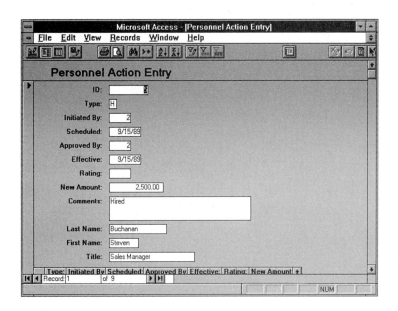

Fig. 12.18
The basic Personnel Action Entry form created by the Form/Subform Form Wizard.

14. Access gives your form the default name Form1. To give it a different name, choose Save Form As from the File menu and type **frmPersonnelActions** as the name of the form in the Save As dialog (see fig. 12.19). Click OK to assign the new name to the form.

Fig. 12.19
Entering a name for your main form in the Save As dialog.

No matter how expert you become in the design of Access forms, using the Form Wizards to create the basic form design saves you time.

Using the Form Design Window

To modify the design of your new form, click the Design View button on the toolbar. The Form Design window appears as shown in figure 12.20. Using the toolbox to add new control elements to the form is one of the subjects of the next chapter. Click the Toolbox button of the toolbar, or double-click the window menu symbol at the upper left corner of the toolbox to make the toolbox temporarily disappear.

III

Forms and Reports

Fig. 12.20

The basic Personnel Action Entry form in design mode.

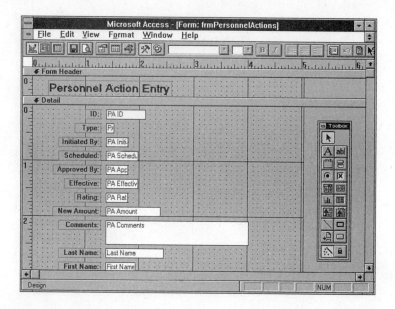

The Personnel Action Entry (frmPersonnelActions) form enables you to experiment with the methods of modifying forms and their content described in the sections that follow.

Caution

Do not save the form with the changes you make when following the instructions contained in this section. These changes are for demonstration purposes only. Saving the changes you make permanently modifies the form you created in the preceding section.

Elements of the Form Design Window

Forms can be divided into three sections: Form Header, Detail, and Form Footer. Headers and footers are optional. The Form Design window includes the following basic elements:

- A toolbar with buttons that are shortcuts for menu selections in form design mode. The functions of the buttons and their equivalent menu choices are listed in tables in the next section.

- A set of vertical and horizontal rulers, calibrated in inches for the United States version of Access. Centimeters is the default for versions of Access supplied in countries where the metric system is used.

■ A vertical line, shown to the left of the toolbox in figure 12.21, that establishes the right margin of the form. You can move the margin indicator line by clicking and dragging it to the desired location.

■ A horizontal line (not shown in fig. 12.21) that establishes the bottom margin of the form. You can drag the line to a new location with the mouse. Margins are important when you are designing a subform to fit within a rectangle of a predetermined size on the main form.

■ Vertical and horizontal scroll bars that enable you to view portions of the form outside the boundaries of the form window.

■ A Form Header bar that defines the height of the form's header section, if you choose to add a header and footer to your form. Headers and footers are added in pairs. The Form Header section contains static text, graphic images, and other controls that appear at the top of the form. If you print a multipage form, the Form Header appears only at the top of the first page.

■ A Form Detail bar that divides the Form Header from the rest of the form. Controls that display data from your tables and queries, plus static data elements such as labels and logos, are on the Form Detail bar.

■ A Form Footer bar (not shown in fig. 12.20) that defines the height of the form's footer section. The Form Footer section is similar in function to the Form Header. If you print a multipage form, the Form Footer appears only at the bottom of the last page.

You can add Form Header and Form Footer sections to a form or delete these sections by choosing Form Hdr/Footer from the Layout menu. (If the form has Header and Footer sections, a check mark appears to the left of the Form Hdr/Footer menu choice.) Delete the Header and Footer sections of the form. A dialog warns you that you lose the content of the title in the current header when you take this action. Because you don't save the changes you make when following the instructions in this and the following sections, the temporary loss of the title text is not significant. Click OK.

Form Design Toolbar Buttons and Menu Choices

The Form Design toolbar of Access 2.0 introduces several new buttons that apply only to the design of forms: the Field List and Palette buttons. Table 12.1 lists the function and equivalent menu choice for each of the standard toolbar buttons in form design mode, except for the buttons that relate to text formatting.

Access

2.0

	Table 12.1	Standard Toolbar Buttons in Form Design Mode	
Button	**Function**		**Menu Choice**
	Selects form design mode.		**View** Form **Design**
	Displays the form in run mode.		**View** Form
	Displays the table or query that is the source of data for the main form.		**View** Datasheet
	Saves the current form.		**File** S**ave**
	Selects Print Preview to display how your form appears if printed. You can print the form from the Print Preview window.		**File** Print Preview
	Displays the Properties dialog for one of the two sections of the form when you click the section bars, or displays the properties of a control when you select it.		**View** Properties
	Displays a list of fields in the query or table that is the data source for the main form.		**View** Field **List**
	Opens the code editing window for Access Basic code contained in a module as integral part of the form (Code Behind Forms, or CBF).		**View** Code
	Displays or closes the toolbox.		**View** Toolbox
	Displays a palette from which you can choose the color of the text, background (fill), and border of a control. The palette also enables you to add special effects (raised or sunken) that affect the appearance of the control and enables you to choose the width of the control's border.		**View** Palette
	Displays the Database window.		**Window** 1 Database
	Returns the form to its state preceding the last modification.		**Edit** U**ndo**
	Displays the main Cue Card.		**Help** Cue Cards
	Displays the Help menu for the form design user interface.		F1 key

The appearance of the Form Design window after clicking the Properties and Palette buttons is shown in figure 12.21.

You can close the palette and the Properties dialog by double-clicking their Document Control-menu boxes, or by clicking the appropriate buttons on the toolbar.

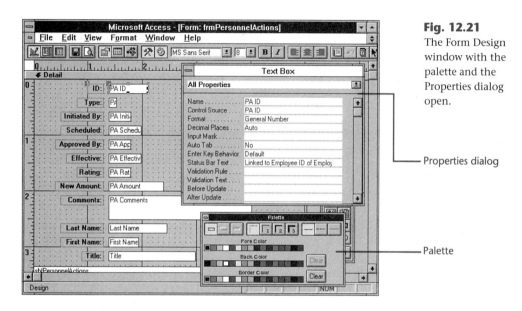

Fig. 12.21
The Form Design window with the palette and the Properties dialog open.

Properties dialog

Palette

Text-Formatting Toolbar Buttons and Lists

When you choose a text-type control, such as a text box, two drop-down lists appear in the toolbar, with an additional set of six toolbar buttons. (The General text alignment button of Access 1.x is not available in Access 2.0.) The lists enable you to choose the desired typeface and type size for the text. The additional buttons, used to format the text, are similar to those buttons found on the toolbar ribbon of Microsoft Word for Windows and other Windows word processing applications.

The default typeface for forms is the same as that for tables and queries, MS Sans Serif in an 8-point font. You can select any bit-mapped or TrueType family installed on your computer from the type family drop-down list. (If you are using a PostScript printer, PostScript type families, such as Helvetica and Palatino, do not appear.) You can choose from a drop-down list of preset type sizes or enter a size in points in the Size combo list. You apply attributes and formatting with the text buttons. Table 12.2 lists the function of each toolbar's text-formatting buttons and its equivalent text-property setting.

III

Forms and Reports

	Table 12.2	Toolbar Buttons for Text Controls in Form Design Mode	
Button		**Function**	**Property and Value**
B		Sets text style to bold (default for titles and labels).	Font Bold = Yes
I		Sets italic (or slanted) text style.	Font Italic = Yes
U		Underlines text.	Font Underline = Yes
▤		Left-justifies text within border.	Text Align = Left
▤		Centers text horizontally within border.	Text Align = Center
▤		Right-justifies text within border.	Text Align = Right

Default Values for Forms

You can change the default values used in the creation of all forms by choosing Options from the View menu and then selecting Form & Report Design from the Categories list (see fig. 12.22). You can create a form to use as a template and to replace the standard template, determine whether control objects snap to a 0.1-inch grid (visible or invisible) when you move them, and determine how objects are displayed when chosen. The effect of each of the options is described in the sections that follow. The options you or other users of Access choose in the Options dialog are saved for each user ID in the MSysOptions table of the SYSTEM.MDA file.

Fig. 12.22
Displaying Form &
Report options in
the Options dialog.

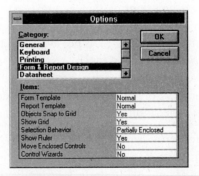

You can change the default values for the current form, section, or controls by choosing the object as described in the following section and then changing the default values displayed in the Properties dialog for that object.

Using the Palette Window

The Palette window of Access 2.0 differs markedly from that of Access 1.x. Toggle buttons replace the Appearance option buttons; you can choose from solid, dashed, or dotted lines for borders; and the buttons that choose the border line width have been moved and reduced in number. The following sections describe how to use the controls of the Palette window to change the background and foreground colors of form sections and control objects, as well as the border properties of control objects.

Background Colors

The background color (`BackColor` property) of a form's section applies to all areas of the section except those occupied by control objects. The default background color of all sections of forms created by the Form Wizard is light gray. This new standard has been adopted by Microsoft for the background color of dialogs of Excel 4+ and other applications introduced after the launch of Windows 3.1 in the spring of 1992.

The default color choices of the Palette window are 16 of the standard *system* colors of Windows 3.1. If you are creating a form that you intend to print, a gray background is distracting and consumes substantial amounts of laser printer toner. Data-entry operators may prefer a white background rather than a gray or colored background. Colored backgrounds do not aid text visibility.

To change the background color of a section of a form, follow these steps:

1. Select the section of the form (Header, Detail, or Footer) whose back-ground color you want to change by clicking an empty area within the section.

2. Click the Palette button on the toolbar to display the Palette window, if necessary.

3. Click the box that contains the color you want to use in the Back Color row of the palette.

Because the background color of each form section is independent, you must repeat the process for other sections of your form. The Clear button of the Back Color row is disabled when a form section is chosen because a clear background color isn't applicable to forms.

You choose the background color of a control object, such as a label, as you do for forms. In most cases, the chosen background color of labels is the same as that of the form, so choose Clear to allow the background color to appear. The default value of the BackColor property of text boxes is white (16777215 in the decimal equivalent of Windows' color coding method) so that text boxes contrast with the form's background color.

Foreground Color, Border Color, and Border Style

Foreground color (the ForeColor property) is applicable only to control objects. (The ForeColor row is disabled when you select a form section.) Foreground color specifies the color in which the text of labels and text boxes appears. The default value of the ForeColor property is black (0). You choose border colors for control objects that have borders in the Border Color row.

The toggle buttons of the Palette window enable you to simulate special effects for control objects, such as a raised or sunken appearance, as well as control the width and style of the border of controls. Table 12.3 lists the function of each button in the Palette window's top row and the button's corresponding property and property value.

Table 12.3 Palette Buttons for Control Style and Border Properties		
Button	**Function**	**Property and Value**
	Controls have normal appearance.	Special Effect = Normal
	Controls have raised appearance.	Special Effect = Raised
	Controls have sunken appearance.	Special Effect = Sunken
	Controls have hairline border.	Border Width = Hairline
	Controls have 1-point border.	Border Width = 1 pt
	Controls have 2-point border.	Border Width = 2 pt
	Controls have 3-point border.	Border Width = 3 pt
	Controls have solid border.	Border Line Style = Solid
	Controls have dashed border.	Border Line Style = Dashes
	Controls have dotted border.	Border Line Style = Dots

The Border Width and Border Line Style drop-down lists offer a number of selections not available from the Palette window. For example, you can choose short dashes, sparse dots, dot-dashes, and other Morse code derivatives for Border Line Style and Border Width property values up to six points.

Creating Custom Colors with the Color Builder

If you are not satisfied with one of the 16 Windows system colors for your form sections or control objects, you can create your own custom color by following these steps:

1. Place the caret in the Back Color, Fore Color, or Border Color text box of the Properties window for a control.

2. Click the ellipsis button to display the Color Common dialog. The basic colors dialog enables you to choose from a set of 48 colors. If one of these colors suits your taste, click OK to assign the color as the value of the property and close the dialog. If not, proceed to step 3.

3. Click the Define Custom Colors button to expand the Color dialog to include the Hue/Saturation and Luminance windows, as shown in figure 12.23.

4. Position the cursor in the square Hue/Saturation window to choose the color you want.

5. Move the arrow at the right of the luminance rectangle while observing the Color block to set the luminance (brightness) value you want.

6. Click Add to Custom Colors to add your new color to the first of the 16 Custom Colors blocks.

7. Click the Custom Color block to select it; then click OK to add the color value to the property and close the Color dialog.

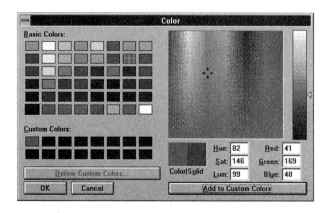

Fig. 12.23
The Color dialog expanded to display the custom color selection control.

III

Forms and Reports

The majority of PCs used for data entry and editing applications run in conventional 16-color VGA mode. In 16-color VGA mode, any colors you choose or create, other than the standard Windows system colors, are simulated by the *dithering* process. Dithering alternates pixels of differing colors to create the usually imperfect illusion of a solid color. Thus, it is a good programming practice to stick with the 16 Windows system colors unless you have a very good reason to do otherwise.

Selecting, Editing, and Moving Form Elements and Controls

The techniques for selecting, editing, and moving the elements that comprise Access 2.0 forms were derived from the form-design system refined by Microsoft for Visual Basic 3.0. If you have used Visual Basic, you will find the selection, relocation, and sizing techniques for Access controls to be similar. Several subtle differences exist between Access and Visual Basic, however. These differences quickly become apparent when you edit your first form.

 The properties that apply to the entire form, each of the five sections into which an Access form can be divided, and each control object on the form are determined by the values shown in the Properties window. To view the Properties dialog for a control, select the control by clicking anywhere on its surface and then click the Properties button of the toolbar. The sections of an Access form are shown in figure 12.24.

The following descriptions tell you how to choose and display the properties of the entire form, its sections, and its control objects:

■ *Form.* Click the area of the form to the right of the right-margin indicator line or choose Select Form from the Edit menu. Selecting the form enables you to set properties for the form as a whole by entering values from the properties listed in the Form Properties dialog.

■ *Header section only.* Click the Form Header or Page Header bar. A set of properties applies to the Form Header or Page Header section only. A Form Header and Footer appear only if you choose Form Hdr/Ftr from the Layout menu. A Page Header and Footer appear if you choose **Page** Hdr/Ftr from the Layout menu. Page Headers and Footers are used primarily in conjunction with printing forms. You delete headers and footers by choosing Form Hdr/Ftr or **Page** Hdr/Ftr a second time.

■ *Detail section only.* Click the Detail bar. A set of properties that duplicates those of the Form Header section applies to the Detail section of the form.

■ *Footer section only.* Click the Form Footer or Page Footer bar. A set of properties identical to the Form Header apply. A Form Footer appears only if a Form Header has been added. The same applies to Page Headers and Footers.

■ *Control object* (or both elements of a control with an associated label). Click the surface of the control. Each type of control has its own set of properties. Choosing one or more control objects is the subject of a subsequent section.

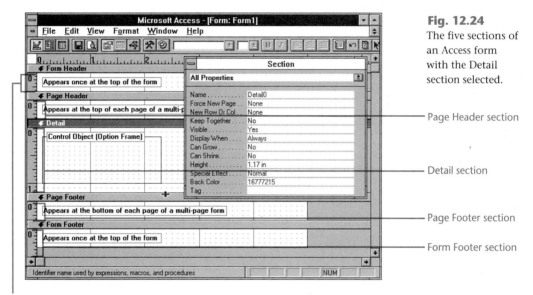

Fig. 12.24
The five sections of an Access form with the Detail section selected.

Changing the Size of the Form Header and Form Footer

You can change the height of the Form Header or Form Footer sections by dragging the Detail or Form Footer bar vertically with the mouse. When you position the mouse pointer at the top edge of a section divider bar, it turns into a line with two vertical arrows, as shown in figure 12.24. You drag the pointer with the mouse to adjust the size of the section above the mouse pointer.

The height of the Detail section is determined by the vertical dimension of the window in which the form is displayed, less the combined heights of the

Form Header and Form Footer (and/or Page Header and Footer) sections, that are fixed in position. When you adjust the vertical scroll bar, only the Detail section scrolls.

Selecting, Moving, and Sizing a Single Control

When you select a control object by clicking its surface, the object is enclosed by a shadow line with an anchor rectangle at its upper left corner and five smaller rectangular sizing handles, as shown in figure 12.25. Text boxes, combo lists, check boxes, and option buttons have an associated (attached) label. When you select one of these objects, the label and the object are selected as a unit.

Fig. 12.25
The appearance of a control object selected for relocation and resizing.

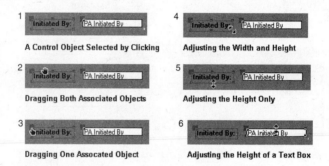

The following choices are available for moving or changing the size of a control object (the numbered choices correspond with the numbers in fig. 12.25):

1. *To select a control (and its associated label, if any),* click anywhere on its surface.

2. *To move the control (and its associated label, if any) to a new position,* move the mouse pointer within the outline of the object at any point other than the small resizing handles or within the confines of a text box (where the cursor can become an editing caret). The mouse pointer becomes a hand symbol when it is on an area that you can use to move the entire control. Press the left mouse button while dragging the hand symbol to the new location for the control. If the control doesn't have an associated label, you can use the control's anchor handle at the upper left corner to move the control. An outline of the control indicates its position as you reposition the mouse. Release the mouse button to drop the control in its new position.

3. *To move the elements of a control with an associated label separately*, position the mouse pointer on the anchor handle (upper left corner) of the control you want to move. The mouse pointer becomes a hand with an extended finger. Drag the individual element to its new position.

4. *To adjust the width and height of a control simultaneously*, click the small sizing handle at one of the three corners of the outline of the control. The mouse pointer becomes a diagonal two-headed arrow. Drag the two-headed arrow to the new position with the mouse.

5. *To adjust only the height of the control*, click the sizing handle on one of the horizontal surfaces of the outline. The mouse pointer becomes a vertical two-headed arrow. Drag the two-headed arrow to the new position with the mouse.

6. Same as item 5 for a text box.

Selecting and deselecting controls is a *toggling* process. Toggling is repeating an action that causes the effect of the action to alternate between the on and off conditions. The Properties, Field List, and Palette buttons on the toolbar and their corresponding menu choices are toggles. The Properties dialog, for example, appears and disappears as you repetitively click the Properties button.

Aligning Controls to the Grid

The Form Design window includes a grid consisting of one-pixel dots with a default spacing of 0.1 inch. When the grid is visible, you can use the grid dots to assist in maintaining the horizontal and vertical alignment of rows and columns of controls. Even if the grid isn't visible, as is the case with forms created by the Form Wizard, you can cause controls to "snap to the grid" by choosing Snap to Grid from the Layout menu. Snap to Grid is a toggle; when Snap to Grid is active, the menu choice is checked. When you move a control, the upper left corner of the object jumps to the closest grid dot.

You can cause the size of control objects to conform to grid spacing by toggling Size to Grid from the Layout menu. You also can choose to have the size of the control fit its content by choosing Size to Fit from the Layout menu.

Toggling the Grid command on the View menu controls the visibility of the grid. You can control whether the grid is visible or invisible when you create a new form by choosing Options from the View menu and setting the View Grid option of the Form & Report Design category to Yes or No. If the grid

Tip
If Snap to Grid is on and you want to locate or size a control without reference to the grid, press Ctrl when you move or resize the control.

III

Forms and Reports

spacing is set to more than 16 per inch or 10 per centimeter, the dots aren't visible. To change the grid spacing for a form, follow these steps:

1. Choose Select Form from the Edit menu.

2. Click the Properties button of the toolbar to make the Properties dialog appear.

3. Change Grid X to 10 and Grid Y to 12 dots per inch (the default) or both values to 16 (if you want controls to align with inch ruler ticks). Users with metric rulers are likely to prefer a value of ten for both the Grid X and Grid Y values.

Selecting and Moving a Group of Controls

You can select and move more than one object at a time by using one of the following methods:

- Enclose the objects with a rectangle created by clicking the surface of the form outside the outline of a control object. Press the left mouse button while dragging the mouse pointer to create an enclosing rectangle that includes each of the objects you want to select (see fig. 12.26). Release the mouse pointer. You may move the group of objects by clicking and dragging the anchor handle of any one of them.

- Select one object and hold down Shift while you use the mouse to select the next object.

- Delete a member from the group by clicking its anchor with the mouse to deselect it. To deselect the group, click any inactive area of the form. An inactive area is an area outside the outline of a control.

Fig. 12.26
A collection of control objects enclosed with a selection rectangle.

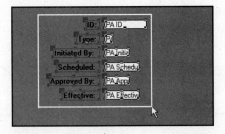

If you select or deselect a control with an associated label, the label is selected or deselected with the control.

> **Note**
>
> The selection rectangle selects a control if any part of the control is included within the rectangle. This behavior is unlike many drawing applications in which the entire object must be enclosed to be selected. You can change the behavior of Access's selection rectangle to require enclosure of the entire object by choosing **Options** from the **View** menu, selecting Form & Report Design from the list, and changing the value of the Selection Behavior option from Partially Enclosed to Fully Enclosed.

Aligning a Group of Controls

You can align selected individual controls or groups of controls to the grid or to each other by choosing Align from the Layout menu and completing the following actions:

- To align a selected control or a group of controls to the grid, choose To Grid from the submenu.

- To adjust the positions of controls within a selected columnar group so that their left edges fall into vertical alignment with the far-left control, choose Left from the submenu.

- To adjust the positions of controls within a selected columnar group so that their right edges align with the right edge of the far-right control, choose Right from the submenu.

- To align rows of controls by their top edges, choose Top from the submenu.

- To align rows of controls by their bottom edges, choose Bottom from the submenu.

Your forms have a more professional appearance if you take the time to align groups of controls both vertically and horizontally.

Using the Windows Clipboard and Deleting Controls

All the conventional Windows Clipboard commands apply to control objects. You can cut or copy a selected control or group of controls to the Clipboard. You then can paste the control or group to the form by using Edit menu commands and relocate the pasted control(s) as desired. Access uses the new Windows 3.1 keyboard shortcut keys: Ctrl+X to cut and Ctrl+C to copy selected control(s) to the Clipboard, and Ctrl+V to paste the selected controls. The traditional Shift+Delete, Ctrl+Insert, and Shift+Insert commands perform the same operations.

You can delete a control by selecting it and then pressing Delete. If you accidentally delete a label associated with a control, select and copy another label to the Clipboard and then select the control with which the label is to be associated and paste the label to the control.

Changing the Color and Border Style of a Control

As mentioned earlier in this chapter, the default color for the text and border of controls is black. Borders are one pixel wide (called *hairline* width); some objects, such as text boxes, have default borders. Labels have a gray background color by default, but a better choice for the default label color would have been *transparent*. Transparent means that the background color appears within the control except in areas occupied by text or pictures. You control the color and border styles of a control from the Palette dialog.

Access
2.0

To change the color or border style of a selected control or group of controls, follow these steps:

1. Select the control(s) whose color you want to change.

2. Click the Palette button on the toolbar to display the palette.

3. Click a color box in the Back Color row to change the background color of the control(s) that aren't transparent (clear). Click the Clear button to make the background transparent.

4. Click a color box in the Border Color row to change the border color of the control(s) that have borders.

5. Click a border width button to change the thickness of the border for control(s) whose borders are enabled.

6. Click a border line style button to change the type of line for the border from solid to dashed or dotted.

7. Click a color box in the Fore Color row to change the color of the text element of the control(s).

PDOX **xBase**

> **Note**
>
> The DOS versions of dBASE and Paradox use reverse video as the default to indicate editable text. The general practice for Windows database entry forms is to indicate editable elements with borders and clear backgrounds. You can create the effect of reverse video by choosing black or a dark color for the fill of a text-box control and choosing a light color for its text. Reverse text is more difficult to read than normal text. If you decide to implement reverse text, use a larger font and the bold text attribute to ensure legibility.

Changing the Content of Text Controls

You can edit the content of text controls by using conventional Windows text-editing techniques. When you place the mouse pointer within the confines of a text control, the mouse pointer becomes the Windows text-editing caret (insertion point) that you use to insert or delete text. You can select text by pressing Shift and moving the caret with the mouse; all Windows Clipboard operations are applicable to text within controls. Keyboard text selection and editing techniques using the arrow keys in combination with Shift are applicable, also.

If you change the name of a field in a text box and make an error in naming the field, you receive a #Name?? error message in the offending text box when you select run mode. Following is a better method of changing a text box with an associated label:

1. Delete the existing label.

2. Click the Field List button in the Properties bar to display the Field List dialog.

3. Scroll the entries in the Field List dialog until you find the field name you want.

4. Click the field name; press the left mouse button; and drag the field name to the location of the deleted control. Release the mouse button to drop the new control.

5. Close the Field List dialog when you are finished.

You then can relocate the new field caption and text box and edit the caption as necessary.

Rearranging the Personnel Actions Form

The objective of the following set of instructions is to rearrange the controls on the Personnel Actions form so that all the form's elements fit in a maximized window of a standard VGA display (640 x 480 pixels). When you complete the following steps, your form appears as shown in figure 12.27.

III

Forms and Reports

Fig. 12.27
The Personnel
Actions form after
relocating and
resizing its control
objects.

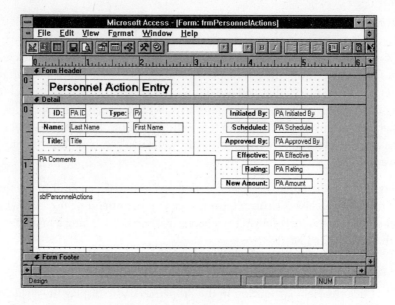

To change the color of form objects and rearrange the controls of the Personnel Actions form to correspond with the positions shown in figure 12.27, follow these steps:

1. Close the Personnel Actions form by double-clicking the Document Control-menu box. Do not save the changes you made in the preceding section.

2. Choose Personnel Actions from the Forms list in the Database window, and click the Design button.

3. Click the Palette button on the toolbar to display the palette.

4. Click the Form Header bar to select the Form Header section, and click the white color square in the Back Color row to change the background color to white.

5. Click the Detail bar to select the Detail section and change its background color to white by the method used in step 5.

6. Enclose all the labels with a selection rectangle; then click the Clear button in the Back Color row of the Palette window to make the labels' background transparent.

7. Choose Select Form from the Edit menu, and then click the Properties button on the toolbar.

8. Scroll the entries in the Properties dialog to display Grid X and Grid Y. Verify that the Grid X property is set to 10 and the Grid Y property value is 12. (Metric users may prefer a 5-by-5 grid providing 2 mm resolution.)

   Figure 12.28 shows the Personnel Actions Entry form after the background color changes and the addition of a 10-by-12 grid in English units.

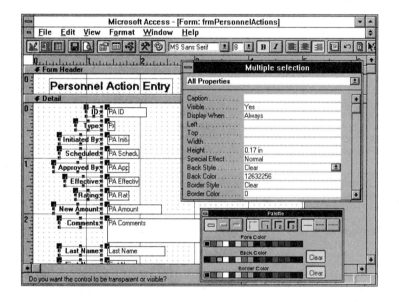

Fig. 12.28

The Personnel Actions Entry form with new background colors.

9. Close the Properties window by clicking the Properties button again.

10. Drag the right margin of the form from its present position (5 inches) to 5.5 inches.

11. Place the mouse pointer at the upper left of the Initiated By control. Enclose Initiated By, Scheduled, Approved By, Effective, Rating, and New Amount by pressing the left mouse button and dragging the lower right corner of the rectangle. Release the mouse button when the six controls are enclosed.

12. Click the surface of one of the selected controls and, with the mouse pointer in the shape of a hand, drag the group to the upper right area of the form.

13. Delete the Comments label; the size of its text box is sufficient to identify it.

III

Forms and Reports

14. Drag the remainder of the controls to the positions shown in figure 12.27.

15. Delete the First Name label and edit the Last Name label to read **Name:**.

16. Adjust the widths of the labels and text boxes to suit their content. The Initiated By and Approved By boxes are made large enough to contain the names of the supervisor and manager, respectively, rather than just their ID numbers.

17. Click and drag the Form Footer bar to approximately 2.7 inches. For the present, the dimensions of your form are 5.5 by 2.7 inches.

18. Click the Save button of the toolbar or choose **Save** from the **File** menu to save your changes to the Personnel Actions form.

You may need to adjust the sizes of some of the controls individually to make their appearance consistent with the other controls. When you complete your rearrangement, click the Form Run Mode button. Your form appears as shown in figure 12.29.

Fig. 12.29

The revised Personnel Action Entry form in run mode.

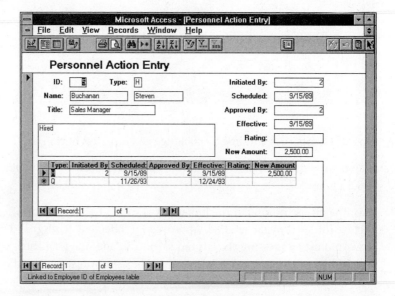

Setting the Properties of a Subform

You can modify the properties of the subform used to create the history of prior Personnel Actions for an employee to suit its intended purpose. In this

case, editing of entries in the subform should not be allowed. To change the
properties of the Personnel Actions subform, follow these steps:

1. Close the frmPersonnelActions form.

2. Open the sbfPersonnelActions subform from the Database window to
   examine its appearance in Datasheet View.

3. Click the Design View button of the toolbar so that you can change the
   properties of the form. You need not be concerned with the design of
   the form; it displays in Datasheet View as a subform. (Datasheet View is
   the default view for subforms.)

4. Click the Properties button on the toolbar to display the Properties
   window for the subform. (Form appears in the Window's title bar.)
   Open the property type drop-down list and select Other Properties.

5. Scroll to the Default Editing entry; open the list; and choose Read Only.
   (Displaying only Other Properties makes the editing properties easier to
   find.)

6. Choose the Allow Editing entry; open the list; and choose Unavailable.
   When you don't allow editing in a subform datasheet, the "tentative
   append" record no longer appears. Your Personnel Actions subform
   appears as shown in figure 12.30.

7. Close the sbfPersonnelActions subform and save your changes.

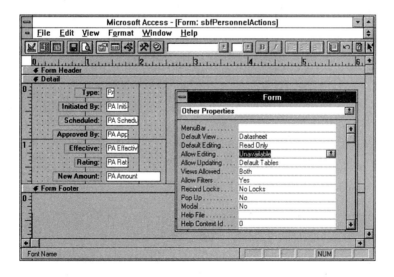

Fig. 12.30

The Personnel
Actions subform
shown in design
mode.

III

Forms and Reports

You can change the default view of the subform to a Continuous form that you can modify to display the data in another format. When displaying historical data, the Datasheet View is usually the best initial choice because it is the easiest to implement.

Modifying Linkages between Main Forms and Subforms

When you add a subform to the main form, Access automatically creates links between the two forms if it can find a likely relationship. Relationships between main forms and subforms are based on the following factors:

- The relationship you have set between tables when both the data sources are from tables.

- The primary-key field of the table that is the data source for the main form and any field with the same name in the subform.

In this example, the Form/Subform Wizard was unable to establish a default relationship between the data source of the form (qryPersonnelActions) and that of the subform (tblPersonnelActions) because the PA ID field is not included in the subform.

To display all the Personnel Actions records for the chosen employee, the linkage must be on the PA ID field. Microsoft calls the main form the *Master* form and the subform the *Child* for the purposes of linkage. The term Child is used because the subform is a Windows multiple document interface (MDI) child window. MDI child windows are conventional windows you can open inside other windows, called *parent windows*.

To change the linkage between the main form and the subform's table or query, follow these steps:

1. Open the frmPersonnelActions form from the Database window in design mode, and click the sbfPersonnelActions control to select the subform.

2. Click the Properties button to display the Subform/Subreport Properties dialog for the subform.

3. Type **PA ID** in the Link Child Fields and Link Master Fields properties text boxes, as shown in figure 12.31.

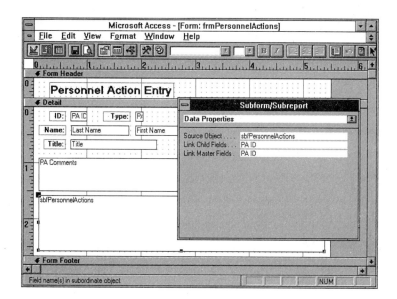

Fig. 12.31
The Properties dialog for the Personnel Action Entry history subform.

4. Click the Form View button of the toolbar to return to run mode so that you can test the linkage.

5. Click the Next Record button at the bottom of the form (just above the status bar) to display records for other employees. Confirm that the record that appears in the subform changes as you move the record pointer for the main form. (Compare the value of the Scheduled field in the main form with the Scheduled field in the subform to verify that the linkage is operating.)

Using Transaction Processing Forms

As noted near the beginning of this chapter, the purpose of transaction processing forms is to add new records to, delete records from, or edit data in the table(s) that underlie the form. This section describes how to add new records to the Personnel Actions table with the Personnel Action Entry form.

Toolbar Buttons in Form View

When you display your form in run mode (Form View), four new buttons for selecting records appear on the toolbar. Table 12.4 lists all the buttons that appear on the toolbar in form run mode, with their functions and equivalent menu choices.

III

Forms and Reports

Table 12.4   Standard Toolbar Buttons in Form Run Mode

Button	Function	Menu Choice
	Selects form design mode.	View Form Design
	Displays the form in run mode.	View Form
	Displays the table or query that is the source of data for the main form.	View Datasheet
	Saves changes made to the current record.	File Save Record
	Prints the form.	File Print
	Selects Print Preview to display how your form will appear if printed. You can print the form from the Print Preview window.	File Print Preview
	Finds (searches for) a value in the selected field or all fields. Displays the Find dialog.	Edit Find
	Goes to the tentative append.	Records Go To New
	Sorts records ascending.	Records Quick Sort Ascending
	Sorts records descending.	Records Quick Sort Descending
	Creates or edits filter/sort criteria to display only selected records in an order other than that in which they appear in the data source.	Records Edit Filter/Sort
	Applies the current filter/sort criteria to the records of the source of the data for the main form.	Records Apply Filter/Sort
	Removes the filter/sort criteria and displays all records.	Records Show All Records
	Gives the Database window the focus.	Window 1 Database
	Undoes changes to the current record.	Edit Undo
	Returns the form to its state before the last modification.	Edit Undo
	Displays the Help menu for forms in run mode.	F1 key

The Find button serves the same purpose in form run mode as it does for tables and queries. You enter characters in the Find dialog, using wild cards if needed, and the first record that matches your entry displays.

The Edit Filter/Sort button displays a query form (a subquery) in which you can select a field(s) on which to sort or enter record-selection criteria. You make the entries in the same manner as for conventional queries. Sorting specified in the subquery overrides the sort criteria of the primary query used as the source of the data. The filter or sort criteria you specify doesn't take effect until you click the Apply Filter/Sort button or make the equivalent menu choice.

Using the Personnel Actions Form

Forms you create with the Form Wizard use the standard record-selection buttons located at the bottom of the form. The record-selection buttons perform the same functions with forms as with tables and queries. You can select the first or last records in the table or query that is the source of data for your main form, or you can select the next or preceding record. Subforms employing Datasheet View always include their own set of record-selection buttons that operate independently of the set for the main form.

Navigation between the text boxes used for entering or editing data in the form is similar to that for queries and tables in Datasheet View, except that the up-arrow and down-arrow keys cause the caret (insertion point) to move between fields, rather than between records. You accept the values you enter by pressing Enter or the Tab key.

To edit or append new records to a table in Form View, the Allow Editing property must be set to Yes, the default. You can toggle this property by choosing Editing Allowed from the Records menu. A check mark next to Editing Allowed indicates that you can edit the records in the table. Make sure that the check mark is present before attempting to append new records or edit existing ones.

Appending New Records to the Personnel Actions Table

In Datasheet View of a table or query, the last record in the datasheet is provided as a *tentative append* record (indicated by an asterisk on the record-selection button). If you enter data in this record, the data automatically is appended to the table, and Access adds a new tentative append record. Because a form doesn't provide a tentative append record automatically, you must create one by using the record-selection buttons.

To append a new record to the Personnel Actions table and enter the required data, follow these steps:

1. Open the Personnel Action Entry form if it is not already open, or click the Form View button if you are in design mode. Data for the first record of the query appears in the text-box controls of your form.

2. Click the New Record button of the toolbar or click the Last Record button to select the last record in the qryPersonnelActions query; then click the Next Record button to advance the record pointer beyond the end of the query. Either action creates a tentative append record and places the record pointer at this new record.

4. All the controls of your form become empty, as illustrated by figure 12.32. (Access 1.x displayed default values for table fields in the tentative append record. With Access 2.0, default values do not display until you enter at least one value in a text box or change the value of another type of control.) The subform datasheet is empty because you haven't entered the employee ID number required to link the subform data.

Fig. 12.32

The blank Personnel Actions form when appending a new record.

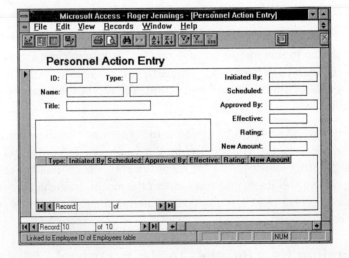

5. Access places the caret in the first text box of the form, the ID text box. Enter a valid Employee ID number (1 to 9, because you have added records the Personnel Actions table for only nine employees) in the ID field. This example uses Steven Buchanan, whose employee ID is 5, so type 5 in the ID field. Use the Tab or Enter key to accept the ID number and move the caret to the next data-entry text box, Type. When you

leave the ID field, the default values for the Type and Scheduled fields appear, Q and today's date, respectively.

The pencil symbol, which indicates that you are editing a record, replaces the triangle at the top of the Record Selector bar to the left of Detail section of the form. The Description property you entered for the field in the table underlying the query appears in the status bar and changes as you move the caret to the next field. (To change a previous entry, use Shift+Tab or the up-arrow and down-arrow keys to maneuver to the text box whose value you want to change.)

6. Because data from the Employees table is included in the query, the name and title of the employee appear in the text boxes below the ID text box after you enter the ID number. Access 2.0 lets you the edit Last Name, First Name, or Title data, although these fields are incorporated in the one table (Employees) of a one-to-many relationship. The editing capability of a form is the same as that for the underlying table or query that serves as its source of data.

If you added an entry for the chosen employee ID when you created the Personnel Actions table in Chapter 4, "Working with Access Databases and Tables," the entry appears in the subform datasheet because you now have created the required link to the Personnel Actions table.

7. Mr. Buchanan was hired on September 15, 1989, and you want to bring his personnel records up-to-date by adding data from previous quarterly and yearly performance reviews. You can accept the default Q for quarterly reviews, or override the default by typing **Y** for yearly reviews in the Type text box. Press Tab or Enter to move to the Initiated By field.

8. Mr. Buchanan reports to the Vice President of Sales, Andrew Fuller, whose employee ID is 2. Enter **2** in the Initiated By text box, and press Enter.

9. Your first entry should be dated about three months after Mr. Buchanan was hired, so a date near 1/15/90 is appropriate for the Scheduled text box. Today's date is the default for the scheduled date. Edit the date, or press F2 to select the default date and replace the default value with a new date.

10. Because Mr. Fuller is a vice president, he has the authority to approve salary increases. Enter Mr. Fuller's employee ID, **2**, in the Approved By text box.

III

Forms and Reports

11. The effective date for salary adjustments for Northwind Traders is the first or fifteenth of the month in which the performance review is scheduled. Enter the appropriate date in the Effective text box.

12. You can enter any number from 0 (terminated) to 9 (excellent) in the Rating text box, which reflects the employee's performance.

13. You can be as generous as you want with the salary increases that you enter in the New Amount text box. The value of the New Amount is a new monthly salary (or a new commission percentage), not an incremental value.

14. Add any comments you care to make concerning how generous or stingy you were with the salary increases in the Comments multiline text box below the Title text box. Multiline text boxes include a scroll bar that appears when the caret is within the text box.

15. When you complete your entries, Access stores them in a memory buffer but does not add the new record to the Personnel Actions table. You can add the record to the table by clicking the Save Record button of the toolbar, choosing Save Record from the File menu, clicking the New Record button, or changing the position of the record pointer with the Prior or Next records selector button. If you want to cancel the addition of a record, click the Undo Current Record button. In this case, click the New Record button to append another record.

16. Repeat steps 7 through 14 to add a few additional records. If you click the New Record button of the toolbar or the Next record selector button and don't make any entries, you can click the Prior button and no record is added to the table.

After you add several records, your form appears like the one shown in figure 12.33. Each record for an employee appears in the subform datasheet in the order of the primary key fields of the Personnel Actions table.

If you don't enter an ID number (or delete the ID number value), but other values have been entered, the new record has no link to the Employees table that is a member of the Personnel Actions query. In this case, you receive the message box shown in figure 12.34. If you receive this message, add the appropriate ID number.

The key fields of the Personnel Actions table are PA ID, PA Type, and PA Scheduled Date; duplicate values of the combination of the three fields aren't allowed. If you try to enter a duplicate of another record, the message box shown in figure 12.35 appears. In this case, change the Type or Scheduled Date entries so that they do not duplicate another record.

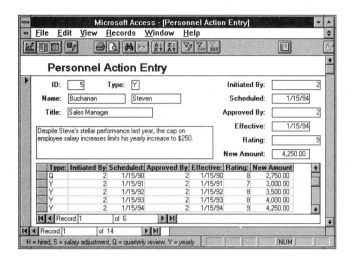

Fig. 12.33
The form after appending several Personnel Actions records for a single employee.

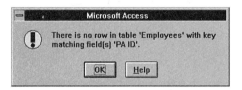
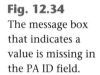

Fig. 12.34
The message box that indicates a value is missing in the PA ID field.

Fig. 12.35
The message box that results from a duplicated entry.

Editing Existing Data

You can edit existing records in the same way you add new records. Use the Next button to find the record you want to edit and then make your changes. You can use the toolbar's Find button to locate records by employee number or by one of the dates in the record. If you prefer that the records be ordered by Effective date to find records for which an effective date hasn't been entered, use the Edit Filter/Sort button and specify an Ascending Sort to the Effective field. Click the Apply Filter/Sort button to apply the sort to the records.

Committing and Rolling Back Changes to Tables

As with tentative append records, Access does not apply record edits to the underlying table until you move the record pointer with the record-selection buttons or choose Save Record from the File menu. Either action is the equivalent of the **CommitTrans** instruction in transaction-processing terminology.

 Rollback reverses a **CommitTrans** instruction. You can accomplish the equivalent of rolling back a single transaction by clicking the Undo Current Record button on the toolbar immediately after you save the record to the table or by choosing Undo Saved Record from the Edit menu if Undo Saved Record is offered as a choice.

Deleting a Record in Form View

In Datasheet View, no direct method exists (such as a "delete record" button) for deleting a record from the Personnel Actions table. To delete the current record underlying the form, choose Select Record from the Edit menu. The vertical Record Selection bar to the left of the Detail section of the form becomes a darker shade of gray, and the triangle used to identify a selected record appears at the top of the bar. Press Delete, and the message box shown in figure 12.36 appears. Click OK to delete the record, or click Cancel if you change your mind.

Fig. 12.36
The message box that asks you to confirm or cancel deletion of a record.

Modifying the Properties of a Form or Control after Testing

The entries you added and edited gave you an opportunity to test your form. Testing a form to ensure that it accomplishes the objectives you establish usually takes much longer than creating the form and the query that underlies it. During the testing process, you may notice that the order of the fields isn't what you want or that records in the subform aren't displayed in an appropriate sequence. The following two sections deal with modifying the properties of the form and the subform control.

Changing the Order of Fields for Data Entry

The order in which the editing caret moves from one field to the next is determined by the TabOrder property of each control. The Form Wizard established the tab order of the controls when you created the original version of the form. The default TabOrder property of each field is assigned, beginning with the value 0, in the sequence in which you add the fields. Because the Form Wizard created a single-column form, the order of the controls in Personnel Actions is top to bottom. The order originally assigned doesn't change when you relocate a control.

To change the sequence of entries—to match the pattern of entries on a paper form, for example—follow these steps:

1. Click the Design Mode button on the toolbar.

2. Choose Ta**b** Order from the **E**dit menu to display the Tab Order dialog shown in figure 12.37. The order of entry is shown by the sequence of field names in the Custom Order list. (In this example, changing the sequence of the entries is unnecessary because the sequence is logical, even after moving the controls to their present location on the Personnel Actions form.)

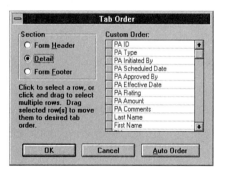

Fig. 12.37
The Tab Order dialog used to change the sequence of data-entry fields.

3. Click the Auto Order button to reorder the entry sequence to left to right by rows and then top to bottom.

4. Drag a control by clicking the button to the left of its name and dropping it at the new location that represents the desired sequence.

5. Click OK if you decide the changes you made can be implemented; click Cancel to retain the original entry sequence.

Removing Fields from the Tab Order

The Tab Order dialog is a major improvement over the technique used by Visual Basic 1+ in which you must select each control and manually edit the value of its Tab Order property. Visual Basic, however, offers the capability to remove a control from the tab order. Prior to Access 2.0, you could not prevent controls from being selected in a tab order sequence. Access 2.0 enables you to set the value of the TabStop property to **False** (No) to prevent controls from receiving the focus in the tab order. To remove a control from the tab order, select the control; open the Properties window; select Other Properties; and change the value of Tab Stop to No (see fig. 12.38). You cannot edit the First Name, Last Name, or Title controls, or the subform, so set the TabStop property to **False** (No) for each of these controls. (Setting the TabStop property value to No does not disable the control; the control only is removed from the tab sequence.)

Fig. 12.38

Removing a field from the tab order.

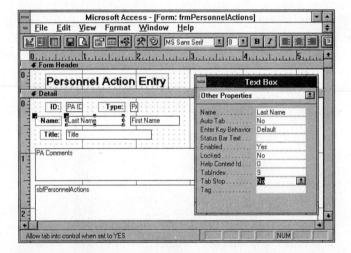

Changing the Source of Data for the Subform and Sorting the Subform Data

The Personnel Actions table is indexed by PA Type and PA Scheduled Date, but the sequence of the records appears in the order of the primary key—PA ID, PA Type, and PA Scheduled Date. Because only PA ID is used to link the records, records for a particular employee appear in the order of the remaining key fields, PA Type and PA Scheduled Date. Eventually, the number of records for an employee can become quite large, so having the records appear in type and date order is convenient. Because only a few records can be displayed in the subform datasheet, the latest entries should appear by default.

This result requires a reverse (descending) sort on the Personnel Actions table. You can establish a descending sort only by substituting a sorted query containing all the records of the Personnel Actions table, as described in the following two procedures.

To create a new sorted query, follow these steps:

1. Close the Personnel Action Entry form.

2. Click the New Query button of the toolbar or click Query button in the Database window, and then click the New button to create a new query.

3. Select Personnel Actions as the table on which to base the query; click Add and then click Close.

4. Drag the * field to the Query grid, and drop it in the first column.

5. Drag the PA Scheduled Date field to the Query grid, and drop it in the second column.

6. Click the Show box in the new PA Scheduled Date column to remove the diagonal cross so that you don't duplicate a field name in the query. Add a descending sort to the PA Scheduled Date column.

7. Click the Run Query button to check that the records are sorted in reverse date order.

8. Close your query and name it **qryPersonnelActionsSubform**.

To change the data source for the subform to the new sorted query, complete the following steps:

1. Click the Form button in the Database window, and open the sbfPersonnelActions subform in design mode.

2. Select the Click the Properties button to display the Properties window and select Data Properties.

3. Click the Record Source box, open the list, and select qryPersonnelActionsSubform as the new data source for the subform, as shown in figure 12.39.

4. If you want to review the design of the table or query you select as the value of the RecordSource property, click the ellipsis button to display the source object in design mode.

5. Close the Properties box, and click the Form View button on the toolbar to verify that the datasheet display is correct.

6. Close the sbfPersonnelActions subform.

Fig. 12.39

The Form Properties dialog entry to change the *RecordSource* property.

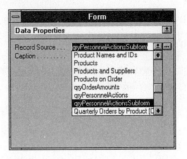

7. Reopen the Personnel Actions form. If you didn't use Steven Buchanan, the first Northwind employee in alphabetical order, enter the number of the employee for whom you added additional records. The history now appears sorted in reverse date sequence.

8. To verify that the sort is active when you add new entries, add a new record with today's date and then click the Prior button to save the new entry. Click Next to display the new entry and verify that the sorting operation is functional.

You can use the same method described in the preceding steps to change the data source of a main form.

Troubleshooting

I receive an error message in the Scheduled column of the subform datasheet every time I try to run the query.

You didn't click the Show box in step 6 of the preceding set of instructions. When a field is duplicated in a query, Access doesn't know which of the two fields to use if the Show check box of both fields is marked.

> **Note**
>
> Clicking the Save Record button or choosing Save Record from the File menu does not update the subform, and the new entry is not displayed in the subform. You must choose Refresh from the Records menu to update the subform's display. The Refresh command doesn't requery the database, but it does cause any updates that may have occurred before the last automatic refreshing operation to appear. The best approach, therefore, is to use the record position buttons to commit the new or edited record. The Refresh command is discussed in Chapter 25, "Securing Multiuser Network Applications."

From Here...

This chapter demonstrated the capabilities of relatively simple Access forms, created by the Form Wizards, to add and edit data. You learned to relocate, resize, and edit control objects that the Main/Subform Form Wizard added to the form for you. The chapter also explained the basic steps involved in using a form to add, edit, and delete records. After testing your form, you made changes to the form's design to make it more effective. Database application developers use this process to create the forms that ultimately comprise a full-scale database application.

When you specify a Single-column or Main/Subform Wizard, the Wizard uses only text-box control with associated labels to create the basic form. The Access toolbox provides many other types of controls you can add to a basic or a blank form that you create without the Form Wizard's help.

- Chapter 8, "Using Query by Example," shows you how to create queries to serve as the RecordSource property of forms.

- Chapter 13, "Designing Custom Multitable Forms," describes how to use the Access toolbox to design a form starting with a blank form.

- Chapters 14, "Printing Basic Reports and Mailing Labels," and 15, "Preparing Advanced Reports," apply the techniques you learned in this chapter to creating Access reports.

III

Forms and Reports

Chapter 13

Designing Custom Multitable Forms

The controls that the Form Wizards add to the forms they create are only a sampling of the 16 control functions offered by Access. Until now, you used the Form/Subform Wizard to create the labels, text boxes, and subform controls for displaying and editing data in the Personnel Actions table. These three kinds of controls are sufficient to create a conventional transaction processing form; you can duplicate a conventional dBASE III/IV or Paradox 3+ DOS data entry screen by using only Access labels and text boxes.

The remaining 13 controls described in this chapter enable you to take full advantage of the Windows graphical user environment. List boxes and combo boxes increase data entry productivity by enabling you to choose from a list of predefined values rather than requiring that you type the value. Option buttons, toggle buttons, and check boxes supply values to Yes/No fields. If you place option buttons, toggle buttons, and check boxes in an option frame, these controls can supply the numeric values you specify. Page breaks control how forms print. Command buttons enable you to execute Access macros or Access Basic procedures. You add controls to the form by using the Access toolbox.

In this chapter, you learn to

■ Create a form from a blank form

■ Use the Access toolbox

■ Use Access Control Wizards

■ Add an option group to a form

■ Add combo boxes to a form

Understanding the Access Toolbox

The Access toolbox is based on the toolbox created for Microsoft Visual Basic. Several Access toolbox buttons are the same as the buttons employed by Visual Basic 3.0, and the method of adding controls to the form also is similar, but not identical, to the method used in Visual Basic 3.0. You choose one of the 16 tools to add a control, represented by the tool's symbol, to the form.

When you create a report, the toolbox serves the same purpose—although the tools that require user input, such as a combo box, are seldom used in reports.

Control Categories

Three control object categories exist in Access forms and reports:

■ *Bound controls* are associated with a field in the data source for the form or subform. The data source can be a table or a query. Bound controls display and update values of the data cell in the associated field of the currently selected record. Text boxes are the most common bound control. You can display the content of graphic objects or play a waveform audio file with a bound OLE object. You can bind toggles, check boxes, and option buttons to Yes/No fields. All bound controls have associated labels that display the caption property of the field; you can edit or delete these labels without affecting the bound control.

■ *Unbound controls* display data you provide that is independent of the data source of the form or subform. The label used as the title for the Personnel Actions form is an example of an unbound control. You use the unbound OLE object to add a drawing or bit-mapped image to a form. You can use Lines and rectangles to divide a form into logical groups or to simulate the boxes used on the paper form. Unbound text boxes are used to enter data not intended to update a field in the data source but are used for other purposes, such as establishing a value used in an expression. Some unbound controls, such as unbound text boxes, include labels; others, such as unbound OLE objects, don't include labels.

■ *Calculated controls* use expressions as their source of data. Usually, the expression includes the value of a field, but you also can use values created by unbound text boxes in calculated control expressions.

The Toolbox

You use the Access toolbox to add control objects to forms and reports. The toolbox appears only in design mode for forms and reports and appears only if you click the Toolbox button of the toolbar or toggle **T**oolbox from the **V**iew menu. When the toolbox is visible, the **T**oolbox menu choice is checked. You can choose from the 16 controls and the one wizard button whose names and functions are listed in table 13.1.

Table 13.1 Control Objects of the Access Toolbox

Tool	Name	Function
	Pointer	Deselects a previously selected tool and returns the mouse pointer to normal function. Pointer is the default tool when you display the toolbox.
	Label	Creates a box that contains fixed descriptive or instructional text.
	Text Box	Creates a box to display and edit text data.
	Option Group	Creates a frame of adjustable size in which you can place toggle buttons, option buttons, or check boxes. Only one of the objects within an object group frame may be selected. When you select an object within an option group, the previously selected object is deselected.
	Toggle Button	Creates a button that changes from on to off when clicked with the mouse. The **On** state corresponds to Yes (-1), and the **Off** state corresponds to No (0). When used within an option group, toggling one button on toggles a previously selected button off. You can use toggle buttons to select a value from a set of values.
	Option Button	Creates a round button (originally called a *radio button*) that behaves identically to a toggle button. Option buttons are most commonly used within option groups to select between values in a set.
	Check Box	Creates a check box that toggles on and off. The behavior of check boxes is identical to toggle and option buttons. Multiple check boxes are most often used outside of option groups so that you can select more than one check box at a time.
	Combo Box	Creates a drop-down combo box with a list from which you can select an item or enter a value in a text box.
	List Box	Creates a drop-down list box from which you may make a choice. A list box is a combo box without the editable text box.
	Graph	Launches the Graph Wizard to create a graph object based on a query or table.
	Subform	Adds a subform or subreport to a main form or report. The subform or subreport you intend to add must exist before you use this control.
	Unbound Object	Adds an OLE object, created by an OLE server application, such as Microsoft Graph or Microsoft Draw, to a form or report. You also add Access 2.0's new OLE Custom Controls in unbound object frames.

(continues)

Table 13.1 Continued		
Tool	**Name**	**Function**
	Bound Object	Displays the content of an OLE field of a record if the field contains a graphic object. If the field contains no graphic object, the icon that represents the object appears, such as the Sound Recorder's icon for a linked or embedded .WAV file type.
	Line	Creates a straight line that you can size and relocate. The color and width of the line can be changed by using the Palette.
	Shape	Creates a rectangle that you can size and relocate. The border color, width, and fill color of the rectangle are determined by selections from the palette.
	Page Break	Causes the printer to start a new page at the location of the page break on the form or report. Page breaks don't appear in form or report run mode.
	Command Button	Creates a command button that, when clicked, triggers an event that can execute an Access macro or an Access Basic event-handling procedure.
	Control Wizards	Turns the Control Wizards on and off. Control Wizards are a new feature of Access 2.0 that aid you in designing complex controls, such as option groups, list boxes, and combo boxes.
	Tool Lock	Maintains the currently selected tool as the active tool until you select another tool, click Lock again, or click the pointer. Without the lock, Access reselects the pointer tool after you use a tool.

Using controls in the design of reports is discussed in the following two chapters, which are devoted entirely to the subject of Access reports. The use of bound and unbound OLE objects is described in Chapter 20, "Adding Graphics to Forms and Reports." Using command buttons to execute macros is covered in Part IV of this book, which deals with Access macros. Writing Access Basic code to respond to command button clicks is included in Part VII. You learn how to use the remaining 13 controls on your forms in the following sections.

Access 2.0's Control Wizards, Builders, and Toolbars

Access 2.0 provides a number of new features to aid you in designing and using more complex forms. Three of these new features, Control Wizards, Builders, and customizable toolbars are described in the three sections that follow.

Access Control Wizards

Much of the success of Access 1.x is attributable to the Form Wizards, Report Wizards, and Graph Wizards that simplified the process of creating database objects. The first wizard appeared in Microsoft Publisher, and most of the new Microsoft productivity applications include a variety of wizards. Chapter 12, "Creating and Using Forms," introduced the Form Wizards; Report Wizards are discussed in the Chapter 14, "Printing Basic Reports and Mailing Labels;" and the Graph Wizard is described in Chapters 19, "Using OLE 2.0," and 20, "Adding Graphics to Forms and Reports." Developers can create custom wizards to perform a variety of duties. You can expect a wide range of wizards to become available from independent software vendors (ISVs) as Access 2.0 gains adherents.

Access 2.0 expands the version 1.x wizards repertoire to include Control Wizards that lead you step-by-step through the design of more complex control objects, such as option groups, list boxes, and combo boxes. Designing and populating list and combo boxes requires several steps. In this chapter, you are introduced to each wizard as you add a control for which one of the Control Wizards is available.

Access Builders

Builders are another feature that Microsoft added to Access 2.0. (The builders in Access 1.x were hidden and undocumented.) You use the new Expression Builder, introduced in Chapter 4, to create expressions that supply values to calculated controls. The Query Builder creates the SQL statements you need when you create list boxes or combo boxes whose RowSource property is an SQL statement that executes a select query. Using the Query Builder to insert SQL statements created by graphical QBE is much simpler than the method used with Access 1.x: you had to create a query, open the SQL window, copy the SQL statement to the clipboard, and then paste it to the RowSource property's text box. Using the Query Builder is described in the section, "Using the Query Builder to Populate a Combo Box," near the end of this chapter.

Customizable Toolbars

The preceding chapters demonstrated that the toolbars of Access 2.0 include many new buttons to expedite the design and use of Access database objects. Access 2.0, like other newly released Microsoft applications, now lets you customize the toolbars to your own set of preferences. If you use Excel 5.0, you'll find Access 2.0's toolbar customization process to be quite familiar. Access 1.x stored toolbars as forms in UTILITY.MDA. Access 2.0 uses the new

III

Forms and Reports

common toolbar dynamic link library, COMMTB.DLL, to manipulate toolbars and stores definitions of your customized versions of standard toolbars in the MSysToolbars table of SYSTEM.MDA. The significance of storing your preferences in SYSTEM.MDA is discussed in Chapter 25, "Securing Multiuser Network Applications."

You can convert conventional floating design tools, such as the Toolbox and Palette windows, to conventional toolbars by the drag-and-drop method. To anchor the toolbox as a second toolbar, also called *docking* the toolbar, follow these steps:

1. Click the title bar of the toolbox to select it, hold the left mouse button down, and drag the toolbox toward the top of Access's parent window.

2. When the toolbox reaches the toolbar area, the dotted outline changes from a rectangle that is approximately the size of the toolbox into a wide rectangle with a depth approximately equal to a toolbar.

3. Release the left mouse button to change the toolbox to an anchored toolbar positioned below the standard Form Design toolbar.

> **Note**
>
> You can anchor or dock a toolbar to any edge of Access's parent window. Click an empty area of the toolbar (not covered by a button), and then drag the toolbar until its outline appears along the left, right, or bottom edge of the window. If you drop the toolbar within the confines of Access's main window, it becomes a floating toolbar.

You can add or delete buttons from toolbars with the Customize Toolbars dialog. If you are using the conventional VGA display format (640 by 480 pixels), there is no room to add new buttons to the Form Design toolbar. However, the Toolbox toolbar has room to add seven or eight additional buttons when Access's main window is maximized. To add form design utility buttons to the Toolbox toolbar you created in the preceding steps, do the following:

1. Choose Toolbars from the **V**iew menu to display the Toolbars dialog.

2. Click the Customize button to display the Customize Toolbars dialog.

3. Select Form Design from the Categories list. The optional buttons applicable to form design operations appear in the Buttons window, as shown in figure 13.1.

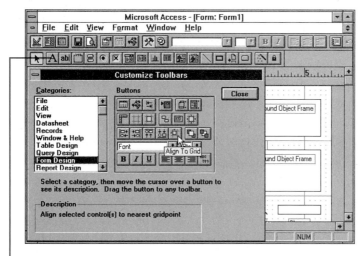

Anchored toolbox toolbar

Fig. 13.1

The toolbox docked as an anchored toolbar at the top of Access's main window with the Customize Toolbar dialog open.

4. The most useful optional buttons for form design are control alignment and sizing buttons. Click the Align to Grid button (see fig. 13.1) and, holding the left mouse button down, drag the button to the Toolbox toolbar and drop it to the right of the Lock button. The right margin of the Toolbox toolbar expands to accommodate the new button. You can drag the Snap to Grid button slightly to the right to create a gap between the new button and the Lock button.

5. Repeat step 4 for the Size to Fit, Size to Grid, Align to Grid, and Align Left buttons, dropping each button at the right edge of the preceding button. Your Toolbox toolbar appears as illustrated by figure 13.2.

The Toolbars and Customize Toolbars dialogs provide the following additional capabilities:

■ To *remove buttons* from the toolbar, open the Customize Toolbars dialog; then click and drag the buttons you don't want and drop them in the Buttons window of the dialog.

■ To *reset* the toolbar to its default design, open the Toolbars dialog, select the toolbar you want to reset in the Toolbars list, and then click the Reset button. A message box asks you to confirm that you want to abandon any changes you made to the toolbar.

III

Forms and Reports

■ To *create a button that opens or runs a database object*, open the Customize Toolbars dialog and scroll the Categories list to display the All Objects items. When, as an example, you select All Tables, the table of the current database appears in the Objects list. Select a table name, such as Employees, and drag the selected item to an empty spot on a toolbar. The tooltip for the new button displays "Open Table 'Employees'." (If you select All Macros and drag a macro object to the toolbar, the button you add runs the macro when clicked.)

■ To *substitute text or a different image for the toolbar picture* of buttons you add to a toolbar, open the Customize Toolbar dialog; then click the button you want to change with the right mouse button to display the button shortcut menu. Choose the Choose Button Face option to display the Choose Button Face dialog. Click one of the images offered, or click the Text check box and type the text you want to display in the text box.

■ To *create a new empty toolbar* that you can customize with any set of the supplied buttons you want, open the Toolbars dialog and select Utility 1 or Utility 2. If there is space to the right of an existing toolbar, the empty toolbar appears in this space. Otherwise, Access creates a new toolbar row for the empty toolbar.

■ To *create a custom toolbar* that becomes a part of your database, open the Toolbars dialog and click the New button. The New Toolbar dialog appears, requesting a name for the new toolbar (Custom Toolbar 1 is the default). Access creates a new floating tool window to which you add buttons from the Custom Toolbars dialog. You can anchor the custom tool window to the toolbar if you want.

■ To *delete a custom toolbar*, open the Toolbars dialog, select the custom toolbar, and click the Delete button. You are requested to confirm the deletion. The Delete button is disabled when you select one of Access's standard toolbars in the list.

Custom toolbars to which you assign names are stored in the current database file, not in SYSTEM.MDA. Custom toolbars become a part of your database application.

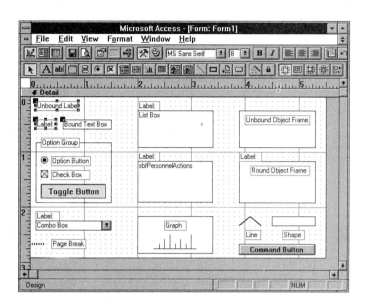

Fig. 13.2
The 16 controls of
the toolbox in
design mode (with
five custom
buttons added).

The Appearance of Controls in Design and Run Modes

The appearance in form design mode of the 16 different controls you can create with the toolbox is shown in figure 13.2. Labels were added to the graph, unbound object, bound object, line, and rectangle controls to identify them in the illustration; the labels aren't actually components of the controls.

When you click the Form View button, the controls appear as shown in figure 13.3. The text box displays a "#Name?" error message because no value is assigned to the content of the text box. The list and combo boxes are empty, as are the unbound and bound objects because no values for their content is assigned to them. A value, Personnel Actions Subform, is assigned to the subform control because a subform control isn't created unless you enter the name of an existing form as the value.

III

Forms and Reports

Fig. 13.3
The toolbox
controls without
assigned values,
displayed in Form
Design View.

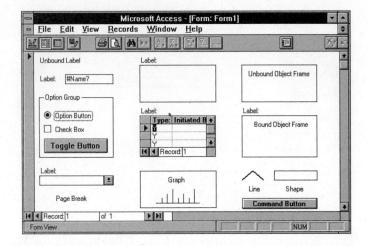

Using the Toolbox to Add Controls

◀ "Creating the
Personnel
Actions Table,"
p.158

◀ "Creating the
Query on
Which to Base
the Form,"
p. 443

Experimenting is the best way of learning how to use a new computer application. No matter how well the product's documentation or a book, such as
this one, describes a process, no substitute exists for trying the methods. This
axiom holds true whether you are designing a form or writing programming
code. The Microsoft programmers who created Access cleverly designed the
user interface for creating custom forms so that the interface is intuitive and
flexible. When you complete the examples in this chapter, you probably will
agree with this statement.

The examples in this chapter use the Personnel Actions table that you created
in Chapter 4, "Working with Access Databases and Tables," and the two queries, qryPersonnelActions and qryPersonnelActionsSubform, that formed the
basis of the Personnel Action Entry form (frmPersonnelActions) and subform
(sbfPersonnelActions) of Chapter 12, "Creating and Using Forms." The
data dictionary needed to create the Personnel Actions table appears in
Appendix C.

Creating a Blank Form with a Header and Footer

When you create a form without using the Form Wizards, Access provides
a default blank form to which you add controls that you choose from the
toolbox. To create a blank form with which to experiment with Access controls, perform the following steps:

1. With the Database window active, click the New Form button of the toolbar; or click the Form button in the Database window, and then click the New button.

2. Even an experimental form requires a data source, so choose qryPersonnelActions from the drop-down list, and then click the Blank Form button of the New Form dialog.

3. Access creates a new blank form with the default title Form1. Click the Maximize button to expand the form to fill the document window. (The illustrations of this chapter show the window in normal mode so that the illustrations can be reproduced at larger scale, making the forms more legible.)

4. If the toolbox isn't visible, click the Toolbox button of the toolbar or choose **T**oolbox from the **V**iew menu to display the toolbox. Drag the toolbox to the top or bottom of the form to anchor it there as a toolbar.

5. From the F**o**rmat menu, choose Form **H**eader/Footer. The blank form appears as shown in figure 13.4. If the grid doesn't appear on the form, choose **G**rid from the **V**iew menu.

   The default width of blank forms is 5.0 inches. The default height of the Form Header and Footer sections is 0.25 inch, and the Detail section is 1 inch high.

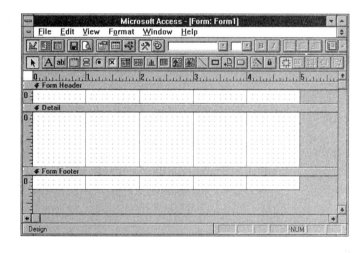

Fig. 13.4
Access's default blank form with a Form Header and Form Footer section added.

III

Forms and Reports

6. To adjust the depth of the Detail section of the form, place the mouse pointer on the top line of the Form Footer bar. The mouse pointer becomes a double-headed arrow with a line between the heads. Hold down the left mouse button and drag the bar to create a depth of about 2.5 inches, measured by the left vertical ruler. The active surface of the form, which is white with the default 10 by 12 grid dots, expands vertically as you move the Form Footer bar, as shown in figure 13.5.

7. Minimize the Form Footer section by dragging the bottom margin of the form to the bottom of the Form Footer bar.

8. Drag the right margin of the form to 5.5 inches as measured by the horizontal ruler at the top of the form. Your blank form now appears as illustrated by figure 13.5.

Fig. 13.5
Expanding the
Detail section of
the blank form.

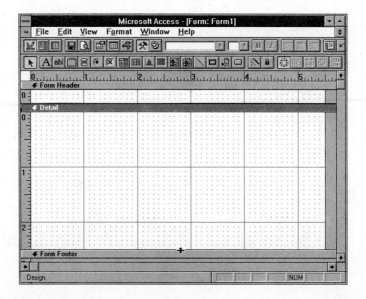

You use the blank form to create a form similar to the Personnel Actions form that you created in Chapter 12, "Creating and Using Forms."

Adding a Label to the Form Header

The label is the simplest control in the toolbox to use. Labels are unbound and static, and they display only text you enter. *Static* means that the label retains the value you assigned for as long as the form is displayed. To add a label to the Form Header section, complete the following steps:

1. Click the Label button of the Toolbox toolbar. When you move the mouse pointer to the active area of the form, the pointer becomes the symbol for the Label button, combined with a position indication crosshair at its upper left. The center point of the crosshair defines the position of the upper left corner of the control.

2. Locate the crosshair pointer at the upper left of the Form Header section, and then press and hold down the left mouse button. Drag the crosshair pointer to the position for the lower right corner of the label, as shown in figure 13.6.

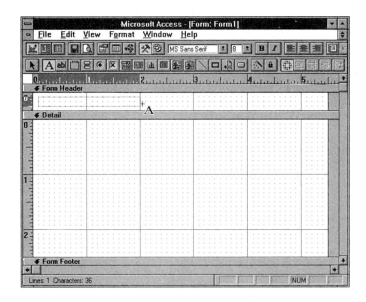

Fig. 13.6
Adding a label
control to the
Form Header.

As you drag the crosshair pointer, the outline of the container for the label follows your movement. The number of lines and characters that the text box can display in the currently selected font is shown in the status bar.

3. If you move the crosshair pointer beyond the bottom of the Form Header section, the Form Header bar expands to accommodate the size of the label. When the label is the size you want, release the mouse button.

4. The mouse pointer becomes the text editing caret inside the outline of the label. Enter **Personnel Action Entry** as the text for the label. If you don't type at least one text character in the label after creating the label, the box disappears the next time you click the mouse.

III

Forms and Reports

◀ "Selecting,
Moving, and
Sizing a Single
Control,"
p. 462

You use the basic process described in the preceding steps to add most of the other types of controls to a form. (Some toolbox buttons, such as the graph and command buttons, launch a Control Wizard to help you create the control if the Wizards button is activated.) After you add the control, you use the anchor and sizing handles described in Chapter 12 to move the control to the desired position and to size the control to accommodate the content. The location of the anchor handle determines the Left (horizontal) and Top (vertical) properties of the control. The sizing handles establish the control's Width and Height properties.

Formatting Text and Adjusting Text Control Sizes

When a control is selected that accepts text as the value, the typeface and font size combo boxes appear on the toolbar. To format the text that appears in a label or text box, complete the following steps:

1. Click the Personnel Action Entry label you created in the previous section to select the label.

2. Double-click the label or click the Properties button of the toolbar to display the Properties window.

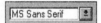

3. Open the Typeface list on the toolbar and select the typeface family you want. MS Sans Serif, the default, is recommended because all users of Windows 3.1 have this bit-mapped font. (MS Sans Serif is quite similar to Linotype Company's Helvetica typeface.) Sans serif faces are easier to read on forms than faces with serifs, such as MS Serif or Times New Roman. (Serif faces are easier to read when a large amount of text is involved, such as in newspapers or the body text of this book.)

4. Open the Font Size list, and select 14 points.

5. Click the Bold attribute button on the toolbar. The label now appears as shown in figure 13.7.

6. The size of the label you created isn't large enough to display the larger font. To adjust the size of the label to accommodate the content of the label, click the Size to Fit button, if you added it to the Toolbox toolbar, or choose Size to Fit from the Format menu. If one or more control is selected, one of the two sizing commands (Size to **G**rid or Si**z**e to Fit) of the F**o**rmat menu is applied to the selected control(s). If no controls are selected, the chosen sizing command applies as the default to all objects you subsequently create, move, or resize.

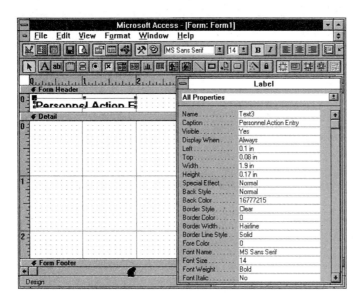

Fig. 13.7
The form title label
and its Properties
window.

When you change the properties of a control, the new values are reflected in the Properties window for the control, as shown in figure 13.7. If you move or resize the label, you see the label's Left, Top, Width, and Height values change in the properties' box. You usually use the Properties window to change the characteristics of a control for which a toolbar button or a menu choice isn't available.

You can choose different fonts and the bold, italic, and underline attributes (or a combination) for any label or caption for a control. You can assign the text content of list boxes and combo boxes to a typeface or size other than the default, but this practice is uncommon in Windows applications.

Creating Bound, Multiline, and Calculated Text Boxes

Access uses the following four basic kinds of text boxes:

- *Single-line* text boxes usually are bound to controls.

- *Multiline* text boxes usually are bound to Memo field types and include a vertical scroll bar to allow access to text that doesn't fit within the dimensions of the box.

III

Forms and Reports

- *Calculated* text boxes obtain values from expressions that begin with the = (equal) sign and usually are a single-line. If you include a field value, such as [PA Scheduled Date], in the expression for a calculated text box, the text box is bound to the PA Scheduled Date field. Otherwise, calculated text boxes are unbound. You cannot edit the value of a calculated text box.

- *Unbound* text boxes that aren't calculated text boxes can be used to supply values, such as limiting dates, to macros or Access Basic procedures. Using unbound text boxes is described in Chapter 18, "Creating Macros for Forms and Reports."

The following sections show you how to create the first three of these basic kinds of text boxes.

Adding a Text Box Bound to a Field

The most common text box used in Access forms is the single-line bound text box that comprised the majority of the controls of the Personnel Actions form you created in Chapter 12. To add a text box that is bound to a field of the form's data source with the Field List window, complete the following steps:

1. Click the Field List button on the toolbar. The Field List window appears.

2. Click the PA ID field in the Field List window. Hold down the left mouse button and drag the field to the upper left of the Detail section of the form. When you move the mouse pointer to the active area of the form, the pointer becomes a field symbol but no crosshairs appear. The position of the field symbol indicates the upper left corner of the text box, not the label, so drop the symbol in the approximate position of the text box anchor handle, as shown in figure 13.8.

3. Drag the text box by the anchor handle closer to the ID label and decrease the box's width.

4. Small type sizes are more readable when you set the bold attribute on. Choose the ID label and click the Bold button, and do the same for the PA ID text box.

Steps 3 and 4 in the preceding example are included to show how to make minor design adjustments to controls that improve the appearance of forms.

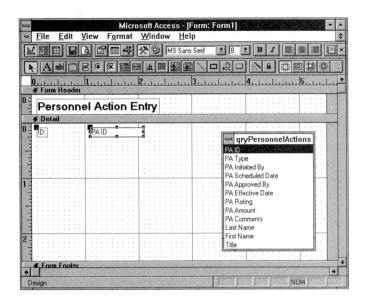

Fig. 13.8
Adding a text box
control bound to
the PA ID field.

Adding a Multiline Text Box with Scroll Bars

Although you can use a conventional text box to display comments or other
text fields with lengthy content, you must scroll the caret through the text
box to read the content. Multiline text boxes enable you to display long
strings of text as a series of lines whose width is determined by the width of
the multiline text box. To create a multiline text box, perform the following
steps:

1. Choose PA Comments from the Field List window. Drag the Field List
   pointer to about the middle of the Detail section and drop the pointer.

2. Relocate the Comments label, and size the text box as shown in figure 13.9.

3. Click the Properties button of the toolbar, and select Layout Properties.
   Scroll the Layout Properties list for the text box until the Scroll Bars
   property appears.

4. Open the Scroll Bars drop-down list and choose Vertical to add a vertical scroll bar to the Comments text box.

III

Forms and Reports

Fig. 13.9
Adding the
multiline Com-
ments text box.

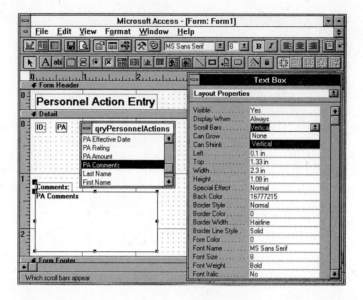

5. If you plan to print the form, change the Can Grow and Can Shrink properties from No to Yes, for the height of the printed version of the form to vary with the number of lines of text in the box. The Can Grow and Can Shrink properties don't affect the appearance of the form in run mode.

> **Note**
>
> The vertical scroll bar of a multiline text box is visible only in form run mode, and then only when the multiline text box has the focus (when the caret is within the text box).

Creating a Calculated Text Box

You can display the result of all valid Access expressions in a calculated text box. An expression must begin with an = (equal) sign and may use Access functions to return values. As mentioned in the introduction to this section, you can use calculated text boxes to display calculations based on the values of fields. To create a calculated text box that displays the current date and time, complete the following steps:

1. Close the Field List window. Click the Text Box tool of the toolbox to add an unbound text box at the upper right of the Detail section of the form.

2. Edit the label of the new text box to read **Date/Time:** and relocate the label so that it is adjacent to the text box.

3. Type **=Now( )** in the text box to display the current date and time from your computer's clock.

4. Adjust the length of the text box to accommodate the number of characters in the default DD/MM/YY HH:MM:SS PM format used for dates and times. The entry appears as shown in the Date/Time text box of figure 13.10. You add the other two text boxes in the following section.

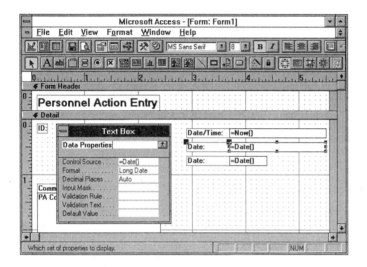

Fig. 13.10
Creating a calculated text box to display the date and time.

Formatting Values

You can use the Format property you learned about in Chapter 4 to determine how dates, times, and numbers are displayed in a text box. To format a date entry, perform the following steps:

1. Using the Text Box tool, add a second unbound text box under the first, and adjust the new box's dimensions to correspond to the other text box.

2. Edit the label to read **Date:** and enter **=Date()** in the text box.

3. Select the text box and click the right mouse button to display the floating menu. Then click Properties, or click the Properties button of the toolbar. Choose Data Properties.

4. Click the Format property and open the list. Choose Long Date from the list.

A Format property applied to a bound text box overrides the format assigned to the field in the table design that supplies the value to the text box.

> **Note**
>
> When you display a form in run mode, the value displayed in the Date/Time text box is the time that you open the form. To update the time, choose **Refresh** from the **Records** menu. The refreshing process that occurs at an interval determined by the Refresh Interval property of the Multiuser Options (the default value is 15 seconds) doesn't update unbound text boxes.

Using the Clipboard with Controls

You can use the Windows Clipboard to easily make copies of controls and their properties. As an example, create a copy of one of the Date/Time controls by using the Clipboard, by performing the following steps:

1. Select the label and the text box by holding down the Shift key and clicking the label associated with the second date text box you added in the preceding section. Both the label and the text box are selected, as indicated by the selection handles on both controls.

2. Press Ctrl+C, or choose **C**opy from the **E**dit menu to copy the control to the Clipboard.

3. Press Ctrl+V, or choose **P**aste from the **E**dit menu to paste the copy of the control below the original version.

4. Click the Format property in the Properties window for the copied control, and choose Short Date from the drop-down list.

5. To display the controls you created, click the Form View button on the toolbar. The form appears as shown in figure 13.11.

6. Delete the two Date text boxes and labels by enclosing both with a selection boundary, created by dragging the mouse pointer from the upper left to the lower right of the text boxes and then pressing the Delete key.

Text boxes (and the associated labels) are the most commonly used control objects on Access forms.

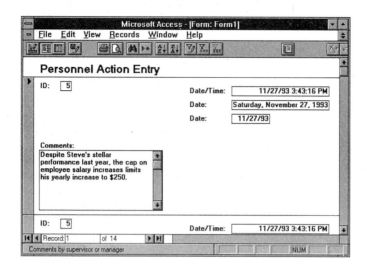

Fig. 13.11
The form title
and text boxes
displayed in
Form View.

Changing the Default View and Obtaining Help for Properties

A form that fills Access's Design window may not necessarily fill the window in form run mode. Run mode may allow the beginning of a second copy of the form to appear, as shown at the bottom of figure 13.11. The second copy is created because the Default View property has a default value of Continuous Forms. Forms have the following three Default View properties (in the Forms Properties window) from which you can choose:

- *Single Form* displays one record at a time in one form.

- *Continuous Forms* displays multiple records, each record having a copy of the Detail section of the form. You can use the vertical scroll bar or the record selection buttons to select the record to display. Continuous Forms view is the default value.

- *Datasheet* displays the form fields arranged like a spreadsheet (in rows and columns).

To change the Default View property of the form to Single Form, complete the following steps:

1. Click the Design View button on the toolbar.

2. Choose Select Form from the Edit menu.

3. Click the Properties button on the toolbar if the Properties dialog isn't visible. The Properties dialog appears. Choose Layout Properties.

III

4. Click the Default View property to open the list.

5. Select Single Form from the list.

6. While Default View is selected, press F1. The help window for the DefaultView property appears. This help window also explains how the DefaultView and ViewsAllowed properties relate to one another.

   The vertical scroll bar disappears from the form in run mode if a single form fits within its MDI child window.

 You can verify that the Default View property has changed to Single Form by clicking the Form View button to review the form's appearance. Only a single copy of the form appears, as shown in figure 13.12.

Fig. 13.12
The appearance of the Personnel Actions Entry form, with the Default View property set to Single Form.

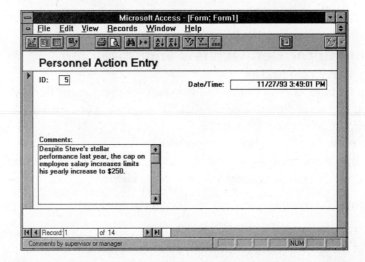

Adding Option Groups, Binding Controls, and Using the Lock Tool

Option buttons, toggle buttons, and check boxes can return only Yes/No (-1/0 or **True**/**False**) values when used by themselves on a form. Here, their use as bound controls is limited to providing values to Yes/No fields in a table. When you place any of these controls within an option group, the buttons or check boxes can return a number you specify for the OptionValue property of the control.

The capability of assigning numbers to the OptionValue property enables you to use one of these three controls inside an option group frame to assign values to the PA Ratings field of the Personnel Actions table. Option buttons are most commonly employed in Windows applications to select one value from a limited number of values.

Note

Placing check boxes within option groups violates the Windows user interface design guidelines. According to the guidelines, a group of check boxes provides multiple additive choices. Thus, if you have more than one check box in a group, any or all of the check boxes can be marked. Use the shape control to create a frame around check boxes. Only option buttons and toggle buttons should be added to option groups.

By default, all the tools you add with the toolbox are unbound controls. You can bind a control to a field by choosing the control you want to use and then clicking the field name in the Field List window to which you want the control bound. Another way of binding a control is to create an unbound control with a tool, and then type the name of a field in the Control Source text box of the Data Properties collection of the Properties window.

Access 2.0 offers two means of creating an option group: using the Option Group Wizard, one of the Control Wizards, or manually adding option buttons or toggle buttons to the option group. The following two sections describe both of these methods.

Using the Option Group Wizard

The Option Group Wizard is one of three Control Wizards that take you step-by-step in the creation of complex controls. To create an option group for the PA Ratings field of the Personnel Actions table with the Option Group Wizard, follow these steps:

1. Click the Control Wizards tool to turn on the wizards, if the toggle button is not on (the default value). Toggle buttons indicate the On (**True**) state with a depressed (sunken) appearance.

2. Click the Option Group tool, position the option group mouse pointer where you want the upper left corner of the option group, and then click the left mouse button to display the first dialog of the Option Group Wizard.

3. Type 5 of the 9 ratings in the Option Name datasheet: **Excellent**, **Good**, **Acceptable**, **Fair**, and **Poor**. Your Option Name datasheet appears as shown in figure 13.13. Click the Next > button to display the second dialog of the series.

Fig. 13.13
The opening
dialog of the
Option Group
Wizard.

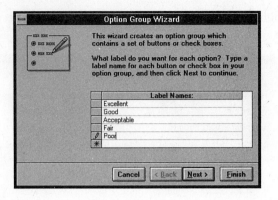

Tip
You can use
accelerator keys
with captions of
option buttons
if you precede
the letter for the
accelerator key
combination
(Alt+*Letter*) with
an ampersand
(&).

4. The second dialog lets you set an optional default value for the option group. Click the Yes, the default is option button, and then open the Default Value combo box. Select Good, as shown in figure 13.14, and then click the Next > button. You can return to the prior step by clicking the < Back button.

Fig. 13.14
Choosing a default
value for the
option group.

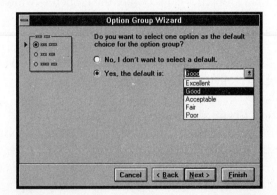

5. The third dialog provides for the assignment of option values to each option button of the group. Type **9**, **7**, **5**, **3**, and **1** in the five text boxes, as illustrated by figure 13.15, and then click the Next > button.

The domain integrity rule for the PA Rating field provides for nine different ratings. Nine option buttons, however, occupy too much space on a form. Thus, only five of the nine ratings are provided here. Later in the chapter, you add a drop-down combo list that has all nine ratings to this form.

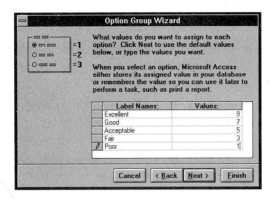

Fig. 13.15
Assigning the numeric *OptionValue* property to the option buttons.

6. The fourth dialog allows you to bind the option frame to a field of a table or a column of a query that acts as the RecordSource of the bound form. Select the PA Rating column of the qryPersonnelActions query to which your form is bound (see fig. 13.16).

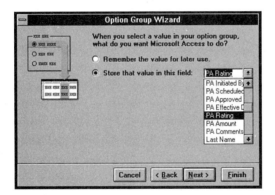

Fig. 13.16
Binding the option group to a column of the *RecordSource* of the form.

7. The fifth dialog lets you determine the style of the option group, as well as the type of controls (option buttons, check boxes, or toggle buttons) to add to the option group. You can preview the appearance of your option group and button style choices in the Sample pane. For this example, accept the defaults, Normal and Option Buttons (see fig. 13.17).

The sunken and raised styles of option groups, option buttons, and check boxes are applicable only to control objects on forms with a BackColor property other than white. Light gray is used to aid in the three-dimensional simulation and neither option buttons nor check boxes have a BackColor property. Thus, option buttons and check boxes with special effects are best suited for light gray backgrounds (BackColor = 12632256).

III

Forms and Reports

Fig. 13.17
Selecting a style
for the option
group and the
type of button to
add.

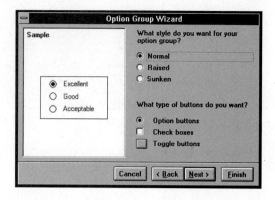

8. The last dialog provides a text box to enter the value of the Caption property of the label for the option group. Type **Rating**, as shown in figure 13.18, and then click Finish to let the Wizard complete its work. Your completed Rating option group appears as illustrated by figure 13.19.

  To test your new bound option group, add a text box bound to the PA Rating column of the query that underlies the form. Figure 13.20 shows the option group in Form View with the space between the buttons closed up, the bold attribute applied to the option group label, and the Rating text box added. Click the option buttons to display the rating value in the text box.

Fig. 13.18
Assigning the
value of the
Caption property
for the option
group's label.

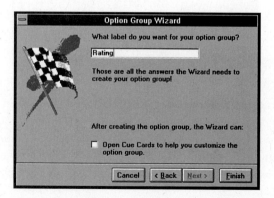

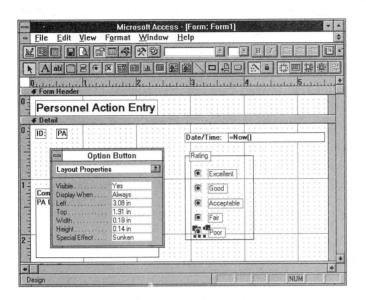

Fig. 13.19
The option group created by the Option Group Wizard.

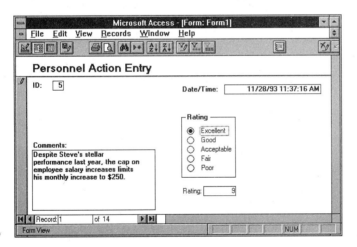

Fig. 13.20
The new option group in Form View.

Creating an Option Group Manually

Although the Option Group Wizard does a good job of creating option groups, it's useful to know how to create a bound option group on your own. To bind an option group frame to the PA Rating field of the Personnel Actions query without taking advantage of the Control Wizard, complete the following steps:

1. Click the Control Wizards toggle button of the toolbox to deactivate the wizards (raised appearance), and then click the Option Group tool of the toolbox.

2. Click the Field List button on the toolbar to display the Field List window and choose the PA Rating column of your query.

3. Hold down the left button of the mouse and drag the Field pointer to a position under the Date/Time text box, adjacent to the Rating option group you created in the preceding section, and then release the mouse button to create an option group of the default size.

   When you create a bound option group by dragging a field from the Field List window, the Option Group name is assigned to the Caption property of the associated label automatically.

4. Resize the option group frame so that it is the same size as the other Rating option group. Apply the bold attribute to the option group's label.

Option buttons, toggle buttons, and check boxes within bound frames inherit many of their properties, such as Control Source, from the frame. The option frame provides the binding of these tools when they are inside a frame. Therefore, you don't use the Field List with these controls. Adding multiple copies of controls is easier if you set the Lock tool in the toolbox on. To add five option buttons to assign values to the PA Rating field, perform the following steps:

1. Click the Lock tool in the toolbox.

2. Click the Option Button tool.

3. Using the crosshair as a reference to the upper left corner of an imaginary rectangle that surrounds the option button, drop the option button at the appropriate location in the option group frame. When the option button symbol enters the option group frame, the button, the frame, and contents appear in reverse video as shown in figure 13.21.

4. Repeat step 3 four more times to include a total of five Rating option buttons inside the Rating option group frame. The labels of the buttons are assigned numbers in the sequence of addition.

5. Click the Lock button in the toolbox again to unlock the Option Button tool, and click the Pointer.

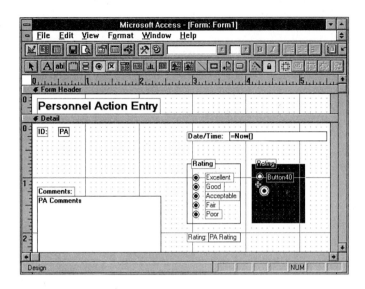

Fig. 13.21
Manually adding a second option button to an option frame.

6. Edit the labels to read, from top to bottom: **Excellent**, **Good**, **Acceptable**, **Fair**, and **Poor**, corresponding to option values of 9, 7, 5, 3, and 1, respectively.

7. Double-click the option button at the top and replace 1 with 9 as the Option Value in the Data Properties list. Default Option Values are assigned in sequence from 1 to the number of buttons in the frame.

8. Repeat step 7 for the four remaining buttons, replacing the default values 2, 3, 4, and 5 with 7, 5, 3, and 1, respectively. No two buttons in an option frame can have the same value.

9. To test the entries, click the Run Mode button on the toolbar. The form appears as shown in figure 13.22.

11. Using the record selection buttons, choose a record to edit. If you previously assigned ratings with odd-numbered values, the option button that corresponds to the value is selected.

12. Click the option buttons in sequence to verify that the proper numeric values appear in the Rating text box.

If you have a Yes/No field in the table, you can use a single option button bound to a field (not inside an option frame) to create the Yes/No values, -1/0, for the user.

Fig. 13.22

The option group frame and option buttons, displayed in run mode.

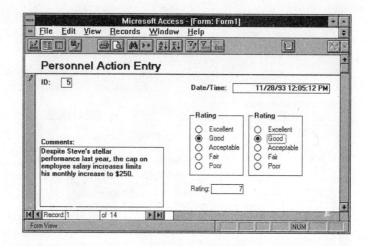

> **Note**
>
> If you add a button or a check box within a frame with the Field List drag-and-drop method, the button is independently bound to the selected field, rather than to the field through the option frame. In this case, the button's Properties dialog doesn't include the `OptionValue` property, and the button assigns Yes/No values to the field.
>
> An independently bound button inside an option frame doesn't follow the rules of the option frame; you can choose this button and another button simultaneously.
>
> Adding independently bound buttons within option frames results in assignment of inconsistent values to fields.

Using the Clipboard to Copy Controls to Another Form

Access's capability of copying controls and their properties to the Windows Clipboard enables you to create controls on one form and copy them to another form. If you use a standard header style, you can copy the controls in the header of a previously designed form to a new form and edit the content as necessary. The form that contains the controls to be copied need not be in the same database as the destination form in which the copy is pasted. You can create a library of standard controls in a dedicated form used only for holding standard controls.

The Rating option group and the Time/Date calculated text box are candidates to add to the Personnel Action Entry form you created in Chapter 12, "Creating and Using Forms." You may want to add a Time/Date text box to the header of all your transaction forms. To add the Rating option group you created in the preceding section and Time/Date controls to the Personnel Action Entry form, perform the following steps:

1. Click the Design View button, and select one of the Ratings option group frame and all the controls within it by dragging a selection frame around it with the mouse.

2. Press Ctrl+C, or choose **C**opy from the **E**dit menu to copy the group of controls to the Clipboard.

3. Click the Show Database Window button of the toolbar; then open the frmPersonnelActions form from the Database window in design mode.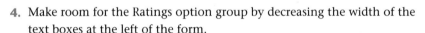

4. Make room for the Ratings option group by decreasing the width of the text boxes at the left of the form.

5. Click the Detail section selection bar, and then press Ctrl+V, or choose **P**aste from the **E**dit menu. A copy of the control appears at the upper left corner of the Detail section.

    Controls are pasted to the section of the form that is presently selected. You cannot select and then drag controls between sections of a form.

6. Position the mouse pointer over the copied option group so that the pointer becomes a hand symbol.

7. Click the left mouse button and drag the option group to the position shown in figure 13.23, and then release the mouse button.

8. Choose **2** Form:Form 1 from the **W**indow menu to reopen Form1.

    The number assigned to Form1 in the Windows menu may differ, depending on the sequence in which you opened the MDI child windows.

9. Select the label and the text box of the Date/Time calculated text box and copy the controls to the Clipboard.

10. Choose **3** Form:frmPersonnelActions from the **W**indow menu.

11. Click the Form Header section selection bar, and then paste the Date/Time control and relocate it to the right in the Form Header section.

Fig. 13.23
Copying the option group to the Personnel Actions form by using the Clipboard.

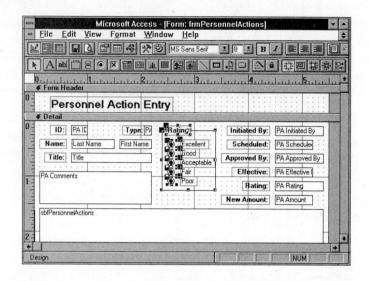

12. You cannot edit the value in the Date/Time calculated text box, so do not add a border. Usually, only text boxes that display data from a table or query that you can edit should have a border. Double-click the Date/Time text box to open the Layout Properties dialog and change the value of the BorderStyle property to Clear.

13. Click the Form View button on the toolbar. The Personnel Action Entry form appears as shown in figure 13.24.

Fig. 13.24
The Rating option group and Date/Time text box displayed in run mode.

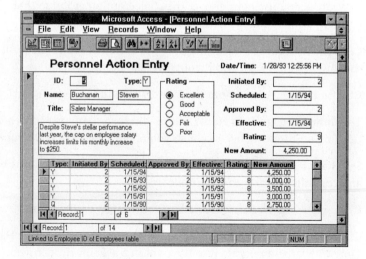

14. Return to design mode, and click the Save button to save your changes.

15. You won't need the Form1 example form again, so close Form1 without saving changes.

Troubleshooting

I copied a control to another form, but when I attempt to use the form, I get an error message when the control gets the focus.

When you copy a control to a form that uses a data source different from the one used to create the original control, you need to change the `ControlSource` property to correspond with the field to which the control is to be bound. Changing the `ControlSource` property doesn't change the `StatusBarText`, `ValidationRule`, or `ValidationText` properties for the new `ControlSource`; you must enter the appropriate values manually.

Using List Boxes and Combo Boxes

List boxes and combo boxes both serve the same basic purpose by enabling you to pick a value from a list, rather than type the value in a text box. These two kinds of list boxes are especially useful when you need to enter a code that represents the name of a person, firm, or product. You don't need to refer to a paper list of the codes and names to make the entry. The differences between list boxes and combo boxes are shown in the following list:

- *List boxes* don't need to be opened to display their content; the portion of the list that fits within the size of the list box you assign is visible at all times. Your choice is limited to values included in the list.

- *Drop-down combo boxes and drop-down lists* consume less space than list boxes in the form, but you must open these controls to select a value. Combo boxes in Access are drop-down lists with a text box, not traditional combo boxes that display the list at all times. You can allow the user to enter a value in the text box element of the drop-down combo list or limit the selection to the members in the drop-down list. If you limit the choice to members of the drop-down list (sometimes called a *pick list*), the user can type the beginning of the list value, and Access searches for a matching entry. This feature reduces the time needed to locate a choice in a long list.

III

Forms and Reports

Drop-down lists and combo boxes are two of the most powerful controls that the Microsoft programmers developed for Access. The data source for these controls may be a table, a query, a list of values you supply, or the names of Access Basic functions. The boxes may have as many columns as you need to display the data needed to make the correct choice.

Adding a Combo Box with a Table or Query as the Data Source

In the majority of cases, you bind the drop-down list or combo box to a field so that the choice updates the value of this field. Two-column controls are the most commonly used. The first column contains the code that updates the value of the field to which the control is bound, and the second column contains the name associated with the code. An example of where a limit-to-list, multiple-column drop-down list is most useful is the assignment of supervisor and manager employee ID numbers to the PA Initiated By and PA Approved By fields in the Personnel Actions form. The Combo Box Wizard is used to add the PA Initiated By drop-down list, and then you employ manual methods to add the PA Approved By drop-down list in the two sections that follow.

Using the Combo Box Wizard

Designing combo boxes is a more complex process than creating an option group, so you're likely to use the Combo Box Wizard for most of the combo boxes you add to forms. Follow these steps to use the Combo Box Wizard to create the PA Initiated By drop-down list that lets you select from a list of Northwind Traders' employees:

1. Open the frmPersonnelActions form from the Database window, in design mode, if it is not presently open.

2. Click the Initiated By text box to select it, and then press Delete to delete the text box from the form.

3. Click the Control Wizards button to turn on the wizards if necessary.

4. Click the Combo Box tool of the toolbox. The mouse pointer turns into a combo box symbol while on the active surface of the form.

5. Click the Field List button to display the Field List window.

6. Drag the PA Initiated By field to the position previously occupied by the Initiated By text box, and drop it there. The first Combo Box Wizard dialog appears.

7. You want the combo box to look up values in the Employees table, so accept the default option button with the query and table symbols and click the Next button (see fig. 13.25). Your selection specifies `Table/Query` as the value of the `RecordSource` property of the combo box. The second Combo Box Wizard dialog appears.

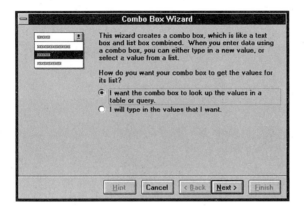

Fig. 13.25
The opening dialog of the Combo Box Wizard.

8. Select Employees from the list of tables in the Tables/Queries list as shown in figure 13.26. Click the Next > button to display the third dialog. A message box advises that the table has more than 15 fields and that only the first 15 fields will appear in the combo box design. Click OK.

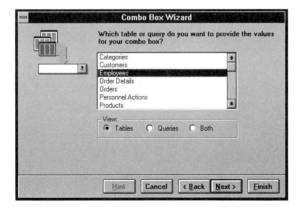

Fig. 13.26
Selecting the *RecordSource* property of the combo box.

III

Forms and Reports

9. You need the Employee ID and the Last Name fields of the Employees table for your combo box. Employee ID serves as the bound field and your combo box displays the Last Name field. Employee ID is selected in the Available Fields list by default, so click the > button to move Employee ID to the Fields in combo box list. Last Name is selected automatically, so click the > button again to move Last Name to the Fields in combo box list. Your Combo Box Wizard dialog appears as illustrated by figure 13.27. This selection specifies the SQL SELECT query that serves as the value of the RowSource property and populates the combo box's list. Click the Next > button to display the fourth dialog.

Fig. 13.27

Selecting the fields of the table with which to populate the combo box.

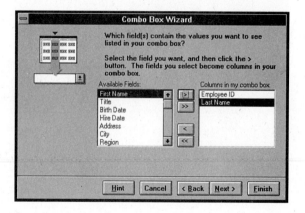

10. The data cells for the two fields you selected in step 7 appear in the datasheet as shown in figure 13.28. The Hint button is enabled, so click the button to display the hint.

Fig. 13.28

Assigning a value to the *BoundColumn* property.

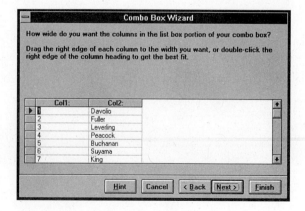

11. The Hint shown in figure 13.29 suggests that you reduce the column width of columns you do not want to appear in the combo box list to 0 by dragging the width of the column to the left until the column disappears. Click OK to close the Hint dialog.

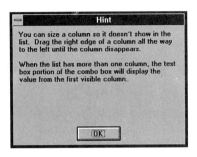

12. Take the hint and drag the right edge of the Col1 column header to the left edge of the datasheet so Col1 disappears. Drag the left edge of the Col2 header to reduce the width of the column to accommodate the last names, as shown in figure 13.30. This establishes the value of the ColumnWidths property. Click the Next > button to display the sixth dialog.

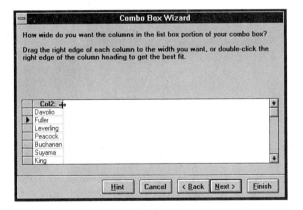

Fig. 13.30
Assigning the *ColumnWidths* property value.

13. Employee ID, the default (first) selection is the field value of the Employees table that you want the combo box selection to supply to the field (see fig. 13.28). Your selection specifies the value (1) of the BoundColumn property. Accept the default, and click the Next > button to display the next dialog.

III

Forms and Reports

Fig. 13.31
Specifying the
bound field for the
combo box.

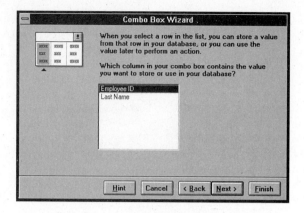

14. Your combo box supplies the Employee ID value corresponding to the
name you select to the PA Initiated By field. You previously specified
that the ControlSource property is the PA Initiated Field when you
dragged the field symbol to the form in step 4. The Combo Box Wizard
uses your prior selection as the default value of the ControlSource property (see fig. 13.32), so accept the default value clicking the Next > button to display the seventh and final dialog.

Fig. 13.32
Assigning the
ControlSource
property value.

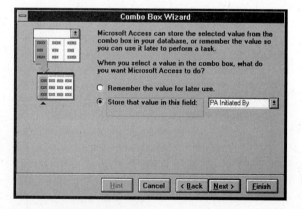

15. The last dialog lets you edit the label associated with the combo box
(see fig. 13.33). Accept the default value, Initiated By:, and click Finish
to add the combo box to your form. Your combo box in design mode
appears as in figure 13.34.

Fig. 13.33
The final Combo
Box Wizard dialog.

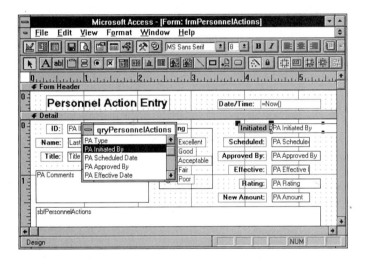

Fig. 13.34
The new combo
box in design
mode.

16. Click the Form View button of the toolbar to test your combo box (see
    fig. 13.35). Change the Initiated By value to another person, such as Mr.
    Brid, the marketing director, and then move the record pointer to make
    the change permanent. Return to the original record, and open the
    combo box to verify that the combo box is bound to the PA Initiated By
    field.

III

Forms and Reports

Fig. 13.35

The Initiated By combo box in run mode.

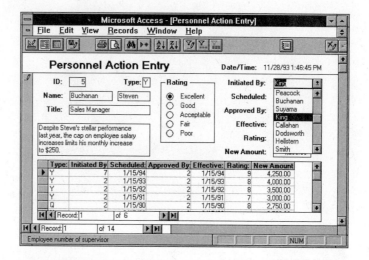

Adding a Combo Box Manually

As mentioned previously in this chapter, it is a good practice to create control objects manually so that you learn the properties associated with the control. To substitute a two-column combo box that you create yourself for the PA Approved By text box in the Personnel Actions form, complete the following steps:

1. Open the frmPersonnelActions form from the Database window in design mode, if it is not presently open.

2. Click the Control Wizards button of the toolbox to disable the wizards if necessary. (Disabled is the button up state.)

3. Select the Approved By text box and its associated label, and then press the Delete key to remove this text box from the form.

4. Click the Field List button of the toolbar to open the Field List window.

5. Click the Combo Box tool in the toolbox. Then click PA Approved By, and drag and drop the field symbol at the preceding location of the Approved By text box. Size the combo box and its label to the approximate dimensions of the text box and label that it replaces.

6. Double-click the combo box to display the Properties window, and select Data Properties.

7. The source of the data for the combo box is the Employees table, so the default value of the RowSourceType property, Table/Query, is correct. Open the Row Source combo list and select the Employees table as the value of the RowSource property.

8. When you choose the name of a table or a query as the RowSource property, all of the fields of the table or columns of the query are included automatically as combo box columns. The first two columns of the Employees table provide the Employee ID to be assigned as the value of the PA Approved By field and Last Name to identify the supervisor. Select Layout Properties, and enter **2** as the Column count to create a two-column combo box.

9. The default width of each column of the combo box is 1 inch. The Employee ID column can be less than 1 inch wide because it consists of only one digit. Enter **0.2** as the width of the first column, followed by a semicolon separator (or a comma), and enter **0.8** as the width of the second column. Access adds inch units (in) for you.

10. The first column of the Employees table, Employee ID, contains the value to assign to the PA Approved By field, so the default value of the BoundColumn property, column 1, is correct. You can choose any column by its number (in left-to-right sequence) as the value to be assigned to the field to which the combo box is bound.

11. Only an employee included in the Employees table can initiate or approve a Personnel Action, so open the Limit to List list and select Yes. (If you want to allow the user to add a value not included in the list, accept the default No value. Adding a user-defined value is not applicable in this case). The Personnel Actions form appears as shown in figure 13.36.

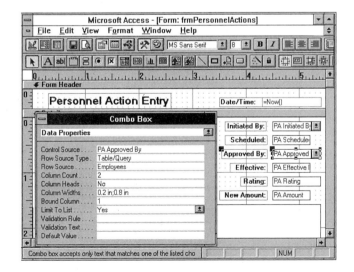

Fig. 13.36
Setting the values of the data properties of the combo box.

III

Forms and Reports

12. Click the Form View button of the toolbar to test the combo boxes. When you open the Approved By combo box, the display appears as in figure 13.37.

Fig. 13.37
The Approved By multiple-column combo box in Form View.

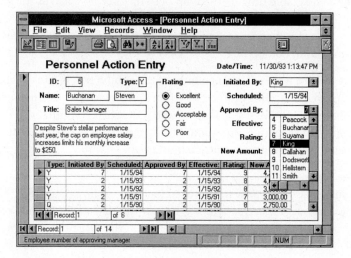

Notice that the Employee ID field value appears in the text element of the combo box, rather than the Last Name field value as in the Initiated By combo box. If the bound column appears in the list element, the value of the bound column appears in the text element.

13. To display only the name of the supervisor or manager in the list and text boxes, return to design mode and change the value of the ColumnWidths property of the first column from 0.2 to 0 inches. This action causes only the second column to appear in the text box and list elements of the combo box, making the two combo boxes of your form consistent.

As an example, if the fourth column of the table or query is the column you want to display in the combo box, type three zero-width columns preceding the width you want for the column that you want to display (**0,0,0,** and **1**).

List and combo boxes are a boon to developers because Access does all the work. Users who, in early versions of Clipper or later versions of dBASE, wrote the code necessary to create a pop-up window that contains a drop-down list will appreciate the ease of creating a combo box in Access.

Using the Query Builder to Populate a Combo Box

If the RowSourceType property for a combo box is Table/Query, you can substitute an SQL statement for a named table or query as the value of the RowSource property. In the case of queries, the advantage of the substitution is that this process prevents the list of queries in the Database window from becoming cluttered with named queries used to create a multitude of combo boxes. For either tables or queries, you can choose only the fields or columns you want for the text box, eliminating the need to hide columns. In addition, you can specify a sort order for the list element of your combo box.

Access

2.0

To invoke Access 2.0's new Query Builder to create an SQL statement to populate the Approved By combo box, follow these steps:

1. Return to or open frmPersonnelActions in design mode and double-click the PA Approved By combo box to open the Properties window. Select Data Properties if necessary.

2. Select the RowSource property, and click the Ellipsis button to launch the Query Builder. You previously selected the Employees table as the value of the RowSource property, so the message box of figure 13.38 appears. Click Yes to confirm the replacement and open the Query Builder's window.

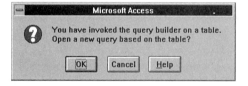

Fig. 13.38
Confirming you want to replace the Employees table with an SQL statement.

3. The Query Builder's window is identical in most respects to the Query Design window, but its title and behavior differs. The Employees table automatically appears in the upper pane. Drag the Employee ID and Last Name fields to columns 1 and 2 of the Query Design grid.

4. You want an ascending sort on the Last Name field, so click the Sort check box. Your query design appears as shown in figure 13.39.

   When you use the Query Builder, you can't execute the query to test it. (The Datasheet View and Run Query buttons are disabled.)

III

Forms and Reports

Fig. 13.39
The design of the query to create the SQL statement for the Approved By combo box.

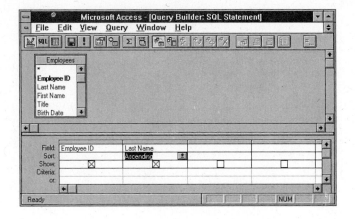

5. Double-click the Document Control-menu box to close the Query Builder. The message box of figure 13.40 appears for confirmation of your change to the RowSource property value, instead of asking if you want to save your query. Click Yes and the SQL statement derived from the graphical QBE design appears as the value of the RowSource property.

Fig. 13.40
Confirming your change to the *RowSource* property value.

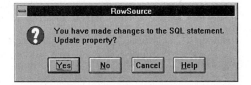

6. SQL statements, especially those created by Access, have a tendency to be lengthy. With the caret in the RowSource property text box, press Shift+F2 to display the SQL statement in the Zoom box, as shown in figure 13.41.

In this case, the field name prefix is applied in each field reference, although it is only necessary in the FROM clause because one table is involved in the query.

Switch to Form View to test the effect of adding the sort (the ORDER BY clause) to the query. Writing your own SQL statements to fill combo boxes with values is discussed in Chapter 24, "Working with Structured Query Language."

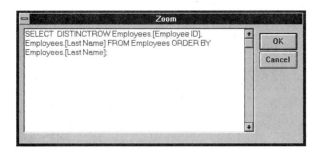

Fig. 13.41
Displaying the SQL
statement in the
Zoom box.

Creating a Combo Box with a List of Static Values

Another application for list boxes and combo boxes is picking values from a static list of options that you create. A drop-down list to choose a Rating value saves space in a form compared with the equivalent control created with option buttons within an option frame. As you design more complex forms, you find that display "real estate" becomes increasingly valuable.

The option frame you added to the Personnel Action Entry form provides a choice of only 5 of the possible 10 ratings. To add a drop-down list to allow entry of all the possible values with the Combo Box Wizard, perform the following steps:

1. Click the Design View button on the toolbar. Click the Control Wizards button of the toolbox, if necessary, to enable the Combo Box Wizard. (Enabled is the button down state.)

2. Select and delete the Rating text box and label.

3. Open the Field List window, and select PA Rating.

4. Click the Combo Box tool in the toolbox. Then drag and the PA Rating field symbol at the former location of the Rating text box. The first Combo Wizard dialog appears.

5. Click the I Will Type in the Values I Want in the Combo Box button, and then click the Next > button to display the second dialog.

6. The Rating combo box requires two columns, the first column containing the allowable values of PA Rating, 0 through 9, and the second column containing the corresponding description of the rating code. Enter 2 as the number of columns. Access assigns RowSource property values in column-row sequence; you enter each of the values for the columns of the first row, and then do the same for the remaining rows. Type **9**, **Excellent**; **8**, **Very Good**; **7**, **Good**; **6**, **Average**; **5**, **Accept-**

able; **4**, **Marginal**; **3**, **Fair**; **2**, **Sub-par**; **1**, **Poor**; **0**, **Terminated**, as shown in figure 13.42 (Don't type the commas or semicolons in the preceding list). Click the Next > button to display the third dialog.

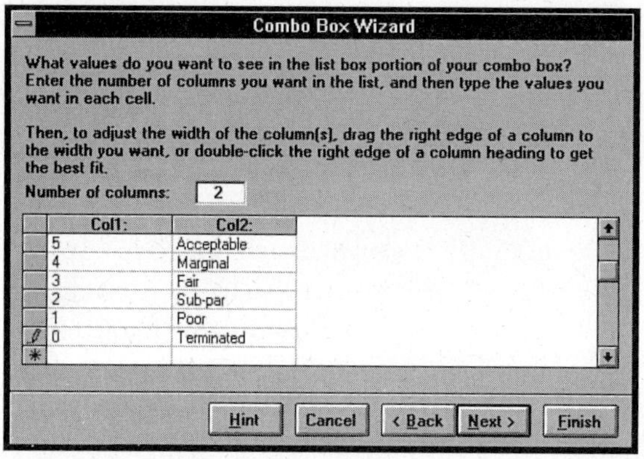

Fig. 13.42
Entering static values in the Combo Box Wizard's datasheet.

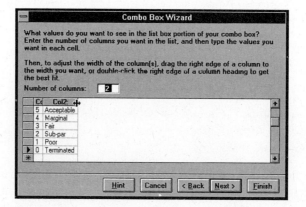

7. Set the widths of the columns you want by dragging the edge of the column header buttons to the left, as shown in figure 13.43. If you don't want the rating number to appear, drag the left edge of column 1 fully to the left to reduce its width to 0. Click the Next > button.

Fig. 13.43
Setting the column widths of the combo box.

8. Select Column 1, the rating number code, as the bound column for your value list. Click the Hint button to display the suggestion for selecting a bound column (see fig. 13.44). Click OK of the Hint dialog, and then click the Next > button to display the next dialog.

9. Accept the default values in the next two dialogs to complete the combo box specification and return to form design mode.

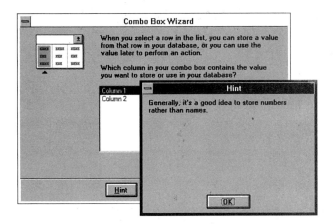

Fig. 13.44
A useful hint when choosing a column to bind to a field of a table or column of a query.

10. Open the Properties window for the combo box and select Data Properties. Set Limit to List to Yes to convert the drop-down combo to a drop-down list. The Personnel Action Entry form in design mode appears as shown in figure 13.45. Notice that Access has added commas after the numbers and semicolons between the row entries, plus double-quotes to surround the text values. This is the format you use when you enter list values manually.

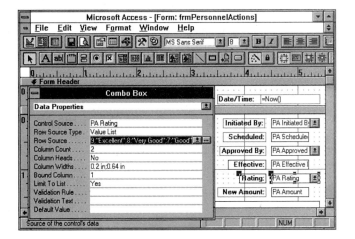

Fig. 13.45
The Data Properties for the value list combo box.

11. Click the Form View button of the toolbar to display the form. The open Rating static-value combo box appears as shown in figure 13.46.

Fig. 13.46
The Rating static-value combo box opened in run mode.

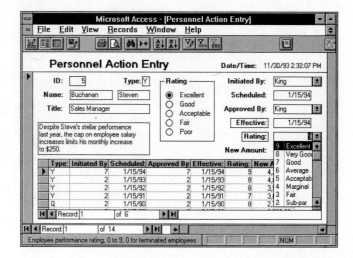

Another opportunity to use a static-value combo box is as a substitute for the Type text box. Several kinds of performance reviews exist: Quarterly, Yearly, Bonus, Salary, Commission, and so on, each represented by an initial letter code.

> **Note**
>
> You can improve the appearance of columns of labels and associated text, list, and combo boxes by right-aligning the text of the labels and left-aligning the text of the boxes. Select all the labels in a column with the mouse, and click the Right Justify button on the toolbar. Then select all the boxes, and click the Left Justify button.

Creating and Using Continuous Forms

Continuous forms are useful for displaying data contained in multiple records of a table or query in a format other than Datasheet View. The Personnel Actions subform, for example, is designed only to display the most recent Personnel Action records for an employee. Editing isn't allowed in the subform, so you don't need the field headers, record selection buttons, and scroll bars associated with Datasheet View. These graphic elements focus more attention on the subform than deserved. You need a *plain vanilla* display of the history for the employee; this plain display requires a continuous form.

The Form Wizard offers the choice of creating a continuous tabular form, so using the Form Wizard is the quickest method of creating a plain vanilla subform. To create a continuous tabular form with the Form Wizards, complete the following series of steps:

1. Close the frmPersonnelActions form, and save the changes you made in the preceding section.

2. Click the Form tab, and then the New button in the Database window to create a new form.

3. Select the qryPersonnelActionsSubform query as the source of data for the new form.

4. Click the Form Wizard button. The Form Wizard Selection dialog appears.

5. Choose Tabular as the type of Form Wizard to use, and click OK. The field selection Form Wizard window appears.

6. Add all the fields to the form with the >> button. Then remove the PA ID and the PA Comments fields with the < button, and click the Next > button. The Form Wizard displays the Style window.

7. Choose Standard as the style for the form, and click the Next > button.

8. Type **frmTest** as the name of the form. Click the Design option button to modify the design of the form, and then click the Finish button.

The Form Wizard created the Standard tabular form by using the frmPersonnelActionsSubform query the data source. To customize the form to make the size and appearance compatible with the Personnel Action Entry form, follow these steps:

1. Click the frmTest title label in the header to select it, and then press the Delete key, leaving the labels for the field names, as shown in figure 13.47.

2. Click the Palette button on the toolbar, click the Form Header bar, and change the background color (BackColor property) to white.

3. Click the Detail header bar, and change the background color to white. Select all of the labels in the header and change the labels' background color to white.

4. Choose Select For**m** from the **E**dit menu, and then click the Properties button of the toolbar.

Fig. 13.47

The Form Wizard's tabular form in design mode.

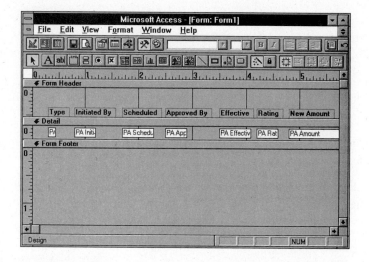

5. Select All properties, and set the value of the DefaultEditing property to Read Only, AllowEditing to Unavailable, ScrollBars to Neither, and RecordSelectors and NavigationButtons to No. These settings disable all editing capability. The default GridX and GridY property values of 10 and 12, respectively, correspond to the grid spacing of frmPersonnelActions. (The ability to independently display the horizontal scroll bar and navigation buttons is a new feature of Access 2.0.)

6. Choose Select **A**ll from the **E**dit menu to select all of the controls on the form. Then choose Hori**z**ontal Spacing from the F**o**rmat menu, and **D**ecrease from the submenu, to reduce the horizontal distance between the controls. The ability to adjust the spacing of controls automatically is a new feature of Access 2.0.

7. Select all of the labels and drag the group to the upper left corner of the Form Header section. Set the BackStyle property to Transparent (Clear). Then drag the Detail section header bar to the bottom of the labels.

8. Select all of the text boxes and drag the group to the top left of the Detail section. Set the BackColor property to white and the BorderColor property to Clear. Drag the Form Footer section header bar to the bottom of the text boxes.

9. Adjust the position and size of the text boxes as shown in figure 13.48.

10. Click the Form View button on the toolbar. The continuous form displays all the records in the Personnel Actions subquery, as shown in figure 13.49.

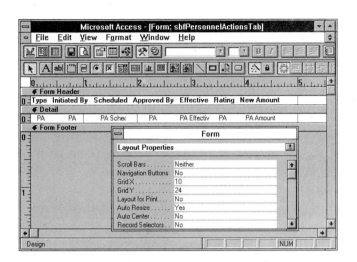

Fig. 13.48
Modifying a
continuous form
created by the
Form Wizard.

11. Close the new subform and assign the new name,
sbfPersonnelActionsTab.

Fig. 13.49
The appearance of
the continuous
form of figure
13.48 in run mode.

Now, you need to replace the Personnel Actions subform with the new Personnel Actions Tabular subform that you created in the preceding steps. To perform this procedure, take the following steps:

1. Open the Personnel Actions form, and click the Design View button of
the toolbar.

2. Click the subform control to select it and, after waiting half a second,
click the control again so that you can edit the ControlSource property.

III

Forms and Reports

3. Add **Tab** to the text in the subform so that it reads
   sbfPersonnelActionsTab. (This is an alternative method of changing the
   value of the ControlSource property of a bound control, such as a
   subform or text box.)

4. On the toolbar, click the Run Mode button. The form appears as shown
   in figure 13.50. If the subform displays scroll bars or a record selector,
   close the Personnel Action Entry form and reopen it from the Database
   window to remove these features (called *adornments*).

Fig. 13.50

The Personnel
Action Entry form
with a continuous
subform substi-
tuted for the
Datasheet
subform.

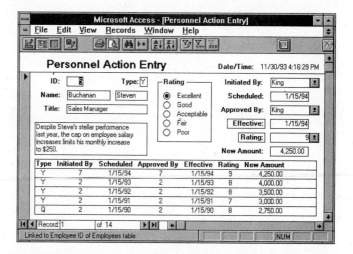

Note

Delete the vertical scroll bar when all the control objects of the noncontinuous form
fit in a maximized form window. The horizontal scroll bar need not be present when
record selectors are used. You can eliminate both the horizontal scroll bar and the
record selection buttons when you substitute command buttons for the record selection buttons in Part IV, "Powering Access with Macros." Unnecessary graphic elements are distracting and have a negative influence on the overall appearance of the
form.

Overriding the Field Properties of Tables

Access uses the table's property values assigned to the fields as defaults. The
form or subform *inherits* these properties from the table or query on which

the form is based. You can override the inherited properties, except for the ValidationRule property, by assigning a different set of values in the Properties dialog for the control. Properties of controls bound to fields of tables or queries that are inherited from the table's field properties are shown in the following list:

- Format

- Decimal Places

- Status Bar Text

- Validation Rule

- Validation Text

- Default Value

- Typeface characteristics, such as Font Name, Font Size, Font Bold, Font Italic, and Font Underline

Values of field properties that you override with properties in a form apply only when the data is displayed and edited with the form. Here, the Format, Decimal Places, and Validation Rules you apply in forms are similar to xBase PICTURE and VALID instructions appended to the GET command.

You can establish validation rules for controls bound to fields that differ from properties of the field established by the table; but you can only narrow the rule. The table-level validation rule for the content of the PA Type field, for example, limits entries to the letters H, S, Q, Y, B, and C. The validation rule you establish in a form cannot broaden the allowable entries; if you add T as a valid choice by editing the validation rule for the PA Type field to **InStr("HSQYBCT",[PA Type])>0**, you receive an error when you enter **T**. However, you can narrow the range of allowable entries by substituting **InStr("SQYB",[PA Type])>0**. Notice that you can use expressions that refer to the field name in validation rule expressions in forms; such expressions are not permitted in table validation rule expressions in Access 2.0.

Adding Page Headers and Footers for Printing Forms

Access enables you to add a separate pair of sections, Page Header and Page Footer, that appear only when the form prints. You add these sections to the form in pairs, by choosing **P**age Header/Footer from the F**o**rmat menu. The following list shows the purposes of Page Headers and Footers:

- *Page Header* sections enable you to use a different title for the printed version. The depth of the Page Header can be adjusted to control the location where the Detail section of the form is printed on the page.

- *Page Footer* sections enable you to add dates and page numbers to the printed form.

Page Header and Page Footer sections appear only in the printed form, not when you display the form in run mode. The Personnel Actions form with Page Header and Page Footer sections added is shown in figure 13.51. The subform control was deleted so that the Form Footer and Page Footer sections appear in the window. Usually, you need to use the vertical scroll bar to display these sections in design mode.

Fig. 13.51

The Personnel Actions form with Page Header and Page Footer sections added.

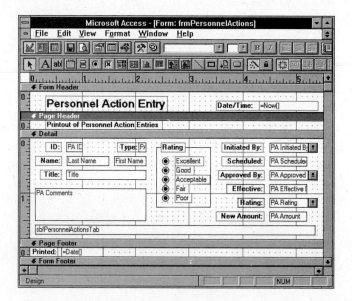

You can control whether the Form Header and Form Footer appear in the printed form with the `DisplayWhen` Layout property of the Properties dialog for each section. In figure 13.51, the Form Header duplicates the information in the Page Header (except for the Date/Time label and text box), so you don't want to print both. To control when a section of the form prints or is displayed, perform the following steps:

1. Double-click the title bar of the section of the form that you want to change to open the related Properties dialog. (The Page Header and Page Footer sections don't have a `DisplayWhen` property; the sections only appear when printing.)

2. Open the Display When list.

3. To display, and not print, the section in run mode, select Screen Only.

4. To print, but not display, the section, select Print Only.

From Here...

The examples presented in this chapter demonstrate the ease with which you can add productivity features to an Access form created by the Form Wizard or build a custom form from ground zero. The toolbox and the related methodology suffice to create forms that satisfy the majority of your database transaction and decision support applications.

- Chapters 14, "Printing Basic Reports and Mailing Labels," and 15, "Preparing Advanced Reports," describe how to use the toolbox to add control objects to reports.

- Chapter 18, "Creating Macros for Forms and Reports," shows you how to add command buttons to forms and attach macros to the command buttons.

- Chapter 20, "Adding Graphics to Forms and Reports," describes how you add bound and unbound object frames containing graphic images to forms.

Chapter 14

Printing Basic Reports and Mailing Labels

The final product of most database applications is a report. In Access, a *report* is a special kind of continuous form designed specifically for printing. Access combines data in tables, queries, and even forms to produce a report that you can print and distribute to people who need or request it. A printed version of a form may serve as a report, which often occurs with reports designed for decision support, one of the topics of Chapter 20, "Adding Graphics to Forms and Reports." Printing a continuous form can create a report that displays some or all the values of fields in a table or query.

This chapter describes how you create relatively simple reports, including multicolumn mailing labels, using the Report Wizards, and how to modify the design of the Wizard's reports to suit your particular needs. The next chapter describes how you design a report from scratch, without using the Report Wizards.

Differences and Similarities between Forms and Reports

Most methods of creating transaction-processing forms, which you learned in Chapter 11, "Using Action Queries," and Chapter 12, "Creating and Using Forms," also apply to reports. The principal differences between reports and forms are detailed in the following list:

- Reports are intended for printing only and, unlike forms, aren't designed for display in a window. When an 8 1/2-by-11-inch report is viewed in Print Preview, its content is not legible. In the zoomed (full-page) view, only a portion of the report is visible in the Print Preview window.

In this chapter, you learn to

- Create an AutoReport from a table or query

- Customize Report Wizard styles

- Use the Report Wizard to create a group-totals report

- Modify a report created by the Report Wizard

- Print multi-column reports as mailing labels

III

Forms and Reports

■ You cannot change the value of the underlying data for a report with a control object from the toolbox, as you can with forms. With reports, Access disregards user input from option buttons, check boxes, and the like. You can use these controls, however, to indicate the status of Yes/No option buttons and check boxes and of fields with values derived from multiple-choice lists.

■ No Datasheet View of a report is available. Only Print Preview and Report Design Views are available.

■ You can create an *unbound* report that isn't linked to a source of data. Unbound reports are used as "containers" for individual subreports that use unrelated data sources.

■ In a report, minimum left, right, top, and bottom printing margins are controlled by the Printer Setup dialog. If a report is less than the printable page width, the report's design determines the right margin. You can increase the left margin over the default setting by positioning the print fields to the right of the left margin of the display.

■ In multicolumn reports, the number of columns, column width, and column spacing are controlled by settings in the Printer Setup dialog, not by controls you add or properties you set in design mode.

Access reports share many characteristics of forms, as shown in the following list:

Access
2.0

■ *Report Wizards* can create the three basic kinds of reports: single-column, groups/totals, and mailing labels. You can modify the reports that the Report Wizard creates as necessary. The Report Wizard is similar in function to the Form Wizard discussed in Chapter 9, "Understanding Operators and Expressions in Access."

■ *Sections* include report headers and footers that appear once at the beginning and at the end of the report and page headers and footers that print at the top and bottom of each page. The report footer often is used to print grand totals. Report sections correspond to similarly named form sections.

■ *Group sections* of reports as a whole comprise the equivalent of the Detail section of forms. Groups often are referred to as *bands*, and the process of grouping records is known as *banding*. You can add Group Headers that include a title for each group, and Group Footers to print group subtotals. You can place static (unbound) graphics in header and footer sections and bound graphics within group sections.

- *Controls* are added to reports from the Access toolbox and then moved and sized with their handles.

- *Subreports* can be incorporated into reports the same way you add subform controls within main forms.

Types of Access Reports

Reports created by Access fall into six basic types, also called *layouts*, detailed in the following list:

- *Single-column reports* list in one long column of text boxes the values of each field in each record of a table or query. A label indicates the name of a field, and a text box to the right of the label provides the values. Access 2.0's new Quick Report feature creates a single-column report with a single click of the AutoReport button of the toolbar. Single-column reports are seldom used because this format wastes paper.

- *Tabular reports* provide a column for each field of the table or query and print the value of each field of the records in rows under the column header. If you have more columns than can fit on one page, additional pages print in sequence until all the columns are printed; then the next group of records is printed.

- *Multicolumn reports* are created from single-column reports by using the "newspaper" or "snaking" column approach of desktop publishing and word processing applications. The format of multicolumn tables wastes less paper, but has limited uses because the alignment of the columns is unlikely to correspond to how you want them.

- *Groups/totals reports* are the most common kind of report. Access groups/ totals reports are similar to reports created by other database managers, such as dBASE and Paradox. You summarize data for groups of records, and then add grand totals at the end of the report.

- *Mailing labels* are a special kind of multicolumn report designed to print names and addresses (or other multifield data) in groups. Each group of fields constitutes a cell in a grid with a number of rows and columns on a page determined by the design of the stock adhesive label on which you are printing.

- *Unbound reports* contain subreports based on unrelated data sources, such as tables or queries.

III

Forms and Reports

The first four types of reports use a table or query as the data source, as do forms; these kinds of reports are said to be *bound* to the data source. The main report of an unbound report is not linked to a table or a query as a data source. The subreports contained by an unbound report, however, must be bound to a data source. Unbound reports enable you to incorporate subreports bound to independent tables or queries.

Creating and Customizing an AutoReport

The simplest method of creating an Access report is to select the table or query to serve as the RecordSource property of the report in the Database window and then click the AutoReport button of the toolbar. (AutoReport is one of the Access Report Wizards in disguise.) Access quickly displays a standard, tabular report in presentation format. Figure 14.1 shows, in print preview mode, an AutoReport created from the Customers table of NWIND.MDB. The length of the report is 23 pages in the standard format.

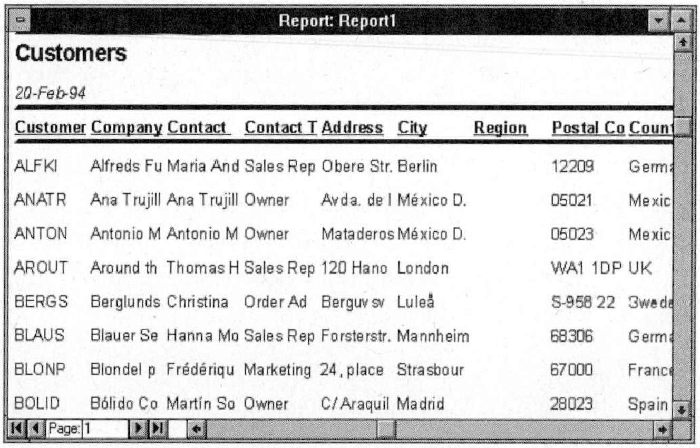

Fig. 14.1

Part of an AutoReport created from the Customers table.

Report: Report1

Customers

20-Feb-94

Customer	Company	Contact	Contact T	Address	City	Region	Postal Co	Count
ALFKI	Alfreds Fu	Maria And	Sales Rep	Obere Str.	Berlin		12209	Germa
ANATR	Ana Trujill	Ana Trujill	Owner	Avda. de l	México D.		05021	Mexic
ANTON	Antonio M	Antonio M	Owner	Mataderos	México D.		05023	Mexic
AROUT	Around th	Thomas H	Sales Rep	120 Hano	London		WA1 1DP	UK
BERGS	Berglunds	Christina	Order Ad	Berguv sv	Luleå		S-958 22	Swede
BLAUS	Blauer Se	Hanna Mo	Sales Rep	Forsterstr.	Mannheim		68306	Germa
BLONP	Blondel p	Frédériqu	Marketing	24, place	Strasbour		67000	France
BOLID	Bólido Co	Martín So	Owner	C/ Araquil	Madrid		28023	Spain

Page: 1

You can change the type and style of the report by customizing the AutoReport Wizard. To customize the AutoReport Wizard, follow these steps:

1. Choose Add-ins from the File menu; then choose Add-In Manager from the submenu to display the Add-In Manager dialog shown in figure 14.2.

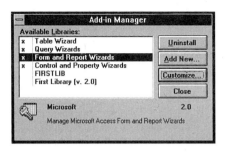

Fig. 14.2
Selecting the
Wizards to
customize with the
Add-In Manager.

2. Select Form and Report Wizards, and click the Customize button to
   display the Customize Add-In dialog (see fig. 14.3).

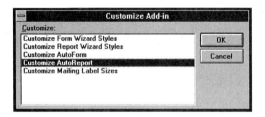

Fig. 14.3
Selecting
AutoReport to
customize.

3. Double-click the Customize AutoReport entry in the Customize list or
   select this item, and click OK to display the AutoReport Style dialog
   shown in figure 14.4.

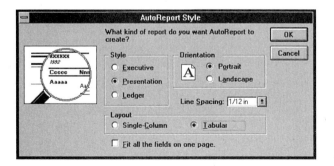

Fig. 14.4
Customizing the
AutoReport style
and layout.

4. Select the style, layout (type of report), line spacing, and print orientation you want with the controls of the Customize AutoReport dialog;
   then click OK to return to the Add-In Manager dialog.

III

Forms and Reports

Tip
You can fit
more records
on a single
page or set of
pages by
changing the
Line Spacing
from 1/12 inch
to 0 inch with-
out affecting
readability of
the report.

The Fit All Fields on One Page check box does exactly what it says, no matter how many fields exist in the RecordSource for the report. If you mark this check box for an AutoReport created from the Customers form, the field columns are truncated severely. Printing in landscape mode alleviates the severity of the truncation, but the report remains difficult to read and some critical data, such as complete telephone numbers, are lost.

5. Click Close to close the Add-In Manager dialog.

6. Select the Customers table in the Database window, and click the AutoReport button to see the effect of your changes to the AutoReport style and layout. The report shown in figure 14.5 results from the selections shown in figure 14.4.

Fig. 14.5
Part of the
customized
AutoReport from
the Customers
table.

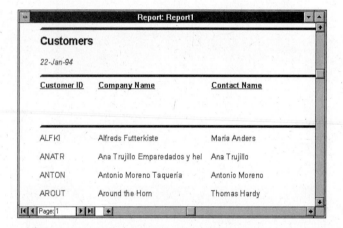

You use the same method described in the preceding steps to customize the

Tip
You can in-
crease the
number of
fields that
display on a
single sheet by
decreasing the
Font Size value
from 10 to 8 or
even 7 points.
Reports are
readable by
most persons
with a 7-point
Arial font.

You use the same method described in the preceding steps to customize the style of the reports created by the individual Report Wizards, including AutoReport. Double-click Report Wizards in step 3, instead of double-clicking AutoReport, to display the Customize Report Styles dialog shown in figure 14.6. You can change the font family and font size, as well as the attributes, of the label and text box components of the bound controls. The changes you make to the style apply to all reports with which the customized style is used.

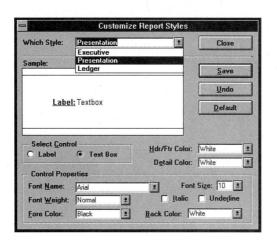

Fig. 14.6

Customizing a style for reports created with the Report Wizard.

Creating a Groups/Totals Report with the Report Wizard

The remainder of this chapter uses an example query, Products and Suppliers, from the Northwind Traders sample database as the underlying RecordSource to create a groups/totals report. This report displays the quantity of each specialty food product in inventory, grouped by product category.

You modify the basic report created by the Report Wizard to create an inventory report. The process of creating a basic report with the Report Wizard is similar to the process you used to create a form in Chapter 12. An advantage of using the Groups/Totals Report Wizard to introduce the topic of designing Access reports is that the steps for this process parallel the steps you take when you start with a default blank report. Starting with a blank report and creating more complex reports are covered in Chapter 15, "Preparing Advanced Reports."

To create a Product on Hand by Category report, follow these steps:

1. Click the Report tab in the Database window, and then click the New button.

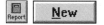

2. Like forms, reports require a data source that can be a table or a query. Select the Products and Suppliers query from the choices offered in the New Report dialog's drop-down list (see fig. 14.7). Then click the Report Wizards button. The Products and Suppliers query includes most of the fields from both the Products table and the Suppliers tables.

Forms and Reports

III

Fig. 14.7
The New Report
dialog used to
select the source of
data for a report.

3. You want a report that groups individual products by category and then totals the product on hand for the group comprising each product category. Click the Groups/Totals Wizard entry in the list, as shown in figure 14.8, and then click OK. The Field Selection dialog appears.

Fig. 14.8
The dialog from
which you select
the Report Wizard
to create.

4. The fields you choose to display represent rows of the report. You need the report to print the product name and supplier so that users do not have to refer to another report to associate codes with names. The fields that you need for this report are Category ID, Product ID, English Name, Supplier ID, Company Name, and Units in Stock. With the > button, select these fields in sequence from the Available Fields list (see fig. 14.9). As you add fields to the Field Order on Report list, the field name is removed from the Available Fields list. The fields appear from left to right in the report, based on the top-to-bottom sequence in which the fields appear in the Field Order on Report list. Click the Next > button when you've completed your entries.

If you add the wrong field to the Field Order on Report list, use the < button to move the field back to the Available Fields list. You can retrace your steps to correct an error by clicking the < Back command button any time this button is activated. The Finish command button accepts all defaults and jumps to step 9, so using this button is not recommended.

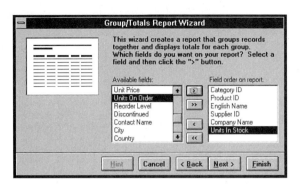

Fig. 14.9
The list from
which you select
the fields to print
in the report.

5. The groups of products are based on the product category, so select
Category ID as the field to group by (see fig. 14.10). Then click the Next
> button. Access enables you to group fields in an outline format with
up to three levels of nesting: group, subgroup, and sub-subgroup.

Fig. 14.10
The Category ID
selected as the
field by which
Access groups
records.

6. The Report Wizard enables you to group data by a coded field, using the
Group drop-down list (see fig. 14.11). Select Normal—the default and
only choice for a number field—and click the Next > button.

III

Fig. 14.11
The Report Wizard
dialog that enables
you to group
records by coded
categories.

Forms and Reports

Access
2.0

> **Note**
>
> If your application uses a text coding scheme, such as BEVA for alcoholic beverages and BEVN for nonalcoholic beverages, you can combine all beverages in a single group by selecting 1st 3 Characters from the list. With Access 2.0, this option is available for fields of the Text data type but not for numeric fields.

7. You can sort the records within groups by any field you choose (see fig. 14.12). Category ID is not offered as a choice because this field is where the records are grouped. Select Product ID with the > button, and click the Next > button.

Fig. 14.12
The Product ID field selected as the sort field.

8. You can select from three different styles for the report: Executive, Presentation, and Ledger (see fig. 14.13). An inventory report deserves the *plain vanilla* ledger presentation favored by accountants. The report has only a few fields, so Portrait orientation (the default) is suitable. Click the Ledger option button, and then click the Next > button. (Line Spacing adjustment is not available for the Ledger style.)

Fig. 14.13
The styles available for a Product on Hand by Category report.

9. In the Report title text box, type **Product on Hand by Category** as the name for the report (see fig. 14.14). You want all the fields to fit across a single 8 1/2-inch wide page, so mark the check box Fit All Fields on One Page. Mark Access 2.0's new Calculate Percentages of the Total check box to show percentages with the category totals.

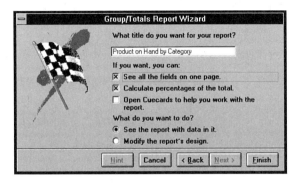

Fig. 14.14
Assigning a title to your report.

10. Click the See the Report with Data in It option button to display how the report appears in print. (If you click the Modify the Report's Design option button, the report appears in design mode.) Click Finish to display the report in print preview mode.

The basic report created by the Report Wizard appears in figure 14.15. Use the vertical and horizontal scroll bars to position the preview as illustrated. (Leave the report in print preview mode for now because you use this report as the basis for examples in subsequent sections of this chapter.)

Fig. 14.15
The basic report created by the Report Wizard.

III

Forms and Reports

The Access Report Wizard is not omniscient. The Wizard has mistakenly assumed that, because three columns have numeric values, you wanted to sum the Category ID, Product ID, and Supplier ID columns. With a few simple modifications, you can obtain a finished report with the information necessary to analyze Northwind's current inventory. (See "Modifying a Basic Report Wizard Report" later in this chapter.)

Using Access's Report Windows

The windows you use to design and run Access reports are easier to use than those windows you use for other basic Access functions. To open an existing Access report, click the Report button in the Database window, and then select a report name from the Database window. If you click the Design button or the New button to create a new report, the design mode toolbar appears with the buttons listed in table 14.1. Access 2.0 adds many new buttons to Access 1.x's report toolbar; the new buttons are indicated by the Access 2.0 icon in the margin.

Table 14.1		**Standard Toolbar Buttons in Report Design Mode**	
Button	**Function**		**Menu Choice**
⬚	Indicates design mode.		Not applicable
⬚	Opens the Print Preview window to show the way the report appears if printed. You can print the report from the Print Preview window.		File Print Preview
⬚	Prints a quick sample report with test data.		File Sample Preview
⬚	Saves the report.		File Save or Save As
⬚	Displays the Sorting and Grouping dialog used to establish the structure of reports and the order in which the data is presented.		View Sorting and Grouping
⬚	Displays the Properties dialog for the entire report, the sections of the report when you click the section divider bars, or the properties of a control when a control is selected.		View Properties

Button	Function	Menu Choice
	Displays a list of fields in the query or table that is the data source for the main report.	View Field List
	Opens the event handling code editing window.	View Code
	Toggles display of the toolbox.	View Toolbox
	Displays a palette from which you can select the color of the text, background (fill), and border of a control.	View Palette
	Opens the Database window.	Window 1:Database
	Returns the report to the state prior to the last modification.	Edit Undo
	Displays the Help menu for reports.	F1

The buttons not listed in table 14.1 serve the same purposes for both forms and reports. As is the case for form design mode, the report text formatting tools are enabled only when a control object that can contain text is selected.

If you double-click the name of an existing report, or click the Open button in the Database window, the report is displayed in print preview mode, which is the run mode for reports. The buttons on the toolbar in print preview mode are listed in table 14.2.

Table 14.2 Standard Toolbar Buttons in Report Print Preview Mode

Button	Function	Menu Choice
	Closes Print Preview and returns to Report Design View or to the Database window.	File Print Preview
	Displays the standard Windows Print dialog that enables you to select the number of pages and copies to print, and other basic printing parameters.	File Print

(continues)

III

Forms and Reports

Table 14.2	Continued		
Button	**Function**		**Menu Choice**
	Displays the Print Setup dialog. You set printing margins and other printing parameters in this dialog.		File Print Setup
	Toggles between full-page and full-size views of the report. Clicking the mouse when its pointer appears as the magnifying glass symbol produces the same effect.		None
 	Creates a rich-text format file that you can import into Word or other Windows word processor applications that support the .RTF format.		File Output To Rich-Text Format
 	Creates a .XLS file in Excel 2.1 (BIFF) format that you can import into Excel 2.1+.		File Output To Microsoft Excel
 	Adds the report as an attachment to a Microsoft Mail message in .RTF, .XLS, or .TXT (ASCII text) format.		File Send (Format)
 	Opens the Database window.		Window 1:Database
	Display the Cue Cards for reports.		Help Cue Cards
	Displays the Help menu for reports.		F1

(Margin icons labeled "Access 2.0" appear beside the rich-text, Excel, Mail, and Database rows.)

Printing reports as files in rich-text format is discussed in Chapter 22, "Using Access with Microsoft Word and Mail Merge"; and printing files in Excel BIFF format is discussed in Chapter 21, "Using Access with Microsoft Excel." Attaching files created from reports to Microsoft Mail messages is described in the next chapter.

Modifying a Basic Report Wizard Report

The Report Wizard creates the best possible final report in the first pass. Usually, the Wizard comes close enough to a finished product that you spend far less time modifying a Wizard-created basic report than you spend creating a report from the default blank template.

In the following sections, you use Access's report design features to make the report easier to read and more attractive.

Deleting, Relocating, and Editing Existing Controls

The first step in modifying the Wizard's report is to modify the existing controls on the report. You don't need to align the labels and text boxes precisely during the initial modification; control alignment is covered in "Aligning Controls Horizontally and Vertically," later in this chapter. To modify the Wizard's report to create space to add additional controls, follow these steps:

1. Click Cancel on the Print Preview toolbar to enter report design mode. The Wizard's report design appears in figure 14.16.

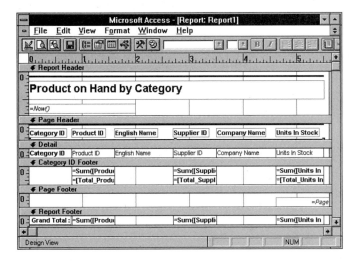

Fig. 14.16
The basic report in design mode.

2. Eliminate the unnecessary subtotals of fields with numeric field data types that the Wizard mistakenly totaled. Click the =Sum([Product ID]) text box in the Category ID Footer section, and press Delete to remove the subtotal. Select the =Sum([Supplier ID]) text box and also delete this subtotal.

3. The Report Wizard also adds two unnecessary percent of total text boxes. Repeat step 2 to delete the =[Total_Product ID]/[GrandTotal_ Product ID] and =[Total_Supplier ID]/[GrandTotal_Supplier ID] text boxes.

4. Repeat step 2 for the same text boxes in the Report Footer section of the report, but do not delete the Grand Total label. The report now creates category totals and grand totals only for Units in Stock.

III

Forms and Reports

5. This report is more useful if you include the value of both the inventory and the number of units on hand. To accommodate one or two additional columns, you must compress the widths of the fields. Category ID occupies a column, but you can display this column's content in the Category ID footer. Select and delete the Category ID label from the Page Header section and the Category ID text box from the Detail section. Your report appears as shown in figure 14.17.

Fig. 14.17
The basic report, after deleting the Category ID label and text box.

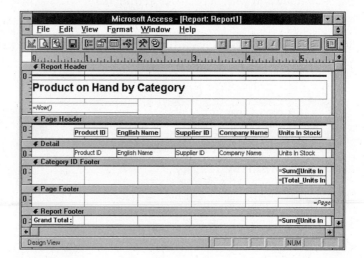

6. All the Page Header labels, Detail text boxes, and Totals text boxes in the Category ID Footer and Report Footer sections must be moved to the left as a group. Click the Product ID label to select it, and then press and hold down Shift. Click the remaining Page Header labels, each of the Detail text boxes, the two Totals text boxes in the Category ID Footer section, and the Grand Total text box in Report Footer section, and then release Shift.

7. Position the mouse pointer over the Product ID label at a location where the pointer turns into the symbol of the palm of a hand. Hold down the left mouse button and drag the selected fields to the left margin. Your report appears as shown in figure 14.18.

8. Editing and positioning the labels is easier if you left-justify the labels. Click a blank area of the report to deselect the group; select all the Page Header labels; and click the Left Justify button on the toolbar. Do the same for the Grand Total label.

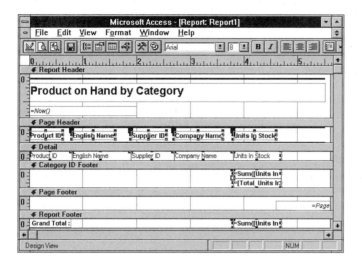

Fig. 14.18
Selected labels and
text boxes, moved
to the left margin
of the report.

9. The borders that create the ledger lines around the text boxes in the
Detail section are unnecessary for this report. Click the Palette button
on the toolbar to display the palette. Select each text box and set the
border color to Clear by clicking the Clear command button, as shown
on the palette in figure 14.19.

You also can hold down Shift and select all the text boxes in the Detail
section, and then mark the Clear Border check box to change all text
boxes at once.

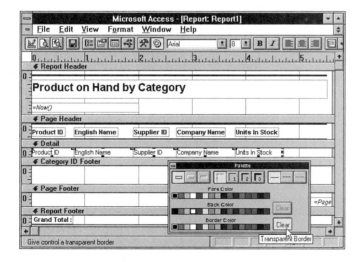

Fig. 14.19
Changing the
borders of the
Detail section
fields that you
want to clear.

III

Forms and Reports

10. The heavy ledger lines that enclose groups of five product lines are created by a rectangle control hidden under the text boxes in the Detail section. Temporarily increase the depth of the Detail section by dragging the Category ID Footer bar down 1/2 inch. Move the Product ID text box down to expose the rectangle control, as shown in figure 14.20. Select and delete the rectangle. Return the Product ID text box and the Category ID Footer bar to their original positions.

Fig. 14.20
Exposing and selecting the rectangle control under the Product ID field for deletion.

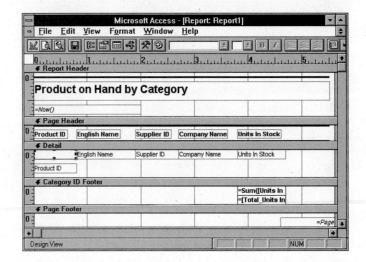

11. Edit the Product ID and Supplier ID labels to remove "ID," and decrease the width of each label. Edit the Units in Stock label to read only "Units." Reduce the width of the Product ID, Supplier ID, and Units in Stock text boxes to match the width of the labels. Relocate the labels to provide more space on the right side of the report, as shown in figure 14.21.

12. You now need to add a bound text box to identify the subtotal in the Category ID Footer section. Click the Field List button on the toolbar. Select Category ID from the list in the Field List window.

Click and drag the field symbol mouse pointer to the left margin of the Category ID Footer. Click the Bold button on the toolbar to add the bold attribute to the Category ID text box.

13. Click and drag the =[Total_Units In Stock]/[GrandTotal_Units In Stock] text box from its present location to the left of the =Sum([Units In Stock]) text box, and then move the Page Footer divider bar up to reduce the footer's depth (see fig. 14.21).

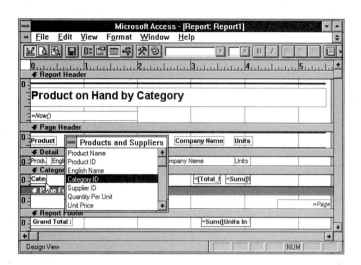

Fig. 14.21
The Product on
Hand by Category
report after
editing, resizing,
and relocating
existing controls.

14. Choose Select **R**eport from the Edit menu; click the Properties button of
the toolbar; and select Layout Properties in the drop-down list of the
Properties window. Type **Product on Hand by Category** as the `Caption`
property of the report.

15. Click the Save button of the toolbar to save your report. Type
rptProductOnHand in the Save As dialog, and then click OK.

Troubleshooting

*When I preview or print my report, a blank page is shown or printed after each
page with data.*

If the width of a report becomes greater than the net printable width (the
paper width, minus the sum of the left and right margins), the number of
report pages doubles. Columns of fields that do not fit the width of a page
print on a second page, similar to the printing method used by spreadsheet
applications. If your right margin is set beyond the right printing margin, or
the right edge of any controls on the report extend past the right printing
margin, the added pages often are blank. Change the printing margins or
reduce the width of your report so that it conforms to the printable page
width. (See "Adjusting Margins and Printing Conventional Reports" later in
this chapter.)

To check the progress of your work, periodically click the Print Preview button on the toolbar to display the report prior to printing. You can click the

Sample Preview button to display a report based on sample data more quickly. At this point, your Product on Hand by Category report appears in print preview mode as shown in figure 14.22.

Fig. 14.22
Previewing the
Product on Hand
by Category
report.

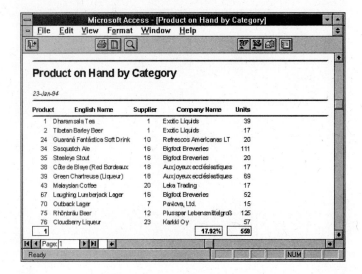

Using the *DLookUp()* Domain Aggregate Function to Print Product Category Names

All the employees of Northwind Traders may not have memorized the eight product category numbers that appear at the extreme left in the Category ID Footer section of the report. The query on which the report is based does not include the Category Name field of the Categories table. You can add the Category Name field to the Product and Suppliers query; however, adding a new field may cause problems with other objects that use the query. You can use Access's domain aggregate function, `DLookUp()`, to add the Category Name to your report.

To add the new Category Name field to the Category ID Footer section of the Product on Hand by Category report, follow these steps:

1. In report design mode, click the Toolbox button to display the toolbox.

2. Click the text box tool and add a new unbound text box to the right of the Category ID text box with the approximate dimensions shown in figure 14.23.

3. Click the new text box and type

   =DLookUp("[Category Name]","Categories","[Category ID] = Report!txtCategoryName") & "Category"

as the value of the text box.

[Category Name] is the value you want to return to the text box. Categories is the table that contains the Category Name field. [Category ID] = Report!txtCategoryName is the criteria that selects the record in the Categories table with a Category ID value equal to the value in the Category ID text box of your report. The Report prefix is necessary to distinguish between the Category ID field of the Categories table and a control object of the same name. (Report is not necessary in this example, but is included to show the general form of the DLookUp() syntax).

4. Select the Category ID text box, and click the Properties button of the toolbar. Select Other Properties in the drop-down list of the Properties window and type **txtCategoryName** as the value of the Name property of the control (see fig. 14.23).

5. Click the Print Preview button of the toolbar. Your Product on Hand by Category report appears as shown in figure 14.24.

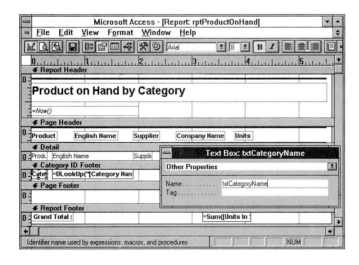

Fig. 14.23
Adding an unbound text box to display the Category Name.

Fig. 14.24

The Product on Hand by Category report with the Category Name text box added.

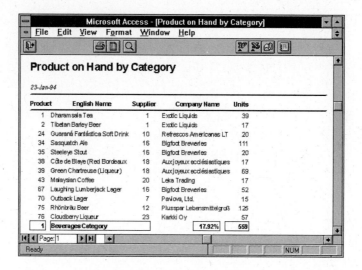

Troubleshooting

#error appears in the Category Name text box when I preview or print the report.

Your DLookUp() expression contains a typographical error, or one of the objects you specified does not exist. Make sure that the entry in the Category Name text box is typed exactly as shown in the preceding step 3. If the name of the field in the table or query being searched is the same as the name of the control, make sure that you add the Report! prefix to the control name. For example, you need to add Report! if you assign "Category Name" as the name of the new control added in the preceding example.

Adding Other Calculated Controls to the Report

Calculated controls, such as the DLookUp() control you added in the preceding section, are quite useful in reports. You use calculated controls to determine extended values, such as quantity times unit price or quantity times cost. Now you have enough space at the right of the report to add a column for the Unit Cost field and a column for the extended inventory value, which is Unit Price multiplied by Units on Hand. To add these controls, follow these steps:

1. Click the Toolbox button of the toolbar to display the Access toolbox if it isn't already displayed.

2. Click the Label tool in the toolbox and place the label to the right of the Units label in the Page Header section. Type **Price** as the label.

3. Add another label to the right of Price, and type **Value**.

4. Click the Field List button on the toolbar to display the Field List dialog. Select Unit Price, and drag the field symbol to a position under the Price label in the Detail section. Drop the text box.

5. Select the Unit Price text box and the Price and Value labels. Change their border color to Clear by clicking the Clear button of the palette. The new columns appear as in figure 14.25.

Fig. 14.25
Adding the Price and Value columns to the report.

6. To create the calculated Value text box, click the Text Box button in the toolbox and add the text box to the right of the Unit Price text box.

7. Type **=[Units in Stock]*[Unit Price]** as the expression for the Value text box. Set the Border Color of the text box to Clear.

8. Repeat steps 6 and 7 to create the Value subtotal text box in the Category ID Footer section, but type **=Sum([Units in Stock]*[Unit Price])** as the subtotal expression. Click the Bold button on the toolbar to set the FontBold property to **Yes**. Set the Name property of this text box in the Other Properties window to **txtTotalValue**.

9. Repeat step 8 to create the Value grand total box in the Report Footer section. Set the Name property of this text box in the Other Properties window to **txtGrandTotalValue**.

Tip

Entering expressions is easier if you press Shift+F2 to open the Zoom box or double-click the text box to display the Properties dialog and enter the expression as the ControlSource property.

III

Forms and Reports

10. Add another unbound text box to the left of the txtTotalValue text box. Type **=[txtTotalValue]/[txtGrandTotalValue]** as the value of the ControlSource property and set the value of the Format property to **Percent**. The report design appears, as shown in figure 14.26.

Fig. 14.26
Controls added to calculate the value of products, plus value subtotals and grand totals.

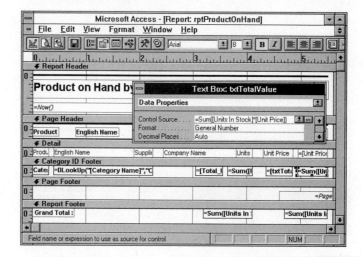

11. Click the Print Preview button on the toolbar to check the result of your additions. The report appears as in figure 14.27; use the vertical scroll bar, if necessary, to display the category subtotal. You can correct any misaligned values and the spacing of the rows of the Detail section in the next section.

Tip
If the Enter Parameter Value dialog appears, you misspelled one or more field names in the expressions; click Cancel and check the properties you added in steps 7 through 9.

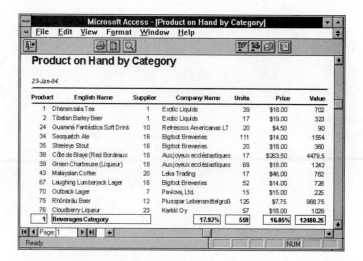

Fig. 14.27
Page 1 of the report, with calculated product values and value subtotals.

12. Click the Bottom of Report page selector button to display the grand totals for the report (see fig. 14.28). The record selector buttons become page selector buttons when you display reports in run mode.

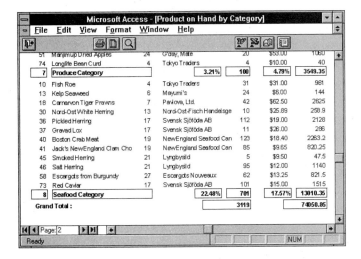

Fig. 14.28
The last page of the report, with grand totals for Units and Value.

Aligning and Formatting Controls; Adjusting Line Spacing

On reports, the exact alignment of label and text box controls is more important than alignment on forms because in the printed report, any misalignment is obvious. Formatting the controls further improves the appearance and readability of the report.

The spacing of the report's rows in the Detail section is controlled by the depth of the section. White space above and below headers and footers is controlled by the depth of their sections and the vertical position of the controls within the sections. You need to adjust the alignment and formatting of controls and line spacing of sections to create a professional-looking report.

Aligning Controls Horizontally and Vertically

Alignment of controls is accomplished by first selecting rows to align, and then aligning the columns. Access 2.0 provides several new control sizing and alignment options to make the process easier. The Align menu of Access 1.x is replaced by the Format menu in Access 2.0; this brings Access's menu bar into conformance with other members of the Microsoft Office suite. To size and align the controls you created, follow these steps:

Access

2.0

1. Click the Close button of the toolbar to return to design mode.

III

Forms and Reports

2. You can adjust the height of all the text boxes simultaneously to fit the font used for their contents. Choose Select All from the Edit menu to select all the controls in the report.

3. Choose Size from the Format menu to display the submenu with the new size adjustment options of Access 2.0, as shown in figure 14.29. Choose To Fit from the submenu to adjust the height of the selected controls. All the controls are adjusted to the proper height. To deselect all the controls, click a blank area of the report.

Fig. 14.29
Access 2.0's new sizing options.

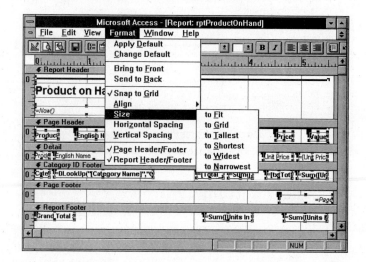

Tip
The title of the report in design mode may have one or more characters missing as a result of the size-to-fit operation. The missing characters reappear when you change to print preview mode.

4. Select all the labels in the Page Header sections. Choose Align from the Format menu, and then click Top in the submenu. This process aligns the tops of each selected label with the uppermost selected label. Click a blank area of the report to deselect the labels.

5. Select all the text boxes in the Detail section, and repeat step 4 for the text boxes.

6. Select the labels and text boxes in the Category ID Footer and Report Footer sections, and repeat step 4.

7. Select all the controls in the Units column. Choose Align from the Format menu, and then click Right so that the column is aligned to the right edge of the text farthest to the right of the column.

8. Select all controls in the Values column (except the Page Footer text box) and repeat step 7.

9. Click the Print Preview button on the toolbar to display the report with the improved alignment of rows and columns.

Formatting Controls

Preceding figure 14.27 shows that you need to revise the formatting of several controls. Product ID and Supplier ID values are right-aligned. Center or left justification is more appropriate for values used as codes rather than as numbers to total. The repeated dollar signs in the Unit Price field detract from readability, and the format of the Value column is inappropriate here.

To change the Format property of these fields, follow these steps:

1. Click the Close button of the toolbar to return to design mode.

2. Select the Product ID text box in the Detail section and click the Center-Align Text button on the toolbar.

3. Select and then center-justify the Supplier ID text box in the detail section. Do the same for the Category ID text box in the Category ID Footer section.

4. Double-click the Unit Price text box to open its Properties dialog.

5. Move to the Format text box and type **#,#00.00**. This procedure eliminates the dollar sign, but preserves the monetary formatting.

6. Repeat steps 4 and 5 for the Values text box. Dollar signs aren't required in the Detail section.

7. Select the Values subtotal in the Category ID Footer. Click Format in the Properties dialog and type **$#,#00.00**. Accountants use dollar signs to identify subtotals and totals in ledgers.

8. Select the Values grand total in the report footer and type **$#,#00.00** as the Values grand total's Format property.

9. The Values grand total in the Report Footer is the most important element of the report, so click the Palette button on the toolbar and click the 2-point border button. This procedure increases the thickness of the border around the grand total.

10. Click the Print Preview button on the toolbar to check formatting modifications. Click the Bottom of Report page selector button to display the last page of the report (see fig. 14.30).

Tip

If you select Currency formatting, instead of entering **$#,#00.00**, to add a dollar sign to the value, your totals do not align. Currency formatting offsets the number to the left to provide space for the parenthesis that accountants use to specify negative monetary values.

III

Forms and Reports

Fig. 14.30
The last page of
the report, with
the correct *Format*
property assigned
to the values.

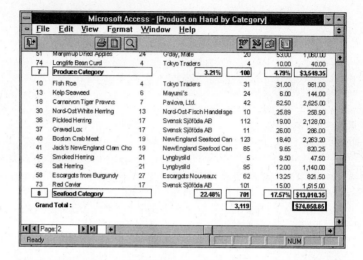

Adjusting Line Spacing

The spacing of controls in the Page Header section, shown in preceding figure
14.27, is greater than necessary, and the depth of the controls in Report
Header is out of proportion to the size of the text. The line spacing of the
remainder of the report's sections is satisfactory, but you can change this
spacing, too. Minimizing line spacing enables you to print a report on fewer
sheets of paper.

To change the spacing of the Page Header and Detail sections of the report,
follow these steps:

1. Click the Close button of the toolbar to return to design mode.

2. Select all the labels in the Page Header, and move the group as close to
   the top of the section as possible.

3. Click the bottom line of the Page Header, and move the line as close to
   the bottom of the text boxes as possible. (You may need to temporarily
   move the Detail section header to be able to select the line.)

4. Click a blank area of the report and then move the Detail section
   header to the bottom of the labels. You cannot reduce the depth of a
   section to less than the Height property of the label with the maximum
   height in the section.

5. Select all the text boxes in the Detail section, and move those boxes as a
   group to the top of the section. Move the Category ID footer up to the
   bottom of the text boxes.

Tip

You may need
to return to
design mode
and adjust the
width or posi-
tion of the Sub-
totals and Grand
Totals text boxes
to align these
values with the
values for the
individual
products.

Tip

You can make
more precise
adjustment to
the size of
controls and
line spacing if
you choose
Snap to Grid
from the For-
mat menu to
toggle Snap to
Grid off.

6. Move the label and the text box in the Report Header section upward to minimize the amount of white space in the Report Header.

7. Click the Print Preview button on the toolbar to check the Page Header depth and Detail line spacing. The spacing shown in figure 14.31 is close to the minimum you can achieve. You cannot reduce the line spacing of a section to less than the spacing required by the tallest text box or label by reducing the section's Height property in the Properties box because Access rejects the entry and substitutes the prior value.

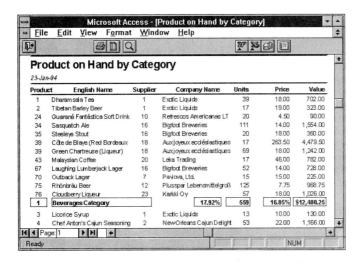

Fig. 14.31
The report in print preview mode after the depth of the Report Header, Page Header, and Detail sections is adjusted.

8. Click the Zoom button on the toolbar to display the report in full-page view. Clicking the mouse when the pointer is the magnifying glass symbol accomplishes the same results as the Zoom button. Alternate clicks toggle between full-size and full-page views.

9. Choose Save from the File menu to save your changes.

Adjusting Margins and Printing Conventional Reports

The full-page Print Preview of the report shows the report as it would print, using Access's default printing margins of one inch on the top, bottom, and sides of the report (see fig. 14.32). To change the default printing margins, choose Options from the View menu, and then select Printing from the list.

III

Forms and Reports

The rest of the adjustments to the printed version of the report are made in the Print Setup dialog. The procedure for printing a report also applies to printing the data contained in tables and queries, as well as single-record or continuous forms.

Fig. 14.32
The report in full-page view.

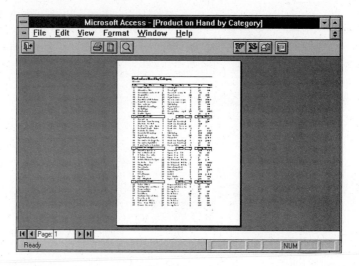

To change the printing margins for a report, follow these steps:

1. Open the Print Setup dialog of figure 14.33 by clicking the Setup button on the toolbar in report run mode. You also can display the Print Setup dialog at any time by choosing Print Setup from the File menu.

Fig. 14.33
The Print Setup dialog for printing data sheets, forms, and reports.

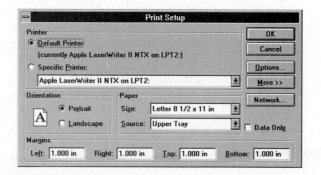

2. The Print Setup dialog is similar to the Print Setup dialog of other Windows applications, but an additional section for printing margins is included. To increase the amount of information on a page, decrease the top and bottom margins. Marking the Data Only check box enables you to print only the data in the report. Report and Page Headers and Footers do not print when Data Only is specified.

3. Enter **2.0** inches for the left margin and substitute **0.75** inches for the right, top, and bottom margins. Click OK. The full-page view of the report with the revised margins appears (see fig. 14.34).

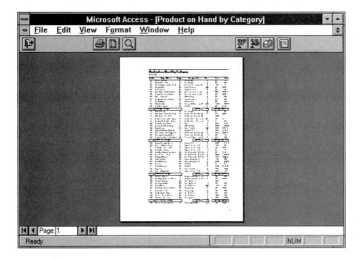

Fig. 14.34
The full-page view of the report with new printing margins applied.

4. To print the report, click the Print button on the toolbar, or choose Print from the File menu. The standard Print dialog appears for the printer specified in Windows as the default printer. Figure 14.35 shows the Print dialog for a PostScript printer, as an example.

5. You can choose to print all or part of a report, print the report to a file for later printing, and select the number of copies to print. Clicking Options enables you to change the parameters applicable to the printer you are using. Click OK to print the report.

The Print Setup dialog includes a More button that expands the basic Report Setup dialog to establish specifications for printing mailing labels and other multiple column reports. These specifications, and the way these specifications are set, are described in the next section.

Tip
The printing margins you establish in the Print Setup dialog for a report apply to the active report only; each report has a unique set of margins. The margin settings are saved when you save the report.

III

Forms and Reports

Fig. 14.35
The Print dialog
controls printing
of data sheets,
forms, and reports.

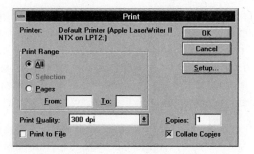

Using the Group *KeepTogether* Property to Prevent Widowed Records

Access 2.0 includes a new KeepTogether property for groups that prevents widowed records from appearing at the bottom of the page. Depending on your report section depths, you may find that a few records of the next group appear at the bottom of the page. You can force a page break when an entire group does not fit on one page by following these steps:

1. Click the Sorting and Grouping button of the toolbar to open the Sorting and Grouping dialog.

2. Select the field with the group symbol in the selection button that corresponds to the group you want to keep together. In this example, select Category ID.

3. Open the Keep Together drop-down list and select Whole Group, as shown in figure 14.36.

4. Close the Sorting and Grouping dialog, and click Print Preview to see the result of applying the group KeepTogether property.

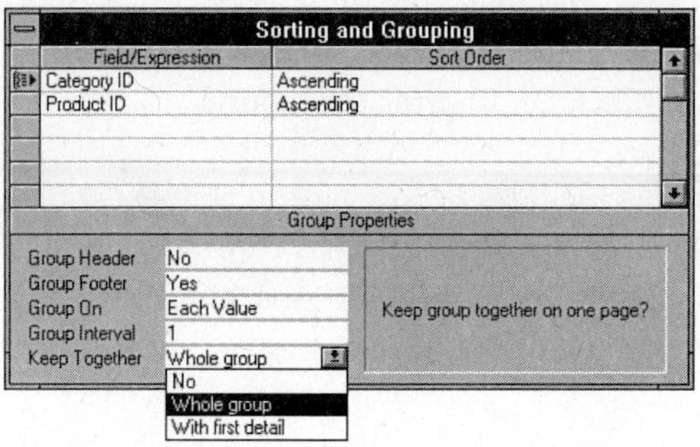

Fig. 14.36
Setting the group
KeepTogether
property.

The Report Wizard made the other entries in the Sorting and Grouping dialog for you. The next chapter describes how to use the Sorting and Grouping dialog for reports you design without the aid of the Wizard.

Printing Multicolumn Reports as Mailing Labels

Access provides the capability of printing multicolumn reports. You can create a single-column report with the Report Wizard, for example, and then arrange the report to print values from the Detail section in a specified number of columns across the page. The most common application of multi-column reports is the creation of mailing labels.

You can create mailing lists with the Report Wizard, or you can start with a blank form. The Report Wizard's advantage is that it includes the dimensions of virtually every kind of adhesive label for dot matrix or laser printers made by the Avery Commercial Products division. You select the product number of the label you plan to use, and Access determines the number of columns and rows per page and the margins for the Detail section of the report. You can also customize the Mailing Label Wizard for odd-size labels or labels produced by other manufacturers.

The Northwind Traders database includes a Customer Mailing Labels report, which you can modify to suit the design of any mailing label. Figure 14.37 shows the Detail section of the Customer Mailing Labels report with the font changed to Courier New in a 10-point font and the size of the label adjusted to 2.5 by 0.833 inches.

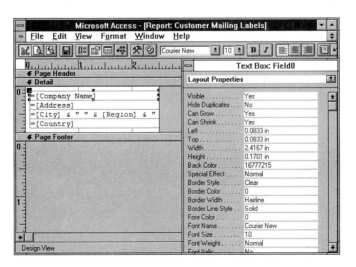

Fig. 14.37

The modified Customer Mailing Labels report in design mode.

The number of columns in a row and the number of rows on a page are determined by settings you select in the lower sections of the expanded Print Setup dialog, shown in figure 14.38. This dialog appears when you click the Setup button on the toolbar in print preview mode. (Click the All Countries option button of the Country Filter dialog; then click OK to get from design to print preview mode.) Then click the More button.

Fig. 14.38
The expanded version of the Print Setup dialog, displayed when you click the More button.

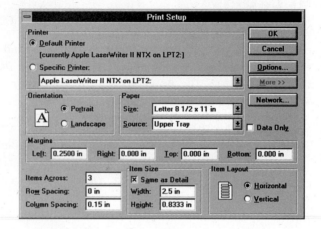

The text boxes, check boxes, and option buttons enable you to perform the following procedures:

- The ItemsAcross property sets the number of labels across the page; in this example, this property changed from 2 to 3.

- The Left and Top margin properties determine the position at which the upper left corner of the first label on the page is printed. These values cannot be less than about 0.2 inch for most laser printers. Labels designed for laser printers are die-cut so that the marginal areas remain on the backing sheet when you remove the individual labels.

- The Width property in the Item Size group overrides the left margin, and the Height property overrides the bottom margin you establish in Report Design View if you don't select Same as Detail to use the margins you set in the Detail section.

- ColumnSpacing determines the position of the left edge of columns to the right of the first column.

- RowSpacing and the Height property determine the number of labels that fit vertically on a page and the vertical distance between successive labels. If you set RowSpacing to zero, the vertical spacing of the labels is determined by the depth of your Detail section.

■ Horizontal Item Layout causes the labels to print in columns from left to right, and then in rows from the top to the bottom of the page.

■ Vertical Item Layout causes the labels to print in *snaking* column style, in the first column, top to bottom, and then the next column, top to bottom, and so on.

The values of these properties are set for three columns of 11 labels per page and appear in the expanded Print Setup dialog.

After you set the dimensions of the mailing labels and click OK, the full-size view of the labels appears as shown in figure 14.39.

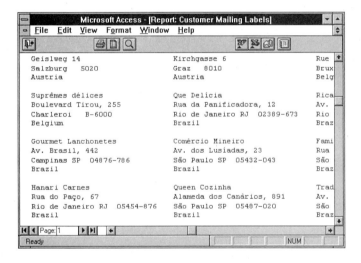

Fig. 14.39
Three-across mailing labels shown in Print Preview's full-size view.

Click the Zoom button on the toolbar to display the full-page layout. To test the label layout properties you set, print only the first page of the labels on standard paper or a xerographic duplicate of the label template supplied with labels designed for laser printing.

You may need to make minor alignment adjustments because the position of the upper left corner of the printer's image and the upper left corner of the paper may not correspond exactly.

If you select Vertical Item Layout, the technique used to print successive Detail rows is identical to the technique used by word-processing applications and page layout applications, such as Aldus PageMaker, to create newspaper (*snaking*) columns. When the first column fills to the specified Height property, Detail rows fill the next column to the right.

III

Forms and Reports

> **Note**
>
> Newspaper columns are suitable for mailing labels but are difficult to format correctly when you convert other kinds of single-column reports to multiple-column. For newspaper columns to operate at all, you need to set the KeepTogether property of the Detail section of the report to No and then set the Height property so that the field data for a single record appears in a single set of rows. If the Detail data includes Memo fields with variable amounts of text in a text box with the CanGrow property set to Yes, formatting newspaper columns properly becomes almost impossible. The easier approach is to lay out the Detail section with multiple columns in design mode, rather than having Access attempt to create newspaper columns.

From Here...

Access 2.0's report generation capability is unrivaled by any other desktop database management application or client-server front-end design tool. Access's report design capabilities are one of the principal incentives for using Access 2.0, rather than Visual Basic 3.0, for database applications. This chapter introduced you to the basic elements of creating reports using the Report Wizards and how to modify the reports the Wizards create for you. Refer to the following chapters for related information:

- Chapter 15, "Preparing Advanced Reports," describes how to sort and group reports, create reports from a blank report, and send reports as files attached to Microsoft Mail messages.

- Chapter 18, "Creating Macros for Forms and Reports," shows you how to write macros that print reports automatically.

- Chapter 20, "Adding Graphics to Forms and Reports," leads you through the methods of using object frame controls to add graphic images, such as logos, to reports.

Chapter 15

Preparing Advanced Reports

Access 2.0's Report Wizards are capable of creating reports that you use "as is" or modify to suit most of your database reporting requirements. In some cases, however, you may need to create reports that are more complex than, or differ from, those offered by the Report Wizards. As an example, you may need to apply special grouping and sorting methods to your reports. Including subreports within your reports requires that you start from a blank report form, rather than using one of the Report Wizards.

To fully understand the process of designing advanced Access reports, you should be familiar with Access functions, one subject of Chapter 9, "Understanding Operators and Expressions in Access." You also need to understand the methods used to create and design forms, which are covered in Chapters 12 and 13. Access functions, such as Sum(), and expressions like ="Subtotal of" & [*Field Name*] & ":" are used extensively in reports. The toolbox used to add controls to forms also adds controls when you create or modify reports. You assign properties of controls, such as labels and text boxes, with the methods you use with forms. If you skipped over Chapter 9 or Chapters 12 and 13, you may want to refer to the sections of those chapters that cover unfamiliar subjects or terminology in this chapter.

Grouping and Sorting Report Data

Most reports you create require that the data in the reports are organized in groups and subgroups, in a style similar to the outline of a book. The Report Wizards let you establish the initial grouping and sorting properties for your data, but you may want to change the arrangement of your report's data after reviewing the Report Wizards' first draft.

Some of the main topics covered in this chapter are

- Grouping and sorting report data

- Starting from a blank report

- Controlling report page breaks

- Printing headers and footers

- Incorporating subreports

- Sending a report as a file attached to a Microsoft Mail message

III

Forms and Reports

You can modify these report properties in design mode with the Sorting and Grouping dialog (see fig. 15.1). This section uses the Product on Hand by Category report you created in the preceding chapter. The sorting and grouping methods described here, however, apply to any report you create. To display the dialog, open the report in Design View and click the Sorting and Grouping button on the toolbar.

Fig. 15.1
The Sorting and Grouping dialog for the report.

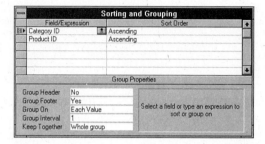

The Sorting and Grouping dialog enables you to determine the field(s) or expression(s) on which the products are grouped, for a maximum of three levels. You can sort the grouped data in ascending or descending order, but you must select one or the other; "unsorted" is not an option. The Sorting and Grouping symbol in the selection button at the left of the window indicates that the field or expression in the adjacent column is used to group the records.

Grouping Data

The method you use to group data depends on the data in the field by which you group. You can group by categories, in which case each category must be represented by a unique value. You can group data by a range of values, which usually are numeric, but you also can group by an alphabetic range. You can use the data in a field to group the data, or you can substitute an expression as the basis for the grouping.

Grouping by Category

You elected to group by category when you told the Report Wizard to use Category ID as the field by which to group. You can alter the grouping sequence easily with the Sorting and Grouping window. To group by Supplier ID, for example, select Supplier ID as the first group field. Change the title label in the Report Header to **Product on Hand by Supplier**, and change the expression for the leftmost text box in the Supplier ID Footer to

=**"Subtotal for** " & **[Company Name]** & ":". Delete the text box with the DLookUp() function and increase the width of the =Subtotal... text box. The report appears as shown in figure 15.2.

> **Note**
>
> You cannot limit the number of rows of detail data in a report by the properties or the controls of reports, unless you write a Top*N* or Top*N*Percent query using Access SQL. (Search on-line help for the TopValues property to learn more about Top*N* and Top*N*Percent queries.) All the rows of a table or query appear somewhere in the Detail section of the report, provided the report includes a Detail section with at least one control. To include only a selected range of dates in a report, for example, you need to base the report on a query with the criteria necessary to select the Detail records. If the user is to choose the range of records to include in the report, use a parameter query as the data source for the report.

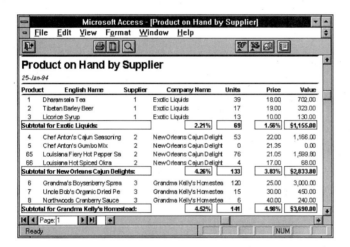

Fig. 15.2
The effect of changing the report grouping so that it displays records by Supplier ID.

If you use a systematic code for grouping, you can group by the first five or fewer characters of the code. With an expression, you can group by any set of characters within a field. To group by the second and third digits of a code, for example, use the expression =Mid([*Field Name*],2,2).

◄ "Text-Manipula-
tion Func-
tions," p. 332

If your table or query contains appropriate data, you can group reports by more than one level by creating subgroups. The Employee Sales by Country report (one of the Northwind Traders sample reports), for example, uses groups (Country) and subgroups (Employee) to organize orders received within a range of dates. Open the Employee Sales by Country report in design mode to view the additional section created by a subgroup.

III

Forms and Reports

Grouping by Range

You often need to sort reports by ranges of values. (If you opened the Employee Sales by Country report, close this report and reopen the Product on Hand by Category report in design mode.) If you want to divide the Product on Hand by Category report into a maximum of six sections, each beginning with a five-letter group of the alphabet (A through E, F through J, and so on) based on the English Name field, the entries in the Sorting and Grouping dialog should look like the entries in figure 15.3.

Fig. 15.3
The Sorting and Grouping criteria to group records in alphabetical intervals.

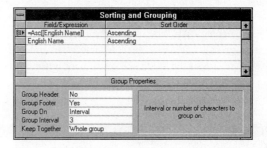

The =Asc([English Name]) function of Access Basic returns the ASCII (numeric) value of the first character of its string argument, the English Name field. You set the Group On specification to Interval, and then set the Group Interval to 3. This setup groups the data into names beginning with A through C, D through F, and so on (see fig. 15.4). You delete all of the text boxes in the group footer, because subtotals by alphabetic groups are not significant. Although of limited value in this report, an alphabetic grouping often is useful for grouping long, alphabetized lists to speed entry location.

◀ "Functions for Date and Time," p. 330

If you group data on a field with a Date/Time data type, Access enables you to set the GroupOn property in the Sorting and Grouping dialog to Year, Qtr (quarter), Month, Week, Day, Hour, or Minute. To group records so that values of the same quarter for several years print in sequence, type **=DatePart("q",[*Field Name*])** in the Field/Expression column of the Sorting and Grouping dialog.

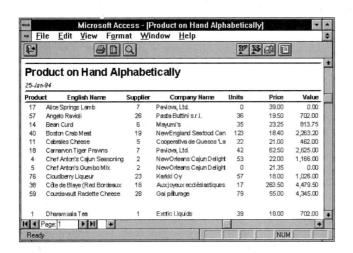

Fig. 15.4
A report in which
products are
categorized by
three-letter
alphabetic
intervals.

Sorting Data Groups

Although most data sorting within groups is based on the values contained in a field, you also can sort by expressions. When compiling an inventory valuation list, the products with the highest inventory value are the most important, and users of the report may want these products listed first in a group. This decision requires a sort of the records within groups on the expression `=[Units in Stock]*[Unit Price]`, the same expression used to calculate the Value column of the report. The required entries are shown in the Sorting and Grouping window of figure 15.5.

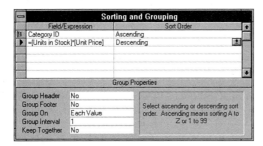

Fig. 15.5
Grouping data by
interval on an
expression.

The descending sort on the inventory value expression results in the report shown in figure 15.6. As expected, the products with the highest inventory value appear first in each field.

III

Forms and Reports

Fig. 15.6

The Product on Hand by Category report, with groups sorted by inventory value.

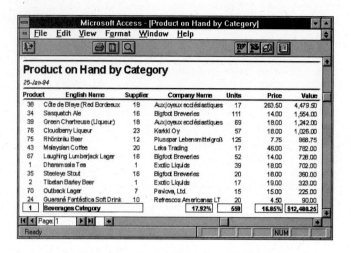

Working from a Blank Report

Usually, the fastest way to set up a report is to use one of the Report Wizards to create a basic report and then modify the basic report as described in the previous sections of this chapter. If you create a simple report, however, the time needed to modify a standard report style created by the Report Wizard may be more than you need to create a report by using the default blank report provided by Access.

◄ "Creating a Monthly Product Sales Crosstab Query" p. 393

The Basis for a Subreport

To create a report to use as the Monthly Sales by Category subreport (sbr1993MonthlyCategorySales) in the following section of this chapter, follow these steps:

1. Close the Product on Hand by Category report, and click the Query tab in the Database window.

2. Select the qry1993MonthlyProductSales query that you created in Chapter 10, and click the Design button. A slightly modified version of this crosstab query serves as the data source for the report of the same name.

3. Change the field name of the first column from Product ID to Category ID by opening the Field list and double-clicking the Category ID field name. You need the Category ID field to link with the Category ID field in the Products on Hand query that is used as the data source for the Products on Hand by Category report.

4. Delete the English Name column. The modified query appears as shown in figure 15.7.

5. From the **F**ile menu, choose Save **A**s and name the modified query **qryMonthlyCategorySales**. Your query result set appears as shown in figure 15.8.

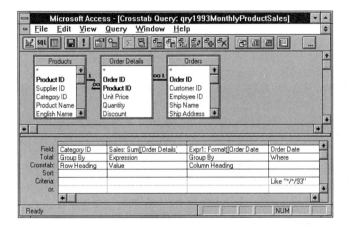

Fig. 15.7
The modified crosstab query for the Monthly Sales by Category subreport.

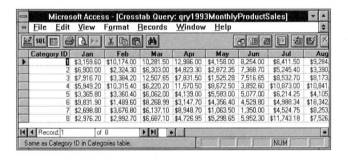

Fig. 15.8
The result set returned by the crosstab query of figure 15.7.

6. Click the New Report button of the toolbar. The New dialog appears.

7. The qryMonthlyCategorySales query is selected automatically as the query on which to base the report. Click the Blank Report button. Access creates the default blank report shown in figure 15.9.

III

Forms and Reports

Fig. 15.9
The starting report
presented by
Access after you
click Blank Report
in the New dialog.

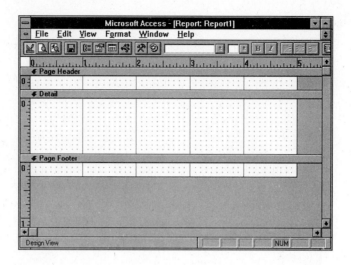

Adding and Deleting Sections of Your Report

When you create a report from a blank template or modify a report created
by the Report Wizard, you may want to add a new section to the report by
using the following guidelines:

- To add Report Headers and Footers as a pair, choose Report **H**eader/
Footer from the F**o**rmat menu.

- To add Page Headers and Footers as a pair, choose **P**age Hdr/Ftr from
the F**o**rmat menu.

 - To add a group Header or Footer, select [Category ID]; then click the
Sorting and Grouping button on the toolbar and set the GroupHeader or
GroupFooter property value to Yes.

A blank report, with the headers and footers for each section that you can
include in a report, appears in figure 15.10.

If you group the data in more than one level (group, subgroup, sub-subgroup), you can add a group header and footer for each level of grouping.
This action adds another pair of sections for each subgroup level to your
report.

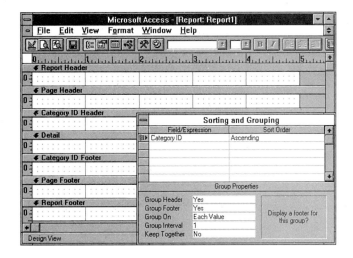

Fig. 15.10
A blank report
with all sections
added.

You delete sections from reports by using methods similar to those used to create the sections. To delete unwanted sections, use the following guidelines:

■ To delete the Detail section or an individual Report Header, Report Footer, Page Header, or Page Footer section, delete all the controls from the section, and then drag the divider bar below up so that the section has no depth. To delete a report footer, drag the bottom margin of the report to the Report Footer border. These sections aren't actually deleted but sections with no depth do not print or affect the report's layout.

■ To delete report headers and footers as a pair, choose Report **H**eader/ Footer from the F**o**rmat menu. If the report header or footer includes a control, a message box warns you that you will lose the controls in the deleted sections.

■ To delete page headers and footers as a pair, choose **P**age Header/Footer from the F**o**rmat menu. A warning message box appears if either section contains controls.

■ To delete a group header or footer, click the Sorting and Grouping button on the toolbar and set the value of the GroupHeader or GroupFooter property to No.

III

Forms and Reports

> **Note**
>
> Page and report headers and footers that incorporate thin lines at the upper border of the header or footer can be difficult to delete individually. Executive-style reports created by the Form Wizard use thin lines difficult to distinguish from the edges of borders. To make these lines visible, choose Select **A**ll from the **E**dit menu to add sizing anchors to the lines. Hold down the Shift key and click the controls you want to save to deselect these controls, and then press the Delete key to delete the remaining selected lines.

Controlling Page Breaks and the Printing of Page Headers and Footers

Manual page breaks are controlled by the Force New Page and Keep Together properties of the group Header, Detail section, and group Footer sections of the report. To set these properties, double-click the section border of the group to display the Properties dialog for the section. ForceNewPage causes an unconditional page break immediately before printing the section. If you set the KeepTogether property to Yes, and insufficient room is available on the current page to print the entire section, a page break occurs and the section prints on the next page.

 To control whether page headers or footers print on the first or last page of a report, choose Select **R**eport from the **E**dit menu and then click the Properties button on the toolbar. You then select a Page Headers and Page Footers printing option in the Layout Properties window (see fig. 15.11).

Fig. 15.11
The Properties window for a report, displaying page-section printing options.

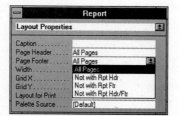

Creating the Monthly Sales by Category Report

The Monthly Sales by Category report is an example of a report that lends itself to starting with a blank report. This report includes information about total monthly sales of products by category. Comparing the monthly sales to the inventory level of a category enables the report's user to estimate inventory turnover rates. This report serves two purposes—as a report and as a subreport within another report. You add the Monthly Sales by Category report as a subreport in the Incorporating Subreports section.

The crosstab query that acts as the report's data source is closely related to a report, but the crosstab query doesn't include detail records (see Chapter 10, "Creating Multitable and Crosstab Queries"). Each row of the query consists of subtotals of the sales for a category for each month of the year. One row appears below the inventory value subtotal when the subreport is linked to the main report, so this report needs only a Detail section. Each detail row, however, requires a *header* label to print the month. The Category ID field is included so you can verify that the data is linked correctly.

To create the Monthly Sales by Category report (and sub-report), follow these steps:

1. Delete all sections of your blank report except the Detail section. Snap to Grid is selected, and 10 by 12 grid dots appear by default in blank reports.

2. Drag the bottom margin of the detail section down so that you have an inch or two of depth in the section. You need maneuvering room to relocate the text boxes and associated labels that you add in the following steps.

3. Click the Sorting and Grouping button on the toolbar to display the dialog, and select Category ID as the field to use to sort the data with a standard ascending sort. Close the Sorting and Grouping dialog.

4. Click the Field List button on the toolbar, select Category ID, and drag the field symbol to the Detail section.

5. Click the Category ID label, and relocate the label to the upper left of the detail section and the Category ID test box to the lower left. Adjust the depth of the label and the text box to 0.2 inches (two grid dots) and the width to 0.5 inches (five dots). Edit the text of the label to read **ID**.

6. Click and drag the Jan field in the field list to the right of the Category ID field. Move the label to the top of the section, adjacent to the right border of the field to its left. Move the text box under the label. Adjust the label and text box depth to 2 dots, the label width to 3 dots and the text box width to 8 dots. Edit the text of the label to delete the colon.

7. Repeat step 6 for the months of Feb through Jun. The report design now appears as shown in figure 15.12.

Fig. 15.12

The report with labels and text boxes added for the first six months of 1993.

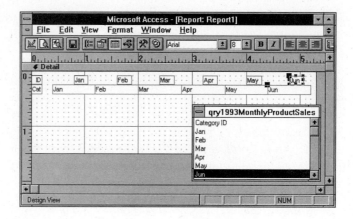

8. Click each label while holding down the Shift key so that all the labels (and labels only) are selected.

9. Click the Bold button of the toolbar to add the bold attribute to the labels. Then click the Center Text button to center the labels above the text boxes.

10. Select the Category ID text box, and click the Bold button on the toolbar.

11. Choose Select **A**ll from the **E**dit menu, and drag the labels and text boxes down one dot from the top of the Detail section. Click a blank area of the report to deselect the controls.

12. If the toolbox is invisible, click the Toolbox button of the toolbar. Click the Line tool and add a line at the top edge of the labels. Drag the line's right-end handle to the right edge of the Jun text box.

13. Click the Palette button, and click the 2-point line thickness button.

14. Repeat steps 12 and 13 for another identical line, but add the new line under the labels.

15. Drag the margins of the Detail section to within one dot of the bottom and right edge of the controls. The design of the report appears as shown in figure 15.13.

16. Click the Print Preview button on the toolbar to verify the design. The full-size view of the report appears (see fig. 15.14).

17. Choose Save **A**s from the **F**ile menu, and type **rptMonthly CategorySales** as the name of the report.

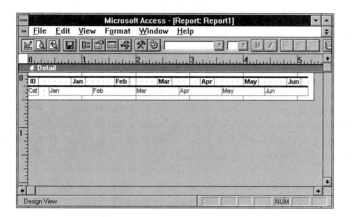

Fig. 15.13

The layout of the detail section of the report.

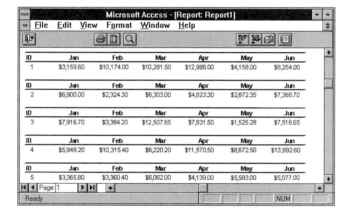

Fig. 15.14

The report in print preview mode.

To add the remaining months of the year to your report, follow these steps:

1. To accommodate another row of labels and text boxes, increase the depth of the Detail section by dragging the bottom margin down (about one inch).

2. Choose Select **A**ll from the **E**dit menu.

3. Press Ctrl+C to copy the labels and text boxes to the Clipboard.

4. Press Ctrl+V to paste a copy of the labels and text boxes to the Detail section.

5. Move this copy under the original labels and text boxes, spaced one grid dot below the originals, as shown in figure 15.15.

III

Forms and Reports

Fig. 15.15
The report design, with a copy of the labels and text boxes added.

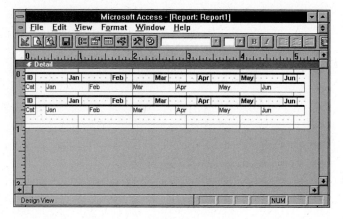

6. Click a blank area of the report to deselect the controls, and then select the new Category ID text box. Delete the Category ID text box. Deleting this text box also deletes the associated label.

7. Edit the labels and text boxes to read **Jul** through **Dec**.

8. Delete the ID label in the first row, and add a new text box in its place. Type **=DLookUp("[Category Name]","Categories","[Category ID] = Report![Category ID]")** as the value of the text box. This entry looks up the Category Name for the Category ID in the Categories table.

9. Set the Visible property of the Category ID text box to No.

10. Drag the bottom margin up to within one dot of the bottom of the text boxes in the second row. The final design appears in figure 15.16.

11. Click the Print Preview button on the toolbar to display the double-row report (see fig. 15.17).

Fig. 15.16
The final design of the Monthly Sales by Category report.

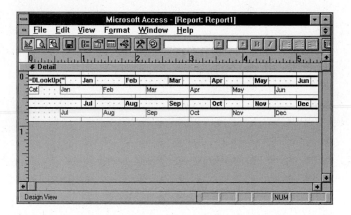

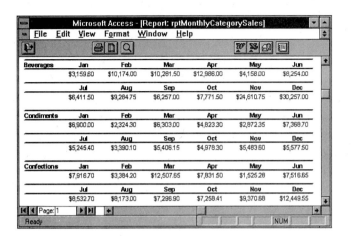

Fig. 15.17
The Monthly Sales by Category report with data for 12 months.

12. Close the Monthly Sales by Category report and save the changes.

Copying controls to the Clipboard, pasting copies to reports, and then editing the copies is often faster than creating duplicate controls that differ from one another only by the text of labels and text boxes.

Incorporating Subreports

Reports, like forms, can include subreports. Unlike the Form Wizard, however, the Report Wizard offers no option of automatically creating reports that include subreports. You can add subreports to reports that you create with the Form Wizard, or you can create subreports from blank reports, as shown in the preceding section.

Adding a Linked Subreport to a Bound Report

If a main report is bound to a table or a query as a data source and the data source for the subreport can be related to the data source of the main report, you can link the data in the subreport to the data in the main report.

To add and link the Monthly Sales by Category report as a subreport to the Product on Hand by Category report, for example, follow these steps:

1. Open the Product on Hand by Category report (rptProductOnHand) in design mode.

2. Drag down the top of the Page Footer border to make room for the subreport in the Category Footer section.

3. Click the Show Database Window button of the toolbar. If the Database window is maximized, click the Document Control-menu box and choose **R**estore.

4. Click and drag the small Report icon from the left of the rptMonthlyCategorySales report to a location inside the Category Footer section. Drop the icon below the Category ID text box.

5. A subreport box similar to a text box, with an associated label, is created at the point where you drop the icon (see fig. 15.18). Delete the label.

Fig. 15.18
Dragging and dropping a report as a subreport within another report.

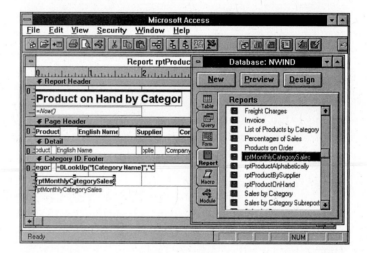

6. Click the Maximize button to restore the Report Design window.

7. Adjust the depth of the Category ID footer to provide about 0.1-inch margins above and below the controls in the section. The report appears in Design View as shown in figure 15.19.

8. You need to link the data in the subreport to the data of the main report so that only the sales data that corresponds to the Category ID value of a specific group appears on-screen. Select the subreport box and click the Properties button to display the Properties window for the subreport. Choose Data Properties and enter Category ID as the value of the `LinkMasterFields` property and Category ID as the value of the `LinkChildFields` property.

Access attempts to create the link. If the main report and subreports are based on tables, and a relationship is set between the tables, Access

creates the link to the related fields. If the main report is grouped to a
key field and the subreport's table or query contains a field of the same
name and data type, Access creates the link.

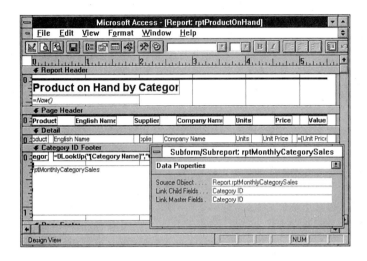

Fig. 15.19
Adding the
Monthly Sales by
Category report as
a subreport of the
Product on Hand
by Category
report.

9. Click the Print Preview button on the toolbar to display the report in
   the full-size view. The subreport appears as shown at the bottom of
   figure 15.20. Click the page selector buttons to view other parts of the
   subreport to confirm that the linkage is correct.

10. Choose **S**ave from the **F**ile menu to save the changes.

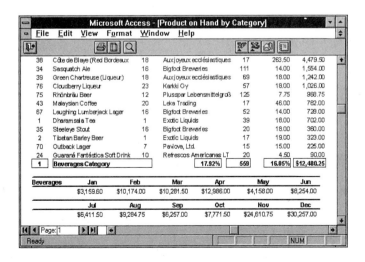

Fig. 15.20
The Monthly Sales
by Category
subreport linked to
the Product on
Hand by category
report.

III

Forms and Reports

You can add and link several subreports to the main report if each subreport has a field in common with the data source of the main report.

> **Note**
>
> You can use calculated values to link main reports and subreports. Calculated values often are based on time: months, quarters, or years. To link main reports and subreports by calculated values, you must create queries for both the main report and the subreport that include the calculated value in a field, such as Month or Year. You create the calculated field in each query by using the corresponding Access date function, **Month()** or **Year()**. To group by quarters, select Interval for the GroupOn property and set the value of the GroupInterval property to 3. You cannot use Qtr as the GroupOn property because the calculated value lacks the Date/Time field data type.

Troubleshooting

When I attempt to create a link between the main report and the subreport, I get a "Can't evaluate expression" error message.

The most likely cause is attempting to create a master-child (more properly parent-child) link with an incompatible data type. The parent-child linkage is similar to joins of queries using the WHERE Subreport.FieldName = Report.FieldName criterion. As with joins, the data types of the linked fields of tables or columns of queries must be identical. You cannot, as an example, link a field of the text data type with a field of the integer data type, even if your text field contains only numbers. If you used an expression to create the link, the data type returned by the expression must match the field value. You can use the data type conversion functions described in Chapter 9, "Understanding Operators and Expressions in Access," to change the data type returned by the expression to that of the linked field. As an example, you can link a text field that contains numbers to a field of the Long Integer data type by entering =**CLng**(TextField) as the linking value.

Using Unlinked Subreports and Unbound Reports

Most reports you create use subreports linked to the data source of the main report. You can, however, insert independent subreports within main reports. Here, you don't enter values for the LinkChildFields and LinkMasterFields properties—or, if Access added values, you delete these values. The data source of the subreport can be related to or completely independent of the main report's source of data. Figure 15.21 shows how a portion of page 2 of the Monthly Sales by Category subreport appears within the Product on Hand by Category report when you delete the Category ID values of the LinkChildFields and LinkMasterFields properties.

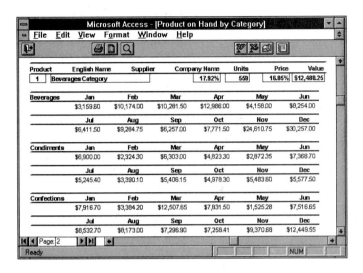

Fig. 15.21

The complete Monthly Sales by Category subreport inserted in the Product on Hand report.

You can add multiple subreports to an unbound report, if all the subreports fit on one page of the report or if all the subreports fit across the page. In the latter case, you can use landscape mode to increase the available page width. To create an unbound report with multiple subreports, follow these steps:

1. Click the Report tab in the Database window, and then click the New button.

   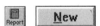

2. Keep the text box of the New Report dialog blank, and click Blank Report. This action creates an unbound report.

3. Click the Show Database Window button of the toolbar to display the Database window, and drag the Report icon for the first subreport to the Detail section of the blank form.

4. Drag the Report icon for the second subreport to the Detail section of the blank form. If the two subreports fit vertically on one page, place the second subreport below the first subreport. If either of the two subreports requires more than a page, place the second subreport to the right of the first. In this case, you need to add column labels for the subreports in the Page Header section of the main report so that the columns are identified on each page.

III

Forms and Reports

Adding Other Controls to Reports

Access places no limit on the toolbox controls that you add to reports. Up to this point, the controls you have modified or added have been limited to labels, text boxes, and lines. These three kinds of controls are likely to comprise more than 90 percent of the controls used in the reports you create. Controls that require user interaction, such as lists and combos, can be used in a nonprinting section of the report, but practical use of these controls in reports is limited. The other controls you may want to add to reports are described in the following list:

- *Bound object frames* print the contents of the OLE Object field data type. An OLE object can be a still or animated graphic, a video clip, waveform or CD audio, or even MIDI music. Reports are designed only to be printed, so animated graphics and sound are inappropriate for reports.

- *Unbound object frames* display OLE objects created by OLE server applications, such as Microsoft Graph 5 (included with Access), Windows Paintbrush, Excel, or the Microsoft WordArt or Equation OLE applets included with Microsoft Word. Usually, unbound objects are placed in the Form Header or Form Footer section of the report, but you can add a logo to the top of each page by placing the image object in the Page Header section. A graph or chart created by the Chart Wizard is a special kind of unbound OLE object.

- *Lines* and *rectangles* (also called *shapes*) create decorative elements on reports. Lines of varying width can separate the sections of the report or lend emphasis to a particular section.

- *Check boxes* and *option buttons* can be used to indicate the values of Yes/No fields or within group frames to indicate multiple-choice selections. Group frames, option buttons, and check boxes used in reports indicate only the value of data cells, and do not change the values. Toggle buttons are seldom used in reports.

- *Command buttons* execute Access macros and Access Basic procedures.

Bound and unbound object frames are the subject of Chapter 20, "Adding Graphics to Forms and Reports." Using Access Basic macros is covered in Part IV of this book, and Access Basic programming is the topic of Part VII.

Sending Reports by Microsoft Mail

If you have installed Microsoft Mail, you can send a report to others as an attachment to a Microsoft Mail message. A Microsoft Mail client application is included with Windows for Workgroups 3.1+ and Microsoft Windows NT 3.1. To send a report as a Mail attachment, follow these steps:

1. In print preview mode, open the report you want to send. (You do not need to have Microsoft Mail running when you create the message.)

2. Click the Mail-It button of the toolbar to display the Send dialog.

3. Select the format in which you want to send the report file in the Select Format list box (see fig. 15.22). This example sends the Product on Hand by Suppliers report in Microsoft Excel 3.0 (.XLS) format.

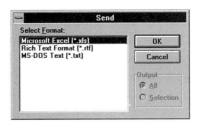

Fig. 15.22
Choosing the format for the Microsoft Mail attachment.

4. Click OK to create the message. A progress-reporting dialog appears while the OutputTo Wizard creates the REPORT_.XLS file. When the process is complete, Microsoft Mail's Send Note window appears.

5. Enter the recipients' names, a subject, and an optional transmittal message, as shown in figure 15.23. Click the Send button to send the message with the attached report file.

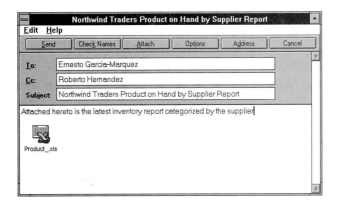

Fig. 15.23
Completing the Microsoft Mail message.

III

Forms and Reports

You cannot view the attachment in a message that is created by an application. (A "nocando" message box appears if you double-click the REPORT_.XLS icon at this point.) Once you send the message, however, you can view the message in your Outbox. Double-click the REPORT_.XLS icon to display the report. The Product on Hand by Supplier report file shown in Excel 5.0 has additional formatting applied (see fig. 15.24).

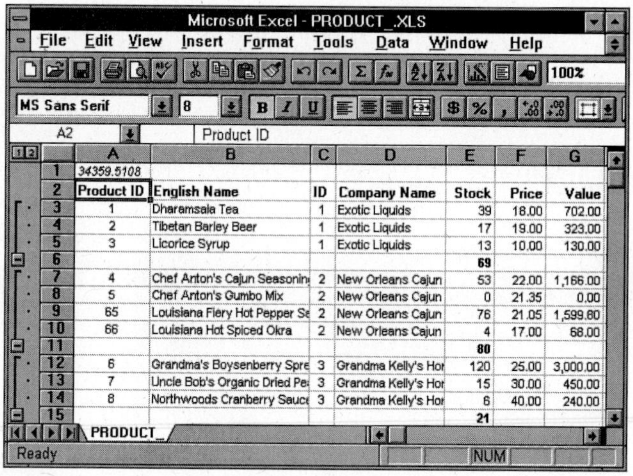

Fig. 15.24

The appearance of the report attachment in Microsoft Excel 5.0.

Note

Depending on the formatting of your report, not all of the field values may appear in an Excel worksheet file. For example, the subtotals for the Values fields, as well as both percentage fields, are missing. These fields, however, can easily be reconstructed in Excel. The OutputTo Wizard cannot incorporate subreports contained in reports printed to files of any of the three available formats. You need to provide individual columns for subtotals and other section footers to assure that the values appear in a .XLS file.

From Here...

This chapter completes Part III of this book, which includes all the basic functions of Access that duplicate the capabilities of database front ends. In Parts II and III, you learned the basic steps to create queries, forms, and reports. Although the Northwind Traders sample database was used in all examples, the queries, forms, and reports you created can be applied to tables attached to Access, rather than within the .MDB structure. If the Access or attached tables are on a network server rather than on the computer's fixed disk, the same procedures you learned in the preceding eight chapters apply.

For information related to the topics discussed in this chapter, refer to the following chapters:

- Chapter 9, "Understanding Operators and Expressions in Access," describes how to use the DLookUp() domain aggregate function and how to create expressions for calculating field values and linking subreports.

- Chapter 20, "Adding Graphics to Forms and Reports," shows you how to print images contained in OLE Object fields of tables or queries and how to add logos or other decorative graphics to reports.

III

Forms and Reports

Part IV

Powering Access with Macros

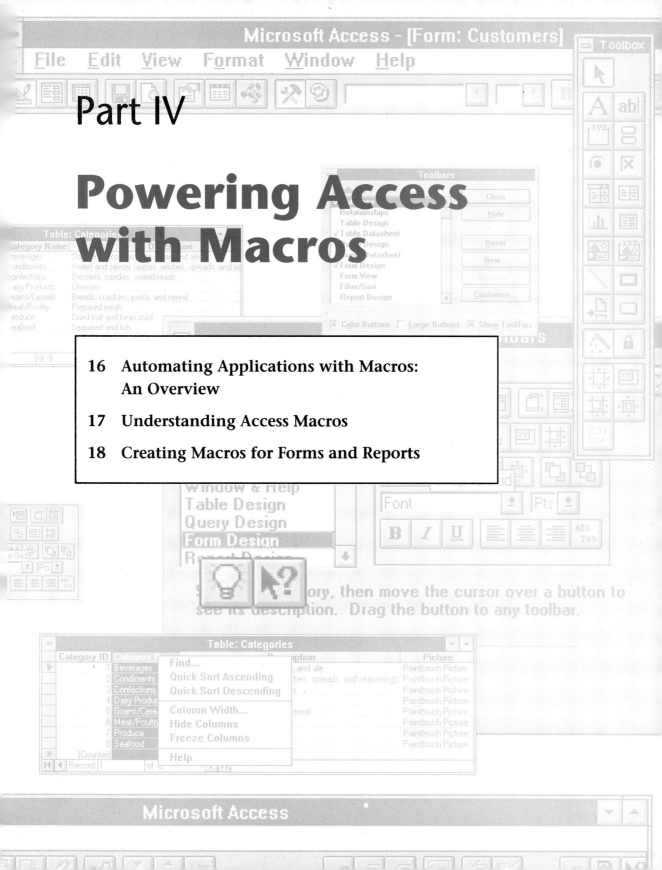

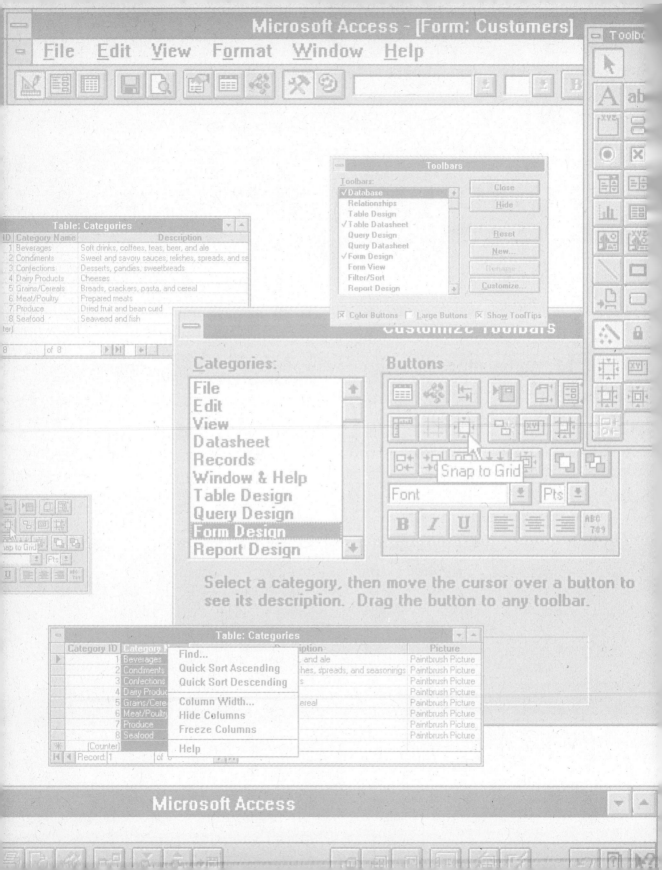

Chapter 16

Automating Applications with Macros: An Overview

Access macros make your database applications more productive. A few simple macros can automate mundane, repetitive procedures. Access lets you use macros to do work that otherwise requires extensive programming with other database applications, such as dBASE, FoxPro, or Paradox.

Macros are lists of actions that are to occur in response to *events*, a process often called "attaching a macro." Some events are occurrences of user actions, such as clicking a command button, opening or closing a form, or typing a value in a text box. Other events are generated by Access itself. A macro's actions are listed in the order you want them to occur. Nearly all the commands in the menu bars, and also other features, are available through actions.

Most of the macro actions have easily recognized names, such as OpenForm or Beep. Most actions require *arguments*. Arguments specify how an action works. Two arguments for the OpenForm action, for example, are Form Name and View. You set these arguments to specify the name of the form being opened and the view in which the form appears.

This chapter provides an overview of Access macros by guiding you through the steps of creating a simple macro that executes when you click a command button that you add to an existing form.

In this chapter, you learn to

- Open the Macro Design window

- Create a simple macro that runs a query

- Modify an existing macro

- Attach a macro to a form's command button

Opening, Running, and Creating Macro Objects

You enter macro actions in *macro datasheets* (often called *macrosheets*) in the Macro Design window. When you save a macro you write, you create a new **Macro** database object. Unlike other Microsoft applications that use macros, such as Excel and Word, you cannot record a series of keystrokes to create an Access macro. The following list describes the four methods of manipulating Access macro objects:

- You open an existing macrosheet from the Macros list of the Database window by selecting the macro and then clicking the Design button. Alternatively, select an event property of a form, report, or control object whose value is a macro name, and then click the ellipsis button to the right of the macro's name to open the macrosheet for the event.

- You execute an existing macro by double-clicking the name of the macro in the Macros list of the Database window; selecting the name of the macro and clicking the Run button; or choosing Run Macro from the File menu and entering the name of the macro in the Run Macro dialog.

- You create a new macro by clicking the Macro tab of the Database window and then clicking the New button to open an empty macrosheet. Alternatively, you can attach a new macro to an event by selecting the event in the Properties window of a form, report, or control object, and then clicking the ellipsis button to display the Choose Builder dialog. Double-clicking the Macro Builder item in the list of the Choose Builder dialog opens an empty macrosheet.

- You execute a macro in Access Basic code with the **DoCmd** RunMacro *MacroName* instruction. You also can use the **DoCmd** *MacroActionName* statement to execute a specific macro action.

Creating a Command Button Macro to Run a Query

The macro you create in this chapter runs a query that displays the content of a **Recordset** object. You assign the macro to a button on the Customers form of NWIND.MDB so that when you click the button, the macro displays all the products purchased by the customer. Figure 16.1 shows the Customers form on which you create a button that runs the macro. Figure 16.2 shows the result of clicking the button.

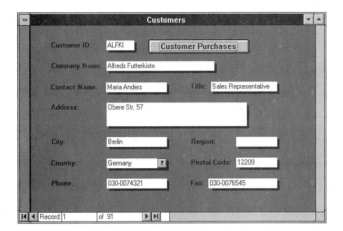

Fig. 16.1
The Customer form with a Customer Purchases command button that runs the macro.

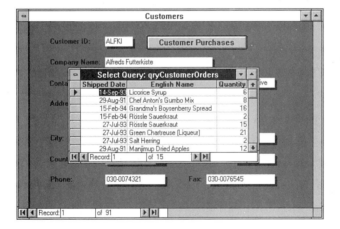

Fig. 16.2
The completed macro opening a query on the current customer's purchase history.

You build this macro in the following three stages:

■ In the first stage, you learn how to open or activate a form and turn off the screen display to prevent screen flashing. In the process, you learn how to enter macro actions and arguments. These first steps ensure that the Customers form is active when the remainder of the macro runs.

■ In the second stage of building this macro, you learn how to add to the existing macro so that the macro opens and refreshes a query that shows all products purchased by the customer.

■ In the third stage, you learn how to assign the macro to a button on a form.

The list of all actions and arguments for the completed macro is in table 16.1, in the "Seeing the Complete Macro Listing" section near the end of this chapter.

Creating a New Macro

You create the macro in a new macrosheet. Although you can put more than one macro in a macrosheet, in this example, the macrosheet contains this macro only. To open a new macrosheet, follow these steps:

1. Open NWIND.MDB, if it is not currently open.

2. Activate the Database window, if necessary, and then click the Macro tab or choose **M**acro from the **V**iew menu. Either action displays the list of existing macros in the Database window.

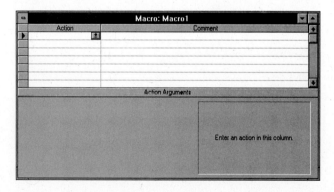

3. Click the New button of the Database window. A new macrosheet appears (see fig. 16.3).

Fig. 16.3
The macrosheet in which you create the macro.

A macrosheet can have up to four columns: Names, Conditions, Action, and Comments. In the example, Access defaults are set so that only the Action and Comments are displayed. (You can toggle display the Names and Conditions columns by clicking the Macro Names and Conditions buttons of the toolbar.) Your macrosheet title bar number may differ from the number shown in figure 16.3 if you have saved macros previously with the default name provided by Access (Macro1...MacroN).

Opening a Form

The next step to creating a macro is to enter the actions you want the macro to perform. Place actions in the Action column in the order in which you want the actions to occur. You can enter actions in three ways. You can type an action, select an action from a combo list in the cell, or, in some cases, drag and drop a database object into the action cell. Because the macro sheet is similar to a Microsoft Excel worksheet, you later can edit, insert, delete, or rearrange macro actions on the sheet.

To enter the OpenForm action by selecting actions and arguments, follow these steps:

1. The macrosheet still should be active. If the macrosheet is not active, press Ctrl+F6 until the window is activated.

2. Use arrow keys to move the insertion point to the uppermost cell of the Action column.

3. Click the pull-down list or press F4 to pull down the combo list. Select the OpenForm action by clicking OpenForm or pressing the arrow keys to highlight OpenForm, and then press Enter.

4. Press F6 to move to the Form Name argument in the lower portion of the macrosheet.

5. Press F4 to pull down the combo list. Then select Customers and press Enter.

To enter the action that opens the Customers form by using the drag-and-drop method, follow these steps:

1. Click the Database window to make this window active.

2. Click the Form tab in the Database window.

3. Select the Customers form name from the Database window, drag the form name to the first cell in the Action column, and release the mouse button. As you drag the Customers form name, the mouse pointer changes to the Form icon.

Releasing the Form icon over the uppermost cell in the action column inserts the OpenForm action and enters the appropriate arguments that open the Customers form. Figure 16.4 shows how the macrosheet appears. Notice that the arguments were entered by Access. Dragging and dropping from the Database window to the macrosheet works for the `OpenTable`, `OpenQuery`, `OpenForm`, `OpenReport`, and `RunMacro` actions.

Fig. 16.4

The *OpenForm* action in the Action column of the macrosheet opening the form specified by the *Form Name* argument.

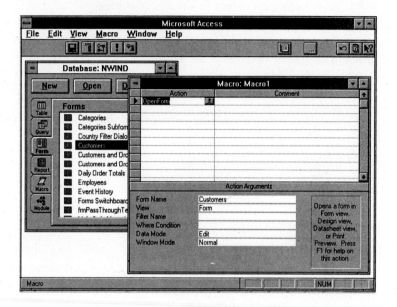

Leave the remaining arguments with the default settings. The macrosheet should appear as shown in figure 16.4; however, the Database window will show Forms.

Running the Macro

Before you can run a macro that you just created or edited, you must save the macrosheet. To save the macrosheet, follow these steps:

1. Choose Save **A**s from the **F**ile menu.

2. Type the name **mcrCustomerPurchases** in the Macro Name text box.

3. Click OK.

You can run a macro in several ways. To run a macro, you can select it from the Database window and click the Run button; double-click the item in the Macros list of the Database window; choose R**u**n Macro from the **F**ile menu; click a button to which the macro is assigned; run the macro from one or more of many kinds of *events* (changes to a Database object, record, or field); or run the macro from another macro.

To run the new macro from the Database window, follow these steps:

1. Click the Show Database Window button of the toolbar, or choose **1** Database: NWIND from the **W**indow menu.

2. Click the Macro tab in the Database window, or choose **M**acros from the **V**iew menu.

3. Select the mcrCustomerPurchases macro name from the list.

4. Click the Run button from the Database window.

The macro opens the Customers form. If the macro doesn't open the form, activate the macrosheet and make sure that the arguments for the OpenForm command specify the Customers form to open in the Edit View.

Polishing the Process of Opening a Form

The one-line macro demonstrates how easily you can create a simple macro. This section tells you how to open the form and give it a more professional appearance by performing the following actions:

- Reducing screen flicker while the form opens

- Ensuring that the form opens and sizes correctly

- Displaying an hourglass as the pointer until the form is completely opened and sized

During the process, you learn more ways to enter actions and arguments and ways to insert rows for new actions.

The first two actions you add to the macro you created need to come before the OpenForm action. To insert two blank rows before the OpenForm action in the macrosheet, follow these steps:

1. Activate the mcrCustomerPurchases macrosheet.

2. Select the cell that contains OpenForm.

3. Click the row selector button to the left of OpenForm to select the row and then press the Insert key twice.

The mcrCustomerPurchases macrosheet now appears as shown in figure 16.5.

Fig. 16.5

The mcrCustomer-
Purchases
macrosheet, with
two blank rows
inserted above
OpenForm.

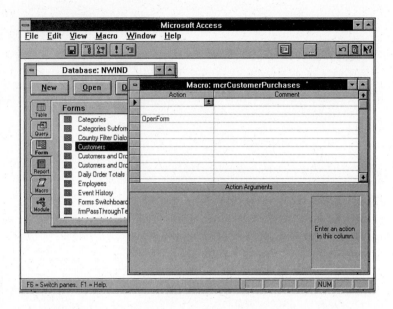

In the two blank Action cells above the OpenForm action, you enter an Echo
action that turns off the screen display until the macro is complete and then
enter an Hourglass action that changes the mouse pointer to an hourglass so
that the operator knows to wait. To enter these two actions and the related
arguments, follow these steps:

1. Select the uppermost cell in the Action column.

2. Choose the Echo action from the combo list in the first cell. (Click the
    down arrow to the right of the cell or press F4 to display the list.)

3. Click the Echo On argument cell in the lower portion of the macrosheet,
    or press F6 to move the insertion point to the lower portion.

4. Choose the No argument from the combo list in the Echo On argument.
    This argument turns off screen refresh until the macro finishes or until
    the macro reaches an Echo On that uses the Yes argument.

5. Select the blank cell under the Echo action by clicking the cell, or by
    pressing F6 and using the arrow keys to move to the cell.

6. Type **Hourglass** in this cell and press Enter. You do not need to
    change the Hourglass On argument.

Now you know three ways to enter actions: by dragging and dropping, by
selecting the action from a combo list, or by typing the action. If you incorrectly type the action, Access displays an alert box. You can enter arguments

the same way: dragging and dropping for Database object names, selecting from a list in certain arguments, or typing an argument name.

The next action that you enter ensures that the Customers form is correctly positioned and sized on-screen. The Size to Fit Form choice of the **W**indow menu on the Form menu bar adjusts the form.

Nearly all Access commands are available as macro actions. You can use the DoMenuItem action to enter actions that duplicate a menu command. The arguments for DoMenuItem specify the menu bar, menu, and command the action performs.

In the following steps, you enter the DoMenuItem action after the form has opened. To enter the equivalent DoMenuItem action to the Size to Fit Form choice of the **W**indow menu, follow these steps:

1. Select the blank Action cell under the OpenForm action. Click the cell with a mouse or press the arrow keys to move the insertion point.

2. Choose the DoMenuItem action from the action cell's combo list.

3. Move to the Action Arguments half of the window by clicking Action Arguments or pressing F6.

   The Menu Bar argument already shows that Form will be active and the Form menu bar will be displayed.

4. Select or type **Window** in the Menu Name argument.

5. Select or type **Size to Fit Form** in the Command argument.

Save this macro by choosing **S**ave from the **F**ile menu. Run the macro from the Database window by using the procedure described in the "Running the Macro" section earlier in this chapter. The screen may have less flicker, and the hourglass is displayed on-screen rather than the standard mouse pointer. Before you start the following section, you may want to minimize the macrosheet to an icon in order to reduce the clutter on-screen.

Creating a Query Object

The second stage of this macro requires a query that creates a **Recordset** object to show the purchase history of the customer displayed in the Customers form. In this section, you create a query object you run with macro actions you add later. This query joins three tables to find the following information: Shipped Date, English Name (of the product), and Quantity. To restrict the query to only shipments that involve the customer name shown in the Customers form, the Customer ID field is included in the query. See **Chapters 8 through 11** for more information on queries.

The query that you build looks like the query in figure 16.6.

Fig. 16.6
The complete query to create a *Recordset* of the customer's purchase history.

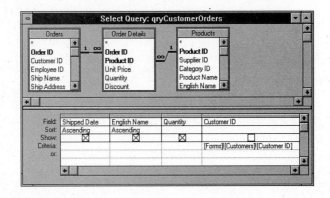

Creating the Query

To create this query, follow these steps:

1. Make the Database window the active window and then click the New Query button of the toolbar.

2. Click the New Query button of the New Query dialog to bypass the Query Wizard.

3. Select the Orders table from the Table/Query scrolling list and click the Add button. The Query Design window appears as shown in figure 16.7.

Fig. 16.7
Selecting the tables you need to query.

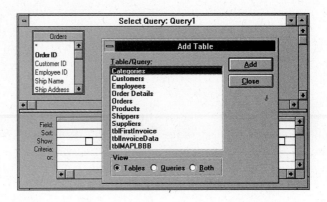

4. Select the Order Details table and then click the Add button; select the Products table and click the Add button.

5. Click the Close button to close the Add Table dialog.

The query window with joined tables should look like the window in figure 16.8. Notice that Access has recognized fields that have previously defined relationships. These fields enable Access to join the information between tables as though all the information resides in a single, large database.

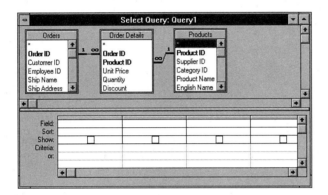

Fig. 16.8
Joining tables to access the information for the customer purchase histories.

Enter the field names across the top of the query window for the fields you want to include in the query. The fields to be included and the order of those fields from left to right across the Field row of the query are shown in the following list and in figure 16.6.

Order in Field	RowTable	Field of Query
1	Orders	Shipped Date
2	Products	English Name
3	Order Details	Quantity
4	Orders	Customer ID

To enter a field name by using the mouse, follow these steps:

1. Drag the field name from the scrolling list of the appropriate table.

2. Drop the field name onto the Field cell in the query.

Alternatively, you can double-click the field name in the table list to add the field in sequence to the query.

To enter a field name from the keyboard, follow these steps:

1. Move to the Field cell in which you want to enter a field.

    Press Tab or Shift+Tab, or press the arrow keys to move between cells.

2. Press F4 to display the list of tables and fields. If you have not previously selected a field in this cell, fields appear as `table.fieldname`: `Orders.Shipped Date`, for example.

3. Select the `table.fieldname` for each Field cell.

To sort the query results so that reading the purchase history is easy, follow these steps:

1. Select the Sort cell under the Shipped Date field and choose Ascending from the combo list.

2. Select the Sort cell under the English Name field and choose Ascending from the combo list.

To enter the criteria for the query, select only the history for the current customer displayed in the Customers form, and enter a criterion under the Customer ID field that specifies that the match will occur for records that have the same customer ID as the customer ID in the form. To enter this criteria, follow these steps:

1. Select the Criteria cell under the Customer ID field.

2. Type the following control name:

    [Forms]![Customers]![Customer ID]

3. Click the Show check box of the Customer ID field so that Customer ID values do not appear in the query result set.

This entry makes the query compare the Customer ID field of the query with the contents of the Customer ID control on the Customers form.

The query you created now should look like figure 16.6. Save this query by choosing Save **As** from the **F**ile menu and typing **qryCustomerPurchases**.

Testing the Query

Before testing the query, you may want to minimize the Query window in order to reduce screen clutter.

To test the query before you run it from a macro, follow these steps:

1. Open the Customers form and select a customer name. Note the Customer ID, such as AROUT.

2. Activate the Database window and click the Query button, or choose **Q**ueries from the **V**iew menu.

3. Select the qryCustomerPurchases query from the list.

4. Click the Open button.

> Open

A datasheet window opens, displaying a sorted list of all purchases made by the same company as the company displayed in the form. Check the Customer ID field in the query to make sure that the ID matches the same company as the company in the form. Close the query and the form after testing.

Running the Query from a Macro

The Customer Purchases macro now opens the Customers form. The following final additions to the macro open the query on top of the form:

1. The result set of the query shows the purchase history of the company.

2. After the query is complete, the MoveSize command adjusts the size of the query window.

3. The query is refreshed.

The present mcrCustomerPurchases macro opens the Customers form. The changes you make to the macro open a query after the form opens. Usually, this macro runs when the Customers form already is open. In this case, the OpenForm command doesn't reopen the Customers form; it makes the Customers form the active window. Placing the OpenForm action before the OpenQuery action is a good way to ensure that the correct form is active and the correct menu bar is displayed. This placement also ensures that the macro will run correctly, even if the macro is not run from the button.

To modify the mcrCustomerPurchases macro, follow these steps:

1. Open the mcrCustomerPurchases macro to make it appear in a window.

2. Move to the blank action cell under the DoMenuItem action by clicking the cell, or press F6 and move to the cell by using the arrow keys.

3. Select the Echo action from the combo list. Change the Echo On argument to Yes.

4. Select the next blank action cell and enter an Echo action, but use an Echo On argument of No.

These two Echo actions are used to refresh the screen at the correct time so you can see the opened Customers form before you start the query. The first Echo action refreshes the screen so you can see the Customers form after the form opens. The second Echo action turns off the screen refresh again while the query works. After you complete this macro, try running the macro without using Echo actions so you can see the difference in appearance.

The following steps add the OpenQuery, Requery, MoveSize, and Beep actions. The OpenQuery action opens the Customer Purchases query you created in the previous section. This query's Data Mode argument is specified as read-only so that the operator cannot change the purchase history. The Requery action ensures that the query is up-to-date. If the operator doesn't close the past query window, but moves to a new customer record and then runs the macro, the Requery action repeats the query to make sure that the query window is current. MoveSize positions the query window, and Beep notifies the operator.

To make the final additions to the macro, follow these steps:

1. Select the blank action cell under the last Echo action.

2. Select the OpenQuery action from the combo list. Switch to the Action Arguments, and select the qryCustomerPurchases as the Query Name (the query you built). Change the Data Mode argument to read-only.

3. Select the next action cell.

4. Select the Requery action, but do not enter a Control argument; leaving Control empty causes the entire query to rerun if necessary.

5. Select the next blank action cell.

6. Select the MoveSize action and enter the following measurements. (Your measurements may need to be different, depending on the screen's resolution.) The result is shown in figure 16.9.

Right   1.6 in

Down   1.1 in

Width   3.57 in

Height   1.75 in

7. Select the next blank action cell and type **Beep** as the action.

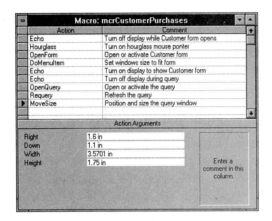

Fig. 16.9

The *MoveSize* action and the on-disk related arguments, which position the active window.

8. Choose **S**ave from the **F**ile menu, or press F12, and save the macro with the same name.

The Customer Products macrosheet now appears as shown in figure 16.10.

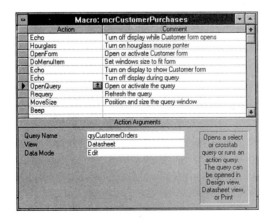

Fig. 16.10

The complete macro activating the Customers form and then running a customer purchase history query.

Test the macro. If the macrosheet is active and you use a mouse, click the Run button on the Macro toolbar. If you use a keyboard, choose **R**un Macro from the **F**ile menu when any window is active. Type the name of the macro, **mcrCustomerPurchases**, and press Enter.

Attaching a Macro Button to a Form

You can make the macro convenient to run by adding a button to the Customers form. You then can click the button to run the macro.

To use the mouse to add a button to the Customers form, follow these steps:

1. Open the Customers form in Design View, and activate the Database window.

2. Click the Macro tab of the Database window or choose **M**acros from the **V**iew menu to display the list of macros in the Database window. Figure 16.11 shows the two windows in preparation to create a button.

Fig. 16.11
Creating a macro button by dragging the macro name onto the form while in Design View.

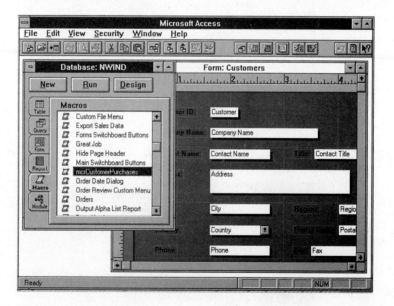

3. Drag the name of the mcrCustomerPurchases macro onto the form where you want the button to appear. Release the mouse button. Figure 16.12 shows the Customer Purchases button in the top right corner of the form.

4. Select and delete the button's text label.

5. Click the button.

6. Display the Form Properties window and change the Control Name property for the button to Button Customer Purchases. The caption is the name of the macro. You can change the button's caption by editing the Caption property. Figure 16.12 shows the completed button on the form.

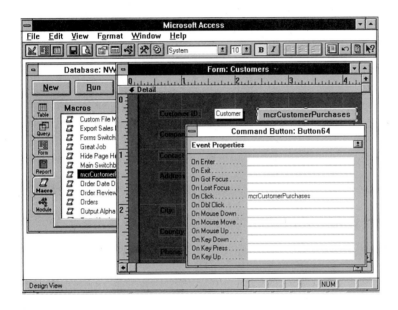

Fig. 16.12
The completed button with the related properties list.

7. Click the Form View button on the toolbar, or choose **F**orm from the **V**iew menu to display the form as the operator sees it during normal operation.

8. Choose **S**ave from the **F**ile menu to save the form with the button.

To run the macro from the button, display the Customers form in Form View and click the command button. The macro reactivates the Customers form, changes the pointer to an hourglass, and beeps when the completed query appears. After the macro is complete, the screen resembles figure 16.2, near the beginning of this chapter.

Troubleshooting

When I run my macro, a message box appears followed by an Action Failed dialog.

The most likely cause of an error in executing an Access macro is a typographic error when you enter or edit the names of database objects in the arguments for macro actions. In this case, the message is "There is no *ObjectType* named '*BadName*'." The Action Failed dialog displays the action name and the arguments. Return to the macrosheet and correct the erroneous object name. Similar errors occur if you type an invalid entry for the arguments of other macro actions.

Seeing the Complete Macro Listing

Table 16.1 shows the complete listing of all actions and the related arguments. Abbreviated comments also are listed for each action. You may want to enter these comments in the macro to make the lines of the macro easier to understand.

Table 16.1   Complete Macro Actions and Arguments

Action	Argument	Argument Entry	Comment
Echo	Echo On	No	Turns off display while Customers form opens.
	Status Bar Text	(none)	
Hourglass	Hourglass On	Yes	Turns on hourglass as pointer.
OpenForm	Form Name	Customers	Opens Customers form if closed; activates if form is open.
	View	Form	
	Filter Name	(none)	
	Where Condition	(none)	
	Data Mode	Edit	
	Window Mode	Normal	
DoMenuItem	Menu Bar	Form	Fits window to the form size.
	Menu Name	Window	
	Command	Size to Fit Form	
Echo	Echo On	Yes	Refreshs the display to show the Customers form.
	Status Bar Text		

Action	Argument	Argument Entry	Comment
Echo	Echo On Status Bar Text	No	Turns off the display during query.
OpenQuery	QueryName View Data Mode	Customer Purchases Datasheet Read Only	Opens or activates the query to show current Customer ID's purchases.
Requery	Control Name	(none)	Redoes the query to make it current in case query was activated and not opened.
MoveSize	Right Down Width Height	1.6 in 1.1 in 3.57 in 1.75 in	Moves and sizes the query window.
Beep			Notifies operator query is complete.

From Here...

Macros can make mundane tasks disappear with the click of a mouse or the press of a key. Many people find macros fun to create. If you create a database system for others to use, you may want to use macros to make Access operation easier for other users who may not know all the Access commands.

Refer to the following chapters to learn more about making macros:

- Chapter 17, "Understanding Access Macros," describes how to create simple or more complex macros, using step-by-step procedures.

- Chapter 18, "Creating Macros for Forms and Reports," provides examples of many of the most frequently used macros.

- Chapter 27, "Writing Access Basic Code," describes how to use the **DoCmd** instruction to execute macros with Access Basic.

Chapter 17

Understanding Access Macros

Macros give you the power to automate your work and to create systems that others can use without your assistance. Macros are well worth taking the time to learn.

Macros help you with repetitive tasks such as opening a collection of forms together and arranging them on-screen. They also help you automate your forms and reports. For example, you may need new records that appear with default values already entered, or you may want forms to open and display information from the same records.

Most of the database tasks you do manually can be duplicated by a macro action. A *macro action* is a single task being performed within a larger procedure. Even the commands you choose from the menu can be used as actions within a macro. You enter macro actions in the Macro Design window, called the *macrosheet* in this book (for consistency with the term *datasheet*).

In addition to completing tasks or procedures for you, macros can make decisions. Macros or a sequence of actions within a macro can *decide* to work depending on some condition you specify. If a user enters an incorrect value, for example, your macro can display a unique alert message for each type of error.

Macros also enable you to customize Access. Your macros can be assigned to custom shortcut keys for frequently used actions. Novice users may want to add buttons to forms or reports so that the click of a mouse runs the macro. For a professional look, systems you create with Access can even have their own custom menus and commands.

In this chapter, you learn

- About features of the Macro Design window

- To add actions to a macro

- To enter action arguments

- To find the macro action you need

- To use the SendKeys action

- About troubleshooting macros

The following list gives you some ideas about how you can effectively use macros in your system:

- **Open and arrange forms and screens used on startup.** Display custom menus by creating a macro that runs automatically when a database opens.

- **Open forms and reports.** Opening one form can automatically open related forms and reports and arrange them on-screen.

- Synchronize forms so that updating one form displays the appropriate record in another form.

- Automate queries and finds.

- Print forms and reports by clicking a button that runs a print macro.

- Ensure data accuracy with macros that perform greater error checking than is possible with the error checking done with a control's properties.

- Transfer data between Access and other Windows applications by clicking a button that runs an import or export macro.

- Close the system gracefully when the user clicks a button or closes a main form.

Understanding the Macrosheet and Toolbar

Whenever you are creating, testing, or editing macros, you work with the macrosheet and the macrosheet toolbar. You need to understand how to use the buttons on the toolbar and parts of the Macro Design window before you learn how to create macros.

The Macrosheet

You create macros within a macrosheet. Open a new macrosheet from the Database window by clicking the Macro tab and then clicking the New button. The new macrosheet opens in Design View (see fig. 17.1).

You can open a macrosheet to read, edit, or copy existing macros. To open an existing macro, click the Macro tab in the Database window. Select a macro from the list in the Database window. Click the Design button in the Database window to open the macrosheet. Figure 17.2 shows a simple macro, the

Review Employee Orders macro from NWIND.MDB. The actions in the Action column define the action the macro performs. Each action has one or more associated arguments that define the way the action works. An OpenTable action, for example, has to know the name of the table to open. Comments are optional and require you to manually type them, but they are worth completing. They can help you or others understand how the macro works.

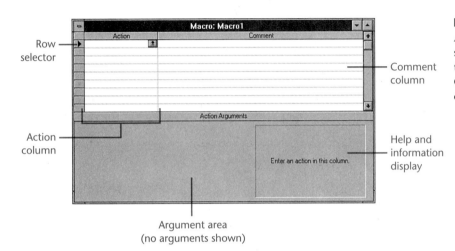

Fig. 17.1
A new macrosheet showing only the Action and Comment columns.

Figure 17.3 shows a more complex macro in a macrosheet. The Macro Name column identifies the start of each macro when the macrosheet contains more than one macro. This capability enables you to group related macros

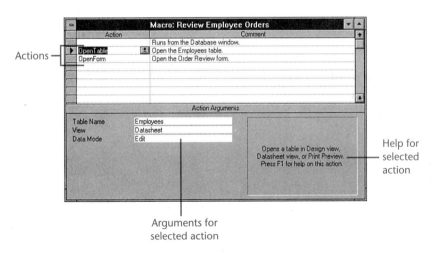

Fig. 17.2
Using arguments to define the way an action works.

in the same macrosheet. The Condition column specifies a condition that controls when a portion of the macro runs. This capability is useful when you want to run a macro only if a specific form is open already or to test for ranges of values the operator has typed into form controls.

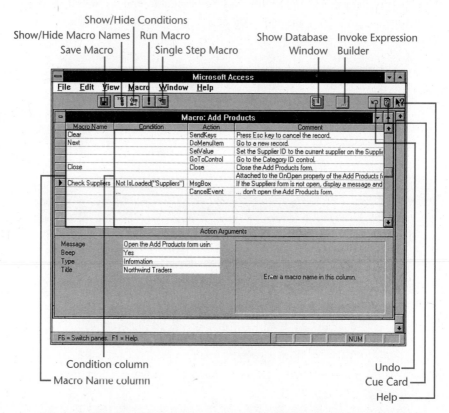

Fig. 17.3

A macrosheet showing the Name and Condition columns for an existing macro.

The Macro Design Window Toolbar

The Macro toolbar is displayed under the menu bar whenever a macrosheet is active. This toolbar contains 10 tools to help you program, run, and test macros (refer to fig. 7.3). The Macro Names and Condition tools toggle on and off the Names and Condition columns in the macrosheet. The Run tool runs the active macro, and the Single Step tool is used to troubleshoot macros that aren't operating correctly. The Invoke Expression Builder button opens the Expression Builder dialog. These tools are described in later sections of this chapter.

Creating a Macro

You create macros by starting with an empty macrosheet (refer to fig. 17.1) and adding the actions and arguments that make your macro do its work. Creating a macro consists of four steps:

1. Opening a new or existing macrosheet.

2. Entering an action for each command or task you want the macro to accomplish. (The term *action* is referred to as a "script," "macro code," or "program code" in other applications or macro/script languages.) For most actions, you also must enter arguments that specify what or how an action works.

3. Saving the macrosheet. A macrosheet must be saved before the new or edited macro can be run.

4. Running the macro to test it.

Inserting Actions and Arguments

To create a new macro, you open a macrosheet and then enter the actions you want to occur in the order you want each action to occur. You can enter actions in the Action column by choosing them from a combo list in each action cell or by typing them in the action cell. As you enter each action, you should enter the arguments for the action in the Arguments window in the lower half of the macrosheet.

To create a macro, follow these steps:

1. Click the Macro tab of the Database window. This action displays a list of existing macros.

2. Click the New button. A new macrosheet appears (refer to fig. 17.1).

3. Click the first cell of the Action column if it isn't selected already. Notice the pull-down arrow in the active cell of the Action column. Figure 17.4 shows the pull-down arrow that displays the combo list.

4. Click the down arrow to the right of the action cell (or press F4) and select the action you want from the combo list that appears. When you select an action, notice that action arguments for the action you have chosen in the lower part of the window change. Figure 17.5 shows the arguments for opening a form.

Or click to display a list of actions

Fig. 17.4
The combo list
arrow enables you
to type or select
actions from a list.

Type in
the cell

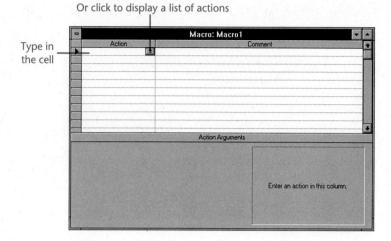

Fig. 17.5
Arguments
specifying how an
action works.

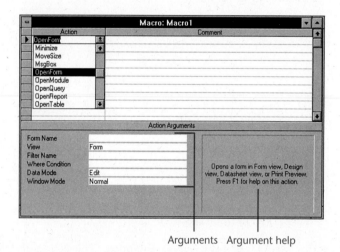

Arguments   Argument help

5. Click the first argument edit box or press F6 to move to the Action Arguments portion of the window.

6. Type or select the arguments for the current action.

   Enter arguments down the column starting from the topmost edit box. Arguments you select in upper boxes may change the alternatives for lower boxes. You can select many arguments from combo lists. If you select an argument's edit box and a combo list arrow appears to the right, you can select an argument from the combo list; otherwise, you must type the argument.

7. If you have to enter additional actions, click the next blank cell of the Active column or press F6 and press the arrow keys to select the next blank active cell. Return to step 4 to enter the action and its argument.

   If you don't need to enter additional actions, continue with step 8.

8. Click the Save button of the toolbar, choose Save As from the File menu, or press F12. In the Save As dialog, type a descriptive name for the macro. Because the macro isn't saved as a separate file, the name can have spaces and doesn't need a file extension. Click OK.

> **Note**
>
> If you are entering a long macro action or argument and have difficulty seeing all the material you are typing, use the Zoom box shown in figure 17.6. The Zoom box expands the action cell or argument to display multiple lines. In the figure, the Zoom box displays the complete IsLoaded() condition in the second condition cell. To display the Zoom box, move the caret into the action cell or argument in which you want to type or edit. Press Shift+F2, and the Zoom box appears, showing the action cell or argument contents. When you are finished editing, click OK or Cancel.

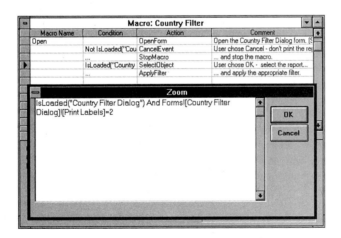

Fig. 17.6
Displaying the Zoom box for easier editing.

Entering Actions

You can enter actions in the Action column in three ways: type the action, select the action from a combo list, or drag a database object into the cell. Each of these methods has advantages and disadvantages.

If you want to enter an action quickly, type it into the Action column. When you press Enter or an arrow key, the action is entered if you spelled it correctly. If you misspell the action, a warning message notifies you. The list of available actions is displayed, making it easy for you to select the action you want.

If you want to browse through a list or are unfamiliar with how to spell an action, select the cell in the Action column and click the down arrow (or press F4) to display the combo list. Scroll to the action and click it or press Enter.

Tip

You can find actions quickly in the action combo list by typing the first letter of the action in the cell and then clicking the down arrow for the combo list. The list scrolls to the item that starts with the letter you typed.

Two different actions can be inserted by dragging and dropping. Dragging and dropping a table, query, form, or report object from the Database window to an action cell inserts the Open. . . action for that object—OpenTable, for example. Dragging and dropping a macro object from the Database window to an action cell inserts a RunMacro action. Figure 17.7 illustrates how windows can be arranged to drag and drop.

To insert an action using drag and drop, follow these steps:

1. Display both the Database window and the macrosheet.

2. Click a tab in the Database window to display the name of the object you want the action to open.

3. Drag the name of the object from the Database window to the cell in the Action column in which you want the action inserted. As you drag the name, the mouse pointer becomes an icon representing the type of object you selected.

4. Release the mouse button when the mouse pointer (an object icon) is over the cell in which you want the action.

If you drag a table, form, query, or report, an OpenTable, OpenForm, OpenQuery, or OpenReport action, respectively, appears in the cell over which you released the object icon. If you dragged a macro, the RunMacro action appears. Examine the arguments for the OpenObject or RunMacro action created to make sure that the appropriate arguments also were entered by the drag-and-drop operation.

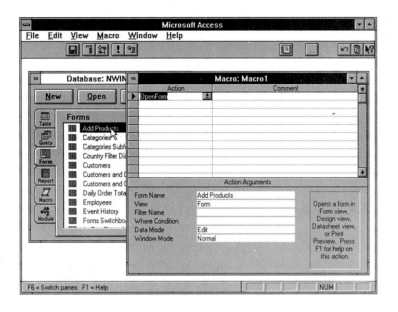

Fig. 17.7
Dragging the object from the Database window to the Action cell in which you want the action inserted.

Entering Arguments

Arguments define the way an action works. The MsgBox action, for example, has the arguments Message, Beep, Type, and Title. These arguments define how the MsgBox action works. Some arguments must be typed into an edit box in the lower half of the macrosheet. Other arguments have a combo list from which you can select valid argument values. A help message and description of the selected argument appear in the lower right corner of the macrosheet. Examples of these arguments and their meanings are shown in table 17.1.

Table 17.1   Arguments for the *MsgBox* Action

Argument Name	Entry Method	Defines
Message Name	Manually typed	The message you type appears in the message dialog.
Beep	Combo list: Yes No	The box either beeps or doesn't beep when displayed.
Type	Combo list: None Critical Warning? Warning! Information	The type of icon appears in the message box.

(continues)

Table 17.1 Continued		
Argument Name	**Entry Method**	**Defines**
Title	Manually typed	The title for the title bar of the dialog.

When you enter arguments, either manually or from a combo list, begin with the first argument and work downward. Selections for some arguments are affected by the settings of earlier arguments.

Tip
You can enter arguments that call for the name of a database object, such as a table or form name, by dragging the database object from the Database window and dropping its icon on the argument's edit box.

Most arguments can be set with an expression beginning with an equal sign. Examples of arguments set by expressions are shown in the examples in Chapter 18, "Creating Macros for Forms and Reports." The arguments that cannot be set by expression are the ObjectType for the Close, GoToRecord, RepaintObject, SelectObject, DeleteObject, or TransferDatabase actions. No item from the DoMenuItem action can use an expression as an argument.

Entering Comments

Don't ignore comments in your macros. They can save you or someone else time when your macro must be reviewed or modified. Enter comments in the Comment column to identify the macro and what it does, identify the event or other macro that runs this macro, and identify what the individual macro actions do. In addition, you can insert blank rows as spaces to separate macros visually when you have more than one macro in a macrosheet. Figure 17.8 shows a macrosheet that contains macros and their documenting comments. Notice how comments are used on lines with blank action cells as the title of the macro and to document how the macro is run or called.

Fig. 17.8
Using comments and blank rows to document macros and make them easier to read.

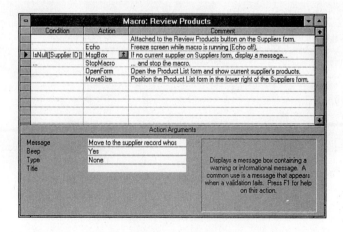

Understanding the Available Macro Actions

Access macro actions can duplicate the commands you choose from menus, as well as control many processes such as synchronizing the records that forms display. There are 46 Access 2.0 macro actions from which you can choose. The following sections describe how you find the macro action you need to perform a particular task.

Getting On-Line Help and Examples for Actions

Use Help for in-depth information about macro actions. To see the entire list of macro actions for which help is available, follow these steps:

1. Choose Contents from the Help menu to display the Microsoft Access Help Contents window.

2. Click the green "Language and Technical Reference" hot spot to display the named window.

3. Click the "Actions programming topic" hot spot in the Language and Technical Reference window to display the Actions Reference window.

4. To learn more about a macro action shown in the window in figure 17.9, click the initial letter of the action to display a list of macro actions that begin with the letter.

5. Click the green hot spot with the name of the action for which you want help. Alternatively, use the Tab key to select the action topic and then press Enter.

If you already know what action you want information for, choose Search from the Help menu. Type in the top edit box the name of the action. As you type, the list scrolls to match as many characters as you have typed. Click the Show Topics button to display subtopics in the lower list. Select one of the subtopics and then click the Go To button. Figure 17.10 shows OpenTable typed in the top edit box.

Fig. 17.9
Selecting an action
from the Help
window to learn
about the action
and see an
example.

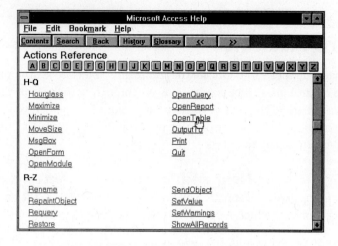

Fig. 17.10
Using the Help
system to search
for macro
commands.

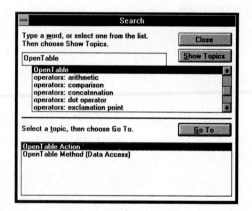

Figure 17.11 shows an example of the help for the OpenTable action. In the
Help window, underlined words are called *hot spots* and are linked to additional help topics. You can jump to this related help topic by clicking an
underlined word or pressing Tab until the underlined word is selected and
then pressing Enter. Return to the Help document from which you started
by clicking the Back button or pressing Alt+B. Click the underlined word
Example at the top of the window to see an example of the action or how its
arguments are completed.

Access Help is a separate Windows application (WINHELP.EXE) that runs in a
separate window. To close the window when you are finished, press Alt+F4
(the shortcut key for closing a Windows application) or double-click the
Control-menu box.

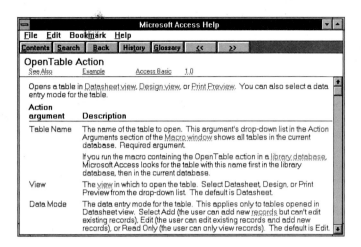

Fig. 17.11
Using Help to
learn about actions
and see examples.

IV

Macros

Finding the Appropriate Action

Macro actions can duplicate most of the actions needed in an automated
database. Before you begin to automate your work, you should read table 17.2
to understand the actions available. Macro actions satisfy most of your application programming needs. If you need a feature or expression that isn't
available as a macro action, you can create it with Access Basic.

For more explicit information about these actions, their syntaxes, and arguments, use the Help command as described earlier to display information
about an action. Chapter 18, "Creating Macros for Forms and Reports," shows
the use of many actions in actual macros. Table 17.2 is a complete list of
macro actions, their arguments, and their functions. Access 1.x provided 42
macro actions; Access 2.0 adds four more. Macro actions listed in table 17.2
that are new to Access 2.0 are indicated by the Access 2.0 icon.

Access

2.0

Table 17.2 Macro Actions		
Action	**Argument**	**Function**
AddMenu	Menu Name Menu Macro Name Status Bar Text	Creates a menu bar containing drop-down menus. The menu bar appears when the form to which AddMenu has been assigned is active.

(continues)

Table 17.2 Continued

Action	Argument	Function
ApplyFilter	Filter Name Where Condition	Filters the data available to a form or report using a filter, query, or SQL WHERE clause.
Beep	(no arguments)	Produces a beep tone for use in warnings or alerts.
CancelEvent	BeforeUpdate OnClose OnDelete OnInsert OnOpen	Cancels an event. This action is useful if a user enters invalid data in a record; then the macro can cancel the update of the database.
Close	Object Type Object Name	Closes the active (default) or a specified window.
CopyObject	Destination Database New Name	Duplicates the specified database object in another database or in the original database using a different name.
Delete Object	Object Type Object Name	Deletes the specified object.
DoMenuItem	Menu Bar Menu Name Command Subcommand	Runs any command on the standard Access menu bars.
Echo	Echo On Status Bar Text	Turns on or off the screen refresh during macro operation. Hides results until they are complete and speeds macro operation.
FindNext	(no arguments)	Finds the next record specified by the FindRecord action or the Find command.
FindRecord	Find What Where Match Case Direction Search As Formatted Search In Find First	Finds the next record after the current record meeting the specified criteria. Searches through a **Table**, **Form**, or **Recordset** object.
GoToControl	Control Name	Selects the control named in the argument. Used to select a control or field when a form opens.

Access
2.0

Action	Argument	Function
GoToPage	Page Number Right Down by Tab	Selects the first field on the designated page in a multi-page form. The first field is the first field as designated order.
GoToRecord	Object Type Object Name Record Offset	Displays the specified record in a **Table**, **Form**, or **Recordset** object.
Hourglass	Hourglass On	Displays an hourglass in place of the mouse pointer while the macro runs. Use it while long macros run.
Maximize	(no arguments)	Maximizes the active window.
Minimize	(no arguments)	Minimizes the active window to an icon within the Access window.
MoveSize	Right Down Width Height	Moves or changes the size of the active window.
MsgBox	Message Beep Type Title	Displays a warning or informational message box.
OpenForm	Form Name View Filter Name Where Condition Data Mode Window Mode	Opens or activates a form in one of its views. Form can be restricted to data-matching criteria, different modes of editing, and whether the form acts as a modal or pop-up dialog.
OpenModule	Module Name Procedure Name	Opens the specified module and displays the specified procedure.
OpenQuery	Query Name View Data Mode	Opens or activates a **Recordset** or cross tab query. You can specify the view and data entry mode.

Access

2.0

(continues)

Table 17.2 Continued

Action	Argument	Function
OpenReport	Report Name View Filter Name Where Condition	Opens a report in the view you specify and filters the records before printing.
OpenTable	Table Name View Data Mode	Opens or activates a table in the view you specify. You can specify the data entry or edit mode for tables in Datasheet View.
OutputTo	Object Type Object Name Output Format Output File Autostart	Copies the data in the specified object to a Microsoft Excel (.XLS), rich-text format (.RTF), or DOS text (.TXT) file. Autostart = Yes starts the application with the association to the extension.
Print	Print Range Page From Page To Print Quality Copies Collate Copies	Prints the active datasheet, report, or form.
Quit	Options	Exits from Access and saves unsaved objects according to the command you specify.
Rename	New Name	Renames the object selected in the Database window.
RepaintObject	Object Type Object Name	Completes recalculations the for controls and updates specified or active database object.
Requery	Control Name	Updates the specified control by repeating the query of the control's source.
Restore	(no arguments)	Restores a maximized or minimized window to its previous window.
RunApp	Command Line	Runs a Windows application.
RunCode	Function Name	Runs a user-defined function written in Access Basic.

Access
2.0

Action	Argument	Function
RunMacro	Macro Name Repeat Count Repeat Expression	Runs the specified macro.
RunSQL	SQL Statement	Runs an action query as specified by the SQL statement.
SelectObject	Object Type Object Name In Database Window	Selects a specified database object.
SendKeys	Keystrokes Wait	Sends keystrokes to any active Windows application.
SendObject	Object Type Object Name Output Format To Cc Bcc Subject Message Text Edit Message	Sends the specified object as an attachment to a Microsoft Mail 3.x message. You enter the Recipient(s) of the message with the values of the To, Cc, and Bcc arguments. You can specify the subject header for the message, add text to the message, and edit the message in Microsoft Mail.
SetValue	Item Expression	Changes the value of a field, control, or property.
SetWarnings	Warnings On	Turns warning messages on or off.
ShowAllRecords	(no arguments)	Removes any filters or queries and displays all records in the current table or query.
StopAllMacros	(no arguments)	Stops all macros.
StopMacro	(no arguments)	Stops the current macro.
Transfer Database	Transfer Type Database Type Database Name Object Type Source Destination Structure Only	Imports, exports, or attaches non-Access databases.

IV

Macros

Access

2.0

(continues)

Table 17.2 Continued		
Action	**Argument**	**Function**
Transfer Spreadsheet	Transfer Type Spreadsheet Type Table Name File Name Has Field Names Range	Imports or exports Access data to a worksheet or spreadsheet file.
TransferText	Transfer Type Specification Name Table Name File Name Has Field Names	Imports or exports Access data to a text file.

Duplicating a Menu Command with an Action

After you work with Access, you know how to manually do many of the jobs you want to automate. These manual tasks usually use commands from the Access menus. To enter macro actions or create an entire macro that duplicates a series of menu commands, you use the DoMenuItem macro action. Keystrokes you enter in dialogs displayed by a command can be entered by the macro using the SendKeys macro action.

The DoMenuItem action duplicates commands on the standard Access menu bars. The arguments for a DoMenuItem action are shown in table 17.3.

Table 17.3 *DoMenuItem* Arguments	
Argument	**Description**
Menu Bar	Each menu bar corresponds to a view. Select from the combo list the view that will be in use when this command runs. If you use DoMenuItem when a form is active, for example, choose Form.
Menu Name	Select from the combo list the menu heading that contains the command you want.
Command	Select from the combo list the command you want.
Subcommand	If a subcommand is required, select the subcommand. On a form, for example, the GoTo choice of the Records menu requires a subcommand such as First.

> **Note**
>
> Macros halt if an action attempts to run and the incorrect object or view is displayed. If you are unsure of the view or object that is active when an action runs, use the single-step method of running the macro. By running a macro in single-step mode, you can step through the macro's actions one at a time. When you run a macro in single-step mode, note which menu bar (Database object) is active when the DoMenuItem action attempts to run. Click the Step button of the Macro toolbar to single-step a macro. This process is described later in this chapter, in the section "Troubleshooting Macros."

You can enter predefined information in a dialog displayed by the DoMenuItem action. To do this, use the SendKeys action. SendKeys sends characters to an open Access dialog or the active Windows application just as though you had typed the characters. The arguments for the SendKeys action are shown in table 17.4.

Table 17.4   *SendKeys* Action Arguments

Argument	Description
Keystrokes	As many as 255 characters can be sent through this argument. Some keyboard characters are replaced by symbols, as described in the next table.
Wait	Enter Yes to make the macro pause until the keystrokes are executed. The default is No.

> **Note**
>
> Send keystrokes to a dialog displayed by DoMenuItem by putting the SendKeys action before the DoMenuItem and specifying No for the Wait argument of the SendKeys action. If the string of characters you want to send is more than the 255-character limit, use multiple SendKeys actions. Chapter 18, "Creating Macros for Forms and Reports," shows examples of how to use DoMenuItem and SendKeys to enter information in a dialog.

To send alphanumeric characters used as text, such as *a, A, b, B* or *1, 2,* or *3*, enclose in quotation marks the characters you want to send—"Denver", for example. Text characters sent to some arguments don't require quotation marks.

Tip
Use Echo No and StopMacro to see interim results from SendKeys.

If a long macro is running and you are sending text and keystrokes to a dialog, in the middle of the macro you will want to see whether the characters are accepted correctly, whether the correct options are chosen, and whether quotation marks around text are needed. To see the SendKeys action work, change the Echo On argument to Yes for any preceding Echo actions. This step lets you see what is happening. Insert a StopMacro action after the DoMenuItem action that opens the dialog that is to receive the keystrokes. When you run the macro, you can see the characters as they are entered in the dialog.

Keystrokes that have no symbol, such as Enter or Esc, are described with a code. Table 17.5 shows the codes you should use to send keystrokes such as Tab, Delete, and arrow movements.

Table 17.5 *SendKeys* Codes for Special Keys

Key to Send	Use in Keystroke Argument
Command Keys	
Backspace	{BACKSPACE} or {BS} or {BKSP}
Break	{BREAK}
Caps Lock	{CAPSLOCK}
Clear	{CLEAR}
Delete	{DELETE} or {DEL}
End	{END}
Enter	{ENTER} or ~
Esc	{ESCAPE} or {ESC}
Help	{HELP}
Home	{HOME}
Insert	{INSERT}
Num Lock	{NUMLOCK}
Print Screen	{PRTSC}
Function Keys	
F1	{F1}
F2	{F2}

Key to Send	Use in Keystroke Argument
F3	{F3}
F4	{F4}
F5	{F5}
F6	{F6}
F7	{F7}
F8	{F8}
F9	{F9}
F10	{F10}
F11	{F11}
F12	{F12}
F13	{F13}
F14	{F14}
F15	{F15}
F16	{F16}
Movement Keys	
Down Arrow	{DOWN}
Left Arrow	{LEFT}
Page Down	{PGDN}
Page Up	{PGUP}
Right Arrow	{RIGHT}
Scroll Lock	{SCROLLLOCK}
Tab	{TAB}
Up Arrow	{UP}

Many actions in Access require the use of keystroke combinations—keys used in combination with Shift, Ctrl, or Alt keys. These codes are listed in table 17.6.

IV

Macros

Table 17.6   *SendKeys* Codes for Shift, Ctrl, and Alt

To Use	Use in the Keystroke Argument
Shift	+
Ctrl	^
Alt	%

When you press two keys in combination, such as Alt+S, specify this action as

%S

To press Alt+S, followed by R (without the Alt), use

%SR

If a key is held down while two or more keys are pressed, enclose the group of following keys in parentheses. The following example is the equivalent of Alt+D+V:

%(DV)

When you want to send the same keystroke many times, add to the keystroke a number specifying how many times to repeat. To move down three times, for example, use the following:

{DOWN 3}

Some characters are used as symbols for keys or are reserved for use in programming features such as dynamic data exchange. To use these characters, enclose them in braces ({ }). These characters are shown in table 17.7.

Table 17.7   *SendKeys* Codes for Reserved Characters

To Use	Use in the Keystroke Argument
+ (plus)	{+}
^ (caret)	{^}
% (percent)	{%}
~ (tilde)	{~}
[or] (brackets)	{[} or {]}
{ or } (braces)	{{} or {}}

> **Note**
>
> Beware of using movement keys such as {Down} or {Tab} as arguments of the SendKeys action to select commands or dialog items. Future versions of Access may include additional menu commands that will change the order of menu items or may involve dialogs with a different structure. There is less chance that you will have to modify your SendKeys argument for future versions if you use an Alt+*Letter* combination to choose commands or dialog items.

Editing and Copying Macro Actions and Arguments

You may need to edit a macro to change its actions or to correct an error. You also may want to copy all or part of a macro from one macrosheet to another to eliminate having to repeat work you already have done. You can even copy macros between databases.

Editing Macros

Using a mouse to edit a macro requires fewer steps than editing from the keyboard. To edit an action or argument, click the mouse pointer in an edit box in which you want to edit and then use normal Windows editing actions.

If you are using a keyboard, press Tab or Enter to move right and then down through the macrosheet. Press Shift+Tab or Shift+Enter to move left and then up. You can move in any direction with the four directional arrows.

As you move between cells, the entire cell contents are selected. You can type or select an item from a combo list to replace all of the selected entry. To edit, press F2 and then press the left- or right-arrow keys, Delete, or Backspace to edit. If the contents you are editing are too long to edit conveniently in the active column cell or the argument cell, press Shift+F2 to display the Zoom box. This box displays the entire cell contents in an edit window. Table 17.8 shows some other useful keys.

Table 17.8   Editing Keys

Key	Movement
Esc	Cancels edit before moving caret out of cell.
Home	Moves to far left cell in the same row.
End	Moves to far right cell in the same row.
Ctrl+Home	Moves to far left cell in the top row.
Ctrl+End	Moves to far left cell in the last row.
Shift+← Shift+→	Selects characters as caret moves.
Ctrl+← Ctrl+→	Moves left one word at a time. Moves right one word at a time.
Shift+Ctrl+← Shift+Ctrl+→	Selects one word at a time.

Deleting, Inserting, or Moving Rows

You should delete rows in a macro when you no longer need the action or condition in that row. You can delete one or more rows by first selecting the rows by clicking the row selector arrow to the left of the macrosheet. To select multiple rows, click the top row selector and drag down as many rows as you want selected. After the rows are selected, press Delete.

Insert rows in a macro when you want to insert an action between existing actions or when you want a blank space between macros to make them more readable. To insert a row, move the caret into a row. (The inserted row appears above the row containing the caret.) Click the row selector or drag across multiple row selectors and then press Insert.

To move one or more rows with the mouse, click the row selector or drag across multiple row selectors so that the rows you want to move are selected. Release the mouse button. Then move the mouse pointer over one of the selected row selectors and hold down the mouse button. As you hold down the button, the pointer becomes a pointer overlying a shaded square box.

Drag the mouse pointer to the row in which you want to move the selected rows. Notice that a horizontal line appears where the moved rows will appear. Release the mouse pointer at the location in which you want the moved rows.

Tip
To undo an insertion or deletion that has just occurred, choose the Edit Undo command or press Ctrl+Z.

Copying Macros

You can copy all or a portion of a macro from one macrosheet to another. This capability can help you reuse macros or use portions of a macro more than once.

To copy a single cell, such as an action, select all the characters in the cell and press Ctrl+C. Move the caret to the location where you want to paste and then press Ctrl+V.

To copy entire rows or an entire macro, click the row selector arrows to select the rows you want to copy and then press Ctrl+C. Open a new or existing macro. Select the cell in which you want to paste the copied data and press Ctrl+V.

To copy a macro from one database to another, copy the macro rows you want to move using the methods described. Choose **O**pen from the File menu while the Database window is active, and open the database in which you want to move the macro. Open an existing or new macrosheet in this database. Select the cell in which you want to paste the first macro cell and press Ctrl+V. Save the new macro.

Tip

Copying rows from a macro and pasting them into another macro doesn't change the arguments for the actions. Make sure that you check arguments after pasting to ensure that they reflect what you want them to do in the new location.

Referring to Form or Report Controls

You must know how to refer to a control name from within a macro for many reasons. You must know how to refer to control names if you want to perform such tasks as the following:

- Synchronizing records in two forms by matching values of controls.

- Setting a control to a specific value.

- Changing a macro's action based on the value of a control.

- Checking data entries values using complex checks and responding with a message.

- Moving the focus to a control on a form when the form opens or a record changes.

- Entering SQL statements in macro actions that filter or query.

Chapter 18, "Creating Macros for Forms and Reports," has numerous examples of how controls are referenced from within macros.

The syntax for referring to controls follows:

For a form:

```
Forms!FormName!ControlName
```

For a report:

```
Reports!ReportName!ControlName
```

Examples for these controls follow:

For a form:

```
Forms!Orders!Quantity
```

For a report:

```
Reports!MonthEnd!Item
```

This syntax has two variations. First, when the macro containing the reference is run from the form or report containing the control, you don't have to specify the full control name. For example, consider a form named Orders that contains a button that runs a macro. In the macro run by the button on the form, you don't have to use the full syntax:

```
Forms!Orders!Quantity
```

You have to refer only to the following:

```
Quantity
```

Tip

If you are in doubt as to which syntax to use, use the full syntax. If you use the short syntax in an inappropriate situation, the macro cannot run. Using full syntax also makes macros run faster.

Second, if a form, report, or control name contains spaces, you must enclose the name in square brackets. If you want to reference the control named Amount Shipped on the Product Shipments form, for example, you must use this syntax:

```
Forms![Product Shipments]![Amount Shipped]
```

If a macro run from the Product Shipments form had to reference the Amount Shipped control, it would use the following syntax:

```
[Amount Shipped]
```

The macro contains this syntax because of the first rule that the full syntax doesn't have to be used when the macro is run from the form or report containing the control that is referenced.

Using Conditional Tests to Change Macro Actions

Your macros can have the capability to make decisions about how they operate. Macros can test whether a condition is true and, when that condition is true, they run actions you specify.

So far, you have seen a macrosheet containing two columns: Action and Comment. You can add to this window a third column on the left in which you can put a conditional test (see fig. 17.12). You enter in this Condition column expressions that can be evaluated as **True** or **False**. If the expression evaluates as **True**, the macro action on the right runs. If the expression evaluates as **False**, the macro action doesn't run.

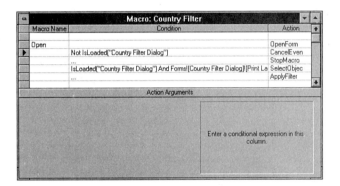

Fig. 17.12

Using tests in the Condition column to determine whether the adjacent macro action runs.

Create conditions in the Condition column with the use of expressions and control names. Table 17.9 lists some examples of typical conditions.

Table 17.9 Typical Conditions for Executing an Action.	
Condition Being Tested	**Description**
[Last Name]="Smith"	**True** when the value of the Last Name control is *Smith*.
Forms!Orders!Quantity<10	**True** when the value of the control named Quantity on the Orders form is less than 10.
[Quantity]>5 **And** [Quantity]<20	**True** when the value of the control named Quantity on the current form is between 5 and 20.

If you want macro actions to run when a condition evaluates as **True**, display the Condition column in the macrosheet and enter the condition. Display the Condition column by clicking the Show/Hide Condition button on the toolbar. Put in the adjacent Action column the macro action you want to run when the condition is **True**. If you want multiple actions to run when a condition is **True**, type an ellipsis (...) in the Condition column next to each action that also should be run. If you want actions to be executed when the condition is **False**, precede the condition with the reserved word **Not**. Figure 17.13 shows a macrosheet with a condition and multiple actions that run when the condition evaluates to **False** and when the condition evaluates to **True**. Conditions can control whether one action runs, an entire macro runs, or a portion of a macro runs.

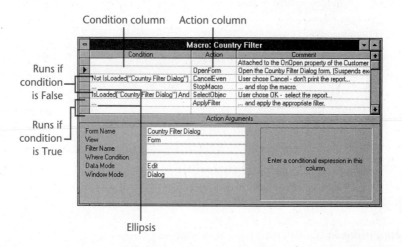

Fig. 17.13
Indicating additional actions that run when a condition is *True*.

To create macro actions that run when the condition evaluates as **True**, follow these steps:

1. Click the Show/Hide Condition button on the Macro toolbar to display the Condition column in the macrosheet.

2. Enter the condition in the Condition column.

3. Enter in the Action column the action you want to run when the condition is **True**.

4. If you want to run additional actions when the condition is true, enter them down the Action column below the action in step 3.

5. If you entered additional actions in step 4, put an ellipsis (...) in the Condition column next to each action. All these actions run when the condition is **True**.

If you save a macrosheet with the Condition column displayed, the next time you open the window in Design View, the Condition column is visible. If you want the Condition column for all macrosheets to be displayed, choose the **View** **O**ptions command and then select Macro Design from the Category list. Enter **Yes** in the Show Condition Column text box.

> **Note**
>
> The conditional If test in Access macros is different from the test in most macro and programming languages. Access macros run actions if a test is **True**, but there is no **False** or Else portion of the test. Access Macros use an If *condition* and then *action* syntax. If *condition* evaluates to **True**, the *action* runs. If *condition* returns **False**, the *action* is skipped and Access jumps to the next action that doesn't have an ellipsis.

Grouping Multiple Macros in a Macro Window

When you have many related macros, you probably will find it most conve- nient to put all the related macros in a single macrosheet. Each macro in the macrosheet must have its own unique name. You enter these names by dis- playing the Macro Name column and then typing in the names. Display the Macro Name column by choosing the **Display N**ames command or by click- ing the Show/Hide Macro Names button on the toolbar. Like the Condition column, this column is displayed to the left of the Action column (see fig. 17.14).

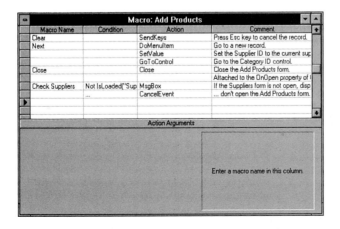

Fig. 17.14
Using the Macro Name column to name individual macros in a macrosheet.

Each unique macro in a macrosheet begins with the action to the right of the name. The macro ends when it reaches the beginning of the next macro or runs out of actions. You don't have to end a macro with a particular *end* action, as you might in many macro or programming languages.

Each macrosheet is a database object. If the macrosheet contains one macro, you can reference that macro or run the macro by using just the name of the macrosheet. In the NWIND database that comes with Access, for example, the Export Sales Data macrosheet contains a single macro. You can run this macro by referring to Export Sales Data.

When a macrosheet contains multiple macros (refer to fig. 17.14), you must reference a specific macro using the following syntax:

```
macrogroupname.macroname
```

where a period separates the *macrogroupname* from the *macroname*. The third macro in the figure, for example, can be run using the following syntax:

```
Country Filter.Cancel
```

To run this third macro, for example, by choosing the File **Ru**n Macro command, you type **Country Filter.Cancel** in the Run Macro dialog. To reference this macro from an event, you use the same syntax to reference one macro from the entire group.

Running Macros

Tip
If you run or reference a macro group, but identify only the group and not a name within it, the first macro within the group runs.

You can execute (run) macros in many ways. If you are creating quick macros for your own immediate use, you may want to run them by choosing them from the macrosheet or the Database window. To create a system that is more automated or one that is easier to use, you can run a macro as shown in table 17.10.

Table 17.10 Ways to Run a Macro	
Macros Can Run When	**Sample Use**
The operator clicks a button	Buttons on form to open other forms or print reports.
A specified event occurs	Operator moves between fields; records change; form or table opens or closes.

Macros Can Run When	Sample Use
The operator presses shortcut key	Shortcut key for frequently used operations.
The operator chooses a custom command from a custom menu	A database system needs its own custom menus.

Running Macros from the Macro Design Window

You can run macros from the macrosheet of the macro you want to run. This capability is useful when you want to test a macro. Figure 17.15 shows the mouse pointer poised over the Run button on the toolbar. Clicking the Run button runs the first macro in the active macro window, Country Filter.

To run a macro when the macro's window is active, click the Run button of the toolbar. You can choose the **Macro Run** command also. If the macro doesn't run as expected or if an Action Failed dialog appears (see fig. 17.16), you may not have had the correct forms, reports, or windows open for the macro to work correctly. Some macros may require a specific form to be active when they run. In this case, open or activate the necessary objects and run the macro using the **File Run** Macro technique described in the following section.

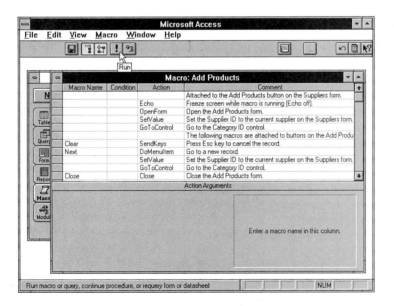

Fig. 17.15
Clicking the Run button on the toolbar to run the first macro in the active macrosheet.

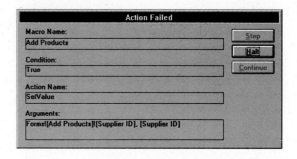

If the active macrosheet contains a group of macros, only the first macro in a macrosheet runs when you click the Run button on the toolbar. Choosing the Macro **Run** command and specifying only the name of the macrosheet is another way of running the first macro in a macrosheet. To run a specific macro within a group, use the File **Run** Macro command described in the following section.

Running Macros with Any Window Active

Choose **Run** Macro from the File menu to run macros when the macrosheet isn't active or to run a macro in a macro group. To run a macro using the **Run** Macro menu command, follow these steps:

1. Choose **Run** Macro from the File menu. The Run Macro dialog appears (see fig. 17.17).

2. To run the first or only macro within a macrosheet, select the name of the macro from the combo list. To run a specific macro from within a group, select the name of the macro group from the combo list, move the insertion point to the end of the name, and type a period followed by the name of the macro within the group: PrepareForm.PrepDate, for example.

3. Click OK, or press Enter.

Running Macros from the Database Window

Another convenient method of running the first or only macro within a macrosheet is to run it from the Database window. To run a macro from the Database window, follow these steps:

1. Open any database objects named as values of the macro's arguments, such as forms or reports.

2. Click the Macro tab to display the list of macros.

3. Double-click the macro name or select the macro name and click the Run button at the top of the Database window.

Running Macros from Another Macro

You can run a macro from within another macro by calling the macro you want to run with the RunMacro action. After the called macro runs, Access returns control to the next action in the first macro. To run a macro from within another macro, enter macro actions within a macrosheet to the point where you want the other macro to run. At that point, enter the RunMacro action in the Action column. In the Macro Name argument, select the name of the macro from the combo list. If you want one macro from within a group to run, select the name of the macro group, type a period, and type the name of the macro within the group. In figure 17.18, the RunMacro action runs one macro that loads all the forms, tables, and queries needed during initial startup. Another RunMacro action sets the default values used when the forms are initially displayed.

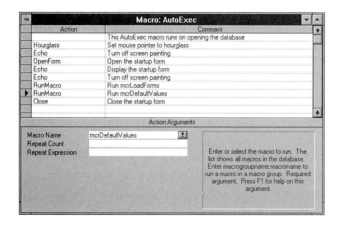

Fig. 17.18

Running a macro from within a macro.

Table 17.11 shows the arguments used with the RunMacro action.

Table 17.11 *RunMacro* Arguments	
Argument	**Description**
Macro Name	Selects the name of the macro to run from the combo list. If you are using one macro from a macro group, select the macro group name from the combo list, and type a period and then the name of the macro as described earlier in this chapter.
Repeat Count	Types the number of times you want the macro to repeat. If you don't enter a number, the macro runs once. If you are familiar with programming constructs, this process is similar to a FOR. . .NEXT loop.
Repeat Expression	Creates an expression that can be evaluated as **True** or **False**. The macro repeats until the Repeat Expression evaluates as False. If you are familiar with programming constructs, this process is similar to a WHILE loop.

Running Macros from an Event

Macros can be *triggered* when specific events in forms and reports occur. For example, you may want a macro to run when a form is opened, when the user selects or exits from a field, or when a field is double-clicked. Macro events can make your system easier to use and make it use the same operating procedures as commercially developed applications. Event-driven macros also are useful for opening multiple forms together, printing reports using specific queries, or creating error checks that are more extensive than those available through control properties.

Access 2.0

Access 2.0 has added a substantial number of new events to the original set of events offered by Access 1.x. Many of the new events, such as those related to mouse operations, are derived directly from the events offered by Visual Basic forms and controls. Other new events are specific to Access forms, reports and controls. Only 20 of the 27 events applicable to Access 2.0 forms appear in the Event Properties window for Forms, shown in figure 17.19. Increasing the number of events that can be triggered by an object is called increasing the *granularity* of events.

In addition to adding new events, the names of three Access 1.x events (OnInsert, OnMenu, and OnPush) have changed. To review the changes to property names from Access 1.x to Access 2.0, follow these steps:

1. Choose Search from the Help menu to display the Search dialog.

2. Enter **what's new** in the combo text box to bring up the What's New in Microsoft Access version 2.0 topic.

3. Double-click the highlighted entry in the upper text box, and then double-click the highlighted entry in the lower text box to display the What's New help topic.

4. Click the "Converting Macros and Code from Version 1.x to Version 2.0" hot spot to display the help topic.

5. Click the Changed Property Names to display this help topic, shown in figure 17.20.

6. Click the hot spot in the Version 2.0 Property Name column to display the help topic for the newly named property.

Fig. 17.19
Some of the events that can be triggered by *Form* objects.

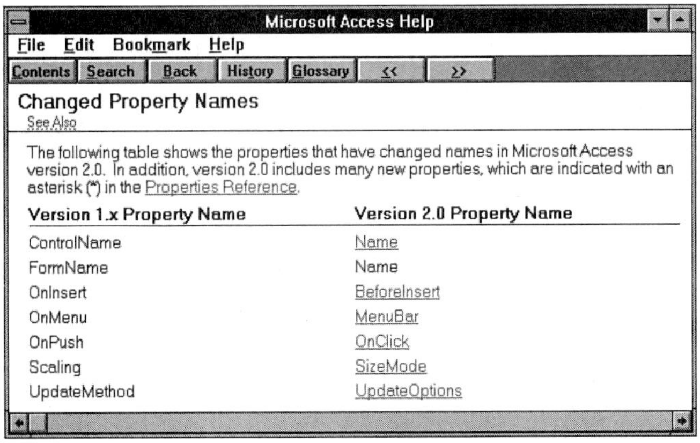

Fig. 17.20
The help topic for properties whose names have changed in Access 2.0.

Both forms and reports have events to which you can assign a macro. These events are specified within the Event Properties window for the object. Many of the events for forms, reports, and control objects are of interest primarily to Access application developers who write event-handling code in Access Basic. The tables that follow list only those events that are the most important for authors of Access macros. The events that apply to forms that are based on a **Recordset** object are listed in table 17.12.

Table 17.12 Events Triggered by a Form Based on a *Recordset* Object		
Form Property	**Event Description**	**Use**
OnOpen	Runs the macro when the form opens but before displaying a record.	Opens or closes other forms when a form is opened.
OnCurrent	Runs the macro before a record becomes current or is displayed in the form.	Moves the focus to a specific control every time the record is updated.
BeforeInsert	Runs the macro when you begin entering data in a new record (was OnInsert in Access 1.x).	Displays needed data or a warning when the user begins to enter data.
BeforeUpdate	Runs the macro after you leave a record but before the record is updated in the database; *see also* BeforeUpdate for control-level events.	Asks the operator for confirmation that the record should be updated.
AfterUpdate	Runs the macro after you leave a record and after changes in the record have been recorded in the database; *see also* AfterUpdate for control-level events.	Transmits changed records to other applications or updates other forms using the new data.
BeforeInsert	Runs the macro before you add a new record to a table or query (was OnInsert in Access 1.x).	Requests confirmation of the addition before adding the new record.
OnDelete	Runs the macro when you attempt to delete a record but before the record is deleted.	Asks the operator to confirm that the record should be deleted before deleting it.

Access
2.0

Access
2.0

IV

Form Property	Event Description	Use
OnClose	Runs the macro before the form disappears.	Asks the operator to confirm that the form should be closed or transmits data to another application when the form is closed.

Events of control objects on forms depend on the type of control object and whether the control object is bound to a field of a **Recordset** object. The events of primary interest associated with bound controls in a **Form** object are shown in table 17.13.

Table 17.13   Events in a Bound Form Control

Form Control Property	Event Description	Use
OnEnter	Runs the macro when you move the focus to a control but before focus is on the control.	Asks the operator for a password for that field or displays information about how to enter in the field.
OnClick	Runs the macro when you click a command button in a form; *see also* OnDblClick in this table (was OnPush in Access 1.x).	Runs any type of macro associated with button operations, such as opening other forms, printing a form, or updating records.
BeforeUpdate	Runs the macro after you leave a control but before the control is changed; *see also* BeforeUpdate for form events.	Validates the entry for this control using more extensive validation than is available with control properties.
AfterUpdate	Runs the macro after you leave a control and after the control changes; *see also* AfterUpdate for form-level events.	Updates other controls depending on the entry in the control that has just changed.
OnDblClick	Runs the macro when you double-click a control or control label.	Displays help information or forms that help the user with data entry.

Access
2.0

(continues)

Table 17.13   Continued

Form Control Property	Event Description	Use
OnExit	Runs the macro when you attempt to move to another control but before the focus moves away.	Uses the GoToControl action to move the focus to a specific control; uses conditions to define different controls to go to depending on the values entered.

The events that occur in a **Report** object are shown in table 17.14.

Table 17.14   Events That Occur in a Report

Report Event	Event Description	Use
OnOpen	Runs a macro when the report opens but before printing.	Asks the user to enter the criteria for a query.
OnClose	Runs a macro when the report closes.	Writes the data and time of the report to a logging file.

Within a report, events are controlled by what happens to a report section. The primary events that control macros are shown in table 17.15.

Table 17.15   Events That Occur in a *Report Section*

Section Events	Event Description	Use
OnFormat	Runs a macro after Access has accumulated or calculated the data for the section but before printing the section.	Changes the appearance or layout of a section depending on data in one of the controls.
OnPrint	Runs a macro after the data in a section is laid out but before printing.	Changes the headers, footers, or page numbers in a section.

To obtain a description of events not included in the preceding tables, place the caret in the event's text box and press F1 to display on-line help for the event.

IV

Macros

Attaching a Macro to an Event

To attach (assign) an existing macro to a specific event associated with a
form, report, or control, follow these steps:

1. Open the form or report and switch to Design View.

2. Select the form, report, section, or control to which you want to assign
   a macro using one of these procedures:

   Select a form or report by clicking in the gray background, or in a report
   by clicking outside a report section, or by choosing Select Form or Select Report from the Edit menu.

   Select a report section by clicking the section header.

   Select a control by clicking the control.

3. Display the property sheet by clicking the Properties button on the
   toolbar or by choosing Properties from the View menu.

4. Open the combo list at the top of the Properties window and select
   Event Properties.

Access

2.0

5. Select the event in the property sheet that you want to run the macro.
   These events are listed in the preceding tables: OnOpen and OnEnter, for
   example. Different events are triggered by forms, reports, and controls.

6. If you have already written the macro for the event, select from the
   event's combo list the macro you want to run, as shown in figure 17.21.
   If the macro is part of a group, select the group's name from the list,
   move the insertion point to the end of the name and then type a period
   and the macro name: **NewRecord.GotoName**, for example. (The first
   entry in the list, [Event Procedure], is intended for creating Access Basic
   event-handling procedures, rather than assigning macros.)

7. To create a new macro, click the ellipsis button to display the Choose
   Builder dialog. Double-click the Macro Builder item in the list to display
   an empty macrosheet that is automatically attached to the currently-
   selected event.

Fig. 17.21
Selecting an
existing macro to
attach to an event.

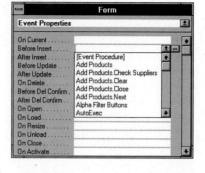

Fig. 17.22
Selecting the
Macro Builder
from the Choose
Builder dialog.

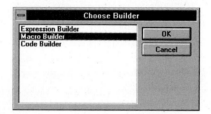

Running Macros from Custom Menu Commands

Your database system should be easy and convenient to use. Although the buttons described in the preceding section are convenient for frequent procedures, they are inappropriate when many commands or options are available in a form. In that case, you probably want to build a custom menu system containing commands that run your macros. One of the advantages of a custom menu is that you can provide the user only those menu choices that can be applied to your Access application. Menu macros are the only method offered by Access to create custom menus.

Creating custom menus with Access 1.x was a time consuming process. You had to write an AddMenu macro (called a *menu bar macro*) to create the menu bar; then write additional macros (called *menu choice macros*) to create the menu choices and supply the menu commands for each menu bar item. The SOLUTION.MDB example database includes a set of menu macros that creates a custom menu. (The menu macros have names beginning with Edit Products Menu Bar.) Access 2.0's new Menu Builder add-in makes creating custom menus easy. The appearance and operation of Menu Builder are quite similar to Visual Basic 3.0's Menu Design window. Making a menu choice in Access, however, does not generate a trappable event, such as mnuFileSave_Click. Instead, making a menu choice executes the macro action associated with the choice.

To replace the standard Access menu with a custom menu for your application, follow these steps:

1. Choose Add-Ins from the File menu to display the Menu Builder's opening dialog, shown in figure 17.23. You can choose an existing menu bar to edit by selecting the menu bar macro in the Edit Menu Bar list box.

2. This example creates a new set of menus, so click the New button to display the second Menu Builder dialog (see fig. 17.24). You can use any of Access's standard menus as a template that you can edit to create a new menu bar. Using a template saves you time by creating most of the entries for you.

Fig. 17.23
The Menu Builder dialog displays all macro objects.

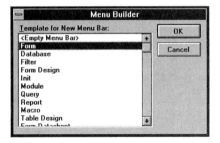

Fig. 17.24
Selecting the template from which to create a new menu bar.

3. Double-click the Form item in the Template for New Menu Bar list to open Menu Builder's main dialog for the new menu bar, as shown in figure 17.25. Access 2.0's standard menu choices for forms in run mode appear in the list.

Menu bar items appear at the left margin of the list box. Menu choices are indented by three hyphens; submenu choices are indented by six hyphens. A menu divider line is represented by a bold hyphen; a divider line appears below the &Close choice. Accelerator keys (Alt+*Key* combinations) are specified by preceding the *Key* letter with an ampersand (&). Menu choices that open dialogs have an ellipsis (...) suffix.

Fig. 17.25
The standard
menu structure
for forms in run
mode.

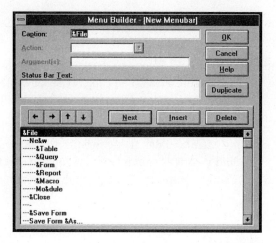

4. Most custom menus require only a few menu bars and choices. Delete the menu bar items and the menu choices not needed by your application by selecting the item and clicking the Delete button. The first few menu choices of a typical custom menu appear in figure 17.26. You can type a description of the purpose of the menu choice in the Status Bar Text box. The text you type appears in the status bar when the user selects the choice.

Each of the menu choices has a default macro action and set of arguments that corresponds to the standard function of the menu choice in Access 2.0. You can change the default action by opening the Action combo list and selecting the DoMenuItem, RunMacro, or RunCode action. The Menu Builder supports only these three macro actions.

5. To Add a new menu bar or menu choice, select item that follows the new menu choice, and then click the Insert button to add an empty row above the selection. If you want a new menu bar, click the left-arrow button to move the choice to the left margin of the list box. If you want a new menu choice of a menu bar, click the right-arrow button (if necessary). Then select the action for the new item, and add the appropriate arguments for the action in the Argument(s) text box, separated by semicolons.

To use the *argument builder* to select the arguments for the action, click the ellipsis button to open the *ActionName* Arguments dialog shown for the DoMenuItem action in figure 17.26. Each argument has a drop-down list that you can choose argument values from.

To move a menu item to a different location with respect to other menu items, select the item and click the up- or down-arrow button.

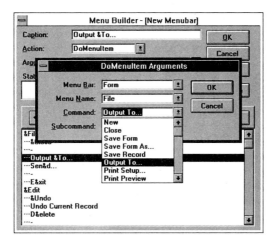

Fig. 17.26
Adding or changing the arguments for a menu macro action.

6. When you've completed the design of your custom menu, click the OK button to create the menu macros. Type the name of your menu bar macro in the Save As dialog. Menu Builder writes the menu bar macro and each menu choice macro for you. Figure 17.27 shows the new menu macros added to the Database window's list of macros for NORTHWIND.MDB.

It is an Access convention to name menu macros by adding an under-score (_) and the menu bar name to the menu bar macro, as in mcr*AppMenuBar*_File. Submenu menu-choice macro names have an additional underscore followed by the name of the submenu choice.

Fig. 17.27
The Database window with the new custom menu macros added.

7. Open the menu bar macro and the menu choice macros to check the menu structure. Figure 17.28 shows the macrosheet for the mcrAppMenuBar_File macro.

Fig. 17.28

The macrosheet
for the
mcrAppMenuBar_File
menu choice
macro.

You can't run a menu bar or menu choice macro from the Database Container or by clicking the Run Macro button of the Macro Design window's toolbar. You receive an error message if you try. You attach the menu bar macro to the MenuBar property of the first form that opens in your application. (In Access 1.x, the MenuBar property is called the OnMenu event.) In the Northwind Traders sample database, the opening form is the Main Switchboard.

To attach the mcrAppMenuBar macro to the MenuBar property of the Main Switchboard form, follow these steps:

1. Open the Main Switchboard form in Design View.

2. Click the Properties button of the toolbar to display the Form Properties window.

3. Open the drop-down list box, and select Other Properties.

4. Place the caret in the text box of the MenuBar property, open the drop-down list, and select mcrAppMenuBar or the name you gave your custom menu bar macro (see fig. 17.29).

5. Click the Form View button of the toolbar. Your custom menu bar replaces Access 2.0's standard menus (see fig. 17.30).

6. Close the Main Switchboard form without saving the changes.

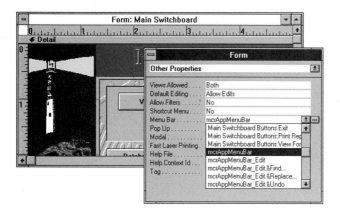

Fig. 17.29
Attaching the menu bar macro to the *MenuBar* property of a form.

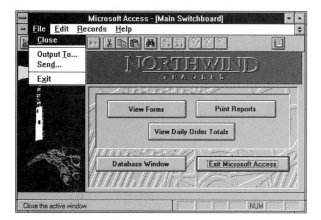

Fig. 17.30
The custom menu bar and its new File choices.

IV

Macros

Note

Custom menus only appear when the form to which the menu bar macro is attached is active. Menu bar and menu choice macros are likely to differ for most of the forms of your application. You can write your own menu bar and menu choice macros, but using the Menu Builder add-in is a much faster process in most cases.

Running Macros from a Shortcut Key

You may want to assign macros you use frequently to a shortcut keystroke. This capability enables you to press a shortcut key such as Ctrl+N to see the next record or Ctrl+P to print.

Macros are assigned to keystrokes using a three-step process:

1. Create the macros you want assigned to shortcut keys in one macro group.

2. In the macrosheet's Name column adjacent to the first macro action for each macro, type the shortcut key code for that macro.

3. Enter the name of the macro group into the Key Assignment Macro field of the Keyboard Category of the View Options command.

Figure 17.31 shows a macro group containing shortcut key codes in the Macro Name column and the macros those codes run. Figure 17.32 shows the Options dialog and the Key Assignment Macro property into which you type the name of the macro group containing shortcut key assignments.

Fig. 17.31
Codes in the Macro Name column specifying which key combination runs a macro.

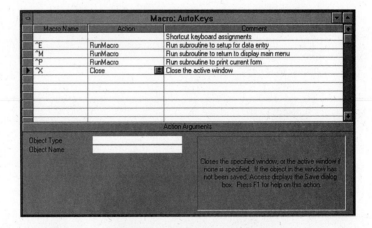

Fig. 17.32
The Key Assignment Macro property specifying which macro group identifies shortcut keys.

Access uses the name AutoKey by default in the Key Assignment Macro property of the Options dialog. You can save the macro group containing shortcut keys with the name AutoKey, or you can change AutoKey in the Key Assignment macro to name any macro group.

The list of shortcut key codes is a subset of the key codes described for the SendKeys action. These codes also use a caret (^) to indicate the Ctrl key and a plus sign (+) to indicate the Shift key. The keys and key codes to which you can assign macros are shown in table 17.16.

Table 17.16   Keys and Key Codes to Which You Can Assign Macros

Shortcut Key or Combination	Key Code for the Macro Name Column
Ctrl+*Letter*	^*letter*
Ctrl+*Number*	^*number*
Function key	{F1} and so on
Ctrl+*Function key*	^{F1} and so on
Shift+*Function key*	+{F1} and so on
Insert or Ins	{Insert}
Ctrl+Insert or Ctrl+Ins	^{Insert}
Shift+Insert or Shift+Ins	+{Insert}
Delete or Del	{Delete} or {Del}
Ctrl+Delete or Ctrl+Del	^{Delete} or ^{Del}
Shift+Delete or Shift+Del	+{Delete} or +{Del}

Note

Shortcut key combinations involving letters that are predefined in Access, such as Ctrl+C and Ctrl+X, can be assigned to your own macros. Your macro takes precedence, however, over the predefined meaning of the shortcut combination. Beware of using Ctrl+C, Ctrl+V, Ctrl+X, and Ctrl+Z for this reason.

IV

Macros

Changing Shortcut Keys during Operation

If your Access system always uses the same shortcut keys for all forms, reports, and operators, you can put all your shortcut keys in a single macro group. As described, you can use the default name AutoKey to name that macro group or give the macro group any name and change the Key Assignment Macro property in the View Options dialog. The name of the macro in the Key Assignment Macro property is read by Access when you first open the database.

To use different sets of shortcut keys for different forms, reports, or operators, you have to create a macro that changes the macro name in the Key Assignment Macro property of the View Options dialog. The macro uses SendKeys and DoMenuItem to do this. The macro necessary for changing shortcut key assignments during database operation is shown in table 17.17.

The macro in table 17.17 works as follows. The SendKeys action sends the keystrokes to the computer's keyboard buffer before the View Options dialog opens. Those keystrokes wait for the dialog to open, and then they stream into the dialog as though you just typed them.

The keystrokes listed in the Keystrokes argument select the Categories list in the View Options dialog and move down to the second item, Keyboard. The keystrokes then select the Items list and move down three cells to the Key Assignment Macro property. In this property edit box, the keystrokes type *newkeymacro*. The name of your macro, *newkeymacro,* contains the new shortcut keys. Using the tilde (~) is the same as pressing Enter to close the View Options dialog. The DoMenuItem action displays the View Options dialog, and the keystrokes from the buffer stream into the dialog as though you typed them, changing the Key Assignment Macro property and closing the box. From that point, Access looks at the macro named in the Key Assignment Macro property whenever it has to find the macro that matches a shortcut key.

This macro renames shortcut keys to the new set specified in the macro, *newkeymacro*—where *newkeymacro* is the name of the macro you have written that contains a new set of shortcut keys.

Table 17.17   A Macro to Change Shortcut Keys

Action	Argument	Argument Entry
SendKeys	Keystrokes	%C{Down}%I{Down 3}*newkeymacro*~
	Wait	No
DoMenuItem	Menu Bar	Form
	Menu Name	View
	Command	Options

Remember that the *newkeymacro* name shown in the table should be replaced with the name of the macro you have created that specifies new shortcut keys.

When you create this macro, you see the keystrokes typed in the Options dialog. If you want the macro to run faster and not display the dialog, insert an Echo action with a No argument at the beginning of the list of actions.

> **Note**
>
> Be careful about frequently changing numerous shortcut keys. It can make your programs difficult to learn. One way to help users learn shortcut keys is to type the shortcut key combination into the command name if there is a custom menu. Another way is to display an abbreviated list of shortcut keys at the bottom of the form.

Running Macros at Startup

Polished systems use a startup macro to prepare the database before the user sees the first screen. Some of the things you may want to happen automatically during startup are changing display settings, arranging forms, setting defaults, and importing data from files or servers. After you write a macro that performs these tasks, you can make it run at startup by saving it with the name AutoExec. The next time you open your database, the macro with the name AutoExec runs immediately.

To prevent an AutoExec macro from running at startup, hold down the Shift key when you choose OK or press Enter in the Open Database dialog.

Troubleshooting Macros

Like other forms of programming, building macros is a continuous process of testing and refining. Building a macro usually begins with creating a simple macro, checking to ensure that it works, and then adding more actions to it. You repeat this process until the macro is complete. The process continues from simple to complex functionality. At each stage, the macro operation is checked so that problems can be resolved while they are small. This section describes some of the troubleshooting aids available in Access and gives you tips about how to resolve problems.

Handling Failed Macros

When a macro reaches an error that causes it to halt operation, Access displays an Action Failed dialog (refer to fig. 17.16 earlier in the chapter). This dialog shows you the name of the macro that failed, the action on which it failed, and the arguments for that action. Note the macro name and action that caused the problem. Note also which form or report is displayed and what action was occurring on-screen; you may find a clue as to why the action failed. Click the Halt button.

Switch to the macrosheet of the macro that failed. Examine the action that failed. Some things to check are whether the action matched the displayed view and object at the time of failure, whether the logic was correct for the procedure the macro was attempting, and whether the data in the arguments is correct.

Single-Stepping through Macro Operation

When a macro fails, its cause may not be readily apparent. Then, it often helps to operate the macro one step at a time. This process enables you to see clearly, for example, what is happening on-screen, which view is present, and what characters are sent with the SendKeys action. To run a macro using the single-step method, follow this procedure:

1. Open the macrosheet.

2. Choose the Macro Single Step command, or click the Single Step button (a footprint) on the Macro toolbar.

3. Arrange the screen and database system as it appears when the macro runs.

4. Run the macro.

In single-step mode, the macro displays a Macro Single Step dialog before each action. Once a single-step mode is turned on, it stays on until you turn it off. Figure 17.33 shows a Macro Single Step dialog. This dialog is similar to the Action Failed dialog, but the Step and Continue buttons are available.

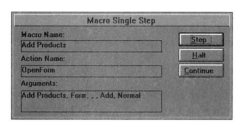

Fig. 17.33
The Macro Single Step dialog.

Choosing the Step button runs the action displayed in the dialog and then stops at the next action and displays that action in the dialog. If one of the arguments involves an expression, the Macro Single Step dialog displays the result of that expression.

When the macro reaches a point at which you want it to continue without stepping through each action, choose the Continue button. Then the macro runs at normal speed.

Troubleshooting Common Macro Issues

The troubleshooting tips in this section may help you correct problems with your macros more quickly.

Run with the Incorrect Object Active

When a macro runs and then halts with the warning that a database object or control isn't available, the macro probably hasn't activated the correct database object.

This commonly happens when the macro needs to run with a specific form active. The macro may be looking for a control that doesn't exist on the active object, for example. To prevent this situation, get in the habit of inserting an OpenObject action to open or activate the proper form, query, table, or report before the macro runs. Misspelled control names also may cause this problem.

Display All Actions during a Single-Step Operation

Remove or remark out Echo actions so that you can see screen changes while running with Single Step.

Echo with the Echo On argument of No hides screen changes. This action prevents you from seeing what is happening during a single-step operation. Change the No argument to Yes to see what the macro is doing. After you have found and resolved the problem, change the value of the Echo On argument from Yes to No. Another technique for tricking an Echo action into not running is to type **False** in the Condition column next to the Echo action you want not to run.

Alert Yourself to Critical Points in Operation

Insert message boxes at critical points in a macro to tell yourself what the macro is doing at that point.

A message box, created with the MsgBox action, can display which portion of the macro is ready to run or what should happen on-screen. This capability enables you to run the macro at normal operating speed and receive notices about which operations are taking place.

Insert Breaks to Check Intermediary Results

Insert a StopMacro action so that you can run a macro at normal speed and stop at a specific point.

If a long macro takes a while to run, you may not want to single-step through its actions to the point where you suspect a problem. Rather, insert a StopMacro action after the action you suspect is causing the problem. You then can run the macro at normal speed. When it stops, you can check results to see whether the macro worked correctly to that point. Move the StopMacro action forward or backward in the macro to pinpoint the area causing a problem. You also can use a condition in the Conditional column to stop the macro for a specific condition. A condition can check the value of a control, for example, and stop the macro if the value is incorrect.

Use Segments of Reusable Macros

Learn to write reusable macros or to write large macros as collections of smaller macros. Run the reusable or small segments with the RunMacro action.

Troubleshooting a small macro is much easier than troubleshooting a large one. If you build small subroutine macros that work correctly, you can join them into a larger macro by running them in the order you want with the RunMacro action. Use the comment lines at the beginning of subroutine macros to document which larger macros or events call the subroutine. This practice helps if you have to change the subroutine. The comments help you determine how changes to the macro may affect other parts of the database.

IV

Macros

Monitor How the Macro Is Related to Other Macros and Objects

Take care in changing macros that may be used in numerous locations.

After changing a macro that seems to work correctly, other parts of your database may not work correctly. The macro you changed may have been used by other parts of the database application. Changing the macro to meet the requirements for one part of the program may have changed it so that it doesn't work correctly in another part of the program.

Watch That *SendKeys* Sends Characters to the Correct Location

If you see menus pull down by themselves, or if data is entered as though it is being typed by a ghost, you have an errant SendKeys action.

SendKeys sends keystrokes to Access just as though you were typing the keys. If you have the Wait argument set incorrectly, or if there is no dialog that opens to receive the sent keys, the keystrokes may be sent directly to the menu bar or into a form, just as though you had typed them.

Be Careful about the Full Macro Name

If only one macro from a macro group runs, check the macro name.

If you specify only the name of a macrosheet, only the first macro in the macro group runs. To run a specific macro in a group, you must specify the macro group name, a period, and the name of the specific macro in the group. The syntax is

```
macrogroupname.macroname
```

When you copy a macro to a new database or macrosheet, the action arguments don't change. In its new environment, arguments such as form, query, or control names may be different. Check the arguments. Even though the actions may be in the correct order, the arguments may be wrong.

Limit the Use of Macros in Run-Time Applications

Minimize the number of macros you employ in applications that you run with MSARN200.EXE, the run-time version of Access 2.0. If an error occurs during the execution of a macro under run-time Access, the Action Failed dialog does not appear. Instead, your application unceremoniously quits without warning you. It takes a major testing effort to ensure that all your macros are *bulletproof*, especially in complex macro-driven applications.

An application ideally designed for use with MSARN200.EXE should include only two types of macros:

- A single AutoExec or startup macro with a RunCode action to execute the main function (called the *entry-point*) to your Access Basic code.

- Menu bar macros with the necessary AddMenu actions to create the custom menu bars and menu choice macros that your application needs. You cannot execute the AddMenu action with a DoCmd AddMenu instruction in Access Basic.

All macro actions or their equivalents, with the exception of RunCode and AddMenu, are available in Access Basic. You should convert all other macros in your application to their equivalent in Access Basic code. Re-create each macro as an Access Basic function, and then substitute *=FunctionName( )* for the *MacroGroup.MacroName* entry in the text box for the event to which the macro is attached. Substituting Access Basic for macros also aids in documenting your application—you can print your Access Basic code. The macro documentation created by the Database Documentor is not as understandable as code, at least to persons who are familiar with one of the dialects of Object Basic.

Each Access Basic function you substitute for macros must include full error trapping with On Error GoTo *LabelName* statements and corresponding labels. In Chapter 27, the "Handling Run-Time Errors" section shows you how to write error-handling routines. Untrapped errors in Access Basic functions and procedures also cause abrupt exits from applications running under MSARN200.EXE.

> **Note**
>
> Andrew Miller, a member of the Microsoft Access quality assurance team, has created an Access library, FIRSTLIB.MDA, that includes an effective macro-to-module converter function. The converter translates your macros to a text file of Access Basic code. When you execute the converter function, a list lets you choose the macro to convert. Each macro is converted into a function named for the macro, and full error-trapping code is added. Download FIRST.ZIP from the MSACCESS forum on CompuServe. When you expand the ZIP file, FIRSTLIB.TXT gives you instructions for using FIRSTLIB.MDA.

From Here...

Microsoft designed Access 2.0's macro language so that you don't need to learn Access Basic and write code to automate your Access applications. The 46 macro actions are surprisingly versatile; you can create quite complex database applications using only macros to respond to events. Even if you write Access Basic event-handling procedures, you are likely to execute many of the macro actions described in this chapter in your code.

The following chapters provide additional information on creating and using event-handling macros:

- Chapter 16, "Automating Applications with Macros: An Overview," describes the process of creating a simple macro to display a form and run a query.

- Chapter 18, "Creating Macros for Forms and Reports," provides examples of many of the most frequently used macro actions.

- Chapter 27, "Writing Access Basic Code," shows you how to use the DoCmd instruction to execute macros with Access Basic.

Creating Macros for Forms and Reports

Whether you use macros as simple productivity aids or to create a complete system that includes menus, command buttons, and event-driven actions, the ability to use macros makes a valuable addition to your skills. In Chapter 17, you saw the fundamentals involved in creating different kinds of macros. In this chapter, you see examples of frequently used macros. Reading and experimenting with the macros in this chapter helps you better understand how macros work and how to create new macros by synthesizing and recombining what you learn in these examples.

In this chapter, many of the macros are designed to augment the Personnel Action Entry form used in other chapters of the book. If you have built the Personnel Action Entry form, you can add many of these macros to make the form easier to use. The Personnel Action Entry form, with command buttons that run the macros described in this chapter, is shown in figure 18.1.

Note

Before working through the examples in this chapter, copy the Northwind Traders database to a separate directory where you can experiment without altering the original database. Use File Manager to copy the NWIND.MDB file to a new file named MYWIND.MDB, or the like, in the \ACCESS directory.

In this chapter, you learn to write Access macros that

- Control forms

- Select a particular record

- Set the focus to a control

- Add and delete records

- Set values of control objects

- Synchronize **Recordset** objects of two forms

- Print a form

Fig. 18.1
The Personnel
Action Entry form
with added
command
buttons.

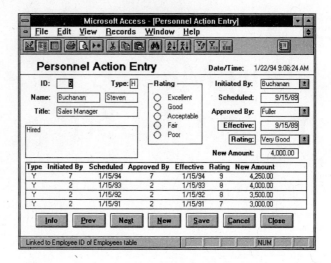

Fig. 18.1
The Personnel
Action Entry form
with added
command
buttons.

Controlling Forms with Macros

Forms lend themselves to the use of macros. Data entry operators spend a high percentage of their time working in forms—entering and editing data or choosing options from pop-up forms that look like dialogs.

Opening and Sizing a Form

One of the more frequently needed and easiest to create macros is a macro that opens and sizes a form. You created just such a macro in Chapter 16, "Automating Applications with Macros: An Overview." Figure 18.2 shows a macro that opens a form. The OpenForm action is selected so that you can see the related arguments in the Action Arguments pane of the Macro window. The OpenForm arguments specify the name of the form to open, whether the form can be edited or is read-only, and in which view the form appears. The Where Condition specifies the record on which the form opens. The Zoom window is shown in the lower part of the screen so that you can see the full Where Condition argument.

You enter the OpenForm action in the cell of the Macro window by selecting OpenForm from the Action list or by dragging the form's name from the Database window into the action cell of the Macro window. Dragging the form's name enters the appropriate arguments. Chapters 16 and 17 describe how to do these two procedures.

Opening a form with a macro gives you greater control than when you open a form manually. With the addition of the actions described in the following tables, the macros can open a form and reduce the screen flicker, change the pointer to an hourglass, size the form, and set the focus to a specific control. Examples that show how to use most of these actions are provided in Chapter 16 and are not duplicated here.

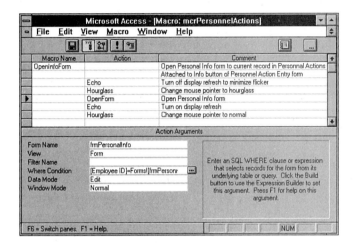

Fig. 18.2
Macro actions that open a form.

Table 18.1 lists the Echo and Hourglass actions you can use to reduce screen flicker and to let the operator know to pause during operation.

Table 18.1	Using the *Echo* and *Hourglass* Actions
Action	**Function**
Echo	Reduces screen flicker during opening. Set the Echo On argument to No before OpenForm to freeze the screen. After the form is opened and sized, and the focus is positioned on a control, set the Echo On argument to Yes to display the completed form. Echo turns on automatically at the end of a macro.
Hourglass	Set the Hourglass On argument to Yes to indicate that the user needs to wait. This is helpful when running long macros or opening large files.

Use the MoveSize, DoMenuItem, and Maximize actions to control the size of the form when it opens. Add the Echo action with the value of the Echo On argument set to Yes after the form has resized. Table 18.2 describes these actions.

Table 18.2	Using the *MoveSize* and *DoMenuItem* Actions
Action	**Function**
MoveSize	Positions and sizes a form using inches measured from the top left corner of the form display area. Use Form Design View with **View Ruler** turned on to see the relative size of inch measurements on-screen.
DoMenuItem	Uses the equivalent of the Size to Fit Form choice of the **Window** menu to exactly fit the window around the form. Set the values of the following arguments: Menu Bar to Form, Menu Name to Window, and Command to Size to Fit Form.

Access
2.0

You have a number of ways to open a form and display the results of a query or filter that limits the records shown in the form. You can use the Filter Name and Where Condition arguments of the OpenForm action to specify the filter or statement that limits records. You also can use the ApplyFilter and ShowAllRecords actions to apply and remove a filter for the records in the current form. Following sections of this chapter describe some of these methods.

Selecting a Control in a Form

One action that macros need frequently is the capability of moving to a specific control, page, or record. You often may use the GoToControl action after performing another action to move the focus to a specific control on the form—the control where the user expects to enter data.

Tip

If you set the value of Access 2.0's new AutoCenter property of the form to Yes, the form is automatically centered horizontally and is positioned vertically above the center of your display.

The simple macro described by table 18.3 opens a form and then uses the GoToControl action to move the focus to the Last Name control. Use only the control name in the Control argument. The control must be on the active form when the GoToControl action runs. You also can use GoToControl to move to a control in a form datasheet, table datasheet, or query result set.

Table 18.3	A Macro to Open a Form and Set the Focus to a Control		
Action	**Argument**	**Argument Entry**	**Explanation**
OpenForm	Form Name	frmPersonalInfo	Opens the Personal Info form.
GoToControl	View Control	Form Last Name	Moves to the control on which the FindRecord action searches.

If you are working in a report, the GoToPage action enables you to move to the first control on a specific page. The GoToRecord action enables you to move to the first, last, next, previous, or new record. You also can move to a specific record number. The record number is the number indicated in the horizontal scroll bar when you scroll through the **Recordset** of a table or form.

Selecting a Record in a Form

The macros described in this section use the GoToRecord action to change the current record in a form. You will probably want to attach these record-selecting macros to command buttons, menu commands, or shortcut keys to make it easy to move between records. You can use the GoToRecord action to select a record in a table, form, or report.

The macro listed in table 18.4 shows you how to make the first record current in a form, table, or report. You generally want a macro like this to run whenever you open the form. The directions for attaching a macro so that the macro runs whenever the form opens are given at the end of this section.

Table 18.4 Making a Form's First Record the Current Record			
Action	**Argument**	**Argument Entry**	**Explanation**
GoToRecord	Object Type	Form	Moves to the first record. (Attach to the On Open event of the form so that the form displays the first record when the form opens.)
	Object Name	Personnel Actions	
	Record	First	
	Offset	(none)	

The following macro moves the current record to the next record by using the GoToRecord action, with the Record argument specified as Next. This macro is attached to the Next command button on the Personnel Action Entry form (refer to fig. 18.1). The Personnel Action Entry form is assumed to be active because the macro runs only when you choose the Next command button. The GoToRecord action is straightforward and moves the current record to the next record in the form.

Tip

When you open a **Recordset** object, the record pointer is placed on the first record automatically. It is a good programming practice, however, to use the explicit `GoToRecord` *ObjectName*, `First` action.

One potential problem with this macro, however, is that the operator may click the Next command button while a new (tentative append) record is current. This situation can occur if you click the New command button to move to the last record and then click the Next command button. Attempting to move to the next record beyond the last one causes a macro error. The macro of table 18.5 illustrates one method of checking for the empty record and avoiding a macro error.

Table 18.5	Testing for an Empty Record			
Condition	**Action**	**Argument**	**Argument Entry**	**Explanation**
`IsNull(Forms![frmPersonnel Actions]![PA ID])`	MsgBox	Message	This is the last record	Checks whether already on a blank record.
		Beep	Yes	
		Type	None	
		Title	Add Record	
...	StopMacro			Stops macro if `IsNull()` is **True**.
	GoToRecord	Object Type Object Name	Form frmPersonnelActions	Goes to next record.
		Record	Next	
		Offset	(none)	

This macro needs the **IsNull()** condition and the MsgBox and StopMacro actions to resolve the problem that occurs when you attempt to select the next record while you are on the last record. The Personnel Action Entry form is designed so that the PA ID control always contains a value. The only record in which PA ID is **Null** is the last (tentative append) record. The condition, **IsNull**(Forms![Personnel Actions]![PA ID]), is true only when the current record is the tentative append. When the condition returns **True**, the MsgBox action displays a warning to the operator and the StopMacro action stops the macro. Notice that the ellipsis (...) in the cell under the `IsNull()` condition indicates that the `StopMacro` action should also run when the condition is true.

To attach a macro to a form's `OnOpen` property so that the macro runs whenever the form opens, perform the following steps:

1. Create and save the macro.

2. Open the form in Design View. Display the Properties window.

3. Scroll to the `OnOpen` property.

4. Select from the `OnOpen` property list the name of the macro that you want to run when the form opens. Access 2.0 displays the name of each macro contained in a macro group, so you don't have to type the macro name manually.

Access

2.0

5. Save the form.

Adding a New Record

Adding a new record uses a macro very similar to the macro that moves to the next record. In the following example, the macro runs when you click the New command button on the Personnel Action Entry form. Clicking the command button opens the Select Employee form shown in figure 18.3 so that you can add a new personnel action for any Northwind Traders employee.

The macro described in table 18.6 is attached to the `OnClick` property of the New command button on the Personnel Action Entry form. The macro begins with an `IsNull()` condition that checks to see whether the current record contains a PA ID (Employee ID) value or is **Null**. If the PA ID field value is **Null**, the macro stops. If the current record in the Personnel Action Entry form does contain employee information, then the rest of the macro runs.

The `Echo` action turns off the screen display so that the opening process runs faster and with less flicker. The display is turned back on when the macro finishes running. The `DoMenuItem` action moves the form to the tentative append record. The `OpenForm` action then opens the Select Employee form, frmSelectEmployee (see fig. 18.3).

Fig. 18.3
The Select
Employee form.

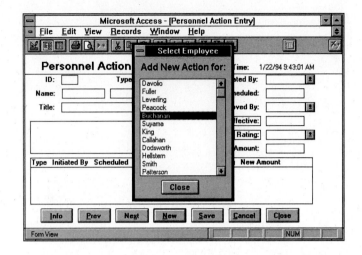

Table 18.6 Adding a New Record and Opening a Form

Condition	Action	Argument	Argument Entry	Explanation
IsNull ([PA ID])	MsgBox	Message	Move to a record that has an employee to add an action.	Checks whether on a blank record.
		Beep	Yes	
		Type	None	
		Title	Add Record	
...	StopMacro			Stops macro if **IsNull()** is **True**.
	Echo	Echo On	No	Stops screen flicker by not refreshing display until done.
	GoToRecord	Object Type Object Name Record	Form frmPersonnelActions New	Goes to the tentative append record of the Personnel Action Entry form.
	OpenForm	Form Name	frmSelectEmployee	Opens the Select Employee form.
		View	Form	
		Filter Name	(none)	

Condition	Action	Argument	Argument Entry	Explanation
		Where		
		Condition	(none)	
		Data Mode	Edit	
		Window Mode	Normal	

The Select Employee form (frmSelectEmployee) is a *modal pop-up form*, a synonym for dialog. You create a modal pop-up form by setting the values of the Modal and PopUp properties of the form to Yes. It is a convention that modal pop-up forms use the Dialog value for the BorderStyle property. Modal pop-up forms retain the focus until you close them. The record source for the list box of the Select Employee form in the Employees table. The Close command button of the Select Employee form executes the CloseForm macro, listed in table 18.7, that passes the Employee ID value from the list selection to the PA ID text box of the Personnel Action Entry form.

Condition	Action	Argument	Argument Entry	Explanation
Table 18.7 The CloseForm Macro for the Select Employee Form				
Not IsNull ([lstEmployee])	Set Value	Item	Forms! [frmPersonnelActions] ![PA ID]	Sets the value of the PD ID field of the Personnel Action Entry form.
		Value	[lstEmployee].Value	
IsNull ([lstEmployee])	Run Macro	Macro Name	mcrPersonnelActions. CancelEdit	Runs the macro to cancel the record addition.
		Repeat Count	(none)	
		Repeat Expression	(none)	
	Close	Object Type	Form	Closes the Select Employee form.
		Object Name	frmSelectEmployee	

Access 2.0

If a selection is made in the employee list, the SetValue action transfers the Employee ID value from the list to the PA ID text box of the Personnel Action Entry form. Using Access 2.0's new Value property of control objects is optional; the name of the control object also returns its value. Notice that because the macro was run from the Select Employee form, the PA ID on the frmPersonnelActions form must be referred to as

    Forms![frmPersonnelActions]![PA ID].

If no selection is made in the employee list, the CancelEdit macro, included in the macro group (mcrPersonnelActions) for the Personnel Action Entry form, executes. The CancelEdit macro uses the DoMenuItem action to execute the Undo Current Record choice of the Edit menu (see table 18.9).

Deleting a Record

Tip

When entering a new record from a data entry form, you get an error when the values in key field(s) are the same as values in existing records.

You need to be able to delete records that are no longer valid. The Delete command button on the Personnel Action Entry form is attached to a Delete macro that deletes the current record. The form shows more than one personnel action record in the subform. The macro deletes the current record of the Personnel Action Entry form.

In the macro shown in table 18.8, the first DoMenuItem action selects the current record and then the second DoMenuItem deletes the selected record. An Access warning box displays when you attempt to delete a record and asks whether you are sure you want to delete the record. Click OK to delete the record. The final DoMenuItem runs the Refresh choice of the Records menu to update the display. Always use the Refresh choice to update the display for deleted or edited records.

Table 18.8   A Macro to Delete the Current Record

Action	Argument	Argument Entry	Explanation
DoMenuItem	Menu Bar	Form	Selects the current record using menu commands.
	Menu Name	Edit	
	Command	Select Record	
	Subcommand	(none)	
DoMenuItem	Menu Bar	Form	Deletes the current record using menu commands.
	Menu Name	Edit	

Action	Argument	Argument Entry	Explanation
	Command	Delete	
	Subcommand	(none)	
DoMenuItem	Menu Bar	Form	Refreshes the display after deleting record. (**Refresh** does not work when adding records.)
	Menu Name	Records	
	Command	Refresh	
	Subcommand	(none)	

Canceling Changes

You can undo the most recent edit to the Personnel Action Entry form by clicking the Cancel command button. The OnClick event for the command button runs the CancelEdit macro shown in table 18.9. This macro runs a DoMenuItem action that replicates the Undo Current Record choice of the **Edit** menu. A final action, RepaintObject, ensures that the entire Personnel Action Entry form is updated.

Tip

If you need the equivalent of pressing the Esc key, use the SendKeys action to send the keystrokes {Esc}.

Table 18.9   A Macro to Cancel Edits to the Current Record

Action	Argument	Argument Entry	Explanation
DoMenuItem	Menu Bar	Form	Undoes the last change to the current record.
	Menu Name	Edit	
	Command	Undo Current	
		Record	
	Subcommand	(none)	
RepaintObject	Object Type	Form	Refreshes the screen without redoing any queries.
	Object Name	frmPersonnelActions	

Setting Values in a Form

Through the SetValue action, you can set values in a form or a property, just as though you typed them. A few of the ways you can use SetValue include the following:

- Set control values in a form

- Set default values in custom dialogs

- Change the appearance of a control or form by changing the values of its properties (Access 2.0 lets you change most of the properties of database objects.)

The SetValue action transfers the result of an expression to the Value property of the control you specify. The result of the expression can be text, a number, or a reference to another control. If the control used in the expression is on the form from which the macro ran, you do not have to use the full syntax to identify the control.

Table 18.10 shows the SetValue action as used in the "Adding a New Record" section earlier in this chapter. Clicking the Close command button of the Select Employee form runs the macro. In that example, the SetValue action transfers the Employee ID value from the currently open Select Employee form into another form, Personnel Action Entry. The transfer ensures that the newly entered record used the same Employee ID value that you select when you click the command button.

Table 18.10	A Macro to Delete the Current Record	
Action	**Argument**	**Argument Entry**
SetValue	Item	Forms![frmPersonnelActions]![PA ID]
	Expression	[lstEmployee].Value

The Item argument is the name of the control being set to a new value. Because the Item is not on the form containing the command button that started the macro, you must specify the argument using the full syntax.

Expression is the value being placed into the control. Because the control containing the Expression, lstEmployee.Value, is on the form containing the command button from which the macro ran, you can specify only lstEmployee, instead of using the full control identifier syntax.

You also can use the SetValue action to change the property of a control. You might want to use the Select Employee form for a variety of applications. Thus you need to change the Caption property of the label above the list of employee names to suit the purpose for which the form is used. To change a control's property, enter as the Item argument the name of the control, a period, and then the property name. In the following macro, the label caption is set to "Add New Action for:" (see table 18.11). (It was not possible to change the value of the Caption property of a label with Access 1.x in run mode.) You must use the full syntax for lblListCaption because the macro starts from the Personnel Action Entry form, not the Select Employee form. Note that you enclose literal strings used as values of the Item argument in double quotation marks.

Access

2.0

Troubleshooting

When I run a macro that sets the value of a property, I get a "Can't set value" error message.

Most likely, the property you specified is not valid or is read-only for the object. As an example, label control objects don't have a Value property; you use the Caption property to enter the caption text. Most properties of Access 2.0 database objects are read-write in run mode, but others remain read-only in run mode. If the property name you specified is valid, check on-line help to determine whether the property value is read-write in run mode. Remember that you must open the form to which your Item entry refers before you can change the value of a form property or the property of a control on the form.

Table 18.11   A Macro to Set the Value of a Control Property

Action	Argument	Argument Entry	Explanation
SetValue	Item	Forms![frmSelectEmployee] !lblListCaption.Caption	Specifies the control property.
	Expression	"Add New Action for:"	Specifies the value for the control property.

In some cases, you may need to change a property for an entire form. For example, you may want a form that is normally visible to disappear. This change can be useful so that the form does not appear, but its controls are still available so that your macros can read the values of the invisible form's controls.

Note

Showing and hiding forms, rather than opening and closing forms, speeds up the operation of your application at the expense of added resource requirements.

Synchronizing Forms to the Same Record

In earlier chapters of this book, you learned how a main form can display information and also a subform of related information. The subform of the Personnel Action Entry form displays the last four personnel actions for the person listed in the main part of the form. Although this subform gives you an information-packed view into your database, it does restrict some of the flexibility of seeing related data. You are limited to seeing the number of records that fit in the subform.

Another, more flexible method of viewing, adding, and editing information related to the current form is to open a second form. This second form displays only data related to the first form. The following macro demonstrates how to keep the record in the second form (Personal Info) synchronized with the record displayed in the first form (Personnel Action Entry). You need to use macros that use the values from the first form to specify which record should be opened in the second form.

Table 18.12   A Macro to Synchronize Two Forms to the Same Record

Action	Argument	Argument Entry	Explanation
OpenForm	Form Name	Personal Info	Opens the Personal Info form.
	View	Form	
	Filter	(none)	
	Where Condition	[Employee ID]= Forms![frmPersonnel Actions]![PA ID]	
	Data Mode	Read Only	
	Window Mode	Normal	

This example runs from the Personnel Action Entry form shown in figure 18.1, near the beginning of the chapter. Clicking the Info command button in the lower left corner runs the macro shown in table 18.12. This macro opens the Personal Info form shown in figure 18.4.

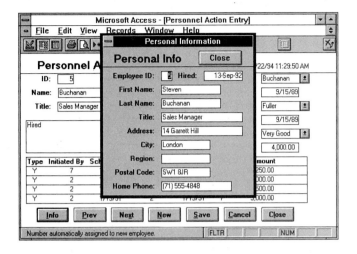

Fig. 18.4
The Personal Info
form synchronized
with another form
to show related
data.

The macro is attached to the OnClick event of the Info command button. The OpenForm action opens the Personal Info form, which was created by the Form Wizard from the Employee table to show personal information such as address and phone number. The form opens with the Data Mode argument in Read Only. This mode limits the user to reading, but not changing personal information.

The Where Condition argument makes the Personal Info form open and display information about the person shown in the current Personnel Action Entry form. The Where Condition argument uses the following condition:

```
[Employee ID]=Forms![Personnel Actions]![PA ID]
```

This condition sets the Employee ID control in the Personal Info form to the same value as the PA ID in the Personnel Action Entry form. Employee ID and PA ID are the same for each individual.

Using the Expression Builder to Enter Expressions

In the preceding examples of expressions used as macro argument values, you type the expression in the text box. Access 2.0's Expression Builder lets you create expressions by pasting selections, made in one to three outline-style list boxes, to an expression text box. Using the Expression Builder is one of the subjects of Chapter 9, "Understanding Operators and Expressions in Access." Click the ellipsis button to the right of the Expression text box to display Expression Builder's dialog. When you close the Expression Builder, the expression you create is pasted into the Expression text box. Figure 18.5 shows the selections you make in Expression Builder to create the highlighted

Tip
If you need a control such as Employee ID on a form, but do not want the control to display, set its Visible property to No. Although the control becomes invisible, you can still use the value it contains.

Access

2.0

portion of the expression in the text box. (The <Value> selection in the right-hand text box uses the name of the control to specify the control's value. Alternatively, you can select the Value property in the list.)

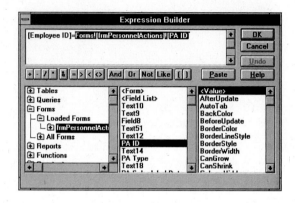

Tip
You can use
Expression
Builder, instead
of the Zoom
box, to edit
Expression
and other
argument
values. If the
ellipsis button
appears next to
an argument-
value text box,
click the but-
ton to open
Expression
Builder with
the expression
displayed for
editing.

Printing a Form

You have to print copies of forms whenever you need filing copies, invoices for mailing, or data for distribution. Printing forms is easy. Use the OpenForm or Print actions to print your forms.

The OpenForm action in table 18.13 enables you to open or activate a form and immediately display that form in the Print Preview window.

Table 18.13   A Macro to Print a Form

Action	Argument	Argument Entry	Explanation
OpenForm	Form Name	frmPersonnelActions	Displays print preview onto the current form.
	View	Print Preview	

From the Print Preview window, you can manually change the page setup options or options in the Print dialog. Clicking the Print or Setup button, shown in figure 18.6, displays the Print or Setup dialog. When you do not specify a Filter or Where Condition, all the current records print, even if the form's DefaultView property is set to Single Form.

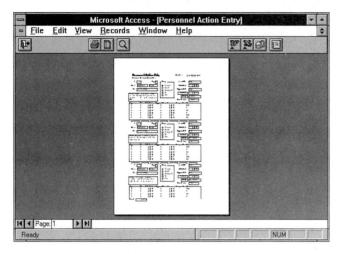

Fig. 18.6

The Print Preview window for the Personnel Action Entry form.

Another method of printing is to use the SelectObject action to select the object you want to print, and then use the Print action to do the actual printing. The Print action gives you the capability of specifying printing details, such as the page numbers and number of copies. The following table shows the SelectObject-Print macro.

Table 18.14   An Alternative Macro to Print a Form

Action	Argument	Argument Entry	Explanation
SelectObject	Object Type	Form	Specifies the opened or closed object to be printed.
	Object Name	frmPersonnel Actions	
	In Database Window	No	
Print	Print Range	(All records, the current Selection, or the specified Pages)	Specifies printing parameters and then prints pages without showing the Print Preview or Print Setup dialog.
	Page From	(starting page)	
	Page To	(ending page)	

(continues)

Table 18.14 Continued			
Action	**Argument**	**Argument Entry**	**Explanation**
	Print Quality	(High, Medium, Low)	
	Copies	(default 1)	
	Collate Copies	(Yes/No)	

From Here...

This chapter has shown you some simple yet timesaving macros. You learned how some of the easy-to-use actions—such as OpenForm, Echo, and DoMenuItem—can reduce your repetitive work load. With the DoMenuItem action, you can replicate frequently used menu commands.

You can use Access Basic code in place of, or to supplement, macros to handle events. Refer to the following chapters to learn more about Access Basic:

- Chapter 27, "Writing Access Basic Code," describes how to use Access 2.0's new Code Behind Forms feature to write event-handling code for forms and reports.

- Chapter 28, "Understanding the Data Access Object Class," explains Access 2.0's new hierarchy of objects created by Access and the Jet database engine.

- Chapter 29, "Exchanging Data with OLE Automation and DDE," gives examples of code for programming objects created by other OLE 2.0-compliant applications, as well as the new OLE Custom Controls.

Part V

Integrating Access with Other Applications

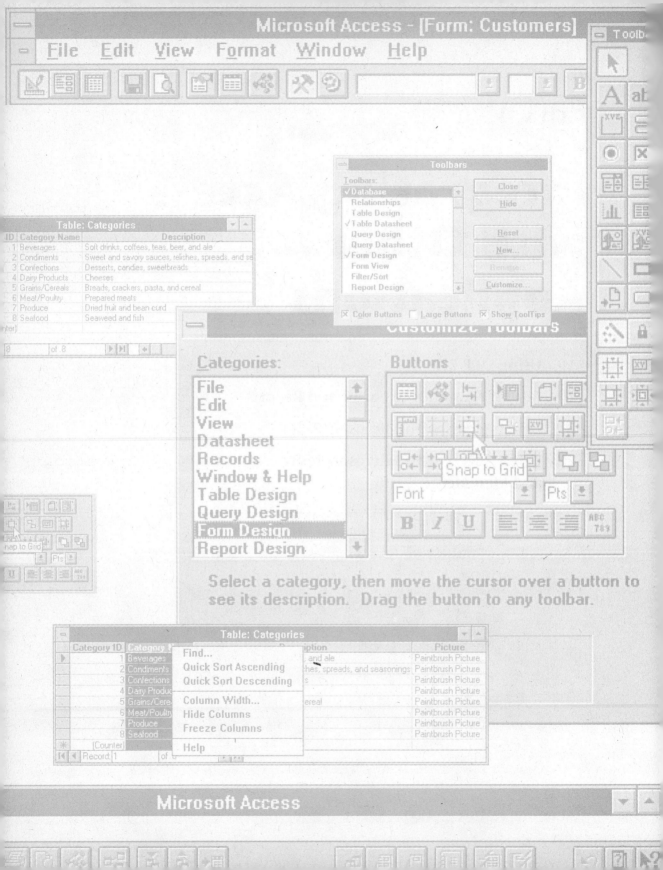

Chapter 19

Using OLE 2.0

Windows 3.1 formally introduced Object Linking and Embedding (OLE, pronounced as the Spanish ¡olé!) 1.0 to the PC. The new versions of members of the Microsoft Office suite, Access 2.0 (in the Professional Edition only), Excel 5.0, Word 6.0, and PowerPoint 4.0 provide a variety of new capabilities with OLE 2.0. OLE is a method of transferring information in the form of *objects* between different Windows applications. This method is similar in concept to, although more sophisticated than, copying text or graphics to the Clipboard and pasting the copied text or graphic to other applications. This chapter introduces you to the principles of OLE and how your Access 2.0 applications can take advantage of the additional features offered by OLE 2.0.

Earlier implementations of OLE, such as in Microsoft Excel 3.0 and PowerPoint 2.0, existed before the release of Windows 3.1. At that time, OLE was implemented from within the application, not by the Windows operating environment. Windows 3.1 made OLE a function of Windows by providing two new files, OLECLI.DLL and OLESVR.DLL, that orchestrate OLE. OLE 2.0-compliant applications add a substantial collection of supporting dynamic link libraries (DLLs) to your \WINDOWS\SYSTEM directory. Although OLE 2.0 employs a much more sophisticated methodology than OLE 1.0, OLE 2.0, in many respects, is easier to use than version 1.0. OLE 2.0 sets the course of future Windows applications and operating systems. As with OLE 1.0 and Windows 3.1, OLE 2.0 will be an integral component of future versions of Windows. OLE 2.0 provides full support of existing OLE 1.0 applications. OLE 2.0 is based on Microsoft's Component Object Model (COM), which is likely to become the *de facto* industry standard for object-oriented application programming in the Windows environment.

In this chapter, you

- Get an overview of OLE 1.0 and OLE 2.0

- Learn how OLE 1.0 and 2.0 compare with DDE for interprocess communication

- Get an introduction of OLE Automation and OLE Custom Controls

- Learn to use the verbose mode of the Registration Database Editor application

- Learn about repairing a damaged registration database file

V

Integrating Access

Understanding the Importance of OLE

Understanding OLE principles is important because OLE is the sole method by which you may add graphic images to your Access forms and reports and add or edit data in OLE Object fields of Access. Using OLE as the method of applying and storing nontext information holds the following advantages over built-in graphics processing offered by some RDBMSs:

- You can use any image-processing application that functions as an OLE server to create and edit bit-mapped graphics: from the simple Windows 3.1 Paintbrush applet to photographic-quality editors, such as Micrografx Picture Publisher.

- You can embed or link vector-based images from simple OLE 1.0 applets, such as Microsoft Draw, or from full-fledged illustration packages, such as CorelDRAW! 4.0, an OLE 2.0 server, or Micrografx Designer. Microsoft Chart 5.0, called MSGraph5 in this book, is included with Access 2.0. MSGraph5 is an OLE 2.0 server applet.

- The added overhead associated with bit-map editors incorporated in the application is eliminated. Self-contained bit-map editors and drawing functions are seldom as capable as stand-alone, shrink-wrapped OLE server applications.

- You don't need to install a collection of import and export filters for different kinds of files. OLE server applications provide file import from, and export to, a variety of file types.

- You can export objects stored in OLE Object fields in Access tables or stored within bound or unbound object frames to other applications via the Clipboard. Bound object frames display the presentation of OLE objects stored in OLE Object fields of Access tables. Unbound object frames display the presentation of static OLE objects, such as company logos used to embellish forms and reports.

- You can store a variety of OLE objects in one OLE Object field. You can link or embed in one OLE Object field waveform audio (.WAV), MIDI music (.MID), animation (.FLI and .MMM), and audio/video interleaved (.AVI) files. You need a large-capacity fixed disk to embed .AVI and long-duration .WAV files, however.

■ You can choose between embedding the data within a table, form, or report or linking the OLE object to a file that contains the data. The behavior of an OLE 2.0 object differs, depending on whether you link or embed an object.

The most common kinds of OLE objects used in Access applications are 16-color and 256-color embedded bit-map graphic images. Figure 19.1 shows a portion of a page from the Northwind Traders Catalog report that includes an embedded bit-map image. The image is a Windows 3.1 Paintbrush bit map embedded by OLE in the Picture field of the Categories table.

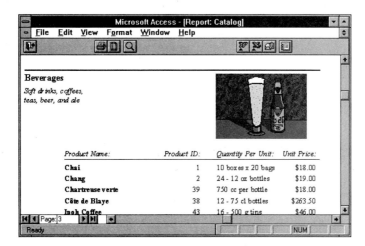

Fig. 19.1
One page of the Northwind Traders Catalog report in print preview mode.

V

Defining OLE

OLE is a member of a class of computer operations known as interprocess communication (IPC). IPC operations enable different applications to send data to and receive data from other applications by an agreed-on procedure. The Clipboard is the primary IPC path for Windows; most present-day communication of data between running applications (other than by reading or writing to disk files) involves using the Windows Clipboard. Windows defines a set of standard data types that you can copy to or paste from the Clipboard. OLE uses these standard Windows data types: bit-mapped and vector-based graphic images, plain and formatted text, digital audio sound, and so on. You may have used (or tried to use) Dynamic Data Exchange (DDE) as an IPC method to transfer data between Windows applications. OLE is a major improvement over DDE because OLE is easier to implement than DDE. OLE 2.0 is expected ultimately to replace DDE.

OLE operations differ from conventional Windows copy-and-paste operations—performed with Ctrl+C and Ctrl+V or by way of DDE—because OLE includes a substantial amount of information about the source of the data, along with the actual data. An OLE object copied to the Clipboard by Excel 5.0, for example, includes the following information:

- The name of the application from which the data originated (in this case, Excel).

- The type of data, such as worksheet, macro sheet, or chart (Excel worksheet).

- The full path to the file, beginning with the drive letter and the file name, if the data is derived from a file or was saved to a file.

- A name assigned to the sheet or chart that contains the data, if the data isn't derived from or saved to a file. The name usually is a long combination of numbers and letters.

- The name or coordinates of the range of the data, if only a portion of an object is included.

- The presentation of the object in Windows metafile (.WMF) format. If the object is not an image, the icon of the application that created the object is the object's presentation.

When you paste data copied to the Clipboard from an Excel worksheet and then double-click the cells' surface, Excel pops up to enable you to edit the data and disappears when you finish. With OLE, you paste complete objects, rather than just data, into an element of the application.

Classifying OLE 2.0-Compliant Applications

OLE 2.0-compliant applications fall into the following six categories:

- *Container applications.* These applications, such as Access 2.0, are stand-alone products that are capable of linking or embedding objects created by other OLE 2.0-compliant applications. Container applications, however, cannot create OLE objects for linking to or embedding in other OLE 2.0 applications. OLE container applications are client applications in OLE 1.0 terminology.

■ *Server-only applications.* These stand-alone applications create OLE objects for embedding in and linking to other applications, but you cannot embed an OLE object in or link an OLE object to them. Visio 2.0, a template-based OLE 2.0 drawing application, is an example of an OLE 2.0 server-only application.

■ *Mini-server applications.* Mini-servers (also called OLE applets) are similar to server-only applications, but mini-servers are not stand-alone products. You can execute an OLE mini-server only from within an OLE container application. MSGraph5 is an OLE 2.0 mini-server. Shapeware Corporation offers a mini-server version of Visio 2.0 called Visio Express.

■ *Full-server applications.* OLE full-servers are stand-alone applications that are capable of creating OLE objects for use by other applications and can embed or link objects created by other OLE servers. Excel 5.0, Word 6.0, and Project 4.0 are OLE 2.0 full-servers.

■ *OLE Automation-compliant applications.* OLE Automation (OA) lets an OLE 2.0 container application manipulate an embedded or linked object by sending programming instructions to the OLE 2.0 server that created it. OA server applications are said to create *programmable objects*. Excel 5.0 and Project 4.0 are both OA-compliant container and server applications. Shapeware's Visio 2.0 is an OA server. Word 6.0 has limited, but useful, OA server capabilities. OLE Automation client applications, such as Access 2.0, use their programming language to send instructions to programmable objects. Using OLE Automation is the subject of Chapter 29, "Exchanging Data with OLE Automation and DDE."

Access

2.0

■ *OLE Custom Controls.* One of the advantages of Visual Basic as a Windows programming environment is its extensibility through custom controls (called VBXs, Visual Basic extensions). Microsoft and third-party software publishers supply a variety of specialized control objects for Visual Basic 3.0, including mini-spreadsheets, image editors, and report writers. Access 2.0 is the first product to offer extensibility through OLE Custom Controls (OCXs, OLE Control extensions). Future versions of Visual Basic and other Microsoft productivity applications, as well as future versions of Windows, undoubtedly will take advantage of OCXs.

▶ "Adding OLE Custom Controls to Your Application," p. 1074

Access

2.0

All OLE 1.0 applications fall into one of the first four categories of the preceding list. When this edition was written, there were very few OLE 2.0 applications available, and even fewer OCXs. All the major software publishers, however, have committed to incorporating OLE 2.0 features in their mainstream products. Suppliers of VBXs also can be expected to provide OCX versions of their more popular custom controls for Visual Basic. By the end of 1994, you can expect to be able to choose from a wide variety of OLE 2.0-compliant products.

Introducing Object Building Blocks

When the term *object* is used in conjunction with a computer application or programming language, the term doesn't refer to a tangible object, such as a rock, a saxophone, or a book. Objects in computer programming and applications are intangible representations of real-world objects. A computer object combines properties, such as the properties you assign to an Access control object in a form or report, and methods that define the behavior of the object. Text box properties—such as text the box contains, the size, typeface, and font the text uses, and the colors and borders employed—vary widely. The ways text box controls behave when you type new text or edit existing text are the methods associated with text box objects of forms and reports. All text boxes in Windows applications share similar, but not identical, methods.

Properties and Methods Encapsulated in Objects

A musical instrument, such as a saxophone, can serve as an example of a tangible object that has an intangible representation: sound. Some properties of a saxophone are size (soprano, alto, tenor, bass, and baritone), kind of fingering, materials of construction, and the name of the instrument's manufacturer.

The methods applicable to saxophones are the techniques used to play these instruments: blowing into the mouthpiece, biting the reed, and fingering the pads that determine the note that you play. Figure 19.2, a vector-based drawing created with CorelDRAW! 3.0, illustrates the properties and methods of a tenor saxophone object.

If you create a programming object that simulates all the properties and all the methods of a particular kind of saxophone, and have the proper audio hardware for a computer, you can create an object that imitates the sound of Charlie Parker's, Art Pepper's, or Stan Getz's style. Stanford University's new WaveGuide acoustic synthesis computer programs create objects capable of this kind of imitation. The properties of a particular saxophone and the methods of the artist playing it are said to be encapsulated in a particular kind of saxophone object. The object acts as a container for the properties and methods that comprise the object.

Properties   Methods

Fig. 19.2

A graphic representation of the properties and methods of a tenor saxophone object.

One more item is found in the container of an OLE object: presentation. Presentation is how the user perceives the object—how the object looks or sounds. The presentation of a WaveGuide saxophone is a musical sound. If the saxophone object is used in a Windows 3.1+ application, the sound probably is reproduced through digital audio techniques by an audio adapter card. The presentation of a large graphic image may be a miniature copy, or thumbnail. At first glance, presentation may appear to be a property. Presentation isn't a property in the true sense, however, because the presentation of an object is dependent on factors outside the object, such as the kind of hardware available, the computer operating system used, and the application in which the object is employed. The presentation of a 256-color bit map on a 16-color VGA display, for example, is quite different from the presentation on a 256-color display driver.

Object-Oriented Applications

Applications and the programming languages—which also are applications—that programmers used to create these applications are object-oriented if the applications can encapsulate properties and methods within an object container. Before object-oriented programming was developed, programmers considered properties and methods as two separate entities. Programmers wrote code that defined the methods of an application. Separate data files contained the properties that the programmer's application manipulated. A classic example of this separation is xBase; a set of .DBF files contains properties (data), and a separate collection of .PRG files contains the methods (programs) applicable to the set of .DBF files.

In contrast to the conventional programming technique, Access takes an object-oriented approach to database management. Access combines the data (tables) and the methods (queries, forms, reports, macros, and Access Basic code) in a single, often massive .MDB container, known as the **Database** object. **Form** and **Report** objects act as containers for **Control** objects. **QueryDef** objects consist of Structured Query Language (SQL) methods applied to **Table** objects. Although lacking some characteristics of a truly object-oriented programming language, Access Basic comes close enough to the mark that you can consider Access Basic to be an object-oriented application programming language.

The Advantages of Objects

Combining properties and methods into an object and then adding a standard presentation provides the following advantages to users of—and the programmers who create—applications:

■ Objects combine data (properties) and the program code that deals with the data (methods) into one object that you can treat as a black box. You need not understand the internal elements of the box to use a box in an application. This characteristic of objects aids in the programming of large-scale applications in which many programmers participate. You can modify an object without affecting how the object is used by other programmers.

■ Objects can be reused when needed. You can create and use a library of objects in many programs or applications. If you create a library of vector-based images created by CorelDRAW! in an Access table, for example, you can edit these images from within Access and then save a copy of the edited drawing in a separate file.

■ Objects can be used with any Windows application that supports OLE. You can use the same graphic or sound object with Access, Excel, or Word for Windows. If you copy an embedded drawing in an Excel spreadsheet to the Clipboard, you can paste the drawing as an unbound object in an Access form or report, or in a data cell of an OLE Object field in a table. Windows for Workgroups and Windows NT enable you to share the content of Clipboard as a Clipbook with other users on the network.

■ Objects are easy to create with OLE. If you copy all or a portion of the data you create in an OLE-compliant application, you create a temporary OLE object in the Clipboard.

Object Classes, Types, Hierarchies, and Inheritance

Programming objects, like real-world objects, are organized in hierarchies of classes and subclasses and in types that have no subclasses. The hierarchy of classes of musical instrument synthesis objects is shown in figure 19.3 (the subclasses are shown for woodwinds only). At the top of the hierarchical structure, you see the master class, Simulated Musical Instruments, for example, that defines the presentation of all the subclasses as digital audio sound.

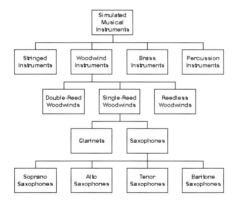

Fig. 19.3

A hierarchy diagram of objects that represents the sound of simulated musical instruments.

Musical instruments are classified by the method used to create the sounds. Saxophones are members of the general woodwind class, which you can further subclass as single-reed woodwinds (see fig. 19.3). Single-reed woodwinds include clarinets and saxophones and share many playing methods. Saxophones can be subclassed further by size and the musical key in which these instruments play. At the bottom of the hierarchy are types that have no further subclasses.

A B-flat (tenor) saxophone has a unique set of property values (data), but the kinds of properties are common to all saxophones. Similarly, the tenor saxophone's playing methods are common to all saxophones. The Tenor Saxophone type inherits both the methods and the list of properties from the Saxophone subclass, which in turn inherits properties from the Single-Reed Woodwind class. Parent classes are a level above child classes in the genealogy of classes, and siblings are members of the same class or type. Access uses the term *Master* to indicate a parent class object, as in the Link Master Fields and Link Child Fields properties of subform and subreport controls.

▶ "Understanding Objects and Object Collections," p. 1037

Figure 19.4 illustrates the hierarchy of the objects within Access that are described up to this point in the book. **Table**, **Form**, and **Report** objects have distinctive properties and methods. **Form** and **Report** objects share the same group of **Control** objects, but some **Control** objects have different behavior when contained in **Form** or **Report** objects. Queries (called **QueryDef** objects) aren't true objects; **QueryDef** objects comprise a set of methods applied to **Table** objects. **Control** objects can be classified further into bound and unbound **Control** objects. Only object frames can incorporate OLE objects and only a bound object frame can display or provide access to editing capability for OLE data in tables or queries.

Fig. 19.4
A simplified hierarchy of database objects in Access.

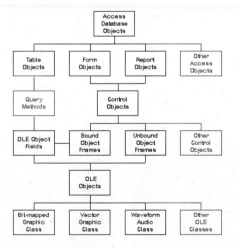

The **Control** objects in Access inherit some methods from the object that contains the control objects. Subform and subreport controls inherit all related methods and many properties from **Form** and **Report** objects, respectively. OLE child objects inherit a large number of their properties and methods from the parent OLE class that defines how OLE objects behave (or should behave). Each OLE child, however, has a complement of properties and methods that apply only to that child. OLE object subclasses at the bottom of figure 19.4 aren't types because each subclass may have different OLE object types. The Bit-mapped Graphic Class, for example, may include Paintbrush Picture, CorelPhotoPAINT! Picture, and PicturePublisher Picture OLE object types.

Containing Objects in Other Objects

OLE is designed to allow a single container document to be built with contributions, known as source documents, from foreign applications. (Container documents are destination documents in OLE 1.0 terminology.) The container document may be created by most applications that are OLE compliant; Access forms and reports, proposals created in Word for Windows, Excel worksheets, and PowerPoint presentation visuals are common destination documents. When more than one application contributes to the content of a document, the document is referred to as *compound*. The application that creates the compound document is the OLE container application (formerly OLE client), and the foreign applications that contribute source documents to the compound document are OLE servers. Access is an OLE client and creates the compound container documents; Access forms, reports, and tables that incorporate OLE objects are compound documents.

Each source document created with OLE servers and contributed to a destination document is an individual, identifiable object that possesses properties, behavior, and has its own presentation. You can choose to *embed* the source document within an Access destination document that acts as a container for one or more source document objects. Embedding includes the object's data in the source document. You also can link the source document; in this case, the data resides in a separate file. The difference between embedding and linking objects is the subject of the next section.

Note

OLE 1.0 let you *activate* an embedded or linked object within the container document, but you could not activate any objects contained within the first embedded or linked object. (To activate an OLE object means to open the object for editing in the source application.) OLE 2.0 eliminates this restriction. Thus, if you embed a Word 6.0 document containing an embedded Excel 5.0 worksheet in the OLE object field of an Access table, you can activate the Word document in Word 6.0 and then activate the worksheet object in Excel 5.0. There is no limit on how deeply you can nest embedded or linked OLE 2.0 objects. (You can, however, run out of system resources during this process if you're using Windows 3.1.)

Whether you embed or link the source document, the code to perform the server's methods isn't incorporated in the compound document. Consider the size of an Access table that contains several copies of EXCEL.EXE. Instead, the server's methods are incorporated by a reference to the application's name, known as the OLE type, in the source document. You need a local copy of the server application that created the source document to edit an embedded source document or to display most linked source documents. Information about OLE server applications is incorporated in your Windows registration database file, REG.DAT. The importance of REG.DAT with OLE 2.0 is explained in "The Registration Database" section at the end of this chapter.

Understanding Differences between OLE and DDE

If you previously used dynamic data exchange between Windows applications, OLE gives you the opportunity to add a new dimension to DDE operations. The differences between OLE and DDE techniques to transfer data are illustrated by figure 19.5. DDE transfers data (properties) from the server to Access text boxes, labels, or other controls that can accommodate text and numbers; OLE transfers data and methods from the server only to unbound or bound object frames.

Fig. 19.5
A diagrammatic representation of the differences between DDE and OLE data transfer in Access.

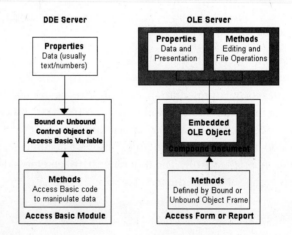

▶ "Using DDE Links with Excel," p. 802

Access includes a function, DDE(), that you can use to create a DDE link to data in any Windows application with DDE server capability. To fully explore the capabilities of DDE with Access, you need to write an Access Basic function or procedure that includes a series of DDE functions, beginning with **DDEInitiate**(). You then execute the Access Basic function or procedure from the `OnClick` event of a command button or the function from a `RunCode` action in an Access macro. Writing code to make full use of DDE with Access (one of the subjects of Chapter 29) or any other Windows application, is and always was a difficult process. In specific cases discussed in the following chapter, Access creates a DDE link to an element in the source application and embeds the data transferred through the link in an OLE Object field.

Using the basic features of OLE requires no programming. Simple OLE operations in Access use the Paste **S**pecial or Insert Ob**j**ect choices of the **E**dit menu. You can copy OLE objects in Access to the Clipboard from the **E**dit menu so that other OLE client applications can use the objects. There are relatively few Access Basic reserved words that apply exclusively to OLE objects; Microsoft deliberately designed OLE for use by nonprogrammers.

You must edit a linked or embedded OLE 1.0 object manually. There is no equivalent in OLE 1.0 of the Access Basic **DDEExecute** instruction that lets you manipulate the data in an OLE 1.0 document with macros or Access Basic code. **DDEExecute** sends instructions to the DDE Server application that can modify the content of an Excel worksheet cell or of a paragraph in a Word document. The syntax of the instructions you send with **DDEExecute** are specific to each DDE client application. OLE 2.0 substitutes a new programming methodology, OLE Automation, for the **DDEExecute** instruction. The advantage of OLE Automation is that you can alter the values of the properties of the object and apply methods to the object using conventional Access Basic syntax. OLE Automation is the foundation upon which OLE Custom Controls are built. OLE Automation and OLE Custom Controls are discussed in the "Taking Advantage of OLE Automation" section later in this chapter.

Embedding versus Linking Source Documents

When you embed a source document, Windows creates a copy of the source document data and embeds the copy permanently in the container document. The source document retains no connection to the embedded data. Subsequent editing or deletion of the file or data from which the source document was created has no effect on the embedded copy in the table or displayed on the forms and reports.

Embedding is the only option if you do not or cannot save the source document as a file. The Microsoft Graph 5.0 and Visio Express OLE 2.0 miniservers allow you only to embed a file. These applets have no **S**ave or Save **A**s choices in their **F**ile menus. When you choose E**x**it from an applet **F**ile menu, a dialog appears, asking whether you want to update the destination document with the edited source document.

Windows 3.1 Paintbrush is the source application for all graphics displayed in bound or unbound objects of the Northwind Traders sample database. Paintbrush enables you to import and save images in .BMP or .PCX files, so you can use Paintbrush to embed or link all bit-mapped graphics you possess or create in either of these file formats.

Open the Categories form, and then double-click the picture. Paintbrush, an OLE 1.0 server, appears so that you can edit the image, as shown in figure 19.6. All bit maps in the Northwind Traders sample database are Paintbrush Picture Objects, embedded in OLE Object fields of tables and in unbound object frames on forms and reports. The title bar of Paintbrush's window in figure 19.6 indicates that the data is embedded in an Access object. You can use the Save **As** choice from Paintbrush's **F**ile menu to save the image as a .BMP or .PCX file.

Fig. 19.6

Windows Paintbrush editing an embedded bit map, displayed in a bound object frame.

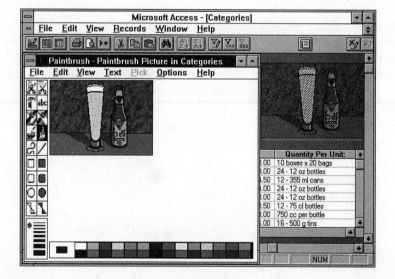

If you link an object, you create a reference to the data of the source document, the name of a file. When you or others change the data in a file linked to the object, the data in the source document permanently changes. The next time you display the data, if you set the value of the UpdateOptions property feature of Access 2.0 to Automatic, the presentation of the object incorporates all changes made to the data in the file. In version 1.x of Access, the Automatic value of the UpdateMethod property was applicable only to OLE objects in unbound frames. You can use Access 2.0's UpdateOptions property to update objects in bound object frames. The capability of updating everyone's linked objects at once is useful in a networked Access application that displays data that periodically is updated by others who share these files on the network.

To link rather than embed an object created by an OLE server, perform the following steps:

1. Open the OLE server, Paintbrush in this example.

2. Load the file that contains the data you want to link. A bit map from the Beverages picture of the Categories form, saved in Paintbrush as \ACCESS\BEVR.BMP, is used in this example.

3. Select the data to copy to the Clipboard. Most image editors use a selection tool to select a section of the graphic. You can select all or part of the image with Paintbrush's rectangular selection tool.

4. Press Ctrl+C to copy the data to the Clipboard.

5. Activate the container application, in this case Access 2.0.

6. Choose Paste **S**pecial from the **E**dit menu of the container application. If the application supports OLE 2.0, the Paste Special dialog shown in figure 19.7 appears.

7. Click the Paste Link option button, and then click OK to paste the image into the container document. In this case, the container is the Picture field of the first record of the Categories table.

Fig. 19.7

The standard OLE 2.0 Paste Special dialog.

Note

Before creating an OLE link in the destination application, you must open the source application and load the file because opening a file in most OLE servers breaks the existing OLE connection.

When you double-click to edit a linked Paintbrush Picture Object, the title bar of Paintbrush's window displays the name of the file that created the image, as shown in figure 19.8. This method is one way that you quickly can determine whether an OLE object is linked, rather than embedded in most OLE client applications (including Access).

Fig. 19.8
Paintbrush, editing a graphic object linked to the file BEVR.BMP.

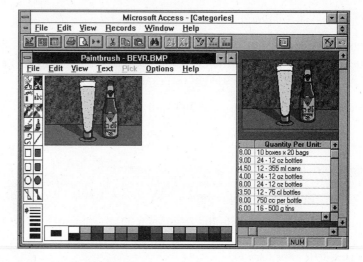

Another advantage of linking some objects whose data resides in files is that you don't waste disk space with duplicate copies of the files in the database. Access creates a copy of the source document's presentation in the table, so you don't save disk space when you link graphic images, spreadsheets, or other source documents whose presentation consists of the data. The presentation of animation, waveform audio, and digital video files is either an icon or the first image of a sequence, so the presentation is small in size. Here, the disk space saved by linking, rather than embedding, is substantial.

> **Note**
>
> Linking a bit-mapped image doesn't save disk space; the presentation stored in .BMP format is the same size in bytes as the original image. If your OLE image server application lets you substitute a *thumbnail* image, the saving in file space often is substantial. A thumbnail image is a smaller version of the original image, often with less color depth (8-bit instead of 24-bit color data, for instance).

The disadvantage of linking is that the linked files must be available to all users of the application. The files must reside in the same directory for their lifetime unless you edit the linkage to reflect a new location. A fully specified path, including the drive designator, is included with the file name in the linking information. The presentation of the source document appears in the form or report, but when you double-click the bound object frame to edit the linked object, you see an error message that the linked file is not found.

> **Note**
>
> OLE 2.0 provides a limited capability to update the links to files that have moved, but it is not a wise practice to depend on the present version of OLE 2.0 to maintain links to relocated files. If the object is contained in an unbound object frame, you can change the value of the SourceDoc property to point to the file in its new location. If the object is contained in a bound object frame, you need to open the file, copy its data to the Clipboard, and then re-create the link by using Paste **S**pecial to create a new link to the file.

Activating OLE 2.0 Objects in Place

Access
2.0

One of the advantages of embedding, rather than linking, objects is that you can activate OLE 2.0 objects in place. In-place activation (also called in-situ editing or in-place editing) causes the source application for the embedded object to "take over" the container application. You activate an OLE object for editing by double-clicking the surface of the object frame that displays a simplified presentation of the worksheet. Figure 19.9 shows an Excel worksheet embedded in an unbound object frame of a form. The worksheet has been activated in place for editing. When an object is activated in place for editing, the object is surrounded by a frame consisting of alternating blue and white diagonal hash marks. Eight sizing handles (black squares at each corner and at the midpoints of the frame) let you adjust the size of the editing frame.

When you activate an embedded OLE 2.0 object, the menu bars of the application with which you created the object replace Access's menus that have the same name. If the source application has addition menus, they are added to Access's menu bar. In figure 19.9, the **F**ile, **E**dit, **V**iew, **F**ormat, and **H**elp menus are replaced by Excel's menus of the same name. Excel adds its own **I**nsert, **T**ools, and **D**ata menus to the menu bar. Excel's anchored toolbars become floating toolbars that you can reposition or hide. Column and row headers, sheet tabs, and scroll bars (called *adornments*) become visible when you activate an Excel worksheet. You have full control over the embedded Excel worksheet and can perform almost any operation on the worksheet that is possible if you had opened a file containing the worksheet in Excel 5.0.

Fig. 19.9
An Excel 5.0
worksheet
activated for
editing in an
Access 2.0 form.

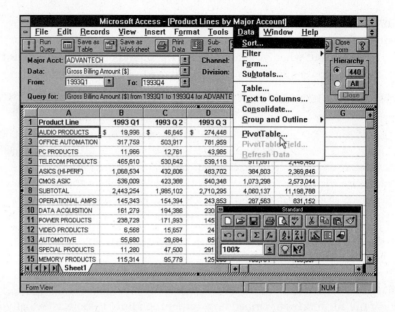

> **Note**
>
> In-place activation is available only for embedded, not linked, OLE 2.0 objects. When you double-click the presentation of a linked OLE 2.0 object, the source application's window appears. In this respect, linked OLE 2.0 objects behave identically to linked or embedded OLE 1.0 objects.

Taking Advantage of OLE Automation

▶ "Manipulating
an Excel 5.0
Workbook
Object,"
p. 1060

OLE 2.0 server and mini-server applications that support OLE Automation *expose programmable objects*. As an example, Excel 5.0 is an OLE Automation server application that creates programmable Excel objects. Thus, when you activate an Excel worksheet object embedded in or linked to an Access 2.0 object frame, you can gain access to the worksheet through the Object property of the object frame control. The Object property is available only with Access Basic code; the Object property does not appear in the Properties window for object frames. The Object property provides access to all the objects, and the properties and methods of the objects, that are exposed by the application that created the embedded or linked object.

Using OLE Automation requires that you learn to program in Access Basic and that you understand the hierarchy of the collections of objects that you intend to program. Collections of objects are groups of objects of the same class that are contained within another object. As an example, the collection of Excel Worksheet objects are contained in Workbook objects. Collections of OA objects follow the same general structure as Access 2.0's data access objects (DAOs) described in Chapter 28, "Understanding the Data Access Object Class." Excel 5.0, for example, has more than 100 different types of objects and several hundred properties and methods that apply to its objects. Access 2.0's **DBEngine** object is the top of Access DAO pyramid; the OA Application object of Excel 5.0 (and most other OA servers) is the equivalent of the **DBEngine** object. All other Excel objects are subclasses of the Application object.

OLE Automation lets you construct applications using the building block approach; if you need a worksheet in your Access application, insert an Excel Worksheet object in an unbound object frame. You then set the values of properties of and apply methods to the Worksheet object with Access Basic code. If you want word processing features, insert a Word 6 Document object in an unbound object frame. You add command buttons or other controls to the form to execute the procedures or functions that contain the required OLE Automation commands.

OLE Custom Controls are a special class of OLE 2.0 mini-servers that use OA to provide access to their properties, methods, and events. (Conventional OA objects don't expose their own events when activated.) When you embed an OLE Custom Control in an unbound object frame, the Control object's events are not added to the Property window's list of events for unbound object frames. However, you can write Access Basic event-handling code for the events exposed by the OCX as procedures in code contained in forms.

The preceding brief discussion of OLE Automation may appear out of context at this point in the book because writing Access Basic code is the subject of Part VII, "Programming with Access Basic." However, future Windows operating systems and applications will make extensive use of OLE 2.0 and OA, and a general description of OLE 2.0 without including OA would be incomplete, at best. As mentioned at the beginning of this section, taking advantage of OA and OLE Custom Controls requires that you write Access Basic code. Mastering OA programming requires a very retentive memory and much experimentation. If you need interprocess communication in your Access 2.0 applications, use OLE 2.0 and OA, not DDE, whenever you can. Your investment astride the OLE 2.0 learning curve will return substantial dividends as more and better OA applications and, especially, OLE Custom Controls become available.

V

Integrating Access

The Registration Database

The WIN.INI file of Windows 3+ has the section [Extensions] that includes a series of entries like bmp=pbrush.exe ^.bmp and wri=write.exe ^.wri. This section of WIN.INI creates the associations between applications and file extensions used by File Manager to launch an application when you double-click a file name. If you double-click a file with a .BMP extension, File Manager launches Windows Paintbrush (PBRUSH.EXE) and opens the chosen file.

The addition of OLE to Windows 3.1 and the improvements made to File Manager required more information about applications than the simple associations of file name extensions with applications in WIN.INI. Rather than expand WIN.INI beyond an already considerable size, Microsoft added a new file, REG.DAT, the registration database, to provide file extension association and other details about applications needed by File Manager and OLE-compliant applications.

When you install Windows 3.1, REG.DAT is added to the \WINDOWS directory. When you install new applications or upgrades designed for use with Windows 3.1, the application appends records to REG.DAT. Most of these applications add a file extension association to REG.DAT during the installation process, usually at the beginning of the REG.DAT file. If the application is an OLE server, the application adds information about its OLE capabilities and presentations to REG.DAT.

The registration process for OLE 1.0 servers is relatively simple. Only a few entries in REG.DAT are required; the most important entries are those that create an association between individual file extensions and the OLE server for the type of file. The registration process for OLE 2.0 servers is not so simple; much more information is required to register OLE 2.0 servers, and even more entries are added for applications that support OLE Automation. OLE Custom Controls also register themselves in REG.DAT. Although the setup program registers each OLE server automatically, you must understand the use of the registration database and the registration database editor application in case you encounter a problem when you attempt to insert an OLE 2.0 object in an Access 2.0 object frame. The following two sections are devoted to REG.DAT and concentrate on the OLE 2.0 aspects of server registration.

The Registration Database Editor

The registration database editor, RegEdit, is included with Windows so that users can display and edit the registration database. The Windows 3.1 User's Guide refers you to a Windows help file that provides some help, and the

Windows 3.1 Resource Kit includes only a cursory explanation of the contents of REG.DAT and the use of RegEdit. None of this information provides even a hint about the new REG.DAT structure required by OLE 2.0. If you plan to use the OLE Object field data type, use MSGraph5 to create graphs, or add sophisticated graphic images to your forms and reports, you need to know more about REG.DAT and RegEdit than appears in the Windows 3.1 and Access 2.0 documentation.

When you launch RegEdit from the Accessories group, using the Program Item properties that Windows 3.1 assigned, a Registration Info Editor window similar to figure 19.10 appears. If RegEdit isn't installed in the Windows Accessories group, choose **R**un from Program Manager's **F**ile menu, type **regedit.exe** in the Command Line text box, and press Enter.

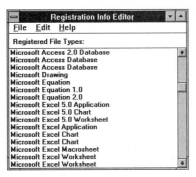

Fig. 19.10
RegEdit's editing window for the registration database file.

Each Windows 3.1 applet and most of the applications designed for Windows 3.1 that you added since you installed Windows 3.1 appear in the window. Entries also exist for some applications that you may not have installed; entries for popular pre-Windows 3.1 applications are included in REG.DAT by Microsoft. Installing new applications updated to Windows 3.1 standards adds new entries to REG.DAT. When you double-click an entry, such as a Word for Windows document, the Modify File Type dialog shown in figure 19.11 appears.

The entries in the Modify File Type dialog are used by File Manager when you double-click a file name with an extension associated with the application whose executable file name appears in the Command text box. Word for Windows uses DDE to open the file; when you double-click a file with a .DOC extension, the entry in RegEdit causes DDE to send a `FileOpen` (`FileName`) instruction to Word. Most applications use a command with the file name appended as a replaceable command line parameter to open a file.

An example of this kind of command is WRITE.EXE %1, where %1 is replaced by the file name you double-click in File Manager. This syntax is identical to the syntax used in DOS batch files.

Fig. 19.11
The Modify File Type dialog of RegEdit for editing REG.DAT commands used by File Manager.

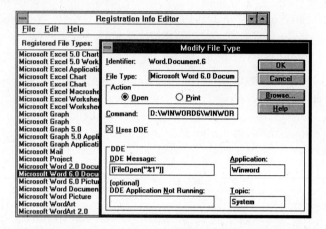

RegEdit hides the information pertinent to OLE. To view the entire content of REG.DAT, you need to add a parameter to the command line that Windows 3.1 uses to launch REG.DAT by completing the following steps:

1. Close RegEdit if it's open.

2. Click the appropriate icon in Program Manager's Accessories group to select RegEdit.

3. From the **F**ile menu, choose **P**roperties.

4. Edit the Command Line entry of the Program Item Properties dialog to read **d:\windows\regedit.exe –v**, where **d:** is the drive in which Windows is installed. The **–v** (or **/v**) parameter stands for verbose mode. Click OK to close the dialog.

5. Double-click the RegEdit button to relaunch RegEdit. RegEdit's display now appears in a format similar to the format shown in figure 19.12.

6. Use the vertical scroll bar or the down-arrow key to locate the first entry for MSGraph, shown in figure 19.12.

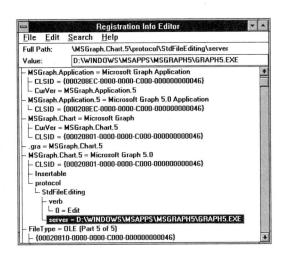

Fig. 19.12
The verbose
display of RegEdit
that includes OLE
server expressions.

The entries for Microsoft Graph 5.0, an OLE 2.0 mini-server supplied with Access 2.0, are treated as though they are file names preceded by a path. Levels in REG.DAT's hierarchy of expressions are separated by backslashes, as shown in the Full Path label at the top of RegEdit's window. The first level of expressions from the left of RegEdit's window is the root. The level at which the selected expression is located is shown by the entry in the Full Path label. Values follow an equal (=) sign; values appear or are entered in the Value text box. The primary registration expressions for Microsoft Graph 5.0 have the following meanings:

- There are a total of four registration entries for MSGraph, two each for MSGraph's Application and Graph objects. Two entries are provided so that you can specify a particular version of MSGraph (MSGraph.*Object*.5; 5 is the current version) or simply specify MSGraph.Chart or MSGraph.Application and rely on the CurVer = MSGraph.Chart.5 or CurVer = MSGraph.Application.5 entries to select the current version. MSGraph.Chart.5 is called the programmatic ID (ProgID) for a Microsoft Graph 5.0 chart.

- The \.gra = MSGraph.Chart.5 entry associates graph files with the .GRA extension with REG.DAT's code for the Microsoft Graph 5.0's Chart object, MSGraph.Chart.5. The association is valid only for a full-server version of MSGraph5 that can save files. In this case, File Manager would launch the full-server version of MSGraph5 when you double-click the icon of a file with the .GRA extension. The version of GRAPH5.EXE supplied with Access 2.0 is an OLE 2.0 mini-server and does not save files.

- MSGraph5 is an OLE server; you can identify OLE server applications by a *ProgID*\protocol entry in the hierarchy of the related REG.DAT expressions.

- An OLE server must have at least one protocol, usually the default OLE protocol, StdFileEditing. OLE protocols determine what action the server takes when it opens the linked file or embedded data. Standard file editing usually displays the chosen file or embedded data in the server's standard presentation.

- Some OLE servers enable you to make a choice of standard file editing presentations chosen by a verb. Sound Recorder, as an example, enables you to choose between playing or editing the sound file as the standard file editing presentation by using the following expressions:

```
\...\StdFileEditing\verb\0 = &Play
\...\StdFileEditing\verb\1 = &Edit
```

- OLE servers capable of performing actions, such as playing a waveform audio file with Sound Recorder, can include a second protocol, StdExecute, that executes the application with embedded or linked data. With Sound Recorder, StdExecute is equal to StdFileEditing with the &Play verb added.

- The server = *d:\path\appname*.{exe¦dll¦ocx} entry provides the full path to the executable file of a server, or an OLE 2.0 dynamic link library (DLL) or an OLE Custom Control (OCX) file. Thus, if you move rather than reinstall one of these types of files, you need to change the path entry to point to the file's new location.

Applications that support OLE 2.0 add a variety of other entries to REG.DAT; an explanation of the purpose of each of these entries is beyond the scope of this book. However, what is important is your ability to recover from problems that result from improper entries for OLE 2.0 servers in your REG.DAT.

How Access and Other OLE Applications Use REG.DAT

The primary REG.DAT entries for each OLE server appear in the Object Type list box of the Insert Object dialog that appears when you choose Insert Object from Access 2.0's Edit menu. Figure 19.13 shows the new Insert Object dialog that is standard for all OLE 2.0-compliant applications with the Microsoft Graph 5.0 entry (MSGraph.Chart.5 ProgID) selected. If you have installed prior versions of current OLE 2.0 servers, such as Excel 4.0 and Word for Windows 2.0, entries may appear for these servers, even if you have deleted the applications from your fixed disk.

> **Note**
>
> Microsoft Access 2.0, Excel 5.0, Word 6.0, and Project 4.0 install their setup program in *APPNAME*\SETUP directories on your fixed disk. The setup program includes an option to remove all or parts of an application. When you remove all of an application, the application's entries in REG.DAT also are removed. Prior versions of these and other OLE servers did not provide for removal of their REG.DAT entries.

Fig. 19.13
The OLE 2.0 Insert Object dialog that enables you to select an available object type, based on REG.DAT.

Each Object Type in the Object Type list box is a specific type of the OLE object. The entries in the list box are derived from REG.DAT's value of each registered OLE server. The Microsoft Graph 5.0 type, for example, is entered from the `MSGraph.Chart.5 = Microsoft Graph 5.0` in REG.DAT. If you double-click the Microsoft Graph 5.0 entry (or select the entry and click OK), GRAPH5.EXE opens with the empty graph shown in figure 19.14. The graph is empty because no source of data has been specified for the graph. You can enter data in the datasheet at the upper left of Microsoft Graph's window, but doing so creates a static graph. You can import an Excel 4.0 *GRAPH*.XLC file or a graph object from an Excel 5.0 *WORKBOOK*.XLS file, but that's about all you can do without having a working knowledge of how graphs obtain data from Access 2.0. Creating graphs from Access data is one of the subjects of Chapter 20, "Adding Graphics to Forms and Reports."

Repairing Your REG.DAT File

If your REG.DAT file is corrupted, some or all of the OLE data types provided by the OLE server applications are missing from the list. In most cases, you can repair the REG.DAT entry by merging the *APPNAME*.REG file that is located in the *APPNAME* directory. As an example, if you have installed Excel 5.0 and Excel objects no longer appear when you open the Insert Object dialog, your REG.DAT file is likely to be corrupted. In most cases, you can repair the entries by taking these steps:

Tip
If you want to move an OLE 2.0 server application to a new location, run the Setup application from the application's program group and click the Remove All button. Then reinstall the application from the distribution disks.

V

Integrating Access

Fig. 19.14

An empty graph created by opening a new *MSGraph5.Chart* object in Form Design View.

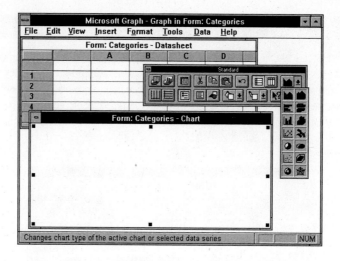

1. Close Access and launch RegEdit.

2. Choose **M**erge Registration File from RegEdit's **F**ile menu to display the Merge Registration File dialog shown in figure 19.15.

Fig. 19.15

RegEdit's Merge Registration File dialog.

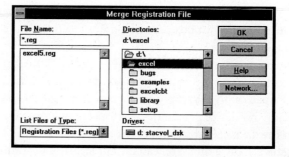

3. Select your \EXCEL directory and double-click the excel5.reg entry to merge EXCEL5.REG with REG.DAT.

4. Choose E**x**it from the **F**ile menu to close RegEdit. Save the changes to your REG.DAT file.

Access

2.0

5. Launch Access, and check for the reappearance of the missing object in the Insert Object dialog.

You can use the preceding steps to repair the registration records for any application that provides an *APPNAME*.REG file. If these steps do not solve the problem, the best course is to remove the application and reinstall it.

> **Note**
>
> Make periodic disk backups of the REG.DAT file with backups of WIN.INI and SYSTEM.INI. If the REG.DAT file becomes corrupted and you don't have a backup, you must reinstall all the OLE server applications so that the REG.DAT entries are added to the list, which is a major task because you need to start with the REG.DAT file supplied with Windows 3.1 and expand the file from compressed form on the Windows 3.1 distribution disk. Restoring a backup REG.DAT file is much easier than re-creating REG.DAT from scratch.

From Here...

In this chapter, you learned the principles of creating OLE 1.0 and 2.0 objects and the concepts behind OLE Automation and OLE Custom Controls. A basic understanding of how OLE works and how to merge application registration files is quite useful when you see an Access message box informing you that your registration database is corrupted. Although this chapter is directed to using OLE 2.0 with Access 2.0, these principles are the same with all OLE 2.0-compliant applications.

For information related to the topics discussed in this chapter, refer to the following chapters:

- Chapter 20, "Adding Graphics to Forms and Reports," shows you how to use Windows Paintbrush and other OLE 2.0 servers to add bit-mapped and vector images to your forms and reports, as well as to embed image data in or link image files to records of the OLE Object data type in Access tables.

- Chapter 21, "Using Access with Microsoft Excel," describes how to embed or link Excel Workbook objects in forms, reports, and tables.

- Chapter 22, "Using Access with Microsoft Word and Mail Merge," discusses adding OLE 2.0 word-processing prowess to your Access 2.0 applications.

- Chapter 29, "Exchanging Data with OLE Automation and DDE," provides examples of manipulating Excel 5.0 and Word 6.0 objects with Access Basic and OLE Automation code.

Chapter 20

Adding Graphics to Forms and Reports

One of the principal incentives for using a Windows desktop database manager is the ability to display graphic images contained in (or linked to) database tables. Early Windows RDBMSs could display images stored in individual bit-mapped graphic files with common formats such as .BMP, .PCX, and .TIF, but could not store the bit-map data within the database file. A few publishers enhanced some of these early desktop products with BLOB (binary large object) field data types. A BLOB field is of variable length and can hold any type of data, regardless of its format. Other Windows desktop RDBMSs use auxiliary files (similar to dBASE's .DBT memo files) to store graphic images and other types of nontext data. When an auxiliary file is used, a field in a database table provides a reference (called a *pointer*) to the location of the data in the auxiliary file.

Many Windows graphic images are stored as combinations of lines, shapes, and patterns, rather than as copies of the pixel pattern of an image on your video display unit. Images of this type are called *vector-based graphics*. Windows illustration applications (such as Corel Systems' CorelDRAW!, Shapeware Corporation's Visio 2.0, and Micrografx's Windows Draw and Designer) create vector-based graphics. Microsoft Graph 5.0 (MSGraph5) uses vector-based graphics to create graphs from data in Access tables. Although each of these products has a proprietary file format, the illustration applications communicate with other applications through the Clipboard in standard Windows metafile format.

This chapter describes how to use both bit-mapped and vector-based graphics in conjunction with Access forms and reports. It also describes how you use MSGraph5 to create graphs and charts from Access 2.0 data.

In this chapter, you learn to

- Add graphic images stored in tables to forms

- Manipulate bit-mapped images in bound controls

- Add vector-based graphic objects to forms and reports

- Use MSGraph5 to create graphs and charts from Access data

V

Integrating Access

Adding a Bound Object Control to a Form or Report

Graphic images and other OLE objects stored in OLE Object fields of Access tables require a bound object control to display their presentation. The *bound object control* is a frame within which a bit-mapped or vector-based image can be displayed; bound object controls are called *bound object frames* in this book.

In the case of still graphic images, the presentation within the bound object frame is a copy of the object's data property. Animated images and video objects may be presented as the icon of the application that created (or supplied) the image or as the first image in the animation sequence or video clip. Sound objects substitute the icon of the OLE server with which their file type is associated in REG.DAT. Double-clicking the bound object frame launches the OLE server that was used to add the object to a data cell in an OLE Object field of your table.

In the following sections, you are introduced to one example of adding a bound object frame to an Access form. You learn how to display a photograph in the Personnel Action Entry form you have built in the preceding chapters. You also learn how to scale the photograph within the bound object frame, so that you get exactly the look you want.

Including Photos in the Personnel Actions Query

The majority of Access applications use the OLE Object field data type to store only graphic images. The Northwind Traders Employees table includes a photograph for each employee as one such graphic image. You can use the OLE Object field data type to add the photograph to your Personnel Actions form. The first step is to incorporate the Photo field of the Employees table in your Personnel Actions query by following these steps:

1. Click the Query button in the Database window, and select the qryPersonnelActions query. Then click the Design button to open the query in Design View.

2. Use the Horizontal Scroll Bar button to position the Query Design grid so that the blank column after the Title column is visible.

3. Select the Photo field of the Employees table.

4. Click and drag the Photo field symbol to the Field row of the column (to the right of the Title column). Your query appears as shown in figure 20.1.

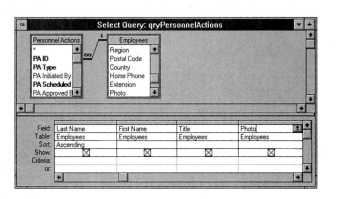

Fig. 20.1
Modifying the design of the qryPersonnelActions query.

Next, run the query so you can view one of the photographs in the Paintbrush window; follow these steps:

1. Click the Run Query button on the toolbar to run the query.

2. Drag the Horizontal Scroll Bar button to the right to display the Photo field in the resulting table.

3. Double-click one of the Paintbrush Picture data cells to display the image in Windows Paintbrush. The chosen image appears in the Paintbrush window (see fig. 20.2).

Fig. 20.2
Testing the Picture field of the qryPersonnelActions query.

4. Choose E<u>x</u>it & Return to Microsoft Access from Paintbrush's <u>F</u>ile menu to close the editing window.

5. Choose <u>C</u>lose from Access's <u>F</u>ile menu and save your changes to the query.

V

Integrating Access

◄ "Repairing
Your Reg.Dat
File," p. 725

Troubleshooting

An "insufficient memory" or "application not properly registered" message appears after double-clicking a data cell in the OLE Object field.

Either of the two messages can occur under low memory conditions. First, try closing all other running applications and then double-clicking the data cell again. If you continue to receive registration error messages, exit and restart Windows. If this doesn't solve the problem, open the Registration Database Editor (RegEdit), choose **F**ind Key from the **S**earch menu, and search for the `.bmp` key. If the `.bmp` key is missing, select the root of the file (\) and then choose **A**dd Key from the **E**dit menu. Type **.bmp** in the Key text box and **PBrush** in the Value text box. Close RegEdit, and save the changes to your REG.DAT file. (There is no registration file for Paintbrush, so you can't use RegEdit's merge feature to reregister Paintbrush.)

The behavior of Paintbrush is similar to that of other OLE 1.0 server applications used to add or edit the values (contents) of data cells in OLE Object fields.

Displaying the Employee's Picture in the Personnel Actions Form

You can edit OLE objects in Access tables and queries only through the window of the OLE server you used (Paintbrush, in this example) to add the objects to the table. The presentation of OLE objects is, however, stored in the OLE field, and is displayed automatically in a bound or unbound object frame. You double-click within the object frame to edit the object.

To add a bound object frame to the Personnel Action Entry form, so you can display the Photo field of your qryPersonnelActions query, follow these steps:

1. Click the Form tab of the Database window, and select the frmPersonnelActions form. If the frmPersonnelActions form is open, you must close it and then reopen it; the reason for this action is explained in the note at the end of this section.

2. Click the Design button of the Database window to open the form in design mode.

3. Position the mouse pointer near the upper left corner of the Rating group frame.

4. Hold down the left mouse button and drag the mouse pointer to the lower right of the frame so that the entire frame is enclosed within the gray rectangle.

5. Release the mouse pointer. The frame and all the objects within it are selected.

6. To make room for the image, press the Delete key to remove the frame and its contents from your form.

7. Click the Field List button, and select Photo from the Field List window.

8. Select the Photo field and drag the Field symbol to the approximate position of the upper left corner of the deleted Rating object frame. Access creates a bound object frame rather than a text box when you create a control directly from the Field List dialog.

9. Select the Photo label, and press the Delete key. A caption is not required for the employee photograph.

10. Position and size the new bound object frame as shown in figure 20.3.

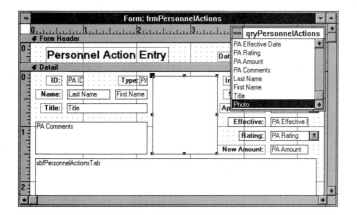

Fig. 20.3
Adding a bound object frame to frmPersonnelActions.

11. Click the Form View button to display your form with the photograph. The form appears as in figure 20.4. Note that only a portion of the photograph appears within the frame. You still need to scale the image, which is the subject of the next section.

Fig. 20.4

Viewing the
Personnel Action
Entry form with
the added Photo
bound object
frame.

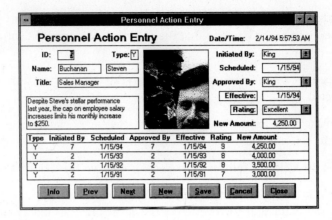

Troubleshooting

The employee's photo does not appear in Form View.

If you add the Photo field to your query and follow the procedure for adding a
bound object frame while the Personnel Action Entry form is open, your frame is
likely to be empty when you display the form in run mode. In this case, the Photo
field is added to the Datasheet View of your form, but the field's cells have **Null**
values. Pressing Shift+F9 (Requery) does not replace the **Null** values with Paintbrush
pictures. If this problem occurs, you must close the form and then reopen it from the
Database window. Access runs the modified query when you open the form, and the
pictures appear.

An alternative method for creating a bound object frame is to click the bound
object frame tool of the toolbox, click the Photo field, and drag the Field
symbol to the form. The extra step involved in this process serves no purpose
because Access chooses a bound object frame for you when you choose a field
in the Field list that is of the OLE Object data type. When you use the bound
object frame tool, the value of the Enabled property is set to No and the Locked
property is set to Yes. The effect of these two properties is as follows:

- When an object frame is disabled, you can't double-click the object to
  launch the OLE server that created the object's content. The setting of
  the Locked property has no effect in this case.

- When an object is enabled and locked, you can launch the OLE server,
  but any edits you make to the content of the object are discarded when
  you close the server application.

The opposite property settings are set by default when you add a bound object from the field list: the object frame is enabled and not locked.

Scaling Graphic Objects

Access provides three methods for scaling graphic objects within the confines of a bound object frame. You select one of these methods by choosing the value of the SizeMode property in the Bound Object Frame Properties dialog displayed in figure 20.5.

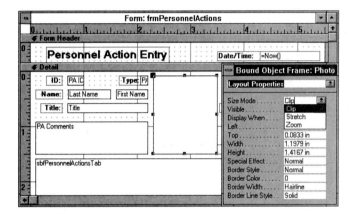

Fig. 20.5
Allowable values of the *SizeMode* property of object frames.

The three options offered for the value of the SizeMode property display the image in the following ways:

- *Clip*, the default, displays the image in its original aspect ratio. The *aspect ratio* is the ratio of the width to the height of an image, measured in pixels or inches. A *pixel* is the smallest element of a bit map that your computer can display, a single dot. The aspect ratio of the standard VGA display, for example, is 640/480 pixels, which is 1.33:1. If the entire image does not fit within the frame, the bottom or right of the image is cropped. *Cropping* an image is a graphic arts term that means cutting off the portions of an image so it fits within a window of a specified size, as shown in the left-hand picture of figure 20.6.

- *Stretch* independently enlarges or shrinks the horizontal and vertical dimensions of the image to fill the frame. If the aspect ratio of the frame is not identical to that of the image, the image is distorted, as illustrated by the center image of figure 20.6. (Access 1.x used the term *Scale* instead of *Stretch*.)

Access

2.0

■ *Zoom* enlarges or shrinks the horizontal or vertical dimension of the image so the image fits within the frame, and the original aspect ratio is maintained. If your frame has an aspect ratio different from that of the image, a portion of the frame is empty, as shown in the right-hand image of figure 20.6.

The bound object frames in figure 20.6 are expanded horizontally to accent the effects of the Stretch and Zoom property values.

Fig. 20.6
Comparing the *Clip*, *Stretch*, and *Zoom* values of the *SizeMode* property.

Clip   Stretch   Zoom

Access does not include the capability to specify a particular area of the image to be clipped, so zooming to maintain the original aspect ratio is the best choice in this case. When you scale or zoom a bit-mapped image, the apparent contrast is likely to increase, as shown in the center and right-hand images of figure 20.6. This increase results from deleting a sufficient number of pixels in the image to make it fit the frame. The increase in contrast is less evident if you choose a 256-color display driver, but doing so may slow the operation of Access significantly.

To apply the Zoom property to your bound object frame in design mode, follow these steps:

1. Select the Photo bound object frame.

    2. Click the Properties button on the toolbar to open the bound object frame Properties window. Select Layout Properties.

3. Click the Size Mode text box, and open its list box.

4. Select Zoom.

To display the form so that you can view the photograph with its new property, follow these steps:

    1. Click the Form View button of the toolbar to display your form, which now appears as shown in figure 20.7.

2. If your frame includes an empty area, as illustrated in figure 20.7, return to design mode, adjust the size of the frame, and rerun the form to verify that the frame has the correct dimensions.

3. Choose **C**lose from the **F**ile menu, and save your changes to the Personnel Action Entry form.

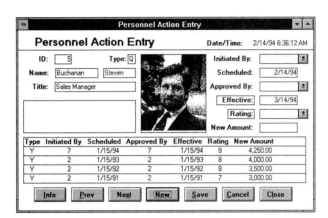

Fig. 20.7
The bound object frame with *Zoom SizeMode* applied.

The technique described in this section allows you to add a bound object frame containing a vector image created with a drawing application, a sound clip from a .WAV or .MID file, or any other OLE object type.

To add a bound object frame to the Detail section of a report, you also use the same method outlined here. The quality of the printed image depends on the type of image, and the laser or inkjet printer you use. Vector-based images (such as drawings created in CorelDRAW!, Micrografx Designer, or Windows DRAW!) result in more attractive printed reports than do bit-mapped images, especially when the bit map is scaled. The contrast problem discussed previously may be aggravated when color images are printed.

Examining Bit-Map Image File Formats

Graphics files are identified by generally-accepted file extensions; these serve to define most (or all) of the format's basic characteristics. The following file extensions identify bit-map image files that have achieved the status of "industry standards" for the PC. Most commercial bit-map image editing applications support these formats, though some do not import .GIF files. The "standard" extensions follow:

■ *.BMP* is for Windows bit-map files in 1-, 2-, 4-, 8-, and 24-bit color depths. .BMP files contain a bit-map information *header* defining the size of the image, the number of color planes, the type of compression used (if any), and information on the palette used. A header is a block of data in the file that precedes the image data.

- *.DIB* is for device-independent bit-map files. The .DIB file format is a variant of the .BMP format; to define the .RGB values of the colors used, it includes a color table in the header.

- *.PCX* is for files that are compatible with ZSoft Paint applications. The .PCX file format is the common denominator for most bit-map file format conversions; almost every graphics application created in the past five years can handle .PCX files, including Windows Paintbrush. .PCX files are compressed by a method called *run-length encoding* (RLE) that can decrease the size of bit-map files by a factor of 3 or more, depending on their contents.

- *.TIF* (an abbreviated form of TIFF) is for tagged image format files. The TIFF format was originally developed by Aldus Corporation, and now is managed by Microsoft Corporation. Originally, TIFF files were used primarily for storing scanned images, but now they are used by a substantial number of applications (including those for Windows) as the preferred bit-map format. A special version of TIFF that uses file compression is used for fax transmission. TIFF files for conventional bit maps are found in both uncompressed and compressed formats. A tag in the header of the file defines information similar to that found in the information header of .BMP files.

- *.JPG* is for files created by applications that offer compression and decompression options for *JPEG* graphics. (Such applications include Micrografx Picture Publisher 3.1.) JPEG is an acronym for the Joint Photographic Experts Group, which has developed a standard methodology to compress and decompress still color images. Special JPEG adapter cards are available to speed the compression and decompression processes. JPEG compression often is used for video images, but MPEG (Moving Pictures Experts Group) compression is expected to predominate in the video field; it provides better compression ratios for video images than does the JPEG method. MPEG compression requires special adapter cards to display live-motion video images at the standard 30 frames-per-second rate.

- *.PCD* (an abbreviation for Photo CD, a Kodak trademark) is for photographic images that are digitized and stored on CD-ROMs by photofinishers. .PCD files use a special compression system devised by the Eastman Kodak Company; you need Kodak's Photo CD Access application for Windows or an image editor such as Picture Publisher 3.1 to display the images and save them to .PCD files.

- *.GIF* is for the graphics interchange file format used to archive bitmapped images on CompuServe. Shareware and freeware .GIF file conversion applications for all popular types of personal computers are available for downloading from CompuServe's Graphic Support forum (GO GRAPHSUP). Graphic Workshop for Windows, GWSWIN.ZIP in Library x of the Zenith forum (GO ZENITH), is a Shareware Windows graphics application that enables you to edit and convert compressed .GIF files to .BMP format. .GIF is the standard bit-map format for background images used by Autodesk Animator.

- *.TGA* is for files in the TARGA file format developed by True Vision for its TARGA product line of graphics adapter cards. TARGA cards were the first to offer relatively high-resolution, wide-spectrum color images with PCs by employing a separate video monitor. TARGA cards were the unchallenged standard for professional graphic artists until the advent of large-screen super-VGA displays.

- *.IMG* is for files created by applications that use Digital Research's GEM application, a graphical interface used by many applications that pre-date Windows 3.0, such as early versions of Ventura Publisher.

If you do not have a Windows image-editing application with OLE file server capability, you need to convert bit-map files in .TIF, .GIF, .TGA, or .IMG format to .BMP or .PCX format; you need to use Windows 3.1's Paintbrush applet to import images and copy them to the Clipboard as OLE objects. You can use Microsoft Word's bit-map file-conversion capability to insert a .TIF file in a new document and then copy the image to the Clipboard as a picture. You cannot edit the Word picture that you paste into an Access table with Paste **S**pecial because the image is not an OLE object; it is a bit-map picture created from a DDE link to Word.

V

Integrating Access

> **Note**
>
> Store individual bit-map images in .PCX and not .BMP files for use with Windows Paintbrush. Using .PCX files saves disk space compared with the .BMP format because .PCX uses RLE file compression. Line-art files (black on a white background) compress the most; 24-bit full-color photographic images compress the least. The JPEG (Joint Photographic Experts Group) compression offered by Micrografx Picture Publisher 3.1 works best for color images, especially images with more than 256 colors (16-bit, 18-bit, or 24-bit color).
>
> If your use of images is intended primarily for printing (as in desktop publishing) and you do not have a color printer, use shades of gray for vector-based images. The 256-grayscale palette is preferred for printing bit-mapped images; change color images to grayscale if your image-editing application supports this conversion.

Adding an Unbound Object Frame to a Form or Report

◀ "Modifying Linkages between Main Forms and Subforms," p. 472

◀ "Adding a Linked Subreport to a Bound Report," p. 593

Instead of using OLE Object fields, images in unbound object frames store their properties as data in the area of your .MDB file devoted to forms or reports. Like the methods you use with bound object frames, the methods that create (or edit) unbound objects are contributed temporarily by the OLE server. After you embed or link the unbound object, the Access application supplies the methods used to display the images.

The use of unbound object frames differs from that of bound object frames in the following ways:

- You set the `Enabled` property of most unbound object frames to `No` so that the OLE server that supplied those unbound objects does not appear if you double-click the object in run mode. The `Enabled` property does not affect your ability to edit the object in design mode. A bound object's `Enabled` property is usually set to `Yes` (the default value when the bound object frame is created from the Field List window).

- Unbound object frames have properties (such as `RowSource`, `LinkChildFields`, `LinkMasterFields`, and `ColumnCount`) that are not applicable to bound object frames. Graphs and other unbound objects use these properties to obtain or present data in an unbound object field.

- You can create a master-child linkage between the content of an unbound object frame and the value of a field in the underlying table or query (or the value entered in a text box on your form).

- Multimedia objects, such as sound or animated graphics, are seldom useful in unbound object frames.

The following sections provide examples that utilize the important additional properties available when you use unbound object frames.

Creating a New Logo for Your Personnel Actions Form

Logotypes and symbols that identify an organization are among the most common graphic objects on forms and in reports. The bit-map example in this section uses the image of a lighthouse from the Northwind Traders database, but you can substitute your organization's logo if you have a bit-map file or a scanner to create an image of suitable dimensions.

To add an image to a new form the easiest way, you copy to the Clipboard an existing unbound object frame of a form or report that contains the image. You then duplicate the image by pasting it into another form. This process is similar to the process for copying OLE objects that are to be used by other applications. You can edit the image as necessary with Windows Paintbrush or another OLE-compliant image editor.

Northwind Traders' Forms Switchboard form contains an image that almost fits the space that now contains the employee photograph on your Personnel Actions form. Follow these steps to copy the Northwind Traders logo to your Personnel Action Entry form:

1. Click the Form View button in the Database window. Choose Forms Switchboard from the list, and then click the Design button.

2. Select the Northwind logo by clicking the lighthouse in the logo.

3. Press Ctrl+C or choose **C**opy from the **E**dit menu to copy the logo to the Clipboard. Close the Forms Switchboard form.

4. Select the frmPersonnelActions form in the Database window, and click the Design button.

5. Select the Photo bound object frame (that you added in the preceding sections), delete it to make room for the new logo, and then click the Detail header bar to select the detail section of the form.

6. Choose **P**aste from the **E**dit menu to create a copy of the logo on your form. Position the logo's unbound object frame as shown in figure 20.8.

Fig. 20.8
Copying an
unbound control
from another
form.

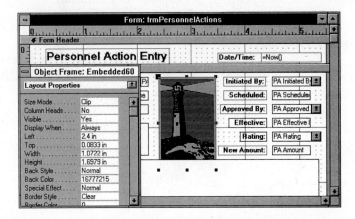

Access applies the SizeMode property to the presentation of the image; SizeMode does not modify the image itself. The copied image extends into the area occupied by the subform; this problem is corrected after you edit the image in the next section.

Editing the Logo with Windows Paintbrush

Because your form's background is white, the dark cyan background of the copied image is inappropriate. You need to change the image's background color to white. Fortunately, Windows Paintbrush includes a Color Eraser tool that can change occurrences of one color to another.

To change the background color of the logo to white and create a .BMP file from the logo, follow these steps:

1. Double-click the logo to launch Paintbrush with the image contained in the unbound object frame.

2. Click the dark cyan (blue-green) color of the palette at the bottom of Paintbrush's window, and then double-click the Color Eraser tool (in the left column) to change the background color to white. Your logo appears as shown in figure 20.9.

3. To save the bit-map logo to disk for use in the next section, choose Save **A**s from Paintbrush's **F**ile menu. The dialog shown in figure 20.10 appears, giving you the opportunity to save the changes you made to the image.

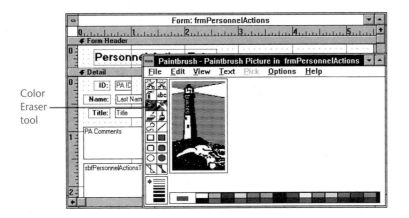

Color
Eraser
tool

Fig. 20.9
Changing the
background color
of the logo with
Paintbrush's Color
Eraser tool.

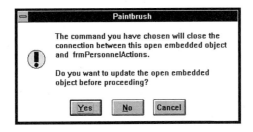

Fig. 20.10
Paintbrush's dialog
that lets you save
your changes
before breaking
the OLE link with
Access.

4. Click Yes to save the changes in your Access form before you create the
   file. Give the bit map a file name (such as **NWIND1.BMP)** in the Save
   As dialog, and click OK.

5. Click Exit from the File menu to return to Access. (The link to Access
   has been broken, so Exit and Return to Microsoft Access does not appear in the File menu.)

6. Drag the bottom of the logo's object frame up, and align it with the
   bottom of the Comments text box.

7. Click the Form View button of the toolbar to display your new logo in
   the form (see fig. 20.11).

8. If you want to save your form with the new logo, choose Save **A**s from
   Access's **F**ile menu, and give the form a name such as
   frmPAwithBitMap.

9. Close the form. If you did save the form with a new name, do not save
   changes so that your original version of frmPersonnelActions is preserved.

Fig. 20.11

The monochrome version of the Northwind Traders logo in the Personnel Action Entry form.

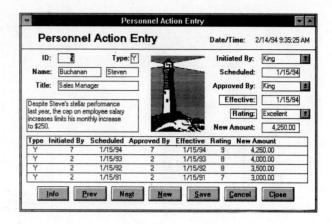

Importing a Bit-Map File into an Unbound Object Box

You can import a bit-mapped image from a file as a new unbound object with the Import Object choice from the **E**dit menu. This technique is a quick way to add a graphic image to your form, provided the image is contained in a .BMP or .PCX file and has dimensions appropriate to your form's design. Most Windows applications for scanners create files in .TIF format but can convert the .TIF files to both .BMP and .PCX formats.

To add an unbound object that contains a bit-mapped image derived from a file to a form in design mode, follow these steps:

1. Open frmPAwithBitMap in Design View. Delete the unbound object frame containing the logo, and click the Detail section header to select the Detail section.

2. Choose Insert Object from the **E**dit menu to display the Insert Object dialog.

3. Click the Create from File option button to use a file as the source of the image data.

4. Open the file you want to use in the Insert Object dialog. Specify NWIND1.BMP, the file you created in step 3 of the preceding example, to use the black-and-white Northwind logo (see fig. 20.12). If you want to create a link the NWIND1.BMP file, mark the Link check box.

5. Click OK. Access creates an unbound object box the size of the image on your form.

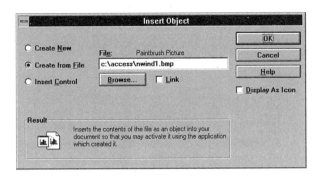

Fig. 20.12
The Insert Object dialog for embedding or linking a .BMP file.

6. Position and size the image. Access sets the `SizeMode` property to `Clip` by default.

7. Open the Properties window; verify that `Enabled` property of the unbound object frame is set to `No` so that Paintbrush does not appear when you double-click the image in run mode.

8. Click the Form View button of the toolbar to verify that the logo appears identical to the copied version you added in the preceding section.

Using Visio Express to Add a Vector-Based Image to a Form or Report

Visio Express is the mini-server version of Shapeware Corporation's Visio 2.0, a template-based drawing application. Visio Express has many of the same features as Visio 2.0, but you cannot run Visio Express (unlike Visio 2.0) as a stand-alone application. Like most OLE mini-servers, Visio Express does not include a built-in printing capability, nor can you save a Visio Express drawing to a file. Visio Express compensates, however, by being much less costly than the full-featured, stand-alone Visio 2.0.

> **Note**
>
> Visio Express includes a feature that is missing from the first crop of OLE 2.0 mini-servers and full servers alike: it can reregister itself in REG.DAT in the event your registration database file becomes corrupted. You register Visio Express in REG.DAT by executing VISIO.EXE with the /R command line parameter. To reregister Visio Express (you can do so at any time), type **\visio\visio.exe /r** in the Command Line text box of Program Manager's Run dialog, and click OK.

Both Visio 2.0 and Visio Express are designed for the majority of Windows users who are not professional graphic designers. You use Visio and third-party templates or stencils to create drawing objects; you can scale or alter these to suit your particular application. Shapeware supplies a variety of sample templates with Visio, and you can download Shareware (as well as public-domain templates) from the Shapeware section of the Windows Third-Party forum (GO VISIO). Both Visio 2.0 and Visio Express are OLE 2.0 server applications, and support in-place activation in most OLE 2.0 client applications. The versions of Visio 2.0 and Visio Express available when this edition was written use anchored toolbars and do not support floating toolbars. Floating toolbars are required for in-place activation in Access 2.0. In-place activation is less suited for drawing and illustration applications because the vast majority of users work with these applications maximized.

Like other drawing and illustration products (CorelDRAW! and Micrografx Designer are examples of Windows illustration applications), Visio 2.0 and Express create vector-based images. Compared with bit maps, vector images have two primary advantages:

- Vector image files are almost always much smaller than a bit-mapped image file of the same object, especially if the image makes use of 256 or more colors.

- Vector image files can be scaled without the degradation of image quality (called *pixelization* or *pixelation*) that occurs when you scale bit maps by factors other than a power of 2 (1/8, 1/4, 1/2, 2, 4, 8, and so on).

The following example demonstrates using the Zoom value of the SizeMode property to scale a vector image contained in a bound object frame of a form. Adding a vector image to a report is an identical process. To embed a Visio Express image in a bound object frame, follow these steps:

1. Create a new form, and choose Insert Object from the **E**dit menu to display the Insert Object dialog.

2. Visio drawings use the extension .VSD, which is associated with Visio 2.0 or Visio Express in REG.DAT. Click the Browse button, and select one of the .VSD sample drawings in the \VISIO\SAMPLES directory (see fig. 20.13). Click OK to close the Browse dialog.

3. Click OK to close the Insert Object dialog and create the unbound object frame. When the object frame containing the Visio drawing is created in a form or report, it defaults to the full size of the original drawing (see fig. 20.14).

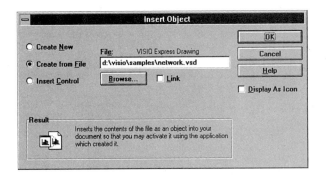

Fig. 20.13
The Insert Object dialog for a Visio Express drawing.

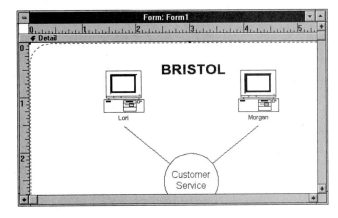

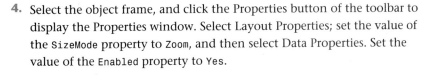

Fig. 20.14
The unbound object frame, containing a full-size Visio drawing.

V

Integrating Access

4. Select the object frame, and click the Properties button of the toolbar to display the Properties window. Select Layout Properties; set the value of the SizeMode property to Zoom, and then select Data Properties. Set the value of the Enabled property to Yes.

5. Relocate and resize the object frame to approximately 2.5 by 2.5 inches, as shown in figure 20.15. Reduce the margins of the form to 3 by 5 inches.

6. Click the Form View button of the toolbar to display the Visio image (see fig. 20.16).

7. Double-click the unbound object frame to launch Visio Express. If the Locked property of the object frame is set to No (the default), you can use Visio Express to edit the drawing (see fig. 20.17).

8. To return to Access, choose E**x**it and Return to Form: Form1 from Visio Express's **F**ile menu.

Fig. 20.15
Scaling the Visio drawing to fit the form.

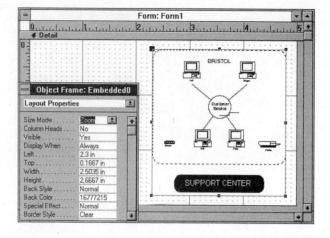

Fig. 20.16
The scaled Visio drawing in Form View (selected).

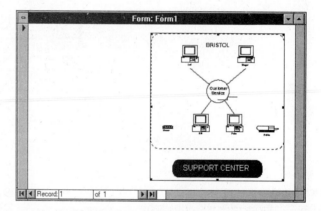

Fig. 20.17
The drawing window of Visio Express with the template window displaying the stencils for PC networks.

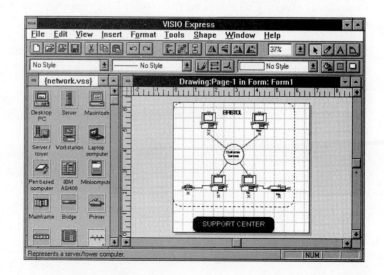

Creating Graphs and Charts with Microsoft Graph 5.0

Microsoft Graph 5.0 (called by its OLE 2.0 programmatic ID, *MSGraph5*, in this book) is an OLE 2.0 mini-server application that is almost indistinguishable from the graphing application native to Excel 5.0. Access 2.0 is the first Microsoft application to include MSGraph5 as one of a suite of OLE 2.0 mini-servers; ultimately these will provide graphing (and other commonly-required capabilities) to all Microsoft productivity applications. The sections that follow describe how to use the Graph Wizard to add MSGraph5 graphs and charts to Access 2.0 forms and reports.

Creating the Query on Which to Base the Graph

Most graphs required by management are the time-series type; these track the history of financial performance data, such as orders received, product sales, gross margin, and the like. In smaller firms, this data comes from tables that store entries from the original documents (such as sales orders and invoices) that underlie the summary information. This type of data often is called a *line-item* source. Because a multi-billion-dollar firm can accumulate several million line-item records in a single year, larger firms usually store summaries of the line-item source data in tables; this technique improves the performance of queries. Summary data are referred to as *rolled-up* data, or simply *rollups*. Although rolling up data from relational tables violates one of the guiding principles of relational theory, tables of rolled-up data are very common in mainframe database environments.

◀ "Creating a Monthly Product Sales Crosstab Query," p. 393

Northwind Traders is a relatively small firm, so it is not necessary to roll up line-item data to obtain acceptable query performance on an Intel 80486-based or faster computer. Thus, you can use one of the queries you created in Chapter 10, qry1993QuarterlyCategorySales, and modify this query to create the qry1993MonthlyCategorySales query that provides more granularity to the graph.

◀ "Decreasing the Level of Detail in Crosstab Queries," p. 397

To create the qry1993MonthlyCategorySales query, follow these steps:

1. Open the qry1993QuarterlyCategorySales query in design mode.

2. Add the Categories table to the query. A join is created between the Category ID fields of the Categories and Products tables.

3. Delete the Category ID column that provided the Row Heading.

4. Drag the Category Name field from the Categories table to the first column of the query, and select Row Heading in the Crosstab row.

V

Integrating Access

5. Alias the Category Name field by typing **Categories:** at the beginning of the field text box.

6. Change the Expr1 statement in the Fields row to **Expr1:Format([Order Date], "mmm")** to use three-letter month abbreviations. Your query appears as shown in figure 20.18.

Fig. 20.18
The design of a query that displays monthly sales by product category.

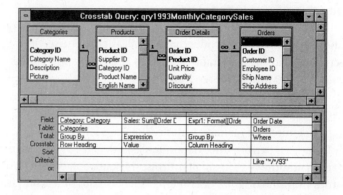

7. Click the Properties button of the toolbar, delete the current entry in the Column Headings text box of the Query Properties window. Enter the 12 month abbreviations, **Jan, . . . Dec**, separating the month abbreviations with commas. Access adds the double quotation marks for you.

Fig. 20.19
Adding fixed column headings for 12 months.

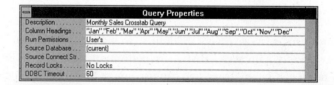

8. Choose Save **A**s from the **F**ile menu, and save your query as **qry1993MonthlyCategorySalesGraph**.

9. Click the Run Query button of the toolbar to check your query result set (see fig. 20.20).

Fig. 20.20
The result set of the qry1993-MonthlyCategory-Sales query.

Category	Jan	Feb	Mar	Apr	May	Jun	Jul
Beverages	$3,159.60	$10,174.00	$10,281.50	$12,986.00	$4,158.00	$8,254.00	$6,411.50
Condiments	$6,900.00	$2,324.30	$6,303.00	$4,823.30	$2,872.35	$7,368.70	$5,245.40
Confections	$7,916.70	$3,384.20	$12,507.65	$7,831.50	$1,525.28	$7,516.65	$8,532.70
Dairy Products	$5,949.20	$10,315.40	$6,220.20	$11,570.50	$8,672.50	$13,892.60	$10,873.00
Grains/Cereals	$3,365.80	$3,360.40	$6,062.00	$4,139.00	$5,583.00	$5,077.00	$6,214.25
Meat/Poultry	$9,831.90	$1,489.60	$8,268.99	$3,147.70	$4,356.40	$4,529.80	$4,988.34
Produce	$2,698.80	$3,676.80	$6,137.10	$8,948.70	$1,063.50	$1,350.00	$4,524.75
Seafood	$2,976.20	$2,992.70	$6,687.10	$4,726.95	$5,298.65	$5,952.30	$11,743.18

Record: 1 of 8

Using the Graph Wizard to Create an Unlinked Graph

Although it is possible to create a graph or chart using the Insert Object method and selecting the Microsoft Graph 5.0 object type, the Graph Wizard makes this process much simpler. You can use the Graph Wizard to create two different classes of graphs and charts:

- *Unlinked*. Unlinked (also called *non-linked*) line graphs display a line for each of the rows of your query. You can also create unlinked stacked column charts and multiple-area charts.

- *Linked*. A linked graph or chart is bound to the current record of the form on which it is located and displays only a single set of values from one row of your table or query at a time.

This section shows you how to create an unlinked line graph based on a query. The next section described how to use MSGraph5 to display alternative presentations of your data in the form of bar and area charts. In the last section of this chapter, you create a graph linked to a specific record of a query result set.

To create an unlinked graph that displays the data from the qry1993MonthlyCategorySalesGraph query, follow these steps:

1. Open a new blank form without selecting a table or query, and click the Toolbox button of the toolbar.

2. Click the Graph button. Position the caret at the upper left of the form, click the left mouse button, and drag the rectangle for the graph to about 3 by 7 inches.

3. When you release the mouse button, the first dialog of the Graph Wizard appears. Click the Queries option button, and select your qry1993MonthlyCategorySalesGraph query (see fig. 20.21). Click the Next > button to display the Graph Wizard's second dialog.

4. Click the line graph button (third from the left in the top row of the buttons that display the available graph styles). The miniature image of your graph displays the month abbreviations in the legend. You want the Category Names to appear in the legend, so click the Rows option button in the Data Series In group. A distorted miniature version of your graph appears, as shown in figure 20.22. Click the Next > button to display the final Graph Wizard dialog.

Fig. 20.21
Selecting the table
or query on which
to base the graph.

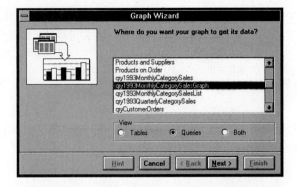

Fig. 20.22
Selecting the type
of graph and the
orientation for the
data series.

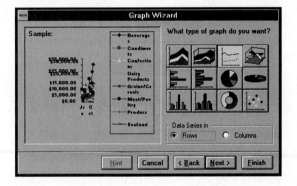

5. Type **1993 Monthly Sales by Category** in the text box to add a title
   to your graph, and click the Yes option button to display the Category
   Name legend (see fig. 20.23).

Fig. 20.23
Adding a title
and legend to
your graph.

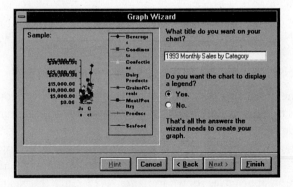

6. Click the Finish button to display your graph in Design View. If your
   graph is less than about eight inches wide, it appears as shown in figure
   20.24, with alternate month labels missing.

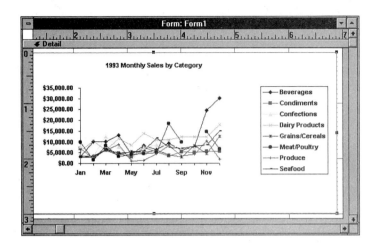

Fig. 20.24
The final un-
bound graph in
Design View.

7. Click the Properties button of the toolbar, select Data Properties, and set the value of the `Enabled` property to `Yes` so you can activate the graph in Form View.

8. Click the Form View button of the toolbar to display your graph in run mode (see fig. 20.25). The graph is the only control on the form, so it receives the focus at all times.

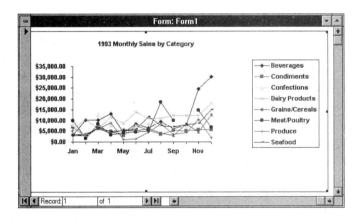

Fig. 20.25
The 1993
Monthly Sales by
Category graph in
Form View.

V

Integrating Access

Tip
When you
complete your
design, set the
value of the
`Enabled` prop-
erty to `No` so
that users of
your applica-
tion can't
activate the
graph and alter
its design.

Note

The Graph Wizard is part of the Access 2.0 wizard library, FRMRPTWZ.MDA. Each of the Graph Wizard's dialogs is a modal, pop-up form. The Chart Wizard's dialogs are created by MSChart5 and have a sculpted, 3-D appearance. Operating the Chart Wizard of MSChart5 is identical to operating Excel 5.0's Chart Wizard.

Modifying the Design Features of Your Graph

▶ "Understanding OLE Automation," p. 1057

MSGraph5 is an OLE 2.0 mini-server; you can activate MSGraph5 in place, and modify the design of your graph. MSGraph5 also supports OLE Automation, so you can use Access Basic code to automate design changes. This section shows you how to use MSGraph5 to edit the design of the graph and how to change the line graph to an area or column chart.

To activate your graph and change its design with MSGraph5, follow these steps:

1. Double-click the graph to activate MSGraph5 in place. A diagonally-hashed border surrounds the graph; MSGraph5's menus replace and supplement those of Access 2.0.

2. Choose **D**atasheet from MSGraph5's **V**iew menu to inspect the data series that Access has transmitted to MSGraph5.

3. Choose **G**ridlines from the **I**nsert menu to display the Gridlines dialog. Mark the Major Gridlines check box of the Value (Y) Axis group to add horizontal grid lines to your graph (see fig. 20.26). Click OK to close the Gridlines dialog, and then double-click the Document Control-menu box to close the datasheet.

Fig. 20.26
Adding horizontal grid lines to the graph.

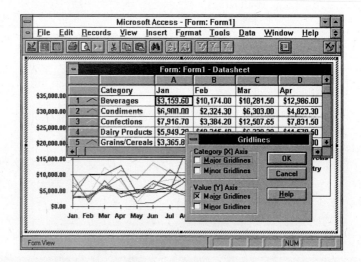

4. You can change the type family and font size of your chart's labels and legend. Select the graph title, and then choose **F**ont from the F**o**rmat menu to open the Format Chart Title dialog. Set the size of the chart title to 12 points (see fig. 20.27), and then click OK to close the dialog.

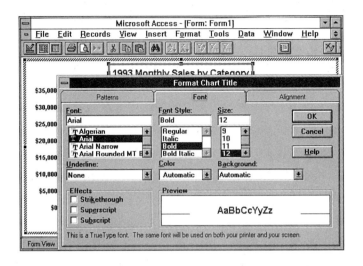

Fig. 20.27
Changing the font size of the graph's title.

5. The decimal "cents" values of the y-axis labels are not needed, so click one of the y-axis labels to select the y-axis. Then choose S**e**lected Axis from the F**o**rmat menu to display the Format Axis dialog.

6. Select the currency format without cents (see fig. 20.28), and click OK to close the dialog and apply the new format. Your line graph appears as shown in figure 20.29.

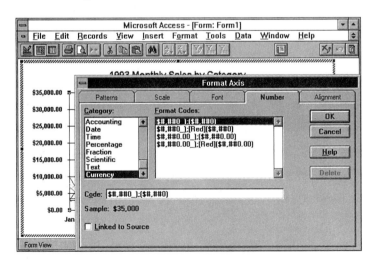

Fig. 20.28
Formatting the numeric values of the y-axis.

V

Integrating Access

Fig. 20.29
The line graph
with reformatted
y-axis labels and a
larger graph title.

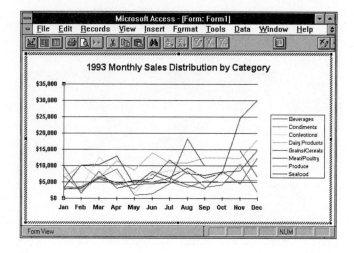

You may want to change the line graph to some other type of chart (such as
area or stacked column) for a specific purpose. Area charts, for example, are
especially effective as a way to display the contribution of individual product
categories to total sales. To change the line graph to another type of chart,
follow these steps:

1. Choose **C**hart Type from the F**o**rmat menu to open the Chart Type
   dialog.

2. Select the Area chart picture in the Chart Type dialog (see fig. 20.30).
   Click OK to change your line graph into an area chart, as shown in figure 20.31. The contribution of each category appears as an individually-
   colored area, and the uppermost line segment represents total sales.

Fig. 20.30
Changing the
line graph to an
area chart.

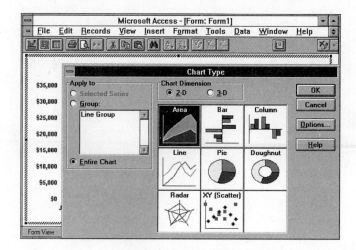

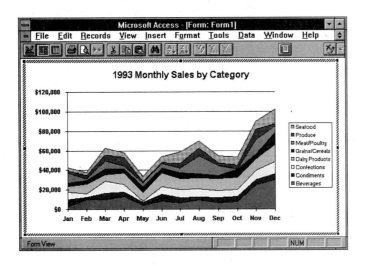

Fig. 20.31
The area chart in
Form View.

3. To convert the area chart into a stacked column chart, choose **C**hart
Type from the F**o**rmat menu, select the Column picture, and then click
the Options button to display the Format Column Group dialog.

4. Click the Stacked Column picture to create the column equivalent of
the area chart (see fig. 20.32). The multiple-column chart subtype,
shown behind the Format Column Group dialog, is the default column
chart subtype.

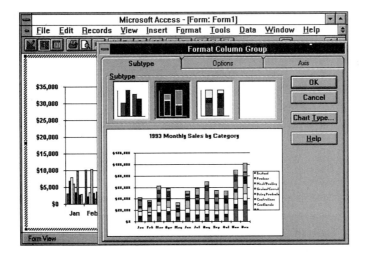

Fig. 20.32
Selecting a stacked
column subtype.

V

Integrating Access

5. Click OK to close the Format Column Group dialog, and then click OK again to close the Chart Type dialog. Your stacked column chart appears as shown in figure 20.33.

Fig. 20.33
The stacked column chart in Form View.

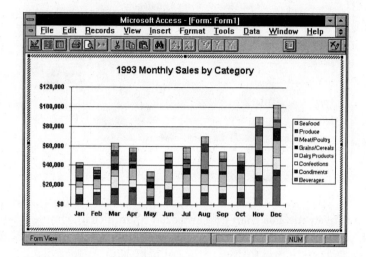

6. Another subtype of the area chart and the stacked column chart is the *percentage distribution* chart. To create the distribution of sales graph shown in figure 20.34, repeat steps 3 through 5, but select the Percent Column picture in the Format Column Group dialog. Because you set the format of the y-axis previously to eliminate the decimals, you need to change the format of the y-axis to Percent manually.

Fig. 20.34
The percentage distribution column chart.

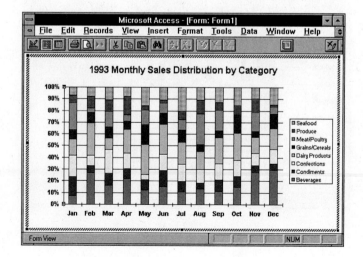

7. Select the final type of graph or chart you want, and save your form
   with a descriptive name such as **frm1993MonthlyCategorySalesGraph**.

> **Note**
>
> The process of adding an unbound graph to an Access report is identical to
> that for forms. Unless you have a color printer, you need to select a line graph
> subtype that identifies data points with a different symbol for each category.
> For area and stacked column charts, select a series of hatched patterns to
> differentiate the product categories.

In addition to the MSGraph3 OLE 1.0 mini-server provided with Access 1.x,
MSGraph5 offers many additional formatting features. However, MSGraph5
is not demonstrably faster in operation than MSGraph3. Each time you
change from Design View to Form View, Access runs the query, launches
MSGraph5 in the background, and passes the query data to MSGraph5. This
process, using the qry1993MonthlyCategorySales query, takes about 13 to 15
seconds on a 80486DX2-66 computer with a video local bus and a fast fixed-
disk drive. The graph custom control of Visual Basic is much faster in operation than MSGraph5.

Another problem with MSGraph5 is that you cannot easily transfer data to
MSGraph5's datasheet with Access Basic code. (MSGraph5 does not expose its
DataSeries object for manipulation by OLE Automation.) You can expect
third-party suppliers to provide faster-operating graphing applications, in the
form of OLE 2.0 mini-servers and OLE Custom Controls. You need to write
Access Basic code, however, to send the data series to these applications.

Linking the Graph to a Single Record of a Table or Query

You create a linked graph or chart by setting the values of the MSGraph5
object's `LinkChildFields` and `LinkMasterFields` properties. The link is similar
to that between a form and a subform. A linked graph displays the data series
from the current row of the table or query that serves as the `RecordSource` of
the form. As you move the record pointer, the graph is redrawn to reflect the
data values in the selected row.

To change the frm1993MonthlyCategorySalesGraph form to accommodate a linked graph, follow these steps:

1. Open frm1993MonthlyCategorySalesGraph in Design View; then click the Properties button of the toolbar to open the Properties window for the form.

2. Select Data Properties; type **qry1993MonthlyCategorySalesGraph** as the value of the RecordSource property, which binds the form to the query.

3. If your form does not have record-navigation buttons, select Layout Properties and set the value of the NavigationButtons property to Yes.

4. Select the graph, and then select Data Properties. Type **Categories** as the value of the LinkChildFields and LinkMasterFields properties (see fig. 20.35). Using this technique, you create the link between the current record of the form and the row of the query that serves as the RowSource property of the graph (through the Categories field).

Fig. 20.35
Linking the graph's *RowSource* property to the current record of the form.

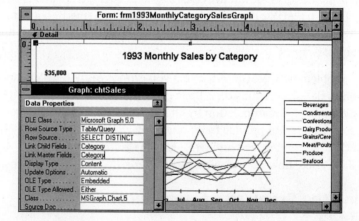

5. To test your linked graph, click the Form View button of the toolbar. If (in the preceding section) you saved the line graph version of the form, your graph appears as shown in figure 20.36.

6. The single line appears a bit anemic for a graph of this size, so double-click the graph to activate it in place. Double-click anywhere on the line to display the Format Data Series dialog. Open the Weight drop-down

list, and choose the thickest line it offers. To add a data-point marker, open the Style drop-down list and select the diamond shape. Use the drop-down lists to set the Foreground and Background colors of the marker to a contrasting hue, such as red (see fig. 20.37). Click OK to close the dialog and implement your design changes.

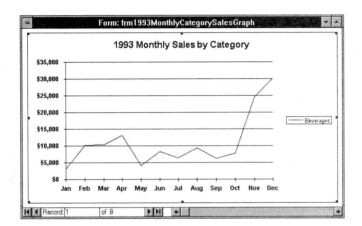

Fig. 20.36
The linked version of the 1993 Monthly Sales by Category graph.

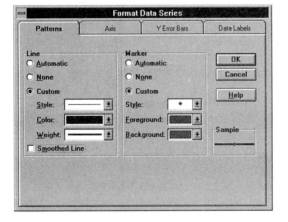

Fig. 20.37
Increasing the thickness of and adding markers to the data series line.

7. Double-click the legend box to open the Format Legend dialog. Click the None option button in the Border frame to remove the border from the legend (see fig. 20.38). Click the Font tab, set the Bold attribute on, and change the font size to 11 points. Click OK to close the dialog and apply your modification to the legend.

Fig. 20.38
Removing the
border from
the legend.

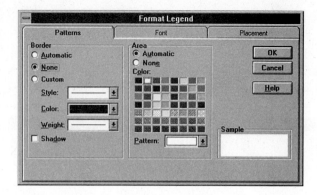

8. To use your enhanced legend as a subtitle for the chart, click and drag the legend to a location under the chart title. Click the Form View button of the toolbar to display your chart in run mode. Access executes the query, and then MSGraph5 draws the revised graph, as shown in figure 20.39. Click the record selection buttons to display a graph of the sales for each of the eight categories.

Fig. 20.39
The Form View
of the graph with
added design
features.

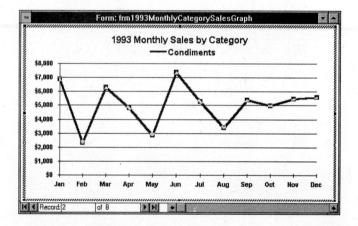

9. You can smooth the data series line by activating the graph and double-clicking the line. Mark the Smoothed Line check box in the Line frame, and then click OK. Your graph now appears as shown in figure 20.40.

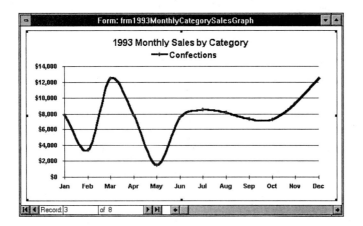

Fig. 20.40
Smoothing
applied to the data
series line using
best-fit curves.

10. MSGraph5 offers a variety of three-dimensional chart formats. Figure 20.41 illustrates a 3-D column chart. You can change the perspective of the graph by activating the chart and clicking either of the two axes to select labels. Click one of the selection squares of the axes, and drag the square to change the perspective.

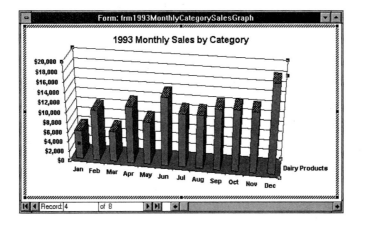

Fig. 20.41
The line graph
converted to a 3-D
column chart.

11. Choose Save **A**s from the **F**ile menu, and save your bound form with a new name.

From Here...

This chapter introduced you to using bound and unbound object frames to contain bit-mapped and vector-based images. The graphs and charts you created with MSGraph5 are dynamic vector images. Once you comprehend the operating principles of MSGraph5, you can create a variety of attractive charts and graphs based on information derived from your database application.

The following chapters expand on the subjects covered in this chapter:

- Chapter 13, "Designing Custom Multitable Forms," describes the process of linking form (master) and control (child) objects in greater detail.

- Chapter 19, "Using OLE 2.0," provides you a general overview of in-place activation of OLE 2.0 servers.

- Chapters 21 and 22, "Using Access with Microsoft Excel" and "Using Access with Microsoft Word and Mail Merge," describe how your Access 2.0 applications can interact with these two popular members of the Microsoft Office 4.0 suite.

- Chapter 29, "Exchanging Data with OLE Automation and DDE," describes the basic principles of using Access Basic to manipulate objects exposed by OLE Automation servers, such as MSGraph5.

Chapter 21

Using Access with Microsoft Excel

Spreadsheet and word processing applications dominate the Windows productivity application software market. According to industry reports, more than 70 percent of all Windows installations in the business environment include a spreadsheet application. Microsoft Office 4.0, which includes Excel 5.0 and Word 6.0, is now reported to represent more than 50 percent of Microsoft's sales of Windows productivity applications. Spreadsheets include the capability to emulate some of the features of database managers, such as sorting ranges of cells defined as a worksheet "database."

One of the principal uses of Access 2.0 is the conversion of worksheet data to tables in a relational database structure. Some of the primary justifications for converting from the familiar worksheet model to an Access 2.0 database include the following:

- ■ Access queries provide much greater flexibility in selecting and sorting data than is offered by the limited sort and selection criteria of spreadsheet applications.

- ■ You can create Access forms to simulate common business forms, which is difficult or impossible to do with present-day Windows spreadsheet applications. Excel 5.0 dialog sheets, for example, offer the choice of only a few simple control objects. Data-entry validation is much easier in Access than in worksheets.

- ■ Access offers many more options for printing formatted reports from your data than are available with worksheets.

- ■ Access macros are easier to implement than macros written in the application languages of spreadsheet programs.

In this chapter, you learn to

- ■ Import data from an Excel worksheet to a table

- ■ Restructure the data using temporary tables

- ■ Return the restructured data to an Excel worksheet

- ■ Use Excel as an OLE 2.0 server

- ■ Use Access's DDE() and DDESend() function with Excel

■ Access Basic enables you to write programs in a full-featured language and does not restrict you to using a set of predetermined worksheet functions.

■ Properly designed Access relational databases minimize the duplication of information and reduce disk file storage requirements for large aggregations of data.

In many situations, however, changing a worksheet to a database is impractical. You may need to be able to view, import, or edit data contained in a worksheet within an Access application. In this case, linking the spreadsheet as an OLE object is the best method. You can attach worksheet files in Excel 4.x formats to Access 2.0 tables with the Excel ODBC driver that is supplied with the Microsoft ODBC Desktop Database Driver kit. The limited utility of attached worksheet files is demonstrated in the first section of this chapter by the conversion process necessary to restructure the data. The second section of this chapter, "Using Excel as an OLE Server," describes how to link or embed worksheet data as OLE objects in bound or unbound object frames.

► "Using Access Basic for DDE," p. 1086

This chapter also includes a brief example of the use of Access's DDE() function to paste the values of individual cells of a Microsoft Excel worksheet into unbound text boxes on an Access form. This technique is useful when you want to obtain the value of a specified data cell or range of cells to display or update values in Access tables. You can use the DDE() function with any Windows spreadsheet application that has DDE server capability. To fully exploit the DDE capabilities of Access, you need to write Access Basic functions that you execute with macros.

> **Note**
>
> Microsoft Excel is used in the following examples, but you can use any Windows spreadsheet application that has OLE server capability. The first series of examples—which shows you how to reorganize spreadsheet data into Access tables—doesn't require a spreadsheet application; you only need a suitable file in Excel .XLS or Lotus .WKS, .WK1, or .WK3 format to import.

Importing and Reorganizing Worksheet Data

Worksheets created by Excel and other spreadsheet applications often contain data suitable for processing with relational database techniques. The worksheet usually is organized for viewing the data quickly; however, this organization seldom is appropriate for manipulation of the data by a RDBMS.

STK_21_1 (described in the next section) is an example of a worksheet formatted for viewing data. Four rows of 22 columns each contain the equivalent of a database record—all available data for a single stock. This type of structure, where a group of individual rows constitute a database record, is common in worksheet design. This structure differs from the design of a true worksheet database in which all the data for a single entity (in this case a stock) is contained in a single row. The examples that follow in this section illustrate how to import a spreadsheet of this type and convert the data it contains to related Access tables. Make-table and update queries assist in the reorganization of the data into relational form.

Obtaining and Converting the Example Worksheet

The file used to create many of the examples in this chapter contains the high and low prices and the trading volume of more than 300 individual stocks for a 21-day period beginning on April 10, 1992. This file was created as a Lotus 1-2-3 worksheet file (STK_21.WK1) by Ideas Unlimited and is available for downloading as STOCK.ZIP (146K in size) from the Excel for the PC Library 3 of the Microsoft Excel forum on CompuServe (GO MSEXCEL).

If you download the worksheet file to use in the following examples, you can import it directly into Access as a Lotus 1-2-3 .WK1 file. The following example uses Excel 5.0. If you have an earlier version of Excel or are using Lotus 1-2-3, the process is similar. Convert the file to worksheets of three different sizes by using the following steps:

1. Expand the file to STK_21.WK1 with PKUNZIP.EXE. (Type **PKUNZIP STOCK** at the DOS prompt.) If you don't have PKUNZIP.EXE, download PK204G.EXE from the IBM New User Library 2, Library Tools (GO IBMNEW).

   After downloading PK204G.EXE, execute the file (type **PK204G** at the DOS prompt) to obtain PKUNZIP.EXE and several other accompanying files, including user documentation.

2. Launch Excel, choose **Open** from the File menu, and open STK_21.WK1 as a Lotus 1-2-3 file (.WK*) in any version of Excel. The worksheet appears in Excel 5.0 as shown in figure 21.1 when you click the Maximize button.

V

Integrating Access

Fig. 21.1

The STK_21.WK1
worksheet opened
in Excel 5.0.

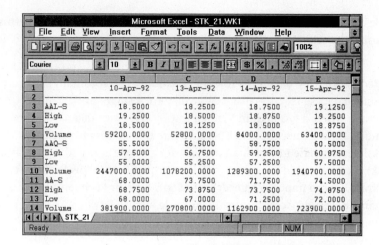

3. Choose Save As from the File menu, and select Microsoft Excel Workbook in the List Files of Type drop-down combo list to save the file as
   an Excel 5.0 workbook, STK_21.XLS, in your \ACCESS directory.

4. Make A1 the selected cell of the STK_21 worksheet, and press
   Shift+Ctrl+End to select the entire worksheet. Choose Copy from the
   Edit menu, or press Ctrl+C to copy its content to the Clipboard.

5. Choose Worksheet from the Insert menu to open a new worksheet,
   Sheet 1. With A1 as the selected cell, choose Paste from the Edit menu,
   or press Ctrl+V to copy the Clipboard contents to the new worksheet.
   Click OK when Excel asks whether you want to continue without Undo.

6. Select the STK_21 worksheet, and choose Delete Sheet from the Edit
   menu. Click OK when the message box asks you to confirm the deletion.

7. Double-click the Sheet1 tab to display the Rename Sheet dialog and
   name the worksheet **STK_21_1**.

8. Press Shift+Ctrl+End to select the entire worksheet, if it is not fully selected, and choose Cells from the Format menu to open the Format
   Cells dialog. Enter **#,###.000** as the format expression in the code text
   box, and click OK. (Three decimal digits are adequate to display fractional prices.) Click OK if you receive a message that Excel cannot undo
   your changes.

9. With the entire worksheet selected, choose Column from the Format
   menu, and then choose AutoFit Selection from the submenu. Click OK
   if asked to confirm the change.

10. The first row of the worksheet is used to provide field names for the table. Enter **Day** in cell A1, and replace the dates (now in Excel numeric format) in the first row of the worksheet with the numbers **1** through **21**. Follow the procedure of step 8, and select row 1 by clicking the row number button and format this row with no decimal digits (format **0**).

11. Select row 2, and choose Delete from the Edit menu to remove the row of hyphens. The worksheet appears as shown in figure 21.2.

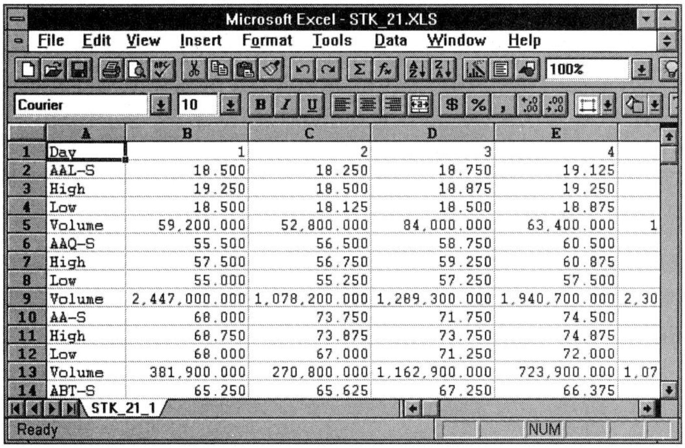

Fig. 21.2

The modified STK_21_1 worksheet in Excel 5.0.

Now you need to make some smaller versions of the worksheet to use in the examples that follow. To create STK_21_2 (201 rows and 50 stocks) and STK_21_3 (17 rows and 4 stocks) worksheets, follow these steps:

1. Use the mouse, or the Shift key with the arrow keys to select the first 201 rows of STK_21. Choose Copy from the Edit menu, or press Ctrl+C to copy the selection to the Clipboard.

2. Insert a new worksheet. Choose Paste from the Edit menu, or press Ctrl+V to paste the 201 rows to the new worksheet. Rename the worksheet **STK_21_2**.

3. With the entire worksheet selected, choose Column from the Format menu and then choose AutoFit Selection from the submenu.

4. Copy the first 17 rows of STK_21_2 to the Clipboard; then insert a new worksheet and paste the cells. Set AutoFit Selection for this worksheet, and rename the worksheet **STK_21_3**.

5. Exit Excel 5.0, and save your changes to the STK_21.XLS workbook file. Don't save the large Clipboard selection.

If you are using another spreadsheet application, the procedure is likely to be quite similar. The two smaller worksheets, STK_21_2 and STK_21_3, demonstrate the effect of worksheet size on Access's performance in sections related to OLE later in this chapter. (You don't need to create the smaller files if you don't have a spreadsheet application that can act as an OLE server.)

The organization of these worksheets is especially well suited to the first example in the next section, which shows you how to reorganize a worksheet to create a properly designed table. Alternatively, you can use for the examples any Excel or .WK* file you have that contains multiple series of numbers.

Importing the Example Worksheet

◀ "Creating a New Database," p. 129

◀ "Creating a Table by Importing an Excel Worksheet," p. 246

The first step in the importing process is to create a new database in which to import the worksheet data. Follow these steps:

1. Launch Access if it is not open, or select the Database window if Access is open. Choose New Database from the File menu. The New Database dialog appears.

2. In the New Database dialog, enter **STOCKS.MDB** as the name of your new database; then click OK.

3. Choose Import from the File menu. The Import dialog opens (see fig. 21.3).

Fig. 21.3

Access 2.0's Import Dialog.

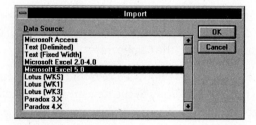

4. Select Microsoft Excel 5.0 from the Data Source list box; then click OK. (Support for importing Excel 5.0 files is new with Access 2.0.) The Select File dialog appears.

5. Select STK_21.XLS in the Select File dialog. Click the Import button to display the Import Spreadsheet Options dialog (see fig. 21.4).

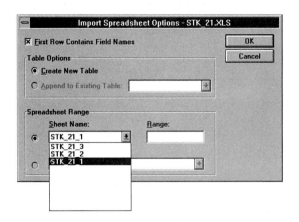

Fig. 21.4
Access 2.0's Import
Spreadsheet
Options dialog for
Excel 5.0 files.

6. Choose the First Row Contains Field Names option in the Import
   Spreadsheet Options dialog, and select STK_21_1 from the Sheet Name
   drop-down list. (Select one of the smaller sheets if you want to save disk
   space.) Click OK. Access imports your worksheet as a table and reports
   the number of records imported in the message box shown in figure 21.5.

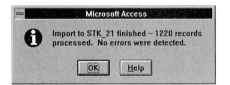

Fig. 21.5
The message box
that confirms the
importation
process.

7. Click OK, and then click the Close button of the Select File dialog.

8. Access assigns the imported worksheet's file name to the imported
   table. Select the STK_21 table, choose Rename from the File menu, and
   name the imported table STK_21_1.

9. Make sure the imported table is selected, and click the Open button to
   display the table in Datasheet View.

10. Select all 22 fields by clicking the Day column header button, holding
    down the mouse button, and dragging the mouse to the right. Choose
    Column Width from the Format menu to display the Column Width
    dialog (see fig. 21.6).

11. Set column width to **15**. Click OK, and then click anywhere in the table
    window to deselect the fields. Manually reduce the width of the Day
    column.

Fig. 21.6

Setting the column
widths of the
STK_21_1 table.

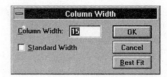

Access has interpreted the field type of the Excel 5.0 data as double-precision, which is not required for any of the values in the table. Single-precision numbers can accommodate all of the numeric values in the table. Using single-precision, rather than double-precision, values saves about 33 percent disk space.

To change the FieldSize property of the numeric fields of the STK_21_1 table, follow these steps:

1. Click the Design View button.

2. Select the first Currency field—the field named 1. Change the Field Size value from Double to Single.

3. Repeat step 2 for the remaining 20 numeric fields.

4. Click the Datasheet button to return to Datasheet View. Click Yes when asked whether you want to save your changes. Access converts the field sizes in the STK_21_1 table from Currency to Single at this point. Your table appears as shown in figure 21.7.

Fig. 21.7

The revised
version of the
STK_21_1 table.

Day	1	2	3	4	5	6
AAL-S	18.5	18.25	18.75	19.125	19	19
High	19.25	18.5	18.875	19.25	19.125	19.125
Low	18.5	18.125	18.5	18.875	18.875	18.875
Volume	59200	52800	84000	63400	16700	16700
AAQ-S	55.5	56.5	58.75	60.5	59	59
High	57.5	56.75	59.25	60.875	60.75	60.75
Low	55	55.25	57.25	57.5	58.5	58.5
Volume	2447000	1078200	1289300	1940700	2309700	2309700
AA-S	68	73.75	71.75	74.5	76.625	76.625
High	68.75	73.875	73.75	74.875	76.75	76.75
Low	68	67	71.25	72	74.375	74.375
Volume	381900	270800	1162900	723900	1079600	1079600
ABT-S	65.25	65.625	67.25	66.375	64.875	64.875
High	66.125	65.75	67.875	67.75	66	66
Low	64.625	64.875	65.625	65.625	64.375	64.375
Volume	1328400	561800	739900	898900	894700	894700

Record: 1   of 1220

Developing a Conversion Strategy

► "Normalizing
Data to the
Relational
Model," p. 852

The second step in the conversion process is to define the tables to be created. Very few worksheets can be converted to a single table that meets relational database standards. Designing the tables to contain the data and establishing the relationships of these tables to each other is the most important element of the conversion process. Following are the two objectives of your design strategy:

- *A design optimized for data display, entry, and editing.* This objective is primary if you plan to use Access for data entry. In the stock prices example, data entry and editing aren't a consideration because the data is supplied in worksheet format by Ideas Unlimited and other purveyors of stock price data.

- *A design that enables you to extract the imported data with the fewest steps.* If you obtain periodic updates to your stock price data in worksheet format, for example, ease of importing the data is the principal consideration.

The initial design usually is a compromise between these two objectives. The stock price example does not involve a compromise because data entry and editing are unnecessary.

When planning the initial design of the tables to contain the stock price and volume data, use this strategy:

- *The data for each element of the group—Close, High, Low, and Volume—is incorporated in an individual table.* A table with the 84 fields required to hold all the data for a stock is unwieldy at best. Reconstructing a worksheet from a table with such a design results in a cumbersome worksheet. One of the principles of relational database design is that you should be able to reconstruct your database with the data (see Chapter 19, "Using OLE 2.0").

- *The key field of each table, Symbol, is the ticker symbol of the stock.* (Ticker symbol is the abbreviation for the name of the stock assigned by the New York Stock Exchange.) This key field enables the tables to be linked in a one-to-one relationship based on the unique values of the ticker symbols. One-to-one relationships are uncommon in relational databases, but in this example, a one-to-one relationship is quite useful.

- *Queries organize the data in the tables as required for Access forms and reports.* Because each field in the query is prefaced by the table name, the names of the tables should be short to save keystrokes.

- *When multiple tables are combined in a query, the records in each table must be identified by type.* The second field, Type, is a single-letter abbreviation of the type of data: C(lose), H(igh), L(ow), and V(olume).

V

Integrating Access

■ The tables must be designed so that the data can be viewed in tabular or graphical form.

Now you need to develop the tactics to create the required tables in accordance with your strategy. The conversion plan involves these elements:

■ The records to be included in the individual tables are extracted from the STK_21_1 table by make-table queries with criteria based on the values in the Day field.

■ The Symbol field from the Close table must be added to the High, Low, and Volume tables.

■ In the query used to create the final table, adding the Symbol field to a table requires a unique key to link the Close table and the tables that don't have symbol values. A Counter field added to the Close, High, Low, and Volume tables can serve as a temporary key field.

■ Creating the new tables is a two-step process. First, the data is extracted to a temporary set of tables (Hi, Lo, and Vol). The second step combines these three tables with the Symbol field of another temporary table, Close, to create the final High, Low, and Volume tables. You need temporary tables in this case because make-table queries cannot alter tables on which they are based.

■ Because the Close table lacks a type identifier field, a Type field must be added to this table. The remaining tables have a type identifier word that can be replaced by the corresponding code letter.

Now that you have a conversion strategy and have decided the tactics to carry it out, you are ready to test merits of both, as described in the next section.

Extracting Data

◀ "Creating New Tables with Make-Table Queries," p. 409

Make-table queries are designed specifically for creating new tables from data in existing tables that meets a specified set of criteria. For STK_21_1, you use make-table queries to create one final table (Close) and three temporary tables (Hi, Low, and Vol). To create these four tables with make-table queries, follow these steps:

1. With the STK_21_1 table open, click the New Query button of the Database window to create a new query based on STK_21_1.

2. Click the New Query button of the New Query dialog to create Query1.

3. Click the Day field, and drag the field symbol to the first column of the query.

4. Click the asterisk (*, all fields), and drag the field symbol to the second column of the query.

5. Click the Show check box in the Day field. (Day is included in the fields in the second column of the query. You cannot include two fields of the same name in a make-table query.)

6. In the Criteria row of the Day field, enter **High** to include only records for the high price of the stock in the temporary Hi table. Your query appears as shown in figure 21.8.

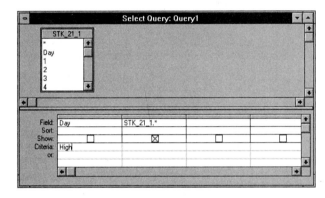

Fig. 21.8

Creating the temporary Hi table with a make-table query.

7. Click the Make-Table Query button of the toolbar, or choose Make Table from the **Query** menu to display the Query Properties dialog.

8. Enter **Hi** in the Table Name text box, and then click OK (see fig. 21.9). The default values for the remaining elements in the Query Properties dialog are satisfactory.

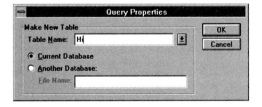

Fig. 21.9

Entering the temporary table name in the Query Properties dialog.

9. Click the Run Query button of the toolbar to create the temporary Hi table. Access displays a message box that indicates the number of records to be added to the new table (see fig. 21.10). Click OK.

Fig. 21.10

The message box that confirms the number of rows added to the new table.

10. Open the Database window, click the Table tab, and double-click the Hi entry in the list to view the table (see fig. 21.11).

Fig. 21.11

The temporary Hi table created by the make-table query.

Day	1	2	3	4	5	6	7	8
High	19.25	18.5	18.875	19.25	19.125	19.125	19	19.125
High	57.5	56.75	59.25	60.875	60.75	60.75	59	57.25
High	68.75	73.875	73.75	74.875	76.75	76.75	78.25	77.375
High	66.125	65.75	67.875	67.75	66	66	64.5	64
High	12.5	12.375	12.5	12.375	12.25	12.25	12.375	23.125
High	62.625	62.75	64.375	64.75	64.75	64.75	62.375	61.75
High	25.125	25.5	26	25.875	24.5	24.5	24.125	23.5
High	31.375	31.25	31.875	32	32.25	32.25	32.25	32.25
High	43.75	44.5	44.25	43.75	43.25	43.25	43.25	43.75
High	42	42	42.25	42.375	42.625	42.625	42.375	42.5
High	40.5	40.125	41.5	42.375	42.625	42.625	42.375	41.875
High	16.625	16.625	16.75	16.875	17	17	16.875	17
High	77.75	77.75	82	81.875	80	80	77.875	77.25

Record: 11 of 305

11. Change the Criteria value to **Low** and repeat steps 6 through 10, substituting **Lo** for the table name in steps 6 and 10.

12. Change the Criteria value to **Volume** and repeat steps 6 through 10, using **Vol** for the table name.

13. The closing prices are in the row with the ticker symbol. Each of the symbols has a hyphen followed by a character that identifies the type of security; –S represents a common stock. Change the Criteria value to **Like "*-*"** to select these rows and repeat steps 6 through 10, using **Close** for the table name. The expression *-* selects all records containing a hyphen. You don't need to create a temporary table in this case because the Close table includes the ticker symbols, as illustrated by figure 21.12.

Tip

Counter fields are the fastest way of adding a primary-key field to a table that does not contain unique values on which to base a primary key.

Modifying the Table Structure

Each table you created in the preceding section requires additional fields so that you can design an append query to create a properly-structured table. A Counter field is used as a temporary key field for each of the four tables. The Close table needs a Type field added, and the Day field of each temporary table needs the name changed to Type. Follow these steps to make the changes:

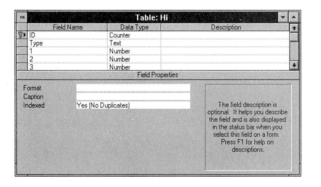

Fig. 21.12
The Close table with the ticker symbol of the stocks.

1. Click the Table button in the Database window, select the Hi table, and click the Design View button.

2. Change the name of the first field from Day to **Type** and set the FieldSize property to **1**, as shown in figure 21.13. This action truncates the Type field value, High, to the required single-letter code H.

Fig. 21.13
Modifications to the design of the temporary Hi table.

3. Click the field selector button of the Type field, and press Insert to add a field at the beginning of the table. Type **ID** in the Field Name column, and select Counter in the Data Type column. Click the Primary Key button of the toolbar to make the ID field the primary-key field.

4. Click the Datasheet View button on the toolbar. Save the changes to the table. A message box advises you that some data may be lost due to truncating the length of the Type field (see fig. 21.14). Click Yes to approve the change.

The table appears as shown in figure 21.15. The primary key that Access creates is a Counter field with the default name ID.

V

Integrating Access

Fig. 21.14
The warning that some data may be lost due to truncating the Type field.

Fig. 21.15
The temporary Hi table with the ID key field added.

ID	Type	1	2	3	4	5	6	7	8
1	H	19.25	18.5	18.875	19.25	19.125	19.125	19	19.125
2	H	57.5	56.75	59.25	60.875	60.75	60.75	59	57.25
3	H	68.75	73.875	73.75	74.875	76.75	76.75	78.25	77.375
4	H	66.125	65.75	67.875	67.75	66	66	64.5	64
5	H	12.5	12.375	12.5	12.375	12.25	12.25	12.375	23.125
6	H	62.625	62.75	64.375	64.75	64.75	64.75	62.375	61.75
7	H	25.125	25.5	26	25.875	24.5	24.5	24.125	23.5
8	H	31.375	31.25	31.875	32	32.25	32.25	32.25	32.25
9	H	43.75	44.5	44.25	43.75	43.25	43.25	43.25	43.75
10	H	42	42	42.25	42.375	42.625	42.625	42.375	42.5
11	H	40.5	40.125	41.5	42.375	42.625	42.625	42.375	41.875
12	H	16.625	16.625	16.75	16.875	17	17	16.875	17
13	H	77.75	77.75	82	81.875	80	80	77.875	77.25
14	H	86	85.625	87.75	87.5	87.5	87.5	86.375	86.375
15	H	58.875	59.375	59.5	59.625	60.75	60.75	61.125	61.5
16	H	54.125	54.375	55.75	55.5	57.125	57.125	56.5	57.125
17	H	18.125	18	17.75	17.875	18.25	18.25	18.25	18

Table: Hi — Record: 1 of 305

5. Repeat steps 1 through 4 for the Lo and Vol tables.

6. Open the Close table in design mode. Change the Day field name to **Symbol**, and change its FieldSize property to **10** to accommodate longer ticker symbols.

7. Click the Selection button for the Symbol field, and press Insert to add an ID counter field. Click the Primary Key button of the toolbar to create the primary-key index.

8. Select the first of the Number fields, and then press Insert to add a new field. Enter **Type** as the Field Name of the new field (added fields default to the Text data type) and set its FieldSize property to **1**. Figure 21.16 shows the design of the Close table.

9. Click the Datasheet View button of the toolbar, save your changes, and accept the truncated field. Figure 21.17 shows the resulting Close table.

The extraction of data from STK_21_1 to the required tables is a relatively simple process because the labels used to identify the data are consistent throughout the worksheet. You may need to write a worksheet macro that creates consistent labels for rows to be included in a specific table if the labels don't exist or aren't consistent in the original version of the worksheet.

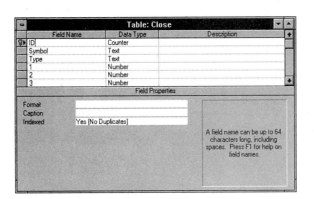

Fig. 21.16 Modifications made to the design of the Close table.

ID	Symbol	Type	1	2	3	4	5	6	7
1	AAL-S		18.5	18.25	18.75	19.125	19	19	18.75
2	AAQ-S		55.5	56.5	58.75	60.5	59	59	56.75
3	AA-S		68	73.75	71.75	74.5	76.625	76.625	77.75
4	ABT-S		65.25	65.625	67.25	66.375	64.875	64.875	63.25
5	ABY-S		12.375	12.375	12.5	12.125	12.25	12.25	12.375
6	ACY-S		61.875	62.375	64.375	64.5	62.625	62.625	60.25
7	ADM-S		25	25.375	25.625	24.375	23.875	23.875	23.375
8	AEP-S		31.25	31.125	31.625	32	32.25	32.25	32.25
9	AET-S		43.5	44	43.625	43.125	43.25	43.25	43.125
10	AGC-S		41.875	41.375	42.125	42.375	42.625	42.625	42.25
11	AHC-S		39.375	40	41.375	42.375	42.375	42.375	41.875
12	AHM-S		16.375	16.625	16.625	16.625	16.75	16.75	16.75
13	AHP-S		76.875	77.75	81.625	80	78.25	78.25	76.125
14	AIG-S		85.375	85.5	86.75	87.25	86.75	86.75	86
15	AIT-S		58.75	58.875	59.375	59.625	60.75	60.75	61.125
16	ALD-S		53.75	53.75	54.625	55.5	57	57	56.5
17	ALK-S		18.125	17.75	17.5	17.875	18.125	18.125	18

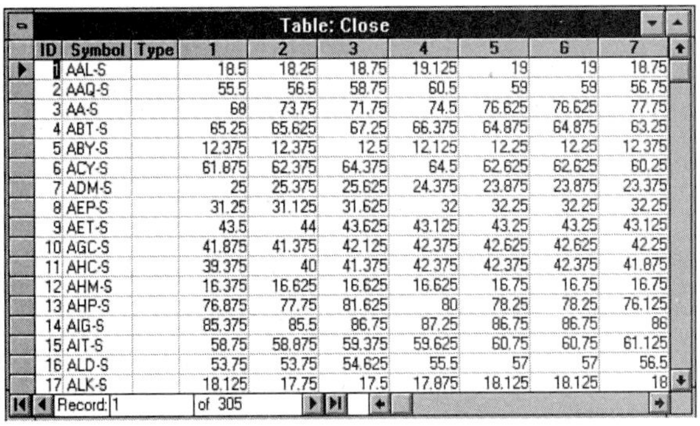

Fig. 21.17 The Close table with the ID and type fields added.

Adding the Type Value to the Close Table

When you need to replace data in a field containing values, the Replace command on the Edit menu is usually a faster process than creating an update query. Because the Replace What text box in the Replace in Field dialog doesn't accept a **Null** value, however, you cannot use the Replace command on the Edit menu to add the C code (for "Close") to the Type field of the Close table. Instead, you must use an update query to change the Type field value. Follow these steps:

◀ "Updating Values of Multiple Records in a Table," p. 422

1. Make the Close table active, and click the New Query button of the toolbar.

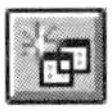

2. Click the New Query button of the New Query dialog to create a new query with the Close table added.

3. Click the Update Query button of the toolbar or choose Update from the Query menu.

4. Select the Type field and drag the field symbol to the first column of the query.

5. Type C in the Update To row. This action changes the Type field value in all records from the default **Null** to C. Figure 21.18 shows the update query design at this point.

Fig. 21.18
The update query used to add C to the Type field of each record in the Close table.

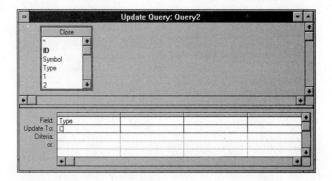

6. Click the Run Query button on the toolbar to update the Type field of the Close table. When the message box shown in figure 21.19 appears, click OK.

Fig. 21.19
The message box that indicates the number of records to be updated.

Tip
If you are creating an application that uses macros to automate the conversion process, save each query with a unique name so that the query can be run by a macro.

Creating the Final Tables

Now you need to combine the Symbol field of the Close table with the data in the Hi, Lo, and Vol tables to create the final High, Low, and Volume tables. In this example, you use the same query each time, changing the temporary table name to create the three final tables.

To create your final High, Low, and Volume tables with make-table queries, follow these steps:

1. With the Close table active, click the New Query button of the toolbar, then click the New Query button of the New Query dialog to create a new query based on the Close table.

2. Click the Make-Table Query button of the toolbar to open the Query Properties dialog. Enter **High** in the Table Name text box as the name of the final table to create, and click OK.

3. Select the Symbol field of the Close table, and drag it to the first column of the make-table query.

4. Click the Add Table button of the toolbar or choose Add Table from the Query menu. Select Hi from the Table/Query list and click OK. Then choose the Close button. Access creates the relationship between the ID fields of the Close and Hi tables for you.

> **Caution**
>
> *This is a very important step.* If Access fails to establish this relationship and you don't add the relationship, you create a *Cartesian product* instead of the result you want. The *Cartesian product* is all possible combinations of all the field values contained in the two tables. In this case, the Cartesian product contains about 95,000 (305 * 305) rows.

5. Click the asterisk (*, all fields) of the Hi table, and drag the field symbol to the second column of the query. The make-table query appears as shown in figure 21.20.

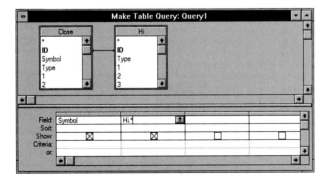

Fig. 21.20
The make-table query that creates the final High table.

6. Click the Run Query button of the toolbar to create the final High table. Click OK from the message box that appears.

7. Select the Hi table field list, and press Delete to remove the field list from the query. Repeat steps 4 through 6 for the Lo table, substituting **Low** as the name for the new final table.

8. Repeat step 7 for the Vol table, entering **Volume** as the name of the final table.

9. Close the query, and don't save the changes.

You must remove the temporary key field, ID, from the Close table so that you can make Symbol the key field. Follow these steps:

1. Open the Database window, click the Table tab, and select the Close table. Click the Design button.

2. Click the field select button of the ID field; then press Delete. When Access displays message boxes asking you to confirm deletion of the field and deletion of the key field, click OK.

3. Select the Symbol field; then click the Primary Key button of the toolbar to make the Symbol field the primary-key field. Figure 21.21 shows the Design View of the Close table.

Fig. 21.21
The Close table, with Symbol as the primary-key field.

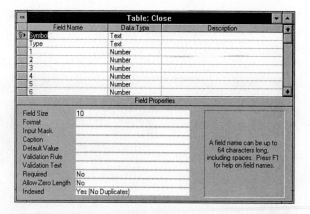

4. Click the Datasheet View button on the toolbar to display the contents of the table. Click OK when asked to confirm your changes.

5. Select all columns of the table by dragging the mouse pointer over the column's field name buttons.

6. Choose **C**olumn Width from the **F**ormat menu; the Column Width dialog appears. Enter **9** in the Column Width text box (see fig. 21.22); then click OK.

Figure 21.23 shows the resulting Close table.

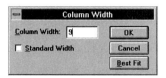

Fig. 21.22
Setting the column widths of the Close table.

Symbol	Type	1	2	3	4	5	6	7	8
AA-S	C	68	73.75	71.75	74.5	76.625	76.625	77.75	76.25
AAL-S	C	18.5	18.25	18.75	19.125	19	19	18.75	19.125
AAQ-S	C	55.5	56.5	58.75	60.5	59	59	56.75	56.25
ABT-S	C	65.25	65.625	67.25	66.375	64.875	64.875	63.25	62.875
ABY-S	C	12.375	12.375	12.5	12.125	12.25	12.25	12.375	23.125
ACY-S	C	61.875	62.375	64.375	64.5	62.625	62.625	60.25	61.5
ADM-S	C	25	25.375	25.625	24.375	23.875	23.875	23.375	23.375
AEP-S	C	31.25	31.125	31.625	32	32.25	32.25	32.25	32.25
AET-S	C	43.5	44	43.625	43.125	43.25	43.25	43.125	43.75
AGC-S	C	41.875	41.375	42.125	42.375	42.625	42.625	42.25	42.5
AHC-S	C	39.375	40	41.375	42.375	42.375	42.375	41.875	41.5
AHM-S	C	16.375	16.625	16.625	16.625	16.75	16.75	16.75	16.875
AHP-S	C	76.875	77.75	81.625	80	78.25	78.25	76.125	77.125
AIG-S	C	85.375	85.5	86.75	87.25	86.75	86.75	86	85.25
AIT-S	C	58.75	58.875	59.375	53.625	60.75	60.75	61.125	61.125
AL-S	C	19.625	20.625	20.125	20.25	20.875	20.875	21.125	20.875
ALD-S	C	53.75	53.75	54.625	55.5	57	57	56.5	56.75
ALK-S	C	18.125	17.75	17.5	17.875	18.125	18.125	18	17.875

Record: 1 of 305

Fig. 21.23
The final version of the Close table.

7. Choose **S**ave Table from the **F**ile menu to save the column width change.

At this point, you can delete the Hi, Lo, and Vol tables. Deleting temporary tables conserves disk space, but only after you compact the database.

Verifying the Tables by Re-Creating the Worksheet

An important step when creating tables from external data sources is to verify that the tables contain the correct information. In most cases, the best method of testing is to use the tables to re-create the data in its original format—or as close to the original format as possible. This strategy enables you to make a direct comparison of the source data and the data contained in the tables.

◄ "Copying and Pasting Tables," p. 180

To create a replica of the original STK_21_1 worksheet, follow these steps:

1. Make the Database window active, click the Table tab, and select the Close table.

2. Press Ctrl+C to copy the table to the Clipboard; then press Ctrl+V to create a copy of the table. The Paste Table As dialog appears.

3. Type **tblStockPrices** as the name of the new table in the Paste Table As dialog (see fig. 21.24). Make sure that the default Structure and Data options button is selected, and then click OK. Access creates a new tblStockPrices table.

Fig. 21.24
Entering the table name in the Paste Table As dialog.

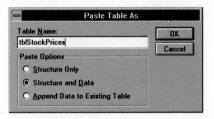

4. Select the tblStockPrices table in the Tables list of the Database window, and then click the Design View button of the toolbar.

5. Click the Indexes button of the toolbar to display the Indexes dialog.

6. Select both the Symbol and Type fields by holding down the Shift key and clicking the two field selection buttons. Then click the Primary Key button of the toolbar.

7. Select the Symbol field and click the Indexed text box in the Field Properties section of the Design window. Choose Yes (Duplicates OK) from the Indexed drop-down list. If you choose No (No Duplicates), you cannot append records. Indexing the Symbol field can speed up queries based on a specific symbol or set of symbols. Figure 21.25 shows the design for the Stock Data table.

Fig. 21.25
Modifying the key field and indexing properties of the tblStockPrices table.

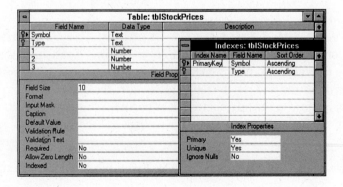

8. Click the Datasheet View button of the toolbar, and click OK when asked whether you want to save your changes. Review the data in the table, and then close the tblStockPrices window.

To add the data in the High, Low, and Volume tables to the Stock Data table, follow these steps:

1. Select the High table in the Database window; then click the New Query button of the toolbar to display the New Query dialog.

2. Click the New Query button to open a new query based on the High table.

3. Click the Append Query button of the toolbar to display the Query Properties dialog. Open the Table Names drop-down list and choose tblStockPrices (see fig. 21.26). The tblStockPrices table is the table to which you want to append the records. Click OK.

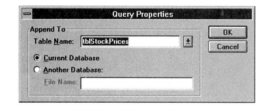

Fig. 21.26
The Query Properties dialog for an append query.

4. Select the asterisk field of the High table field list and drag the field list symbol to the first column of the query. Figure 21.27 shows the append query design.

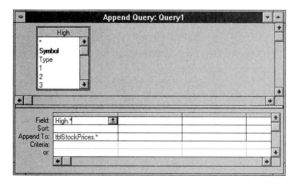

Fig. 21.27
The append query design to add records to tblStockPrices from the High table.

V

Integrating Access

5. Click the Run Query button on the toolbar to append the High records to Stock Data. The message box shown in figure 21.28 indicates the number of records to be appended. Click OK.

Fig. 21.28
The message box
confirming the
append operation.

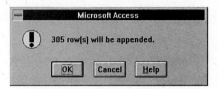

6. Delete the High table's field list from the query, and then click the Add Table button of the toolbar and repeat steps 4 and 5 to append the Low and Volume table data to tblStockPrices.

7. After you have appended the data from the High, Low, and Volume tables to tblStockPrices, open the tblStockPrices table from the Database window. The table appears as shown in figure 21.29. The data for Close, High, Low, and trading Volume appears in the same sequence as in the worksheet because the table is indexed on the combination of the Symbol and the Type fields. Access creates a no-duplicates index on the key field(s).

If you did not close the Stock Data table in step 7 of the preceding series of steps, the High, Low, and Volume data does not appear. You need to close and then reopen the table for the added records to appear in the correct order. Choosing **Refresh** from the **Records** menu is not a substitute for closing and reopening the table.

Fig. 21.29
The final version
of the
tblStockPrices
table with all
records appended.

Symbol	Type	1	2	3	4	5	6	7	8	9
AA-S	C	68	73.75	71.75	74.5	76.625	76.625	77.75	76.25	75
AA-S	H	68.75	73.875	73.75	74.875	76.75	76.75	78.25	77.375	76.375
AA-S	L	68	67	71.25	72	74.375	74.375	75.625	75.5	75
AA-S	V	381900	270800	1162900	723900	1079600	1079600	531000	297500	219000
AAL-S	C	18.5	18.25	18.75	19.125	19	19	18.75	19.125	19
AAL-S	H	19.25	18.5	18.875	19.25	19.125	19.125	19	19.125	19.125
AAL-S	L	18.5	18.125	18.5	18.875	18.875	18.875	18.625	18.75	19
AAL-S	V	59200	52800	84000	63400	16700	16700	21200	73400	44100
AAQ-S	C	55.5	56.5	58.75	60.5	59	59	56.75	56.25	57.625
AAQ-S	H	57.5	56.75	59.25	60.875	60.75	60.75	59	57.25	58
AAQ-S	L	55	55.25	57.25	57.5	58.5	58.5	56	56	56.25
AAQ-S	V	2447000	1078200	1289300	1940700	2309700	2309700	1839700	1610400	1531500
ABT-S	C	65.25	65.625	67.25	66.375	64.875	64.875	63.25	62.875	63.375
ABT-S	H	66.125	65.75	67.875	67.75	66	66	64.5	64	63.375
ABT-S	L	64.625	64.875	65.625	65.625	64.375	64.375	63	62	62.5
ABT-S	V	1328400	561800	739900	898900	894700	894700	738300	907600	525300
ABY-S	C	12.375	12.375	12.5	12.125	12.25	12.25	12.375	23.125	12.125
ABY-S	H	12.5	12.375	12.5	12.375	12.25	12.25	12.375	23.125	12.125

Table: tblStockPrices — Record: 1 of 1220

8. Click the Document Control-menu box in the tblStockPrices Data window, and choose **Restore** from the Document Control menu. Open the

STK_21_1 table; then click the exposed surface of the tblStockPrices window to compare it with the original version (see fig. 21.30).

Indexing tblStockPrices has changed the order of some of the entries. Confirm that the data for a few stocks in both tables are the same.

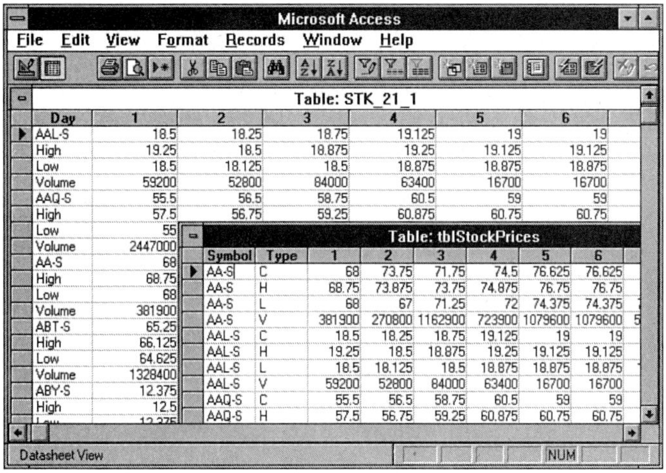

Fig. 21.30
Comparing the tblStockPrices table with the original version.

You can add stock price data for later dates by consecutively numbering the fields in successive Excel tables. As an example, the next 21 days of prices and trading volumes would use field names 22 through 42 for the numeric values. You could name the tables you create Close2, High2, Low2, and Volume2, and then add these tables to your queries to extend the range of dates to be included. Alternatively, you could create tables that have the high, low, close, and volume data for a given stock on a specific date. Making this type of transformation, however, requires that you write Access Basic code to restructure the tables.

Note

The structure of the tblStockPrices table does not conform to the rules of relational databases, although its structure is an improvement over the original Excel worksheet. Using individual fields for dates constitutes "repeating groups," a violation of first normal form for relational tables. A fully normalized table would consist of a single record for the high, low, close, and volume data for a single stock on a single date. The composite primary key of such a table would be the stock ticker symbol and the date. Creating a fully-normalized table from STK_21.XLS requires the use of a complex DDE operation or the use of OLE Automation. Both of these operations require a substantial amount of Access Basic code.

Using the Tables You Created

◄ "Establishing
Relationships
between
Tables," p. 164

◄ "Enforcing
Referential
Integrity,"
p. 169

In this section, queries combine the data in the tables to create forms and reports that display the data in tabular or graph form. The relationships between the tables should be established automatically for the queries you create. In addition, you need to maintain referential integrity; that is, you shouldn't be able to delete a closing price for a stock for which you have high, low, and volume data. This obligation requires that you include relationships as properties of the tables.

To establish the relationships between the tables, follow these steps:

1. Make the Database window active, and then click the Relationships button of the toolbar or choose **R**elationships from the Edit menu. The empty Relationships window opens with the Add Table dialog active.

2. Select the High table in the Table/Query list box, and click the Add button.

3. Repeat step 2 for the Low, Close, and Volume tables, and then click the Close button. Your Relationships window appears as shown in figure 21.31.

Fig. 21.31
The Relationships window with the four tables added.

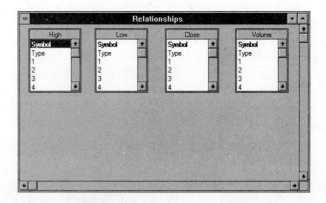

4. Drag the Symbol field from the High table field list to the Symbol field of the Low table field list to create a join, and open the Relationships dialog.

5. Mark the Enforce Referential Integrity check box, and then click the One option button in the One To frame. The relationship between each table is one-to-one.

6. Mark the Cascade Update Related Fields check box. This lets you change the Symbol value for a stock if its NYSE ticker symbol should change, an unlikely (but conceivable) event. If you change one Symbol value, the Symbol values for all of the related tables change in unison.

7. Mark the Cascade Delete Related Records check box. This lets you remove all of the records for a stock that is delisted from the NYSE, a more likely event. Your Relationships dialog appears as shown in figure 21.32.

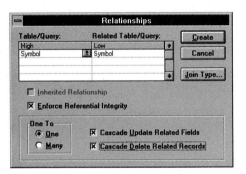

Fig. 21.32
Setting referential integrity enforcement rules in the Relationships dialog.

8. Click the Create button to create the join.

9. Repeat steps 4 through 8 for the join between the Low and Close tables and the join between the Close and Volume tables. The Relationships window appears as shown in figure 21.33.

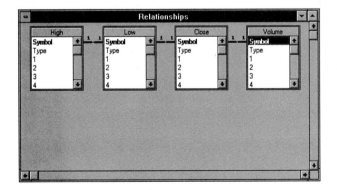

Fig. 21.33
The Relationships window with one-to-one relationships between each table.

10. Double-click the Document Control-menu box to close the Relationships window and save your changes.

> **Note**
>
> Always establish default relationships between the tables of your database so that these relationships are added automatically to the queries you create. If you don't establish default relationships and then Access doesn't create or you forget to add relationships to your query, you may obtain the Cartesian product (described earlier in this section) instead of the result you want. The Cartesian product of large tables can be large and take several minutes to create. Pressing Esc or Ctrl+Break may not halt the process, and Windows may exhaust its resources in creating the Cartesian product, creating an out-of-memory error.

To create a test query that includes all the data in your tables, follow these steps:

1. Select the High table in the Database window, and then click the New Query button of the toolbar to display the New Query dialog.

2. Click the New Query button to create a query with the High table added.

3. Click the Add Table button of the toolbar to add the Low, Close, and Volume tables. The joins between the tables are established automatically (by the relationships you established in the preceding series of steps) as you add each table, as shown by the lines connecting the Symbols fields in figure 21.34. Click the Close button.

Fig. 21.34
Part of the query design for the 21-day stock prices query.

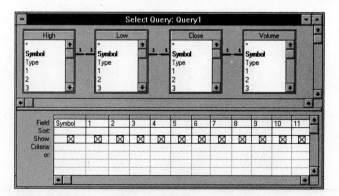

4. Double-click the header of the High table's field list to select all of the fields, and drag the multiple field column to the first column of the query.

5. Select and delete the Type column. Then use the horizontal scroll bar slider to display the first empty column after the 22 columns devoted to the High field.

6. Repeat steps 4 and 5 for the Low, Close, and Volume tables, but also delete the Symbol field for these three tables.

7. Click the Run Query button of the toolbar to display the query. You can drag the columns of the query to reorder the columns in a logical sequence, as shown in figure 21.35.

8. Click the SQL button of the toolbar to display the SQL statement for the query (see fig. 21.36).

Symbol	High.1	Low.1	Close.1	Volume.1	High.2	Low.2	Close.2
AAI-S	19.25	18.5	18.5	59200	18.5	18.125	18.25
AAQ-S	57.5	55	55.5	2447000	56.75	55.25	56.5
AA-S	68.75	68	68	381900	73.875	67	73.75
ABT-S	66.125	64.625	65.25	1328400	65.75	64.875	65.625
ABY-S	12.5	12.375	12.375	2900	12.375	12.375	12.375
ACY-S	62.625	61.5	61.875	199400	62.75	61.75	62.375
ADM-S	25.125	24.5	25	1819500	25.5	24.875	25.375
AEP-S	31.375	31	31.25	214300	31.25	31	31.125
AET-S	43.75	42.5	43.5	160700	44.5	43.75	44
AGC-S	42	41.75	41.875	66400	42	41.25	41.375
AHC-S	40.5	39.25	39.375	213300	40.125	39.25	40
AHM-S	16.625	16.125	16.375	266000	16.625	16.25	16.625
AHP-S	77.75	76.75	76.875	561800	77.75	77	77.75
AIG-S	86	84.75	85.375	226200	85.625	84.875	85.5
AIT-S	58.875	58.625	58.75	336700	59.375	58.5	58.875
ALD-S	54.125	53	53.75	368100	54.375	53	53.75
ALK-S	18.125	17.5	18.125	37400	18	17.625	17.75
AL-S	19.625	19.5	19.625	184200	20.625	19.5	20.625

Record: 1   of 305

Fig. 21.35
The query result set with the columns reordered.

```
SELECT DISTINCTROW High.Symbol, High.[1], High.[2], High.[3], High.[4], High.[5],
High.[6], High.[7], High.[8], High.[9], High.[10], High.[11], High.[12], High.[13],
High.[14], High.[15], High.[16], High.[17], High.[18], High.[19], High.[20], High.[21],
Low.[1], Low.[2], Low.[3], Low.[4], Low.[5], Low.[6], Low.[7], Low.[8], Low.[9], Low.[10],
Low.[11], Low.[12], Low.[13], Low.[14], Low.[15], Low.[16], Low.[17], Low.[18],
Low.[19], Low.[20], Low.[21], Close.[1], Close.[2], Close.[3], Close.[4], Close.[5],
Close.[6], Close.[7], Close.[8], Close.[9], Close.[10], Close.[11], Close.[12], Close.[13],
Close.[14], Close.[15], Close.[16], Close.[17], Close.[18], Close.[19], Close.[20],
Close.[21], Volume.[1], Volume.[2], Volume.[3], Volume.[4], Volume.[5], Volume.[6],
Volume.[7], Volume.[8], Volume.[9], Volume.[10], Volume.[11], Volume.[12],
Volume.[13], Volume.[14], Volume.[15], Volume.[16], Volume.[17], Volume.[18],
Volume.[19], Volume.[20], Volume.[21]
FROM [[High INNER JOIN Low ON High.Symbol = Low.Symbol] INNER JOIN Close
ON Low.Symbol = Close.Symbol] INNER JOIN Volume ON Close.Symbol =
Volume.Symbol;
```

Fig. 21.36
The SQL statement for the query of figures 21.34 and 21.35.

Note

The square brackets surrounding the numbered field names in the SQL statement shown in figure 21.36 are required to prevent the numbers from being interpreted by Jet as numeric values. Enclosing the field names in square brackets assures that the field names are treated as literals.

Access
2.0

V

Integrating Access

You can use queries of the preceding type to display or edit any data in the four tables by using a form or to print part or all of the stock data with an Access report. You might design other queries that display only stocks that meet a specific criterion, such as minimum trading volume or a range of stock closing prices. The ability to rearrange data in almost any desired row and column sequence quickly, using simple queries, demonstrates that Access query datasheets are at least as flexible as worksheets.

Exporting Stock Data as a Worksheet

When you are collecting data on the same set of common stocks, you can simplify the conversion process by modifying the design of the Excel worksheet to correspond to the design of the tables. You can avoid making a large number of changes to the worksheet in Excel by exporting the Access tblStockPrices table back to Excel in Excel 5.0 format.

To export the Stock Data table to an .XLS workbook file, follow these steps:

1. Activate the Database window, and choose Export from the File menu to display the Export dialog.

2. Select Microsoft Excel 5.0 in the Data Destination list of the Export dialog, and then click OK. The Select Microsoft Access Object dialog appears.

3. Select tblStockPrices in the Objects in STOCKS list, and click OK. The Export to File dialog appears. The first eight characters of the table name, with an .XLS extension, is the default file name.

4. Type **STK_DATA.XLS** in the File Name text box of the Export to File dialog; then click OK. Access exports the data in Excel 5.0's .XLS workbook format.

5. Launch Excel 5.0, and open the STK_DATA.XLS file. The rows in the tblStockPrices worksheet display in the order in which they were added to the Stock Data table (see fig. 21.37). Access doesn't export data from a table in the order in which the table is indexed. (The primary-key's index is based on the Symbol and Type fields.)

6. With cell A1 selected, choose Sort from Excel's Data menu to open the Sort dialog. Excel detects that the first row is a header and automatically selects Header Row in the My List Has option group. Select Symbol in the Sort By drop-down list and Type in the Then By list (see fig. 21.38).

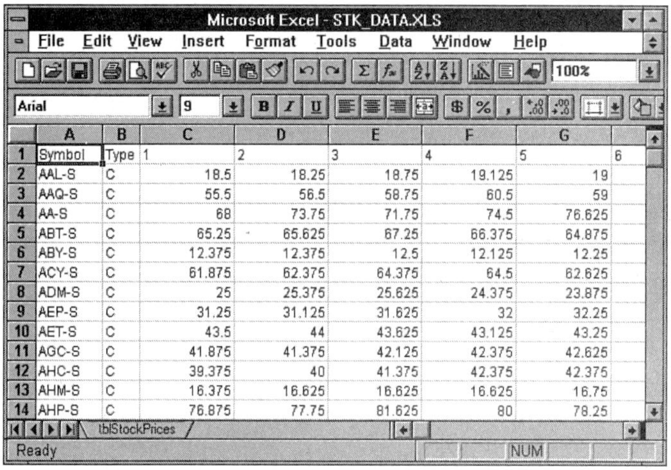

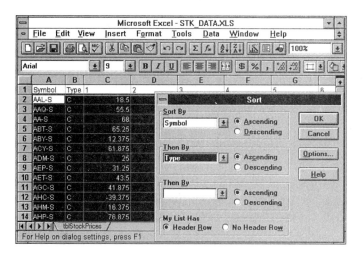

Fig. 21.37
The unsorted
version of
tblStockPrices in
Excel 5.0.

Fig. 21.38
Specifying the
columns on which
to sort the stock
price data.

7. Click OK; the sorted worksheet appears as shown in figure 21.39.

8. Choose **S**ave from the **F**ile menu to save the sorted worksheet and close
Excel.

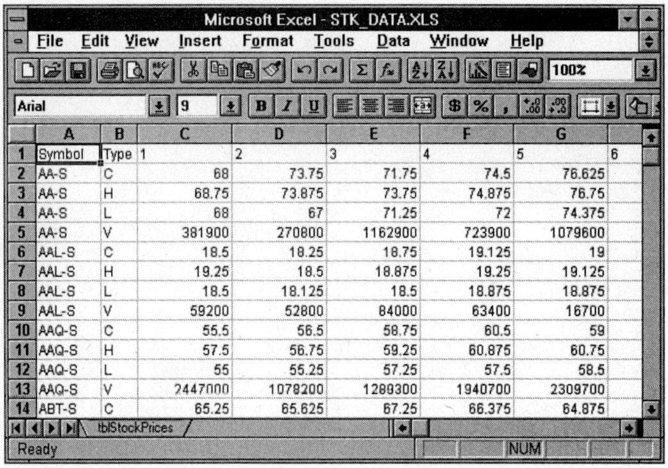

Fig. 21.39
The stock price data sorted in the order of the table's primary-key fields.

	A	B	C	D	E	F	G	
1	Symbol	Type	1	2	3	4	5	6
2	AA-S	C	68	73.75	71.75	74.5	76.625	
3	AA-S	H	68.75	73.875	73.75	74.875	76.75	
4	AA-S	L	68	67	71.25	72	74.375	
5	AA-S	V	381900	270800	1162900	723900	1079600	
6	AAL-S	C	18.5	18.25	18.75	19.125	19	
7	AAL-S	H	19.25	18.5	18.875	19.25	19.125	
8	AAL-S	L	18.5	18.125	18.5	18.875	18.875	
9	AAL-S	V	59200	52800	84000	63400	16700	
10	AAQ-S	C	55.5	56.5	58.75	60.5	59	
11	AAQ-S	H	57.5	56.75	59.25	60.875	60.75	
12	AAQ-S	L	55	55.25	57.25	57.5	58.5	
13	AAQ-S	V	2447000	1079200	1289300	1940700	2309700	
14	ABT-S	C	65.25	65.625	67.25	66.375	64.875	

tblStockPrices

Ready   NUM

Note

You can export the worksheet data in the order in which it is indexed by creating a make-table query that includes the Symbol and Type fields (with the Show check box not marked) and the asterisk field. Sort the Symbol and Type fields in ascending order. Run the query and export the sorted table you create to Excel.

You can use the new worksheet as a template for entry or import of stock price and trading volume data for other ranges of dates. Using the new format eliminates the necessity of creating temporary tables during the conversion process.

Using Excel as an OLE Server

This section describes methods of creating links between data cells in OLE Object fields and worksheets created with Excel 5.0. You can duplicate some examples with Excel 3.0 and 4.0, but version 5.0, with its OLE 2.0 compatibility, has several added features that simplify the process. The step-by-step examples in this section are based on the assumption that you are familiar with the use of Excel 5.0.

You can embed or link an Excel worksheet, macrosheet, or graph as a bound or unbound OLE object. You can copy data from the OLE worksheet object to the Clipboard and then paste the data into a bound or unbound text box. The following sections provide examples of these techniques.

Embedding an Excel Worksheet in a Form

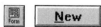

You can embed an entire Excel worksheet in an unbound object frame using the simple process that follows. In this case, the presentation of an Excel worksheet (or what you can display of the worksheet in a bound object frame) is the entire content of the worksheet. Large embedded worksheets occupy considerable disk space and may require a substantial period of time to display their presentation; you may want to use a small worksheet (5K or less file size, such as a workbook file created from the STK_21_3 worksheet) if you are short on disk space.

To embed an Excel worksheet in an unbound object frame of a new form, follow these steps:

1. Open the STOCKS.MDB database, if necessary, and create a new blank form. Initially, size the form to about 3.33 inches high by 6 inches wide.

2. Click the Toolbox button of the toolbar and select the unbound object frame tool. Create a frame with the left corner at about .5 inches from the form's left edge and about .25 inches from the top. (The dimensions of these margins are important; see the troubleshooting note at the end of this section.) The Insert Object dialog appears.

3. Click the Create from File option button and type **c:\access\stk_21.xls** (or the name of any other Excel 5.0 workbook file you want to embed) in the File text box, and then click OK (see fig. 21.40).

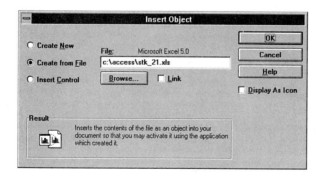

Fig. 21.40
Inserting an unbound object from an Excel 5.0 file.

Troubleshooting

A message box appears, indicating that the Excel worksheet is corrupted, that Excel is not properly registered, or that there is not enough memory to open Excel.

Close other open applications and try again. If the procedure continues to display error messages, exit Windows and start over. (An application has failed to release its global memory blocks on closing.) If you continue to receive error messages that refer to the registration database, you need to merge EXCEL5.REG with REG.DAT. See the "Repairing Your REG.DAT File" section, near the end of Chapter 19 for detailed instructions.

---

4. Select the unbound object frame and drag the right border to about 5.8 inches. Drag the bottom border to about 3.1 inches.

5. Click the Properties button of the toolbar. Select Data Properties and set the value of the Enabled property to Yes. If you don't enable the object frame, you can't activate the object (see fig. 21.41).

Fig. 21.41
Setting the *Enabled* property of the object to allow in-place activation.

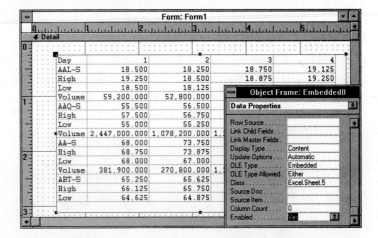

6. Select Other Properties and set the value of the Locked property to No. If the object is locked, you can't edit the values in the worksheet.

7. Click the Form View button of the toolbar to display the presentation of your worksheet (see fig. 21.42). If only part of a column displays, return to Design View and adjust the width of your object frame so that

a full column is displayed with a .25-inch border at the right. You also may need to adjust the height of the form to provide a 0.25-inch border at the bottom. (The borders inside the object frame are necessary; see the following troubleshooting note.)

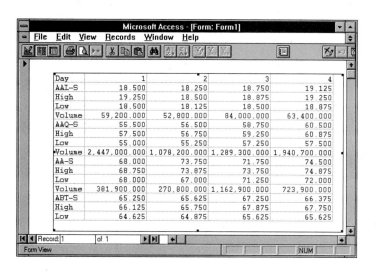

Fig. 21.42
The presentation of a worksheet in an unbound object frame.

V

Integrating Access

8. Double-click the object frame to activate the worksheet in place. If you have set the left and top positions of your object frame and provided the proper internal borders, your activated worksheet appears as shown in figure 21.43. Excel 5.0's Edit and View menus replace Access's Edit and View menus, and Excel's Insert, Format, Tools, and Data menus are added to Access's menu. The toolbars that normally appear when you open Excel are floating toolbars in Access 2.0. Activated mode is indicated by a blue hashed border around the object frame.

You can perform any operation that is possible in Excel 5.0 when the object is activated, except operations that require use of Excel's **File** menu, such as saving the workbook to a file or printing the worksheet.

9. Click outside the bound object frame to de-activate the object and return to presentation mode so that Access's menu bar is active.

10. Choose Spreadsheet Object from Access's Edit menu, and then choose Open from the submenu to open Excel 5.0's window with the embedded data as the source of Excel's current workbook (see fig. 21.44). When you open Excel, you can print the worksheet or save the embedded workbook to a file.

Fig. 21.43
The worksheet
activated in place.

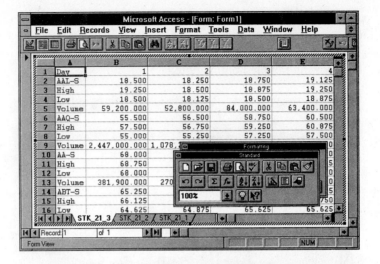

Fig. 21.44
Opening Excel 5.0
in its own window
(from presentation
mode).

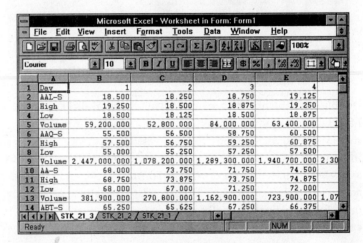

11. Choose Exit from Excel's File menu to close the instance of Excel and return to presentation mode.

12. Close your form and save the changes.

Troubleshooting

Excel's column selection buttons, row selection buttons, worksheet tabs, horizontal scroll bar, or the vertical scroll bar don't appear when the object is activated.

Two sets of critical factors determine the visibility of *adornments*, as the preceding objects are called, when you activate an object in place. The top position of the object frame must provide room for the column selector buttons in the form area (.25 inch), and the left position of the frame must provide space for the row selector buttons (.5 inch). The visibility of the horizontal and vertical scroll bars is determined by the internal margin of the object, the space between the edge of the worksheet presentation and the bottom and right edge of the object frame (.25 inch each). If, after setting these values, all of the adornments shown in figure 21.43 do not appear, position the mouse pointer on the upper left corner of the activation border and drag the corner diagonally downward to reduce the size of the activation frame. You may need to make repeated adjustments to the size of the object frame and the activation frame to ensure that all adornments appear.

Extracting Values from an OLE Object

You can copy individual numeric or text values from a linked or embedded Excel OLE object and place the values in a text box. To add the close, high, and low values of the AAL-S stock to a multiline text box added to the form you created in the preceding section, follow these steps:

1. Reduce the size of your unbound object frame containing the Excel worksheet object, and move the frame down to make room for a multiline text box at the top of the form.

2. Add a text box to the form, and set the value of the Scrollbars property to Vertical.

3. Double-click the unbound object frame to activate the workbook object.

4. Select the cell or range of cells you want to import to a text control object. In this case, select A2:I5 to return 8 days of price data for the AAL-S stock

5. Choose Copy from the Edit menu, or press Ctrl+C to copy the A2:I5 range to the Clipboard.

6. Select the text box, deactivating the object frame, and then choose Paste Special from Access's Edit menu to display the Paste Special dialog. When you copy data items from an embedded object, you only have the option of pasting them as text (see fig. 21.45). Click OK.

Fig. 21.45

Pasting a selection from an embedded Excel worksheet.

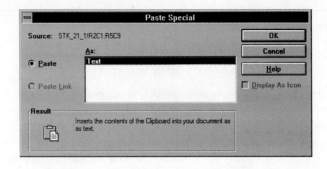

7. The pasted data items appear as shown in figure 21.46. The vertical bars between the values in the Describe text box represent the tab characters that Excel uses to separate data columns in a row.

Fig. 21.46

A selection from an embedded Excel worksheet pasted into an unbound text box.

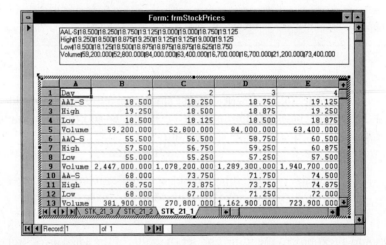

▶ "Manipulating an Excel 5.0 Workbook Object," p. 1060

▶ "Using Access Basic for DDE," p. 1086

If you create one or more bound text boxes with a numeric data type, you can paste a number from a selected single cell to each text box and then use the values to update the fields of the table to which the text box is bound. A more efficient method, however, is to use OLE Automation or Access Basic **DDE**. . . instructions to update values in tables with data from another application. (Using a simplified version of DDE is described later in this chapter.)

Linking to a Range of Cells of an Excel Worksheet

Embedding Excel objects is useful if you want to use OLE Automation to transfer data from a **Recordset** object to embedded worksheet cells. In most cases, however, creating an OLE link to all or a range of cells in a worksheet is a more common practice. Linking enables you to display or edit the most recent version of the worksheet's data from its source file. Any changes you make in Access are reflected when you close Excel if you save the changes.

The conventional process of linking a file in Excel is similar to that for using OLE 1.0 to link graphics files; in-place activation is not available with linked objects. To create a link with a range of cells in an Excel file, perform the following steps:

1. Open a new, blank Access form.

2. Launch Excel independently of Access.

3. Choose **O**pen from Excel's File menu, and in Excel's Open dialog, select the file you want to link.

4. Select the cells of the worksheet to be included in your Access table; then copy the selected cells to the Clipboard with Ctrl+C. Cell range A1:E17 of the STK_21_3 worksheet is used in this example.

5. Choose Paste **S**pecial from the Access Edit menu to display the Paste Special dialog. Click the Paste Link option button. Your only choices for a linked object are the object or the text contained in the selected data items. The data source, STK_21_3.R1C1:R13C5, appears in the Source label (see fig. 21.47).

Fig. 21.47
The Paste Link dialog for a linked range of cells in an Excel worksheet.

6. Click OK to create the unbound object frame containing the presentation of the selected cells. You don't need to provide for margins in the design because in-place activation is not available with linked objects.

7. Set the value of the `Enabled` property of the frame to `Yes` and the `Locked` property of the frame to `No`.

8. Click the Form View button of the toolbar. The presentation of your linked object appears as shown in figure 21.48.

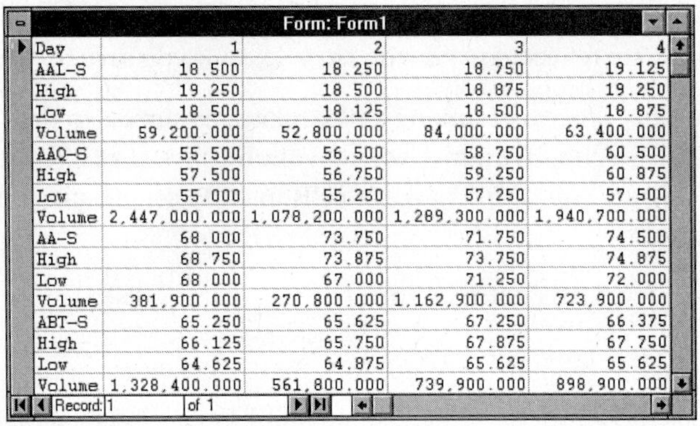

Day	1	2	3	4
AAL-S	18.500	18.250	18.750	19.125
High	19.250	18.500	18.875	19.250
Low	18.500	18.125	18.500	18.875
Volume	59,200.000	52,800.000	84,000.000	63,400.000
AAQ-S	55.500	56.500	58.750	60.500
High	57.500	56.750	59.250	60.875
Low	55.000	55.250	57.250	57.500
Volume	2,447,000.000	1,078,200.000	1,289,300.000	1,940,700.000
AA-S	68.000	73.750	71.750	74.500
High	68.750	73.875	73.750	74.875
Low	68.000	67.000	71.250	72.000
Volume	381,900.000	270,800.000	1,162,900.000	723,900.000
ABT-S	65.250	65.625	67.250	66.375
High	66.125	65.750	67.875	67.750
Low	64.625	64.875	65.625	65.625
Volume	1,328,400.000	561,800.000	739,900.000	898,900.000

Fig. 21.48 The presentation of a linked range of worksheet cells.

9. Double-click the presentation of the worksheet to launch Excel in its own window with the linked cells selected (see fig. 21.49).

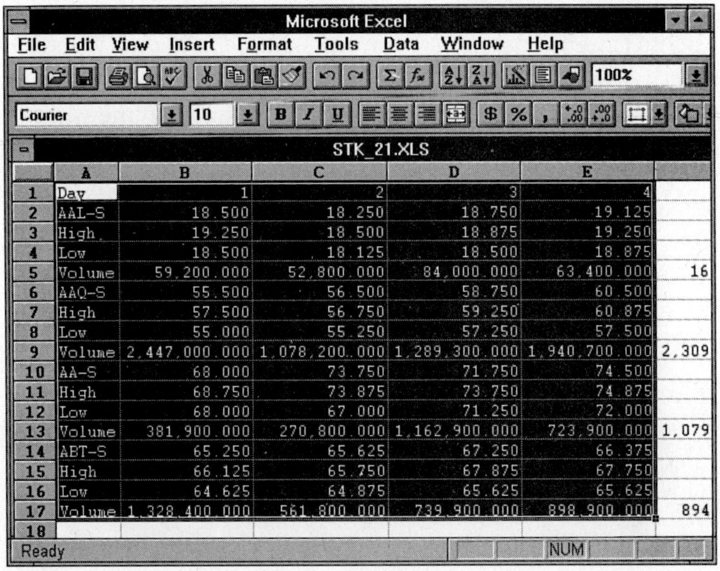

	A	B	C	D	E	
1	Day	1	2	3	4	
2	AAL-S	18.500	18.250	18.750	19.125	
3	High	19.250	18.500	18.875	19.250	
4	Low	18.500	18.125	18.500	18.875	
5	Volume	59,200.000	52,800.000	84,000.000	63,400.000	16
6	AAQ-S	55.500	56.500	58.750	60.500	
7	High	57.500	56.750	59.250	60.875	
8	Low	55.000	55.250	57.250	57.500	
9	Volume	2,447,000.000	1,078,200.000	1,289,300.000	1,940,700.000	2,309
10	AA-S	68.000	73.750	71.750	74.500	
11	High	68.750	73.875	73.750	74.875	
12	Low	68.000	67.000	71.250	72.000	
13	Volume	381,900.000	270,800.000	1,162,900.000	723,900.000	1,079
14	ABT-S	65.250	65.625	67.250	66.375	
15	High	66.125	65.750	67.875	67.750	
16	Low	64.625	64.875	65.625	65.625	
17	Volume	1,328,400.000	561,800.000	739,900.000	898,900.000	894
18						

Fig. 21.49 The instance of Excel launched by double-clicking the linked cells' presentation.

10. Choose Exit from Excel's File menu to return the focus to Access. If you have made changes to the data, you can elect to save the changes at this point.

Using DDE Links with Excel

If you need to extract individual numeric or text values from a worksheet to update values in your database, *dynamic data exchange* (DDE) is a better method than OLE. DDE enables you to transfer data from a specific cell within a worksheet to a bound or unbound text box on a form or report. Figure 21.48 shows the design of a form that displays the data from the STK_21_3.XLS worksheet, using Access's DDE() function.

The syntax of the DDE() function follows:

```
=DDE(AppName, TopicName, ItemName)
```

AppName, *TopicName*, and *ItemName* are enclosed within quotation marks when you use *string literals* (the actual names). The following list describes these arguments:

- *AppName* is the Windows task name of the DDE server application, assigned by its publisher. *AppName* consists of a single word (no spaces allowed) and is often a contraction of the full name of the product, such as *WinWord* for Word for Windows. You usually can find the DDE *AppName* for an application in documentation for that application.

- *TopicName* is, in the majority of cases, the full path and file name of the file that contains the data to be sent to Access.

- *ItemName* is the name of the location of the data to be sent within *TopicName*. For a worksheet, *ItemName* can be a range of cells in Excel's row-column format (R1C1) or the name of a range of cells. In Word for Windows, *ItemName* is usually a bookmark.

If the worksheet file is located in the C:\ACCESS directory, for example, and you want to extract the data from cells A2:F5, the function is as follows:

```
=DDE("Excel","c:\access\stk_21.XLS","R2C1:R5C6")
```

Cell A2 corresponds to column 1 of row 2, and cell F5 is located in column 6 of row 5. You can substitute a named range from the worksheet for the R#C# coordinates as the DDE topic.

Figure 21.50 illustrates the design of a simple form that uses the DDE() function to retrieve the stock ticker symbol, plus high, low, close, and volume data, for the stock specified by the coordinates of the cells in the STK_21.XLS workbook. The elements of the design of the form of figure 21.50 are

- The value of the ControlSource property of each text box is =DDE("Excel", "c:\access\stk_21.xls", "RrCc"), where *r* and *c* are the row and column coordinates of the required cell.

- The stock prices are formatted with the $#,###.000 mask, and the volume is formatted with #,### to eliminate the trailing zeros.

■ When you display the form in Form View and Excel is not running with the specified topic, the message box of figure 21.51 appears. Click OK to launch Excel, minimized to an icon. (If Excel is running with another topic, a second instance of Excel is launched.)

■ Excel opens the STK_21.XLS workbook to the currently selected worksheet and returns the values to the text boxes (see fig. 21.52).

Fig. 21.50

The design of a simple form using the *DDE( )* function to return cell values.

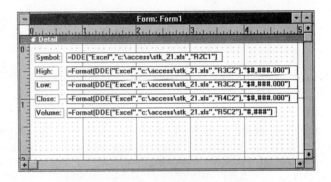

Fig. 21.51

The message box that appears if Excel is not running with the specified topic.

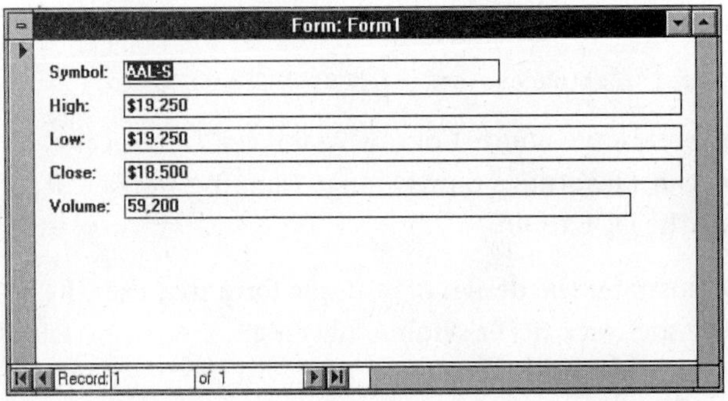

Fig. 21.52

Data returned by Excel via DDE to an Access form.

Using the DDE() function is cumbersome because of the amount of typing necessary to supply the argument values. You can use copy and paste methods to add additional cells. After pasting an additional set of cells, you change the column number in each DDE() expression. Figure 21.53 shows five days of stock price data for the AAL-S stock.

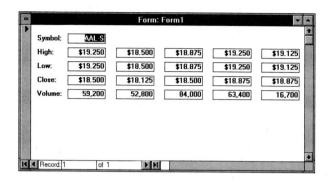

Fig. 21.53
The form design of
figure 21.49 with
four additional
days of stock
prices.

You can use the Access DDE() function to obtain and display specific data
items from worksheets more quickly and easily than by copying them from
an OLE server that supplies worksheet objects in bound or unbound object
frames. You only need to open Excel or another DDE-compliant spreadsheet
application once; the server runs minimized to an icon. After loading the
spreadsheet application, data transfer to the form or report is rapid, and DDE
consumes much less memory than OLE during the process.

You cannot edit data in a text box supplied by the =DDE() expression. To use
the full capabilities of DDE, you need to create an Access Basic function and
then call the function from a command button or with an Access macro.

Access provides a second DDE function, DDESend(), that enables you to transfer data, usually from a text box, from an Access form to an Excel worksheet
or any other document in a Windows application that supports DDE. The
syntax of the DDESend() function is as follows:

    =DDESend(*AppName*, *TopicName*, *ItemName*, *Data*)

AppName, *TopicName*, and *ItemName* are the same as the arguments for the
DDE() function. *Data* is a string that can be a literal value enclosed within
quotation marks, a function that returns a string, or the value of a text box
control. For example, if you want to change "Day" in cell A1 of the
STK_21.XLS worksheet in your C:\ACCESS directory to "Date," you add
a text box control to your form and type **=DDESend("Excel",
"c:\access\stk_21.xls", "R1C1", "Date")** as the value of the ControlSource
property of the text box.

You can send the value of another text box on your form by substituting the
control Name of the other text box for the literal string in the preceding example. If you have a text box with the Name Close 1, whose data you want to

send to cell B2, the syntax of the DDESend() statement for value of the ControlSource property of the DDESend() text box is:

```
=DDESend("Excel", "c:\access\stk_21_3.xls", "R2C2", [Close 1])
```

The value of the ControlSource property of a DDESend() text box must be that of another text box because text boxes with =DDESend() expressions as their ControlSource property are read-only in run mode. The text box that contains the DDESend() function appears blank in Form View; thus, you set the Visible property of =DDESend() text boxes to No. You can specify the DDESend() function as the ControlSource property of an Option Group, Check Box, or Combo Box control, but these controls are also read-only and are disabled (dimmed) in run mode.

Both the DDE() and DDESend() functions execute immediately upon the opening of the form in which they are used. If your Access application includes multiple *TopicNames*, an instance (copy) of the application specified by *AppName* is opened for each *TopicName* you add to your forms. Thus, you can rapidly deplete the resources available to Access with multiple copies of Excel (or other DDE servers), resulting in out-of-memory messages from Access. You must close each instance of the DDE server application manually by choosing the instance in Task Manager's list and clicking End Task or by clicking the DDE server's icon and choosing Close from the Application Control menu. Using the Access Basic **DDE**. . . statements, explained in Chapter 29, is the preferred method of implementing the equivalent of the DDE() and DDESend() functions.

From Here...

This chapter provided typical examples of the ability of Access to interact with data in worksheets. Importing and reorganizing data formerly contained in worksheets is one of the most common tasks you encounter if you are using Access for business applications. If conversion isn't practical or desirable, you can use OLE to display and edit worksheet data in Access. If you only need to display values of a few specific data cells in a worksheet, DDE is the quickest and easiest approach.

The following chapters provide further information on the subject discussed in this chapter:

- Chapter 7, "Attaching, Importing, and Exporting Tables," provides additional information on importing and exporting data to and from Excel workbook files.

- Chapter 19, "Using OLE 2.0," provides an overview of OLE and the new capabilities of OLE 2.0.

- Chapter 22, "Using Access with Microsoft Word and Mail Merge," shows you how the Access Mail Merge Wizard uses DDE to create merge data sources for Microsoft Word 6.0.

- Chapter 29, "Exchanging Data with OLE Automation and DDE," describes how to use Access Basic to perform operations that are more flexible than those afforded by the `DDE()` and `DDESend()` functions.

Chapter 22

Using Access with Microsoft Word and Mail Merge

Members of the Microsoft Office software suite are specifically designed to make constructing cooperative applications easy. One of the principal applications for database applications is creating mailing lists for use in conjunction with form letters. Thus, Access 2.0, a member of the Professional Edition of Microsoft Office, includes a Mail Merge Wizard that not only automates the process of creating Word 6.0 merge data files, but also aids you in creating new form letters. You also can use the reverse process and create form letters using Word 6.0's new mail merge process. Creating form letters from Word 6.0 accommodates users who do not have access to a copy of retail Access 2.0 on their computer. Word 6.0 uses Microsoft Query and the Open Database Connectivity (ODBC) application programming interface (API) to connect to Access 1.1 and a variety of other desktop database types.

As with Excel worksheets, you can embed or link Word documents in bound or unbound object frames and add a complete word processing system to your Access application. If you embed the Word document in the object frame, you can take advantage of OLE 2.0's in-place activation to make the operating environment of Access almost identical to that of Word. Word's menu supplements the Access menu, and Word's anchored toolbars appear as floating toolbars on your display. Word's document editing window, in Page View, appears within the confines of your object frame.

In this chapter, you learn to

- Use Access's Mail Merge Wizard to create Word 6.0 form letters

- Use Access databases as the data source for the Word 6.0 mail merge process

- Embed and link Word 6.0 documents in Access tables and forms using OLE 2.0

- Create a simple form to display and edit embedded or linked documents

Using the Access Mail Merge Wizard

Access 2.0's Mail Merge Wizard can help you create a new main merge document or employ an existing main merge document from which to create form letters. The Mail Merge Wizard uses a table or a query as the data source for the merge data file. The sections that follow describe the following two methods of creating a form letter:

■ Using the Mail Merge Wizard to create a new main merge document whose merge data source is an Access table

■ Using an existing main merge document with a merge data source from an Access select query.

Creating and Previewing a New Form Letter

When you first try a new Wizard, it's customary to create a new object rather than use the Wizard to modify an existing object, such as a main merge document. The following steps use the Mail Merge Wizard to create a new main merge document from records in the Customers table of NWIND.MDB.

1. Open NWIND.MDB, if necessary, and select the Customers table in the Database window.

2. Click the Merge-It button of the toolbar to launch the Mail Merge Wizard. The Wizard's first and only dialog appears as shown in figure 22.1.

Fig. 22.1
The dialog of the Microsoft Word Mail Merge Wizard.

3. Click the Create a New Document and Then Link the Data to It option button to create a new main merge document using fields from the Customers table.

4. If you want to display Word 6.0's on-line help for mail merge operations during the document creation process, mark the Open Microsoft Word Help on How to Complete Your Mail Merge check box.

5. Click OK to launch Word 6.0 if it is not running, and open a new mail merge main document. Click the Insert Merge Field button to verify the fields from the Customers table appear in the drop-down list, as shown in figure 22.2.

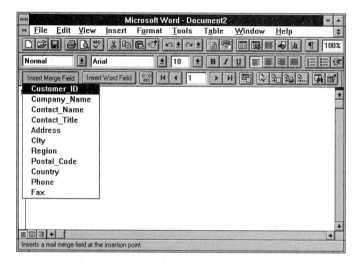

Fig. 22.2
Displaying the available merge fields in Word 6.0's mail merge window.

6. With the caret at the top of the document, choose Date and Time from Word's Insert menu to add a date field to the main document.

7. Add a blank line, click the Insert Merge Field button to display the drop-down list, and insert the fields from the Customers table to create the address section of the main document (see fig. 22.3).

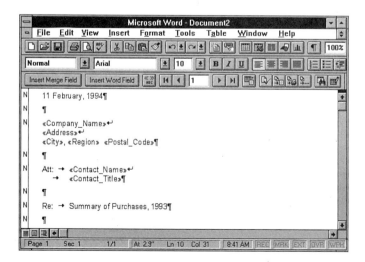

Fig. 22.3
Adding the merge fields to the main merge document.

> **Note**
>
> Spaces and other punctuation in merge data field names are not permitted by Word. The Mail Merge Wizard substitutes underscores (_) for spaces and other illegal characters in Access field names.

8. Click the View Merged Data button of the Mail Merge toolbar to preview the appearance of your form letter.

Tip

Click the Find Record button of the toolbar, type **USA** in the Find What text box, and select Country from the In Field drop-down list. Click OK to find the first U.S. record.

9. The form letters go only to customers in the United States, so repeatedly click the next record button of the mail merge toolbar to find the first U.S. record. Alternatively, type **32** in the text box of the toolbar. The preview of the form letter for Great Lakes Food Market appears as shown in figure 22.4.

10. You want to send letters to U.S. customers, so you need to create a query that returns only records whose Country column has the value "USA". Close Word, and save your main merge document with an appropriate file name, such as **PURC_SUM.DOC** for Purchases Summary. This file is used in the next section, as well as later in the chapter where you open the Access data source from Word.

Fig. 22.4
Displaying a preview of a form letter to a U.S. customer.

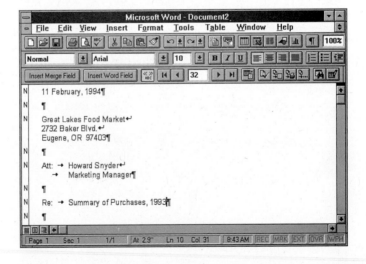

> **Note**
>
> The Mail Merge Wizard uses dynamic data exchange (DDE) to communicate with Word, so you cannot use Word 6.0's query features to select and sort the merge data. If you attempt to do so, you break the DDE link between Word and Access. Thus, you need to base your final mail merge document on an Access query if you want to select or sort your records.

Using an Existing Main Merge Document with a New Data Source

Once you've created a standard main merge document, the most common practice is to use differing data sources to create form letters by category of addressee. Take the following steps to use the main mail merge document you created in the preceding section, PURC_SUM.DOC, with a new data source based on a simple Access query:

V

1. Open a new query, and add the Customers table.

2. Add the Company Name, Contact Name, Contact Title, Address, City, Region, Postal Code, and Country fields to the query.

3. Enter **USA** as the criterion for the Country field, and clear the Show check box to prevent Country from appearing in the query. Add an ascending sort to the Postal Code field. Your query design appears as shown in figure 22.5.

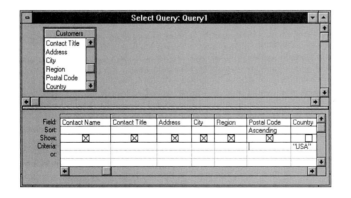

Fig. 22.5
The query design for the U.S. customers mailing list.

4. Click the Run Query button of the toolbar to verify the query result set (see fig. 22.6). Choose **S**ave or Save As from Access's File menu, and save the query with an appropriate name, such as **qryCustomersUSA**.

Fig. 22.6

The query result set for U.S.-based customers.

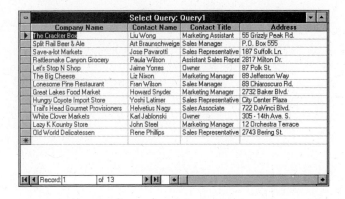

5. With the Query open, click the Merge-It button of the toolbar to launch the Mail Merge Wizard. With the Link Your Data to an Existing Microsoft Word Document option button marked (the default), click OK to display the Select Microsoft Word Document dialog (see fig. 22.7).

Fig. 22.7

Selecting the main merge document.

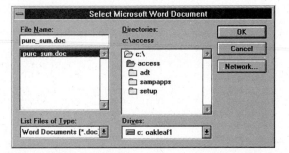

6. Select your main merge document in the File Name list and click OK. A message box, shown in figure 22.8, appears when you change the data source for a merge document. Click Yes to launch Word with the new data source.

Fig. 22.8

The message box that appears when you change the merge data source.

7. You can confirm that your query is the new merge data source by clicking the Insert Merge Field button and checking the field list. (The Country field should not appear.)

Alternatively, you can click the Edit Data Source button of Word's mail merge toolbar to display the query in Access, as shown in figure 22.9. (Click the Minimize button of Access's Query Datasheet window to return the focus to Word.)

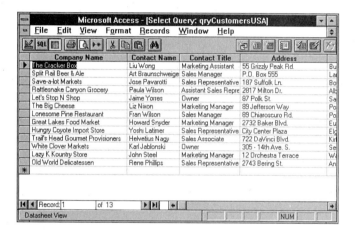

Fig. 22.9
Displaying the query result set from Word.

8. You can merge the main document and the data source directly to the printer or create a series of form letters in a new document. The latter choice lets you inspect the letters before you print them. Click the Merge To New Document button to create the new form letter. The top of the first form letter, in ZIP code sequence, appears as shown in figure 22.10.

If you close Word at this point, make sure you save your changes to PURC_SUM.DOC. PURC_SUM.DOC is used as the main merge document in the sections that follow.

V

Integrating Access

Fig. 22.10

The final form
letter addressed to
U.S. customers.

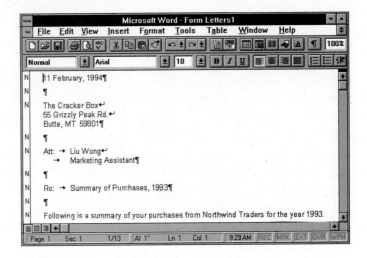

Using Word 6.0's Mail Merge Feature with Access Databases

▶ "Understanding
ODBC Drivers,"
p. 961

In many cases, Access 2.0 isn't available to users of Word who need to create
form letters from data contained in Access .MDB files. Like Excel 5.0, Word
6.0 includes a copy of Microsoft Query and the necessary ODBC drivers to
connect to Access 1.1 .MDB files, plus dBASE, FoxPro, and Paradox 3+ table
files. The version of the Access ODBC driver included with Word 6.0 when
this edition was written, RED110.DLL, does not support the Access 2.0 .MDB
format. Thus, the examples in the following two sections use the NWind data
source, which consists of a collection of dBASE files derived from the Access
1.1 version of NWIND.MDB. If you have the Access 1.1 version of
NWIND.MDB, you can substitute it for the NWind data source. Using the
dBASE data source, however, has the advantage of demonstrating the error
correction capabilities of Word 6.0's mail merge feature.

Word 6.0 includes the Mail Merge Helper, which is similar in concept to an
Access wizard. The following two sections use the Mail Merge Helper to create
a new Microsoft Query (MSQuery) data source and to use an existing
MSQuery data source.

Creating a New Mail Merge Data Source with Microsoft Query

To use Microsoft Query to create a merge data source from a Microsoft Access
1.1 database, follow these steps:

1. Launch Word 6.0, if necessary, and open the PURC_SUM.DOC main merge document you created earlier in this chapter.

2. Click the Mail Merge Helper button of the mail merge toolbar to open the Mail Merge Helper dialog (see fig. 22.11). The entry in the Data label of the Data Source section is NWIND.MDB!Query qryCustomersUSA. This is the syntax for specifying the topic of a DDE conversation when you use Access as a DDE server.

▶ "Using Access as a DDE Server," p. 1090

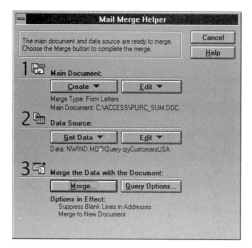

Fig. 22.11
The Mail Merge Help dialog with an Access DDE merge data source specified.

3. Click the Get Data button, and select Create Data Source from the drop-down list to open the Create Data Source dialog. Word includes a set of default field names you can use to create merge data files (see fig. 22.12).

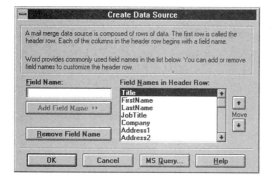

Fig. 22.12
Word 6.0's Create Data Source dialog.

V

Integrating Access

4. This example uses MSQuery to create the data source, so click the MS Query button to launch MSQuery. MSQuery opens with the Select Data Source dialog active (see fig. 22.13).

Fig. 22.13
Microsoft Query launched with the Select Data Source dialog open.

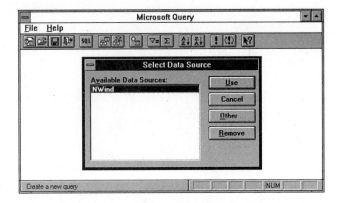

5. MSQuery comes with a default ODBC data source, NWind, that points to a set of dBASE IV sample .DBF files that are located in your \WINDOWS\MSAPPS\MSQUERY directory. Click the Use button with NWind selected in the Available Data Sources list to select the .DBF file to use in the Add Tables dialog.

   If you have an updated version of MSQuery that includes the new ODBC driver for Access 2.0 .MDBs, or if you have the Access 1.1 version of NWIND.MDB, you can click the Other button to open the ODBC Data Sources dialog. Select MS Access Databases in the list (see fig. 22.14). Click OK to display the Select Database dialog. Select the .MDB file you want in the Files list, and click OK. The Add Tables dialog for the selected .MDB file is similar to that for .DBF and other desktop database files.

Fig. 22.14
Selecting an ODBC data source or the driver for a type of desktop database.

6. In the Add Tables dialog, double-click the CUSTOMER.DBF item of the Table Name list (see fig. 22.15) to add the CUSTOMER.DBF table to MSQuery's graphical QBE panel. MSQuery is quite similar in use to the Query Design window of Access.

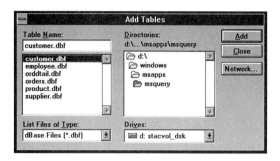

Fig. 22.15
Selecting the CUSTOMER.DBF table file in the Add Tables dialog.

7. Click and drag the following fields to the columns of the Query Result panel: COMPANY, CONTACT, CON_TITLE, ADDRESS, CITY, REGION, ZIP_CODE, and COUNTRY. (The sequence in which the columns appear is not significant.)

8. Click the header bar of the ZIP_CODE column to select the column, and then click the Sort Ascending button of MSQuery's toolbar to sort the query in ZIP code sequence.

9. Place the caret in the Criteria Field text box, and open the drop-down list of fields. Select COUNTRY, and type **USA** in the Value text box. (MSQuery adds the single quote marks for you; MSQuery uses single quotes in place of Access 2.0's default double-quote marks to identify literal string values.) Your query design appears as shown in figure 22.16.

10. Choose Save As from MSQuery's File menu to display the Select Data Source dialog. Select the QRY File item in the list, and click the Save button to open the Save As dialog. Assign your query a name, such as **CUSTS_US.QRY**, and click OK. You use the saved query in the section that follows.

11. Choose **Return Data to Microsoft Word** from MSQuery's File menu to close MSQuery and return to the Mail Merge Helper. The entry in the Data label of the Data Source section is now `D:\WINDOWS\MSAPPS \MSQUERY\CUSTOMER.DBF`, where $D:\backslash$ is the drive on which you have Windows installed (see fig. 22.17). Click the Cancel button of Mail Merge Helper to return to Word.

V

Integrating Access

Fig. 22.16
The query design
for the U.S.
mailing list.

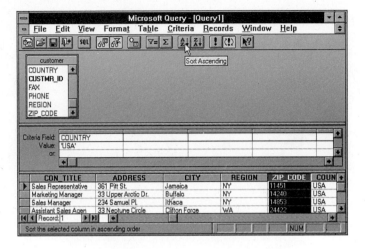

Fig. 22.17
The Mail Merge
Helper dialog with
a dBASE file
specified as the
merge data source.

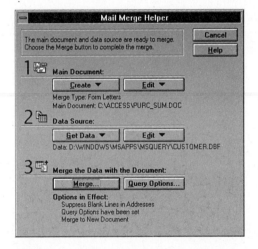

At this point you have assigned a new merge data source for the main merge document, PURC_SUM.DOC. If you used the NWind data source, however, several of the field names of the query do not correspond to the merge fields in your main merge document. The following steps test the merge operation and let you fix the orphaned merge field entries created when you used qryCustomersUS as the merge data source:

1. Click the Test for Errors button of the mail merge toolbar to display the Checking and Reporting Errors dialog (see fig. 22.18). Select the Complete the Merge, Pausing to Report Each Error as It Occurs option button (the default), and click OK.

Fig. 22.18
Specifying a
method for testing
for errors in a form
letter.

2. Word begins the mail merge test. When it encounters the first instance of the Company_Name merge field, the Invalid Merge Field dialog appears. Select the COMPANY field from the drop-down list to replace the Company_Name entry, as shown in figure 22.19.

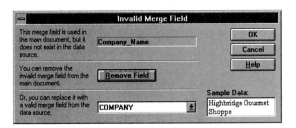

Fig. 22.19
Correcting a merge
field entry with
the Invalid Merge
Field dialog.

V

Integrating Access

3. Repeat step 2 for each of the invalid merge fields, Contact_Name (CONTACT), Contact_Title (CON_TITLE), and Postal_Code (ZIP_CODE). After you fix each field, the preview of the merged form letter appears as shown in figure 22.20.

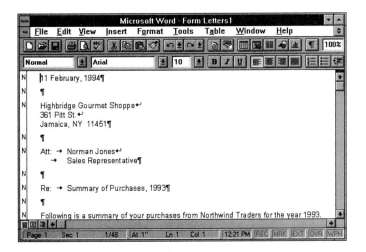

Fig. 22.20
The result of the
error testing
process when
merge field errors
are corrected.

4. Click the View Merged Data button to display the changes made by your entries in the Invalid Merge Field dialog (see fig 22.21). Merge field matches are not case-sensitive, so merge field-field name combinations such as Address-ADDRESS are valid.

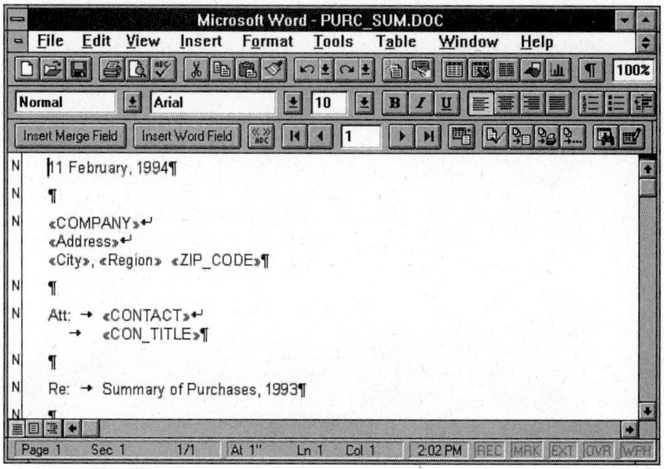

Fig. 22.21

Corrections made to the merge field entries in the main merge document.

5. Click the Merge To Document button to review the final form letter. The final form letter is designated Form Letters 2 to distinguish it from the preview version, Form Letters 1.

Creating Form Letters from an Existing Query

Once you've created and saved a query with MSQuery, you can use the saved query to create another set of form letters. MSQuery's saved queries are similar to Access queries saved as `QueryDef` objects in .MDB files. To use an existing .QRY file as the data source for a merge document, follow these steps:

1. Click the Mail Merge Helper button to display the dialog.

2. Click the Get Data button, and select Open Data Source from the drop-down list to display the Open Data Source dialog.

3. Choose the MS Query Files (*.qry) item in the List Files of Type drop-down list.

4. Select the CUSTS_US.QRY file you saved in the preceding section, and click OK (see fig. 22.22). The message box shown in figure 22.23 appears.

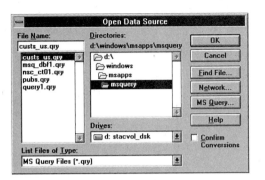

Fig. 22.22
Choosing an existing MSQuery .QRY file in the Open Data Source dialog.

Fig. 22.23
Making the .QRY file the permanent source of data for the main merge document.

5. To make the CUSTS_US.QRY the permanent source of data for the PURC_SUM.DOC main merge document, click the Yes button of the message box to return to the Mail Merge Helper Dialog (see fig. 22.24). *D:\PATH*\CUSTS_US.QRY appears in the Data label of the Data Source section.

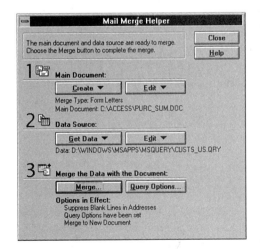

Fig. 22.24
The Mail Merge Helper dialog with the .QRY file specified as the data source.

Embedding or Linking Word Documents in Access Tables

Many word processing documents are a collection of individual paragraphs, each of which may change depending on the purpose of the document. If the document is a contract, many of the paragraphs are likely to be *boilerplate*, standard paragraphs that are added based on the jurisdiction and purpose of the contract, and the relationship between the parties. Similarly, books are collections of chapters; when an author is writing a book, each chapter may go through several editing stages. Keeping track of boilerplate files and maintaining collections of book chapter files in various editing stages can be a daunting project. Even if you establish a workable DOS file-naming convention, you can easily lose track of the relationship between the file name and the content of the file.

Tip
Windows NT's
long file
names, which
are available
only when you
use the New
Technology
File System
(NTFS), can aid
in providing a
better descrip-
tion of the
content of files.

Applications that track documents and maintain revision records for documents fall into the category of *document management systems*. Document management systems differ from image management systems; the latter handle static bit-mapped images (usually created by scanners), rather than dynamic document content (editable data). With its OLE 2.0 capability, Access 2.0 is a logical candidate for the creation of document management applications.

You can create a simple document management system by designing a table with one or more fields of the OLE Object data type to contain embedded documents or links to individual document files. You need a minimum of two other fields: one to identify the source file name of the document and the other to provide a document description. Additional fields can be added to indicate document ownership, track document status, hold key terms, and control who can modify the document. Figure 22.25 shows the design of a simple table designed to store the manuscript of this edition in the form of individual chapters in an OLE Object field.

Fig. 22.25
The design of the table for a simple document management system.

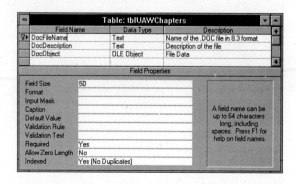

Once you define the fields for your document table, you need to determine whether you want to embed the document's data in the table or link the documents to their source files. Make your choice based on the following criteria:

- Embedding the document lets you use in-place activation to review the document within Access. In-place activation is a less intrusive process.

- Activating a linked document launches Word 6.0 in its own window.

- Embedding the document provides an independent copy of the document that can serve as an archive. You can set the value of the Locked property of the object to Yes to allow the object to be activated, but not altered.

- Linking the document allows you to view changes to the document as they occur.

- Linking requires that the document remain in the same location. In most cases, moving the document to another drive or directory breaks the link.

- You cannot save an embedded Word 6.0 or Excel 5.0 document to a file or print the embedded document using File menu choices in the in-place activated mode. The file menus of these applications do not replace the File menu of Access 2.0 when the embedded objects are activated. However, you can open Word's window to make the Word File menu accessible.

> **Note**
>
> You can use OLE Automation instructions in Access Basic modules to save an embedded Word 6.0 document to a file or print the document. The Object property of the object frame lets you manipulate embedded or linked objects with Access Basic code. Chapter 29, "Exchanging Data with OLE Automation and DDE," describes how to apply OLE Automation methods to Word documents.

Embedding or Linking a Word 6.0 Document in a Table

To embed or link a Word 6.0 document in an OLE Object field of a table with a design similar to that shown in figure 22.25, follow these steps:

1. Place the caret in the OLE Object field, and choose Insert Object from the Edit menu to display the Insert Object dialog (see fig. 22.26).

Fig. 22.26

The Insert Object dialog.

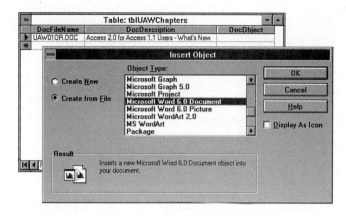

2. You can create an empty Word document by accepting the default, Create New. To link or embed an existing document, click the Create from File option button and then click OK. (You don't need to select Microsoft Word 6.0 Document when you insert an object from a file.) The Object Type list changes to the File text box.

3. You can type the path and file name in the File text box or click the Browse button to display the Browse dialog (see fig. 22.27). Select the file you want to use in the File Name list, and then click OK to close the Browse dialog and return to the Insert Object dialog.

Fig. 22.27

Selecting a source document file in the Browse dialog.

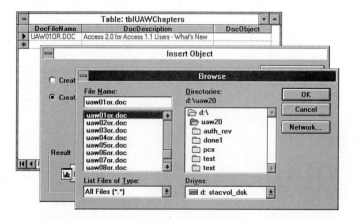

4. The file you selected in the preceding step appears in the File text box. At this point you can choose between linking and embedding the file. The example that follows uses embedded objects to demonstrate in-place activation (see fig. 22.28). If you want to link the file, mark the Link text box. Click OK.

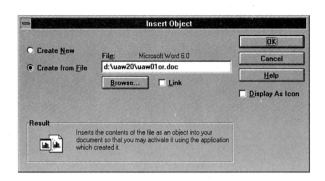

Fig. 22.28
Embedding a
Word 6.0 docu-
ment object from a
file.

5. Position the record selector of the table to a different record to save the embedded object or link to the object's file in your table, together with its OLE presentation.

Repeat the above steps for each document you want to add to the table. You can activate the document object in Word 6.0's window by double-clicking the OLE Object cell. Viewing the documents you insert in the file lets you verify that their contents correspond to their description.

Troubleshooting

The Microsoft Word 6.0 Document entry does not appear in the Insert Object dialog's Object Type list, or attempting to insert a Word 6.0 document results in a message box stating that the registration database entry is invalid or corrupted.

Registration database entries for Word 6.0 are missing or invalid. If the Word 6.0 entry is missing, it is likely that Word's Setup program did not complete its operation. (The last step of Setup adds entries to REG.DAT). If the "corrupted" message appears, it is likely that you moved the Word files from the original directory in which Setup installed the files into a different directory. In either case, you need to merge WINWORD6.REG with your registration database to correct the problem. See the instructions for merging registration files in the "Repairing Your REG.DAT File" section of Chapter 19, "Using OLE 2.0."

Creating a Form to Display the Document

If your table contains only a few fields, you can use the AutoForm Wizard to create a simple form to display and edit your linked or embedded object. To create the document display form, follow these steps:

1. With the Database window active, click the New Form button of the toolbar to display the New Form dialog.

2. Select the table that contains your linked or embedded documents, and click the Form Wizards button to display the Form Wizards dialog.

3. Double-click the AutoForm item in the Which Wizard Do You Want? list to create the new form.

4. Click the Design View button of the toolbar, and then relocate and resize the controls as necessary. Your bound object frame should occupy most of the display area. To view the entire document in its original format, set the Height property of the object frame to 11 inches and the Width property to 8.5 inches.

5. Return to Form View to display the presentation of the document. Figure 22.29 shows the presentation of the initial version of the manuscript for the first chapter of this edition. The size of the bound object frame of figure 22.29 is about 3.5 by 6 inches.

Fig. 22.29

The presentation of a Word 6.0 document in a bound object frame.

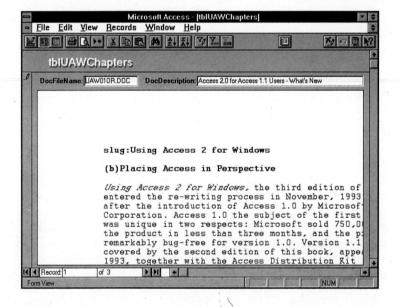

6. Double-click the surface of the object frame to activate the object. Activating the object launches Word 6.0 if it is not running. If you embedded the document, activation adds Word's toolbars to the display as floating toolbars. Word's menu choices take over Access's Edit and View menus, and Word adds its Insert, Format, Tools, and Table menus to the menu bar (see figure 22.30). You can move through the document with the Page Up and Page Down keys. All the editing features of Word 6.0 are available when the document object is activated.

7. Click the surface of the form, outside of the area of the bound object frame, to deactivate the object and return to presentation view of the document.

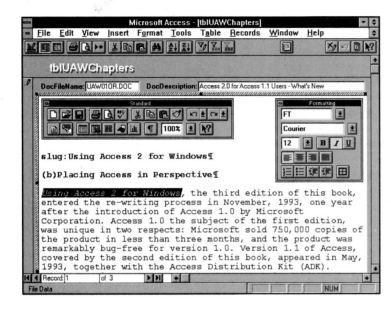

Fig. 22.30
A Word 6.0 document activated in a bound object frame.

8. To save the document to a file, alter the page layout or print an embedded document, choose Document Object from the Edit menu, and then choose **O**pen from the submenu. Word's window takes over your display, and the File menu of Word appears as shown in figure 22.31.

9. Choose Close and Return to *FormName* from the File menu to close Word's window and return to Access.

> **Note**
>
> The only view of a Word document available when the object is embedded is Page Layout View. You can change the layout of the embedded document by opening the document in Word (see preceding step 8), choosing Page Setup from Word's File menu, and then making the required adjustments.

You also can insert additional document objects directly in the form. To embed or link an object in Form View, change to presentation mode if necessary. Position the record pointer on the blank (tentative append) record. An empty presentation appears in the bound object frame. Choose Insert **Object** from the Edit menu, and follow the steps 2 through 5 of the preceding section to embed or link additional document objects.

Fig. 22.31
Opening the embedded document in Word 6.0's window.

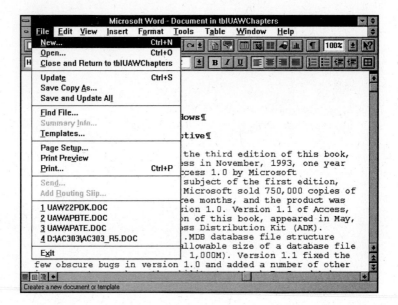

From Here...

This chapter concentrated on the methodology for creating form letters based on data in Access tables because creating form letters is one of the most common applications for database management systems. You learned how to use Access 2.0's Mail Merge Wizard and the Mail Merge Helper of Word 6.0 to create merge data sources from database tables. The chapter concluded with a description of how to create a simple Access document management system that takes advantage of in-place activation to display and edit Word 6.0 documents.

For information on topics related to those in this chapter, refer to the following chapters:

■ Chapter 4, "Working with Access Databases and Tables," shows you how to design tables for a variety of database applications.

■ Chapter 8, "Using Query by Example," introduces you to the design of simple queries, similar to those used for creating most merge data sources.

- Chapter 12, "Creating and Using Forms," describes the use of other Access Form Wizards to create more complex forms.

- Chapter 29, "Exchanging Data with OLE Automation and DDE," shows you how to manipulate Word 6.0 documents using the Word.Basic object and Access Basic OLE Automation code.

Part VI

Using Advanced Access Techniques

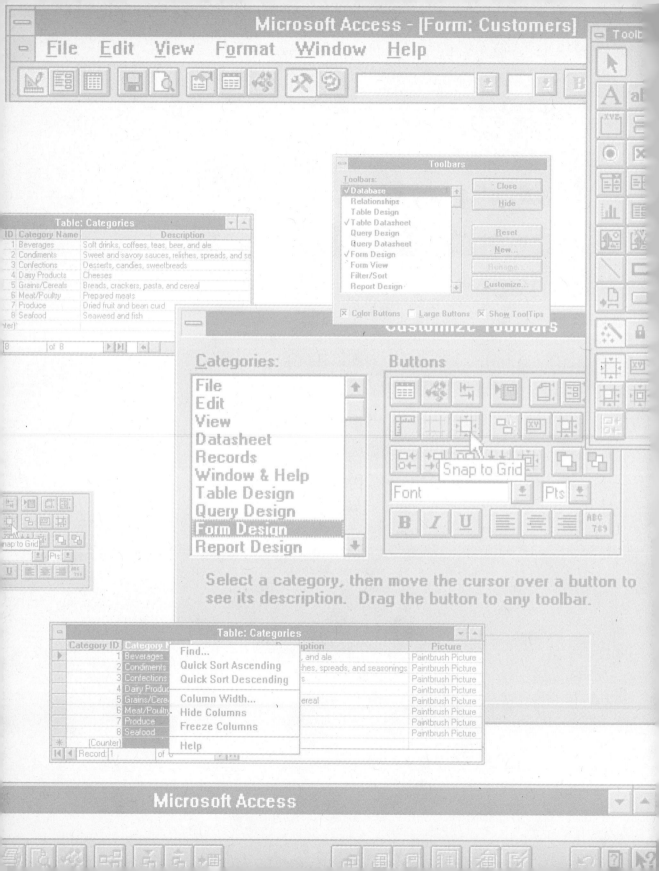

Chapter 23

Exploring Relational Database Design and Implementation

You were introduced to a few of the elements of relational database design when you created the Personnel Actions table and joined it with the Employees table of the Northwind Database. Chapter 21, "Using Access with Microsoft Excel," gave you a bit more insight into how to create a relational database from information contained in a worksheet. When you're presented with the challenge of designing a database from ground zero, however, especially a complex or potentially complex database, you need to understand the theory of relational database design and its terminology.

This chapter takes a step back and starts with the definition of data objects and how you identify them. Because Access is object-oriented, the concepts of database design presented in this chapter have an object-oriented bent. The reason for this approach is twofold:

- Access's relational tables incorporate many of the features of client-server databases. Properties, such as validation rules and indexes, and methods that include preventing duplicate primary key entries, are combined in the table object. Details of relations between tables and methods of enforcing referential integrity are stored in the database object.

- Access Basic treats the database itself and each of Access's database elements—tables, queries, forms, and reports—as programming objects.

In this chapter, you learn to

- Design a relational database system

- Create tables that comply with the rules of relational database design

- Document your Access database application with a data dictionary

- Understand how Access uses indexes to speed queries

- Prevent deletion of records in tables on which other tables depend

VI

Advanced Techniques

After you've identified the data objects that are to be included in the tables of your database, you need to design the tables to contain the data objects. You use a process called *data normalization* to create tables that conform to the relational database model. Normalization is the process of eliminating duplicate information in tables by extracting the duplicate data to new tables that contain records with unique data values. You then join the tables you create by fields with common data values to create a relational database structure. Normalizing data is the subject of the "Normalizing Data to the Relational Model" section of this chapter.

The role of indexes in maintaining unique values in primary-key fields and organizing data tables was described briefly in preceding chapters. This chapter provides an explanation of how indexes are constructed and maintained with Access. Properly designed indexes improve the performance of your applications without consuming excessive amounts of disk space or slowing the appending of new records to a crawl.

This chapter also deals with the rules that establish and maintain referential integrity, one of the most important considerations in designing a database. Referential integrity enforces uniqueness in primary keys and prevents the occurrence of orphaned records, such as records of invoices whose customer data records have been deleted.

Understanding Database Systems

Prior to this chapter, you have used the Northwind Traders demonstration database, created a few simple databases, and perhaps imported your own data in another database format into an Access table. No formal theories were presented to aid or hinder your understanding of the underlying design of the database examples. Now that you have gained some experience using Access, the more theoretical concepts of database design should be easier to understand.

This section takes a systems approach to database design, starting with a generalized set of objectives, outlining the steps necessary to accomplish the objectives, and then explaining the theory and practice behind each step.

The Objectives of Database Design

The strategy of database design is to accomplish the following objectives:

- Fulfilling your own needs or the needs of the organization for information in a timely, consistent, and economical manner.

- Eliminating or minimizing the duplication of database content across the organization. In a large organization, eliminating duplication may require a *distributed database*. Distributed databases use multiple servers to store individual databases. The individual databases are attached to one another, to use Access terminology, through a local-area network (LAN) or wide-area network (WAN) so that they appear as a single database to the user.

- Providing rapid access to the specific elements of information in the database required by each user category. Operating speed is a function of the relational database management system (RDBMS) itself, the design of the applications you create, the capabilities of the server and client computers, and network characteristics.

- Accommodating expansion of databases to adapt to the needs of a growing organization, such as the addition of new products and processes, complying with governmental reporting requirements, and incorporating new transaction and decision-support applications.

- Maintaining the integrity of the database so that it contains only validated, auditable information. Some client-server databases, such as Microsoft SQL Server, provide built-in *triggers* to maintain database integrity. Triggers are a set of rules that are included in the database. If you violate a rule, the trigger sends an error message instead of performing the transaction. The Enforce Referential Integrity check box in Access's Relationships dialog creates the equivalent of a trigger.

- Preventing access to the database by unauthorized persons. Access provides a security system that requires users to enter a password to use a particular database.

- Permitting access only to those elements of the database information that individual users or categories of users need in the course of their work. You can permit or deny users the right to view the data in specific tables of the database.

- Allowing only authorized persons to add or edit information in the database. Permissions in Access are multilevel; you can selectively allow users to edit tables or alter their structure, as well as edit or create their own applications.

- Easing the creation of data entry, editing, display, and reporting applications that efficiently serve the needs of the users of the database. The design of the RDBMS's front-end features determines the ease with which new applications are created or existing ones can be modified. You have seen in the preceding chapters that Access is especially adept as a front-end application generator.

The first two objectives are independent of the database manager you choose. The RDBMS influences or determines the other objectives. Operating speed, data validation, data security, and application creation are limited by the capabilities built into the RDBMS and the computer environment under which it operates. If your database is shared on a network, you need to consider the security features of the network operating system and the client-server database system (if one is used) in the security strategy.

The Process of Database Design

The process of designing a relational database system consists of 10 basic steps:

1. Identifying the objects (data sources) that the database system is to represent

2. Discovering associations between the objects (when you have more than one object)

3. Determining the significant properties and behaviors of the objects

4. Ascertaining how the properties of the objects relate to one another

5. Creating a preliminary data dictionary to define the tables that comprise the database

6. Designating the relationships between database tables based on the associations between the data objects contained in the tables, and incorporating this information in the data dictionary

7. Establishing the types of updates and transactions that create and modify the data in the tables, including any necessary data integrity requirements

8. Determining how to use indexes to speed up query operations without excessively slowing down the addition of data to tables or consuming excessive amounts of disk space

9. Deciding who can access and who can modify data in each table (data security), and altering the structure of the tables if necessary to assure data security

10. Documenting the design of the database as a whole, completing data dictionaries for the database as a whole and each table it contains; and writing procedures for database maintenance, including file backup and restoration

Each step in the design process depends on preceding steps. The sections in this chapter follow steps 1 through 8 in sequence. Database security is the subject of Chapter 25, "Securing Multiuser Network Applications."

The Object-Oriented Approach to Database Design

Databases contain information about objects that exist in the real world. These objects may be people, books in a library, paper invoices or sales orders, maps, money in bank accounts, or printed circuit boards. Such objects are *tangible*. Whatever the object, it must have a physical representation, even if only an image on a computer display that never finds its way to the printer, as in the mythical "paperless office." References to objects in this book, not preceded by a word describing the type of object such as "table object" or "OLE object," indicate real-world, tangible objects.

Tangible objects possess *properties* and *behavior*, just as the OLE objects discussed in Chapter 19, "Using OLE 2.0," have properties and methods. This combination might appear to be applicable only to databases of persons, not books or bank balances; however, all database objects other than those in archival databases have both properties and behavior. Archival databases are used to store information that never changes—new data is simply added to such databases. An example of an archival database is one containing the text of previously published newspapers.

Considering Static and Dynamic Properties of Objects

An object's properties determine the content of a database or table that contains object representations of the same type. Books are assigned subject codes, derived from the Dewey decimal system. Modern books have an identifying ISBN code, and most now have a Library of Congress catalog number. These numbers are properties of a book, as are the title, author, number of pages, and binding type. Such properties are *static*: they are the same whether the book is in the stacks of a library or checked out by a cardholder. Customer information for a bank account, such as account number, name, and address, also is considered static, even though customers occasionally change addresses. Book check-out status and bank account balances are *dynamic* properties: they change from day to day or hour to hour.

Describing Data Entities and Their Attributes

A single object, including all of its static properties, is called a *data entity*. Each individual data entity must be unique so that you can distinguish it from others. A bank's checking account customer is a data entity, for example, but money in the customer's account is not, because the money cannot be uniquely identified. Because a customer may have more than one account, a social security number or federal employer identification number doesn't suffice as a unique identifier; an account number must be assigned to ensure the uniqueness of each customer data entity.

Deposit slips and checks are objects that are represented in the database as other data entities that *relate* to the customer entity. Check numbers aren't unique enough to distinguish them as entities; many different customers might have checks numbered 1001. Combining the customer number and the check number doesn't suffice as a unique identifier because different banking firms might use the same customer number to identify different people. The bank identification number, customer number, and the check number together uniquely identify a debit entity. Each check contains this information printed in magnetic ink. The amount property of each debit (check) or credit (deposit) entity is used to adjust the balance in the customer's account by simple subtraction and addition, a process called a *transaction*.

You wouldn't want to wait while an Automated Transaction Machine (ATM) calculated your balance by processing every transaction since you opened your account. Therefore, a *derived* static property, the last statement balance, can be included in the customer data entity and updated once per month. Only last-statement-to-date transactions need be processed to determine the current balance—a dynamic, *calculated* property. In figure 23.1, lines connect static properties of bank account objects to the data entities derived from them. Properties of objects included in data entities, such as account number and customer name, are called *attributes*.

Accounting for the Behavior of Objects with Methods

The behaviors of related database objects determine the characteristics of transactions in which their data entities participate. Books in a library may be acquired, checked out, returned, and lost. Bank account behavior is very easy to describe: A customer opens the account, deposit transactions and interest accumulations (credits) increase the account balance, and writing checks, withdrawing cash from an ATM, and incurring bank charges (debits) reduce the balance. Crediting or debiting a bank account is an example of a transaction. Transactions occur in response to *events*, such as making a deposit or withdrawal at an ATM. Access implements transactions by using *methods* in response to events initiated by the user, such as opening a form or clicking a command button.

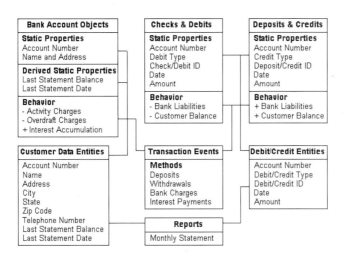

Fig. 23.1
Relationships between objects, entities, events, and methods in a banking database.

In conventional relational databases, you can represent tangible objects and object properties as data entities, but not object's real-world behavior. The OLE Object field data type, described in Chapter 13, "Designing Custom Multitable Forms," is an exception to this rule. The behavior of an OLE data object is determined by the methods available in the OLE server that were used to create it or add it to the OLE Object field. With conventional data entities, you emulate the behavior of tangible objects by using the methods that you incorporate into your applications.

Programs that you write using the RDBMS's native language implement database methods. In the case of Access, macros consisting of one or more *actions*, or Access Basic functions and procedures, implement the methods. A macro action is a prepackaged set of methods designed for a specific purpose. If one of the standard actions doesn't fit your requirements, you can use the RunCode() macro action to use Access Basic functions that include the methods you need. Alternatively, you can execute an Access function or invoke an event-handling procedure directly from the event property. As you learned in Part IV, "Powering Access with Macros," the events that you can use to initiate macro action methods are listed in the properties windows of forms, reports, and control objects.

Access is unique among today's PC database managers because it saves the macros and programs that you create for a database within the database file itself, not in separate .SC, .PRG, or .EXE files as do other PC RDBMSs. Access tables have self-contained properties and methods; other PC RDBMSs require separate programs to validate data, display status text, and create indexes. Therefore, Access database files and the tables they contain conform to the object "paradigm"—a synonym for the word "model" that has become an object-oriented cliché.

Combining Different Entities in a Single Table

You can include representations of different types of objects in a single table as long as you can represent their properties and behavior in the same manner and yet distinguish the different object types. For example, checks and debits are shown as a single data-object type in figure 23.1, although one originates from a paper check and the other from an Electronic Funds Transfer debit. A Debit Type field can indicate the different sources. You can combine cash deposits and transfers from a savings account into a single data-entity type in a Credits table. You might want to combine both Debits and Credits in a single table, which you can do by using different codes for Debit Types and Credit Types. To identify a debit or credit uniquely, you need to include fields for bank ID, customer number, debit/credit type, and a transaction number. Although a check number can serve as the transaction number, the system must assign transaction numbers to other types of transactions, such as those conducted at ATMs. Access can use a counter field to add a unique transaction number to each data entity, including checks. The check number becomes another attribute.

Database Terminology

The terms used to describe formally a database and the elements that comprise it derive from four different sources. The data-description language, of which *entity* and *attribute* are members, derives from the terminology of statistics. Another set of terms, which describe the same set of elements, is based on computer terminology and relates to how the elements are stored within disk files. Query by example introduced new terms to the language of databases—for example, row, column, and cell—and Structured Query Language adopted these terms. Table 23.1 compares words that are used for data description, in QBE and SQL, and for describing data-storage methodologies employed by Access, xBase, and Paradox. The Access Basic language takes an object-oriented approach to programming, so table 23.1 also includes terms applicable to object-oriented programming (OOP).

Table 23.1   A Comparison of Data-Description and Data-Storage Terminology

Data Description	QBE and SQL	Object-Oriented	Access Storage	xBase/Paradox
Heterogeneous Universe	Database	Base Object Class	File	Directory
Universe (homogeneous)	Table	Object Class	Table (Sub-File)	Data File
Entity (object, instance)	Row	Data Object	Record	Record
Attribute	Cell	Object Property	Field	Field
Attribute Data Type	Datatype	Data Type	Field Data Type	Field Type
Attribute Domain	Validation Rule	Enumeration	Validation Rule	Valid Statement
Attribute Value	Cell Value	Property Value	Field Value	Field Value
Identifier	Primary Key	Property Value	Key, Index	Index File

The real-world object is the basic source of information that is represented in a database as an entity. In explaining the terms included in table 23.1, therefore, the following definition list begins with an entity, breaks it down into its component parts, and then establishes its position in the hierarchy of databases and tables.

- *Entity.* A unique representation of a single real-world object, created using the values of its attributes in computer-readable form. To ensure uniqueness, one or more of an entity's attributes must have values unlike the corresponding values of any other entity of the same class. An entity corresponds to a *row* in QBE and SQL, or a *record* in data-storage terminology. Entities are also called *data entities, data objects, data instances,* or *instances.*

- *Attribute.* A significant property of a real-world object. Every attribute carries a value that assists in identifying the entity of which it is a part and distinguishing the entity from other members of the same entity class. Attributes are contained in *fields* (data-storage terminology) or *columns* (QBE and SQL). An attribute also is called a *cell* or *data cell,* terms that describe the intersection of a row and a column or a field and a record.

■ *Attribute data type.* Basic attribute data types consist of all numeric (integer, floating-point, and so forth) and string (text or alphanumeric) data types without embedded spaces or separating punctuation. The string data type can contain letters, numbers, and special characters (such as those used in languages other than English). An attribute with a basic attribute data type is indivisible and is called an *atomic* type. Text data types with spaces or other separating punctuation characters are called *composite attribute data types*. You can divide most composite types into basic data types by *parsing*. Parsing means to separate a composite attribute into basic attributes. For example, you can parse "Smith, Dr. John D., Jr." to Last Name (Smith), Title (Dr), First Name (John), Middle Initial (D), and Suffix (Jr) basic attribute types. Special field types, such as Memo, Binary Large Object (BLOB), and OLE, are composite attribute data types that cannot be parsed to basic data types by conventional methods. You cannot, therefore, create Access indexes that include Memo and OLE attribute data types; only attributes with basic attribute data types can be indexed.

■ *Attribute domain.* The allowable range of values for an attribute of a given attribute data type. The attribute data type determines the domain unless the domain is limited by a process external to the data in the table. As an example of attribute domain limitation, the domain of an employee age attribute that has an integer data type might be limited by a data validation method to any integer greater than 13 and less than 90. In object-oriented terms, the domain consists of an *enumeration* of acceptable values. A days-of-the-week enumeration (the domain of days) consists of a list of its members: Monday, Tuesday, Wednesday, and so forth. Access validation rules, stored in tables, maintain *domain integrity*, limiting data entry to limits set by the data validation expression.

■ *Attribute value.* The smallest indivisible unit of data in an entity. Attribute values are limited to those within the attribute domain. *Cell value* and *data value* are synonyms for attribute value.

■ *Identifier.* An attribute or combination of attributes required to uniquely identify a specific entity (and no others). Identifiers are called *primary-key field(s)* in Access and are used to create the primary index of the entities. When an entity's attribute values are duplicated in other entities' corresponding attributes, you need to combine various attributes to ensure a unique identifier for the entity. When more than one attribute is used as an identifier, the key fields are called a *composite* or *compound* primary key.

■ *Homogeneous universe.* The collection (set) of all data entities of a single data entity type. The data entities must have an identical set of attributes, attribute data types, and attribute domains. This set corresponds to an Access or Paradox *table*, or a *data file* in xBase. The set also is called an *entity class* or *entity type*, and its members are sometimes called *entity instances*, or just *instances*.

■ *Heterogeneous universe.* The collection (set) of related entity classes comprising related homogeneous universes—the *database*. A database is stored as a single file in Access and most client-server databases. Paradox and xBase store databases as collections of related files, usually in a single directory. A dBASE catalog is a file that includes records to identify the individual files that comprise the entire database. Access databases include a special table that catalogs the objects that the databases contain. You can reveal the content of the catalog by using the techniques described in the "Access's Integrated Data Dictionary System" section, near the end of this chapter.

Much of the formal terminology used to describe data objects in relational databases is quite technical and rather abstract. You need to understand the meaning of these terms, however, when you create the data models that form the basis of the design of your database.

Types of Tables and Keys in Relational Databases

Specific to relational databases are certain types of tables and keys that enable relationships between tables. Understanding these tables and keys is essential to comprehending relational databases and the rules of data normalization, which are discussed in the "Normalizing Data to the Relational Model" section. The following list defines the various relational keys and tables:

■ *Base table.* In a relational database, a base table is the table that incorporates one or more columns of an object's properties and contains the primary key that uniquely identifies that object as a data entity. A base table must have a primary key. Base tables are often called *primary tables* because of the requirement for a primary key.

■ *Relation table.* A table that is used to provide linkages between other tables and isn't a base table (because it doesn't incorporate properties of an object or because it doesn't have a primary key field) is called a *relation table*. Key fields in relation tables each must be foreign keys, related to a primary key field in a base table.

Technically, a true relation table is comprised wholly of foreign keys and contains no independent data entities. The Order Details table of the Northwind Traders database is an example of a relation table that contains data values that aren't foreign keys (the Unit Price and Quantity fields, for example). Its Order ID field is related to the field of the same name in the Orders table. Likewise, the Product ID field is related to the Product ID field of the Products table. Although Order Details has a composite key, it isn't a true primary key; its purpose is to prevent duplication of a product entry in a specific order.

- *Primary key*. A primary key consists of a set of values that uniquely specifies a row of a base table, which in Access is the primary table. For any primary-key value, one and only one row in the table matches this value. You can base the primary key on a single field if each data cell's value is unique at all times.

- *Candidate keys*. Any column or group of columns that meets the requirements for a primary key is a candidate to become the primary key for the table. Name and social security number are candidate keys to identify a person in the United States; however, social security number is the more appropriate choice because two people can have the same name but not the same valid social security number.

- *Composite keys*. If you need data from more than one column of the table to meet the uniqueness requirement of a primary key, the key is said to be a composite or a *concatenated key*.

- *Foreign keys*. A foreign key is a column whose values correspond to those contained in a primary key, or the far left portion of a composite primary key, in another related table. A foreign key can consist of one column or a group of columns (a *composite foreign key*). If the length of a foreign key is less than the corresponding primary key, the key is called a *partial* or *truncated foreign key*.

Examples of the preceding keys and tables occur in the discussions of normal forms in the "Normalizing Data to the Relational Model" section, later in this chapter. But first, the following sections examine the process of data modeling.

Data Modeling

The first step in designing a database is to determine which objects to represent within the database and which of the objects' properties to include. This process is called *data modeling*. The purpose of a data model is to create a logical representation of the data structure that is used to create a database.

Data modeling can encompass an entire organization, a division or department, or a single type of object. Models that deal with objects, rather than the tables that you later create from the objects, are called *conceptual data models*.

Figure 23.2 illustrates two different approaches (conceptual data models) to database design: the bottom-up approach to create an application database and the top-down method to develop subject databases. These two approaches, discussed in the following sections, result in databases with quite different structures.

Application Databases

You can base data models on specific needs for data presented in a particular manner. For such a needs-based model, you can use the *bottom-up* approach and start with a view of the data on a display, a printed report, or both, as shown in the left-hand example of figure 23.2. This approach results in an *application database*. If you are creating a simple database for your own use or dealing with a single type of data object, the *bottom-up* approach may suffice because the presentation requirements and the properties of the objects involved are usually well defined. The problem with the bottom-up approach is that it leads to multiple individual databases that may duplicate each other's information. Several persons or groups within an organization might have a requirement for an application database that includes, for example, a customers table. When a new customer is added or data for an existing customer is changed in one application database, you need to update each of the other application databases. The updating process is time-consuming and subject to error.

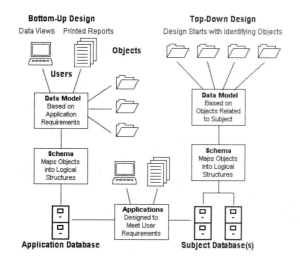

Fig. 23.2

A comparison of bottom-up and top-down database designs.

VI

Advanced Techniques

Conceptual data models, such as those shown in figure 23.2, are independent of the database manager you use and the type of database files it accesses. Therefore, the same data model accommodates databases in Access's native format, as well as the others with which Access is compatible. Data models aren't connected with any programming language or tools used to create applications. The applications box in figure 23.2 isn't a component of conventional data models, but is added to show where application design fits into the overall picture.

Subject Databases

A better approach is to base the design of the database on groups of objects that are related by subject matter. For a manufacturing firm, tables are usually grouped into databases devoted to a single department or function. The following lists some database examples:

- *Sales* database consisting of customer, sales order, sales quota, product discount, and invoice tables

- *Production* database including product, price, parts, vendor, and cost accounting tables

- *Personnel* database with employee, payroll, and benefits tables (large firms may include tables relating to health care providers and employment applicants)

- *Accounting* database incorporating general ledger and various journal tables

Databases that consist of tables relating to a single class of subjects or functions are called *subject databases*. Even if you are creating the first database application for a small organization, starting with an overall plan for the organization's total information requirements in subject databases pays long-term dividends. If you decide or are assigned to create an invoicing application, for instance, you can establish sales, production, and personnel databases from the beginning, rather than have to split up a single invoice database at a later time and rewrite all your applications to access tables within multiple databases.

Subject databases require *top-down* design, depicted in the right-hand diagram of figure 23.2. In this case, the properties of the data objects, not the applications used with them, determine the design. Designing subject databases involves creating a diagram of the relevant objects and the associations between them, and then creating models for each database involved. You distribute the model diagrams to users and then interview them to determine their information needs based on the content of the model databases.

Diagrammatic Data Models

Large, complex data models resemble the work-flow and paper-flow diagrams commonly used in analyzing organizations' administrative procedures. If you have such diagrams or descriptions, they make the data-modeling process much easier. Generating an organization-wide data model may involve a substantial amount of research to determine the needs of the organization as a whole and of individuals using specialized applications. In many cases, users and potential users aren't able to define what information they need or how they want to see it presented.

Many methods exist of creating diagrams to represent data models. One of the more useful methods is the Entity-Relationship (E-R) diagram, developed by Peter Chen in 1976 and expanded on by David R. McClanahan in a series of articles entitled "Database Foundations: Conceptual Designs" in *DBMS* magazine (see fig. 23.3). You can use E-R diagrams to represent relationships between objects and depict their behavior.

Fig. 23.3
An Entity-Relationship diagram of two data entities from figure 23.1.

Data entities are enclosed within rectangles, data attributes within ovals, and relations between entities within diamonds. Relations between database objects, at the conceptual stage, can be defined by their behavior; therefore, E-R diagrams include at least one verb whose object, unless otherwise indicated, is to the right of the diamond relation symbol. You add symbols to the diagram as the model's detail increases. One of the advantages of the E-R diagram is that you can use it to represent the conceptual design of very large systems with multiple databases in a relatively small amount of space.

Database Schema

A graphic description of the layout of tables in the form of bars that contain their field names and show a simplified version of relationships between them can be employed to aid users to grasp the concept of the database. A diagram that shows the logical representation of data is called a *schema*. A schema, such as the one shown in figure 23.4 for an ocean shipping line, is independent of the RDBMS used to implement the database.

VI

Advanced Techniques

In figure 23.4, the primary keys are shaded, and the relations between the table keys are indicated by lines that connect the keys. Foreign keys are unshaded, except when they correspond to a component of a composite primary key. The descriptions shown between the bars are optional; they are useful in describing the relationships to users. You can expand a schema of this type to include the source documents involved, the reports to be generated, and the applications that pertain to all or a portion of the tables.

Fig. 23.4
The schema for the operations database of a shipping line.

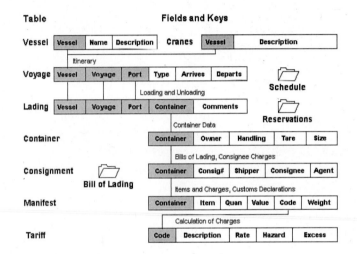

External Determinants of Database Design

Finding the data objects that provide the information to meet all of an organization's requirements may require extensive detective work. Many objects may not be available within the organization itself. For instance, if you are developing a database application that involves geographic positioning (called *geocoding*), you may need map tables such as the U.S. Census Bureau's TIGER/Line files or tables derived from them by others. Images to be incorporated as OLE objects may not be available in file formats that are compatible with your OLE server applications and require file-type conversion. If the accounting department is using packaged accounting software, you need to incorporate representations of the structure of its database into your model. In this case, you also need to plan how to exchange information with the accounting data, but you need not include the access methodology in your conceptual data model.

Using CASE Tools to Create Access Databases

Computer-aided software engineering (CASE) tools are available from several publishers for designing and then automatically creating the structure of client-server relational databases, such as SQL Server, ORACLE, and SQLBase. CASE tools that run under Windows let you use graphic techniques, such as Entity-Relationship diagrams, to design the structure of the tables and establish relationships between the tables. Database CASE tools save much time and prevent many errors when you implement a large and complex relational database.

Most case tools contain a *repository* that stores information about table design, primary and foreign key fields, constraints (validation rules) for fields, and types of relations between the tables. The repository is a database maintained by the CASE application itself. You can print database schema and generate data dictionaries from records in the repository. When your database design appears satisfactory, the CASE tool translates the data in the repository to an SQL Data Definition Language (DDL) statement. You send the DDL statement to the client-server RDBMS on the server. This RDBMS can be used to create the entire database or just add tables to the database. SQL's DDL commands are one of the subjects of the next chapter.

At the time of this edition's printing, only one commercial CASE tool was available for creating Access databases; InfoModeler, published by Asymetrix, Incorporated, of Bellevue, Washington, uses a new approach to designing databases called *Object Role Modeling* (ORM). ORM lets you express the design of a database in simple, English terms through a language called *Formal Object Role Modeling Language* (FORML). InfoModeler translates FORML statements into a graphic schema, related to but more flexible than E-R diagrams. Figure 23.5 shows a portion of the ORM database diagram for the tutorial application of InfoModeler, a classic Instructor-Course-Student database.

InfoModeler lets you print the ORM graphic schema and creates a data dictionary for the database. This reduces the time required to describe the structure of the database to others, as well as much of the drudgery of creating a comprehensive data dictionary.

Fig. 23.5
An Object Role
Modeling diagram
for an Access
database.

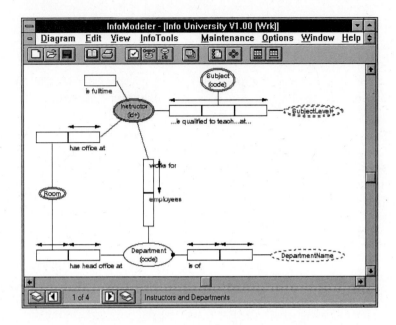

Normalizing Data to the Relational Model

Up to this point, most of the subject matter in this chapter has been applicable to any type of database—hierarchical, relational, or even the new class of object database systems. However, because Access is a relational database management system, the balance of the chapter is devoted to relational databases. Because Access fully implements the relational model in its native database structure and you can attach tables from other relational RDBMSs, including client-server tables, to Access databases, the discussion that follows is general in nature and applies to any database system with which Access is compatible or for which you have the appropriate Open Database Connectivity (ODBC) driver.

The theory of relational database design is founded in a branch of mathematics called *set theory*, with a great deal of combinatorial analysis and some statistical methodology added. The set of rules and symbols by which relational databases are defined is called *relational algebra*. This chapter doesn't delve into the symbolic representation of relational algebra, nor does it require you to comprehend advanced mathematics. The chapter does, however, introduce you to many of the terms used in relational algebra for the sake of consistency with advanced texts that you may want to consult on the subject of database design.

Normalization Rules

Normalization is a formalized procedure by which data attributes are grouped into tables and tables are grouped into databases. The purposes of normalization include the following:

- Eliminating duplicated information in tables

- Accommodating future changes in the structure of tables

- Minimizing the impact of change on user applications that access the data

Normalization is done in steps, the first three and most common steps Dr. E. F. Codd described in his 1972 paper, "Further Normalization of the Data Base Relational Model." These steps are depicted in figure 23.6. The following sections describe each of the five steps that comprise the normalizing process.

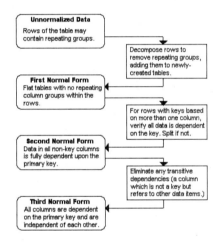

Fig. 23.6

A graphic representation of relational database normalization to the third normal form.

First Normal Form

First normal form requires that tables be flat and contain no repeating groups. A flat table has only two dimensions—length (number of records or rows) and width (number of fields or columns)—and cannot contain data cells with more than one value. For a single cell to contain more than one data value, the representation of the cell's contents requires a third dimension, depth, to display the multiple data values. Flat tables and the flat-file databases referred to in prior chapters are similar in that both have two dimensions. Flat-file databases, however, consist of only one table and have no restrictions on the content of the data cells within the table.

VI

Advanced Techniques

An example of unnormalized data for a shipping line appears in figure 23.7. This presentation often is seen in the schedules published by transportation firms where the stops are displayed across the page. This example is representative of a schedule created by importing the worksheet file that was used to create the printed version of the schedule. In the various examples of tables that follow, missing borders are the equivalent of an ellipsis; that is, a missing right border indicates that additional columns (fields) exist beyond the far right column, and a missing bottom border means that more rows (records) follow. (Those readers who are mariners will recognize the example as a mythical schedule for the vessels of the former Pacific Far East Lines.)

Fig. 23.7

A partial schedule of voyages for a shipping line.

Vessel	Name	Voyage	Embarks	From	Arrives	Port	Departs	Arrives	Port	Departs
528	Japan Bear	9203W	5/31/92	SFO	6/6/92	HNL	6/8/92	7/15/92	OSA	7/18/92
603	Korea Bear	9203W	6/05/92	OAK	6/19/92	OSA	6/21/92	6/25/92	INC	6/28/92
531	China Bear	9204W	6/20/92	LAX	7/10/92	PAP	7/11/92	8/28/92	SYD	9/2/92
528	Japan Bear	9204W	8/20/92	SFO	8/27/92	HNL	8/29/92	9/30/92	OSA	10/2/92

Because the vessels stop at a number of ports, the Arrives, Port, and Departs columns are duplicated for each stop in the voyage. This type of data structure is allowed in COBOL, where the repeating group (Arrives, Port, and Departs) OCCURS any number of TIMES, but not in relational databases. The data in the preceding schedule isn't in first normal form because it contains repeating groups. The table must be *decomposed* (divided) into two tables, therefore, with the repeating groups (shown in shaded type in figure 23.7) removed from the Schedule table and placed in two new tables, Ports and Vessel Voyages, as shown in figure 23.8.

Fig. 23.8

The Vessel Voyages and Ports tables created from the Schedule table.

Vessel	Name	Voyage	Embarks	From
528	Japan Bear	9203W	5/31/92	SFO
603	Korea Bear	9203W	6/5/92	OAK
531	China Bear	9204W	6/20/92	LAX
528	Japan Bear	9204W	8/20/92	SFO

Arrives	Port	Departs
6/6/92	HNL	6/8/92
6/19/92	OSA	6/21/92
7/10/92	PAP	7/11/92
8/27/92	HNL	8/29/92
7/15/92	OSA	7/18/92
6/25/92	INC	6/28/92
8/28/92	SYD	9/2/92
9/30/92	OSA	10/2/92

Now you need to provide for a link between the Ports and Vessel Voyages tables to retain the relationship between the data. Because this shipping line numbers voyages for each vessel with the year and voyage for the year, as well as the general direction of travel (9204W is the fourth voyage of 1992, westbound), both Vessel and Voyage need to be used to relate the two tables. Neither Vessel nor Voyage is sufficient in itself because a vessel has multiple voyages during the year and the voyage numbers used here recur for other vessels. Because you must create a new Ports table to meet the requirements of the first normal form, you have the chance to order the columns in the order of their significance. Columns used to establish relations are usually listed first, in the sequence in which they appear in the composite primary key, when more than one column is included in the key (see fig. 23.9).

Vessel	Voyage	Port	Arrives	Departs
528	9203W	HNL	6/6/92	6/8/92
603	9203W	OSA	6/19/92	6/21/92
531	9204W	PAP	7/10/92	7/11/92
528	9204W	HNL	8/27/92	8/29/92
528	9203W	OSA	7/15/92	7/18/92
603	9203W	INC	6/25/92	6/28/92
531	9204W	SYD	8/28/92	9/2/92
528	9204W	OSA	9/30/92	10/2/92

Fig. 23.9
Linking fields added to the Ports relation table.

Next, you establish the key field(s) for the Ports table that uniquely identify a record in the table. Clearly, Vessel and Voyage must be included because these columns constitute the relation to the Vessel Voyages table. You need to add the Port field to create a unique key (Vessel + Voyage can have duplicate values). Vessel + Voyage + Port creates a unique composite primary key because the combination takes into account stopping at a port twice—when returning eastbound, the voyage carries an "E" suffix. You need a primary key for the Ports table because other tables may be dependent on this table.

> **Note**
>
> A spreadsheet application, such as Microsoft Excel, can speed up the process of normalizing existing data, especially when the data contains repeating groups. Import the data into a worksheet; then cut and paste the data in the repeating groups into a new worksheet. When the data for both of the tables is normalized, save the worksheets and then import the files to Access tables. This process is usually faster than creating make-table queries to generate normalized tables.

Second Normal Form

Second normal form requires that data in all nonkey columns be fully dependent on the primary key and on each element (column) of the primary key when it is a composite primary key. *Fully dependent* means that the data value in each nonkey column of a record is determined uniquely by the value of the primary key. If a composite primary key is required to establish the uniqueness of a record, the same rule applies to each value of the fields that comprise the composite key of the record. Your table must be in first normal form before examining it for conformity to the second normal form. The second normal form removes much of the data redundancy that is likely to occur in a first-normal table.

Returning to the Vessel Voyages table, you can see that it requires a composite key, Vessel + Voyage, to create a unique key because the vessel number (and vessel name) recurs. However, when you create such a key, you observe that the Vessel and Name aren't dependent on the entire primary key because neither is determined by Voyage. You also find that the vessel name occurs for each of a vessel's voyages; for example, the *Japan Bear* appears twice. This lack of dependency violates the rules of the second normal form and requires Vessel Voyages to be split into two tables, Vessels and Voyages. One row is required in the Vessels table for each ship and one row in the Voyages table for each voyage made by each ship (eastbound and westbound directions are considered separate voyages for database purposes). As was the case for Ports, a unique key is required to relate voyages to the vessel, so the vessel number column is added to the Voyages table, as shown in figure 23.10.

Fig. 23.10

The Vessels and Voyages tables created from the Vessel Voyages table.

Vessel	Vessel Name
528	Japan Bear
603	Korea Bear
531	China Bear

Vessel	Voyage	Embarks	From
528	9203W	5/31/92	SFO
603	9203W	6/5/92	OAK
531	9204W	6/20/92	LAX
528	9204W	8/20/92	SFO

Third Normal Form

The third normal form requires that all nonkey columns of a table be dependent on the table's primary key and independent of one another. Tables must conform to the first and second normal forms to qualify for third-normal-form status.

Your Vessels and Voyages tables are now in third normal form because there are no repeating groups of columns and the data in nonkey columns is dependent on the primary key field. The nonkey columns of Ports, Arrives, and Departs are dependent on the composite key (Vessel + Voyage + Port) and independent of one another. Ports, therefore, meets the requirements of first, second, and third normal forms. The departure date is independent of the arrival date because the difference between the two is based on the vessel's lading into and out of the port, the availability of berths and container cranes, and the weather.

To demonstrate normalization to the third normal form, suppose that you want to identify the officers of the vessel, including the master, chief engineer, and first mate, in the database. Your first impulse might be to add their employee numbers, the primary key of an Employee table, to the Vessels table (see fig. 23.11).

Vessel	Vessel Name	Master	Chief	1st Mate
528	Japan Bear	01023	01155	01367
603	Korea Bear	00955	01203	00823
531	China Bear	00721	00912	01251

Fig. 23.11

A table with a transitive dependency between vessels and crew members.

This table violates the third normal rule because none of the officers assigned to a vessel is dependent on the vessel itself. This type of dependency is called *transitive*. The master's, chief's, and first mate's maritime licenses allow them to act in their respective capacities on any vessel for which the license is valid. Any officer may be assigned to other vessels as the need arises, or remain on board for only a portion of the voyage.

One method of removing the transitive dependency might be to add the employee number columns to the Vessel Voyages table. This method doesn't provide a satisfactory solution, however, because the vessel may arrive at a port with one group of crew members and depart with another group. In addition, you need to specify the crew members who remain with the vessel while it is in port. A relation table, such as that shown for the *Japan Bear* in figure 23.12, solves the problem. Duplicate values in the Port and To (destination port) fields designate records for crew members responsible for the vessel while in port. The Crew table of figure 23.12 qualifies as a relation table because all of its fields correspond to primary keys or parts of primary keys in the base tables—Vessels, Voyages, Ports, and Employees.

Vessel	Voyage	Port	To	Master	Chief	1st Mate
528	9203W	SFO	HNL	01023	01156	01367
528	9203W	HNL	HNL	01023	01156	01367
528	9203W	HNL	OSA	01023	01156	01367
528	9203W	OSA	OSA	01023	01156	01367
528	9203W	OSA	INC	01023	01156	01367

Fig. 23.12

Removing transitive dependency with a relation table.

All of your tables are now flat, contain no duplicate information other than that in the columns used for keys, and conform to the first through third normal form.

Fourth Normal Form

Many database designers disregard the fourth and fifth normal forms; those designers consider the fourth and fifth forms too esoteric or applicable only in specialized cases. Disregarding the fourth normal form often results in poorly designed databases, but not necessarily malfunctioning ones.

The fourth normal form requires that independent data entities not be stored in the same table when many-to-many relationships exist between these entities. The table of figure 23.12 violates the fourth normal form because many-to-many relationships exist between the Vessel and the fields that identify crew members. The fourth normal form is discussed in the "Many-to-Many Relations and the Fourth Normal Form" section later in this chapter because it is the only normalization rule that is dependent on a specific type of relationship.

Fifth Normal Form and Combined Entities

The fifth normal form requires that you be able to reconstruct exactly the original table from those tables into which it was decomposed. Re-creating the Excel spreadsheet from the tables in the example in Chapter 15 demonstrates compliance with the fifth normal form. Fifth normal form requires that the tables comply with the rules for third normal form and, when many-to-many relationships are present, with the rule for the fourth normal form.

The Voyages table appears quite similar to that of Ports. The From column is equivalent to Port, and Embarks is the same as Departure. Therefore, you can move the data in the Voyages table to the Ports table and delete the Voyages table. Figure 23.13 shows the new Ports table. The rows from the Voyages table don't have values in the Arrives column because they represent points of departure.

Fig. 23.13

Records from the Voyages table appended to the Ports table.

Vessel	Voyage	Port	Arrives	Departs
528	9203W	HNL	6/6/92	6/8/92
603	9203W	OSA	6/19/92	6/21/92
531	9204W	PAP	7/10/92	7/11/92
528	9204W	HNL	8/27/92	8/29/92
528	9203W	OSA	7/15/92	7/18/92
603	9203W	INC	6/25/92	6/28/92
531	9204W	SYD	8/28/92	9/2/92
528	9204W	OSA	9/30/92	10/2/92
528	9203W	SFO		5/31/92
603	9203W	OAK		6/5/92
531	9204W	LAX		6/20/92
528	9204W	SFO		8/20/92

However, you cannot explicitly reconstruct the original table from the combined Voyages and Ports tables in all cases because you cannot distinguish an embarkation row from the other rows by a value in the table. A Null value in the Arrives field is a candidate to distinguish an embarkation, but most PC RDBMSs don't support null values. You eliminate any ambiguity that using a Null value might cause and bring the table into fifth normal form by adding a single-character field, Type, with single-letter codes to define the type of call. In figure 23.14, the codes E and S represent Embarkation and Scheduled call, respectively. Other codes might include M for Maintenance stop and R for Return voyage.

Vessel	Voyage	Port	Type	Arrives	Departs
528	9203W	HNL	S	6/6/92	6/8/92
603	9203W	OSA	S	6/19/92	6/21/92
531	9204W	PAP	S	7/10/92	7/11/92
528	9204W	HNL	S	8/27/92	8/29/92
528	9203W	OSA	S	7/15/92	7/18/92
603	9203W	INC	S	6/25/92	6/28/92
531	9204W	SYD	S	8/28/92	9/2/92
528	9204W	OSA	S	9/30/92	10/2/92
528	9203W	SFO	E		5/31/92
603	9203W	OAK	E		6/5/92
531	9204W	LAX	E		6/20/92
528	9204W	SFO	E		8/20/92

Fig. 23.14
The Type field added to comply with the fifth normal form.

Figure 23.15 demonstrates that you can reconstruct the content of the original Schedule table from the Vessels and Ports tables. Query1 creates the first five columns of the Schedule table by adding the criterion E for the Type field, which isn't shown. You can re-create the remaining columns of the Schedule table from Query2 that uses the S criterion for the Type field.

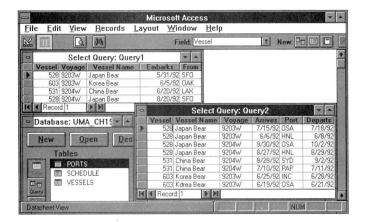

Fig. 23.15
The datasheets of the two queries required to reconstruct the Schedule table.

Types of Relationships

The subject of relationships between entities usually precedes discussions of normalization. Relationships are reserved for the second step in this book, however. You can only create valid relationships between tables that have been structured in accordance with at least the first three normalization rules of relational database design described in the preceding sections. This section describes the four basic types of relationships between tables and employs Entity-Relationship diagrams to depict the relationships graphically.

One-to-One Relations

The simplest relationship between tables is a one-to-one relationship. In such a relationship, the tables have exact one-to-one row correspondence; no row

VI

Advanced Techniques

in one table has more than one corresponding row in the other table. You can combine one-to-one-related tables into a single table consisting of all the tables' columns.

One-to-one relations are often used to divide very wide base tables into narrower ones. You might want to divide a wide table to reduce the time needed to view fields containing specific sets of data, such as the stock prices table in the example of Chapter 15. Often you need to control access to the parts of tables that contain sensitive or confidential data. An example is an employee file; everyone might have read-only access to the employees' names, but only members of the personnel department are authorized to view salary and other payroll information (see fig. 23.16).

Fig. 23.16

Two tables with a one-to-one relationship.

Employee	Position	Last	First	MI
00668	Master	Johansson	Lars	F.
00721	Master	Karlsson	Bo	B.
00885	Chief	MacGregor	Paul	C.
00912	Chief	McDemott	John	R.
00955	Master	Olafson	Karl	T.
01023	Master	Kekkonen	Eino	K.
01156	Chief	McDougal	William	U.
01203	Chief	Kashihara	Matsuo	

Employee	Salary
00668	6500.00
00721	6250.00
00885	5100.00
00912	5000.00
00955	6100.00
01023	6050.00
01156	4900.00
01203	4850.00

If you are sharing tables on a network, dividing large tables can improve response time when many users are updating the tables' data. Chapter 25, "Securing Multiuser Network Applications," explains the reason for the speed improvement.

Figure 23.17 shows the Entity-Relationship diagram for the Employees and Salaries tables. The 1s added to each side of the relation diamond indicate the one-to-one relationship. The participation of entities in relations can be mandatory or optional. Optional relations are symbolized by a circle drawn on the line connecting the optional entity with the relation diamond. In the figure, the Paid-Salaries relation is optional because some employees can be paid on an hourly basis and linked to a Wages table. Tables with mandatory one-to-one relationships are base tables. A table with an optional one-to-one relation to a base table is a related table. Multiple tables with one-to-one relations where the corresponding records in the other tables are optional can reduce the database's disk space requirement.

Fig. 23.17

An E-R diagram for an optional one-to-one relationship.

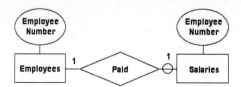

Another example of a one-to-one relationship is that between an xBase memo field and a corresponding entry in a memo (DBT) file. Access treats free-text as the content of a data cell in the table, so no relationship is involved.

One-to-Many Relations

One-to-many relations link a single row in one table with two or more rows in another through a relation between the primary key of the base table and the corresponding foreign key in the related tables. Although the foreign key in the table containing the many relationships may be a component of a composite primary key, it is a foreign key for the purposes of the relationship. One-to-many relations are the most common type of relation.

The one-to-many relation shown in figure 23.18 links all records in the Ports table to one record in the Vessels table. The one-to-many relation enables you to display all records in the Ports table for scheduled ports of call of the *Japan Bear*.

Vessel	Vessel Name		Vessel	Voyage	Port	Type	Arrives	Departs
528	Japan Bear		528	9203W	HNL	S	6/6/92	6/8/92
			528	9204W	HNL	S	8/27/92	8/29/92
			528	9203W	OSA	S	7/15/92	7/18/92
			528	9204W	OSA	S	9/30/92	10/2/92
			528	9203W	SFO	E		5/31/92
			528	9204W	SFO	E		8/20/92

Fig. 23.18
A one-to-many relationship between the Vessels and Ports tables.

The E-R diagram of figure 23.19 expresses this relationship, where the degree of the Vessel entity relations between the two tables are indicated by the "1" and "m" adjacent to their entities.

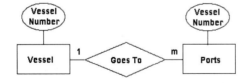

Fig. 23.19
The E-R diagram for the one-to-many relation of figure 23.17.

Many-to-One Relations

Many-to-one relations are the converse of the one-to-many type. The many-to-one relation enables you to display the vessel name for any record in the Ports table. If the roles of the participating entities are simply reversed to create the many-to-one relation, the relationship is said to be *reflexive*; that is, the many-to-one relation is the reflection of its one-to-many counterpart (see fig. 23.20). All many-to-one relations in Access are reflexive; you can specify only a one-to-one or one-to-many relation between the primary table and the related table with the two option buttons in Access's Relationship dialog.

Fig. 23.20

The Ports and Vessels tables in a reflexive many-to-one relationship.

Vessel	Voyage	Port	Type	Arrives	Departs
528	9203W	HNL	S	6/6/92	6/8/92
528	9204W	HNL	S	8/27/92	8/29/92
528	9203W	OSA	S	7/15/92	7/18/92
528	9204W	OSA	S	9/30/92	10/2/92
528	9203W	SFO	E		5/31/92
528	9204W	SFO	E		8/20/92

Vessel	Vessel Name
528	Japan Bear

If you select a record on the many side of the relationship, you can display the record corresponding to its foreign key on the one side. E-R diagrams for reflexive relationships are often drawn like the diagram in figure 23.21. Reflexive relationships are indicated by the appropriate form of the verb placed outside the diamond that defines the relation.

Fig. 23.21

The E-R diagram for a reflexive many-to-one relationship.

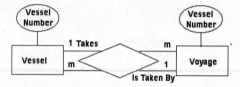

Many-to-Many Relations and the Fourth Normal Form

Many-to-many relationships cannot be expressed as simple relations between two participating entities. You create many-to-many relationships by making a table that has many-to-one relations with two base tables.

The Crews relation table created in the "Third Normal Form" section to assign crew members to legs of the voyage is shown again in figure 23.22. The Crews table creates a many-to-many relationship between the Vessels table, based on the Vessel entity, and the Employees table, based on the employee number entities in the Master, Chief, and 1st Mate fields.

Fig. 23.22

The first version of the Crews relation table.

Vessel	Voyage	Port	To	Master	Chief	1st Mate
528	9203W	SFO	HNL	01023	01156	01367
528	9203W	HNL	HNL	01023	01156	01367
528	9203W	HNL	OSA	01023	01156	01367
528	9203W	OSA	OSA	01023	01156	01367
528	9203W	OSA	INC	01023	01156	01367

The table in figure 23.22 has a many-to-one relation with the Vessels table and a many-to-one relation with the Employees table. This version of the Crews table creates a many-to-many relation between the Vessels and Employees tables. The employees who crew the vessel are independent of one another; any qualified employee can, in theory, be assigned to fill a crew position on any leg of a voyage. The table in figure 23.22 violates the fourth normal form, therefore, because it contains independent entities.

Figure 23.23 shows the restructured Crews relation table needed to assign employees to legs of voyages. The table has one record for each employee for each leg of the voyage.

Employee	Vessel	Voyage	Port	To
01023	528	9203W	SFO	HNL
01156	528	9203W	SFO	HNL
01367	528	9203W	SFO	HNL
01023	528	9203W	HNL	HNL
01156	528	9203W	HNL	HNL
01367	528	9203W	HNL	HNL
01023	528	9203W	HNL	OSA
01156	528	9203W	HNL	OSA
01367	528	9203W	HNL	OSA
01023	528	9203W	OSA	OSA
01156	528	9203W	OSA	OSA
01367	528	9203W	OSA	OSA
01023	528	9203W	OSA	INC
01156	528	9203W	OSA	INC
01367	528	9203W	OSA	INC

Fig. 23.23

The Crews table restructured to fourth normal form.

You can add new entities to this table, provided that the entities are wholly dependent on all the foreign-key fields. An example of a dependent entity is payroll data that might include data attributes such as regular hours worked, overtime hours, and chargeable expenses incurred by each employee on each leg of a voyage. Such entities are called *weak* or *associative* entities because they rely on other base tables for their relevance. The Crews table is no longer considered strictly a relation table when you add associative entities because it no longer consists wholly of fields that constitute foreign keys.

The E-R diagram for the many-to-many relation table relating employees and the legs of a voyage to which the employees are assigned is shown in figure 23.24. The encircled Date connected to the Assigned Crew relation expresses *cardinality:* one employee can be assigned to only one voyage on a given date. The cardinality of the relation, therefore, is based on the departure and arrival dates for the leg. Automatically enforcing the condition that employees not be in more than one place at one time can be accomplished by creating a no-duplicates index consisting of all the Crews table's fields. Associative entities are shown in E-R diagrams as a relation diamond within an entity rectangle. If you add payroll data to the Crews table, an associative entity is

VI

Advanced Techniques

created. Assignment of an employee to a voyage is optional, as indicated by the circled lines; employees may have shore leave, be indisposed, or be assigned to shoreside duties.

Fig. 23.24
An E-R diagram for a many-to-many relationship with an associative entity.

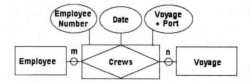

Using graphic schema and Entity-Relationship diagrams when you design an Access database helps ensure that the database meets your initial objectives. Schema also are useful in explaining the structure of your database to its users. E-R diagrams can uncover design errors, such as the failure to normalize tables at least to fourth normal form. Few experiences are more frustrating than having to restructure a large table when you realize its design wasn't fully normalized. Forethought, planning, and diagramming are the watchwords of success in database design.

Working with Data Dictionaries

After you have determined the individual data entities that comprise the tables of your database and established the relations between them, the next step is to prepare a preliminary written description of the database, called a *data dictionary*. Data dictionaries are indispensable to database systems; an undocumented database system is almost impossible to administer and maintain properly. Errors and omissions in database design often are uncovered when you prepare the preliminary data dictionary.

When you have completed and tested your database design, you prepare the final detailed version of the data dictionary. As you add new forms and reports to applications, or modify the existing ones, you update the data dictionary to keep it current. Even if you are making a database for your personal use, a simplified version of a data dictionary pays many dividends on your time investment.

Conventional Data Dictionaries

Data dictionaries contain a text description of the database as a whole, each table it contains, the fields that comprise the table, primary and foreign keys, and values that may be assigned to fields when they contain coded or enumerated information. The purpose and description of each application that uses the database is included. Data dictionaries shouldn't be dependent on the particular RDBMS used to create and manipulate the database. Because data dictionaries are hierarchical in nature, they lend themselves to the use of traditional outline formats that are implemented in Windows word processing applications. The following illustrates the structure of a conventional data dictionary using legal-style outline headings:

1. DATABASE - Proper name and filename

    A text description of the purpose and general content of the database and who may use it. A list of applications that operate on the database is useful, along with references to any other databases that use the information that the database contains. If a graphic schema of the database has been prepared, it appears in this section.

    1.1. DATA AREA - Name of the group of which tables are a member

    When tables are classified by group, such as the Payroll group within the Human Resources database, a description of the group

    1.1.1. TABLE - Individual tables that comprise the data area

    1.1.1.1. PERMISSIONS - User domains with access to the table

    1.1.1.2. RECORD - General definition of the data entities

    1.1.1.2.1. PRIMARY KEY - Field(s) in the primary key

    1.1.1.2.1.1. INDEX - Primary key index specification

    1.1.1.2.2. FOREIGN KEY(S) - Other key fields

    1.1.1.2.2.1 INDEX - Indexes on foreign keys

    1.1.1.2.3. FIELDS - Nonkey fields

    1.1.1.2.3.1 ENUMERATIONS - Valid codes for fields.

Text follows each heading and describes the purpose of the database element to which the heading refers. Subsequent headings include descriptions of the applications that use the database tables, with subheadings for queries, forms, and reports. Captured images of displays and copies of reports add to the usefulness of the data dictionary. Printouts of programming code usually are contained in appendixes. Complete data dictionaries are essential for database maintenance. An alternative format consists of content descriptions of each table in tabular form.

VI

Advanced Techniques

Access's New Integrated Data Dictionary System

Access

2.0

Access 2.0's new Database Documentor add-in library replaces the Database Analyzer library included with Access 1.x. The Documentor creates a report that details the objects and the values of the properties of the objects in the current database. Thus Documentor is a substantial improvement over Analyzer, which only created tables that contained lists of objects and their properties; you had to design your own reports based on the *@ObjectName* tables created by Analyzer, or export the table data to Excel or Word tables to create the dictionary.

> **Note**
>
> The present version of Documentor prints reports but can't export its data to tables or files. You can use the generic printer (TTY.DRV) and print the report to an ASCII text file and then import the file into a word processing application. You need to do a substantial amount of formatting of the resulting text, however, to create a readable data dictionary.

In many cases, Documentor tells you more than you want to know about your database; the full report for all of the objects in NWIND.MDB, for example, generates *hundreds* of pages. Most often, you only want to document your tables and, perhaps, your queries to create a complete data dictionary. The following steps show you how to create a data dictionary with Database Documentor:

1. Open the database you want to document, and then choose Add-Ins from the **F**ile menu and click **D**atabase Documentor. Database Documentor's opening dialog appears, as shown in figure 23.25 for NWIND.MDB.

Fig. 23.25
Database Documentor's opening window.

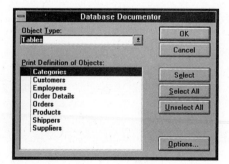

2. Choose the type of object you want to document from the Object Type drop-down list. The All Object Types item adds every object in the database to the Print Definition of Objects list.

3. Click the Options button to display the Print Table Definition dialog. The most detailed set of information for both tables and indexes is the default. If your Access database is not secure, you can click the Permissions by User and Group check box to eliminate reporting permissions data (see fig. 23.26). Click OK to return to the opening dialog.

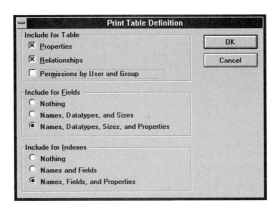

Fig. 23.26
Setting options for documenting tables.

4. Select the table you want to document in the Print Definition of Objects list, and then click the Select button. This marks the table with an "x" as shown in figure 23.27. (Double-clicking the list item has the same effect.) Alternatively, if you want to document all of the tables of your database, click the Select All button. For this example, only the Orders and Order Details tables are documented.

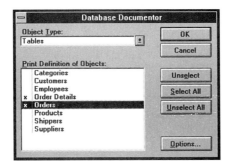

Fig. 23.27
Two tables selected for documenting.

5. Select Queries from the Object Type drop-down list to display the **QueryDef** objects in your database. Click the Options button to display the Print Query Definition dialog. Click the Permissions by User and Group check box to eliminate security data from the report (see fig. 23.28).

Fig. 23.28
Selecting the options for printing query definitions.

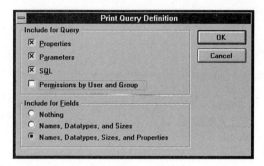

6. Double-click the Order Information query entry to add this query to the documentation, and then click OK to create the report.

7. After a short period, the Object Definition print-preview window appears as shown in figure 23.29. Note that the report for three objects is 13 pages in length. Click the last page button to view the documentation for the Order Information query.

Fig. 23.29
The first page of Database Documentor's report.

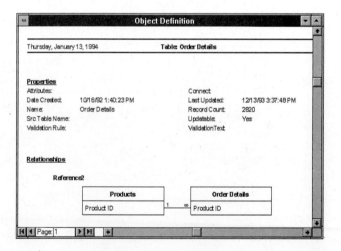

8. Click the Print button of the toolbar to print the report, and then click the Close button of the toolbar or double-click the Document Control-menu box to close the Object Definition print-preview window.

Documenting other objects in your database follows the same method outlined in the preceding steps. You can print data for the database itself (<Current Database> in the Object Type list) or for selected forms, reports, macros, and modules.

Using Access Indexes

Database managers use indexes to relate the values of key fields to the location of the data entity on the disk. The basic purpose of an index is to speed up access to specific rows or groups of rows within a database table. You also use indexes to enforce uniqueness of primary keys and establish upper and lower limits for queries. Using an index eliminates the necessity of re-sorting the table each time you need to create a sequenced list based on a foreign key.

Each PC database manager creates and uses indexes in a variety of ways. Paradox uses a mandatory primary index (.PX) to speed up queries and to ensure nonduplicate keys. Secondary indexes on nonprimary-key fields are permitted by Paradox (.X## and .Y##), created either by the QuerySpeedUp menu choice or the PAL INDEX instruction. dBASE and some of its xBase dialects enable any number of indexes to be created in the form of individual .NDX files, for a single file or table. The number of xBase indexes that you can have open at any one time, so as to keep them current, is determined by the xBase RDBMS you choose. You select the index you want to use with the SET ORDER TO *IndexFileName* instruction. Several xBase languages have their own index structures, such as Clipper's .NTX and FoxPro's .IDX. dBASE IV and FoxPro 2 go one step beyond, with their multiple index, .MDX and .CDX, structures that combine several indexes in a single file. You specify a TAG name to identify which index is to be used to find the records you want.

Indexed Sequential Access Method (ISAM)

ISAM stands for Indexed Sequential Access Method, a term that describes a file structure in which the records are logically located (sorted) in the sequence of the values of their primary key, with an index used to provide random access to individual records. The term *logically* is applied to record location because the records' physical location on the disk may not be sequential; their physical location is determined by the disk's file allocation table (FAT) and the degree of file fragmentation on the drive. ISAM is often used to describe any database structure that uses indexes for searching. This book adheres to the original definition in which the records must be in the order of their primary key.

VI

Advanced Techniques

Classic mainframe ISAM databases have file structures that use overflow sectors, space reserved on the disk to handle insertion of new records. The database administrator periodically sorts the file to insert the data from the overflow sectors into the body of the table structure at appropriate locations. The periodic sorting clears the overflow sectors for future additions. The process is called *file maintenance*. Improved insertion techniques have been applied to databases created by PC and client-server RDBMSs. These methods are described in the sections that follow.

DOS RDBMSs duplicate ISAM structures by using an insertion technique. For instance, many xBase dialects enable you to INSERT a record in the middle of a file (the ISAM method), rather than APPEND a BLANK to the end of a file (the *heap* technique). When you INSERT a record near the top of a large, indexed xBase file, you can catch up on your sleep while the RDBMS moves all the following records to make room for the new one, adjusting all of the index entries to refer to new locations. Figure 23.30 shows the difference between a record INSERT and APPEND. Paradox's native mode is ISAM, which explains why some of its operations, such as canceling an edit on a large table, take so long to complete.

Fig. 23.30
Inserting versus appending new records in an xBase file.

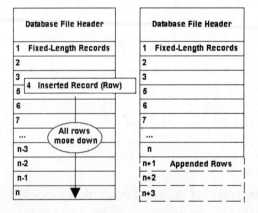

Certain types of files created by DOS RDBMSs inherently fit the ISAM mold—sales order and invoice records with a numeric key incremented by one for each addition are the best examples; Access's Counter field data type performs the numbering function automatically. Other types of tables, such as lists of customers, are often sorted alphabetically. You have to INSERT each record in the proper location or re-sort the file each time you add a new customer to maintain a true ISAM structure. The faster method with xBase is to APPEND BLANKS and REPLACE the blanks WITH data; this procedure adds the new records in a heap at the bottom of the file. Periodically, DOS adds another cluster to the file to accommodate the newly added data. Some xBase dialects, such as Clipper, don't include the INSERT command.

The header of an xBase .DBF file, such as the one in figure 23.30, includes the name of each field, its field data type, its length in bytes, and some additional data. All data records in the file are the same length, representing the sum of the field lengths plus one byte to indicate whether the record is marked for deletion. xBase files are called the *fixed-length record* type. Values that don't fill the length of a field are padded with spaces; character fields are padded with spaces to the right of the text, and numbers are right-justified by padding to the left. xBase files often incorporate much more padding than data.

The record numbers shown in figure 23.30 aren't present in the data, but are deduced by calculating the offset (the intervening number of bytes) of the record from the beginning of the file. If the header is 300 bytes long, record 1 begins at offset 300, corresponding to the 301st byte (the offset of the first byte is 0). Assuming the fields total 80 bytes in width, record 2 begins at offset 380, 3 at offset 460, and so forth. The location of a data item's value is determined by calculating the offset of the desired record, and then adding the offset to the beginning of the column (field) containing the data.

Access Data Pages and Variable Length Records

Access, like Microsoft SQL server and many other SQL databases, divides the data stored in its table structures into 2K *data pages*, corresponding to the size of a conventional DOS fixed-disk file cluster. A header, similar to the one in figure 23.31, is added to each page to create the foundation for a *linked list* of data pages. The header contains a reference, called a *pointer*, to the page that precedes it as well as to the one that follows. Linked lists use pointers to link the data pages to one another in order to organize the data table. If no indexes are in use, new data is added to the last page of the table until the page is full, and then another page is added at the end. The process is much like the heap method used by xBase and the manner in which DOS creates entries that link fixed-disk data clusters in its file allocation table (FAT).

Data pages contain only integral numbers of rows. The space that remains after the last row that fits in the page is called *slack*. You may be familiar with the concept of slack from the characteristic of current DOS versions that allocate fixed-disk file space in 2K clusters. A small batch file, for example, may be displayed as having a file size of 120 bytes, but the file actually occupies 2,048 bytes of disk space; the unused space is slack. Access uses variable-length records for its data rows instead of the fixed-length record structure of xBase. Variable-length records don't require padding for data that is shorter than the designated field size.

Fig. 23.31

The structure of a
data page in an
Access table.

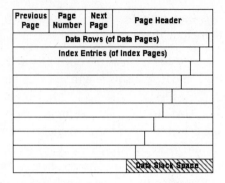

Data rows longer than 2K are contained in multiple pages. Avoid long rows if possible, as they may reduce storage efficiency by increasing the percentage of slack space in the data pages. Access files with relatively short rows store data, especially character-based data, more efficiently than xBase or Paradox. Special fields containing text and images are stored in separate data structures linked to the data item in the data page. The storage concept is similar to that for xBase memo files, but the implementation differs in Access.

The advantage of data pages with their own headers, over the single-header, record-based xBase structure of figure 23.30, is that you can keep a table's data pages in ISAM order by altering only the pointers in the page header and not the structure of the file itself. This process, which uses a *nonclustered index* (discussed in the "Nonclustered and Clustered Indexes" section), is much faster than the INSERT method for xBase files and usually matches the speed of the APPEND technique.

Balanced Binary Trees, Roots, and Leaves

Most database managers use an indexing method called a *binary tree* that is referenced by its abbreviated form, B-tree. In describing an index structure, the tree is inverted, with its root and trunk at the top, progressing downward to branches and leaves, the direction taken by the searching process. A binary tree is defined as a tree in which the trunk divides into two branches, with each branch dividing into two sub-branches and further twofold divisions until reaching the leaves, which are indivisible. The points of the two-way divisions are called *nodes*. Binary trees for computer-based searching were first proposed by John Mauchly, one of the pioneers of electronic computers, in 1946.

When you make many insertions and deletions in a database, conventional B-tree structures can become very lopsided, with many sub-branches and leaves stemming from one branch and few from another. The reason for this is explained by mathematical theory that is beyond the scope of this book. Lopsided B-trees slow the searching process for records that are in an especially active area of the database. This situation causes undesirable effects in, for example, an airline reservation system where passenger reservations are being added to or deleted from a flight at a rapid rate immediately prior to its scheduled departure.

To solve the lopsided B-tree problem, two Russian mathematicians, G. M. Adelson-Velski and E. M. Landis, proposed a balanced B-tree structure in 1963. In a balanced B-tree structure, the length of the search path to any leaf is never more than 45-percent longer than the optimum. Each time a new row is added to the index, a new node is inserted and the tree is rebalanced if necessary. A small balanced B-tree structure appears in figure 23.32. Its nodes are labeled + (plus) or – (minus), called the *balance factor*, according to whether the right subtree height minus the left subtree height is +1 or –1. If the subtrees are the same height, the node is empty. Balance factors are used to determine how a new node is added to maintain the tree in balance.

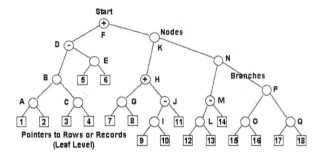

Fig. 23.32
A diagram of a simple balanced B-tree index.

Access and most other modern RDBMSs use the balanced B-tree structure to create indexes. Balanced B-trees improve search speed, at the expense of increasing the time necessary to add new records, especially when the table is indexed on several keys. In a multitasking or client-server environment, however, the server conducts the addition process independently. The user can then perform other client operations, such as entering the key to search for another record, while the server's insertion and index rebalancing operations are going on.

Nonclustered and Clustered Indexes

Most RDBMSs, including Access, use nonclustered indexes to locate records with specific key values. Nonclustered means that the RDBMS adds data by the heap or APPEND method, and the rows of the table aren't in the sequence of their primary key—that is, the table isn't structured as an ISAM table.

Figure 23.33 shows the structure, compressed and truncated, of a nonclustered Access index. xBase indexes have a similar structure, substituting records for data pages.

Fig. 23.33

A diagram of a conventional nonclustered index.

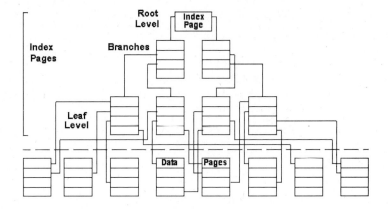

Notice the more-or-less random association of the data pages to the location of the pointers at the leaf level of the index. This lack of order is typical for indexes on foreign keys in all types of databases and for indexes on primary keys in non-ISAM files. If organized into an ISAM structure with the index created on the primary key, the file would have the more organized appearance of the diagram in figure 23.34.

Fig. 23.34

A diagram of a clustered index.

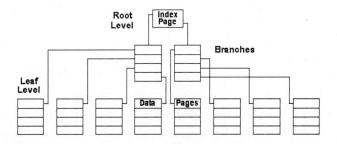

Many client-server databases, such as Microsoft and Sybase SQL Server, can use a clustered index to create ISAM order out of heap-induced chaos. When you use a clustered index, its table converts from heap-based row-insertion structure to the balanced B-tree structure in figure 23.34. In this case, the leaf level of the index consists of the data pages themselves. This organization is accomplished by rewriting the pointers in each data page's header in the order of the key on which the clustered index is based. Because the header can have only one set of pointers, fore and aft, you can have only one clustered index per table. In almost all cases, you create the clustered index from the primary key.

To retain the balanced B-tree organization of data pages, a RDBMS needs a balancing technique for insertions. Instead of using overflow sectors, the RDBMS adds a new page, readjusts the header pointers to include the new page in the linked list, and then moves the last half of the rows in the original page to the new page. The RDBMS then updates the index to reflect the changes. This process speeds up data access, but slows updating; therefore, the process is practical only for a RDBMS running on a high-speed server computer under an advanced operating system, such as Windows NT or OS/2, and having large amounts of RAM.

Query Speed versus Update Performance

Access, like Paradox, automatically creates an index on the primary-key field. Adding other indexes to Access tables, which is similar to using Paradox's QuerySpeedUp menu command, is a two-edged sword. You can speed up the performance of queries because the index assists the sort sequence; you don't need to sort the query's **Recordset** on a primary-key index, and sorts in the order of other indexes you specify are speeded. On the other hand, when you append a new record, Access must take the time to update all the table's indexes. When you edit a field of a record that is included in one or more indexes, Access has to update each of the indexes affected by the edit.

Access 2.0 now incorporates FoxPro's Rushmore technology that optimizes query operations on indexed tables with large numbers of records. Many decision-support queries can be speeded by a factor of 10 to 25 or more by adding the appropriate indexes, in addition to the index on the primary-key field that is created for you. You can improve the performance of Access applications, especially when tables with large numbers of records or queries that join several tables are involved, by observing these guidelines:

Access

2.0

- Minimize the number of indexes used with transaction-based tables, especially in networked multiuser applications that share tables. Access locks pages so that they aren't editable by other users while you are editing records, and for the time it takes Access to update the indexes when you are finished.

- Minimize the number of indexes in tables that are used regularly with append and delete queries. The time required to update indexes is especially evident when making changes to the data in bulk.

- Add indexes judiciously to tables that have large numbers of records and are used primarily in decision-support applications.

VI

Advanced Techniques

■ Add indexes to foreign-key fields of tables that participate in joins with primary tables. However, when specifying a selection criterion on the key field, always use the key field of the primary table rather than the foreign-key field of the related table.

■ Add indexes to fields on which you set criteria. If transaction processing performance is more important than the speed of decision support applications, only add indexes to those fields that occur most often in the criteria of your select queries.

Indexing becomes more important as the number of records in your tables increases. You may find that you need to experiment to determine whether an index is effective in significantly increasing the speed of a query. If you find the index is warranted by improved query performance, check the speed of transaction processes with the new index before committing to its use.

> **Note**
>
> If you are using a shared database on a peer-to-peer network, such as Windows for Workgroups, and the database is located on your computer, use another workgroup member's computer to test the effectiveness of indexes. Network characteristics may affect the performance of indexes significantly. Try to make the test during periods of maximum network traffic, not during off hours when no one is contributing to network congestion.

Enforcing Database Integrity

The integrity of a database is comprised of two elements: entity integrity and referential integrity. Entity integrity requires that all primary keys must be unique within a table, and referential integrity dictates that all foreign keys must have corresponding values within a base table's primary key. Although the normalization process creates entity and referential integrity, either the RDBMS itself or your application must maintain that integrity during the data-entry process. Failure to maintain database integrity can result in erroneous data values and ultimately in widespread corruption of the entire database.

Ensuring Entity Integrity and Auditability

Database managers differ widely in their capabilities to maintain entity integrity through unique primary-key values. Paradox, for instance, enforces unique primary keys within the RDBMS by flagging as a *key violation* any attempt to insert a row with an identical primary key and placing the offending record in the KeyViol table. Access uses a similar technique when you specify a no-duplicates index; if you paste or append records that have duplicate primary keys, Access appends those records to a Paste Errors or Append Errors table.

In xBase, you can add as many records with duplicate index keys as you want. Then if you use SET UNIQUE ON, a SEEK finds only the first record with the same key; however, any duplicate keys remain in the file and, for example, appear in an indexed LIST operation. Indexed DELETEs affect only the first undeleted record found for the SEEK parameter; you must perform a DELETE for each duplicate. You need to write xBase code, therefore, to test for data duplicates before you APPEND the record that adds the data to the file.

Enforcing entity integrity within the table itself, the process used by Access and Paradox, is more reliable than using application programming code to prevent duplication of primary-key values. Access provides two methods of ensuring entity integrity that are independent of the applications employing the tables:

- A key field that uses the Counter data type that creates unique values based on an automatically incremented long integer. You cannot create a duplicate primary key in this case because you cannot edit the values in fields of the Counter data type.

- An index on the primary-key field with the NoDuplicates property. If you attempt to enter a duplicate value in the key field, Access displays an error message.

Either of these methods ensures unique key fields, but a Counter field is necessary so that documents, such as sales orders, invoices and checks, are sequentially numbered. Sequential numbering is necessary for internal control and auditing purposes. Counter fields normally begin with 1 as the first record in a table, but rarely does a real-world cash disbursements or invoice table need 1 as a starting number. You cannot create a table with a Long Integer Number field, enter the beginning number, and then change the field data type to Counter. Access issues a warning message if you attempt this procedure. You can use an append query, however, to establish a specific beginning Counter value.

VI

Advanced Techniques

> **Note**
>
> Access 2.0 increments the value of the counter field even if Access prevents you from adding a record to a table with a counter field. Such a situation can occur if domain or referential integrity rules are violated when addition of a record is attempted. For this reason, Access 2.0's counter field may not be satisfactory for applications where sequential documents must be accounted for.

To create a starting Counter value of 123456 in the Invoice field of a tblInvoiceData table's first record, perform the following steps:

1. Open the Database window, select the Orders table, and press Ctrl+C to copy the table to the Clipboard.

2. Press Ctrl+V, and enter **tblInvoiceData** as the name of the table to create. Then click the Structure Only option button to create the new Invoice Data table with no records.

3. Open the tblInvoiceData table in design mode, click the select button of the Order ID field, and then press Insert to add a new field.

4. Enter **Invoice** as the Field Name, and choose Counter as the Data Type.

5. Click the Indexes button on the toolbar. Delete the PrimaryKey index on Order ID, which enables you to append a record that doesn't have a value for the key field (**Null** values aren't allowed in key fields). Close the Indexes window.

You also need to set the value of the Required property of the Customer ID field to No and the AllowZeroLength property to Yes. Otherwise the append query that follows will not execute. The tblInvoiceData table design appears as shown in figure 23.35.

Fig. 23.35
A table designed for adding a Counter-type field with an arbitrary starting number.

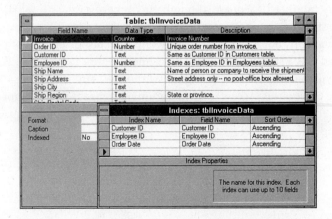

6. Close the tblInvoiceData table and save your changes. Don't create a primary-key field at this point.

7. Create a temporary table called tblFirstInvoice with one field called Invoice.

8. Set the Invoice field's DataType property to Number and the FieldSize property to LongInteger.

9. Change to Datasheet View and enter a value in Invoice 1 less than the starting number you want (for this example, type **123455**).

10. Close the tblFirstInvoice table, save your changes, and don't create a primary-key field.

11. Create a new query and add the tblFirstInvoice table. Click and drag the Invoice field symbol to the first column of the Query Design grid.

12. Choose **A**ppend from the **Q**uery menu and enter **tblInvoiceData** as the table to which to append the record. Click OK. Invoice automatically appears as the Append To field. Click the Run Query button on the toolbar to add the single record in tblFirstInvoice to the tblInvoiceData table.

13. Close Query1 without saving your changes.

The next record you append to tblInvoiceData is assigned the value 123456 in the Invoice (Counter) field. To verify that this technique works properly for appended records, perform the following steps:

1. Create a new query, and add the Orders table. Click and drag the asterisk (all fields) symbol to the first column of the Query Design grid.

2. Choose **A**ppend from the **Q**uery menu and enter **tblInvoiceData** as the table to which to append the records from the Orders table. Click the Run Query button on the toolbar to add the records from the Orders table.

3. Close Query1 and don't save the changes.

4. Open the tblInvoiceData table.

   Access has added numbers beginning with 123456 to the new Invoice field, corresponding to Order ID values of 10000 and higher, as shown in figure 23.36.

VI

Advanced Techniques

Fig. 23.36

The Invoice Data table with counter values starting with 123456.

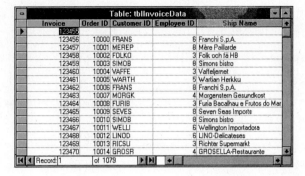

Invoice	Order ID	Customer ID	Employee ID	Ship Name
123456				
123456	10000	FRANS	6	Franchi S.p.A.
123457	10001	MEREP	8	Mère Paillarde
123458	10002	FOLKO	3	Folk och fä HB
123459	10003	SIMOB	8	Simons bistro
123460	10004	VAFFE	3	Vaffeljernet
123461	10005	WARTH	5	Wartian Herkku
123462	10006	FRANS	8	Franchi S.p.A.
123463	10007	MORGK	4	Morgenstern Gesundkost
123464	10008	FURIB	3	Furia Bacalhau e Frutos do Mar
123465	10009	SEVES	8	Seven Seas Imports
123466	10010	SIMOB	8	Simons bistro
123467	10011	WELLI	6	Wellington Importadora
123468	10012	LINOD	6	LINO-Delicateses
123469	10013	RICSU	3	Richter Supermarkt
123470	10014	GROSR	4	GROSELLA-Restaurante

Record: 1 of 1079

If you were adding a Counter-type field to real-world data, you would delete the first blank record and then make the Invoice field the primary-key field. Access creates a no-duplicates index when you assign a Counter-type field as a primary-key field.

Troubleshooting

When I try to execute the append query that provides the starting value minus 1 to my table structure, I get an error message.

You have constraints on your the fields of your destination table that do not allow **Null** values or empty strings in fields. Open your destination table in design mode, and make sure that the Required property of each field is set to No and that the AllowZeroLength property of each field of the Text data type is set to Yes. Also make sure that your destination table does not have a primary-key field specified.

Maintaining Referential Integrity

Prior chapters have discussed use of Access 2.0's new database-level referential integrity enforcement capabilities. Maintaining referential integrity requires strict adherence to a single rule: *Each foreign-key field in a related table must correspond to a primary-key field in a base or primary table.* This rule requires that the following types of transactions be prevented:

- Adding a record on the many side of a one-to-many relationship without the existence of a corresponding record on the one side of the relationship

- Deleting a record on the one side of a one-to-many relationship without first deleting all corresponding records on the many side of the relationship

- Deleting or adding a record to a table in a one-to-one relationship with another table without deleting or adding a corresponding record in the related table

- Changing the value of a primary-key field of a base table on which records in a relation table depend

- Changing the value of a foreign-key field in a relation table to a value that doesn't exist in the primary-key field of a base table

A record in a relation table that has a foreign key with a value that doesn't correspond to the value of a primary key in a relation table is called an *orphan record*.

Whenever possible, use Access 2.0's built-in join features to maintain referential integrity at the database level and don't rely on applications to test for referential integrity violations when adding records to relation tables or deleting records from base tables. Access gives you the opportunity to enforce referential integrity automatically between tables in a database by marking the Enforce Referential Integrity check box in the Relationships dialog. As noted in Chapter 11, "Using Action Queries," you also can specify cascading updates and cascading deletions when you use Access's referential integrity enforcement capabilities. Access 2.0 also enforces referential integrity in attached Access tables.

Paradox versions 3.0 and later automatically enforce referential integrity between master and detail table records. Paradox handles changes to the values of primary-key (link) fields with dependent records in relation (detail) tables in a different manner than Access. When you change a value in a Paradox link field, the corresponding fields of linked records in detail tables change automatically. This process is identical to Access 2.0's cascade update feature.

Most xBase RDBMSs don't have the capability to enforce referential integrity automatically. You need to write xBase code that tests for the required records with SEEK commands on indexed files.

From Here...

This chapter covered the fundamental principles of relational database design and how to restructure tables so that they conform to these principles. Methods of documenting your database design, both in the preliminary and final stages, with text and graphical descriptions of data structures and

VI

Advanced Techniques

relationships was emphasized. Many entire books have been written on each of these two subjects. Indexing techniques were covered in detail because of the differences between Access's approach to indexes and that of xBase and other desktop databases. Indexes also play a critical role in maintaining entity integrity by preventing duplication of key-field values. Access 2.0's automatic enforcement of relational integrity at the database level, combined with cascading updates and deletions, provides protection against orphan records in your relation tables.

- Chapter 24, "Working with Structured Query Language," describes how to write queries in SQL, instead of using Access's graphical QBE design window.

- Chapter 25, "Securing Multiuser Network Applications," shows you how to share databases between workgroup members and how to secure your Access applications and data.

- Chapter 26, "Connecting to Client-Server Databases," covers the use of Access for creating front-end applications for database server back-ends, such as Microsoft and Sybase SQL Server, ORACLE, Informix, and other popular client-server RDBMSs.

Chapter 24

Working with Structured Query Language

This chapter describes Structured Query Language (SQL), the structure and syntax of the language, and how Access translates queries you design with Access's graphical query-by-example technique into SQL statements. An SQL background helps you understand the query process and design more efficient queries. A knowledge of SQL syntax is necessary to use the new Subquery and UNION query capabilities of Access 2.0 and for many of the applications you write in Access Basic. Examples of SQL have been presented in other chapters in this book. These examples, usually figures that illustrate an SQL statement created by Access, demonstrate what occurs *behind the scenes* when you create a query or a graph.

Access is a useful learning tool for gaining fluency in SQL. This chapter shows you how to create Access query-by-example (QBE) queries from SQL statements entered in the SQL dialog. If you use SQL with another DBM, such as dBASE IV or Microsoft SQL Server, this chapter can help you make the transition from ANSI SQL or Transact-SQL, the extended version of SQL used by the Microsoft and Sybase versions of SQL Server, to Access's implementation of SQL.

Many users of Access decision-support applications want to be able to define their own queries. When you open an Access database with MSARN200.EXE, the query design window is hidden. Thus, you need to design forms that include control objects that users can manipulate to construct an Access SQL statement to return the query result set they need. You write Access Basic code to translate users' choices on the form into an Access SQL statement; then create a `QueryDef` object (a query definition whose name appears in the Database window) in the current database.

In this chapter, you learn

- The categories of SQL reserved words

- The syntax of SQL statements

- To write SELECT statements

- To join tables with an SQL statement

- To write SQL action queries

VI

Advanced Techniques

What Is Structured Query Language?

Structured Query Language, abbreviated SQL (usually pronounced "sequel" or "seekel," but more properly "ess-cue-ell") is the common language of client-server database management. The principal advantage of SQL is that this language is standardized—you can use a common set of SQL statements with all SQL- compliant database management systems. The first U.S. SQL standard was established in 1986 as ANSI X3.135-1986. The current version is ANSI X3.135-1992, usually known as SQL-92.

> **Note**
>
> ANSI, an acronym for the American National Standards Institute, is an organization devoted to establishing and maintaining scientific and engineering standards. ANSI-standard SQL was first adopted as a worldwide standard in 1987 by the International Standards Organization (ISO), a branch of the United Nations.

SQL is an application language for relational databases, not a system or programming language. SQL is a set-oriented language; thus, ANSI SQL includes neither a provision for program flow control (branching and looping) nor keywords to create data entry forms and print reports. Programming functions usually are implemented in a system language such as xBase, PAL, C, or COBOL. Some implementations of SQL, such as Transact-SQL used by Microsoft and Sybase SQL Server, add flow control statements (IF. . .ELSE and WHILE) to the language. Publishers of ANSI SQL-compliant DBMs are free to extend the language if the basic ANSI commands are supported. The ANSI/ISO implementation of SQL is independent of any system language with which it might be used.

**Access
2.0**

ANSI SQL includes a set of standard commands (keyword verbs) that are broadly grouped into six categories: data definition, data query, data manipulation, cursor control, transaction processing, and administration or control. Provisions for SQL keywords that maintain data integrity were added in a 1989 revision of the original standard as ANSI X3.135-1989, *Database Language—SQL with Integrity Enhancement*. Access 2.0's implementation of SQL includes the data integrity keywords.

SQL has three different methods of implementation: Direct Invocation, Module Language, and Embedded SQL. Direct Invocation sends a series of SQL statements to the DBM. The DBM responds to the query by creating a table that contains the result and displays the table. Entering SQL commands at the dBASE IV SQL prompt is an example of Direct Invocation. Embedded SQL is the most common implementation; the SQL statements are generated by the application or included as strings of text in a command of an application language. Access queries—whether created by graphical QBE, by an SQL property in Access Basic, or by the Row Source property of a graph—use Embedded SQL.

Looking at the Development of SQL

SQL was created because, early in the 1970s, IBM wanted a method with which nonprogrammers could extract and display the information they wanted from a database. Languages that can be used by nonprogrammers are called *fourth generation*, or 4GL, and sometimes are referred to as *structured English*. The first commercial result of this effort was *query by example* (QBE), developed at IBM's laboratories in Yorktown Heights, New York. QBE was used, beginning in the late 1970s, on terminals connected to IBM System 370 mainframes. A user could obtain a result with less than an 80-character line of QBE code that required 100 or more lines to implement in COBOL or the other 3GL languages of the day.

Virtually any language developed by IBM, at least before the rise of Microsoft Corporation in the PC market, became the standard to which all other languages are compared. These languages often are adopted and improved on by others; Access, dBASE IV, and Paradox use QBE to display selected data from tables.

At the other end of the country, programmers at IBM's San Jose facility were developing System R, the progenitor of SQL/DS and IBM's DB2 relational database. In the mid-1970s, IBM scientist Dr. E.F. Codd proposed SQL (then known as SEQUEL for *S*tructured *E*nglish *Q*uery *L*anguage) as a means of accessing information from the relational database model he had developed in 1970. Relational databases based on the Codd model that use the SQL language to retrieve and update data within them have become, like QBE, computer-industry standards.

SQL has achieved the status of being the exclusive language of client-server databases. A database server (the back end) application holds the data. Client applications (front ends) add to or edit the data. SQL statements are generated by the client application. If you deal regularly with databases of any type, the odds are great that you ultimately will need to learn SQL. You need to learn Access SQL *now* if you plan to create applications with user-defined queries that are usable with MSARN110.EXE.

VI

Advanced Techniques

Comparing ANSI and Access SQL

Access SQL is designed for creating queries, not for creating or modifying tables. SQL, therefore, doesn't include many of the approximately 100 keywords incorporated in the ANSI standard for SQL. Few, if any, commercial SQL-compliant DBMs for the PC implement much more than half of the standard SQL keywords. The majority of the common SQL keywords missing from Access's implementation are provided by the expressions you create with operators, built-in Access functions, or user-defined functions you write in Access Basic. The effect of many unsupported ANSI SQL keywords related to tables is achieved by making selections from Access's Database window or from menus.

When you learn a new language, it is helpful to categorize the vocabulary of the language by usage and then into the familiar parts of speech. SQL commands, therefore, first are divided into six usage categories:

- *Data Query Language* (DQL) commands, sometimes referred to as *data retrieval* commands, obtain data from tables and determine how the results of the retrieval are presented. The SELECT command is the principal instruction in this category. DQL commands often are considered members of the Data Manipulation Language.

- *Data Manipulation Language* (DML) commands provide INSERT and DELETE commands, which add or delete entire rows, and the UPDATE command, which can change the values of data in specified columns within rows.

- *Transaction Processing Language* (TPL) commands include BEGIN TRANSAC-TION, COMMIT [WORK], and ROLLBACK [WORK], which group multiple DML operations. If one DML operation of a transaction fails, the preceding DML operations are canceled (rolled back).

- *Data Definition Language* (DDL) commands include CREATE TABLE and CREATE VIEW instructions that define the structure of tables and views. DDL commands are used also to modify tables and to create and delete indexes. The keywords that implement data integrity are used in conjunction with DDL statements.

- *Cursor Control Language* (CCL) commands can select a single row of a query table for processing. Cursor control constructs, such as UPDATE WHERE CURRENT, are implemented by the Jet database engine, so these commands are not discussed in this chapter.

■ *Data Control Language* (DCL) commands, such as GRANT and REVOKE, perform administrative functions that grant and revoke PRIVILEGES to use the database, a set of tables within the database, or specific SQL commands. Access SQL does not include DCL; instead, you use Access's security objects for implementing security.

Keywords that comprise the vocabulary of SQL are identified further in the following categories:

■ *Commands,* such as SELECT, are verbs that cause an action to be performed.

■ *Qualifiers,* such as WHERE, limit the range of values of the entities that comprise the query.

■ *Clauses,* such as ORDER BY, modify the action of an instruction.

■ *Operators,* such as =, <, or >, compare values and are used to create joins when JOIN syntax is not used.

■ *Group aggregate functions,* such as MIN( ), return a single result for a set of values.

■ *Other* keywords modify the action of a clause or manipulate cursors that are used to select specific rows of queries.

> **Note**
>
> As in dBASE and PAL programming, SQL keywords usually are capitalized, but the keywords aren't case-sensitive. The uppercase convention is used in this book and SQL keywords are set in the monospace type. You use *Parameters,* such as *column_list,* to define or modify the action specified by keywords. Names of replaceable parameters are printed in lowercase italicized monospace type.

SQL Reserved Words in Access

Access doesn't support all the ANSI SQL keywords with identical reserved words in the Access SQL language. In this chapter, *keywords* are defined as the commands and functions that comprise the ANSI SQL language. Access SQL commands and functions, however, are referred to here as *reserved words* to distinguish them from ANSI SQL.

VI

Advanced Techniques

The tables in the following section are intended to acquaint readers who are familiar with ANSI or similar implementations of SQL in other DBMs or database front-end applications, with the Access implementation of SQL. If you haven't used SQL, the tables demonstrate that SQL is a relatively sparse language, which has far fewer keywords than programming languages like Access Basic, and that Access SQL is even more sparse: Access SQL has few keywords you have to learn. You learned in earlier chapters to use the Access operators and functions in expressions that Access substitutes for ANSI SQL keywords.

Access SQL Reserved Words Corresponding to ANSI SQL Keywords

Access supports the ANSI SQL keywords listed in table 24.1 as identical reserved words in Access SQL. Don't use Access SQL reserved words that correspond to SQL reserved words as the names of tables, fields, or variables. The reserved words in table 24.1 appear in all capital letters in the Access SQL statements Access creates for you when you design a query or when you add a graph to a form or report. Reserved words in table 24.1 marked with an asterisk are only available with Access 2.0.

Table 24.1 ANSI SQL-92 Keywords Corresponding to Access SQL Reserved Words				
ADD*	CONSTRAINT*	HAVING	MAX	REFERENCES*
ALL	COUNT	IN	MIN	RIGHT
ALTER*	CREATE*	INDEX*	NOT	SELECT
ANY*	DELETE	INNER	NULL	SET
AS	DESC	INSERT	ON	SOME*
ALIAS	DISALLOW*	INTO	OR	UNION*
ASC	DISTINCT	IS	ORDER	UNIQUE*
AVG	DROP*	JOIN	OUTER	UPDATE
BETWEEN	EXISTS*	KEY*	PARAMETERS	VALUE*
BY	FOREIGN*	LEFT	PRIMARY*	VALUES*
COLUMN*	FROM	LIKE	PROCEDURE	WHERE

The keywords that relate to data types—CHAR[ACTER], FLOAT, INT[EGER], and REAL—aren't included in table 24.1 because Access SQL uses a different reserved word to specify these SQL data types (refer to table 24.3 later in this chapter). The comparison operations (=, <, <=, >, and =>) are common to both ANSI SQL and Access SQL. Access substitutes the < > operator for ANSI SQL's not-equal (!=) operator.

As in ANSI SQL, the IN reserved word in Access SQL can be used as an operator to specify a list of values to match in a WHERE clause or a list created by a subquery. Access 2.0 SQL now supports subqueries. IN is used also to identify a table in another database; this use is discussed near the end of this chapter, in the "Adding *IN* to Use Tables in Another Database" section.

Access Functions and Operators Used in Place of ANSI SQL Keywords

Table 24.2 shows reserved words in Access that correspond to ANSI SQL keywords but are operators or functions used in Access expressions. Access doesn't use ANSI SQL syntax for its aggregate functions; you cannot use the SUM(DISTINCT *field_name*) syntax of ANSI SQL, for instance. Access, therefore, distinguishes between its use of the SUM() aggregate function and the SQL implementation, SUM(). Expressions that use operators such as **And** and **Or** are enclosed in parentheses in Access SQL statements; Access uses uppercase AND and OR (refer to table 24.1) when criteria are added to more than one column.

Table 24.2 Access Reserved Words that Substitute for ANSI SQL Keywords			
Access	**ANSI SQL**	**Access**	**ANSI SQL**
And	AND	Max()	MAX()
Avg()	AVG()	Min()	MIN()
Between	BETWEEN	Not	NOT
Count()	COUNT()	Null	NULL
Is	IS	Or	OR
Like	LIKE	Sum()	SUM()

The Access **IsNull**( ) function that returns **True** (–1) or **False** (0), depending on whether **IsNull**( )'s argument has a **Null** value, has no equivalent in ANSI SQL, and isn't a substitute for Is Null or Is Not Null qualifiers in WHERE clauses. Access SQL does not support distinct aggregate function references, such as AVG(DISTINCT *field_name*); the default DISTINCTROW qualifier added to the SELECT statement by Access serves this purpose.

Access SQL Reserved Words, Operators, and Functions Not in ANSI SQL

Access SQL contains a number of reserved words that aren't ANSI SQL keywords (see table 24.3). Most of these reserved words define Access data types; some reserved words have equivalents in ANSI SQL and others don't. You use Access DDL reserved words to modify the properties of tables. Access Basic's SQL property DISTINCTROW is described in the following section. PIVOT and TRANSFORM are used in creating crosstab queries that are unique to Access.

Table 24.3   Access SQL Reserved Words Not in ANSI SQL

Access SQL	ANSI SQL	Category	Purpose
BINARY	No equivalent	DDL	Not an Access data type
BOOLEAN	No equivalent	DDL	Access Yes/No data type
BYTE	No equivalent	DDL	Byte data type, 1-byte integer
CURRENCY	No equivalent	DDL	Access Currency data type
DATETIME	No equivalent	DDL	Access Date/Time data type
DISTINCTROW	No equivalent	DQL	Updatable Access **Recordset** objects
DOUBLE	REAL	DDL	REAL in ANSI SQL
LONG	INT[EGER]	DDL	Long Integer data type
LONGBINARY	No equivalent	DDL	OLE Object data type
LONGTEXT	VARCHAR	DDL	Memo data type
OWNERACCESS	No equivalent	DQL	Run with owner's privileges parameters
PIVOT	No equivalent	DQL	Used in crosstab queries

Access SQL	ANSI SQL	Category	Purpose
SHORT	SMALLINT	DDL	Integer data type, 2 bytes
SINGLE	No equivalent	DDL	Single-precision real number
TEXT	CHAR[ACTER]	DDL	Text data type
TRANSFORM	No equivalent	DQL	Creates crosstab queries
? (LIKE wild card)	_ (wild card)	DQL	Single character with LIKE
* (LIKE wild card)	% (wild card)	DQL	Zero or more characters
# (LIKE wild card)	No equivalent	DQL	Single digit, 0–9
# (date specifier)	No equivalent	DQL	Encloses date/time values
<> (not equal)	!=	DQL	Access uses ! as a separator.

Access provides four statistical aggregate functions that aren't incorporated in ANSI SQL. These functions are listed in table 24.4.

Table 24.4   Aggregate SQL Functions Added in Access SQL

Access Function	Category	Purpose
StdDev()	DQL	Standard deviation of a population sample
StdDevP()	DQL	Standard deviation of a population
Var()	DQL	Statistical variation of a population sample
VarP()	DQL	Statistical variation of a population

VI

Advanced Techniques

◄ "Creating Queries from Tables with Indirect Relationships," p. 362

Access's *DISTINCTROW* and SQL's *DISTINCT* Keywords

The DISTINCTROW keyword that follows the SQL SELECT keywords causes Access to eliminate duplicated rows from the query's result. The effect of DISTINCTROW is especially dramatic in queries used to display records in tables that have indirect relationships. To create an example of a query that you can use to demonstrate the effect of Access DISTINCTROW SQL keyword:

1. Open a new query in NWIND.MDB by clicking the Query button and then clicking the New button. Click the New Query button to bypass the Query Wizards.

2. Add the Customers, Orders, Order Details, Products, and Categories tables to the query, in sequence. Access automatically creates the required joins.

3. Drag the Company Name field from the Customers field list to the Field row of the first column of the query design grid. Select the Sort cell, open the drop-down list with F4, and choose Ascending Sort Order.

4. Drag the Category Name from the Categories field list to the Field row of the second column of the grid. Add an ascending sort to this field.

5. Click the SQL button of the toolbar. The SQL statement that creates the query is shown in the SQL window in figure 24.1.

Fig. 24.1
The SQL statement that creates the query to determine customers purchasing categories of products.

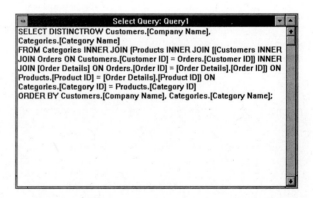

```
Select Query: Query1
SELECT DISTINCTROW Customers.[Company Name],
Categories.[Category Name]
FROM Categories INNER JOIN [Products INNER JOIN [[Customers INNER
JOIN Orders ON Customers.[Customer ID] = Orders.[Customer ID]] INNER
JOIN [Order Details] ON Orders.[Order ID] = [Order Details].[Order ID]] ON
Products.[Product ID] = [Order Details].[Product ID]] ON
Categories.[Category ID] = Products.[Category ID]
ORDER BY Customers.[Company Name], Categories.[Category Name];
```

6. Click the Run Query button on the toolbar to execute the query.

7. Click the End of Table button to determine the number of rows in the query table. At the time of this writing, the number of rows (Records) returned by the query is 643.

To demonstrate the effect of removing the DISTINCTROW keyword from the SQL statement and to verify, in this case, that the effect of ANSI SQL's DISTINCT and Access SQL's DISTINCTROW keywords is the same, follow these steps:

1. Click the SQL button of the toolbar to edit the SQL statement.

2. Delete the DISTINCTROW keyword from the SQL statement, and choose OK to close the SQL window.

3. Click the Run Query button. The new query result table contains many duplicated rows.

4. Click the End of Table button to check the number of rows in the result. The number of rows, 2,820, is more than four times the number of rows that results when the duplicate removal process of DISTINCTROW is applied to the query.

5. Click the SQL button of the toolbar to edit the SQL statement again. Add DISTINCT after the keyword SELECT.

6. Click the Run Query button again, and then click the End of Table button. You get the same result of 643 records that you obtain when you use the DISTINCTROW keyword.

7. Close, but do not save, the query.

DISTINCTROW is a special Access SQL keyword and is unavailable in standard (ANSI) SQL; DISTINCTROW is related to, but not the same as, the DISTINCT keyword in ANSI SQL. Both keywords eliminate duplicate rows of data in query result tables but differ in execution, as shown in the following list:

■ DISTINCT in ANSI SQL eliminates duplicate rows based only on the values of the data contained in the rows of the query, from left to right. You cannot update values from multiple-table queries that include the keyword DISTINCT.

■ DISTINCTROW, available only in Access, eliminates duplicate rows based on the content of the underlying table, regardless of whether additional field(s) that distinguish records in the table are included. DISTINCTROW allows values in special kinds of multiple-table **Recordset** objects to be updated.

To distinguish between these two keywords, assume that you have a table with a Last Name field and a First Name field and only 10 records, each with the Last Name value, *Smith*. Each record has a different First Name value. You create a query that includes the Last Name field but not the First Name field.

- DISTINCTROW returns all 10 Smith records because the First Name values differ in the table.

- DISTINCT returns 1 record because the First Name field that distinguishes the records in the table that contains the data is absent in the query result table.

All SQL statements created by Access include the default keyword DISTINCTROW, unless you purposely replace this keyword by the DISTINCT keyword, using the Query Properties dialog's Unique Values Only option. The only way of eliminating DISTINCTROW from queries is to delete it by editing the SQL statement. The circumstances that require you to delete DISTINCTROW are rare, possibly nonexistent.

Access

2.0

Creating Tables with Access DDL

You can create new tables in your current database with Access 2.0's new Data Definition Language reserved words. Using SQL to create new tables is of primary interest to developers of Access applications because it is much easier to create new tables with the Access user interface. For the sake of completeness, however, a brief description of Access 2.0 SQL DDL statements follows:

- CREATE TABLE *table_name* (*field_name data_type* [*field_size*]
  [, *field_name data_type*...]) creates a new table with the fields specified by a comma-separated list. Properties of fields are space-delimited, so you need to enclose *field_name* entries for field names with spaces in square brackets ([]). The *data_type* can be any valid Access SQL field data types, such as TEXT or INTEGER. The *field_size* entry is optional for TEXT fields only. (The default value is 50 characters.)

- CONSTRAINT *index_name* {PRIMARYKEY¦UNIQUE¦REFERENCES *foreign_table*
  [(*foreign_field*)]} creates an index on the field name whose entry the expression follows. You can specify the index as the PRIMARYKEY or as an UNIQUE index. You also can establish a relationship between the field and the field of a foreign table with the REFERENCES *foreign_table* [*foreign_field*] entry. (The [*foreign_field*] item is required if the foreign_field is not a primary-key field.)

- ALTER TABLE allows you to add new fields (ADD COLUMN *field_name*...) or delete existing fields (DROP COLUMN *field_name*...).

- **DROP INDEX** *index_name* **ON** *table_name* deletes the index from a table specified by *table_name*.

- **DROP TABLE** *table_name* deletes a table from the database.

Common ANSI SQL Keywords and Features Not Supported by Access SQL Reserved Words

The majority of the ANSI SQL keywords that aren't supported by Access 2.0 are elements of SQL's Data Control Language. Transactions, which are implemented automatically for most operations by the Jet database engine, only can be explicitly declared in Access Basic code. The record position buttons of Access queries and forms substitute for most cursor-control (CCL) statements in ANSI SQL that choose a particular row in a query. These substitutes are listed in table 24.5.

Table 24.5   Common ANSI SQL Keywords Not Supported in Access SQL

Reserved Word	Category	Substitute
AUTHORIZATION	DCL	Privileges dialog
BEGIN	TPL	Access Basic **BeginTrans** method
CHECK	DQL	Table Validation Rule property
CLOSE	CCL	Document Control menu of query
COMMIT	TPL	Access Basic **CommitTrans** method
CREATE VIEW	DDL	Query design mode and filters
CURRENT	CCL	Query run mode, record position buttons
CURSOR	CCL	Query run mode
DECLARE	CCL	Query run mode (cursors are automatic) Database window
DROP VIEW	DDL	Query design mode
FETCH	DQL	Text boxes on a form or report
GRANT	DCL	Privileges dialog

(continues)

Table 24.5 Continued		
Reserved Word	**Category**	**Substitute**
PRIVILEGES	DCL	Privileges dialog
REVOKE	DCL	Privileges dialog
ROLLBACK	TPL	Access Basic **RollbackTrans** method
TRANSACTION	TPL	Access Basic transaction methods
VALUES	DML	Data values entered in tables or forms
WORK	TPL	Access Basic **BeginTrans** method
: (variable)	DQL	Access Basic **Dim** statement prefix
!= (not equal)	DQL	Access <> not-equal operator

The Jet database engine uses transaction processing for all Access DML commands executed by action queries. You implement transaction processing (COMMIT and ROLLBACK [WORK]) on **Recordset** objects you create with code by writing Access Basic functions or procedures that contain the **BeginTrans**, **CommitTrans**, and **Rollback** reserved words. Many other less commonly used SQL keywords, such as COBOL and PASCAL, don't have Access SQL reserved word equivalents.

Writing Select Queries in SQL

When you create a select query in query design mode, Access translates the QBE query design into an Access SQL statement. You can view the Access SQL equivalent of your design by clicking the SQL button of the toolbar. Displaying and analyzing the SQL statements that correspond to queries you design or queries in the Northwind Traders sample database is useful when you are learning SQL.

The heart of SQL is the SELECT statement used to create a select query. Every select query begins with the SELECT statement. The following lines of syntax are used for a SQL SELECT statement that returns a query table (called a result set, usually a **Recordset** object of the **Dynaset** type) of all or selected columns (fields) from all or qualifying rows (records) of a source table:

```
SELECT [ALL¦DISTINCT¦DISTINCTROW] select_list
    FROM table_names
[WHERE search_criteria]
[ORDER BY column_criteria[ASC¦DESC]]
```

The following list shows the purpose of the elements in this basic select query statement:

- SELECT is the basic command that specifies a query. The *select_list* parameter determines the fields (columns) that are included in the result table of the query. When you design an Access QBE query, the *select_list* parameter is determined by the fields you add to the Fields row in the Query grid. Only those fields with the Show check box marked are included in *select_list*. Multiple field names are separated by commas.

  The optional ALL, DISTINCT, and DISTINCTROW qualifiers determine how rows are handled. ALL specifies that all rows are to be included, subject to subsequent limitation. DISTINCT eliminates rows with duplicate data. As discussed earlier in the chapter, DISTINCTROW is an Access SQL keyword, similar to DISTINCT, that eliminates duplicate rows but also enables you to modify the query table.

- FROM *table_name* specifies the name or names of the table or tables that form the basis for the query. The *table_names* parameter is created in Access QBE by the entries you make in the Add Table dialog. If fields from more than one table are included in *select_list*, each table has to be specified in *table_names*. Commas are used to separate the names of multiple tables.

- WHERE *search_criteria* determines which records from the selection list are displayed. The *search_criteria* parameter is an expression with a text (string) operator, such as LIKE, for text fields or a numeric operator, such as >=, for fields with numeric values. The WHERE clause is optional; if you don't add a WHERE clause, all the rows that meet the SELECT criteria are returned.

- ORDER BY *column_criteria* specifies the sorting order of a **Recordset** object of the **Dynaset** or **Snapshot** type created by the query. A **Recordset** object of the **Snapshot** type is a query result set that is not updatable. Like the WHERE clause, ORDER BY is optional. You can specify an ascending or descending sort by the optional ASC or DESC keywords. If you don't specify a sort direction, ascending sequence is the default.

VI

Advanced Techniques

The following lines show an example of a simple SQL query statement:

```
SELECT [Company Name],[Customer ID],[Postal Code]
    FROM Customers
WHERE [Postal Code] LIKE "9*"
ORDER BY [Company Name];
```

You must terminate an Access SQL statement by adding a semicolon immediately after the last character on the last line.

> **Note**
>
> Examples of SQL statements in this book are formatted to make the examples more readable. Access doesn't format the SQL statements. When you enter or edit SQL statements in the Access SQL window, formatting these statements so that commands appear on individual lines makes the SQL statements more intelligible. Use Ctrl+Enter to insert newline pairs before SQL keywords. Spaces and newline pairs are ignored when Access processes the statement.

The preceding query results in an Access **Recordset** object of three columns and as many rows as the number of records in the Customers table for companies located in ZIP codes with values that begin with the character 9, sorted alphabetically by the company name. You don't have to specify the table name with the field name in the *select_list* because only one table is used in this query. When Access creates an SQL statement, the table name always precedes the field name. Usually, Access processes queries you write in either ANSI SQL or Access SQL syntax. This example differs from ANSI SQL only in the substitution of the Access SQL asterisk for ANSI SQL's % wild card.

Programming Statements in xBase Equivalent to SQL

If you are accustomed to using the dot prompt—with xBase dialects that include interactive capability—or writing xBase programs, you can use much of your xBase experience in learning SQL. In xBase, you achieve a result identical to the preceding simple SQL query by the following set of statements, assuming that the CustName index exists:

```
USE Customers INDEX CustName
LIST FIELDS Company, CompanyID, PostalCode
FOR SUBSTR(PostalCode,1,1) = "9"
```

The CustName index is needed to provide the equivalent of the ORDER BY clause so that the list appears in customer name sequence, unless the Customer table was sorted previously by customer name, which is unlikely. The dot-prompt commands in xBase are closely related to SQL statements invoked directly. Many of the keywords differ between the two languages, but you can achieve similar results with either language. The advantage of SQL over xBase dialects is that SQL syntax is simpler and usually requires fewer keywords to obtain the same result.

Using SQL Punctuation and Symbols

SQL uses relatively few symbols, other than the comparison operators for expressions mentioned earlier. SQL uses commas, periods, semicolons, and colons as punctuation. The following list of symbols and punctuation is used in ANSI SQL and the Access SQL dialect; differences between the two forms of SQL are noted where appropriate:

- Commas are used to separate members of lists of parameters, such as multiple field names, as in Name, Address, City, ZIP.

- Square brackets surrounding field names are required only when the field name includes spaces or other symbols, including punctuation, not allowed by SQL, as in [Company Name].

- A period is used to separate the table name from the field name, if fields of more than one table are involved in the query, as in Customers.[Company Name].

- ANSI SQL uses the single quote symbol (') to enclose literal string values. You can use the double quote (") or the single quote symbol to enclose literal values in Access SQL statements.

- ANSI SQL uses % and _ (underscore) symbols as the wild cards for the LIKE statement, rather than the * (asterisk) and ? used by Access SQL to specify zero or more and a single character, respectively. The Access wild cards correspond to the wild cards used in specifying DOS group file names.

- Access provides the # wild card for the LIKE statement to represent any single digit. Access also uses the # symbol to enclose date/time values in expressions. This symbol isn't available in ANSI SQL.

- The end of an Access SQL statement is indicated by a mandatory semicolon.

- Colons cannot be used in Access as prefixes to indicate user-declared variables you create in ANSI SQL. You cannot create variables with Access SQL; user-declared variables in Access are limited to the Access Basic functions and procedures you write.

VI

Advanced Techniques

■ The exclamation mark is used by Access and ANSI SQL as a *not in* operator for character lists used with LIKE. ANSI SQL uses != for not equal;
Access SQL uses <>.

As the preceding list demonstrates, relatively minor differences exist in the
availability and use of punctuation and symbols between ANSI and Access
SQL. Indentation often is used in writing multiple-line SQL statements. Indented lines indicate continuation of a preceding line or a clause that is dependent on a keyword in a preceding line.

Using SQL Statements to Create Access Queries

You can enter SQL statements in query design mode to create simple Access
queries that are reflected in changes to the design of the Query grid. This
method is another useful way to learn the syntax of SQL. If your entries contain errors in spelling or punctuation, Access displays a message box that
describes the error and its approximate location in the statement. When you
choose OK in the SQL dialog, Access translates your SQL statement into a
QBE query design.

To create an Access QBE select query with the SQL statement, break and
repeat the previous query marked INSERT, as shown in the following lines:

```
SELECT [Company Name],[Customer ID],[Postal Code]
    FROM Customers
WHERE [Postal Code] LIKE "9*"
ORDER BY [Company Name];
```

To create the Access QBE select query, follow these steps:

1. Open the Northwind Traders database, and then open a new query.

2. Close the Add Table dialog without adding a table name.

3. Click the SQL button of the toolbar to open the SQL window.

4. Delete any text, such as DISTINCTROW, that may appear in the SQL
   Text box in the SQL dialog.

5. Enter the SQL statement in the SQL window. Use Ctrl+Enter to create
   new lines. Your SQL statement appears as shown in figure 24.2.

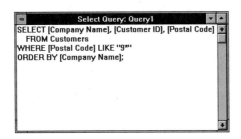

Fig. 24.2
An SQL statement
for a simple select
query.

6. Click the Design View button of the toolbar. Access creates the equivalent of your SQL statement in graphical QBE (see fig. 24.3).

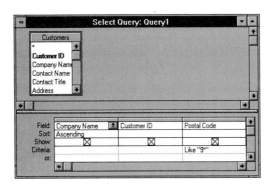

Fig. 24.3
The QBE design
created by Access
from the query in
figure 24.2.

7. Click the Run Query button on the toolbar. The result of your query in Datasheet View appears as shown in figure 24.4.

Fig. 24.4
The query in figure
24.3 in Datasheet
View.

To change the order by which the query result is sorted, follow these steps:

1. Click the SQL button of the toolbar.

2. Change ORDER BY [Company Name] to **ORDER BY [Postal Code]**, and click the Design View button.

VI

Advanced Techniques

3. The query grid in design mode displays Ascending in the Postal Code column rather than in the Company Name column, indicating that the query result set is sorted by ZIP code.

4. Click the Run Query button of the toolbar to display the result set sorted in ZIP code sequence (see fig. 24.5).

Fig. 24.5
The query of figure 24.4 in ZIP code order.

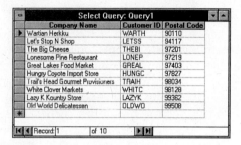

Select Query: Query1

Company Name	Customer ID	Postal Code
Wartian Herkku	WARTH	90110
Let's Stop N Shop	LETSS	94117
The Big Cheese	THEBI	97201
Lonesome Pine Restaurant	LONEP	97219
Great Lakes Food Market	GREAL	97403
Hungry Coyote Import Store	HUNGC	97827
Trail's Head Gourmet Provisioners	TRAIH	98034
White Clover Markets	WHITC	98128
Lazy K Kountry Store	LAZYK	99362
Old World Delicatessen	OLDWO	99508

Record: 1 of 10

Using the SQL Aggregate Functions

If you want to use the aggregate functions to determine totals, averages, or statistical data for groups of records with a common attribute value, you add a GROUP BY clause to your SQL statement. You can further limit the result of the GROUP BY clause with the optional HAVING qualifier:

```
SELECT [ALL¦DISTINCT¦DISTINCTROW]
    aggregate_function(field_name) AS alias
    [,select_list]
    FROM table_names
[WHERE search_criteria]
GROUP BY group_criteria
    [HAVING aggregate_criteria]
[ORDER BY column_criteria]
```

The *select_list* includes the *aggregate_function* with a *field_name* as its argument. The field used as the argument of an aggregate function must have a numeric data type. The additional SQL keywords and parameters required to create a GROUP BY query are shown in the following list:

■ AS *alias* assigns a caption to the column. It is created in an Access QBE query by the *alias:aggregate_function(field name)* entry in the Field row of the Query grid.

■ GROUP BY *group_criteria* establishes the column on which the grouping is based. In this column, GROUP BY appears in the Totals row of the Query grid.

■ HAVING *aggregate_criteria* is one or more criteria applied to the column that contains the *aggregate_function*. The *aggregate_criteria* of HAVING is applied after the grouping is completed. WHERE *search_criteria* operates before the grouping occurs; at this point, no aggregate values exist to test against *aggregate_criteria*. Access substitutes HAVING for WHERE when you add criteria to a column with the *aggregate_function*.

The following GROUP BY query is written in ANSI SQL, except for the # symbols that enclose date and time values:

```
SELECT [Ship Region], SUM([Freight]) AS [Total Freight]
    FROM Orders
WHERE [Ship Country]="USA"
    AND [Order Date] BETWEEN #01/1/91# AND #12/31/93#
GROUP BY [Ship Region]
    HAVING SUM([Freight]) >50
ORDER BY SUM([Freight]) DESC;
```

The query returns a result set that consists of two columns: Ship Region (states) and the totals of Freight for each Ship Region in the United States, for the years 1991 through 1993. The result set is sorted in descending order.

To create an SQL GROUP BY query in Access, follow these steps:

1. Open a new query, click the SQL button of the toolbar and enter the preceding GROUP BY example code in the SQL dialog (see fig. 24.6).

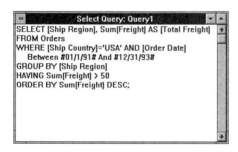

Fig. 24.6
An SQL statement, using the *SUM()* aggregate function.

2. Click the Design View button of the toolbar. Your QBE GROUP BY query design appears as shown in figure 24.7.

Fig. 24.7
Access's QBE
design for the
query in
figure 24.6.

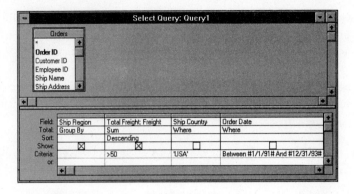

   3. Click the Run Query button on the toolbar. The states in which total
orders exceeding $10,000 were received in 1991 are shown ranked by
order volume and displayed in Datasheet View (see fig. 24.8).

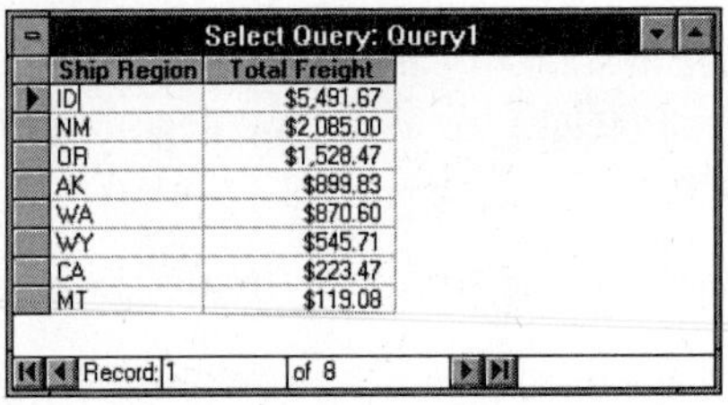

Fig. 24.8
The aggregate
query design in
figure 24.7 in
Datasheet View.

Creating Joins with SQL

Joining two or more tables with Access QBE uses the JOIN...ON structure that
specifies the table to be joined and the relationship between the fields on
which the JOIN is based:

```
SELECT [ALL|DISTINCT|DISTINCTROW]select_list
    FROM table_names
{INNER|LEFT|RIGHT} table_name JOIN join_table ON
    join_criteria
[{INNER|LEFT|RIGHT} table name JOIN join_table ON
    join_criteria]
[WHERE search_criteria]
[ORDER BY column_criteria]
```

The elements of the JOIN statement are shown in the following list:

■ *table_name* JOIN *join_table* specifies the name of the table that is
joined with other tables listed in *table_names*. Each of the tables participating in a join must be included in the *table_names* list and before and

after JOIN. When you specify a self-join by including two copies of the field list for a single table, the second table is distinguished from the first by adding an underscore and a digit to the table name.

One of the three types of joins—INNER, LEFT, or RIGHT—must precede the JOIN statement. INNER specifies an equi-join; LEFT, a left outer join; and RIGHT, a right outer join. The type of join is determined in Access QBE by double-clicking the line connecting the joined fields in the table and clicking option button 1, 2, or 3 in the Join Properties dialog.

- ON *join_criteria* specifies the two fields to be joined and the relationship between the joined fields—one field in *join_table* and one in another field in a table in *table_names*. The *join_criteria* expression contains an equal sign (=) comparison operator and returns a **True** or **False** value. If the value of the expression is **True**, the record in the joined table is included in the query.

The number of JOIN statements you can add to a query usually is the total number of tables participating in the query minus one. You can create more than one JOIN between a pair of tables, but the result is often difficult to predict.

The Access SQL statement for the equi-join between the Personnel Actions and Employees tables based on ID values in each table is shown in figure 24.9, and Employees is repeated in the FROM clause. The copy of Employees is associated with the JOIN statement and is required in Access SQL joins. The JOIN reserved word in Access SQL creates the lines that connect the joined fields in Query Design View.

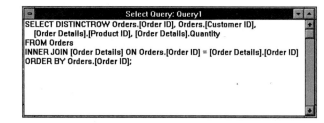

Fig. 24.9
The Access SQL implementation of an equi-join.

You create equi-joins in ANSI SQL with the WHERE clause, using the same expression to join the fields as that of the ON clause in the JOIN command. The WHERE clause is more flexible than the JOIN...ON structure because you can use other operators such as BETWEEN...AND, LIKE, >, and <. These operators result in error messages when they are substituted for the equal sign (=) in the ON clause of the JOIN statement. You don't have to repeat the Employees field in this case. The ANSI SQL statement in figure 24.10, and in the following text, gives the same result as the Access SQL statement in figure 24.9:

```
SELECT DISTINCTROW Orders.[Order ID], Orders.[Customer ID],
    [Order Details].[Product ID], [Order Details].Quantity
FROM Orders
INNER JOIN [Order Details] ON Orders.[Order ID] = [Order
Details].[Order ID]
ORDER BY Orders.[Order ID];
```

Fig. 24.10

The equi-join in figure 24.9, created by a *WHERE* clause.

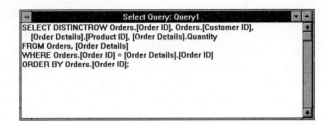

You create multiple joins with WHERE clauses by separating each join expression with an AND operator. When you use the WHERE clause to create joins in Access, the join lines don't appear between the fields in query design mode.

Access
2.0

Using *UNION* Queries

UNION queries let you combine the result set of two or more SELECT queries into a single result set. NWIND.MDB includes an example of a UNION query, which has a special symbol, two overlapping circles, in the Database window. You can create UNION queries only with SQL statements; if you add the UNION keyword to a query, the query design mode button of the toolbar and the Query **D**esign choice of the **V**iew menu are disabled. The general syntax of UNION queries is as follows:

```
SELECT select_statement
UNION SELECT select_statement
    [GROUP BY group_criteria]
    [HAVING aggregate criteria]
[UNION SELECT select_statement
    [GROUP BY group_criteria]
    [HAVING aggregate criteria]]
[UNION...]
[SORT BY sort_criteria]
```

The restrictions on statements that create UNION queries are the following:

■ The number of fields in the *field_list* of each SELECT and UNION SELECT query must be the same. You receive an error message if the number of fields in not the same.

■ The sequence of the field names in each field_list must correspond to similar entities. You don't receive an error message for dissimilar entities, but the result set is likely to be unfathomable. The field data types in a single column need not correspond; however, if the column of the result set contains both numeric and Text data types, the data type of the column is set to Text.

■ Only one SORT BY clause is allowed, and it must follow the last UNION SELECT statement. You can add GROUP BY and HAVING clauses to each SELECT and UNION SELECT, if needed.

Figure 24.11 shows the SQL statement to create a UNION query derived from the Union Query included in NWIND.MDB. The syntax of the SQL statement illustrates the ability of UNION queries to include values from two different field data types, Text (Customer ID) and Long Integer (Supplier ID), in the single, aliased ID column. The query result set appears in figure 24.12.

Tip

You can specify a UNION query, which causes the union symbol to appear in the Database window when you save the query, by choosing **SQL** Specific from the **Query** menu, and then choosing **U**nion from the submenu.

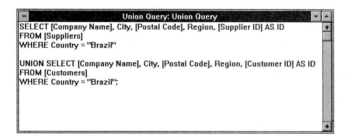

Fig. 24.11

Creating a multi-column *UNION* query.

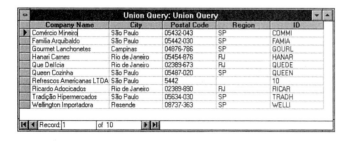

Fig. 24.12

The result of the *UNION* query of figure 24.11.

VI

Advanced Techniques

Implementing Subqueries

Versions of Access prior to 2.0 used nested queries to emulate the subquery capability of ANSI SQL. (A nested query is a query executed against the result set of another query.) Access 2.0 lets you write a SELECT query that uses another SELECT query to supply the criteria for the WHERE clause. The general syntax of subqueries is

```
SELECT field_list
FROM table_list
WHERE [table_name.]field_name IN SELECT select_statement
[GROUP BY group_criteria]
    [HAVING aggregate_criteria]
[ORDER BY sort_criteria];
```

Figure 24.13 shows the SQL statement for the example Subquery query included in NWIND.MDB, with formatting added for clarity. This query returns names and addresses of customers who placed orders between April 1, 1993, and June 30, 1993. The SELECT subquery that begins after the IN predicate returns the Customer ID values from the Orders table against which the Customer ID values of the Customers table are compared.

Fig. 24.13

The SQL statement for a subquery.

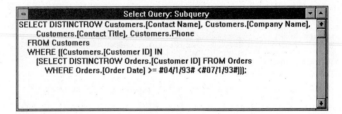

Tip

Depending on the complexity of your query, using a subquery instead of nested queries often improves performance.

Unlike UNION queries, you can create a subquery in query design mode. You type **IN**, followed by the SELECT statement as the criterion of the appropriate column. Figure 24.14 shows the query design with part of the IN SELECT statement in the Criteria row of the Customer ID column. Figure 24.15 shows the result set returned by the SQL statement of figure 24.13.

Specifying Action Query Syntax

Data Manipulation Language (DML) commands are implemented by Access's action queries: append, delete, make-table, and update. Access SQL reserved words that create crosstab queries, TRANSFORM and PIVOT, are included in this section because crosstab queries are related to DML queries. The syntax for each type of Access action query is shown in this section.

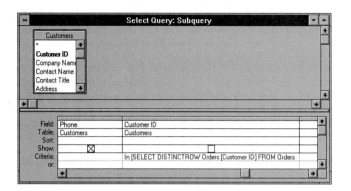

Fig. 24.14
Entering the SQL statement for a subquery in the Criteria row.

Fig. 24.15
The query result set from the subquery of figures 24.13 and 24.14.

Append queries use the following syntax:

```
INSERT INTO dest_table
    SELECT [ALL¦DISTINCT¦DISTINCTROW] select_list
        FROM source_table
    [WHERE append_criteria]
```

If you omit the WHERE clause, all the records of *source_table* are appended to *dest_table*.

Delete queries take the following form:

```
DELETE FROM table_name
    [WHERE delete_criteria]
```

If you omit the optional WHERE clause in a delete query, you delete all data in *table_name*.

Make-table queries use the following syntax:

```
SELECT [ALL¦DISTINCT¦DISTINCTROW] select_list
    INTO new_table
    FROM source_table
        [WHERE append_criteria]
```

VI

Advanced Techniques

To copy the original table, substitute an asterisk (*) for *select_list* and omit the optional WHERE clause.

Update queries use the SET command to assign values to individual columns:

```
UPDATE table_name
    SET column_name = value [, column_name = value]
    [WHERE update_criteria]
```

Access 2.0

Separate multiple *column_name* entries and corresponding values by commas if you want to update the data in more than one field. Access 2.0 SQL supports the ANSI SQL VALUES keyword for adding records to tables the hard way (specifying the VALUE of *each* column of *each* record.)

Crosstab queries use the Access SQL keywords TRANSFORM and PIVOT. The following syntax applies to time-series crosstab queries:

```
TRANSFORM aggregate_function(field_name) [AS alias]
    SELECT [ALL¦DISTINCT¦DISTINCTROW] select_list
        FROM table_name
    PIVOT Format(field_name),"format_type")
        [IN (column_list)]
```

TRANSFORM defines a crosstab query, and PIVOT specifies the GROUP BY characteristics plus the fixed column names specified by the optional IN predicate. Crosstab queries, like queries with multiple or nested JOINs, are better left to Access QBE to create the query. You can edit the query as necessary after Access has written the initial SQL statement.

Troubleshooting

When I try to execute a query from my SQL statement, an Enter Parameter dialog appears.

You misspelled one of the table names in your *table_list*, one of the field names in your *field_list*, or both. If the Jet engine's query parser can't match a table name or a field name with those specified in the FROM clause, Jet assumes that the entry is a parameter and requests its value. Check the spelling of the database objects in your SQL statement. (If you misspell an SQL keyword, you usually receive a syntax error message box.)

Adding *IN* to Use Tables in Another Database

Access enables you to open only one database at a time, unless you write code to open another table with an Access Basic function or procedure. You can use Access SQL's IN clause, however, with a make-table, append, update, or delete query to create or modify tables in another database. Access provides only the capability to make a table or append records to a table in another Access database through graphical QBE. You click the Another Database option in the Query Properties dialog for the make-table or append query and type the file name of the other database.

You have to write an SQL query or edit a query created by Access to update data or delete records in tables contained in another database of any type, or to perform any operation on a dBASE, Paradox, or Btrieve file that isn't attached to your database. The SQL query uses the IN clause to specify the external database or table file. The advantage of using the IN clause is simplicity: you don't have to attach the table before using it. The disadvantage of using the IN clause is that indexes associated with dBASE and Paradox tables aren't updated when the content of the table is modified.

Working with Another Access Database

You can create a table in another Access database, delete all the records, and then append the records back to the table from which the records were deleted, using the IN clause to specify the name of the other database that contains the table. To try an example of using the IN clause, open a new query or an existing query and follow these steps:

1. Click the SQL button of the toolbar, delete any existing text if you have a query open, and type the following line in the SQL window (see fig. 24.16).

   SELECT * INTO Customers IN "OLE_OBJS.MDB"
   FROM Customers;

   SELECT...INTO creates a make-table query. If you haven't created OLE_OBJS.MDB, choose **N**ew Database from the **F**ile menu and create a new database named OLE_OBJS.MDB or whatever you like in your \ACCESS directory. If the new database is in a different location, you need to add the path to the IN string.

Fig. 24.16
A query that
creates a table in
another database.

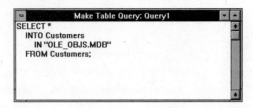

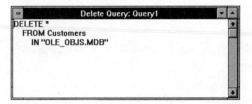

2. Click the Run Query button of the toolbar to make the new Customers table in your OLE_OBJS database. Click OK when the message box advises you of the number of records that are copied to the new Customers table created in OLE_OBJS. You can open OLE_OBJS.MDB to verify the existence of the new table.

3. Click the SQL toolbar button again, delete the existing text, and type the following line (see fig. 24.17):

   DELETE * FROM Customers IN "OLE_OBJS.MDB"

   DELETE. . .FROM creates a delete query.

Fig. 24.17
Deleting all
records from a
table in another
database.

4. Click the Run Query button of the toolbar to delete the records in the OLE_OBJS Customers table. Click OK to confirm the deletion of the records.

Tip
You cannot use
the IN identi-
fier with Access
DDL state-
ments, such as
DROP TABLE or
CREATE TABLE.

To append the records you deleted back into the Customers table of the OLE_OBJS database, follow these steps:

1. Choose **O**pen from the **F**ile menu, and select your OLE_OBJS database, which contains the Customers table with no records.

2. Click the Query button on the Database window, and then click the New button. Close the Add Table dialog without adding a table.

3. Click the SQL button of the toolbar and type the following line in the SQL Text box (see fig. 24.18):

INSERT INTO Customers SELECT * FROM Customers IN "C:\ACCESS\SAMPAPPS\NWIND.MDB"

`INSERT INTO` creates an append query.

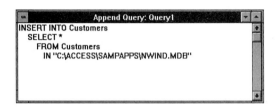

Fig. 24.18
A query to append records to a table in another database.

4. Click the Run Query button on the toolbar to add the records from NWIND's customers table. Confirm the append by clicking OK in the message box.

Although you accomplish the same objectives by attaching a table from another database or copying tables to the Clipboard and pasting the table into another database, using an SQL query for this purpose is a more straightforward process.

Using the *IN* Clause with Other Types of Databases

You can create or modify dBASE, Paradox, and Btrieve tables by specifying in an IN statement the path to the file and the file type, using the following special Access SQL syntax reserved for foreign database file types:

```
IN "[drive:\]path" "database_type"
```

The *path* to the file is required, even if the database is located in your \ACCESS directory; you receive an error if you omit the path entry. You can use an empty string, `""`, to identify the current directory.

The *database_type* expression must be enclosed in quotation marks. It consists of one of the seven foreign file types supported by ISAM DLLs supplied with Access 2.0, followed by a semicolon: dBASE III;, dBASE IV;, FoxPro 2.0;, FoxPro 2.5;, Paradox 3.x;, Paradox 4.x;, or Btrieve;. (The capability to manipulate Paradox 4.x files is a feature of Access 2.0.) The semicolon after the file type name is required, but the database file type names are not case-sensitive—*dbase iii*; is acceptable to Access.

Access 2.0

You can create a dBASE III table from a query by using the syntax shown in figure 24.19.

VI

Advanced Techniques

Fig. 24.19
Creating a dBASE
III table from an
SQL query.

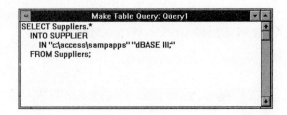

You can append records to a dBASE III file with the syntax shown in figure 24.20. In deleting and updating records in foreign tables, use the syntax shown in the "Specifying Action Query Syntax" section, with the IN clause added. When you append records to or delete records from a foreign database type that does not support transaction processing, you receive the warning message shown in figure 24.21.

Fig. 24.20
Appending records
to a dBASE III
table with an SQL
query.

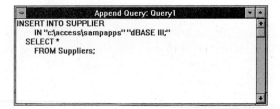

Fig. 24.21
The warning
message that
appears when
appending records
to an attached
table of a foreign
database type.

Using SQL Statements in Forms, Reports, and Macros

If you create a large number of forms and reports based on queries or that use queries, or if you use macros to run select and action queries, the query list in your Database window can become cluttered. You can use SQL queries you write or copy from the SQL dialog in place of the names of query objects and then delete the query from your database. SQL statements can be used for the following purposes:

- *Record Source property of forms and reports.* Substitute the SQL query text for the name of the query in the Record Source text box.

- *Row Source property in lists and drop-down combo lists on a form.* Using an SQL statement rather than a query object gives you greater control over the sequence of the columns in your list.

- *Argument of the* RunSQL() *macro action.* Only SQL statements that create action queries can be used with the RunSQL() macro action.

- *Parameter of the SQL property of an Access Basic function that creates a select query or modifies an existing query.* You use the RunCode() macro action to create the query and then display it with the OpenQuery() macro action. Using this technique creates the equivalent of the RunSQL() macro action for select queries. The technique is described in Part IV, "Powering Access with Macros."

You can create and test your Access SQL statements in query design mode and then copy the statement to the Clipboard. Paste the text into the text box for the property or into your Access Basic module. Then close the test query design without saving it.

From Here...

This chapter described the basic details of the use of Structured Query Language in Access. Important differences between the ANSI and Access implementations of SQL were outlined for readers who have used SQL in other database management applications. The syntax of the SQL example statements in this chapter adhere to ANSI standard syntax as much as possible. Using WHERE clauses rather than JOIN statements can save substantial amounts of typing when you write your own SQL statements. Writing your own SQL statements frees you from having to use some of the rigid conventions of the QBE methods implemented by Access.

- Chapter 9, "Understanding Operators and Expressions in Access," describes how to use all of the operators discussed in this chapter.

- Chapter 10, "Creating Multitable and Crosstab Queries," shows you how to use Access's graphical QBE window to create the Access SQL statements that underlie all Access queries.

- Chapter 25, "Securing Multiuser Network Applications," introduces the use of Access in a network environment. Both client-server and peer-to-peer network applications are described.

VI

Advanced Techniques

Chapter 25

Securing Multiuser Network Applications

Personal computer networking is one of the fastest-growing areas in the PC marketplace. Many large organizations are engaged in downsizing database applications to personal computer networks. *Downsizing* means moving a database system that runs on a costly large-scale computer such as a mainframe, to smaller, lower-priced computers such as PCs. Small- to moderate-size organizations have discovered that installing a PC network can increase productivity and reduce the required investment in computing hardware. An organization need purchase only a single laser printer if all users can share it on a network. The cost of fixed disk drives is reduced when users share large files rather than keep multiple independent copies on local disk drives.

Reducing operating costs is the principal incentive for installing PC networks. In many cases, savings in the investment for required PC peripheral components is the sole consideration in the decision to install a network. When you use a database application, however, productivity plays the most important role in the network decision-making process. The capability to share up-to-date information contained in a database system among many users is a strong incentive to install a PC network because it increases productivity. Increasing productivity with a networked database system can, in turn, reduce operating costs by many times the savings offered by the reduction of the investment when you share computer peripheral equipment.

Another improvement in productivity when using a PC network is the capability of networked computers to send electronic messages (e-mail) to one another. E-mail applications such as Microsoft Mail 3+ and Lotus cc:Mail can improve productivity by reducing the never-ending flow of paper memoranda between members of larger organizations. You can attach files to e-mail

VI

Advanced Techniques

messages and include graphic images or sounds in them. A new class of software, called *workgroup* or *scheduling* applications, enables users to schedule appointments and meetings jointly and contribute to jointly authored documents.

Access will be the first networked Windows application used by many readers of this book. Windows for Workgroups 3.11, a version of Windows 3.1 that provides highly simplified installation of very low-cost and easy-to-administer PC networks, should appeal to first-time network users. If you don't have a network now and you plan to create Access applications to be shared by other users, Windows for Workgroups 3.11 is a logical choice as a "starter" network.

Microsoft Corporation designed Access specifically for use in a networked, workgroup environment. Many of Access's features, especially the security system, were added primarily for network operation. If your network is already set up, you can choose to install Access on the network or install only the files you intend to share. If you don't have a network when you begin using Access, the process is simple to change your database files from single-user to shared status when you install a network. This chapter explains how to set up and use Access in a variety of network environments, share database files, establish database security, and administer a multiuser database system.

Installing Access on a Network

Tip
Use the Custom installation option if you want to connect to client-server databases with Open Database Connectivity (ODBC). The Typical option does not install the ODBC files.

If you are using a network operating system with application server capabilities, such as Novell NetWare 3.x/4.x or Windows NT Advanced Server, two ways exist to install Access in a network environment:

- Install Access on the network server. All workstations run the server's copies of Windows and Access and don't require a copy of either Windows or Access on their local disk drives. This approach saves disk space on the workstations but usually results in slower operation of both Windows and Access. The degree of impairment of operating speed depends on your network's performance and the number of users accessing the network simultaneously. A full installation of Access requires about 20M of server disk space.

- Install a copy of Access on each workstation that will use the application from an individual set of distribution disks or from the network server. Access requires between about 8M and 20M of disk space, depending on the features you include in the workstation installation and whether you previously installed OLE 2.0 server applications such as Excel 5.0. This is the only installation method recommended for computers connected in a peer-to-peer network.

You need an individual copy of the Access software for each workstation that uses Access or a license for each workstation that runs an Access application with the retail version of Access 2.0. For additional details, refer to the license information that Microsoft supplies with Access.

The Microsoft Access Developer's Toolkit (ADT) includes a run-time version of Access. Run-time Access 2.0, MSARN200.EXE, enables users to run applications you create but not to create or modify applications. Run-time Access enables multiple workstations to run Access applications without an individual license for each workstation. You can install run-time Access on the server or local workstations; installation of run-time Access on each workstation is recommended because you gain operating speed. The amount of disk space consumed by run-time Access is less than that for the retail version of Access because the Access help file and the Access wizards and builders are not components of run-time Access.

> **Note**
>
> Do not attempt to share the complete or run-time version of Access on a peer-to-peer network. Peer-to-peer networks are designed for sharing printers and data files, not the executable (.EXE) and help (.HLP) files of applications. The computer and network resources required to run Access from a peer server slow applications running on the server to a crawl and greatly increase network traffic.

Tip
If many users need to install or upgrade to Access 2.0, it usually is faster to use the "administrator's installation" on a network server and then install Access 2.0 on the workstations from the administrator's installation, rather than from the distribution diskettes. (See ACREADME.HLP on Setup diskette 1.)

Sharing Your Access Database Files with Other Users

▶ "Examining the Content of the Access Developer's Toolkit," p. 1099

While you are learning to use Access and designing your first Access applications, you use Access in single-user mode and maintain exclusive use of the database files you create. If your application is designed for use on a single computer, using files exclusively is satisfactory. If your application is designed for use in a networked environment, you need to set up a workgroup for the users who will share the database that includes the application you created.

VI

Advanced Techniques

Tip

If you intend to share your Access applications, make a backup copy of SYSTEM.MDA. Use the backup copy to make new SYSTEM.MDA files for applications you create for other workgroups.

Creating Database Applications for File Sharing

Sharing a database application requires that each user of the database share a common system file, SYSTEM.MDA, which contains information on the members of the workgroup, such as their log-on names, passwords, and the groups of which they are members. Permissions for users to open and modify objects are stored in the .MDB file. Permissions are discussed in a later section, "Maintaining Database Security."

When you develop an application intended for shared use, create a new SYSTEM.MDA file specifically for the application and develop the application in its own directory. When the application is completed, you can copy the files in this directory to the workgroup directory of the network or peer-to-peer server that is used to share them.

The location of the SYSTEM.MDA file that Access uses when it is launched is specified by the SystemDB= entry of the [Options] section of the MSACC20.INI file in your \WINDOWS directory. The options section of MSACC20.INI contains two entries, typically the following:

```
[Options]
UtilityDB=C:\ACCESS\UTILITY.MDA
SystemDB=C:\ACCESS\SYSTEM.MDA
```

Change the SystemDB= entry to specify the name and location of the new SYSTEM.MDA file for the application you develop.

Tip

You can use Access 2.0's Workgroup Administrator application in place of Notepad to make the required changes to the SystemDB= entry of MSACC20.INI.

To establish a directory for the development of a shared database application, complete the following steps:

1. Launch File Manager and add a subdirectory, called **\SHARED** in this example, to your \ACCESS directory.

2. Copy SYSTEM.MDA from your \ACCESS directory to the \ACCESS\SHARED subdirectory.

3. If you already created the database file you intend to share, copy the database file from the \ACCESS directory to \ACCESS\SHARED.

4. Close File Manager, launch Notepad, and open MSACC20.INI.

5. Locate the [Options] section of MSACCESS.INI and edit the SystemDB= entry to specify the SYSTEM.MDA file in the new subdirectory:

```
SystemDB=C:\ACCESS\SHARED\SYSTEM.MDA
```

Close Notepad, and close Access if it is running.

6. Launch Access. Access reads the MSACC20.INI file only during the loading process.

7. If you copied an existing database file from the \ACCESS directory, open the file to verify its operation with the new SYSTEM.MDA file. Otherwise, choose **N**ew Database from Access's **F**ile menu to create the new database file.

Troubleshooting

After changing the SystemDB= *entry, Access opens with a* "'d:\path\system.mdb' isn't a valid path" *message, and then Access closes.*

The SystemDB= entry isn't valid, or you cannot connect to the server share specified by d:[\path]. You cannot use UNC (Uniform Naming Convention) syntax, \\servername\directory, to specify the location of SYSTEM.MDA. Use File Manager to verify that your entry is correct and that your network connection to the server is working. Choose **R**efresh from File Manager's **W**indow menu to verify that the server connection currently is valid.

The dedicated SYSTEM.MDA file contains information pertaining only to the database application to be shared and the Northwind sample database. You can develop the application using Access's default operating options and then change the options to provide for file sharing when the application is completed.

You can change the SYSTEM.MDA file that Access uses when launched with the Access Setup application. The procedure is described in the section, "Choosing Workgroups with the Workgroup Administrator," later in this chapter.

Note

Minimize the number of database objects you create when you develop applications to be shared. Use SQL statements to replace query objects when possible (see Chapter 24, "Working with Structured Query Language"). Combine related Access macros so that you have as few individual macro objects as possible (see Chapter 17, "Understanding Access Macros"). Criteria for combining macros are the subject of a tip in the "Granting and Revoking Permissions for Database Objects" section, later in this chapter. Minimizing the number of objects reduces the number of entries you need to make when you establish database security restrictions (permissions) for your application.

VI

Advanced Techniques

Preparing to Share Your Database Files

Setting up Access to share database files requires several changes to the operating options for Access that are determined by settings in the Multiuser Options dialog. You open this dialog by choosing **O**ptions from the **V**iew menu and then choosing Multiuser from the list of options presented. The changes you make to the default multiuser settings, which apply to all databases you open thereafter, follow:

- Access opens database files for exclusive use by a single user in its default operating mode. Change the file-opening mode of your workgroup database to shared mode so that more than one user can open the file.

- You can gain additional area on the display by removing the toolbar from view. Users are unlikely to be allowed to modify your application, so you can remove the toolbar if your applications don't require that users employ any of its actions or you have created your own custom toolbars. When you use run-time Access, MSARN200.EXE automatically hides the toolbar unless you specify that it appear.

- You can set the locking mode and adjust the refresh interval and the number of update retries from their default values, if necessary. *Record locking* prevents more than one user from making simultaneous changes to the same record. *Refresh interval* determines how often the data displayed in a datasheet or form is rewritten automatically to reflect changes made by other members of the workgroup. Access attempts to update a locked record for the number of times specified as retries, before issuing a message box that the record is locked and cannot be updated. Access doesn't lock records in a SQL Server table attached with the ODBC API, but the records in the table you attach can be locked by users of SQL Server.

Tip
The options you set apply only to your user record in SYSTEM.MDA. Have all users who are sharing the same SYSTEM.MDA file set their options to the same value as yours.

To set the operating options of the system database you are using (SYSTEM.MDA) for shared use of Access database files, complete the following steps:

1. Choose **O**ptions from the **V**iew menu. The Options dialog appears.

2. Select Multiuser/ODBC from the Category list, as shown in figure 25.1.

3. Open the Default Record Locking drop-down list, and select either No Locks or Edited Record. No Locks is the preferable setting because the record is locked only during the interval while the record is being

replaced, which is usually a very short time. If you choose Edited
Record, no other user can update the record (or any other record in the
page that contains the record) while a user is performing an edit on the
record. If you select All Records, no other user can make changes to a
table when another user opens the table, and you cannot view or query
tables attached by ODBC, such as SQL Server tables. Selecting All
Records is the equivalent of table locking in xBase or Paradox.

Fig. 25.1
The Options dialog
for setting the
multiuser values.

4. Open the Default Open Mode for Databases drop-down list, and select
   Shared to make the databases you open shareable.

5. You edit the values for Refresh Interval, Update Retry Interval, Number
   of Update Retries, and ODBC Refresh Interval in the remaining text
   boxes. The default values, except for Number of Retries, are adequate
   for most network installations. You can set the Number of Update Retries to a more conservative value of 5; this results in a 1.25-second wait
   before you receive the Can't Update message box if your Update Retry
   Interval is 250 milliseconds.

6. When you complete your entries as shown in figure 25.1, click OK. The
   values you entered are saved in your record of the SYSTEM.MDA system
   database file.

Now that you have set up the database files for shared use, you need to set up
the workstations so that they can join the workgroup for the application.

VI

Advanced Techniques

Note

Record locking is a misnomer in Access. An Edited Record lock is applied to a 2K page that may contain many records if the fields of the records have small Size property values. Use of No Locks, the default, speeds operation of Access in a multiuser environment because the time required to lock and unlock table pages is saved. No Locks is called *optimistic locking*; optimistic locking assumes that the probability is low that two or more users might attempt to alter the same record simultaneously. If you attempt to update a record in a table with No Locks that is being updated simultaneously by another user, Access displays a message box that lets you choose to accept or overwrite the other user's changes. The conservative approach is to use Edited Record locking, but doing so may impair performance when many users simultaneously update data in a single table.

Creating Workgroup Directories for Database Files

Workgroups are established by creating directories to hold the database file(s) and a copy of the workgroup's system file, SYSTEM.MDA. Each member of the workgroup shares the copy of the SYSTEM.MDA file in the workgroup directory. Members of the workgroup use the database(s) in the workgroup directory, but they can attach, import, or export tables located in other workgroup directories, depending on their permissions to use the foreign files.

Note

You can rename a workgroup's SYSTEM.MDA to a name more representative of the workgroup's function, such as SALES.MDA. If you rename SYSTEM.MDA, you need to change the `SystemDB=` entry in the `[Options]` section of MSACC20.INI.

If you create separate Access databases for the Accounting, Sales, and Production departments, for example, you may locate the database and dedicated SYSTEM.MDA files in \ACCESS\ACCOUNT, \ACCESS\SALES, and \ACCESS\PRODUCT directories of the network or peer-to-peer server. These directories appear to workstations as separate drives, perhaps D, E, and F. To use the same drive designator for all databases at the workstation level, you add another layer to the server directory structure, \ACCESS\DATABASE\ACCOUNT, for example. The DATABASE subdirectory is then shared as drive D on the workstations.

To create a workgroup directory on a network or peer-to-peer server, complete the following steps:

1. Create the directory on the server computer that is shared with the members of the database workgroup.

2. Designate the names of the workstation computers authorized for access to the new directory. Make sure that you designate read-write access for each workstation, even if the workstation isn't to be allowed to modify data. Any directory that contains a SYSTEM.MDA file must not be made read-only.

3. Copy the files from the directory in which you developed the application to the new server directory. The server directory must contain SYSTEM.MDA and at least one database file.

4. Edit the workstation's MSACCESS.INI file so that the `SystemDB=` entry of the `[Options]` section designates the path to the workgroup directory, as in the following example:

   ```
   SystemDB=d:\account\system.mda
   ```

5. Launch Access from the workstation and open the database file on the server.

6. Run your application and make a temporary modification to one of the tables to verify that you have read-write authorization in the new directory.

7. Make a backup copy of the database and the SYSTEM.MDA file from the development directory in which you created it. The purpose of the backup is to maintain a copy of the original application in case you encounter problems when you establish database security.

8. You now can safely delete the development copy of the database file on your computer. You may, however, want to keep the file as a local copy for modification and further development as required.

Note

Always make a backup copy of the related SYSTEM.MDA file when you back up a database file. If your SYSTEM.MDA file or the file for a workgroup becomes corrupted and cannot be repaired, you may not be able to open the database, even from a restored backup copy. Backing up database files is discussed in the "Administering Databases and Applications" section near the end of this chapter.

You also can create a new workgroup with the Workgroup Administrator application described in the next section.

Access

2.0

Choosing Workgroups with the Workgroup Administrator

Access 2.0's application group includes a Workgroup Administrator icon that lets users choose a workgroup to join. The Workgroup Administrator application, WRKGADM.EXE, replaces Access 1.x's workgroup option of the Setup application that you executed with the command line, SETUP.EXE /W. Workgroup Administrator changes the SystemDB= entry in the [Options] section of MSACC20.INI to point to the SYSTEM.MDA (or *WRKGROUP*.MDA) file in the directory you select.

To use the Workgroup Administrator to change workgroups, follow these steps:

1. Launch the Workgroup Administrator by double-clicking its icon in Program Manager's Microsoft Access application group. The opening dialog shown in figure 25.2 appears.

Fig. 25.2

Starting the change workgroups process.

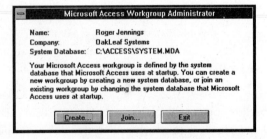

2. Click the Join button to open the Join Workgroup Database dialog. The current SystemDB= entry in the [Options] section of MSACC20.INI appears in the Database text box (see fig. 25.3).

Fig. 25.3

Your current workgroup displayed in the Join Workgroup Database dialog.

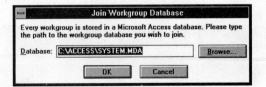

3. Enter the well-formed path to the SYSTEM.MDA or *WRKGROUP*.MDA file in the text box, or click the Browse button to display the Select Workgroup System Database dialog shown in figure 25.4.

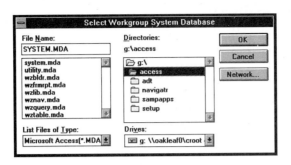

Fig. 25.4
Selecting the
SYSTEM.MDA
file for the new
workgroup.

4. Select the drive and directory in which the SYSTEM.MDA file for the new workgroup is located and click OK to close the Select Workgroup System Database dialog. Your selection appears in the Join Workgroup Database dialog shown in figure 25.5.

5. Click OK to confirm your new SystemDB= entry; click OK when the message box confirms that you have joined the workgroup (see fig. 25.9); then click the Exit button of the Microsoft Workgroup Administrator's dialog (see fig. 25.10) to complete the process.

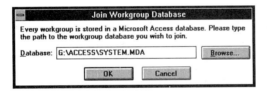

Fig. 25.5
Confirming the
SYSTEM.MDA
file for the new
workgroup.

You also can use the Workgroup Administrator to create a new workgroup directory and add the workgroup's SYSTEM.MDA file to the directory. To automate the process of creating the new workgroup, follow these steps:

1. Launch the Workgroup Administrator, and click the Create button of the opening dialog to display the Workgroup Owner Information dialog.

2. Change the entries in the Name and Organization text boxes if you want, and enter a descriptive name and code for the workgroup in the Workgroup ID text box (see fig. 25.6). Click OK to display the Workgroup System Database dialog.

3. Enter the well-formed path to the new workgroup directory in the Database text box of the Workgroup System Database dialog as shown in figure 25.7. If the directory does not exist, Workgroup Administrator creates it for you. Click OK to display the Confirm Workgroup Information dialog.

VI

Advanced Techniques

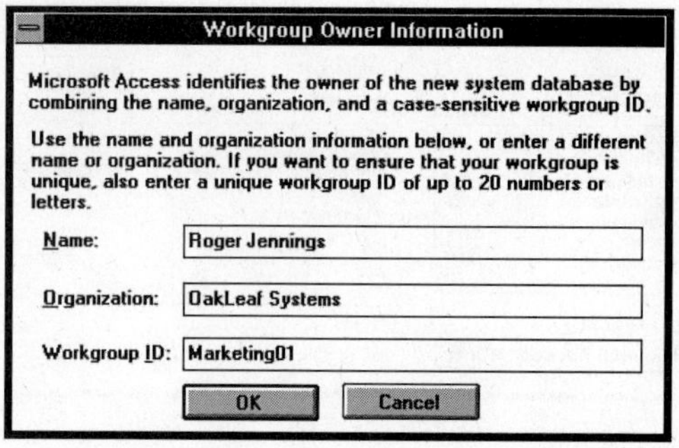

Fig. 25.6
Entering the
description of your
new workgroup.

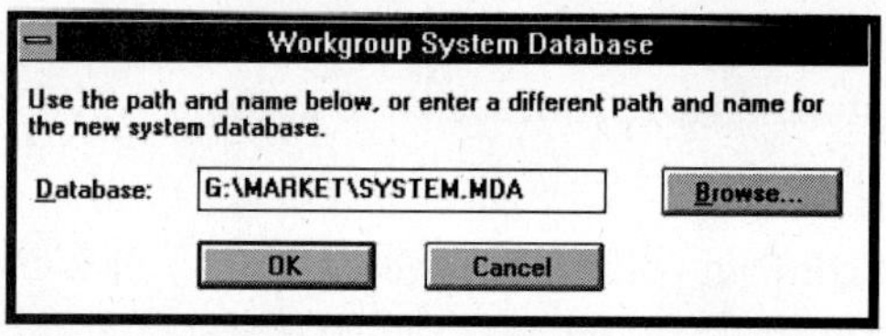

Fig. 25.7
Creating the new
workgroup
directory.

4. If the information in the Confirm Workgroup Information dialog (see
   fig. 25.8) is correct, click OK. The message box of figure 25.9 confirms
   that you have created the new workgroup directory.

5. Click OK to display the Workgroup Administrator dialog shown in
   figure 25.10.

Fig. 25.8
Confirming the
description of your
new workgroup
directory.

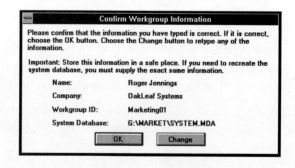

Fig. 25.9
The message box
that indicates your
new workgroup
directory has been
created.

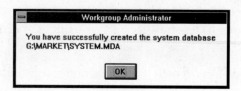

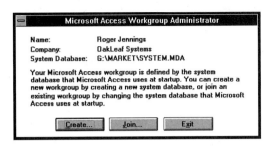

Fig. 25.10
Workgroup
Administrator's
dialog with the
final confirmation
message.

6. Click Exit to close the Workgroup Administrator dialog.

Using Command Line Options to Open a Database

Access provides a number of options that you can employ to customize how Access starts for each user. All users in a workgroup may share a common database, but you may want individual users to start Access with a different form. You can open a workgroup database automatically, execute a macro that opens a specific form, and supply a user name or password when you start Access by entering options on the command line that you use to start Access for each workgroup member, as in the following example:

```
d:\msa_path\msaccess.exe [n:\mdb_path\mdb_name.mdb ]
[/User user_name ][/Pwd pass_word ][/X macro_name ]
    [/Ro ][/Excl ]
[/Cmd cmd_value]
```

Table 25.1 describes the elements of the Access startup command line options.

Table 25.1 Command Line Options for Launching Access	
Command Line Element	**Function**
d:\msa_path\msaccess.exe	Command to launch Access
n:\mdb_path\mdb_name.mdb	Path and name of startup database file
/User user_name	Start with user_name as user name
/Pwd pass_word	Start with pass_word as password
/X macro_name	Run macro_name on startup

(continues)

VI

Advanced Techniques

Table 25.1   Continued

Command Line Element	Function
/Ro	Open *mdb_name* for read-only use
/Excl	Open *mdb_name* for exclusive use
/Cmd *cmd_value* Basic Command function	Specify a value to be returned by the Access

Tip
Opening the local application .MDB with the /Excl parameter speeds operation of the application. The /Excl option applies to the local database, not the attached tables of the shared data .MDB file.

The run-time version of Access recognizes an additional parameter, /ini, whose argument specifies the path to and the name of a custom .INI file for the application (see Chapter 30, "Using the Access 2.0 Developer's Toolkit," for details).

Note

Do not use the /Ro option if you want some members of the workgroup to be able to modify the tables of the database. If you specify the /Ro option for one workstation, all workstations in the workgroup are restricted to read-only use of the database. Use the permissions features of Access, described in the "Maintaining Database Security" section of this chapter, to designate those users who can update the data in tables and those who cannot.

The sequence in which you enter the command line options doesn't affect the options' operation; however, a convention is that the name of the file to open always immediately follows the command that launches the application. Do not use the /Excl option if you want other users to be able to share the database. When you omit the /Excl option, shared or exclusive use of databases is determined by the Default Open Mode for Databases choice of the Multiuser Options, discussed in a previous section, "Preparing to Share Your Database Files."

Tip
When changing an icon, you can choose from a wide range of interesting icons by clicking the Browse button and selecting \WINDOWS \MORICONS.DLL.

The following example starts Access, opens the Northwind Traders sample database using *Gabriel* as the user name and *Marquez* as the password, and runs the PA Open Form macro. Access is assumed to be located in network directory E:\ACCESS, and SALES.MDB and SYSTEM.MDB are located in the network directory N:\SALES. The procedure also assigns a special icon for the application. To create an icon that uses these command line parameters to open Access, follow these steps:

1. Open or select the Windows program group in which you want to install the icon for Access.

2. Choose **N**ew from Program Manager's **F**ile menu, and select Program Item in the New Program Object dialog. Click OK; the Program Item Properties dialog appears.

3. Type a short title of your application, such as **PA Form**, in the Description text box of the Program Item Properties dialog.

4. Type the following in the Command Line text box; then press Tab:

```
e:\access\msaccess.exe n:\sales\sales.mdb /User
Gabriel /Pwd Marquez /X PA Open Form
```

5. Type **n:\sales** in the Working Directory text box and press Tab. This entry establishes the workgroup directory as the working directory when the user launches Access.

6. Click the Change Icon button. The Change Icon dialog appears, as shown in figure 25.11.

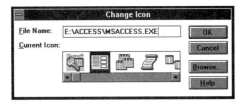

Fig. 25.11

The Change Icon dialog displaying Access icons.

7. Click the Form icon from those offered in the Current Icon box, and click OK to close the dialog. Icons are provided for forms, tables, reports, queries, macros, and modules. The icons from which you can choose correspond to the icons used by Access when you minimize the window of a database object.

8. Your application now is assigned the new icon in the Program Items Properties dialog, as shown in figure 25.12.

9. Click OK to accept your entries.

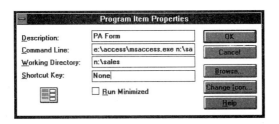

Fig. 25.12

The Program Item Properties dialog for automatic startup of Access.

VI

Advanced Techniques

You need to repeat these steps for each workstation in the workgroup, changing the /X macro_name entry as necessary to start each workstation with the appropriate form.

> **Note**
>
> Adding a user's password as an option to the startup command line violates one of the basic rules of database security: do not disclose your password to any other person. The preceding example that uses a password as a command line option does so only for the purpose of completely defining the options available. You should not use the /Pwd command line option under any circumstances.

Maintaining Database Security

Database security prevents unauthorized persons from accidentally or intentionally viewing, modifying, deleting, or destroying information contained in a database. Database security is of primary concern in a multiuser environment, although you may want to use Access's security features to prevent others from viewing or modifying databases stored on your single-user computer. This section describes the multilayered security features of networked Access databases and how you use these features to ensure a secure database system.

Specifying the Principles of Database Security on a LAN

Ten basic principles of database security exist for databases installed on a LAN. Five of these principles are associated with the network operating system:

1. Each user of a network must be positively identified before they can gain access to the network. Identification requires a unique user name and secret password for each user. Users must not share their passwords with one another, and all passwords used should be changed every 60 to 90 days.

2. Each identified user of the network must be authorized to have access to specific elements of the network, such as server directories, printers, and other shared resources. Each user has a network *account* that incorporates the user's identification data and authorizations. The network file that contains this information is always encrypted and is accessible only by the network administrator(s).

3. Actions of network users should be monitored to determine whether users are attempting to access elements of the network for which they don't have authorization. Users that repeatedly attempt to breach network security should be locked out of the network until appropriate administrative action can be taken.

4. The network should be tamper-proof. Tamper-proofing includes installing security systems immune to *hacking* by ingenious programmers and testing routinely for the presence of viruses.

5. Data stored on network servers must be protected against hardware failure and catastrophic destruction (fires, earthquakes, hurricanes, and so on) by adequate and timely backup. Backup systems enable you to reconstruct the data to its state at the time the last backup occurred.

   The measures required to establish the first five principles are the responsibility of the network administrator for a server-based system. In a peer-to-peer network, network security measures are the responsibility of each person that shares his or her resources with others.

   The remaining five principles of database security are determined by the security capabilities of the database management system and the applications you create with it.

6. The contents of tables in a database should be encrypted to prevent viewing the data with a file-reading or other *snooping* utility.

7. Users must be further identified before they are allowed to open a database file. A secret password, different from the user's network access password, should be used. The database file that contains user identification and password data (database user accounts) must be encrypted. The encryption technique used should be sophisticated enough to prevent hackers from deciphering it. Only the database administrator(s) have access to this file.

8. Users must be assigned specific permission to use the database and the tables it contains. If users are to be restricted from viewing specific columns of a table, access to the table should be in the form of a query that includes only the fields that the user is authorized to view. The database management system must provide for revoking specific permissions as the need arises.

9. The data in tables should be auditable. Lack of auditability is an incentive to computer-based embezzling. Updates made by users to tables that contain financial data should be maintained in a log, preferably in

another database, that identifies the user who made the entry and the date and time the update was made. Logs are useful in reconstructing database entries that occurred between the time the database was last backed up and the time data was restored from the backup copy.

10. Operations that update records in more than one table should be accomplished by transaction techniques that can be reversed (rolled back) if updates to all the tables involved cannot be completed immediately.

Most network operating systems in use on PCs provide for the first five database security principles, but enforcement of password secrecy, monitoring of user transgressions, and virus surveillance often are ignored, especially in peer-to-peer networks. Access provides all five of the database security principles, but you must take specific actions to invoke and maintain these principles.

> ### Note
>
> One of the most frequent breaches of database security occurs when a temporary worker is hired to stand in for a user who is ill or on vacation. Instead of establishing a new network account, including a user name, password, and new user (or guest) account for the database, the employee's user names and passwords are divulged to the temporary worker for the sake of expediency. A temporary worker should be assigned his or her own identification for the network and database; the temporary worker's authorizations should be removed when the regular employee returns to the job.

Managing Groups and Users

Access and most client-server databases establish the following three groups of database users:

- *Administrators* (Admins) who have the authority to view and update existing tables and add or delete tables and other database objects from the database. Members of the Admins group usually have permission to modify the applications contained in databases.

- *Regular members of workgroups* (Users) who are assigned permission to open the database and are granted permissions to view and modify databases on a selective basis. Users ordinarily aren't granted permissions to modify Access applications.

- *Occasional users of databases* (Guests) who are granted limited rights to use a database and the objects it contains but aren't assigned a user account. Guest privileges often are assigned to persons being trained in the use of a database application.

When you install Access, you automatically are made a member of the Admins group with the name Admin and have all permissions granted. You have an empty password and Personal ID Number (PIN); this means that you don't need to enter a password to log on to the database(s) associated with the SYSTEM.MDA installed in the \ACCESS directory. When you are learning Access, you have little reason to establish database security. After you begin to create a useful database application, you should implement basic security provisions on your own computer.

Establishing Your Own Admins Name, Password, and PIN

Access has two levels of security: *application* level and *file* level. The application-level security system requires that each user of Access enters a user name and a password to start Access. Establishing single-user application-level security and preparing for multiuser security requires that you perform the following tasks:

1. Activate the log-on procedure for Access. This action requires that you add a password for the Admin user. To remain Admin, you need not complete the remaining steps, but the only security is your password.

2. Create a new account for yourself as a member of the Admins group.

3. Log on to Access using your new Admin user account.

4. Delete the default Admin user account. The Admins group should include entries for active database administrators only.

Note

Before you begin the following procedure, make a disk backup copy of the SYSTEM.MDA file in use and any database files that you created or modified while using this SYSTEM.MDA file. If you forget the user name or password you assigned to yourself after deleting the Admin user, you cannot log on to Access. In this case, you must restore the original version of the SYSTEM.MDA file. Then you may not be able to open the database files with which the original version of the SYSTEM.MDA file is associated unless you restore the backed-up versions.

VI

Advanced Techniques

To activate the log-on procedure for Access, complete the following steps:

1. A temporary password to the Admin user is necessary to activate Access's log-on procedure. Open a database so that the Security menu choice is displayed. Choose **C**hange Password from the **S**ecurity menu to display the Change Password dialog shown in figure 25.13.

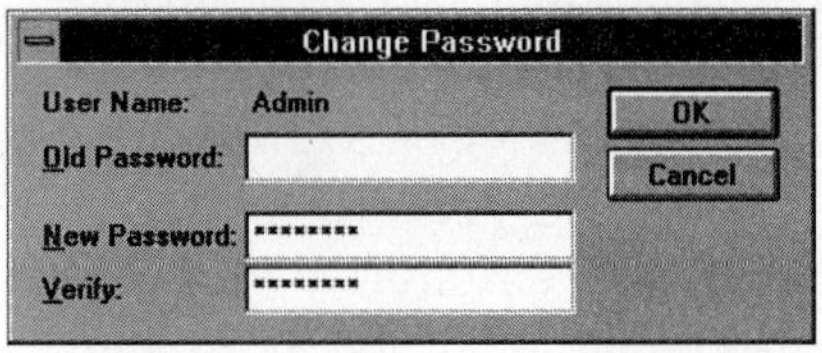

Fig. 25.13
The Change Password dialog used to establish your new password.

Tip

If you don't change the Admin user's password, you automatically are logged on as Admin with a blank password each time you start Access.

2. Press the Tab key to bypass the Old Password text box (this enters the equivalent of an empty password) and enter a temporary password, such as **Temp**, in the New Password text box. Your entry is shown as a series of asterisks to prevent disclosing your password to others as you enter it. Passwords are case-sensitive, so *Temp* is a different password from *temp*.

3. Type the password in the Verify text box to test your entry. The verification test is not case-sensitive.

   Click OK. If you receive the message "No permissions for Admin user," click OK because you delete the Admin user in the steps that follow.

4. Exit Access and launch it again from Program Manager. The Logon dialog shown in figure 25.14 appears.

Fig. 25.14
The Logon dialog that appears when you start Access with a user name and password.

5. Type **admin** in the Name text box, press Tab, and enter the password, exactly as you typed it in step 2. Press Enter or click OK. If you enter the password correctly, Access continues the startup procedure.

To add your new user account in the Admins group, perform the following steps:

1. Open a database so that the **S**ecurity menu choice appears. Choose **U**sers from the **S**ecurity menu. The Users dialog shown in figure 25.15 appears. All members of the Admins group automatically are included (and must be included) in the Users group. Both Admins and Users appear in the Member Of list.

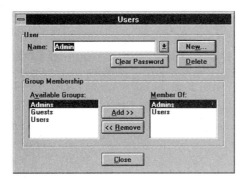

Fig. 25.15
The Users dialog for adding, changing, or deleting Access user accounts.

2. Click the New button to add your new account. The New User/Group dialog appears.

3. Type the name you want to use to identify yourself to Access in the Name text box and a four-digit PIN in the Personal ID Number text box as shown in figure 25.16. The PIN, with the Name entry, uniquely identifies your account. This precaution is necessary because two people may use the same log-on name; the Name and PIN values are combined to create a no-duplicates index on the Users table in SYSTEM.MDA. Click OK to close the New User/Group dialog and return to the Users dialog.

Fig. 25.16
The New User/ Group dialog.

VI

Advanced Techniques

4. *This is a critical step.* Select Admins in the Available Groups dialog and click the Add button to add the Admins group to your new user name (see fig. 25.17). If you fail to do this, you cannot delete the Admin user. (Access requires that there be at least one member of the Admins group in each SYSTEM.MDA file.)

Fig. 25.17
Adding the
Admins group to
your new user
account.

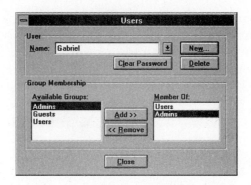

5. You don't enter a password for the new user at this time because you still are logged on to Access as Admin. Click the Close button to close the Users dialog and exit Access.

Tip
When you log on with your new user name, you can't see the names of the last four databases you opened as Admin when you choose **O**pen from the **F**ile menu. Prior database selections are specific to each user.

6. Launch Access, type your new user name in the Logon dialog, and press Enter or click OK. Do not enter a password because you have an empty password at this point. User names aren't case-sensitive; Access considers *NewAdmin* and *newadmin* to be the same user.

7. Open a database and choose **C**hange Password from the **S**ecurity menu. The Password dialog appears. Press Tab to bypass the Old Password text box and type the password you plan to use until it is time to change your password (to maintain system security). Passwords can be up to 14 characters long and can contain any character, except ASCII character 0, the Null character. Verify your password, and then press Enter or click OK to close the Password dialog.

8. Choose **U**sers from the **S**ecurity menu. The Users dialog appears. Open the Users list and select your new user name from the list. Verify that you are a member of the Admins and Users group. Open the Users list again and select Admin; then click Delete. You are asked to confirm deletion by the message box shown in figure 25.18. Click OK to confirm deletion.

Fig. 25.18
The message box
requesting
confirmation of
account deletion.

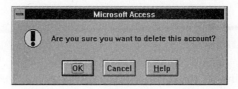

9. Exit Access, and then launch it again from Program Manager. Test your new password during the log-on procedure.

You use the same procedure to add other users as members of the default Admins, Users, or Guests group or of new workgroups you create.

Note

Be sure to write down and save your own PIN, and the PIN of every user you add to the workgroup, for future reference. User names and PINs aren't secure elements, so you can safely keep a list without compromising system security. This list should be accessible only to database administrators. You need a user's PIN so that the user can be recognized as a member of another workgroup when the need arises. (See the "Granting Permissions for a Database in Another Workgroup" section near the end of this chapter.)

Establishing Members of Access Groups

Groups within Access's security system are not the same as workgroups. As discussed previously, a workgroup shares the same SYSTEM.MDA file that is located in a specific directory. The entries you made in the preceding steps were saved in the SYSTEM.MDA file located in your \ACCESS directory (unless you specified a different directory in a previous section of this chapter). Workgroups have their own SYSTEM.MDA files in different directories.

To add a new user to a group, you must be logged on to Access as a member of the Admins group and complete the following steps:

1. Choose Users from the Security menu to open the Users dialog.

2. Click New. The New User/Group dialog appears. Type the new user's name and PIN. Click OK to create the account and close the dialog. The Users dialog reappears. Make a note of the PIN you used to add the new user. You need to know the user's PIN so that you can duplicate an entry for the new user in other workgroups.

3. The default group for all new users is Users. To add the user to the Admins group, select Admins in the Available Groups list and click the Add button to add Admins to the Member Of list (see preceding fig. 25.15). All users must be members of the Users group, except for members of the Guests group. To change the group membership of a current user to the Guests group, delete the user's account and then add the user with only Guests appearing in the Member Of list. Use the Remove

button to delete the User group assignment. Click Close to return to Access's main window when your selections are complete.

4. Request the new user to log on to Access with the user name and change their password from the default empty value to a legitimate password.

5. You can improve the level of security by typing the new user's password yourself, so that users cannot bypass the password step by leaving their passwords blank.

To enter a password for a new user, close Access, log on as the new user, choose **C**hange Password from the **S**ecurity menu, and enter the user's chosen password.

Before you add a significant number of users, decide whether you need additional groups and determine the permissions that should be assigned to each group other than Admins. These aspects of database security are discussed in the sections that follow.

> **Note**
>
> When requesting new users to enter their first password, emphasize the advantage of the use of longer passwords that combine upper- and lowercase characters and numbers because they improve system security. Users should not use their initials, names of spouses or children, birth dates, or nicknames; these are the entries that unauthorized users try first to gain access to the system.

Adding a New Group

In most cases, Admins, Users, and Guests are the only groups necessary for each workgroup you create. Members of a group usually share the same permissions to use database objects (which is the subject of the next section). Adding a new Access group is not necessary, therefore, unless you have a category of users who are to have a different set of permissions than members of the Users or Guests groups. Such a category may distinguish Users (who may be limited to viewing data) from members of "Data Entry" who have permission to update the data in tables.

To add a new group, perform the following steps:

1. Choose **G**roups from the **S**ecurity menu. The Groups dialog shown in figure 25.19 appears.

Fig. 25.19
Adding a new
user group to
a database.

2. Click the New button to open the New User/Group dialog (see preceding fig. 25.16).

3. Type the name of the Group in the Name dialog and a four-digit Personal ID Number, and then press Enter or click OK. The Groups dialog reappears.

   Group names can be up to 20 characters long and can contain spaces, but punctuation symbols aren't allowed. You don't need to make a note of the PIN in the case of groups because the PIN is used only for indexing purposes.

4. Click Close from the Groups dialog. You can delete the newly added group by clicking the Delete button now.

After you add a new group, you need to assign the default permissions that apply to all members of the group by the procedure outlined in the "Granting and Revoking Permissions" section that follows.

Deleting Users and Groups

Members of the Admins group have the authority to delete users from any group and to delete any group except Admins, Users, and Guests. To delete a user or group, choose **U**sers or **G**roups from the **S**ecurity menu, select the user or group to delete from the list box, and click Delete. You are asked to confirm the deletion. Admins, Users, and Guests groups must each contain one user account; you cannot delete all users for any of these groups.

Clearing Forgotten Passwords

If a user forgets their password and you are logged in to Access as a member of the Admins group, you can delete the user's password, so that you or the user can enter a new password.

To clear a user's password, complete the following steps:

1. Choose **U**sers from the **S**ecurity menu.

2. Open the Name list and select the user whose password you want to clear.

3. Click the Clear Password button (refer to fig. 25.15).

4. Make sure that the user whose password you cleared enters a new password, or log on to Access as the new user and enter a new password for the user.

As mentioned previously, entering the user's password as the database administrator is the only means of ensuring that the database security is enforced. There is no other means of ensuring that users assign themselves a password. (Of course, perverse users can change their own password to an empty string if they choose to do so.)

Understanding Database Object Ownership

The user who creates an object becomes the *owner* of the object. (Access calls the owner of an object the object's *creator*). Object owners have special status within the Access security system. The following two sections briefly describe owners' permissions and how to change the ownership of database objects. A more detailed description of object ownership is contained in the file SECURE.ZIP that you can download from the MSACCESS Forum of CompuServe.

Owner Permissions for Objects

The owner of an object has full (Administer) permissions for the object. No other user, including members of the Admins group can alter the object owner's permissions for the object. For example, the Admin user is the owner of all the database objects in NWIND.MDB. Thus, anyone who uses the Admin user account has full permissions for all objects in NWIND.MDB.

When a user other than the object's creator adds a new object to the database or to one of the existing objects in the database, this user becomes the owner of the object. For example, if user Margaret adds a control object to a form created by Larry, Margaret is the owner of the control object, not Larry. Mixed ownership of objects can lead to bizarre situations, such as the inability of the owner of a query to execute the query because the owner of the underlying tables has changed. (You can overcome this problem, however, by adding the WITH OWNERACCESS OPTION to the SQL statement for the query.)

When you create new database objects using the default Admin user ID, anyone else who has a retail copy of Access 2.0 and uses the default Admin user

ID also has full permissions for these objects. Thus, when you begin development of an application that you intend to share with others or that you want to prevent others from using or modifying, create a new account in the Admins group as described earlier in the chapter. Use your new Admins account when you create new applications.

Changing the Ownership of Database Objects

You can change the ownership of all the objects in a database for which you have Administer permissions by importing all the database objects into a new database you create with a user ID other than Admin. Access 2.0 makes it easy to import all the database objects from one .MDB file into another .MDB file with the Import Database add-in. The Import Database add-in automatically imports every object in the source database into the destination database.

Access

2.0

To test the Import Database add-in, follow these steps:

1. Launch Access and log on with your new user ID that includes Admins group membership.

2. Choose **N**ew Database from the **F**ile menu and give your database a name, such as **TEST.MDB**.

3. Choose Add-Ins from the **F**ile menu and then choose Im**p**ort Database from the submenu to display the Import Database dialog.

4. Select the source database whose objects you want to import. The \ACCESS\SAMPAPPS\SOLUTION.MDB file is a good choice for a test because it is relatively small (see fig. 25.20).

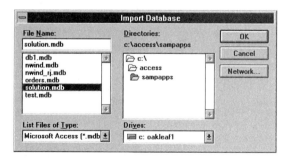

Fig. 25.20
Selecting the source database for importing objects.

VI

Advanced Techniques

5. Click OK to import all the objects from the source database into your new database. (This may take some time if your source database contains a large number of objects.)

The owner of all the objects in the new database is the user ID you used when you opened the new database.

> **Note**
>
> This chapter uses the term *user ID* to identify users of Access. Internally, Access uses a *system ID* (SID) to identify users. The SID is a value that Access computes from the user ID, password, and PIN. The SID is stored in the MSysUsers table of SYSTEM.MDA as an encrypted binary value in a field of the Binary (varbinary) data type. The Binary field data type is only supported by the retail and run-time Access for this purpose. Only Microsoft Corporation presently can create a field of the Binary data type.

Granting and Revoking Permissions for Database Objects

The second layer of Access security is at the database level. Access lets the database administrator grant or revoke *permissions* to use specific database objects to all members of a group or to specific members of a group. Permissions grant authority for users to view or alter specific database objects. The permissions granted to the group are inherited by each member as he or she is added to the group. You can grant additional permissions to individual members of a group, but you cannot revoke permissions that individual members inherit from the group. Permissions are stored within the database file as properties of individual database objects. Only members of the Admins group or users who have Administer permission can grant or revoke permissions for database objects.

> **Note**
>
> When you modify permissions for objects within a database, you establish accounts for users in the database file. If you delete the Admin user and assign yourself a new user name and PIN in the Admins group, any changes you make to the permissions by clicking the Assign button in the Permissions dialog are made a permanent element of the database. You must log on to Access with your new user name and password. Do not use the Assign button unless you are satisfied with the user name(s) you created in previous sections of this chapter. Click Cancel after making any changes to permissions you do not want to make permanent.

Table 25.2 lists the permissions offered by Access for database objects, ranked in descending level of authority. Full Permissions allow the user to use all the features of Access, including design functions. The description of the specific action allowed by a permission is listed in the Explicit Permissions column. Permissions at an authority level below Full Permissions require other permissions to operate; these required permissions are called *implicit permissions*.

Table 25.2 Permissions to Use Access Database Objects			
Permission	**Database Objects**	**Explicit Permissions**	**Implicit Permissions**
Open/Run	Forms, reports, macros	Use or run objects	Read Data
Read Design	All	View objects	Execute for macros only
Modify Design	All	Alter, replace, or delete objects	Update Data and Execute
Administer	All database objects	All permissions	Not applicable
Read Data	Tables, queries, forms	View data in objects	Read Design
Update Data	Tables, queries, forms	Edit table data	Read Data
Insert Data	Tables, queries, forms	Append data in tables	Read Data
Delete Data	Tables, queries, forms	Delete data in tables	Read Data

If, for example, you allow a user to modify design, this user also must be able to modify data and execute objects. Therefore, Update Data and Open/Run permissions are implied by the Modify Design permission. This user, and any other users allowed to modify data, must be able to read data. All users having permission to read data must be able to read designs. When you establish permissions for a database object, Access adds the implicit permissions automatically.

The Admins and Users groups have full permissions, and the Guests group has Read Design and Read Data permissions for any new database objects you create. If you intend to share the database with other users, it is not likely that you want all members of the Users group to have permission to update database tables nor should all Guests be able to view all objects. A more conservative set of permissions for the three groups follows:

- *Admins.* Full permissions for all objects. Admins privileges should be assigned to as few individuals as possible, consistent with the availability of backup database administrators to cover for the absence of the primary administrator. Members of the Admins group also must be members of the Users group.

- *Users.* Execute and Read Data permissions. Update, Insert, and Delete Data permissions are granted for specific forms and reports. Users ordinarily aren't granted Modify Design permission in databases.

- *Guests.* No group permissions. All permissions are granted to each guest on an *ad hoc* basis. Members of the Guests group are deleted when they no longer need access to the database.

You can add new groups with specific group permissions, such as DataEntry or Developers, to make assigning user permissions for database objects simpler.

> **Note**
>
> You can use the Run with Owner's Permissions check box or add the `WITH OWNERACCESS OPTION` to SQL statements to enable users without the required permissions to execute a query or to prevent them from doing so.

Altering Group Permissions

After you design your hierarchy of permissions and add any new user groups you need, you are ready to assign group permissions for each of the objects in your database. Only members of the Admins group can alter permissions for Groups or Users. The Permissions check boxes that are enabled depend on the type of object you choose. Open/Run, for example, is enabled only for database, form, report, and macro objects.

To change the permissions for a group, complete the following steps:

1. Open the database for which group permissions are to be granted or revoked.

2. Choose **P**ermissions from the **S**ecurity menu. The Permissions dialog appears.

3. Click the Groups option button to display the permissions for groups of users; then select Users in the User/Group Name list.

4. Open the Object Type drop-down list and select the type of database object whose permissions you want to change.

5. Select the specific object to which the new permissions will apply in the Object Name list.

6. Open the User/Group list and select the Group whose permissions you want to revise, Users for this example. Figure 25.21 shows the full permissions that Access assigns by default to the Users group.

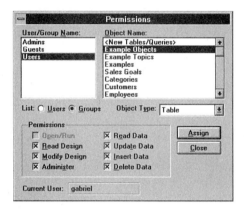

Fig. 25.21
The default permissions for the Users group.

7. Permissions currently granted to the group are shown by an X in the Permissions check boxes. Click the Modify Design, Update Data, Insert Data, and Delete Data check boxes to allow the users groups only to display forms and read table data. When you remove a permission, Access automatically removes the Administer permission. Your Permissions dialog appears as shown in figure 25.22.

8. Click the Assign button to make the new permissions effective for the selected database object.

9. Repeat steps 4 through 8 for each database object whose user permissions you want to change.

VI

Advanced Techniques

Fig. 25.22

Revising permissions for the Example Objects table for the Users group.

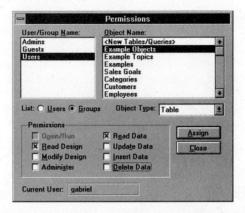

Granting Additional Permissions to Specific Users

The process of granting additional permissions to a specific user is similar to the process used to alter Group permissions. Permissions inherited by the user from the group to which the user is assigned are *not shown* in the Permissions dialog. To grant additional permissions to a specific user, complete the following steps:

1. Choose **P**ermissions from the **S**ecurity menu. The Permissions dialog appears.

2. Click the Users option button to display the permissions for a specific user, and then open the User/Group list and select the user, as shown in figure 25.23.

   TestUser is a member of the Users group. As mentioned in the introduction to this section, the Read Definitions and Read Data permissions that were inherited by TestUser from the modified permissions of the Users group aren't shown in the Permissions check boxes.

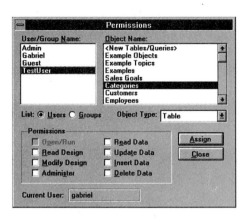

Fig. 25.23
The Permissions dialog for a user with inherited permissions.

3. To assign Modify Data permission to a specific user so that the user can update data for an object, select the object using the Type and Name lists, and then click the Update Data, Insert Data, and Delete Data check boxes. The implicit permissions—Read Design and Read Data—associated with the explicit permission, Update Data, are marked automatically by Access, as shown in figure 25.24. Click the Assign button after selecting each object whose permissions you want to change.

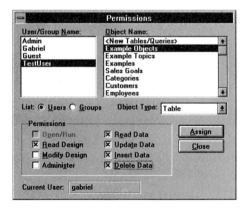

Fig. 25.24
The Permissions dialog for a new user, with the new data permissions added.

Implicit permissions for individual users are displayed in the Permissions check boxes, regardless of whether the implicit permissions also were inherited from group membership.

4. Repeat step 3 for each user that requires permissions for an object that aren't inherited from the user's group permissions. Click the Close button when you complete the permission changes for all users who require such changes.

VI

Advanced Techniques

> **Note**
>
> You can use the /Ro command line option, described in the preceding section, "Using Command Line Options to Open a Database," to revoke Update Data, Insert Data, and Delete Data permissions for the database on specific workstations. This isn't a secure method because the user can edit the command line option, remove the /Ro entry, and log on again with read-write privileges. If you use this method, Access displays a message box indicating that the database is being opened in read-only mode and that the user cannot modify data.

Granting Permissions for a Database in Another Workgroup

If your application requires that you attach a table in a secure database used by a different workgroup, the user needs to be a member of a group in the other workgroup and needs to be assigned appropriate permissions for the attached table. At this point, you need the list of PINs for users, mentioned in the "Establishing Your Own Admins Name, Password, and PIN" section earlier in this chapter.

To grant permission for a user to modify data in a table attached from another workgroup's database, perform the following steps:

1. Close Access; you need to relaunch Access when you select another workgroup.

2. Launch the Workgroup Administrator application and specify the path to the SYSTEM.MDA file of the workgroup that uses the database that contains the table to be attached.

3. Launch Access and open the database that contains the table to be attached.

4. Add an account for the user to the Users group with exactly the same user name and PIN as was used to add the user account to his or her workgroup.

5. If you don't want this user to join the other workgroup, enter a password and don't disclose the password to the user.

6. Open the Permissions dialog, select the table object to be attached, and assign the appropriate data permission for the table for the user.

You need to use the same PIN for the user in both workgroups because the account for the user is created from the user name and PIN, and the accounts must be identical in both databases. You also must use the same PIN number to reinstate the user's account if your SYSTEM.MDA file becomes corrupted; you don't have a current backup; and Access cannot repair it.

Administering Databases and Applications

Administering a multiuser database involves a number of duties besides adding and maintaining user accounts. The most important function of the database administrator is to ensure that periodic valid backup copies are made of database and system files. The database administrator's other responsibilities consist of routine database maintenance, periodic compacting of database files, and repairing databases.

Backing Up and Restoring Databases

The following maxims relate to maintaining backup copies of database files:

- The time interval between successive backups of databases is equal to the amount of data you are willing and able to reenter in the event of a fixed disk failure. Except in unusual circumstances, such as little or no update activity, daily backup is the rule.

- Rotate backup copies. Make successive backups on different tapes or disk sets. One of the tapes or disks may have defects that prevent restoring the backup. The backup device, such as a tape drive, can fail without warning you that the recorded data isn't valid.

- Test backup copies of databases periodically. You should test one different copy in the backup rotation sequence for restorability. If you rotate five daily backup tapes, for example, you should randomly choose one of the tapes, restore the database file from the tape, and open it with Access to ensure its validity every fifth day. Access tests each database object for integrity when you open the database file.

- Maintain off-site backups that you can use to restore data in case of a disaster, such as a fire or flood. The copy of the backup tape or disk that you test for restorability is a good candidate for an off-site backup copy.

You can back up database files on a network server by copying them to a workstation that has a fixed disk, but this technique doesn't provide backup security. The user of the workstation can erase or damage the backup copy if you don't create the off-site copy required for security against disasters.

Backing up data on network and peer-to-peer servers usually is accomplished with a tape drive device. These devices usually include an application that backs up all data on a network server or selected files on peer-to-peer servers at intervals and times you select. The simpler the backup operation, the more likely you are to have current backups. Regardless of how automated the backup procedure, however, you need to manually restore the test copy.

Compacting and Repairing Database Files

Compacting and repairing database files was discussed in Chapter 3, "Navigating within Access." You should compact database files in which applications add and delete data to recover the disk space occupied by the deleted data. The procedure for compacting a database is similar to that described for encrypting and decrypting databases, except that you choose **C**ompact Database rather than **E**ncrypt/Decrypt Database from the **F**ile menu.

If you have a fixed disk defragmentation utility, such as Norton Utilities' SpeedDisk or Allen Morris's Shareware Disk Organizer (DOG), you can improve the operating speed of Access if you periodically defragment database files. Most defragmentation utilities tell you whether a disk drive has sufficient fragmentation to justify running the utility.

If you receive a message that a database is corrupted or if the database behaves in an irregular manner, one or more of the objects it contains may be corrupt as the result of a hardware error. Databases can become corrupt as the result of a power failure when the computer is writing to the database file. The **R**epair Database choice of Access's **F**ile menu attempts to repair the damage. If Access cannot repair the corruption, you must restore the latest backup copy. Test the backup copy with the existing SYSTEM.MDA file; in some cases, you may need to restore the prior SYSTEM.MDA file that contains the user account data for the database.

Encrypting and Decrypting Database Files

File-level security isn't complete until you encrypt the database. Encrypting the database prevents others from reading its contents with a text editing or disk utility application, such as is included with Symantec's Norton Utilities. Encryption of databases causes Access's operations on tables to slow perceptibly because of the time required to decrypt the data. Only members of the Admins group can encrypt or decrypt a database.

> **Note**
>
> If you are using Stac Electronics' Stacker, DOS 6.0+'s DoubleDisk, or a similar fixed disk data-compression utility, you will find that encrypting your database files reduces the percentage of compression to zero or a very small number. Encrypting files eliminates the groups of repeating characters that form the basis of most data-compression algorithms.

To encrypt or decrypt an Access database file, complete the following steps:

1. Make sure that the disk drive of the computer on which the database is stored has sufficient free space to create a copy of the database you intend to encrypt or decrypt. Access makes a new copy of the file during the process.

2. All other workstations, including your own, need to close the database file to be encrypted. You cannot encrypt or decrypt a database file that is in use on any workstation.

3. Activate the Database window and choose **E**ncrypt/Decrypt Database from the **F**ile menu. The Encrypt/Decrypt dialog appears.

4. Select the name of the database file to be encrypted and click OK.

5. If the file already is encrypted, it is decrypted, and vice versa. The title bar of the dialog that opens indicates whether the file will be encrypted or decrypted in this operation. If you are interested only in whether the file has been encrypted, you can click Cancel now.

6. Type the name of the encrypted or decrypted file to create, and click OK. Normally, you type the same name as the original file; Access does not replace the original copy of the file if the process does not succeed.

Databases are compacted by Access when they are encrypted or decrypted.

> **Note**
>
> You do not need to encrypt files while you're developing applications using files that aren't shared with others unless the files contain sensitive information. After the files are made shareable, a good security practice is to encrypt them, even if they don't contain confidential data.

VI

Advanced Techniques

◄ "Compacting
    Databases,"
    p. 117

◄ "Encrypting
    and Decrypting
    Databases,"
    p. 120

Modifying and Updating Multiuser Applications

As mentioned in earlier chapters of this book, it is a recommended database design practice to create two database files for multiuser applications. One file contains the data objects (tables), and the other file contains the application objects. The queries, forms, and reports you create when you develop a multiuser application are likely to be altered in response to suggestions from users and the needs of a growing organization.

If you combine data and application objects in a single file, modifying an existing application requires that you make a temporary unshared copy of the database file, make the modifications to the test file, and then test the modifications or additions you made. Then you need to export the modifications to the multiuser database.

To modify or update the multiuser copy of the single database file, perform the following steps:

1. Have all users close the database file to be updated or modified.

2. Make a backup copy of the multiuser database file and the related SYSTEM.MDA file.

3. If you made changes to the structure of any tables, import the corresponding table with a different name to your temporary database, and then append the data from the table to your new table structure (only) with an append query.

4. Export the objects you added or altered to the multiuser database.

5. Test the operation of the updated multiuser application.

The procedure for importing and exporting individual database objects is covered in Chapter 7, "Attaching, Importing, and Exporting Tables."

From Here...

Although this chapter was devoted primarily to using Access in a multiuser environment, many elements of database security discussed apply to single-user applications. Even if you don't have a network now, if you use Access in an organization of more than ten employees, multiuser applications will likely be a part of your future.

■ Chapter 3, "Navigating within Access," explains the processes of encrypting, converting, and compacting Access databases.

- Chapter 7, "Attaching, Importing, and Exporting Tables," describes how you attach tables contained in shared Access databases to local application .MDBs.

- Chapter 26, "Connecting to Client-Server Databases," discusses the special techniques you use to attach tables of client-server RDBMSs using the ODBC Administrator application. Access 2.0's new SQL pass-through methods also are described.

VI

Advanced Techniques

Chapter 26

Connecting to Client-Server Databases

One of the computer buzz words of the mid-1990s, *downsizing*, was mentioned in the context of local area networks (LANs) in the preceding chapter. Downsizing has another element: moving database management systems from mainframe computers to client-server RDBMSs running on PCs and RISC (reduced instruction set computing) workstation-servers. Another newly minted term, *rightsizing*, means choosing the best combination of platforms to ensure maximum available of corporate data to those who need it. Rightsizing often involves retaining mainframe computers as giant database servers, but moving the applications that access and manipulate the data from the mainframe to PCs. The final member of the ...sizing trio is *upsizing*. Upsizing means moving from a desktop database, such as Access, dBASE, or Paradox, to a client-server RDBMS.

Regardless of the linguistic legitimacy of terms such as rightsizing, these words have become ingrained in today's *computerese*. Each of these expressions relates to the *scalability* of applications; scalable applications can run on a variety of platforms, communicate by industry-standard LAN protocols, and access data stored in a variety of different types of databases. Access 2.0 presently runs under Windows 3+ or Windows NT 3+, and Windows NT runs on PCs and RISC workstations, so Access itself is moderately scalable.

The Microsoft Windows network operating system (NOS) and Novell NetWare both offer their own NOS protocols (NetBEUI and IPX/SPX respectively) but also offer TCP/IP (Transport Control Protocol/Internet Protocol). TCP/IP rapidly is becoming the worldwide standard for heterogeneous networks—networks that connect servers and workstations using different hardware and operating systems. Several vendors offer add-on TCP/IP networking

In this chapter, you learn to

■ Understand the Open Database Connectivity API

■ Install the Microsoft ODBC driver for SQL Server

■ Add and remove ODBC data sources

■ Attach client-server tables to Access databases

■ Use Access 2.0's SQL pass-through queries

VI

Advanced Techniques

capability for DOS and Windows. Thus, the scalability of Access applications can be enhanced by the NOS that connects a multiuser Access application to the shared database files. For example, it is a relatively simple process to use TCP/IP to share database files located on a NFS (Network File System) server running under UNIX.

The third element of scalability, the capability to access data that resides in a variety of SQL-compliant databases, is provided by Microsoft Corporation's Open Database Connectivity (ODBC) products. Access 2.0 includes the ODBC Administrator application and an ODBC driver for the Microsoft and Sybase versions of SQL Server. When this edition was written, there were 76 suppliers of ODBC drivers, and the number of individual drivers numbered in the hundreds. ODBC provides Access with the capability to connect to virtually any popular mainframe-, minicomputer-, RISC-, and PC-resident SQL-compliant database. This chapter describes how ODBC works and how you connect to client-server databases with ODBC drivers.

Defining the Client-Server Environment

Client-server databases are designed specifically for use on application server-based networks. An application server uses a network operating system, such as Windows NT Advanced Server, optimized specifically for running applications rather than sharing files or peripheral devices. Client-server databases have many advantages over conventional database systems, including increased database security, incorporation of all components of the database (and often all databases) in a single file, and faster access to data. The clients of a client-server database are workstations, often called *front-ends*, connected to the server, the *back-end*. In these respects, Access databases and client-server databases are similar. The principal difference between Access and a typical client-server database manager, such as Microsoft SQL Server, is that the client-server application performs many operations on the server that traditionally are done by database applications running on the client workstation.

Client-server database managers accept SQL statements from client applications. The CSDBM interprets the SQL statement and executes the actions specified in the statement. If you send a SELECT query SQL statement to the CSDBM, the CSDBM returns only the result table to the client; processing of the query occurs on the server computer. This action speeds query generation two ways: The amount of information traveling over the network is reduced, and server computers often have much more powerful and faster microprocessors than do the workstation clients.

To understand many of the examples of this chapter, you need to know how the computers that created the examples are set up. The following list describes the computers and the network used to create this chapter's examples of employing ODBC for connecting to client-server databases:

- The server (\\OAKLEAF0) is an 80486DX2-66 ISA clone with local bus video, 32M of RAM, and a 1.2G Maxtor SCSI-2 fixed disk drive (8 ms. average access time). An Ultrastor 34F SCSI fixed disk controller on the local bus uses Corel SCSI to provide ASPI services when running under DOS 5.0. Dual-boot DOS/Windows NT is installed on the 600M C:\ drive (a FAT partition). Windows for Workgroups 3.11 is installed on the C:\ drive. The D:\ drive is a Texel DM-3024 double-speed SCSI CD-ROM drive. The remaining 600M of the fixed drive is an E:\ partition using NTFS (Windows NT's New Technology File System.)

- Microsoft SQL Server 4.2 for Windows NT (Enterprise Edition, SQLSNT for short) runs under Windows NT Advanced Server 3.1 (NTAS) on the \\OAKLEAF0 server. This combination was selected because it represents the highest price-performance value of any full-fledged client-server RDBMS/NOS available at the time this edition was written. SQLSNT is a multi-threaded, symmetrical multiprocessing (SMP) server that achieves very high data throughput with 250 or more simultaneous users. The 16-bit versions of SQLSNT's SQL Administrator, SQL Object Manager, SQL Client Configuration Utility, and ISQL/w, the Windows version of the ISQL command line utility, are installed on each client.

- The client used to write this edition (\\OAKLEAF1) is an 80486DX2-66 ISA clone with local bus video, 16M of RAM, and a 300M disk with a conventional FAT C:\ partition, a D:\ partition compressed with Stac Electronics Stacker 3.0 drive, and a Sony CDU-431 CD-ROM (F:\; Stacker 3.0 occupies the E:\ partition). Thus, *server shares* (logical drives attached from the server) begin as drive G:\.

- Another client (\\OAKLEAF2) is an 80386DX33 ISA clone with a 300M disk used primarily for composing and sequencing music. It is equipped with a variety of sound cards and synthesizer modules. The 80386 client is used for testing the performance of Access applications on the average client workstation.

VI

Advanced Techniques

- The server and the clients are equipped with Intel EtherExpress 16 network interface cards (NICs) connected via thin Ethernet coaxial cabling. Both NetBEUI (NetBIOS Extended User Interface, the native protocol for Windows for Workgroups and Windows NT networks) and TCP/IP network protocols are used. Remote Access Services (RAS), which allow dial-up (modem) connection to the NTAS server, also are implemented.

If the preceding description appears to be written in Greek, don't despair; knowing the computer setup is only necessary to explain the entries in the text boxes of the dialogs illustrated in this chapter.

Defining Open Database Connectivity

Access uses the Microsoft Open Data Base Connectivity (ODBC) application programming interface (API) to provide access to any database system for which ODBC drivers are available. An application programming interface is a standardized method by which an application communicates with elements of the computer's operating system or environment. For example, applications use the Windows API in GDI.EXE, a Windows DLL, to perform all display operations. The ODBC API enables a standard set of SQL statements in any application to be translated to commands recognized by the database. The role of ODBC drivers is explained in the following section.

The ODBC API is the first element of Microsoft's Windows Open Services Architecture (WOSA) that is intended to be used to create commercial Windows applications. MAPI (Messaging API) and TAPI (Telephony API) also are members of WOSA. Ultimately, WOSA will include a group of APIs that enable Windows applications to manipulate data residing in any format on any type of computer located anywhere in the world. Enterprise-wide data sharing through local and wide area networks, using LAN cabling, dial-up and dedicated telephone lines, and microwave or satellite transmission, now primarily employs large mainframe computers as centralized database servers.

One of today's trends in enterprise-wide computing is the use of distributed database systems. Distributed database systems enable elements of a large database to be stored on servers in different locations that act as if they were a single large server. As advanced Windows operating systems are developed and additional members of WOSA become a reality, PCs using Intel 80x86 architecture and RISC processors will capture a larger share of the server market. Access is designed to play an important role in enterprise-wide, distributed database systems: creating the applications users need to view and update the myriad databases to which they can connect.

Understanding ODBC Drivers

The ODBC API consists of a driver manager and one or more ODBC drivers, as illustrated by the shaded boxes in figure 26.1. Windows uses drivers to adapt its standard API to specific combinations of hardware such as displays, keyboards, and printers. Likewise, the ODBC API uses drivers to translate instructions passed from the application through the driver manager to instructions compatible with various RDBMSs. When the ODBC driver manager receives instructions from Access intended for a data source, such as a SQL Server database, the driver manager opens the appropriate ODBC driver for the database. The relationship of the ODBC driver manager and drivers parallels Access's built-in Jet (originally Joint Engine Technology, JET) database engine and the drivers used to connect to Access, dBASE, FoxPro, Paradox, and Btrieve files.

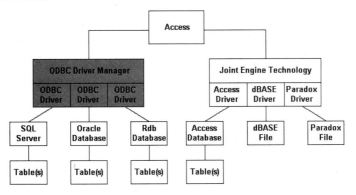

Fig. 26.1
A comparison of the ODBC and Jet driver systems used with Access.

ODBC drivers are classified as one of the following two types:

- *Single-tier* drivers translate SQL statements into low-level instructions that operate directly on files. Single-tier drivers are required for RDBMSs that don't process SQL statements directly. The widely used PC RDBMSs fall into this category. The drivers included with Access for connecting to dBASE, Paradox, and Btrieve databases are single-tier drivers (but they aren't ODBC drivers).

- *Multiple-tier* drivers process ODBC actions but pass SQL statements directly to the data source. All popular client-server RDBMSs that can run on PCs and most mini- and mainframe RDBMSs process SQL statements directly. The ODBC drivers shown in the list that follows are multiple-tier drivers because the client-server RDBMSs with which the drivers are used process SQL statements directly.

VI

Advanced Techniques

One ODBC driver is required for each type of client-server database whose tables you want to attach to an Access database, but a single driver can be used to connect to several databases of the same type. Each connection to a database is called an *instance* of a driver.

Access

2.0

The ODBC API is based on a standard called the X/Open SQL Call Level Interface (CLI) developed by the SQL Access Group, an organization comprised of hardware manufacturers, software suppliers, and users of SQL databases. Microsoft published the standards for creating ODBC drivers, so any RDBMS supplier can make its database product compatible with Access by writing the appropriate driver. Microsoft provides a single ODBC driver that is compatible with the following client-server databases:

■ Microsoft SQL Server databases on Windows NT, Microsoft LAN Manager, IBM LAN Server, Novell, and Banyan networks.

■ Sybase SQL Server databases up to, but not including Sybase System 10, running on UNIX servers and as NetWare-Loadable Modules (NLMs) on Novell servers. (You can use the SQL Server driver with Sybase System 10, but you cannot avail yourself of many of the new System 10 features with this driver.)

Most publishers of major client-server database management systems provide ODBC drivers for their database products. Prior versions of Access included a driver for ORACLE databases through version 6.0; this driver is not included with Access 2.0. Oracle Corporation (Redwood Shores, CA) now provides and supports ODBC drivers for its Oracle Server RDBMSs. Q+E Software (formerly Pioneer Software, Raleigh, NC), supplies a variety of third-party ODBC drivers for client-server and other databases. Microsoft Corporation offers the ODBC Desktop Database Drivers kit and includes these drivers with Microsoft Excel 5.0 and Word 6.0. If the client-server RDBMS you are using is not included in the preceding list, check with the supplier to determine whether an ODBC-compliant driver is available for the RDBMS and whether the driver is compatible with Access.

Installing the Access ODBC Driver for SQL Server

Installing the Access ODBC driver for Microsoft SQL Server is a three- or four-stage process, depending on the version of Microsoft or SQL Server installed. Following are the basic steps in the process:

- Add a special set of stored procedures to each SQL Server to which workstations running Access are connected if you are running a SQL Server version prior to 4.2 or Sybase SQL Server. You do not need to run the stored procedure if you are using SQLSNT.

- Grant permissions to the users of workstations that access tables or columns of tables of SQL Server databases. (SQL Server does offer column-level permissions.)

- Install the Access ODBC driver on each workstation that needs to attach SQL Server tables to Access databases. If all workstations are to share the same SQL Server files, you can install the ODBC driver on the network server rather than on each workstation. (If you use the Custom installation and specify that the ODBC drivers be installed, you can skip this step.)

- Establish connections to specific SQL Server databases with the Access ODBC Administrator application.

Each of these stages, except the second stage, is described in the sections that follow. SQL Server's documentation covers granting permissions to users of SQL Server databases. Granting permissions usually is performed by the database administrator or the database owner.

Configuring Microsoft and Sybase SQL Server

Microsoft SQL Server versions earlier than 4.2 and Sybase SQL Server do not include all the stored procedures necessary to provide information about the SQL Server system catalog that is required by the ODBC driver. Use the batch file INSTCAT.SQL, included on the ODBC distribution disk, with SQL Server's isql command line utility. INSTCAT.SQL installs the required catalog-stored procedures. Type the following statement at the DOS command line of a workstation connected to SQL Server:

```
isql -Usa -Ppass_word -Sserver_name < d:\instcat.sql
```

VI

Advanced Techniques

In this case, d is the drive in which the ODBC disk is located. This isql statement adds the stored procedures to SQL Server listed in table 26.1.

Table 26.1 SQL Server Stored Procedures Required for Use with the ODBC APIs	
Procedure Name	**Purpose of Stored Catalog Procedure**
sp_column_privileges	Provides column privileges for the specified table(s).
sp_columns	Provides information about the columns in the table(s).
sp_databases	Supplies a list of databases.
sp_fkeys	Provides information about foreign keys in tables(s).
sp_pkeys	Supplies data on primary keys of table(s).
sp_server_info	Provides attribute names and values for the server.
sp_special_columns	Gives information on columns in a table that have special attribute types.
sp_sproc_columns	Supplies data on columns for a stored procedure.
sp_statistics	Lists the indexes for a table.
sp_stored_procedure	Lists the stored procedures for the system.
sp_table_privileges	Describes the privileges for the table(s).
sp_tables	Lists the table(s) that can be queried.

The stored procedures listed in table 26.1 are included in version 4.2+ of Microsoft SQL Server for OS/2 and SQL Server for Windows NT.

Installing the ODBC Administrator on Workstations

Each workstation that needs to attach SQL Server tables to Access databases must be connected to the SQL Server through the network operating system, Microsoft Windows Network, Microsoft LAN Manager, IBM LAN Server, Banyan VINES, or Novell NetWare. If you are running Windows 3.0+, the connection to Windows is made with the Networks option of the Windows Setup application.

To install the ODBC Administrator application for Access 2.0 on a workstation on which Access 2.0 is installed, but ODBC was not specified during installation, perform the following steps:

1. Close all open Windows applications. If the MS Access Setup icon appears in the Microsoft Access program group, double-click the icon to launch the maintenance setup operation and skip to step 5.

2. Insert disk 1 of the Access distribution disk set into drive A or drive B.

3. Choose **R**un from Program Manager's **F**ile menu.

4. Type *d:***setup** in the Command Line text box, where *d* is the disk drive in which the ODBC disk is located, and press Enter or click OK. The opening setup dialog of figure 26.2 appears for workstations on which Access 2.0 is installed.

Tip
You don't need to install the ODBC Administrator if you previously installed Microsoft Excel 5.0 or Word 6.0 with the database options. Open Control Panel and check to see whether the ODBC icon is present. If it is, proceed to the next section.

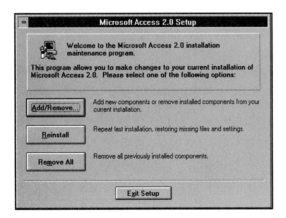

Fig. 26.2
Starting the maintenance installation of ODBC drivers.

5. Click the Add/Remove button to display the Maintenance Installation dialog shown in figure 26.3.

VI

Advanced Techniques

Fig. 26.3

The Maintenance Installation dialog that adds the ODBC drivers and Administrator.

6. The ODBC Support check box is cleared if you did not install the ODBC Support files. ODBC Support installs both the ODBC Administrator application and the SQL Server ODBC driver. Click the ODBC Support check box; then click Continue.

Tip

If you installed the ODBC Administrator application (ODBCADM.EXE) from a previous version of Access, delete the icon for ODBCADM.EXE, or you can encounter GPFs if you try to run ODBCADM.EXE with the newly installed ODBC files.

The Access 2.0 Setup process automatically installs the SQL Administrator application, ODBCINST.DLL, as a component of the Windows Control Panel application. Figure 26.4 shows the appearance of Control Panel's application group after installing the ODBC Administrator. Setup also installs the SQL Server ODBC driver and creates the required entries for SQLSRVR.DLL in your new ODBCINST.INI file in your \WINDOWS directory. The next section describes how to add an SQL Server data source.

Adding and Removing SQL Server Data Sources

You use Control Panel's ODBC Administrator application to add or remove SQL Server data sources. You need at least one SQL Server data source to enable Access to attach, export, or import SQL Server tables. To add an SQL Server data source, follow these steps:

1. Double-click the ODBC icon in Control Panel to launch the ODBC Administrator. ODBC Administrator's Data Sources dialog appears, as shown in figure 26.5.

Fig. 26.4
Control Panel
with the ODBC
Administrator
application
installed.

Figure 26.5 shows a multitude of ODBC data sources. If you have not previously installed ODBC data sources, the ODBC Data Sources (Driver) list is empty. If you are installing the SQL Server data source on another user's workstation, there may be a variety of ODBC data sources installed for use with other applications such as Microsoft Excel 5.0, Project 4.0, and Word 6.0.

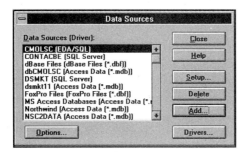

Fig. 26.5
The Data
Sources dialog
of the ODBC
Administrator.

2. Click the Add button to add a new ODBC data source with the Add Data Source dialog. If there is more than one ODBC driver in the Installed ODBC Drivers list, select the SQL Server item, as shown in figure 26.6.

Figure 26.6 is representative of the appearance of the Add Data Source dialog after installing one of the Microsoft applications that include the Microsoft Query DDE server applet.

VI

Advanced Techniques

Fig. 26.6
Choosing the SQL
Server ODBC
driver in the Add
Data Source server
dialog.

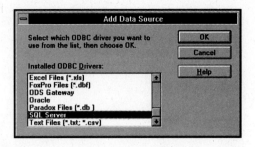

3. Click OK to display the ODBC SQL Server Setup dialog. Enter a short descriptive name of the SQL Server database in the Data Source Name dialog. Unless you have a particular database that contains the tables you want to attach to Access, type **pubs** to specify the pubs sample database supplied with SQL Server. Type a description of the database, such as **SQL Server Sample Database**, in the Description text box.

4. Select the name of the server that holds the SQL Server database you want to use from the Server combo list. If no entries appear in the combo list, type the name of the server (without the preceding \\) in the text box. Unless you are using TCP/IP as your network protocol or using a special network library (netlib) for the data source, accept the (Default) entries for the Network Address and Network Library text boxes (see fig. 26.7). The default network library for SQL Server is DBNMP3.DLL. Click the Options button to expand the dialog to specify a default database.

Fig. 26.7
Beginning the
definition of a
new ODBC data
source.

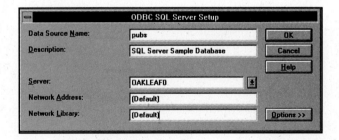

5. Type **pubs** in the Database Name text box, as shown in figure 26.8.

The Language Name drop-down list displays the National languages that the database supports. (National language is not necessarily the same as the Locale.)

The Convert OEM to ANSI check box changes special characters in SQL Server database tables to their Windows (ANSI) equivalents, when an ANSI equivalent is available. If you or the database administrator installed SQL Server with the default code page, you don't need to be concerned with OEM to ANSI conversion.

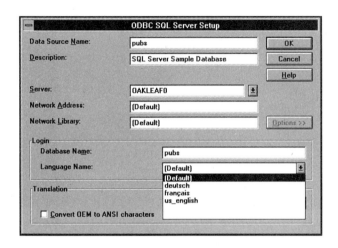

Fig. 26.8
Completing the definition of the ODBC data source.

6. Click OK to add the new data source and close the Data Source dialog. Your new data source is added to the Data Sources (Driver) list of the Data Sources dialog, as shown in figure 26.9.

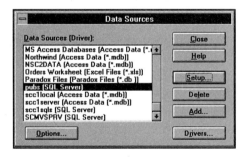

Fig. 26.9
The new SQL Server data source installed for use with the ODBC API.

VI

Advanced Techniques

7. Click Exit to close the ODBC Administrator application, and then close Control Panel.

You can add additional SQL Servers data sources for a workstation by repeating steps 1 through 4 before exiting the ODBC Administrator application. The entries you make for each new data source are added to the ODBC.INI file located in the \WINDOWS directory of the workstation.

Using Databases Connected by ODBC

After you add the SQL Server database as a data source, you can attach, import, or export tables in the SQL Server database to your Access database, depending on the permissions granted by SQL Server to each connected workstation. You use tables in the client-server database in the same manner you use attached Access, dBASE, FoxPro, Paradox, or Btrieve tables. (See Chapter 7, "Attaching, Importing, and Exporting Tables.") You don't specify indexes to be used with client-server tables because indexes are automatically opened when you open the table for which indexes have been created, just as with Access tables.

Pubs is a demonstration database, supplied with Microsoft and Sybase SQL Server, that contains tables for a fictional book distributor. Pubs' tables include information on imaginary book publishers, titles, and authors. (Using all lowercase names for SQL Server objects is a long-standing convention, thus the name "pubs"). To attach the tables in the pubs SQL Server database to an Access database, NWIND.MDB in this example, follow these steps:

1. Launch Access and open the Northwind Traders sample database. Choose **A**ttach Table from the **F**ile menu. The Attach dialog appears.

2. Use the vertical scroll bar to expose the <SQL Database> entry in the Data Source list, as shown in figure 26.10. Double-click the <SQL Database> entry or select the entry and click OK. The SQL Data Sources dialog appears.

Fig. 26.10
The Attach dialog with the <SQL Database> data source added.

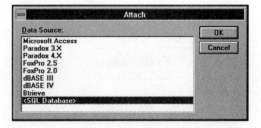

3. Double-click or select the data source name in the Select Data Source list as shown in figure 26.11. The SQL Server Login dialog appears.

Fig. 26.11
Choosing the a network host name as an SQL data source.

4. Type your login identification and password in the Login ID and Password text boxes. **sa** (system administrator) is used as the Login ID, and no Password is used in this example (see fig. 26.12).

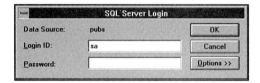

Fig. 26.12
Logging in to the SQL Server pubs database as the system administrator.

5. Click the options button to display additional login options, as shown in figure 26.13. Open the Database drop-down list of the Options section of the SQL Server Login dialog to display other databases installed on the server. The entries in the Application Name and Workstation ID text boxes are added automatically for you by Access. Select pubs and click OK to log in to SQL Server.

After you are connected to the Pubs database with the ODBC API, the Attach Tables dialog appears.

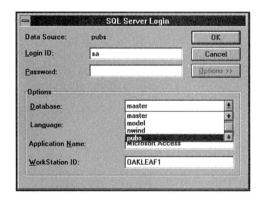

Fig. 26.13
The extended version of the SQL Server Login dialog.

VI

Advanced Techniques

6. Select the dbo.authors table (dbo is an SQL Server abbreviation for database owner), as shown in figure 26.14, and click the Save Login ID and Password Locally check box. Click the Attach button to attach the table to NWIND.MDB.

Fig. 26.14
Attaching the dbo.authors table from the pubs database to the Northwind Traders database.

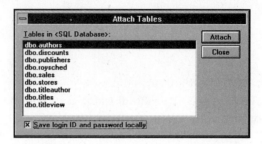

Checking the Save Login ID check box eliminates the need to reenter your login ID and password each time you attach another table. If the database administrator adds additional security provisions to a database (by adding a special MSysConf table to the database), the Save Login ID check box is disabled.

7. The message box of figure 26.15 indicates that you successfully attached the table. An underscore substitutes for the period between dbo and the table name because periods are not allowed within Access table names. (Periods are separators between table names and fields in Access.)

Fig. 26.15
The message box that indicates that an SQL Server table was attached.

8. Repeat steps 6 and 7, adding the dbo.titleauthor, dbo.titles, and dbo.publishers tables from the pubs database to the tables attached to NWIND.MDB. The Tables list of the Database window appears as shown in figure 26.16. (You can attach all the tables, if you want.)

Fig. 26.16
The Tables list
of the Database
window with four
tables attached
from the pubs
database.

Double-click the dbo_*table_name* item you want to examine. To create a
query that joins the tables and displays the author name, book title, and
book publisher, follow these steps:

1. Create a new query and add the dbo_authors, dbo_titleauthor,
   dbo_titles, and dbo_publishers tables to your query. Then click the
   Close button of the Add Tables dialog.

   Key fields of SQL Server tables are indicated in bold type, the same way
   Access emphasizes key fields in its tables. Access creates and joins automatically based on the key fields and identically named foreign-key
   fields of the SQL Server tables.

2. Click and drag the au_lname field from the dbo_authors table to the
   field row of the first column of the query.

3. Repeat step 2 for the title field of the dbo_titles table and the pub_name
   field of the dbo_publishers table. Your Query Design window appears,
   as shown in figure 26.17.

4. Click the Run Query button on the toolbar to display your query result
   set, as shown in figure 26.18.

VI

Advanced Techniques

Fig. 26.17
The Query Design window for the example based on tables attached from the pubs database.

Select Query: Query1

au_lname	title	pub_name
White	Prolonged Data Deprivation: Four Case Studies	New Moon Books
Green	The Busy Executive's Database Guide	Algodata Infosystems
Green	You Can Combat Computer Stress!	New Moon Books
Carson	But Is It User Friendly?	Algodata Infosystems
O'Leary	Cooking with Computers: Surreptitious Balance Sheets	Algodata Infosystems
O'Leary	Sushi, Anyone?	Binnet & Hardley
Straight	Straight Talk About Computers	Algodata Infosystems
Bennet	The Busy Executive's Database Guide	Algodata Infosystems
Dull	Secrets of Silicon Valley	Algodata Infosystems
Gringlesby	Sushi, Anyone?	Binnet & Hardley
Locksley	Net Etiquette	Algodata Infosystems
Locksley	Emotional Security: A New Algorithm	New Moon Books
Blotchet-Halls	Fifty Years in Buckingham Palace Kitchens	Binnet & Hardley
Yokomoto	Sushi, Anyone?	Binnet & Hardley
del Castillo	Silicon Valley Gastronomic Treats	Binnet & Hardley
DeFrance	The Gourmet Microwave	Binnet & Hardley

Record: 1 of 25

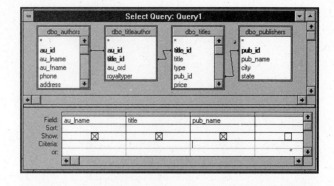

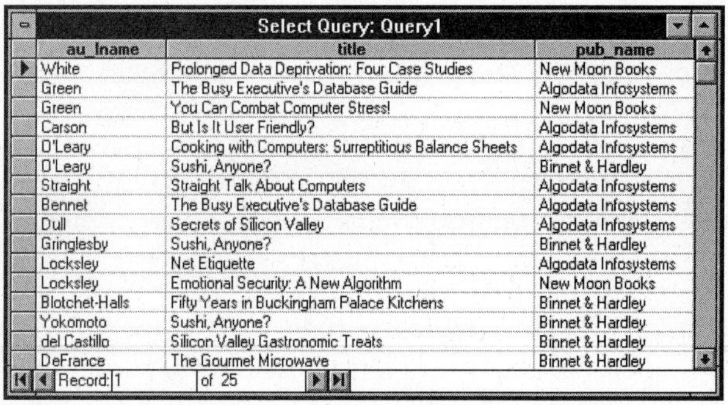

Fig. 26.18
The query result set from the query design shown in figure 26.17.

5. To remove the attached tables from the Northwind Traders database, close your query and save it for the example of the next section. Click the Show Database window button of the toolbar, click the Tables button in the Database Window, and select the name of the attached table to delete. Press Delete. A message box appears that requests you to confirm that you want to delete the attachment to the table (see fig. 26.19). Click Cancel because you use the attached SQL Server tables in the next section.

Fig. 26.19
The message box that confirms deletion of an attachment to a table.

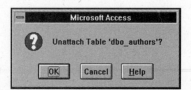

> **Note**
>
> You can eliminate the need to add the dbo_ prefix to table names by renaming the attachments to the table name without the dbo_ prefix. Close any open attached tables, select the table, and then choose Rename from the File menu to enter the new name.

The preceding example, using the pubs and Northwind Traders databases, is typical of the procedure that you use to attach tables from any client-server database for which an ODBC driver is available.

Troubleshooting

A "Cannot connect to server" or similar error messages occur when attempting to attach to SQL Server.

There are a variety of problems that can lead to the inability to connect to SQL Server. The most common cause is the lack of or an outdated version of the DBNMP3.DLL library on your computer. DBNMP3.DLL is the named pipes library that is required to connect to SQL server. Choose Search from File Manager's File menu and verify that DBNMP3.DLL is installed in \WINDOWS\SYSTEM. (The size of the version of DBNMP3.DLL that was current when this edition was written is 10,704 bytes. The date should correspond to the dates of other files installed by Access of other applications that install DBNMP3.DLL, such as CTL3D.DLL or CTL3DV2.DLL.) If you have additional copies of DBNMP3.DLL with earlier dates in directories other than \WINDOWS\SYSTEM, delete these unneeded copies.

Using Access 2.0's SQL Pass-Through Queries

Access
2.0

SQL pass-through queries enable you to write queries in the dialect of SQL used by the server RDBMS. SQL Server, as an example, lets you write stored procedures that you can execute by name, instead of by sending SQL statements to the server. Executing a stored procedure query is faster than executing the query through Access's Jet database engine because of reduced network traffic and faster execution of the query by the server. (Stored procedure queries are pre-compiled by SQL Server.) You also need to use SQL pass-through if you want to take advantage of special Transact-SQL reserved words not included in Access SQL.

Access 1.x required that you use Access Basic to declare the functions of MSASP110.DLL, an SQL pass-through library available for downloading from CompuServe. Access 2.0 has built-in SQL pass-through capability, similar to that offered by Visual Basic 3.0. You can convert the query you created in the preceding section to an SQL pass-through query by following these steps:

1. Open the saved query in Query Design View, and choose SQL-Specific from the **Q**uery menu; then choose **P**ass-through from the submenu.

2. The SQL window opens with the SQL statement behind your query, as shown in figure 26.20. The Query Design button is disabled when you convert a conventional Access query to the SQL pass-through type.

3. Click the Run Query button of the toolbar to execute your pass-through query. You receive the same query result set as that from the conventional query executed through the Jet database engine.

Fig. 26.20

The SQL window for an SQL pass-through query.

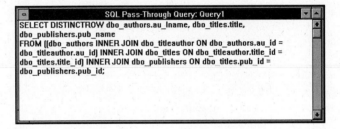

When you save an SQL pass-through query, the ODBC symbol (the Western Hemisphere), appears in the Queries list of the Database window, as shown in figure 26.21.

Fig. 26.21

The Queries list of the Database window with a saved SQL pass-through query.

Note

SQL pass-through queries bypass the Jet database engine, but Access SQL and ANSI SQL-92 INNER JOIN statements are not accepted by version 4.x of SQL Server. (SQL Server uses WHERE clauses to create joins.) The Microsoft ODBC driver for SQL Server traps the INNER JOIN statement and converts the Access/ANSI SQL statements to an equivalent SQL WHERE clause.

Troubleshooting

I receive error messages when I attempt to log in or run queries on client-server tables attached by ODBC.

You can change two entries in the [ODBC] section of your MSACCESS.INI file if you are having difficulty logging on the SQL Server or processing queries based on SQL Server tables. Following are the entries and their default values, in seconds:

```
[ODBC]
QueryTimeout=605
LoginTimeout=20
```

You can change these entries, if necessary, with Windows Notepad to provide additional time to process a query or to connect to SQL Server. Unless you are processing very large queries or network traffic is especially intense, the default values ordinarily suffice.

Exporting Access Tables to a Client-Server Database

Creating the definition of tables in a client-server database can be a very lengthy process, especially if you need to write SQL DDL statements at the ISQL prompt to create the tables. Tools for SQL Server, such as SQL Object Manager, simplify the process of creating new client-server tables. It's even easier, however, to export your existing Access tables to a database in SQL Server. When you export Access tables to SQL Server, you ensure that the SQL Server table's field data types correspond to the data types of the your Access table.

VI

Advanced Techniques

To export a table from NWIND.MDB to the pubs database, follow these steps:

1. Select the table you want to export to the SQL data source in the Tables list of the Database window.

2. Choose **E**xport from the **F**ile menu to display the Export dialog. Select <SQL Database> in the Data Destination list as shown in figure 26.22. Click OK to display the Select Microsoft Access Object dialog.

Fig. 26.22
Initiating the export of an Access table to SQL Server.

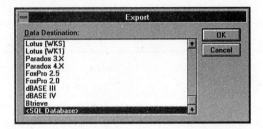

3. Your selection from step 1 automatically is selected in the Objects in *DATABASE* list, as shown in figure 26.23. Click OK to display the Export dialog.

Fig. 26.23
Selecting the table object to export.

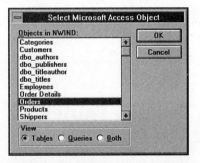

4. Click OK to Export the table to the server with the same name as used in NWIND.MDB (see fig. 26.24). You don't need to add the dbo_ prefix for SQL Server tables. The Select SQL Data Sources dialog appears.

Fig. 26.24
Specifying the table name in the SQL Server database.

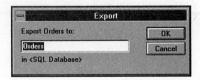

5. Double-click pubs, or any other data source to which you want to export the table, to display the SQL Server Login dialog. Your name and password are stored internally, so click the OK button.

The status bar shows the progress of exporting the table to the server. Exporting an Access table with a large number of records is not as fast as importing the content of the table to SQL Server from an ASCII text file with a bulk copy program (BCP). However, exporting the table is much quicker when the table contains less than 10,000 records. You can view the result of the export operation with SQL Object Manager or a similar application.

Figure 26.25 shows SQL Object Manager displaying the structure of the Orders table of NWIND.MDB exported to the pubs database. Notice that the SQL Server ODBC driver replaces spaces in field names of the Orders table with underscores. (Spaces are not allowed in SQL Server table or field names.)

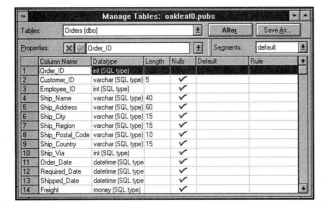

Fig. 26.25
Displaying the structure of the dbo_Orders table with SQL Object Manager.

> **Note**
>
> When you export an Access table to SQL Server, the indexes, rules (validation rules), default values, and other properties of the table are not exported. You need to use SQL Object Manager or a similar tool to add indexes and other properties to the new server table. Alternatively, you can use ISQL and SQL ALTER TABLE statements to add the indexes and other properties.

VI

Advanced Techniques

From Here...

This chapter provided you with a brief introduction to the use of the ODBC Administrator application with Microsoft SQL Server for Windows NT version 4.2. The examples included in this chapter also are applicable to Sybase SQL Server. Adding data sources for other client-server RDBMSs for which ODBC drivers are available is similar, but the dialog(s) to specify the details of the data source differ.

For information on programming with Access Basic and related topics, refer to the following chapters:

- Chapter 27, "Writing Access Basic Code," describes how to use Access 2.0's new Code Behind Forms feature to write event-handling code for forms and reports.

- Chapter 28, "Understanding the Data Access Object Class," explains Access 2.0's new hierarchy of objects created by Access and the Jet database engine.

- Chapter 29, "Exchanging Data with OLE Automation and DDE," gives examples of code for programming objects created by other OLE 2.0-compliant applications, as well as the new OLE Custom Controls.

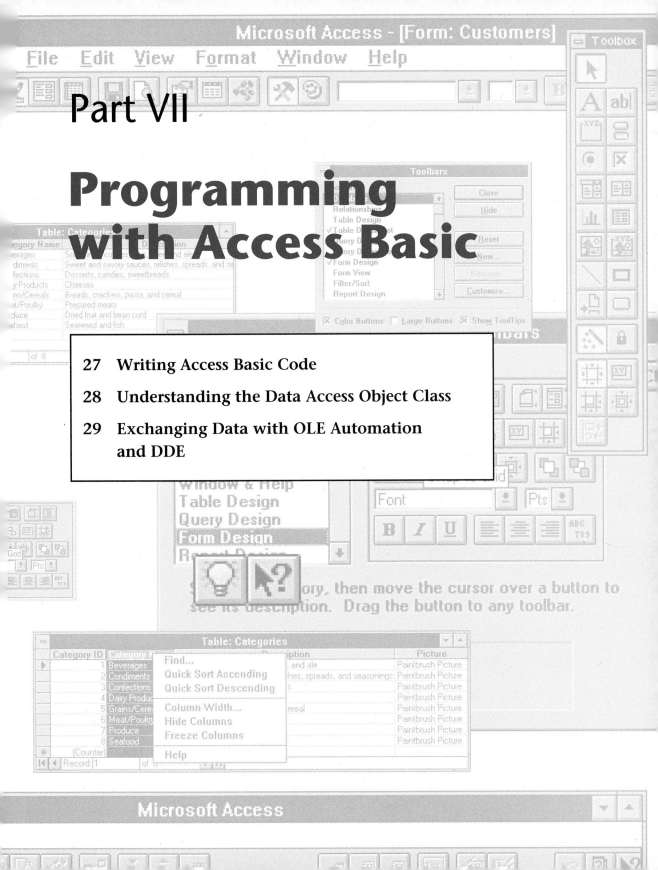

Part VII

Programming with Access Basic

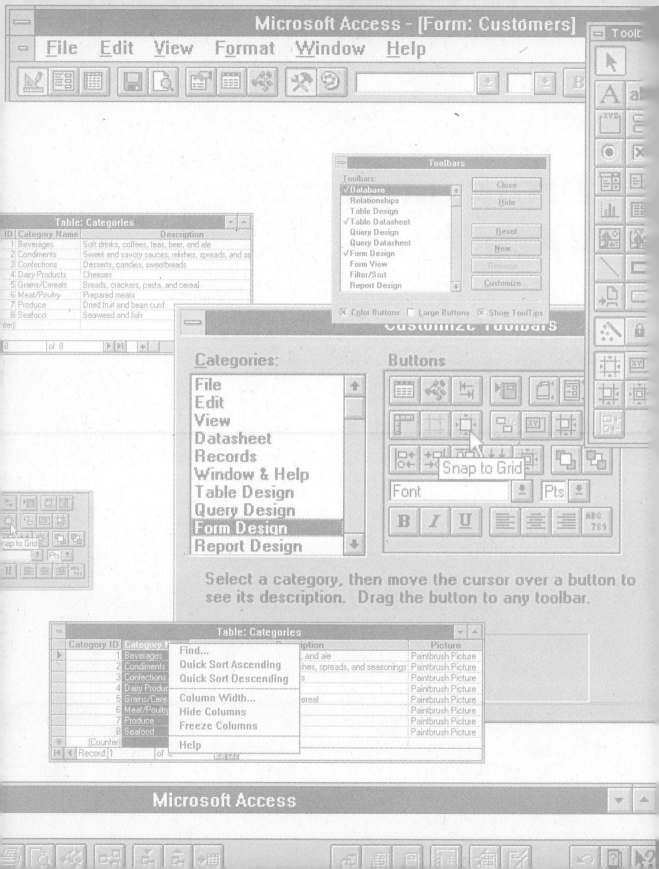

Chapter 27

Writing Access Basic Code

Most Access applications you create do not require you to write a single line of Access Basic code. Many commercial Access applications, such as MTX International's Accounting SDK for Access, rely primarily on macros rather than Access Basic code for automating applications. Sequences of Access actions, contained in macro objects, usually are sufficient to provide the methods you need to respond to events, such as running queries, displaying forms, and printing reports. The built-in functions of Access enable you to perform complex calculations in queries. You may, however, want or need to use Access Basic code for any of the following reasons:

- To create user-defined functions (UDFs) that substitute for complex expressions you use repeatedly to validate data, compute values for text boxes, and perform other duties. Creating a UDF that you refer to by a short name minimizes potential typing errors and enables you to document the way your expression works.

- To write expressions that include more complex decision structures than allowed by the standard **IIf()** function (in an **If...Then...Else ...End If** structure, for example), or to write expressions that need loops for repetitive operations.

- To perform actions not available from standard Access macros, such as transaction processing with the Access Basic equivalents of SQL COMMIT and ROLLBACK statements.

- To execute DDE operations that you cannot perform with the standard DDE() and DDESend() functions of Access, or to execute DDE operations over which you need more control than is offered by these functions.

In this chapter, you learn to

- Modify a sample Access Basic function

- Use the Immediate Window to evaluate Access Basic functions

- Use the **Debug.Print** object to print values of Access Basic variables

- Write and test your own user-defined function

- Use the Code Builder to create an event-handling procedure

Using Access Basic's DDE capabilities is one of the subjects of Chapter 29, "Exchanging Data with OLE Automation and DDE."

■ To open more than one database in an application where attaching a table or using the SQL IN statement is not sufficient for your application.

■ To provide hard-copy documentation for your application. If you include actions in Access Basic code rather than macros, you can print the Access Basic code to improve the documentation for your application. Well-documented code is likely to be easier to understand than the documentation for macros created by the Database Documentor.

■ To create run-time applications that substitute Access Basic functions for macros so that execution errors do not cause your application to quit without warning.

This chapter describes Access Basic, introduces you to Access Basic modules and procedures, shows you how to use the Module window to enter and test Access Basic code, and helps you start writing user-defined functions. The chapter also includes examples of Access Basic programs.

Introducing Access Basic

Several years ago, Bill Gates, the founder and chairman of Microsoft Corporation, stated that all Microsoft applications that use macros would share a common macro language built on BASIC. BASIC is the acronym for Beginners All-Purpose Symbolic Instruction Code. Gates's choice of BASIC is not surprising when you consider that Microsoft was built on the foundation of Gates's BASIC interpreter that ran in 8K on the early predecessors of the PC. He reiterated his desire for a common macro language in an article that appeared in *One-to-One with Microsoft* in late 1991.

Before Access 1.0 was released, the results of Gates's edict were observed in only one Microsoft product, Word for Windows. If you have created Microsoft Word macros, or just made minor changes to macros you recorded, you will find that Access Basic is very similar to WordBasic. With the arrival of Excel 5.0, Visual Basic, Applications Edition (more commonly known as Visual Basic for Applications or VBA), has become the *lingua franca* for programming Microsoft's productivity applications. As you see in the following section, Access 2.0 Basic is very similar to VBA.

Access Basic is a programming language, not a macro language; Access has its own macro "language." You create the equivalent of macros with Access Basic functions and procedures. To execute the Access Basic functions and procedures that you write, you use Access's macro language or specify the name of an Access Basic function as the value of an event. You can execute any macro action from Access Basic by preceding the keyword with a **DoCmd** and a space. The names of many macro actions appear to be the same as Access Basic reserved words. Except for MsgBox and SendKeys, macro action names and Access Basic reserved words that are identical in name use a different syntax and perform different but usually related functions.

The Object Basic Root Language

Access

2.0

Access Basic, Visual Basic (version 2.0 and higher), and Visual Basic for Applications are three members of a family of languages collectively called Object Basic in this book. Ultimately, all the dialects of Object Basic are likely to be replaced by a single version of VBA, the equivalent of a macro Esperanto. A sea change may not occur immediately, but the decision has been made: future versions of all of Microsoft's productivity applications will use VBA for application programming. Microsoft Excel 5.0 and Project 4.0 use VBA in place of their former macro languages; the next major releases of Microsoft Access, Word, Visual Basic, and FoxPro undoubtedly will employ VBA.

In the process of upgrading existing applications, Microsoft has taken evolutionary steps down the path to VBA. Although Access 2.0 does not use VBA, many of the additions and modifications to Access 1.x Basic have been made to conform the language to VBA syntactical requirements. Similarly, the changes from version 2.0 to 3.0 of Visual Basic reflect increased compatibility with VBA. Thus, if you have used Visual Basic, writing Access Basic code is a snap. Version 2.0 of Visual Basic, the language on which Access 1.x Basic was modeled, included many of the new keywords added by Access to the Object Basic root language. In return, version 2.0 of Access Basic has adopted several reserved words from Visual Basic 3.0. Access 2.0 also has adopted Visual Basic 3.0's model for writing code to process events triggered by forms and reports, and control objects on forms, called Code Behind Forms (CBF) by Access.

Although programmers who use "more sophisticated" languages, such as C++ and Pascal, heaped derision on the original dialects of BASIC, Access Basic is a full-featured language. Like other programming languages, Access Basic offers a full set of constructs, such as conditional statements and loops. Access Basic also provides the freedom to use any of the functions of the Windows API, as well as other members of the Windows Open System Architecture (WOSA), such as the Messaging API (MAPI) and the Telephony API (TAPI). The most important addition to Access 2.0, however, is the capability to declare and manipulate objects created by other applications through OLE Automation (OA). Using OA is one of the subjects of Chapter 29.

Access Basic Compared with xBase, PAL, and Visual Basic

Programmers who have experience with dBASE III, dBASE IV, or other xBase dialects, such as Clipper and FoxBase, will find that Access Basic uses many of the same xBase keywords or minor variations of familiar xBase keywords. Borland's PAL is related to xBase, so PAL programmers will also find the translation of PAL to Access Basic keywords straightforward.

User-defined functions are almost identical in structure in Access Basic, xBase, and PAL. This similarity in code structure ends, however, with user-defined functions. Writing code for Windows applications in general, and for Access in particular, requires an entirely different code structure. Applications for DOS RDBMSs use top-down programming techniques, which means that a main program calls (executes) other sub-programs or procedures that perform specific actions. The user of the application makes choices from a menu that determine which sub-programs or procedures are invoked. Menus that let the application remain idle are enclosed within DO WHILE. . .ENDDO loops while the user decides what menu command to choose next. Your code is responsible for all actions that occur while the application is running.

The situation with Windows and Access differs from that of top-down programming. Access itself is the main program, and Windows is responsible for many functions that you must code in DOS RDBMS languages. This fact is a blessing for new programmers because Windows and Access simplify the development of complex applications. However, Access's and Windows' contributions are a curse for top-down DOS programmers because Access and Windows require an entirely new approach to writing RDBMS code. The guiding principles for DOS RDBMS developers writing Access Basic applications are the following:

■ Don't even *think* about writing Access Basic code during the development stage of your first applications; use macros. Most applications do not need any code other than an occasional user-defined function. Those applications that do need code usually do not require very much of it. The exception is for run-time Access applications, where using Access Basic code is preferred.

■ Use command buttons and associated macro actions to substitute for the traditional menu commands of DOS RDBMSs. In most applications, you create a menu that gives the user only the **Q**uit command from a **F**ile menu. All other user-initiated choices in the application are handled by control objects on forms.

■ Concentrate on using macro actions to respond to user- and application-initiated events, such as opening forms. Study the event-oriented properties of form and control objects and the macro actions available to respond to the event properties. Learn the full capabilities of each macro action native to Access before you write your own actions in Access Basic. Event properties combined with the appropriate macro actions usually can substitute for about 95 percent of the code you write for DOS RDBMSs.

■ After your application is up and running, consider writing Access Basic code to add the nuances that distinguish professionally written database applications. If you are a programmer, you may find that implementing macro actions in code is preferable to using macro objects to contain those actions, because you can print the code to document your application.

Where You Use Access Basic Code

You probably will first use Access Basic to create functions that make complex calculations. Creating an Access Basic function to substitute for calculations with many sets of parentheses is relatively simple and a good introduction to writing Access Basic code. Writing expressions as Access Basic functions enables you to add comments to the code that make the purpose and construction of the code clear to others. Also, comments aid your memory when you decide to revise an application after using it for a few months.

Your next step is to create Access Basic event-handling procedures in form or report modules to replace macros. You use event-handling procedures to perform operations that are cumbersome to implement with or that cannot be accomplished by macro actions. For example, the RunCode macro action executes Access Basic functions, but the RunCode action ignores the function's return value if it has one. In Access 1.x, you entered the name of a function, preceded by an equal sign, as the value of an event, replacing the name of a macro. Access 2.0 gives you the choice of calling a function contained in an Access module, or executing an event-handling procedure contained in a form or report module.

Typographic and Naming Conventions Used for Access Basic

This book uses a special set of typographic conventions for references to Access Basic keywords and object variable names in Access Basic examples:

- `Monospace` type is used for all Access Basic code in the examples, as in `lngItemCounter`.

- **`Bold monospace`** type is used for all Access Basic reserved words and type-declaration symbols, as in **`Dim`** and **`%`**. Standard function names in Access Basic, as described in Chapter 9, "Understanding Operators and Expressions in Access," also are set in bold type so that reserved words, standard function names, and reserved symbols stand out from variable and function names and values you assign to variables.

- *`Italic monospace`* type indicates a replaceable item, as in **`Dim`** *`DataItem`* **`As String`**.

- ***`Bold italic monospace`*** type indicates a replaceable reserved word, such as a data type, as in **`Dim`** *`DataItem`* **`As`** ***`DataType`***; ***`DataType`*** is replaced by a keyword corresponding to the desired Access Basic data type.

- Names of variables that refer to Access objects, such as forms or reports, use a three-letter prefix derived from the object name, as in `frmFormName` and `rptReportName`. The prefixes for object variables are listed in Appendix B, "Naming Conventions for Access Objects."

- Names of other variables are preceded by a one-letter or three-letter data type identifier, such as `varVariantVariable` and `intIntegerVariable`. Boolean variables (flags) that return only **`True`** or **`False`** values use the `f` prefix, as in `fIsLoaded`.

- Optional elements are included within square brackets, as in `[OptionItem]`. Square brackets also enclose object names that contain spaces or special punctuation symbols.

- An ellipsis (. . .) substitutes for code not shown in syntax and code examples, as in `If...Then...Else...End If`.

> **Note**
>
> Names of macro actions that serve as arguments of the **DoCmd** *MacroName* statement are not set in bold type because macro action names are not reserved words in Access Basic. When a keyword in Access Basic is used in Access database objects other than modules, the typeface is determined by the context in which the word is presented.

Modules, Functions, and Procedures

Access

2.0

A *module* is a container for Access Basic code, just as a form is a container for control objects. Access 2.0 provides the following three types of modules:

Module

- *Access Modules*. You create an Access module to contain your Access Basic code the same way that you create any other new database object: click the Module tab in the Database window, and then click the New button. No significant differences exist between Access modules in versions 1.x and 2.0. Figure 27.1 shows the IsLoaded() function.

- *Form Modules*. Form modules contain code to respond to events triggered by forms or controls on forms. You open a form module by selecting a form in the Database window and then clicking the Code button of the toolbar. Alternatively, choose **C**ode from the **V**iew menu. Either of these methods opens a module that Access automatically names Form.*FormName*, where *FormName* is the name of the selected form. In addition to opening the module, the selected form also opens in Design View. Another method of opening a form module is to click the ellipsis button for one of the event properties for a form or a control object on a form. Selecting Code Builder from the Choose Builder dialog displays a the Form.FormName module with a procedure stub, **Sub** *ObjectName_EventName*...**End Sub**, written for you. Figure 27.2 shows the stub created for the Change event of the Product ID text box of the Add Products form. (The comments between **Sub**... and **End Sub** were added manually.)

Tip
Using Access modules to contain all your Access Basic code speeds opening of forms and reports, but slows initial opening of your application.

- *Report Modules*. Report modules contain code to respond to events triggered by reports. (Control objects on reports do not trigger events.) You open report modules in the same way you open form modules. Report modules are named Report.*ReportName* automatically.

Fig. 27.1
The Access module window for the *IsLoaded()* function.

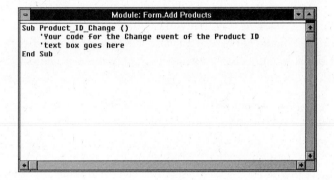

```
Module: Utility Functions
Function IsLoaded (MyFormName)
' Accepts: a form name
' Purpose: determines if a form is loaded
' Returns: True if specified the form is loaded;
'          False if the specified form is not loaded.
' From: User's Guide Chapter 25

    Dim i

    IsLoaded = False
    For i = 0 To Forms.Count - 1
        If Forms(i).FormName = MyFormName Then
            IsLoaded = True
            Exit Function        ' Quit function once form has been
        End If
    Next

End Function
```

Fig. 27.2
A Code Behind Forms event-handling procedure stub created with the Code Builder.

```
Module: Form.Add Products
Sub Product_ID_Change ()
    'Your code for the Change event of the Product ID
    'text box goes here
End Sub
```

A module consists of a *Declarations section* and usually one or more *procedures* or *functions*. As the name suggests, the Declarations section of a module is used to declare items (usually variables and constants, the subjects of following sections) used by the procedures and functions contained in the module. You can use a module without functions or procedures to declare **Global** variables and constants that can be used by any function or procedure in any module.

Procedures are typically defined as subprograms referred to by name in another program. Referring to a procedure by name *calls* or *invokes* the procedure; the code in the procedure executes, and then the sequence of execution returns to the program that called the procedure. Another name for a procedure is *subroutine*. Procedures can call other procedures, in which case the called procedures are called *subprocedures*. Procedures are defined by beginning (**Sub**) and end (**End Sub**) reserved words, as in the following example:

```
Sub ProcName
    [Start of procedure code]
    . . .
    [End of procedure code]
End Sub
```

Note

You can refer to the procedure name to invoke the procedure, but Access Basic provides a keyword, **Call**, that explicitly invokes a procedure. Prefixing the procedure name with **Call** is a good programming practice because this keyword identifies the name that follows as the name of a procedure rather than a variable.

Functions are a class of procedures that return values to their names, as explained in Chapter 9. C programmers would argue that procedures are a class of functions that do not return values, called *void* functions. Regardless of how you view the difference between functions and procedures, keep the following points in mind:

■ Access modules require that you write Access Basic functions (not procedures) to act in place of macro actions and as user-defined functions. Functions are the entry point to all the Access Basic code in Access modules.

■ The only way you can call a procedure in an Access Basic module is from an Access Basic function or from another procedure. You cannot directly execute a procedure in an Access module from any Access database object.

■ Unlike Access modules, form and report modules use procedures (not functions) to respond to events. Using form- and report-level procedures for event-handling code mimics Visual Basic's approach for events triggered by forms and controls on forms.

■ Function names in Access modules are global in scope with respect to Access modules. Thus you cannot have duplicate function names in any Access module in your application. However, form and report modules can have a function with the same name as a function in a module, because form and report function and procedure names have form- or report-level scope. A function in a form module with the same name as a function in an Access module function takes priority over the Access module version. Thus if you include the IsLoaded() function in a form module and you call the IsLoaded() function from a procedure in the form module, the IsLoaded() function in the form module executes.

VII

Programming Access

■ To execute an Access Basic function in Access Basic code, you must use the function in an expression, such as

```
intReturnValue=nilFunctionName([Arguments])
```

even when the function returns no value.

Functions are created within a structure similar to procedures, as in the following example:

```
Function FuncName([Arguments])
    [Start of function code]
    ...
    [End of function code]
End Function
```

You cannot use **Call** to execute a function; you must refer to the function by name. Function calls are identified by the parentheses that follow the function name, even if the function requires no arguments.

You can add as many individual procedures and functions as you want to a module. If you write a substantial amount of Access Basic code, you should take one of the following two approaches:

■ Use form and report modules to contain the code that responds to the events on forms. Procedures common to several forms, however, should be incorporated in Access modules. As mentioned in the tip earlier in this chapter, adding substantial amounts of code to form modules slows the opening of the form.

■ Create separate Access modules for code associated with a particular class of object, such as forms. A form that requires an appreciable amount of code usually deserves its own module. When you take the Access module approach, your application opens more slowly, but forms open more rapidly. Users are likely to favor applications that respond more quickly after they are launched.

Access modules are assigned names and stored in the current database, like all other Access database objects. Form and report modules are stored with the **Form** or **Report** object. Access 2.0 enables you to open a module with Access Basic code and insert text in the module. Obtaining access to modules is discussed in the next chapter, "Understanding the Data Access Object Class."

Data Types and Database Objects in Access Basic

When you create Access Basic tables, all data types that you use to assign field data types and sizes (except for OLE and Memo field data types) have counterparts in Access Basic. With the exception of the **Variant** and **Currency** data types, Access Basic data types are represented in most other dialects of BASIC, such as Microsoft QuickBASIC and the QBasic interpreter supplied with MS-DOS 5+. All these data types, including **Variant**, are supported by Visual Basic 2.0 and higher.

Traditional BASIC dialects use a punctuation symbol called the *type-declaration character*, such as **$** for the **String** data type, to designate the data type. The Access Basic data types, the type-declaration characters, the corresponding field data types, and the ranges of values are shown in the AB Type, Symbol, Field Type, Minimum and Maximum Value columns of table 27.1, respectively. The Field Types Byte, Integer, Long Integer, Counter, Single, and Double correspond to the Field size property of the Number data type in tables, queries, forms, and reports.

Table 27.1 Access Basic and Corresponding Field Data Types				
AB Type	**Symbol**	**Field Type**	**Minimum Value**	**Maximum Value**
Integer	%	Byte, Integer, Yes/No	–32,768	32,767
Long	&	Long Integer, Counter	–2,147,483,648	2,147,483,647
Single	!	Single	–3.402823E38 1.401298E–45	–1.401298E–45 3.402823E38
Double	#	Double	–1.79769313486232E308 4.94065645841247E–324	4.9406564841247E–324 1.79769313486232E308
Currency	@	Currency	–922,337,203,685, 477.5808	922,337,203,685, 477.5807
String	$	Text	0 characters	65,500 characters (+/–)
Variant	None	Any	January 1, 0000 (date) Same as **Double** (numbers) Same as **String** (text)	December 31, 1999 (date) Same as **Double** (numbers) Same as **String** (text)

Tip
All data re-
turned from
fields of tables
or queries is of
the **Variant**
data type by
default. If you
assign the field
value to a
conventional
data type, such
as **Integer**, the
data type is said
to be *coerced*.

You can dispense with the type-declaration character if you explicitly declare your variables with the **Dim...As** *DataType* statement, discussed later in this section. If you do not explicitly declare the variables' data type or use a symbol to define an implicit data type, Access Basic variables default to the **Variant** data type.

The # sign is also used to enclose values specified as dates, as in varNewYears = #1/1/95#. In this case, bold type is not used for the enclosing # signs, because these symbols are not intended for the purpose of the # reserved symbol that indicates the **Double** data type.

Database objects, such as tables, queries, forms, and reports, all of which you used in prior chapters, also have corresponding data types in Access Basic. Here Access Basic departs from other BASIC languages, with the exception of Visual Basic. The most commonly used database object types of Access 2.0 Basic are listed in table 27.2.

Access 2.0

Table 27.2 The Most Common Database Object Data Types Supported by Access Basic

Object Data Type	Corresponding Database Object
Database	Access databases
Form	Forms, including subforms
Report	Reports, including subreports
Control	Controls on forms and reports
QueryDef	Query definitions (SQL statement equivalents)
Recordset	A virtual representation of a table or the result set of a query (Access 2.0)
Table	Tables of databases (Access 1.x)
Dynaset	Results of queries that are updatable (Access 1.x)
Snapshot	Results of queries that are not updatable (Access 1.x)

The **Table**, **Dynaset**, and **Snapshot** object data types of Access 1.x have been replaced by the all-encompassing **Recordset** data type of Access 2.0. You distinguish the type of **Recordset** object (**Table**, **Dynaset**, or **Snapshot**) by the **Recordset** object's Type property. The **Table**, **Dynaset**, and **Snapshot** object types are supported by Access 2.0 for backward compatibility with Access 1.x code. However, it is a good practice to use the new **Recordset** data type, because there is no guarantee that the obsolescent Access 1.x object data types will be supported in future versions of Access. The new object data types and object collections introduced by Access 2.0 are discussed in the next chapter.

> ### Note
>
> The **Recordset** data type of Access Basic and the Recordset property of Visual Basic 3.0 are not the same. Visual Basic 3.0's Recordset property refers to the records in the underlying table or query that serves as the data source for a data control object.

Access
2.0

Variables and Naming Conventions

Variables are named placeholders for values of a specified data type that change when your Access Basic code is executed. You give variables names, as you name fields, but the names of variables cannot include spaces or any other punctuation except the underscore character (_). The other restriction is that a variable cannot use an Access Basic keyword by itself as a name; keywords are called *reserved words* for this reason. The same rules apply to giving names to functions and procedures. Variable names in Access Basic typically employ a combination of upper- and lowercase letters to make them more readable.

Implicit Variables

You can create variables by assigning a value to a variable name, as in the following example:

```
NewVar = 1234
```

A statement of this type *declares* a variable, which means to create a new variable with a name you choose. The statement in the example creates a new implicit variable, NewVar, of the **Variant** data type with a value of 1234. (Thus NewVar would be more appropriately named varNewVar.) When you do not specify a data type for an implicit variable by appending one of the type-declaration characters to the variable name, the **Variant** data type is assigned by default. The following statement creates a variable of the Integer data type:

```
NewVar% = 1234
```

Declaring variables of the **Integer** or **Long** type when decimal fractions are not required speeds the operation of your code. Access takes longer to compute values for **Variant**, **Single**, and **Double** variables.

Explicit Variables

It is better programming practice to declare your variables and assign those variables a data type before you give variables a value. Programming languages such as C, C++, and Turbo Pascal require you to declare variables before you use them. The most common method of declaring variables is by using the **Dim...As** structure, where **As** specifies the data type. This method declares explicit variables. An example follows:

```
Dim intNewVar As Integer
```

If you do not add the **As Integer** keywords, intNewVar is assigned the **Variant** data type by default.

You can require that all variables must be explicitly declared prior to their use by adding the statement, **Option** Explicit, in the Declarations section of a module. The advantage of using **Option** Explicit is that Access will detect misspelled variable names and display an error message when misspellings are encountered. If you do not use **Option** Explicit and you misspell a variable name, Access creates a new implicit variable with the misspelled name. Resulting errors in your code's operation can be difficult to diagnose.

Scope and Duration of Variables

Variables have a property called *scope*, which determines when they appear and disappear in your Access Basic code. Variables appear the first time you declare them and then disappear and reappear on the basis of the scope you assign to them. When a variable appears, it is said to be *visible*, meaning that you can assign the variable a value, change its value, and use it in expressions. Otherwise, the variable is *invisible*; if you use a variable's name while it is invisible, you create a new variable with the same name instead.

The following lists the four scope levels in Access Basic:

- *Local (procedure-level) scope.* The variable is visible only during the time when the procedure in which the variable is declared is executed. Variables that you declare, with or without using the **Dim...As** keywords in a procedure or function, are local in scope.

Access
2.0
- *Form-level and report-level scope.* The variable is visible only when the form or report in which it is declared is open. You declare form-level and report-level variables in the Declarations section of form and report modules.

- *Module-level scope.* The variable is visible to all procedures and functions contained in the module in which the variable was declared. You declare variables with module scope in the Declarations section of the module, using the **Dim...As** keywords.

■ *Global scope.* The variable is visible to all procedures and functions within all modules. You declare variables with global scope in the Declarations section of a module, using the **Global...As** keywords.

The scope and visibility of variables declared in two different Access modules of the same database, both having two procedures, are illustrated by the diagram in figure 27.3. In each procedure, variables declared with different scopes are used to assign values to variables declared within the procedure. Invalid assignment statements are shown crossed out in the figure. These assignment statements are invalid because the variable used to assign the value to the variable declared in the procedure is not visible in the procedure.

Variables also have a property called *duration,* or lifetime. The duration of a variable is your code's execution time between the first appearance of the variable (its declaration) and its disappearance. Each time a procedure or function is called, local variables declared with the **Dim...As** statement are set to default values, with 0 for numeric data types and the empty string (" ") for string variables. These local variables ordinarily have a duration equal to the lifetime of the function or procedure—from the time the function or procedure is called until the **End Function** or **End Sub** statement is executed.

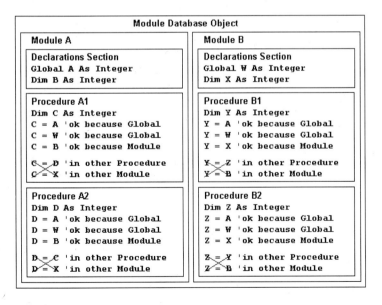

Fig. 27.3
Valid and invalid assignment statements for variables of different scopes.

To preserve the values of local variables between occurrences (called *instances*) of a procedure or function, you substitute the reserved word **Static** for **Dim**. Static variables have a duration of your Access application, but their scope is determined by where you declare them. Static variables are useful when you want to count the number of occurrences of an event. You can make all variables in a function or procedure static variables by preceding **Function** or **Sub** with the **Static** keyword.

> **Note**
>
> Minimize the number of local variables that you declare **Static**. Local variables do not consume memory when they are not visible. This characteristic of local variables is especially important in the case of arrays, discussed in the "Access Basic Arrays" section that follows shortly, because arrays are often very large.

User-Defined Data Types

You can create your own data type consisting of one or more Access data types. User-defined data types are discussed in this section pertaining to variables because you need to know what a variable is before you can declare a user-defined data type. You declare a user-defined data type between the **Type...End Type** keywords, as in the following example:

```
Type DupRec
    Field1 As Long
    Field2 As String * 20
    Field3 As Single
    Field4 As Double
End Type
```

User-defined data types are particularly useful when you create a variable to hold the values of one or more records of a table that uses fields of different data types. The **String * 20** statement defines Field2 of the user-defined data type as a *fixed-length* string of 20 characters, usually corresponding to the Size property of the Text field data type. String variables in user-defined data types are always specified with a fixed length. You must declare your user-defined data type (called a *record* or a *structure* in other programming languages) in the Declarations section of a module.

You must explicitly declare variables to be of the user-defined type with the **Dim**, **Global**, or **Static** keywords because there is no reserved symbol to declare a user-defined data type, as in **Dim** CurrentRec **As** DupRec. To assign a value to a field of a variable with a user-defined data type, you specify the name of the variable and the field name, separating them with a period, as in CurrentRec.Field1 = 2048.

Access Basic Arrays

Arrays are variables that consist of a collection of values, called *elements* of the array, of a single data type in a regularly ordered structure. Implicitly declared arrays are not allowed in Access Basic (or in Visual Basic). You declare an array with the **Dim** statement, adding the number of elements in parentheses to the variable name for the array, as in the following example:

```
Dim NewArray (20) As String
```

This statement creates an array of 21 elements, each of which is a conventional, variable-length string variable. You create 21 elements because the first element of an array is the 0 (zero) element, unless you specify otherwise by adding the **To** modifier, as in the following example:

```
Dim NewArray (1 To 20) As String
```

The preceding statement creates an array with 20 elements.

You can create multidimensional arrays by adding more values, separated by commas. The statement

```
Dim NewArray (9, 9, 9) As Long
```

creates a three-dimensional array of 10 elements per dimension. This array, when visible, occupies 4,000 bytes of memory (10 * 10 * 10 * 4 bytes/long integer).

You can create a dynamic array by declaring the array using **Dim** without specifying the number of elements and then using the **ReDim** reserved word to determine the number of elements the array contains. You can **ReDim** an array as many times as you want; each time you do so, the values stored in the array are reinitialized to their default values, determined by the data type, unless you follow **ReDim** with the reserved word, **Preserve**. The following sample statements create a dynamic array:

```
Dim NewArray ( ) As Long             'In Declarations sections
ReDim Preserve NewArray (9, 9, 9)    'In procedure, preserves prior values
ReDim NewArray (9, 9, 9)             'In procedure, reinitializes all elements
```

Dynamic arrays are useful when you don't know how many elements an array requires when you declare it. You can **ReDim** a dynamic array to zero elements when you no longer need the values it contains; this enables you to recover the memory that the array consumes while it is visible. Arrays declared with **Dim** are limited to eight dimensions. You can use the **ReDim** statement within a procedure without preceding it with the **Dim** statement to create local-scope arrays with up to 60 dimensions.

Scope, duration rules, and keywords apply to arrays in the same way in which they apply to conventional variables. You can declare dynamic arrays with global and module-level scope by adding the **Global** or **Dim** statement to the Declarations section of a module, and then use the **ReDim** statement by itself in a procedure. If you declare an array with **Static**, rather than **Dim**, the array retains its values between instances of a procedure.

> **Note**
>
> Do not use the **Option** Base keywords to change the default initial element of arrays from 0 to 1. **Option** Base is included in Access Basic for compatibility with Visual Basic. In Visual Basic, **Option** Base is for compatibility with other BASIC dialects. Many arrays you create from Access Basic objects must begin with element 0. If you are concerned about the memory occupied by an unused zeroth element of an array, use the **Dim ArrayName (1 To N) As DataType** declaration. In most cases, you can disregard the zeroth element.

Named Database Objects as Variables in Access Basic Code

Properties of database objects you create with Access can be treated as variables and assigned values within Access Basic code. You can assign a new value to the text box that contains the address information for a customer by name, for example. Use the following statement:

```
Forms!Customers!Address = "123 Elm St."
```

The keyword **Forms** defines the type of object. The exclamation point (called the *bang* symbol by programmers) separates the name of the form and the name of the control object. The ! symbol is analogous to the \ path separator that you use when you are dealing with DOS files. If the name of the form or the control object contains a space or other punctuation, you need to enclose the name within square brackets, as in the following statement:

```
Forms!Customers![Contact Name] = "Joe Hill"
```

Alternatively, you can use the **Set** keyword to create your own named variable for the control object. This procedure is convenient when you need to refer to the control object several times; it is more convenient to type txtContact than the full "path" to the control object, in this case a text box.

```
Dim txtContact As Control
Set txtContact = Forms!Customers![Contact Name]
txtContact = "Joe Hill"
```

You can assign any database object to a variable name by declaring the variable as the object type and using the **Set** statement to assign the object to the variable. You do not create a copy of the object in memory when you assign it a variable name; the variable refers to the object in memory. Referring to an object in memory is often called *pointing* to an object; many languages have a pointer data type that holds the value of the location in memory where the variable is stored. Access Basic does not support pointers. The next chapter deals with creating variables that point to the new Access 2.0 database objects.

Variable Naming Conventions

In the event that you need to write large amounts of Access Basic code, you probably will employ a large number of variable names and many different data types. On forms and reports, many different types of named control objects can be used, each of which you can assign to a variable name with the **Set** keyword in your Access Basic code. As your code grows in size, remembering the data types of all the variables becomes difficult.

Stan Leszynski, a Seattle database consultant, and Greg Reddick, an independent programmer and author, have proposed a set of variable-naming conventions for Access Basic. Their proposed naming conventions employs *Hungarian notation*, which is used primarily in the C and C++ languages. Hungarian refers to the nationality of the method's inventor, who was involved in the development of Access, and the fact that only Hungarians are likely to be able to correctly pronounce some of the abbreviations involved, such as "sz." Leszynski and Reddick adapted Hungarian notation for use in the Access Basic environment; their convention is commonly called *L-R naming*.

Hungarian notation uses a set of codes for the data type. You prefix the variable name with the code in lowercase letters. For example, the prefix code for a text box is txt, so the variable name for the text box in the preceding example is txtContact. Strings in C code are identified by the prefix lpsz, an abbreviation for long pointer to a string, zero-terminated (with Chr$(0) or ASCII Null). Access Basic does not support the pointer data type (but it does use pointers for the location of string variables), and it does not use zero-terminated strings. Thus, str is a more appropriate prefix for Object Basic strings.

The data type identifier of a user-defined data type is called a *created tag*. In Hungarian notation, created tags are capitalized as in the following:

```
Type REC
    lngField1 As Long
    strField2 As String
    sngField3 As Single
    dblField4 As Double
End Type
```

A variable of type REC is declared with the lowercase rec prefix, such as in the following:

```
Dim recCurRecord As REC
```

Created tags should be short, but should not duplicate one of the standard data type prefix codes.

Using standard data type prefixes makes your code easier to read and understand. Many of the code examples in this book use the new proposed naming conventions. The complete list of the original L-R notation for Access Basic objects and variables appears in Appendix B.

Symbolic Constants

Symbolic constants are named placeholders for values of a specified data type that do not change when your Access Basic code is executed. You precede the name of a symbolic constant with the keyword, **Const**, as in **Const** sngPI = 3.1416. You declare symbolic constants in the Declarations section of a module or within a function or procedure. Precede **Const** with the **Global** keyword if you want to create a global constant visible to all modules, as in **Global Const** sngPI = 3.1416. **Global** constants only can be declared in the Declarations section of an Access Basic module.

Typically, symbolic constants take names in all capital letters to distinguish them from variables. Often underscores are used to make the names of symbolic constants more readable, as in sngVALUE_OF_PI.

You do not need to specify a data type for constants, nor is a data type tag necessary, because Access Basic chooses the data type that stores the data most efficiently. Access Basic can do this, because it knows the value of the data when it "compiles" your code.

> **Note**
>
> Access is an intepreted language, so the term "compile" in an Access Basic context is a misnomer. When you "compile" the Access Basic source you write in code editing windows, Access creates a tokenized version of the code (called *pseudo-code* or *p-code*). This subject is discussed in the section, "The Access Basic Compiler," later in the chapter.

Access System-Defined Constants

Access includes seven system-defined constants, **True**, **False**, **Yes**, **No**, **On**, **Off**, and **Null**, that are created by Access when launched. Of these seven, you can use **True**, **False**, and **Null** in Access Basic code. The remaining four are valid for use with all database objects except modules. When the system-defined constants **True**, **False**, and **Null** are used in Access Basic code examples in this book, they appear in bold monospace type.

> **Note**
>
> The global constants TRUE and FALSE must be explicitly declared in Visual Basic 2.0 and earlier. You cannot declare these constants in Access Basic. If you attempt to declare TRUE, FALSE, or NULL as constants in Access Basic, you receive the error message, "Expected: identifier."

Access Intrinsic Constants

Access Basic provides a number of pre-declared intrinsic symbolic constants for actions (prefixed with A_), databases (prefixed with DB_), and the **Variant** data type (prefixed with V_). The names appear in the Help window for the Constants subject. You may not use any of these intrinsic constants' names as names for constants that you define.

Controlling Program Flow

Useful procedures must be able to make decisions based on the values of variables and then take specified actions based on those decisions. Blocks of code, for example, may need to be repeated until a specified condition occurs. Statements used to make decisions and repeat blocks of code are the fundamental elements that control program flow in Access Basic and all other programming languages.

All programming languages require methods of executing different algorithms based on the results of one or more comparison operations. You can control the flow of any program in any programming language with just three types of statements: conditional execution (If...Then), repetition (Do While...Loop and related structures), and termination (End...). The additional flow control statements in Access Basic and other programming languages make writing code more straightforward.

The code examples used in this section do not include **Dim** statements, so Hungarian notation is not used here, and data type identification symbols are used for brevity to indicate the data types of variables.

Branching and Labels

◄ "Assignment and Comparison Operators," p.319

If you have written DOS batch files or WordPerfect macros, you are probably acquainted with branching and labels. Both the DOS batch language and the WordPerfect macro language include the GoTo *Label* command. DOS defines any word that begins a line with a colon as a label; WordPerfect requires use of the keyword LABEL and then the label name.

When BASIC was first developed, the *only* method of controlling program flow was through its GOTO *LineNumber* and GOSUB *LineNumber* statements. Every line in the program required a number that could be used as a substitute for a label. GOTO *LineNumber* caused the interpreter to skip to the designated line and continue executing the program from that point. GOSUB *LineNumber* caused the program to follow that same branch, but when the BASIC interpreter that executed the code encountered a RETURN statement, program execution jumped back to the line following the GOSUB statement and continued executing at that point.

Skipping Blocks of Code with *GoTo*

Procedural BASIC introduced named labels that replaced the line numbers for GOTO and GOSUB statements. Access Basic's **GoTo** *Label* statement causes your code to branch to the location named *Label:* and continue from that point. Note the colon following *Label:*, which identifies the single word you assigned as a label. However, the colon is not required after the label name following the **GoTo**. In fact, if you add the colon, you get a "label not found" error message.

A label name *must* begin in the far left column (1) of your code. This often interferes with orderly indenting of your code, explained in the next section, just one more reason, in addition to those below, for not using **GoTo**.

Avoiding "Spaghetti Code" by Not Using *GoTo*

The sequence of statements in code that uses multiple **GoTo** statements is very difficult to follow. It is almost impossible to understand the flow of a large program written in line-numbered BASIC because of the jumps here and there in the code. Programs with multiple **GoTo**s are derisively said to contain "spaghetti code."

Access

2.0

The **GoTo** statement is required for only one purpose in Access Basic: handling errors with the **On Error GoTo** *Label* statement. Although Access Basic supports BASIC's ON...GOTO and ON...GOSUB statements, using those statements is not considered good programming practice. You can eliminate all **GoTo** statements in form and report modules by using Access 2.0's new Error event described in the "Handling Run-Time Errors" section later in this chapter.

Conditional Statements

A conditional statement executes the statements between its occurrence and the terminating statement if the result of the relational operator is true. Statements that consist of or require more than one statement for completion are called *structured statements*, *control structures*, or just *structures*.

The *If...Then...End If* Structure

The syntax of the primary conditional statement of procedural BASIC is as follows:

```
If Condition1% [= True] Then
    Statements to be executed if Expression1 is true
[Else[If Condition2%[ = True] Then]]
    Optional statements to be executed if Condition1%
    is false [and Condition2% is true]
End If
```

The `= True` elements of the preceding conditional statement are optional and typically not included when you write actual code. `If Condition1% Then` and `If Condition1% = True Then` produce the same result.

You can add a second condition with the `ElseIf` statement that must be `True` to control execution of the statements that are executed if `Condition1%` is false. Note that no space is used between `Else` and `If`. An `If...End If` structure that incorporates the `ElseIf` statement is the simplified equivalent of the following:

```
If Condition1% Then
    Statements to be executed if Expression1 is true
Else
    If Condition2% Then
        Statements to be executed if Condition1% is
        false and Condition2% is true]
    End If
End If
```

Whether a statement is executed is based on the evaluation of the immediately preceding expression. This expression may include additional `If...End If` or other flow control structures `If...End If` structures within other `If...End If` structures are said to be *nested*, as in the preceding example. The number, or *depth*, of `If...End If`s that can be nested within one another is unlimited.

Note that the code between the individual keywords that make up the flow control structure is indented. Indentation makes code within structures easier to read. You usually use the tab key to create indentation.

To evaluate whether a character is a letter and to determine its case, you can use the following code:

```
If Asc(Char$) > 63 And Asc(Char$) < 91 Then
    CharType$ = "Upper Case Letter"
ElseIf Asc(Char$) > 96 And Asc(Char$) < 123 Then
    CharType$ = "Lower Case Letter"
End If
```

> **Note**
>
> You have seen a single-line version of the **If...End If** statement, **IIf( )**, in the "Assignment and Comparison Operators" section of Chapter 9. The single-line version does not require the terminating **End If** statement. Although acceptable for simple statements, the single-line version's use is questionable (not necessarily poor) programming practice, so this book avoids it.

You use the **If...End If** statement more often than any other flow control.

The *Select Case...End Select* Structure

When you must choose among many alternatives, **If...End If** structures can become very complex and deeply nested. The **Select Case...End Select** structure was added to procedural BASIC to overcome this complexity. In addition to testing whether an expression evaluates to true or false, **Select Case** can evaluate variables to determine whether those variables fall within specified ranges. The generalized syntax is in the following example:

```
Select Case VarName
    Case Expression1[, Expressions, ...]
        (Statements executed if the value of VarName
        = Expression1 or Expressions)
    [Case Expression2 To Expression3
        (Statements executed if the value of VarName
        is in the range of Expression2 to Expression3)]
    [Case Is RelationalExpression
        (Statements executed if the value of
        VarName = Expression1)]
    [Case Else
        (Statements executed if none of the
        above cases is met)]
End Select
```

Select Case evaluates *VarName*, which can be a string, a numeric variable, or an expression. It then tests each **Case** expression in sequence. **Case** expressions can take one of the following four forms:

- A single or list of values to which to compare the value of *VarName*. Successive members of the list are separated from the predecessor by commas.

- A range of values separated by the keyword **To**. The value of the first member of the range limits must be less than the value of the second. Strings are compared by the ASCII value of their first character.

- The keyword **Is**, followed by a relational operator, such as <>, <, <=, =, >=, or >, and a variable or literal value.

- The keyword **Else**. Expressions following **Case Else** are executed if no prior **Case** condition is satisfied.

The **Case** statements are tested in sequence, and the code associated with the first matching **Case** condition is executed. If no match is found and the **Case Else** statement is present, the code following the statement is executed. Program execution then continues at the line of code following the **End Select** terminating statement.

If *VarName* is a numeric type, all expressions with which it is to be compared by **Case** are forced to the same data type.

The following example is of **Select Case** using a numeric variable, *Sales#*:

```
Select Case Sales#
    Case 10000 To 49999.99
        Class% = 1
    Case 50000 To 100000
        Class% = 2
    Case Is < 10000
        Class% = 0
    Case Else
        Class% = 3
End Select
```

Note that because Sales# is a double-precision real number, all the comparison literals also are treated as double-precision (not the default single-precision) real numbers for the purposes of comparison.

A more complex example that evaluates a single character follows:

```
Select Case Text$
    Case "A" To "Z"
        CharType$ = "Upper Case"
    Case "a" To "z'
        CharType$ = "Lower Case"
    Case "0" To "9"
        CharType$ = "Number"
    Case "!", "?", ".", ",", ";"
        CharType$ = "Punctuation"
    Case ""
        CharType$ = "Empty String"
```

```
        Case < 32
              CharType$ = "Special Character"
        Case Else
              CharType$ = "Unknown Character"
   End Select
```

This example demonstrates that **Select Case**, when used with strings, evaluates the ASCII value of the first character of the string, either as the variable being tested or the expressions following **Case** statements. Thus **Case < 32** is a valid test, although Text$ is a string variable.

Repetitive Operations—Looping

In many instances you must repeat an operation until a given condition is satisfied, whereupon the repetitions terminate. You may want to examine each character in a word, sentence, or document, or assign values to an array with many elements. Loops are used for these and many other purposes.

Using the *For*. . .*Next* Statement

Access Basic's **For**. . .**Next** statement enables you to repeat a block of code a specified number of times, as shown in the following example:

```
For Counter% = StartValue% To EndValue% [Step
    Increment%]
    Statements to be executed
    [Conditional statement
        Exit For
    End of conditional statement]
Next [Counter%]
```

The block of statements between the **For** and **Next** keywords is executed (EndValue%-StartValue% + 1) / Increment% times. As an example, if StartValue% = 5, EndValue% = 10, and Increment% = 1, execution of the statement block is repeated six times. You need not add the keyword **Step** in this case—the default increment is 1. Although **Integer** data types are shown, **Long** (integers) may be used. The use of real numbers (**Single** or **Double** data types) as values for counters and increments is possible, but uncommon.

The dividend of the above expression must always be a positive number if execution of the internal statement block is to occur. If EndValue% is less than StartValue%, Increment% must be negative; otherwise, the **For**...**Next** statement is ignored by Access Basic.

The optional **Exit For** statement is provided so that you can prematurely terminate the loop using a surrounding **If**...**Then**...**End If** conditional statement. Changing the value of the counter variable within the loop itself to terminate its operation is discouraged as a dangerous programming practice. You might make a change that would cause an infinite loop.

> **Note**
>
> If you use a numeric variable for `Increment%` in a **For...Next** loop and the value of the variable becomes 0, the loop repeats indefinitely and locks up your computer, requiring you to reboot the application or Access Basic. Make sure that your code traps any condition that could result in `Increment%` becoming 0.

The repetition of `Counter%` following the `Next` statement is optional, but is considered good programming practice, especially if you are using nested **For...Next** loops. Adding `Counter%` keeps you informed of which loop you are counting. If you try to use the same variable name for a counter of a nested **For...Next** loop, you receive an error message.

When the value of `Counter%` exceeds `EndValue%` or the **Exit For** statement is executed, execution proceeds to the line of code following **Next**.

Using *For. . .Next* Loops to Assign Values to Array Elements

One of the most common applications of the **For...Next** loop is to assign successive values to the elements of an array. If you have declared a 26-element array named `Alphabet$()`, the following example assigns the capital letters A through Z to its elements:

```
For Letter% = 1 To 26
    Alphabet$(Letter%) = Chr$(Letter% + 63)
Next Letter%
```

The preceding example assigns 26 of the array's 27 elements if you used **Dim** `Alphabet$(26)` rather than **Dim** `Alphabet$(1 To 26)`. 63 is added to `Letter%` because the ASCII value of the letter A is 64, and the initial value of `Letter%` is 1.

Understanding *Do While. . .Loop* and *While. . .Wend*

A more general form of the loop structure is **Do While...Loop**, which uses the following syntax:

```
Do While Condition% [= True]
    Statements to be executed
    [Conditional statement
        Exit Do
    End of conditional statement]
Loop
```

This loop structure executes the intervening statements only if `Condition%` equals **True** (–1), and continues to do so until `Condition%` no longer equals **True** or the optional **Exit Do** statement is executed. Note that `Condition%`

need not equal **False** (0) for the loop to terminate; the **False** condition in Access Basic is defined as Not **True**.

From the preceding syntax, the previous **For. . .Next** array assignment example can be duplicated by the following structure:

```
Letter% = 1
Do While Letter% <= 27
    Alphabet(Letter%) = Chr$(Letter% + 63)
    Letter% = Letter% + 1
Loop
```

Another example of a **Do** loop is the **Do Until. . .Loop** structure, which loops as long as the condition is not satisfied, as in the following example:

```
Do Until Condition% <> True
    Statements to be executed
    [Conditional statement
        Exit Do
    End of conditional statement]
Loop
```

The **While. . .Wend** loop is identical to the **Do While. . .Loop** structure, but you cannot use the Exit Do statement within it. The **While. . .Wend** structure is provided for compatibility with QBasic and QuickBASIC and should be abandoned in favor of **Do {While¦Until}. . .Loop** in Access Basic.

Making Sure Statements in a Loop Occur at Least Once

You may have observed that the statements within a **Do While. . .Loop** structure are never executed if Condition% is **Not True** when the structure is encountered in your application. You also can use a structure in which the conditional statement that causes loop termination is associated with the **Loop** statement. The syntax of this format is in the following example:

```
Do
    Statements to be executed
    [Conditional statement then
        Exit Do
    End of conditional statement]
Loop While Condition%[ = True]
```

A similar structure is available for **Do Until. . .Loop**:

```
Do
    Statements to be executed
    [Conditional statement
        Exit Do
    End of conditional statement]
Loop Until Condition%[ = False]
```

These structures ensure that the loop executes at least once *before* the condition is tested.

Avoiding Infinite Loops

You have already received warnings about infinite loops in the descriptions of each of the loop structures. If you create a *tight* loop, (one with few statements between **Do** and **Loop**) that never terminates, executing the code causes Access Basic to appear to freeze. You cannot terminate operation, and you must use Ctrl+Alt+Delete to reboot, relaunch Access Basic, and correct the code.

These apparent infinite loops are often created intentionally with code such as the following:

```
Temp% = True
ExitLoop% = False
Do While Temp% [= True]
    Call TestProc(ExitLoop%)
    If ExitLoop%[ = True] Then
        Exit Do
    End If
Loop
```

The preceding example repeatedly calls the procedure TestProc, whose statements are executed, until ExitLoop% is set **True** by code in TestProc. Structures of this type are the equivalent of DO WHILE .T. ... ENDDO structures in dBASE. You must make sure that ExitLoop% eventually becomes **True**, one way or another, no matter what happens when the code in TestProc is executed.

> **Note**
>
> To avoid locking up Access Basic with tight infinite loops, include the **DoEvents** command in loops during the testing stage, as in the following example:
>
> ```
> Do While Temp%[ = True]
>     Call TestProc(ExitLoop%)
>     If ExitLoop% Then
>         Exit Do
>     End If
>     DoEvents
> Loop
> ```
>
> **DoEvents** tests the Windows environment to determine whether any other event messages, such as a mouse click, are pending. If so, **DoEvents** allows the messages to be processed and then continues at the next line of code. You can then remove **DoEvents** to speed up the loop, after your testing verifies that infinite looping cannot occur.

Typically, you can write the **Do While** line as **Do While** Temp%, not **Do While** Temp% = **True**. Displaying the relational operator, as in Temp% = **True**, however, makes your code more readable and is used in this chapter's examples for clarity.

Handling Run-Time Errors

No matter how thoroughly you test and debug your code, run-time errors appear eventually. Run-time errors are errors that occur when Access executes your code. Use the **On Error GoTo** instruction to control what happens in your application when a run-time error occurs. **On Error** is not a very sophisticated instruction, but it is your only choice for error processing in Access modules. You can branch to a label, or you can ignore the error. The general syntax of **On Error**. . . follows:

```
On Error GoTo LabelName
On Error Resume Next
On Error GoTo 0
```

On Error GoTo LabelName branches to the portion of your code with the label LabelName:. LabelName must be a label; it cannot be the name of a procedure. The code following LabelName, however, can (and often does) include a procedure call to an error-handling procedure, such as ErrorProc:

```
On Error GoTo ErrHandler
...
[RepeatCode:
(Code using ErrProc to handle errors)]
...
GoTo SkipHandler
ErrHandler:
Call ErrorProc
[GoTo Repeat Code]
SkipHandler:
...
(Additional code)
```

In this example, the **On Error GoTo** instruction causes program flow to branch to the ErrHandler label that executes the error-handling procedure ErrorProc. Ordinarily, the error handler code is located at the end of the procedure. If you have more than one error handler, or if the error handler is in the middle of a group of instructions, you need to bypass it if the preceding code is error-free. Use the GoTo SkipHandler statement that bypasses ErrHandler instructions. To repeat the code that generated the error after ErrorProc has done its job, add a label such as RepeatCode: at the beginning of the repeated code, and then branch to the code in the ErrHandler: code.

Alternatively, you can add the keyword **Resume** at the end of your code to resume processing at the line that created the error.

On Error Resume Next disregards the error and continues processing the succeeding instructions.

After an **On Error GoTo** statement executes, it remains in effect for all succeeding errors until another **On Error GoTo** instruction is encountered or until error processing is explicitly turned off with the **On Error GoTo 0** form of the statement.

If you do not trap errors with an **On Error GoTo** statement, or if you have turned error trapping off with **On Error GoTo 0**, a dialog with the appropriate error message appears when a run-time error is encountered.

If you do not provide at least one error-handling routine in your Access Basic code for run-time applications, your application quits abruptly when the error occurs.

Detecting the Type of Error with the *Err* Function

The **Err** function (no arguments) returns an integer representing the code of the last error, or 0 if no error occurs. This function is ordinarily used within a **Select Case** structure to determine the action to take in the error handler based on the type of error incurred. Use the Error$() function to return the text name of the error number specified as its argument, as in the following example:

```
ErrorName$ = Error$(Err)
Select Case Err
    Case 58 To 76
        Call FileError 'procedure for handling file errors
    Case 281 To 297
        Call DDEError 'procedure for handling DDE errors
    Case 340 To 344
        Call ArrayError 'procedure for control array errors
End Select
Err = 0
```

Some of the error codes returned by the **Err** function are listed in the Error Codes topic of the Access help file. Choose **S**earch from the **H**elp menu to display the Search dialog. Then type **Error Codes** in the text box and press Enter. The Error Codes Help window displays a list of code numbers and their descriptions. Click the underlined description text to display a window that describes each error code in detail.

You can substitute the actual error processing code for the Call instructions shown in the preceding example, but using individual procedures for error handling is the recommended approach. The **Err** *statement* is used to set the error code to a specific integer. This statement should be used to reset the error code to 0 after your error handler has completed its operation, as shown in the preceding example.

The **Error** statement is used to simulate an error so that you can test any error handlers you have written. You can specify any of the valid integer error codes or create a user-defined error code by selecting an integer not included in the list. A user-defined error code returns "User-defined error" to **Error$()**.

Using the *Error* Event in Form and Report Modules

Access 2.0 includes a new event, Error, triggered when an error occurs on a form or report. You can use an event-handling procedure in a form or report to process the error, or you can assign a generic error-handling function in an Access module to the Error event with an =ErrorHandler() entry. (You also can attach a macro to the Error event, but macros have limited means of dealing with run-time errors.)

When you invoke an error-handling procedure or function from the Error event, you need to use the **Err** function to detect the error that occurred and take corrective action, as described in the preceding section.

Exploring the Module Window

You write Access Basic functions and procedures in the Module window. To display a Module window, click the Module tab of the Database window. Then double-click the name of the module you want to display. To open a new Access Basic module, click the New button. A Module code editing window appears as shown in figure 27.4. Figure 27.4 displays the Proper() function of the Utility Functions module included in NWIND.MDB. You choose the function or procedure to display from the procedures drop-down list. The Module window incorporates a text editor, similar to Windows Notepad, in which you type your Access Basic code. Unlike Visual Basic 3.0 and Visual Basic for Applications, the Access 2.0 code editing window does not color-code keywords and comments.

The Access Basic code in figure 27.4 demonstrates two principles of writing code in any language: add comments that explain the purpose of the statements, and use indentation to make your code more readable. Comments in Access Basic are preceded with an apostrophe ('); alternatively, use the prefix

Rem (for "remark" in earlier versions of BASIC) to indicate that the text on the line is a comment. **Rem** must be the first statement on a line (unless preceded by a colon that separates statements), but the apostrophe prefix can be used anywhere in your code. Comments that precede the code identify the procedure, explain its purpose, and indicate the macro or other procedure that calls the code. If the function returns a value, a description of the returned value and its data type is included.

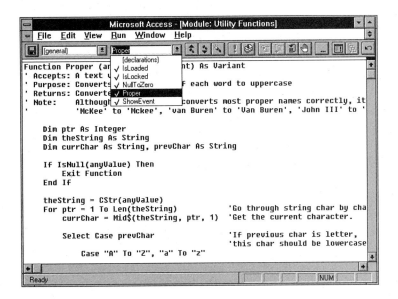

Fig. 27.4
Opening an Access Basic function in the Module window.

The Toolbar of the Module Window

Table 27.3 lists the purpose of each item in the toolbar of the Module window, and the menu commands and key combinations that you can substitute for toolbar components. Buttons marked with an asterisk (*) in the Items column are new with Access 2.0.

Access
2.0

Button	Item	Alternate Method	Purpose
Table 27.3	**Elements of the Module Window's Toolbar**		
🖫	Save Button*	**F**ile **S**ave	Save changes to the current procedure.
N/A	Object List*	None	Displays a list of objects in form or report modules. (Only (general) appears for Access modules.)

(continues)

Table 27.3 Continued

Button	Item	Alternate Method	Purpose
N/A	Procedure List	**V**iew **P**rocedures or press F2	Displays a procedure in an Access module or an event that is applicable to the selected object in a form module or report module. Select the procedure or event name from the drop-down list. Procedures are listed in alphabetical order by name.
	Previous Procedure	**V**iew P**r**evious Procedure or Ctrl + Cursor Up	Displays the procedure with the next name higher in the list, if one exists.
	Next Procedure	**V**iew **N**ext Procedure or Ctrl+Cursor Down	Displays the procedure with the next name lower in the list, if one exists.
	New Procedure*	**E**dit Ne**w** Procedure	Opens the New Procedures dialog that lets you select **Function** or **Sub** and name the new procedure.
	Run	**R**un **C**ontinue or press F5	Continues execution of the procedure after execution of a procedure has been halted by a break condition or after use of the Single Step or Procedure Step button.
	Compile * Loaded Modules	**R**un **C**ompile Loaded Modules	Creates pseudo-code (p-code) from the text version of all Access modules and all form and report modules currently open.
	Step Into*	**R**un **S**tep Into or press F8	Moves through an Access Basic procedure one statement (line) at a time.
	Step Over*	**R**un Ste**p** Over or press Shift+F8	Moves through an Access Basic procedure one subprocedure at a time.
	Reset	**R**un **R**eset	Terminates execution of an Access Basic procedure and reinitializes all variables to their default values.

Button	Item	Alternate Method	Purpose
	Breakpoint	**R**un **T**oggle Breakpoint or press F9	Toggles a breakpoint at the line of the code in which the caret is located. Breakpoints are used to halt execution at a specific line. If a breakpoint is set, the Breakpoint button turns it off.
	Build*	None	Opens the Choose Builder dialog to use a builder to create an expression.
	Immediate Window*	**V**iew **I**mmediate Window	Opens the Immediate Window.
	Calls*	**V**iew **C**alls	Displays the Calls dialog that lists all procedures called prior to reaching a breakpoint in your code.
	Undo	**E**dit **U**ndo	Rescinds the last keyboard or mouse operation performed, if possible.
	Help	F1 key	Displays help for the user interface of the Module window.

The View Procedures dialog, which appears when you press F2 (see fig. 27.5), enables you to select any Access module or open form/report module in the database and then choose to display a function or procedure of the selected module. (The Form_Load procedure and IsLoaded() function of the Add Products form that appear in figure 27.5 were added to the Add Products form for demonstration purposes.)

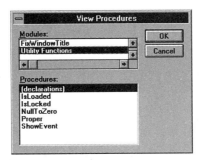

Fig. 27.5
The View Procedures dialog for selecting a function or procedure to edit.

Module Shortcut Keys

Additional shortcut keys and key combinations listed in table 27.4 can help you as you write and edit Access Basic code. Two key combinations, Ctrl+N and Ctrl+Y, are not commonly used in Windows applications. These two combinations were implemented in the original version of the WordStar application and were later adopted by Borland International for its code-editing applications.

Table 27.4   Key Combinations for Entering and Editing Access Basic Code

Key Combination	Purpose
F3	Finds next occurrence of a search string.
Shift+F3	Finds previous occurrence of a search string.
F9	Clears all breakpoints.
Tab	Indents a single line of code by four (default value) characters.
Tab with selected text	Indents multiple lines of selected code by four (default) characters.
Shift+Tab	Unindents a single line of code by four characters.
Shift+Tab with selected text	Unindents multiple lines of selected code by four characters.
Ctrl+N	Inserts a new blank line above the caret.
Ctrl+Y	Deletes the line on which the caret is located.

You can change the default indentation of four characters per tab stop by choosing **O**ptions from the **V**iew menu; choosing Module Design from the Category list; and entering the desired number of characters in the Tab Stop Width text box.

Menu Commands in the Module Window

Menu commands to perform operations not included in table 27.3 are listed in table 27.5. Menu commands common to other database objects, such as **F**ile **S**ave, are not included in the table.

Table 27.5   Module Window Menu Commands

Menu	Commands	Purpose
File	**L**oad Text	Displays the Load Text dialog to select a text file (ASCII format) of Access Basic code to replace or merge with the existing module's code.
	Save **T**ext	Displays the Save Text dialog to save the module's code to a text file in ASCII format.
	Print	Displays the Print dialog to print all or part of the code contained in the module.
	Run Macro	Displays a dialog with a list of macro objects so you can run the code from the macro that calls the Access Basic function.
Edit	**F**ind	Displays the Find dialog to search for specific text strings or regular expressions entered in the Find text box.
	Find **N**ext	Locates and highlights the next occurrence of the search string entered in the Find dialog.
	Find Pre**v**ious	Locates and highlights the previous occurrence of the search string entered in the Find dialog.
	Replace	Replaces all or selected occurrences of the text entered in the Find text box with the text in the Replace text box.
View	Split **W**indow	Divides the Module window into two windows that can display the code of individual procedures.
	C**l**ear All	Clears all breakpoints set in the Breakpoints module. (Active only when breakpoint(s) are set. See "Adding a Breakpoint to the IsLoaded() Function" in this chapter.)
	Modify	Displays a dialog with a Command$ text box into which you enter command line parameters to simulate Access Basic parameters added to the startup command line.

The Access Basic Help System

Microsoft provides an extensive, multilevel help system to help you learn and use Access Basic. If you place the caret on a keyword or select a keyword and then press the F1 key, or click the Help button on the toolbar, for example, a help window for the keyword appears. If you click the "Example" hot spot under the name of the keyword, you see an example of the keyword used in Access Basic (see fig. 27.6).

Fig. 27.6

A help window for a method, and an example window showing how to use that method.

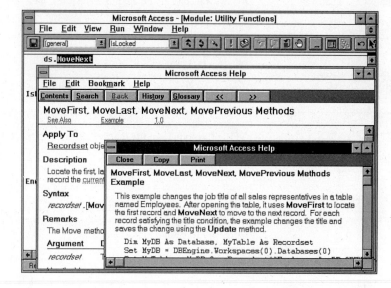

If you press F1 when the caret is not located on a keyword, the help system presents you with an alphabetic list of Access Basic keywords and reserved symbols (see fig. 27.7). You can narrow the list to a particular keyword class by clicking the "Actions", "Functions", "Properties", or "Methods Reference" hot spots. A list of error messages and the message meanings also is available when you click the "Error Messages Reference" hot spot.

Fig. 27.7

The Programming Topics help window for Access Basic.

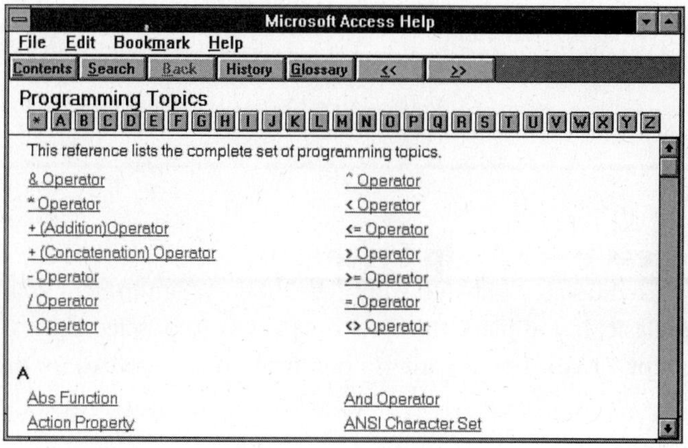

The Access Basic Compiler

Programming languages, such as Pascal and C, use compilers. *Compilers* are applications that convert the code statements—*source code*—you write into instructions the computer can understand—*object code*. These languages use punctuation symbols to identify where statements begin and end; Pascal, for example, uses a semicolon to tell the compiler that a statement is complete. Separating code into individual statements and determining which words in a statement are keywords is *parsing* the code.

After you compile Pascal or C code, you link the code with *libraries* to create an *executable* file. *Libraries* are additional object code that perform standard operations, such as mathematical calculations. Libraries in Access Basic, such as WIZARD.MDA, have a similar purpose. An executable file for a Windows application has the extension .EXE; you run executable files as independent applications. Compiling and linking an application, especially a Windows application, can be a complex process. Microsoft Visual C++, Professional Edition, for example, requires 50M for a typical installation. (A minimum installation consumes 9M.)

Traditional BASIC languages, such as QBasic and also the native dBASE and Paradox programming languages, employ interpreters to execute code. An *interpreter* is an application that reads each line of code, translates the code into instructions for your computer, and then tells the computer to execute these instructions. The interpreter parses code line by line, beginning with the first nonblank character on a line and ending with the newline pair, carriage return (CR, Chr$(13)), and line feed (LF, Chr$(10)). A *newline pair* is created by pressing the Enter key. Compilers for the dBASE language, such as the Borland dBASE compiler and CA-Clipper, also use the newline pair to indicate the end of a statement.

You must execute interpreted code within the application in which the code was created. You run QBasic code, for example, from QBasic, not as a stand-alone application. An interpreter's advantage is that it can test the statements you enter for proper syntax as you write them. Compiled languages don't issue error messages until you compile the source code to object code. Another advantage of interpreters is that you don't need to go through the process of compiling and linking the source code every time you make a change in the code. Unfortunately, interpreters usually execute code more slowly than the computer executes a compiled (.EXE) application.

Access combines the features of both a compiler and an interpreter. Access interprets the code you write when you terminate a line with the Enter key.

If possible, Access corrects your syntax; otherwise you receive a syntax error message, which usually is accompanied by a suggestion for correcting the mistake. Each line of code, therefore, must contain a syntactically correct statement. Some languages, such as xBase and Paradox, enable you to continue a statement; xBase, including Clipper, uses the semicolon for this purpose. VBA offers a statement continuation character, but no statement continuation character exists in Access Basic. No matter how long your Access Basic statement is, it must be written on a single line. (The maximum length of a line of code is 255 characters.)

After you write the source code, Access compiles this code into a cross between interpreted and object code known as *pseudo-code*, or p-code. Pseudo-code runs faster than conventional interpreted code. Access compiles to p-code the code you write or modify the first time the code is used in an application. Access discovers most errors not caught during entry as the code compiles. You can choose Compile **A**ll Loaded Modules from the **R**un menu to force Access to compile all the code in Access modules and open form/report modules. Forcing compilation before running the code—especially if the form or macro that executes the code takes a long time to load—can save substantial time during development.

Examining the Utility Functions Module

One recommended way to learn a new programming language is to examine simple examples of code and analyze the statements used in the example. Microsoft includes some useful code examples in the Utility Functions module of the Northwind Traders sample database. Some of these examples are called by macros in NWIND.MDB.

This section shows how to open a module, display a function in the Module window, and then relate the function to the macro action that calls the function and the database object with which the macro is associated. Examples of the use of the Immediate Window, breakpoints, and the **Debug** object also are provided.

Viewing the *IsLoaded()* Function and the Country Filter Macro

To view the IsLoaded() user-defined function used in the example in the "Synchronizing Forms to the Same Record" section of Chapter 18, "Creating Macros for Forms and Reports," follow these steps:

1. Open the Database window and click the Module button.

2. Double-click in the Module list. The Declarations section of the module appears (see fig. 27.8). When you open a module, the Declarations section appears in the Procedure list.

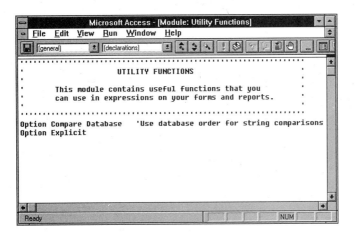

Fig. 27.8

The Declarations section of the sample module supplied with Access.

The **Option** Compare Database keyword is explained in the following section, "Using Text Comparison Options." Option Explicit establishes the requirement that all variables are declared before the variables are assigned a value. Module-level variables are not declared for use by the Utility Functions module's procedures.

3. Open the Procedures drop-down list and select the IsLoaded function. The Module window for the IsLoaded() function appears (see fig. 27.1 at the beginning of this chapter).

The purpose of the IsLoaded() function is to determine whether an application loaded a form with a name specified by the argument, MyFormName, passed in the expression that calls IsLoaded().

4. IsLoaded() is called by the Country Filter macro that responds to the OnOpen event of the Customer Mailing Labels report. To see this macro, open the Database window, click the Macro button, select the Country Filter macro, and click the Design button. The macrosheet for the Country Filter macro appears as shown in figure 27.9.

The IsLoaded() function returns **True** if the Country Filter Dialog pop-up form is loaded and **False** if this pop-up form is not loaded. In this macro, IsLoaded() is used to return a condition to control the execution of two sets of macro actions. If IsLoaded() returns **False**, the CancelEvent and StopMacro actions execute. If IsLoaded() returns **True**, execution continues with the SelectObject and ApplyFilter actions.

Fig. 27.9
The Country Filter
macro that calls
the *IsLoaded()*
function.

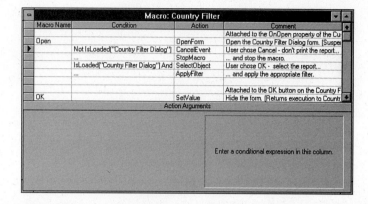

5. To see how the Country Filter macro works, open the Database window; click the Report button; and double-click Customer Mailing Labels. When you run the Customer Mailing Labels report, a modal dialog appears (see fig. 27.10). *Modal* dialogs are boxes that you must close by clicking a button before you can perform further actions. If you click the Specific Country option button, you can enter in the text box the name of the country for which you want mailing labels.

If you click Cancel or press Escape, the Country Filter dialog closes. The Country Filter macro tests the condition **Not** IsLoaded ("Country Filter Dialog") to determine if the user canceled the request for mailing labels.

Fig. 27.10
The Country Filter
dialog that runs
the Country Filter
macro.

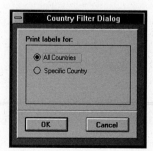

Adding a Breakpoint to the *IsLoaded()* Function

When you examine the execution of Access Basic code written by others, and when you debug your own application, breakpoints are very useful. This section explains how to add a breakpoint to the `IsLoaded()` function so that the Customer Mailing Labels Report stops executing when the Country Filter macro calls the `IsLoaded()` function and Access displays the code in the Module window.

To add a breakpoint to the `IsLoaded()` function, follow these steps:

1. Choose Module: Utility Functions from the **W**indow menu to make the Module window active.

2. Place the caret on the line `IsLoaded = ` **`True`**.

3. Click the Breakpoint button of the toolbar, choose **T**oggle Breakpoint from the **R**un menu, or press F9. The breakpoint you create is indicated by changing the attribute of the line to bold (see fig. 27.11).

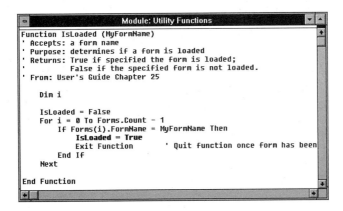

Fig. 27.11
The *IsLoaded()* function with a breakpoint set.

4. Choose Report:Customer Mailing Labels from the **W**indow menu, or click the Report button of the Database window. Then double-click Customer Mailing Labels to run the Customer Mailing Labels report.

5. Click the All Countries option button, and then click OK. When execution of the Country Filter macro reaches the `IsLoaded()` function, execution of `IsLoaded()` begins with the `Dim i` line that assigns variable `i` the **Variant** data type. (The **Integer** data type is more appropriate for counter variables.)

The value that IsLoaded() returns, unless changed later, is specified by the line IsLoaded = **False**. The function name is used as the variable name so that a return value is assigned to the function name.

The **For** i = 0 **To** Forms.Count -1...**Next** loop tests each of the forms loaded to determine if the name of a specific form exists in the Forms collection. The Forms collection of **Form** objects is a predefined *enumeration* (similar to an array) whose members consist of all loaded forms, beginning with the zeroth member. The Count property of Forms returns the number of forms currently loaded. Collections of database objects are discussed in the next chapter.

The element of the Forms collection tested is specified by Forms(i), and the value of the FormName property of each form, returned by Forms(i).FormName, is compared with the value of MyFormName, Country Filter Dialog in this case. If the result of the comparison is **True**, the line that contains the breakpoint is reached, execution halts, and the Module window displays the module code. The line with the breakpoint is enclosed in a highlighting rectangle (see fig. 27.12).

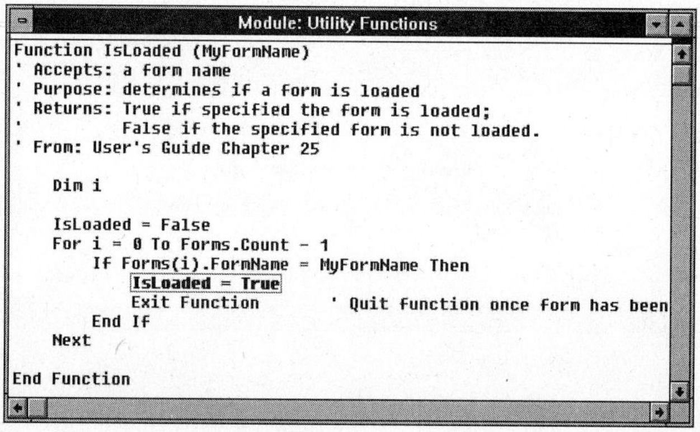

Fig. 27.12

The *IsLoaded()* procedure when the breakpoint is reached and the Immediate Window is opened.

```
Module: Utility Functions

Function IsLoaded (MyFormName)
' Accepts: a form name
' Purpose: determines if a form is loaded
' Returns: True if specified the form is loaded;
'          False if the specified form is not loaded.
' From: User's Guide Chapter 25

    Dim i

    IsLoaded = False
    For i = 0 To Forms.Count - 1
        If Forms(i).FormName = MyFormName Then
            IsLoaded = True
            Exit Function        ' Quit function once form has been
        End If
    Next

End Function
```

Using the Immediate Window

In Chapter 9's "Using the Immediate Window" section, you learned to use the Immediate Window to display the results of computations and values returned by functions. The Immediate Window also is useful when you want to display the value of variables when the breakpoint is encountered. To display the value of local (procedure-level) variables, execution of your code must be halted at a breakpoint beyond the point at which the variables are assigned their values.

To open the Immediate Window and display the value of a variable while execution is halted at the breakpoint shown in preceding figure 27.12, follow these steps:

1. Click the Immediate Window button of the toolbar or choose **I**mmediate Window from the **V**iew menu.

2. Type **? MyFormName** and press Enter to display the value of this variable (see fig. 27.12). The **?** symbol is shorthand for the reserved word `Print`.

3. You can display the value of the variable, i, by typing **? i** and pressing Enter. You cannot, however, type **? IsLoaded** to determine the value of the function; you receive an error message if you try.

4. Type **? IsLoaded(MyFormName)** and press Enter. The Immediate Window executes the function again (creating a second instance of the function), but execution stops at the breakpoint.

5. Click the Step Into button of the toolbar, choose **S**ingle Step from the **R**un menu, or press F8 to continue execution of the function. The `Exit Function` statement is encountered, and execution jumps to the `End Function` line. Click the Single Step button, or press F8 again. `IsLoaded()` then returns -1 (`True`) in the Immediate Window.

6. Continue clicking the Step Into button. Execution of the first instance of the function continues until `Exit Function` is reached; then you see the Customer Mailing List report in print preview mode.

7. Choose C**l**ear All Breakpoints from the **R**un menu to toggle the breakpoint off.

When you write your own code, the Immediate Window is *very* handy for debugging purposes.

Printing to the Immediate Window with the *Debug* Object

When you need to view the values of several variables, you can use the `Debug` object to automate printing to the Immediate Window. If you add the `Debug` object to the `IsLoaded()` function, you can create a list in the Immediate Window of all the forms that are open.

To modify the IsLoaded() function to list all open forms, follow these steps:

1. Load three or four additional forms by repeatedly opening the Database window, clicking the Form button, and double-clicking a form name in the list. The Customers, Categories, Forms Switchboard, and Main Switchboard forms are good choices because these forms load quickly.

2. Choose Module: Utility Functions from the **W**indow menu to make the IsLoaded() function's window active.

3. Place the caret on the line that contains **If** Forms(i)... and press Ctrl+N to insert a new line above this line.

4. Type the following text in the new line and press Enter:

   ```
   Debug.Print Forms(i).FormName
   ```

   This statement prints the name of each open form in the Immediate Window.

5. Add an apostrophe in front of the line **Exit Function** to turn the statement into a comment. Without **Exit Function**, all forms are listed, regardless of when Country Filter Dialog is encountered during execution of the loop.

6. Place the caret on the last line of the function, **End Function**, and press F9 to create a breakpoint. This causes the Module window to appear when the function is run by the macro.

7. Open the Database window; click the Report button; and double-click Customer Mailing Labels. Click OK in the Country Filter Dialog.

 8. Click the Immediate Window button to display the Immediate Window. The name of each form is added to the Immediate Window by the **Debug.Print** statement (see fig. 27.13).

9. Double-click the Document Control-menu box, or choose **C**lose from the **F**ile menu. Do not save changes to the Utility Function module. Then close the other forms that you opened for this example.

The **Debug.Print** statement is particularly useful in displaying the values of variables that change when you execute a loop. When you have completed testing of your procedure, you delete the **Debug** statements.

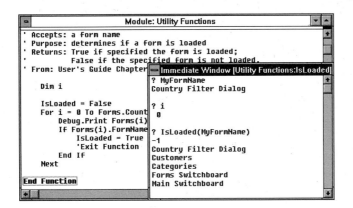

Fig. 27.13
The *Debug* object used to print values of variables to the Immediate Window.

Using Text Comparison Options

The comparisons that the IsLoaded() function made between the values of MyFormName and Forms(i).FormName in the preceding examples are based on the value of the **Option** Compare Database statement, which appears in the Declarations section of the Utility Functions module. To determine how text comparisons are made in the module, you can use any of the following statements:

■ **Option** Compare Binary comparisons are case-sensitive. Lowercase letters are not equivalent to uppercase letters. To determine the sort order of characters, Access uses the character value assigned by the Windows ANSI character set.

■ **Option** Compare Text comparisons are not case-sensitive. Lowercase letters are treated as the equivalent of uppercase letters. The sort order of characters is determined by the sCountry= setting in the [intl] section of your WIN.INI file. For most North American users, the sort order is the same as **Option** Compare Binary, ANSI. Unless you have a reason to specify a different comparison method, use **Option** Compare Text.

■ **Option** Compare Database comparisons are case-sensitive and the sort order is that specified for the database.

Option Compare Binary is the default if you do not include an **Option** Compare statement in the Declarations section of the module. However, Access adds **Option** Compare Database and a comment to the Declarations section when you create a new module, overriding the default. **Binary** and **Database** are reserved words in Access Basic, but these words do not have the same meaning as the reserved words when used in the **Option** Compare statement. For compatibility with changes in possible future releases of Access, you should not use Compare or Text as names of variables.

Writing Your Own Functions and Procedures

You do not need to be an Access Basic expert to write a user-defined function. The information you learned about operators and expressions in Chapter 9, as well as the introduction to Access Basic statements presented in this chapter, enable you to create UDFs that supplement Access Basic's repertoire of standard functions. After you master user-defined functions, you can try your hand at writing functions—actually, procedures in the form of functions—executed by the RunCode action of macro objects. Access Basic procedures offer flexibility in manipulating database and control objects, but require more knowledge of programming techniques than is needed to create UDFs. This section describes how you write a simple user-defined function.

User-defined functions are required when you need a conditional statement more complex than that accommodated by the **IIf**() function. An example is a fixed set of quantity discounts that apply to all or a group of products. You can create a table of quantity discounts; however, a user-defined function that returns the discount is easier to implement and faster to execute.

For this example, the discounts are 50 percent for 1,000 or more of an item; 40 percent for 501 to 999; 30 percent for 100 to 499; 20 percent for 50 to 99; 10 percent for 10 to 49; and no discount for purchases of fewer than 10 items. Discount structures of this type lend themselves well to **Select Case...End Select** structures.

To create the user-defined function sngDiscount() that returns a fractional percent discount based on the value of the argument, Quantity, follow these steps:

1. Click the Modules button of the Database window, and double-click the Utility Functions module.

2. Position the cursor on the line following **Option** Explicit and type **Function sngDiscount(intQuantity As Integer)**. After you press Enter, Access opens a new Module window with the function name on

the first line and adds the `End Function` statement. This process is quicker than clicking the New Procedure button or choosing Ne**w** Procedure from the **E**dit menu.

The `sng` prefix of the function name indicates that the function returns the **Single** data type. The **As Integer** modifier for the `intQuantity` argument specifies that the function treats `intQuantity` as an **Integer** data type. If you do not specify the data type, your function assigns the default **Variant** data type to `intQuantity`.

3. Position the caret at the beginning of the blank line and press Tab. To establish the discount schedule, enter the following lines of code:

```
Select Case intQuantity
    Case Is >= 1000
        sngDiscount = .5
    Case Is >= 500
        sngDiscount = .4
    Case Is >= 100
        sngDiscount = .3
    Case Is >= 50
        sngDiscount = .2
    Case Is >= 10
        sngDiscount = .1
    Case Else
        sngDiscount = 0
End Select
```

Tip

You don't need to enter the **Is** keyword because Access checks the syntax of each statement you write when you press Enter. If you omit the **Is** keyword, Access adds it for you.

Use the Tab key to duplicate the indentation illustrated in the preceding example. **Case** statements are executed from the first statement to the last, so quantities are entered in descending sequence. If `sngQuantity = 552`, the criterion is not met for **Case Is >= 1000**, so the next **Case** statement is tested. **Case Is >= 500** is satisfied, so `sngDiscount` receives the value .4 and execution proceeds directly to the **End Select** statement.

4. To make sure that the function is acceptable to Access Basic's compiler, click the Compile All button of the toolbar or choose Compile **A**ll Loaded Modules from the **R**un menu. Access converts the entries to a form that it can process. When you compile the code, Access indicates any errors not caught by line-by-line syntax checking.

5. You do not need to create a table or macro to test the function; the Immediate Window performs this task adequately for sample code. If the Immediate Window is not open, click the Immediate Window button of the toolbar or choose **I**mmediate Window from the **V**iew menu.

6. Test the sngDiscount() function by entering **?**
sngDiscount(*Quantity*) in the Immediate Window, and then press
Enter. Substitute numeric values for *Quantity*, (see fig. 27.14).

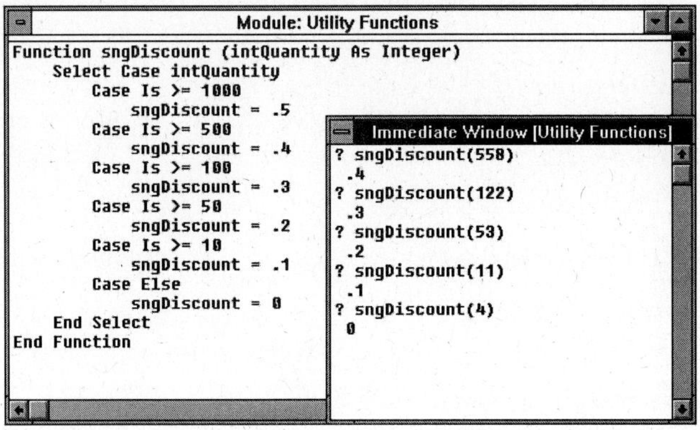

Fig. 27.14
Code for the
sngDiscount() user-
defined function.

```
Function sngDiscount (intQuantity As Integer)
    Select Case intQuantity
        Case Is >= 1000
            sngDiscount = .5
        Case Is >= 500
            sngDiscount = .4
        Case Is >= 100
            sngDiscount = .3
        Case Is >= 50
            sngDiscount = .2
        Case Is >= 10
            sngDiscount = .1
        Case Else
            sngDiscount = 0
    End Select
End Function
```

Module: Utility Functions

Immediate Window [Utility Functions]
```
? sngDiscount(558)
 .4
? sngDiscount(122)
 .3
? sngDiscount(53)
 .2
? sngDiscount(11)
 .1
? sngDiscount(4)
 0
```

7. To save the UDF, click the Save button of the toolbar or choose **S**ave
from the **F**ile menu.

You can employ user-defined functions in expressions to compute values for
calculated fields, validate data entry, construct queries, and other purposes
where an expression can be used.

Troubleshooting

An "Expected Shared or variable" message box appears when entering a **Dim**
VariableName **As** **DataType** *statement.*

You attempted to name a variable with a reserved word. For example, you receive
the preceding error message if you attempt to create a **Dim** Option **As** **Integer**
statement. **Option** is an Access Basic reserved word. Change the name of the object,
preferably using the data type tag prefix, as in intOption.

Access
2.0

Writing Code Behind Forms with the Code Builder

This section describes the process you use to write event-handling code in
form or report modules. Simple event-handling procedures (*event-handlers*)
can take the place of macros. This example replaces the Country Filter.OK

macro, which hides the Country Filter Dialog form, with an event-handling procedure that performs the same function.

To create an event-handler to replace the Country Filter.OK macro, follow these steps:

1. Close any forms or modules you have open; then open the Country Filter Dialog form in Design View.

2. Pull down the bottom of the Country Filter Dialog's window to expose the OK button; then click OK to select it.

3. Click the Properties button of the toolbar and select Event Properties.

4. Place the caret in the On Click event text box (see fig. 27.15) and click the ellipsis button to display the Country Filter macrosheet.

Fig. 27.15
The Country Filter.OK macro assigned to the *OnClick* event of the OK button.

5. Place the caret in the OK cell of the macrosheet to display the arguments of the SetValue action (see fig. 27.16.) Clicking the OK button of the Country Filter Dialog hides the form (SetValue Visible = No).

6. Close the Country Filter macrosheet to return to the Country Filter Dialog form's Design View.

7. Delete the Country Filter.OK entry for the OnPush event, and then click the ellipsis button to display the Choose Builder dialog (see fig. 27.17).

8. Select Code Builder and click OK to open the Form.Country Filter Dialog module. Access creates a **Sub** Button15_Click()...**End Sub** event-handler stub for you.

9. Type **Me.Visible = False** between the **Sub**... and **End Sub** lines (see fig. 27.18). The **Me** reserved word refers to the Form object in which the

module is contained, not the OK command button. `Me.Visible = False` is the Access Basic equivalent of the `SetValue Visible = No` macro action.

Fig. 27.16

The OK macro shown in the Country Filter macrosheet.

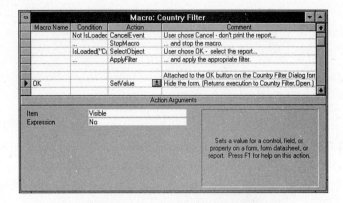

Fig. 27.17

Selecting the Code Builder with the Choose Builder dialog.

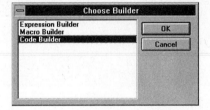

Fig. 27.18

Writing the event-handling code to hide the Country Filter Dialog.

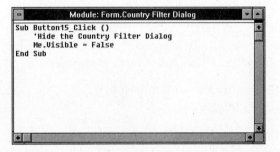

10. Close the Form.Country Filter Dialog module. The event-handling procedure you wrote ([Event Procedure]) is attached to the `OnPush` event of the OK command button (see fig. 27.19).

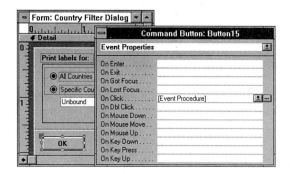

Fig. 27.19
The *Button15_Click* event handler attached to the *OnPush* event of the OK button.

11. Close the Country Filter Dialog form and save your changes.

12. Open the Customer Mailing Labels report in print preview mode. Click OK to print labels for all countries. Your event-handler for the OK button performs identically to the Country Filter.OK macro.

Many Access developers choose to use event-handling procedures, rather than macros, to process all events triggered on forms and reports. This is especially true of developers who are accustomed to programming in Visual Basic. An advantage of using macros is that all the event-handling macros can be located in a single macrosheet so that all the event processing for a form appears in a single window. Event-handling procedures are best suited to situations where the event requires complex operations, such as manipulating database objects "behind the scene."

From Here...

This chapter introduced you to Access Basic code so that you can create user-defined functions and replace macros with simple event-handling procedures. This chapter described ways to use the Module window to enter and edit code, and explained the compiling process for Access Basic in the context of compilers and interpreters for other programming languages. The use of conditional statements and different types of loops were covered. You combined the expressions you learned in Chapter 9 with the Access Basic keywords presented here so you could write short examples of Access Basic code. The methods you use to handle run-time errors were explained briefly.

- Chapter 9, "Understanding Operators and Expressions in Access," provides a thorough description of Access's operators and functions that you can employ in Access Basic code.

- Chapter 17, "Understanding Access Macros," lists all the macro actions of Access 2.0. Each of these actions is a candidate for replacement by Access Basic event-handling code.

- Chapter 28, "Understanding the Data Access Object Class," describes Access 2.0's new set of database objects and the collections in which they are contained.

Understanding the Data Access Object Class

Access 2.0 offers Access Basic programmers the opportunity to change the values of almost all properties of its database objects in run mode. The majority of Access 1.x object properties were read-only in run mode; you could alter the property values only in design mode. (The term *run-time* often is used in this context; however, this book uses *run mode* to avoid confusion with the term *run-time*, which is applied to applications that use run-time Access, MSARN200.EXE.) In addition, Access 2.0 lets you create new database objects, including **Database** and **Table** objects, with Access Basic code. Microsoft calls this ability *creating objects programmatically*. Access 1.x required that you employ the user interface to create new databases and tables. (You could use a special library, MSADDL11.DLL, to create tables programmatically, albeit with difficulty.)

This chapter introduces you to the many new data access objects (DAOs) of Access 2.0 and explains how you can manipulate the DAOs with Access Basic code. There is no "Data Access Object," *per se*; the term refers to all the collections of Access 2.0 objects. The structure of the hierarchy of DAOs is, to a major extent, designed to conform to the requirements and recommendations of the Object Linking and Embedding (OLE) 2.0 specification. Thus, much of this chapter uses OLE 2.0 terminology.

Understanding Objects and Object Collections

The specification for Object Linking and Embedding (OLE) 2.0 requires that OLE 2.0-compliant applications, such as Access 2.0, organize programmable

Access
2.0

The principal topics in this chapter include

■ The hierarchy of the data access objects of Access 2.0

■ Referring to the current **Database** object

■ Creating new **Recordset** objects in the Immediate Window

■ Creating a **QueryDef** object

■ Writing a function to display a **QueryDef** result set.

objects into a hierarchical structure of *classes* of objects. The two members of Access object classes that you have used are Forms and Reports. You use these class names as identifiers, such as Forms!*FormName.PropertyName* and Reports!*ReportName!ControlName.PropertyName*, in expressions. In these expressions, Forms or Reports is the class name, and *FormName* or *ReportName* is the literal name of the member object of the class.

In OLE 2.0 jargon, groups of objects of the same class are called *collections*. Forms is the collection of open **Form** objects and Reports is the collection of open **Report** objects. Collections are similar to arrays, except that collections consist of references (called *pointers*) to member objects whereas Access Basic arrays consist of elements that have assigned values. Unlike arrays, the members of collections may appear or disappear without your intervention. As an example, the members of the Forms collection change as you open and close the **Form** objects of your application.

Naming Standards for Object Collections

To conform to OLE 2.0 standards for creating programmable objects, collections are named by the English-language plural of the class name of objects contained in the collection. As an example, Microsoft Graph 5 (MSGraph5) has **Axis** objects; the collection of these objects is called the Axes collection. Collections have relatively few properties; the most common property is Count. The IsLoaded() function discussed in the preceding chapter made use of the value of the Count property in the **For** i = 0 **To** Forms.Count - 1 statement to *iterate* or *enumerate* the Forms collection. To iterate or enumerate a collection usually means to test all (or a particular set of) members of a collection for values of a specified property. The IsLoaded() function tests the FormName property of members of the Forms collection in the **If** Forms(i).FormName = MyFormName **Then** statement.

Figure 28.1 shows the hierarchy of the data access objects of Access 2.0. The topmost member of the hierarchy is the **DBEngine** object, representing the Jet database engine, which contains the Workspaces collection. The Workspaces collection contains Databases, Users, and Groups collections. None of these collections were *exposed* by Access 1.x. Exposing a collection makes the members of the collection accessible to Access Basic code. Notice that the Forms and Reports collections do not appear in figure 28.1. The Forms and Reports collections of Access 1.x and 2.0, like the Scripts (macros) and Modules collections added by Access 2.0, are not DAOs. The Forms and Reports collections are defined by Access, not by Jet, and have two distinct identities:

■ Documents collections, which consist of all saved forms and reports, are members of the Containers collection

■ Forms and Reports collections, which contain only members of the Forms and Reports Containers collection that are currently open in your application

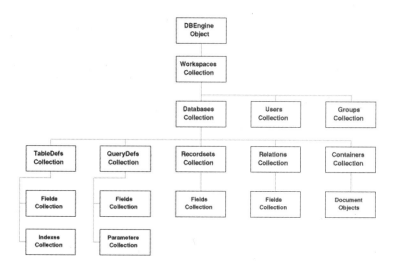

Fig. 28.1
The hierarchy of Access 2.0's data access objects.

In the case of Containers and Documents, Access 2.0 departs from the OLE 2.0 rules for naming collections. Documents are collections that are members of the Containers collection; there are no "Container" objects in the collection. The list in the Database window enumerates the Name property of members of the class of the Documents collection you select by clicking a tab. When you refer to **Form** and **Report** objects in expressions, you use the Forms and Reports collections, *not* the member of the Containers collection with the same name.

Referring to Data Access Objects

Knowing the hierarchy of data access objects is critical to their manipulation by your Access Basic code. As an example, if you want to refer to the currently open database, you specify the full "path" through the hierarchy to your object with the following statement:

```
DBEngine.Workspaces(0).Databases(0)
```

The zeroth member of the Workspaces collection is the current **Workspace** object, also called the current *session* or *instance* of the Jet database engine. The current session comes into existence when you first launch Access. Similarly, Databases(0) specifies the database you open after launching Access, called the *current database*. You can open additional **Workspace** objects and add one or more **Database** objects to the newly created **Workspace** object with Access Basic code. Adding new members to collections is described in sections that follow.

> **Note**
>
> The Database object specified by **DBEngine**.Workspaces(0).Databases(0) is the same object identified by the **CurrentDB**() function of Access 1.x. Using the Container(*i*) syntax, as in
>
> **Set** dbCurrent = **DBEngine**.Workspaces(0).Databases(0)
>
> rather than the Access 1.x form, **Set** dbCurrent = **CurrentDB**(), is advisable to assure compatibility with future versions of Access. (See the "Creating Object Variables" section that follows.)

Tip
You can minimize typing by using the shorthand notation
Set dbCurrent =
DBEngine(0)(0)
to specify the current workspace and open database.

A **Database** object can contain **TableDef**, **QueryDef**, **Recordset**, and **Relation** objects, as well as Documents collections in the Containers collection. Following is a brief description of each of these objects, except the Containers collection:

- **TableDef** objects represent the definition of tables. **TableDef** objects contain Fields and Indexes collections, which contain one member for each field and index of the table represented by the **TableDef** object. **TableDef** objects have several properties such as Name, RecordCount, and ValidationRule, that apply to the table as a whole. The **Field** and **Index** objects have their own sets of properties.

- **QueryDef** objects represent the definition of queries and contain Fields (which might better have been named Columns) and Parameters collections. **QueryDef** objects have properties, such as Name, SQL, and Updatable. **QueryDef** objects were exposed by Access 1.x.

- **Recordset** objects, which have been mentioned throughout this book, represent virtual tables (images) that are stored in RAM. **Recordset** objects are said to be "created over" a table or a query result set. **Recordset** objects, which mimic the behavior of the underlying object, can be of the **Table**, **Dynaset**, or **Snapshot** type. As mentioned in earlier chapters of this book, the **Table**, **Dynaset**, and **Snapshot** data types appear in Access 2.0 for compatibility with Access 1.x code. You should use Access 2.0's **Recordset** objects to assure compatibility with future versions of Access.

- **Relation** objects represent default relationships between fields of tables that, in most cases, you create in the Relationships window. **Relation** objects contain a Fields collection.

> **Note**
>
> If the size of a **Recordset** object exceeds the available RAM, the remainder of the object is placed in a temporary "spill file" in the directory specified by the SET temp= entry in your AUTOEXEC.BAT file.

Following are the three different methods of creating a reference to a member of a collections:

- The *index* method uses conventional array subscripts to specify a particular member of a collection by its position in the collection: `CollectionName(i)`, where *i* ranges from 0 to `CollectionName.Count - 1`. Using the index to the object is the fastest method of referring to members of collections. The problem with the index method is that the index of a particular member object is likely to change as you open and close objects in the collection.

- The *argument* method uses a literal identifier, either a quoted string or a variable holding the value of a literal identifier: `CollectionName("ObjectName")` or `CollectionName(strObjectName)`. This method is preferred when you know the name of the member object.

- The *literal* method uses the bang operator to separate the literal name of the object from the collection name: `CollectionName!ObjectName`. If the literal name contains spaces, enclose the literal in square brackets, as in `CollectionName![Object Name]`. This method is used primarily with **Form** and **Report** objects, but is applicable to members of any collection. In this case, you can't use a variable in place of the name of the member object. The literal method is the least flexible of the three.

Properties of and Methods Applicable to DAOs

Most objects have a `Properties` collection that you can use to enumerate the properties of the object. You can read (get) the value of properties and set the value of most properties of an object in run mode.

DBEngine.Workspaces(0).Count returns **4**, the number of properties of the **Workspace** object. You can obtain the name of a property with the `CollectionName(i).Properties(i).Name` statement, where *i* = 0 to Count - 1. As an example, **DBEngine**.Workspaces(0).Properties(0) returns the value of the Name property. Name is the zeroth property of almost all DAOs. **DBEngine**.Workspaces(0).Properties(0) returns #DefaultWorkspace#, ...Properties(1) returns the value of UserName, admin for unsecure databases, and ...Properties(3) returns the value of the IsolateODBCTrans property, 0.

> **Note**
>
> `DBEngine.Workspaces(0).Properties(2)` holds the Password property of the user. This property is write-only; you can set this value but not read it. You receive an "Invalid Operation" message if you attempt to execute the following:
>
> `DBEngine.Workspaces(0).Properties(2).`

To read or set property values of objects lower in the hierarchy than `Workspaces`, you need to declare an object variable, and then assign the object variable the object you want to manipulate from its collection. Creating object variables is the subject of the next section.

You can apply methods to members of collections, such as **Append** to add a new member to a collection. The `Properties` collection is interesting in this respect: Access 2.0 allows you to append user-defined properties to the `Properties` collection. Some properties of objects are called Access-defined properties; you must append the Access-defined property to the collection in order for Access to assign the property a value. (This obscure methodology is of principal interest to Access developers using SQL pass-through queries, one of the subjects of Chapter 26, "Connecting to Client-Server Databases.")

> **Note**
>
> Publishing limitations preclude listing the properties and methods for each DAO. Use the search feature of Access's on-line help to obtain a list of the properties and methods for the object in which you are interested. Choose **S**earch from the **H**elp menu and enter the name of the collection or object in the text box; then select the Summary entry that appears in the lower list of the Search dialog.

Creating Object Variables

You need to declare *object variables* to represent a specified object lower than **Workspace** objects in the DAO hierarchy. All object variables must be declared explicitly. Object variables are declared with **Dim** *objName* **As** *ObjectType* statements in the Declarations section of a module to create an object variable with module-level scope or in a procedure to create a local object variable. The following code creates an object variable, dbCurrent, that refers to the current database:

```
Dim dbCurrent As Database
Set dbCurrent = DBEngine.Workspaces(0).Databases(0)
```

The **Set** reserved word is used to assign values to variables of object data types. The value of the variable is a reference (pointer) to a block of memory in which the object is located. Thus, dbCurrent is said to *point to* the current database.

> **Note**
>
> Names of object classes that are object data types in Access Basic are set in **bold monospace** type because these names are Access Basic reserved words. Names of collections are set in regular monospace type because these names are keywords but not reserved words. For example, you can assign a value to a variable named Databases; however, this is not a recommended practice. You cannot assign a value to a variable named **Database**. You receive an "Expected: statement" error message if you try.

Once you have declared a **Database** variable, such as dbCurrent, you can use dbCurrent as a shorthand method of assigning pointers to the database objects. To refer to the TableDefs collection of the current database, which is a *subclass* of the **Database** object, use the following statements:

```
Dim tdfCategories As TableDef
Set tdfCategories = dbCurrent.TableDefs("Categories")
```

As a general practice, you create a module-level variable of the **Database** type to point to the current database. If more than one module contains DAO manipulation code, substitute **Global** dbCurrent **As Database** for **Dim** dbCurrent **As Database**. The scope of subclasses of your dbCurrent object depends on your use of the object subclasses in your code.

Using the Immediate Window to Explore DAOs

The Immediate Window is a useful tool to explore the hierarchy of database objects and a few of their properties. Figure 28.2 shows a group of entries in the Immediate Window that report the value of members of the Properties collection of the current **Workspace** object. You can obtain the Name and Value property of each of the **Workspace** object's properties with the syntax shown in figure 28.2. Value is the default property of DAOs, so its use is optional; if you omit the property name, the value of the specified property is returned.

You cannot declare variables explicitly in the Immediate Window; thus, you need to declare object variables in the Declarations section of a module and then enter **Set** statements in the Immediate Window to assign object pointers to the variables. Figure 28.3 provides examples of declaring object variables at the module level and of assigning pointer values to the variables in the Immediate Window. Database objects contain one `TableDef` object for each table listed in the Database window, and each `TableDef` object contains one `Field` object for each field of the table.

Fig. 28.2
Obtaining
property values of
collections and
objects of
NWIND.MDB in
the Immediate
Window.

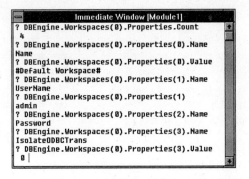

Fig. 28.3
Declaring and
assigning values to
object variables.

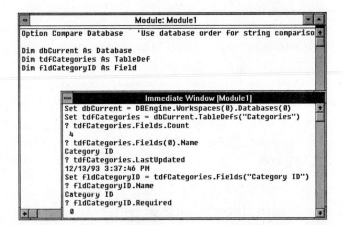

Creating New Data Access Objects

As mentioned earlier in this chapter, Access 2.0 lets you create new DAOs with Access Basic code. The most common DAOs you create with Access Basic are `Recordset` and `QueryDef` objects. `QueryDef` objects, like `TableDef` objects, are called *persistent* objects because `QueryDef` and `TableDef` objects also are `Document` objects. `QueryDef` and `TableDef` objects are stored as elements of your .MDB file and appear in the Queries and Tables lists, respectively, of the Database window. `Recordset` objects are *impersistent* objects; `Recordset` objects exist in memory only from the time you open them until they are closed. You can close a `Recordset` object by applying the `Close` method; `Recordset` objects are closed automatically when the variable that points to them goes out of scope. When you close a **Recordset** object, the memory the object consumes is released to your application.

> ### Note
>
> Using Access Basic to create new **Workspace**, **Database**, **User**, **Group**, **TableDef**, and **Relation** objects is beyond the scope of this book. You can create these objects, with the exception of the **Workspace** object, much easier with Access's user interface. You also can create new **TableDef** objects with make-table queries or by using Access 2.0's new SQL Data Definition Language statements.

Opening a New *Recordset* Object

You create a new **Recordset** object with the **OpenRecordset** method of **Database**, **TableDef**, and **QueryDef** objects. The general syntax of the **OpenRecordset** method has two forms:

    Set rsdName = dbName.OpenRecordset(strSource[, intType[, intOptions]])

    Set rsoName = objName.OpenRecordset([intType[, intOptions]])

The first form, which is applicable only to **Recordset** objects created over **Database** objects requires a value for the str*Source* argument. The value of the str*Source* argument can be the name of a **TableDef** or **QueryDef** object, or an Access SQL statement. Tables 28.1 and 28.2 list values allowed for the int*Type* and int*Options* arguments for both of the preceding syntax examples. The values shown in the table are the names of intrinsic global constants that are defined by Access. In the case of the int*Options* values listed in table 28.2, you can combine the options you want with the **Or** operator, as in DB_DENYWRITE **Or** DB_DENYREAD.

Table 28.1   Values for the int*Type* Argument of the *OpenRecordset()* Method

int*Type*	Description of Type
DB_OPEN_TABLE	**Table** (default value for **TableDef** source)
DB_OPEN_DYNASET	**Dynaset** (default value for **Database**, **QueryDef**, **Recordset**, or an attached **TableDef**)
DB_OPEN_SNAPSHOT	**Snapshot** (not updatable)

Table 28.2   Values for the *int*Options Argument of the *OpenRecordset()* Method

int*Options*	Purpose of Option
DB_DENYWRITE	Prevents others from making changes to any records in the underlying table(s) while the **Recordset** is open.
DB_DENYREAD	Prevents others from reading any records in the underlying table while the **Recordset** is open. This option, which applies to **Table**-type **Recordset** objects only, should be used for administrative purposes only in a multiuser environment.
DB_READONLY	Does not allow updates to records in the table. Read-only access increases the speed of some operations.
DB_APPENDONLY	Only allows appending new records. (Applies to **Dynaset**-type **Recordset** objects only.)
DB_INCONSISTENT	You can update the one-side of a one-to-many relationship. (Applies to **Dynaset**-type **Recordset** objects only.)
DB_CONSISTENT	You cannot update the one-side of a one-to-many relationship, the default. (Applies to **Dynaset**-type **Recordset** objects only.)
DB_FORWARDSCROLL	Creates a **Recordset** object of the forward-scrolling-only **Snapshot** type.

The following two sections show how to create two different types of **Recordset** objects.

A *Recordset* Object That Represents the Image of a Table

You can create the following two types of **Recordset** objects over a table, both of which create a virtual table in memory:

- A **Recordset** object of the **Dynaset** type created from the current **Database** object. To open a **Dynaset Recordset** object over the Orders table, add the **Dim** rstOrders **As Recordset** variable declaration statement to the Declarations section of the module; then use the following statement to assign the pointer:

      Set rstOrders = dbCurrent.**OpenRecordset**("Orders")

  A more appropriate object tag for rstOrders is rsdOrders, representing the **Dynaset Recordset** object.

■ A **Recordset** object of the **Table** type created from a **TableDef** object. To open a **Table Recordset** object over the Orders table, add the **Dim tdfOrders As TableDef** variable declaration statement to the Declarations section of the module; then use the following statements to assign the pointers:

```
Set tdfOrders = dbCurrent.TableDefs("Orders")
Set rstOrders = tdfOrders.OpenRecordset().
```

Figure 28.4 illustrates the creation of both of the preceding types of **Recordset** objects in the Immediate Window.

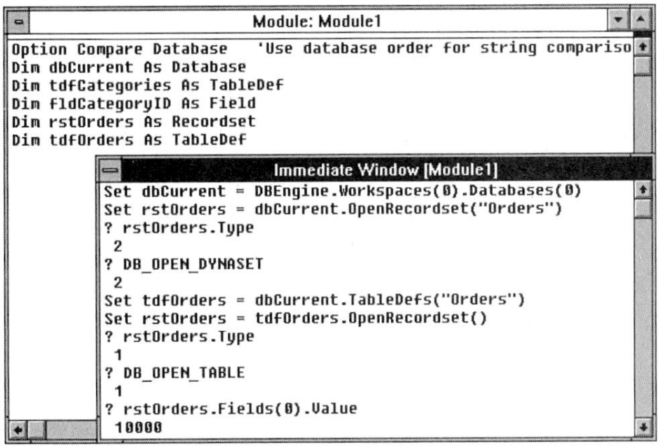

Fig. 28.4
Creating *Recordset* objects of the *Dynaset* and *Table* type in the Immediate Window.

Moving to a Specific Record in a *Recordset* Object

Opening a **Recordset** of the **Table** type lets you quickly find a record in a table with the **Seek** method. This method is applicable only to **Table**-type **Recordset** objects whose underlying table contains an index on the field in which the value you want to find is located. To apply the **Seek** method, you first must specify the index name. The following example sets the record pointer to the record in the Orders table of NWIND.MDB with a value of 10233 in the Order ID field, the primary key of the table:

```
Set tdfOrders = dbCurrent.TableDefs("Orders")
Set rstOrders = tdfOrders.OpenRecordset()
rstOrders.Index = "PrimaryKey"
rstOrders.Seek "=", 10233
If rstOrders.NoMatch Then
    'Record not found, display message box
Else
    'Record found, add code to process the record here
End If
```

Note

You can't enter conditional statements in the Immediate Window, but you can test the preceding code by typing the entries up to and including the **Seek** line, and then executing **? rstOrders.NoMatch** to determine if the **Seek** method was successful in finding a matching record. If **0** is returned, the record pointer rests on the matching record.

If the field in which you are **Seek**ing the value is not the primary key field, you specify the field's name. The NoMatch property returns **False** if the value specified by the **Seek** expression is found; it returns **True** if a matching record is not found. Note that the behavior of the NoMatch property is the opposite of the FOUND() function of xBase. Figure 28.5 shows typical entries to test the **Seek** method in the Immediate Windows. The seek method allows the use of a variety of other operators, such as < or >= in place of the = operator. Thus the **Seek** method is more flexible than xBase's FOUND() function.

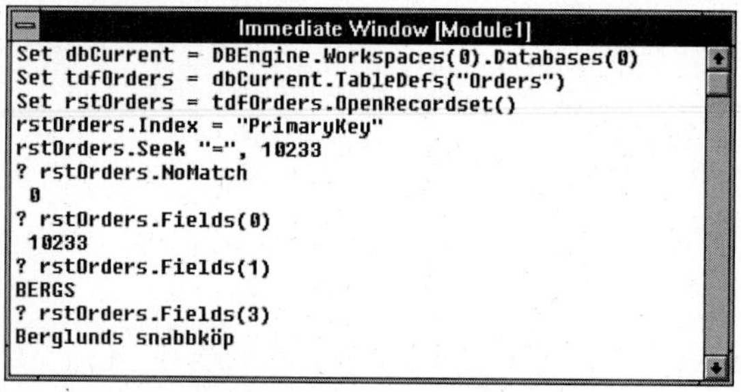

Fig. 28.5

Applying the *Seek* method to *Recordset* objects of the *Table* type.

```
                  Immediate Window [Module1]
Set dbCurrent = DBEngine.Workspaces(0).Databases(0)
Set tdfOrders = dbCurrent.TableDefs("Orders")
Set rstOrders = tdfOrders.OpenRecordset()
rstOrders.Index = "PrimaryKey"
rstOrders.Seek "=", 10233
? rstOrders.NoMatch
  0
? rstOrders.Fields(0)
 10233
? rstOrders.Fields(1)
BERGS
? rstOrders.Fields(3)
Berglunds snabbköp
```

Tip

You cannot apply the **Find**. . .methods to a forward-scrolling-only **Recordset** object of the **Snapshot** type. The only method applicable to such objects is **MoveNext**.

You use the **Find**. . .methods to locate a specific record in **Recordset** objects of the **Dynaset** and **Snapshot** type. There are four **Find**. . .methods: **FindFirst**, **FindNext**, **FindLast**, and **FindPrevious**. Not surprisingly, each method does what its name indicates. The general syntax of the **Find**. . .methods is

> **Find{First¦Next¦Last¦Previous}** strCriteria

The single strCriteria argument of the **Find**. . .methods must be a valid SQL WHERE clause, without the WHERE reserved word. As with the **Seek** method, the NoMatch property returns **False** if a match occurs. Figure 28.6 shows examples of the use of three of the four **Find**. . .methods.

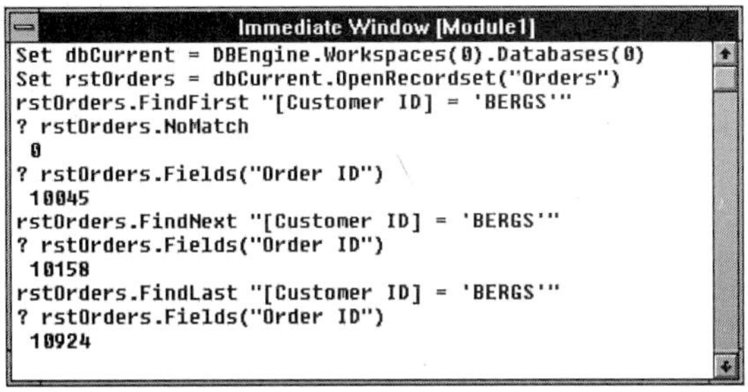

Fig. 28.6
Applying the
Find... methods to
Recordset objects of
the *Dynaset* or
Snapshot type.

A Recordset That Emulates a *QueryDef* Object

You can substitute a valid Access SQL statement for a table or query name as
the value of the strSource property to create a **Recordset** object of the **Dynaset**
or **Snapshot** type over selected records of o᠎ ᠎e or more tables. Such a **Recordset**
is the equivalent of an "impersistent **QueryDef**" object (a **QueryDef** object is
not a **Document** object). Figure 28.7 shows you how to create a **Recordset** object using an SQL statement in the Immediate Window. You must add a **Dim**
strSQL **As String** statement to the Declarations section of the module if the
Option Explicit statement has been executed. The entire strSQL = ... statement is

```
strSQL = "SELECT * FROM Orders, [Order Details]
    WHERE [Order Details].[Order ID] = Orders.[Order ID]
        AND Orders.[Customer ID] = 'BERGS'"
```

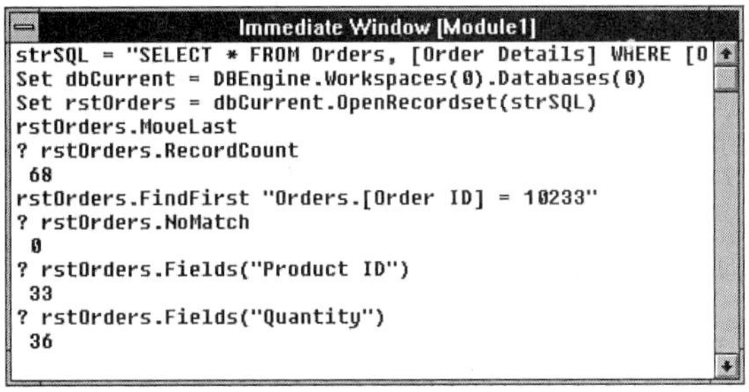

Fig. 28.7
Creating a
Recordset object
with an Access
SQL statement.

If you only need to manipulate a **Recordset**'s records temporarily, creating
the "impersistent **QueryDef**" **Recordset** is faster than creating a legitimate,
persistent **QueryDef** object.

Defining a New *QueryDef* Object

You use the **CreateQueryDef** method to create a new, persistent **QueryDef** object and add it to the QueryDefs collection. One of the advantages of creating
a **QueryDef** is that you can use the name you give the **QueryDef** in place of a

Tip
You need to apply
the **MoveLast**
method before
testing the
value of the
RecordCount
property. If you
omit the
MoveLast method,
you may receive
an erroneous
RecordCount
value (usually 1).

table name in an Access SQL statement. The name of the **QueryDef** must not
duplicate the name of an existing **QueryDef** *or* **TableDef** object. The syntax for
creating a new **QueryDef** object is

> **Set** qdf*Name* = db*Name*.CreateQueryDef(str*Name*, str*SQL*)

QueryDef objects are what their object class name implies, the definition of a
query. If str*SQL*'s SQL statement represents an action query, you apply the
Execute method to the **QueryDef** object to execute the query. You must create
a **Recordset** over **QueryDef** objects that define select queries. Figure 26.8 illustrates how you create a new **QueryDef** object and open a **Recordset** object
based on the **QueryDef**. You need to add **Dim** qdfOrderData **As QueryDef** and
Dim rsqOrderData **As Recordset** to the Declarations section of your code before you can execute the code in the Immediate Window.

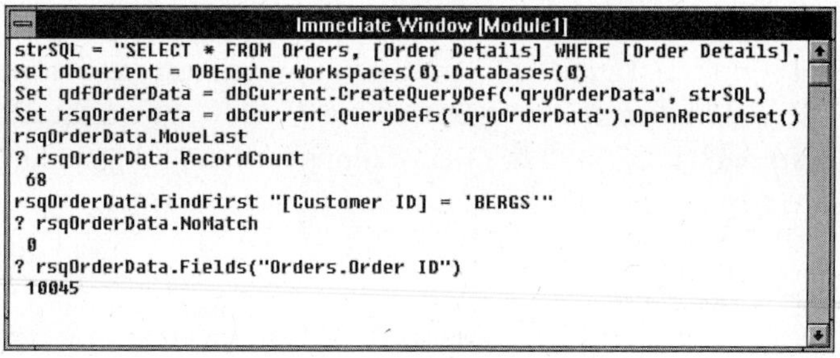

Fig. 28.8
Creating a new
QueryDef object
and opening a
Recordset over the
QueryDef.

```
Immediate Window [Module1]
strSQL = "SELECT * FROM Orders, [Order Details] WHERE [Order Details].
Set dbCurrent = DBEngine.Workspaces(0).Databases(0)
Set qdfOrderData = dbCurrent.CreateQueryDef("qryOrderData", strSQL)
Set rsqOrderData = dbCurrent.QueryDefs("qryOrderData").OpenRecordset()
rsqOrderData.MoveLast
? rsqOrderData.RecordCount
 68
rsqOrderData.FindFirst "[Customer ID] = 'BERGS'"
? rsqOrderData.NoMatch
 0
? rsqOrderData.Fields("Orders.Order ID")
 10045
```

Writing a Function That Uses Database Objects

All database objects that you can create and manipulate with Access's graphical development environment also can be created and manipulated with
Access Basic code. You can use Access Basic to create a new table, add records
to the table, define a query to select records from the table, create a form to
display the data, and then print a report. In other words, you can use Access
Basic to create an application exactly the same way you use the dBASE language or PAL. The purpose of Access's graphical development environment,
however, is to minimize the need for code in applications.

The nilTestQuery() function you write in the following example uses the
QueryDef and **Database** object data types to create a query with an SQL statement and then display that query in Datasheet View.

The `nilTestQuery()` function contains a number of Access Basic reserved words that have been explained in the preceding sections of this chapter, but an example of one reserved word (**DoCmd**) has not yet been provided. Describing every Access Basic reserved word requires a book in itself, as you can see by the length of the *Access Basic Language Reference*, if you have the Access Developer's Toolkit. As you enter the keywords in this example, place the caret inside the keyword and press the F1 key to obtain a detailed explanation of the keyword and its use from Access Basic's Help system.

To create the `nilTestQuery()` function, follow these steps:

1. Close any module you have open; then make the Database window active, click the Module tab, and click the New button to create a new module.

2. You can accept the default **Option** Compare Database statement that Access adds to the Declarations section of a new module, or change the compare modifier to Text to make comparisons not case-sensitive. Add the **Option** Explicit statement to force explicit declaration of variables.

3. To create the new procedure, type **Function nilTestQuery()** below the **Option** Explicit statement. Access Basic procedures called by macros must be written as functions, although these procedures do not return usable values to the macro action; thus the `nil` prefix.

4. You need to declare and assign data types to the variables that the procedure uses. Below **Function** nilTestQuery(), enter the following statements to create object variables with local (procedure-level) scope:

```
Dim dbNWind As Database
Dim qdfTestQuery As QueryDef
```

5. You need to specify the database, NWIND.MDB, that contains the table for the query. Type the following statement:

```
Set dbNWind = DBEngine.Workspaces(0).Databases(0)
```

6. You cannot have two **QueryDef** objects of the same name, so you need to delete the **QueryDef** created by multiple executions of the procedure with the **DeleteQueryDef** method. Enter the following statements:

```
On Error Resume Next
dbNWind.DeleteQueryDef ("qryTestQuery")
On Error GoTo 0
```

An error is generated if the **QueryDef** you attempt to delete doesn't exist. qryTestQuery doesn't exist the first time you run the function, so an error occurs. The **On Error Resume Next** statement causes Access to disregard errors that occur in code below the statement. **On Error GoTo 0** resumes run-time error checking.

7. You need a variable to hold (point to) the definition of the query. Enter the following:

   ```
   Set qdfTestQuery = dbNWind.CreateQueryDef("qryTestQuery")
   ```

8. Now you enter the SQL statement that you use to create and run the query. You can add the SQL statement as the optional second argument of the **CreateQueryDef** method, instead of by setting the value of its SQL property. Enter the following:

   ```
   qdfTestQuery.SQL = "SELECT * FROM Suppliers WHERE [Supplier
   ID] < 11;"
   ```

   In this case, you use the square brackets to enclose Supplier ID because you are specifying a field name, not assigning an object name. Database object names with spaces or other punctuation must be enclosed between square brackets in Access Basic SQL statements.

9. Finally, you need to execute the query and display the **Recordset** object created over the **QueryDef** in a datasheet. The macro action, OpenQuery, creates a **Recordset** and displays the rows of the **Recordset** in Datasheet View. You use the **DoCmd** reserved word to execute macro actions in Access Basic. Enter the following statement:

   ```
   DoCmd OpenQuery "qryTestQuery"
   ```

10. Your Module window appears as shown in figure 28.9, but without the explanatory comments.

Fig. 28.9

Code for the *nilTestQuery()* function.

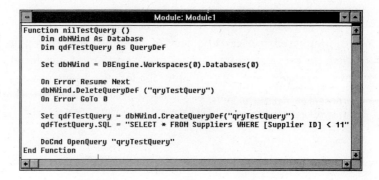

```
Function nilTestQuery ()
    Dim dbNWind As Database
    Dim qdfTestQuery As QueryDef

    Set dbNWind = DBEngine.Workspaces(0).Databases(0)

    On Error Resume Next
    dbNWind.DeleteQueryDef ("qryTestQuery")
    On Error GoTo 0

    Set qdfTestQuery = dbNWind.CreateQueryDef("qryTestQuery")
    qdfTestQuery.SQL = "SELECT * FROM Suppliers WHERE [Supplier ID] < 11"

    DoCmd OpenQuery "qryTestQuery"
End Function
```

11. Click the Compile Loaded Modules button of the toolbar or choose Compile Lo**a**ded Modules from the **R**un menu to verify the syntax of the statements you entered.

12. Click the Save button of the toolbar or choose **S**ave from the **F**ile menu, and give the new module a name, such as **Test Query Module**.

13. Open the Immediate Window and delete any existing entries. Type **? nilTestQuery()** and press Enter. Your query result set appears in the datasheet (see fig. 28.10).

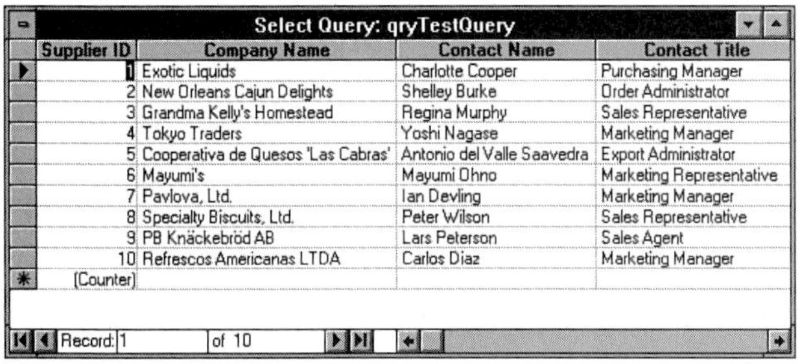

Supplier ID	Company Name	Contact Name	Contact Title
1	Exotic Liquids	Charlotte Cooper	Purchasing Manager
2	New Orleans Cajun Delights	Shelley Burke	Order Administrator
3	Grandma Kelly's Homestead	Regina Murphy	Sales Representative
4	Tokyo Traders	Yoshi Nagase	Marketing Manager
5	Cooperativa de Quesos 'Las Cabras'	Antonio del Valle Saavedra	Export Administrator
6	Mayumi's	Mayumi Ohno	Marketing Representative
7	Pavlova, Ltd.	Ian Devling	Marketing Manager
8	Specialty Biscuits, Ltd.	Peter Wilson	Sales Representative
9	PB Knäckebröd AB	Lars Peterson	Sales Agent
10	Refrescos Americanas LTDA	Carlos Diaz	Marketing Manager

Select Query: qryTestQuery — Record: 1 of 10

Fig. 28.10
The Datasheet View of the query result set created by the *nilTestQuery()* function.

From Here...

This chapter introduced you to the data access objects of Access 2.0. Exploring all of the properties and methods of every type of DAO and giving examples of their use requires a book in itself. Thus the examples of this chapter were limited to creating and manipulating the most commonly used DAOs, **Recordset** and **QueryDef** objects.

For information related to the topics discussed in this chapter, refer to the following chapters:

- Chapter 17, "Understanding Access Macros," provides a complete list of all of the macro actions you can execute with Access Basic's **DoCmd** reserved word.

- Chapter 27, "Writing Access Basic Code," explains the structure and syntax of Access Basic.

- The next chapter, "Exchanging Data with OLE Automation and DDE," describes how you manipulate with Access Basic code the objects you create from other applications' repertoires of objects.

Chapter 29

Exchanging Data with OLE Automation and DDE

One of the major challenges that faced Microsoft Corporation during the early development of Windows was to establish a standard method of *interprocess communication*. Interprocess communication (IPC) means the ability to transfer data, including graphic images, and to operate commands between two different applications running on the same computer. Microsoft elected to use the Windows Clipboard as the intermediary in the process and named the IPC methodology *dynamic data exchange* (DDE). Almost all commercial Windows productivity applications, such as word processors, spreadsheets, and project managers, implement DDE to transfer data. Windows for Workgroups and Windows NT let you implement DDE conversations over a network using NetDDE. DDE's principal problems are the independence of the source of the data and its destination, and the need for rather complex application programming to implement the DDE process.

The next major step in IPC technology was OLE 1.0, originally implemented by Excel 3.0, Word for Windows 2.0, and PowerPoint 2.0. Windows 3.1 included the DLLs necessary to implement OLE 1.0, OLECLI.DLL, and OLESVR.DLL. Providing OLE 1.0 client and server capability became *de rigeur* for all mainstream Windows applications. The primary advantage of OLE 1.0 is that you can create compound documents in which a document (source data) created by one application, the OLE server, is embedded within a destination document created by another application, the OLE client. Thus, there is a much closer relationship between the source and destination documents when you use OLE. Creating compound documents is one of the primary

In this chapter, you learn to

- Send data to an Excel 5.0 worksheet and Word 6.0 document using OLE Automation

- Add OLE Custom Controls to an Access application

- Manipulate OLE Custom Controls

- Use Access Basic DDE to retrieve data from an Excel worksheet

- Employ Access as a DDE server

subjects of Chapter 19, "Using OLE 2.0." OLE 1.0 overcame the need for most of the application programming requirements of DDE. On the other hand, OLE 1.0 did not provide programmers the ability to easily manipulate individual pieces of data, such as a specific cell value in a worksheet. Thus, OLE 1.0 was unable to replace DDE in many applications that required IPC. OLE also lacks DDE's ability to operate over a network; both the OLE client and OLE server application must reside on the same computer.

Access 2.0

Microsoft's solution to the IPC limitations of OLE 1.0 is OLE Automation (OA), an optional component of the OLE 2.0+ specification. (OLE 2.01 was the current version of the OLE 2.0 specification when this book was written.) Applications that implement OA expose their objects so that these objects can be manipulated by code contained in other applications. Microsoft calls the objects exposed by an OA server *programmable objects*. Programmable objects let you assemble customized applications using the "cinder block" approach; programmable objects are the blocks and code acts as the mortar. OLE 2.0 and OA still require that both the client and server application reside on a single computer. When this edition was written, however, Microsoft Corporation and Digital Equipment Corporation announced a joint development program to add network transportability and cross-platform compatibility to programmable objects using Digital's ObjectBroker technology.

Microsoft's Bill Gates has stated that future versions of Windows and Windows NT will include OLE 2.0 as part of the operating system and also will make extensive use of programmable objects. Building applications with reusable, programmable objects will minimize the development time for (and thus the cost of) creating custom Windows applications. Common programmable objects, such as drawing, graphing, and spell-checking objects, ultimately will reduce the fixed disk space required by the mega-apps that can share these objects. Another advantage to shared programmable objects is that upgrades to multiple applications can be implemented by releasing a single improved version of the shared object.

This chapter has two objectives: to show you how to best take advantage of OA in your Access 2.0 applications and to use DDE for IPC with applications that are not OA-compliant. The first part of this chapter covers OA and Access 2.0's new OLE Custom Controls. Examples that demonstrate Access's capabilities as a DDE client and server, which have not changed significantly in version 2.0, complete the chapter.

Understanding OLE Automation

Access 2.0 is an OLE 2.0 client application with OA client capability. Thus, to implement OA, you need OLE 2.0 servers. When this edition was written, there were few OA servers available. OLE Automation servers are of three basic types:

- *Full servers,* such as Microsoft Excel 5.0 and Project 4.0, and Shapeware Visio 2.0, that are stand-alone productivity applications with OLE Automation capability added. Excel 5.0 and Project 4.0 expose their object to their own application programming (macro) language, Visual Basic for Applications (VBA). Microsoft Word 6.0 exposes its menu commands, rather than objects, and uses WordBasic, not VBA, as its macro language. The next version of Word is expected to become a full server and substitute VBA for WordBasic.

- *Mini-servers,* such as Microsoft Graph 5.0 (MSGraph5) and Shapeware Visio Express, that only can be executed from within an OLE Automation client application. Mini-servers are similar to the OLE 1.0 applets supplied with Word for Windows 2.0 and other Microsoft OLE 1.0 applications, such as Microsoft Draw. (Visio Express is a mini-server version of Visio 2.0.) Mini-servers that display a particular class of objects, such as video clips, are called *viewers.* Using the Graph Wizard to create MSGraph5 charts is one of the subjects of Chapter 20, "Adding Graphics to Forms and Reports." You also can create custom graphs and charts by programming MSGraph5 with Access Basic code.

- *OLE Custom Controls* (OCXs) that are a special type of mini-server. OLE Custom Controls, which use the .OCX file extension, expose events in addition to properties and methods. OLE Custom Controls are the object-oriented equivalent of Visual Basic's .VBX custom controls. As mentioned in Chapter 1, "Access 2.0 for Access 1.1 Users—What's New?" and Chapter 19, "Using OLE 2.0," Access 2.0 is the first Microsoft application that is compatible with OCXs. You need the Access Developer's Toolkit (ADT) to add OCXs to your Access applications; the ADT includes sample custom controls and the other files that provide the "glue" between Access's unbound object frames and OCXs.

One of the advantages of OA is that you can manipulate programmable objects without creating a visible instance of the OA server. Unlike DDE, which requires that the server application be launched in a window or as an icon, OA launches the application for you. Unless you instruct the server to activate its window, the server is invisible; the server's name does not appear in the Windows Task List.

> **Note**
>
> Although the OA server's window is not visible, OA full servers can consume a substantial percentage of the available resources of your computer. This is particularly true of mega-apps, such as Excel 5.0 and Word 6.0, when used as OA servers. You can speed the opening of Excel 5.0 as an OA server and minimize the resources Excel consumes by not loading unneeded add-ins. If you plan to make extensive use of OA in your applications, you should have a minimum of 12M of RAM (preferably 16M) and make sure that the amount of RAM plus the size of your permanent swap file total at least 20M (preferably 25M).

The sections that follow show you how to write Access Basic code to program objects created by each of these three types of OA servers.

Using OLE Automation Servers

To use OLE Automation, you must first write the code to create an instance in your application of the object you plan to program. Access 2.0 Basic contains the following three, new, reserved words that you use to create an instance of a programmable object with Access Basic code:

- The **Object** data type for the programmable object variables you declare with **Dim** *objName* **As Object** statements. The Object property of a programmable OA object contained in a bound or unbound object frame control points to the instance of the object. You can assign the OA object to a variable with the general syntax:

  Set *objName* = Forms!frmName!uofName.Object

- The **CreateObject**() function that assigns a pointer to a new instance of an empty programmable object, such as a blank Excel 5.0 worksheet. The general syntax of the CreateObject() function is:

  Set *objName* = **CreateObject**("*ServerName.ObjectType*")

- The **GetObject**() function that assigns a pointer to a new instance of a programmable object whose data is contained in an existing file, str*FilePathName*, in the following syntax example:

  Set *objName* = **GetObject**(strFilePathName[, "*ServerName.ObjectType*"])

■ You can omit the *ServerName.ObjectType* argument if an entry in your REG.DAT file associates the file's extension with the object of the application you want to program. In the case of Excel 5.0, the default object type for .XLS files is Excel.Workbook. If you substitute an empty string ("") for strFilePathName, the preceding statement assigns a pointer to an object of *ServerName.ObjectType* if such an object is open. If an object of the specified type is not open when the statement is executed, a trappable error occurs.

Note

Names of programmable objects created by OA server applications appear in regular (not bold) monospace type because the names of these objects are not Access Basic object data types.

Leszinsky-Reddick naming conventions for variable prefixes (tags) of programmable objects were not established when this edition was written. This book uses the common lowercase file extensions as the prefix to identify objects created by full servers. Examples are xla*App* for the Excel application, xlw*Book* for Excel 5.0 workbooks, xls*Sheet* for worksheets, xlc*Chart* for Excel charts, and xlm*Module* for Excel VBA modules (although Excel 5.0 does not create .XLA, .XLW, .XLC, or .XLM files in Excel 5.0 format). Word 6.0 Document objects are identified by *docName*, and pseudo-objects of the Word.Basic menu command type are identified by doc*Command*. Visio 2.0 drawings are identified by vsd*Name*.

These three reserved words also are used by VBA to program objects of other applications. To write OA code, you need to know the server name of the OA server and the names of the object types created by the server. Excel 5.0 includes a 300+ page manual, *Visual Basic User's Guide*, with descriptions of many of Excel 5.0's objects and the VBA syntax to manipulate them. Excel 5.0 also has an object browser, described in the following section, that lists Excel's exposed objects and collections. Word 6.0 users are not so lucky; you need to purchase the WordBasic manual (see the note that follows). The two sections that follow show you how to create and manipulate Excel 5.0 Workbook and Worksheet objects, and the Cells collection, as well as a Word 6.0 Document object.

> **Note**
>
> A printed version of the Excel 5.0 on-line help file for VBA, *Microsoft Excel Visual Basic for Applications Reference* (ISBN 1-55615-624-3), and a guide to WordBasic, *Microsoft Word Developer's Kit* (ISBN 1-55615-630-8), are available from Microsoft Corporation. The *Function Reference* is no longer included with the retail or Microsoft Office versions of Excel; you now must purchase the *Microsoft Excel Worksheet Function Reference* (ISBN 1-55615-637-5) from Microsoft.

Manipulating an Excel 5.0 Workbook Object

Learning to write OLE Automation code is a much quicker process if you use the Immediate Window to try OA instructions before you begin writing OA code. The hierarchy of Excel 5.0 programmable objects is at least as complex as that of Access 2.0. Fortunately, the concepts of addressing objects in all OA-compatible applications is nearly identical. Thus, the techniques you learned in Chapter 28, "Understanding the Data Access Object Class," stand you in good stead when you encounter Excel 5.0's `Excel.Application` object. The following sections describe how to create a test workbook, CUSTOMER.XLS, with a single worksheet, CUSTOMER, and transfer data to and from the worksheet using Access Basic and OLE Automation.

Creating CUSTOMER.XLS

The examples that follow use the CUSTOMER.XLS workbook file with data from the Customers table of NWIND.MDB. The example of OLE Automation with Excel 5.0 in this chapter uses the `GetObject()` function to open the CUSTOMER.XLS file and manipulate the data in the worksheet. To create CUSTOMER.XLS, follow these steps:

1. Select the Customers table in the Database window, and click the Analyze It with MS Excel button of the toolbar to export the data in the table to Excel 5.0 in Excel 3.0 format (see fig. 29.1).

2. When the content of the Customers table appears in a new Excel worksheet, select cells A2 through D9. Choose **N**ame from Excel's **I**nsert menu, and then choose **D**efine from the submenu. Type **TestRange** in the Names in Workbook text box, and click OK. This creates a named range that you use in the examples that follow.

3. Choose Save **A**s from Excel's **F**ile menu, and select Microsoft Excel Workbook in the Save File As Type drop-down list to save the file in Excel 5.0 format.

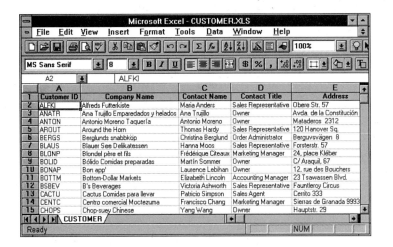

Fig. 29.1
The data of the
Customers table
exported to a
Microsoft Excel 5.0
workbook.

4. Accept the default directory, C:\ACCESS, and the default name for the
   file, CUSTOMER.XLS, unless you have a reason to do otherwise. Click
   OK to save the file and close the dialog.

5. Choose Add-**I**ns from Excel's **F**ile menu and clear all of the check boxes
   in the Add-In dialog's Add-Ins Available list. Eliminating add-ins decreases the time required to launch Excel. Click OK to close the Add-Ins
   dialog.

6. Close Microsoft Excel.

The Hierarchy of Basic Excel 5.0 Objects

The following list describes the hierarchy of the most commonly used programmable objects exposed by Excel 5.0:

- Application represents an instance of Excel 5.0. Using the Application
  object, you can execute almost all of Excel's menu commands by applying methods to the Application object. The Application object has
  properties such as ActiveWorkbook and ActiveSheet that specify the current Workbook and Worksheet objects. You can specify Excel.Application
  as the value of the *ServerName.ObjectType* argument of the
  CreateObject() and **GetObject**() functions.

- Workbook is the primary object of Excel 5.0. Workbook objects are files
  that contain the other objects you create with Excel 5.0: Worksheet and
  Chart objects. Worksheet and Chart objects are contained in Worksheets
  and Charts collections, respectively. The Excel implementation of VBA
  does not distinguish between collections and objects; for example, the
  VBA help file calls the Worksheets collection an object.

- Worksheet objects are elements of the Workbook object that contain data. The primary interaction between Access 2.0 and Excel 5.0 takes place with Worksheet objects. You can transfer data contained in rows and columns of an Access **Recordset** object to cells in an Excel Worksheet object, and vice versa. If you specify Excel.Sheet as the value of the *ServerName.ObjectName* argument of the **GetObject**() function, the first member of the Worksheets collection, the ActiveSheet property of the Workbook object, is opened by default.

- Range objects are groups of cells specified by sets of cell coordinates. You can get or set the values of a single cell or a group of cells by specifying the Range object. If the cells are contained in a named range, you can use the range name to refer to the group of cells. (A group of cells is not the same as a collection of cells; there is no "Cells" collection in Excel 5.0.)

  The Cells method specifies the coordinates of a Range object. There is no "Cell" object in Excel 5.0, but you can use the Cells method to read or set the value of a single cell or group of cells, specified by coordinate sets.

Excel 5.0 exposes a variety of other objects. The preceding four objects, however, are those that you use most often in conjunction with OA operations executed with Access Basic code.

Using Excel's On-Line Help File for VBA

If you don't have a copy of the *Microsoft Excel Visual Basic for Applications Reference*, you can open the VBA_XL.HLP on-line help file to act as a reference for the objects, methods, and properties exposed by Excel 5.0. To open VBA_XL.HLP while running Access and display objects and methods references, follow these steps:

1. Choose **C**ontents from Access's **H**elp menu to open the help window.

2. Choose **O**pen from the help window's **F**ile menu to display the Open dialog.

3. Select your Excel 5.0 directory and double-click VBA_XL.HLP in the File Name list to open the on-line help file for Excel's implementation of VBA.

4. Click the Objects hot spot to display an alphabetic list of objects exposed by Excel 5.0. Objects exposed to VBA also are exposed to OA client applications.

5. Click the W button to display the part of the list that includes the
Workbook object (see fig. 29.2).

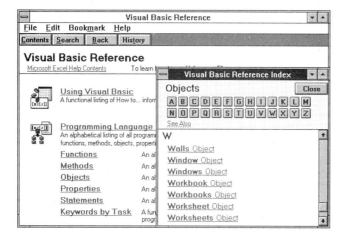

Fig. 29.2

The opening
window of the
VBA_XL.HLP file
with the W entries
of the objects
Reference Index
activated.

6. Click the "Worksheet" hot spot to display the help window for the
Worksheet object, and then click the Methods hot spot to display the list
of methods applicable to the Worksheet object. You can obtain a list of
properties of the object by clicking the Properties hot spot.

7. Click the "Cells" hot spot to display the help window for the Cells
method (see fig. 29.3).

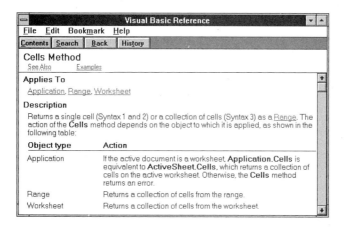

Fig. 29.3

The syntax reference for
the *Cells* method.

8. Click the Examples hot spot to display an example of VBA code applicable to the `Cells` method (see fig. 29.4). Some VBA constructs, such as `With…End With`, and named arguments (argument values specified with the `:=` operator) are not available in Access Basic. Most of the VBA code examples, however, are compatible with Access Basic.

Fig. 29.4
Visual Basic for Applications example code for the *Cells* method.

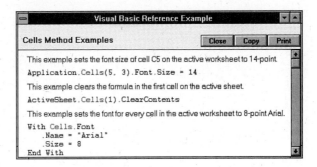

Opening and Manipulating an Existing Excel Worksheet Object

You can specify any object listed in your registration database (REG.DAT) file that is identified by a *ServerName.ObjectType*[*.Version*] entry at the root level of REG.DAT. Figure 29.5 shows most of the REG.DAT entries for Excel 5.0 displayed by the registration database editor (RegEdit) in verbose mode (opened with the REGEDIT.EXE /v command line). The option *Version* suffix indicates the version number of *ServerName*; if you have two versions of the same OA server, you can use *Version* to specify one of the two.

Fig. 29.5
Primary registration database entries for Excel 5.0 *Application*, *Worksheet*, and *Chart* objects.

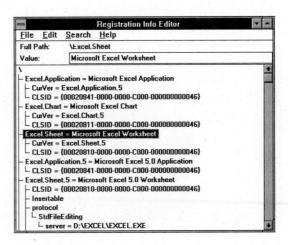

In addition to the primary entries for Excel 5.0 objects you can open, additional data for creating or opening programmable objects appear in the

`CLSID = OLE (Part 1 of 5)` section of REG.DAT, near the end of the REG.DAT file. A part of the additional REG.DAT entries for the `Excel.Application` and `Excel.Worksheet` objects appears in Figure 29.6. The `/automation` command line parameter for the `LocalServer` entry for the `Excel.Application.5` object specifies that Excel executes without opening a window. The `/automation` parameter is implied for the `Excel.Worksheet.5` object.

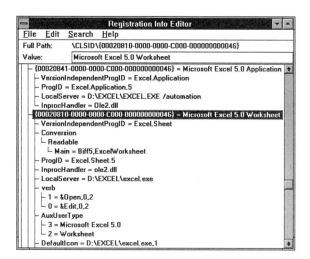

Fig. 29.6
Additional registration database entries for Excel 5.0 *Application* and *Worksheet* objects.

> **Note**
>
> In all examples of this chapter that use the Immediate Window, pressing the Enter key after typing **? *Expression*** is implied.

To open the `Worksheet` object of the CUSTOMER.XLS `Workbook` object, follow these steps:

1. Close Excel if it is running. Open a new module in the Northwind Traders database and add the following **Object** variable declarations in the Declarations section:

   ```
   Dim xlaAppXL5 As Object 'Application object
   Dim xlwCust As Object   'Workbook object
   Dim xlsCust As Object   'Sheet object
   ```

2. Open the Immediate Window and type the following statement to create an Object of the `Excel.Sheet` (`Worksheet`) type. When you press Enter, Excel 5.0 is launched in `/automation` mode.

   ```
   Set xlsCust = GetObject("customer.xls", "Excel.Sheet")
   ```

Depending on the speed of your computer, opening Excel 5.0 may take an appreciable period. (When the hourglass mouse pointer returns to a caret in the Immediate Window, Excel has finished loading.) CUSTOMER.XLS only includes one Worksheet object, so the CUSTOMER worksheet is the ActiveSheet object.

3. Verify that you have a valid Worksheet object by typing **?** **xlsCust.Cells(1, 1)**. After a brief interval, the expected result, Customer ID, appears.

4. You can test the ability of the Cells method to return the values of other cells by typing **? xlsCust.Cells(R, C)**, where *R* is the row and *C* is the column of the cell coordinates (see fig. 29.7).

Fig. 29.7

Command to read and set the values of a single cell in the CUSTOMERS worksheet.

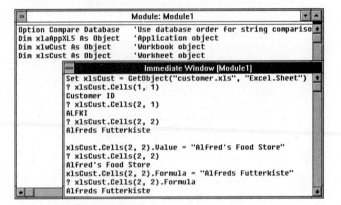

5. You can alter the content of a cell by entering an expression such as **xlsCust.Cells(2, 2).Value = "Alfred's Food Shop"**. Like many Access control objects, in which the name of an object returns its value, the Cells method does not require that you explicitly specify the Value property. Verify that the content changed by typing **? xlsCust.Cells (2, 2)**, with and without appending **.Value** (see fig. 29.7).

You also can use the Formula property to set the value of a cell. The advantage of the Formula property is that you also can use this property to enter a formula using Excel A1 syntax, such as `"=A10+B15"`.

Using Named Ranges of Cells

If you created the named range, TestRange, in CUSTOMER.XLS, you can return the values of the cells in the range by referring to the Range object of the Worksheet object. Figure 29.8 shows typical expressions that operate on the `Range` object of a `Worksheet` object and the `Ranges` collection of a `Workbook` object.

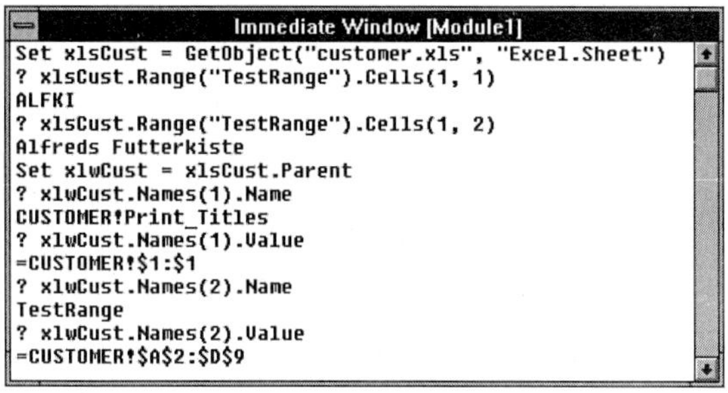

```
Immediate Window [Module1]
Set xlsCust = GetObject("customer.xls", "Excel.Sheet")
? xlsCust.Range("TestRange").Cells(1, 1)
ALFKI
? xlsCust.Range("TestRange").Cells(1, 2)
Alfreds Futterkiste
Set xlwCust = xlsCust.Parent
? xlwCust.Names(1).Name
CUSTOMER!Print_Titles
? xlwCust.Names(1).Value
=CUSTOMER!$1:$1
? xlwCust.Names(2).Name
TestRange
? xlwCust.Names(2).Value
=CUSTOMER!$A$2:$D$9
```

Fig. 29.8

Expressions that return the values in *Range* objects and the *Ranges* collection.

To specify a cell within a named `Range` object, use the following general syntax:

```
wksWorksheet.Range(strRangeName).Cells(intRow, intCol)
```

Because named ranges are global for all worksheets in an Excel workbook, the `Names` collection is a member of the `Workbook` object. Thus, you need to refer to the `Workbook` object that contains the `Worksheet`. The *Worksheet*.`Parent` property returns the `Workbook` object that contains the `Worksheet`, as in the following example:

```
Set xlwWorkbook = xlsWorksheet.Parent
```

You then can refer to the `Ranges` collection of the `Workbook` object with statements such as

```
strRangeName = xlwWorkbook.Names(intIndex).Name
strRangeValue = xlwWorkbook.Names(intIndex).Value
```

Unlike Access Basic collections, which begin with an index value of 0, the first member of a VBA collection has an index value of 1. When you use Access 2.0's OutputTo feature to export the data in a table to an Excel worksheet, the field names are placed in a named range called Print_Titles (`Names(1)`). The TestRange range you added earlier in the chapter (`Names(2)`) does not have the CUSTOMER! worksheet identifier prefix (unless you added it when you created the named range).

Closing a Workbook and the *Application* Object

Just as a `Workbook` object is the value of the `Parent` property of a `Worksheet`, the `Application` object is the `Parent` property of a `Workbook`. The value of

Excel 5.0's `Application` object is `Microsoft Excel`. Figure 29.9 illustrates expressions that work their way upward in Excel's object hierarchy, from `Worksheet` to `Application` objects. You can shortcut the process by using `xlsCust.Parent.Parent` to point to the `Application` object from a `Worksheet` object.

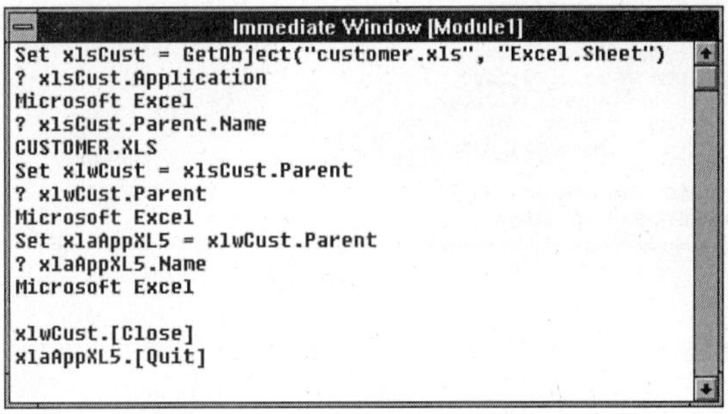

Fig. 29.9

Assigning objects higher in the hierarchy, and closing *Workbook* and *Application* objects.

```
Immediate Window [Module1]
Set xlsCust = GetObject("customer.xls", "Excel.Sheet")
? xlsCust.Application
Microsoft Excel
? xlsCust.Parent.Name
CUSTOMER.XLS
Set xlwCust = xlsCust.Parent
? xlwCust.Parent
Microsoft Excel
Set xlaAppXL5 = xlwCust.Parent
? xlaAppXL5.Name
Microsoft Excel

xlwCust.[Close]
xlaAppXL5.[Quit]
```

You use the `Close` method to close an Excel `Workbook` object (you can't close a `Worksheet` object) and the `Quit` method to exit the application. It is a good practice to explicitly exit the OA server application to conserve scarce system resources. If you attempt to apply the `Close` or `Quit` methods in Access Basic code (or in the Immediate Window), you receive an error message, "Method not applicable to this object." This error occurs because `Close` and `Quit` also are Access Basic keywords. To prevent the Access Basic interpreter from intercepting the keyword, you enclose it with square brackets. For example, the following statements close the `Workbook` object and then exit the application:

```
Set xlaAppXL5 = xlsCust.Parent.Parent
xlsCust.Parent.[Close](False)
xlaAppXL5.[Quit]
```

The **False** argument of the `Close` method closes the `Workbook` without displaying the message box that asks if you want to save changes to the `Workbook`. When using the `Quit` method to exit the application, you receive the preceding message, regardless of whether you modified the worksheet. To avoid this message when reading Excel 5.0 worksheets, close the worksheet before applying the `Quit` method. You must create an `Application` object because you cannot execute the `xlsCust.Parent.Parent.[Quit]` statement after closing the `xlsCust` object. (You receive an "Object has no value" error message if you try.)

Creating a New Excel Worksheet with Access Basic Code

You can emulate the OutputTo feature of Access 2.0 with Access Basic OLE Automation code. The following function, CreateCust(), creates a new Workbook object, CUST.XLS, and copies the data from the Customers table to a Worksheet named CUSTOMERS. One of the primary incentives for writing your own version of the OutputTo feature is the ability to format the Worksheet object the way you want. You also can add custom column headers. (The code to add column headers is not included in the CreateCust() function.)

```
Function CreateCust() As Integer
    'Purpose: Create new Excel 5.0 worksheet from Customers table

    'Declare local variables (Object variables are module-level)
    Dim dbNWind As Database     'Current database
    Dim rstCust As Recordset    'Table Recordset over Customers
    Dim intRow As Integer       'Row counter
    Dim intCol As Integer       'Column counter

    'Assign DAO pointers
    Set dbNWind = DBEngine.Workspaces(0).Databases(0)
    Set rstCust = dbNWind.OpenRecordset("Customers")

    DoCmd Hourglass True

    'Create a new Excel Worksheet object
    Set xlsCust = CreateObject("Excel.Sheet")
    DoEvents

    'Give the new worksheet a name
    xlsCust.Name = "CUSTOMERS"

    'Get the Application object for the Quit method
    Set xlaAppXL5 = xlsCust.Parent.Parent

    intRow = 1
    intCol = 1

    rstCust.MoveFirst              'Go to the first record (safety)
    Do Until rstCust.EOF
        'Loop through each record
        For intCol = 1 To rstCust.Fields.Count
            'Loop through each field
            xlsCust.Cells(intRow, intCol).Value = _
rstCust.Fields(intCol - 1)
        Next intCol
```

```
                      rstCust.MoveNext
                      intRow = intRow + 1
                      'DoEvents        'For safety, delete after testing for speed
                  Loop

                  For intCol = 1 To xlsCust.Columns.Count
                      'Format each column of the worksheet
                      xlsCust.Columns(intCol).Font.Size = 8
                      xlsCust.Columns(intCol).AutoFit
                      If intCol = 8 Then
                          'Align numeric and alphanumeric postal codes left
                          xlsCust.Columns(intCol).HorizontalAlignment = -4131
                      End If
                  Next intCol

                  DoCmd Hourglass False

                  xlsCust.SaveAs ("CUST.XLS")
                  xlaAppXL5.[Quit]
              End Function
```

The value, -4131, assigned to the value of the HorizontalAlignment property of the eighth column (H) is the value of the xlLeft intrinsic global constant. This constant is intrinsic and global for VBA code in Excel 5.0 modules, but it is undefined in Access. To determine the numerical values of the xlConst constants, you must open a module in Excel, open the Debug window, and then type **? xlConst** to obtain the numerical value of the constant. Figure 29.10 shows the values of xlLeft and xlRight, two of the constant values that are valid for the HorizontalAlignment property.

Fig. 29.10

Obtaining values of xlConst intrinsic constants in Excel's Debug window.

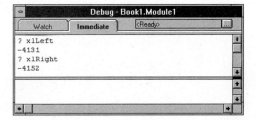

Run the function shown in the preceding listing by entering **? CreateCust()** in the Immediate Window. Figure 29.11 shows the CUST.XLS workbook with the CUSTOMER worksheet created by the CreateCust() function opened in Excel 5.0.

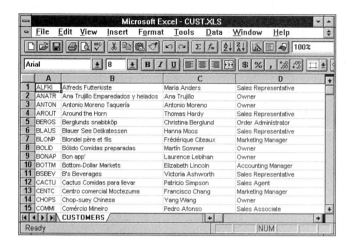

Fig. 29.11
Part of the Excel
5.0 worksheet
created from the
Customers table.

VII

Programming Access

Sending Data to Microsoft Word 6.0 with OLE Automation

Chapter 22, "Using Access with Microsoft Word and Mail Merge," demonstrates that Access 2.0's Mail Merge Wizard does a very competent job of creating merge data files for use with Microsoft Word 6.0. The Mail Merge Wizard uses DDE, rather than OLE Automation, to communicate with Word. Although Word 6.0 is not a full-fledged OA server application, Word exposes one programmable object with two names: Word.Basic alias WordBasic. You use the Word.Basic object type with the **CreateObject**() function; the Word.Basic object type corresponds to Excel's Excel.Application object. You use the WordBasic object when you want to manipulate the Object of a bound or unbound object frame. The WordBasic object is a member of the Application class. An object of either the Word.Basic or WordBasic type lets you use WordBasic document manipulation commands as methods of the object.

To create an independently programmable Word document object (a Word document that is not contained in an object frame of your application), you use the following generic code:

```
Dim docName As Object
Set docName = CreateObject("Word.Basic")

docName.FileOpen "d:\path\filename.doc"        'Open a file
'…Code to manipulate document
docName.FileClose(1)                           'Save and close
                                                the file

Set docName = Nothing                          'Close Word
```

Tip
You cannot use the **GetObject**("*docname*.doc") function to open an existing Word 6.0 document from a file.

> **Note**
>
> Even if you do not make changes in the document file, use the `FileClose(1)` statement to save the file. The version of Word 6.0 available when this edition was written sets the "dirty" flag even when the code does not change the content of the document.

The **Set** *objName* = **Nothing** statement closes the instance of the server application and frees the resources the server consumes. This statement is similar to the **Quit** method applied to the `Application` object; a Word object does not support the **Quit** method or the `FileExit` WordBasic command. Figure 29.12 shows an example of using the Immediate Window to test the preceding example code. The document opened by the WordBasic `FileOpen` command of figure 29.12 is the manuscript for this chapter with the section heading identified by the bookmark "WordHead."

Fig. 29.12

Using the Immediate Window to manipulate a Word 6.0 document object.

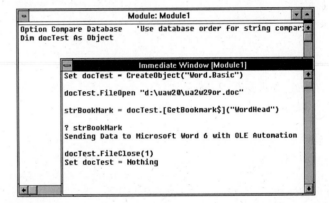

Most persons who alter word processing documents want to view the modifications before final acceptance. Thus, the majority of Access applications that use OA with Word 6.0 are more likely to involve Word documents contained in bound or unbound object frames. Chapter 22 explains how to add an unbound object frame containing an embedded Word document. The following generic code lets you apply WordBasic commands to the document contained in a bound or unbound object frame:

```
Dim uofName As Control
Dim docName As Object
Set uofName = Forms!FormName!ControlName
uofName.Action = 7    'Activate the object
Set docName = uofName.Object.Application.WordBasic
'Code to manipulate object
Set docName = Nothing
```

The uof*Name*.Action = 7 statement is required if the object has not been activated when you execute the preceding code example. An object in a frame must be activated before you can refer to its Object.Application.*ObjectType* property.

Figure 29.13 shows an example of activating an embedded Word 6.0 object and then reading and setting the value of bookmarked text. To execute the code shown in figure 29.13, you must first insert an unbound Word 6.0 object, uofObject, with a bookmark named "WordHead" in a form named frmWordDoc. When you execute the docTest.EditGoTo "WordHead" statement, Word selects the bookmark. The docTest.Insert "New Section Head" statement replaces the existing bookmarked text with "New Section Head". Figure 29.14 shows the result of executing the Insert command.

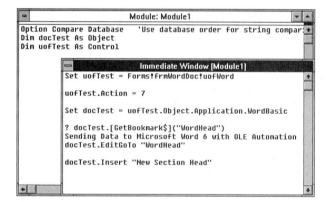

Fig. 29.13
Replacing the text of a bookmark in an embedded OLE object.

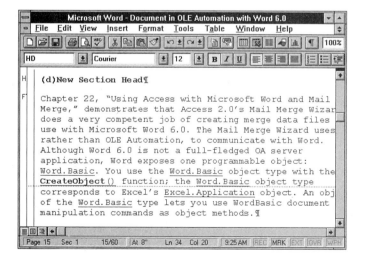

Fig. 29.14
The result of executing the code shown in Figure 29.13.

Using OLE Automation and code similar to that shown in figure 29.13, you can create a document that consists of nothing but empty bookmarks and then fill the bookmarks with text contained in Text or Memo fields of tables or from the Value property of control objects on forms. Using OLE Automation, Access's Mail Merge feature, provides a much more flexible method of creating specialized documents.

Adding OLE Custom Controls to Your Application

OLE Custom Controls (OCXs) are a special class of programmable OA objects that expose their own events, in addition to their properties and methods. You embed the OCX in an unbound object frame and program the Object property of the control, employing the same types of statements used with other embedded programmable objects. OCXs are similar to Visual Basic custom controls (VBXs) in concept and use; the principal difference between OCXs and VBXs is that OCXs are embedded within object frames, while VBXs create independent controls on Visual Basic forms.

Example OLE Custom Controls Included in the ADT

The Access Developer's Toolkit (ADT) includes the following custom controls designed specifically for use with Access:

- *Calendar* (MSACAL20.OCX) provides a programmable calendar object. When the calendar opens, its date is set to the value of **Now**. You can change the date by applying **NextPeriod** and **PreviousPeriod** methods or by setting the Calendar Control's Value property. A list of the properties, methods, and events of the Calendar Control is contained in the MSACAL20.HLP on-line help file.

- *Scrollbar* (MSASB20.OCX) supplies a programmable scroll bar you can use to set values. The Scrollbar Custom Control is modeled on the native scroll bar control of Visual Basic. The Value property represents the position of the slider between two extreme values set by Scrollbar's Min and Max property values. Scrollbar's on-line help file is MSASB20.HLP.

- *Data Outline* (OUTL1016.OCX) provides a means of displaying data contained in tables or queries in an outline structure. The Data Outline Control, also known as the Navigator Control, is derived from the design of the outline custom control (MSOUTLIN.VBX) of the Professional Edition of Visual Basic 3.0. When you double-click an entry in the Control, the form associated with the data item appears. Figure 29.15

shows the Data Outline Control displaying part of the Categories-Products-Suppliers table hierarchy of NWIND.MDB.

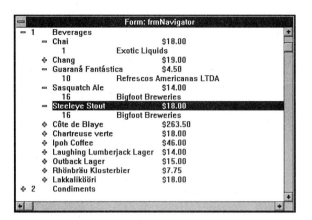

Fig. 29.15
The Navigator Custom Control displaying data from tables in NWIND.MDB.

Each of the .OCX and associated .HLP files for the example Controls are located in your \ACCESS\HLP directory. Linking OCXs to Access requires three additional DLLs—OC1016.DLL, MFCOLEUI.DLL, and STDTYPE.DLL—which are installed in your \WINDOWS\SYSTEM directory.

The Calendar and Scrollbar Controls are *distributable components*; that is, you can include MSACAL20.OCX and MSASB20.OCX with applications you distribute with run-time Access (MSARN200.EXE). Navigator, however, is not a distributable component. Refer to the license agreement in the ADT for the terms under which you can employ Navigator in applications you create for others to use.

Adding the Calendar Custom Control to a Form

You need to register an OCX in your registration database (REG.DAT) file before you can add the Control to a form. Once the OCX is registered, you add OLE Custom Controls in unbound object frames to single (not continuous) forms. To add a Calendar Control to a form, follow these steps:

1. Create a new blank (unbound) form about 5 inches wide and 3 inches deep.

2. Choose Insert Object from the **E**dit menu to display the OLE 2.0 Insert Object dialog (see fig. 29.16).

3. Click the Insert Control option button, and then click the Add Control button to display the Add Control dialog. The Custom Controls supplied with the ADT are located in the \ACCESS\ADT directory (see fig. 29.17).

Fig. 29.16
The appearance of the Insert Object dialog before registering OCXs.

Fig. 29.17
The Add Control dialog for registering OCXs.

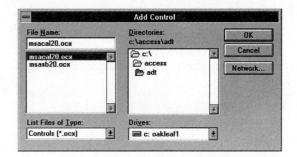

4. Double-click MSACAL20.OCX in the File Name list to add the Calendar Control to your form (see fig. 29.18).

Fig. 29.18
Adding the Calendar Control to a form.

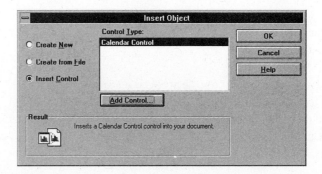

5. Size the Calendar Control to about 2.75 by 2 inches, position the mouse pointer on the Control, and then click the right mouse button to display the floating menu for the unbound object frame.

6. Choose Calendar Control **O**bject from the floating menu with the left mouse button to open the object's submenu (see fig. 29.19). Choose **P**roperties to open the Properties dialog for the Control.

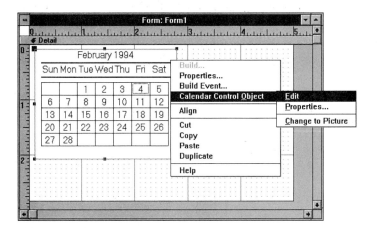

Fig. 29.19
The floating menus for an OLE Custom Control.

7. The first Properties dialog lets you set the current date and the first day of the week. (The defaults are your computer's system date and Sunday.) Open the drop-down list at the top of the dialog, and select Font to open the Font Properties dialog.

> ### Note
>
> Technically speaking, the Properties dialog of an OCX is called a *Property Frame* and the content of the Property Frame is stored in *Property Pages*. Entries for the Property Frame and Property Page(s) are added to the entries for the OCX in your REG.DAT file. To see these entries, you need to add the **/v** parameter to the Command Line entry for REGEDIT.EXE (**c:\windows\regedit.exe /v**) in Program Manager's Program Item Properties dialog for RegEdit.

8. Select Arial from the Font combo list, apply the Bold attribute, and set the font size to 11 points (see fig. 29.20). Click the Check Mark button to apply your selection to the Control.

Fig. 29.20
The Font Properties dialog of the Calendar Control.

9. Select Color from the Properties drop-down list to display the color dialog. With the `BackColor` property selected, click the light gray button to apply a gray background to the Control. You can change the `ForeColor` property from black to another color if you want. You also can use the Windows system colors for the background and foreground colors (see fig. 29.21).

Fig. 29.21
The Color
Properties dialog
of the Calendar
Control.

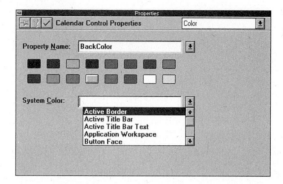

10. Click the Control-menu box to close the Properties dialog. Double-click a blank area of the form to display the Form Properties dialog, and then set the `DefaultView` property value to `Single Form`, and name the control **ocxCalendar**. Your Calendar control appears as shown in figure 29.22.

11. Save your form with a descriptive name, such as **frmCalendarControl**.

Fig. 29.22
The Calendar
Control with the
values of the *Font*
and *BackColor*
properties altered.

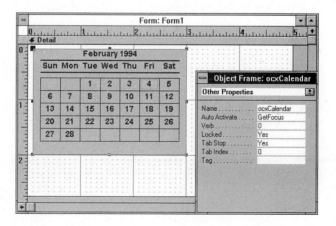

The procedure for adding the Scrollbar (MSASB20.OCX) and Data Outline (OUTL1016.OCX) control supplied with the ADT and third-party custom controls is similar to the preceding process.

Troubleshooting

The Insert Control option button does not appear in the Insert Object dialog.

The Insert Control option button only appears if the MFCOLEUI.DLL, OC1016.DLL, and STDTYPE.TLB files, required for OLE Custom Controls, are properly installed in your \WINDOWS\SYSTEM directory. These files are installed when you run the ADT's Setup program or when you run Setup for a third-party OCX. The dates of the three files usually are the same. If you have installed the ADT or a third-party OCX, check for the presence of each of these files in \WINDOWS\SYSTEM. If the files are missing or have wrong dates, try running Setup again. If the second installation attempt fails, contact the vendor's technical support group.

Programming the Calendar Control

Each OCX has its own collection of properties, methods, and events. Each of the three OCXs supplied with the ADT has an on-line help file to assist you in programming the control. You can open the help file from Access or click the help (?) button of a Control's Properties dialog. Figure 29.23 shows the help topic for the methods applicable to the Calendar Control. As is the case for any object contained in a bound or unbound OLE object frame, you apply methods to the `Object` property of the frame.

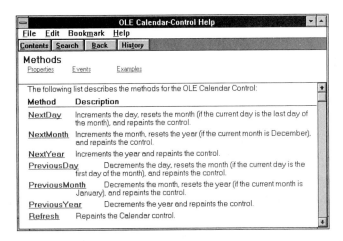

Fig. 29.23
The on-line help topic for the Calendar Control's methods.

To program the Calendar Control and complete the design of the frmCalendarControl form, follow these steps:

1. Add six command buttons, stacked vertically to the right of the calendar. Assign **Next Week**, **Last Week**, **Next Month**, **Last Month**, **Next Year**, and **Last Year** as the value of the Caption property for the six buttons in sequence. Name the buttons **cmdNextWeek**, **cmdLastWeek**, and so forth.

2. Add an unbound text box under the calendar. Assign **lblDate** and **txtDate** as the values of the Name property of the label and text box, respectively (see fig. 29.24).

Fig. 29.24

The final design of the Calendar Control form.

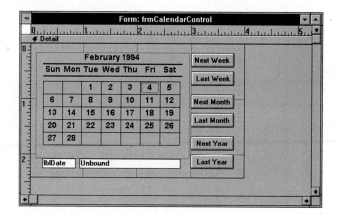

3. Click the Calendar Control with the right mouse button and choose Build Event from the floating menu to open the code editing window for ocxCalendar. Select the GotFocus event from the events drop-down list to create the **Sub** ocxCalendar_GotFocus()...**End Sub** stub.

4. Enter the following code (see fig. 29.25) for the GotFocus event to display the date when the form opens:

```
Sub ocxCalendar_GotFocus ()
'Purpose: Update the text boxes
lblDate.Caption = Format(ocxCalendar.Object.Value,
"mm/dd/yy")
txtDate.Value = Format(ocxCalendar.Object.Value, "dddddd")
End Sub
```

The ocxCalendar control must be the first control in the tab order for the form for the preceding code to execute when you open the form.

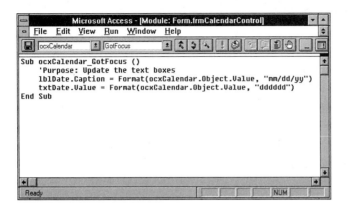

Fig. 29.25
Entering the code
for the *GotFocus*
event.

5. Select and copy the three lines of code to the Clipboard, and then select
the Updated event from the events drop-down list. Paste the code in
the **Sub** `ocxCalendar_Updated()`...**End Sub** stub.

6. MSACAL20.OCX does not have a "NextWeek" or "LastWeek" method, so
you add or subtract 7 days from the Value property of the object as a
substitute for the missing methods. Select the cmdNextWeek button,
and click the right mouse button. Choose Build Event from the floating
menu. Double-click Code Builder in the Choose Builder dialog to open
the code editing window. Add the following code:

```
Sub cmdNextWeek_Click ()
'Purpose: Advance the current date by one week
ocxCalendar.Object.Value = ocxCalendar.Object.Value + 7
End Sub
```

7. Repeat step 6 for the cmdLastWeek button, but change + 7 to - 7.

8. Because MSACAL20.OCX does have methods for changing the month
and year (see preceding fig. 29.23), you can add the following code to
apply the appropriate method to the Calendar Control with each Click
event of the remaining four buttons:

```
Sub cmd{Next|Previous}{Year|Month}_Click ()
'Purpose: Use the Next or Previous Month or Year method
 to increment or decrement the month
ocxCalendar.Object.{Next|Previous}{Month|Year}
End Sub
```

9. Complete the design of the form by adding a gray background to the
Detail Section of the form. Set the value of the PopUp and Modal properties of the form to Yes, and the value of the MinButton and MaxButton
properties to No.

10. Click the Form View button of the toolbar to open your Calendar Control form (see fig. 29.26). Verify your event-handling procedures by testing the action of each of the six buttons.

Fig. 29.26

The Calendar Control in Form View.

Exploring Dynamic Data Exchange

Chapter 21, "Using Access with Microsoft Excel," demonstrated how you can use Windows' dynamic data exchange (DDE) capabilities, the DDE() and DDESend() functions in particular, to transfer data between Excel and Access using the Clipboard as an intermediary. Access Basic has its own set of DDE methods that provide more flexibility than the DDE() and DDESend() functions. Using Access Basic for DDE data transfers is faster than using the DDE() and DDESend() functions because you can make multiple requests for data after you establish a DDE communications channel. The sections that follow describe how DDE works and how to use the DDE... statements and functions of Access Basic to exchange information with other Windows applications.

Principles of Dynamic Data Exchange

DDE is Windows' traditional method of interprocess communication; DDE allows applications that are not OLE 2.0 compliant to exchange data on a real-time basis. The process of exchanging data is called a DDE *conversation*. The application that initiates the conversation is called the DDE *client*, and the application that provides the data is called the DDE *server*. DDE clients also can supply unsolicited data to DDE servers (called *poking* data) and can send commands for servers to execute. An application can engage in several DDE conversations simultaneously, acting as a server in some and a client in others.

The basic elements of a DDE conversation consist of a request from a client to a server to initiate a conversation, exchange of information between the server and the client, and termination of the conversation. These elements, called DDE *transactions*, comprise the DDE protocol. DDE transactions take place between windows in each of the participating applications that are dedicated to the DDE conversation. These windows are usually invisible. Figure 29.27 is a diagram of a DDE conversation; optional transactions of the conversation are shown in gray type.

To execute the DDE protocol, the client and server send a series of Windows messages to the message queue maintained by the Windows operating system. Windows processes the messages and then removes each message from the message queue in first-in, first-out (FIFO) sequence.

The six elements of the conversation shown in figure 29.27 involve many Windows messages. Several messages may be passed between the client and server to implement one element of the conversation. To maintain the proper timing of messages, the client can request that the server acknowledge all request messages. This type of conversation is called an *asynchronous* DDE conversation.

Tip

The client usually initiates the Terminate Conversation transaction, but the server also can terminate a transaction.

Fig. 29.27
The elements of a
DDE conversation.

In an asynchronous conversation, the client waits until it receives an acknowledgment from the server, indicating that it has processed a request message, before the client sends the server the next message. Most DDE conversations are asynchronous. *Synchronous* conversations use a time-out method; the client sends a series of messages and then awaits a response. If the expected response isn't received within the time-out period, an error message results.

Understanding Service Names, Topics, and Items

DDE uses a three-level hierarchy to identify the data that the client transmits to the server:

- *Service name*. Identifies the server application. Prior to Windows 3.1, *service name* was called *application name*. The service name is usually the name of the application's executable file, less the .EXE extension, such as EXCEL, WINWORD, or MSACCESS. An application may have more than one service name; the application's documentation usually provides the application's DDE service name(s).

- *Topic*. Identifies the context of the information that is the subject of the conversation. In most cases, the topic is the name of a file, such as an Excel worksheet or a Word for Windows document. If an application doesn't use files, the topic is usually a string that is specific to the application. A third type of topic, the System topic, is described in the following section.

- *Item*. A specific piece of data contained in a topic, such as text specified by a bookmark in a word processing document.

Understanding the *System* Topic

Most applications that support DDE provide an additional topic called System. If the server application fully supports the System topic, you can use SysItems to obtain information about the server and its status. SysItems returns a comma-separated list of all valid items that you can use in conjunction with the System topic. In most cases, at least the following two SysItems are supported:

- *Topics*. Provides a list of the files that are open in the application, if the application is file-based. Otherwise, it provides a list of the names of application-specific strings.

- *Formats*. Supplies a list of the Clipboard formats that the server application supports. Excel, for example, supports 11 different Clipboard formats for DDE data. The client application automatically selects the format that suits it best. Access requires that the format be plain text (the Clipboard's CF_TEXT format). Access cannot, for instance, process graphic images (using Clipboard's CF_BITMAP format) with DDE. You cannot alter the DDE Clipboard format in Access Basic.

Many applications don't include the information returned by SysItems in the product documentation. You must write a short DDE application to find out this information. The SysItems supported by Access as a DDE server are listed in the section, "Using the *System* Topic," near the end of this chapter.

Choosing between DDE and OLE Automation

Access is biased toward the use of OLE 2.0 and OLE Automation for interprocess communication because OLE 2.0 is easier to implement and OA is a more reliable method of interprocess communication than DDE. OLE Automation overcomes OLE 1.0's inability to manipulate individual data items contained in an OLE object. OLE is the only practical method of transferring large blocks of data, such as graphic images, between Access and other applications. The maximum length of a DDE string in Access is about 32K, and Access, as noted previously, cannot handle graphic formats with DDE.

If you need to communicate with applications that are not OLE 1.0 or 2.0 servers, DDE is your only option. Most major publishers of Windows applications were in the process of adapting their products to OLE 2.0 when this edition was written. If your access application must address specific data items in a container document, and the OLE 2.0 server you want to use with Access does support OLE Automation, you must use DDE. It is likely that software publishers will give priority to adding OLE 2.0's improved user interface to their applications and then add OA features based on user demand. Implementing OA in a mega-app, such as Excel 5.0, is a major undertaking; the fact that Microsoft's own Word 6.0 does not conform to the object structure of OA is ample testimony to the complexity of the code required.

As mentioned at the beginning of this chapter, you must currently use DDE if you need to use interprocess communication between two computers on a network. The NetDDE features of Windows for Workgroups and Windows NT let users share a single Clipbook. Thus, you can obtain data via DDE from a remote computer. As a rule, however, NetDDE operations usually are confined to DDE links you create with the built-in DDE features of applications, rather than with the **DDE**... functions of Access Basic.

> **Tip**
> You can use the Access Basic **GetChunk** and **AppendChunk** methods to transfer data that exceeds 32K in length to and from fields of the Memo and OLE Object field data types.

Choosing between *DDE()* and *DDESend()* and Access Basic DDE

If you are faced with using Access as a DDE client, you must determine the best way of implementing DDE. When you used the DDE() and DDESend() functions in Chapter 21, "Using Access with Microsoft Excel," to obtain data from or send data to an Excel spreadsheet, you specified the service name, topic, and item for each transaction. When you use these functions, Access does most of the work for you. DDE() initiates a conversation, specifies the topic, requests the particular data item, and then terminates the conversation with a single command. Similarly, DDESend() transfers a data item to a server with a single function.

If you need to transfer substantial numbers of data items between two applications, using DDE() or DDESend becomes quite cumbersome. In the majority of cases, you need a separate control object to hold the value of each data item. The alternative is to use a table with records that contain the values to identify the data item; this technique was used for the Stock Prices example of Chapter 21. Creating a table to specify the addresses of a large number of data items is, at best, a tedious process. If the data items are properly organized, you can write an Access Basic procedure to append the data to a table.

Using Access Basic for DDE

Access Basic includes a set of six keywords that are used to initiate, process, and terminate DDE conversations. The four statements and two functions that comprise the DDE keywords of Access Basic are listed in table 29.1.

If you have written macros using DDE in Word for Windows' WordBasic language, you already know how to use these commands. The one difference is the lack of the string type identification character in the **DDERequest**() function; **DDERequest**() in Access Basic returns data of the Variant data type; **DDERequest$**() in WordBasic always returns a string. Pre-Excel 5.0 DDE macro functions dispense with the DDE prefix, but otherwise use similar commands. Visual Basic for Applications uses the same DDE... reserved words as Access Basic. Visual Basic substitutes Link... for DDE... and requires more statements to process a DDE conversation, but the overall approach of Visual Basic to DDE is similar to that of other Microsoft applications.

Table 29.1	DDE Keywords of Access Basic	
Keyword	**Type**	**Purpose**
DDEExecute	Statement	Sends a command recognized by a DDE server over an open DDE channel.
DDEInitiate()	Function	Initiates a conversation with a DDE server and returns an integer that serves as the DDE channel number.
DDEPoke	Statement	Sends unsolicited data to a DDE server.
DDERequest()	Function	Requests a specific item of information from a DDE server over an open DDE channel.
DDETerminate	Statement	Closes an open DDE channel specified by number.
DDETerminateAll	Statement	Closes all open DDE channels.

Understanding the Structure and Syntax of Access Basic DDE Statements

The structure of a simple Access Basic generic DDE code that requests a data item (*ItemName*) from a topic (*TopicName*) of an application (*ServiceName*) follows:

```
intChannel = DDEInitiate("ServiceName", "TopicName")
DDERequest(wChannel, "ItemName")
DDETerminate wChannel
```

The **DDEInitiate**() function returns an integer, int*Channel*, that all succeeding DDE statements use to identify the communication channel for the service name and topic. This set of instructions assumes the application is loaded before the **DDEInitiate**() function is called. Unlike OLE, if the application isn't loaded, you receive an error message. You then must start the application with Access Basic's **Shell**() function.

Using the *Shell()* Function to Load an Application

The operation of the **Shell**() function is similar to running an application from the **R**un command of the Program Manager's **F**ile menu. The syntax of the **Shell**() function is as follows:

```
hTask = Shell("AppFile", intStyle)
```

In this case, *AppFile* is the full file name, including the .EXE extension, of the application you want to run, EXCEL.EXE, for example. If *AppFile* isn't on your DOS path, you need to add the well-formed path to the file name.

The int*Style* argument specifies the presentation of the application when it is loaded. Assigning an int*Style* of 6 is the equivalent of checking the Run Minimized check box in the Run dialog; Windows starts the application in iconic style without the focus. Unless you have a specific reason to display the server in a window, always use the iconic style without the focus when opening a DDE server.

If you call the **Shell**() function when an application is already running, you launch another instance of most applications. This consumes resources that you may need to keep Access operating. To determine whether the application is presently running, you can use the **On Error GoTo** instruction, but the most straightforward method is to test the error value with the **Err** function and then use **Shell**().

◀ "Exporting Data in Other File Formats," p. 283

Experimenting with DDE in the Immediate Window

The CUSTOMER.XLS workbook you created earlier in this chapter provides an Excel 5.0 worksheet, CUSTOMER, that you can use to experiment with Access Basic **DDE...** functions. If you didn't create CUSTOMER.XLS, export the Customers table of NWIND.MDB to CUSTOMER.XLS in a format appropriate for your present version of Microsoft Excel. The sequence of **DDE...** instructions shown in figure 29.28 requires that an instance of Excel be open with the CUSTOMER.XLS worksheet active.

Fig. 29.28
Communicating with an open application and topic using DDE.

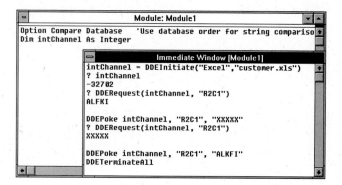

The first statement in figure 29.28, intChannel = **DDEInitiate**("Excel", "customer.xls"), opens a DDE channel to Excel and the worksheet. An intChannel value of 0 indicates an error; the most likely cause of the error is that Excel is not open or the topic you specified is not one of the items that is returned by the System topic. You can obtain a list of valid topics with a ? **DDERequest**(intChannel, "Topics") statement with a channel opened to the System topic. This statement returns [CUSTOMER.XLS]CUSTOMER System, specifying the CUSTOMER worksheet of the CUSTOMER.XLS workbook.

Unlike the prior OLE Automation example, you use Excel's RC (row, channel) nomenclature to specify the cell coordinates in DDE conversations. Thus, the ? **DDERequest**(intChannel, "R2C1") statement returns the value in cell A2. You can send unrequested data to a DDE server with the **DDEPoke** statement. For example, the **DDEPoke** intChannel, "R2C1", "XXXXX" statement replaces "ALKFI" with "XXXXX", as shown in figure 29.29. Using the **DDETerminateAll** instruction is recommended when you have completed the conversation, unless you need to maintain other DDE channels in use. In the latter case, use the **DDETerminate** intChannel statement to terminate a specific channel.

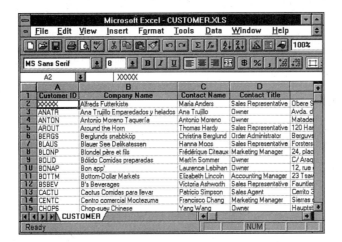

Fig. 29.29
Using the *DDEPoke*
statement to
change a cell value
in a worksheet.

Figure 29.30 illustrates the use of the **Shell**() function to launch the DDE server application. To experiment with the **Shell**() function, close Excel and don't save the changes to your worksheet. The **Shell**() function launches the application and returns the Windows Task Manager's task handle (hTask) to the instance of the application. With Excel 5.0, the ? **Shell**("excel.exe") function, without the optional *intStyle* parameter, opens an iconized instance of Excel 5.0 with an empty workbook (Book1) and worksheet (Sheet1). (Earlier versions of Excel open with an empty worksheet.)

You must use a valid topic to open a DDE channel; the System topic is valid for almost all DDE server applications. Most DDE servers accept commands from DDE client applications via a channel to their System topic. You use Excel's function syntax with the **DDEExecute** statement to perform Excel's menu commands. Thus, the statement **DDEExecute** intChannel, "[OPEN(""c:\access\customer.xls"")]" opens the CUSTOMER.XLS workbook. You must open another DDE channel, identical to the one you use when Excel is already open, to communicate with the worksheet in the workbook.

Tip
Your Excel
directory must
be on your DOS
path for the
Shell() func-
tion to execute
correctly.
? **Shell**
("excel.exe")
returns 0 and
an error mes-
sage if the
statement can't
open Excel.

> **Note**
>
> The double quotation marks (" ") that surround the path and file name create the single quotation mark required by Excel's function syntax. Most applications require commands passed by DDE to be enclosed within square brackets.

Fig. 29.30

Using the *Shell()* function and the *DDEExecute* statement to open a channel to a worksheet.

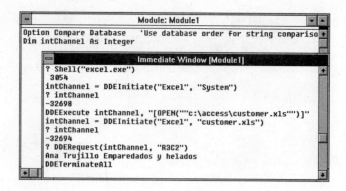

Although the examples of this section are devoted to communicating with Microsoft Excel, the process is similar for almost all other DDE servers. You can use DDE to provide interprocess communication with Lotus 1-2-3, WordPerfect for Windows, and even fax applications, such as WinFax PRO. As mentioned earlier in this chapter, the Mail Merge feature of Access relies solely on DDE to communicate with Word.

Using Access as a DDE Server

Access can act as a DDE server to other DDE client applications. Access recognizes a set of DDE instructions issued by the client applications that is more versatile than the set offered by most DDE server applications. The flexibility of Access's DDE server instruction set compensates for the application's inability to act as an OLE server. In the majority of cases, DDE is a better choice than OLE for transferring columnar data to a client spreadsheet application.

Using the *System* Topic

When a client application initiates a DDE channel on the System topic and specifies Topics as the data item in a **DDERequest**() statement, Access returns a list of the topics it currently supports. With Access running and NWIND.MDB open, type and then execute the following Word macro:

```
Sub MAIN
    Channel = DDEInitiate("MSAccess", "System")
    Topics$ = DDERequest$(Channel, "Topics")
    DDETerminate(Channel)
    Insert Topics$
End Sub
```

Access returns a tab-separated string and Word inserts this string, similar to that in the following example, at Word's current insertion point:

```
System C:\ACCESS\SYSTEM.MDA  C:\ACCESS\UTILITY.MDA
C:\ACCESS\WZLIB.MDA
C:\ACCESS\WZBLDR.MDA  C:\ACCESS\WZNAV.MDA     C:\ACCESS\WZFRMRPT.MDA
C:\ACCESS\SAMPAPPS\NWIND.MDB
```

As mentioned in the preceding section, the System topic is supported by all Windows DDE servers. Unlike Access 1.1, which returned UTILITY, WIZARD, and NWIND, Access 2.0 returns the path, file name, and extension of all open topics.

The System topic supports the SysItems data item that returns a list of valid data items that you can use to determine additional information about Access's capabilities as a server. Run the following Word for Windows macro:

```
Sub MAIN
    Channel = DDEInitiate("MSAccess", "System")
    SysItems$ = DDERequest$(Channel, "SysItems")
    DDETerminate(Channel)
    Insert SysItems$
End Sub
```

The macro inserts the following comma-separated list of valid data items for the System topic:

```
Status,Formats,SysItems,Topics
```

If you substitute Formats for SysItems in the preceding macro, Access 2.0 returns the three types of Clipboard formats it supports:

```
Text    CSV    XLTable
```

CSV is an abbreviation for comma-separated values, the format in which Access returns the examples shown previously. XLTable is a new Excel 5.0 format added to Access 2.0.

The data items supported by the System topic are summarized in table 29.2.

Table 29.2 Data Items Supported by Access's *System* Topic	
Data Item	**Purpose**
Status	Returns Ready or Busy.
Formats	Returns a list of the formats Access can copy onto the Clipboard, presently CSV, Text, and XLTable.

(continues)

Table 29.2 Continued	
Data Item	**Purpose**
SysItems	Returns a list of the data items, except *MacroName*, supported by the System topic.
Topics	Returns a list of all open databases, including libraries.
MacroName	Enables a macro in the current database to be executed with the **DDEExecute** statement using the System topic.

Returning Information about Other Topics

You can obtain four different sets of data by specifying the name of the open database:

- *Database object lists*. To obtain these lists, use the name of the database as the topic in the **DDEInitiate**() statement and use one of the following keywords as the data item in a **DDERequest**() statement: TableList, QueryList, FormList, ReportList, MacroList, and ModuleList.

- *Data from tables*. To obtain this data, specify the database (followed by a semicolon), the keyword TABLE, and the name of the table as the topic in the **DDEInitiate**() statement. Then use one of the following keywords as the data item in a **DDERequest**() statement: All, Data, FieldNames, FirstRow, NextRow, PrevRow, LastRow, and FieldCount.

- *Data from a query*. To obtain this data, specify the database (followed by a semicolon), the keyword QUERY, and the name of the query as the topic in the **DDEInitiate**() statement. Then use one of the same keywords for the TABLE topic as the data item in a **DDERequest**() statement.

- *Data from an SQL statement*. To obtain this data, specify the database (followed by a semicolon), the keyword SQL, and a valid SQL statement in the **DDEInitiate**() statement. Then use one of the same keywords for the TABLE topic as the data item in a **DDERequest**() statement.

The sections that follow give the syntax and an example of an Excel 4.0 macro that executes each of these DDE client processes. The information in these sections assumes some familiarity with the command macros features of Excel 4.0. Excel 5.0 is backwardly compatible with Excel 4.0 macros, so these macros also are operable in Excel 5.0.

You can execute macros over DDE channels initiated with the *DatabaseName* topic in the same manner as those initiated with the System topic. You specify the *MacroName* of a macro contained in the open database as the data item in a DDERequest() statement.

Listing Database Object Names with the *DatabaseName* Topic

You can obtain lists of all database objects in an Access database you specify with the *DatabaseName* topic. *DatabaseName* can be NWIND or NWIND.MDB, for example, if NWIND.MDB is open. Otherwise, you need to include the Shell() function command in your macro.

After initiating the DDE conversation with the *DatabaseName* topic, you can use the data items listed in table 29.3 with the DDERequest() request function to return a CSV string listing the names of database objects in the database.

Table 29.3 Data Items Recognized with the *DatabaseName* Topic	
Data Item	**Purpose**
TableList	A list of tables in *DatabaseName*
QueryList	A list of queries in *DatabaseName*
MacroList	A list of macros in *DatabaseName*
ReportList	A list of reports in *DatabaseName*
FormList	A list of forms in *DatabaseName*
ModuleList	A list of modules in *DatabaseName*

For example, the following Excel 4.0 macro returns the first three entries in a list of the tables in the Northwind Traders sample database, assuming NWIND.MDB is open:

```
=INITIATE("MSAccess","NWIND")
=INDEX(REQUEST(A2,"TableList"),1)    Categories
=FORMULA(A3,B3)
=INDEX(REQUEST(A2,"TableList"),2)    Customers
=FORMULA(A5,B5)
=INDEX(REQUEST(A2,"TableList"),3)    Employees
=FORMULA(A7,B7)
=TERMINATE(A2)
=RETURN()
```

Enter the macro statements of the example in a macrosheet in rows 1 through 9 of column A. Select cell A1, and then choose **R**un from Excel's **M**acros menu. Choose OK or press Enter when the Run Macro dialog appears. The values appear in cells B3, B5, and B7.

Using the *TableName* and *QueryName* Topics to Obtain Data

You can add a qualifier to *DatabaseName* to specify a table or query object contained in *DatabaseName* as the topic. The syntax is as follows:

```
DatabaseName;TABLE TableName
DatabaseName;QUERY QueryName
```

Table 29.4 lists the data items that are valid for use with both the *TableName* and *QueryName* topics, plus the *SQLStatement* topic discussed in the next section.

Table 29.4   Data Items Recognized by the *TableName*, *QueryName*, and *SQLStatement* Topics

Data Item	Purpose
All	Returns all data in the table, preceded by a row of field names.
Data	Returns all rows of data without a row of field names.
FieldNames	Returns a list consisting of all field names.
FirstRow	Returns the data in the first row of the table or query.
NextRow	Returns the data in the next row in the table or query. If NextRow is the first request, the data in the first row is returned. NextRow fails if the current row is the last record.
PrevRow	Returns the previous row in the table or query. If PrevRow is the first request, the data in the last row of the table or query is returned. PrevRow fails if the current row is the first record.
LastRow	Returns the data in the last row of the table or query.
FieldCount	Returns the number of fields in the table or query.
MacroName	Enables a macro in the current database to be executed with the DDEExecute() statement using the System topic.

The following Excel 4.0 macro returns the first three fields of the first row of the Categories table:

```
=INITIATE("MSAccess","NWIND;TABLE Categories")
=INDEX(REQUEST(A2,"FirstRow"),1)          BEVR
=FORMULA(A3,B3)
=INDEX(REQUEST(A2,"FirstRow"),2)          Beverages
=FORMULA(A5,B5)
=INDEX(REQUEST(A2,"FirstRow"),3)          Soft drinks, …
```

```
=FORMULA(A7,B7)
=TERMINATE(A2)
=RETURN()
```

Enter and run the macro using the procedure described previously in the *DatabaseName* section.

Running a Query with the *SQLStatement* Topic

The SQLStatement topic returns a valid SQL statement following the SQL keyword. The syntax for the SQLStatement topic is as follows:

```
DatabaseName;SQL SQLStatement;
```

The SQL statement must end with a semicolon.

An Excel 4.0 macro that executes the SQL statement, SELECT * FROM Customers, and lists the names of the first three customers in the resulting **Recordset** object is as follows:

```
=INITIATE("MSAccess","NWIND;SQL SELECT * FROM Customers;")
=INDEX(REQUEST(A2,"FirstRow"),2)    Alfreds Futterkiste
=FORMULA(A3,B3)
=INDEX(REQUEST(A2,"NextRow"),2)     Ana Trujillo Emparedados y
                                    helados
=FORMULA(A5,B5)
=INDEX(REQUEST(A2,"NextRow"),2)     Antonio Moreno Taquería
=FORMULA(A7,B7)
=TERMINATE(A2)
=RETURN()
```

In the majority of cases, you write macros in the client application's macro language that contain loops to process multiple rows of data. Excel 5.0's Visual Basic for Applications, and even WordBasic, makes writing macros with loops and conditional branching easy. However, the design of macros in the languages of applications other than Access is beyond the scope of this book.

From Here...

The primary emphasis of this chapter is on Access 2.0's OLE Automation capabilities and OLE Custom Controls because OA and OCXs represent the future direction of interprocess communication for Windows applications, as well as for applications running under a variety of other operating systems. Many Windows applications do not support OLE 1.0 and, thus, are not likely to support OLE 2.0, either. Therefore, the chapter provided you with the basics using Access 2.0 as a DDE client. Finally, because Access is not an OLE server, you must use DDE if you want to use Access 2.0 as the source of data for a client application. This chapter demonstrates that Access 2.0 has a much richer set of DDE server capabilities than most other Windows database applications.

The following chapters provide additional information on the use of OLE 2.0 and the simplified version of DDE offered by Access's DDE() and DDESend() functions:

■ Chapter 19, "Using OLE 2.0," gives an overview of Access 2.0's implementation of OLE 2.0 and OLE Automation.

■ Chapter 20, "Adding Graphics to Forms and Reports," shows you how to use OLE 1.0- and OLE 2.0-compliant applications with Access 2.0 and describes how to use the Graph Wizard with Microsoft Graph 5.0 to create bound and unbound graphs and charts.

■ Chapter 21, "Using Access with Microsoft Excel," and Chapter 22, "Using Access with Microsoft Word and Mail Merge," describe the use of the DDE() and DDESend() functions with these two popular productivity applications.

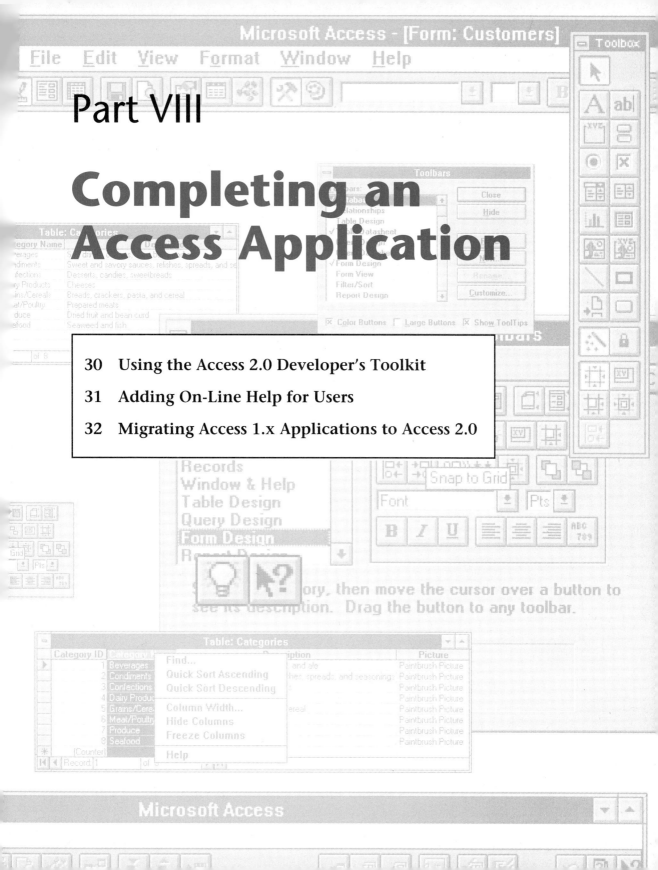

Part VIII

Completing an Access Application

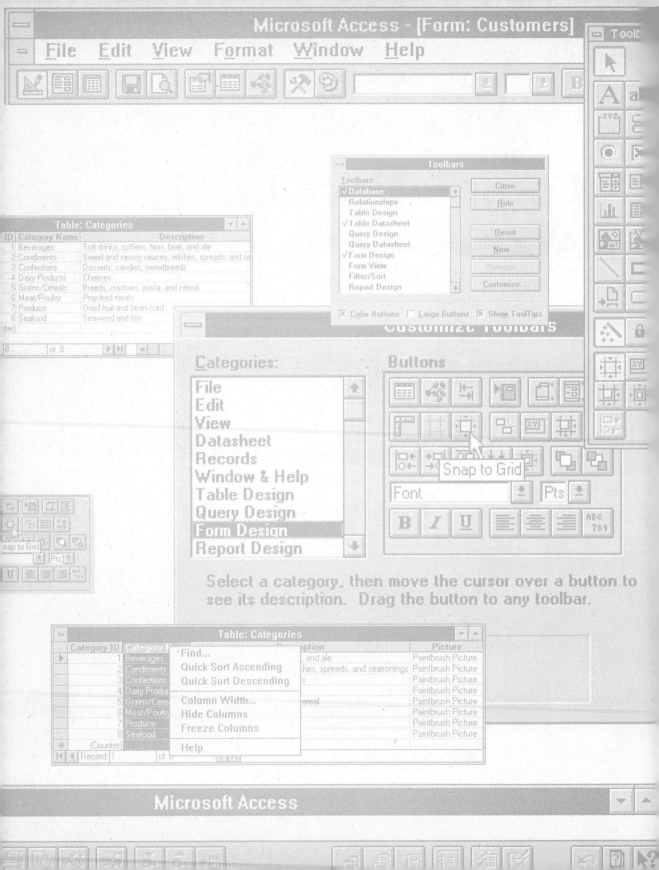

Chapter 30

Using the Access 2.0 Developer's Toolkit

The Access Developer's Toolkit (ADT) for Access 2.0 replaces the Access Distribution Kit (ADK) of version 1.1. The Access 1.1 ADK consisted of the run-time version of Access 1.1 (MSARN110.EXE) and the files required to create distribution disks using run-time Access. The ADK's Setup Wizard was included to aid you in creating the complex STFSETUP.IN_ file required to orchestrate the setup operation based on the content of your distribution disks. The ADK also included the Microsoft Help Compiler (HC31.EXE), a *Help Compiler Guide*, and an example on-line help file for the Visual Basic 3.0 sample application, IconWorks. Manuals, in the form of pamphlets, described how to use the ADT and explained the syntax of many of the then undocumented Access Basic reserved words for creating forms and reports "programatically." Thus, the ADK was of interest primarily to application developers, rather than end-users.

Microsoft changed the description of the ADK from a "Distribution Kit" to a "Developer's Toolkit" because the content of the ADT has expanded greatly. This chapter describes what's in the ADT and how to use the Setup Wizard to create run-time distribution disks for your Access 2.0 applications.

In this chapter, you learn to

- Modify the design of your Access applications for run-time execution

- Create custom *APPNAME*.INI files for run-time applications

- Use the Setup Wizard to create distribution disks

- Understand the function of Setup's information files

VIII

Completing Applications

Examining the Content of the Access Developer's Toolkit

The new ADT for Access 2.0 is directed at both the Access developer and power-user communities. The new ADT contains the following components:

■ The executable run-time Access file, MSARN200.EXE, and the run-time version of Microsoft Graph 5.0 (MSGraph5). A license from Microsoft Corporation to distribute these files, plus the other Access 2.0 files needed by users of your run-time applications, is included in the ADT.

■ An improved version of the Setup Wizard you use to create images of the distribution disks for your application. The Setup Wizard also writes the SETUP.INF file (formerly STFSETUP.IN_) required by SETUP.EXE. SETUP.INF is a more complex version because of the additional files required to implement OLE 2.0 and OLE Automation with Windows 3.1+.

■ The *Microsoft Access 2.0 Language Reference* manual. The *Language Reference* no longer is included with the retail version of Access. If you don't purchase the ADT, you need to buy the *Language Reference* from Microsoft Corporation. (The content of the *Language Reference* is included in Access 2.0's on-line help file, but most Access power users are likely to want a printed version.)

■ The *Advanced Topics* manual that describes how to create distributable Access applications. In addition, *Advanced Topics* supplements the *User's Guide* of retail Access 2.0 with chapters that cover application design and optimization, using the ODBC API, creating Access add-ins, implementing OLE Automation, and programming OLE Custom Controls.

◀ "Adding OLE Custom Controls to Your Application," p. 1074

■ The three OLE Custom Controls described in Chapter 29, "Exchanging Data with OLE Automation and DDE." You can distribute two of these Controls, the Calendar Control (MSACAL20.OCX) and the Scrollbar Control (MSASB20.OCX), with run-time applications. Refer to the license agreement for restrictions on distributing the Data Outline (Navigator) Control.

■ A replacement for Visual Basic 3.0's VBDB300.DLL that provides Visual Basic developers with a *mapping layer* between Visual Basic 3.0 and Access 2.0's new .MDB file structure. The mapping layer detects whether the .MDB file is version 1.1 or 2.0, and automatically uses the appropriate Jet DLLs for the .MDB. The Jet version 2.0 DLL required by Visual Basic 3.0 developers, MSAJT112.DLL, also is included.

■ Versions of the wizards supplied with retail Access that include comments in their Access Basic code. You need to be very conversant with

Access Basic to understand the operation of the wizards' code because the comments are terse at best.

■ The Microsoft Help Compiler, HC31.EXE, the *Help Compiler Guide*, and the files needed to create ICONWRKS.HLP, an example help file.

▶ "Compiling Your Help Files," p. 1134

Except for the Help Compiler components, all of the preceding components are new for version 2.0.

Differences between Run-Time and Retail Access

The behavior of your Access applications differs when you execute the applications under retail (MSACCESS.EXE) and run-time (MSARN200.EXE). Following are the principle differences that distinguish run-time execution:

■ Many design-related menu choices are removed. Your run-time applications should use menu macros to create the menu bars and menu items your application requires.

■ The Database window is not visible. You specify the database to open as the first parameter of the command line that executes MSARN200.EXE. Run-time applications also need an AutoExec macro to display an opening "splash screen" or the first form of your application.

■ Special-purpose keys and combinations are disabled. Shift is disabled during the database opening process. Ctrl+Break is disabled so that users cannot halt Access Basic code or macro operation. (Ctrl+Break remains active during query execution so that users can halt a "runaway" query that returns very large numbers of records.)

■ Pressing F1 for on-line help results in a "Can't open help file" error message if you don't supply a custom on-line help file for your application. Supplying even a very simple help file is a better practice than allowing an error to occur when the user presses F1. (You are not allowed to distribute the Access on-line help file.)

■ All errors that occur in the execution of macros and untrapped errors that occur while executing Access Basic code result in an instantaneous exit of Access. The user receives no warning of the impending disappearance of your application. As mentioned in the previous chapters of

VIII

Completing Applications

this book, you cannot trap macro errors. Thus, you should use Access Basic code rather than macros for all event-handling operations. Macros should be limited to the AutoExec macro to open your first form and the AutoKeys macro to assign key combinations to execute functions and to add custom menu bars and menu choices to your application's user interface.

■ Run-time applications expect to find a private *APPNAME*.INI file that replaces retail Access's MSACC20.INI. You are not allowed to distribute MSACC20.INI itself, but you are allowed to create your own clone of MSACC20.INI. Writing private .INI files for your application is the subject of the next section.

◀ "The Microsoft Access Solutions Pack," p. 63

■ If you use separate data and application .MDB files, you need to provide Access Basic routines that test to determine if the data .MDB file is on the expected drive and in the specified directory. If not, a special form and another routine is required to specify the location of the data .MDB file. Each of the applications included with the Microsoft Access Solutions Pack contains an example of a "reattach the tables" form and the required Access Basic code to perform the reattachment process.

No significant change in the preceding list has occurred with MSARN200.EXE. Thus, the Access 1.1 run-time applications you convert to Access 2.0 are likely to behave identically. Chapter 32, "Migrating Access 1.x Applications to Access 2.0," describes the changes you need to make to execute your applications with MSARN200.EXE. These changes also are necessary for the applications to execute with the retail version of Access 2.0.

Writing *APPNAME*.INI Files for Run-Time Applications

Before you create distribution disks, you create a custom information file, *APPNAME*.INI, that serves the same purpose as MSACC20.INI. Following are the differences between run-time .INI files and MSACC20.INI:

■ The name of your custom .INI file does not need to be the same as the name of your application .MDB file, but it is the usual practice to make the file name parts identical.

■ *APPNAME*.INI files for run-time applications have an additional [Run-Time Options] section that accepts the following entries:

```
[Run-Time Options]
TitleBar=Proper Name of Your Application
Icon=[d:\path\]iconfile.ico
HelpFile=[d:\path\]helpfile.hlp
```

You need not include the drive and path of the files if the files are located in the user's current directory (the same directory as your application .MDB file).

- If your application is designed for a workgroup, you need to specify the location of SYSTEM.MDA or *APPNAME*.MDA that replaces SYSTEM.MDA. The Setup Wizard automatically installs UTILITY.MDA in the directory you specify; the Wizard only installs SYSTEM.MDA if you specify that it is to be installed. The usual practice is to install SYSTEM.MDA, or its surrogate, in the same server directory as the shared data .MDB file. Thus, the entries in the [Options] section of your *APPNAME*.INI file are

◀ "Creating Workgroup Directories for Database Files," p. 924

```
[Options]
SystemDB=s:\[sharedir\]sysfile.mda
UtilityDB=[d:\path\]utility.mda
AllowCustomControls=1
AllowOLE1LinkFormat=0
```

where *s* is the drive designator of the server share, *sharedir* is the subdirectory of the server share (if applicable), and *sysfile*.mda is the name of your applications system file (usually named SYSTEM.MDA or *WRKGROUP*.MDA). You can change the SystemDB entry value with the Workgroup Administrator application.

- You are not allowed to distribute the Wizards supplied with retail Access. Thus, you eliminate all sections that contain the word *Wizard(s)*, unless you have created your own wizard or have a license to distribute a third-party wizard. Delete the entire [Menu Add-Ins] section. You also eliminate all entries in the [Libraries] section, unless your application requires a library database. If you fail to eliminate the libraries entries, MSARN200.EXE generates an error when loading and run-time Access's window disappears when you click OK.

- Eliminate the entries in the [Installable ISAMs] section that specify foreign database types that are not needed by your application, and then delete the corresponding section, such as [Paradox 4.x]. If your application does not require any foreign database types, you can delete the [Installable ISAMs] section entirely.

- If your application does not rely on the ODBC API to connect to client-server databases, you can remove the entire [ODBC] section.

VIII

Completing Applications

Following is the beginning of the NSC_ASK.INI file that is specified in the "Creating Distribution Disks with the Setup Wizard" section of this chapter:

```
[Options]
SystemDB=s:\nsc_ask.mda
UtilityDB=utility.mda
AllowCustomControls=1
AllowOLE1LinkFormat=0

[Run-Time Options]
TitleBar=Proper Name of Your Application
Icon=nsc_ask.ico
HelpFile=nsc_ask.hlp

[Libraries]

[Microsoft Access]
Filter=Microsoft Access (*.mdb)¦*.mdb¦All Files (*.*)¦*.*¦
Extension=mdb
OneTablePerFile=No
IndexDialog=No
Maximized=1
CreateDbOnExport=No

[ISAM]
PageTimeout=5
LockedPageTimeout=5
CursorTimeout=10
LockRetry=20
CommitLockRetry=20
MaxBufferSize=512
ReadAheadPages=16
IdleFrequency=10
```

The remainder of the NSC_ASK.INI file consists of formatting sections for importing and exporting data in text and spreadsheet formats.

Creating Distribution Disks with the Setup Wizard

Microsoft Corporation's standard Setup program changed with the introduction of early 1994's round of Microsoft productivity application upgrades. The Setup application for users of your Access 2.0 run-time applications is derived from the new standard Setup program. The Access 2.0 Setup Wizard (SETUPWIZ.MDB, a database, not a library) also has been given a major facelift.

The description of using the Setup Wizard that follows assumes that you have created or appropriated an icon file for your application and have both on-line help and *APPNAME*.INI files. To create images of the distribution disks on your fixed disk (or a server drive), follow these steps:

1. Launch retail Access and open the SETUPWIZ.MDB database in your \ACCESS\ADT directory. The Setup Wizard's AutoExec macro displays the opening dialog shown in figure 30.1.

2. Click the Add File button to open the Add File dialog. Enter the path and file name of your application database in the File Name box. The destination entry, $(AppPath), points to the default drive and directory for your application on the user's computer.

3. Click the Show in Program Manager Group check box so that the icon for your application appears in its Application Group window.

Tip
Make sure you have at least 8M of free disk space on the drive that you use to store the disk images before you start creating distri-bution disks.

Fig. 30.1
The opening dialog of the Setup Wizard.

4. The Wizard writes the Command Line entry for the Program Item for you. Marking the Run with MSARN200 check box adds the name of your application database as the first command line parameter. The /Excl parameter, which causes Access to open the application database in exclusive mode is added as the default. Unless your application itself (not a separate shared data .MDB file) is to be shared, the /Excl param-eter contributes to better performance of your application. You can add the /Ini parameter, which specifies the name of your *APPNAME*.INI file, or the Wizard adds it for you from the entry you make in the INI File text box.

5. Check the Always Overwrite File check box to eliminate version testing of prior versions of your application. Your first Add File dialog appears as shown in figure 30.2. Click OK to accept the command line, data-base, and *APPNAME*.INI file entries and close the Add File dialog.

◄ "Using Com-mand Line Options to Open a Data-base," p. 929

VIII

Completing Applications

Fig. 30.2
Adding the
specification for
your application
.MDB file.

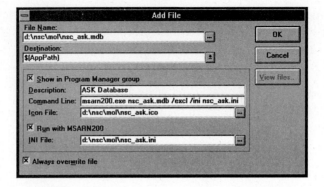

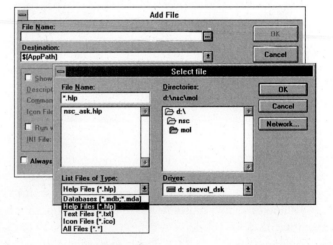

6. Click the Add File button to add your on-line help file. Click the ellipsis button adjacent to the File Name text box to display the Select File dialog. The List Files of Type drop-down list lets you choose from .MDB, .MDA, .HLP, .TXT, and .ICO files, as well as files of any type (see fig. 30.3). Select your on-line help file, and click OK to close the Select File dialog.

Fig. 30.3
The Select File
dialog for adding
standard file types.

7. Repeat step 6 for your icon file.

◄ "Maintaining
Database Secu-
rity," p. 932

8. If your application is designed to be used in a workgroup environment, repeat step 6 for the SYSTEM.MDA file or your *APPNAME*.MDA file. Make sure that the SYSTEM.MDA file you use is not the same SYSTEM.MDA file you used when developing the application if you

want to prevent users from being able to view the design of your application by using a copy of retail Access. When you complete your additions, the initial dialog of the Setup Wizard appears as shown in figure 30.4. Click the Next > button to open the Optional Features dialog.

Fig. 30.4
The Setup Wizard's initial dialog with the list of application files to include.

VIII

Completing Applications

9. Select the ISAM drivers you want to install, if any, in the Available Options list box, and click the Install button. (Uninstall replaces the Install caption when you select an installed option.)

10. If your application uses Microsoft Graph 5.0, repeat step 9 for the run-time version of MSGraph5 (see fig. 30.5). You do not have a license to install the full version of MSGraph5 located in your \WINDOWS\MSAPPS\MSGRAPH directory.

11. If your application is designed for use by a workgroup, repeat step 9 for the Change Workgroup Program Manager Item. (The Change Workgroup application is added to your setup disks even if you do not add the Program Item.) Click the Next > button to proceed to the program group and destination directory dialog.

Tip
If your application uses the ODBC API, you must add the required ODBC files to your list. See Chapter 26, "Connecting to Client-Server Databases," which describes these files.

Fig. 30.5
Adding optional features for your application.

12. Enter the title you want for the program item group in the Application Name text box; then enter the default drive and directory in which to install your application in the Default Installation directory text box (see fig. 30.6). Click OK to display the optional executable file dialog.

Fig. 30.6
Adding the Program Group title and the default installation directory.

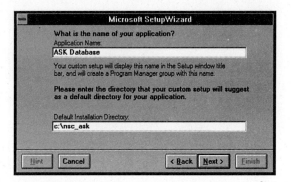

13. You can specify that an executable Windows application run before the setup process is fully completed (see fig. 30.7).

Fig. 30.7
The dialog in which to specify an executable file to run in conjunction with the setup operation.

Tip
If you save the Template File when you open the Setup Wizard again, the Load Template button is enabled. You can use the Template File instead of re-entering the specifications to re-create your disk images.

If your application is shared on a network using the TCP/IP protocol, you might want to run a Windows ping program to verify the location of the server. In most cases, you don't make an entry at this point. Click the Next > button to display the disk image specification dialog.

14. Enter the drive and directory in which you want to create the disk image files in the Application Setup Directory text box. Click the option button for the type of disks you want to make (see fig. 30.8). If you want to make both 1.44M and 1.2M disks, click 1.2M to create image files that fit on disks of either capacity. You can save your specification as a Template File by clicking the Save Template button. Click the Finish button to proceed with creation of the image files.

Fig. 30.8
Specifying the location and disk capacity of the distribution disk image files.

15. The Setup Wizard now begins to seriously go about her work. The Create Disk Images dialog informs you of the progress of the process of creating compressed copies of the distributable files and the files you specified for your application (see fig. 30.9). You can disregard the indication that all of the files are being added to the image of DISK1. Distributing the files across the individual disk image files takes place after the size of the compressed file is determined.

16. When the lengthy process is completed, the understated message box of figure 30.10 appears.

Tip

You may want to get a cup of coffee (or have lunch) while the Setup Wizard creates the images. The process takes at least 15 minutes on an 80486DX2/66 computer with an 8ms fixed disk.

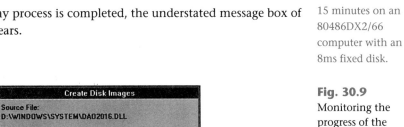

Fig. 30.9
Monitoring the progress of the disk image creation process.

Fig. 30.10
The notice that the Wizard has finally completed her task.

VIII

Completing Applications

Four 1.44M disks are required to hold an Access application of nominal size. Most applications that use MSGraph5 require five 1.44M disks. It's up to you to copy the files in the image directories (*PATH*\DISK1...*PATH*\DISK*n*) to each distribution disk. (Unfortunately, the Setup Wizard does not do this for you.)

ADT 2.0 Understanding the Setup Information Files

The new Setup Wizard of Access 2.0 creates SETUP.INF, SETUP.STF and SETUP.LST files in the *PATH*\DISK1 directory. The purpose of these three SETUP.??? files, called *setup scripts* by Microsoft, is as follows:

- *SETUP.LST* is used by the main Setup program (SETUP.EXE) to specify the setup message, setup window title, and the name of the temporary directory into which the setup files are placed. SETUP.EXE launches ACMSETUP.EXE with the command parameters specified in the `CmdLine` entry of the `[Params]` section. Figure 30.11 shows all of the entries in SETUP.LST.

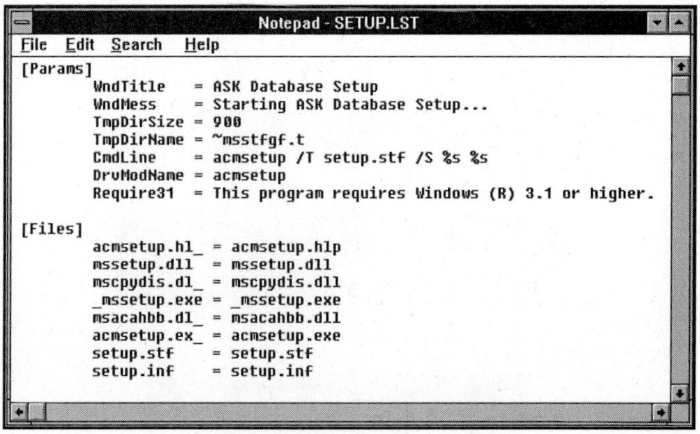


```
[Params]
        WndTitle    = ASK Database Setup
        WndMess     = Starting ASK Database Setup...
        TmpDirSize  = 900
        TmpDirName  = ~msstfgf.t
        CmdLine     = acmsetup /T setup.stf /S %s %s
        DrvModName  = acmsetup
        Require31   = This program requires Windows (R) 3.1 or higher.

[Files]
        acmsetup.hl_  = acmsetup.hlp
        mssetup.dll   = mssetup.dll
        mscpydis.dl_  = mscpydis.dll
        _mssetup.exe  = _mssetup.exe
        msacahbb.dl_  = msacahbb.dll
        acmsetup.ex_  = acmsetup.exe
        setup.stf     = setup.stf
        setup.inf     = setup.inf
```

Fig. 30.11 The SETUP.LST script file.

- *SETUP.INF* is read by ACMSETUP.EXE and specifies the names, disk number, file sizes, and other properties of each of the files to be installed on the user's fixed disk. SETUP.INF supplies data about the files to SETUP.STF. Figure 30.12 shows the part of SETUP.INF that specifies the properties of files for your application.

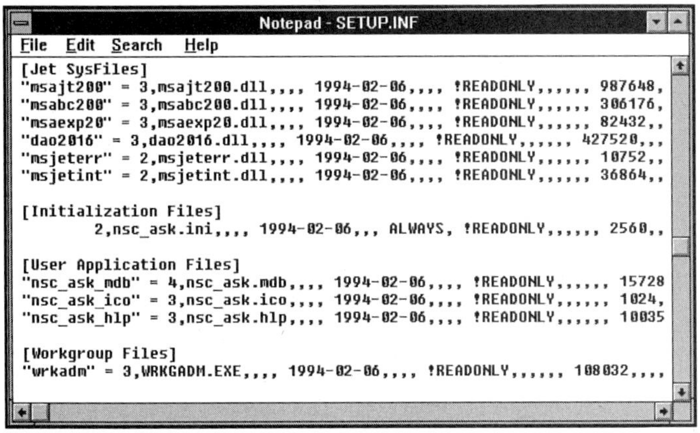

```
[Jet SysFiles]
"msajt200" = 3,msajt200.dll,,,, 1994-02-06,,,, !READONLY,,,,,, 987648,
"msabc200" = 3,msabc200.dll,,,, 1994-02-06,,,, !READONLY,,,,,, 306176,
"msaexp20" = 3,msaexp20.dll,,,, 1994-02-06,,,, !READONLY,,,,,, 82432,,
"dao2016" = 3,dao2016.dll,,,, 1994-02-06,,,, !READONLY,,,,,, 427520,,,
"msjeterr" = 2,msjeterr.dll,,,, 1994-02-06,,,, !READONLY,,,,,, 10752,,
"msjetint" = 2,msjetint.dll,,,, 1994-02-06,,,, !READONLY,,,,,, 36864,,

[Initialization Files]
        2,nsc_ask.ini,,,, 1994-02-06,,, ALWAYS, !READONLY,,,,,, 2560,,

[User Application Files]
"nsc_ask_mdb" = 4,nsc_ask.mdb,,,, 1994-02-06,,,, !READONLY,,,,,, 15728
"nsc_ask_ico" = 3,nsc_ask.ico,,,, 1994-02-06,,,, !READONLY,,,,,, 1024,
"nsc_ask_hlp" = 3,nsc_ask.hlp,,,, 1994-02-06,,,, !READONLY,,,,,, 10035

[Workgroup Files]
"wrkadm" = 3,WRKGADM.EXE,,,, 1994-02-06,,,, !READONLY,,,,,, 108032,,,,
```

Fig. 30.12 Part of the SETUP.INF script file.

- *SETUP.STF* also is read by ACMSETUP.EXE and controls how the files are installed. Figure 30.13 shows two parts of the SETUP.STF file created by the Setup Wizard. (Intervening lines are indicated by an ellipsis.)

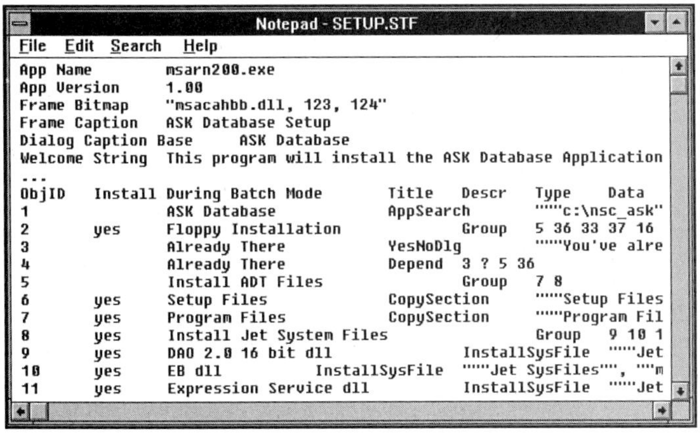

```
App Name          msarn200.exe
App Version       1.00
Frame Bitmap      "msacahbb.dll, 123, 124"
Frame Caption     ASK Database Setup
Dialog Caption Base      ASK Database
Welcome String    This program will install the ASK Database Application
...
ObjID   Install During Batch Mode      Title   Descr   Type    Data
1               ASK Database           AppSearch       """"c:\nsc_ask"
2       yes     Floppy Installation            Group   5 36 33 37 16
3               Already There          YesNoDlg        """"You've alre
4               Already There          Depend  3 ? 5 36
5               Install ADT Files              Group   7 8
6       yes     Setup Files            CopySection     """"Setup Files
7       yes     Program Files          CopySection     """"Program Fil
8       yes     Install Jet System Files       Group   9 10 1
9       yes     DAO 2.0 16 bit dll             InstallSysFile  """"Jet
10      yes     EB dll          InstallSysFile """"Jet SysFiles""", """m
11      yes     Expression Service dll         InstallSysFile  """"Jet
```

Fig. 30.13 Two parts of the SETUP.STF script file.

It is a relatively simple matter to customize the STFSETUP.IN_ script created by the Access 1.1 ADK's Setup Wizard to accommodate additional files and to customize the installation process. Figures 30.11 through 30.13 give evidence that customizing the scripts by editing the SETUP.??? script files is not for the faint of heart. Fortunately, the limitation on the number of files you can add imposed by Access 1.1's ADK has been lifted with Access 2.0, so you can install a large number of special files in the directories pointed to by the Setup Wizard's. If any of your files must be installed in directories other than the application's directory, \WINDOWS, or \WINDOWS\SYSTEM, you need to edit the script file. To do so requires Microsoft documentation for the script file formats that is not included in the *Advanced Topics* manual.

> **Note**
>
> When this edition was written, information on the new setup script file formats had not been published by Microsoft. You can expect this information to appear on the CD-ROMs distributed to members of the Microsoft Developer's Network (MSDN) during 1994. Search for the SETUP topic with the Title Text Only check box marked to determine if the MSDN CD-ROM contains the required information.

From Here...

Refer to the following chapters to learn more about the subjects discussed in this chapter:

- Chapter 25, "Securing Multiuser Network Applications," describes the entries in your *APPNAME*.INI file required for users to share a common SYSTEM.MDA file.

- Chapter 26, "Connecting to Client-Server Databases," provides information on the content of the ODBC.INI and OCBCINST.INI files that you need to include when your application is a front-end for a client-server database.

- Chapter 29, "Exchanging Data with OLE Automation and DDE," lists the files that are required to be supplied on distribution disks for applications that use OLE Custom Controls.

Chapter 31

Adding On-Line Help for Users

On-line Help is an indispensable element of the Access applications you create for others to use, especially if the applications are complex. Users of Windows applications are reported to take advantage of on-line Help more frequently than those using the same applications under DOS. The reason is undoubtedly the easy-to-use WinHelp engine, as well as its navigation and search features.

This chapter explains how to create Windows Help files to provide context-sensitive Help for your applications. To create Help files, you need a word processing application that creates Rich Text Format (.RTF) files, such as Word for Windows 2.0+. (.RTF is a method of including formatting instructions with text in a readable ASCII file; .RTF is described in "Taking a Brief Look at the Rich Text Format" later in this chapter.) You also need HC31.EXE, the Microsoft Help compiler that converts the .RTF files to a form readable by the Windows 3.1 Help engine, WinHelp. HC31.EXE is not included with Access but is included with the Access Developer's Toolkit (ADT) and the Professional Edition of Visual Basic 2.0. Recent versions of most language compilers designed for creating Windows applications, such as Microsoft Visual C++ and Borland C++, also include HC31.EXE.

> **Note**
>
> Word for Windows 2.0 is used in the examples of this chapter because many of the help-authoring tools that were available when this edition was written were designed for use with Word for Windows 2.0. Updated versions of all help-authoring tools designed to take advantage of the features of Word 6.0 are likely to be available by the time you read this edition.

In this chapter, you learn to

- Use a typical help authoring tool to create help files

- Add ContextID values for context-sensitive on-line help

- Add bit-mapped images to help files

- Create a Program Information File for the help compiler

- Compile your help file with the Microsoft Help Compiler

VIII

Completing Applications

> **Note**
>
> The information in this chapter is intended to be a supplement to, not a substitute for, the *Help Compiler Guide* or other documentation accompanying HC31.EXE, the Microsoft Help compiler application. That documentation also deals with advanced topics such as Help macros, which are not covered in this chapter.

Understanding How the WinHelp Engine Works

The WinHelp engine, WINHELP.EXE, is used by all applications to display the contents of Help files. WINHELP.EXE contains a single function, WinHelp(), whose arguments determine the name of the Help file to use and the topic to display. WinHelp files are a special type of file, with the extension .HLP, designed for use with the WinHelp engine. WinHelp files are created from .RTF files that use special codes, embedded as footnote markers, to create indexes to topics. These indexes then are used by WinHelp() to locate the topics in the file, find keyword search entries, enable the user to browse topics in sequence, and create a history of the Help screens viewed by the user.

The techniques for creating Help files that use WinHelp features are explained in this chapter. However, first you need to understand the features of the WinHelp engine, and how links between help topics are created. These subjects are included in two sections that follow.

Using the Features of the WinHelp Engine

Creating Help files for Windows applications is a more complex process than writing Help text files for DOS applications. You need to create an .RTF file with special topic, browsing, and keyword entries; create a *project file* (also called a *make file*); and then compile your .RTF files to WinHelp.HLP with the Help compiler.

With the WinHelp engine, you have much more flexibility than you have with the simple text files that you use for Help for DOS-based database management applications. WinHelp enables you to illustrate your Help files with bit maps and meta files, add music or sound to the Help windows, and format your text in any typeface and font available on the user's computer. This chapter shows you how to create WinHelp files that use the following methods to display Help windows explaining specific topics:

■ *Context strings* enable you to use *hot spots* to display a window identified by the context string. Hot spots add hypertext-like capabilities to your application's Help system. (Hypertext is explained in the next section, "Understanding Hypertext Links in Help Files.") Context strings are names that identify a particular Help window. When the user clicks a green hot spot with which a context string is associated, a new Help window identified by the context string appears. You can choose between conventional nonmodal windows for Help text and graphics and modal pop-up windows that usually provide definitions of terms.

■ *Keywords* assigned to a topic enable the user to search the WinHelp file for other topics that include the same word in a keyword list. A list box of all topics identified with the chosen keyword enables the user, rather than the WinHelp file, to make the navigation decisions.

■ *Browse-sequence numbers* establish the sequence in which windows for topics appear when the user clicks the << and >> buttons of the Help window.

■ *Context-sensitive Help* uses context ID numbers coupled to the context strings associated with individual topics. You can specify the WinHelp file to be used for a form or report by assigning the file name to the Help File property of a form or report or a control object on a form or report. Then you assign the context ID value to the Help Context ID property of a control object. You select the control to give it the focus, press the F1 key, and the Help window with the designated topic appears.

Context strings, keywords, browse-sequence numbers, and context ID numbers are placed in footnotes in the Help text files. The Help compiler uses the footnote text to create the indexes needed to make the WinHelp file operable.

Understanding Hypertext Links in Help Files

Hypertext was invented to make related items in complex documents easily accessible. A table of contents presents the topics of a book in an orderly, linear form, telling you where to find topics from the front to the back of the book. Hypertext works differently. Hypertext links are nonlinear and are similar to the nonclustered indexes for database tables described in Chapter 23, "Exploring Relational Database Design and Implementation." Hypertext links, also called *jumps*, save you the trouble of looking up the topic in the index and turning to the appropriate pages. The green hot spots of the Access

VIII

Completing Applications

Help windows are hypertext links to other related topics. These related topics have hot spots that link to even more related topics. Glossary-type hot spots provide jumps to definitions of unfamiliar terms in a pop-up window.

Planning Help Files for Your Applications

Creating a Help file is much like writing a book. You determine your intended audience, develop a master outline of the parts of the Help system, and then fill in the lower outline levels of each part with the topic titles covering each aspect of your application. This process creates the hierarchy of your Help file. Finally, you add the text for each topic, written to accommodate the user's level of familiarity with computers in general, the operating system in use, and similar applications. With the advent of the CD-ROM, you can expect Help files to grow to encyclopedic length. Microsoft's Multimedia Works and Lotus's SmartHelp for Lotus 1-2-3 for Windows are early examples of this trend—the Help files are contained in CD-ROM tracks and consist of 500M to 600M of text and images.

The Help file and your application's operating manual usually cover much of the same material. A good Help file can reduce by more than half the time needed to prepare printed documentation. You can use standardized Help files for various, related applications because WinHelp can find topics in any file that you include in your final Help file list.

Build your Help file as you develop the Access application. One of the advantages of this approach is that you can evaluate the application's ease of use. If you can explain a step clearly in a paragraph or two of a Help file, the user probably will understand what you intend; otherwise, consider altering the application to clarify the actions required of the user. Simultaneous creation of Help files also aids in eliminating the omission of important topics. The topic you forget to include in your WinHelp file is always the one that users don't understand. Another benefit is the Help file's capability to document your application as you proceed with its development. When you return to writing code after your vacation, use the Help file to refresh your recollection of what the application was intended to accomplish and to remind you of where you were when you left.

Aiming at the User's Level of Expertise

You should direct the structure and contents of your Help file to the experience level of your audience, not only with computers in general and

Windows in particular, but also with applications that are similar to the one you are creating. If you are developing a database front end for your firm, for example, your users may be experienced data entry persons or management colleagues who are familiar with the terminology of your industry and the content of your databases. But what happens when a temporary replaces your vacationing data entry person, and you are in Teaneck training sales representatives?

Users can be classified within five basic groups with increasing levels of competence:

1. *Computing novice.* A person who has never used a personal computer or who is making the transition from use of a mainframe terminal to a self-contained or networked PC. Special applications often are written for trainees or employees in transition from one job classification to another.

2. *Windows novice.* An individual who is familiar with DOS or uses an Apple Macintosh, but is new to the Windows GUI. Your Help file should include details on effective use of the mouse and keyboard shortcuts. A glossary of Windows terminology is a definite requirement, and diagrams for menu choices are Helpful. Simple diagrams created with the Microsoft Draw applet usually suffice.

3. *Application novice.* One who is experienced with Windows but not with the type of application you are creating. An example is a word processing operator assigned to use your database front end. You may not need to include information on how to use the keyboard and mouse for these users.

4. *Application-familiar user.* A person who is familiar with Windows and the type of application you are developing. Such a person may be a data entry operator who regularly uses the database features of a Windows spreadsheet application, or an executive who has used applications developed with a client-server front end for Windows. The Help file need only explain those elements of the application that are not intuitive or that differ from commercial implementations of similar applications. You may be able to dispense with printed documentation for application-familiar users.

5. *Power user.* A person who does not read the documentation or use your Help file. Power users believe no application has ever left the beta stage. They find warts (anomalies) and bugs in version 7.6 of your application.

VIII

Completing Applications

The first four classifications require distinctly different contents in their Help files. One way of accomplishing this differentiation is to create a different Help file for each user level and supply the appropriate file or include a dialog to select the appropriate Help file at startup. An alternative is to create a single Help file and change the topic name of the entry point in the file for each subject at different skill levels. You can create a browse sequence to enable the user to obtain information about the subject at a higher or lower level of detail.

Examining the Standard Structure of Help Topics

Most Help files are arranged in a structure corresponding to the basic subject matter covered by the application and include assistance to users in the translation of menu commands. The structure of a typical Help file for a full-scale Access application appears in figure 31.1. Solid lines show the topic selection paths in a linear, hierarchical structure. Topic windows comprise the lowest level of the hierarchy. Dashed lines show nonlinear, hypertext links.

Fig. 31.1
A sample Help file structure for an order entry and billing application.

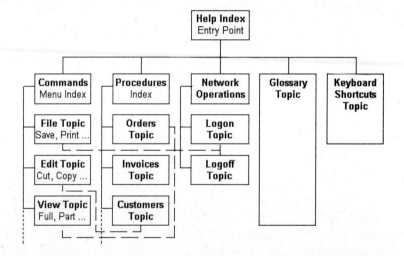

In this example, the Commands Menu Index and Procedures Index are secondary indexes that list the topics within each category and provide quick access to a specific topic. Individual topics in different categories, however, may be related, so they are joined by dashed lines in figure 31.1. The dashed lines do not follow the usual top-to-bottom sequence in a category of related topics. You can provide hot spots to create cross-category jumps or use common keywords that give the user quick access to a related topic in another category.

All Help files have an entry point, usually called a *Help Index*, which is where you select the Help category you want. In some cases, selecting a category, such as Commands, leads to another Help window that enables you to access commands through the main menu. You choose the command for which you need Help, and a window appears explaining the command. You make choices in Index windows and receive Help, textual or graphic, in topic windows.

If you plan to create a number of related applications, you may want to create individual Help files for each category or for a particular category that is the same for all the applications. As an example, if you are writing a number of database front ends for your firm, the glossary portion of the Help file may be the same for all applications. You therefore can create the glossary as a separate .RTF file and then compile it with other .RTF files written specifically for the particular applications. The project file for the Help compiler, described in this chapter's section "Creating the Project File," can include as many .RTF Help files as you want to include in the compiled WinHelp .HLP file.

Creating the Text for Help Files

As mentioned at the beginning of this chapter, you must create Windows Help files in a word processing application that exports files in Rich Text Format (.RTF) and is capable of creating hidden text. Alternatively, you can manually add the required .RTF control words and symbols to unformatted text with a conventional text editor such as Windows Notepad, but this process is extremely laborious. Word for Windows 2.0, Microsoft Word 6.0, Ami Pro, and WordPerfect for Windows provide .RTF export capability.

The following paragraphs take a look at the Rich Text Format needed for Help files and familiarize you with many of the common codes used in a Help file. Then you learn how to create Help files by using a commercial Help authoring system and by building the Help file manually.

Taking a Brief Look at the Rich Text Format

.RTF (rich text format) is a Microsoft Corporation standard for interprocess communication (IPC) transfer of formatted text and graphics. .RTF is a valid Windows Clipboard format for many applications. You can use .RTF files for IPC transfers between Windows applications and DOS, OS/2, or Apple Macintosh applications created by Microsoft and many other software publishers.

An .RTF file consists of control words, symbols, and groups combined with unformatted text in ANSI (Windows), PC-8 (used by Hewlett-Packard laser printers), Macintosh, or IBM PC character sets. An .RTF file of the first two sentences of the preceding paragraph (less most of the header section added by Word for Windows) appears as

```
\paperw12240\paperh31680\margl1800\margr1800\margt1440
\margb1440\gutter0\deftab360\widowctrl\ftnbj{\*\templa
te F:\\WINWORD2\\QUE_BOOK.DOT}\sectd \linex0\endnhere
\pard\plain \qj\fi504\sa120\keep \f4\fs21\lang1033
.RTF (rich text format) is a Microsoft Corporation standard for
interprocess communication (IPC) transfer of formatted text and
graphics. .RTF is a valid Windows Clipboard format for many
applications.\par
```

A backslash character precedes .RTF control words and symbols, which are used to indicate text formatting. Double backslashes are used to include a backslash in the text. The original version of *Microsoft Word for Windows Technical Reference*, published by Microsoft Press to accompany Word for Windows 1.0+ versions, includes a complete description of the format of .RTF files. .RTF is not discussed in *Using WordBasic*, a manual offered by Microsoft with the purchase of Word for Windows 2.0+. Fortunately, you do not need a full understanding of .RTF syntax to write Windows Help files.

Examining the Basic Elements of Help Files

Windows Help files consist of a combination of formatted text, double-underlined hot spots that specify hypertext jumps, single-underlined hot spots for pop-up windows, footnote symbols and text, and hidden text. Footnote symbols serve as codes to tell HC31.EXE how to use the information included in the footnotes and hidden text. Context strings (hidden text used to identify hot spots), footnote symbols, and footnote text do not appear in the Help window viewed by the user. Table 31.1 lists common footnote codes.

Table 31.1 Common Footnote Codes Used in .RTF Help Documents		
Help Element	**Footnote Code**	**Description**
Context string	#	Identifies each topic in a Help file. Context strings are optional and are used by WinHelp to find a specific topic when the user initiates a jump to it.
Topic title	$	Displays topics in the dialogs for the Search and History buttons, as well as those topics marked by using the Bookmark menu.

Help Element	Footnote Code	Description
Keyword	K	Provides entries for lists that appear in the Search dialog, enabling the user to jump to any topic that contains the keyword.
Browse sequence	+	Displays groups of topics in a predetermined sequence. These topics are accessed in sequence by the << and >> buttons of the Help menu.

Each of the commonly used .RTF codes for WinHelp files is described in table 31.2. Lowercase codes shown in bold type are .RTF formatting instructions (**v** stands for hidden text, for example).

Table 31.2 Common .RTF Codes Used in .RTF Help Documents		
Help Element	**.RTF Code**	**Description**
Jump	**uldb** *JumpText* **v** *TopicName*	Links related topics in a manner similar to hypertext. When the user clicks a coded word or bit map, *JumpText*, WinHelp moves to *TopicName*. You identify a jump by double-underlining the text. With HC31.EXE, users can jump to topics in different files.
Pop-up window topic	**ul** *JumpText* **v** *TopicName*	Displays the text identified by *TopicName* in a modal dialog when the user clicks a single-underlined hot spot, *JumpText,* in the Help file.
16-color bit-map reference	bmc *picture.ext*	Inserts a 16-color bit map (BMP or DIB) or meta-file (WMF) image, *picture.ext,* into a Help file. Images are positioned as if they were characters or may

(continues)

Help Element	.RTF Code	Description
		be formatted with optional parameters. You also may copy a bit map to the Clipboard with CopyBmp if the bit map is identified as a hot spot. (If you are using Word for Windows, you can simply use Insert Picture to insert the bit map in the text.)
Nonscrolling region	\keepn	Keeps a region containing text immediately below the menu bar from scrolling with the balance of the text when the scroll bar is used.
Nonwrapping text	\keep	(Keep with next formatting.) Prevents an area of the screen from wrapping if the user reduces the width of the Help window. This option is frequently used with tabular information.
Embedded window	ew ...	Enables the display of 256-color bit maps or animation sequences and can play sound files.

Depending on the Windows word processing program (and its version) that you use, the program usually inserts most or all of the preceding codes when you save a file as an .RTF file. You can use many other codes in addition to those shown in tables 31.1 and 31.2 when authoring WinHelp files, but the use of special-purpose codes is beyond the scope of this book. The documentation accompanying the Help compiler explains the use of special-purpose codes not listed here.

Using Commercial Help Authoring Systems to Create Help Files

You can speed up the process of creating Help files by using a commercial Help authoring system. One example is RoboHelp, which is offered by Blue Sky Software Corporation of La Jolla, California. Specifically designed for use with Word for Windows 2.0+, RoboHelp uses a sophisticated template, ROBOHELP.DOT, and includes the additional files required to automate the Help file-creation process. In the following sections, you learn how to use these templates to Help you create your Help files.

Using the RoboHelp Template

The main advantage of using a commercial Help authoring system is that you can create WinHelp files quickly. RoboHelp also does most of the housekeeping for you, such as adding footnotes and assigning Help context strings, which can save up to 50 percent of the time needed to create a Help file.

To create a Help file with RoboHelp, follow these steps:

1. Launch Word for Windows, open the **F**ile menu, and choose **N**ew. The Use Template dialog appears.

2. Choose the ROBOHELP template from the Word 5 Use Template list box; then choose OK or press Enter. The Save File As dialog appears.

3. Save the file with the name that you want to give your Help file— **NWIND**, for example. This step establishes the name of your Help file as a variable in the RoboHelp macro.

   RoboHelp automatically inserts the Help Index topic for you when you start a new Help file and opens its Help Index window.

4. Click RoboHelp's Topic button to add a topic to the Help Index window. RoboHelp displays an Insert New Help Topic dialog.

5. Click the Advanced >> button to display additional data about the topic in the New Help Topic dialog.

6. Enter the topic title, such as **Commands**, in the Topic Title text box. RoboHelp automatically adds the same title to the Search Word(s) text box, as shown in figure 31.2. You can add more search words if you prefer; separate each word from the preceding word with a semicolon. Search words appear in the list box in the Search dialog that appears when you choose **S**earch from the **H**elp menu.

   RoboHelp creates entries in the Context String, Browse Sequence, and Build Tag text boxes. The browse-sequence numbers are incremented by 5 each time you add a topic. Choose OK, and RoboHelp adds a hard page break and the new topic title, Commands, to a new page.

Fig. 31.2

RoboHelp's dialog
for adding a new
Help topic.

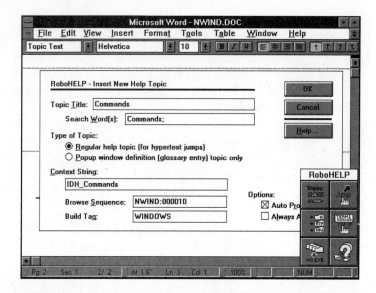

7. Position the caret on the line in the Help Index page where you want to create the hot spot for the new topic (Commands, in this example). Click the Jump button to create a hypertext link between the hot spot and the topic. The Create New Hypertext Jump to Help Topic dialog appears.

8. In the Click Text text box, enter the text that you want the user to click (or select with the Tab key) to display the Help window for the Help topic; **Commands** is a good choice for this example. Choose the context string (IDH_Commands, in this example) from the Jump To list box. (The IDH_ prefix is an abbreviation for Index Help.) Your completed Create New Hypertext Jump to Help Topic dialog appears as shown in figure 31.3.

   You can create as many levels in your Help file structure as you want by repeating this step to add new subtopics to the main topic (Commands, in this example). Figure 31.4, for example, shows the beginning of a Help file with a three-level hierarchy—index, category, and topic—based on the structure of figure 31.1 at the beginning of this chapter. The footnotes that RoboHelp creates for you are shown in the Footnotes pane of figure 31.4. The footnote that uses the asterisk (*) symbol is called the *build tag*, which enables you to compile the Help file with or without topics identified by the build tag. The use of build tags is optional.

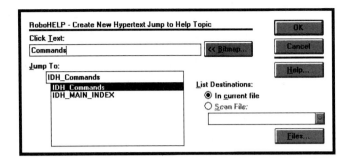

Fig. 31.3
The Create New
Hypertext Jump to
Help Topic dialog.

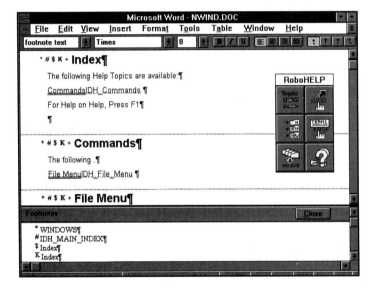

Fig. 31.4
The beginning of a
Help file in Word
for Windows 2.0+.

VIII

Completing Applications

9. Add the Help text to your topic. You can add bit-map graphics files, drawings created in Microsoft Draw, or other objects created by OLE servers by choosing **P**icture or **O**bject from Word's **I**nsert menu and then selecting the appropriate graphics file or object.

10. When you have created the basic structure of your Help system, choose Save and **G**enerate Code from Word's **F**ile menu. RoboHelp adds several of its own menu items to Word's **F**ile, **E**dit, **V**iew, **I**nsert, and **T**ools menus.

11. Enter a descriptive title, such as **Northwind Traders Help System**, when RoboHelp requests a title for the title bar of your Help windows.

RoboHelp has created NWIND.RTF, the file that serves as the source code for your NWIND.HLP file. To use HC31.EXE to compile NWIND.RTF to NWIND.HLP, follow these steps:

1. Click the HC.EXE button, or choose **M**ake Help System from the **F**ile menu. RoboHelp runs HC31.EXE in a DOS window from a PIF file that is created when you install RoboHelp.

2. Click the Run Help button, or choose **R**un the Help System from the **F**ile menu. Your new WinHelp file appears. Figure 31.5 shows the Help window created from the sample structure given in figure 31.1.

Fig. 31.5
A Help window created with the aid of RoboHelp.

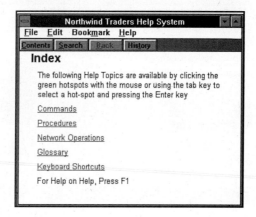

From this Help file, you can click the green Commands hot spot to display the topic, such as File Menu, that you entered at lower levels in the hierarchy.

RoboHelp takes most of the drudgery out of creating a WinHelp file, but the organization and contents of the file are up to you. RoboHelp does not include HC31.EXE, so you need to purchase it or a compiler that includes it, such as Visual Basic 2.0.

Creating Help Text Files Manually

Using RoboHelp or the VBHELP.DOT template to write WinHelp files is convenient but not necessary. You can create your text file with any Windows word processor that creates .RTF files, with any template, and in any format you want. The rules for inserting footnotes and codes, designating hot spots, and separating individual topics with page breaks are described in the steps that follow.

To create a Help file manually, using Word for Windows 2.0 and beginning with the index, follow these steps:

1. Choose **N**ew from Word for Windows' **F**ile menu and choose the template you want to use for your Help file text. Choose the Normal template if you have not created a template for Help files.

> **Note**
>
> When creating Help text files with Word for Windows 2.0, choose **O**ptions from the **T**ools menu and click the View button. Choose the Hidden Text, Paragraph Marks, Tabs, Line Breaks and Fonts as Printed, and Table Grid lines check boxes to mark them. You need to view hidden text entries, and the other settings aid you in formatting the text. Choose Page Set**u**p from the Forma**t** menu and then click the Size and Orientation option button. Set the height to 22 inches, the maximum allowed by Word. You then can create long topics without inserting soft page breaks. Space paragraphs 0.5 lines apart by choosing **P**aragraph from the Forma**t** menu and then clicking Before or After so that .5 appears in the text box. Using half a line instead of inserting a full line between paragraphs not only saves space in the screen, but also improves readability.

2. Choose Foot**n**ote from the **I**nsert menu. The Footnote dialog appears.

3. In the **C**ustom Footnote Mark text box, type **$**, the symbol used to identify the title of the topic (see fig. 31.6). The purpose of the footnote symbols is described in table 31.1, in the earlier section, "Examining the Basic Elements of Help Files."

Fig. 31.6
The Word for Windows Footnote dialog.

4. The footnote pane opens with the caret positioned after the $ footnote symbol. Enter the title of the topic, **Index**.

5. Repeat steps 2 through 4, substituting the # footnote symbol in the Custom Footnote Mark text box to indicate a context string and then entering the context string **IDH_MAIN_INDEX**. (The context strings used in this example follow RoboHelp conventions; IDH is an abbreviation for Index Help.)

6. Repeat steps 2 through 4, substituting the **K** footnote symbol that denotes members of the keywords list. Then enter **Index;Help;** as the footnote text.

7. Repeat steps 2 through 4 again, entering the + footnote symbol and then a browse-sequence number in the footnote pane. Enter a number with a low value for the index, such as **000005**. The leading zeroes, used by RoboHelp, are optional. You can precede the browse-sequence number with a Help file name and a colon, as in NWIND:000005, to identify the .RTF file if you are using more than one file.

8. Enter the text for your Help window, beginning with the title, **Index**, and then entering the text that explains how to use the Help index. Enter the names of each topic that you want to create hot-spot jumps for, each on a separate line, but do not apply special formatting to these names yet.

9. Each topic that comprises an individual window in a Help text file needs to be separated from the next topic by a hard page break. When you have completed the text portion of your Help Index window, press Ctrl+Enter (or choose **B**reak from the **I**nsert menu, and then choose **P**age Break). The hard page break causes the footnote markers in the text ($, #, K, and +) to be associated only with the index topic. Soft page breaks do not divide topics. Figure 31.7 shows an example of how your Help window might look.

10. Create the additional category index and topic Help windows that you need by repeating steps 2 through 9, substituting body and footnote text appropriate to the topic. When you are writing Help files manually, you first create the topic text and then add the formatting and context ID strings to create the hypertext links between the topics.

Now you need to create the hypertext links to the topic names that you added for each category in step 8 of the preceding example. To create hot spots and the links, follow these steps:

1. Add the context ID string of the topic to which you want to link immediately after the name of the topic in the text of the index page. As an example, type **CommandsIDH_Commands**, as your first entry in which Commands is the hot spot and IDH_Commands is the context string.

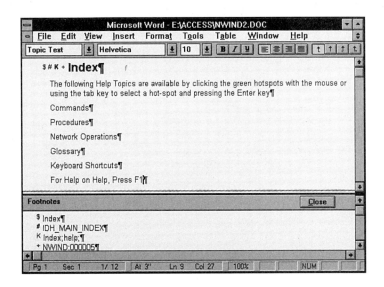

Fig. 31.7

A Help topic page prior to applying formatting.

VIII

2. Select (highlight) the name of the topic—Commands, for example— and press Ctrl+D to add the double-underline attribute.

3. Select the context ID string and press Ctrl+H to make the context ID string hidden text.

4. Repeat steps 1 through 3 for each of the names of the topics for which you want jumps. When you complete your entries for the Index topic, the index page appears as shown in figure 31.8.

The double-underlined text shown in figure 31.8 indicates a hot-spot jump to the topic identified by the context ID that follows, formatted as hidden text. The hot spot appears in green underlined type when you execute the Help file. Hidden text does not display. The footnote text contains the indexing information that HC31.EXE uses to create the required hypertext links, browse sequences, and keyword lists that the user can search.

You can substitute a pop-up window for a hypertext jump by formatting a word with the single-underline attribute and then adding a hidden-text context string immediately after the word. Single-underlined text appears in the Help window, green and without the underline. After you (or the users for whom you have created the Help file) click this type of hot spot, the topic appears in a modal window. Clicking the pop-up window makes it disappear.

Fig. 31.8

The Help index page after hot spots have been formatted.

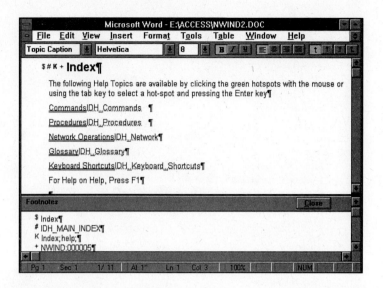

When you have completed your entries to the point where you want to test the Help file with your application, follow these steps:

1. Choose **S**ave from Word for Windows' **F**ile menu to save your Help file in Word format.

2. Choose Save **A**s from the **F**ile menu.

3. Choose Rich Text Format from the Save File As Type drop-down list.

4. Give your file the same name as the database file with which it is to be used, **NWIND** for example, and add the .RTF extension.

   The Save As dialog appears, as shown in figure 31.9.

5. Choose OK to save your file.

Creating the Help project file and running HC31.EXE to compile your WinHelp file, the next two tasks needed to complete the Help file-creation process, are covered in "Compiling Your Help Files," later in this chapter.

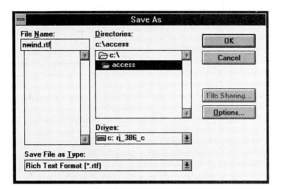

Fig. 31.9

The Save As dialog for a Rich Text Format text file.

Adding Illustrations to Your Help Files

You can use the (**bmc** *BitmapName*) tab, formatted as hidden text, to incorporate a bit map into your Help file by reference. Inserting a bit map directly into your Word for Windows Help document, however, is a much simpler process. If you have a commercial screen capture application, such as Inner Media's Collage Plus or Horizon Technologies' SnagIt, you can use it to create .BMP files of your application's windows that you then can insert into Help topic windows. Otherwise, you can use Windows Paintbrush to create the .BMP illustrations. First you need to retrieve the image you want to use. Follow these steps:

1. Set up the application that includes the image you want and display the image. If the window is less than one full screen, minimize any windows that appear underneath it to provide a neutral gray background, and position the window you want to copy at the upper left corner of the display.

2. Press the Print Screen key to copy the entire display to the Clipboard.

With the image in your Clipboard, you're ready to use Paintbrush to edit the image and add it to your Help file. Follow these steps:

1. Launch Windows Paintbrush, and choose **P**aste from the **E**dit menu to copy the Clipboard image to Paintbrush's editing window. A dashed line surrounds the image, indicating that the entire image is selected.

◀ "Using Visio Express to Add a Vector-Based Image to a Form or Report," p. 745

◀ "Editing the Logo with Windows Paintbrush," p. 742

VIII

Completing Applications

2. Click anywhere within the screen image, and while holding down the left mouse button, drag the image diagonally downward about one-fourth inch to expose a blank margin at the top and left edges of the image.

3. Click the blank margin to deselect the image. The dashed selection lines disappear.

4. Using the Scissors tool with the rectangular box, drag a selection box around the area you want to incorporate in the illustration, as shown in figure 31.10. Because enclosing precisely the area you want to save is difficult, add a margin to be edited (cropped) later.

Fig. 31.10
Selecting the bit-map image to copy to a file.

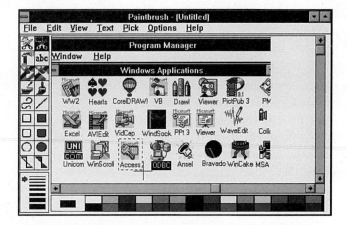

5. Choose Copy To from the Edit menu to save your bit map in a file. The Copy To dialog appears.

6. In the File Name text box, enter the path to your Help file and the file name for the bit map (with the extension .BMP), as shown in figure 31.11. Do not use the Save or Save As command of the File menu; these commands save the entire image.

7. Choose New from the File menu and do not save the existing image.

8. Choose Paste From from the Edit menu and enter the path and file name you used in step 6. You paste the image, rather than open the file, so that you can position the image where you want it in Paintbrush's editing window.

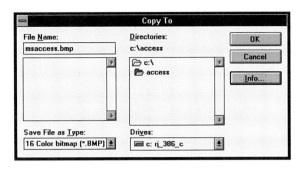

Fig. 31.11
Copying the selected bit-map image to a 16-color .BMP file.

9. Edit the image as required. You can use Paintbrush's line and text tools to add callouts or to modify the image.

10. When you are satisfied with the illustration, use the Scissors tool to enclose the area you want to save. Choose C**o**py To from the **E**dit menu. In the Copy To dialog, enter the path to your Help file and the file name for the bit map (with the extension .BMP).

To add the bit-map image to your Help file, open the Help file in Word for Windows and position the caret where you want to place the bit map. Choose **P**icture from the **I**nsert menu and double-click the name of your bit-map file. Figure 31.12 shows an example of a Help Page file with a bit-map icon for Access added at the top of the window.

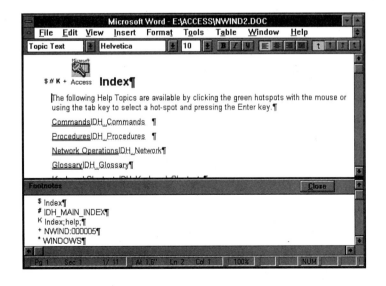

Fig. 31.12
The Help topic page with a bit-map icon added.

When you compile your WinHelp file with HC31.EXE (see "Using the Help Compiler" later in this chapter), the image you inserted appears as shown in figure 31.13.

Fig. 31.13
The WinHelp
window displaying
the Access icon.

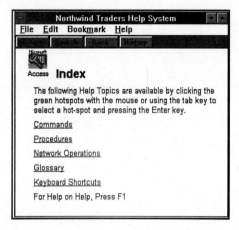

You also can insert drawings in the form of Windows meta files (.WMFs). If you have Microsoft Draw and HC31.EXE, you can import the bit-map file, add callouts or other graphic elements to it, and embed the resulting .WMF file in your text or add a {**bmp** ... } reference to it.

Compiling Your Help Files

As you have learned in this chapter, Windows requires that you compile .RTF files to a specific format with the Microsoft Help compiler. If you want to use Word for Windows 2.0, incorporate tables in your Help files, or use the other new WinHelp 3.1 features described in the preceding sections, you must use a Help compiler that has a version number of 3.10 or higher. You can determine the version number by running the compiler without command line parameters.

In the sections that follow, you learn how to create a Help project file, use the Help project file with the Help compiler, and understand error messages you may receive from the Help compiler.

Creating the Project File

Before you can create, using the Help compiler, a WinHelp.HLP file from your .RTF file, you need to create a project file. This file provides instructions that tell HC.EXE or HC31.EXE which files to compile and which indexes you want the Help compiler to create. Project files are similar in concept to the .MAK files of Visual Basic and C compilers.

The Help compiler uses a project file with the extension .HPJ, such as HELPFILE.HPJ. The compiled Help file has the same name as the project file, but with the extension HLP, as in HELPFILE.HLP. You create Help project files with a standard text editor such as Windows Notepad. The only entry *required* in the project file for a simple WinHelp file is the FILES section header, enclosed in square brackets and followed by the names of your .RTF files on separate lines, as in this example:

```
[FILES]
hlpfile1.rtf
hlpfile2.rtf
hlpfile3.rtf
```

You need to enter the full path to the files if you do not set the path with the ROOT= line in the [OPTIONS] section of your Help project file. The sections that you may include in your Help project file, and some of the common [OPTIONS] keywords used, are listed in table 31.3. Values shown for [OPTIONS] keywords in the table are those most commonly used in creating conventional WinHelp files. (You also can include comments in the Help project file by preceding each comment line with a semicolon.)

VIII

Completing Applications

Table 31.3 Required and Optional Sections of a Help Project File		
Section of File	**Required?**	**Description**
[OPTIONS]	No	Defines any options required to control the Help compilation process. Some of the more common options include the following:
OPTIONS Keywords		
	ROOT=d:\path	Defines the path to your Help files.
	INDEX=ContextString	Sets the context string for the index topic. Valid only when you're using HC.EXE (Windows 3.0).

(continues)

Table 31.3 Continued		
Section of File	**Required?**	**Description**
	CONTENTS=*ContextString*	Sets the context string for the index topic with the Windows 3.1 Help compiler, HC31.EXE.
	TITLE=*AppName Help*	Sets the title for the Help file, which appears in the Help title bar.
	ICON=*IconFile.ICO*	Sets the icon that is displayed when the Help window is minimized.
	COMPRESS=0 ¦ FALSE	Controls file compression. 0, or False, means do not compress files. 1, or True, compresses the file. Compressing .HLP files saves disk space at the expense of speed in displaying Help windows (due to the time required to decompress the file). HC31.EXE supports varying degrees of compression.
	WARNING=3	Determines what errors are reported. 0 through 3 control the level of error reporting: 0 = no error reports; 1 = most severe warnings; 2 = intermediate warning level; and 3 = report all warnings.
	REPORT=1|ON	Determines whether progress reports of the compilation are provided. 1, or On, = Report progress of compile; 0, or Off, = no report.
[FILES]	Yes	Specifies the Help files included in the compilation.
[BUILD]	No	Specifies topics to include in or exclude from the compiled file.
[BUILDTAGS]	No	Names valid build tags, enabling the selection of topics to be compiled within a file.

Section of File	Required?	Description
[CONFIG]	Yes, if DLLS	Registers DLLs used with WinHelp macros in the Help file. Must include the BrowseButtons macro if they are to appear in the Help menu bar.
[BITMAPS]	No	Specifies bit-map files used in the compilation and not inserted into the text of your Help document. This element is required if you used the ROOT option to specify the path to the files.
[MAP]	No	Associates context strings with context ID numbers. You need a map section to use the Context ID property of Access forms, reports, and control objects.
[ALIAS]	No	Assigns more than one context string to a subject.
[WINDOWS]	No	Describes the main Help window and any secondary window types in the Help file. HC31.EXE enables you to define the size, placement, and color of Help windows.
[BAGGAGE]	No	Names any additional data files that are to be incorporated within the WinHelp file.

Although only the [FILES] section is needed for simple WinHelp files created with Word for Windows or another Windows words processor, adding the [OPTIONS] section and the following keyword entries to all .HPJ files is common practice:

```
[OPTIONS]
ROOT=c:\access
BUILD=WINDOWS
CONTENTS=IDH_Main_Index (substitute INDEX= for HC.EXE)
TITLE=Northwind Traders Help
WARNING=3
REPORT=1
```

VIII

Completing Applications

The BUILD=WINDOWS line suppresses a noncritical error message that appears if you do not specify a BUILD name. (You can substitute any name you want for WINDOWS.) If you add BUILD=WINDOWS to the [OPTIONS] section to suppress the error message, you need to add another section with the following entries:

```
[BUILDTAGS]
WINDOWS
```

The COMPRESS keyword is optional because COMPRESS=0 is the default value. You change the ROOT, INDEX, and TITLE entries to values that are appropriate to the WinHelp file you are creating.

You need a [MAP] section in your .HPJ file to assign context ID numbers to context strings. The value you assign to Help category and topic windows is discussed in the section that follows. The other sections listed in table 31.3 seldom are required in WinHelp files created with Windows word processing applications.

Adding a *[MAP]* Section for Context ID Numbers

Applications, such as Access and Visual Basic 2.0, that enable you to add context-sensitive Help with Help File and Context ID properties require that you add a [MAP] section to your project file. This procedure enables you to assign a context ID number to each of the Help windows that you want to associate with an object in the application you create. Using the Help File and Context ID properties of Access forms, reports, and control objects is the subject of a following section, "Linking Help Topics to Your Access Application."

The numbers that correspond to context strings can be arbitrary, but following a regular pattern is a good practice. As an example, the .RTF file used as a demonstration in the preceding sections has a Help Index window and four categories of Help windows, as shown in table 31.4. You assign the Index window a low value, such as 1 or 10. You give Help categories numbers such as 100 or 1000 so that you can assign numbers such as 110 to topics belonging to the 100 category. Using even hundreds to identify categories enables you to establish a four-level hierarchy: index, category, subcategory, and topic. Four levels is usually sufficient for even the most complex application. Adding a Help context ID number to the Help Index window lets you set the Help Index window as the context when there is no Help window applicable to the object you select in Access.

Using a Help file-tracking database can assist in preventing duplication of context ID numbers if you assign the Context ID field as the primary key or create a No Duplicates index on the Context ID field.

Table 31.4   Sample Context ID Numbers Assigned to Context Strings

Category Context String	Context ID	Topic Context String	Context ID
IDH_Main_Index	10		
IDH_Commands	100		
IDH_File	110	IDHfile_new	111
		IDHfile_open	113
		IDHfile_close	115
		IDHfile_exit	119
IDH_Edit	120	IDHedit_undo	121
IDH_Procedures	200	IDHproc_orders	211...219
		IDHproc_invs	221...229
		IDHproc_custs	231...239
IDH_Network	300	IDHnet_logon	311
		IDHnet_logoff	321
IDH_Keyboard _Shortcuts	400		

After you determine the context ID values for each of your Help windows, you add the [MAP] section to your Help project file and then add the context ID strings, a space (you also can use a Tab as a separator), and the corresponding context ID value, as in the following example:

```
[MAP]
IDH_Main_Index 10
IDH_Commands 100
IDH_Procedures 200
IDH_Network 300
IDH_Keyboard_Shortcuts 400
```

You can add the lines to complete the context ID assignment for Help topic windows under the category entries or in groups that follow the category assignments; the entries do not need to be in numerical sequence.

Figure 31.14 shows TEST.HPJ, the Help project file used to compile the test version of this chapter's examples, as the file appears in Windows Notepad.

VIII

Completing Applications

Fig. 31.14
The project file
used to create the
TEST.HLP file.

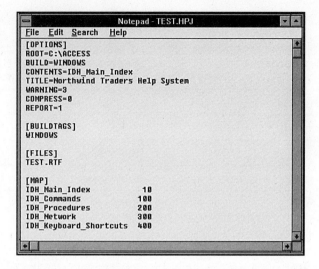

```
[OPTIONS]
ROOT=C:\ACCESS
BUILD=WINDOWS
CONTENTS=IDH_Main_Index
TITLE=Northwind Traders Help System
WARNING=3
COMPRESS=0
REPORT=1

[BUILDTAGS]
WINDOWS

[FILES]
TEST.RTF

[MAP]
IDH_Main_Index            10
IDH_Commands             100
IDH_Procedures           200
IDH_Network              300
IDH_Keyboard_Shortcuts   400
```

Using the Help Compiler

You execute HC31.EXE, a DOS application, from the DOS command line. The
following lines show the two appropriate syntaxes:

```
HC HELPFILE[.HPJ]

HC31 HELPFILE[.HPJ]
```

The file name of the Help project file is a required parameter, but the .HPJ
extension is optional and thus enclosed in brackets in the preceding examples.

The messages displayed by HC31.EXE when you compile the test WinHelp
file with TEST.HPJ are shown in figure 31.15. The message lines describe each
phase of the compilation process as it occurs. If you set Report = 0 or Report =
Off, only the name of the project file appears when you run the Help compiler.

Fig. 31.15
Compiling
TEST.HPJ, with
HC31.EXE and the
REPORT keyword
set to 1.

```
Microsoft (R) Help Compiler Version 3.10.358
Copyright (c) Microsoft Corp 1990 - 1991. All rights reserved.
e:\access\test.HPJ

Compiling file E:\ACCESS\TEST.DOC...
Resolving browse sequences.
Resolving context strings.
Resolving keywords.
```

Creating a Program Information File (PIF) for the Help Compiler

When you are developing a Help file, create an HC.PIF program information file so that you can run the Help compiler in a DOS window. Using a .PIF file and running the Help compiler in a window accelerates the inevitable edit-compile-test sequence when you are creating a new WinHelp file.

To create HC.PIF for HC.EXE or HC31.EXE, follow these steps:

1. Launch the PIF Editor from Program Manager's Accessories group. PIF Editor's dialog appears.

2. Type **hc.exe** or **hc31.exe** in PIF Editor's Program Filename text box. Add the path to the directory in which the Help compiler is located if the directory is not on your path.

3. Type **HC3.0** or **HC3.1** in the Window Title text box, depending on the version of the Help compiler you are using.

4. Type the name of your project file, for example **test.hpj**, in the Optional Parameters text box.

5. Type the name of the directory where your Help project file is located, such as **c:\access**, in the Startup Directory text box, if you are not using RoboHelp, VBHELP.DOT, or another Help file authoring application that supplies the name of the current Help project file as a DOS command line parameter.

6. Type **256** in the KB Required and **384** in the KB Desired text boxes of the Memory Requirements section. HC.EXE and HC31.EXE run in 256K of DOS memory.

7. Click the Windowed option button in the Display Usage section and the Background check box of the Execution section. This second selection allows HC.EXE or HC31.EXE to run while you are using other Windows applications.

8. Mark the Close Window on Exit check box. (If you want the DOS window to remain open to display error messages, do not mark the Close Window on Exit check box.) Your PIF Editor window (for HC31.EXE, not used with a Help file authoring application in this example) appears as shown in figure 31.16.

9. Choose Save **A**s from the **F**ile menu. The Save As dialog appears.

VIII

Completing Applications

10. Type **hc.pif** in the File Name text box (regardless of the version of the Help compiler you are using); then choose OK. PIF Editor saves your file, and the dialog closes.

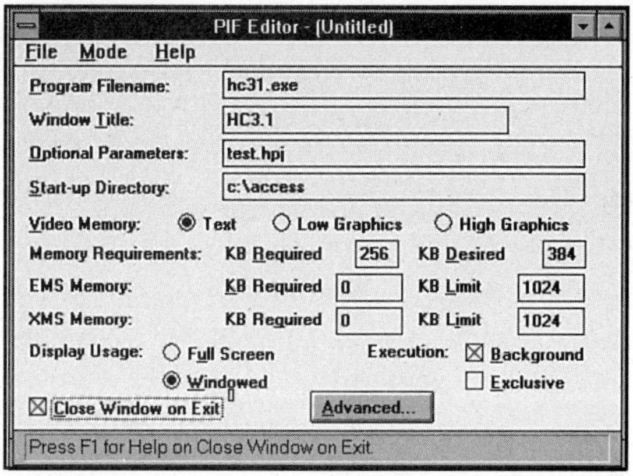

Fig. 31.16
The HC.PIF file
used to run
HC31.EXE in a
DOS window.

Fig. 31.16
The HC.PIF file used to run HC31.EXE in a DOS window.

Now you need to add an icon to run HC.PIF in one of Program Manager's groups. If you have an Access program group, this is a logical place to add the icon for HC.PIF.

To add HC.PIF to your Access program group, follow these steps:

1. Open the Access program group; or if the Access program group is open, click its window to activate it.

2. Choose **N**ew from Program Manager's **F**ile menu. The New Program Object dialog appears.

3. Click the Program Item option button, if it is not selected, and then choose OK. The Program Item Properties dialog appears.

4. Type **Help Compiler 3.1** (or **3.0** if you are using HC.EXE) in the Description text box, and type **hc.pif** in the Command Line text box.

5. Click the Change Icon button. A message box appears advising you that HC.PIF does not have an icon and that you can select one from those supplied with Program Manager.

6. Choose OK; the Change Icon dialog appears.

7. Use the horizontal scroll bar to expose the icon for the Swiss Army knife, or choose another likely candidate from the selection of icons. Click the icon to select it, and then choose OK. The Program Item Properties dialog appears with the icon you selected.

8. Choose OK to add the icon for HC.PIF to your Access program group and close the Program Item Properties dialog. Your Access program group appears as shown in figure 31.17.

9. Double-click the Help Compiler icon to test your HC.PIF file. If you added the BUILD= option and the [BUILDTAGS] section, your HC31.EXE DOS window appears as shown in figure 31.18.

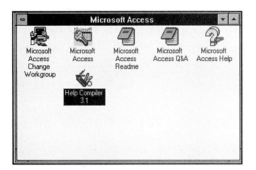

Fig. 31.17
The Microsoft Access program group with the Help compiler icon added.

Fig. 31.18
HC31.EXE compiling TEST.RTF in a DOS window.

If you did not mark the Close Window on Exit check box when you created HC.PIF, remember to use Task Manager (press Ctrl+Esc) and close the inactive windows created by successive compilations of your Help file. In this case, Windows adds a new Help Compiler window each time you compile your Help file.

Examining Help Compiler Error Messages

HC.EXE and HC31.EXE display error messages if errors are encountered in creating the WinHelp file. The sequence number of the topic in the file or the file name that contains the error is included in the error message. If your text file does not contain soft page breaks, the error number corresponds to the page number. Messages that begin with "Error" are fatal. Fatal errors are reported regardless of the value of the REPORT keyword, and no WinHelp file is created. Messages beginning with "Warning" do not prevent the creation of a WinHelp file, but the file may not operate properly. Most Help compiler messages are quite specific in identifying the error in the .RTF file being compiled.

The most typical messages you receive from the Help compiler are the result of typographical errors in context strings. Some of the warning messages (4098 and 4056) you receive as a result of misspelling context strings in the TEST.HPJ file are shown in figure 31.19. If you don't include the BUILD= assignment and the [BUILDTAGS] section, you receive a warning message (3178) that you can safely ignore. Messages prefaced with "Warning" do not prevent the Help compiler from creating a new .HLP file.

Fig. 31.19

Warning messages resulting from missing build information and errors in context string designation.

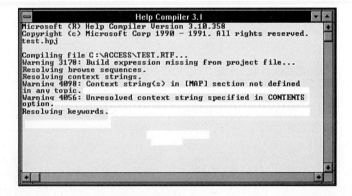

Errors result from the inability of the Help compiler to locate an .RTF file, omitting the [FILES] section, or errors of similar magnitude. Figure 31.20 shows the error messages resulting from typing the wrong file name in the [FILES] section of the .HPJ file. Messages prefaced with "Error" are fatal, and a new .HLP file is not created.

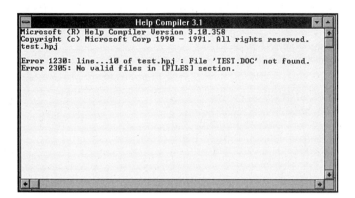

Fig. 31.20
Fatal errors that
result from the
inability of the
Help compiler to
find a required file.

Troubleshooting

*Whether I run the help compiler from a PIF file in a Window or from the DOS prompt, I
receive "Insufficient memory" errors.*

Large help files that include bit-mapped images, such as ICONWRKS.HLP that is
supplied with the ADT, require a substantial amount of DOS low memory (often in
excess of 400K) to compile. If you receive low memory errors, exit Windows and run
HC31.EXE from the DOS command line. If you still receive "Insufficient memory"
errors, you may need to modify your AUTOEXEC.BAT and CONFIG.SYS files to reduce
the memory occupied by device drivers and memory-resident applications.

Linking Help Topics to Your Access Application

You can create context-sensitive Help for your Access applications, similar to
that used by Access's own Help system, by using one of two methods:

- You can use the HelpFile property of a form or report to designate the
  WinHelp file that is to be used. You then assign the context ID number
  as the value of the ContextID property of a control to display a specific
  Help window when the user selects the control and presses F1 for Help.

- You can use the WinHelp() function of the WinHelp engine in Access
  Basic procedures and functions. The Access Basic code you use to declare and then use WinHelp() in Access Basic is typical of the method
  for using any of the functions of Windows and third-party dynamic
  link libraries (DLLs).

The following sections give you more details about these two procedures.

Assigning Help Files and Context IDs to Access Objects

You can specify a Help file and a Help Context ID value to be used for a form or report, plus each control object on the form or report. The capability to assign a specific Help file to a form or report enables you to write smaller Help files that load faster.

To assign a Help file and a context ID number to a form and a control on a form, follow these steps:

1. Open the Customers form for this example, and click the Design View button.

2. Click the Properties icon of the toolbar to display the Properties window; then choose Select Form from the **E**dit menu to select the form as a whole, rather than one of its sections.

3. Select Other Properties in the drop-down list. In the Help File text box of the Other Properties window, type the name of your WinHelp file. For this example, type **ICONWRKS.HLP**, the Help file created by compiling ICONWRKS.RTF with ICONWRKS.HPJ. These three files are included with the ADT. ICONWRKS.HLP must be located in the same directory as your database file.

4. In the Help Context ID text box, type the value of the Help Context ID of the Help topic that applies to the form as a whole. In this example, the value 1 is used for the Contents section, so type **1** in the Help Context ID text box. Your properties window appears as shown in figure 31.21.

5. Select the Customer ID bound text box and enter the Context ID value for the Help topic that applies to the control object in the Help Context ID text box, as shown in figure 31.22. The value assigned to the Color Palette topic is 1905 in this example, so enter **1905** in the Help Context ID text box. Properties dialogs for control objects do not have a Help File text box because the value of the `HelpFile` property applies to the form and all the control objects it contains.

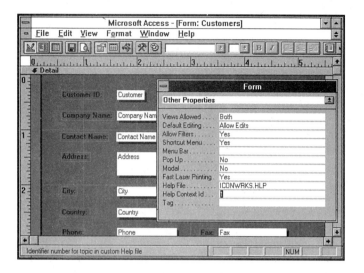

Fig. 31.21
The Properties window when assigning a Help file and Context ID value.

VIII

Completing Applications

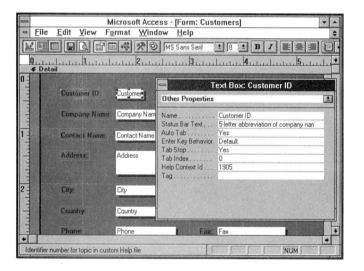

Fig. 31.22
The Text Box properties window when you're assigning Context ID value to a control object.

6. Click the Run Mode button on the toolbar. The Customer ID field is selected when the Customers form loads. Press the F1 key, and the Editor: Color Palette topic is displayed in the IconWorks Help System window, as shown in figure 31.23.

Fig. 31.23
The help topic
selected by the
HelpContextID
value of the
Customer ID
text box.

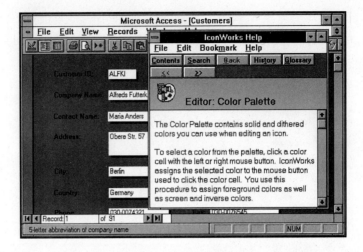

You can create Help topics for each of the form's fields by assigning different `HelpContextID` property values to each text box or other control object on the form. Alternatively, you can assign to control objects a `HelpContextID` value of 0 so that all control objects on the form display the Help topic with the `HelpContextID` value assigned to the form. If you set the `HelpContextID` value of the form to 0, Access displays its own Help window when you press the F1 key. The procedure described in the preceding steps also applies to reports.

Adding Calls to WinHelp in Access Basic Code

Assigning Help files to forms and reports and `HelpContextID` values to forms, reports, and control objects provides all the WinHelp capabilities you need for most applications. If you use Access Basic procedures that change how control objects behave, however, you may need to set the `HelpContextID` values in your Access Basic procedures.

To control the action of the WinHelp engine with Access Basic code, you call the `WinHelp()` function when you need to change a Help file name or context ID value. The syntax of the `WinHelp()` function is as follows:

```
intHelpOK = WinHelp(hWnd, strHelpFile, intCommand, lngData)
```

In the preceding syntax, wHelpOK is an integer variable used to receive the return value of the WinHelp() function. The arguments of the WinHelp() function are explained in the following sections.

◀ "Data Types and Database Objects in Access Basic," p. 993

Declaring Windows Functions in Access Basic

You call Windows functions in the same manner that you call Access Basic functions within Access Basic procedures. You need to inform Access Basic of your intention to use an external function, however, before using that function in your code. For this task, which is called *declaring a function prototype*, you use the Declare keyword. The syntax of the declaration statement follows:

▶ "Naming Conventions for Access Objects," p. 1205

```
Declare Function WinHelp Lib "User" (ByVal hWnd As
Integer, ByVal strHelpFile As String, ByVal intCommand
As Integer, lngData As Any) As Integer
```

The following list explains the statement's components:

- **ByVal**. A keyword that tells Access to transfer the data in the argument to the Windows function with a data type that is compatible with the C language in which Windows is written.

- hWnd. A Windows handle (code number or integer) to the window that is active when the Help function is called with the F1 key.

- strHelpFile. The name of the Help file, including the .HLP extension.

- intCommand. Table 31.5 lists and describes the intCommand constant values for you.

- lngData. An argument whose data type depends on the value of the wCommand argument you choose; so the lngData argument is declared an As Any data type and is not prefixed with the ByVal keyword.

Table 31.5   *WinHelp()intCommand* Constant Values and Their Actions

intCommand Constant	Value	Description
HELP_CONTEXT	1	Causes a specific Help topic, identified by a Long integer and specified as the lngData argument, to be displayed.

(continues)

VIII

Completing Applications

Table 31.5 Continued		
intCommand Constant	**Value**	**Description**
HELP_QUIT	2	Notifies WinHelp() that the specified Help file is no longer in use and can be closed. The lngData argument is ignored.
HELP_INDEX	3	Displays the index of the specified Help file, as designated by the author. The lngData argument is ignored.
HELP_HELPONHELP	4	Displays Help for using the WinHelp application itself. The lngData argument is ignored.
HELP_SETINDEX	5	Sets the context number specified by the lngData argument, a long integer, as the current index for the specified Help file.
HELP_KEY	257	Displays the first corresponding topic found in a search for the keyword specified by the dwData argument, in this case, As String (as a string variable).
HELP_MULTIKEY	513	Displays Help for a keyword found in an alternate keyword table. The lngData argument is a data structure containing the size of the string, the letter of the alternate table, and the keyword string.

Table 31.5 describes how the data type of the lngData argument changes with the value of intCommand. The lngData argument may be a long integer, a string, or a user-defined data type. Therefore, lngData is declared As Any and is passed by reference, not by value. When you want lngData to be ignored by WinHelp(), you should set lngData to &H0 (null, rather than decimal 0) in your application.

The additions to the Declarations section of your module to take advantage of all the features WinHelp() offers follow:

```
'Declare WinHelp function prototype
Declare Function WinHelp Lib "User" (ByVal hWnd As Integer,
ByVal strHelpFile As String, ByVal intCommand As Integer,
lngData As Any) As Integer
```

```
'Declare global constants for wCommand
Global Const HELP_CONTEXT = &H1          'Display a specified topic
Global Const HELP_QUIT = &H2             'Terminate WinHelp for application
Global Const HELP_INDEX = &H3            'Display the Help index
Global Const HELP_HELPONHELP = &H4       'Display Help on using Help
Global Const HELP_SETINDEX = &H5         'Set the current Help index
Global Const HELP_KEY = &H101            'Display a topic for keyword
Global Const HELP_MULTIKEY = &H201       'Use the alternate keyword table
Global Const KEY_F1 = &H70               'Key code for Help key

'Declare the multikey Help user-defined variable type
(structure)
Type MKH 'Multikey Help
    wSize           As Integer      'Size of record
    sfKeylist       As String * 1   'Code letter for keylist
    sfKeyphrase     As String * 100 'String length is arbitrary
End Type

'Declare global Help variables
Global strHelpFile   As String      'Name of Help file
Global ingCommand    As Integer     'Help command constant
Global lngHelpCtx    As Long        'Help context value when numeric
Global strHelpKey    As String      'Help keyword for search when string
Global intHelpOK     As Integer     'Return value from WinHelp()
```

You do not need to add the constants to the Declarations section of your module if you want to substitute the integer values shown in table 31.5 as the wCommand argument when you use the WinHelp() function. You must, however, declare the MKH (multikey Help) structure in your global module, declare a record variable, and assign values to its fields in your code if you plan to use more than one Help key in your application. A good practice is to make the name of your Help file a global variable.

Using the WinHelp API Function in Your Access Basic Code

Assign the name of your Help file to szHelpFile and default values to wCommand and dwHelpCtx in the Declarations section of the module. These variables are made global so that they retain the last value set to all modules contained in your Access database. You set dwHelpCtx to the value of the context ID of the topic you want to display when the user requests Help at a particular point in your code. For example,

```
'Assign initial values to Help variables
strHelpFile = "TEST.HLP"
intCommand = HELP_CONTEXT
lngHelpCtx = 255
```

Completing Applications

VIII

To display Help, create the function `AppHelp()` as shown in this example:

```
Function AppHelp()
    HelpOK = WinHelp(hWnd, strHelpFile, intCommand, ByVal
        lngHelpCtx)
End Function
```

Add a Help button to your form or report and assign `=AppHelp()` as the value of the `OnClick` event. When you click the Help button, `WinHelp()` displays the appropriate topic.

`lngHelpCtx` must be passed by value to `lngData`, but the prototype did not include `ByVal`, so you must include `ByVal` with the argument when you call the function. `lngHelpCtx` is set to `&H0` when `lngData` is ignored.

If `intCommand` is set to the value of `HELP_KEY` for a keyword search, the syntax of the call to `WinHelp()` is as follows:

```
intCommand = HELP_KEY
lngHelpKey = "Invoice"
intHelpOK = WinHelp(hWnd, strHelpFile, intCommand, ByVal
    strHelpKey)
```

If you want to use the `Multikey` command to select an entry in a multikey table, you need to create a variable of the `MKH` data type, *mkhMultiKey*, and assign values to each of its fields as shown in the following example:

```
Dim mkhMultiKey As MKH
mkhMultiKey.mkSize = Len(mkhMultiKey)
mkhMultiKey.mkKeyList = "A"
mkhMultiKey. strKeyphrase = "A Keyphrase in Keylist A"
```

Then call `WinHelp()` with the following code in your multikey Help function:

```
intHelpOK = WinHelp(hWnd, strHelpFile, intCommand, mkhMultiKey)
```

You need an individual macro for each type of Help function you want to use.

From Here...

This chapter showed you the basic steps for creating custom Help files for your Access applications. You learned how to create the Help file document with a commercial Help file authoring application, and you saw an example of a simple Word for Windows 2.0+ template that streamlines housekeeping for Help files. The chapter explained how to create Help project files and use them with HC31.EXE, the Microsoft Help compiler, to compile documents in rich text format to WinHelp files. You also learned the methods for assigning custom Help files to forms and reports and setting the `HelpContextID` values for control objects to display specific topics. A description of how you use the `WinHelp()` function of Windows with your Access Basic code concluded the chapter.

For information on manipulating graphic images, naming of Access Basic variables, and upgrading your Access 1.x applications to Access 2.0, refer to these chapters:

- Chapter 20, "Adding Graphics to Forms and Reports," includes examples of how you edit bit-map and vector images with Windows Paintbrush and Microsoft Draw.

- Chapter 32, "Migrating Access 1.x Applications to Access 2.0," describes the process of converting Access 1.1 applications to Access 2.0 and helps you avoid some of the pitfalls that may occur when you make the conversion.

- Appendix B, "Naming Conventions for Access Objects," describes the Leszynski-Reddick (L-R) naming conventions for the Access Basic variables used in the examples of this chapter.

VIII

Completing Applications

Chapter 32

Migrating Access 1.x Applications to Access 2.0

Each version of Access—1.0, 1.1, and 2.0—has a different database file structure at the binary (byte) level. The differences between .MDB files created with versions 1.0 and 1.1 were relatively minor; thus you could use the Compact feature of Access to convert version 1.0 .MDBs to version 1.1, or *vice versa*. Microsoft made substantial changes to the structure of Access 2.0's .MDB file structure. These changes are beyond the capability of the Compact feature, so Microsoft added the Convert Database choice to the File menu to re-create version 1.0 and 1.1 .MDB files in 2.0 format. The Convert Database process is *not reversible*; once you've converted a database to the Access 2.0 .MDB structure, you can't convert it back to version 1.x. However, you can open and use version 1.x .MDB files with Access 2.0. Thus, this chapter begins with the ramifications of continuing to use version 1.x .MDB files with Access 2.0 and then explains how to convert your existing .MDB files to Access 2.0's structure.

In this chapter, you learn to

■ Convert version 1.x application .MDBs to Access 2.0

■ Use version 2.0 application .MDBs with version 1.x data .MDBs

■ Detect and correct import errors

■ Eradicate elusive run-time and compile-time errors

Using Access 1.x Application .MDB Files with Access 2.0

Access 2.0 was designed to be backwardly compatible with Access 1.x .MDB files. However, the compatibility is not totally complete. When you open a version 1.x file in Access 2.0, you receive the message shown in figure 32.1. The following list describes the principal limitations of using version 1.x .MDB files with Access 2.0:

- You cannot save any changes you make to the design of any object contained in a version 1.x .MDB file.

- You cannot change ownership of or permissions for objects contained in a version 1.x .MDB file.

Caution

You must use the new Version argument of the **DoCmd** DoMenuItem action with the A_MENU_VER20 constant to specify the new Access 2.0 menu structure in Access Basic code.

- DoMenuItem macro actions that refer to menu choices that have changed in Access 2.0 occasionally produce an unexpected result.

- SendKeys operations that execute Access 2.0 menu choices and make selections in dialogs are likely to fail due to changes in the Access 2.0 menu structure and the design of Access 2.0 dialogs.

- Access Basic statements that use the dot (.) separator to refer to a table field called "Name" fail, because Name is now a property of a field. (You can use the bang (!) separator to refer to the Name field's value.)

If you don't need to change the design of your Access 1.x application, and the application does not contain any of the specific problem areas in the preceding list, you can continue to use the 1.x application with Access 2.0. The message shown in figure 32.1 will appear each time you open the application.

Fig. 32.1

The message that displays when you open an Access 1.x .MDB file in Access 2.0.

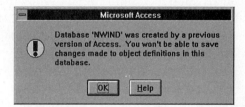

Using Access 1.x Data .MDB Files with Access 2.0

If you use the recommended two-database method (storing application objects and data objects in two separate .MDB files), you can convert your application .MDB file to version 2.0, but leave the database .MDB as a version 1.x file. When you attach tables contained in Access 1.x .MDB files, you don't receive a warning message. You cannot use Access 2.0 features, such as enforcing referential integrity between attached version 1.x tables and local tables. Figure 32.2 shows the appearance of the Relationships window with a table attached from an Access 1.x database. The check boxes that let you enforce referential integrity are disabled.

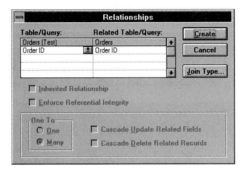

Fig. 32.2
The Relationships window for a join between an attached Access 1.x table and a local Access 2.0 table.

VIII

Completing Applications

You need to retain the version 1.x structure for your data .MDB files if any of the following conditions apply:

- You are using the database .MDB with a Visual Basic 3.0 application and you have not purchased the Access Developer's Toolkit that contains the updated version of VBDB300.DLL that is compatible with both version 1.x and version 2.0 .MDB files.

◄ "Examining the Content of the Access Developer's Toolkit," p. 1099

- You are converting a series of different application .MDB files from version 1.x to version 2.0 and need to maintain compatibility with all application .MDBs until the conversion process is complete.

- You are using the Access ODBC driver (RED110.DLL) with the Simba ODBC driver manager that implements the database connectivity features of Excel 5.0, Word 6.0, and Project 4.0. The RED110.DLL driver is compatible only with Access version 1.x databases. At the time this edition was written, Microsoft had committed to providing an updated Access 2.0 driver for use with Excel 5.0 and Word 6.0.

If you have developed several workgroup applications using Access 1.x, you must maintain the shared data .MDB file in version 1.x format until you have converted all of the application databases to Access 2.0. The only penalty you pay for this is the temporary inability to use the new table design features offered by Access 2.0.

Converting versus Importing .MDB Files

You have the following options for converting version 1.x application, data, or combined application-data .MDB files:

◀ "Converting
Databases to
Access 2.0
Format," p. 119

- Use the Convert Database choice of the File menu to perform the conversion. This is the fastest method of performing the conversion. The ownership of objects in the converted database does not change. Make sure to specify a different file name or directory for the converted .MDB file so you don't overwrite the existing version 1.x file. If the conversion process fails, the source database file might become corrupted and unrepairable.

◀ "Converting
Databases to
Access 2.0
Format," p. 119

- Use the Import Wizard to import all of the objects from the version 1.x .MDB to a newly created version 2.0 .MDB file. When you import the objects, you become the owner (Creator) of the objects.

Tip
Check for the presence of the ConvertErrors table when you use the Import Wizard. The Import Wizard does not display an error message upon encountering a conversion error.

The database object permissions assigned to users and groups are not affected by either converting or importing the objects.

Handling Conversion and Import Errors

If the Access Convert feature encounters a property value that is invalid in Access 2.0, you receive an error message similar to that shown in figure 32.3. You are most likely to encounter errors in field-level ValidationRule expressions that include references to other fields of the table. Field-level ValidationRule expressions in Access 2.0 refer only to the values of the field to which the ValidationRule applies. References to other fields of the table are not permitted. You need to use the table-level ValidationRule property to compare the value of one field against the value of another field of the current record.

Fig. 32.3
A message indicating an error in the conversion process.

When conversion errors occur, Access 2.0 creates a table called ConvertErrors and appends one record to the table for each conversion error encountered. Table 32.1 lists the field names and field values for a typical entry in the ConvertErrors table. This error occurred as a result of the reference to the PA Scheduled Date field in the `ValidationRule` expression for the PA Effective Date field of the Personnel Actions table.

Tip
If Access generates several conversion errors, print a Quick Report from the table to serve as a reference to correct the errors in your new database object.

Table 32.1   Field Names and Typical Field Values of the ConvertErrors Table

Field Name	Field Value
Error	Unknown or invalid reference 'PA Scheduled Date' in validation expression or default value in table 'Personnel Actions'
Field	PA Effective Date
Property	Validation Rule
Table	Personnel Actions
Unconvertible Value	>=[PA Scheduled Date] Or Is Null

After inspecting the errors in the ConvertErrors table, you must replicate the unconvertible value in a form accepted by Access 2.0. As an example, you change the >=[PA Scheduled Date] `Or Is Null` expression to a table-level `ValidationRule` expression, [PA Effective Date] >=[PA Scheduled Date] `Or IsNull`([PA Effective Date]).

Exterminating Access Basic Compilation Bugs

If the Access Basic modules contain any code that cannot be compiled without error by Access 2.0, you cannot use any of the Access wizards or open the Add-In Manager. If you attempt to open the Add-In Manager, as an example, you receive the error message shown in figure 32.4. The most likely source of such an error is reference to a property name that is valid in Access 1.1, but not in Access 2.0. A conflict between a Name field name and the property `Name` creates a run-time, not a compile-time error. Figure 32.5 shows an example of real Access 1.1 Basic code (from a book about developing Access 1.1 applications) that illustrates both problems. The term *apparent* is used in the caption of figure 32.5 because the *real* problem is use of the `ColumnWidth` property.

VIII

Completing Applications

Fig. 32.4

A message box indicating that Access 2.0 can't compile imported Access 1.1 code.

Fig. 32.5

A message box indicating an apparent conflict with a field called Name.

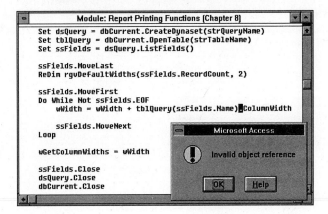

Replacing `ssFields.Name` with `ssFields!Name` does not solve the compilation problem, because the `ColumnWidth` property of a field of a table is not a property of a **Field** object of a **Table** object that is defined by the Jet 2.0 database engine. You continue to receive the same error message from the Access interpreter. (The Access 1.1 `ColumnWidth` property was not documented in Access 1.1's on-line help file.) `ColumnWidth` is, however, an Access-defined property of a **TableDef** object. To use an Access-defined property, you need to open the **TableDef** object for the table and then apply the **Append** method to add the `ColumnWidth` property to the `Properties` collection of the **TableDef** object. This requires that you execute the following statements before you refer to the value of the `ColumnWidth` property of a **Field** object:

```
Dim tdfTable As TableDef
Dim prpColWidth As Property
. . .
prpColWidth.Name = "ColumnWidth"
Set tdfTable = dbCurrent.TableDefs("TableName")
tdfTable.Properties.Append prpColWidth
```

Once your code has executed the preceding statements, you can obtain the value of the `ColumnWidth` property for a field of a **TableDef** or **QueryDef** object's datasheet. It is obscure new features, such as Access-defined properties, that often cause the conversion process to become quite time-consuming.

Using the Import Wizard to Convert Databases

The Import Wizard creates a list of all the objects in the Access 1.x database and then imports each of the objects into a new or existing database. You open the Import Wizard's sole dialog by choosing Add-Ins from the File menu, and then Import Database from the submenu. Select the version 1.x database whose objects you want to import (see fig. 32.6), and then click the OK button. The Wizard imports each of the objects. Using the Import Wizard is much faster than choosing Import from the File menu and then importing each object in a database.

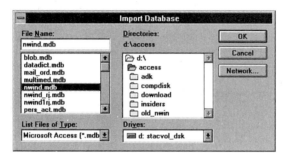

Fig. 32.6
Selecting the source database from which to import database objects.

VIII

Completing Applications

Converting Data .MDBs from Version 1.x to 2.0

Once all of your application database files have been converted to Access 2.0, you can convert the data .MDBs to version 2.0. (This assumes the lack of the other constraints listed in the earlier "Using Access 1.x Data .MDB Files with Access 2.0" section of this chapter.) Data .MDBs don't include macros or Access Basic code, so you won't encounter problems with missing menus, run-time errors, or compile-time bugs. The principal advantage of converting data .MDBs is to gain access to version 2.0's new field-level and table-level ValidationRule properties and to be able to enforce referential integrity between local and attached tables. A third advantage of converting all your .MDBs to Access 2.0's structure is that you can recover the space used by Access 1.1 on your computer.

You can use either the Convert feature or the Import Manager add-in of Access 2.0 to handle the conversion. The Convert feature is faster and also provides the benefit of warning you when convert errors occur. These error messages, however, require your attendance during the conversion process to click the OK button. If you are converting very large files, you can use Import Manager to perform an unattended conversion.

From Here...

You're on your own with Access 2.0.

This book's objective has been to provide you with the information you need to master the development of Access database applications at the beginning and intermediate levels. Access 2.0 is a very sophisticated application, and publishing limitations preclude complete descriptions of its every function and keyword. Access 2.0, however, has an exceptionally complete on-line help system. Thus any feature or function that you find missing here undoubtedly can be located as a topic or cross-reference entry in MSACC20.HLP.

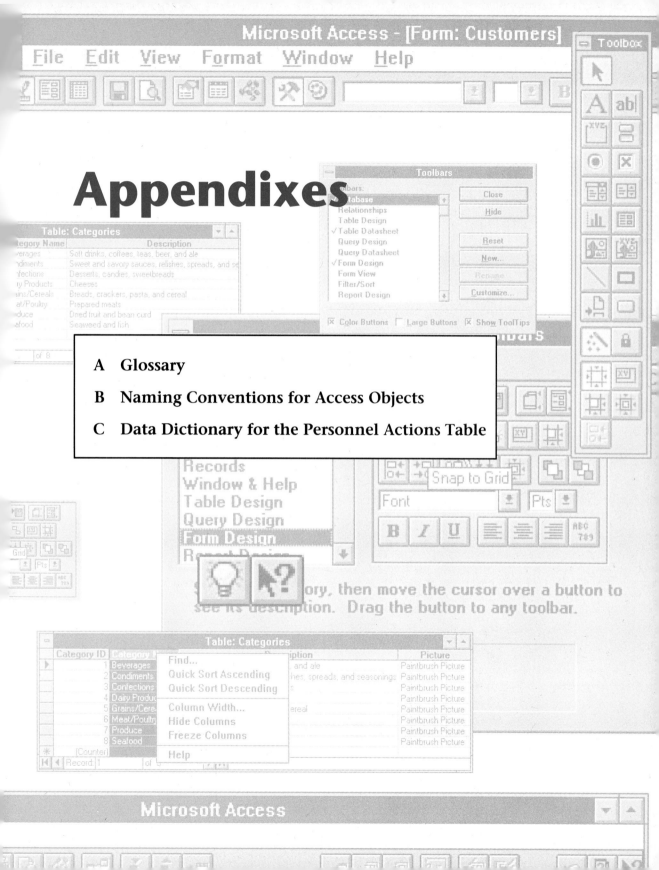

Appendixes

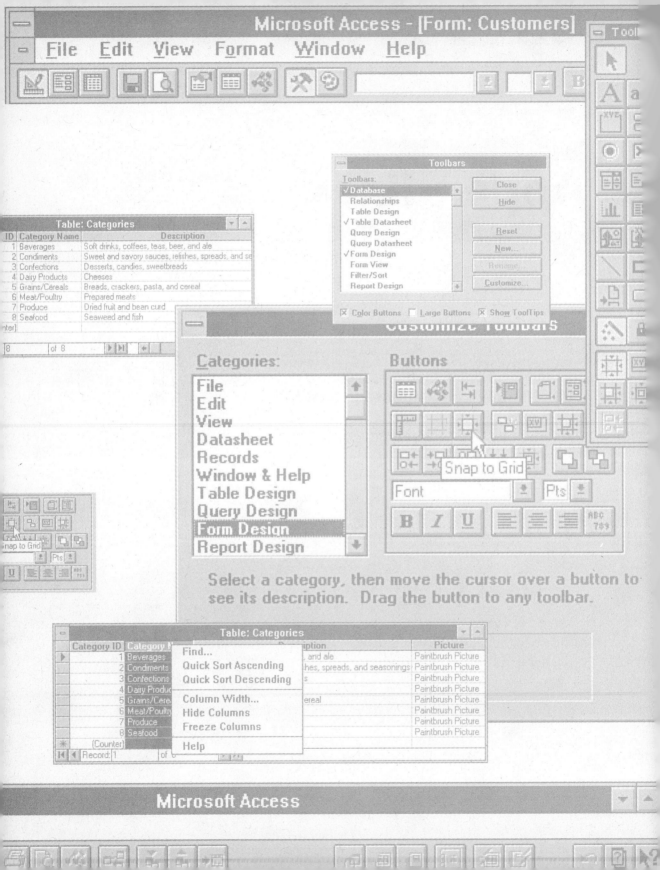

Appendix A

Glossary

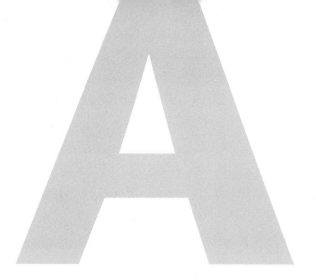

Accelerator key   A key combination that provides access to a menu choice, macro, or other function of the application in lieu of selection with the mouse, usually combining Alt+*Key*. Sometimes called a shortcut key, but shortcut keys usually consist of Ctrl+*Key* combinations.

Activation   An OLE 2.0 term meaning to place an object in a running state, which includes binding the object, or to invoke a method of the object. See also *Binding*.

Active   In Windows, the currently running application or the window to which user input is directed; the window with the focus. See also *Focus*.

Add-in   A wizard (such as the Query Wizard) or builder (such as the Menu Builder) that aids users of Access to create or run database applications. You use Access 2.0's Add-In Manager to install wizards and builders. (Choose Add-Ins from the **F**ile menu.) See also *Wizard* and *Builder*.

Address   The numerical value, usually in hexadecimal format, of a particular location in your computer's random-access memory (RAM).

Aggregate functions   The ANSI SQL functions AVG(), SUM(), MIN(), MAX(), and COUNT() and Access SQL functions StDev(), Var(), First(), and Last(). Aggregate functions calculate summary values from a group of values in a specified column. They are usually associated with GROUP BY and HAVING clauses. See also *Domain aggregate functions*.

Aggregate object   An OLE 2.0 term that refers to an object class that contains one or more member objects of another class.

Alias   A temporary name assigned to a table in a self join, to a column of a query, or to rename a table. **Alias** is also an embedded keyword option for the Access Basic **Declare** statement. The **Alias** keyword is used to register prototypes of DLL functions so that the function can be called from programs by another name.

ANSI   An abbreviation for the American National Standards Institute. ANSI in the Windows context refers to the ANSI character set that Microsoft decided to use for Windows (rather than the IBM PC character set that includes special characters such as those used for line drawing, called the OEM character set). The most common character set is ASCII (the American Standard Code for Information Interchange), which for English alphabetic and numeric characters, is the same as ANSI.

API   An abbreviation for Application Programming Interface. Generically, a method by which a program can obtain access to or modify the operating system. In Windows, the 750 or so functions provided by Windows 3.1 DLLs that allow applications to open and close windows, read the keyboard, interpret mouse movements, etc. Programmers call them *hooks*. Access Basic provides access to these functions with the **Declare** statement. See also *DLL*.

Applet   A Windows application that is supplied as a component of another Windows application, rather than a retail product. The Notepad, Write, and Character Map applications supplied with Windows 3.1 are applets.

Application   The software product that results from creation of a program, often used as a synonym for the program code that creates it. Microsoft Word for Windows, Microsoft Excel, WordPerfect for Windows, and Lotus 1-2-3 are called *mainstream* Windows applications in this book. Applications are distinguished by the environment for which they are designed (e.g. Windows, DOS, Macintosh, UNIX) and their purpose. Windows applications carry the DOS executable file extension, .EXE.

Application Control-menu box   The small, square button at the extreme left of the title bar of an application. Clicking the Application Control-menu box displays the Application Control menu. Double-clicking the Application Control-menu box closes the application.

Argument   Data supplied to a function and upon which the function acts or uses to perform its task. Arguments are enclosed in parentheses. Additional arguments, if any, are separated by commas. Arguments passed to procedures usually are called *parameters*.

Array   An ordered sequence of values (elements) stored within a single named variable, accessed by referring to the variable name with the number of the element (index or subscript) in parentheses, as in `strValue = strArray(3)`. Arrays in Access Basic may have more than one dimension, in which case, access to the value includes indexes for each dimension, `strValue = strArray(3,3)`.

ASCII   Abbreviation for the American Standard Code for Information Interchange. A set of standard numerical values for printable, control, and special characters used by PCs and most other computers. Other commonly used codes for character sets are ANSI (used by Windows) and EBCDIC (Extended Binary-Coded Decimal Interchange Code, used by IBM for mainframe computers.)

Assign   To give a value to a named variable.

Attached table   A table that is not stored in the currently open Access database (native table), but which you can manipulate as if the table were a native table. You use Access's Attachments Manager to attach tables in other databases. (Choose A**d**d-Ins from the **F**ile menu, and choose the A**t**tachments Manager from the submenu.)

Asynchronous   A process that can occur at any time, regardless of the status of the operating system or applications that are running.

Authentication   The process of verifying a user's login ID and password.

Automation   An OLE 2.0 term that refers to a means of manipulating another application's objects. See also *OLE Automation*.

Back up   To create a file (backup file) that duplicates data stored in one or more files on a client or server computer.

Background   In multitasking computer operations, the application or procedure that is not visible on-screen and that does not receive user generated input. In Windows, an application that is minimized and does not have the focus is in the background.

Base date   A date used as a reference from which other date values are calculated. In the case of Access Basic and SQL Server, the base date is January 1, 1900.

Base tables   The permanent tables from which a query is created. A synonym for underlying tables. Each base table in a database is identified by a name unique to the database.

Appendixes

Batch   A group of statements processed as an entity. DOS batch files, such as AUTOEXEC.BAT, and SQL statements are examples of a batch process.

Binary file   A file whose content does not consist of lines of text. Executable (.EXE), dynamic link library (.DLL), and most database files are stored in binary format.

Binary string   A string consisting of binary, not text, data that contains bytes outside the range of ANSI or ASCII values for printable characters. Bit-field. See also *Mask*.

Binding   Attaching a `Form` or `Report` object to a table, or a control object to a field of a table or the column of a query result set so that the `Form` or `Report` object determines the current record of the table or that the control object reflects the value of the data cell or field of the current record or row.

Bit   The smallest piece of information processed by a computer. A bit, derived from the contraction of BInary digiT (or Binary digIT) has two states, on (1) or off (0). Eight bits make up a byte, and 16 bits combined is called a *word*.

Bitwise   A process that evaluates each bit of a combination, such as a byte or word, rather than processing the combination as a single element. Logical operations and masks use bitwise procedures.

Bit map   The representation of a screen or printed image, usually graphic, as a series of bytes.

Blitting   The process of using the `BitBlt()` function of Windows' GDI.EXE to modify a bit map using bit block transfer.

Boolean   A type of arithmetic in which all digits are bits; that is, the numbers may have only two states, on (true or 1) or off (false or 0). Widely used in set theory and computer programming, Boolean, named after the mathematician George Boole, also is used to describe a data type that may only have two states, true or false. In Access Basic, true is represented by `&HFF` (all bits of an 8-bit byte set to 1) and false by `&H0` (all bits set to 0). Access Basic does not have a native Boolean or BOOL type.

Bound   See *Binding* and *Object frame*.

Break   To cause an interruption in program operation. Ctrl+C is the standard DOS break-key combination but seldom halts operation of a Windows application. Esc is more commonly used in Windows to cause an operation to terminate prior to completion.

Breakpoint   A designated statement that causes program execution to halt after executing the statement preceding it. Breakpoints may be toggled on or off by an Access Basic menu selection, **R**un **T**oggle Breakpoint, or the F9 function key.

Buffer   An area in memory of a designated size (number of bytes) reserved, typically, to hold a portion of a file or the value of a variable. When string variables are passed as arguments of DLL functions, you must create a buffer of sufficient size to hold the returned string. This is accomplished by creating a fixed-length string variable of the necessary size, using the `String$()` function, prior to calling the DLL function.

Builder   A component of Access that provides assistance in creating expressions (Expression Builder) or control objects (Menu Builder).

Built-in functions   Functions that are included in a computer language and need not be created by the programmer as user-defined functions.

Cache   A block of memory reserved for temporary storage. Caches usually store data from disk files in memory to make access to the data faster.

Caption   The title that appears in the title bar of a window. Access Basic calls the text of a label, check box, frame, and command or option button control object the `Caption` property.

Caret   The term used by Windows to indicate the cursor used when editing a text field, usually shaped as an I-beam. The caret, also called the insertion point, can be positioned independently of the mouse pointer.

Cartesian product   Named for René Descartes, a French mathematician. Used in `JOIN` operations to describe all possible combinations of rows and columns from each table in a database. The number of rows in a Cartesian product is equal to the number of rows in table 1 times that in table 2 times that in table 3, and so on. Cartesian rows that do not satisfy the `JOIN` condition are disregarded.

Cascading delete   A trigger that deletes data from one table based on a deletion from another table. Usually used to delete detail data (e.g. invoice items) when the master record (invoice) is deleted.

Case sensitivity   A term used to define whether the interpreter or compiler treats lowercase and uppercase letters as the same character. Most are case-insensitive. C is an exception; it is case sensitive, and all of its keywords are in lower case. Many interpreters, Access Basic included, reformat keywords to its standard: all uppercase for BASIC, a combination of upper- and lowercase letters in Access Basic. Access Basic does not distinguish between upper- and lowercase letters used as names for variables.

Channel   In Windows, channel ordinarily refers to a unique task ID assigned to a dynamic data exchange (DDE) conversation. Access, Word for Windows, and Excel assign integer channel number aliases starting with 1 for the first DDE channel opened and numbered sequentially thereafter. Channel is also used to identify an I/O port in mini- and mainframe computers

Check box   A windows dialog and Access Basic object that consists of a square box and an associated caption. A diagonal cross in the box is created or erased (toggled) by alternate clicks on the box or the label with the mouse or by pressing an assigned hot key.

Child   In Windows, usually an abbreviation for an MDI child window. Child is also used in computer programming in general to describe an object that is related to but lower in hierarchical level than a parent object. See also *MDI Child*.

Chunk   A part of either a RIFF or standard MIDI file that is assigned to a particular function and may be treated as a single element by an application. Access Basic uses the term chunk to refer to a part of any file that you read or write with the `GetChunk` and `AppendChunk` instructions.

Class identifier   See *CLSID*.

Clause   The portion of an SQL statement that begins with a keyword that names a basic operation to be performed.

Client   The device or application that receives data from a server device or application. The data may be in the form of a file received from a network file server, an object from an OLE server, or values from a DDE server assigned to client variables.

Clipboard   Windows' temporary storage location for text and graphic objects, as well as Access objects, such as control objects, forms, tables, reports, and so on. The Clipboard is the intermediary in all copy, cut, and paste operations. You can view and save the contents of the Clipboard using the Program Manager's Clipboard applet.

CLSID   An identification tag that is associated with an OLE 2.0 object created by a specific server. CLSID values are registered in REG.DAT and must be unique for each OLE 2.0 server and each type of object that the server can create.

Clustered index   An index in which the physical and index order are the same. Equivalent to INDEX ON RECNO() TO ... in xBase.

Code   Short for source code. The text you enter in your program to create an application. Code consists of instructions and their parameters, functions and their arguments, objects and their events, properties and methods, constants, variable declarations and assignments, and expressions and comments.

Code template   Self-contained groups of modules and resources that perform a group of standard functions and that may be incorporated within other applications requiring these functions, usually with little or no modification.

Code Window   In Access Basic, the window that appears when you select Module from the Database window or click the Ellipsis button of an event property to create or edit an event-handling subprocedure. Also called the code editing window.

Collection   A group of objects of the same class that are contained within another object. Collections are named as the plural of their object class. As an example, the Forms and Reports collections are groups of **Form** and **Report** objects contained in the **Database** object.

Color palette   A means of establishing a foreground or background color in Windows by selecting a color from those displayed with the mouse. The color palette then converts the selection to the standard Windows RGB (red/green/blue) color format. The color palette provides the set of colors for graphic objects of 256 colors or less. Access 2.0 allows you to specify a particular palette for individual forms. Also called *palette* or *Windows palette*.

COM   An acronym for component object model, the name of Microsoft's design strategy to implement OLE 2.0.

Combo list   A Windows object that combines text box and list elements into a single object. In Access Basic, combo lists are of the drop-down type by default. The list element of a drop-down combo list appears when a downward-pointing arrow to the right of the text box is clicked.

Command   A synonym for instruction. Specifies an action to be taken by the computer.

Command button   A Windows object that causes an event when clicked. Command buttons are ordinarily a gray rectangle surrounded by a border with rounded corners.

Comment   Explanatory material within source code not designed to be interpreted or compiled into the final application. In Access Basic, comments are usually preceded by an apostrophe (`'`), but can also be created by preceding them with the `Rem` keyword.

Common Dialog   A standardized dialog box, provided by Windows 3.1+, that may be created by a Windows API function call to functions contained in CMDIALOG.DLL. Common dialogs include FileOpen, FileSave, Print and Printer Setup, ColorPalette, Font, Search and Replace. Using the common dialogs in Access applications requires that you use the `Declare` statement to create function prototypes for the functions in CMDIALOG.DLL that you plan to use.

Common User Access   See *CUA*.

Comparison operators   See *Operator*.

Compile   To create an executable or object (machine-language) file from source (readable) code. In Access, compile means to create pseudo-code (tokenized code) from the source code you write in the code editing windows.

Component object model   See *COM*.

Composite key or index   A key or index based on the values in two or more columns. Equivalent to an `INDEX ON field1 + field2 + ... TO index_filename` statement in xBase. See also *Key* and *Index*.

Composite menu   A menu that includes menu choices from an OLE 2.0 server application that uses in-place (in-situ) activation (editing).

Composite moniker   The location within a container document or object where the compound document is located.

Compound   In computer programming, a set of instructions or statements that requires more than one keyword or group of related keywords to complete. `Select Case...Case...End Select` is an example of a compound statement in Access Basic.

Compound document   A document that contains OLE objects created by an application other than the application that originally created or is managing the document.

Concatenation   Combining two expressions, usually strings, to form a longer expression. The concatenation operator is `&` in Access Basic and SQL, although Access Basic also permits the `+` symbol to be used to concatenate strings.

Concurrency   The condition when more than one user has access to a specific set of records or files at the same time. Concurrency is also used to describe the ability of a database management system to handle simultaneous queries against a single set of tables.

Container   An object or application that can create or manipulate compound documents. The OLE 2.0 custom control of Access Basic is called the OLE container control.

Control   A synonym for a dialog object in Access Basic. Controls include labels, text boxes, lists, combo lists, option buttons, and command buttons. Access 2.0 also provides compatibility with OLE Custom Controls.

Control array   In Visual Basic, the term given to multiple controls on a single form with the same Name property. (Access Basic does not support control arrays.) Individual controls (elements) of a control array are designated by their index, starting with 0, up to one less than the number of controls with the same name.

Control-menu box   See *Application Control-menu box* and *Document Control-menu box*.

Conversation   In DDE operations, the collection of Windows messages that are passed between two different applications, the client and server, during an interprocess communication.

Correlated subquery   A subquery that cannot be independently evaluated. Subqueries depend on an outer query for their result. See also *Subquery* and *Nested query*.

Counter   A special field data type of Access tables that numbers each new record consecutively. Fields of the counter field data type usually are used to create primary keys in cases where an unique primary key cannot be created from data in the table.

CUA   An abbreviation for Common User Access, an element of IBM's SAA (Systems Application Architecture) specification, which establishes a set of standards for user interaction with menus, dialogs, and other user-interactive portions of an application. The CUA was first implemented in Windows and OS/2 and has been an integral part of these GUIs since their inception.

Current database   The database opened in Access with the **O**pen Database choice of the **F**ile menu (or the equivalent) that contains the visible objects of an Access application.

Current record   The record in a `Recordset` object whose values you modify. The current record supplies values of the current record's data cells to control objects that are bound to the table's fields.

Current statement   The statement or instruction being executed at a particular instance in time. In debugging or stepwise operation of interpreted applications such as Access Basic, the next statement that will be executed by the interpreter when program operation is resumed.

Custom control   A control object not native to the application. Access 2.0 supports OLE Custom Controls (OCXs). Visual Basic 3.0 and Visual C++ use Visual Basic Extension custom controls (VBXs).

Data access object   The container for all of the objects that can be embodied in an Access application. The top member of the data access object hierarchy of Access is the `DBEngine` object, which contains `Workspace`, `User`, and `Group` objects. `Database` objects are contained in the `Workspace` object.

Data definition   The process of describing databases and database objects such as tables, indexes, views, procedures, rules, default values, triggers, and other characteristics.

Data dictionary   The result of the data definition process. Also used to describe a set of database system tables that contain the data definitions of database objects.

Data element   The value contained in a data cell, also called a data item, or simply an element. A piece of data that describes a single property of a data entity, such as a person's first name, last name, social security number, age, sex, or hair color. In this case, the person is the data entity.

Data entity   A distinguishable set of objects that is the subject of a data table and usually has at least one unique data element. A data entity might be a person (unique social security number), an invoice (unique invoice number), or a vehicle (unique vehicle ID number; license plates are not necessarily unique across state lines).

Data integrity   The maintenance of rules that prevent inadvertent or intentional modifications to the content of a database that would be deleterious to its accuracy or reliability.

Data modification   Changing the content of one or more tables in a database. Data modification includes adding, deleting, or changing information with the INSERT, DELETE, and UPDATE SQL statements.

Data sharing   The ability to allow more than one user to access information stored in a database from the same or a different application.

Data type   The description of how the computer is to interpret a particular item of data. Data types are generally divided into two families: strings that usually have text or readable content, and numeric data. The types of numeric data supported varies with the compiler or interpreter used. Most programming languages support a user-defined record or structure data type that can contain multiple data types within it. Field data types, which define the data types of database tables, are distinguished from Access Basic data types in this book.

Database   A set of related data tables and other database objects, such as a data dictionary, which are organized as a group.

Database administrator   The individual(s) responsible for the administrative functions of client-server databases. The database administrator (DBA) has privileges (permissions) for all commands that may be executed by the RDBMS and is ordinarily responsible for maintaining system security, including access by users to the RDBMS itself and performing back up and restoration functions.

Database device   A file in which databases and related information, such as transaction logs, are stored. Database devices usually have physical names (e.g. a DOS or OS/2 file name) and a logical name (the parameter of the USE statement).

Database object   A component of a database. `Database` objects include tables, views, indexes, procedures, columns, rules, procedures, triggers, and defaults. The `DBEngine` object in Access Basic is the topmost member of the class of Access objects. All objects within a single database are subclasses of the `Database` object.

Database owner   The user who originally created a database. The database owner has control over all of the objects in the database but may delegate control to other users. Access calls the database owner the Creator. The database owner is identified by the prefix "dbo" in SQL Server.

Database window   The window that appears when you open an Access database and lists the objects (tables, queries, forms, reports, macros, and modules) that are contained in the `Database` object.

Date function   A function that provides date and time information or manipulates date and time values.

DDE   An abbreviation for *dynamic data exchange*, an Interprocess Communication (IPC) method used by Windows and OS/2 to transfer data between different applications.

Deadlock   A condition that occurs when two users with a lock on one data item attempt to lock the other's data item. Most RDBMSs detect this condition, prevent its occurrence, and advise both users of the deadlock situation.

Debug   The act of removing errors in the source code for an application.

Declaration   A statement that creates a user-defined data type, names a variable, creates a symbolic constant, or registers the prototypes of functions incorporated within dynamic link libraries.

Declaration section   A section of an Access Basic module reserved for statements containing declarations.

Declare   In text and not as a keyword, to create a user-defined data type, data holder for a variable, or constant. As an Access Basic keyword, to register a function contained in a dynamic link library in the global module.

Default   A value assigned or an option chosen when no value is specified by the user or assigned by a program statement.

Default database   The logical name of the database assigned to a user when he logs in to the database application.

Demand lock   Precludes more shared locks from being set on a data resource. Successive requests for shared locks must wait for the demand lock to be cleared.

Dependent   A condition in which master data in a table (e.g., invoices) is associated with detail data in a subsidiary table (invoice items). In this case, invoice items are dependent upon invoices.

Design mode   One of three modes of operation of Access, also called Design View. Design mode allows you to create and modify tables, queries, forms, reports, and control objects, and enter macro actions and Access Basic code. The other two modes are run mode, also called run time, when the application is executing, and startup mode before you open an Access database.

Destination document   A term used by OLE 1.0 to refer to a compound document.

Detail data   Data in a subsidiary table that depends on data in a master table to have meaning or intrinsic value. If one deletes the master invoice records, the subsidiary table's detail data for items included in the invoice lose their reference in the database—they become "orphan data."

Detail table   A table that depends on a master table. Detail tables usually have a many-to-one relationship with the master table. See also *Detail data*.

Device   A computer system component that is capable of sending or receiving data, such as a keyboard, display, printer, disk drive, or modem.

Device context   A Windows term that describes a record (struct) containing a complete definition of all of the variables required to fully describe a window containing a graphic object. These include the dimensions of the graphic area (viewport), drawing tools (pen, brush) in use, fonts, colors, drawing mode, etc. Windows provides a handle (hDC) for each device context.

Dialog   A pop-up modal child window, also called a dialog box, that requests information from the user. Dialogs include message boxes, input boxes, and user-defined dialogs for applications such as choosing files to open.

DIB   An acronym for device-independent bit map, a Windows-specific bitmap format designed to display graphic information. DIB files take the extension .DIB and uses a format similar to the .BMP format.

Difference   In data tables, data elements that are contained in one table but not in another.

Directory list   An element of a file selection dialog that selectively lists the subdirectories of the designated directory of a specified logical drive.

DLL   An abbreviation for *dynamic link library*, a file containing a collection of Windows functions designed to perform a specific class of operations. Functions within DLLs are called (invoked) by applications as necessary to perform the desired operation.

Docfile   The file format for creating persistent OLE objects. Docfiles usually have the extension .OLE.

Document   A programming object that contains information that originates with the user of the application, rather than created by the application itself. The data for documents usually is stored in disk files. Access tables, forms, and reports are documents, as are Excel or Lotus 1-2-3 worksheets.

Document Control-menu box   The small, square button at the upper left of the menu bar of an application that uses the multiple document interface (MDI). Clicking the Document Control-menu box displays the Document Control menu. Double-clicking the Document Control-menu box closes the document (but not the application). See also *MDI.*

Domain   A group of workstations and servers that share a common security account manager (SAM) database and that allow a user to log on to any resource in the domain with a single user ID and password. In Access, a domain is a set of records defined by a table or query.

Domain aggregate functions   A set of functions, identical to the SQL aggregate functions, that you can apply to a specified domain, rather than to one or more `Table` objects. See also *Aggregate functions.*

Drag-and-drop   A Windows process whereby an icon representing an object, such as a file, can be moved (dragged) by the mouse to another location (such as a different directory) and placed (dropped) in it. You can use drag-and-drop techniques in Access 2.0's design mode. Access does not provide the drag-and-drop capabilities for control objects that are associated with Visual Basic control objects.

Drive   The logical identifier of a disk drive, usually specified as a letter. When used as a component of a path, the drive letter must be followed by a colon and backslash, as in C:\.

Dynamic data exchange   See *DDE.*

Dynamic link library   See *DLL.*

Dynaset   A set of rows and columns in your computer's memory that represent the values in an attached table, a table with a filter applied, or a query result set. You can update the values of the fields of the underlying table(s) by changing the values of the data cells of a `Dynaset` object. In Access 2.0 `Dynaset` is a type of `Recordset` object.

Embedded object   A source document stored as an OLE object in a compound document.

Empty   A condition of an Access Basic variable that has been declared but has not been assigned a value. `Empty` is not the same as the `Null` value nor is it equal to the empty or zero-length string (`""`).

Enabled   The ability of a control object to respond to user actions such as a mouse click, expressed as the `True` or `False` value of the `Enabled` property of the control.

Environment   A combination of the computer hardware, operating system, and user interface. A complete statement of an environment follows: a 486DX2-66 computer with a VGA display and two-button mouse, using the DOS 5.0 operating system, and running the Windows 3.1 Graphical User Interface in its Enhanced Mode with the Multimedia Extensions 1.0.

Environmental variable   A DOS term for variables that are declared by PATH and SET statements, usually made in an AUTOEXEC.BAT file, and stored in a reserved memory location by DOS. These may be used by applications to adjust their operation for compatibility with user-specific hardware elements or directory structures.

Equi join   A JOIN where the values in the columns being joined are compared for equality and all columns in both tables are displayed. This results in two identical columns in the result.

Error trapping   A procedure by which errors generated during the execution of an application are re-routed to a designated group of lines of code (called an error handler) that performs a predefined operation, such as ignoring the error. If errors are not trapped in Access Basic, the standard modal message dialog with the text message for the error that occurred appears.

Event   The occurrence of an action taken by the user and recognized by one of Access's event properties, such as OnClick or OnDblClick. Events are usually related to mouse movements and keyboard actions; however, events also can be generated by code using the Timer control object, for example.

Event-driven   The property of an operating system or environment that implies the existence of an idle loop. When an event occurs, the idle loop is exited and event-handler code, specific to the event, is executed. After the event handler has completed its operation, execution returns to the idle loop, awaiting the next event.

Exclusive lock   A lock that prevents others from locking data items until the exclusive lock is cleared. Exclusive locks are placed on data items by update operations, such as SQL's INSERT, UPDATE, and DELETE.

Executable   Code, usually in the form of a disk file, that can be run by the operating system in use to perform a particular set of functions. Executable files in Windows carry the extension .EXE and may obtain assistance from dynamic link libraries (DLLs) in performing their tasks.

Exponent   The second element of a number expressed in scientific notation, the power of 10 by which the first element, the mantissa, is multiplied to obtain the actual number. For +1.23E3, the exponent is 3, so you multiply 1.23 by 1,000 (10 to the third power) to obtain the result, 1,230.

Expression   A combination of variable names, values, functions, and operators that return a result, usually assigned to a variable name. `Result = 1 + 1` is an expression that returns 2 to the variable named `Result`. `DiffVar = LargeVar - SmallVar` returns the difference between the two variables to `DiffVar`. Functions may be used in expressions, and the expression may return the value determined by the function to the same variable as that of the argument. `strVar = Mid$(strVar, 2, 3)` replaces the value of strVar with three of its characters, starting at the second character.

Family   One or more typefaces having a related appearance. Courier roman (standard), italic, and bold constitute the Courier family.

Field   Synonym for a column that contains attribute values. Also, a single item of information in a record or row.

Fifth normal form   The rule for relational databases that requires that a table that has been divided into multiple tables must be capable of being reconstructed to its exact original structure by one or more JOIN statements.

File   The logical equivalent of a table. In dBASE, for instance, each table is a single .DBF file.

File moniker   The location of the well-formed path to a persistent OLE 2.0 object.

First normal form   The rule for relational databases that dictates that tables must be flat. Flat tables can contain only one data value set per row. Members of the data value set are called data cells, are contained in one column of the row, and must have only one value.

Flag   A variable, usually Boolean (true/false), that is used to determine the status of a particular condition within an application. The term set is often used to indicate turning a flag from false to true, and reset for the reverse.

Flow control   In general usage, conditional expressions that control the sequence of execution of instructions or statements in the source code of an application. `If...Then...End If` is a flow control statement. The term is also used to describe diagrams that describe the mode of operation of an application.

Focus   A Windows term indicating the currently selected application, or one of its windows, to which all user-generated input (keyboard and mouse operations) is directed. The title bar of a window with the focus is colored blue for the default Windows color scheme.

Font   A typeface in a single size, usually expressed in points, of a single style or having a common set of attributes. Font often is misused to indicate a typeface family or style.

Foreground   In multitasking operations, the application or procedure that is visible on-screen and to which user-generated input is directed. In Windows, the application that has the focus is in the foreground.

Foreign key   A column or combination of columns whose value must match a primary key in another table when joined with it. Foreign keys need not be unique for each record or row. See also *Primary key*.

Form   A synonym for a user-defined window in Access. A `Form` object contains the control objects that appear on its surface and the code associated with the events, methods, and properties applicable to the form and its control objects.

Form-Level   Variables that are declared in the Declarations Section of an Access form. These variables are said to have form-level scope, and are not visible to procedures outside the `Form` object in which the variables are declared.

Fourth normal form   The rule for relational databases that requires that only related data entities be included in a single table and that tables may not contain data related to more than one data entity when many-to-one relationships exist among the entities.

Frame   In Windows, an enclosure, usually with a single-pixel-wide border, that encloses a group of objects, usually of the dialog class. When referring to SMPTE timing with MIDI files, it is one image of a motion picture film or one complete occurrence of a television image (1/30 of a second).

Front-end   When used in conjunction with database management systems, an application, a window, or a set of windows by which the user may access and view database records, as well as add to or edit them. Front-end sometimes is used to describe application launchers that function similarly to Windows Program Manager.

Appendixes

Function   A subprogram called from within an expression in which a value is computed and returned to the program that called it through its name. Functions are classified as internal to the application language when their names are keywords. You may create your own, user-defined functions in Access Basic by adding code between `Function` *FunctionName*`...End Function` statements.

Global   Pertaining to the program as a whole. `Global` variables and constants are accessible to, and `Global` variables may be modified by, code at the form, module, and procedure level.

Global module   A code module (container) in Access Basic in which all global variables and constants are declared and in which the prototypes of any external functions contained in DLLs are declared. Use of a global module in Access applications is common but is not required.

Grid   A preset group of visible or imaginary vertical and horizontal lines used to assist in aligning the position of graphic objects. In Access, the intersection of the imaginary lines is shown as dots on forms and reports in design mode. Control objects automatically align their outlines to these dots if the snap-to-grid option is enabled.

Group   In reports, one or more records that are collected into a single category, usually for the purpose of totaling. Database security systems use the term group to identify a collection of database users with common permissions. See also *Permissions*.

Handle   An unsigned integer assigned by Windows to uniquely identify an instance (occurrence) of a module (application, `hModule`), task (`hTask`), window (`hWnd`), or device context (`hDC`) of a graphic object. Handles in 32-bit Windows applications, including applications for Windows NT, are 32-bit unsigned integers (`dw` or double-words). Also used to identify the sizing elements of control object in design mode. See also *Sizing handle*.

Header file   A file type used by C and C++ programs to assign data types and names to variables and to declare prototypes of the functions used in the application. C header files usually carry the extension .H.

Hierarchical menu   A menu with multiple levels, consisting of a main menu bar that leads to one or more levels of submenus from which choices of actions are made. Almost all Windows applications use hierarchical menu structures.

Hot-link   A term used to describe a DDE (dynamic data exchange) operation in which a change in the source of the DDE data (the server) is immediately reflected in the object of the destination application (the client) to which has requested it.

Icon   A 32 by 32-pixel graphic image used to identify the application in the program manager window, when the application is minimized, and in other locations in the application chosen by the programmer (such as the **H**elp **A**bout dialog).

Identifier   A synonym for "name" or "symbol," usually applied to variable and constant names.

Idle   In Windows, the condition or state in which both Windows and the application has processed all pending messages in the queue from user- or hardware-initiated events and is waiting for the next to occur. The idle state is entered in Access Basic when the interpreter reaches the `End Sub` statement of the outermost nesting level of procedures for a form or control object.

Immediate Window   In Access Basic, a non-modal dialog in which you may enter expressions and view results without writing code in a code editing window. You may also direct information to be displayed in the Immediate Window by use of the `Debug` object.

In-place activation   The ability to activate an object (launch another application) and have the container application take on the capabilities of the other application. The primary feature of in-place activation (also called in-situ activation) is that the other application's menu choices merge with or replace the container application's menu choices in the active window.

Index   For arrays, the position of the particular element with respect to others, usually beginning with 0 as the first element. When used in conjunction with database files or tables, index refers to a lookup table, usually in the form of a file, that relates the value of a field in the indexed file to its record or page number and location in the page (if pages are used.)

Infinite loop   A `Do While`...`Loop`, `For`...`Next`, or similar program flow control structure in which the condition to exit the loop and continue with succeeding statements is never fulfilled. In `For`...`Next` loops, infinite looping occurs when the loop counter is set to a value less than that assigned to the `To` embedded keyword within the structure.

Appendixes

Initialize   In programming, setting all variables to their default values and resetting the point of execution to the first executable line of code. Initialization is accomplished automatically in Access Basic when you start an application.

Inner query   Synonym for subquery.

Insertion point   The position of the cursor within a block of text. When the cursor is in a text field, it is called the caret in Windows.

Instance   A term used by Windows to describe the temporal existence of a loaded application or one or more of its windows.

Instantiate   The process of creating an instance of an object in memory.

Integer   A whole number. In most programming languages, an integer is a data type that occupies two bytes (16 bits). Integers may have signs (as in Access Basic), taking on values from –32,768 to +32,767, or be unsigned. In the latter case, integers can represent numbers up to 65,535.

Interface   A noun describing a connection between two dissimilar devices. A common phrase is "user interface," meaning the "connection" between the display-keyboard combination and the user. Adapter cards constitute the interface between the PC data bus and peripheral devices such as displays, modems, CD-ROMs, and the like. Drivers act as a software interface between Windows and the adapter cards. A bridge is an interface between two dissimilar networks. Use of interface as a verb is jargon.

Intersection   The group of data elements that are included in both tables that participate in a JOIN operation.

Invocation path   The route through which an object or routine is invoked. If the routine is deeply nested, the path may be quite circuitous.

Invoke   To cause execution of a block of code, particularly a procedure or subprocedure.

Item   The name given to the elements contained in a list or the list component of a combo.

Join   A basic operation, initiated by the SQL JOIN statement, that links the rows or records of two or more tables by one or more columns in each table. Equivalent to the xBase SET RELATION TO. . . command.

Jump   In programming, execution of code in a sequence that is not the same as the sequence in which the code appears in the source code. In most cases, a jump skips over a number of lines of code, the result of evaluation of a conditional expression. In some cases, a jump causes another subroutine to be executed.

Key or key field   A field that identifies a record by its value. Tables are usually indexed on key fields. For a field to be a key field, each data item in the field must possess an unique value. See also *Primary key* and *Foreign key*.

Key value   A value of a key field included in an index.

Keyword   A word that has specific meaning to the interpreter or compiler in use and causes predefined events to occur when encountered in source code. Keywords differ from reserved words because you can use keywords as variable, procedure, or function names. Using keywords for this purpose, however, is not a good programming practice.

Label   In Access Basic programming, a name given to a target line in the source code at which execution results upon the prior execution of a `GoTo` `LabelName` instruction. A label also is an Access control object that displays, but cannot update, text values.

LAN   An acronym for *local area network*. A LAN is a system comprising multiple computers that are physically interconnected through network adapter cards and cabling. LANs allow one computer to share specified resources, such as disk drives, printers, and modems, with other computers on the LAN.

Launch   To start a Windows application. The Windows Program Manager is an application launcher.

Leaf level   The lowest level of an index. Indexes are "botmorphic" and derive the names of their elements from the objects found on trees, such as trunks, limbs, and leaves.

Library   A collection of functions, compiled as a group and accessible to applications by calling the function name, together with any required arguments. DLLs are one type of library; those used by compilers to provide built-in functions are another type.

Library database   An Access database that is automatically attached to Access when you launch it. Access library databases usually have the extension .MDA.

Linked object   A source document in a compound document that is included by reference to a file that contains the object's data, rather than by embedding the source document in the compound document.

Appendixes

List   A dialog object that provides a list of items from which the user may choose with the mouse or the cursor keys.

Livelock   A request for an exclusive lock on a data item that is repeatedly denied because of shared locks imposed by other users.

Local   The scope of a variable declared within a procedure, rather than at the form, module, or global level. Local variables are visible (defined) only within the procedure in which they were declared.

Local area network   See *LAN*.

Lock   A restriction of access to a table, portion of a table, or data item imposed to maintain data integrity of a database. Locks may be shared, in which case more than one user can access the locked element(s), or exclusive, where the user with the exclusive lock prevents other users from creating simultaneous shared or exclusive locks on the element(s).

Logical   A synonym for Boolean. Logical is a data type that may have true or false values only. Logical is also used to define a class of operators whose result is only `True` or `False`.

Loop   A compound program flow control structure that causes statements contained between the instructions that designate the beginning and end of the structure to be repeatedly executed until a given condition is satisfied, at which point program execution continues at the source code line after the loop termination statement.

LRPC   An acronym for lightweight remote procedure call used for OLE 2.0 operations on a single computer. LRPC requires that both applications involved in the procedure call be resident on the same computer. Presumably HRPC (heavyweight remote procedure call) will someday allow transfer of OLE 2.0 objects between two or more computers over a network.

Machine language   Program code in the form of instructions that have meaning to and can be acted upon by the computer hardware and operating system employed. Object files compiled from source code are in machine language, as are executable files that consist of object files linked with library files.

Macro   A set of one or more instructions, called actions by Access, that respond to events. Macros and Access Basic code, which can substitute for Access macros, are used to automate applications.

Mantissa   The first element of a number expressed in scientific notation that is multiplied by the power of 10 given in the exponent to obtain the actual number. For +1.23E3, the exponent is 3, so you multiply the mantissa, 1.23, by 1,000 (10 to the third power) to obtain the result, 1,230.

MAPI   Acronym for the Windows Messaging API created by Microsoft for use with Microsoft Mail.

Master database   A database that controls user access to other databases, usually in a client-server system.

Master table   A table containing data on which detail data in another table is dependent. Master tables have a primary key that is matched to a foreign key in a detail table. Master tables often have a one-to-many relationship with detail tables.

MDI server   An OLE 2.0 server that supports multiple compound documents within a single running instance of the application.

Memo   A field data type that can store text with a length of up to about 64,000 bytes. (The length of the Text field data type is limited to 255 bytes.)

Menu   A set of choices from which the user determines the next set action to take. The design of menus in Windows is governed by the CUA or Common User Access specification developed by IBM.

Metafile   A type of graphics file, used by Windows and other applications, that stores the objects displayed in the form of mathematical descriptions of lines and surfaces. Windows metafiles, which use the extension .WMF, are a special form of metafiles.

Method   One of the characteristics of an object and a classification of keywords in Access Basic. Methods are the procedures that are applicable to an Access form, report, or control object. Methods that are applicable to a class of objects are inherited by other objects of the same class and may be modified to suit the requirements of the object by a characteristic of an object called polymorphism.

Mini-server   An applet with OLE server capabilities that you cannot run as a stand-alone application.

Mission-critical   A cliché used in software and hardware advertising to describe the necessity of use of the promoted product if one wishes to create a reliable database system.

Modal   A dialog that must be closed before further action can be taken by the user.

Modeless   A window or dialog that may be closed or minimized by the user without taking any other action—the opposite of modal.

Module   A block of code, consisting of one or more procedures, for which the source code is stored in a single location (a Module object in Access). In a compiled language, a code module is compiled to a single object file.

Module level   Variables and constants that are declared in the Declarations section of a module. These variables have module-level scope and are visible (defined) to all procedures that are contained within the module.

Moniker   A handle to the source of a compound document object.

Monitor   A name often used in place of the more proper terms, display or video display unit (VDU).

Multitasking   The ability of a computer with a single CPU to simulate the processing of more than one task at a time. Multitasking is effective when one or more of the applications spends most of its time in an idle state waiting for a user-initiated event such as a keystroke or mouse click.

Multimedia   The combination of sound and graphic images within a single application for the purpose of selling new computer hardware and software. Related outcomes are the creation of animated presentations that incorporate sound effects and graphics, as well as expansion of the market for PCs in the music industry.

Multiuser   Concurrent use of a single computer by more than one user, usually through the use of remote terminals. UNIX is inherently a multiuser operating system.

Natural join   A SQL JOIN operation in which the values of the columns engaged in the join are compared, with all columns of each table in the join that do not duplicate other columns being included in the result. Same as an equi join except that the joined columns are not duplicated in the result.

Nested   An expression applied to procedures that call other procedures within an application. The called procedures are said to be nested within the calling procedure. When many calls to subprocedures and sub-subprocedures are made, the last one in the sequence is said to be deeply nested.

Nested object   An OLE 2.0 compound document incorporated in another OLE 2.0 compound document. You can nest OLE 2.0 documents as deeply as you wish. OLE 1.0 does not supported nested objects.

Nested query   An SQL SELECT statement that contains subqueries. See *Subquery*.

Newline pair   A combination of a carriage return, the Enter key (CR or Chr$(13)), and line feed (LF or Chr$(10)) used to terminate a line of text on-screen or within a text file. Other characters or combinations may be substituted for the CR/LF pair to indicate the type of newline character (soft, hard, deletable, etc.).

NFS   An abbreviation for Network File Server, a file format and set of drivers created by Sun Microsystems Incorporated, that allows DOS/Windows and UNIX applications to share a single server disk drive.

Non-clustered index   An index that stores key values and pointers to data based on these values. In this case, the leaf level points to data pages rather than to the data itself, as is the case for a clustered index. Equivalent to SET INDEX TO *field_name* in xBase.

Normal forms   A set of five rules, the first three of which originally were defined by Dr. E. F. Cobb, that are used to design relational databases. Five normal forms are generally accepted in the creation of relational databases. See also *First normal form*, *Second normal form*, etc.

Normalization   Creation of a database according to the five generally accepted rules of normal forms. See also *Normal forms*.

Not-equal join   A JOIN statement that specifies that the columns engaged in the join do not equal one another.

NT   An abbreviation for New Technology when applied to Windows. Microsoft's competitors have advertised that NT stands for "not there" or "never through." Windows NT Advanced Server and SQL Server for Windows NT were used extensively in the preparation of the two networking chapters of this book without incidents of any kind.

Null   A variable of no value or of unknown value. The default values, 0 for numeric variables and an empty string ("") for string variables, are not the same as the Null value. The NULL value in SQL statements specifies a data cell with no value assigned to the cell.

Appendixes

Object   In programming, elements that combine data (properties) and behavior (methods) in a single container of code called an object. An Access **Form** or **Report** object is a member of the class of Access **Database** objects; a particular control object is a subclass of the control objects class. Objects inherit their properties and methods from the classes above them in the hierarchy and can modify the properties and methods to suit their own purposes. The code container may be part of the language itself, or you may define your own objects in source code.

Object code   Code in machine-readable form that can be executed by your computer's CPU and operating system, usually linked with libraries to create an executable file.

Object frame   An Access control object that contains and displays or plays an OLE object. Bound object frames display or play OLE objects contained in OLE Object fields of Access tables. Unbound object frames display or play objects that are either embedded in a **Form** or **Report** object or are linked to a file that supplies the object's data.

Object permissions   Permissions granted by the database administrator for others to view and modify the values of database objects, including data in tables. See also *Statement permissions*.

Offset   The number of bytes from a reference point, usually the beginning of a file, to the particular byte of interest. The first byte in a file, when offset is used for location, is always 0.

OpenDoc   A unimplemented "standard" proposed by Apple Computer, Borland International, Lotus Development, WordPerfect Corporation, and other competitors of Microsoft to supplant or replace OLE 2.0.

Operand   One of the variables or constants upon which an operator acts. In 1 + 2 = 3, both 1 and 2 are operands; + and = are the operators.

Operating system   Applications that translate basic instructions, such as keyboard input, to language understood by the computer. The most common operating systems used with personal computers are DOS (Disk Operating System), UNIX, and OS/2.

Operator   A keyword or reserved symbol that, in its unary form, acts on a single variable, otherwise on two variables, to give a result. Operators may be of the conventional mathematic type such as +, - (subtract), /, and * (multiply), as well as logical such as **And** or **Not**. The unary minus (-), when applied to a single variable in a statement such as intVar = - intVar inverts the sign of intVar from - to + or from + to -.

Optimistic locking   A method of locking a record or page of a table that makes the assumption that the probability of other users locking the same record or page is low. With optimistic locking, the record or page is locked only when the data is updated, not during the editing process (`LockEdits` property set to **False**).

Option button   A synonym for radio button, the original terminology in the CUA specification. Option buttons are circular control objects whose center is filled when selected. If grouped, only one option button of a group may be selected.

Outer join   An SQL `JOIN` operation in which all rows of the joined tables are returned, whether or not a match is made between columns. SQL database managers that do not support the OUTER JOIN reserved words use the *= operator to specify that all of the rows in the preceding table return and =* to return all of the rows in the succeeding table.

Outer query   A synonym for the primary query in a statement that includes a subquery. See also *Subquery*.

Page   In tables of client-server and Access databases, a 2K block that contains records of tables. Client-server and Access databases lock pages, while DOS desktop databases usually lock individual records. Page-locking is required when variable-length records are used in tables.

Parameter   The equivalent of an argument but associated with the procedure that receives the value of an argument from the calling function. The terms parameter and argument, however, are often used interchangeably.

Parse   The process of determining if a particular expression is contained within another expression. Parsing breaks program statements into keywords, operators, operands, arguments, and parameters for subsequent processing of each by the computer. Parsing string variables involves searching for the occurrence of a particular character or set of characters in the string and then taking a specified set of actions when found or not found.

Permissions   Authority given by the system administrator, database administrator, or database owner to perform operations on a network or upon data objects in a database.

Persistent (graphics)   A Windows graphic image that survives movement, resizing, or overwriting of the window in which it appears. Persistent images are stored in global memory blocks and are not released until the window containing them is destroyed.

Appendixes

Persistent (objects)   An object that is stored in the form of a file or an element of a file, rather than only in memory. `Table` and `QueryDef` objects are persistent because these objects are stored in .MDB files. `Recordset` objects of the `Snapshot` and `Dynaset` type, on the other hand, are stored in memory. Such objects are called *temporal* or *impersistent* objects.

Pessimistic locking   A method of locking a record or page of a table that makes the assumption that the probability of other users locking the same record or page is high. With pessimistic locking, the record or page is locked during the editing and updating process (`LockEdits` property set to `True`).

Point   In typography, the unit of measurement of the vertical dimension of a font, about 1/72 of an inch. The point is also a unit of measurement in Windows, where it represents exactly 1/72 of a logical inch or 20 twips.

Pointer   A data type that comprises a number representing a memory location. Near pointers are constrained to the 64K default local data segment. Far pointers can access any location in the computer's memory. Pointers are used extensively in C-language applications to access elements of arrays, strings, structures, and the like. Access Basic has only one pointer data type—to a zero-terminated string when the `ByVal...As String` keywords are applied to an Access Basic string passed to an external function contained in a dynamic link library.

Poke   In DDE terminology, the transmission of an unrequested data item to a DDE server by the DDE client. In BASIC terminology, placing a byte of data in a specific memory location. Access Basic does not support the BASIC POKE keyword and uses the `DDEPoke` method for DDE operations.

Precedence   The sequence of execution of operators in statements that contain more than one operator.

Primary key   The column or columns whose individual or combined values (in the case of a composite primary key) uniquely identify a row in a table.

Primary verb   The default verb for activating an OLE 2.0 object. Edit is the default verb for most OLE objects except multimedia objects, whose default verb is usually Play.

Print zone   The area of a sheet of paper upon which a printer can create an image. For most laser printers and standard dot-matrix printers, this is 8 inches in width. The vertical dimension is unlimited for dot-matrix printers and usually is 13.5 inches for a laser printer with legal-size paper capabilities.

Printer object   An Access Basic object representing the printer chosen as the default by the Control Panel Printers function's Set Default choice.

Procedure   A self-contained collection of source code statements, executable as an entity. All Access Basic procedures begin either with the reserved word `Sub` or `Function`, which may be preceded by the `Private` or `Static` reserved words, and terminate with `End Sub` or `End Function`.

Program   All of the code required to create an application, consisting basically of declarations, statements, and in Windows, resource definition and help files.

Projection   A projection identifies the desired subset of the columns contained in a table. You create a projection with a query that defines the fields of the table you want to display but without criteria that limit the records that are displayed.

Properties window   A window that displays the names and properties of Access table, form, report, and control objects.

Property   One of the two principal characteristics of objects (the other is methods). Properties define the manifestation of the object, for example, its appearance. Properties may be defined for an object or for the class of objects to which the particular object belongs, in which case they are said to be inherited.

Pseudo object   Objects that are contained within other OLE 2.0 objects, such as the cells of a spreadsheet object.

Qualification   A search condition that data values must meet to be included in the result of the search.

Qualified   To precede the name of a database object with the name of the database and the object's owner or to precede the name of a file with its drive designator and the path to the directory in which the file is stored. The terms well-qualified path and well-formed path to a file appear often in documentation.

Query   A request to retrieve data from a database with the SQL SELECT instruction.

QueryDef   A persistent Access object that stores the Access SQL statements that comprise a query. `QueryDef` objects are optimized, when applicable, by the Access database engine's query optimizer and stored in a special optimized format.

RDBMS   An abbreviation for relational database management system. An RDBMS is an application that is capable of creating, organizing, and editing databases; displaying data through user-selected views; and printing formatted reports. Most RDBMSs include at least a macro or macro language, and most provide a system programming language. dBASE III and IV, Paradox, and FoxPro are RDBMSs. Nantucket's Clipper is not because Clipper does not incorporate a user interface—Clipper is a database program compiler.

Record   A synonym for a user-defined data type, called a structure in C and C++. Record also is used in database applications to define a single element of a relational database file that contains each of the fields defined for the file. Records need not contain data to exist—the xBase command, APPEND BLANK, adds a record to a database that contains default data for strings (all spaces), numeric and date fields (zeroes) but **Null** data (?) for logical fields. A record is the logical equivalent of the row of a table. A set of related fields or columns of information that are treated as a unit by an RDBMS application.

Recursion   A condition in which a procedure or function calls itself. As a general rule, you should avoid recursive procedures and functions in Access Basic unless you are an experienced programmer.

Referential integrity   Rules governing the relationships between primary keys and foreign keys of tables within a relational database that determine data consistency. Referential integrity requires that the values of every foreign key in every table be matched by the value of a primary key in another table.

Refresh   To redisplay records in Access's datasheet views or in a form or report so as to reflect changes others in a multiuser environment have made to the records.

Relation   Synonym for a table or a data table in an RDBMS.

Relational database   See *RDBMS*.

Relational operators   Relational operators consist of operators such as >, <, <>, and = that compare the values of two operands and return true or false depending on the values compared. They are sometimes called comparative operators.

Remote procedure call (RPC)   An interprocess communication method that allows an application to run specific parts of the application on more than one computer in a distributed computing environment.

Reserved word   Words that comprise the vocabulary of a programming language and that are reserved for specific use by the programming language.

You cannot assign a reserved word as the name of a constant, variable, function, or subprocedure. Although the terms reserved word and keyword often are used interchangeably, they do not describe an identical set of words. See also *Keyword*.

Restriction   A query statement that defines a subset of the rows of a table based on the value of one or more of its columns.

RGB   A method of specifying colors by using numbers to specify the individual intensities of its red, green, and blue components, the colors created by the three "guns" of the CRT of a color display.

RIFF   An acronym for the Windows Resource Interchange File Format used in conjunction with the Multimedia Extensions to Windows 3.1. Depending upon their definition, these files may contain MIDI sequence, sample dump or system exclusive data, waveform files, or data to create graphic images. RIFF is the preferred file format, at least by Microsoft Corporation, for multimedia files; however, few applications yet create RIFF files.

Rollback   A term used in transaction processing that cancels a proposed transaction that modifies one or more tables and undoes changes, if any, made by the transaction prior to a COMMIT or COMMIT TRANSACTION statement.

Routine   A synonym for procedure.

Row   A set of related columns that describes a specific data entity. A synonym for record.

Row aggregation functions   See *Aggregate functions*.

Rule   A specification that determines the type of data and value of data that may be entered in a column of a table.

Run mode   The mode of Access operation when Access is executing your database application. Run mode is called run-time by Microsoft; however, the term run-time normally refers to errors that occur when running the executable version of an application.

Running state   An OLE 2.0 object is in the running state when the application that created the object is launched and has control of the object.

Scope   In programming terminology, the extent of visibility (definition) of a variable. Access Basic has global (visible to all objects and procedures in the application), form/report (visible to all objects and procedures within a single form or report), module (visible to all procedures in a single module file), and local (visible only within the procedure in which declared) scope. The scope of a variable depends upon where it is declared. See also *Global*, *Form-Level*, *Module-Level*, and *Local*.

Screen object   An Access Basic object and object class defined as the entire usable area of the video display unit. All visible form and control objects are members of subclasses of the `Screen` object.

Scroll bar   Vertical and horizontal bars at the right side and bottom, respectively, of a multiline text box that allow the user to scroll the window to expose otherwise hidden text. Access also provides scroll bars for tables and queries in run mode (datasheet view) and for forms or reports that exceed the limits of the display.

SDI server   An OLE 2.0 server that supports only a single compound document (Single Document Interface) within an instance of the application.

Second normal form   The rule for relational databases requiring that columns that are not key fields each be related to the key field. That is, a row may not contain values in data cells that do not pertain to the value of the key field. In an invoice item table, for instance, the columns of each row must pertain solely to the value of the invoice number key field.

Seek   To locate a specific byte, record, or chunk within a disk file. The `Seek` method of Access Basic can only be used in conjunction with `Recordset` objects of the `Table` type and requires that the table be indexed.

Select list   The list of column names, separated by commas, that specify the columns to be included in the result of a `SELECT` statement.

Selection   In Windows, one or more objects that have been chosen by clicking the surface of the object with the mouse or otherwise assigning the focus to the object. When used in conjunction with text, selection means the highlighted text that appears in a text box or window. See also *Restriction*.

Self-join   An SQL `JOIN` operation used to compare values within the columns of one table. Self-joins join a table with itself, requiring that the table be assigned two different names, one of which must be an alias.

Separator   A reserved symbol used to distinguish one item from another, as exemplified by the use of the exclamation point (`!`, bang character) in Access to separate the name of an object class from a specific object of the class, and an object contained within specified object.

Sequential access file   A file in which one record follows another in the sequence applicable to the application. Text files, for the most part, are sequential.

Server   A computer on a LAN that provides services or resources to client computers by sharing its resources. Servers may be dedicated, in which case they share their resources but do not use them themselves except in performing administrative tasks. Servers in client-server databases are ordinarily dedicated to making database resources available to client computers. Servers may also be used to run applications for users; in which case, the server is called an application server. Peer-to-peer or workgroup servers, such as servers created by using Windows for Workgroups to share disk directories, are another class of server.

Session   The period between the time that a user opens a connection to a database and the time that the connection to the database is closed.

Shared application memory   Memory that is allocated between processes involved in an LRPC call. See also *LRPC*.

Shared lock   A lock created by read-only operations that does not enable the user who creates the shared lock to modify the data. Other users can place shared locks on data so they can read it, but no user may apply an exclusive lock on the data while any shared locks are in effect.

Shortcut key   A key combination that provides access to a menu choice, macro, or other function of the application in lieu of selection with the mouse.

Single-stepping   A debugging process by which the source code is executed one line at a time to allow you to inspect the value of variables, find infinite loops or remove other types of bugs.

Sizing handle   The small black rectangles on the perimeter of Access control objects that appear on the surface of the form or report in design mode when the object is selected. You drag the handles of the rectangles to shrink or enlarge the size of control objects.

Source code   The readable form of code that you create in a high-level language. Source code is converted to machine-language object code by a compiler or interpreter.

Source document   A term used by OLE 1.0 to refer to a compound object in a container document.

SQL An acronym, pronounced either as "sequel" or "seekel," for Structured Query Language, a language developed by IBM Corporation for processing data contained in mainframe computer databases. (Sequel is the name of a language, similar to SQL, developed by IBM but no longer in use.) SQL has now been institutionalized by the creation of an ANSI standard for the language.

SQL aggregate functions See *Aggregate functions*.

Statement A syntactically acceptable (to the interpreter or compiler of the chosen language) combination of instructions or keywords and symbols, constants, and variables that, in Access Basic, must appear on a single line. Other languages use symbols to define the termination of a statement, such as semicolon terminators used by Pascal.

Statement permissions Permissions granted by the owner of a database or the database administrator for other users to execute specified SQL statements that act on the database's objects.

Static When applied to a variable, a variable that retains its last value until another is assigned, even though the procedure in which it is defined has completed execution. All global variables are static. Variables declared as `Static` are similar to global variables; however, their visibility is limited to their declared scope. Static is also used to distinguish between statically linked (conventional) executable files and those that use DLLs.

Stored procedure A set of SQL statements (and with those RDBMSs that support them, flow control statements) that are stored under a procedure name so that the statements can be executed as a group by the database server. Some RDBMSs, such as Microsoft and Sybase SQL Server, pre-compile stored procedures so that they execute more rapidly.

String A data type used to contain textual material, such as alphabetic characters and punctuation symbols. Numbers may be included in or constitute the value of string variables, but cannot be manipulated by mathematical operators.

Structure Two or more keywords that are used together to create an instruction, which is usually conditional in nature. In C and C++ programming, a user-defined data type. See also *Compound*.

Structured Query Language See *SQL*.

Stub A procedure or user-defined function that, in Access Basic, consists only of `Sub SubName`...`End Sub` or `Function FnName`...`End Function` lines with no intervening code. Stubs are created automatically by Access for event-handling code stored in **Form** and **Report** objects. Stubs are used to block out the procedures required by the application that can be called by the **Main** program. The intervening code statements are filled in during the programming process.

Style   In typography, a characteristic or set of attributes of a member of a family of typefaces created by an outline or bit map designed specifically to implement it. Styles include bold, italic, bold-italic, bold-italic-condensed, and so forth. Styles may contain attributes for weight (bold, demi-bold, black), form (italic, roman), and spacing (compressed or extended) in various combinations.

Submenu   A set of choices presented when a main menu choice is made. In Windows, the first-level submenus are similar to drop-down dialogs. Second-level submenus usually appear horizontally at the point of the first submenu choice.

Subform   A form contained within another form.

Subprocedure   A procedure called by another procedure other than the main procedure (WinMain in Windows.) In Access, all procedures except functions are subprocedures because MSACCESS.EXE or MSARN200.EXE contains the WinMain procedure.

Subquery   A SQL SELECT statement that is included (nested) within another SELECT, INSERT, UPDATE, or DELETE statement, or nested within another subquery.

Subreport   A report contained within another report.

Syntax   The rules governing the expression of a language. Like English, Spanish, Esperanto, or Swahili, programming languages each have their own syntax. Some languages allow much more latitude (irregular forms) in their syntax. Access Basic has a relatively rigid syntax, while C provides more flexibility at the expense of complexity.

System administrator   The individual(s) responsible for the administrative functions for all applications on a LAN or users of a UNIX cluster or network, usually including supervision of all databases on servers attached to the LAN. If the system administrator's (SA's) responsibility is limited to databases, the term database administrator (DBA) is ordinarily assigned.

Appendixes

System colors The 20 standard colors used by Windows for elements of its pre-defined objects such as backgrounds, scroll bars, borders, and title bars. You may change the system colors from the defaults through Control Panel's Color and Desktop functions.

System databases Databases that control access to databases on a server or across a LAN. Microsoft SQL Server has three system databases: the master database that controls user databases, tempdb that holds temporary tables, and model that is used as the skeleton to create new user databases. Any database that is not a user database is a system database.

System function Functions that return data about the database rather than from the content of the database.

System object An object defined by Access rather than by the user. Examples of system objects are the **Screen** and **Debug** objects.

System table A data dictionary table that maintains information on users of the database manager and each database under the control by the system.

Tab order The order in which the focus is assigned to multiple control objects within a form or dialog with successive depression of the Tab key.

Table A database object consisting of a group of rows (records) divided into columns (fields) that contain data or **Null** values. A table is treated as a database device or object.

Text box A Windows object designed to receive printable characters typed from the keyboard. Access Basic provides two basic types: single- and multi-line. Entries in single-line text boxes are terminated with an Enter keystroke. Multi-line text boxes accept more than one line of text, either by a self-contained word-wrap feature (if a horizontal scroll bar is not present) or by a Ctrl+Enter key combination.

Text file A disk file containing characters with values ordinarily ranging from **Chr$**(1) through **Chr$**(127) in which lines of text are separated from one another with newline pairs (**Chr$**(13) **&** **Chr$**(10)).

Theta join A SQL JOIN operation that uses comparison or relational operators in the JOIN statement. See also *Operator*.

Third normal form The rule for relational databases that imposes the requirement that a column that is not a key column may not be dependent upon another column that is not a key column. The third normal form is generally considered the most important because it is the first in the series that is not intuitive.

Thread   A part of a process, such as an executing application, that can run as an object or an entity.

Time stamp   The date and time data attributes applied to a disk file when created or edited. Time stamp is a database type for SQL Server and the ODBC API.

Timer   An Access Basic object that is invisible in run mode and that is used to trigger a Timer event at preselected intervals.

Title bar   The heading area, usually blue, of a window in which the title of the window appears, usually in bright white (reverse).

Toggle   A property of an object, such as a check box, that alternates its state when repeatedly clicked with the mouse or activated by a shortcut key combination.

Toolbar   A group of command button icons, usually arranged horizontally across the top of a window, that perform functions that would ordinarily require one or more menu choices. Floating toolbars can be located anywhere on your display.

Toolbox   A collection of command buttons designated as tools, usually with icons substituted for the default appearance of a command button, that choose a method applicable to an object (usually graphic) until another tool is selected. An example is the Access Basic Toolbox.

Topic   In DDE conversations, the name of the file or other identifying title of a collection of data. When used in conjunction with help files, the name of the subject matter of a single help screen display.

TRANSACT-SQL   A superset of ANSI SQL used by Microsoft and Sybase SQL Server. TRANSACT-SQL includes flow control instructions and the capability to define and use stored procedures that include conditional execution and looping.

Transaction   A group of processing steps that are treated as a single activity to perform a desired result. A transaction might entail all of the steps necessary to modify the values in or add records to each table involved when a new invoice is created. RDBMSs that are capable of transaction processing usually include the capability to cancel the transaction by a rollback instruction or to cause it to become a permanent part of the tables with the COMMIT or COMMIT TRANSACTION statement.

Trigger A stored procedure that occurs when a user executes an instruction that may affect the referential integrity of a database. Triggers usually occur prior to the execution of INSERT, DELETE, or UPDATE statements so that the effect of the statement on referential integrity can be examined by a stored procedure prior to execution. See also *Stored procedure*.

Twip The smallest unit of measurement in Windows and the default unit of measurement of Access Basic. The twip is 1/20 of a point, or 1/1440 of a logical inch.

Type See *Data type*.

Typeface Synonym for face. A set of fonts of a single family in any available size possessing an identical style or set of attributes.

Unary See *Operator*.

UNC An abbreviation for uniform naming convention, the method of identifying the location of files on a remote server. UNC names begin with \\.

Unicode A replacement for the 7-bit or 8-bit ASCII and ANSI representations of characters with a 16-bit model that allows a wider variety of characters to be used.

Uniform data transfer (UDT) The interprocess communication (IPC) method used by OLE 2.0. OLE 1.0 uses DDE for IPC.

Unique index An index in which no two key fields or combinations of key fields upon which the index is created may have the same value.

UNIX Registered trademark of Novell, Incorporated (formerly of AT&T) for its multiuser operating system, now administered by the Open Systems Foundation (OSF). Extensions and modifications of UNIX include DEC Ultrix, SCO UNIX, IBM AIX, and similar products.

Update A permanent change to data values in one or more data tables. An update occurs when the INSERT, DELETE, UPDATE, or TRUNCATE TABLE SQL commands are executed.

User-defined A data type, also called a record, that is specified in your Access Basic source code by a **Type. . .End Type** declaration statement in the Declarations Section of a module. The elements of the user-defined record type can be any data type valid for the language and may include other user-defined types.

User-defined transaction A group of instructions combined under a single name and executed as a block when the name is invoked in a statement executed by the user.

Validation The process of determining if an update to a value in a table's data cell is within a pre-established range or is a member of a set of allowable values. Validation rules establish the range or set of allowable values.

Variable The name given to a symbol that represents or substitutes for a number (numeric), letter, or combination of letters (string).

View The method by which the data is presented for review by the user, usually on the computer display. Views can be created from subsets of columns from one or more tables.

WAN An acronym for *wide area network*. A WAN is a system for connecting multiple computers in different geographical locations through the use of the switched telephone network or leased data lines, by optical or other long-distance cabling, or by infra-red or radio links.

WAVE file A file containing waveform audio data, usually with a .WAV extension.

Waveform audio A data type standard of the Windows Multimedia Extensions that defines how digitally sampled sounds are stored in files and processed by Windows API functions calls.

Wild card A character that substitutes for and allows a match by any character or set of characters in its place. The DOS ? and * wild cards are similarly used in Windows applications.

Win32 An API for creating 32-bit applications that run both on the present 16-bit (DOS) version of Windows and on Windows NT. Applications that are written to the Win32 API provide substantially improved performance when run under Windows NT. At the time this book was written, Microsoft was attempting to consolidate several versions of the Win32 API (such as Win32s and Win32c) into a single Win32 API.

WinHelp A contraction used to describe the Windows help engine of Windows 3.1 and the files that are used in the creation of Windows 3.1 help systems.

Workstation A client computer on a LAN or WAN that is used to run applications and is connected to a server from which it obtains data shared with other computers. It is possible, but not common, for some network servers to be used as both a server and a workstation. Microsoft LAN Manager and Windows NT, for instance, permit this. Workstation is also used to describe a high-priced PC that uses a proprietary microprocessor and proprietary architecture to create what some call an "open" system.

WOSA Acronym for the Windows Open Services Architecture that is the foundation for such APIs as ODBC, MAPI, and TAPI. Microsoft also develops special vertical-market WOSA APIs for the banking, financial, and other industries.

WOW An acronym for Windows on Win32, a subsystem of Windows NT that allows 16-bit Windows applications to run in protected memory spaces called virtual DOS machines (VDMs).

xBase Any language interpreter or compiler or a database manager built upon the dBASE III+ model and incorporating all dBASE III+ commands and functions. Microsoft's FoxPro and Computer Associates' Clipper are xBase dialects. Most xBase database managers add a substantial number of commands and functions to the dBASE III+ vocabulary. xBase RDBMSs often do not use the same index file structure as dBASE III+, but all use the same database file (.DBF) structure.

Yes/No field A term used by Access to describe a field of a table whose allowable values are Yes (**True**) or No (**False**). Called a logical or Boolean field by other RDBMSs.

Appendix B

Naming Conventions for Access Objects

Many Access developers use a standardized method of assigning names to Access database objects and to Access Basic variables that refer to these objects. Standardized object and variables names, called *naming conventions*, make the design of Access applications easier for others to understand. The naming conventions for Access objects and variables in this book use a modified form of *Hungarian notation* that commonly is used in C and C++ programming. The term Hungarian derives from the nationality of the naming convention's inventor, Charles Simonyi, who at one time worked on the development of Access 1.0 at Microsoft. One of the prefixes that defines a zero-terminated string variable in C, *sz*, is a combination of letters that is commonly found in the Hungarian language.

Microsoft first proposed the use of Hungarian notation for naming objects in dialects of Object Basic in the *Programmer's Guide* for Visual Basic 2.0. Greg Reddick, an independent software developer and a former Microsoft employee, and Stan Leszynski of Leszynski and Company, a database consulting firm, extended the Visual Basic object-naming conventions to include the database objects of Access 1.0. Leszynski and Reddick also expanded the naming conventions to include names of variables that refer to Access objects. This book uses the Leszynski-Reddick (L-R) naming conventions in all Access Basic code examples, with the specific exceptions that are noted in the sections that follow.

Most of the information and much of the text in the sections that follow in this appendix are derived from the original naming conventions that appeared in the file NAMING.DOC, which at one time was posted in the MSACCESS forum. Reddick dedicated the content of this file to the public domain. Subsequently, Leszynski and Reddick compiled a copyrighted version of the naming conventions that appeared in the February 1993 (Charter) issue of *Smart Access*, a monthly technical journal published by Pinnacle Publishing, Inc.

Using Tags

Tags generally are short (typically three letters, but ranging from one to four letters) and mnemonic. Some of the tag names in the original version of the naming convention derive from the C programming language, so the mnemonic connections were somewhat stretched in Access. For example, w was used for the **Integer** data type because integers are stored internally as a word (16 bits, 2 bytes). A word (w) in C, however, represents an unsigned integer. You could not use i to indicate the **Integer** data type because i was used as a data type prefix for indexes. Subsequently, the three-letter prefixes int and lng have come to be used in lieu of the w and dw (double-word) tags. The f prefix, indicating an **Integer** variable used as a flag, which only can have the values **True** or **False**, remains in common usage.

> ### Note
>
> No standard naming convention for the classes and sub-classes of objects created by applications that support OLE Automation had appeared when this book was written. It is likely that prefixes, such as xlw, doc, and vsd, will be used to identify the source of OA objects created in Excel 5.0, Word 6.0, and Visio 2.0, respectively. The problem involved in creating tags for sub-classes of OA objects is the profusion of objects defined by OA-compliant applications. One look at the Object Browser of Excel 5.0 is enough to discourage anyone from attempting to define standard tags for all of Excel 5.0's objects. Eventually, it is likely that someone (hopefully Microsoft) will attempt to establish naming conventions for VBA and OA objects.

Table B.1 lists the proposed naming conventions for Access 2.0 objects and provides examples of their use. The majority of the tags listed in table B.1 follow the naming conventions assigned by Microsoft Corporation to Visual Basic objects because Access and Visual Basic 3.0 have many object names in common. Object names that are followed by an asterisk (*) were introduced with Access 2.0 and are not included in the original version of the L-R naming conventions. All of the new objects of Access 2.0 are members of the data access object base class.

Table B.1   Access 2.0 Objects and Their Corresponding Tags

Object	Tag	Example with Qualifier
Bound object frame	bof	bofAudioFile
Chart	cht	chtSales
Check box	chk	chkReadOnly
Combo list	cbo	cboEnglish
Command button	cmd	cmdCancel
Container*	cnt	cntApplication
Database	db	dbAchievers
Document*	doc	docApplication
Dynaset	ds	dsOverAchiever (Access 1.x)
Field*	fld	fldLastName
File list	fil	filSource
Form	frm	frmFileOpen
Frame	fra	fraLanguage
Graph		See Chart
Group*	grp	grpUsers
Horizontal scroll bar	hsb	hsbVolume
Index*	idx	idxPrimaryKey
Label	lbl	lblHelpMessage
Line	lin	linVertical
List box	lst	lstPolicyCodes
Macro	mcr	mcrMain
Menu	mnu	mnuFileOpen
Module	mod	modLibrary
OLE object	ole	oleObject1
Option button	opt	optFrench

(continues)

Table B.1 Continued		
Object	**Tag**	**Example with Qualifier**
Option group	grp	grpChoices
Page break	brk	brkForm1
Parameter*	prm	prmStartDate
Property*	prp	prpLockEdits
Query object	qry	qryOverAchiever
QueryDef object (persistent)	qdf	qdfOverAchiever
Recordset*	rs	rsQuerySet
Report	rpt	rptFireList
Shape (for example, a rectangle)	shp	shpCircle
Snapshot	ss	ssThisQuery (Access 1.x)
Subform	sbf	sbfMany
Subreport	sbr	sbrNewReport
Table	tbl	tblCustomer (Access 1.x)
TableDef*	tdf	tdfCustomer
Text box	txt	txtGetText
Unbound object frame	uof	uofLogo
User	usr	usrCurrent
Vertical scroll bar	vsb	vsbRate
Workspace	ws	wspCurrent

Note

The original tags proposed for **Dynaset** and **Snapshot** objects, rsd and rss, respectively, included rs because both objects are types of **Recordset** objects. In Access 2.0, the **Recordset** object, introduced in Visual Basic 3.0, replaces the **Table**, **Dynaset**, and **Snapshot** objects. (**Table**, **Dynaset**, and **Snapshot** objects remain defined by Access 2.0 for compatibility with Access 1.x applications.)

When you declare a variable with one of the object data types listed in table B.1, the tag defines the variable's data type, and the qualifier is the name of the object (without spaces or punctuation). The section that follows describes the use of tags with variable names that point to objects or represent values.

Tags for Access Basic Variables

Tags commonly are used to identify the data type and size property of Access Basic variables that have corresponding data types in other languages. The tags replace the data type identifier characters of the original dialects of BASIC. In the majority of cases, C or Windows programming conventions originally were used for these tags. C doesn't support the `Currency` and `Variant` data types of Access Basic and treats fixed-length strings as an array of the `char` type. C and Windows use `LP` to indicate a pointer of the long type, but Access Basic does not support pointer variables. Therefore, the `dw` tag, an abbreviation for double-word, is used to indicate a long integer, as is common in specifying the data type of arguments passed to Windows functions. Table B.2 lists the tags that specify data types not listed in table B.1. Both the Access Basic data type tag as used in this book and the original C-style tag appear in table B.2.

Note

As mentioned in Chapter 29, "Exchanging Data with OLE Automation and DDE," OA requires that the data types of arguments passed to OA functions be of the `Variant` data type. Applications that support OLE 2.0 and OLE Automation include the C user-defined data type, `variant`.

Table B.2 Proposed Variable Tags Based on Data Type

Data Type	Tag	C Tag	Example with Qualifier
Integer	int	w	intRetValue, wRetValue
Long	lng	dw	lngParam, dwParam
Single	sng	s	sngLoadFactor, sLoadFactor
Double	dbl	d	dblPi, dPi
Currency	cur	mny	curSalary, mnySalary

(continues)

Table B.2 Continued			
Data Type	**Tag**	**C Tag**	**Example with Qualifier**
String (fixed length)	str	sf	strContact, sfContact
String (variable length)	str	sz	strName, szName
Variant	var	v	varInput, vInput

Tags for User-Defined Data Types

When creating a user-defined data type (also called a record type in Pascal and a structure in C), you always use a created tag. By convention, the created tag is capitalized. When you create a user-defined data type with a **Type...End Type** declaration such as the following:

```
Type NAM
    strFirst   As String * 15
    strMiddle  As String * 15
    strLast    As String * 20
End Type
```

you declare variables of type NAM with the created tag in lowercase, as in the following:

```
Dim namAdd As NAM
```

This convention removes any ambiguity about the data type of namAdd, as long as you use one of the standard object tags. When you refer to a field of the record, as in the following:

```
strLastName = RTrim$(namAdd.strLast)
```

the data types of the record and the field are identified properly.

Context Tags

When you use a value in a context other than a simple variable, you should use a different tag, even if the data type is one listed in table B.2. Table B.3 provides examples of context-based prefixes that you substitute for the data type tags of table B.2. The tag f, for flag, is used to identify the Boolean or logical variable, typed as an integer in Access Basic.

Table B.3 Tags Based on Use or Context of a Variable

Use of Variable	Prefix	Example with Qualifier
Boolean (Yes/No)	f	fReturnValue
Character	ch	chLetterLastPressed
Handle	h	hCursor
Handle to a window	hwnd	hwndForm
Handle to a device context	hdc	hdcPrinter
Bit	b	bMin

To expand further on context tags, assume that you have written Access Basic code that determines the validity of an address. 1 is a valid address, 2 is the last known address, 3 is no address, and so on. If this code is used frequently, then you invent a new tag, rather than using int or w. For example, vad may indicate a valid address; therefore, vadShipTo would contain the validity code for the Ship To address.

Using Prefixes

Prefixes modify data type tags to provide additional information about the variable. Tags and prefixes are concatenated to create the variable name, as shown in the examples of common prefixes in table B.4.

Table B.4 Common Prefixes for Types of Variables

Data Type	Access Prefix	C Prefix	Example	Description
Array	a	rg	aintStock, rgwStock	Array of integers
	i	i	iaintStock, irgwStock	Index into aintStock or rgwStock
	i	i	ilstPickList	Index into a list
Count	c	c	cchstrName	Count of chars in strName
	c	c	clstPickList	Count of items in a list

(continues)

Table B.4	Continued			
Data Type	**Access Prefix**	**C Prefix**	**Example**	**Description**
Group	gr	gr	grbClass	Group of Class bits
Unused	zz	zz	zzfrmNames	An unused form

The difference between a group and an array is that you can use an index into an array, but you must use code to specify a particular member of a group. Indexes are integers unless specified otherwise.

Using Common Variable Qualifiers

Although the prefix and tag are sufficient to fully specify a variable's type, they may not be sufficient to distinguish one variable from another. When two variables of the same type are within the same scope, further specification is required to remove ambiguities. This specification is achieved with qualifiers. A qualifier is a short, descriptive word that indicates the variable's use. You can use multiple words. The first letter of the qualifier is capitalized, as is the first letter of each additional word. You concatenate the qualifier without using intervening spaces.

The data type prefix aint or rgw is a perfectly valid and complete variable name for an array, as are frm for a form and str or sz for a string; however, you can have only one distinct variable of each type in a procedure. Table B.5 lists some common qualifiers.

Table B.5	Common Qualifiers for Variable Names		
Purpose	**Qualifier**	**Access Example**	**C Example**
First element of set	First	iaintFirst	irgwFirst
Last element of set	Last	iaintLast	irgwLast
Lower limit of set	Min	iastrNamesMin	irgszNamesMin
Upper limit of set	Max	iastrNamesMax	irgszNamesMax

Purpose	Qualifier	Access Example	C Example
Invalid value	Nil	hwndNil	hwndNil
Temporary variable	T	intT	wT
Source	Src	lngBufferSrc	dwBufferSrc
Destination	Dest	lngBufferDest	dwBufferDest

The common qualifiers usually are appended to the rest of the qualifier name.

When you are constructing a database, you can use the same qualifier name for the following elements: the table, the main form for accessing the table, and the main query for the table. In the case of a database with a table called tblCustomerName, for example; the form for entering the customers would be called frmCustomerName.

> **Note**
>
> Using tags to prefix table names is becoming a relatively common practice in Access applications, but the proposed extension of naming conventions to tag field names with their field data types, proposed in the L-R Access naming conventions, has not been widely accepted.

Using Tags with Function Names

You construct function names just as you construct variable names, with the exception that the first letters are the tag of the return type of the function. The function, strGetFormName(), for example, returns a variable-length string. A function name with the nil prefix or without a tag prefix indicates that the function doesn't return a value.

Appendix C

Data Dictionary for the Personnel Actions Table

You use the Personnel Actions table in examples in the following chapters:

The step-by-step procedures for creating the Personnel Actions table and adding the first nine records to the table are included in Chapter 4, "Working with Access Databases and Tables."

Tables C.1 through C.5 provide a tabular data dictionary for the Personnel Actions table.

Table C.1 lists the values of the FieldName, Caption, DataType, FieldSize, and Format properties of the Personnel Actions table. These values are entered in the Properties text boxes for each field.

Table C.1   Field Properties for the Personnel Actions Table

Field Name	Caption	Data Type	Field Size	Format
PA ID Number	ID	Number	Long Integer	General
PA Type	Type	Text	1	@> (all caps)
PA Initiated By Number	Initiated By	Number	Integer	General
PA Scheduled Date	Scheduled	Date/Time	N/A	Short Date
PA Approved By Number	Approved By	Number	Integer	General
PA Effective Date	Effective	Date/Time	N/A	Short Date
PA Rating Number	Rating	Number	Integer	General
PA Amount	Amount	Currency	N/A	##,##0.00#
PA Comments	Comments	Memo	N/A	None

Table C.2 lists the entries you make to assign default values to each field for which default values are required. You enter these values in the Default Values text box of the indicated field.

Table C.2   Default Field Values for the Personnel Actions Table

Field Name	Default Value	Comments
PA Type	Q	Quarterly performance reviews are the most common personnel action.
PA Scheduled Date	=Date()	The expression to enter today's (DOS) date.
PA Effective Date	=Date() +28	Four weeks from today's date.

Table C.3 lists the values you enter as Validation Rules and the accompanying Validation text that is displayed in the status bar if an entry violates one of the rules. Only those fields with validation rules are shown in table C.3.

Field Name	Validation Rule	Validation Text
Table C.3 Validation Criteria for Fields of the Personnel Actions Table		
PA ID	>0	Please enter a valid employee ID number.
PA Type	"H" Or "S" Or "Q" Or "Y" Or "B" Or "C"	Only H, S, Q, Y, B, and C codes may be entered.
PA Initiated By	>0	Please enter a valid supervisor ID number.
PA Scheduled Date	Between Date() -3650 And Date() +365	Scheduled dates cannot be more than 10 years ago nor more than 1 year from now.
PA Approved By	>0 Or Is Null	Please enter a valid manager ID number or leave blank if not approved.
PA Rating	Between 0 And 9 Or Is Null	Rating range is 0 for terminated employees, 1 to 9, or blank.

Table C.4 lists the key fields, indexes, and relationships for the Personnel Actions table. A composite key field is used so that duplication of an entry of a record for an employee is precluded. The default index that Access creates on the primary key field is shown for completeness; you do not add this index because Access creates indexes on key fields automatically. Index1 is for demonstration purposes only and is not used in the examples. You establish the relationship with the Employees table by opening the Database window, choosing **R**elationships from the **E**dit menu, and making the selections that are listed for the Relationships property in table C.4 in the Relationships dialog.

Table C.4   Key Fields, Indexes, and Relationships for the Personnel Actions Table

Property	Value
Primary Key Fields	PA ID;PA Type;PA Scheduled Date
Primary Key Index	PA ID;PA Type;PA Scheduled Date
Relationships	Primary table: Employees Related table: Personnel Actions Enforce Referential Integrity: True (checked) Cascade Deletions: True (checked) Cascade Updates: True (checked)

Table C.5 lists the first nine entries in the Personnel Actions table that are used to demonstrate use of the table. The (PA) Scheduled (Date) and (PA) Effective (Date) entries are based on the Hired Date information in the Employees table. Enter these values after you have created the composite primary key for the table. Assigning performance ratings (except 0, terminated) to the records is optional.

Table C.5   First Nine Entries for the Personnel Actions Table

ID	Type	Initiated By	Scheduled	Approved By	Effective	Rating Amount	Comments
1	H		01-Apr-87		01-Apr-87	2,000	Hired
2	H		15-Jul-87		15-Jul-87	3,500	Hired
3	H	2	01-Mar-88	2	01-Mar-88	2,250	Hired
4	H	2	01-Apr-88	2	01-Apr-88	2,250	Hired
5	H	2	15-Sep-89	2	15-Sep-89	2,500	Hired
6	H	5	15-Sep-89	2	15-Sep-89	4,000	Hired
7	H	5	01-Dec-89	2	01-Dec-89	3,000	Hired
8	H	2	01-Feb-90	2	01-Feb-90	2,500	Hired
9	H	5	15-Oct-91	2	15-Oct-91	3,000	Hired

Index

X–Y–Z